International Trade and Customs Law
of the European Union

International Trade and Customs Law of the European Union

Francis Snyder   BA(Yale), JD(Harvard), CDEPA,
DS(Paris I [Panthéon-Sorbonne])

Officier de l'Ordre des Palmes Académiques;
Member of the Bar of Massachusetts;
Professor of European Community Law,
European University Institute, Florence;
Co-Director, Academy of European Law, Florence;
Professor of Law, College of Europe, Bruges;
Honorary Visiting Professor of Law, University College London

With the assistance of
Leonard W N Hawkes   BA(Kent)
Solicitor;
LeBoeuf Lamb Greene & MacRae, London and Brussels

Butterworths
London, Charlottesville, Dublin, Durban, Edinburgh,
Hong Kong, Kuala Lumpur, New Delhi, Singapore, Sydney,
Toronto, Wellington
1998

United Kingdom	Butterworths, a Division of Reed Elsevier (UK) Ltd, Halsbury House, 35 Chancery Lane, LONDON WC2A 1EL and 4 Hill Street, EDINBURGH EH2 3JZ
Australia	Butterworths, a Division of Reed International Books Australia Pty Ltd, CHATSWOOD, New South Wales
Canada	Butterworths Canada Ltd, MARKHAM, Ontario
Hong Kong	Butterworths Asia (Hong Kong), HONG KONG
India	Butterworths India, NEW DELHI
Ireland	Butterworth (Ireland) Ltd, DUBLIN
Malaysia	Malayan Law Journal Sdn Bhd, KUALA LUMPUR
New Zealand	Butterworths of New Zealand Ltd, WELLINGTON
Singapore	Butterworths Asia, SINGAPORE
South Africa	Butterworths Publishers (Pty) Ltd, DURBAN
USA	Lexis Law Publishing, CHARLOTTESVILLE, Virginia

Typeset by Ponting–Green Publishing Services, Chesham, Buckinghamshire
Printed by Antony Rowe Ltd, Chippenham, Wiltshire

Visit us at our website: http://www.butterworths.co.uk

Preface

This book is a comprehensive guide to the international trade and customs law of the European Union (EU). It covers EU customs law, general commercial policy, specific economic sectors, and preferential arrangements and bilateral agreements. Its primary objective is to provide a clear, precise and thorough statement of the law on these subjects. Consequently, the book deals with the provisions of the Treaty on European Union (TEU), the European Community (EC) Treaty, the European Coal and Steel Community (ECSC) Treaty and the European Atomic Energy Community (EAEC) Treaty; acts under the TEU and EC, ECSC and EAEC secondary legislation; multilateral and bilateral agreements; decisions of the European Court of Justice and the Court of First Instance regarding EU international trade and customs law; and decisions of the World Trade Organization (WTO). It also refers to selected secondary literature, though a more complete discussion of the relevant secondary literature on the wide range of subjects dealt with in this book must await another occasion.

My main purpose in writing this book has been to provide a treatment of EU international trade and customs law in a form that can and would be used everyday, as an indispensable resource, by interested people in any part of the world who wish or need to learn more about this important subject. The book is intended mainly for practising lawyers, lawyers in public service, government officials, and staff of regional and international organisations. However, it should also be of interest to teachers, researchers, students, politicians, lobbyists, importers, exporters and others in economic and social life and any other people who, for whatever reason, are attracted by EU international trade and customs law and need a clear and comprehensive treatment of it.

For many reasons, this book has been a very long time in the making. As a result, I am more than usually indebted to numerous people and various institutions for their help and support. I am grateful for the assistance of Leonard Hawkes, who contributed Chapters 13, 14 and part of Chapter 6. I wish to give special thanks to Candido Garcia Molyneux, who prepared the first draft of Chapters 1–5, 8 and much of Chapter 6. Without his invaluable contribution, the book would have taken considerably longer to complete. During the preparation of the book I have benefited enormously from the help of a number of excellent research assistants, some of whom now enjoy distinguished academic, legal, political or diplomatic careers. They include Song Ying, Jason Coppel, Wolf Sauter (who prepared a first draft of Chapter 9) and Candido Garcia Molyneux, as well as (in alphabetical order) Vassil Breskovski, Nicholas Emiliou, Katarzyna Gromek Broc, Miguel Poiares Maduro, Jasper Snyder, John Tillotson, Nuno Venade Ribeiros Mato and Angela Ward. Additional help on specific matters was provided by

Maria do Ceu Esteves, Niklas Fagerlund, Anna Lixi, Cosimo Monda, Marcelo J Oviedo and Filip Tuytschaever. In preparing his chapters, Leonard Hawkes benefited from the assistance of Francesco Malatesta, Carol McDiarmid and in particular Candido Garcia Molyneux, who prepared the first draft of Chapters 13 and 14. The book would not have been possible without the help of the staff of the library of the European University Institute, notably Elspeth Fehilly, Machteld Nijsten and especially Emir Lawless, to whom I wish to express here my sincere thanks for her constant help, thoughtfulness and efficiency. I owe a special debt of gratitude to Anne-Lise Strahtmann, whose kindness, encouragement and support have contributed so much to the making of this book.

While writing this book, I have been most closely associated with three institutions: the European University Institute in Florence, the College of Europe in Bruges and the Faculty of Laws, University College London. All have encouraged the research on which this book is based. I wish to thank the Faculty of Laws, University College London and subsequently the Research Council of the European University Institute for financial support. The European Commission, the Council of the European Union, the European Parliament and the European Court of Justice have been uniformly helpful in providing documents and other information. I am grateful also to several institutions for allowing me to present parts of the book at conferences or seminars. They include the Academy of European Law, Florence; College of Europe, Bruges; Chinese Academy of Social Sciences, Beijing; European University Institute, Florence; Fudan University, Shanghai; Research Committee on the Sociology of Law of the International Sociological Association; University of Hong Kong; Peking University; Instituto de Estudos Europeus de Macau; University of Tokyo; University College London; University of Wisconsin at Madison; and Wuhan University. I also wish to thank the EU–China Higher Education Co-operation Programme, which in 1998 awarded me the first Robert Schuman Professorship. This enabled me to spend a month in spring 1998 at the Chinese Academy of Social Sciences in Beijing and, in addition to lecturing, to discuss many of the themes of the book.

In view of the long gestation period of this book, very special thanks are due to the excellent staff at Butterworths for their encouragement, support, patience and skill in seeing this book through to publication.

I have endeavoured to state the law as of 1 May 1998, though it has also been possible to take account of some subsequent developments. Nevertheless, in a subject area that is changing so rapidly, and in a work of this length and complexity, it is almost inevitable that, despite one's best efforts, some of the material may be out of date by the time of publication. Despite one's firm intentions, it is also likely that there are gaps in the coverage of certain topics or omissions which need eventually to be rectified. We live in the age of globalisation, so the medium of a book, as that of a still photograph, is hardly adequate to capture the dynamic nature of the international trade and customs law of the European Union. Indeed, as informed readers will know, currently the European Union itself does not have legal personality, so most of the law discussed in this book concerns not the EU strictly speaking, but rather the EC, ECSC and the EAEC. This state of affairs may change in the future. For the moment the EU, in addition to its importance in intergovernmental matters, remains a convenient way of designating the totality composed of the three legally distinct Communities and various forms of intergovernmental co-operation, in other words the evolving legal structure created by the Maastricht Treaty on European Union as amended by the Amsterdam Treaty.

The best counsel for anyone who pretends to write a comprehensive book about the international trade and customs law of the European Union is modesty. During the writing of this book, I have tried to bear this counsel firmly in mind. Consequently, while knowing that any attempt to be comprehensive and absolutely up-to-date must inevitably fall short, I have tried to provide at least an introduction to the subject, which could serve both as a reference source for practising lawyers and as a solid foundation for future academic research. I would be most grateful for any suggestions for improving the book and increasing its usefulness to its readers.

Francis Snyder   26 June 1998
Florence

Contents

Table of Commission and Council Regulations

Table of Commission and Council Directives

Table of Commission and Council Decisions

Table of Treaties

Table of cases

Decisions of the European Court of Justice are listed below numerically. These decisions are also
included in the preceding alphabetical list.

Part I

Customs

Chapter 1

Classification of goods

INTRODUCTION

The Community is based upon a customs union which must cover all trade in goods and which must involve the prohibition between Member States of customs duties on imports and exports and of all charges having equivalent effect, and the application of a Common Customs Tariff in their relations with third countries.[1] A Common Customs Tariff is necessary so that the same duty or measure can be applied to the same imported or exported product on a Community-wide basis. The Common Customs Tariff is composed of the Combined Nomenclature, together with the rates of duty and other relevant charges, and the tariff measures included in the Taric or in other Community arrangements.[2]

THE COMBINED NOMENCLATURE

The Combined Nomenclature meets, at one and the same time, the require-ments of both the Common Customs Tariff and of the external trade statistics

---

1 Art 9 of the Treaty. The Court has consistently held that the justification for the prohibition of customs duties and charges having equivalent effect is based on the fact that any pecuniary charge imposed on goods by reason of the fact that they cross a frontier constitutes an obstacle to the movement of such goods. See Joined Cases 2/69 & 3/69 *Diamantarbeiders v Brachfeld* [1969] ECR 211, paragraph 14; see also Joined Cases C-363/93, C-407/93, C-408/93, C-409/93, C-410/93 & C-411/93 *Rene Lancry SA v Direction Generale des Douanes* [1994] ECR I-3957. The prohibition of restrictions in intra-Community trade has the same scope as regards products imported from another Member State after being in free circulation there as for those originating in the same Member State. See Case 119/78 *Peureux v Services Fiscaux de la Haute-Saone et du Territoire de Belfort* [1979] ECR 975. Products in free circulation are to be understood as meaning those products which, coming from third coun-tries, were duly imported into any one of the Member States in accordance with the require-ments laid down by Art 10 of the Treaty. See Case 41/76 *Donckerwolcke v Procureur de la Republique* [1976] ECR 1921. Furthermore, a charge levied at a regional frontier by reason of the fact that goods are brought into one region of a Member State undermines the unity of the Community customs territory and constitutes an obstacle to the free movement of goods at least as serious as a charge levied at a national frontier on products entering a Member State as a whole. See Case C-163/90 *Administration des Douanes et Droits Indirects v Legros* [1992] ECR I-4625; see also Joined Cases C-363/93, C-407/93, C-408/93, C-409/93, C-410/93 & C-411/93 *Rene Lancry SA v Direction Generale des Douanes* [1994] ECR I-3957.
2 Council Regulation 2658/87 Art 4(1) on the tariff and statistical nomenclature and the Com-mon Customs Tariff, OJ 7.9.87 L256/1, as amended; see also Council Regulation 2913/92 Art 20(3), OJ 19.10.92 L302/1.

of the Community.[3] It is reproduced in Annex I to Council Regulation (EEC) 2658/87 on the tariff and statistical nomenclature and the Common Customs Tariff, which is annually replaced by the Commission with the assistance of the Nomenclature Committee.[4]

The Combined Nomenclature follows closely the harmonized system of the International Convention on the Harmonized Commodity Description and Coding System to which the Community is party.[5] Thus, it comprises the harmonized system nomenclature;[6] Community subdivisions to that nomenclature referred to as 'CN' subheadings, in those cases where a corresponding rate is specified;[7] preliminary provisions, additional section or chapter notes and footnotes relating to the CN subheadings.[8]

The combined nomenclature is divided into 21 sections containing 99 chapters. The chapters are composed of headings and subheadings. Products are grouped in the different chapters according to the material of which they are made. Within each chapter, the headings of the products are placed in the order based upon their degree of processing. The CN sections and chapters and subheadings are generally preceded by section notes, chapter notes and subheading notes, respectively.

The CN is laid down in a tabular form. Column 1 sets the CN code. Each subheading has an eight-digit code number.[9] The first six digits of such code are the code numbers relating to the headings and subheadings of the harmonized system nomenclature.[10] The seventh and eight digit identify the CN subheadings for the Community purposes.[11] Column 2 provides a description of the good. Column 3 establishes the autonomous rate of duty.[12] Column 4 sets the

3 Council Regulation 2658/87 Art 1(1) on the tariff and statistical nomenclature and the Common Customs Tariff, OJ 7.9.87 L256/1, as amended; see also Peter Oliver & Xenophon Yataganas 'The Harmonized System of Customs Classification' 7 YB Eur L 113–129 (1987). Both Art 28 and 113 constitute together the appropriate legal basis for the establishment of the Combined Nomenclature. See also Case 165/87 *Commission of the European Communities v Council of the European Communities* [1988] ECR 5545.
4 See Council Regulation 2658/87 Art 1(3) on the tariff and statistical nomenclature and the Common Customs Tariff, OJ 7.9.87 L256/1, as amended; see also ibid Art 12. As to the functions and procedures of the Nomenclature Committee see ibid Art 7 ; see also ibid Art 8; see also ibid Art 9; see also ibid Art 10. See also Case 795/79 *Handelmaatchappij Pesch & Co BV v Hoofdproduktschap voor Akkerbouwprodukten* [1980] ECR 2705. The last Commission replacement of Annex I was contained in Commission Regulation 2086/97, OJ 14.11.97 L312/1.
5 See International Convention on the Harmonized Commodity Description and Coding System, OJ 20.7.87 L198/3; see also Council Decision 87/369 concerning the conclusion of the International Convention on the Harmonized Commodity Description and Coding System and of the Protocol of Amendment thereto, OJ 20.7.87 L198/1. Both Articles 28 and 113 of the Treaty are the legal bases for the Council's power to conclude the International Convention on the Harmonized Commodity Description and Coding System. See Case 165/87 *Commission of the European Communities v Council of the European Communities* [1988] ECR 5545.
6 Council Regulation 2658/87 Art 1(2)(a) on the tariff and statistical nomenclature and the Common Customs Tariff, OJ 7.9.87 L256/1, as amended.
7 Ibid Art 1(2)(b).
8 Ibid Art 1(2)(c).
9 Ibid Art 3(1).
10 Ibid Art 3(1)(a).
11 Ibid Art 3(1)(b). If a heading or subheading of the harmonized system is not further subdivided for Community purposes, the seventh and eight digits are '00'. Ibid.
12 The duties expressed in columns 3 and 4 are generally *ad valorem* duties. See Rule 4 of the General Rules Concerning Duties, Section I(B) of Part 1 of Annex I to Council Regulation 2658/87 on the tariff and statistical nomenclature and the Common Customs Tariff, OJ 7.9.87 L256/1 as amended by Commission Regulation 2086/97, OJ 14.11.97 L312/1.

conventional rate of duty which is the tariff as bound by the GATT commit-ments.[13] Since the Community applies the conventional duties to both GATT and non GATT members, these are usually the only relevant duties. However, the autonomous rate applies when it is less than the conventional rate or if there is no conventional rate.[14] Nevertheless, the autonomous and conventional rates of columns 3 and 4 do not apply where special autonomous customs duties are provided for in respect of goods originating in certain countries or where pref-erential customs duties are applicable in pursuance of special agreements.[15] Column 5 establishes, if applicable, supplementary units concerning weight, volume, length, etc, with a view to the application of tariff or other measures relating to trade in goods.[16]

THE TARIC

The Commission, assisted by the Nomenclature Committee, must establish the Integrated Tariff of the European Communities (Taric) on the basis of the Com-bined Nomenclature.[17] The Taric must be used by the Commission and the Mem-ber States for the application of Community measures concerning imports and where necessary, exports and trade between Member States.[18] It also serves as a basis for the working tariffs and tariff files in the Member States. The Taric is designed to show the various rules applying to specific products when imported into the customs territory of the Community or, in some cases, when exported from it. It shows all third country and preferential duty rates applicable as well as all commercial policy measures. Hence, it incorporates the provisions of the har-monized system, the provisions of the Community's combined nomenclature and the provisions of specific Community legislation such as tariff suspensions, tariff quotas, tariff preferences, anti-dumping and countervailing measures, levies, import prohibitions, quantitative limits, export prohibitions, etc.[19]

13 The Community may subdivide column 4 in order to apply different duties in different year periods. Thus, in the CN for 1998, the conventional duties reproduced in column 4a are those that will apply from 1 January 1998 to 30 June 1998. The conventional rates of duty in column 4b are applicable from 1 July 1998. See ibid Rule 1.
14 See Rule 1 of the General Rules Concerning Duties, Section I(B) of Part 1 of Annex I to Council Regulation 2658/87 on the tariff and statistical nomenclature and the Common Customs Tariff, OJ 7.9.87 L256/1 as amended by Commission Regulation 2086/97, OJ 14.11.97 L312/1.
15 See Rule 2 of the General Rules Concerning Duties, Section I(B) of Part 1 of Annex I to Council Regulation 2658/87 on the tariff and statistical nomenclature and the Common Customs Tariff, OJ 7.9.87 L256/1 as amended by Commission Regulation 2086/97, OJ 14.11.97 L312/1.
16 Concerning the list of supplementary units see Council Regulation 2658/87 on the tariff and statistical nomenclature and the Common Customs Tariff, OJ 7.9.87 L256/1 as amended by Commission Regulation 2086/97, OJ 14.11.97 L312/1.
17 Council Regulation 2658/87 Art 2(1) on the tariff and statistical nomenclature and the Com-mon Customs Tariff, OJ 7.9.87 L256/1, as amended; see also ibid Art 6; see also Commission of the European Community *Integrated tariff of the European Communities* OJ 15.4.98 L115/1.
18 Council Regulation 2658/87 Art 5(1) on the tariff and statistical nomenclature and the Com-mon Customs Tariff, OJ 7.9.87 L256/1.
19 As to the complete list of specific Community measures to which the Taric applies see Annex II to Council Regulation 2658/87 on the tariff and statistical nomenclature and the Common Customs Tariff, OJ 7.9.87 L256/1, as amended.

The Taric is published annually.[20] The day-by-day changes in Community legislation are recorded in a data base which is continually updated. Member States are given prompt electronic notification of amendments so that they can amend their own working tariffs and tariff files accordingly. The TARIC constitutes an instrument for practical use and information but it does not have a legal status in itself. However, the use of its codes is obligatory in customs and statistical declarations in trade with third countries.[1]

The Taric code consists of eleven digits. It first incorporates the eight digits of the combined nomenclature. The ninth digit is reserved for the Member States' national statistical subdivisions. The tenth and eleventh digits refer to the Taric subheading. An additional code of usually four digits is used to identify certain Community measures such as anti-dumping and countervailing duties, references prices or export refunds.[2]

THE RULES ON THE CLASSIFICATION OF GOODS

Three factors must be taken into account to impose a tariff duty or any other Community measure on the export or import of goods. First, the good must be adequately classified in the combined nomenclature. Second, as different Community measures may apply on the basis of where the good comes from, its origin must be determined. Finally, since most duties and Community measures are applied *ad valorem*, the good must be valued.

Tariff classification governs the application of customs duties and also the application of other trade-related measures including quantitative restrictions, anti-dumping duties, preferential tariff rates, export refunds and suspension of customs duties. It is in essence a matter of factual evaluation in view of the features and properties of the goods to be classified.[3] However, as it is impossible to envisage all possible combinations of features and properties of goods in an exhaustive list of tariff classification provisions, tariff classification is not susceptible to an exhaustive regulation. Nevertheless, certain sources may provide for guidance. First, the basic rules are contained in the General Rules for the Interpretation of the Combined Nomenclature.[4] Second, as the Communi-

---

20 As to the printed version of Taric 1997 see OJ 1.4.97 C102/1; see also OJ 1.4.97 C102A/1.
  1 Council Regulation 2658/87 Art 5(2) on the tariff and statistical nomenclature and the Common Customs Tariff, OJ 7.9.87 L256/1, as amended.
  2 Thus, for example, as a result of Council Regulation 904/98, imposing definitive anti-dumping duties on imports into the Community of personal fax machines originating in the People's Republic of China, Japan, the Republic of Korea, Malaysia, Singapore, Taiwan and Thailand, OJ 30.4.98 L128/1, imports of personal fax machines from the PRC, with a Taric Code 8517 21 00 * 10, are subject to a definitive duty of 51.6% reflected in additional Taric Code 8900. Therefore code 8517 21 00 * 10 8900 should alert the customs authorities of the Member States that personal fax machines from the PRC are subject to an anti-dumping duty of 51.6%.
  3 See Paulette Vander Schueren 'Customs Classification: One of the Cornerstones of the Single European Market, but one which Cannot Be Exhaustively Regulated' 28 CML Rev 855–875 (1991).
  4 *General Rules for the Interpretation of the Combined Nomenclature*, Section I A of Part I of Annex I to Council Regulation 2658/87 on the tariff and statistical nomenclature and the Common Customs Tariff, OJ 7.9.87 L256/1 as last amended by Commission Regulation 2086/97, OJ 14.11.97 L312/1.

ty's Combined Nomenclature follows closely the International Convention on the Harmonized Commodity Description and Coding System, the explanatory notes and comments to the harmonized system of the World Customs Organization provide useful guidance.[5] Third, since agreements regarding the Common Customs Tariff have been reached between the Community and its partners in the WTO, the principles underlying those agreements may be of assistance in interpreting the rules of classification applicable to it.[6] Fourth, the section notes, chapter notes and subheading notes of the combined nomenclature can also play a very important role in the classification of goods.[7] Fifth, the Commission produces both regulations providing detailed rules concerning the classification of specified products,[8] as well as explanatory notes for the general rules of

---

5 The Harmonized System Committee of the World Customs Organization established by the International Convention on the Harmonized Commodity Description and Coding System is in charge of preparing the explanatory notes, classification, opinions or other advice as guides to the interpretation of the Harmonized System. See Art 7(2) of the International Convention on the Harmonized Commodity Description and Coding System, OJ 20.7.87 L198/3; see also ibid Art 8(2); see also World Customs Organization *Harmonized Commodity Description and Coding System: Explanatory Notes*, Brussels, WCO (1996). The European Court of Justice has consistently held that the explanatory notes of the WCO constitute an important means of ensuring the uniform application of the Common Customs Tariff by the customs authorities of the Member States and as such may be considered a valid aid to the interpretation of the tariff. Furthermore, in the absence of relevant Community provisions, the explanatory notes and the classification opinions provided by the WCO are an authoritative source for the purpose of the interpretation of the headings of the Common Customs Tariff. See Case 30/71 *Kurt Siemers & Co v Hauptzollamt Bad Reichenhall* [1971] ECR 919, paragraph 5; see also Case 77/71 *Gervais-Danone AG v Hauptzollamt Munchen-Schwanthalerstrasse* [1971] ECR 1127, paragraph 5; see also Case 14/71 *Gunther Henck v Hauptzollamt Emmerich* [1971] ECR 779, paragraph 7; see also Case 13/71 *Gunther Henck v Hauptzollamt Emmerich* [1971] ECR 767, paragraph 7; see also Case 12/71 *Gunther Henck v Hauptzollamt Emmerich* [1971] ECR 743, paragraph 7; see also Case 12/73 *Claus W Muras v Hauptzollamt Hamburg-Jonas* [1973] ECR 963, paragraph 14; see also Case 185/73 *Hauptzollamt Bielefeld v Offene Handelsgesellschaft in Firma H C Konig* [1974] ECR 607, paragraph 18; see also Case 14/70 *Deutsche Bakels GmbH v Oberfinanzdirektion Munchen* [1970] ECR 1001, paragraph 10; see also Case 35/75 *Matisa-Maschinen GmbH v Hauptzollamt Berlin-Packhof* [1975] ECR 1205, paragraph 2. However, those notes do not have legally binding force so that, where appropriate, it is necessary to consider whether their content is in accordance with the actual provisions of the Common Customs Tariff and whether they alter the meaning of such provisions. See Case C-35/93 *Develop Dr Eisbein GmbH & Co v Hauptzollamt Stuttgart-West* [1994] ECR I-2655, paragraph 18; see also Case 798/79 *Dittmeyer v Hauptzollamt Koln-Rheinau v Chem-Tec* [1980] ECR 2639; see also Case 38/75 *Douaneagent der NV Nederlandse Spoorwegen v Inspecteur der Invoerrechten en Accijnzen* [1975] ECR 1439, paragraph 24. In this sense, when the WCO interpretation of the harmonized system is not binding on the Community or if it has not given an interpretation, the Community has the power to interpret by means of regulation and subject to review by the Court of Justice, the Combined Nomenclature, as it is to be applied by the Community. Yet, when exercising that power, the Community legislator must observe the prohibition of the WCO on making changes in the chapter or section notes in a manner modifying the scope of the chapters, sections and headings. See Case C-233/88 *Gijs van de Kolk-Douane Expediteur BV v Inspecteur der Invoerrechten en Accijnzen* [1990] ECR I-265.
6 See Case 92/71 *Interfood GmbH v Hauptzollamt Hamburg-Ericus* [1972] ECR 231, paragraph 6.
7 See Case 3/71 *Gebruder Bagusat v Hauptzollamt Berlin-Packhof* [1971] ECR 577.
8 As to regulations adopted since 1990 see Commission Regulation 28/90, OJ 6.1.90 L3/9 (starch); see also Commission Regulation 48/90, OJ 11.1.90 L8/16 (electronical industry; office equipment); see also Commission Regulation 313/90, OJ 7.2.90 L35/7 (beef); see also Commission Regulation 542/90, OJ 3.3.90 L56/5 (plastics; paper; paperboard); see

also Commission Regulation 650/90, OJ 17.3.90 L71/11 (plastics; fishing products; chemicals); see also Commission Regulation 1012/90, OJ 25.4.90 L105/5 (electronical industry; office equipment); see also Commission Regulation 1422/90, OJ 30.5.90 L137/5; see also Commission Regulation 1936/90, OJ 7.7.90 L174/25 (electronical industry; office equipment); see also Commission Regulation 1964/90, OJ 11.7.90 L178/5 (electronical industry; office equipment); see also Commission Regulation 2368/90, OJ 14.8.90 L219/26 (pigmeat); see also Commission Regulation 316/91, OJ 9.2.91 L37/25; see also Commission Regulation 440/91, OJ 27.2.91 L52/7 (processed foodstuff); see also Commission Regulation 441/91, OJ 27.2.91 L 52/9 (confectionary; toy industry); see also Commission Regulation 442/91, OJ 27.2.91 L52/11 (decorative items; wood products; radio telecommunications); see also Commission Regulation 546/91, OJ 7.3.91 L60/12 (textile products); see also Commission Regulation 964/91, OJ 20.4.91 L100/14 (mushroom growing; desiccated product; protein products); see also Commission Regulation 1176/91, OJ 7.5.91 L114/27 (clothing); see also Commission Regulation 1214/91, OJ 9.5.91 L116/44 (plastics); see also Commission Regulation 1288/91, OJ 17.5.91 L122/11 (textile products); see also Commission Regulation 1796/91, OJ 25.6.91 L160/40; see also Commission Regulation 2399/91, OJ 8.8.91 L220/5 (ferrous metals; foodstuffs); see also Commission Regulation 2507/91, OJ 22.8.91 L233/9 (clothing); see also Commission Regulation 3425/91, OJ 27.11.91 L325/6 (tobacco); see also Commission Regulation 3640/91, OJ 14.12.91 L344/62 (garment); see also Commission Regulation 3694/91, OJ 19.12.91 L350/17 (clothing); see also Commission Regulation 396/92, OJ 20.2.92 L44/9 (electronic devices; commercial vehicles); see also Commission Regulation 509/92, OJ 29.2.92 L55/80 (cereal products); see also Commission Regulation 597/92, OJ 10.3.92 L64/13 (starch; chemicals); see also Commission Regulation 840/92, OJ 3.4.92 L88/29 (metal furniture); see also Commission Regulation 1035/92, OJ 28.4.92 L110/29 (tobacco; aromatic plants; medical plants); see also Commission Regulation 1340/92, OJ 27.5.92 L145/13 (chemicals); see also Commission Regulation 1533/92, OJ 16.6.92 L162/5 (animal nutrition; meat products; wood residue; milk by-products); see also Commission Regulation 1911/92, OJ 11.7.92 L192/23 (textile products; clothing; knitted and crocheted goods); see also Commission Regulation 2087/92, OJ 24.7.92 L208/24 (toy industry; wood products; publication products); see also Commission Regulation 2812/92, OJ 29.9.92 L284/10 (chemicals); see also Commission Regulation 2933/92, OJ 9.10.92 L293/8 (polymer; confectionary product); see also Commission Regulation 2949/92, OJ 13.10.92 L296/5 (clothing); see also Commission Regulation 3180/92, OJ 31.10.92 L317/64 (household electrical appliances); see also Commission Regulation 3513/92, OJ 15.12.92 L355/12 (vegetable oil; vegetable juice; sugar products); see also Commission Regulation 3801/92, OJ 30.12.92 L384/9 (footwear; sport product); see also Commission Regulation 3802/92, OJ 30.12.92 L384/13 (animal nutrition; cereal products); see also Commission Regulation 350/93, OJ 18.2.93 L41/7 (knitted and crocheted goods); see also Commission Regulation 719/93, OJ 27.3.93 L74/47 (cheese); see also Commission Regulation 731/93, OJ 30.3.93 L75/7 (marine life; traditional fishing); see also Commission Regulation 893/93, OJ 17.4.93 L93/5 (knitted and crocheted goods); see also Commission Regulation 1395/93, OJ 8.6.93 L137/7 (food technology; rice); see also Commission Regulation 1486/93, OJ 18.6.93 L 147/8 (fruit product; nut); see also Commission Regulation 1611/93, OJ 26.6.93 L155/9 (knitted and crocheted goods); see also Commission Regulation 1825/93, OJ 9.7.93 L167/8 (chemicals); see also Commission Regulation 2174/93, OJ 4.8.93 L195/20 (textile product; man-made fibre); see also Commission Regulation 2291/93, OJ 18.8.93 L206/1 (milk; processed foodstuff); see also Commission Regulation 3295/93, OJ 1.12.93 L296/43 (textile products); see also Commission Regulation 536/94, OJ 11.3.94 L68/16 (earths and stones); see also Commission Regulation 754/94, OJ 6.4.94 L89/2 (peripherals; electronic components; microelectronics; radio telecommunications); see also Commission Regulation 869/94, OJ 20.4.94 L101/1 (magnetic mediums); see also Commission Regulation 883/94, OJ 22.4.94 L103/7 (audiovisual materials; motor vehicles); see also Commission Regulation 884/94, OJ 22.4.94 L103/10 (television equipment; satellite communications; telecopy); see also Commission Regulation 1637/94, OJ 7.7.94 L172/3 (non-alcoholic beverages; sugar products); see also Commission Regulation 1638/94, OJ 7.7.94 L172/5 (medical and surgical instruments); see also Commission Regulation 1639/94, OJ 7.7.94 L172/8 (petroleum products); see also Commission Regulation1663/94, OJ 9.7.94 L176/2 (semi-metals); see also Commission Regulation 1966/94, OJ 30.7.94 L198/103 (knitted and crocheted goods); see also Commission Regulation 3056/94, OJ 16.12.94 L323/10 (milk by-products); see also Commission Regulation 3057/94, OJ 16.12.94 L323/12 (soft fruits; frozen fruits); see also Commission Regulation 3176/94, OJ 23.12.94 L335/56 (textile products); see also Commission Regulation 3272/94, OJ 29.12.94 L339/58 (metal products; data processing industry; magnetic mediums; electrical equipment); see

interpretation and the different sections, chapters, headings and subheadings.[9] Sixth, the European Court of Justice has delivered around two hundred cases providing basic principles and guidelines on tariff classification.[10]

also Commission Regulation 3330/94, OJ 31.12.94 L350/52 (poultry cuts); see also Commission Regulation 559/95, OJ 15.3.95 L57/51 (textile products); see also Commission Regulation 834/95, OJ 14.4.95 L84/1 (textile products; rubber industry); see also Commission Regulation 2564/95, OJ 1.11.95 L262/25 (discdrives; microelectronics); see also Commission Regulation 2694/95, OJ 23.11.95 L280/13 (syrups); see also Commission Regulation 2696/95, OJ 23.11.95 L280/17 (prepared foodstuffs; animal nutrition; textile products); see also Commission Regulation 2802/95, OJ 6.12.95 L291/5 (alcoholic beverages; syrups); see also Commission Regulation 2810/95, OJ 6.12.95 L 291/24 (pig carcasses); see also Commission Regulation 214/96, OJ 6.2.96 L28/8 (favouring pharmaceutical products); see also Commission Regulation 215/96, OJ 6.2.96 L28/9 (gaming; toy industry); see also Commission Regulation 241/96, OJ 9.2.96 L31/14 (contraception products); see also Commission Regulation 242/96, OJ 9.2.96 L31/16 (military equipment); see also Commission Regulation 510/96, OJ 26.3.96 L76/7 (composite materials; office supplies); see also Commission Regulation 511/96, OJ 26.3.96 L76/9 (clothing); see also Commission Regulation 617/96, OJ 5.4.96 L88/1 (musical instruments; automatic games); see also Commission Regulation 618/96, OJ 5.4.96 L88/3 (gaming); see also Commission Regulation 691/96, OJ 18.4.96 L97/13 (chemicals; pulp and paper industry substitutes to fuel); see also Commission Regulation 902/96, OJ 22.5.96 L122/1 (agricultural vehicle; spare parts); see also Commission Regulation 955/96, OJ 31.5.96 L130/1 (television equipment; spare parts); see also Commission Regulation 1307/96, OJ 6.7.96 L167/17 (electrical equipment; atmospheric pollution); see also Commission Regulation 1308/96, OJ 6.7.96 L167/19 (clothing); see also Commission Regulation 1510/96, OJ 30.7.96 L189/89 (foodstuff; gaming; confectionary products); see also Commission Regulation 1735/96, OJ 6.9.96 L225/1 (decorative items); see also Commission Regulation 2338/96, OJ 7.12.96 L318/3 (toy industry); see also Commission Regulation 2383/96, OJ 17.12.96 L326/1 (wood products); see also Commission Regulation 2494/96, OJ 28.12.96 L338/38 (thin sheet); see also Commission Regulation 4/97, OJ 7.1.97 L3/1 (dental medicine; toilet article); see also Commission Regulation 92/97, OJ 22.1.97 L19/1 (clothing; toilet article); see also Commission Regulation 286/97, OJ 19.2.97 L48/3 (milk products); see also Commission Regulation 287/97, OJ 19.2.97 L48/5 (foodstuffs; milk products); see also Commission Regulation 1054/97, OJ 12.6.97 L154/14 (textile products); see also Commission Regulation 1196/97, OJ 28.6.97 L170/13 (mushroom growing; prepared foodstuffs); see also Commission Regulation 1458/97, OJ 26.7.97 L199/11 (textile products; clothing); see also Commission Regulation 1509/97, OJ 31.7.97 L204/8 (building materials; decorative items); see also Commission Regulation 2184/97, OJ 4.11.97 L299/6 (electrical equipment; telecommunications; toy industry); see also Commission Regulation 1510/97, OJ 16.12.97 L345/45 (foodstuffs); see also Commission Regulation 201/98, OJ 28.1.98 L21/3 (pharmaceutical products); see also Commission Regulation 823/98, OJ 12.4.98 L117/2 (carcasses of ovine animals). These regulations on the classification of certain products are of legislative nature and cannot have retroactive effect. See Case 30/71 *Kurt Siemers & Co v Hauptzollamt Bad Reichenhall* [1971] ECR 919, paragraph 8; see also Case 77/71 *Gervais-Danone AG v Hauptzollamt Munchen-Schwanthalerstrase* [1971] ECR 1127, paragraph 8; see also Case 158/78 *P Biegi v Hauptzollamt Bochum* [1979] ECR 1103, paragraph 11. Furthermore, such regulations may not amend the combined nomenclature. See Case C-80/96 *Quelle Schickedanz AG und Co v Oberfinanzdirektion Frankfurt am Main* [1998] ECR I-123.

9 See Commission of the European Communities *Explanatory Notes to the Combined Nomenclature of the European Communities*, OJ 5.12.94 C342/1. The explanatory notes drawn up by the Commission may be an important aid to the interpretation of the scope of the various tariff headings but they do not have legally binding force. See Case C-143/97 *Leonhard Knubben Speditions GmbH v Hauptzollamt Mannheim* (1997) Transcript, 9 December, paragraph 14.

10 For a thorough analysis of the Court's case law on the classification of goods See Edwin A Vermulst, 'EC Customs Classification Rules: Should Ice Cream Melt?' 15 Michigan J Int'l L 1241–1327 (1994).

THE GENERAL RULES FOR THE INTERPRETATION OF THE COMBINED NOMENCLATURE

Following the International Convention on the Harmonized Commodity Description and Coding System, the Community's Combined Nomenclature lays down six basic rules for its interpretation.[11]

(1)   *The titles of sections, chapters and sub-chapters are provided for ease of reference only; for legal purposes, classification shall be determined according to the terms of the headings and any relative section or chapter notes and, provided such headings or notes do not otherwise require, according to the following provisions.*

For the interpretation of the nomenclature of the Common Customs Tariff, the titles of sections, chapters and subchapters are provided for ease of reference only, and classification is to be determined according to the terms of the headings and any relevant section or chapter notes.[12] The expression 'provided such headings or notes do not otherwise require' is intended to make clear that the terms of the headings and any relative section of chapter notes are the first consideration of determining classification.[13] Only if such terms do not provide sufficient guidance, reference may be sought in the provisions of rules 2, 3, 4, 5 and 6.

In the interests of legal certainty and ease of verification, the decisive criterion for the classification of goods is in general to be sought in their objective characteristics and properties as defined in the wordings of the relevant headings of the Common Customs tariff and of the notes to the sections or chapters.[14] The objective characteristics and properties must be defined in the wording of the headings and notes to the sections or chapters of the Combined Nomenclature and not in other Community legislation which may classify and define the goods for purposes other than classification.[15] Such objective characteristics

---

11 *General Rules for the Interpretation of the Combined Nomenclature*, Section I A of Part I of Annex I to Council Regulation 2658/87 on the tariff and statistical nomenclature and the Common Customs Tariff, OJ 7.9.87 L256/1 as last amended by Commission Regulation 2086/97, OJ 14.11.97 L312/1.

12 See Case C-1/89 *Ingrid Raab v Hauptzollamt Berlin-Packhof* [1989] ECR I-4423.

13 *See Explanatory Note V to Rule 1* in World Customs Organization *Harmonized Commodity Description and Coding System: Explanatory Notes*, Brussels, WCO (1996).

14 See Case 53/75 *Belgian State v Jean Nicolas Vandertaelen and Dirk Leopold Maes* [1975] ECR 1647; see also Case 62/77 *Carlsen Verlag GmbH v Oberfinanzdirektion Koln* [1977] ECR 2343; see also Joined Cases C-106/94 & C-139/94 *Criminal Proceedings against Patrick Colin and Daniel Dupre* [1996] ECR I-4759, paragraph 22; see also Case C-459/93 *Hauptzollamt Hamburg-St Annen v Thyssen Haniel Logistic GmbH* [1995] ECR I-1381; see also Case 40/80 *Paul F Weber v Milchwerke Paderborn-Rimbeck eG* [1989] ECR 1395; see also Case 145/81 *Hauptzollamt Hamburg-Jonas v Ludwig Wunsche & Co* [1982] ECR 2493, paragraph 9; see also Case 185/73 *Hauptzollamt Bielefeld v Offene Handelsgesellschaft in Firma H C Konig* [1974] ECR 607, paragraph 18; see also Case C-67/95 *Rank Xerox Manufacturing (Netherland) BV v Inspecteur der Invoerrechten en Accijnzen* (1997) Transcript, 9 October, paragraph 17; see also Case C-105/96 *Codisel-Sociedad de Apoio Tecnico a Industria Lda v Conselho Tecnico Aduaneiro* (1997) Transcript, 17 June, paragraph 17; see also Case C-143/97, *Leonhard Knubben Speditions GmbH v Hauptzollamt Mannheim* (1997) Transcript, 9 December, para-graph 14.

15 See Case C-270/96 *Laboratoires Sarget SA v Fonds d'Intervention et de Regulation du Marche du Sucre* [1998] 2 CMLR 1285; see also Case C-201/96 *Laboratoires de Therapeutique Modern (LTM) v Fonds d'Intervention et de Regularisation du Marche du Sucre (FIRS)* (1997) Transcript, 6 November.

and properties must be present at the time of the presentation of the goods for customs clearance.[16] The Court's most commonly used objective factor for the classification of goods is the physical characteristics of the goods, particularly their composition.[17]

The Court has consistently held the predominance for classification purposes of objective criteria over all subjective criteria unless specified in the terms of the headings or in the chapter or section notes.[18] Moreover, the classification for customs purposes of a product cannot be altered by the fact that it has undergone processing if the processed product thereafter contains the essential constituents of the basic product in proportions which do not differ substantially from the content in those constituents which the relevant product exhibits in its natural state. That condition will not be fulfilled if the product contains a substance not found in the product in its natural state in a proportion greater than it is necessary to make the product more like the product in its natural state.[19]

However, the Court will take account of more subjective factors such as flavour,[20] manufacturing process,[1] intended use,[2] or visibility to the naked eye,[3] where the terms of the headings, section or chapter notes expressly require so.

---

16 See Case 175/82 *Hans Dinter GmbH v Hauptzollamt Koln-Deutz* [1983] ECR 969, paragraph 10.

17 See Case 12/73 *Claus W Muras v Hauptzollamt Hamburg-Jonas* [1973] ECR 963; see also Case 158/78 *P Biegi v Hauptzollamt Bochum* [1979] ECR 1103; see also Case C-274/95, C-275/95 & 276/95 *Ludwig Wunsche & Co v Hauptzollamt Hamburg-Jonas* [1997] ECR I-2091, paragraph 15; see also Case C-384/89 *Ministere Public v Gerard Tomatis and Christian Fulchiron* [1991] ECR I-127; see also Joined Cases C-106/94 & C-139/94 *Criminal Proceedings against Patrick Colin and Daniel Dupre* [1996] ECR I-4759.

18 See Case 28/70 *Kommanditgesellschaft in Firma Otto Witt v Hauptzollamt Luneburg* [1970] ECR 1021; see also Case 40/80 *Paul F Weber v Milchwerke Paderborn-Rimbeck eG* [1989] ECR 1395; see also Case C-228/89 *Farfalla Flemming und Partner v Hauptzollamt Munchen-West* [1990] ECR I-3387, paragraph 8; see also Case 222/85 *Hauptzollamt Osnabruck v Kleiderwerke Hela Lampe GmbH & Co KG* [1986] ECR 2449, paragraph 15; see also Case C-1/89 *Ingrid Raab v Hauptzollamt Berlin-Packhof* [1989] ECR I-4423, paragraph 25; see also Case C-35/93 *Develop Dr Eisbein GmbH & Co v Hauptzollamt Stuttgart-West* [1994] ECR I-2655, paragraph 18.

19 See Case 40/80 *Paul F Weber v Milchwerke Paderborn-Rimbeck eG* [1989] ECR 1395; see also Case 164/88 *Ministere Public v J P Rispal* [1989] ECR 2041.

20 See Case 30/71 *Kurt Siemers & Co v Hauptzollamt Bad Reichenhall* [1971] ECR 919, paragraph 7; see also Case 77/71 *Gervais-Danone AG v Hauptzollamt Munchen-Schwanthalerstrasse* [1971] ECR 1127, paragraph 7; see also Case 185/73 *Hauptzollamt Bielefeld v Offene Handelsgesellschaft in Firma H C Konig* [1974] ECR 607, paragraph 19.

1 See Case C-248/92 *Jepsen Stahl GmbH v Hauptzollamt Emmerich* [1993] ECR I-4721, paragraph 10; see also Case 128/73 *Past & Co KG v Hauptzollamt Freiburg* [1973] ECR 1277; see also Case C-377/92 *Felix Koch Offenbach Couleur und Karamel GmbH v Oberfinanzdirektion Munchen* [1993] ECR I-4795; see also Case C-143/97 *Leonhard Knubben Speditions GmbH v Hauptzollamt Mannheim* (1997) Transcript, 9 December, paragraphs 16–20.

2 See Case 38/72 *Arend van de Poll KG v Hauptzollamt Trier* [1972] ECR 1329; see also Case 19/88 *International Container et Transport (ICT) and BFI Electronique SA v Direction Generale des Douanes et Droits Indirects de Roissy* [1989] ECR 577; see also Case C-382/95 *Techex Computer & Grafik Vertriebs GmbH v Hauptzollamt Munchen* (1997) Transcript, 18 December; see also Case C-270/96 *Laboratoires Sarget SA v Fonds d'Intervention et de Regularisation du Marche du Sucre* [1998] 2 CMLR 1285; see also Case C-201/96 *Laboratoires de Therapeutique Modern (LTM) v Fonds d'Intervention et de Regularisation du Marche du Sucre (FIRS)* (1997) Transcript, 6 November, paragraph 29; see also Case C-338/95 *Wiener SI GmbH v Hauptzollamt Emmerich* [1998] 1 CMLR 1110.

3 See Case 317/81 *Howe & Brainbridge BV v Oberfinanzdirektion Frankfurt am Main* [1982] ECR 3257.

The interpretation of a tariff heading must in doubtful cases take into consideration both the function of the Customs Tariff in view of the needs of the system of organization of the markets and its purely customs function.[4] In the absence of an express provision it would be inappropriate for the headings of the Common Customs Tariff to be applied differently for one and the same product depending on whether the classification is for the imposition of customs duties, the application of the rules of common organization of the market or the system of monetary compensatory amounts.[5] However, the same principles of classification need not necessarily apply for classification of goods for the purposes of customs duties and for the purposes of imposing agriculture measures.[6]

If a heading or chapter provides for duty free or preferential treatment, it is important to look at its intent as a factor for the classification of goods within that heading.[7]

Failing any amendments of the Common Customs Tariff by the Community institutions, the interpretation of the tariff cannot vary as and when technology changes.[8]

(2)   (a) *Any reference in a heading to an article shall be taken to include a reference to that article incomplete or unfinished, provided that, as presented, the incomplete or unfinished article has the essential character of the complete or finished article. It shall also be taken to include a reference to that article complete or finished (or failing to be classified as complete or finished by virtue of this rule), presented unassembled or disassembled.*

Rule 2(a) applies to both incomplete or unfinished articles and unassembled or disassembled products.

A reference in a heading to an article must be taken to include a reference to that article incomplete or unfinished. As the uncomplete or unfinished product must have the essential character of the complete or finished product, it is necessary to define what are the essential characteristics of the finished product.[9] The provisions of this Rule also apply to articles not ready for direct use, having the approximate shape or outline of the finished article or part, and which can only be used other than in exceptional cases, for completion

---

4 See Case 14/71 *Gunther Henck v Hauptzollamt Emmerich* [1971] ECR 779; see also Case 12/71 *Gunther Henck v Hauptzollamt Emmerich* [1971] ECR 743; paragraph 9; see also Case 72/69 *Hauptzollamt Bremen-Freihafen v Bremer Handelsgesellschaft* [1970] ECR 427; see also Case 74/69 *Hauptzollamt Bremen- Freihafen v Waren-Import-Gesellschaft Krohn and Co* [1970] ECR 451, paragraph 15.

5 See Case 158/78 *P Biegi v Hauptzollamt Bochum* [1979] ECR 1103, paragraph 18; see also Case 5/78 *Milchfutter GmbH & Co KG v Hauptzollamt Gronau* [1978] ECR 1597.

6 See Case 92/71 *Interfood GmbH v Hauptzollamt Hamburg-Ericus* [1972] ECR 231, paragraph 5.

7 See Case 291/87 *Volker Huber v Hauptzollamt Frankfurt am Main-Flughafen* [1988] ECR 6449, paragraph 16 (where the Court analyzes the intent of a Chapter providing for duty free); see also Case 47/82 *Gebroeders Vismans BV v Inspecteur der Invoerrechten en Accijnzen, Rotterdam* [1982] ECR 3983, paragraph 7 (where the Court takes into account the intent of a GSP provision providing for duty free in order to determine the classification of the goods).

8 See Case C-67/95 *Rank Xerox Manufacturing (Netherland) BV v Inspecteur der Invoerrechten en Accijnzen* (1997) Transcript, 9 October, paragraph 22; see also Case 234/87 *Casio Computer Co GmbH Deutchland v Oberfinanzdirektion Munchen* [1989] ECR 63, paragraph 12.

9 See Case C-66/89 *Directeur General des Douanes et des Droits Indirects v Powerex-Europe* [1990] ECR I-1959, paragraphs 9–10.

into the finished article or part—blanks—unless these are specified in a particular heading.[10]

A reference in a heading to an article must be taken to include that article complete or finished presented unassembled or disassembled. This Rule also applies to incomplete or unfinished articles presented unassembled or disassembled provided that they can be treated as complete or finished.[11] The concept of assembly means the operation whereby the components of a mechanism, device or a complex object are assembled in order to render it serviceable or to make it function. The essential requirement is therefore, on the one hand, that the disassembled product must not be usable for the purposes expected of the finished product and, on the other hand, that the component parts of the products must normally, in order to be of use, be assembled so as to constitute the finished product.[12] An article is to be considered to be imported unassembled or disassembled where the component parts, that is the parts which may be identified as components intended to make up the finished product, are all presented for customs clearance at the same time and no account is to be taken of the assembly technique or the assembly method.[13] Unassembled components of an article which are in excess of the number required for that article when complete must be classified separately.[14]

(2)   (b) *Any reference in a heading to a material or substance shall be taken to include a reference to mixtures or combinations of that material or substance with other materials or substances. Any reference to goods of a given material or substance shall be taken to include a reference to the goods consisting wholly or partly of such material or substance. The classification of goods consisting of more than one material or substance shall be according to the principles of rule 3.*

Rule 2(b) deals with the classification of certain mixtures or substances and goods made wholly or in part of a certain substance.[15] It applies only if the headings or the section or chapter notes do not require otherwise. Mixtures being preparations described as such in a section or chapter note or in a heading text must be classified under the provisions of Rule 1.[16]

Any reference in a heading to a material or substance is extended to include mixtures or combinations of that material or substance with other materials or substances. Furthermore, any heading referring to a material or substance is extended to include goods consisting partly of that material or substance. The headings to which this Rule refers are headings in which there is a reference to

---

10 Semi-manufactures not yet having the essential shape of the finished articles (such as is generally the case with bars, discs, tubes, etc) are not to be regarded as blanks. *Explanatory Note II to Rule 2* in World Customs Organization *Harmonized Commodity Description and Coding System: Explanatory Notes*, Brussels, WCO (1996).
11 See *Explanatory Note VI to Rule 2* in World Customs Organization *Harmonized Commodity Description and Coding System: Explanatory Notes*, Brussels, WCO (1996).
12 Case 295/81 *International Flavours and Fragrances IFF (Deutschland) GmbH v Hauptzollamt Bad Reichenhall* [1982] ECR 3239, paragraphs 10–11.
13 See Case C-35/93 *Develop Dr Eisbein GmbH & Co v Hauptzollamt Stuttgart-West* [1994] ECR I-2655, paragraph 17.
14 See *Explanatory Note VII to Rule 2* in World Customs Organization *Harmonized Commodity Description and Coding System: Explanatory Notes*, Brussels, WCO (1996).
15 See Case 234/81 *E I Du Pont de Nemours Inc and Dewfield v Customs and Excise Comrs* [1982] ECR 3515.
16 See *Explanatory Note X to Rule 2* in World Customs Organization *Harmonized Commodity Description and Coding System: Explanatory Notes*, Brussels, WCO (1996).

a material or substance and headings in which there is a reference to goods of a given material or substance.[17] This Rule, however, does not widen the heading so as to cover goods which cannot be regarded, as required under Rule 1, as answering the description in the headings.[18]

The classification of goods consisting of more than one material or substance if prima facie classifiable under two or more headings must be done according to Rule 3.

(3)   *When by application of rule 2(b) or for any other reason, goods are prima facie classifiable under two or more headings, classification shall be affected as follows.*

This Rule provides three methods—specific description, essential character and heading which occurs last in numerical order—of classifying goods which, prima facie, fall under two or more headings, either under the terms of Rule 2(b) or for any other reason.[19] The Court has consistently held that Rule 3 can only apply provided the terms of headings or section or chapter notes do not otherwise require.[20] The methods laid down in Rule 3(a), Rule 3(b) and Rule 3(c) must be applied in the order in which they are set out in the rule.[1]

(3)   (a) *The heading which provides the most specific description shall be preferred to headings providing a more general description. However, when two or more headings each refer to part only of the materials or substances contained in mixed or composite goods or to part only of the items in a set put up for retail sale, those headings are to be regarded as equally specific in relation to those goods, even if one of them gives a more complete or precise description of the goods.*

Where goods are prima facie classifiable under two or more headings, the heading which provides the most specific description is to be preferred to the headings providing a more general description.[2] A description by name is more specific than a description by class.[3] Similarly if the goods answer to a description which more clearly identifies them, that description is more specific than one where identification is less complete.[4] Where a mixture, composite good or goods put up for retail sale is, prima facie, classifiable under two or more headings of the Common Customs Tariff, each of which relates to one of the materials composing the mixture, composite good or goods set up for retail

---

17 See *Explanatory Note X to Rule 2* in World Customs Organization *Harmonized Commodity Description and Coding System: Explanatory Notes*, Brussels, WCO (1996).

18 This occurs where the addition of another material or substance deprives the goods of the character of goods of the kind mentioned in the heading. See *Explanatory Note XII to Rule 2* in World Customs Organization *Harmonized Commodity Description and Coding System: Explanatory Notes*, Brussels, WCO (1996).

19 See *Explanatory Note I to Rule 3* in World Customs Organization *Harmonized Commodity Description and Coding System: Explanatory Notes*, Brussels, WCO (1996).

20 See Case 137/78 *Henningsen Food Inc v Produkschap voor Pluimvee en Eieren* [1979] ECR 1707, paragraph 8.

 1 See Case 28/75 *Baupla GmbH v Oberfinanzdirektion Koln* [1975] ECR 989, paragraph 4.

 2 See Case C-164/95 *Fabrica de Queijo Eru Portuguesa Lda v Alfandenga de Lisboa* [1997] ECR I-3441.

 3 *See Explanatory Note IV (a) to Rule 3* in World Customs Organization *Harmonized Commodity Description and Coding System: Explanatory Notes*, Brussels, WCO (1996).

 4 An example could be tufted textiles carpets, identified for use in motor cars, which are to be classified not as accessories of motor cars in heading 87.08 but in heading 57.03, where they are more specifically described as carpets. Ibid.

sale, none of the headings can be regarded as more specific than the others on the sole ground that it gives a more precise or more complete description of the product referred to.[5] Furthermore, Rule 3(a) is excluded when the relevant tariff headings fall within different chapters.[6]

(3) (b) *Mixtures, composite goods consisting of different materials or made up of different components, and goods put up in sets for retail sale, which cannot be classified by reference to 3(a) shall be classified as if they consisted of the material or component which gives them their essential character in so far as this criterion is applicable.*

Rule 3(b) applies only where the goods are prima facie classifiable under two or more headings and no specific heading takes precedence over more general headings.[7] It applies to mixtures, composite goods consisting of different materials or made up of different components and goods put up in sets for retail sale.

The expression composite goods includes not only those in which the components are attached to each other to form a practically inseparable whole but also those goods with separable components, provided those components are adapted one to the other and are mutually complementary and that together they form a whole which it would be difficult to sell in different parts.[8]

The expression 'goods set up in sets' is to be interpreted as goods which consist of products or articles having independent or complementary uses, grouped together for meeting a need of carrying out a specific activity and which are set up in retail packings.[9] It implies that the goods are closely linked from the marketing point of view, with the result that they are not only presented together for customs clearance but are also normally supplied together, at the various marketing stages and in particular the retail stage, in a single package in order to satisfy a demand or to perform a specific function.[10] They must consist of at least two different articles which are prima facie, classifiable in different headings, put up together to meet a particular need or carry out a specific activity, and put up in a suitable manner for sale directly to users without repacking.[11]

Under Rule 3(b) classification of goods must be done on the basis of the component which gives them their essential character.[12] This may be done by determining whether the product would retain its characteristic properties if

---

5 See Case 28/75 *Baupla GmbH v Oberfinanzdirektion Koln* [1975] ECR 989, paragraph 7.
6 See Case C-67/95 *Rank Xerox Manufacturing (Netherland) BV v Inspecteur der Invoerrechten en Accijnzen* (1997) Transcript, 9 October, paragraph 30.
7 See Case 163/84 *Hauptzollamt Hannover v Telefunken Fernseh und Rundfunk GmbH* [1985] ECR 3299, paragraph 36.
8 See *Explanatory Note IX to Rule 3* in World Customs Organization *Harmonized Commodity Description and Coding System: Explanatory Notes*, Brussels, WCO (1996); see also Case C-105/96 *Codisel Sociedad de Apoio Tecnico a Industria Lda v Conselho Tecnico Aduaneiro* (1997) Transcript, 17 June, paragraph 23.
9 See Case 60/83 *Metro International Kommanditgesellschaft v Oberfinanzdirektion Munchen* [1984] ECR 671, paragraph 13.
10 See Case 163/84 *Hauptzollamt Hannover v Telefunken Fernseh und Rundfunk GmbH* [1985] ECR 3299, paragraph 35.
11 The term therefore covers sets consisting, for example, of different foodstuffs intended to be used together in the preparation of a ready-to-eat dish or meal. See *Explanatory Note X to Rule 3* in World Customs Organization *Harmonized Commodity Description and Coding System: Explanatory Notes*, Brussels, WCO (1996).
12 See Case 60/83 *Metro International Kommanditgesellschaft v Oberfinanzdirektion Munchen* [1984] ECR 671, paragraph 14.

one or other of its constituents were removed from it.[13] The factor which determines the essential character will vary as between different kinds of goods.[14] The essential character of the product may be established inter alia by the nature of the material or component, its bulk, quantity, weight, value or function.[15]

With regard to Rule 3(b) the Court has used the functional unit principle. The functional unit principle is intended to allow classification under a given heading of machines and appliances made up of components falling under several tariff headings, in cases where those components as a whole are intended to perform the single clearly defined function referred to in the tariff heading in question. The principle does not apply where some of the components making up a product may be used independently of the other components and for functions other than those which may be performed by all the components together.[16]

Rule 3(b) is excluded when the articles in question display no feature enabling their essential character to be determined.[17] It is also excluded where the characteristic property of the mixtures, composite goods or goods put up in sets for retail sale would be removed if either of its components were removed.[18] Moreover, Rule 3(b) does not apply to goods consisting of separately packed constituents put up together, whether or not in a common packing, in fixed proportions for the industrial manufacture of, for example, beverages.[19]

(3)   (c) *When goods cannot be classified by reference to 3(a) or (b), they shall be classified under the heading which occurs last in numerical order among those which equally merit consideration.*

Under Rule 3(c), articles must be classified under the heading which occurs last in numerical order amongst those which equally merit consideration in determining their classification.[20]

(4)   *Goods which cannot be classified in accordance with the above rules shall be classified under the heading appropriate to the goods to which they are most akin.*

This Rule relates to goods which cannot be classified in accordance with Rules 1 to 3. Under this Rule, it is necessary to compare the presented goods

---

13 See Case 253/87 *Sportex GmbH & Co v Oberfinanzdirektion Hamburg* [1988] ECR 3351, paragraph 8; see also Joined Cases C-153/88 to C-157/88 *Ministere Public v Gerard Fauque* [1990] ECR I-649, paragraph 11.

14 See *Explanatory Note VII to Rule 3* in World Customs Organization, *Harmonized Commodity Description and Coding System: Explanatory Notes*, Brussels, WCO (1996).

15 See Case C-105/96 *Codisel Sociedad de Apoio Tecnico a Industria Lda v Conselho Tecnico Aduaneiro* (1997) Transcript, 17 June, paragraph 24; see also Case 130/82 *Naamloze vennoostschap Farr Co v Belgium* [1983] ECR 327, paragraph 5.

16 See Case 163/84 *Hauptzollamt Hannover v Telefunken Fernseh und Rundfunk GmbH* [1985] ECR 3299, paragraphs 33–34; see also Case 60/83 *Metro International Kommanditgesellschaft v Oberfinanzdirektion Munchen* [1984] ECR 671, paragraph 9.

17 See Case C-67/95 *Rank Xerox Manufacturing (Netherland) BV v Inspecteur der Invoerrechten en Accijnzen* (1997) Transcript, 9 October, paragraph 30.

18 See Case C-80/96 *Quelle Schickedanz AG und Co v Oberfinanzdirektion Frankfurt am Main* [1998] ECR I-123.

19 See *Explanatory Note XI to Rule 3* in World Customs Organization *Harmonized Commodity Description and Coding System: Explanatory Notes*, Brussels, WCO (1996).

20 See Case C-67/95 *Rank Xerox Manufacturing (Netherland) BV v Inspecteur der Invoerrechten en Accijnzen* (1997) Transcript, 9 October, paragraph 31.

with similar goods in order to determine the goods to which the presented are most akin. The presented goods are classified in the same heading as the similar goods to which they are most akin.[1] Such kinship can depend on many factors, such as description, character and purpose. The Court has held that the question whether goods are akin one to another is to be decided on the basis not only of their physical characteristics but also of their use and commercial value. In this sense, in the absence of special circumstances the commercial value of goods is normally their market price.[2]

(5)   *In addition to the foregoing provisions, the following rules shall apply in respect of the goods referred to therein.*

(5)   (a) *Camera cases, musical instrument cases, gun cases, drawing instrument cases, necklace cases and similar containers, specially shaped or fitted to contain a specific article or set of articles, suitable for long term use and presented with the articles for which they are intended, shall be classified with such articles when of a kind normally sold therewith. This rule does not, however, apply to containers which give the whole its essential character.*

Rule 5(a) applies only to those containers which (1) are specially shaped or fitted to contain a specific article or set of articles; (2) are suitable for long term use; (3) are presented with the articles for which they are intended, whether or not the articles are packed separately for convenience or transport; (4) are of a kind normally sold with such articles; and (5) do not give the whole its essential character.[3]

(5)   (b) *Subject to the provisions of Rule 5(a), packing materials and packing containers presented with the goods therein shall be classified with the goods if they are of a kind normally used for packing such goods. However, this provision is not binding when such packing materials or packing containers are clearly suitable for repetitive use.*

In this sense, the terms 'packing materials' and 'packing containers' mean any external or internal containers, holders, wrappings or supports other than transport devices (eg transport containers), tarpaulins, tackle or ancillary transport equipment.[4] They include beverage barrels, bottle and plastic crates for the bottles even where these articles are to be returned to the seller of the beverage in another country.[5] Furthermore, the term 'packing containers' does not cover the containers referred to in general rule 5(a).[6] Packing containers normally used for marketing beverages, jam, spices, etc, are to be classified with the goods they contain even if clearly suitable for repetitive use.[7]

---

1 See *Explanatory Note II to Rule 4* in World Customs Organization *Harmonized Commodity Description and Coding System: Explanatory Notes*, Brussels, WCO (1996).
2 See Case 40/69 *Hauptzollamt Hamburg-Oberelbe v Firma Paul G Bollmann* [1970] ECR 69.
3 See *Explanatory Note I to Rule 5* in World Customs Organization *Harmonized Commodity Description and Coding System: Explanatory Notes*, Brussels, WCO (1996).
4 Footnote to Rule 5(b) of the *General Rules for the Interpretation of the Combined Nomenclature*, Section I A of Part I of Annex I to Council Regulation 2658/87 on the tariff and statistical nomenclature and the Common Customs Tariff, OJ 7.9.87 L256/1 as last amended by Commission Regulation 2086/97, OJ 14.11.97 L312/1.
5 See Case 357/87 *Firma Albert Schmid v Hauptzollamt Stuttgart-West* [1988] ECR 6239.
6 Footnote to ibid Rule 5(b).
7 See Commission of the European Communities *Explanatory Notes to the Combined Nomenclature of the European Communities* OJ 5.12.94 C342/1, 9.

(6)   *For legal purposes, the classification of goods in the subheadings of a heading shall be determined according to terms of those subheadings and any related subheading notes and mutatis mutandis to the above rules, on the understanding that only subheadings at the same level are comparable. For the purpose of this rule the relative section and chapter notes also apply, unless the context otherwise requires.*

Classification must be done on the understanding that only subheadings, chapter and section notes at the same level are comparable.[8]

BINDING INFORMATION

The Community provides for an advance ruling procedure for importers and exporters with respect to tariff classification and origin of goods. The Member States' customs authorities must, upon written request, issue binding tariff information or binding origin information which will be binding on the administration of all Community Member States.[9] The aim of the binding information is to enable the trader to proceed with certainty where there are doubts as to the classification or origin of goods, thereby protecting him against any subsequent change in the position adopted by the customs authorities.[10]

Applications for binding information must be made in writing either to the competent customs authorities in the Member State or Member States in which the information is to be used, or to the competent authorities in the Member State in which the applicant is established.[11] An application for binding tariff information must relate to only one type of goods.[12] An application for binding origin information must relate to only one type of goods and one set of circumstances conferring origin.[13] A request for binding information may be refused where it does not relate to an import or export operation actually envisaged.[14] However, if the customs authorities consider that the application does not contain all the particulars required to give an informed opinion, they must ask the applicant to supply the missing information before rejecting the application.[15]

The binding information must be notified to the applicant as soon as

---

8 See Case C-164/95 *Fabrica de Queijo Eru Portuguesa Lda v Alfandenga de Lisboa* [1997] ECR I-3441.

9 Council Regulation 2913/92 Art 12 (1), OJ 19.10.92 L 253/1, as amended by Regulation 82/97 of the European Parliament and of the Council, OJ 21.1.97 L17/1; see also ibid Art 12(2); See also Commission Regulation 2454/93 Art 5(1), OJ 11.10.93 L335/1, as amended by Commission Regulation 12/97, OJ 13.1.97 L9/1. However, only binding tariff information supplied by the customs authorities of a Member State since 1 January 1991 will be binding on a Community wide basis. See ibid Art 11.

10 See Case C-315/96 *Lopex Export GmbH v Hauptzollamt Hamburg-Jonas* [1998] ECR I-317.

11 Commission Regulation 2454/93 Art 6(1), OJ 11.10.93 L335/1, as amended by Commission Regulation 12/97, OJ 13.1.97 L9/1. The list of customs authorities designated by the Member States to receive application for or to issue binding information must be published in the 'C' series of the Official Journal of the European Communities. See ibid Art 6(5).

12 Ibid Art 6(2). As to the particulars which an application for binding tariff information must contain. See ibid Art 6(3)(A).

13 Ibid Art 6(2). Concerning the particulars which an application for binding origin information must include. See ibid Art 6(3)(B).

14 Council Regulation 2913/92 Art 11(1), OJ 19.10.92 L 253/1.

15 Commission Regulation 2454/93 Art 6(4), OJ 11.10.93 L335/1, as amended by Commission Regulation 12/97, OJ 13.1.97 L9/1.

possible.[16] Where it has not been possible to notify the tariff binding information to the applicant within three months of the acceptance of the application, the customs authorities must contact the applicant and explain the reason for the delay and indicate the expected day of notification.[17] In the case of origin of goods, the information must be provided within a time limit of 150 days from the date of acceptance of the application.[18] Applicants may appeal against the advance ruling.[19] A copy of the binding information and the facts must be transmitted to the Commission without delay by the customs authorities of the Member States concerned.[20] This will allow the Community institutions and Member States to avoid any inconsistencies in binding information on a Community wide basis.[1]

The binding information may be invoked only by the holder, or its representative, of such information.[2] The information will be binding only in respect of goods on which customs formalities are completed after the date on which the information was supplied by them.[3] The holder of the binding tariff information may use it in respect of particular goods only where it is established to the satisfaction of the customs authorities that the goods in question conform in all respects to those described in the information presented in the tariff binding information.[4] In the case of origin of goods, the authorities must be satisfied that the goods in question and the circumstances determining their origin conform in all respects to those described in the information presented.[5]

The binding information will be valid for a period of six years in the case of tariff classification and three years in the case of origin from the date of issue.[6] However, a ruling may be annulled where the customs authorities determine that it is based on inaccurate or incomplete information from the applicant.[7]

---

16 Ibid Art 7(1).

17 Ibid Art 7(1)(a).

18 Ibid Art 7(1)(b). The binding tariff and binding origin information will be notified by means of a form conforming to the specimens shown in Annex 1 and Annex 1A to Commission Regulation 2454/93, OJ 11.10.93 L335/1, as amended by Commission Regulation 12/97, OJ 13.1.97 L9/1. See ibid Art 7(2).

19 As to the procedure for such appeal see Council Regulation 2913/92, OJ 19.10.92 L 253/1 Art 243.

20 Commission Regulation 2454/93 Art 8(1), OJ 11.10.93 L335/1, as amended by Commission Regulation 12/97, OJ 13.1.97 L9/1. Conversely, where a Member State so requests, the Commission must send the particulars contained in the copy of the form and the other relevant information. See ibid Art 8(2).

1 As to the procedure applying in the even of inconsistencies in binding information provided by different Member States see ibid Art 9.

2 Ibid Art 10(1). The holder need not necessarily be the applicant. See ibid Art 5.

3 Council Regulation 2913/92 Art 12(2), OJ 19.10.92 L 253/1, as amended by Regulation 82/97 of the European Parliament and of the Council, OJ 21.1.97 L/17/1. The authorities may require the holder, when fulfilling customs formalities, to inform them that it is in possession of binding tariff or binding origin information. See Commission Regulation 2454/93 Art 10(2), OJ 11.10.93 L335/1, as amended by Commission Regulation 12/97, OJ 13.1.97 L9/1.

4 Council Regulation 2913/92 Art 12(3), OJ 19.10.92 L 253/1, as amended by Regulation 82/97 of the European Parliament and of the Council, OJ 21.1.97 L/17/1; see also Commission Regulation 2454/93 Art 10(3)(a), OJ 11.10.93 L335/1, as amended by Commission Regulation 12/97, OJ 13.1.97 L9/1.

5 Council Regulation 2913/92 Art 12(3), OJ 19.10.92 L 253/1, as amended by Regulation 82/97 of the European Parliament and of the Council, OJ 21.1.97 L/17/1; see also Commission Regulation 2454/93 Art 10(3)(b), OJ 11.10.93 L335/1, as amended by Commission Regulation 12/97, OJ 13.1.97 L9/1.

6 Council Regulation 2913/92 Art 12(4), OJ 19.10.92 L 253/1, as amended by Regulation 82/97 of the European Parliament and of the Council, OJ 21.1.97 L/17/1.

7 Ibid.

Furthermore, the binding tariff information will cease to be valid, in the case of tariff information, where a regulation is adopted and the information no longer conforms to the law laid down thereby;[8] where it is no longer compatible with the interpretation of the nomenclatures at the Community level by reason of an amendment to the explanatory notes to the combined nomenclature or by a judgment of the Court, or at the international level, by reason of a classification opinion or an amendment of the explanatory notes of the Harmonized System adopted by the World Customs Organization;[9] where it is revoked or amended because the conditions of the information are no longer met.[10] In the case of origin of goods the binding information will cease to be valid where a regulation is adopted or an agreement is concluded by the Community and the information no longer conforms to the law thereby laid down;[11] where it is no longer compatible with, at Community level, the explanatory notes and opinions adopted for the purposes of interpreting the rules or with a judgment of the Court, or at international level, the Agreement on Rules of Origin established in the WTO or with the explanatory notes or an origin opinion adopted for the interpretation of that Agreement;[12] where it is revoked or amended because its conditions are no longer fulfilled.[13]

However, the holder of binding information which ceases to be valid for reasons other than a revocation or amendment because the conditions are no longer met, may still use that information for a period of six months from the date of publication or notification, provided that it concluded binding contracts for the purchase or sale of the goods in question on the basis of binding information, before that measure was adopted.[14] This exceptional extension will only apply for the purpose of determining import or export duties, calculating export refunds and any other amounts granted for imports or exports as part of the common agricultural policy, using import, export or advance-fixing certificates which are submitted when formalities are carried out for acceptance of the customs declaration concerning the goods in question, provided that such certificates were issued on the basis of the information concerned.[15] Furthermore, the holder of binding information wishing to make use of such extension must notify the customs authorities and provide any necessary supporting

---

8 Ibid Art 12(5)(a)(i).

9 Ibid Art 12(5)(a)(ii).

10 Ibid Art 12(5)(a)(iii). As to the date on which the binding information ceases to be valid see ibid Art 12(5)(a); see also Commission Regulation 2454/93 Art 12(2)(a), OJ 11.10.93 L335/1, as amended by Commission Regulation 12/97, OJ 13.1.97 L9/1. The Court has considered that the cessation of validity of the binding information in all these cases is in accordance with the principle of legal certainty and traders may not claim a legitimate expectation especially since the rules on binding information provided for a system of protection against unforeseeable or irreparable damage. See Case C-315/96 *Lopex Export GmbH v Hauptzollamt Hamburg-Jonas* [1998] ECR I-317.

11 Council Regulation 2913/92 Art 12(5)(b)(i), OJ 19.10.92 L 253/1, as amended by Regulation 82/97 of the European Parliament and of the Council, OJ 21.1.97 L/17/1.

12 Ibid Art 12(5)(b)(ii).

13 Ibid Art 12(5)(b)(iii). Concerning the date on which the binding information ceases to be valid see ibid Art 12(5)(b); see also Commission Regulation 2454/93 Art 12(2)(b), OJ 11.10.93 L335/1, as amended by Commission Regulation 12/97, OJ 13.1.97 L9/1.

14 However, in the case of products for which an import, export or advance fixing certificate is submitted when customs formalities are carried out, the period of six months is replaced by the period of validity of the certificate. See Council Regulation 2913/92 Art 12(6), OJ 19.10.92 L 253/1, as amended by Regulation 82/97 of the European Parliament and of the Council, OJ 21.1.97 L/17/1.

15 Ibid Art 12(7).

documents to enable a check to be made that the relevant conditions have been satisfied.[16] In addition, the exceptional extension may be excluded if the Commission decides that it could jeopardize the operation of the arrangements for certain products laid down under the common agricultural policy.[17]

16 Commission Regulation 2454/93 Art 14(1), OJ 11.10.93 L335/1, as amended by Commission Regulation 12/97, OJ 13.1.97 L9/1.
17 Council Regulation 2913/92 Art 12(7), OJ 19.10.92 L 253/1, as amended by Regulation 82/97 of the European Parliament and of the Council, OJ 21.1.97 L/17/1; see also Art 14(2) Commission Regulation 2454/93, OJ 11.10.93 L335/1, as amended by Commission Regulation 12/97, OJ 13.1.97 L9/1.

Chapter 2

Origin of goods

INTRODUCTION

The second factor on the basis of which duties and other measures prescribed in respect of trade in goods are applied is the origin of such goods.[1] A common definition of the concept of the origin of goods constitutes an indispensable means of ensuring the uniform application of the Common Customs Tariff, of quantitative restrictions and of all other measures adopted in relation to the importation or exportation of goods, by the Community or by the Member States.[2] The Customs Code establishes different rules for preferential and non-preferential origin.

NON-PREFERENTIAL ORIGIN

Introduction

The Customs Code defines the non-preferential origin of goods for the purposes of applying the Customs Tariff of the European Communities with the exception of preferential measures; applying measures other than tariff measures established by Community provisions governing specific fields relating to the trade in goods; and the preparation of certificates of origin.[3] It distinguishes between goods wholly obtained in one country and goods whose production involved more than one country.[4]

---

1 The term 'goods' within the meaning of Art 9 of the Treaty refers to products which can be valued in money and which are capable of forming the subject of commercial transactions. See Case 7/68 *Commission of the European Communities v Italy* [1968] ECR 423.
2 See Case 49/76 *Gesellschaft fur Uberseehandel mbH v Handelskammer Hamburg* [1977] ECR 41, paragraph 5.
3 Council Regulation 2913/92 Art 22, OJ 19.10.92 L302/1. As to the concept of preferential measures see ibid Art 20(3)(d) and (e). The Community rules on non-preferential origin follow closely the WTO *Agreement on Rules of Origin*, OJ 23.12.94 L336/144.
4 For the purposes of the Community rules on non-preferential origin, country means a third country or the Community as appropriate. See Commission Regulation 2454/93 Art 35, OJ 11.10.93 L253/1.

Goods wholly obtained in one country

Goods wholly obtained in one country originate therein.[5] Such goods are mineral products extracted in that country;[6] vegetable products harvested therein;[7] live animals born and raised therein;[8] products derived from live animals raised therein;[9] products of hunting or fishing carried on therein;[10] products of sea fishing and other products taken from the sea outside a country's territorial sea by vessels registered or recorded in the country concerned and flying the flag of that country;[11] goods obtained or produced on board factory ships from the previous products originating in that country, provided that such factory ships are registered or recorded in that country and fly its flag;[12] products taken from the seabed or subsoil beneath the seabed outside the territorial sea provided that country has exclusive rights to exploit the seabed or subsoil;[13] waste and scrap products derived from manufacturing operations and used articles, if they were collected therein and are fit only for the recovery of raw materials;[14] and goods which are produced therein exclusively from any of the goods referred to above or from their derivatives, at any stage of production.[15]

5 Council Regulation 2913/92 Art 23(1), OJ 19.10.92 L302/1. The expression country covers the country's territorial sea. See ibid Art 23(3). A distinction must be established between Community goods and goods of Community origin. Community goods are goods which are wholly obtained or produced in the customs territory of the Community and not incorporating goods imported from countries or territories not forming part of the customs territory of the Community; goods imported from countries or territories not forming part of the customs territory of the Community which have been released for free circulation; and goods obtained in the customs territory of the Community, either from goods wholly obtained or produced in the customs territory of the Community or from goods wholly obtained or produced in the customs territory of the Community and goods imported from countries or territories not forming part of the customs territory and which have been released for free circulation. Community goods lose that status, but not their origin, when they are removed from the customs territory of the Community. See Council Regulation 2913/92 Art 4(7), OJ 19.10.92 L302/1.
6 Ibid Art 23(2)(a).
7 Ibid Art 23(2)(b).
8 Ibid Art 23(2)(c).
9 Ibid Art 23(2)(d).
10 Ibid Art 23(2)(e).
11 Ibid Art 23(2)(f). In this sense, the Court has held repeatedly that the origin of fish is determined by the flag of the vessel which caught it independently of where the fish was caught. See Case C-9/89 *Spain v Council of the European Communities* [1990] ECR I -1383; see also Case C-280/89 *Commission of the European Communities v Ireland* [1992] ECR I-6185. In the exceptional case in which a number of vessels flying different flags or registered in different countries co-operate in a joint fishing operation, it should be held, for the purposes of applying the provisions in question, that the origin of the fish must be made to depend on the flag flown by the vessel which performed the essential part of the operation of catching them. The vessel that locates the fish and separates them from the sea by netting them performs the essential part of such operation. See Case 100/84 *Commission of the European Communities v United Kingdom* [1985] ECR 1169, paragraph 19. Art 23(2)(f) CC only applies in the absence of any processing. Ibid, paragraph 14.
12 Council Regulation 2913/92 Art 23(2)(g), OJ 19.10.92 L302/1.
13 Ibid Art 23(2)(h).
14 Ibid Art 23(2)(i).
15 Ibid Art 23(2)(j).

Goods produced in more than one country

Goods whose production involved more than one country are considered to originate in the country where they underwent their last substantial, economically justified processing or working in an undertaking equipped for that purpose and resulting in the manufacture of a new product or representing an important stage of manufacture.[16] In order to meet the purposes and requirements of the Customs Code, the determination of the origin of goods must be based on a real and objective distinction between raw material and processed product, depending fundamentally on the specific material qualities of each of those products. Therefore the last process or operation is only substantial if the product resulting therefrom has its own properties and a composition of its own, which it did not possess before that process or operation. Activities affecting the presentation of the product for the purposes of its use, but which do not bring about a significant qualitative change in its properties, are not of such a nature as to determine the origin of the said product.[17] Whether a certain operation is the last substantial operation resulting in the manufacture of a product is often a question of a technical nature which must be examined having regard to the definition of the product and to the various processes which result in its formation. In this sense, the last substantial process or operation may be interpreted as being constituted by the combination of operations resulting in the manufacture of a new and original product.[18] In any case, the analysis should not go beyond the last substantial operation. Thus, the requirement that virtually all components of a product must be of a specific origin, even those of little value which are of no use in themselves unless they are incorporated into a whole, would amount to a repudiation of the very objective of the rules on the determination of origin.[19]

Simple assembly operations, which do not require staff with special qualifications for the work in question or sophisticated tools or specially equipped

---

16 Ibid Art 24.
17 See Case 49/76 *Gesellschaft fur Uberseehandel mbH v Handelskammer Hamburg* [1977] ECR 41, paragraphs 5 and 6. In this sense, the grinding of a raw material such as casein to various degrees of fineness cannot be considered as a process or operation for the purposes of Art 24 of the Customs Code because the only effect of doing so is to change the consistency of the product and its presentation for the purposes of its later use but it does not bring about a significant qualitative change in the raw material. Furthermore, the quality control by grading to which the ground product is subjected and the manner in which it is packaged relate only to the requirements for marketing the product and do not affect its substantial properties. Ibid, paragraph 7; see also Case 93/83 *Zentrag v Hauptzollamt Bochum* [1984] ECR 1095, paragraph 14 (where the Court held that boning, trimming, drawing the sinews, cutting into pieces and vacuum-packing of meat facilitates the marketing of meat by enabling it to be sold to the customer through commercial undertakings which do not have their own butcher. Yet, it considered that these operations do not produce any substantial change in the properties and the composition of the meat, and their main effect is to divide the different parts of a carcase according to their quality and pre-existing characteristics and to alter their presentation for the purposes of sale. Furthermore, the Court maintained that a certain increase in the time for which the meat will keep and a slowing down in the maturing process do not constitute a sufficiently pronounced qualitative change in substance to satisfy the requirements mentioned above.)
18 See Case 114/78 *Yoshida GmbH v Industrie-und Handelskammer Kassel* [1979] ECR 151, paragraph 11; see also Case 34/78 *Yoshida v Kamer Van Koophandel En Fabrieken Voor Friesland* [1979] ECR 115, paragraph 11.
19 See Case 114/78 *Yoshida GmbH v Industrie-und Handelskammer Kassel* [1979] ECR 151, paragraph 12; see also Case 34/78 *Yoshida v Kamer Van Koophandel En Fabrieken Voor Friesland* [1979] ECR 115, paragraph 12.

factories for the purposes of assembly, do not come within the definition of a substantial process or operation to be taken into account in determining the origin of goods within the meaning of Art 24 of the Customs Code.[20] However, an assembly operation may be regarded as conferring origin where it represents from a technical point of view and having regard to the definition of the goods in question the decisive production stage during which the use to which the component parts are to be put becomes definitive and the goods in question are given their specific qualities.[1] In view of the variety of operations which may be described as assembly there are situations where consideration on the basis of technical criteria may not be decisive in determining the origin of goods. In such cases, it is necessary to take account of the value added by the assembly as an ancillary criterion.[2] The basis should be that the assembly as a whole must involve an appreciable increase in the commercial value of the finished product, at the ex-factory stage. In that respect, it is necessary to consider in each particular case whether the amount of the value added in the country of assembly in comparison with the value added in other countries justifies conferring the country of assembly as the country of origin.[3]

The Commission implementing regulation lays down specific rules for textiles and textiles articles falling within Section XI of the combined nomenclature, for specific products obtained listed in Annex 11 of the Commission implementing regulation and for spare parts.[4]

For textiles and textiles articles falling within Section XI of the combined nomenclature, a complete process will be considered as a working or processing conferring origin.[5] In this sense, a complete process is a working or processing as a result of which the products obtained receive a classification under a heading of the combined nomenclature other than those covering the various non-originating materials used.[6] However, for those products listed in Annex 10 of

---

20 See Case C-26/88 *Brother International GmbH v Hauptzollamt Giessen* [1989] ECR 4253, paragraph 17.
1 Ibid paragraph 19.
2 Ibid paragraph 20.
3 Ibid paragraph 22. In this sense, it is not necessary to determine whether the assembly operation involves any intellectual contribution. Ibid paragraph 24.
4 The Committee which assists the Commission on the implementation of the origin of goods provisions is the Customs Code Committee. See Council Regulation 2913/92 Art 247, OJ 19.10.92 L302/1. As to the procedure to be followed see ibid Art 249. In adopting implementing provisions on the common definition of the concept of the origin of goods, the Commission is obliged not to exceed the powers which the Council has conferred upon it for the implementation of the rules which it has promulgated in that regulation and, more precisely, it must define specific criteria of origin which comply with the objective criteria of Art 24 of the Customs Code. Although the Commission possesses a discretionary power for the application of the general criteria contained in Art 24 of the Customs Code, it cannot however, in the absence of objective justification, adopt entirely different solutions for similar working or processing operations. See Case 162/82 *Criminal Proceedings Against Paul Cousin* [1983] ECR 1101. If the origin of a product has not been determined by the Commission, the national customs authorities, applying the criteria laid down in the Customs Code, may determine the origin of the imported products. See Case 229/86 *Brother Industries Ltd v Commission of the European Communities* [1987] ECR 3757. In any case, private parties do not have the right to institute proceedings against Commission reports which are sent to the Member States following origin investigations. Ibid.
5 Commission Regulation 2454/93 Art 36, OJ 11.10.93 L253/1.
6 Ibid Art 37. The Commission may use the tariff classification of processed products to define the origin of goods if it takes the change of tariff heading for processed products solely as a basic rule, justified on the one hand by the need for legal certainty and on the other hand by the problems of definition in multiple economic circumstances, and it supplements and adapts

the implementing regulation, only the specific processes referred to in that Annex in connection with each product obtained will be regarded as a complete process, whether or not they involve a change of heading.[7] Furthermore, certain processes are considered as insufficient working or processing to confer the status of originating products whether or not they imply a tariff shift.[8] Such operations are:

(1) operations to ensure the preservation of products in good condition during transport and storage (ventilation, spreading out, drying, removal of damaged parts and like operations);[9]

(2) simple operations consisting of removal of dust, sifting or screening, sorting, classifying, matching (including the making-up of sets of articles), washing, cutting up;[10]

(3) changes of packing and breaking-up and assembly of consignments, simple placing in bags, cases, boxes, fixing on cards or boards, etc and all other simple packing operations;[11]

(4) the affixing of marks, labels or other like distinguishing signs on products or their packaging;[12]

(5) simple assembly of parts of products to constitute a complete product;[13]

(6) a combination of two or more of the above specified operations.[14]

For specific products obtained listed in Annex 11 of the Commission's implementing regulation, the working or processing referred to in the column 3 of such Annex will be regarded as a process or operation conferring origin.[15]

Accessories, spare parts or tools delivered with any piece of equipment, machine, apparatus or vehicle which form part of its standard equipment are considered to have the same origin as that piece of equipment, machine, apparatus or vehicle.[16] Furthermore, essential spare parts for use with any piece of equipment, machine, apparatus or vehicle put into free circulation or previously exported will be deemed to have the same origin as that piece of equipment,

---

that basic rule in order to take into account the particular features of specific working or processing operations. In such case, it is not adopting a method which is in itself incompatible with the general criteria provided by the Customs Code. See Case 162/82 *Criminal Proceedings Against Paul Cousin* [1983] ECR 1101; see also Hironori Asakura *The Harmonized System and Rules of Origin* 27(4) JWT 5–21 (1993).

7 Commission Regulation 2454/93 Art 37, OJ 11.10.93 L253/1. As to the method of applying the rules in Annex 10 see the introductory notes in Annex 9 of Commission Regulation 2454/93, OJ 11.10.93 L253/1. Concerning the concepts of 'value', 'ex-works price' and 'value acquired as a result of assembly operations' of Annex 10 see ibid Art 40.

8 Ibid Art 38.

9 Ibid Art 38(a).

10 Ibid Art 38(b).

11 Ibid Art 38(c).

12 Ibid Art 38(d).

13 Ibid Art 38(e).

14 Ibid Art 38(f).

15 Ibid Art 39. As to the method of applying the rules set out in Annex 11 see the introductory notes in Annex 9 of Commission Regulation 2454/93, OJ 11.10.93 L253/1. As to the concepts of 'value', 'ex-works price' and 'value acquired as a result of assembly operations' of Annex 11 see Commission Regulation 2454/93 Art 40, OJ 11.10.93 L253/1.

16 Commission Regulation 2454/93 Art 41(1), OJ 11.10.93 L253/1, as introduced by Commission Regulation 3665/93, OJ 31.12.93 L335/1. 'Piece of equipment, machine, apparatus, or vehicle' means goods listed in Sections XVI, XVII and XVIII of the Combined Nomenclature. See Commission Regulation 2454/93 Art 43(a), OJ 11.10.93 L253/1.

machine, apparatus or vehicle.[17] These presumptions of origin will be accepted only if this is necessary for importation into the country of destination, and if the incorporation of the said essential spare parts in the piece of equipment, machine, apparatus or vehicle concerned at the production stage would not have prevented the piece of equipment, machine, apparatus or vehicle from having Community origin or that of the country of manufacture.[18]

If an application is presented to the competent authorities or authorized agencies of the Member States for a certificate of origin for essential spare parts, the certificate and the application must include a declaration by the person concerned that the goods mentioned are intended for the normal maintenance of a piece of equipment, machine, apparatus or vehicle previously exported, together with the exact particulars of the said piece of equipment, machine, apparatus or vehicle.[19] Furthermore, whenever possible, the person concerned must also give the particulars of the certificate of origin under cover of which was exported the piece of equipment, machine, apparatus, or vehicle for whose maintenance the parts are intended.[20]

If the origin of the essential spare parts must be proved for their release for free circulation in the Community by the production of a certificate of origin, it must also include a declaration by the person concerned that the goods mentioned therein are intended for the normal maintenance of a piece of equipment, machine, apparatus or vehicle previously released together with the exact particulars of the said piece of equipment, machine, apparatus or vehicle.[1]

Moreover, in order to ensure the rules concerning the origin of spare parts, the competent authorities may require additional proof, in particular the production of the invoice or copy of the invoice relating to the piece of equipment, machine, apparatus or vehicle put into free circulation or previously exported; or the contract or a copy of the contract or any other document showing that delivery is being made as part of the normal maintenance service.[2]

With the purpose of avoiding the circumvention of Community measures, any processing or working in respect of which it is established, or in respect of which the facts as ascertained justify the presumption, that its sole object was to circumvent the provisions applicable in the Community to goods from specific countries will under no circumstances be deemed to confer on the goods thus produced the origin of the country where it is carried out.[3] In this sense, the transfer of an assembly from the country in which the parts were manufactured to another country in which use is made of existing factories does not in itself justify the presumption that the sole object of the transfer was to circumvent the applicable provisions unless the transfer of assembly coincides with the entry into force of the relevant measures. In that case, the manufacturer concerned must prove that there were reasonable grounds other than avoiding the

---

17 Ibid Art 41(2).'Essential spare parts' means parts which are components without which the proper operation of pieces of equipment, machines, apparatus or vehicles which have been put into free circulation or previously exported cannot be ensured, and characteristic of those goods, and intended for their normal maintenance and to replace parts of the same kind which are damaged or have become unserviceable. See ibid Art 43(b).
18 Ibid Art 42.
19 Ibid Art 44.
20 Ibid Art 44.
 1 Ibid Art 45.
 2 Ibid Art 46.
 3 Council Regulation 2913/92 Art 25, OJ 19.10.92 L302/1.

consequences of the provisions in question for carrying out the assembly operations in the country from which the goods were exported.[4]

The certificate of origin

The customs legislation or other Community legislation governing specific fields
may provide that a document must be produced as proof of the origin of goods.[5]
The Commission implementing regulation establishes rules both for the certificate of origin to be produced on importation of a product into the Community
as well as the certificates of Community origin.

When the origin of a product is or has to be proved on importation by the
production of a certificate of origin, the certificate must fulfil the following
conditions:

(1) it must be made out by a reliable authority or agency duly authorized for
    that purpose by the country of issue;[6]
(2) it must contain all the particulars necessary for identifying the products to
    which it relates, in particular: the number of packages, their nature, and
    the marks and numbers they bear, the type of product, the gross and net
    weight of the product,[7] the name of the consignor;[8]
(3) it must certify unambiguously that the product to which it relates origi-
    nated in a specific country.[9]

However, notwithstanding the production of the certificate of origin, the customs authorities may, in the event of serious doubts, require any additional
proof to ensure that the indication of origin does comply with the rules laid
down by the relevant Community legislation.[10]

The certificate of Community origin issued by the competent authorities or
authorized agencies of the Member States must comply also with all the requirements of certificate of origin for the importation of goods other than cer-
tifying the specific country of origin.[11] Such certificates of origin must certify

---

4 See Case C-26/88 *Brother International GmbH v Hauptzollamt Giessen* [1989] ECR 4253,
   paragraph 29.
5 Council Regulation 2913/92 Art 26(1), OJ 19.10.92 L302/1.
6 Commission Regulation 2454/93 Art 47(a), OJ 11.10.93 L253/1.
7 These particulars may, however, be replaced by others, such as the number or volume, when
   the product is subject to appreciable changes in weight during carriage or when its weight
   cannot be ascertained or when it is normally identified by such other particulars. See ibid Art
   47(b).
8 Ibid Art 47(b).
9 Ibid Art 47(c).
10 Council Regulation 2913/92 Art 26(2), OJ 19.10.92 L302/1. The Court has held that a
   customs agent cannot entertain a legitimate expectation with regard to the validly of certificates by virtue of the fact that they were initially accepted by the customs officers of a
   Member State. The role of those officers in regard to the initial acceptance of declarations in
   no way prevents the customs authorities of the Member States from subsequently checking
   their veracity. See Joined Cases 98 & 230/83 *Van Gend & Loos NV and Expeditiebedrijf
   Wim Bosman BV v Commission of the European Communities* [1984] ECR 3763, paragraph
   20.
11 Commission Regulation 2454/93 Art 48(1), OJ 11.10.93 L253/1. Concerning the forms of
   these certificates and applications relating to them see Annex 12 to Commission Regulation
   2454/93, OJ 11.10.93 L253/1.

that the goods originated in the Community.[12] However, when the exigencies of export trade so require, they may certify that the goods originated in a particular Member State. But if the conditions for qualifying for Community origin are met only as a result of a series of operations or processes carried out in different Member States, the goods may only be certified as being of Community origin.[13]

The certificates of Community origin will be issued upon written request of the person concerned.[14] Where the circumstances so warrant, in particular when the applicant maintains a regular flow of exports, the Member States may decide not to require an application for each export operation, on condition that the provisions concerning origin are complied with. Furthermore, where the exigencies of trade so require, one or more extra copies of an origin certificate may be issued.[15]

Each certificate must bear a serial number by which it can be identified. The application for the certificate and all copies of the certificate itself will bear the same number.[16] The competent authorities or authorized agencies of the Member States which have issued the certificates of origin must retain the applications for a minimum of two years.[17]

---

12 Ibid Art 48(3). National legislation prohibiting the retail sale of certain products imported from other Member States unless they bear or are accompanied by an indication of origin must be considered as a measure having equivalent effect to a quantitative restriction prohibited by Art 30 of the Treaty. This rule applies both to goods originating in the EC as well as goods originating outside the Community which are in free circulation in the Community. Manufacturers may, however, wish to introduce such indication of origin. In such cases, the Member States may introduce rules governing such indications to protect consumers. See Case 207/83 *Commission of the European Communities v United Kingdom* [1985] ECR 1201. However, certificates of origin can also be used for intra-Community trade where the products from the third countries are exported from one Member State to another in cases where national restrictive measures such as those provided for in Art 115 of the Treaty apply and a specific authorization has been given. See Case 212/88 *Criminal Proceedings Against F Levy* [1989] ECR 3511. Even if no specific authorization under Art 115 has yet been given, Member States are not prevented from requiring from an importer a declaration concerning the actual origin of goods in question even in the case of goods put into free circulation in another Member State and covered by a Community movement certificate. Nevertheless, the Member States may not require from the importer more in this respect than an indication of the origin of the products in so far as he knows it or may reasonably be expected to know it. In addition, the fact that the importer did not comply with the obligation to declare the real origin of goods cannot give rise to the application of penalties which are disproportionate, taking account of the purely administrative nature of the contravention. See Case 52/77 *Leonce Cayrol v Giovanni Rivoira & Figli* [1977] ECR 2261.

13 Commission Regulation 2454/93 Art 48(3), OJ 11.10.93 L253/1.

14 As to the details concerning the measures and form of the certificate see ibid Art 50(1). As to the languages of the certificate and the application see ibid Art 50(2). Both the application form and the certificate of Community origin must be completed in typescript or by hand in block capitals, in an identical manner, in one for the official languages of the Community or, depending on the practice and requirements of trade, in any other languages. See ibid Art 51. The competent authorities of the Member States must determine what additional particulars, if any, are to be given in the application. Such additional particulars must, however, be kept to a minimum. Furthermore, each Member State must inform the Commission of the provisions it adopts on these particulars. The Commission must immediately communicate this information to other Member States. See ibid Art 53.

15 Such copies shall be made out on forms corresponding to the specimen in Annex 12 to Commission Regulation 2454/93 OJ 11.10.93 L253/1. See ibid Art 49.

16 In addition the competent authorities or authorized agencies of the Member States may number such documents by order of issue. See ibid Art 52.

17 Ibid Art 54. Applications may also be retained in the form of copies thereof provided that these have the same probative value under the law of the Member State concerned.

The Commission implementing regulation lays down specific provisions for use of certificates of origin relating to agricultural products originating in third countries for which special non-preferential import arrangements have been established.[18] Such certificates must only be issued by the competent authorities of the third countries concerned if the products to which the certificates relate can be considered as products originating in those countries within the meaning of the rules in force in the Community.[19] They must consist only of a single sheet identified by the word 'original' next to the title of the document.[20] If additional copies are necessary, they must bear the designation 'copy' next to the title of the document.[1] In any case, the competent authorities in the Community shall accept as valid only the original of the certificate of origin.[2] Each certificate must bear a serial number by which it can be identified and must be stamped by the issuing authority and signed by the person or persons empowered to do so. The certificate must be issued when the products to which it relates are exported.[3] Exceptionally, however, they may be issued after the export of the products to which they relate if the failure to issue them at the time of such export was a result of involuntary error or omission or special circumstances.[4] Unless there are other specific provisions under the specific arrangements in question, their period of validity will be of ten months from the date of issue.[5]

The entitlement to use special import arrangements and applicable certificates of origin for certain agricultural products is subject to the setting up of an administrative co-operation procedure with the Community authorities unless the arrangements concerned specify the contrary.[6] For this purpose, the third countries concerned must send the Commission the names and addresses of the issuing authorities for certificates of origin together with specimens of the stamps used by such authorities and the names and addresses of the government authorities to which request for subsequent verifications of origin should be sent.[7]

The Community authorities may carry out a subsequent verification of the certificates of non-preferential origin for agricultural products subject to import arrangements. Such verifications may be carried out at random and when-

---

18 Ibid Art 55.
19 Ibid Art 56(2). These certificates of origin must be made out on a form conforming to the specimen in Annex 13 to Commission Regulation 2454/93 OJ 11.10.93 L253/1. See Commission Regulation 2454/93 Art 56(1), OJ 11.10.93 L253/1. The certificates must certify all necessary information provided for in the Community legislation governing the special import arrangements. See ibid Art 56(3).
20 Ibid Art 57(1). As to the form and language of the certificate see ibid Art 58.
 1 Ibid Art 57(1).
 2 Ibid Art 75(2). The certificate must be completed in typescript or by means of a mechanical data processing system or similar procedure. See ibid Art 59(1). Entries must not be erased or overwritten. Any changes must be made by crossing out the wrong entry and if necessary adding the correct particulars. See ibid Art 59(2). Any additional particulars which may be required for the implementation of the special import arrangements must be included in Box 5 of the certificate of origin. Unused spaces in boxes 5, 6 and 7 must be struck through in such a way that nothing can be added at a later stage. See ibid Art 60.
 3 Ibid Art 61.
 4 Ibid Art 62. Yet the issuing authorities may not issue retrospectively these certificates of origin until they have checked that the particulars in the exporter's application correspond to those in the relevant export file. Furthermore retrospective certificates must make clear in their Remarks box that they were issued retrospectively.
 5 Ibid Art 56(4).
 6 Ibid Art 63(1).
 7 If the third countries fail to send the Commission this information the competent authorities in the Community must refuse access entitlement to the special import arrangements. See ibid Art 63(2).

ever there is reasonable doubt as to the authenticity of the certificate or the accuracy of the information it contains.[8] In such cases, the Community authorities will return the certificate of origin or a copy thereof to the governmental authority designed by the exporting country, giving, where appropriate, the reasons of form or substance for an enquiry and any information that has been obtained suggesting that the particulars given on the certificates are inaccurate or that the certificate is not authentic.[9]

The results of the subsequent verifications carried out by the designated government authority in the third country in question must be communicated to the competent authorities of the Community as soon as possible. These results must make it possible to determine whether the origin certificates apply to the goods actually exported and whether such goods can benefit from the special importation arrangements concerned.[10] If within a time limit of six months the third country concerned does not reply to the request for subsequent verification, the competent Community authorities will definitively refuse to grant entitlement to the special import arrangements.[11]

PREFERENTIAL ORIGIN

Introduction

The Community distinguishes between rules of origin of goods for the purposes of preferential tariff measures contained in agreements which the Community has concluded with certain countries or group of countries and which provide for the granting of preferential tariff treatment;[12] and rules of origin of goods for the purposes of preferential tariff measures adopted unilaterally by the Community in respect of certain countries, groups of countries or territories.[13] The rules of origin of goods for the purposes of conventional tariff measures are set out in the annexes or protocols to the agreements.[14] The rules of origin of goods for the purposes of unilateral preferential tariff measures are set out in the Commission implementing regulation.[15] This regulation establishes rules for goods from countries falling under the Generalized System of Preferences[16] and goods from the Republics of Bosnia-Herzegovina and Croatia, the Federal

---

8 Ibid Art 64(1).
9 Ibid Art 64(2).
10 Ibid Art 65(1).
11 Ibid Art 65(2).
12 Council Regulation 2913/92 Art 20(3)(d), OJ 19.10.92 L302/1.
13 Ibid Art 20(3)(e).
14 Ibid Art 27(a).
15 Ibid Art 27(b) As to the meaning of goods for the purpose of unilateral preferential tariff measures see Commission Regulation 2454/93 Art 66(d), OJ 11.10.93 L253/1, as amended by Commission Regulation 12/97, OJ 13.1.97 L9/1. In this sense, the Court has maintained that the Commission may where appropriate apply the concept of the origin of goods in a different manner in the field of generalized tariff preferences than in the framework of the common rules drawn for non preferential treatment. Furthermore, such an application may, in fact, be necessary to attain the objective of the generalized tariff preferences of ensuring that the preferences benefit only industries which are established in developing countries and which carry out the main manufacturing process in those countries. See Case 385/85 *SR Industries v Administration des Douanes* [1986] ECR 2929, paragraph 7; see also Case 827/79 *Amministrazione delle Finanze v Ciro Acampora* [1980] ECR 3731.
16 See Commission Regulation 2454/93 Section I, Chapter II, Title IV, OJ 11.10.93 L253/1, as amended by Commission Regulation 12/97, OJ 13.1.97 L9/1.

Republic of Yugoslavia, the Former Yugoslav Republic of Macedonia and the territories of the West Bank and the Gaza Strip.[17]

However, so as to provide a typology it is useful to classify the rules of preferential origin in the following groups:[18]

(1) those for the purpose of the Generalized System of Preferences and for goods coming from the Occupied Territories and the Republics of Bosnia-Herzergovina and Croatia, the Federal Republic of Yugoslavia, the Former Yugoslav Republic of Macedonia;
(2) those included in the Lome IV Convention with regard to the ACP countries and those included in the arrangements relating to the Association of the Overseas Countries and Territories;[19]
(3) those included in the EFTA, EEA and Europe Agreements;
(4) those included in the Mediterranean agreements; and
(5) those included in the preferential arrangments relating to territories with a particular political status such as the Faroe Islands,[20] Ceuta and Melilla and the Canary Islands;[1] and the Principality of Andorra.[2]

As all these rules of preferential origin follow the same basic principles, the system of those for the purposes of the General System of Preferences will be presented first. Thereafter, we shall specify the particularities of the Lome IV, EFTA, EEA, Europe and Mediterranean systems.

General system of preferences

Products originating in a beneficiary country for the purposes of applying the Community generalized tariff preferences are those products wholly obtained in that country;[3] as well as those obtained in that country in the manufacture of which products other than those there wholly obtained are used, provided that the said products have undergone sufficient working or processing.[4] In this sense, products originating in the Community which are subject in a beneficiary

17 See ibid Section II, Chapter II, Title IV.
18 See Nicholas A Zaimis & Clifford Chance *EC Rules of Origin*, Chancery Law Publishing (1992).
19 The rules of origin for goods coming from the OCT are very similar to those of the ACP. See Annex II to Council Decision 91/482, OJ 19.9.91 L263/67, as amended by Council Decision 97/803, OJ 21.11.97 L329/50. Special derogations apply to Montserrat (see Commission Decision 94/724, OJ 9.11.94) and to Saint Pierre and Miquelon (see Commission Decision 96/529, OJ 4.9.96 L223/3).
20 See Protocol 3 to Agreement between the European Community, of the one part, and the Government of Denmark and the House Government of the Faroe Islands of the other part, OJ 22.2.97 L53/2.
1 See Council Regulation 1135/88, OJ 2.5.88 L114/1, as amended by Council Regulation 3902/89, OJ 23.12.89 L375/5.
2 See Appendix to theAgreement in the form of exchange of letters between the European Economic Community and the Principality of Andorra, OJ 31.12.90 L374/13, as amended by Decision 2/95 of the EC-Andorra Joint Committee, OJ 1.12.95 L288/51.
3 Commission Regulation 2454/93 Art 67(1)(a), OJ 11.10.93 L253/1, as amended by Commission Regulation 12/97, OJ 13.1.97 L9/1. Concerning the meaning of product see ibid Art 66(c).
4 Ibid Art 67(1)(b). To determine whether a product is an originating product in a beneficiary country it is not necessary to determine the origin of the energy and fuel, plant or equipment, machines and tools or goods which do not enter, and which are not intended to enter, into the final composition of the product, and which might be used in its manufacture. See ibid Art 75.

country to sufficient working or processing operations will be considered as originating in that beneficiary country.[5] Furthermore, in so far as Norway and Switzerland grant generalized tariff preferences to products originating in developing countries and apply a definition of the concept of origin corresponding to those of the Community, products originating in the Community, Norway or Switzerland exported directly to a beneficiary country where they are thereafter subject to sufficient working or processing operations shall be considered as originating in that beneficiary country.[6]

Products wholly obtained in a beneficiary country

Products wholly obtained in a beneficiary country or in the Community are:[7]

(1) mineral products extracted from its soil or its seabed;[8]
(2) vegetable products harvested there;[9]
(3) live animals born and raised there;[10]
(4) products from live animals raised there;[11]
(5) products obtained by hunting or fishing conducted there;[12]
(6) products of sea fishing and other products taken from the sea outside the territorial waters by their vessels;[13]
(7) products made on board their factory ships exclusively from products taken outside the territorial waters by their vessels;[14]

5 The Community products must have undergone processing or working operations beyond those described in Art 70 of the Commission Regulation. See ibid Art 67(2). In order to establish the origin of the products obtained in the Community the provisions for goods from beneficiary countries apply *mutatis mutandis*. For the purposes of the rules of origin of products from countries falling within the scope of the general system of preferences the term 'Community' does not cover Ceuta and Melilla. See ibid Art 96(1) The Community rules on origin of goods from countries falling within the scope of the generalized system of preferences apply *mutatis mutandis* in determining whether products may be regarded as originating in the exporting beneficiary country benefiting from the generalized system of preferences when imported into Ceuta and Melilla or as originating in Ceuta and Melilla. See ibid Art 96(2) For these purposes, Ceuta and Melilla must be regarded as a single territory. See ibid Art 96(3).
6 The products must have undergone in the beneficiary country processing or working operations beyond those described in Commission Regulation 2454/93 Art 70, OJ 11.10.93 L253/1, as amended by Commission Regulation 12/97, OJ 13.1.97 L9/1. See ibid Art 67(4). This possibility only applies upon condition that Norway and Switzerland grant, by reciprocity, the same treatment to Community products. See ibid Art 76(5).
7 The terms 'beneficiary country' and 'Community' also cover the territorial waters of that country or of the Member States. See ibid Art 68(3).
8 Ibid Art 68(1)(a).
9 Ibid Art 68(1)(b).
10 Ibid Art 68(1)(c).
11 Ibid Art 68(1)(d).
12 Ibid Art 68(1)(e).
13 Ibid Art 68(1)(f).
14 Ibid Art 68(1)(g). In this sense, the term 'their vessels' and 'their factory ships' applies only to vessels and factory ships which are registered or recorded in the beneficiary country or in a Member State; which sail under the flag of a beneficiary country or of a Member State; which are owned to the extent of at least 50% by nationals of the beneficiary country or of the Member States or by a company having its head office in that country or in one of the Member States, of which the manager or managers or chairman of the board of directors or of the supervisory board, and the majority of such boards, are nationals of that beneficiary country or of the Member States and of which, in addition in the case of companies, at least half the capital belongs to that beneficiary country or to the Member States or to public bodies or nationals of

(8)   used articles collected there fit only for the recovery of raw materials;[15]
(9)   waste and scrap resulting from manufacturing operations conducted there;[16]
(10)   products extracted from the seabed or below the seabed which is situated outside their territorial waters but where it has exclusive exploitation rights;[17]
(11)   goods produced there exclusively from any of the products specified above.[18]

Goods obtained from sufficient processing operations on non-originating products

Non-originating materials are considered to be sufficiently worked or processed when the products obtained are classified in a heading which is different from those in which all the non-originating materials used in its manufacture are classified.[19] However, the following operations will be considered as insufficient working or processing to confer the status of originating products, regardless of whether or not a tariff shift takes place:

(1)   operations to ensure the preservation of products in good condition during transport and storage;[20]
(2)   simple operations consisting of the removal of dust, sifting or screening, sorting, classifying, matching (including the making-up of sets of articles), washing, painting, cutting up;[1]
(3)   changes of packing and breaking-up and assembly of packages, simple placing in bottles, flasks, bags, cases, fixing on cards or boards, etc and all other simple packing operations;[2]

that beneficiary country or to the Member States; of which the master and officers are nationals of the beneficiary country or of the Member States; and of which at least 75% of the crew are nationals of the beneficiary country or of the Member States. See ibid Art 68(2). Vessels operating on the high seas, including factory ships on which the fish is caught, is worked or processed will be considered as part of the territory of the beneficiary country or of the Member State to which they belong. See ibid Art 68(4). The Court has held that where on a particular voyage or part of a voyage and in addition to its normal crew, a vessel takes on board a number of third country nationals to work as trainees or as unskilled hands below decks, particular for training purposes, in order to comply with a joint venture agreement entered with an undertaking in a non-member country for the purpose of enabling the vessel to fish inside the exclusive economic zone of that country, such nationals are not to be considered as crew for origin of good purposes. The question whether under the terms of the joint venture agreement, the third country nationals are paid by the operator of the vessel or by the undertaking in the non-member country is immaterial. See Joined Cases C-153/94 & C-204/94 *R v Customs and Excise Comrs, ex p Faroe Seafood Co Ltd* [1996] ECR I-2465, paragraph 45.
15 Commission Regulation 2454/93 Art 68(1)(h), OJ 11.10.93 L253/1, as amended by Commission Regulation 12/97, OJ 13.1.97 L9/1.
16 Ibid Art 68(1)(i).
17 Ibid Art 68(1)(j).
18 Ibid Art 68(1)(k). In this sense, in order to enjoy preferential customs treatment, the products must be kept physically separate during any processing from products from third countries. Where raw materials of a qualifying country have been processed in a factory which also processed those of a third country, it is for the exporter to show proof, by producing all appropriate supporting documents, that the raw materials were physically separated from those of other origins. See Joined Cases C-153/94 & C-204/94 *R v Customs and Excise Comrs, ex p Faroe Seafood Co Ltd* [1996] ECR I-2465, paragraphs 58–62.
19 Ibid Art 69(1). As to the meaning of classified see ibid Art 66(i).
20 Ibid Art 70(a).
 1 Ibid Art 70(b).
 2 Ibid Art 70(c).

(4) the affixing of marks, labels or other like distinguishing signs on products or their packaging;[3]

(5) simple mixing of products, whether or not of different kinds, where one or more components of the mixture do not meet the conditions to be considered as originating products of a beneficiary country or of the Community;[4]

(6) simple assembly of parts of products to constitute a complete product;[5]

(7) a combination of two or more of any of the operations previously specified;[6]

(8) and the slaughter of animals.[7]

Furthermore, for products mentioned in columns 1 and 2 of the list set out in Annex 15 of the Commission implementing regulation, the conditions given in column 3 for the product concerned must be fulfilled instead of the tariff shift.[8]

Exceptionally, however, non-originating materials may be used in the manufacture of a given product without being sufficiently worked or processed provided that their total value does not exceed 5 per cent of the ex-works price of the final product and subject to the conditions laid down in Note 3.4 in Annex 14 of the Commission implementing regulation.[9]

Accessories, spare parts and tools dispatched with a piece of equipment, machine, apparatus or vehicle which are part of the normal equipment and included in the price or not separately invoiced are regarded as one with the piece of equipment, machine, apparatus or vehicle in question.[10] Furthermore, sets will be regarded as originating sets when the component articles are originating products. Nevertheless, when a set is composed of originating and non-originating articles, the set as a whole will be regarded as originating in the beneficiary country, provided that the value of the non-originating articles does not exceed 15 per cent of the ex-works price of the set.[11]

Regional cumulation

The Community establishes special rules on regional cumulation for specific regional groups. These groups are the Association of South-East Asian Nations (ASEAN);[12] the Central American Common Market (CACM);[13] and the Andean Community.[14]

To determine whether the product manufactured in a beneficiary country which is a member of a regional group originates therein, products originating in any of the countries of that regional group and used in further manufacture in another country of the group must be treated as if they originated in the

3 Ibid Art 70(d).
4 Ibid Art 70(e).
5 Ibid Art 70(f).
6 Ibid Art 70(g).
7 Ibid Art 70(h).
8 Ibid Art 69(2).
9 Ibid Art 71(1). Regarding the concept of material see ibid Art 66(b). As to the meaning of manufacture see ibid Art 66(a). Concerning the meaning of value see ibid Art 66(g). As to the concept of ex-works price see ibid Art 66(f). This exception does not apply to products falling within Chapters 50 to 63 of the Harmonized System. See ibid Art 71(2).
10 Ibid Art 73.
11 Ibid Art 74.
12 Ibid Art 72(3)(a). Including Brunei, Darusalam, Indonesia, Malaysia, Philippines, Singapore, Thailand and Vietnam.
13 Ibid Art 72(3)(b). Including Costa Rica, Honduras, Guatemala, Nicaragua and El Salvador.
14 Ibid Art 73(3)(c). Including Bolivia, Colombia, Ecuador, Peru and Venezuela.

country of further manufacture.[15] In this sense, the country of origin of the final product will be that where the last working or processing was carried out provided that

(1) the value added there is greater than the highest customs value of the products used originating in any of the other countries of the regional group;[16] and
(2) the working or processing carried out there exceeds those set out in Art 70 of the Commission implementing regulation and, in the case of textile products, also the operations referred to at Annex 16.[17]

If these two conditions are not satisfied, the products will have the origin of the country of the regional group which accounts for the highest customs value of the originating products coming from the other countries of the group.[18]

To ensure compliance with these special rules for regional groups, the Community requires the production of a certificate of origin Form A or an invoice declaration.[19] The country of origin must be marked in box 12 of the certificate of origin Form A or on the invoice declaration.[20] If the goods are exported from a country of a regional group to another country of the same group to be used in further working or processing, or to be re-exported where no further working or processing takes place, the country of origin shall be the country of manufacture of the goods. If the goods are exported after further working or processing, the country of origin will be determined in accordance with the rules of regional cumulation.

The application of the special rules on regional cumulation is subject, however, to specific conditions. First, the rules relating to trade in the context of regional cumulation, as between the countries of the regional group, must be identical to those of the Community.[1] Second, each country must have undertaken to comply or ensure compliance with the terms of Community rules on origin of goods for the application of the Generalized System of Preferences and to provide the administrative co-operation necessary both to the Community and to other countries of the regional group in order to ensure the correct issue of certificates of origin Form A and the verification of certificates of origin Form A and invoice declarations.[2]

Exceptions for least developed countries

Least developed countries benefiting from the generalized system of preferences may be granted derogations from the rules of origin for the purposes of

---

15 Ibid Art 72(1).
16 Ibid Art 72a(1)(a). As to the concept of valued added see ibid Art 72a(3). As to the meaning of customs value see ibid Art 66(e).
17 Ibid Art 72a(1)(b).
18 Ibid Art 72a(2).
19 Ibid Art 72a(4); see also ibid Art 72a(5).
20 Ibid Art 72a(6).
 1 Ibid Art 72b(1)(a).
 2 Ibid Art 72b(1)(b). This undertaking must be transmitted to the Community through the Secretariat of the regional group. See ibid Art 72b(1)(b).

the generalized system of preferences when the development of an existing industries or the creation of new industries justifies such special treatment.[3] For this purpose, the country concerned must submit to the Community a request for a derogation together with the reasons for the request.[4] The examination of the requests shall take into account, in particular,

(1) cases where the application of existing rules of origin would affect significantly the ability of an existing industry in the country concerned to continue its exports to the Community, with particular reference to cases where this could lead to business closures;[5]
(2) specific cases where it can be clearly demonstrated that significant investment in an industry could be deferred by the rules of origin and where a derogation encouraging implementation of the investment programme would enable the rules to be satisfied by stages;[6]
(3) the economic and social impact of the decision to be taken especially in respect of employment in the beneficiary countries and the Community.[7]

If a derogation has been granted to the products of a country, the certificate of origin Form A or the invoice declaration must refer to such derogation.[8]

Conditions for the acquisition of originating status in a beneficiary country: proof of origin

The rules of origin must be wholly satisfied without interruption in the beneficiary country concerned or in the Community.[9] Originating products exported from the beneficiary country or from the Community to another country which are returned must be considered as non-originating products unless it can be demonstrated that the goods returned are the same goods as those exported and that they have not undergone any operations beyond what is necessary to preserve them in good condition while in that country.[10] Furthermore, products originating in a beneficiary country will benefit from the application of the rules for the generalized system of preferences on submission of either a

3 Ibid Art 76(1) The least developed beneficiary countries are listed in the Council EC regulations and the ECSC decisions applying the generalized tariff of preferences for the current year. See Chapter 22 on GSP. As to derogations granted to textiles from Nepal see Commission Regulation 1715/97, OJ 4.9.97 L 242/19. Concerning derogations granted to textiles from Laos see Commission Regulation 1713/97, OJ 4.9.97 L242/1. Regarding derogations granted to textiles products from Bangladesh see Commission Regulation 2260/97, OJ 14.11.97 L 311/18. As to derogations granted to textiles from Cambodia see Commission Regulation 1714/97 OJ 4.9.97 L 242/10.
4 Concerning the information to be furnished in the request see Commission Regulation 2454/93 Art 76(3), OJ 11.10.93 L253/1, as amended by Commission Regulation 12/97, OJ 13.1.97 L9/1.
5 Ibid Art 76(2)(a).
6 Ibid Art 76(2)(b).
7 Ibid Art 76(2)(c).
8 Ibid Art 76(5).
9 Ibid Art 77. This provision excludes procedures such as outward and inward processing.
10 Ibid Art 77.

certificate of origin Form A,[11] or in specified cases, an invoice declaration, as proof of their origin.[12]

Originating products will be eligible on importation into the Community to benefit from the generalized system of preferences provided that they have been transported directly from the beneficiary country to the Community or from the Community to the beneficiary country,[13] and that a certificate of origin Form A is produced.[14] The certificate of origin must be issued either by the customs authorities or by any governmental authorities of the beneficiary country, provided that the latter country has communicated to the Commission specific information for administrative co-operation with the Community authorities,[15] and assists the Community by allowing the customs authorities of the Member States to verify the authenticity of the document or the accuracy of the information regarding the true origin of the products in question.[16] The certificate of origin must be issued only on written application from the exporter or his authorized representative.[17] It must be issued only if the products to be exported can be considered as products originating in that country within the meaning of the Community rules of origin of goods under the generalized system of preferences.[18] The certifi-

---

11 Ibid Art 80(a). As to the specimen of Form A see Annex 17 to Commission Regulation 2454/93, OJ 11.10.93 L253/1.

12 Commission Regulation 2454/93 Art 80(b), OJ 11.10.93 L253/1, as amended by Commission Regulation 12/97, OJ 13.1.97 L9/1. Special provisions apply for small packages from private persons to private persons or forming part of travellers' personal luggage. See ibid Art 90c.

13 As to the concept of direct transport from the beneficiary country to the Community or from the Community to the beneficiary country see ibid Art 78(1). Special rules apply for regional groups see ibid Art 72b(3). Special exceptions apply for exhibitions see ibid Art 79. As for the evidence of direct transport see ibid Art 78(2). Where the goods are transported through a third country it is necessary to ensure that their final destination is not changed.During their transport the goods must not have been declared through customs, released into free circulation or processed in any way which might undermine the concept of originating products. Yet, legal or commercial operations, which, although not directly related to the transport of the goods, do not change the destination of the goods and are not such as to affect their origin do not conflict with the rule of direct transport laid down in the Article. A commercial operation such as the reinvoicing of goods which are under the surveillance of the customs authorities of the country of transit cannot itself have any effect in relation to the destination of the goods or their origin. See Case 156/85 *Procureur de la Republique v Perles Eurotool* [1986] ECR 1595.

14 Commission Regulation 2454/93 Art 81(1), OJ 11.10.93 L253/1, as amended by Commission Regulation 12/97, OJ 13.1.97 L9/1. However, the Court has maintained that the system of tariff preferences, whilst it may involve the requirement of a certificate of origin in order to justify the application of preferential rates, must not be understood as authorizing excessively restrictive administrative measures in the actual machinery for checking the origin of the goods. See Case 231/81 *Hauptzollamt Wurzburg v H Weidenmann GmbH & Co* [1982] ECR 2259, paragraph 8.

15 See Commission Regulation 2454/93 Art 93, OJ 11.10.93 L253/1, as amended by Commission Regulation 12/97, OJ 13.1.97 L9/1.

16 Ibid Art 81(1).

17 Ibid Art 81(3). The exporter or its authorized representative must submit with the application any appropriate supporting document proving that the products to be exported qualify for the issue of a certificate of origin Form A.

18 Ibid Art 81(5). For this purpose the competent authorities must have the right to call for any documentary evidence or to carry out any check which they consider appropriate. See ibid Art 81(6). Entitlement to benefit from the system of tariff preferences granted by the Community to certain products from developing countries is lost if the certificate of origin Form A issued when products are exported for purposes of the application of the said tariff preferences states the country of destination to be a country other than a Member States of the European Community. See Case C-368/92 *Administration des Douanes v Solange Chiffre* [1994] ECR I-605, paragraph 14.

cate must be made available to the exporter as soon as the export has taken place or is ensured.[19] Exceptionally, a certificate of origin may be issued after exportation of the products to which it relates if it was not issued at the time of exportation because of errors or accidental omissions or special circumstances, or it is demonstrated to the satisfaction of the customs authorities that a certificate of origin Form A was issued but was not accepted on importation for technical reasons.[20] In these cases, the competent governmental authority may issue retrospectively the certificate of origin only after verifying that the particulars contained in the exporter's application conform with those contained in the corresponding export documents and that a certificate of origin Form A satisfying all the conditions of the Community rules of origin was not issued when the products in question were exported.[1]

The certificate of origin must be submitted within 10 months of the date of issue to the customs authorities of the Member State of importation where the products are presented.[2] Certificates of origin submitted to the customs authorities of importation after the expiry of the 10 month period may be accepted for the purpose of applying the tariff preferences where the failure to observe the time limit is due to exceptional circumstances or when the products have been presented to customs authorities within the 10 month period.[3]

When the goods are imported within the framework of frequent and continuous trade flows of a significant commercial value; or are the subject of the same contract of sale, the parties to this contract established in the exporting country and in the Community; or are classified in the same code of the combined nomenclature; or come exclusively from the same exporter, are destined for the same importer, and are made the subject of entry formalities at the same customs office in the Community, a single proof of origin may be submitted to the customs authorities at the importation of the first consignment.[4]

---

19 Commission Regulation 2454/93 Art 81(5), OJ 11.10.93 L253/1, as amended by Commission Regulation 12/97, OJ 13.1.97 L9/1. The date of issue of the certificate must be indicated in box 11 of Form A. See ibid Art 81(9).

20 Ibid Art 86(1). In this sense, the Court has held that provided that the products in question satisfy the Community rules of origin, there is no reason why a fresh certificate may not be issued retrospectively by the competent government authority of the exporting country. The fresh certificate must be taken into account by the competent customs authorities in the Community for the purposes of grant of tariff exemption established by the Community's system of generalized tariff preferences, provided that all the other conditions of validity laid down in the Community rules are satisfied. See Case C-368/92 *Administration des Douanes v Solange Chiffre* [1994] ECR I-605, paragraph 29.

1 Commission Regulation 2454/93 Art 86(2), OJ 11.10.93 L253/1, as amended by Commission Regulation 12/97, OJ 13.1.97 L9/1. Whenever a certificate is issued retrospectively it must contain the endorsement 'issued retrospectively' or 'Delivre a posteriori'. Special rules apply also in the case of loss of the certificate of origin. See ibid Art 87.

2 Ibid Art 82(1).

3 Ibid Art 82(2); see also ibid Art 82(3). In the absence of any express provision to the contrary, an importer may not be denied the right to produce a valid certificate after the expiry of the period during which the regulation establishing the tariff preference was in force provided that the certificate related to a transaction affected during that time. See Case 231/81 *Hauptzollamt Wurzburg v H Weidenmann GmbH & Co* [1982] ECR 2259, paragraph 12. However, this possibility is excluded when the certificate is produced after the customs duties for the goods which benefited previously from a tariff preference have been reintroduced. See Case 321/82 *Volkswagenwerk AG v Hauptzollamt Braunschweig* [1983] ECR 3355, paragraph 11.

4 Commission Regulation 2454/93 Art 82(4), OJ 11.10.93 L253/1, as amended by Commission Regulation 12/97, OJ 13.1.97 L9/1. This procedure will be applicable for the quantities and a period determined by the competent customs authorities which in any case cannot exceed three months. A similar proof or origin may also be requested for the importation of dismantled or non-assembled products. See ibid Art 83.

If originating products in a beneficiary country are placed under the customs control of a customs office in the Community, it will be possible to replace the original proof of origin by one or more certificates of origin Form A for the purpose of sending all or some of these products elsewhere within the Community or in Norway or Switzerland.[5] The replacement certificate will be issued by the customs office under whose control the products are placed on the basis of a written request by the re-exporter and it will be regarded as the definitive certificate of origin for the products to which it refers.[6]

An invoice declaration may serve as proof of origin in a beneficiary country if it is made out by an approved Community exporter,[7] or by any exporter for any consignment consisting of one or more packages containing or originating products whose total value does not exceed Ecu 3000, and provided that authorities of the beneficiary country assist the Community.[8]

The customs authorities of the Community may authorize as an approved exporter any exporter who makes frequent shipments of Community goods and who offers, to the satisfaction of the customs authorities, all guarantees necessary to verify the originating status of the products as well as the fulfilment of the other requirements of the Community rules on the origin of goods.[9] In this sense, the customs authorities must grant to the approved exporter a customs authorization number which must appear on the invoice declaration.[10]

An invoice declaration may be produced if the products concerned can be considered as originating in the Community or in a beneficiary country.[11] The exporter making the invoice declaration must be prepared to submit at any time, at the request of the customs or governmental authorities of the exporting country, all appropriate documents sustaining the originating status of the goods concerned and providing that all conditions are fulfilled.[12]

The evidence of Community origin status of products which are thereafter subject in the beneficiary country to such working or processing operations as to become originating in that beneficiary country must be furnished either by production of a EUR.1 movement certificate[13] or by production of an invoice declaration.[14]

The discovery of slight discrepancies between the statements made in the certificate of origin Form A, in the EUR.1 movement certificate or in an invoice declaration, and those made in the documents produced to the customs office

---

5 Ibid Art 88(2).
6 Ibid Art 88(2). As to the details of the replacement certificate see ibid Art 88(3); see also ibid Art 88(4); see also ibid Art 88(5). For products benefiting from the special derogations for least developed countries, this replacement certificate procedure will only apply when such goods are intended for the Community. See ibid Art 88(6).
7 Ibid Art 90(1)(a).
8 Ibid Art 90(1)(b). Concerning the meaning of consignment see ibid Art 66(j). In this case the use of the invoice declaration is subject to special conditions. See ibid Art 90(6).
9 Ibid Art 90a(1). The customs authorities may grant the status of approved exporter on any conditions which they consider appropriate. See ibid Art 90a(2).
10 Ibid Art 90a(3).
11 Ibid Art 90(a). As to the details of the invoice declaration see ibid Art 80(b); see also ibid Art 90(4); see also ibid Art 90(5); see also Annex 18 to Commission Regulation 2454/93, OJ 11.10.93 L253/1.
12 Commission Regulation 2454/93 Art 90(2), OJ 11.10.93 L253/1, as amended by Commission Regulation 12/97, OJ 13.1.97 L9/1.
13 Ibid Art 90b(1)(a). As to the specimen of such certificate see Annex 21 Commission Regulation 2454/93, OJ 11.10.93 L253/1.
14 Commission Regulation 2454/93 Art 90(1)(b), OJ 11.10.93 L253/1, as amended by Commission Regulation 12/97, OJ 13.1.97 L9/1.

for the purpose of carrying out the formalities for importing the products will not *ipso facto* render the certificate or declaration null and void, provided that it is duly established that the document does correspond to the products concerned.[15]

The entitlement to benefit from the generalized tariff preferences is subject to the setting up of a co-operation procedure between the beneficiary countries and the Community authorities.[16] Subsequent verification of certificates of origin Form A and invoice declarations may be carried out at random or whenever the customs authorities in the Community have reasonable doubt as to the authenticity of the document or as to the accuracy of the information regarding the true origin of the products in question.[17] In such cases, the Community customs authorities will return a copy of the certificate of origin Form A or the invoice declaration to the competent governmental authorities of the exporting beneficiary country, giving the reasons of form or substance of such enquiry and any information that has been obtained suggesting that the particulars given on the said certificate or the invoice declaration are inaccurate.[18] The exporting beneficiary country must communicate the results of its verification within six months. The results must be such as to establish whether the

---

15 Ibid Art 92. Likewise, obvious formal errors such as typing errors on a certificate of origin Form A, EUR.1 movement certificate or an invoice declaration should not cause the document to be rejected if these errors are not such as to create doubts concerning the correctness of the statements made in the document. Ibid.

16 Ibid Art 93. For this purpose the beneficiary countries must inform the Commission of the names and addresses of the governmental authorities which are empowered to issue certificates of origin together with the specimens of stamps used by those authorities and the names and addresses of the governmental authorities responsible for the control of the certificates and the invoice declarations. See ibid Art 93(1). Likewise the Commission must send the beneficiary countries specimens of the stamps used by the customs authorities of the Member States to issue EUR.1 movement certificates.

17 Ibid Art 94(1). The Court has held that the benefit of the preferential system is linked to the origin of the goods and, thus, a verification is a necessary element of the system. The Community rules, however, seek to avoid, for practical reasons, a systematic verification of the origin of the products, which would excessively delay the customs transactions. Thus, the Community rules provide for two kinds of subsequent verification of certificates of origin, namely at random or whenever the customs authorities responsible have reasonable doubts as to the authenticity of the document or the accuracy of its information. Normally, subsequent verification at random can only take place after the production of the certificate and customs clearance which automatically follows such production when there is nothing to cast initial doubt on the authenticity of the certificate. In this sense, the Court has considered that it must be recognized that the possibility of checking after importation without the importer's having been previously warned may cause him difficulties when in good faith he has thought he was importing goods benefiting from tariff preferences in reliance on certificates which, unbeknown to him, were incorrect or falsified. Yet, the Court has held that the Community does not have to bear the adverse effects of the wrongful acts of the suppliers of its nationals, the importer can attempt to obtain compensation from the perpetrator of the fraud and furthermore, in calculating the benefits from trade in goods likely to enjoy tariff preferences, a prudent trader aware of the rules must be able to assess the risks inherent in the market which he is considering and accept them as normal trade risks. See Case 827/79 *Amministrazione delle Finanze v Ciro Acampora* [1980] ECR 3731, paragraphs 7–8. Furthermore, the customs authorities are not required to recognize the assessments made by the customs authorities of the beneficiary exporting country in the case of unilateral tariff preferences. See Joined Cases C-153/94 & C-204/94 *R v Customs and Excise Comrs, ex p Faroe Seafood Co Ltd* [1996] ECR I-2465, paragraph 24.

18 Commission Regulation 2454/93 Art 94(2), OJ 11.10.93 L253/1, as amended by Commission Regulation 12/97, OJ 13.1.97 L9/1. If the Community authorities decide to suspend the tariff preferences pending the results of the verification, they must offer to release the products to the importer subject to any protective measures judged necessary.

certificate of origin Form A or the invoice declaration in question applies to the products actually exported and whether these products are in fact eligible to benefit from the tariff preferences.[19] In cases of reasonable doubt, if there is no reply within six months or such reply does not contain sufficient information to determine the authenticity of the document in question or the real origin of the products, a second communication shall be sent to the competent authorities. If after the second communication, the results are not communicated within a period of four months or these do not contain the necessary information to determine the authenticity of the documents or the origin of the products concerned, the Community authorities must refuse entitlement to the preferential tariff measures except in the case of exceptional circumstances.[20]

Various republics and territories

In general terms, the Commission implementing regulation establishes the same rules of origin for products coming from the Republics of Bosnia-Herzegovina and Croatia, Federal Republic of Yugoslavia, Former Yugoslav Republic of Macedonia, and Territories of the West Bank and the Gaza Strip as those established for the purposes of the Generalized System of Preferences.[1]

ACP rules

The Lome IV Convention establishes non-reciprocal tariff preferences in favour of the ACP countries. Thus, many of the principles of interpretation of the rules of origin for the purpose of the Generalized System of Preferences are applicable to those laid down in Lome IV. However, the ACP rules of origin have certain particularities. Protocol 1 of the Lome IV Convention establishes the definition of the concept of originating products and methods of administrative co-operation.[2]

For the purpose of implementing the trade co-operation provisions of the Lome IV Convention, a product is considered to be originating in the ACP states if it has been either wholly obtained or sufficiently worked or processed in the ACP states.[3] With regard to the concept of products wholly obtained the Protocol establishes specific provisions for fishery products. Products wholly obtained in the ACP countries, in the Community or in the OCT, may include products of sea fishing and other products taken by the sea by their vessels.[4] The term 'their vessels' applies only to vessels which are registered or recorded in a Member State, in an ACP State, or in an OCT, which sail under the flag of a Member State, of an ACP State or of an OCT, which are owned to an extent of at least 50 per cent by nationals of States party to the Convention, or of an

19 Ibid Art 94(3).
20 Ibid Art 94(5). Special rules apply for regional groups see ibid Art 94(5). The Community rules concerning the issue, use and subsequent verification of certificates of origin Form A will apply *mutatis mutandis* to products originating in Ceuta and Melilla. See ibid Art 96(4). For these purposes the Spanish customs authorities are responsible for the application of these rules in Ceuta and Melilla. See ibid Art 96(5).
1 See Commission Regulation 2454/93 Arts 98–123, OJ 11.10.93 L253/1, as amended by Commission Regulation 12/97, OJ 13.1.97 L9/1.
2 See Protocol 1, EC Citation of the Lome IV.
3 Ibid Art 1.
4 Ibid Art 2(1)(f).

OCT, or by a company with its head office in one of these States or OCT, of which the manager or managers, chairman of the board of directors or the supervisory board, and the majority of the members of such boards, are nationals of States party to the Convention or of an OCT and of which, in addition in the case of partnerships or limited companies, at least half the capital belongs to States party to the Convention or to public bodies or nationals of such States or of an OCT, of which 50 per cent of the crew, master and officers included, are nationals of States party to the Convention or of an OCT.[5] Furthermore, where an ACP State offers the Community the opportunity to negotiate a fisheries agreement and the Community does not accept this offer, the ACP State concerned may charter or lease third country vessels to undertake fisheries activities in its exclusive economic zone and request that such vessel be treated as their vessel. The Community will recognize vessels chartered or leased by the ACP State as their vessels under the following conditions. First, the Community must not have availed itself of the opportunity to negotiate a fisheries agreement with the ACP State concerned. Second, at least 50 per cent of the crew, master and officers included, must be nationals of States party to the Convention or of an OCT. Third, the charter or lease must be accepted by the Commission as providing adequate opportunities for developing the capacity of the ACP State to fish on its own account and in particular conferring on the ACP State the responsibility for the nautical and commercial management of the vessel placed at its disposal for a significant period of time.[6]

The Protocol establishes also a value tolerance higher than that established for the Generalized System of Preferences. Non-originating materials may be used in the manufacture of a given product, provided their total value does not exceed 15 per cent of the ex-works price of the final product and subject to the conditions laid down in Note 4.4 in Annex I to the Protocol.[7]

Furthermore, the Protocol provides for liberal cumulation rules. For the purpose of establishing the origin of goods covered by the Lome IV Convention, the ACP States are considered as being one territory.[8] When products wholly obtained in the Community or in the OCT undergo working or processing in the ACP States, they must be considered as having been wholly obtained in the ACP States.[9] Working or processing carried out in the Community or in the OCT must be considered as having been carried out in the ACP States, when the materials undergo working or processing in the ACP States.[10] Moreover, at the request of the ACP States, products originating in a neighbouring country, other than an ACP State, belonging to a coherent geographical entity, will be considered as originating in the ACP State where they undergo further working or processing, provided that the working or processing carried out in the ACP State exceeds the insufficient operations listed in Art 3(3) of the Protocol,[11] and

---

5 Ibid Art 2(2).
6 Ibid Art 2(3).
7 Ibid Art 5.
8 Ibid Art 6(1). As to the information procedure for cumulation purposes see ibid Art 23.
9 Ibid Art 6(2).
10 Ibid Art 6(3). Arts 6(2) and 6(3) apply to any working or processing carried out in the ACP States, including the operations listed in Art 3(3). See ibid Art 6(4).
11 However, products of Chapter 50–63 of the Harmonized System must in addition undergo in the ACP State at least working or processing as a result of which the product obtained receives a classification under a heading of the Harmonized System different from than covering the products originating in the the non-ACP developing country. For products listed in Annex X to the Protocol, only the specific processing referred to in its column 3 will apply, whether or not it involves a change of heading. See ibid Art 6(5).

the ACP States, the Community and the other countries concerned have concluded an agreement on adequate administrative procedures which will insure the correct application of the rules.[12] The ACP–EC Council of Ministers will decide on the ACP requests on the basis of a report drawn up by the ACP–EC Customs Co-operation Committee.[13]

Originating products made up of materials wholly obtained from sufficiently processed products in two or more ACP States will be considered as products originating in the ACP State where the last working or processing took place, provided this working or processing exceeded the insufficient operations listed in Art 3(3)(a), (b), (c) and (d) or a combination thereof.[14]

Finally, the Protocol allows for the derogation of its rules where the development of existing industries or the creation of new industries justifies them at the request of the ACP State or States concerned.[15] The examination of requests will in particular take into account the level of development or the geographical situation of the ACP State or States concerned;[16] cases where the application of the existing rules of origin would significantly affect the ability of an existing industry in an ACP State to continue its exports to the Community, with particular reference to cases where this could lead to cessation of its activities;[17] specific cases where it can be clearly demonstrated that significant investment in an industry could be deterred by the rules of origin and where a derogation favouring the realization of the investment programme would enable these rules to be satisfied by stages.[18] However, in every case an examination will be made to ascertain whether the rules relating to cumulation of origin do not provide a solution to the problem.[19] Where a request for derogation concerns a least-developed or an island ACP State, its examination must be carried out with a favourable bias having particular regard to the economic and social impact of the decision to be taken especially in respect of employment[20] and the need to apply the derogation for a period taking into account the particular situation of the ACP State concerned and its difficulties.[1] Special account will be taken, case by case, of the possibility of conferring originating status on products which include in their composition materials originating in neighbouring developing countries, least developed countries or developing countries with which one or more ACP States have special relations, provided that satisfactory administrative co-operation can be established.[2] The derogation must be granted where the value added to the non-originating products used in the ACP State or States concerned is at least 45 per cent of the value of the finished product, provided that the derogation is not such as to cause serious injury to an economic sector of the Community or of one

---

12 This possibility does not apply to tuna products classified under Harmonized System Chapters 3 or 16, rice products of the HS code 1006 or the textile products listed in Annex XI to the Protocol. See ibid Art 6(5).
13 Ibid Art 6(5). As to the procedure to be followed by the Committee see ibid Art 30.
14 Ibid Art 7.
15 Ibid Art 31(1). As to the content of the request see ibid Art 31(2). Concerning derogations from the definition of originating products to take account of the special situation of Zambia regarding the production of polyester-cotton yarn see Decision 5/97 of the ACP-EC Customs Co-operation Committee, OJ 6.12.97 L335/19.
16 Ibid Art 31(3)(a).
17 Ibid Art 31(3)(b).
18 Ibid Art 31(3)(c).
19 Ibid Art 31(4).
20 Ibid Art 31(5)(a).
 1 Ibid Art 31(5)(b).
 2 Ibid Art 31(6).

or more Member States.[3] Upon request derogations concerning canned tuna and tuna loins will be automatically granted, with an annual quota of 4000 tonnes for canned tuna and with an annual quota of 500 tonnes for tuna loins.[4]

EFTA agreements

Following the amendments made during the last years, the EFTA, EEA and the Europe agreements contain very similar provisions concerning cumulation, the basic origin rule, the general tolerance rule, a prohibition of drawback of or exemption from customs duties, and proof of origin and administrative co-operation.

The rules of origin of goods covered by the EFTA agreements are contained in Protocol 3 to such agreements.[5] The protocol contains special provisions concerning cumulation, the basic origin rule, the general tolerance rule, the principle of territoriality, a prohibition of drawback of or exemption from customs duties, and proof of origin.

For the purposes of the Agreement, products originating in the Community are products wholly obtained in the Community;[6] products obtained in the Community incorporating materials which have not been wholly obtained there, provided that such materials have undergone sufficient working or processing in the Community;[7] and goods originating in the European Economic Area within the meaning of Protocol 4 to the Agreement in the European Economic Area.[8] Similarly products originating in Switzerland are products wholly obtained therein, and products obtained in Switzerland incorporating materials which have not been wholly obtained there, provided that such materials have undergone sufficient working or processing in Switzerland. Materials originating in the Community will be considered as materials originating in Switzerland when incorporated into a product obtained there. In this sense, it will not be necessary that such materials have undergone sufficient working or processing, provided they have undergone working or processing beyond what are considered to be insufficient operations.[9] Likewise, materials originating in Switzerland will be considered as materials originating in the Community when incorporated into a product obtained there even though such materials have not undergone sufficient working or processing, provided they have undergone working or processing beyond what are considered to be insufficient operations.[10]

Moreover, materials originating in Poland, Hungary, the Czech Republic, the Slovak Republic, Bulgaria, Romania, Latvia, Lithuania, Estonia, Slovenia, Iceland or Norway within the meaning of the Agreements between the Community and Switzerland and these countries must be considered as originating in the Community or Switzerland when incorporated into a product obtained

3 Ibid Art 31(7).
4 Ibid Art 31(8). As to the procedure to be followed in the adoption of the derogation see ibid Art 31(9). As to the period of validity and possible extensions see ibid Art 31(10).
5 See Protocol 3, concerning the definition of the concept of originating products and methods of administrative co-operation, to the Agreement between the European Economic Community and the Swiss Confederation, OJ 31.12.72 L300/191, as amended by Decision 1/96 of the EC-Switzerland Joint Committee, OJ 23.7.97 L195/1.
6 Protocol 3 to the Agreement between the European Economic Community and the Swiss Confederation Art 2(1)(a), as amended.
7 Ibid Art 2(1)(b).
8 Ibid Art 2(1)(c).
9 Ibid Art (3)(1). As to the concept of insufficient operations see ibid Art 7.
10 Ibid Art 3(2).

there. In such cases it will not be necessary that such materials have undergone sufficient working or processing.[11] However, such materials will only continue to be considered as originating in the Community or Switzerland when the value added there exceeds the value of the materials used originating in any of the other countries. Otherwise, the products concerned must be considered as originating in the country which accounts for the highest value of originating materials used.[12]

Although the Protocol formally maintains the sufficiently worked or processed rule to determine the origin of goods not wholly obtained in the Community or Switzerland, in practice it has replaced this general rule by a product-specific test. Products are considered to be sufficiently worked or processed when the conditions set out in the list of Annex II are fulfilled.[13] If a product which has acquired originating status by fulfilling the conditions set out in the list is used in the manufacture of another product, the conditions applicable to the products in which it is incorporated do not apply to it, and no account must be taken of the non-originating materials which may have been used in its manufacture.[14] Moreover, all the operations carried out in either the Community or Switzerland on a given product must be considered together when determining whether the working or processing undergone by that product is to be regarded as an insufficient operation to confer origin status.[15]

The protocol contains also special provisions concerning the general tolerance rule.[16] Non-originating materials which, according to the conditions set out in the list of Annex II, should not be used in the manufacture of a product may nevertheless be used provided that:

(1) their total value does not exceed 10 per cent of the ex-works price of the product;
(2) any of the percentages given in the list for the maximum value of non-originating materials are not exceeded as a consequence of the application of this exception.[17]

The Protocol provides for an exception to the principle of territoriality under which all working or processing operations must take place without interruption in the Community or Switzerland for products to benefit from the preferential treatment. The acquisition of originating status must not be affected by working or processing carried out outside the Community or Switzerland on materials exported from the Community or Switzerland and subsequently reimported there, provided that:

(1) the said materials are wholly obtained in the Community or Switzerland or have undergone there working or processing going beyond what are

---

11 Ibid Art 4(1) This cumulation will only apply where the processing requirements for non-originating materials to obtain originating status contained in the Agreements concerned are identical to the requirements contained in Annex II to the Protocol. See ibid Art 4(3).
12 Ibid Art 4(2) In this sense, in the allocation of origin, no account must be taken of the other countries which have undergone sufficient working or processing in the Community or Switzerland.
13 Ibid Art 6(1).
14 Ibid Art 6(1).
15 Ibid Art 7(2).
16 This exception does not apply to products falling within Chapters 50 to 63 of the Harmonized System. See ibid Art 6(2).
17 Ibid Art 6(2).

considered to be in the Protocol insufficient operations prior to their exportation;[18] and

(2) it can be demonstrated to the satisfaction of the customs authorities that
the reimported goods result from the working or processing of the exported materials and the total added value acquired outside the Community or Switzerland carried out through the application of this exception
does not exceed 10 per cent of the ex-works price of the final product for
which originating status is claimed.[19]

The Protocol also contains a prohibition of drawback of or exemption from
customs duties. Non-originating materials used in the manufacture of products
originating in the Community, Switzerland or in one of the other countries for
which diagonal cumulation may apply for which a proof of origin is issued or
made out must not be subject in the Community or Switzerland to drawback of,
or exemption from, customs duties of whatever kind.[20] Furthermore, products
falling within Chapter 3 and heading 1604 to 1605 of the Harmonized System
and originating in the Community within the meaning of the Protocol for which
a proof of origin is issued or made out must not be subject in the Community to
drawback of or exemption from customs duties or whatever kind.[1]

Finally, the Protocol provides for simplified procedures for proof of origin,
special provisions for approved exporters and particular rules of administrative
co-operation.[2]

---

18 Ibid Art 11(3)(a).
19 Ibid Art 11(3)(b). As to the concept of total value added see ibid Art 11(5). This exception
   does not apply to products which do not fulfil the conditions set out in Annex II and which
   can only be considered as sufficiently worked or processed as a result of the application of the
   general tolerance rule. See ibid Art 11(6).
20 Ibid Art 15(1)(a). This prohibition applies to any arrangement for refund, remission or non-
   payment, partial or complete, of customs duties or charges having an equivalent effect, applicable in the Community or Switzerland to materials used in the manufacture and to products
   falling within Chapter 3 and heading 1604 to 1605 of the Harmonized System, where such
   refund remission or non-payment applies, expressly or in effect, when products obtained for
   the said materials are exported and not when they are retained for home use there. See ibid
   Art 15(2). This prohibition applies only in respect of materials which are of the kind to which
   the Agreement applies. They will not preclude the application of an export refund system for
   agricultural products in accordance with the provisions of the Agreement. See ibid Art 15(5).
   The prohibition applies also in respect of packings, accessories, spare parts and tools and
   products in a set within the meaning of the Protocol. See ibid Art 15(4).
 1 Ibid Art 15(1)(b).
 2 See ibid Titles V and VI. In this sense, the Court has distinguished between the principles ruling
   proof of origin and administrative co-operation in those agreements establishing free trade
   areas and in which reciprocal rights and duties are contained and those unilateral or conventional measures where it is the Community alone which grants preferential benefit to third
   countries. With regard to agreements establishing free trade areas the Court has maintained
   that the systems laid down by the Protocols are based on a co-operation between the customs
   authorities of both parties and on the reliance that must be placed on the acts of those authorities and can function only if the customs authorities of the importing state recognize the determinations
   legally made by the authorities of the exporting state. See Case 218/83 *Les Rapides Savoyards
   Sarl v Directeur General des Douanes et Droits Indirects* [1984] ECR 3105; see also Case C-12/
   92 *Criminal Proceedings Against Edmond Huygen* [1993] ECR I-6381. Furthermore, the Court
   has held that in the context of reciprocal trade agreements, exceptions to the obligation to
   present the certificate of proof of origin may be permitted where the trader in question is
   confronted with quite exceptional circumstances which are outside its control and whose consequences could not have been avoided in spite of all care taken. See Case C-12/92 *Criminal
   Proceedings Against Edmond Huygen* [1993] ECR I-6381; see also Case C-334/93 *Bonapharma
   Arzneimittel GmbH v Hauptzollamt Krefeld* [1995] ECR I-319.

The European Economic Area

The rules of origin of goods for the European Economic Area are provided for in Protocol 4 of the agreement.[3] The EEA rules of origin provide for certain particularities concerning cumulation, the basic origin rule, the general tolerance rule, working or processing carried outside the EEA, a prohibition of drawback of or exemption from customs duties, and proof of origin.

A product is considered to be originating in the EEA within the meaning of the EEA Agreement if it has been either wholly obtained there or sufficiently worked or processed in the EEA. For this purpose, the territories of the Contracting Parties to which the Agreement applied must be considered as a single territory.[4] Furthermore, materials originating in Poland, Hungary, the Czech Republic, the Slovak Republic, Bulgaria, Romania, Latvia, Lithuania, Estonia, Slovenia or Switzerland, within the meaning of the Agreements between the Contracting Parties and these countries, must be considered as originating in the EEA when incorporated into a product obtained there without it being necessary that such materials have undergone sufficient working or processing.[5] Products which have acquired such originating status will only continue to be considered as products originating in the EEA when the value added there exceeds the value of the materials used originating in any of the previously referred countries. Where this is not the case, the products concerned will be considered as originating in the country which accounts for the highest value of the originating materials used. In the allocation of origin, no account must be taken of materials originating in the other countries which have undergone sufficient working or processing in the EEA.[6]

Although the sufficiently worked or processed rule is formally maintained, it is in fact replaced by a product-specific test. To determine whether a product originates in the EEA, products which are not wholly obtained are considered to be sufficiently worked or processed when the conditions set out in the list of Annex II to the Protocol are fulfilled.[7] The list contains a test for all products covered by the EEA Agreement.[8] If a product which has acquired originating status by fulfilling the conditions set out in the list is used in the manufacture of another product, the conditions applicable to the product in which it is incorporated do not apply to it, and no account must be taken of the non-originating materials which may have been used in its manufacture.

Furthermore, the Protocol includes a list of insufficient working or processing operations which do not confer status or originating status.[9] However, to

3 See Protocol 4 to the Agreement on the European Economic Area, OJ 3.1.94 L1/1 as replaced by Decision of the EEA Joint Committee 71/96, OJ 23.1.97 L21/12.
4 Protocol 4 to the Agreement on the European Economic Area Art 2(1), OJ 3.1.94 L1/1 as replaced by Decision of the EEA Joint Committee 71/96, OJ 23.1.97 L21/12. Certain exceptions apply to the Principality of Liechtenstein until 1 January 2000. See ibid Art 2(2).
5 Ibid Art 3(1). This cumulation rule may only be applied where the processing requirements for non-originating materials to obtain originating status contained in the Agreements concerned are identical to the requirements contained in Annex II to the Protocol. See ibid Art 3(3).
6 Ibid Art 3(2).
7 Ibid Art 5(1).
8 See List of working or processing required to be carried out on non-originating materials in order that the product manufactured can obtain originating status, Annex II to Protocol 4 to the Agreement on the European Economic Area, OJ 3.1.94 L1/1 as replaced by Decision of the EEA Joint Committee 71/96, OJ 23.1.97 L21/12, at 32.
9 See Protocol 4 to the Agreement on the European Economic Area Art 6(1), OJ 3.1.94 L1/1 as replaced by Decision of the EEA Joint Committee 71/96, OJ 23.1.97 L21/12.

determine whether a processing falls under the definition of insufficient operation all the operations carried out in the EEA on a given product must be considered together.[10]

The EEA rules of origin introduce also a general tolerance rule on the amount of non-originating material which can be used in excess of the origin conditions normally required.[11] Non-originating materials which, according to the conditions set out in the list, should not be used in the manufacture of a product may nevertheless be used, provided that:

(1) their total value does not exceed 10 per cent of the ex-works price of the product;[12]
(2) any of the percentages given in the list of the Annex for the maximum value of non-originating materials are not exceeded through the application of this exception.[13]

The EEA rules of origin also provide for an exception to the principle of territoriality identical to that of the EFTA agreements.[14] It includes also similar provisions to the EFTA rules concerning the prohibition of drawback of or exemption from customs duties.[15]

Finally, the Protocol provides for special rules concerning proof of origin.[16]

Europe Agreements

The rules of origin of goods of the Europe Agreements are laid down in Protocol 4 of each of the agreements.[17] The Europe Agreements' originating rules provide for particularities relating to cumulation, the basic origin rule, the general tolerance rule, the prohibition of drawback of or exemption from customs duties, and the application of a simplified procedure.

For the purposes of the Agreement, products originating in the Community are products wholly obtained in the Community;[18] products obtained in the Community incorporating materials which have not been wholly obtained there, provided that such materials have undergone sufficient working or processing in the Community;[19] and goods originating in the European Economic Area within the meaning of Protocol 4 to the Agreement in the European Economic

---

10 Ibid Art 6(2).
11 This general tolerance rule does not apply to products falling within Chapters 50–60 of the Harmonized System. See ibid Art 5(2).
12 Ibid Art 5(2)(a).
13 Art 5(2)(b).
14 See ibid Art 11(3); see also ibid Art 11(4); see also ibid Art 11(5); see also ibid Art 11(6); see also ibid Art 11(7).
15 See ibid Art 14.
16 See Title V of Protocol 4 to the Agreement on the European Economic Area, OJ 3.1.94 L1/1 as replaced by Decision of the EEA Joint Committee 71/96, OJ 23.1.97 L21/12.
17 See Protocol 4, concerning the definition of the concept of originating products and methods of administrative co-operation, to Europe Agreement establishing an association between the European Communities and their Member States, on the one part, and the Republic of Hungary, on the other part, OJ 31.12.93 L347/2, as amended by Council Decision 3/96 of the Association Council, Association between the European Communities and their Member States, on the one part, and the Republic of Hungary on the other part, OJ 7.4.97 L92/1. Similar rules apply in respect of other Europe Agreements.
18 Protocol of the Europe Agreement with the Republic of Hungary Art 2(1)(a).
19 Ibid Art 2(1)(b).

Area.[20] Similarly, products originating in the Republic of Hungary are products wholly obtained in Hungary;[1] and products obtained in Hungary incorporating materials which have not been wholly obtained there, provided that such materials have undergone sufficient working or processing in Hungary.[2] Yet materials originating in the Community must be considered as materials originating in Hungary when incorporated into a product obtained there. In this sense, it will not be necessary that such materials have undergone sufficient working or processing, provided that they have undergone working or processing going beyond what are considered to be insufficient operations.[3] Likewise, materials originating in Hungary will be considered as materials in the Community when incorporated into a product obtained there without it being necessary that such materials have undergone sufficient working or processing provided they have undergone working or processing going beyond what are considered to be insufficient operations.[4]

Furthermore, the Protocol provides also for the possibility of diagonal cumulation of origin. Thus, materials originating in Poland, the Czech Republic, the Slovak Republic, Bulgaria, Romania, Latvia, Lithuania, Estonia, Slovenia, Iceland, Norway, or Switzerland within the meaning of the Agreements between the Community and Hungary and these countries must be considered as originating in the Community or Hungary when incorporated into a product obtained there. In such case, it will not be necessary that such materials have undergone sufficient working or processing.[5] However, such materials will only continue to be considered as originating in the Community or Hungary when the value added there exceeds the value of the materials used originating in any of the other countries. Otherwise, the products concerned must be considered as originating in the country which accounts for the highest value of originating materials used.[6]

Although the Protocol formally maintains the sufficiently worked or processed rule in order to determine the origin of goods not wholly obtained in Hungary or the Community, it has in practice replaced such rule by a product-specific test. Thus, for the purposes of determining whether a product originates in the Community or Hungary, products which are not wholly obtained are considered to be sufficiently worked or processed when the conditions set out in the list of Annex II are fulfilled.[7] However, if a product which has acquired originating status by fulfilling the conditions set out in the list is used in the manufacture of another product, the conditions applicable to the products in which it is incorporated do not apply to it, and no account must be taken of the non-originating materials which may have been used in its manufacture.[8] Moreover, all the operations carried out in either the Community or Hungary on a given product must be considered together when determining whether the

20 Ibid Art 2(1)(c).
 1 Ibid Art 2(2)(a).
 2 Ibid Art 2(2)(b).
 3 Ibid Art 3(1). As to the insufficient operations see ibid Art 7.
 4 Ibid Art 3(2).
 5 Art 4(1). This cumulation may only be applied where the materials used have acquired the status of originating products by an application of rules of origin identical to the rules in the Protocol. See ibid Art 4(3).
 6 Ibid Art 4(2). In this sense, in the allocation of origin, no account must be taken of the other countries which have undertaken sufficient working or processing in the Community or Hungary.
 7 Ibid Art 6(1).
 8 Ibid Art 6(1).

working or processing undergone by that product is to be regarded as an insufficient operation to confer origin status.[9]

The Protocol contains also special provisions concerning the general tolerance rule identical to those of the EFTA and EEA agreements.[10] It also contains similar provisions concerning the prohibition of drawback of or exemption from customs duties.[11]

Finally, the Europe Agreements provide also for a simplified procedure for approved exporters.[12]

The Mediterranean Agreements

The rules of origin of goods for the purposes of the Mediterranean Agreements are laid down in a protocol to such agreements.[13] These rules of origin provide for particularities relating to bilateral cumulation, special cumulation rules concerning goods from Tunisia, Algeria and Morocco, sufficiently worked or processed products, direct transport and proof of origin.

For the purpose of the Agreement between the Community and Tunisia, products originating in the Community are products wholly obtained in the Community as well as products obtained in the Community which contain materials not wholly obtained there, provided that such materials have undergone sufficient working and processing within the meaning of the Protocol.[14] Likewise, products originating in Tunisia are products wholly obtained in Tunisia together with products obtained in Tunisia which contain materials not wholly obtained there, provided that the said materials have undergone sufficient working or processing in Tunisia within the meaning of the Protocol.[15] Yet the Protocol establishes special bilateral cumulation rules. Thus, materials originating in Tunisia within the meaning of the Protocol must be considered as materials originating in the Community without having undergone sufficient working or processing, provided, however, that they have undergone processing or working going beyond what are considered to be insufficient operations.[16] Similarly, materials originating in the Community must be considered as materials originating in Tunisia without having to undergo sufficient working or processing there, provided that they have undergone working or processing beyond what are considered to be insufficient operations.[17]

Furthermore, the agreements with Tunisia, Morocco and Algeria, contain special cumulation rules concerning goods coming from any of these countries. Hence, in the case of the agreement with Tunisia, material originating in Algeria or Morocco within the meaning of the protocols to the agreements between the Community and these countries must be considered as originating in the Community or in Tunisia without such materials having undergone sufficient working or processing in the latter countries, provided that they have under-

---

9 Ibid Art 7(2).
10 See ibid Art 6(2).
11 See ibid Art 15.
12 See ibid Art 22.
13 See Protocol 4 to Euro-Mediterranean Agreement establishing an association between the European Communities and their Member States, on the one part, and the Republic of Tunisia, on the other part, OJ 30.3.98 L97/2.
14 Ibid Art 2(1).
15 Ibid Art 2(2).
16 Ibid Art 3(1).
17 Ibid Art 2(2).

gone there working or processing beyond what are considered to be insufficient operations.[18] This cumulation will only be applicable to the materials originating in Algeria or Morocco to the extent that trade between the Community and Algeria or Morocco and trade between Tunisia and Algeria or Morocco is governed by identical rules of origin.[19] Where the originating products are obtained in two or more of either the Community, Tunisia, Algeria, or Morocco, they must be considered as originating products of the state or the Community according to where the last working or processing took place, provided that working or processing went beyond what are considered to be insufficient operations.[20]

The Protocol also contains particular rules concerning sufficiently worked or processed products. Non-originating materials are considered to be sufficiently worked or processed when the product obtained is classified in a heading which is different from that in which all the non-originating materials used in its manufacture are classified as long as they have undergone working or processing beyond what are considered to be insufficient operations.[1] However, for products mentioned in columns 1 and 2 of the list in Annex II to the Protocol, the conditions set out in column 3 for the product concerned must be fulfilled. Yet, for products falling under chapters 84 to 91 of the CN, the exporter may opt to apply the conditions set out in column 4 instead of those set out in column 3.[2]

The Protocol also includes special provisions concerning direct transport. Taking into account the special cumulation rules applying to Algeria and Morocco and Tunisia, it provides that preferential treatment provided for under the agreement applies only to products or materials which are transported between the territories of the Community and Tunisia or if applicable, of Algeria and Morocco, without entering any other territory.[3] Furthermore, goods originating in Tunisia or in the Community may be transported by pipeline across territory other than that of the Community or Tunisia.[4]

The Protocol contains also special provisions regarding a simplified procedure for the issue of certificates of origin.[5]

---

18 Ibid Art 4(1); see also ibid Art 4(2).
19 Ibid Art 4(3); see also ibid Art 4(4).
20 Ibid Art 5(3).
 1 Ibid Art 7(1).
 2 Ibid Art 7(2).
 3 Ibid Art 15(1).
 4 Ibid.
 5 See Art 22.

Chapter 3

Valuation of goods

INTRODUCTION

As most customs duties are imposed *ad valorem*, the third factor on the basis of which duties and other measures prescribed in respect of trade in goods are applied is the customs value of such goods. The Customs Code defines the customs value for the purposes of applying the customs tariff and non tariff measures laid down by Community provisions governing specific fields relating to trade in goods.[1] The basic objective of the Community rules on customs valuation is to foster world trade by introducing a fair, uniform and neutral form of customs valuation of goods for the application of the Common Customs Tariff excluding the use of arbitrary or fictitious values.[2]

THE TRANSACTION VALUE

The basic method to determine the customs value of the imported good is its transaction value, that is, the price actually paid or payable for the goods when sold for export to the customs territory of the Community, adjusted where necessary.[3] In this sense, the price actually paid or payable is the total payment made or to be made by the buyer to or for the benefit of the seller for the

---

1 Council Regulation 2913/92 Art 28, OJ 19.10.92 L302/1. Specific provisions apply regarding the determination of the value for customs purposes of goods released for free circulation after being assigned a different customs approved treatment or use. See ibid Art 36(1). The Community rules on customs valuation follow closely the Agreement on the Implementation of Article VII of the General Agreement on Tariffs and Trade 1994, OJ 23.12.94 L336/119. The rules on the valuation of goods for customs purposes are based on the assumption that the imported goods are capable of being put on the market and absorbed into commercial circulation. In this sense, no distinction can be made between illegal products, such as illegal drugs, which have not been discovered and those which are destroyed under the control of the competent authorities. See Case 50/80 *Joszef Horvath v Hauptzollamt Hamburg-Jonas* [1981] ECR 385, paragraph 12; see also Case 221/81 *Wilfried Wolf v Hauptzollamt Dusseldorf* [1982] ECR 3681, paragraph 15.

2 See Case 7/83 *Ospig Textilgesellschaft KGW Ahlers v Hauptzollamt Bremen-Ost* [1984] ECR 609, paragraph 14.

3 Council Regulation 2913/92 Art 29(1), OJ 19.10.92 L302/1. In this regard, the fact that the goods which are subject of a sale are declared for free circulation will be considered as an adequate indication that they were sold for export to the customs territory of the Community. In the case of successive sales before valuation, only the last sale, which led to the introduction of the goods into the customs territory of the Community, or a sale taking place in the customs territory of the Community before entry for free circulation of the goods will be considered as such indication. If a price is declared which relates to a sale taking place before

imported goods and includes all payments made or to be made as a condition of sale of the imported goods by the buyer to the seller or by the buyer to a third party to satisfy an obligation of the seller.[4] The customs value must be calculated on the basis of the conditions on which the individual sale was made, even if they do not accord with trade practice or may appear unusual for the type of contract in question.[5] The price paid or payable must be made to a buyer established in the customs territory of the Community, a buyer who has its residence or place of business therein.[6] However, there is nothing to prevent both parties to such sale from being established in the Community.[7] The price actually paid or payable refers to the price of the imported goods. Thus, the flow of dividends or other payments from the buyer to the seller that do not relate to the imported goods are not part of the customs value.[8]

For the purpose of determining the transaction value, the rules of customs valuation must be interpreted without reference to the rules on the system of export and import licences. Quota charges connected with the acquisition of

---

the last sale on the basis of which the goods were introduced into the customs territory of the Community, it must be demonstrated to the satisfaction of the customs authorities that this sale of goods took place for export to the customs territory in question. See Commission Regulation 2454/93 Art 147(1), OJ 11.10.93 L253/1, as amended by Commission Regulation 1762/95, OJ 21.7.95 L171/8.

4   Council Regulation 2913/92 Art 29(3)(a), OJ 19.10.92 L302/1. An example of indirect payment would be the settlement by the buyer whether in whole or in part of a debt owed by the seller. See Interpretative Note to Art 29(3)(a) in *Interpretative Notes on Customs Value*, Annex 23 of Commission Regulation 2454/93, OJ 11.10.93 L253/1. The payment need not necessarily take the form of a transfer of money. Payment may be made by way of letters of credit or negotiable instrument and may be made directly or indirectly. Ibid. Activities, including marketing activities, undertaken by the buyer on his own account, other than those for which an adjustment is provided in Art 32, are not considered to be an indirect payment to the seller, even though they might be regarded as of benefit to the seller or have been undertaken by agreement with the seller, and their cost will not be added to the price actually paid or payable in determining the customs value of imported goods. See Council Regulation 2913/92 Art 29(3)(b), OJ 19.10.92 L302/1. As to the concept of marketing activities see Commission Regulation 2454/93 Art 149, OJ 11.10.93 L253/1. If the price actually paid or payable includes an amount in respect of any internal tax applicable within the country of origin or export in respect of the goods in question, such amount must not be incorporated in the customs value provided that it can be demonstrated to the satisfaction of the customs authorities that the goods in question have been or will be relieved therefrom for the benefit of the buyer. See ibid Art 146. In most cases, the transaction value will be the invoiced price. In this sense, the Court has held that the customs authorities may not in principle reduce the customs value declared. However, the determination of value for customs purposes cannot have the effect of requiring the fiscal and financial authorities of the Member States to accept that valuation for purposes other than the application of the Common Customs Tariff. See Case 54/80 *Procureur de la Republique v Samuel Wilner* [1980] ECR 3673, paragraph 8; see also Case 65/79 *Procureur de la Republique v Rene Chatain* [1980] ECR 1345, paragraph 16–17.

5   See Case 65/85 *Hauptzollamt Hamburg-Ericus v Van Houten International GmbH* [1986] ECR 447, paragraph 13.

6   See Case 111/79 *Suisse Caterpillar Overseas v Belgium* [1980] ECR 773, paragraph 11. To meet this requirement it is not necessary that the registered office of the buyer in the case of a company must be in the customs territory of the Community. It suffices that the buyer has an establishment there which carries out activities such as may be exercised by an independent undertaking in the same sector and has its own accounts allowing the customs authorities to carry out the necessary inspections and checks. Ibid paragraph 13.

7   See Case C-11/89 *Unifert Handels GmbH Warendorf v Hauptzollamt Munster* [1990] ECR I-2275, paragraph 11.

8   See Interpretative Note to Art 29(1) in *Interpretative Notes on Customs Value*, Annex 23 of Commission Regulation 2454/93, OJ 11.10.93 L253/1.

export quotas in the context of a quota system may not be taken into account for the calculation of the valuation of goods for customs purposes.[9] However, although quotas allocated free of charge to the seller may have a commercial value, they entail no charges. Thus, amounts invoiced in respect of those quotas constitute in reality a disguised element of the price of the goods and, thus, they must be included as part of the customs value.[10] Certificates of authenticity, unlike export licences, are inseparably connected to the goods in question. Hence, the costs of acquisition of such certificates must be regarded as an integral part of the price paid or payable for the goods and therefore of the customs value.[11]

Where the price has not actually been paid at the material time for customs valuation purposes, the price payable for settlement at the said time will as a general rule be taken as the basis for customs valuation.[12] If the goods declared for free circulation are part of a larger quantity of the same goods purchased in one transaction, the price actually paid or payable will be that price represented by the proportion of the total price which the quantity so declared bears to the total quantity purchased.[13] The same proportional rule will apply in the case of loss of part of the consignment or when the goods being valued have been damaged before entry into free circulation.[14] In order to benefit from this proportional rule, the products must have been bought free of defect but arrived in the customs territory of the Community as damaged products.[15] However, if the parties, in their sale contract, have made express provision for the possibility of a discrepancy between the quantity of goods purchased and the quantity unloaded, and the buyer has accepted that risk within the limits of an agreed allowance, the customs value must remain unchanged.[16]

Such transaction value will be adopted as the customs value provided that:

9 The same solution applies whether it is the buyer who buys the quota from a third party or whether it is the seller who buys the quota from a third party. See Case 7/83 *Ospig Textilgesellschaft KGW Ahlers v Hauptzollamt Bremen-Ost* [1984] ECR 609, paragraphs 14–17. Furthermore, whether the export licences are the subject of lawful or unlawful trade is immaterial as there is no difference in economic terms between the two cases. See Case C-29/93 *Ospig Textil-Gesellschaft W Ahlers GmbH & Co KG v Hauptzollamt Bremen-Freihafen* [1994] ECR I-1963, paragraph 15.
10 See Case C-340/93 *Klaus Thierschmidt GmbH v Hauptzollamt Essen* [1994] ECR I-3905, paragraph 19. Quota charges not included in the customs value do not need to be indicated separately in the declaration of customs value. Ibid paragraph 28.
11 See Case C-219/88 *Malt GmbH v Hauptzollamt Dusseldorf* [1990] ECR I-1481, paragraphs 14–15.
12 Commission Regulation 2454/93 Art 144(1), OJ 11.10.93 L253/1.
13 Ibid Art 145(1).
14 Ibid Art 145(2). However, if the goods are used in a third country between the time of sale and the time of entry into free circulation, the customs value need not be the transaction value. See Commission Regulation 2454/93 Art 147(2), OJ 11.10.93 L253/1, as amended by Commission Regulation 1762/95, OJ 21.7.95 L171/8.
15 See Case 183/85 *Hauptzollamt Itzehoe v H J Repenning GmbH* [1986] ECR 1873, paragraph 18. However, no distinction is to be made according to whether the damage or loss occurred before or after the risk passed to the buyer. *See Case C-59/92 Hauptzollamt Hamburg-St Annen v Ebbe Sonnichsen GmbH* [1993] ECR I-2193, paragraph 4.
16 See Case C-11/89 *Unifert Handels GmbH Warendorf v Hauptzollamt Munster* [1990] ECR I-2275, paragraph 36. Furthermore, the excess of total weight of the goods, which is the foreseeable consequence of the obligation to guarantee the agreed minimum weight per unit, must be taken into consideration for the determination of the value of goods. See Case 91/74 *Hauptzollamt Hamburg-Ericus v Hamburger Import-Kompanie GmbH* [1975] ECR 643.

(1)   there are no restrictions as to the disposal or use of the goods by the buyer, other than restrictions which are imposed by a law or by the public authorities in the Community, limiting the geographical area in which the goods may be resold, or not substantially affecting the value of goods;[17]

(2)   the sale or price is not subject to some consideration or consideration for which a value cannot be determined with respect to the goods being valued;[18]

(3)   no part of the proceeds of any subsequent resale, disposal or use of the goods by the buyer will accrue directly or indirectly to the seller, unless an appropriate adjustment can be made;[19] and

(4)   the buyer and seller are not related.[20] Persons will be considered to be related only if: they are officers or directors of one another's business;[1] they are legally recognized partners in business;[2] they are employer and employee;[3] any person directly or indirectly owns, controls or holds 5% or more of the outstanding voting stock or shares of both of them;[4] one of them directly or indirectly controls the other;[5] both of them are directly or indirectly controlled by a third person;[6] together they directly or indirectly control a third person;[7] or they are members of the same family.[8] Yet, persons who are associated in business with one another in that one is the sole agent, sole distributor or sole concessionaire of the other will not necessarily be considered as related.[9]

17 Council Regulation 2913/92 Art 29(1)(a), OJ 19.10.92 L302/1. An example of a restriction which does not substantially affect the value of goods would be the case where a seller requires a buyer of automobiles not to exhibit them prior to a fixed date which represents the beginning of a model year. See Interpretative Note to Art 29(1)(a) in *Interpretative Notes on Customs Value*, Annex 23 of Commission Regulation 2454/93, OJ 11.10.93 L253/1.

18 Council Regulation 2913/92 Art 29(1)(b), OJ 19.10.92 L302/1. An example could be where the seller establishes the price of the imported goods on condition that the buyer will also buy other goods in specified quantities. See Interpretative Note to Art 29(1)(b) in *Interpretative Notes on Customs Value*, Annex 23 of Commission Regulation 2454/93, OJ 11.10.93 L253/1. However, if it is established that the sale or price of the imported goods is subject to a condition or consideration the value of which can be determined with respect to the goods being valued, such value will be considered as an indirect payment by the buyer to the seller and part of the price actually paid or payable provided that the condition or consideration does not relate to other activities, including marketing activities, undertaken by the buyer on his own account; or a factor in respect of which an addition is to be made to the price actually paid or payable under Art 32 of the Customs Code. See Commission Regulation 2454/93 Art 148, OJ 11.10.93 L253/1.

19 Council Regulation 2913/92 Art 29(1)(c), OJ 19.10.92 L302/1. As to the appropriate adjustments to be made see ibid Art 32.

20 Ibid Art 29(1)(d); see also Case 111/79 *Suisse Caterpillar Overseas v Belgium* [1980] ECR 773, paragraphs 18–20.

1 Commission Regulation 2454/93 Art 143(1)(a), OJ 11.10.93 L253/1.

2 Ibid Art 143(1)(b).

3 Ibid Art 143(1)(c).

4 Ibid Art 143(1)(d).

5 Ibid Art 143(1)(e). In this sense, one person will be deemed to control another when the former is legally or operationally in a position to exercise restraint or direction over the latter. See Interpretative Note to Art 143(1)(e) in *Interpretative Notes on Customs Value*, Annex 23 of Commission Regulation 2454/93, OJ 11.10.93 L253/1.

6 Commission Regulation 2454/93 Art 143(1)(f), OJ 11.10.93 L253/1.

7 Ibid Art 143(1)(g).

8 As to persons which are considered to be of the same family see ibid Art 143(1)(h).

9 Ibid Art 143(2).

However, in determining whether the transaction value is acceptable, the fact that the buyer and the seller are related will not in itself be sufficient grounds for regarding the transaction value as unacceptable. Where necessary, the circumstances surrounding the sale will be examined and the transaction value will be accepted provided that the relationship did not influence the price. If in the light of information provided by the declarant or otherwise, the customs authorities have grounds for considering that the relationship influenced the price, they must communicate those grounds to the declarant who must be given a reasonable opportunity to respond.[10] In a sale between related persons, the transaction value will be accepted wherever the declarant demonstrates that such value closely approximates to one of the following occurring at or about the same time:

(1) the transaction value in sales, between buyers and sellers who are not related in any particular case, of identical or similar goods for export to the Community;[11]
(2) the customs value of identical or similar goods as determined by the value based on the unit price at which the imported goods for identical or similar imported goods are sold within the Community in the greatest aggregate quantity to persons not related to sellers;[12]
(3) the customs value of identical or similar goods, as determined by the computed value, consisting of the sum of the cost or value of materials and fabrication or other processing employed in producing the imported goods, an amount for profit and general expenses equal to that usually reflected in sales of goods of the same class or kind as the goods being valued which are made by the producers in the country of exportation for export to the Community, and the costs of transport and insurance of the imported goods, and loading and handling charges associated with the transport of the imported goods to the place of introduction into the customs territory of the Community.[13]

These tests are to be used at the initiative of the declarant and only for comparison purposes to determine whether the transaction value is relevant despite the relationship between the buyer and seller. The tests may not be used to establish substitute values.[14]

---

10 Council Regulation 2913/92 Art 29(2)(a), OJ 19.10.92 L302/1. If the declarant so requests, the communication of the grounds must be in writing; see also Interpretative Note to Art 29(2) in *Interpretative Notes on Customs Value*, Annex 23 of Commission Regulation 2454/93, OJ 11.10.93 L253/1.
11 Council Regulation 2913/92 Art 29(2)(b)(i), OJ 19.10.92 L302/1.
12 Ibid Art 29(2)(b)(ii); see also ibid Art 30(2)(c).
13 Ibid Art 29(2)(b)(iii); see also ibid Art 30(2)(d); see also ibid Art 32(1)(e). As to the meaning of goods of the same class or kind see Commission Regulation 2454/93 Art 142(1)(e), OJ 11.10.93 L253/1. In applying the foregoing tests, due account must be taken of demonstrated differences in commercial levels, quantity levels, the elements enumerated in Art 32CC and costs incurred by the seller in sales in which it and the buyer are not related and where such costs are not incurred by the seller in sales in which it and the buyer are related. See Council Regulation 2913/92 Art 29(2)(b), OJ 19.10.92 L302/1; see also Interpretative Note to Art 29(2)(b) in *Interpretative Notes on Customs Value*, Annex 23 of Commission Regulation 2454/93, OJ 11.10.93 L253/1.
14 Council Regulation 2913/92 Art 29(2)(c), OJ 19.10.92 L302/1.

ADJUSTMENTS TO BE MADE TO THE TRANSACTION VALUE

In determining the transaction value, there must be added to the price actually paid or payable for the imported goods:[15]

(1)   commission and brokerage, except buying commissions,[16] the costs of containers which are treated as being one, for customs purposes, with the goods in question,[17] the costs of packing, whether for labour or materials;[18] to the extent that they are incurred by the buyer but are not included in the price actually paid or payable for the goods;[19]

(2)   the value, apportioned as appropriate, of materials, components, parts and similar items incorporated in the imported goods,[20] tools, dies, moulds and similar items used in the production of the imported goods,[1] materials consumed in the production of the imported goods,[2] engineering, development, artwork, design work, and plans and sketches undertaken elsewhere than in the Community and necessary for the production of the imported goods;[3] where supplied directly or indirectly by the buyer free of

15 Art 32 of the Code contains an exhaustive list of ancillary costs which must be added to the price actually paid or payable for the purpose of determining the customs value. Costs which are not included in this list can be taken into account for the purpose of determining the customs value only if they are regarded as an integral part of the price of the goods. See Case 219/88 *Malt GmbH v Hauptzollamt Dusseldorf* [1990] ECR I-1481, paragraphs 12–13. The general principle is that services and goods included in the list of Art 32 of the Code should not be excluded even if they are provided or produced in the customs territory of the Community. See Case C-116/89 *BayWa AG v Hauptzollamt Weiden* [1991] ECR I-1095, paragraph 15; see also Case C-11/89 *Unifert Handels GmbH Warendorf v Hauptzollamt Munster* [1990] ECR I-2275, paragraph 25.

16 Council Regulation 2913/92 Art 32(1)(a)(i), OJ 19.10.92 L302/1; see also ibid Art 33(1)(e). As to the concept of buying commissions see ibid Art 32(4).

17 Ibid Art 32(1)(a)(ii). Where the containers are to be the subject of repeated importations, their cost must, at the request of the declarant, be apportioned, as appropriate, in accordance with generally accepted accounting principles. See Commission Regulation 2454/93 Art 154, OJ 11.10.93 L253/1.

18 Council Regulation 2913/92 Art 32(1)(a)(iii), OJ 19.10.92 L302/1. The term packings refers to containers which are suitable not only for transporting the product in question but also for storing and marketing them. If the packings are not purchased by the importer but merely placed at its disposal by the seller on condition that they are returned, and where the price payable by the importer does not include the price of packings, their value must not be included in the customs value as it is not part of the transaction value. However, in the case in which the cost of packing is represented by the payment of financial compensation for the loss of containers, to be determined and paid separately after the imported goods have been consumed, it is necessary to adjust ex post facto the value for those goods for customs purposes. See Case 357/87 *Firma Albert Schmid v Hauptzollamt Stuttgart-West* [1988] ECR 6239.

19 Council Regulation 2913/92 Art 32(1)(a), OJ 19.10.92 L302/1.

20 Ibid Art 32(1)(b)(i). Licence fees which are provided to grow harvest seeds thereafter imported into the Community must be considered as materials, components, parts and similar items incorporated in the imported goods. See Case C-116/89 *BayWa AG v Hauptzollamt Weiden* [1991] ECR I-1095.

1 Council Regulation 2913/92 Art 32(1)(b)(ii), OJ 19.10.92 L302/1.

2 Ibid Art 32(1)(b)(iii).

3 Ibid Art 32(1)(b)(iv). This provision concerns only services which are necessary for the production of the imported goods. See Case C-116/89 *BayWa AG v Hauptzollamt Weiden* [1991] ECR I-1095, paragraph 17; see also Interpretative Note to Art 32(1)(b)(iv) in *Interpretative Notes on Customs Value*, Annex 23 of Commission Regulation 2454/93, OJ 11.10.93 L253/1. In this sense, the cost of research and preliminary design sketches is not to be included in the customs value. See Commission Regulation 2454/93 Art 155, OJ 11.10.93 L253/1.

charge or at reduced cost for use in connection with the production and sale for export of the imported goods, to the extent that such value has not been included in the price actually paid or payable;[4]

(3) royalties and licence fees relating to the goods being valued that the buyer must pay, either directly or indirectly, as a condition of sale of the goods being valued, to the extent that such royalties and fees are not included in the price actually paid or payable.[5]

Furthermore, in the case in which the manufactured article and process of use thereof are so closely linked that the manufactured article and the process of use are embodied in one and the same article, the patent rights for the process of use must be included in the customs value of the article.[6] However, charges for the right to reproduce the imported goods in the Community will not be added to the price actually paid or payable for the imported goods in determining the customs value. Furthermore, payments made by the buyer for the right to distribute or resell the imported goods must not be added to the price actually paid or payable for the imported goods if such payments are not a condition of the sale for export to the Community of the goods.[7] Moreover, a royalty or licence fee will be added to the price actually paid or payable only when the payment is related to the goods being value, and constitutes a condition of sale of those goods.[8] If the imported goods are only an ingredient or component of goods manufactured in the Community, an adjustment to the price paid or payable for the imported goods must be made when the royalty or licence fee relates to those goods.[9] If royalties or licence fees relate partly to the imported goods and partly to other ingredients or component parts added to the goods after their importation, or to post importation activities or services, an appropriate apportionment must be made only on the basis of objective and quantifiable data.[10] A royalty or licence fee in respect of the right to use a trade mark

4 Council Regulation 2913/92 Art 32(1)(b), OJ 19.10.92 L302/1.

5 Ibid Art 32(1)(c); see also Interpretative Note to Art 32(1)(c) in *Interpretative Notes on Customs Value*, Annex 23 of Commission Regulation 2454/93, OJ 11.10.93 L253/1. As to the concept of royalties and licence fees see Commission Regulation 2454/93 Art 157(1), OJ 11.10.93 L253/1. In this sense, the country of residence of the recipient of the royalty or licence fee will not be a material consideration. See ibid Art 162. Where the method of calculation of the amount of a royalty or licence fee derives from the price of the imported goods, it may be assumed in the absence of evidence to the contrary that the payment of that royalty or licence fee is related to the goods to be valued. However, where the amount of a royalty or licence fee is calculated regardless of the price of the imported goods, the payment of that royalty or licence fee may nevertheless be related to the goods to be valued. See ibid Art 161; see also Case 82/76 *Farbwerke Hoechst AG v Hauptzollamt Frankfurt-am-Main* [1977] ECR 335.

6 See Case 1/77 *Robert Bosch GmbH v Hauptzollamt Hildesheim* [1977] ECR 1473, paragraph 5; see also Case 135/77 *Robert Bosch GmbH v Hauptzollamt Hildeheim* [1978] ECR 855.

7 Council Regulation 2913/92 Art 32(5), OJ 19.10.92 L302/1.

8 Commission Regulation 2454/93 Art 157(2), OJ 11.10.93 L253/1. When the buyer pays royalties or licence fees to a third party, these conditions will not be considered as met unless the seller or a person related to it requires the buyer to make that payment. See ibid Art 160.

9 Ibid Art 158(1). In this sense, where goods are imported in an unassembled state or only have to undergo minor processing before resale, such as diluting or packing, this will not prevent a royalty or licence fee from being considered related to the imported goods. See ibid Art 158(2).

10 Ibid Art 158(3). Concerning the method of appropriate apportionment see Interpretative Note to Art 32(2) in *Interpretative Notes on Customs Value*, Annex 23 of Commission Regulation 2454/93, OJ 11.10.93 L253/1.

is only to be added to the price actually paid or payable for the imported goods where the royalty or licence fee refers to goods which are resold in the same state or which are subject only to minor processing after importation, the goods are marketed under the trade mark, affixed before or after importation, for which the royalty or licence fee is paid and the buyer is not free to obtain such goods from other suppliers unrelated to the seller.[11]

(4)   the value of any part of the proceeds of any subsequent resale, disposal or use of the imported goods that accrues directly or indirectly to the seller;[12]
(5)   the cost of transport and insurance of the imported goods and loading and handling charges associated with the transport of the imported goods to the place of introduction into the customs territory of the Community.[13]

Where goods are carried by the same mode of transport to a point beyond the place of introduction into the customs territory of the Community, the transport costs must be assessed in proportion to the distance covered outside and inside the customs territory of the Community, unless evidence is produced to the customs authorities to show the costs that would have been incurred under a general compulsory schedule of freight rates for the carriage of the goods to the place of introduction into the customs territory of the Community.[14] If several means of transport are used and if, therefore, different schedules of freight rates have been applied, there is no longer any direct relationship between the proportion of the total distance represented by the journey outside the Community and the proportion of the costs relating thereto. In such cases, the cost of transport must be calculated, either by deducting the costs of transport within the customs territory of the Community, determined on the basis of the schedule of freight rates normally applied, from the price actually paid or payable, or by determining the costs of transport to the place of introduction into the customs territory of the Community on the basis of the rates normally applied.[15]If goods are invoiced at a uniform free domicile price which corresponds to the price at the place of introduction, transport

---

11 Commission Regulation 2454/93 Art 159, OJ 11.10.93 L253/1.
12 Council Regulation 2913/92 Art 32(1)(d), OJ 19.10.92 L302/1.
13 Ibid Art 32(1)(e). Regarding the concept of the place of introduction into the customs territory of the Community see Commission Regulation 2454/93 Art 163, OJ 11.10.93 L253/1. The term cost of transport must be interpreted as including all costs, whether they are main or incidental costs, incurred in connection with moving the goods to the customs territory of the Community. Therefore, demurrage charges, which consist of compensation provided for in the shipping contract to compensate the ship owner for any delays arising during the loading of the vessel, must be considered to be covered by the term cost of transport. See Case C-11/89 *Unifert Handels GmbH Warendorf v Hautzollamt Munster* [1990] ECR I-2275, paragraph 29. The air transport costs to be included in the customs value of goods will be determined by applying the rules and percentages shown in Annex 25 Commission Regulation 2454/93, OJ 11.10.93 L253/1. See Commission Regulation 2454/93 Art 166, OJ 11.10.93 L253/1. As to the rules on postal charges see ibid Art 165.
14 Ibid Art 164(a). A container transport does not constitute a means of transport since it may be effected in different ways and the costs of transport varies depending on the way chosen. See Case C-17/89 *Hauptzollamt Frankfurt am Main-Ost v Deutsch Olivetti GmbH* [1990] ECR I-2301, paragraph 15.
15 See Case C-17/89 *Hauptzollamt Frankfurt am Main-Ost v Deutsch Olivetti GmbH* [1990] ECR I-2301, paragraph 25.

costs within the Community will not be deducted from the price.[16] Yet, such deduction will be allowed if evidence is produced to the customs authorities that the free-frontier price would be lower than the uniform domicile price.[17] Where transport is free or provided by the buyer, transport costs to the place of introduction, calculated in accordance with the schedule of freight rates normally applied for the same modes of transport, must be included in the customs value.[18]

The additions to be made to the price actually paid or payable must be made only on the basis of objective and quantifiable data.[19] However, the customs authorities may, at the request of the person concerned, authorize certain elements which are to be added to the price actually paid or payable, and though not quantifiable at the time of incurrence of the customs debt, are to be determined on the basis of appropriate and specific criteria.[20]

However, provided that they are shown separately from the price actually paid or payable, the following costs will not be included in the customs value:[1]

(1) charges for the transport of goods after their arrival at the place of introduction into the customs territory of the Community;[2]
(2) charges for construction, erection, assembly, maintenance or technical assistance, undertaken after importation of imported goods such as industrial plants, machinery or equipment;[3]
(3) charges for interest under a financing arrangement entered into by the buyer and relating to the purchase of imported goods, irrespective of whether the

---

16 Commission Regulation 2454/93 Art 164(b), OJ 11.10.93 L253/1. A uniform price implies a price which is uniform for every place of destination within the area where it is applied and includes in general a fixed amount intended to cover the average costs of transport of the goods from the place of dispatch to the various places of destination. The concept of uniform free domicile price must be interpreted as meaning that the price in question is not necessarily uniform for all destinations within the customs territory of the Community. See Case 84/79 *Richard Meyer-Uetze KG v Hauptzollamt Bad Reichenhall* [1980] ECR 291, paragraphs 8–9.

17 This exception must be interpreted as meaning that it is not necessary to prove that the same supplier has in fact sold the goods at a free frontier invoice price. Instead, it is necessary to determine the price which a prospective purchaser would have had to pay for a free frontier purchase of the goods which have be assessed, all other conditions of the sale being identical, in the event of importation through the same place of introduction. See Case 84/79 *Richard Meyer-Uetze KG v Hauptzollamt Bad Reichenhall* [1980] ECR 291, paragraph 12.

18 Commission Regulation 2454/93 Art 164(c), OJ 11.10.93 L253/1.

19 Council Regulation 2913/92 Art 32(2), OJ 19.10.92 L302/1.

20 In such cases, the declared customs value is not to be considered as provisional within the meaning of Commission Regulation 2454/93 Art 254, OJ 11.10.93 L253/1. See Art 156a(1) ibid as inserted by Commission Regulation 1676/96, OJ 28.8.96 L218/1. As to the conditions under which this authorization may be granted see ibid Art 156a(2).

1 These costs must be paid by the importer on the basis of a separate invoice or charge and be distinguished in the declaration value from the price actually paid or payable for the goods. The value declaration cannot be corrected by the importer after the time for valuation for customs purposes, which is to say, after the goods have been released to free circulation. However, the Court has considered that the customs authorities may, if the circumstances warrant it, check the invoice relating to the costs in question in order to verify that the costs which have been invoiced are not fictitious. See Case 290/84 *Hauptzollamt Schweinfurt v Mainfrucht Obstverwertung GmbH* [1985] ECR 3909; see also Case C-79/89 *Brown Boveri & Cie AG v Hauptzollamt Mannheim* [1991] ECR I-1853, paragraph 35.

2 Council Regulation 2913/92 Art 33(1)(a), OJ 19.10.92 L302/1.

3 Ibid Art 33(1)(b).

finance is provided by the seller or another person.[4] In this sense, where a seller of goods allows the buyer time to pay, that constitutes a financial arrangement as soon as the buyer accepts the deferred payment. To be a financial arrangement it is not necessary for such deferred payment to be the subject of a specific agreement between the buyer and the seller, separate from the agreement relating to the sale of the imported goods. The price to take into account in determining the value for customs purposes in the case of deferred payment is the price for forward payment, unless a discount for cash payment was provided or the existence of a different price for cash payment was proved at the customs department. In this sense, it is inadequate as proof of the existence of a price different from the price for forward payment to show that the price for forward payment includes credit charges. What must be proved is the existence of another price of a definite amount for which the buyer or other buyers in similar circumstances are entitled to settle in the event of payment before the agreed date.[5] Furthermore, where charges for interest payable as consideration for the deferred payment agreed by the seller are a separate item on the invoice sent to the buyer, it must be considered that, where there is no objection on the part of the buyer, it has in effect agreed to the charges for interest relating to the deferred payment.[6] The same is true where the charges for interest can be inferred from the difference between the prices for payment CAD (cash against documents) and deferred payment respectively and those prices are specified in the agreement between the two parties relating to the sale, rather than on the invoice.[7]

(4)   charges for the right to reproduce imported goods in the Community;[8]

(5)   buying commissions;[9]

---

4 Provided that the financing arrangement has been made in writing and where required, the buyer can demonstrate that such goods are actually sold at the price declared as the price actually paid or payable and the claimed rate of interest does not exceed the level for such transaction prevailing in the country where, and at the time when, the finance was provided. See ibid Art 33(1)(c). This deduction will be applied *mutatis mutandis* where the customs value is determined by applying a method other than the transaction value. See Commission Regulation 2454/93 Art 156, OJ 11.10.93 L253/1.

5 See Case 8/73 *Hauptzollamt Bremerhaven v Massey-Ferguson GmbH* [1973] ECR 897, paragraphs 8–11.

6 See Case C-21/91 *Wunsche v Hauptzollamt Hamburg-Jonas* [1992] ECR I-3647.

7 See Case C-93/96 *Industria e Comercio Textil (ICT) v Fazenda Publica* [1997] ECR I-2881, paragraph 17.

8 Council Regulation 2913/92 Art 33(1)(d), OJ 19.10.92 L302/1.

9 Ibid Art 33(1)(e). The concept of buying commission does not include an amount paid by the buyer to the seller if the amount is calculated in such a way as to permit the seller to cover its administrative costs and other general costs not directly related to the sale in question. See Case C-11/89 *Unifert Handels GmbH Warendorf v Hauptzollamt Munster* [1990] ECR I-2275, paragraph 24. With regard to the situation of a buying agent acting in its own name but on behalf of the importer, the Court has held that since such agent acts on behalf of the importer, its function in relation to the purchase of goods is only one of representation and it bears no financial risks in the purchase. Consequently even if it acts in its own name, its function is limited to participation as indirect representative in a contract of sale concluded in fact between its principal and the supplier. The transaction to which reference must be made in order to determine the customs value in accordance with Art 29 is accordingly the transaction between the manufacturer or supplier of the goods and the importer. The fact that the transaction is carried out through the medium of a buying agent is irrelevant in this regard since the financial risk connected with the transaction is assumed by the importer. Therefore, the sum paid by the importer to the buying agent for the service of representing it in the purchase of the goods in question constitutes a buying commission, which according to Art 33(1)(e) must not be included in the customs value. In this sense, the fact that the importer has entered the agent's name

(6)   import duties or other charges payable in the Community by reason of the importation or sale of the goods.[10]

As a way of derogation, the customs authorities may, at the request of the person concerned, authorize certain charges which are not to be included in the customs value, in cases where the amounts relating to such elements are not shown separately at the time of incurrance of the customs debt, to be determined on the basis of appropriate and specific criteria.[11]

SECONDARY VALUATION METHODS

The Customs Code lays down a list of successive rules to determine the customs value where the transaction value between the exporter and the importer cannot be established or accepted.

First of all, where the transaction value cannot be accepted or defined, the customs value will be determined by taking the transaction value of identical goods sold for export to the Community and exported at about the same time as the goods being valued.[12] The customs value must be determined by reference to the transaction value of identical goods in a sale at the same commercial level and in substantially the same quantity as the goods being valued. If no such sale is found, the transaction value of identical goods sold at a different commercial level and/or in different quantities, adjusted to take account of differences attributable to commercial level and/or quantity must be used, provided that such adjustments can be made on the basis of demonstrated evidence which clearly establishes the reasonableness and accuracy of the adjustment, whether the adjustment leads to an increase or a decrease in the value.[13] If transport and insurance costs are included in the transaction value, an adjust-

as seller in its customs value declaration and has declared the price of the goods invoiced by the agent does not affect the customs value arising from the application of Art 29. See Case C-299/90 *Hauptzollamt Karlsruhe v Gebr Hepp GmbH & Co KG* [1991] ECR I-4301.

10 Council Regulation 2913/92 Art 33(1)(f), OJ 19.10.92 L302/1. This provision concerns only duties or other charges payable in the Community and not those paid elsewhere. See Case 219/88 *Malt GmbH v Hauptzollamt Dusseldorf* [1990] ECR I-1481, paragraph 17. Costs of warehousing are not to be included in the customs value and must be deducted from the transaction value if they are included. See Case 38/77 *Enka BV v Inspecteur der Invoerrechten en Accijnzen, Arnhem* [1977] ECR 2203. Furthermore, the customs value does not include the cost of determining the quantity of goods on arrival at their destination where such goods are paid for by the buyer. See Case 65/85 *Hauptzollamt Hamburg-Ericus v Van Houten International GmbH* [1986] ECR 447, paragraph 14.

11 In such cases, the declared customs value is not to be considered as provisional within the meaning of Art 254. See Commission Regulation 2454/93 Art 156a(1), OJ 11.10.93 L253/1 as inserted by Commission Regulation 1676/96, OJ 28.8.96 L218/1. Concerning the conditions under which the authorization must be granted see ibid Art 156a(2).

12 Council Regulation 2913/92 Art 30(2)(a), OJ 19.10.92 L302/1; see also Interpretative Note to Art 30(2)(a) in *Interpretative Notes on Customs Value*, Annex 23 to Commission Regulation 2454/93, OJ 11.10.93 L253/1. Concerning the meaning of identical goods see Commission Regulation 2454/93 Art 142(1)(c), OJ 11.10.93 L253/1; see also ibid Art 142(2). A transaction value for goods produced by a different person will be taken into account only when no transaction value can be found for identical goods produced by the same person as the goods being valued. See ibid Art 150(4).

13 Ibid Art 150(1). If more than one transaction value of identical goods is found, the lowest such value must be used to determine the customs value of the imported goods. See ibid Art 150(3).

ment must be made to take account of significant differences in such costs and charges between the imported goods and the identical goods in question arising from differences in such costs and charges between the imported goods and the identical goods in question arising from differences in distances and modes of transport.[14]

Second, if it is not possible to determine the transaction value for identical goods, the customs value will be based on the transaction value of similar goods sold for export to the Community and exported at about the same time as the goods being valued.[15] Again the customs value will be determined by reference to the transaction value of similar goods in a sale at the same commercial level and in substantially the same quantity as the goods being valued. If no such sale is found, the transaction value of similar goods sold at a different commercial level and/or in different quantities, adjusted to take account of differences attributable to commercial level and/or to quantity, must be used, provided that such adjustments can be made on the basis of demonstrated evidence which clearly establishes the reasonableness and accuracy of the adjustment, whether this adjustment leads to an increase or a decrease in the value.[16] Where transport and insurance costs are included in the transaction value, an adjustment must be made to take account of significant differences in such costs and charges between the imported goods and the similar goods in question arising from differences in distances and modes of transport.[17]

Third, if the transaction value for similar goods cannot be determined, the customs value will be based on the unit price at which the imported goods for identical or similar imported goods are sold within the Community in the greatest aggregate quantity to persons not related to the sellers.[18] If the imported goods or identical similar goods are sold in the Community in the condition as imported, the customs value of the imported goods must be based on the unit price at which the imported goods or identical similar goods are sold in the greatest aggregate quantity, at about the time of importation of the goods being valued, to persons who are not related to the persons from whom they buy such goods, subject to deductions for either the commissions usually paid or agreed

---

14 Ibid Art 150(2).
15 Council Regulation 2913/92 Art 30(2)(b), OJ 19.10.92 L302/1; see also Interpretative Note to Art 30(2)(b) in *Interpretative Notes on Customs Value*, Annex 23 of Commission Regulation 2454/93, OJ 11.10.93 L253/1. Regarding the meaning of similar goods see Commission Regulation 2454/93 Art 142(1)(d), OJ 11.10.93 L253/1; see also ibid Art 142(2). A transaction value for goods produced by a different person will be taken into account only when no transaction value can be found for similar goods produced by the same person of the goods being valued. See ibid Art 151(4).
16 Ibid Art 151(1). If more than one transaction value of similar goods is found, the lowest of such value must be used to determine the customs value for the imported goods. See ibid Art 151(3).
17 Ibid Art 151(2).
18 Council Regulation 2913/92 Art 30(2)(c), OJ 19.10.92 L302/1. The unit price at which imported goods are sold in the greatest aggregate quantity is the price at which the greatest number of units is sold in sales to persons who are not related to the persons from whom they buy such goods at the first commercial level after importation at which such sales take place. See Commission Regulation 2454/93 Art 152(3), OJ 11.10.93 L253/1; see also Interpretative Note to Art 152(3) in *Interpretative Notes on Customs Value*, Annex 23 to Commission Regulation 2454/93, OJ 11.10.93 L253/1. In this sense, any sale in the Community to a person who supplies directly or indirectly free of charge or at reduced cost for use in connection with the production and sale for export of the imported goods any elements specified in Art 32(1)(b) of the Customs Code must not be taken into account in establishing the unit price. See 152(4) Commission Regulation 2454/93, OJ 11.10.93 L253/1.

to be paid or the additions usually made for profit and general expenses in connection with sales in the Community of imported goods of the same class or kind;[19] the usual costs of transport and insurance associated costs incurred within the Community;[20] the import duties and other charges payable in the Community by reason of the importation or sale of the goods.[1] If neither the imported goods nor identical or similar imported goods are sold at or about the same time of importation of the goods being valued, the customs value of imported goods must be based on the unit price at which the imported goods or identical or similar imported goods are sold in the Community in the condition as imported at the earliest date after importation of the goods being valued but before the expiration of 90 days after such importation.[2] Where neither the imported goods nor identical or similar goods are sold in the Community in the conditions as imported, then, if the importer so requests, the customs value must be based on the unit price at which the imported goods, after further processing, are sold in the greatest aggregate quantity to persons in the Community who are not related to the persons from whom they buy such goods, due allowance being made for the value added by such processing and the necessary deductions.[3]

When this third system is not possible, the customs value will be based on the computed value, consisting of the sum of the cost or value of materials and fabrication or other processing employed in producing the imported goods, and amount for profit and general expenses equal to that usually reflected in sales of goods of the same class or kind as the goods being valued which are made by producers in the country of exportation for export to the Community and the cost of transport and insurance of the imported goods and loading and handling charges associated with the transport of the imported goods to the place of introduction into the customs territory of the Community.[4] In

19 Ibid Art 152(1)(a)(i); see also Interpretative Note to Art 152(1)(a)(i) in *Interpretative Notes on Customs Value*, Annex 23 to Commission Regulation 2454/93, OJ 11.10.93 L253/1.
20 Commission Regulation 2454/93 Art 152(1)(a)(ii), OJ 11.10.93 L253/1.
 1 Ibid Art 152(1)(a)(iii).
 2 Ibid Art 152(1)(b).
 3 Ibid Art 152(2); see also Interpretative Note to Art 152(2) in *Interpretative Notes on Customs Value*, Annex 23 to Commission Regulation 2454/93, OJ 11.10.93 L253/1. The deductions are the same as those of Commission Regulation 2454/93 Art 152(1)(a), OJ 11.10.93 L253/1.
 4 Council Regulation 2913/92 Art 30(2)(d), OJ 19.10.92 L302/1; see also ibid Art 32(1)(e); see also Interpretative Note to Art 30(2)(d) in *Interpretative Notes on Customs Value*, Annex 23 to Commission Regulation 2454/93, OJ 11.10.93 L253/1. If the declarant so requests, the order of application of Art 30(2)(c) and Art 30(2)(d) may be reversed, so that the computed value can be calculated instead of determining the unit price at which the imported goods for identical or similar imported goods are sold within the Community. See Council Regulation 2913/92 Art 30(1), OJ 19.10.92 L302/1. In applying the computed value method, the customs authorities may not require or compel any person not resident in the Community to produce for examination, or to allow access to, any account or other record for the purposes of determining the customs value. However, information supplied by the producer of the goods for the purposes of determining the computed valued may be verified in a non-Community country by the customs authorities of a Member State with the agreement of the producer and provided that such authorities give sufficient advance notice to the authorities of the country in question and the latter do not object to the investigation. See Commission Regulation 2454/93 Art 153(1), OJ 11.10.93 L253/1. Where information other than that supplied by or on behalf of the producer is used for the purposes of determining the computed value, the customs authorities must inform the declarant, if the latter so request, of the source of such information, the data used and the calculation based on such data, subject to the rules of confidentiality under Art 15 of the Customs Code. See ibid Art 153(3).

this sense, the costs or value of materials and fabrication must include the cost of containers which are treated as being one, for customs purposes, with the goods in question, as well as the cost of packing, whether for labour or materials.[5] It must also include the value, duly apportioned, of any specified product or service which has been supplied directly or indirectly by the buyer for use in connection with the production of the imported goods.[6] The general expenses must cover the direct and indirect costs of producing and selling the goods for export which are not included in the cost or value of materials and fabrication or other processing employed in producing the imported goods.[7]

REASONABLE MEANS METHOD

Where the customs value of the imported goods cannot be determined on the basis of any of the previous means, it will be defined on the basis of data available in the Community, using reasonable means consistent with the principles and general provisions of the Agreement on Implementation of Art VII of the General Agreement on Tariffs and Trade of 1994, Art VII of the General Agreement on Tariffs and Trade of 1994, and the provisions of the Customs Code.[8] However, in any case, no customs value will be determined on the basis of:

(1)   the selling price in the Community of goods produced in the Community;[9]
(2)   a system that provides for the acceptance for customs purposes of the higher of two alternative values;[10]
(3)   the price of goods on the domestic market of the country of exportation;[11]
(4)   the cost of production, other than computed values which have been determined for identical or similar goods in accordance with Art 30(2)(d);[12]
(5)   prices for export to a country not forming part of the customs territory of the Community;[13]
(6)   minimum customs values;[14] or
(7)   arbitrary or fictitious values.[15]

---

5 Ibid Art 153(2).
6 As to the specified product or services see Council Regulation 2913/92 Art 32(1)(b), OJ 19.10.92 L302/1. In this sense, the value of the elements specified in Art 32(1)(b)(iv) of the Customs Code which are undertaken in the Community must be included only to the extent that such elements are charged to the producer. See Commission Regulation 2454/93 Art 153(2), OJ 11.10.93 L253/1.
7 Ibid Art 153(4).
8 Council Regulation 2913/92 Art 31(1), OJ 19.10.92 L302/1, as amended by Regulation 82/97 of the European Parliament and of the Council, OJ 21.1.97 L/17/1; see also Interpretative Note to Art 31(1) in *Interpretative Notes on Customs Value*, Annex 23 to Commission Regulation 2454/93, OJ 11.10.93 L253/1.
9 Council Regulation 2913/92 Art 31(2)(a), OJ 19.10.92 L302/1.
10 Ibid Art 31(2)(b).
11 Ibid Art 31(2)(c).
12 Ibid Art 31(2)(d).
13 Ibid Art 31(2)(e).
14 Ibid Art 31(2)(f).
15 Ibid Art 31(2)(g).

SPECIAL RULES FOR DATA PROCESSING EQUIPMENT

Following the Customs Code,[16] the Commission implementing regulation establishes specific rules for the valuation of certain carrier media for use in ADP equipment. In determining customs value of imported carrier media bearing data or instructions for use in data processing equipment, only the cost or value of the carrier medium itself must be taken into account.[17] The customs value of imported carrier media bearing data or instructions will not therefore include the cost or value of the data or instructions, provided that such cost or value is distinguished from the use or value of the carrier medium in question.[18]

RULES ON EXCHANGE RATES

Where factors used to determine the customs value of goods are expressed in a currency other than that of the Member State where the valuation is made, the rate of exchange to be used will be that duly published by the competent authorities of the Member State concerned.[19] The rate to be used must reflect as effectively as possible the current value of such currency in commercial transactions in terms of the currency of such Member State and in principle will be the rate recorded on the second-last Wednesday of a month and published on that or the following day.[20] Where a rate of exchange recorded on the last Wednesday of a month and published on that or the following day differs by 5 per cent or more from the rate recorded on the second-last Wednesday of the month and published on that or the following day, it will replace the latter rate from the first Wednesday of that month as the rate to be applied.[1] If a rate of exchange cannot be established under the previous rules, the rate of exchange to be used will be designated by the Member State concerned and will reflect as effectively as possible the current value of the currency in question in commercial transactions in terms of the currency of that Member State.[2]

If the customs authorities of a Member State authorize a declarant to furnish or supply at a later date certain details concerning the declaration for free

---

16 Ibid Art 34.
17 The expression 'carrier medium' must not be taken to include integrated circuits, semiconductors and similar devices or articles incorporating such circuits or devices. See Commission Regulation 2454/93 Art 167(2)(a), OJ 11.10.93 L253/1. The expression 'data or instructions' will not be taken to include sound, cinematographic or video recordings. See ibid Art 167(2)(b).
18 Ibid Art 167(1).
19 Council Regulation 2913/92 Art 35, OJ 19.10.92 L302/1. Regarding the concept 'published' see Commission Regulation 2454/93 Art 168(b), OJ 11.10.93 L253/1; see also Case C-189/88 *Cartorobica SpA v Ministero delle Finanze dello Stato* [1990] ECR I-1269.
20 Commission Regulation 2454/93 Art 169(1), OJ 11.10.93 L253/1. The rate recorded on the second-last Wednesday of a month will be used during the following calendar month. See ibid Art 169(2). As to the concept of rate recorded see ibid Art 168(a). Where a rate of exchange is not recorded on the second-last Wednesday or if recorded, is not published on that or the following day, the last rate recorded of the currency in question published within the preceding 14 days will be deemed to be the rate recorded on that Wednesday. See ibid Art 169(3).
1 Ibid Art 171(1); see also ibid Art 171(2). Where in a Member State a rate of exchange is not recorded on a Wednesday or, if recorded, is not published on that or the following day, the rate recorded will be that most recently recorded and published prior to that Wednesday. See ibid Art 171(3).
2 Ibid Art 170.

circulation of the goods in the form of a periodic declaration, this authorization may, at the declarant's request, provide that a single rate be used for conversion into that Member State's currency of elements forming part of the customs value as expressed in a particular currency. In this case, the rate to be used will be the rate which is applicable on the first day of the period covered by the declaration in question.[3]

PERISHABLE GOODS

Following the Customs Code, the Commission implementing regulation establishes specific rules and procedures which may be applied, at the request of the declarant, to determine the customs value of certain perishable goods.[4] For this purpose, the Commission must establish for each classification heading a unit value per 100 kg net expressed in the currencies of the Member States.[5] The unit values must be established by the Commission on alternate Tuesdays on the basis of the weighted average of the average free at-frontier unit price, not cleared through customs, expressed in the currency of the Member State in question per 100 kg net and calculated on the basis of prices for undamaged goods in specified marketing centres during a specified reference period,[6] in relation to the quantities entered into free circulation over the period of a calendar year with payment of import duties.[7] The unit values will apply for periods of 14 days, each period beginning on a Friday.[8]

Consignments which at the material time for valuation for customs purposes contain no less than 5 per cent of produce unfit in its unaltered state for human consumption or the value of which has been depreciated by no less than 20 per cent in relation to the average market prices for sound produce must be treated as damaged.[9] Such consignments may be valued either after sorting by application of unit values to the sound portion, the damaged portion being destroyed under customs supervision, or by application of unit values established for sound produce after deduction from the weight of the consignment of a percentage equal to the percentage assessed as damaged by a sworn expert and accepted by the customs authorities, or by application of unit values established for the sound produce reduced by the percentage assessed as damaged by a sworn expert and accepted by the customs authorities.[10]

---

3 Ibid Art 172.
4 Council Regulation 2913/92 Art 36(2), OJ 19.10.92 L302/1. As to the perishable goods, and their classification, subject to these specific rules and procedures see Annex 26 to Commission Regulation 2454/93, OJ 11.10.93 L253/1.
5 Commission Regulation 2454/93 Art 173(1), OJ 11.10.93 L253/1. See Commission Regulation 919/98, OJ 30.4.98 L128/51.
6 Ibid Art 173(2)(a). As to the determination of the average free at-frontier price not cleared through customs see ibid Art 173(3). As to the method of calculating the weighted average of the average free at-frontier unit price see ibid Art 175(2). Concerning the specified marketing centres see Annex 27 to Commission Regulation 2454/93, OJ 11.10.93 L253/1. Regarding the determination of the specified reference period see Commission Regulation 2454/93 Art 174, OJ 11.10.93 L253/1.
7 Ibid Art 173(2)(b). Both the average free at-frontier unit price and the quantities entered into free circulation must be supplied to the Commission by the Member States in relation to each classification heading. See ibid Art 173(2).
8 Ibid Art 173(1).
9 Ibid Art 176(1).
10 Ibid Art 176(2).

In declaring or causing to be declared the customs value of one or more products which it imports by reference to the unit values established in accordance with the rules and simplified procedures for perishable goods, the person concerned will join such simplified procedure system for the current calendar year in respect of the product or products in question.[11]

DECLARATION OF PARTICULARS AND DOCUMENTS TO BE FURNISHED TO ESTABLISH THE CUSTOMS VALUE

If it is necessary to establish a customs value, a declaration of particulars relating to customs value must accompany the customs entry made in respect of the imported goods.[12] Such value declaration must be drawn up on a form D.V.1 supplemented where appropriate by one or more forms D.V.1 bis.[13] The value declaration can be made only by a person who has his residence or place of business in the customs territory of the Community and is in possession of the relevant facts.[14] The lodging with a customs office of a value declaration will, without prejudice to the possible application of the penal provisions, be equivalent to the engagement of responsibility, by the person concerned, in respect of the accuracy and completeness of the particulars given in the declaration, the authenticity of the documents produced in support of these particulars and the supply of any additional information or documents necessary to establish the customs value of the goods.[15] Furthermore, the customs authorities need not determine the customs value of the imported goods on the basis of the transaction value method if they are not satisfied, on the basis of reasonable doubts, that the declared value represents the total amount paid or payable.[16] Yet, the customs authorities must first ask for additional information. If those doubts continue, the customs authorities must, before reaching a final decision, notify the person concerned, in writing if requested, of the grounds of those doubts and provide him with a reasonable opportunity to respond. Thereafter, a final decision and the grounds therefor must be communicated in writing to the person concerned.[17]

However, the customs authorities may waive the requirement of a value declaration if the customs value of the goods cannot be determined on the basis of the transaction value of the imported goods. In such cases, the person concerned must furnish or cause to be furnish to the customs authorities such other information as may be requested for the purposes of determining the customs value under another method.[18] Furthermore, except where it is essential for the

---

11 Ibid Art 177(1).
12 The rules on the value declaration do not apply in respect of perishable goods for which the customs value is determined under the simplified procedures system. See ibid Art 178(5).
13 Ibid Art 178(1). As to the form D.V.1 see the specimen in Annex 28 to Commission Regulation 2454/93, OJ 11.10.93 L253/1; concerning the form D.V.1 bis see the specimen in Annex 29 Commission Regulation 2454/93, OJ 11.10.93 L253/1.
14 Commission Regulation 2454/93 Art 178(2), OJ 11.10.93 L253/1. As to the form and documentation to accompany the value declaration see ibid Art 181.
15 Ibid Art 178(4).
16 Commission Regulation 2454/93 Art 181a(1), OJ 11.10.93 L253/1, as inserted by Commission Regulation 3254/94, OJ 31.12.94 L346/1.
17 Commission Regulation 2454/93 Art 181a(2), OJ 11.10.93 L253/1, as inserted by Commission Regulation 3254/94, OJ 31.12.94 L346/1.
18 Commission Regulation 2454/93 Art 178(3), OJ 11.10.93 L253/1. Such other information must be supplied in such form and manner as may be prescribed by the customs authorities. Ibid.

correct application of import duties, the customs authorities must waive the requirement of all or part of the value declaration where the customs value of the imported goods in a consignment does not exceed Ecu 5000, provided that they do not constitute split or multiple consignments from the same consignor to the same consignee;[19] or where the importations involved are of a non-commercial nature;[20] or where the submission of the particulars in question is not necessary for the application of the Customs Tariff of the European Communities or where the duties provided in the Tariff are not chargeable due to specific customs provisions.[1]

In the case of continuing traffic in goods supplied by the same seller to the same buyer under the same commercial conditions, the customs authorities may waive the requirement that all the particulars of the value declaration be furnished in support of each customs declaration, but must require them whenever the circumstances change and at least once every three years.[2]

---

19 Ibid Art 179(1)(a). As to the determination of the amount in Ecu see ibid Art 179(2).
20 Ibid Art 179(1)(b).
 1 Ibid Art 179(1)(c). These three waivers may be withdrawn and the submission of a D.V.1 may be required where it is found that a condition necessary to qualify for that waiver was not or is no longer met. See ibid Art 179(4).
 2 Ibid Art 179(3). This waiver may be withdrawn and the submission of a D.V.1 may be required where it is found that a condition necessary to qualify for that waiver was not or is no longer met. See ibid Art 179(4).

Chapter 4

Entry of goods

ENTRY OF GOODS

Goods brought into the territory of the Community are, from the time of their entry, subject to customs supervision as long as necessary to determine their customs status, or, in the case of non-Community goods, until their customs status is changed, they enter a free zone or free warehouse or they are re-exported or destroyed.[1] For such purpose, they must be conveyed by the person bringing them into the Community to the customs office designated by the customs authorities or any other place designated or approved by such authorities;[2] or to a free zone, if the goods are to be brought into that free zone direct by sea or air, or by land without passing through another part of the customs territory of the Community, where the free zone adjoins the land frontier between a Member State and a third country.[3] Goods brought into the Community include goods which, although still outside the customs territory of the Community, may be subject to the control of the customs authorities of a Member State by virtue of an agreement concluded between such Member State and a third country.[4] They also include goods already placed under a transit procedure when they are brought into the customs territory of the Community.[5] However, they do not include goods which have temporarily left the customs territory of the Community while moving between two points in that territory by sea or air, provided that carriage has been effected by a direct route and by regular air service or shipping line without a stop outside the Community customs territory;[6] nor goods on board vessels or aircraft crossing the territorial sea or airspace of the Member States without having as their destination a port or airport situated in those Member States.[7] Furthermore, on condition that customs control is not jeopardized, tourist, frontier or postal traffic of negligible economic importance is not included.[8]

If by reason of unforeseeable circumstances or force majeure, the goods cannot be conveyed to the appropriate place, the person bound to do so or any other person acting in his place must inform the customs authorities of such

1 Council Regulation 2913/92 Art 37, OJ 19.10.92 L302/1.
2 Ibid Art 38(1)(a).
3 Ibid Art 38(1)(b).
4 Ibid Art 38(3).
5 Ibid Art 54.
6 Ibid Art 38(5).
7 Ibid Art 38(6).
8 Ibid Art 38(4).

situation without delay.[9] Likewise, where, by reason of unforeseeable circumstances or force majeure, a vessel or aircraft is forced to put into port or land in the customs territory of the Community and the goods cannot be conveyed to the appropriate customs office, the person bringing the vessel or aircraft into the customs territory of the Community or another person acting in its place must inform the customs authorities without delay.[10]

The person who brought the goods into the customs territory of the Community, or any other person who assumes responsibility for carriage of the goods following such entry, must present the goods to the customs authorities.[11] The presentation of the goods must be followed by a summary declaration in order to identify the goods.[12] This declaration must be made on a form corresponding to the model prescribed by the customs authorities. However, the latter may permit the use as a summary declaration of any commercial or official document which contains the particulars necessary for the identification of the goods.[13] A summary declaration will not be necessary in the case of goods imported by travellers and consignments by letter and parcel post. Furthermore, the customs authorities may waive the lodging of a summary declaration on condition that this does not jeopardize customs supervision of the goods, where the formalities necessary for the goods to be assigned a customs-approved treatment or use are previously carried out.[14]

Once presented to customs, the goods may, with the permission of the customs authorities, be examined or samples may be taken, so that they can be assigned a customs-approved treatment or use.[15] The permission to examine the goods must be granted to the person empowered to assign the goods a customs-approved treatment or use at its oral request, unless the customs authorities consider that a written request is required.[16] The examination and the

---

9 Where the unforeseeable circumstances or force majeure do not result in the total loss of the goods, the customs authorities must also be informed of their precise location. See ibid Art 39(1).

10 Ibid Art 39(2).

11 Ibid Art 40. This obligation does not apply to goods carried by travellers or placed under a customs procedure but not presented to customs; or to goods already placed under a transit procedure when they are brought into the customs territory of the Community until they reach their destination and are presented to customs in accordance with the rules governing transit. See ibid Art 41; see also Arts 54 and 55. If goods are brought into the customs territory of the Community from a third country by sea or air and are consigned under cover of a single transport document by the same mode of transport, without transhipment, to another port or airport in the Community, they must be presented to customs only at the port or airport where they are unloaded or transhipped. See Commission Regulation 2454/93 Art 189, OJ 11.10.93 L253/1. Special provisions apply to the cabin baggage and hold baggage of travellers. See ibid Arts 190–197.

12 Such summary declaration must be lodged by the person who brought the goods into the customs territory of the Community, or by any person who assumes responsibility for carriage of the goods following such entry, or the person in whose name either of the preceding persons acted. See Council Regulation 2913/92 Art 44(2), OJ 19.10.92 L302/1. The customs authorities may, however, allow a period for lodging the declaration which must not extend beyond the first working day following the day on which the goods are presented to customs. See ibid Art 43.

13 Ibid Art 44(1). As to the particulars of the summary declaration see Commission Regulation 2454/93 Art 183, OJ 11.10.93 L253/1, as amended by Commission Regulation 3665/93, OJ 31.12.93 L335/1.

14 Council Regulation 2913/92 Art 45, OJ 19.10.92 L302/1.

15 Ibid Art 42.

16 Commission Regulation 2454/93 Art 182(1), OJ 11.10.93 L253/1. However, the taking of samples may be authorized only at the written request of the person concerned. See ibid Art 182(2).

taking of samples must be carried out under the supervision of the customs authorities.[17] The person concerned must bear the risk and costs of unpacking, weighing, repacking, and any other operation involving the goods.[18]

The goods may be unloaded or transhipped from the means of transport carrying them solely with the permission of the customs authorities and in places designated or approved by such authorities.[19] Furthermore, the goods must not be removed from their original position without the permission of the customs authorities.[20] However, for the purpose of inspecting goods and means of transport carrying them, the customs authorities may at any time require that the goods be unloaded and unpacked.[1]

Non-Community goods presented to customs must be assigned a customs-approved treatment or use authorized for such non-Community goods.[2] Where the goods are covered by a summary declaration, the formalities necessary for them to be assigned a customs-approved treatment or use must be carried out within 45 days from the date on which the summary declaration is lodged in the case of goods carried by sea; or 20 days from the date on which the summary declaration is lodged in the case of goods carried otherwise than by sea.[3]

The customs authorities must without delay take all measures necessary, including the sale of the goods, to regularise the situation of goods in respect of which the formalities necessary for them to be assigned a customs-approved treatment or use are not initiated within the required periods.[4]

Until they are assigned a customs approved treatment or use, goods presented to customs will, following such presentation, have the status of 'goods in temporary storage' and be stored only in places approved by the customs authorities, referred to as 'temporary storage facilities', under the conditions laid down by the authorities.[5] 'Goods in temporary storage' may be subject only to such forms of handling as are designed to ensure their preservation in an unaltered state without modifying their appearance or technical characteristics.[6] The person who has made the summary declaration or, where such declaration has not yet been lodged, the person responsible for doing so, will be liable for giving effect to the measures taken by the customs authorities to regularize the situation of the goods and for bearing the costs of such measures.[7]

---

17 Ibid Art 182(3).
18 It must also pay any costs in connection with the analysis of the goods. See ibid Art 182(3).
19 However, such permission will not be required in the event of imminent danger necessitating the immediate unloading of all or part of the goods. In that case, the customs authorities must be informed accordingly forthwith. See Council Regulation 2913/92 Art 46(1), OJ 19.10.92 L302/1.
20 Ibid Art 47.
1 Ibid Art 46(2); see also Commission Regulation 2454/93 Art 184, OJ 11.10.93 L253/1.
2 Council Regulation 2913/92 Art 48, OJ 19.10.92 L302/1.
3 Ibid Art 49(1). If the circumstances so warrant, the customs authorities may set a shorter period or authorize an extension of these periods. Such extension, however, must not exceed the genuine requirements which are justified by the circumstances. See ibid Art 49(2).
4 Ibid Art 53(1).
5 See ibid Arts 50 and 51; see also Commission Regulation 2454/93 Art 185, OJ 11.10.93 L253/1. The goods will be placed in a 'temporary storage facility' on the basis of the summary declaration. However, the customs authorities may require the lodging of a specific declaration made out on a form corresponding to the model they have determined. See ibid Art 186.
6 Council Regulation 2913/92 Art 53, OJ 19.10.92 L302/1.
7 Commission Regulation 2454/93 Art 187, OJ 11.10.93 L253/1.

Where the circumstances so require, the customs authorities may have the goods presented to customs destroyed. In such case, they must inform the holder of the goods who will bear the costs.[8]

If the customs authorities find that goods have been brought unauthorized into the customs territory of the Community, or have been withheld from customs surveillance, they must take any measures necessary, including the sale of the goods, in order to regularize the situation.[9]

PLACING THE GOODS UNDER CUSTOMS PROCEDURE

Save as otherwise provided, goods may at any time, under the conditions laid down, be assigned any customs-approved treatment or use irrespective of their nature or quantity, or their country of origin, consignment or destination.[10] Customs-approved treatments or uses are:

(1)   the placing of the goods under a customs procedure;[11]
(2)   their entry into a free zone or free warehouse;[12]
(3)   their exportation from the customs territory of the Community;[13]
(4)   their destruction;[14] and
(5)   their abandonment to the Exchequer.[15]

Customs procedures are:

(1)   the release of goods for free circulation;[16]
(2)   transit;[17]
(3)   customs warehousing;[18]
(4)   inward processing;[19]
(5)   processing under customs control;[20]
(6)   temporary admission;[1]
(7)   outward processing;[2] and
(8)   exportation.[3]

---

8 Council Regulation 2913/92 Art 56, OJ 19.10.92 L302/1.
9 Ibid Art 57.
10 However, this will not preclude the imposition of prohibitions or restrictions justified on grounds of public morality, public policy or public security, the protection of health and life of humans, animals or plants, the protection of national treasures possessing artistic, historic or archaeological value or the protection of industrial and commercial property. See ibid Art 58.
11 Ibid Art 4(15)(a).
12 Ibid Art 4(15)(b).
13 Ibid Art 4(15)(c).
14 Ibid Art 4(15)(d).
15 Ibid Art 4(15)(e).
16 Ibid Art 4(16)(a).
17 Ibid Art 4(16)(b).
18 Ibid Art 4(16)(c).
19 Ibid Art 4(16)(d).
20 Ibid Art 4(16)(e).
 1 Ibid Art 4(16)(f).
 2 Ibid Art 4(16)(g).
 3 Ibid Art 4(16)(h).

All goods intended to be placed under a customs procedure must be covered by a declaration for that customs procedure.[4] The declaration must be lodged with the customs office where the goods were presented during the days and hours appointed for opening as soon as the presentation of the goods has taken place.[5] It must be made in writing; or using a data-processing technique;[6] or by means of a normal declaration or any other act whereby the holder of the goods expresses its wish to place them under a customs procedure.[7] The official model for a written declaration to customs by the normal procedure is the Single Administrative Document.[8] It must be signed and contain all the particulars necessary for the implementation of the provision governing the customs procedure for which the goods are declared.[9] It must be drawn up in one of the official languages of the Community which is acceptable to the customs authorities of the Member State where the formalities are carried out and be completed in accordance with the explanatory note in Annex 37 Commission Regulation 2454/93 and any additional rules laid down in other Community legislation.[10] The Single Administrative Declaration must be accompanied by a specified list of documents where the goods are released for free circulation;[11] entered into the transit procedure;[12] for the customs warehousing procedure;[13] the inward processing procedure;[14] for processing under customs control;[15] for

4 Ibid Art 59(1). The customs declaration may cover two or more articles but the particulars relating to each article must be regarded as constituting a separate declaration. See Commission Regulation 2454/93 Art 198(1), OJ 11.10.93 L253/1.

5 However, the customs authorities may, at the request of the declarant and at its expense, authorize the declaration to be lodged outside the appointed days and hours. See ibid Art 202. Furthermore the said authorities may authorize the declaration to be lodged before the declarant is in a position to present the goods. In such case, the customs authorities may set a time limit for presentation of the goods. If the goods have not been presented during this time limit the declaration will be considered not to have been lodged. See ibid Art 201(2).

6 Concerning the details of customs declarations made using a data-processing technique see Commission Regulation 2454/93 Arts 222–224, OJ 11.10.93 L253/1, as amended by Commission Regulation 3665/93, OJ 31.12.93 L335/1; see also ibid Art 199.

7 Council Regulation 2913/92 Art 61, OJ 19.10.92 L302/1. As to oral declarations see Commission Regulation 2454/93 Arts 225–229, OJ 11.10.93 L253/1, as amended by Commission Regulation 3665/93, OJ 31.12.93 L335/1 and Commission Regulation 12/97, OJ 13.1.97 L9/1. Concerning customs declaration made by any other act see Commission Regulation 2454/93 Arts 230–234, OJ 11.10.93 L253/1, as amended by Commission Regulation 1762/95, OJ 21.7.95 L171/8. Oral and customs declaration made by an act other than a written declaration or a data-processing technique will not be possible for goods in respect of which the payment of refunds or other amounts or the repayment of duties is sought or which are subject to a prohibition or restriction or to any other special formality. See Commission Regulation 2454/93 Art 235, OJ 11.10.93 L253/1

8 Ibid Art 205(1). Under certain conditions simplified procedures may apply for declarations in writing. See Council Regulation 2913/92 Art 76, OJ 19.10.92 L302/1; see also Commission Regulation 2454/93 Arts 253 and 253a, OJ 11.10.93 L253/1, as amended by Commission Regulation 3665/93, OJ 31.12.93 L335/1.

9 Council Regulation 2913/92 Art 62, OJ 19.10.92 L302/1. As to the particulars of the Single Administrative Document and the information it must contain see Commission Regulation 2454/93 Arts 205–209, OJ 11.10.93 L253/1, as amended by Commission Regulation 3665/93, OJ 31.12.93 L335/1.

10 See Commission Regulation 2454/93 Arts 211 and 212, OJ 11.10.93 L253/1. Annex 37 Commission Regulation 2454/93 contains the maximum and minimum list of boxes to be used for declarations of entry for a particular customs procedure. See ibid Art 216.

11 See ibid Art 218.

12 Ibid Art 219.

13 Commission Regulation 2454/93 Art 220(1)(a), OJ 11.10.93 L253/1, as amended by Commission Regulation 12/97, OJ 13.1.97 L9/1.

14 Ibid Art 220(1)(b).

15 Ibid Art 220(1)(c).

the temporary importation;[16] for the outward processing procedure;[17] and for export or re-export.[18]

The declaration may be made by any person who is able to present the goods in question or have them presented to the competent customs authority, together with all the documents which are required to be produced for the application of the rules governing the customs procedure in respect of which the goods were declared.[19] The declarant must be established in the Community unless it makes a declaration of transit or temporary importation, declares the goods on an occasional basis or where Member States conclude bilateral agreements with third countries or follow customary practices having similar effect, under which nationals of such countries may make customs declarations in the territory of the Member States in question, subject to reciprocity.[20]

The lodging with a customs office of a declaration signed by the declarant or its representative will render it responsible under the provisions in force for the accuracy of the information given in the declaration, the authenticity of the documents attached and compliance with all the obligations relating to the entry of the goods in question under the procedure concerned.[1] Declarations which comply with the required conditions must be accepted by the customs authorities immediately, provided the goods to which they refer are presented to customs.[2] If the declaration has been lodged before the goods have arrived at the customs office, it may be accepted only after the goods in question have been presented to customs.[3] The date of acceptance of the declaration must be noted therein.[4] Save as otherwise expressly provided, the date to be used for the purposes of all the provisions governing the customs procedure for which the goods are declared will be the date of acceptance of the declaration by the customs authorities.[5]

The declarant may at its request, be authorized to amend one or more of the particulars of the declaration after it has been accepted by the customs authority, by the lodging of a new declaration.[6] The amendment will not have the effect of rendering the declaration applicable to goods other than those origi-

---

16 Ibid Art 220(1)(d).
17 Ibid Art 220(1)(e).
18 Commission Regulation 2454/93 Art 221(1), OJ 11.10.93 L253/1.
19 Council Regulation 2913/92 Art 64(1), OJ 19.10.92 L302/1. However, where the acceptance of a customs declaration imposes particular obligations on a specific person, the declaration must be made by that person or on his behalf. See ibid Art 64(2)(a).
20 See ibid Art 64(2)(b); see also ibid Art 64(3).
 1 Commission Regulation 2454/93 Art 199, OJ 11.10.93 L253/1.
 2 Council Regulation 2913/92 Art 63, OJ 19.10.92 L302/1.
 3 Commission Regulation 2454/93 Art 201(3), OJ 11.10.93 L253/1.
 4 Ibid Art 203.
 5 Council Regulation 2913/92 Art 67, OJ 19.10.92 L302/1. In this sense, the date of importation in order to determine the customs debt and the application of any other Community measures is the day on which the import declaration for the goods is accepted by the customs authorities. This acceptance may not take place until the goods have reached the place prescribed by the customs for the process of customs clearance and until the documents which must be produced have been submitted. See Case 113/75 *Giordano Frecassetti v Amministrazione delle Finanze dello Stato* [1976] ECR 983. A delay in the dispatch of goods due to events not attributable to the importer cannot affect the interpretation to be given to day of importation. See Case 113/78 *N G J Schouten B V v Hoofdproduktschap voor Akkerbouwprodukten* [1979] ECR 695.
 6 Council Regulation 2913/92 Art 65, OJ 19.10.92 L302/1. In that case the relevant date for determination of any duties payable and for any other provisions governing the customs procedure in question will be the date of the acceptance of the original declaration. See Commission Regulation 2454/93 Art 204, OJ 11.10.93 L253/1.

nally covered.[7] However, no amendment will be permitted where the authorization is requested after the customs authorities have informed the declarant that they intend to examine the goods; or have established that the particulars in question are incorrect; or have released the goods.[8]

The customs authorities may, at the request of the declarant, invalidate a declaration already accepted where the declarant furnishes proof that the goods were declared in error for the customs procedure covered by that declaration or that as a result of special circumstances, the placing of the goods under the customs procedure for which they were declared is no longer justified.[9] Nevertheless, where the customs authorities have informed the declarant of their intention to examine the goods, a request for invalidation of the declaration must not be accepted until after the examination has taken place.[10] Only under specified circumstances may the declarations be invalidated after the goods have been released.[11]

For the verification of the declarations which they have accepted, the customs authorities may

(1) examine the documents covering the declaration and the documents accompanying it. They may require the declarant to present other documents for the purpose of verifying the accuracy of the particulars contained in the declaration; and

(2) examine the goods and take samples for analysis or for detailed examination.[12]

If the authorities decide to examine the goods or take samples they must so inform the declarant or its representative.[13] Where they choose to examine part of the goods, the customs authorities must inform the persons concerned which items they wish to examine.[14] The goods will be examined in the places designated and during the hours appointed for that purpose by the customs authorities.[15] The transport of the goods to the places where they are to be examined and the samples to be taken, and all the handling necessary for such examination or taking of samples, will be carried out by or under the responsibility of the declarant who must bear all the costs incurred.[16] The declarant will be entitled to be present when the goods are examined and when samples are taken. Furthermore, the customs authorities may require the declarant to be present or represented when the goods are examined or samples are taken in order to provide them with the assistance necessary to facilitate such examination or taking of the goods or samples.[17] If the samples taken are not destroyed

---

7 Council Regulation 2913/92 Art 65, OJ 19.10.92 L302/1.
8 Ibid Art 65.
9 Ibid Art 66(1).
10 Ibid Art 66(1).
11 Ibid Art 66(2); see also Commission Regulation 2454/93 Art 251, OJ 11.10.93 L253/1, as amended by Commission Regulation 3665/93, OJ 31.12.93 L335/1 and Commission Regulation 1427/97, OJ 24.7.97 L196/31.
12 Council Regulation 2913/92 Art 68, OJ 19.10.92 L302/1.
13 Commission Regulation 2454/93 Art 239(1), OJ 11.10.93 L253/1; see also ibid Art 242.
14 The customs authorities' choice will be final. See ibid Art 240(2).
15 Ibid Art 239(1).
16 Council Regulation 2913/92 Art 69(1), OJ 19.10.92 L302/1.
17 Ibid Art 69(2). Regarding the particulars of the assistance and the consequences of its refusal see Commission Regulation 2454/93 Arts 241, 242 and 243, OJ 11.10.93 L253/1, as amended by Commission Regulation 482/96, OJ 20.3.96 L70/5.

by the analysis or more detailed examination, they must be returned upon request.[18] However, where samples are taken, the customs authorities will not be liable for payment of any compensation in respect thereof but only bear the costs of their analysis or examination.[19] In no case will the quantities taken by the customs office as samples be deducted from the quantity declared.[20]

If only part of the goods covered by the declaration are examined, the results of the partial examination must be taken to apply to all the goods covered by that declaration. Nevertheless, the declarant may request a further examination of the goods if it considers that the results of the partial examination are not valid as regards the remainder of the goods declared.[1]

Where the customs authorities verify the declaration and accompanying documents or examine the goods, they must indicate at least in the copy of the declaration retained by them or in a document attached thereto the basis and results of such verification or examination.[2] The results of verifying the declaration will be used for the purposes of applying the provisions governing the customs procedure under which the goods are placed.[3]

The customs authorities must take the measures necessary to identify the goods where identification is required in order to ensure compliance with the conditions governing the customs procedure for which the said goods have been declared.[4]

If the conditions for placing the goods under the procedure in question are fulfilled and provided that the goods are not subject to any prohibitive or restrictive measures, the customs authorities must release the goods as soon as the particulars in the declaration have been verified or accepted without verification.[5] Where the customs authorities take samples for analysis or more detailed examination, they must authorize the release of goods in question without waiting for the results of the analysis unless there are other grounds for not doing so.[6] If the acceptance of a customs declaration gives rise to a customs debt, the goods covered by the declaration must not be released unless the customs debt has been paid or secured.[7] Where appropriate, the granting of release will give rise to the entry in the accounts of the import duties determined according to the particulars in the declaration.[8] Where pursuant to the provisions governing the customs procedure for which the goods are declared, the customs authorities require the provision of a security, the goods will not be released for the customs procedure in question until such security is provided.[9] The customs

---

18 Commission Regulation 2454/93 Art 246, OJ 11.10.93 L253/1.

19 Council Regulation 2913/92 Art 69(3), OJ 19.10.92 L302/1.

20 Commission Regulation 2454/93 Art 245(1), OJ 11.10.93 L253/1.

 1 Council Regulation 2913/92 Art 70(1), OJ 19.10.92 L302/1.

 2 Commission Regulation 2454/93 Art 247(1), OJ 11.10.93 L253/1.

 3 If the declaration is not verified, these provisions will be applied on the basis of the particulars contained in the declaration. See Council Regulation 2913/92 Art 71, OJ 19.10.92 L302/1.

 4 Ibid Art 72(1).

 5 Ibid Art 73(1).

 6 Commission Regulation 2454/93 Art 224, OJ 11.10.93 L253/1.

 7 However, this requirement will not apply to the temporary importation procedure with partial relief from import duties. See Council Regulation 2913/92 Art 74(1), OJ 19.10.92 L302/1.

 8 Special provisions apply for the cases in which the particulars of the declaration and the results of the verification do not correspond. See Commission Regulation 2454/93 Art 248, OJ 11.10.93 L253/1, as amended by Commission Regulation 1427/97, OJ 24.7.97 L196/31.

 9 Council Regulation 2913/92 Art 74(2), OJ 19.10.92 L302/1.

authorities must determine the form of release, taking into account the place in which the goods are located and of the special arrangements for their supervision.[10]

Any necessary measures, including confiscation and sale, may be taken to deal with goods which cannot be released because it has not been possible to undertake or continue examination of the goods within the period prescribed by the customs authorities for reasons attributable to the declarant, or the documents which must be produced before the goods can be placed under the customs procedure requested have not been produced, or payments or security which should have been made or provided in respect of import duties or export duties, as the case may be, have not been made or provided within the period prescribed, or they are subject to bans or restrictions.[11] However, where the documents have not been presented or the declarant has not produced the payment or security in respect of any import or export duties, the customs authorities must give the declarant a time limit to regularize the situation of the goods.[12] If the declarant does not present the documents in the time limit prescribed, the declaration will be deemed invalid and the customs office will cancel it.[13] Where the declarant does not produce the payment or security within the time limit granted to it, the customs authorities may start the preliminary formalities for the sale of the goods. Any necessary measures may also be taken to deal with goods which are not removed within a reasonable period of time after their release.[14]

The customs authorities may, on their own initiative or at the request of the declarant, amend the declaration after release of the goods.[15] Thus, the customs authorities may, after releasing the goods and in order to satisfy themselves as to the accuracy of the particulars contained in the declaration, inspect the commercial documents and data relating to the import or export operations in respect of the goods concerned or to subsequent commercial operations involving these goods. Such inspections may be carried out at the premises of the declarant, of any other person directly or indirectly involved in the said operations in a business capacity or any other person in possession of the said document and date for business purposes. Those authorities may also examine the goods where it is still possible for them to be produced.[16] Where revision of the declaration or post-clearance examination indicates that the provisions governing the customs procedure concerned have been applied on the basis of incorrect or incomplete information, the customs authorities must, in accordance

---

10 If the declaration was made in writing, a reference to the release and its date will be made on the declaration, or where applicable, a document attached, and a copy will be returned to the declarant. See Commission Regulation 2454/93 Art 249, OJ 11.10.93 L253/1.
11 Council Regulation 2913/92 Art 75(a), OJ 19.10.92 L302/1.
12 Commission Regulation 2454/93 Art 250(1), OJ 11.10.93 L253/1. However, the customs authorities may require the payment of a sum, other than the customs duties and any expenses arising from the temporary storage of the goods, for accepting a declaration after the expiry of the required periods, provided that the amount of that sum is determined in accordance with the principle of proportionality and under conditions which are analogous to those applicable in national law to infringements of the same nature and gravity. See Case C-36/94 *Siesse v Director da Alfandega de Alcantara* [1995] ECR I-3573, paragraph 25.
13 Commission Regulation 2454/93 Art 250(2), OJ 11.10.93 L253/1.
14 Council Regulation 2913/92 Art 75(b), OJ 19.10.92 L302/1. Where the customs authorities decide to sell the goods, this must be done in accordance with the procedures in force in the Member States. See Commission Regulation 2454/93 Art 252, OJ 11.10.93 L253/1, as amended by Commission Regulation 3665/93, OJ 31.12.93 L335/1.
15 Council Regulation 2913/92 Art 78(1), OJ 19.10.92 L302/1.
16 Ibid Art 78(2).

with any provisions laid down, take the measures necessary to regularize the situation, taking account of the new information available to them.[17]

In order to simplify the completion of formalities and procedures as far as possible while ensuring that the operations are conducted in a proper manner, the authorities may grant permission for the presentation of a simplified declaration; the presentation of a commercial or administrative document in place of the customs declaration; or an entry in the records without presenting the goods to customs.[18]

RELEASE FOR FREE CIRCULATION

The release for free circulation confers on non-Community goods the customs status of Community goods. It entails the application of commercial measures, completion of the other formalities laid down in respect of the importation of goods and the charging of any other duties legally due.[19]

The customs debt will be incurred at the time of acceptance of the customs declaration for release for free circulation.[20] However, where the rate of the import duty is reduced after the date of acceptance of the declaration for release for free circulation but before the goods are released, the declarant may make an application for the more favourable rate.[1]

If a consignment is made up of goods falling within different tariff classifications, and dealing with each of those goods in accordance with its tariff classification for the purpose of drawing up the declaration would entail a burden of work and expense disproportionate to the import duties chargeable, the customs authorities may, at the request of the declarant, agree that import duties be charged on the whole consignment on the basis of the tariff classification of the goods which are subject to the highest rate of import duty.[2]

The procedure to be followed for the release of the goods for free circulation is the normal procedure for placing the goods under a customs procedure.[3] However, the customs authorities may provisionally accept, at the request of the declarant, incomplete declarations or declarations accompanied with insufficient documents, for a period not exceeding one month from the date of such acceptance.[4] The customs authorities' acceptance of an incomplete declaration

---

17 Ibid Art 78(3).
18 Ibid Art 76(1).
19 Ibid Art 79(1); see also Case 275/85 *Commission of the European Communities v Italy* [1987] ECR 465. As to temporary importation see Council Regulation 2913/92 Arts 137–144, OJ 19.10.92 L302/1; see also Commission Regulation 2454/93 Arts 275, 276, 278 and 670–747, OJ 11.10.93 L253/1, as amended by Commission Regulation 3665/93, OJ 31.12.93 L338/1, Commission Regulation 3254/94, OJ 31.12.94 L346/1, Commission Regulation 1762/95, OJ 21.7.95 L171/8 and Commission Regulation 482/96, OJ 20.3.96 L70/4.
20 See Council Regulation 2913/92 Art 76, OJ 19.10.92 L302/1; see also ibid Art 201(2).
 1 Ibid Art 80. As to the concept of import duty see ibid Art 4(10).
 2 Ibid Art 81.
 3 See Council Regulation 2913/92 Arts 59–78, OJ 19.10.92 L302/1; see also Commission Regulation 2454/93 Arts 198–253a, OJ 11.10.93 L253/1.
 4 As to the conditions and details for the acceptance of the incomplete declaration or declaration not accompanied with all the required supporting documents see Commission Regulation 2454/93 Arts 254 and 255, OJ 11.10.93 L253/1. Where the application of a reduced or zero rate of import duty depends on the production of a missing document, if the customs authorities have good reason to believe that the goods covered by the incomplete declaration may qualify for such reduced or zero rate of duty, a further period not exceeding three months

will not prevent or delay the release of the goods declared, unless other grounds exist for doing so.[5] If the later production of the particulars of the declaration or of the supporting documents cannot affect the amount of duties to which the goods covered by the said declaration are liable, the customs authorities must immediately enter in the accounts the sum payable.[6] If the incomplete declaration contains a provisional indication of value, the customs authorities must enter immediately in the account the amounts of duty determined on the basis of that indication and require, if necessary, the lodging of a security adequate to cover the difference between that amount and the amount to which the goods may ultimately be liable.[7] Otherwise, the late production of the particulars of the declaration or the accompanying documents may affect the amount of duties; where the late production of any missing particulars or documents may lead to the application of a duty at a reduced rate, the customs authorities must immediately enter in the accounts the duties payable at the reduced rate and require the lodging of a security covering the difference between that sum and the sum which would be payable if the import duties were calculated at the normal rate;[8] where the late production of any missing particulars or document may lead to the admission of the goods with total relief from duties, the customs authorities must require the lodging of a security covering the amount which would be payable if the duties were charged at the normal rate.[9] Where at the expiry of the granted period, the declarant has not supplied the details necessary for the final determination of the customs value of the goods, or has failed to provide the missing particulars or documents, the customs authorities must immediately enter in the accounts as duties to which the goods in question are subject the amount of security previously required.[10]

Furthermore, a declarant may request to be authorized to make a declaration for release for free circulation in a simplified form, which may be an incomplete declaration on the Single Administrative Document or an administrative or commercial document accompanied by a request for free circulation or a general request in respect of release operations to take place over a given period.[11] The authorization will be granted on condition that it is possible to guarantee an effective check on compliance with import prohibitions or restrictions or other provisions governing release for free circulation.[12] The authorization must designate the customs office(s) competent to accept the simplified declaration, specify the form and content of the simplified declaration, specify the goods to which it applies and the particulars which must appear on the declaration to identify the goods, make reference to the security to be provided to cover any customs debt which may arise, and specify the form and contents of the supplementary declarations and the time limits within which they must be lodged.[13]

The customs authorities may allow, upon request, the use of the local clearance procedure to any person wishing to have the goods released for free

---

may be allowed for the production of the document in question. The document may be presented after the expiry of the date of the period for which the reduced or zero rate was set, provided that the declaration was accepted before that date. See ibid Art 256.

5 Ibid Art 257(1).
6 Ibid Art 257(2).
7 Ibid Art 257 (3).
8 Ibid Art 257(4)(a).
9 Ibid Art 257(4)(b).
10 Ibid Art 258.
11 Ibid Art 260.
12 Ibid Art 261(1). As to the cases where the authorization should be refused see ibid Art 261(2).
13 Ibid Art 262.

circulation at its premises or at other designated places.[14] The authorization will be granted provided that the applicant's records enable the customs authorities to carry out effective checks, in particular retrospective checks, and it is possible to guarantee an effective check on compliance with import or export prohibitions or restrictions or any other provisions governing the release for free circulation.[15] The authorization must lay down the specific rules for the operation of the procedure and in particular stipulate the goods to which it applies, the obligations of the holder and the reference to the guarantee to be provided, the time of release of the goods, the time limit within which the supplementary declaration must be lodged with the competent customs office designated for that purpose and the conditions under which the goods are to be covered by general, periodic or recapitulative declarations as appropriate.[16]

If Community goods are temporarily exported under an ATA carnet,[17] they may be released for free circulation on the basis of such document.[18]

Where the goods are released for free circulation at a reduced or zero rate of duty on account of their end use, they must remain under customs supervision. Such supervision will end when the conditions laid down for granting the reduced or zero rate of duty cease to apply, where the goods are exported or destroyed, or where the use of the goods for purposes other than those laid down for the application of the reduced or zero rate of duty is permitted subject to payment of the duties due.[19]

Goods released for free circulation will lose their Community goods status if

(1)   the declaration for release for free circulation is invalidated after their release [20] or

(2)   the import duties payable on those goods are repaid or remitted under the inward processing procedure in the form of the drawback system, or in respect of defective goods or goods which fail to comply with the terms of the contract, or in the special circumstances allowing the repayment or remission of duties where repayment is conditional upon the goods being exported or re-exported or being assigned an equivalent customs approved treatment or use.[1]

---

14 Ibid Art 263.

15 Ibid Art 264 (1). As to the cases where the authorization should be refused see ibid Art 264(2). Concerning the operation of the local clearance procedure see Commission Regulation 2454/93 Art 266, OJ 11.10.93 L253/1, as amended by Commission Regulation 2193/94, OJ 9.9.94 L235/6.

16 Commission Regulation 2454/93 Art 267, OJ 11.10.93 L253/1.

17 ATA carnet means the international customs document for temporary importation established by virtue of the ATA Convention. See ibid Art 1(2).

18 Ibid Art 290(1). As to the formalities which the customs office must follow see ibid Art 290(2).

19 Council Regulation 2913/92 Art 82, OJ 19.10.92 L302/1. Concerning the rules on the authorization for the admission of these goods, the duties of the holder of the authorization, the assignment to the end use in question, transfer of the goods, transport, storage and consignment to another Member State see Commission Regulation 2454/93 Arts 290a–304, OJ 11.10.93 L253/1, as amended by Commission Regulation 3665/93, OJ 31.12.93 L335/1, Commission Regulation 1676/96, OJ 28.8.96 L218/1, and Commission Regulation 89/97, OJ 21.1.97 L17/28. Special rules apply for horses for slaughter. See Commission Regulation 2454/93 Arts 305–308, OJ 11.10.93 L253/1.

20 Council Regulation 2913/92 Art 83(a), OJ 19.10.92 L302/1.

1 Ibid Art 83(b). Concerning the rules on the return of the duties as a result of the importer's rejection of the goods see ibid Art 238. Regarding the special circumstances allowing the repayment or remission of duties see ibid Art 239.

Chapter 5

Inward and outward processing

THE INWARD PROCESSING PROCEDURE

Introduction

Inward processing is the system whereby imported goods may be processed in the customs territory of the Community without giving rise to liability for payment of customs duties or other commercial policy measures where such goods are intended for export outside the customs territory of the Community in the form of compensating products.[1] Such arrangements are aimed at promoting exports from Community undertakings, under the international division of labour, by enabling them to import goods from non-member countries without paying import duties where they are to be exported from the Community after processing, but without adversely affecting the essential interests of Community producers.[2] The provisions on the inward processing system are not applicable to intra-Community trade.[3]

The Customs Code provides for two basic procedures under the inward processing arrangement. First, it provides for the suspension system, whereby non-Community goods intended for re-export from the customs territory of the Community in the form of compensating products may be imported without such goods being subject to import duties.[4]

---

1 Council Regulation 2913/92 Art 114(1), OJ 19.10.92 L302/1; see also Commission Europeenne, *Rapport sur le Fonctionnement et l'Avenir du Regime Douanier Economique du Perfectionnement Actif*, Commission Europeenne: DG XXI (1996); see also Case 49/82 *Commission of the European Communities v Kingdom of the Netherlands* [1983] ECR 1195 (where the Court established the boundaries between the inward processing system and the customs warehouse arrangement). As to the processing operations allowed under the inward processing procedure see ibid Art 114(2)(c). For the definition of main compensating products see Commission Regulation 2454/93 Art 549(a), OJ 11.10.93 L253/1. For the definition of secondary compensating products see ibid Art 549(b). For the definition of losses see ibid Art 549(c). For the definition of operators see ibid Art 549(e).
2 See Case C-325/96 *Fabrica de Queijo Eru Portuguesa Lda v Subdirector-Geral das Alfandegas* (16 December 1997, unreported), paragraph 3. Products brought into the Community under the inward processing arrangement are considered to be imported and exported for the purposes of the International Dairy Agreement or any international trade agreement. Inward processing is, thus, subject to the rules of the International Dairy Agreement or other agreements concerning minimum import/ export prices. See Case C-61/94 *Commission of the European Communities v Germany* [1996] ECR I-3989, paragraphs 22–27.
3 Case 260/78 *Maggi GmbH v Hauptzollamt Munster* [1979] ECR 2693.
4 Council Regulation 2913/92 Art 114(1)(a), OJ 19.10.92 L302/1. See also ibid Art 114(2)(a).

Second, the Code allows for the use of a drawback system whereby operators may request the repayment or remission of import duties chargeable on goods released for free circulation in the Community if they are exported from the customs territory of the Community in the form of compensating products.[5] As a general rule, the drawback system may apply to all goods.[6] However, such system cannot be applied to those goods which at the time the declaration of release for free circulation is accepted:

(1) are subject to quantitative import restrictions,[7]
(2) might within quotas qualify for a preferential tariff measure or an autonomous suspensive measure,[8]
(3) are subject to agricultural levy or any other import charge provided for under the common agricultural policy under specific arrangements applicable to certain goods resulting from the processing of agricultural products,[9] or
(4) if an export refund has been set for the compensating products resulting from the processing of the import goods.[10]

Goods entered under the inward processing procedure will also be relieved from specific commercial policy measures which are intended to be applied on the release of goods for free circulation, for such time as they remain under the procedure.[11] Furthermore, the re-export of non-Community goods entered under the drawback system shall not give rise to the application of the commercial policy measures laid down for exports of the goods in the unaltered state or in compensating products.[12]

Under the suspension system of the inward processing procedure, compensating goods may also qualify for exemption from the export duties to which iden-

---

5 Ibid Art 114(1)(b); see also ibid Art 114(2)(b).
6 Ibid Art 124.
7 Ibid Art 124(1).
8 Ibid. As for the meaning of an autonomous suspensive measure see ibid Art 20(3)(d) to (f).
9 Ibid Art 124(1).
10 Furthermore, permission to use the drawback system will be granted only if at the time the declaration of exportation of the compensating products is accepted the import goods are not subject to an agricultural levy or any other import charge provided for under the common agricultural policy or under specific arrangements applicable to certain goods resulting from the processing of agricultural products and no export refund has been set for the compensating products. See ibid Art 124(3).
11 Commission Regulation 2454/93 Art 607(1)(a), OJ 11.10.93 L253/1. However, where Community legislation provides for specific commercial policy measures to be adopted on goods brought into the customs territory of the Community, such measures will apply on import goods entered under the inward processing arrangement. See ibid Art 607(1)(b). Thus, non-Community goods, even where they are not liable to import duties, may be entered for the inward processing procedure under the suspension system with a view to waive any commercial policy measures applying to the release for free circulation, or with view to waive any commercial policy measures applying to exports of the goods in the unaltered state or the compensating products. See ibid Art 607(2)(a). This shall be without prejudice to the commercial policy measures applying to the export of products in the Community. See ibid Art 607(2)(b).
12 Ibid Art 608. However, the exemption from commercial policy measures, both under the suspensions system and the drawback system, is designed to apply only to commercial policy measures not entailing the imposition of tariffs which, like customs duties, are levied on imported goods for the purpose of protecting the Community market. See Case C-61/94 *Commission of the European Communities v Germany* [1996] ECR I-3989, paragraph 55.

tical products obtained from Community goods instead of import goods would be liable.[13] Export duties are not exempted under the drawback system.[14]

Grant of authorization

The use of the inward processing procedure is conditional upon authorization being issued by the customs authorities.[15] An authorization to use the suspension system shall be granted only where the applicant has the actual intention of re-exporting the main compensating products from the customs territory of the Community.[16] The drawback system will be authorized only where opportunities exist for export of the main compensating products from the customs territory of the Community.[17]

The authorization shall be issued at the request of the person who carries out processing operations or who arranges for them to be carried out.[18] The grant of authorization is subject to certain administrative and economic conditions.[19] First, the authorization can be granted only to persons established in the Community.[20] Second, the customs authorities may grant such authorization where the import goods can be identified in the compensating products.[1] Finally the authorization shall be granted only where the inward processing procedure can help to create the most favourable conditions for the export or re-export of compensating products, provided that the essential interests of Community producers are not adversely affected.[2]

Such economic conditions are considered to be fulfilled inter alia where:

13 Council Regulation 2913/92 Art 129, OJ 19.10.92 L302/1.
14 Ibid Art 126.
15 Ibid Art 86.
16 Commission Regulation No 2454/93 Art 551(1), OJ 11.10.93 L253/1.
17 Ibid Art 551(2). Where the conditions for use of both systems are fulfilled, the applicant may request that the authorization be for either the suspension system or the drawback system. See ibid Art 551(3).
18 Council Regulation 2913/92 Art 116, OJ 19.10.92 L302/1. As to the concept of person see ibid Art 4(1). If the processing operation is to be carried out under a job-processing contract between two persons established in the Community, the application will be lodged by or on behalf of the principal. See Commission Regulation No 2454/93 Art 555(3), OJ 11.10.93 L253/1; see also Case C-291/91 *Textilveredlungsunion GmbH & Co KG (TVU) v Hauptzollamt Nurnberg-Furth* [1993] ECR I-579, paragraph 13 (considering also that in a situation of that kind, the competent customs authority must be able to seek from the principal the evidence that the economic conditions to which the issue of authorization is subject have been fulfilled and every guarantee which it considers necessary to that end).
19 Council Regulation 2913/92 Art 117, OJ 19.10.92 L302/1.
20 Ibid Art 117(a). Yet, persons established outside the Community may benefit from such authorization in respect of imports of a non-commercial nature. Ibid Art 117(a). As to the concept of imports of a non-commercial nature see Commission Regulation 2454/93 Art 554(4), OJ 11.10.93 L253/1 and Council Regulation 2913/92 Art 1(6), OJ 19.10.92 L302/1.
 1 Art 117(b). The customs authorities must stipulate the means of identifying the import goods in the compensating products. See Commission Regulation No 2454/93 Art 551(4), OJ 11.10.93 L253/1, as amended by Commission Regulation No 2193/94, OJ 9.9.94 L235/6. As to the particular means which customs authorities shall make use of see Commission Regulation No 2454/93 Art 551(4) letters (a) to (e), OJ 11.10.93 L253/1, as amended by Commission Regulation No 2193/94, OJ 9.9.94 L235/6.
 2 Council Regulation 2913/92 Art 117(c), OJ 19.10.92 L302/1. The interests of the Community producers must be adversely affected and not simply affected. Compare with Art 5 of Council Regulation 1999/85, OJ 20.7.85 L188/1 (85).

(1) the processing consists of operations carried out under a job-processing contract with a person established in a third country,[3] operations involving goods of a non-commercial nature,[4] repairs,[5] usual forms of handling intended to preserve the goods, improve their appearance or marketable quality or prepare them for distribution or resale,[6] operations in which the value of the goods, by eight digit CN code, does not exceed Ecu 300,000 per applicant per calendar year, irrespective of the number of operators carrying out the processing operation,[7] the processing of durum wheat to produce pasta,[8] further processing operations to be applied on compensating goods obtained under an authorization already issued.[9]

(2) No goods comparable to the goods to be processed are produced in the Community;[10] are produced in the Community in sufficient quantity;[11] can be made available to the applicant within a suitable time by producers established in the Community;[12] or can be used either because their price would make the proposed commercial operation economically impossible,[13] they do not have the quality or characteristics necessary for the operator to produce the required compensating products,[14] they do not conform with the requirements of the third country purchaser of the compensating products,[15] or the compensating products must be obtained from import goods in order to comply with provisions concerning the protection of industrial or commercial property rights.[16]

(3) The applicant for an authorization in respect of a particular type of goods to be entered for the procedure within a given period obtains during such period 80 per cent of its total requirements for such goods incorporated in the compensating products in the customs territory of the Community in the form of comparable goods produced in the Community,[17] is trying to guard against supply problems,[18] has tried to obtain the products from Community producers but has met with no response from them,[19] is building civil aircraft for delivery to airline companies,[20] is carrying out repair, modification or conversion of civil aircraft,[1] or is building satellites or parts of satellites.[2]

---

3 Commission Regulation No 2454/93 Art 552(a)(i), OJ 11.10.93 L253/1, as amended by Commission Regulation No 2193/94, OJ 9.9.94 L235/6.
4 Commission Regulation No 2454/93 Art 552(a)(ii), OJ 11.10.93 L253/1.
5 Ibid Art 552(a)(iii).
6 Ibid Art 552(a)(iv).
7 Ibid Art 552(1)(a)(v), as amended by Commission Regulation No 482/96, OJ 20.3.96, L 70/5.
8 Commission Regulation No 2454/93 Art 552(1)(a)(vi), OJ 11.10.93 L253/1.
9 Ibid Art 552(1)(a)(vii), as introduced by Commission Regulation No 1676/96, OJ 28.8.96 L218/1.
10 Commission Regulation 2454/93 Art 552(1)(b), OJ 11.10.93 L253/1, which also defines comparable goods.
11 Ibid Art 552(1)(c).
12 Ibid Art 552(1)(d).
13 Ibid Art 552(1)(e)(i).
14 Ibid Art 552(1)(e)(ii).
15 Ibid Art 552(1)(e)(iii).
16 Ibid Art 552(1)(e)(iv).
17 Ibid Art 552(1)(f)(i). This possibility does not apply in respect of goods listed in Annex II to the EC Treaty. See ibid Art 552(2).
18 Ibid Art 552(1)(f)(ii).
19 Ibid Art 552(1)(f)(iii).
20 Ibid Art 552(1)(f)(iv).
 1 Ibid Art 552(1)(f)(v).
 2 Ibid Art 552(1)(f)(vi).

In all such cases the applicant is to indicate in its application the reasons for which the conditions are considered to be fulfilled.[3] However, in exceptional circumstances, the applicant may state reasons, other than those included in the list, due to which the economic conditions are considered to be fulfilled.[4] In such cases, if the customs authorities consider that the economic conditions are fulfilled, they may grant authorization for a limited period of time which may not exceed nine months.[5] In all cases, neither the fact that the Community producer of comparable goods which could be used to carry out the processing operations is an undertaking in competition with the person applying to use the procedure or the fact that the goods are produced in the Community by a single undertaking, shall in themselves be taken as grounds for granting the authorization.

The application shall be presented to the customs authorities designated by the Member State where the processing operation is to be carried out.[6] However, where it is expected that successive processing operations will be carried out by or on behalf of the applicant in different Member States, application for a single authorization may be made.[7]

If compensating products are to be obtained from other compensating products obtained under an authorization already issued in cases other than successive processing operations in different Member States, the person carrying out the further processing operation or having them carried out must submit a new application.[8]

The authorization will be issued by the authorities to which the application was presented.[9] In exceptional cases, the customs authorities may issue a retroactive authorization.[10] Where successive processing operations will be carried out in different Member States, the authorization may not be issued without the agreement of the customs authorities designated by the Member States in which the places indicated in the application are located.[11]

Where the general simplified procedure of Art 76 does not apply, the Customs Code provides for a simplified procedure for authorizing the use of the suspension system under the inward processing arrangement.[12] Such procedure

---

3 Ibid Art 552(3).
4 Ibid Art 553(1).
5 Ibid Art 553(2). In those cases, the particulars of the application will be communicated to the Commission. The Commission implementing regulation provides for an internal Community procedure in order to ensure that both the interests of the Community operators and those of the Community producers of comparable goods to those imported are protected. See ibid Art 553(3). See also ibid Art 553(4), as amended by Commission Regulation 2193/94, OJ 9.9.94 L235/6.
6 Commission Regulation 2454/93 Art 555(2)(a), OJ 11.10.93 L253/1.Concerning the particularities of the application see ibid Art 555(1); see also ibid Art 497 and Annex 67/B.
7 Ibid Art 552(2)(b). In this case the application will be made to the customs authorities of the Member State where the first operations will be carried out.
8 Ibid Art 557.
9 Ibid Art 556(1). Regarding the particularities of the authorization see ibid Art 500 and Annex 68/B. See also ibid Arts 556(4), 556(5), 556(6), 556(7), 556(8), as amended by Commission Regulation No 2193/94, OJ 9.9.94 L235/6.
10 Commission Regulation 2454/93 Art 556(1), OJ 11.10.93 L253/1. Such authorization may not go back beyond the time when the application was lodged.
11 Ibid Art 556(2). Thus, the Commission implementing regulation provides for a consultation procedure to be followed. See ibid Art 556(2). To ensure the correct application of the provisions governing such procedure, the customs authorities may require the holder for the purposes of facilitating controls to keep inward processing records which shall indicate the quantities of import goods entered for the procedure and of compensating goods to be obtained, and all the particulars needed for the monitoring of the operations and the correct calculation of any import duties which may be payable. See ibid Art 556(3).
12 Ibid Art 568.

will only apply in cases other than the use of the equivalent system, where the processing operations are to take place in a single Member State.[13] In such cases, the customs authorities shall allow the lodging of the declaration of entry for the procedure, under the suspension system, or the declaration for release for free circulation, under the drawback system, to constitute an application for authorization.[14]

Where such simplified procedure does not apply, the declaration of entering import goods for the inward processing procedure under the suspension system must be lodged at one of the offices of entry for the procedure specified in the authorization.[15]

Where a simplified procedure does not apply, the declaration for release for free circulation under the drawback system must be lodged at one of the offices of entry for the procedure specified in the authorization.[16] Such declaration must indicate that such system is being used and provide particulars of the authorization.[17]

The simplified procedure provided in Art 76 of the Code for release for free circulation under the drawback system will apply in accordance with Arts 275 and 276.[18]

Operation of the procedure

The customs authorities must set in the authorization the conditions under which the inward processing procedure may be used.[19] In this sense, the customs authorities must indicate the period of validity of the authorization. In doing so, they must take into account the economic conditions and the specific needs of the applicant.[20]

The customs authorities must also specify the period within which the compensating products resulting from the processing operations must be exported

---

13 Ibid Art 568(1). Certain processing operations are excluded from this simplified procedure. See ibid Art 568(2); see also ibid Art 552(1)(a).

14 Ibid Art 568(2). The declarations must be accompanied by a document made out by the declarant containing the particularities of the inward processing operation, unless such information can be entered in the form used for the declaration itself. See ibid Art 568(3) (laying down the information to be included in the document). The acceptance of the declaration will constitute the authorization. Such acceptance, however, will remain in any event subject to the conditions governing the granting of the authorization. See ibid Art 568(2).

15 Ibid Art 574(1). Such declaration shall be made in accordance with Council Regulation 2913/92 Arts 59–78, OJ 19.10.92 L302/1 and Commission Regulation 2454/93 Arts 198–252, OJ 11.10.93 L253/1 and shall include a description of the goods which shall correspond to the specifications of the authorization. See ibid Art 575(1); see also ibid Art 575(2). For the purposes of Art 62(2) of the Customs Code, the documents to accompany the declaration shall be those provided for in Art 220 of the implementing regulation. See ibid Art 575(3).

16 Ibid Art 625.

17 Council Regulation 2913/92 Art 125(1), OJ 19.10.92 L302/1 .

18 Commission Regulation No 2454/93 Art 627, OJ 11.10.93 L253/1.

19 Council Regulation 2913/92 Art 87, OJ 19.10.92 L302/1.

20 Commission Regulation No 2454/93 Art 558(1), OJ 11.10.93 L253/1, as amended by Commission Regulation No 2193/94, OJ 9.9.94 L235/6. Special rules apply where the period of validity exceeds two years. See ibid Art 558(1). However, in case of products covered by the common organization of the market in milk and milk products which are intended for the manufacture of butter and cheese, or chocolate, biscuits or lemonade, the period of validity must not exceed three months. Ibid Art 558(2); see also Art 1 of Council Regulation No 804/68.

or assigned another customs approved treatment or use.[1] In establishing this period the customs authorities must take account of the time required to carry out the processing operations and dispose of the compensating products.[2] Extensions may be granted upon request where circumstances warrant even when the period has already expired.[3]

However, in the case of certain agricultural products, the period of re-exportation must not exceed six months.[4] The period for re-exportation may not be extended for agriculture products.[5] The period for re-exportation will run from the date on which the non-Community goods are placed under the inward processing procedure.[6]

The customs authorities must also set in the authorization either the quantity or percentage of compensating products to be obtained from the processing of a given quantity of import goods or the method of determining such rate of yield.[7]

Transfer of the import goods or compensating products under the suspension system

The Customs Code allows for the transport or transfer of the import goods entered under the suspension system of the inward processing procedure. When such goods are to be moved within the customs territory of the Community, the transportation of such goods or products shall take place either in accordance with the provisions concerning external transit or in accordance with the transfer procedures.[8] Furthermore, the customs authorities will permit compensating products or goods in the unaltered state to be transferred without customs formalities and without termination of the inward processing procedure from

---

1 Council Regulation 2913/92 Art 118(1), OJ 19.10.92 L302/1.
2 Ibid Art 118(1); see also Commission Regulation No 2454/93 Art 559(1), OJ 11.10.93 L253/1.
3 Council Regulation 2913/92 Art 118(2), OJ 19.10.92 L302/1; see also Commission Regulation No 2454/93 Art 559(2), OJ 11.10.93 L253/1.
4 Council Regulation 2913/92 Art 118(4), OJ 19.10.92 L302/1; see also Commission Regulation No 2454/93 Art 560(1), OJ 11.10.93 L/253/1; see also Art 1 of Council Regulation No 565/80, OJ 7.3.80 L62/5. Furthermore, in the case of products covered by the common organization of the market in milk and milk products which are intended for the manufacture of butter and cheese, or chocolate, biscuits or lemonade, the period of exportation may not exceed four months. Special deadlines apply also for the processing of live animals and meat. See ibid Art 560(3), as introduced by Commission Regulation 1762/95, OJ 21.7.95 L171/8.
5 Case C-325/96 *Fabrica de Queijo Eru Portuguesa Lda v Subdirector-Geral das Alfandegas* (16 December 1997, unreported), paragraphs 18–19.
6 Council Regulation 2913/92 Art 118(2), OJ 19.10.92 L302/1; see also Commission Regulation No 2454/93 Art 562(1), OJ 11.10.93 L253/1.
7 Council Regulation 2913/92 Art 119(1), OJ 19.10.92 L302/1; see also ibid Art 114(2)(f). This rate shall as far as possible be set on the basis of production data and shall be identifiable in the records of the operator's undertaking. See Commission Regulation 2454/93 Art 566(1), OJ 11.10.93 L253/1. The rate or method of determining it shall be subject to retrospective verification by the customs authorities. See ibid Art 566(2). Annex 77 Commission Regulation 2454/93, as amended by Commission Regulation 1427/97, OJ 24.7.97 L196/31, includes standard rates of yield which shall apply to inward processing operations carried out on import goods and resulting in the production of the compensating products listed in such Annex. See Council Regulation 2913/92 Art 119(2), OJ 19.10.92 L302/1; see also Commission Regulation 2454/93 Art 567(2), OJ 11.10.93 L253/1. These standard rates of yield shall apply only to import goods of sound, genuine and merchantable quality which conform to any quality laid down in Community legislation. See ibid Art 567(1).
8 Ibid Art 616, as amended by Commission Regulation No 3665/93, OJ 31.12.93 L335/1.

the plant of one operator to the plant of another operator, with a view to further processing, provided the transfer is entered in the inward processing records.[9] The customs authorities will also permit compensating products or goods in the unaltered state to be transferred from the holder of one authorization to the holder of another authorization, provided the transfer is recorded in the inward processing records of the first holder in accordance with the procedure described in Annex 83.[10]

If permission is given for the use of the transfer procedures they shall be set out in the authorization. In the case of transfer of goods or products from the holder of one authorization to the holder of a second authorization, both of these authorizations shall stipulate the transfer procedures.[11]

Processing operations outside the customs territory of the Community

The Customs Code allows imported goods in the unaltered state or their compensating goods which are under the inward processing procedure to be temporarily exported for the purpose of further processing outside the customs territory of the Community.[12] Such temporary exportation, however, will only be possible after the customs authorities grant authorization in accordance with the rules provided for outward processing.[13] Under the drawback system, the temporary exportation of compensating products will not be considered as exportation for the purposes of repayment or remission of the import duties initially paid except where the products are not reimported into the Community within the period prescribed.[14]

Where a customs debt is incurred in respect of the reimported products, the Code requires the customs authorities to charge the specified import duties.[15]

---

9 Commission Regulation 2454/93 Art 617, OJ 11.10.93 L253/1. In such case the holder of the authorization shall retain the responsibility for the transferred goods or products. See ibid Art 618.

10 Ibid Art 619. In this case, however, responsibility for the transferred goods or products shall pass to the holder of the second authorization at the time at which it takes delivery of the goods or products and enters them in its inward processing records. See ibid Art 620(1). Thus, such entry in the inward processing records shall have the effect of placing the goods or products under the procedure in the name of the holder of the second authorization. See ibid Art 620(2).

11 Ibid Art 616(3), as amended by Commission Regulation No 3665/93, OJ 31.12.93 L335/1. The holder of the authorization shall be responsible for providing the customs authorities with advance notification of the transfers to be carried out in the form and manner which such authorities shall determine. See Commission Regulation No 2454/93 Art 622, OJ 11.10.93 L253/1.

12 Council Regulation 2913/92 Art 123, OJ 19.10.92 L302/1.

13 Ibid Art 86; see also ibid Art 123.

14 Ibid Art 127.

15 First, import duties must be charged on the compensating goods or goods in the unaltered state which had been temporarily exported. The calculation of these import duties will be based on the general rules applicable to import goods and compensating products under the inward processing procedure. See ibid Art 123(2)(a). Second, the customs authorities must also charge import duties on products reimported after processing outside the customs territory of the Community. Such amount must be calculated in accordance with the provisions relating to the outward processing procedure, on the same conditions as would have been applied had the products exported under the latter procedure been released for free circulation before such export took place. See ibid Art 123(2)(b). As to the calculation of the value of the goods on which the import duties must apply see Case C-16/91 *Wacker Werke GmbH & Co KG v Hauptzollamt Munchen-West* [1992] ECR I-6821.

Discharge of the procedure

The suspension system under the inward processing procedure will be discharged in respect of the import goods when the compensating products or goods in the unaltered state have been declared for another customs-approved treatment or use and all other conditions for use of the procedure have been complied with.[16]

In cases where the nature or the characteristics of the import goods or compensating products have been altered as a result of unforeseeable circumstances or force majeure so that it becomes impossible to obtain the final compensating products for which the authorization for the suspension system had been authorized, the holder of the authorizations must inform the supervising customs office of what has happened. In such cases, the provisions on the event of the total destruction or irreversible loss of goods will apply.[17]

The declaration discharging the suspension system under the inward processing procedure must be lodged at one of the offices of discharge specified in the authorization.[18] The simplified procedure provided for in Art 76 may apply in accordance with Art 278 of the implementing regulation.

Any compensating products or goods in the unaltered state to be assigned a customs-approved treatment or use shall be presented to the office of destination in order to undergo the customs formalities specified for the treatment or use in question under the general provisions applicable.[19]

The holder of the authorization must also supply the supervising office with a bill of discharge within 30 days of the expiration of the time limit for re-exportation.[20]

With regard to the discharge of the drawback system, except where the simplified procedure of Art 568 applies, the declaration assigning the compensating products to one of the customs approved treatments or uses referred to in Art 128 of the Code must be lodged at one of the offices of discharge specified in the authorization.[1] Where the simplified procedure

---

16 Commission Regulation 2454/93 Art 577(1), OJ 11.10.93 L253/1. For the purposes of discharging the suspension system under the inward processing procedure, the delivery of the goods in the customs territory of the Community to be used for certain purposes or by certain persons shall be considered as export from the customs territory. See ibid Art 577(2), as amended by Commission Regulation 2193/94, OJ 9.9.94 L235/6 and Commission Regulation No 3665/93, OJ 31.12.93 L335/1 and Commission Regulation No 1676/96, OJ 28.8.96 L218/1. For the purposes of discharging the drawback system under the inward processing procedure, the same situations will be considered as export of compensating products from the Community. The discharge of the procedure will be carried out in accordance either with the quantities of import goods corresponding to the compensating products assigned to one of the treatments which allow for discharge or to the quantities of goods in the unaltered state assigned to such a treatment or use. See ibid Art 577(3).

17 Ibid Art 579(1); see also ibid Art 579(2); see also ibid Art 579(4); see also ibid Art 571(3). However, in cases where the alteration may affect the continuation in force or the substance of the authorization, Art 87(2) of the Code will apply. See ibid Art 579(3).

18 Ibid Art 582(1). In cases, however, where the simplified procedure for authorization of the inward processing arrangement has been used, such declaration shall be lodged with the customs office which issued the authorization. See ibid Art 582(2). Yet, in both cases, the supervising office may allow such declarations to be presented at another customs office. See ibid Art 582(3). As to the details of the declaration see ibid Art 583.

19 Ibid Art 581.

20 Ibid Art 595(1). See also ibid Art 596. However, the supervising office may itself make out the bill of discharge within the same time limit. See ibid Art 596(3). As to the information to be contained in the bill of discharge see ibid Art 595(2).

1 Ibid Art 631(1).

applies, such declaration shall be presented at the office which issued the authorization.[2] The declaration or application to assign compensating products to one of the customs-approved treatments or uses referred to in Art 128 of the Code shall contain all the particulars necessary to support a repayment claim.[3] The proportion of import goods incorporated in compensating products will be calculated when necessary in order to determine the import duties to be repaid or remitted.[4] The repayment or remission of import duties will be subject to the lodging by the holder of the authorization of a claim with the supervising office.[5]

No quotas may be applied when allowing for the discharge of the inward processing system by their transfer to another suspension system.[6]

Release for free circulation under the suspension system

The release for free circulation under the suspension system of goods in the unaltered state or main compensating products will be allowed where the person concerned is unable to assign those goods or products to a customs approved treatment or use under which import duties would not be payable.[7] The customs authorities may authorize release for free circulation on a general basis as long as such authorization does not contravene other Community provisions relating to release for free circulation.[8]

---

2 Ibid Art 631(2). However, in both cases the supervising office may allow the declaration to be presented to another customs office. See ibid Art 631(3).

3 Ibid Art 629.

4 Such calculation shall not be effected when all the compensating products are assigned to one of the treatments or uses referred to in Art 128 of the Code. See ibid Art 634(1). The calculation will be effected in accordance with the quantitative scale method or the value scale method or by any other method giving the same results on the basis of the examples laid out in Annex 80. See ibid Art 634, as amended by Commission Regulation No 3665/93, OJ 31.12.93 L335/1. As to the particularities of the quantitative method to be used in the drawback system see Commission Regulation No 2454/93 Art 635, OJ 11.10.93 L253/1; see also ibid Art 636. Concerning the particularities of the value scale method to be used in the drawback system see ibid Art 636.

5 The claim shall be submitted in duplicate and shall take place at a maximum of six months from the date on which the compensating products were assigned one of the customs-approved treatments or uses referred to in Art 128(1) of the Code. See ibid Art 639(1). In special circumstances, the customs authorities may extend such period even after it has expired. See ibid Art 639(2).

6 Case C-437/93 *Hauptzollamt Heilbronn v Temic Telefunken Microelectronic GmbH* [1995] ECR I-1687, paragraph 28.

7 Ibid Art 580, as amended by Commission Regulation No 2193/94, OJ 9.9.94 L235/6.

8 Commission Regulation No 2454/93 Art 580(2), OJ 11.10.93 L253/1, as amended by Commission Regulation No 3665/93, OJ 31.12.93 L335/1. In such cases, import goods may be put on the Community market in the form either of compensatory products or goods in the unaltered state without the formalities for release for free circulation being completed at the time of being put on the Community market. See Commission Regulation No 2454/93 Art 580(3), OJ 11.10.93 L253/1, as amended by Commission Regulation No 3665/93, OJ 31.12.93 L335/1. These goods put on the market shall be considered to be Community goods forthwith. See Commission Regulation No 2454/93 Art 580(3), OJ 11.10.93 L253/1, as amended by Commission Regulation No 3665/93, OJ 31.12.93 L335/1. Import goods, whether in the form of compensating products or goods in the unaltered state, which are covered by a general authorization for release for free circulation and which upon expiry of the period for re-exportation have not being assigned any of the customs approved treatments or uses referred to in Art 89 of the Code shall be considered to have been released for free circulation and the declaration for release for free circulation being completed at the time of being put on the market. See Commission Regulation No 2454/93 Art 580(4), OJ 11.10.93 L253/1.

Release for free circulation: payment of customs duties and compensatory interest

The release for free circulation of import goods liable to import duties will result in a customs debt.[9] Import goods, however, may benefit from preferential treatment if:

(1) they are eligible for any preferential treatment existing in respect of identical goods at the time of acceptance of the declaration of release for free circulation; and
(2) at the time of acceptance of the declaration of placing the goods under the inward processing procedure the import goods fulfilled the conditions to qualify for preferential tariff treatment within tariff quotas or ceilings.[10]

The proportion of goods incorporated in compensatory products shall be calculated when necessary in order to determine the import duties to be charged.[11]

As a general rule, where a customs debt is incurred, the amount of such debt must be determined on the basis of the taxation elements appropriate to the import goods at the time of acceptance of the declaration of placing of these goods under the inward processing procedure.[12]

The release for free circulation of import goods will also result in the application by the customs authorities of any commercial policy measures in force in the Member State where the goods were entered for the procedure at the time when the declaration for release for free circulation was accepted.[13]

The release for free circulation of compensating products will result in import duties if they appear in the list included in Annex 79, to the extent that they are in proportion to the exported part of the compensating products not included in such list.[14] The release for free circulation of compensating products other than secondary compensating products listed in Annex 79 will also be

---

 9 Council Regulation 2913/92 Art 201(1)(a), OJ 19.10.92 L302/1.
10 Ibid Art 121(2).
11 Such calculation shall be based on a quantitative scale method or on a value scale method or by any other method giving the same results on the basis of the examples set out in Annex 80. See Commission Regulation No 2454/93 Art 591, OJ 11.10.93 L253/1, as amended by Commission Regulation No 3665/93, OJ 31.12.93 L335/1. Concerning the definition of quantitative scale method see Commission Regulation 2454/93 Art 549(d), OJ 11.10.93 L253/1.As to the definition of value scale method see ibid Art 549(e). Regarding the particularities of both methods see ibid Arts 592, 593 and 594.
12 Council Regulation 2913/92 Art 121(1), OJ 19.10.92 L302/1. As to the calculation of import duties on import goods eligible for favourable treatment by reason of their end use see Commission Regulation No 2454/93 Art 585a, OJ 11.10.93 L253/1, as inserted by Commission Regulation No 3665/93, OJ 31.12.93 L335/1.
13 Commission Regulation No 2454/93 Art 609, OJ 11.10.93 L253/1.
14 Yet, the holder of the authorization may ask for the duty of compensating products to be calculated on the basis of the taxation elements appropriate to the import goods at the time of acceptance of the declaration of placing of these goods under the inward processing procedure. See Council Regulation 2913/92 Art 122(a), OJ 19.10.92 L302/1; see also ibid Art 121. See also Commission Regulation 2454/93 Art 588, OJ 11.10.93 L253/1.Special provisions apply for olive oils and olives see Council Regulation 2913/92 Art 122(a), OJ 19.10.92 L302/1; see also Commission Regulation 2454/93 Art 585, OJ 11.10.93 L253/1. In the case of release for home use in the Community goods previously subject to inward processing arrangements, the agricultural levy payable is to bear default interest for the period between temporary importation and definitive importation see Case C-166/94 *Pezzullo Molini Pastifici Mangimifici SpA v Ministero delle Finanze* [1996] ECR I-331, paragraph 18.

subject to the application of any commercial policy measures in force in the Member State where the goods were entered for the procedure at the time when the declaration for release for free circulation is accepted.[15]

Compensating products placed under a suspensive arrangement or in a free zone or free warehouse are subject to import duties calculated in accordance with the rules applicable to the customs procedure in question or to the free zones or warehouses where they have been placed.[16]

In the event of release for free circulation of goods in the unaltered state or compensating products in a Member State other than the one in which the goods were entered for the procedure, such Member State shall collect the import duty which is mentioned in the information sheet INF 1.[17]

The import duties shall be paid at the latest on presentation of the bill of discharge.[18]

Where a customs debt is incurred in respect of compensating products or goods in the unaltered state, compensatory interest must be paid on the import duty applicable.[19] The rate applied must be that of the Member State where the inward processing operation or the first such operation took place or should have taken place and will apply to all customs debts incurred in the course of a six month period.[20] The annual interest rate to be charged shall be set by the Commission on the basis of the arithmetical average of representative short-term rates in each Member State in the same six month period of the previous year.[1]

Under the drawback system, the goods are considered to be in free circulation from the moment they are imported and thus if the operator does not export the compensating products or the import goods in their unaltered state, it will not incur any customs debt.[2] Furthermore, under such system, the holder of the

15 Ibid Art 609. However, compensating goods may also enjoy favourable treatment owing to special use for which they are intended or be admitted free of import duty where provision is made for such treatment in the case of identical imported goods. See Council Regulation 2913/92 Art 122(d), OJ 19.10.92 L302/1. See also ibid Art 122(e). Furthermore, compensating goods may also be made subject to the rules governing assessment of duty laid down under the procedure for processing under customs control where the import goods could have been placed under that procedure. See ibid Art 122(c).

16 Ibid Art 122(b). In such cases the operator may ask the amount of such debt to be calculated on the basis of the taxation elements appropriate to the import goods at the time of acceptance of the declaration of placing of these goods under the inward processing procedure. Yet, the import duty must be at least equal to the amount calculated under this method for all cases other than the processing under customs control.

17 Commission Regulation 2454/93 Art 586, OJ 11.10.93 L253/1.Concerning the details of the information sheet INF 1. See ibid Art 611.

18 Ibid Art 597(1).

19 Ibid Art 589(1). Compensatory interests is also due in cases of agricultural levies. See Case C-166/94 *Pezzullo Molini Pastifici Mangimifici SpA v Ministero delle Finanze* [1996] ECR I-331, paragraph 18. However, implementing regulation provides for certain situations for which no compensatory interest must be paid. See ibid Art 589(2), as amended by Commission Regulation No 3665/93, OJ 31.12.93 L335/1 and Commission Regulation No 1676/96, OJ 28.8.96 L218/1. On the administrative requirements and the Community consultation procedure which may take place in order to waive the compensatory interest see Commission Regulation No 2454/93 Art 589(3), OJ 11.10.93 L253/1.

20 Ibid Art 589(4)(a).

1 Ibid Art 589(4)(a); concerning the interest rates applicable during the first half of 1997 see Commission Regulation No 2252/96, OJ 26.11.96 L302/19. As to the details of the application of the interest rates see ibid Art 589(4)(b)as amended by Commission Regulation No 1676/96, OJ 28.8.96 L218/1. Special provisions may apply for the calculation and accounting of the compensatory interest in the case of processing operations involving two or more Member States. See ibid Art 590.

2 Council Regulation 2913/92 Art 126, OJ 19.10.92 L302/1.

authorization may ask for the import duty to be repaid or remitted if it can establish to the satisfaction of the customs authorities that import goods released for free circulation under the drawback system in the form of compensating products or goods in the unaltered state have been either exported or placed with a view to being subsequently re-exported under the transit procedure, the temporary importation procedure or the suspensive arrangement of the inward procedure or in a free zone or warehouse, and all conditions for use of the drawback system procedure have also been fulfilled.[3] However, if the goods are placed under a customs procedure or in a free zone or free warehouse and thereafter released for free circulation, the amount of the import duties repaid or remitted will be considered to constitute the amount of the customs debt to be paid.[4]

Equivalent compensation, prior exportation and triangular traffic

Under special conditions, the compensating products intended to be exported may be obtained from equivalent Community goods instead of import goods.[5] The use of equivalent goods is an exception to the general rules of inward processing and, thus, must be interpreted restrictively.[6] Such equivalent goods must be of the same quality, have the same technical characteristics as the import goods and fall within the same eight-digit subheading of the combined nomenclature code.[7] Exceptionally, however, equivalent goods may be at a more advanced stage of manufacture than the import goods, provided that the essential part of the processing to which the said equivalent goods are subject is carried out in the undertaking of the holder of the authorization or in the undertaking where the operation is being carried out on his behalf.[8]

The use of the equivalent compensation shall be possible only where it has been requested by the person concerned in the application and where the authorization specifies the factors which the equivalent and the import goods have in common and the means by which these may be checked.[9] If the authorization does not specify use of equivalent compensation but the holder of the authorization wishes to use such system, the said holder must apply for the authorization initially granted to be modified.[10]

---

3 Ibid Art 128(1), as amended by Regulation No 82/97 of the European Parliament and of the Council, OJ 21.1.97 L17/1.
4 Council Regulation 2913/92 Art 128(4), OJ 19.10.92 L302/1, as amended by Regulation No 82/97 of the European Parliament and of the Council, OJ 21.1.97, L 17/1.
5 Council Regulation 2913/92 Art 115(1)(a), OJ 19.10.92 L302/1. See also ibid Art 114(2)(e).
6 Case C-103/96 *Directeur General des Douanes et Droits Indirects v Eridiania Beghin-Say SA* [1997] ECR I-1453.
7 Ibid Art 115(2); see also Commission Regulation No 2454/93 Art 569(1), OJ 11.10.93 L335/1, as amended by Commission Regulation No 3665/93, OJ 31.12.93 L335/1, which adds the requirement that the goods must fall within the same eight-digit subheading of the combined nomenclature; see also Case C-103/96 *Directeur General des Douanes et Droits Indirects v Eridiania Beghin-Say SA* [1997] ECR I-1453, paragraphs 22–27 (upholding such implementation). Special provisions laid down in Annex 78 may apply to goods included in this Annex. See Commission Regulation No 2454/93 Art 569(2), OJ 11.10.93 L253/1.
8 Council Regulation 2913/92 Art 115(2), OJ 19.10.92 L302/1; see also Commission Regulation No 2454/93 Art 570(1), OJ 11.10.93.
9 Ibid Art 569(3). The authorization must also specify the specific measures which must be taken in order to ensure compliance with the provisions applying to the equivalent compensation system. See ibid Art 569(3); see also ibid Art 551(4), as amended by Commission Regulation No 2193/94, OJ 9.9.94 L235/6.
10 Commission Regulation No 2454/93 Art 569(5), OJ 11.10.93.

Furthermore, the Customs Code allows compensating goods to be exported from the Community before the importation of the import goods.[11] Such exportation, however, is not possible under the drawback system,[12] nor can authorizations be issued in certain specified economic conditions.[13]

The procedures governing the entry of goods for the inward processing procedure under the suspension system shall also apply to import goods, under the equivalent compensation system whether with prior exportation or not.[14] In cases of prior exportation, the procedure shall be discharged when the customs authorities have accepted the declaration in respect of the non-Community goods which must be done within the period laid down.[15]

As part of the prior exportation system the customs authorities may allow the triangular traffic system.[16] This system is such whereby the import goods are entered for the procedure in the Community at a customs office other than the one at which the prior exportation of the compensating products took place.[17]

THE OUTWARD PROCESSING PROCEDURE

Introduction

The outward processing procedure is the system whereby Community goods may be exported temporarily from the customs territory of the Community in order to undergo processing operations and the compensating products resulting from those operations be released for free circulation with total or partial

---

11 Council Regulation 2913/92 Art 115(1)(b), OJ 19.10.92 L302/1. The customs authorities shall indicate the period within which the non-Community goods must be declared for the procedure taking account of the time required for the procurement and transport to the Community of the import goods. See ibid Art 118(3); see also Commission Regulation 2454/93 Art 561(1), OJ 11.10.93 L253/1. As a general rule this period must not exceed six months. However, this period may be extended if the holder of the authorization submits a reasoned request, provided that the total period does not exceed twelve months. See ibid Art 561(2). Goods subject to a price regulating mechanism must be granted a three month period. See ibid Art 561(2). Special provisions apply also in the case of raw sugar see ibid Art 561(2); see also Commission Regulation No 2630/81, OJ 11.9.81 L258/16. These periods will run from the date of acceptance of the export declaration. See Art 562(2). If the compensating goods would be liable to export duties were they not being exported or re-exported under an inward processing operation, the holder of the authorization shall provide a security to ensure payment of the duties should the import goods not be imported within the period prescribed. See Council Regulation 2913/92 Art 115(5), OJ 19.10.92 L302/1 .
12 Ibid Art 126.
13 Commission Regulation No 2454/93 Art 572(1), OJ 11.10.93 L253/1, as amended by Commission Regulation No 3665/93, OJ 31.12.93 L335/1. As to the economic conditions which do not allow for the possibility of prior exportation under the suspension system see Commission Regulation No 2454/93 Art 552, OJ 11.10.93 L253/1, as amended.
14 Ibid Art 573(1). However, equivalent goods used under the equivalent compensation procedure, whether with prior exportation or not, will not be subject to the procedures for entry of goods for the procedure. See ibid Art 573(2).
15 Ibid Art 577(1). Joined Cases 244 & 245/85, *Cerealmangimi SpA and Italgrani SpA v Commission of the European Communities* [1987] ECR 1303.
16 Ibid Art 600. Triangular traffic system is only possible as part of the prior exportation system.
17 Ibid Art 549(i). As to the details of the triangular traffic system see ibid Art 575(3); see also ibid Art 601, as amended by Commission Regulation No 3665/93, OJ 31.12.93 L335/1; see also Commission Regulation No 2454/93 Art 602, OJ 11.10.93 L253/1; see also ibid Art 603, as amended by Commission Regulation No 2193/94, OJ 9.9.94 L235/6; see also Commission Regulation No 2454/93 Art 604, OJ 11.10.93 L253/1; see also ibid Art 605.

relief from import duties and non-tariff common commercial policy measures.[18] The purpose of that mechanism is to avoid the levying of customs duty on goods exported from the Commmunity for processing.[19] This procedure may apply to all Community goods other than those whose export gives rise to repayment or remission of import duties, or which prior to export were released for free circulation with total relief from import duties by virtue of end use, for as long as the conditions from granting such relief continue to apply, or whose export gives rise to the granting of export refunds or in respect of which a financial advantage other than such refunds is granted under the common agricultural policy by virtue of the export of the said goods.[20]

The temporary export of Community goods will, however, entail the application of export duties, commercial policy measures and other formalities for the exit of Community goods from the customs territory of the Community.[1]

Grant of authorization

The use of the outward processing procedure is conditional upon authorization being issued by the customs authorities.[2] An authorization to use the outward processing procedure will be granted at the request of the person who arranges for the processing operations to be carried out.[3] However, an authorization may be granted to another person in respect of goods of Community origin where the processing operation consists in incorporating those goods into goods obtained outside the Community and imported as compensating products, provided that use of the procedure helps to promote the sale of export goods without adversely affecting the essential interests of Community producers of products identical or similar to the imported compensating products.[4]

---

18 Council Regulation 2913/92 Art 145(1), OJ 19.10.92 L302/1; see also ibid Art 160; see also Case 49/82 *Commission of the European Communities v Netherlands* [1983] ECR 1195. As to the specific conditions for the application of economic outward processing arrangements to textiles and clothing listed in Chapters 50 to 63 of the Combined Nomenclature and resulting from outward processing operations see Council Regulation No 3036/94, OJ 15.12. 94 L322/1; see also Council Regulation No 1385/94, OJ 18.6.94 L152/4 (opening and providing for the administration of Community tariff quotas for frozen hake fillets and for processing work in respect of certain textile products under Community outward processing arrangmeents). Allowed processing operations under the outward processing procedure are: (1) the working of goods, including erecting or assembling them or fitting them to other goods; (2) the processing of goods; (3) the repair of goods, including restoring them and putting them in order. See Council Regulation 2913/92 Art 145(3)(b), OJ 19.10.92 L302/1; see also ibid Art 114(2)(c).
19 See Case C-16/91 *Wacker Werke GmbH & Co KG v Hauptzollamt Munchen-West* [1992] ECR I-6821.
20 Ibid Art 146.
 1 Ibid Art 145(2). See also Case 118/79 *Gebruder Knauf Westdeutsche Gipswerke v Hauptzollamt Hamburg-Jonas* [1980] ECR 1183 (where the Court considered that in the outward processing system whenever there is an export levy being imposed to compensate for the internal subsidies in the framework of the CAP, such export levy must be applied on those goods which are temporarily exported).Commercial policy measures on export must apply at the time of acceptance of the declaration of entry for the procedure. See Commission Regulation 2454/93 Art 784(1), OJ 11.10.93 L253/1. This however, shall not affect decisions allowing ashes and residues of copper and copper alloys falling within CN code 2620 and waste of copper and copper alloys falling within CN code 7404 00 not to be charged against export quotas. See ibid Art 784(2).
 2 Council Regulation 2913/92 Art 86, OJ 19.10.92 L302/1.
 3 Ibid Art 147(1).
 4 Ibid Art 147(2). Concerning the details of both this application and its resulting authorization see Commission Regulation 2454/93 Art 759, OJ 11.10.93 L253/1.

An application for the use of the outward processing procedure must be made in conformity with Art 497 of the Commission implementing regulation and in accordance with the specimen contained in Annex 67/E.[5] Such application must be made to the customs authorities designated by the Member States where the goods for temporary exportation are located.[6] If it is expected that the goods will be exported from several Member States, application for a single authorization may be made to the customs authorities designated by the Member State where part of the goods are located.[7]

An authorization will be granted only if specified conditions are fulfilled. First, the authorization will only be granted to persons established in the Community.[8] Second, the customs authorities must satisfy themselves that it is possible to establish that the compensating products have resulted from the processing of the temporary export goods.[9] Third, the authorization to use the procedure must not be liable seriously to harm the essential interests of Community processors.[10]

The authorizations will be issued by the customs authorities to which the application was presented and shall be made in conformity with Art 500 and in accordance with the specimen in Annex 68/E.[11]

Operation of the procedure

The period of validity of the authorization shall be set by the customs authorities having regard to the economic conditions and the specific needs of the applicant.[12]

The customs authorities must specify also the period within which the compensating products should be reimported into the customs territory of the Community. Such period must be determined with reference to the time required to complete the processing operations and to transport the temporary export goods and the compensating products.[13] The reimportation of the compensating products will be deemed to have been accomplished when the products are released for

---

5 Ibid Art 750(1).
6 Ibid Art 750(2)(a).
7 Ibid Art 750(2)(b). The application must include particulars of the sequence of the operations and the expected places of temporary exportation. The authorization may not be issued without the agreement of the customs authorities designated by the Member States in which the places indicated in the application are located. As to the internal Community procedure which must be followed see ibid Art 751(2).
8 Council Regulation 2913/92 Art 148(a), OJ 19.10.92 L302/1.
9 Ibid Art 148(b). As to the particular means which can be used for the identification see Commission Regulation 2454/93 Art 749(1), OJ 11.10.93 L253/1. Where the procedure is requested for the repair of goods, the customs authorities must satisfy themselves that the temporary export goods are capable of being repaired. See ibid Art 750(2). If it is not possible to establish whether the compensating products will be manufactured from the temporary export goods and a request is made to the customs authorities for a derogation, the authorities shall submit the application to the Commission. See ibid Art 749(5).
10 Council Regulation 2913/92 Art 148(c), OJ 19.10.92 L302/1.
11 Ibid Art 751(1).
12 Where the period exceeds two years, the economic conditions on the basis of which the authorization was issued shall be reviewed periodically at intervals specified therein. See ibid Art 743. In duly substantiated exceptional cases, the customs authorities may issue a retroactive authorization which, however, may not go back beyond the time when the application was lodged. See ibid Art 751.
13 This period will be calculated from the date of acceptance of the declaration of entry for the procedure. See ibid Art 754(1).

free circulation or placed in a free zone or free warehouse or under the customs warehousing or inward processing procedures or placed under the external Community transit procedure.[14]

The customs authorities must also set either the rate of yield of operation or, where necessary, the method of determining that rate.[15] Such rate of yield must be fixed no later than the time when the goods are entered for the procedure taking into account the technical data concerning the operation or operations to be performed where these are available, or where they are not, data available in the Community relating to operations of the same type.[16]

If the simplified procedures for entry for the procedure laid down in Art 76 of the Code are not applied, and the processing operations concern the repair of goods, a customs office empowered by the customs authorities to issue authorizations using the simplified procedure shall allow the lodging of the declaration of entry for the procedure to constitute an application for authorization. In this case, the acceptance of the declaration shall constitute the authorization.[17] Furthermore, where the processing operations concern repairs of a non-commercial nature, whether for a consideration or free of charge, the customs office designated by the customs authorities will at the request of the declarant, allow the declaration for release for free circulation to constitute the application for authorization.[18]

The customs authorities must permit the use of the triangular traffic system whereby compensating products are released for free circulation with partial or total relief from import duties with a customs administration other than that from which the goods were temporarily exported, in connection with the authorization of the outward processing procedure or at a special request of the holder of the authorization, presented after the authorization has been granted but before the compensating products have been released from free circulation.[19]

The declaration entering temporary export goods for the outward processing procedure shall be lodged at one of the offices of entry for the procedure specified in the authorization.[20] Such declaration must be made in accordance with

---

14 Ibid Art 754(3). However, the customs authorities may extend that period on submission of a duly substantiated request by the holder of the authorization even if the initial period has already expired. See Council Regulation 2913/92 Art 149(1), OJ 19.10.92 L302/1; see also Commission Regulation 2454/93 Art 755, OJ 11.10.93 L253/1.

15 Council Regulation 2913/92 Art 149(2), OJ 19.10.92 L302/1. As to the definition of rate of yield see ibid Art 145(3)(d).

16 Commission Regulation 2454/93 Art 757, OJ 11.10.93 L253/1. However, where circumstances so warrant, the customs authorities may fix the rate of yield after the goods have been entered for the procedure, but not later than the time when the declaration for release for free circulation of the compensating products is accepted. See ibid Art 758.

17 Ibid Art 760(1). Regarding the details and the information to be provided in the declaration see ibid Art 760(2); see also ibid Art 763(2).

18 Ibid Art 761(1). It shall be for the applicant to prove the non-commercial nature of the goods. See ibid Art 761(1). In this sense, repairs of a non-commercial nature are repairs to goods, including restoring them to their original condition and putting them in order, which are carried out on an occasional basis and relate exclusively to goods for the personal use of the importer or his family, which do not by their nature or quantity reflect any commercial interest. See ibid Art 761(2). In such cases the declaration must be presented at a customs office with a customs officer duly empowered by the customs authorities. See ibid Art 767(3).

19 Ibid Art 777(1); see also ibid Art 748(g). As to the details of the triangular traffic system see ibid Arts 778–783.

20 Ibid Art 763(1).

the provisions laid down for exportation.[1] The simplified procedures provided for in Art 76 of the Code will apply in accordance with Art 277.[2]

Relief

The total or partial relief from import duties provided for under the outward processing procedure will be granted only where the compensating products are declared for release for free circulation in the name or on the behalf of the holder of the authorization or any other person established in the Community provided that person has obtained the consent of the holder of the authorization and the conditions of the authorization are fulfilled.[3] The declaration for release for free circulation shall be lodged at one of the offices of discharge specified in the authorization.[4]

In determining the customs relief, the Customs Code adopts the so-called 'differential taxation system'. Thus, the total or partial relief from import duties must be effected by deducting from the amount of the import duties applicable to the compensating products released for free circulation the amount of the import duties that would be applicable on the same date to the temporary export goods if they were imported into the customs territory of the Community from the country in which they underwent processing operations or the last processing operation.[5] The amount to be deducted, however, must be calculated on the basis of the quantity and nature of the goods in question on the date of acceptance of the declaration placing them under the outward processing procedure and on the basis of the other items of charge applicable to them on

1 Ibid Art 764(1). The description of the goods in the declaration must correspond to the specifications laid down in the authorization. See ibid Art 764(2). The provisions of ibid Art 658(3) shall apply. See ibid Art 764(3).
2 Commission Regulation 2454/93, OJ 11.10.93 L253/1: see ibid Art 765.
3 Council Regulation 2913/92 Art 150(1), OJ 19.10.92 L302/1; see also Commission Regulation 2454/93 Art 766, OJ 11.10.93 L253/1. Relief will not be granted if any of the conditions or obligations relating to the outward processing procedure are not fulfilled, unless it is established that the failures have no significant effect on the correct operation of the procedure. See Council Regulation 2913/92 Art 150(2), OJ 19.10.92 L302/1. The rules for customs relief under the outward processing procedure shall be applied without prejudice to the application of provisions, adopted or liable to be adopted in the context of trade between the Community and third countries, which provide for relief from import duties in respect of certain compensating products. See ibid Art 151(5). When the compensating products are released for free circulation, the specific commercial policy measures in force for such products at the time when the declaration for release for free circulation is accepted shall apply only where such products do not originate in the Community within the meaning of Council Regulation 2913/92 Arts 23 and 24, OJ 19.10.92 L302/1. See Commission Regulation 2454/93 Art 785, OJ 11.10.93 L253/1.
4 Ibid Art 767(1). Where the simplified procedure for repairs which are not of a non-commercial nature applies, the declaration shall be lodged with a customs office which issued the authorization. See ibid Art 767(2). However, the supervising office may allow such declarations to be presented at a different customs office. See ibid Art 767(4). As to the details of the declaration see ibid Art 768. Furthermore, the simplified procedures provided for in Art 76 of the Code shall apply to release for free circulation under the procedure in accordance with Arts 254–267 and 278. See ibid Art 769.
5 Council Regulation 2913/92 Art 151(1), OJ 19.10.92 L302/1; see also Case C-16/91 *Wacker Werke GmbH & Co KG v Hauptzollamt Munchen-West* [1992] ECR I-6821; see also Case C-142/96 *Hauptzollamt Munchen v Wacker Werke GmbH & Co KG* (1997) Transcript, 17 July (where the Court established how to determine the customs value of both the compensating products and the temporary export products).

the date of acceptance of the declaration relating to the release for free circulation of the compensating products.[6]

In the calculation of the amount to be deducted no account shall be taken of

(1) the charges provided for in the Council regulations on the market in cereals,[7] pigmeat,[8] eggs,[9] poultry meat,[10] fruit and vegetable sector,[11] wine;[12] and

(2) anti-dumping duties and countervailing duties

which would have been applicable to the temporary exports if they had been imported into the Member State concerned from the country where they underwent the processing operation or the last such operation.[13]

Where the temporary export goods could qualify on their release for free circulation for a reduced or zero rate of duty by virtue of their end use, that rate shall be taken into account provided that the goods underwent operations consistent with such end use in the country where the processing operation or last operation took place.[14] Furthermore, if the compensating products qualify for a preferential tariff measure and the measure exists for goods falling within the same tariff classification as the temporary export goods, the rate of import duty to be taken into account in establishing the amount to be deducted shall be that which would apply if the temporary export goods fulfilled the conditions under which that preferential measure may be applied.[15]

If all the compensating products other than secondary compensating products resulting from a given processing operation are not released for free circulation at the same time,[16] the proportion of temporary goods incorporated in the compensating products will be calculated in the following way. First, if one kind of compensating product only is derived from the outward processing operations from one or more kinds of temporary export goods, the quantitative scale method shall be used to determine the amount to be deducted on release for free circulation of the compensating products.[17] Second, where several kinds of compensating product are derived from the outward processing operations from one or more kinds of temporary export goods and all elements of the said goods are found in each of the different kinds of compensating product, the

---

6 As to the determination of the value of the temporary export goods see ibid Art 151(2); see also Art 77 Commission Regulation 2454/93, OJ 11.10.93 L253/1.
7 Council Regulation 2727/75, OJ 1.11.75 L281/1.
8 Council Regulation 2759/75, OJ 1.11.75 L282/1, as amended.
9 Council Regulation 2771/75, OJ 1.11.75 L282/49, as amended.
10 Council Regulation 2777/75, OJ 1.11.75 L283/77, as amended.
11 Council Regulation 1035/72, OJ 20.5.72 L118/1, as amended.
12 Council Regulation 822/87, OJ 27.3.87 L84/1, as amended.
13 Commission Regulation 2454/93 Art 770, OJ 11.10.93 L253/1.
14 Council Regulation 2913/92 Art 151(3), OJ 19.10.92 L302/1.
15 Ibid Art 151(4).
16 As to the definition of secondary compensating products see Commission Regulation 2454/93 Art 748(b), OJ 11.10.93 L253/1.
17 Ibid Art 773(1). The quantity of each kind of temporary export goods corresponding to the quantity of compensating products released for free circulation to be taken into account for determining the amount to be deducted shall be calculated by applying to the total quantity of each kind of the said goods a coefficient corresponding to the ratio of the quantity of compensating products released from free circulation of the compensating products. See ibid Art 773(2). As to the concept of quantitative scale method see ibid Art 748(d).

quantitative scale method shall be used.[18] Finally, in all other cases, the value scale method must be used.[19]

However, in all cases where an outward processing authorization which does not provide for a repair is used and the customs authorities are able by agreement with the holder of the authorization to set an approximate amount of duty payable under the provisions on partial relief from import duties, the said authority may set an average rate applicable to all processing operations to be carried out under such authorization in the case of undertakings which frequently carry out outward processing operations.[20]

If the purpose of the processing operation is the repair of temporary export goods, such goods shall be released for free circulation with total relief from import duties where it is established to the satisfaction of the customs authorities that the goods were repaired free of charge, either because of a contractual or statutory obligation arising from a guarantee or because of a manufacturing defect unless account was taken of the defect at the time when the goods in question were first released for free circulation.[1] However, if such repair is carried out in return for payment, the partial relief from the import duties shall be granted by establishing the amount of the duties applicable on the basis of the taxation elements pertaining to the compensating products on the date of acceptance of the declaration of release for free circulation of those products and taking into account as the customs value an amount equal to the repair costs, provided that those costs represent the only consideration provided by the holder of the authorization and are not influenced by any links between the holder and the operator.[2] Furthermore, in the case of repairs or of additional processing operations to be carried out under the temporary exportation of the inward processing procedure, no commercial policy measures for imports shall apply.[3]

The standard exchange system and prior importation

Within the outward processing procedure, the Customs Code allows for the use of the standard exchange system whereby an imported good may, as replacement product, replace a compensating product.[4] The standard exchange system may be used where the processing operation involves the repair of Community goods other than those subject to the common agricultural policy or to specific arrangements applicable to certain goods resulting from the processing of

18 Ibid Art 774(1). In deciding whether such method applies, no account shall be taken of losses. See ibid Art 774(2). In this sense, secondary compensating products which constitute waste, scrap, residues, offcuts and remainders shall be taken as losses. See ibid Art 774(3). As to the details of this method see ibid Art 774(4); see also ibid Art 774(5).

19 However, with the agreement of the holder of the authorization and for the purposes of simplification, the customs authorities may apply the quantitative scale method instead of the value scale method where either method would give similar results. See ibid Art 775(1). For the definition of value scale method see ibid Art 748(e). As for the details of this method see ibid Art 775(2); see also ibid Art 775(3); see also ibid Art 775(4).

20 Ibid Art 776 (establishing also the details of such rate).

1 Council Regulation 2913/92 Art 152, OJ 19.10.92 L302/1.

2 Ibid Art 153. As to the definition of such repair costs see Commission Regulation 2454/93 Art 771(3), OJ 11.10.93 L253/1.

3 Ibid Art 785(2).

4 Council Regulation 2913/92 Art 154(1), OJ 19.10.92 L302/1. Where the standard exchange system is used no commercial policy measures for imports shall apply. See Commission Regulation 2454/93 Art 785(2), OJ 11.10.93 L253/1.

agricultural products.[5] Authorization to use this system, however, may be issued only at the request of the person who arranges for the processing operations to be carried out.[6]

Replacement products must have the same tariff classification, be of the same commercial quality and possess the same technical characteristics as the temporary export goods, had the latter undergone the repair in question.[7] In this sense, the customs authorities must satisfy themselves that the use of the standard exchange system is not authorized as means of improving the technical performance of the goods.[8]

Furthermore, the customs authorities must allow the prior importation of replacement products before the temporary export goods are exported.[9] In such case, the export goods must be temporarily exported within a period of two months from the date of acceptance by the customs authorities of the declaration relating to the release of the replacement products for free circulation.[10] For the purposes of determining the customs relief, the amount to be deducted shall be determined on the basis of the items of charges applicable to the temporary export goods on the date of acceptance of the declaration placing them under the procedure.[11]

An authorization for use of the standard exchange system without prior importation may also be used for the reimportation of compensating products instead of the replacement products provided that the conditions are fulfilled.[12]

If the circumstances so warrant and all the conditions for authorizing use of the standard exchange system without prior importation are fulfilled, the customs authorities may allow the holder of an outward processing authorization which does not provide for use of this system to import replacement products if the person concerned submits a request to this effect no later than the time the products are imported.[13]

---

5 Council Regulation 2913/92 Art 154(2), OJ 19.10.92 L302/1.

6 Ibid Art 159.

7 Ibid Art 155(1).

8 Commission Regulation 2454/93 Art 749(4), OJ 11.10.93 L253/1. Moreover, if the temporary export goods have been used before export, the replacement products must also have been used and may not be new products. Yet, the customs authorities may, however, grant derogations from this rule if the replacement products have been supplied free of charge whether because of a contractual or statutory obligation arising from a guarantee or because of a manufacturing defect. See Council Regulation 2913/92 Art 155(2), OJ 19.10.92 L302/1.

9 Ibid Art 154(4). In case of prior importation, however, a security must be provided to cover the amount of the import duties and no retroactive authorization will be granted. See Commission Regulation 2454/93 Art 751, OJ 11.10.93 L253/1. The use of the triangular traffic system shall not be authorized under the standard exchange system with prior importation. See ibid Art 777(2).

10 Council Regulation 2913/92 Art 157(1), OJ 19.10.92 L302/1. In this sense, the placing of goods in a free zone or free warehouse or under the customs warehousing procedure for subsequent export shall be treated as export. See Commission Regulation 2454/93 Art 756(2), OJ 11.10.93 L253/1. However, where circumstances so warrant, such period may be extended even after the original period has expired. See ibid Art 756(1).

11 Council Regulation 2913/92 Art 158, OJ 19.10.92 L302/1.

12 Commission Regulation 2454/93 Art 752(1), OJ 11.10.93 L253/1.

13 Ibid Art 752(2).

Chapter 6

Other customs procedures and specific reliefs

TRANSIT

Introduction

The aim of the transit procedure is to facilitate the transport of goods within the Community and in particular to simplify the formalities which have to be undergone when goods cross Community internal frontiers.[1] The Community rules provide for an internal and an external transit procedure.

The internal transit procedure applies, essentially, to goods which satisfy the conditions laid down in Arts 9 and 10 of the Treaty, namely goods originating in the Member States or goods in free circulation in the Community, referred to as Community goods.[2] It allows the movement of Community goods from one point to another within the customs territory of the Community passing through the territory of a third country without any change in their customs status.[3]

The external transit procedure applies, essentially, to goods which do not satisfy the conditions laid down in Arts 9 and 10 of the Treaty.[4] Thus, it allows the movement from one point to another within the customs territory of the Community of:

---

1 See Case 136/80 *Hudig en Pieters BV v Minister van Landbouw en Visserij* [1981] ECR 2233, paragraph 2; see also Case C-328/89 *Berner Allgemeine Versicherungsgesellschaft v Amministrazione delle Finanze dello Stato* [1991] ECR I-2431; see also Communication from the Commission, *The Future of the Transit Systems*, Brussels 9.10.1996 COM (96) 477 final; see also Communication from the Commission to the European Parliament and the Council, *Action Plan for Transit in Europe: A New Customs Policy*, Brussels 30.4.97 COM (97) 188 final. The Community is bound by Article V of GATT which lays down the principle of freedom of transit through the territory of each contracting party for traffic in transport to or from the territory of other contracting parties. However, such provision cannot have direct effect in the Community law and individuals may not rely upon it. See Case 266/81 *Societa Italiana per l'Oleodotto Transalpino (SIOT) v Ministero delle Finanze, Ministero della Marine Mercantile, Circoscrizione dognale di Trieste and Ente Autonomo del Porto di Trieste* [1983] ECR 731, paragraphs 27–28.
2 See Case C-83/89 *Openbaar Ministerie and Minister van Financien v Vicent Houben* [1990] ECR I-1161, paragraph 14; see also Case 99/83 *Claudio Fioravanti v Amministrazione delle Finanze dello Stato* [1984] ECR 3939.
3 Council Regulation 2913/92 Art 163, OJ 19.10.92 L302/1. As to the Community goods covered by the internal transit procedure see Commission Regulation 2454/93 Art 311, OJ 11.10.93 L253/1, as amended by Commission Regulation 75/98, OJ 13.1.98 L7/3.
4 See Case C-83/89 *Openbaar Ministerie and Minister van Financien v Vicent Houben* [1990] ECR I-1161, paragraph 13.

(1) non-Community goods, without such goods being subject to import duties and other charges or to commercial policy measures;[5] and

(2) Community goods which are subject to a Community measure involving their export to third countries and in respect of which the corresponding customs formalities for export have been carried out.[6]

However, the external transit procedure may also apply to goods passing through the territory of a third country if provision is made to that effect under an international agreement;[7] or carriage through that country is effected under cover of a single transport document drawn up in the customs territory of the Community.[8]

Thus, for a correct application of the transit procedure one must distinguish between Community goods and non-Community goods.[9] All goods in the customs territory of the Community must be deemed to be Community goods unless it is established that they do not have Community status.[10] Goods brought into the customs territory of the Community and goods in temporary storage or in a free zone or free warehouse and goods placed under a suspensive procedure will not be considered to be Community goods unless their Community status is adequately established.[11] However, goods brought into the customs territory of the Community will be considered as Community goods unless it is established that they do not have Community status where, if carried by air the goods have been loaded or transhipped at a Community airport, for consignment to another airport in the customs territory of the Community, and carried under cover of a single transport document drawn up in a Member State; or where, if carried by sea, the goods have been shipped between ports in the customs territory of the Community by an authorized regular shipping service.[12]

5 Council Regulation 2913/92 Art 91(1)(a), OJ 19.10.92 L302/1.
6 Ibid Art 91(1)(b). As to the Community goods covered by this form of external transit see Commission Regulation 2454/93 Art 310, OJ 11.10.93 L253/1.
7 Council Regulation 2913/92 Art 93(a), OJ 19.10.92 L302/1.
8 In such a case the operation of that procedure must be suspended in the territory of the third country. See ibid Art 93(b); see also Commission Regulation 2454/93 Art 312, OJ 11.10.93 L253/1.
9 The rules for proving the Community status of goods are justified by the need to facilitate the movement of goods across the Community's internal frontiers, which is one of the principles of the common market. In this sense, Arts 9 and 10 of the Treaty are silent as to the means of proof and the burden of proof of the Community status of goods and thus they leave it to secondary Community legislation to settle those matters. See Case C-117/88 *Trend-Modern Textilhandels GmbH v Hauptzollamt Emmerich* [1990] ECR I-631, paragraphs 19–20; see also Case 237/96 *Belgian Minister for Financial Affairs v Eddy Amelynck* (1997) Transcript, 25 September, paragraph 19.
10 Commission Regulation 2454/93 Art 313(1), OJ 11.10.93 L253/1, as amended by Commission Regulation 75/98, OJ 13.1.98 L7/3. As to proof of Community or non-Community status of goods where goods are brought into or returned to another part of the customs territory or placed under customs procedure see Council Regulation 2913/92 Art 180, OJ 19.10.92 L302/1; see also Case C-83/89 *Openbaar Ministerie and Minister van Financien v Vicent Houben* [1990] ECR I-1161, paragraph 11.
11 Commission Regulation 2454/93 Art 313(2), OJ 11.10.93 L253/1, as amended by Commission Regulation 75/98, OJ 13.1.98 L7/3. Concerning the establishment of the Community status of goods see Arts 314 to 323 Commission Regulation 2454/93, OJ 11.10.93 L253/1, as amended by Commission Regulation 75/98, OJ 13.1.98 L7/3.
12 Commission Regulation 2454/93 Art 313(2), OJ 11.10.93 L253/1, as amended by Commission Regulation 75/98, OJ 13.1.98 L7/3. Concerning the concept of a regular shipping service and the procedure for granting its authorization see Arts 313a and 313b Commission Regulation 2454/93, OJ 11.10.93 L253/1, as amended by Commission Regulation 75/98, OJ 13.1.98 L7/3. Special provisions apply for products of sea-fishing and other products taken

Provided that the implementation of Community measures applying to goods is guaranteed, Member States may by bilateral or multilateral arrangement establish between themselves simplified procedures consistent with criteria to be set according to the circumstances and applying to certain types of goods traffic or specific undertakings.[13] Furthermore, each Member State may establish simplified procedures in certain circumstances for goods not required to move in the territory of another Member State.[14]

Procedure

All goods intended to be placed under a transit procedure must be covered by a transit declaration.[15] Goods which are to move under the external transit procedure must be subject to a T1 declaration.[16] Likewise, goods which are to move under the internal Community transit procedure are subject to a T2 declaration.[17] In the case of consignments comprising both goods which have to move under the external transit procedure and goods which have to move under the internal Community transit procedure, supplementary forms which bear the symbol 'T1 bis' or 'T2 bis' respectively may be attached to a single Community transit declaration form.[18] Loading lists may be used as the descriptive part of the Community transit operations.[19]

The transit declaration must be signed by the principal and at least three copies thereof must be produced at the office of departure.[20] It must be ac-

---

from the sea by boats. See Commission Regulation 2454/93 Arts 325–340, OJ 11.10.93 L253/1, as amended by Commission Regulation 482/96, OJ 20.3.96 L70/5.

13 Council Regulation 2913/92 Art 97(2)(a), OJ 19.10.92 L302/1. In this sense, Art 233 of the Treaty states that the provisions of the Treaty shall not preclude the existence or completion of regional unions between Belgium and Luxembourg or between Belgium, Luxembourg and the Netherlands, to the extent that the objectives of these regional unions are not attained by application of this Treaty. See Art 233 of the Treaty; see also Case 105/83 *Pakvries BV v Minister for Agriculture and Fisheries* [1984] ECR 2101, paragraph 11.

14 Council Regulation 2913/92 Art 97(2)(b), OJ 19.10.92 L302/1.

15 Ibid Art 59(1). As to the general rules for the placing of goods under a customs procedure, including transit see Council Regulation 2913/92 Arts 59 to 78, OJ 19.10.92 L302/1; see also Commission Regulation 2454/93 Arts 198–253a, OJ 11.10.93 L253/1.

16 A T1 declaration means a declaration on a form corresponding to the specimens in Annex 31–34 of Commission Regulation 2454/93 and used in accordance with the notes referred to in Annex 37–38 of Commission Regulation 2454/93. See Commission Regulation 2454/93 Art 341(1), OJ 11.10.93 L253/1.

17 The provisions on external transit procedure apply *mutatis mutandis* to the internal transit procedure, See Commission Regulation 2454/93 Art 381(2), OJ 11.10.93 L253/1. A T2 declaration is a declaration on a form corresponding to the specimen in Annexes 31 to 34 Commission Regulation 2454/93 and used in accordance with the notice in Commission Regulation 2454/93 Annex 37. See Commission Regulation 2454/93 Art 381(1), OJ 11.10.93 L253/1, as amended by Commission Regulation 75/98, OJ 13.1.98 L7/3.

18 Commission Regulation 2454/93 Art 382(1), OJ 11.10.93 L253/1.

19 Such loading lists must be based on the specimen in Annex 45 to Commission Regulation 2454/93 and used in accordance with Commission Regulation 2454/93 Arts 343–345. See Commission Regulation 2454/93 Art 341(2), OJ 11.10.93 L253/1. In the case of consignments comprising both goods moving under the external transit procedure and goods moving under the internal transit procedure, separate loading lists must be made out and may be attached to a single Community transit declaration form. See Commission Regulation 2454/93 Art 383, OJ 11.10.93 L253/1.

20 Commission Regulation 2454/93 Art 346(2), OJ 11.10.93 L253/1. Office of departure means the customs office where the Community transit operation begins. See Commission Regulation 2454/93 Art 309(b), OJ 11.10.93 L253/1.

companied by the transport document.[1] Furthermore, the customs documents of export/dispatch or re-exportation of the goods from the customs territory of the Community or any other document of equivalent effect must also be presented to the office of departure with the transit declaration to which it relates.[2]

The office of departure will accept and register the transit declaration, prescribe the period within which the goods must be presented at the office of destination and take such measures for identification as it considers necessary.[3] Where the transit operation concerns goods which are the subject of a decision of the Commission by which the goods are considered to present an increased risk of fraud, or whenever the customs authorities consider it necessary, the office of departure may prescribe an itinerary for the consignment.[4] The office of departure must also enter the necessary particulars on the transit declaration, retain its own copy, and return the other to the principal or its representative.[5]

The principal is the holder under the external Community transit procedure.[6] It must be responsible for the production of the goods intact at the customs office of destination by the prescribed time limit and with due observance of the means adopted by the customs authorities to ensure identification;[7] and the observance of the provisions relating to the Community transit procedure.[8]

The goods must be transported under cover of the copies of the transit document returned to the principal or its representative by the office of departure.[9] Copies of the transit documents must be presented as required by the customs authorities.[10] Furthermore, the consignment and the copies of the transit

---

1 The office of departure may dispense with the presentation of this document at the time of completion of the formalities but such document must be presented at the request of the customs office or any other competent authority in the course of the transport. See Commission Regulation 2454/93 Art 219, OJ 11.10.93 L253/1.
2 Commission Regulation 2454/93 Art 219(2), OJ 11.10.93 L253/1. Moreover, the customs authorities may, where appropriate, require production of the document relating to the preceding customs procedure. See Commission Regulation 2454/93 Art 219(3), OJ 11.10.93 L253/1.
3 Commission Regulation 2454/93 Art 348(1), OJ 11.10.93 L253/1. As a general rule identification must be ensured by sealing. See Commission Regulation 2454/93 Art 349(1), OJ 11.10.93 L253/1. However, the office of departure may dispense with sealing if, having regard to the other possibilities of identification, the description of the goods in the transit declaration document or in the supplementary documents make them readily identifiable. See ibid Art 349(4).
4 Commission Regulation 2454/93 Art 348(1a), OJ 11.10.93 L253/1, as amended by Commission Regulation 482/96, OJ 20.3.96 L70/5. In the case of force majeure, the carrier may diverge from the prescribed itinerary but it must present the transit declaration and the consignment without delay to the nearest customs authorities of the Member State in which the consignment is located. See Commission Regulation 2454/93 Art 348(1b), OJ 11.10.93 L253/1, as amended by Commission Regulation 482/96, OJ 20.3.96 L70/5.
5 Commission Regulation 2454/93 Art 348(2), OJ 11.10.93 L253/1.
6 Council Regulation 2913/92 Art 96(1), OJ 19.10.92 L302/1.
7 Ibid Art 96(1)(a).
8 Ibid Art 96(1)(b); see also Case 136/80 *Hudig en Pieters BV v Minister van Landbouw en Visserij* [1981] ECR 2233, paragraph 19. However, a carrier or recipient of goods who accepts goods knowing that they are moving under Community transit must also be responsible for production of the goods intact at the customs office of destination by the prescribed time and with due observance of the measures adopted by the customs authorities to ensure identification. See Council Regulation 2913/92 Art 96(2), OJ 19.10.92 L302/1.
9 Commission Regulation 2454/93 Art 350(1), OJ 11.10.93 L253/1.
10 Commission Regulation 2454/93 Art 350(2), OJ 11.10.93 L253/1.

document must be presented at each office of transit.[11] Where goods are transported via an office of transit other than that mentioned in the transit document, the transit office must without delay inform the office mentioned in the document.[12] The offices of transit must not inspect the goods unless some irregularity is suspected which could result in abuse.[13] Where goods are loaded or unloaded in the presence of intermediate customs authorities the copies of the transit document returned by the office of departure must be presented to those authorities.[14]

The goods described on the transit document may be transferred to another means of transport under the supervision of the customs authorities of the Member State in the territory of which the transfer is to be made, without the need for a new transit declaration.[15]

If seals are broken in the course of the transport for reasons beyond the carrier's control, the carrier must without delay request that a certified report be drawn up by the customs authorities in the Member State in which the means of transport is located.[16] In the case of an accident necessitating transfer to another means of transport, such transfer will take place under the supervision of the customs authorities without the need for a new transit declaration.[17] In the event of imminent danger, necessitating immediate unloading of the whole or part of the load, the carrier may take action on its own initiative and record such action in the transit document.[18] Where if as a result of accidents or other incidents arising in the course of the transport operation, the carrier is not in a position to comply with the period established by the office of departure, it shall inform the customs authorities in the Member State in which the means of transport is located who will then record the relevant details on the transit document.[19]

---

11 Commission Regulation 2454/93 Art 352(1), OJ 11.10.93 L253/1. Office of transit means the customs office at the point of exit from the customs territory of the Community when the consignment is leaving that territory in the course of a Community transit operation via a frontier between a Member State and a third country or the customs office at the point of entry into the customs territory of the Community when the goods have crossed the territory of a third country in the course of a Community transit operation. See Commission Regulation 2454/93 Art 309(c), OJ 11.10.93 L253/1.

12 Commission Regulation 2454/93 Art 352(4), OJ 11.10.93 L253/1.

13 Commission Regulation 2454/93 Art 352(3), OJ 11.10.93 L253/1. The Court, however, has held that this provision should be limited by Art 36 of the Treaty. Thus, it cannot preclude legislation of a Member State, which, on external security grounds, requires special authorization to be obtained for the transit through its territory of goods described as strategic material, irrespective of the Community transit document issued by another Member State. Nevertheless, the measures adopted by the Member State as a consequence of the failure to comply with that requirement must not be disproportionate to the objective pursued. See Case C-367/89 *Criminal Proceedings against Aime Richardt and Les Accessoires Scientifiques SNC* [1991] ECR I-4621, paragraph 26.

14 Commission Regulation 2454/93 Art 353, OJ 11.10.93 L253/1.

15 Commission Regulation 2454/93 Art 354, OJ 11.10.93 L253/1. The customs authorities, on such conditions as they must determine, may authorize such transfer without their supervision. In that case the carrier must record the relevant details on the transit document and inform the customs authorities of the Member State of transfer, for the purposes of obtaining their endorsement. See Commission Regulation 2454/93 Art 354(2), OJ 11.10.93 L253/1. As to the concept of means of transport see Commission Regulation 2454/93 Art 309(a), OJ 11.10.93 L253/1.

16 If possible, the customs authorities concerned must affix new seals. See Commission Regulation 2454/93 Art 355(1), OJ 11.10.93 L253/1.

17 Commission Regulation 2454/93 Art 355(2), OJ 11.10.93 L253/1.

18 Commission Regulation 2454/93 Art 355(3), OJ 11.10.93 L253/1.

19 Commission Regulation 2454/93 Art 355(4), OJ 11.10.93 L253/1.

The external transit procedure will end when the goods and the corresponding documents are produced at the customs office of destination.[20] The office of destination must record on the copies of the transit document the details of controls carried out and send a copy to the office of departure and retain the other copy.[1] Where the goods are presented at the office of destination after expiry of the time limit prescribed by the office of departure and the failure to comply with such time limit is due to circumstances which are explained to the satisfaction of the office of destination and are not attributable to the carrier or the principal, these will be deemed to have complied with the time limit prescribed.[2] The person presenting a Community transit document to the office of destination together with the consignment to which that document relates may obtain a receipt on request.[3]

Simplified and special procedures

The Community provides specific rules for the simplification of transit formalities to be carried out at the office of departure or destination.[4] The aim of these simplified procedures is that customs formalities and controls should be kept to a minimum whilst ensuring that the simplifications provided for are not liable to affect adversely the customs interests of the Community.[5]

The customs authorities of each Member State may allow authorized consignors not to present at the office of departure either the goods concerned or the Community transit declaration in respect of those goods.[6] Authorized consignors may only be persons who frequently consign goods;[7] whose records enable the customs authorities to check their operations;[8] who, where

---

20 Council Regulation 2913/92 Art 92, OJ 19.10.92 L302/1; see also Commission Regulation 2454/93 Art 356(1), OJ 11.10.93 L253/1. Office of destination means the customs office where the goods placed under the Community transit procedure must be produced to complete the Community transit operation. See Commission Regulation 2454/93 Art 309(d), OJ 11.10.93 L253/1. A Community transit operation may be concluded at an office other than that specified in the transit document. The other office will then become the office of destination. See Commission Regulation 2454/93 Art 356(3), OJ 11.10.93 L253/1. Special provisions apply in the case of transit concerning goods which are the subject of a Commission decision by which they are considered to present an increased risk of fraud. See Commission Regulation 2454/93 Art 356(3a), OJ 11.10.93 L253/1, as amended by Commission Regulation 482/96, OJ 20.3.96 L70/5.

1 Commission Regulation 2454/93 Art 356(2), OJ 11.10.93 L253/1.

2 Commission Regulation 2454/93 Art 356(5), OJ 11.10.93 L253/1.

3 Commission Regulation 2454/93 Art 357(1), OJ 11.10.93 L253/1.

4 These simplified procedures do not apply to goods placed under the transit procedure where export of those goods is prohibited or is subject to restrictions, duties or other charges. See Commission Regulation 2454/93 Art 397, OJ 11.10.93 L253/1; see also ibid Art 463. Furthermore, the customs authorities of the Member State of departure or destination may exclude certain categories of goods from these simplified procedures. See Commission Regulation 2454/93 Art 410, OJ 11.10.93 L253/1.

5 See Case C-292/96 *Goritz Intransco International GmbH v Hauptzollamt Dusseldorf* [1998] ECR I-165.

6 Commission Regulation 2454/93 Art 398, OJ 11.10.93 L253/1. Such exception may apply to both obligations or it may be confined to only one of them. Thus it allows the customs authorities to grant the status of authorized consignor even when it is no longer possible to exempt such consignor from the obligation to present the goods at the office of departure because such goods have already been presented to customs. See Case C-292/96 *Goritz Intransco International GmbH v Hauptzollamt Dusseldorf* [1998] ECR I-165.

7 Commission Regulation 2454/93 Art 399(1)(a), OJ 11.10.93 L253/1.

8 Commission Regulation 2454/93 Art 399(1)(b), OJ 11.10.93 L253/1.

a guarantee is required under the Community transit procedure, provide a comprehensive guarantee;[9] and who have not committed serious or repeated offences against customs or tax legislation.[10] The authorizations must specify the office or offices competent to act as offices of departure for the consignments;[11] the period which, and the procedure by which the authorized consignor is to inform the office of departure of the consignments to be sent, in order that the office may carry out any necessary controls before the departure of the goods;[12] the period within which the goods must be presented at the office of destination;[13] and the identification measures to be taken.[14] The authorization must stipulate that the box reserved for the office of departure on the front of the Community transit declaration forms be stamped in advance with the stamp of the office of departure and be signed by an official of that office;[15] or be stamped by the authorized consignor with a special stamp approved by the customs authorities.[16]

Not later than on consignment of the goods, the authorized consignor must enter on the front of copies 1 and 4 of the duly completed transit declaration the period within which the goods must be presented at the office of destination, the identification measures applied and the phrase 'Simplified procedure'.[17] Following the consignment, copy 1 must be sent without delay to the office of departure. The other copies must accompany the goods.[18] This Community transit declaration will be equivalent to an external or internal Community transit document and the authorized consignor who signed the declaration will be considered as the principal.[19]

The customs authorities of each Member State may issue an authorization waiving presentation at the office of destination where transport of goods under the Community transit procedure is intended for an authorized consignee previously authorized by the customs authorities of the Member State to which the office of destination belongs.[20] An authorized consignee may be a person who frequently receives consignments under the Community transit procedure;[1] whose records enable the customs authorities to check the operations;[2] and who has not committed serious or repeated offences against customs or tax legislation.[3] The authorizations must specify the office or offices competent to act as offices of destination for consignments which the authorized consignee receives;[4] and the period within which, and the procedure by which, the author-

9 Commission Regulation 2454/93 Art 399(1)(c), OJ 11.10.93 L253/1.
10 Commission Regulation 2454/93 Art 399(1)(d), OJ 11.10.93 L253/1. The customs authorities may withdraw the authorization where the authorized consignor no longer fulfils these conditions or fails to comply with any other requirements. See Commission Regulation 2454/93 Art 399(2), OJ 11.10.93 L253/1.
11 Commission Regulation 2454/93 Art 400(a), OJ 11.10.93 L253/1.
12 Ibid Art 400(b).
13 Ibid Art 400(c).
14 Ibid Art 400(d).
15 Ibid Art 401(1)(a).
16 Ibid Art 401(1)(b).
17 Ibid Art 402(1).
18 Ibid Art 402(2), OJ 11.10.93 L253/1.
19 Ibid Art 403.
20 Ibid Art 406(1).
 1 Ibid Art 407(1)(a).
 2 Ibid Art 407(1)(b).
 3 Ibid Art 407(1)(c). The customs authorities may revoke the authorization when the authorized consignee no longer fulfils the previous conditions or fails to comply with the requirements of the authorization or the Community transit rules. See ibid Art 407(2).
 4 Ibid Art 408(1)(a).

ized consignee is to inform the office of destination of the arrival of the goods in order that the office may carry out any necessary controls upon arrival of the goods.[5] The principal will have fulfilled its obligations when the copies of the Community transit documents which accompanied the consignment, together with the goods intact, have been delivered within the prescribed period to the authorized consignee at its premises or at the place specified in the authorization and the identification measures have been observed.[6] The authorized consignee must at the request of the carrier issue a receipt in respect of each consignment delivered stating that the document and the goods have been delivered.[7] The authorized consignee must, in respect of consignments arriving at its premises or at the places specified in the authorization, immediately inform the office of destination of any excess quantities, shortages, substitutions or other irregularities such as broken seals;[8] and send the office of destination without delay the copies of the Community transit document which accompanied the consignment, indicating the date of arrival and the conditions of any seals affixed.[9]

The Community rules on transit provide for simplified formalities for goods to be carried by rail,[10] and for goods to be carried by rail in large containers.[11] Furthermore, special provisions apply for transport by air,[12] transport by sea,[13] and transport by pipeline.[14] Special provisions apply to the goods whose export from the Community is prohibited or is subject to restrictions, duties or other charges in so far as the measures introducing the prohibition, restriction, duty or any other charge so provide and without prejudice to any special provisions which that measure may comprise.[15]

Guarantees and irregularities

Under the external transit procedure, the principal must provide a guarantee to ensure payment of any customs debt or other charges which may be incurred in respect of the goods.[16] The guarantee may be comprehensive, covering a number of Community transit operations, or individual, covering a single

5 Ibid Art 408(1)(b). Furthermore, the customs authorities must specify in the authorization whether any action by the office of destination is required before the authorized consignee may dispose of the goods. See ibid Art 408(2).
6 Ibid Art 406(2).
7 Ibid Art 406(3).
8 Ibid Art 409(1)(a).
9 Ibid Art 409(1)(b). The office of destination must enter the required particulars on the copies of the Community transit document. See ibid Art 409(2).
10 See Commission Regulation 2454/93 Arts 412–425, OJ 11.10.93 L253/1 as amended by Commission Regulation 2193/94, OJ 9.9.94 L235/6 and Commission Regulation 75/98, OJ 13.1.98 L7/3.
11 See Commission Regulation 2454/93 Arts 436–442, OJ 11.10.93 L253/1, as amended by Commission Regulation 1762/95, OJ 21.7.95 L171/8, Commission Regulation 1427/97, OJ 24.7.97 L196/31 and Commission Regulation 75/98, OJ 13.1.98 L7/3.
12 See Commission Regulation 2454/93 Arts 443–445, OJ 11.10.93 L253/1, as amended by Commission Regulation 75/98, OJ 13.1.98 L7/3.
13 See Commission Regulation 2454/93 Arts 446–449, OJ 11.10.93 L253/1, as amended by Commission Regulation 75/98, OJ 13.1.98 L7/3.
14 See Commission Regulation 2454/93 Art 450, OJ 11.10.93 L253/1.
15 See Commission Regulation 2454/93 Arts 463–470, OJ 11.10.93 L253/1.
16 Exceptions may apply to journeys by sea and air, carriage of goods on the Rhine and the Rhine waterways, carriage by pipeline and operations carried out by the railway companies of the Member States. See Council Regulation 2913/92 Art 94, OJ 19.10.92 L302/1. The rules on external transit apply *mutatis mutandis* to the procedure for internal Community transit. See Commission Regulation 2454/93 Art 381(2), OJ 11.10.93 L253/1.

Community transit operation.[17] The guarantee may consist of the joint and several guarantees of any natural or legal third person established in the Community and approved by the customs authorities of the Member State, or, in the case of single Community transit operations, a cash deposit lodged by the principal at the office of departure.[18]

The use of the comprehensive guarantee will be granted only to persons who are established in the Member State where the guarantee is furnished;[19] who have been regular users, either as principals or as consignors, of the Community transit system during the previous six months or are known by the customs authorities to have a good financial standing which is sufficient to fulfil the commitments;[20] and who have not committed any serious or repeated infringement of customs or tax laws.[1]

A comprehensive guarantee must be lodged within an office of guarantee which shall determine the amount of the guarantee, accept the guarantor's undertaking and issue an authorization allowing the principal to carry out, within the limits of the amounts guaranteed, any Community transit operation irrespective of the office of departure.[2] Furthermore, each person who has obtained authorization must be issued with one or more guarantee certificates.[3] Reference to the guarantee certificate must be made on each transit document.[4]

The amount of the comprehensive guarantee must be fixed at 100% of the duties and other charges payable with a minimum of ERU 7000.[5] Under special circumstances, the customs authorities may fix at a minimum 30% of the duties

17 Commission Regulation 2454/93 Art 359(2), OJ 11.10.93 L253/1.
18 Ibid Art 359(3). In the performance of external Community transit operations there is a distinction between the principal and the guarantor, particularly in regard to the extent of the obligations which both assume towards the competent national authorities and the conditions on which they are released from them. The obligations which the guarantor assumes as such towards the competent national authorities are not the same as those assumed by the principal but are intended to ensure that the competent authorities receive any duties and charges which one of the Member States is entitled to require in respect of goods carried through its territory. The principal and the guarantor need not be different persons. In the case of cash deposits the guarantor and the principal can be the same person. However, where a comprehensive guarantee is provided in respect of several Community transit operations, the guarantor and the principal cannot be the same person. See Case 136/80 *Hudig en Pieters BV v Minister van Landbouw en Visserij* [1981] ECR 2233, paragraphs 18–34.
19 Commission Regulation 2454/93 Art 360(1)(a), OJ 11.10.93 L253/1, as amended by Commission Regulation 482/96, OJ 20.3.96 L70/5.
20 Commission Regulation 2454/93 Art 360(1)(b), OJ 11.10.93 L253/1, as amended by Commission Regulation 482/96, OJ 20.3.96 L70/5.
 1 Commission Regulation 2454/93 Art 360(1)(c), OJ 11.10.93 L253/1, as amended by Commission Regulation 482/96, OJ 20.3.96 L70/5. The office of guarantee must revoke the authorization for the use of the comprehensive guarantee if these conditions are no longer fulfilled. See Commission Regulation 2454/93 Art 360(6), OJ 11.10.93 L253/1, as amended by Commission Regulation 482/96, OJ 20.3.96 L70/5.
 2 Commission Regulation 2454/93 Art 360(2), OJ 11.10.93 L253/1, as amended by Commission Regulation 482/96, OJ 20.3.96 L70/5; see also ibid Art 360(3). Office of guarantee means the customs office where a comprehensive or flat rate guarantee is lodged. See Commission Regulation 2454/93 Art 309(e), OJ 11.10.93 L253/1.
 3 Commission Regulation 2454/93 Art 360(4), OJ 11.10.93 L253/1, as amended by Commission Regulation 482/96, OJ 20.3.96 L70/5.
 4 Ibid Art 360(5).
 5 Commission Regulation 2454/93 Art 361(1), OJ 11.10.93 L253/1, as amended by Commission Regulation 2153/96, OJ 12.11.96 L289/1. As to the determination of such amount and its annual review see Commission Regulation 2454/93 Arts 361(3) and 361(4), OJ 11.10.93 L253/1, as amended Commission Regulation 482/96, OJ 20.3.96 L70/5.

and other charges payable, with a minimum of ERU 7000.[6] The period of validity of the guarantee must not exceed two years.[7]

The use of the comprehensive guarantee must be temporarily forbidden when it is intended to cover external Community transit operations concerning goods which are the subject of a decision of the Commission by which these goods are considered to present an increased risk of fraud.[8]

On issue of the guarantee certificate or at any time during its validity, the principal must on its own responsibility designate on the reverse of the certificate the person or persons authorized to sign the Community transit declarations on its behalf.[9] Such person named on the reverse of the guarantee certificate will be deemed to be the authorized representative of the principal.[10] If the guarantee is cancelled, the principal must return to the guarantee office all valid guarantee certificates issued to it.[11]

Member States may allow the guarantor to furnish by declaration a single guarantee for a flat rate amount of ERU 7000, guaranteeing payment of duties and other charges which may become chargeable in the course of a Community transit operation carried out under his responsibility, whoever the principal may be.[12]

An individual guarantee furnished for a single Community transit operation must be lodged at the office of departure which must fix the amount of the guarantee.[13] Such guarantee may be a cash deposit which will be returned when the transit document is discharged at the office of departure.[14]

The guarantor must be released from its obligation once the customs debt in respect of which the guarantee was given is extinguished or can no longer arise and upon expiration of a period of 12 months from the date of registration of the transit declaration where it has not been advised by the customs authorities of the Member State of departure of the non-discharge of the transit document.[15] Where, within 12 months, the guarantor has been advised by the

---

6 See Commission Regulation 2454/93 Art 361(2), OJ 11.10.93 L253/1, as amended by Commission Regulation 2153/96, OJ 12.11.96 L289/1.
7 However, that period may be extended by the guarantee office for one further period not exceeding two years. See Commission Regulation 2454/93 Art 365, OJ 11.10.93 L253/1.
8 Commission Regulation 2454/93 Art 362(1), OJ 11.10.93 L253/1, as amended by Commission Regulation 482/96, OJ 20.3.96 L70/5. The maximum period for which use of the comprehensive guarantee must be prohibited in respect of any goods will be 12 months, unless the Commission decides to extend such period. See Commission Regulation 2454/93 Art 362(2), OJ 11.10.93 L253/1, as amended by Commission Regulation 75/98, OJ 13.1.98 L7/3. On the adoption of specific measures to prohibit temporarily the use of the comprehensive guarantee for certain external Community transit operations see Commission Decision 96/743, OJ 29.12.96 L338/105, as amended by Commission Decision 97/583, OJ 28.8.97 L237/41; see also Commission Decision 98/7, OJ 6.1.98 L2/11.
9 Commission Regulation 2454/93 Art 363(1), OJ 11.10.93 L253/1. The principal may at any time delete the name of the authorized person from the reverse of the certificate. See ibid Art 363(2).
10 Commission Regulation 2454/93 Art 364, OJ 11.10.93 L253/1.
11 Ibid Art 366.
12 Ibid Art 367. As to the particulars of these flat-rate guarantees see Commission Regulation 2454/93 Arts 368–372, OJ 11.10.93 L253/1, as amended by Commission Regulation 3254/94, OJ 31.12.94 L346/1 and Commission Regulation 482/96, OJ 20.3.96 L70/5.
13 Commission Regulation 2454/93 Art 373(1), OJ 11.10.93 L253/1.
14 Ibid Art 373(2).
15 Ibid Art 374. This provision seeks to ensure certainty in the law for persons who act as guarantors for transit operations in accordance with the Community rules in question. Thus, it must be interpreted as meaning that unless the guarantor is notified by the customs authorities of the Member State of departure of the non-discharge of the transit declaration, then, in the absence of any fraud of which it may be guilty, the guarantor is in any event released from

customs authorities of the non-discharge of the document, it must in addition be notified that it is or may be required to pay the amounts for which it is liable in respect of the Community transit operation in question within a period of three years after the date of registration of the transit declaration.[16] Otherwise, the guarantor must likewise be released from its obligation.[17]

A principal may obtain from the customs authorities in the Member State where it is established a guarantee waiver for the external transit operations carried out by it from any Member State of departure and through the territory of any Member State.[18] Such waiver will not apply to external transit operations involving goods of total value exceeding ERU 100,000 per consignment;[19] or which are listed in Annex 52 as involving increased risks, where the quantity exceeds that shown in column 3.[20] Furthermore, the waiver must not apply for transit operations concerning goods which are the subject of a decision of the Commission by which these goods are considered to present an increased risk of fraud.[1]

Where by reason of an offence or irregularity committed in connection with a Community transit operation, the duties and other charges payable are not collected, recovery of those duties and charges is to be effected by the Member State in which the offence or irregularity was committed, in accordance with the laws, regulations and administrative provisions of that state.[2]

If a consignment has not been presented at the office of destination and the place where the offence or irregularity occurred cannot be established, the office of departure must notify the principal of this fact as soon as possible and in any case before the eleventh month following the date of registration of the Community transit declaration.[3] The principal may provide proof of the regularity of the transit operation or the place where the offence or irregularity was actually committed within three months from the date of notification.[4]

its obligations. See Case 277/80 *SIC- Societa Italiana Cauzioni v Amministrazione delle Finanze dello Stato* [1982] ECR 629, paragraph 16; see also Case C-367/89 *Criminal Proceedings against Aime Richardt and Les Accessoires Scientifiques SNC* [1991] ECR I-4621. However, Art 374 must be interpreted as meaning that it does not cover the principal but only the person who in the case of the joint and several guarantee acts as guarantor in accordance with Community rules. See Case 136/80 *Hudig en Pieters BV v Minister van Landbouw en Visserij* [1981] ECR 2233, paragraph 28.

16 Commission Regulation 2454/93 Art 374, OJ 11.10.93 L253/1.
17 Ibid.
18 Council Regulation 2913/92 Art 95(1), OJ 19.10.92 L302/1. Such waiver may be granted only to persons who are established in the Member State where the waiver is granted, who are regular users of the Community transit procedure, whose financial situation is such that they can meet their commitments, who have not committed any serious infringement of customs or fiscal laws and who undertake to pay upon the first application in writing by the customs authorities, any sums claimed in respect of their transit operations. See ibid Art 95(2).
19 Ibid Art 95(3)(a); see also 376(1)(a) Commission Regulation 2454/93, OJ 11.10.93 L253/1.
20 Council Regulation 2913/92 Art 95(3)(b), OJ 19.10.92 L302/1; see also Commission Regulation 2454/93 Art 376(1)(b), OJ 11.10.93 L253/1, as amended by Commission Regulation 75/98, OJ 13.1.98 L7/3.
 1 Commission Regulation 2454/93 Art 376(2), OJ 11.10.93 L253/1, as amended by Commission Regulation 482/96, OJ 20.3.96 L70/5.
 2 See Case 99/83 *Claudio Fioravanti v Amministrazione delle Finanze dello Stato* [1984] ECR 3939.
 3 Commission Regulation 2454/93 Art 379(1), OJ 11.10.93 L253/1, paragraph 23; see also Case 252/87 *Hauptzollamt Hamburg-St Annen v Wilhelm Kiwall KG* [1988] ECR 4753, paragraph 10.
 4 Commission Regulation 2454/93 Art 379(2), OJ 11.10.93 L253/1. As to the proof of the regularity of the transit operation see Commission Regulation 2454/93 Art 380, OJ 11.10.93 L253/1, as amended by Commission Regulation 482/96, OJ 20.3.96 L70/5.

Otherwise, where the place of the irregularity cannot be established, such offence or irregularity must be deemed to have been committed in the Member State to which the office of departure belongs or in the Member State to which the office of transit at the point of entry into the Community belongs, to which a transit advice has not been given.[5] The duties and other charges relating to the goods concerned must be levied by the presumed Member State in accordance with Community or national provisions.[6] If the Member State where the offence or irregularity was actually committed is determined before expiry of a period of three years from the date of registration of the transit declaration, that Member State must in accordance with Community or national provisions, recover the duties and other charges (apart from those levied by the previously presumed Member State as own resources of the Community) relating to the goods concerned. In such case, once proof of such recovery is provided, the duties and other charges initially levied (apart from those levied as own resources of the Community) must be repaid.[7]

CUSTOMS WAREHOUSING

Introduction

The essential purpose of the customs warehousing procedure is to provide for the storage of goods.[8] It allows the storage in a customs warehouse of non-Community goods, without such goods being subject to import duties or commercial policy measures which would be applicable on their release for free circulation;[9] and Community goods, where Community legislation governing specific fields provides that their being placed in a customs warehouse attracts the application of measures normally attaching to the export of goods.[10] However, in the case of non-Community goods, it is important to distinguish between release into free circulation and entry of goods into the customs territory of the Community. Thus, where the Community rules provide that commercial policy measures are to apply to the introduction of goods into the customs territory of the Community, they will apply when non-Community goods are entered for the customs warehousing procedure.[11]

Furthermore, where an economic need exists and customs supervision is not adversely affected thereby, the customs authorities may allow Community goods other than those attracting the application of measures normally attaching to the export of such goods to be stored on the premises of a customs warehouse, and the processing under the inward processing procedure or under the processing under customs control of non-Community goods, without such goods being subject to the customs warehousing procedure.[12]

5 Commission Regulation 2454/93 Art 378(1), OJ 11.10.93 L253/1.
6 Ibid Art 378(2).
7 Ibid Art 378(3).
8 See Case 49/82 *Commission of the European Communities v Netherlands* [1983] ECR 1195, paragraph 10.
9 Council Regulation 2913/92 Art 98(1)(a), OJ 19.10.92 L302/1.
10 Ibid Art 98(1)(b).
11 Commission Regulation 2454/93 Art 507(b), OJ 11.10.93 L253/1.
12 In these cases, the customs authorities may require that the goods be entered in the warehouse stock records. See Council Regulation 2913/92 Art 106, OJ 19.10.92 L302/1. As to the details of the use of customs warehouse without entry of Community goods for the procedure see Commission Regulation 2454/93 Arts 535–537, OJ 11.10.93 L253/1, as amended by

Use of the procedure

A customs warehouse is any place where goods may be stored approved by and under the supervision of the customs authorities.[13] It may be either a public warehouse or a private one. A public warehouse is a customs warehouse available for use by any person for the warehousing of goods.[14] A private warehouse is a customs warehouse reserved for the warehousing of goods by the warehousekeeper.[15]

Customs warehouses may be classified into six different types. A type A customs warehouse is a public warehouse which is under the responsibility of the warehousekeeper.[16] A type B customs warehouse is a public warehouse under the responsibility of each depositor.[17] A type C customs warehouse is a private warehouse where the warehousekeeper is the same person as the depositor but is not necessarily the owner of the goods.[18] A type D customs warehouse is a private warehouse where the warehousekeeper is the same person as the depositor but it is not necessarily the owner of the goods and where if the goods are released for free circulation under the simplified procedure, the nature of the goods, the customs value and the quantity of the goods to be taken into account for the purposes of determining the customs debt may be those applicable to the goods at the time when they were placed under the customs warehousing procedure.[19]

Goods may also be placed under the customs warehousing procedure without being stored in a customs warehouse.[20] In this sense, a type E customs warehouse refers to the case where the customs warehousing procedure may apply to goods placed in storage facilities belonging to the warehousekeeper which are not actually a customs warehouse.[1] Finally, a type F customs warehouse is a public warehouse which is operated by the customs authorities.[2]

Commission Regulation 482/96, OJ 20.3.96 L70/5. Concerning the use of a customs warehouse without entry of non-Community goods for the procedure see Commission Regulation 2454/93 Arts 538–548, OJ 11.10.93 L253/1, as amended by Commission Regulation 3665/93, OJ 31.12.93 L335/1.

13 Council Regulation 2913/92 Art 98(2), OJ 19.10.92 L302/1.

14 Ibid Art 99.

15 Ibid Art 99. The warehousekeeper is the person authorized to operate the customs warehouse. See ibid Art 99.

16 Commission Regulation 2454/93 Art 504(1), OJ 11.10.93 L253/1.

17 Commission Regulation 2454/93 Art 504(1), OJ 11.10.93 L253/1. The depositor is the person bound by the declaration placing the goods under the customs warehousing procedure or to whom the rights and obligations of such a person have been transferred. See Council Regulation 2913/92 Art 99, OJ 19.10.92 L302/1.

18 Commission Regulation 2454/93 Art 504(1), OJ 11.10.93 L253/1.

19 Commission Regulation 2454/93 Art 504(1), OJ 11.10.93 L253/1; see also Commission Regulation 2454/93 Art 112(3), OJ 11.10.93 L253/1, as amended by Council Regulation 82/97, OJ 21.1.97 L17/1.

20 Council Regulation 2913/92 Art 98(3), OJ 19.10.92 L302/1.

1 Commission Regulation 2454/93 Art 504(2), OJ 11.10.93 L253/1.

2 Commission Regulation 2454/93 Art 504(4), OJ 11.10.93 L253/1. The placing of imported goods which originate in another Member State or are in free circulation, in temporary storage in the special stores of public warehouses in the interior of the territory of a Member State represents a service rendered to traders. Thus, storage charges commensurate with the service thus rendered and levied on goods presented at such warehouses do not amount to charges having an effect equivalent to customs duties. However, such storage charges would constitute charges having equivalent effect in so far as they were also levied when goods imported into the Member State in question were presented at a special store solely for the completion of customs formalities and when the goods had been exempted from storage and no request for temporary storage had been made by the importer. See Case 132/82 *Commission of the European*

Customs warehouses of type A, B, C and D must consist of premises or any other defined location approved by the customs authorities.[3] If the customs authorities decide to operate a type F customs warehouse, they must designate the premises or location which constitute the warehouse.[4] Warehouses of type A, C, D and E may be approved as victualling warehouses for the application of export refunds in agricultural products.[5]

The operation of a customs warehouse, other than a type F warehouse, is subject to the issue of an authorization by the customs authorities.[6] Thus, any person wishing to operate a customs warehouse must make a request in writing containing the information required for granting the authorization, in particular demonstrating the existence of an economic need for the warehousing.[7] The application for the authorization must conform to Annex 67 of Commission Regulation 2454/93 and be submitted to the customs authorities designated by the Member State where the places to be approved as customs warehouses are situated.[8] If the application for authorization relates to cross-border warehousing, that is, the storage of goods under the customs warehousing procedure of type C, D, or E in more than one Member State, it must be submitted to the customs authorities designated by the Member State where the warehousekeeper's main accounts are kept.[9]

The authorization may be granted only to persons established in the Community who offer every guarantee necessary for the proper conduct of the operations and where customs authorities can supervise and monitor the procedure without having to introduce administrative arrangements disproportionate to the economic needs involved.[10] It will only be granted if the applicant shows that there is a real economic need for warehousing and if the warehouse is intended principally for the storage of goods.[11] In the case of cross-border warehousing, before issuing the authorization, the customs authorities of the

---

Communities v Belgium [1983] ECR 1649, paragraph 10; see also Case 133/82 *Commission of the European Communities v Luxembourg* [1983] ECR 1669, paragraph 10.

3 Commission Regulation 2454/93 Art 505(1), OJ 11.10.93 L253/1.

4 Commission Regulation 2454/93 Art 505(2), OJ 11.10.93 L253/1. Furthermore, a place approved by the customs authorities as a temporary storage facility or operated by the customs authorities may also be approved as a type A, B, C, D warehouse or operated as a type F facility. See ibid Art 505(3). As to the concept of temporary storage facility see ibid Art 185.

5 Commission Regulation 2454/93 Art 506, OJ 11.10.93 L253/1. As to the concept of victualling warehouses see Art 38 Commission Regulation 3665/87, OJ 14.12.87 L351/1.

6 Council Regulation 2913/92 Art 100(1), OJ 19.10.92 L302/1.

7 Ibid Art 100(2); see also Commission Regulation 2454/93 Art 497(1), OJ 11.10.93 L253/1. As to the details of the application see ibid Art 497(2).

8 In the case of a type E customs warehouse, the application must be submitted to the customs authorities designated by the Member State where the warehousekeeper's main accounts are kept. See ibid Art 509(1).

9 Commission Regulation 2454/93 Art 509(2), OJ 11.10.93 L253/1, as amended by Commission Regulation 1762/95, OJ 21.7.95 L171/8; see also Christian Amand 'Cross-Border Warehousing' (1996/1) *EC Tax Revue* 28.

10 See Council Regulation 2913/92 Art 86, OJ 19.10.92 L302/1; see also ibid Art 101(3). The assessment of whether the administrative costs of supervision and control of the customs warehouse are in proportion to the economic needs for customs warehousing must take into account inter alia the type of customs warehouse and procedures which may be applied therein. See Commission Regulation 2454/93 Art 510(2), OJ 11.10.93 L253/1.

11 However, the goods may also undergo usual forms of handling, inward processing or processing under customs control provided that such operations do not predominate over the storage of goods. See ibid Art 510(1). In this sense, without prejudice to the exceptions provided for in Annex 69a Commission Regulation 3254/94, retail sales in the premises, storage area or any other defined location of a customs warehouse will not be allowed. This prohibition also

Member State where the application was submitted must obtain the agreement of the customs authorities designated for that purpose by the other Member States involved. Moreover, in such case, the Member States concerned must lay down a procedure whereby the respective customs officers can ensure the supervision of the procedure, the places of storage themselves and the goods entered for customs warehousing.[12]

The authorization must be issued by the customs authorities designated by each Member State in which an application was made.[13] It must lay down the conditions for operating the customs warehouse.[14] It must contain, inter alia, the customs office responsible for supervising the customs warehouse.[15] If the person concerned asks permission to present the goods or declare them for the procedure at customs offices other than the supervising office and the proper conduct of the operations would not be affected, the customs authorities may empower one or more offices to act as offices of entry for the procedure.[16] In the case of cross-border warehousing, the customs authorities which issued the authorization must send a copy to the customs authorities concerned.[17] Authorizations must be for an unlimited period.[18]

The warehousekeeper is responsible for ensuring that while the goods are in the customs warehouse they are not removed from customs supervision;[19] for fulfilling the obligations that arise from the storage of goods covered by the customs warehousing procedure;[20] and for complying with the particular conditions specified in the authorization.[21] In this sense, the customs authorities may ensure the fulfilment of these responsibilities by demanding the warehousekeeper provide a guarantee.[1] However, where the authorization concerns a type B public warehouse, it may provide that these obligations, other than complying with the particular conditions specified in the authorization, devolve exclusively upon the depositor.[2] In any case, the depositor must at all times be responsible for fulfilling the obligations arising from the placing of the goods under the customs warehousing procedure.[3]

The rights and obligations of the warehousekeeper may with the agreement of the customs authorities be transferred to another person.[4]

---

applies to goods placed under the customs warehousing procedure in a type E warehouse. See Commission Regulation 2454/93 Art 510(3), OJ 11.10.93 L253/1, as amended by Commission Regulation 3254/94, OJ 31.12.94 L346/1.

12 Commission Regulation 2454/93 Art 509(2), OJ 11.10.93 L253/1, as amended by Commission Regulation 1762/95, OJ 21.7.95 L171/8.

13 Commission Regulation 2454/93 Art 511(1), OJ 11.10.93 L253/1. As to the date on which the authorization takes the effect see ibid.

14 Council Regulation 2913/92 Art 100(2), OJ 19.10.92 L302/1.

15 Commission Regulation 2454/93 Art 511(3), OJ 11.10.93 L253/1.

16 Ibid Art 511(4).

17 Ibid Art 511(4).

18 However, the general rules governing annulment, revocation and amendment of authorizations apply. Ibid Art 511(2). Furthermore, the economic need criterion must be considered to be no logger fulfilled where the person concerned asks in writing for the authorization to be revoked. An authorization may also be revoked where the customs authorities consider that the customs warehouse is not or is no longer used to warrant its existence. See ibid Art 512.

19 Council Regulation 2913/92 Art 101(a), OJ 19.10.92 L302/1.

20 Ibid Art 101(b).

21 Ibid Art 101(c).

 1 Ibid Art 104.

 2 Ibid Art 102(1).

 3 Ibid Art 102(2).

 4 Ibid Art 103.

Operation of the procedure

A declaration for the entry of goods for the customs warehousing procedure must be made in accordance with Arts 59–78 of Council Regulation 2913/92[5] and Arts 198–252 of Commission Regulation (EC) 2454/93, governing the normal procedure for customs declarations.[6] The customs authorities may accept incomplete declarations if they contain at least the particulars necessary for identification of the goods to which the declaration relates, including their quantity.[7] Furthermore, the declarant, may, upon request, be authorized to make the declaration of entry for the procedure in a simplified form when the goods are presented to the customs authorities.[8]

The goods placed under the customs warehousing procedure must be entered in the stock records as soon as they are brought into the customs warehouse.[9] The stock records must at all times show the current stock of goods which are still under the customs warehousing procedure.[10] In customs warehouses types A, C, D and E, the customs authorities must designate the warehousekeeper as the person required to keep the stock records which must be made available to the supervising office to enable it to carry out any checks.[11] Goods entered for the customs warehousing procedure in customs warehouses type A, C, or D must be entered in the stock records at the time when they are physically placed in the customs warehouse.[12] In type B customs warehouses, stock records are not kept. However, the supervising office must keep the declarations of entry for the procedure or the administrative documents used for such entry to monitor their discharge.[13] Likewise, in type F warehouses, stock records are not necessary;[14] the customs authorities must keep records of the declarations instead.[15] The stock records and the customs authorities records of type F customs warehouses must contain all the particulars necessary for the proper application and supervision of the procedure.[16] The stock records of a type D warehouse must contain, in addition, the information specified in Annex 37 of Commission Regulation 2454/93.[17]

Import goods may undergo the usual forms of handling intended to preserve them, improve their appearance or marketable quality, or prepare them for

---

5 OJ 19.10.92 L302/1.
6 Commission Regulation 2454/93 Art 514, OJ 11.10.93 L253/1. Special provisions concerning declaration, operation of the procedure, handling and discharge apply in respect of Community prefinanced agricultural products. See Commission Regulation 2454/93 Arts 529–534, OJ 11.10.93 L253/1, as amended by Commission Regulation 3665/93, OJ 31.12.93 L335/1.
7 This exception does not apply to prefinanced agricultural products. See Commission Regulation 2454/93 Art 268, OJ 11.10.93 L253/1.
8 Ibid Art 269(1). As to the details of the simplified procedure see Commission Regulation 2454/93 Arts 269–274, OJ 11.10.93 L253/1, as amended by Commission Regulation 1762/95, OJ 21.7.95 L171/8.
9 Council Regulation 2913/92 Art 107, OJ 19.10.92 L302/1; see also Council Regulation 2913/92 Art 105, OJ 19.10.92 L302/1.
10 Commission Regulation 2454/93 Art 520(3), OJ 11.10.93 L253/1.
11 Ibid Art 517(1).
12 Ibid Art 521(1). Similarly, in a type E customs warehouse, the entry in the stock records must take place at the time the goods arrive at the storage facilities of the holder of the authorization. See ibid Art 521(2).
13 Ibid Art 517(2).
14 Council Regulation 2913/92 Art 105, OJ 19.10.92 L302/1.
15 Commission Regulation 2454/93 Art 517(3), OJ 11.10.93 L253/1.
16 As to the particulars which such records must include see ibid Art 520.
17 Ibid Art 520(2).

distribution or resale.[18] Community goods attracting the application of measures normally attaching to the export of such goods when placed under the customs warehousing procedure and covered by the common agricultural policy may undergo only the forms of handling expressly stipulated for such goods.[19] The allowed forms of handling are not intended in principle to permit the goods to pass from one stage of marketing to another.[20] The person concerned must apply to the supervising office in writing on a case-by-case basis, for authorization to carry out usual forms of handling before such handling is carried out.[1] However, an authorization to operate a customs warehouse or to use the procedure may indicate the usual forms of handling which are expected to be carried out under the procedure.[2]

Provided the proper conduct of operations is not thereby affected, the supervising office will allow both Community goods and non-Community goods to be stored in the same storage area.[3] Where such common storage makes it impossible to identify at all times the customs status of each type of goods, it will only be permitted if the goods are equivalent.[4]

The supervising office may, where it considers necessary to ensure the proper operation of the customs warehouse, require an inventory to be made of all or some of the goods placed under the customs warehousing procedure, periodically or otherwise.[5]

Where the circumstances so warrant, goods placed under the customs warehousing procedure may be temporarily removed from the customs warehouse.[6] However, before temporarily removing the goods from the premises of the customs warehouse, the person concerned must apply to the supervising office in writing, on a case-by-case basis, for authorization to do so.[7] While they are

18 Council Regulation 2913/92 Art 109(1), OJ 19.10.92 L302/1. The list of the usual forms of handling refers to operations to ensure the preservation of the import goods during storage such as ventilation or treatment against parasites; operations improving the presentation or marketability of the import goods such as desalination or dividing goods where simple operations are involved; and operations preparing the import goods for distribution or resale such as sorting, ironing of textiles or anti-rust treatment. See Commission Regulation 2454/93 Annex 69, OJ 11.10.93 L253/1, as amended by Commission Regulation 3254/94, OJ 31.12.94 L346/1. In this sense, change of packings is different from repacking in different units, which should not be considered as a usual form of handling. See Case 276/84 *Gebruder Metelmann GmbH & Co KG v Hauptzollamt Hamburg-Jonas* [1985] ECR 4057, paragraph 9.
19 Council Regulation 2913/92 Art 109(2), OJ 19.10.92 L302/1.
20 See Case 49/82 *Commission of the European Communities v Netherlands* [1983] ECR 1195, paragraph 10.
 1 Council Regulation 2913/92 Art 109(3), OJ 19.10.92 L302/1; see also Commission Regulation 2454/93 Art 523(1), OJ 11.10.93 L253/1. The application must provide all the particulars necessary for application of the provisions governing the customs warehousing procedures. See Commission Regulation 2454/93 Art 523(2), OJ 11.10.93 L253/1, as amended by Commission Regulation 3254/94, OJ 31.12.94 L346/1.
 2 In this case, the person concerned will only need to notify the supervising office before the handling of the goods is carried out. See Commission Regulation 2454/93 Art 523(3), OJ 11.10.93 L253/1.
 3 Commission Regulation 2454/93 Art 524(1), OJ 11.10.93 L253/1, as amended by Commission Regulation 3665/93, OJ 31.12.93 L335/1.
 4 Equivalent goods are those goods falling within the same subheading of the combined nomenclature, having the same commercial quality and the same technical characteristics. See Commission Regulation 2454/93 Art 524(2), OJ 11.10.93 L253/1.
 5 Ibid Art 527.
 6 Council Regulation 2913/92 Art 110, OJ 19.10.92 L302/1.
 7 As to the details of the application and the authorization see Commission Regulation 2454/93 Art 525, OJ 11.10.93 L253/1.

outside the customs warehouse the goods may undergo the same forms of handling as when they are in the warehouse.[8]

The customs authorities may allow goods placed under the customs warehousing procedure to be transferred from one customs warehouse to another.[9] Such transfer will not imply the termination of the customs warehousing procedure.[10] The responsibility for the goods transferred will pass to the warehousekeeper of the customs warehouse in which the goods are to be placed when it receives the goods and enters them in its stock records.[11]

There is no limit to the length of time goods may remain under the customs warehousing procedure.[12] The customs warehousing procedure will be discharged when a new customs-approved treatment or use is assigned to the goods placed under such procedure.[13] Community goods attracting the application of measures normally attaching to the export of goods when placed under the customs warehousing procedure which are covered by the common agricultural policy and are placed under the customs warehousing procedure must be exported or be assigned a treatment or use provided for by the Community legislation governing such goods.[14] If equivalent goods are stored in common, goods declared for a customs-approved treatment or use may be considered to be either Community or non-Community goods, at the choice of the person concerned.[15] The particulars relating to the discharge of the procedure must be entered in the stock records at the time when the goods are released following the presentation of a declaration entering them for a customs approved treatment or use, or by the time the goods leave the customs warehouse's premises, where the simplified procedure is applied.[16]

The release for free circulation of non-Community goods liable to import duties or the placing of such goods under the temporary importation with partial relief from import duties will result in the incurrence of a customs debt.[17] Where a customs debt is incurred in respect of import goods and the customs value of such goods is based on a price actually paid or payable which includes the cost of warehousing and of preserving goods while they remain in the warehouse, such costs need not be included in the customs value if they are shown separately from the price actually paid or payable for the goods.[18] Furthermore, where the import goods have undergone the usual forms of handling, the nature of the goods, the customs value and the quantity to be taken into account in determining the amount of import duties must, at the request of the declarant, be those which would be

8 Council Regulation 2913/92 Art 110, OJ 19.10.92 L302/1.
9 Ibid Art 111. Concerning the details of the procedure to be followed see Commission Regulation 2454/93 Arts 526(1), 526(2) and 526(4), OJ 11.10.93 L253/1, as amended by Commission Regulation 3254/94, OJ 31.12.94 L346/1.
10 This will not be the case where the transfer is from or to a type B customs warehouse. See Commission Regulation 2454/93 Art 526(5), OJ 11.10.93 L253/1.
11 Ibid Art 526(3).
12 However, in exceptional cases, the customs authorities may set a time limit by which the depositor must assign the goods a new customs-approved treatment or use. See Council Regulation 2913/92 Art 108(1), OJ 19.10.92 L302/1.
13 Ibid Art 89.
14 Ibid Art 113.
15 Commission Regulation 2454/93 Art 528(1), OJ 11.10.93 L253/1.
16 Ibid Art 521(4).
17 Council Regulation 2913/92 Art 201(1), OJ 19.10.92 L302/1.
18 Ibid Art 112(1). See Case 38/77 *Enka BV v Inspecteur der Invoerrechten en Accijinzen, Arnhem* [1977] ECR 2203, paragraph 30.

taken into account, for the goods, at the time when the customs debt is incurred, if they had not undergone such handling.[19] Where import goods are released for free circulation under a simplified procedure, the nature of the goods, the customs value and the quantity to be taken into account for the purposes of determining the customs debt must be those applicable to the goods at the time when they were placed under the customs warehousing procedure, provided that the rules of assessment relating to those goods were ascertained or accepted at the time when the goods were placed under the procedure, unless the declarant requests their application at the time when the customs debt is incurred.[20]

No customs debt will be incurred in respect of specific goods where the person concerned proves that the use of the customs warehousing procedure results in the total destruction or irretrievable loss of the said goods as a result of the actual nature of the goods or unforseeable circumstances or force majeure, or as a consequence of authorization by the customs authorities.[1] The Court has held that the extinction of the customs debt must be based on the fact that the goods have not been used for the economic purpose which justified the application of import duties. In the case of theft, it may be assumed that the goods pass into the Community commercial circuit and, thus, such case does not fall within the scope of the derogation from the incurrence of the customs debt, regardless of the circumstances in which the theft was committed.[2] In the event of total destruction or irretrievable loss of goods, the portion of goods entered for the procedure which has been destroyed or lost must be established by reference to the proportion of goods of the same type under the procedure on the premises of the customs warehouse at the time when the destruction or loss occurred, unless the warehousekeeper can produce evidence of the actual quantity of goods under the procedure which was destroyed or lost.[3]

FREE ZONES AND FREE WAREHOUSES

Introduction

Free zones and free warehouses are parts of, or premises within, the customs territory of the Community, separated from the rest of that territory, in which non-Community goods are considered, for the purpose of import duties and commercial policy import measures, as not being on the Community customs territory, provided they are not released for free circulation or placed under another customs procedure or used or consumed under conditions other than those provided for in customs regulations;[4] and in which Community goods for which such provision is made under Community legislation governing specific fields qualify, by virtue of being placed in a free zone or free warehouse, for measures normally attaching to

---

19 Council Regulation 2913/92 Art 112(2), OJ 19.10.92 L302/1.
20 Ibid Art 112(3), OJ 19.10.92 L302/1, as amended by Council Regulation 82/97, OJ 21.1.97 L17/1.
1 Council Regulation 2913/92 Art 206(1), OJ 19.10.92 L302/1.
2 See Joined Cases 186 & 187/82 *Ministero delle Finanze v Esercizio Magazzini Generali SpA and Mellina Agosta Srl* [1983] ECR 2951, paragraph 14.
3 Commission Regulation 2454/93 Art 528(2), OJ 11.10.93 L253/1.
4 Council Regulation 2913/92 Art 166(a), OJ 19.10.92 L302/1.

the export of goods.[5] However, as under the customs warehousing procedure, it is important to distinguish between release of goods for free circulation and their entry into the customs territory of the Community. Where Community rules provide that commercial policy measures are to apply to the entry of goods into the customs territory of the Community, such measures will apply when non-Community goods are placed in a free zone or free warehouse.[6]

Any person may apply for a part of the customs territory of the Community to be designated a free zone or for a free warehouse to be set up. Member States will designate parts of the customs territory of the Community as free zones or authorize the establishment of free warehouses.[7] They must determine the area covered by each zone which must be enclosed.[8] Likewise, premises which are to be considered as free warehouses must be approved by Member States.[9] Furthermore, the construction of any building in a free zone will require the prior approval of the customs authorities.[10]

The perimeter and the entry points of free zones and free warehouses must be subject to supervision by the customs authorities.[11] Thus, the customs authorities may carry out checks on the persons and means of transport entering or leaving a free zone or free warehouse at random or whenever they have reasonable doubts concerning the compliance with the applicable legislation.[12] In this sense, the customs authorities may check goods entering, leaving or remaining in a free zone or free warehouse. To enable such checks to be carried out, a copy of the transport document, which must accompany goods entering or leaving, must be handed to, or kept at the disposal of, the customs authority by any person designated for this purpose by such authorities.[13]

5 Ibid Art 166(b).
6 Commission Regulation 2454/93 Art 800(b), OJ 11.10.93 L253/1. Ibid Art 801, OJ 11.10.93 L253/1, as amended by Commission Regulation 1427/97, OJ 24.7.97 L196/31.
7 Council Regulation 2913/92 Art 167(1), OJ 19.10.92 L302/1. As to the customs authorities relevant for the granting of the authorizations within the framework of the customs procedures with economic impact and within the framework of the free warehouses/free zones see OJ 27.6.96 C187/8.
8 Ibid Art 167(2). As to the particularities of the perimeter and the area immediately outside the perimeter see Commission Regulation 2454/93 Art 802, OJ 11.10.93 L253/1.
9 Council Regulation 2913/92 Art 167(2), OJ 19.10.92 L302/1.
10 Ibid Art 167(4). Authorization will also be necessary when a building in a free zone or a building constituting a free warehouse is converted. See Commission Regulation 2454/93 Art 803(4), OJ 11.10.93 L253/1. As to the details of the application and authorization see ibid Arts 803(1), 803(2) and 803(3). For prefinanced agricultural products, a victualling warehouse may be set up in a free zone or a free warehouse in accordance with Commission Regulation 3665/87 Art 38, laying down common detailed rules for the application of the system of export refunds on agricultural products. See Commission Regulation 2454/93 Art 828, OJ 11.10.93 L253/1.
11 Council Regulation 2913/92 Art 168(1), OJ 19.10.92 L302/1.
12 Ibid Art 168(2); see also Commission Regulation 2454/93 Art 804, OJ 11.10.93 L253/1. The access to a free zone or free warehouse may be denied to persons who do not provide every guarantee necessary for compliance with the rules provided for by the Community customs rules. See Council Regulation 2913/92 Art 168(3), OJ 19.10.92 L302/1.
13 Ibid Art 168(4). The transport document may be any document relating to transport, such as a waybill, delivery note, manifest or dispatch note, provided it gives all the information necessary for identification of the goods. See Commission Regulation 2454/93 Art 812, OJ 11.10.93 L253/1.

Operation of a free zone or free warehouse

Both Community and non-Community goods may be placed in a free zone or a free warehouse.[14] As a general rule, goods, other than prefinanced agricultural products, entering a free zone or free warehouse need not be presented to the customs authorities, nor need a customs declaration be lodged, other than the checks that the customs authorities may carry out on such goods.[15] However, the arrival of goods in the places used for the activity must be entered immediately in stock records.[16] Furthermore, goods must be presented to the customs authorities and undergo the prescribed customs formalities where they have been placed under a customs procedure which is discharged when they enter a free zone or free warehouse;[17] they have been placed in a free zone or free warehouse on the authority of a decision to grant repayment or remission of import duties;[18] or they qualify for measures normally attaching to the export of goods.[19] Moreover, the customs authorities may require goods subject to export duties or to other export provisions to be notified to the customs department.[20]

The customs authorities must certify the Community or non-Community status of goods placed in a free zone or free warehouse at the request of the person concerned.[1]

---

14 However, the customs authorities may require that goods which present a danger or are likely to spoil other goods which, for other reasons, require special facilities be placed in premises specially equipped to receive them. See Council Regulation 2913/92 Art 169, OJ 19.10.92 L302/1.

15 Ibid Art 170(1). As to the presentation of the goods and lodging of a declaration in the case of prefinanced agricultural products see Commission Regulation 2454/93 Art 823, OJ 11.10.93 L253/1. Agriculture goods means goods covered by the Regulations referred to in Art 1 of Council Regulation 565/80 on the advance payment of export refunds in respect of agricultural products. Goods coming under Council Regulation 3448/93 on trade arrangements applicable to certain goods resulting from the processing of agricultural products, or Commission Regulation 1222/94 laying down common detailed rules for the application of the system of granting export refunds on certain agricultural products exported in the form of goods not covered by Annex II to the Treaty, and the criteria fixing the amount of such refunds, will also be treated as agricultural goods. See Commission Regulation 2454/93 Art 503(a), OJ 11.10.93 L253/1, as amended by Commission Regulation 482/96, OJ 20.3.96 L70/5.

16 Council Regulation 2913/92 Art 170(1), OJ 19.10.92 L302/1; see also Commission Regulation 2454/93 Art 811, OJ 11.10.93 L253/1.

17 Council Regulation 2913/92 Art 170(2)(a), OJ 19.10.92 L302/1. In such cases, the relevant documents must be presented with the goods. See Commission Regulation 2454/93 Art 813(1), OJ 11.10.93 L253/1. Where the inward processing procedure or temporary importation procedure is discharged by the placing of the compensating goods or import products under the external transit procedure, followed by entry into a free zone or free warehouse with a view to subsequent export from the customs territory of the Community, the customs authorities must carry out random checks to satisfy themselves that the indications 'Merchandises PA/S', 'Merchandises PA/R' and 'Merchandises AT' are entered in the stock records. See ibid Art 813; see also Commission Regulation 2454/93 Art 817(3)(f), OJ 11.10.93 L253/1, as amended by Commission Regulation 3254/94, OJ 31.12.94 L346/1.

18 Council Regulation 2913/92 Art 170(2)(b), OJ 19.10.92 L302/1. Where a decision to repay or remit import duties authorizes the placing of goods in a free zone or a free warehouse, the customs authorities must issue an adequate certificate. See Commission Regulation 2454/93 Art 814, OJ 11.10.93 L253/1.

19 Council Regulation 2913/92 Art 170(2)(c), OJ 19.10.92 L302/1.

20 Ibid Art 170(3). However these notifications imply neither the presentation of a document on entry nor systematic and general controls on all goods entering. See Commission Regulation 2454/93 Art 815, OJ 11.10.93 L253/1

1 Council Regulation 2913/92 Art 170(4), OJ 19.10.92 L302/1.

Operators must take the necessary precautions to ensure that the persons they employ to carry out their activities comply with customs legislation.[2] They must also keep stock records in a form approved by the customs authorities.[3] Such stock records must enable the customs authorities to identify the goods, and must record their movements.[4]

Any industrial, commercial or service activity may be authorized in a free zone or free warehouse.[5] However, the customs authorities may impose certain restrictions having regard to the nature of the goods concerned or the requirements of customs supervision.[6] Furthermore, the carrying out of such activities must be notified in advance to the customs authorities.[7] Such notification must take the form of presentation of the application for approval of the stock records.[8]

Non-Community goods placed in a free zone or free warehouse may, while they remain in such parts or premises, be released for free circulation;[9] undergo the usual form of handling allowed for non-Community goods in customs warehouses without authorization;[10] be placed under the inward processing procedure under the conditions laid down by that procedure;[11] be placed under the procedure for processing under customs control under the conditions laid down by that procedure;[12] be placed under the temporary importation procedure under the conditions laid down by that procedure;[13] be abandoned;[14] or be destroyed, provided that the person concerned supplies the customs authorities with all the information they judge necessary.[15]

---

2 Commission Regulation 2454/93 Art 806, OJ 11.10.93 L253/1. Operator means any person carrying on an activity involving the storage, working, processing, sale or purchase of goods in a free zone or free warehouse. See ibid Art 799.
3 Council Regulation 2913/92 Art 176(1), OJ 19.10.92 L302/1.
4 Ibid Art 176(1). As to the contents of the stock records see Commission Regulation 2454/93 Art 817, OJ 11.10.93 L253/1, as amended by Commission Regulation 3254/94, OJ 31.12.94 L346/1. In the case of prefinanced agricultural products, the stock records must contain in addition the date on which these goods were placed in the free zone or the free warehouse and reference particulars of the entry declaration. See Commission Regulation 2454/93 Art 824, OJ 11.10.93 L253/1.
5 Council Regulation 2913/92 Art 172(1), OJ 19.10.92 L302/1.
6 Ibid Art 172(2).
7 Ibid Art 172(1).
8 Commission Regulation 2454/93 Art 805, OJ 11.10.93 L253/1. As to the particularities of the application for approval and its approval see ibid Arts 808, 809 and 810.
9 Council Regulation 2913/92 Art 173(a), OJ 19.10.92 L302/1. Concerning the procedure to be followed when non-Community goods are released into free circulation within a free zone or free warehouse see Commission Regulation 2454/93 Art 819, OJ 11.10.93 L253/1.
10 Council Regulation 2913/92 Art 173(b), OJ 19.10.92 L302/1; see also Commission Regulation 2454/93 Art 818, OJ 11.10.93 L253/1, as amended by Commission Regulation 3254/94, OJ 31.12.94 L346/1.
11 However, processing operations within the territory of the old free port of Hamburg, in the free zones of the Canary Islands, Azores, Madeira and overseas departments will not be subject to the economic conditions which are normally required under the inward processing procedure. Specific conditions apply to the old free port of Hamburg. See Council Regulation 2913/92 Art 173(c), OJ 19.10.92 L302/1.
12 Ibid Art 173(d). As to the procedure applicable where the inward processing procedure or the procedure for processing under customs control is used in a free zone or free warehouse see Commission Regulation 2454/93 Arts 829–840, OJ 11.10.93 L253/1, as amended by Commission Regulation 1427/97, OJ 24.7.97 L196/31.
13 Council Regulation 2913/92 Art 173(e), OJ 19.10.92 L302/1.
14 Ibid Art 173(f).
15 Ibid Art 173(g).

Community goods qualifying for measures normally attaching to the export of goods which are covered by the common agricultural policy may undergo only the forms of handling expressly provided for such goods. However, unlike under the customs warehousing procedure, such handling may be undertaken without authorization.[16]

Otherwise, both non-Community goods and Community goods qualifying for measures normally attaching to the export of goods must not be consumed or used in free zones or warehouses.[17] However the consumption or use of goods will be possible when the release for free circulation of such goods would not entail the application of import duties or measures under the common agricultural or commercial policy.[18]

As a general rule, there is no limit to the length of time goods may remain in free zones or free warehouses.[19] However, prefinanced agricultural goods must leave the customs territory of the Community within the time limits laid down in Community agricultural legislation.[20]

Goods leaving a free zone or free warehouse may be exported or re-exported from the customs territory of the Community, or brought into another part of the customs territory of the Community.[1]

Non-Community goods may be re-exported from the customs territory of the Community; destroyed or abandoned to the exchequer where national legislation makes provision to that effect.[2] Re-exportation must, where appropriate, involve application of the formalities laid down for goods leaving, including commercial policy measures.[3]

Community goods qualifying for measures normally attaching to the export of goods which are covered by the common agricultural policy must be assigned a treatment or use provided for by the rules under which they are eligible, by virtue of their being placed in a free zone or free warehouse, for measures normally attaching to the export of such goods.[4] If such goods are returned to another part of the customs territory of the Community, or if no application for their assignment to a treatment or use has been made by the expiry of the specific time limit established for such goods, the customs authorities must take the measures laid down by the relevant legislation governing specific fields relating to failure to comply with the specified treatment or use.[5]

In cases other than those where exports are subject to export duties or commercial policy measures, where goods are taken directly from the customs territory of the Community, neither presentation of the goods nor a customs declaration

---

16 Ibid Art 157. Prefinanced agricultural products may undergo the forms of handling provided for in Annex 73 to Commission Regulation 2454/93. See Commission Regulation 2454/93 Art 825, OJ 11.10.93 L253/1.

17 Council Regulation 2913/92 Art 175(1), OJ 19.10.92 L302/1.

18 In that event, no declaration of release for free circulation or temporary importation will be required unless such goods are subject to a quota or ceiling. See ibid Art 175(2).

19 Ibid Art 171(1).

20 Commission Regulation 2454/93 Art 827, OJ 11.10.93 L253/1; see also Case C-231/91 *Annuss GmbH & Co KG v Hauptzollamt Hamburg-Jonas* [1992] ECR I-6433.

1 Council Regulation 2913/92 Art 177, OJ 19.10.92 L302/1.

2 Ibid Art 182(1).

3 Ibid Art 182(2).

4 Ibid Art 179(1).

5 Ibid Art 179(2).

will be required.[6] Instead, particulars of the removal of goods must be entered immediately in the stock records.[7] In order to satisfy themselves that the provisions on export, re-export or dispatch applicable to the goods removed from the free zone or free warehouse are complied with, the customs authorities may carry out random checks on the operator's stock records.[8]

Where a customs debt is incurred in respect of non-Community goods and the customs value of such goods is based on a price actually paid or payable which includes the cost of warehousing or of preserving goods while they remain in the free zone or free warehouse, such costs must not be included in the customs value if they are shown separately from the price actually paid or payable for the goods.[9] When such goods have undergone, in a free zone or free warehouse, one of the usual forms of handling allowed for customs warehousing, the nature of the goods, the customs value and the quantity to be taken into consideration in determining the amount of import duties must, at the request of the declarant, and provided that such handling was covered by an authorization, be those which would be taken into account in respect of the time in which the customs debt is incurred, had they not undergone such handling.[10]

When goods are brought into or returned to another part of the customs territory of the Community or placed under a customs procedure, the certificate provided by the customs authorities at their entry into the free zone or free warehouse may be used as proof of the Community or non-Community status of such goods.[11] If such status is not proved by such certificate or other means, the goods must be considered to be Community goods, for the purposes of applying export duties and export licences or export measures laid down under the commercial policy; and non-Community goods in all other cases.[12]

PROCESSING UNDER CUSTOMS CONTROL

Introduction

The procedure for processing under customs control allows non-Community goods to be used in the customs territory of the Community in operations which alter their nature or state, without being subject to import duties or commercial policy measures, and thereafter allows the processed products to be released for free circulation at the rate of import duty appropriate to them.[13] It may be used for goods in column I of the list in Annex 87 Commission Regulation 2454/93 which are to undergo the processing referred to in column II of the said Annex.[14]

---

6 Commission Regulation 2454/93 Art 821, OJ 11.10.93 L253/1. However, prefinanced agricultural goods must be declared in accordance with Commission Regulation 2454/93 Art 534. See Commission Regulation 2454/93 Art 827(2), OJ 11.10.93 L253/1.
7 Ibid Art 820.
8 Ibid Art 822; see also ibid Art 827.
9 Council Regulation 2913/92 Art 178(1), OJ 19.10.92 L302/1.
10 Ibid Art 178(2).
11 Ibid Art 180(1).
12 Ibid Art 180(2).
13 Council Regulation 2913/92 Art 130, OJ 19.10.92 L302/1.
14 Commission Regulation 2454/93 Art 650, OJ 11.10.93 L253/1.

Authorization to use the procedure

The use of the procedure for processing under customs control is conditional upon authorization being issued by the customs authorities at the request of the person who carries out the processing or arranges for it to be carried out.[15] The application must be made in writing in accordance with the specimen in Annex 67/C Commission Regulation 2454/93 by the person to whom authorization may be granted.[16] It must be presented to the customs authorities designated by the Member State where the processing operations are to be carried out.[17] However, where it is expected that the processing operations will be carried out in different Member States, an application for a single authorization including particulars of the sequence of operations and the exact places where they will be carried out may be lodged with the customs authorities of the Member States where the first of such operations will take place.[18]

The authorization will be granted only to:

(1) persons established in the Community;[19]
(2) where the imports can be identified in the processed products;[20]
(3) where the goods cannot be economically restored after processing to their description or state as it was when they were placed under the procedure;[1]
(4) where use of the procedure cannot result in circumvention of the effect of the rules concerning origin and quantitative restrictions applicable to the imported goods;[2] and
(5) where the necessary conditions for the procedure to help create or maintain a processing activity in the Community without adversely affecting the essential interests of Community producers of similar goods are fulfilled.[3]

The authorization must be issued by the authorities to which the application was presented and made out in a model conforming to the specimen in Annex 68/C Commission Regulation 2454/93.[4] Where it is expected that processing operations will be carried out by or on behalf of the applicant in different Member States, the authorization may not be issued without the agreement of the customs authorities designated by the Member States in which the places indicated in the application are located.[5]

The conditions under which the procedure may be used must be set out in the authorization.[6] The customs authorities may require the holder of the authori-

---

15 Council Regulation 2913/92 Art 85, OJ 19.10.92 L302/1; see also ibid Art 132.
16 Commission Regulation 2454/93 Art 651, OJ 11.10.93 L253/1; Concerning the details of the application see also ibid Arts 497 and 498 .
17 Commission Regulation 2454/93 Art 651(2)(a), OJ 11.10.93 L253/1.
18 Ibid Art 651(2)(b).
19 Council Regulation 2913/92 Art 133(a), OJ 19.10.92 L302/1.
20 Ibid Art 133(b).
 1 Ibid Art 133(c).
 2 Ibid Art 133(d).
 3 Ibid Art 133(e).
 4 Commission Regulation 2454/93 Art 652, OJ 11.10.93 L253/1. As to the details of the authorization see ibid Art 500 and 501.
 5 As to the consultation procedure to be followed see Commission Regulation 2454/93 Art 652(2), OJ 11.10.93 L253/1.
 6 Council Regulation 2913/92 Art 87(1), OJ 19.10.92 L302/1. The holder of the authorization must notify the customs authorities of all factors arising after the authorization was granted which may influence its continuation or content. See ibid Art 87(2).

zation, in order to facilitate checks, to keep or have kept for it stock records which indicate the quantities of import goods entered for the procedure and of processed products obtained, and all particulars needed for the monitoring of the operations and the correct calculation of any import duties which may be payable.[7] The period of validity of the authorization must be set on a case-by-case basis by the customs authorities, having regard to the specific requirements of the applicant.[8] When issuing the authorization, the customs authorities must specify the period within which the processed goods must be assigned to a customs-approved treatment or use taking into account the time required to carry out the processing operations and to dispose of the processing products.[9] The customs authorities must also set the rate of yield of the operations or, where appropriate, the method determining such rate.[10] This rate of yield must, as far as possible, be established on the basis of production and be identifiable in the records of the holder of the authorization.[11]

A simplified procedure for authorization to use the processing under customs control procedure may be followed if the processing operations are to take place in a single Member State.[12] The customs office empowered by the customs authorities to grant authorizations using the simplified procedure, must allow the lodging of the declaration of entering goods for the procedure to constitute an application for authorization. In this case, the acceptance of such declaration will constitute authorization, the said acceptance remaining in any event subject to the conditions governing the granting of authorization.[13]

The rights and obligations of the holder of the authorization may on the conditions laid down by the customs authorities, be transferred successively to other persons who fulfil any conditions laid down in order to benefit from the processing under customs control procedure.[14]

Entry and discharge of goods

The entry of goods into the processing under customs control procedure must be accompanied by a declaration of entry. Such declaration must be lodged at one of the offices of entry for the procedure specified in the authorization.[15] The

---

7 Commission Regulation 2454/93 Art 652(3), OJ 11.10.93 L253/1.
8 If such period exceeds two years, the conditions on which the authorization was issued must be reviewed periodically at intervals laid down in the authorization. See ibid Art 653.
9 Ibid Art 654(1); see also Council Regulation 2913/92 Art 134, OJ 19.10.92 L302/1; see also Council Regulation 2913/92 Art 118, OJ 19.10.92 L302/1. Where the circumstances so warrant, the period specified in the authorization may be extended even when that originally set has expired. See Commission Regulation 2454/93 Art 654(2), OJ 11.10.93 L253/1.
10 Council Regulation 2913/92 Art 134, OJ 19.10.92 L302/1. See also ibid Art 119.
11 Commission Regulation 2454/93 Art 655(1), OJ 11.10.93 L253/1. The rate or method of determining the rate of yield is subject to retrospective verification by the customs authorities. See ibid Art 655(2).
12 Ibid Art 656(1).
13 This simplified procedure only applies where the general simplified procedure referred to in Art 76 on the assignment of a customs-approved treatment or use does not apply. See ibid Art 656(2). As to the information which the declaration must contain see ibid Art 656(3).
14 Council Regulation 2913/92 Art 90, OJ 19.10.92 L302/1.
15 Commission Regulation 2454/93 Art 657, OJ 11.10.93 L253/1. In the case where authorization to use the procedure is granted under the simplified procedure, the declaration must be lodged at a duly empowered customs office. See ibid Art 657(2).

declaration must be made in accordance with the normal procedure for customs declarations.[16] The description of the goods given in the declaration must correspond to the specifications in the authorization.[17]

The procedure for processing under customs control will be discharged when a new customs-approved treatment or use is assigned either to the goods placed under such arrangement or to the processed products placed under it.[18] The simplified procedures for release for free circulation, export and re-exportation may be applied.[19] The discharge of the procedure must be based either on the quantity of import goods corresponding by application of the rate of yield to the processed products or on the quantity of goods in the unaltered state which have been assigned to customs-approved treatment or use.[20] The declaration discharging the procedure for the processing of goods under customs control must be lodged at one of the customs offices of discharge specified in the authorization.[1] Such declaration must be made in accordance with the provisions laid down for the customs-approved treatment or use concerned.[2] The description of the processed products or import goods in the declaration of discharge must correspond to the specification laid down in the authorization.[3]

The holder of the authorization must supply the supervising office with a bill of discharge within 30 days of the expiry of the time limit for discharge.[4]

Where a customs debt is incurred in respect of goods in the unaltered state or of products that are at an intermediate stage of processing as compared with that provided for in the authorization, the amount of that debt must be determined on the basis of charge elements appropriate to the import goods at the time of acceptance of the declaration relating to the placing of the goods under the procedure for processing under customs control.[5]

Where the import goods qualified for preferential tariff treatment when they were placed under the procedure for processing under customs control, and such preferential treatment is applicable to products identical to the processed products released for free circulation, the import duties to which the processed products are subject must be calculated by applying the rate of duty applicable

---

16 Commission Regulation 2454/93 Art 658(1), OJ 11.10.93 L253/1. As to the rules on the normal procedure of customs declarations see Council Regulation 2913/92 Arts 59–75, OJ 19.10.92 L302. See also Commission Regulation 2454/93 Art 198–252, OJ 11.10.93 L253/1.

17 Ibid Art 658(2). Regarding the documents to accompany the declaration see ibid Art 658(3). Concerning incomplete declarations see ibid Art 275. As to the simplified declaration and local clearance procedures see ibid Art 276.

18 Council Regulation 2913/92 Art 89, OJ 19.10.92 L302/1.

19 In the case of re-exportation, the provisions of Commission Regulation 2454/93 Arts 279–289 will apply *mutatis mutandis*. See Commission Regulation 2454/93 Art 278(1), OJ 11.10.93 L253/1.

20 Ibid Art 660(1). In the case of re-exportation, the provisions of Arts 279–289 Commission Regulation 2454/93 will apply *mutatis mutandis*. See ibid Art 60(2).

1 In the case of a simplified procedure for the authorization to use the processing under customs control procedure, the declaration must be lodged with the customs office which issued the authorization. See Commission Regulation 2454/93 Art 661(2), OJ 11.10.93 L253/1.

2 Ibid Art 662(1).

3 Ibid Art 662(2). As to the documents to accompany the declaration see ibid Art 583(3).

4 Ibid Art 664(1). As to the contents of the bill of discharge see ibid Art 664(2).

5 Council Regulation 2913/92 Art 135, OJ 19.10.92 L302/1. In such case the rules in Commission Regulation 2454/93 Arts 591–594 concerning the proportion of import goods incorporated in the products will apply *mutatis mutandis*. See Commission Regulation 2454/93 Art 660(2), OJ 11.10.93 L253/1.

under that treatment.[6] If such preferential treatment is subject to tariff quotas or tariff ceilings, the application of the rate of duty in respect of processed products must also be subject to the condition that the said preferential tariff treatment is applicable to the import goods at the time of acceptance of the declaration of release for free circulation. In this case, the quantity of import goods actually used in the manufacture of the processed products released for free circulation must be charged against the tariff quota or ceilings in force at the time of acceptance of the declaration of release for free circulation and no quantities must be counted against tariff quotas or ceilings opened in respect of products identical to the processed products.[7]

If the processed products are released for free circulation their customs value may be, at the choice of the person concerned, the customs value determined at or about the same time of identical or similar goods produced in any third country; or the selling price, provided this is not influenced by a relationship between the buyer and the seller; or the selling price in the Community of identical or similar goods, provided this is not influenced by a relationship between buyer and seller; or the customs value of the import goods plus the processing costs.[8]

When commercial policy measures are in force for the import of goods at the time of the acceptance of the declaration for release for free circulation, such measures must not apply to the processed products unless they are also in force for products identical to the processed products, in which case the measures must be applied to the quantity of import goods actually used in the manufacture of the processed products released for free circulation.[9]

SPECIFIC RELIEFS

The Community system of reliefs from import and export duties of specific goods is governed by Council Regulation No 918/83.[10] It provides for those situations in which, when some circumstances are met, relief from import or export duties is to be granted respectively when goods are put into free circulation in or are exported from the Community.

In the preamble of Regulation 918/83 it is explained that taxation of the goods listed in the Regulation is not justified when '… the usual need to protect the economy is absent …'. However, Regulation 918/83 does not preclude the application by Member States of import or export prohibitions or restrictions which are justified on grounds of public morality, public policy or public security, protection of health and life of humans, animals or plants, protection of national treasures possessing artistic, historical or archaeological value or protection of industrial or commercial property.[11]

'Import duties' means customs duties and charges having equivalent effect and also agricultural levies and other import charges provided for under the common agricultural policy or under specific arrangements applicable to

6 Council Regulation 2913/92 Art 136(1), OJ 19.10.92 L302/1.
7 Ibid Art 136(2).
8 Commission Regulation 2454/93 Art 666, OJ 11.10.93 L253/1.
9 Ibid Art 667.
10 Council Regulation 918/83 setting up a Community system of reliefs from customs duty, OJ 24.3.83 L105/1.
11 See Preamble of Council Regulation 918/83.

certain goods resulting from the processing of agricultural products;[12] 'export duties' means agricultural levies and other export charges provided for under the common agricultural policy or under specific arrangements applicable to certain goods resulting from the processing of agricultural products.[13]

Under Regulation 918/83, relief from import duty is granted to personal property[14] which has to be intended, in particular, as household effects,[15] cycles and motor cycles, private motor vehicles and their trailers, camping caravans, pleasure craft and private airplanes.

Chapter I of Regulation 918/83 identifies a series of situations giving rise to a relief from import duties.

Under Title I of the Regulation, relief is granted for personal property belonging to natural persons transferring their normal place of residence from a third country to the Community. The relief is limited to personal property which:

(1) except in special cases justified by the circumstances, has been in the possession of and, in the case of non-consumable goods, used by the person concerned at his former normal place of residence for a minimum of six months before the date on which he ceases to have his normal place of residence in the third country of departure;

(2) is intended to be used for the same purpose at his new normal place of residence.

However, Member States are entitled to make relief conditional upon the payment, either in the country of origin or in the country of departure, of fiscal charges to which the good concerned is normally liable.[16]

Title II of the Regulation provides relief for goods imported on the occasion of a marriage.[17] It include goods belonging to a person transferring the normal place of residence into the customs territory of the Community on the occasion of his or her marriage, as well as presents customarily given on the occasion of a marriage. However, the value of each present shall not exceed 1000 Ecu.[18] Relief is only granted to persons whose normal place of residence has been outside the customs territory of the Community for a continuous period of at least 12 months[19] and who produce evidence of their marriage.[20]

Except under special circumstances, the goods must have entered the Community territory not earlier than two months before the date fixed for the wedding and not later than four months after the date of the wedding.[1]

---

12 Ibid Art 1(2)(A).
13 Ibid Art 1(2)(B).
14 'Personal property' means any property intended for the personal use of the person concerned or for meeting their household needs: ibid Art 1(2)(C).
15 'Household effects' means personal effects, household linen, furnishings and equipment intended for the personal use of the persons concerned or for meeting their household needs: ibid Art 1(2)(D).
16 Council Regulation 918/83 Art 3. For the other provisions concerning Title I of the Regulation, see also ibid Arts 4–10.
17 Ibid Arts 11–15.
18 Ibid Art 2.
19 Derogations from this rule may be granted provided that the intention of the person concerned was clearly to reside outside the customs territory of the Community for a period of at least 12 months. Ibid Art 12.
20 Ibid.
 1 Ibid Art 14.

Relief is also granted to personal property acquired by inheritance,[2] entered for free circulation not later than two years from the date on which the person concerned becomes entitled to the property, unless this period is extended by the competent authorities on special grounds.[3]

Relief to household effects for furnishing a secondary residence[4] concerns goods which:

(1) except in special cases justified by the circumstances, have been owned and used by the person concerned for a minimum of six months before the date on which they were exported; and
(2) are appropriate both by nature and by quantity to the normal furnishing of the said secondary residence.[5]

Title V relates to school outfits, scholastic material and other scholastic household effects representing the usual furnishings for a student's room and belonging to pupils or students coming to stay in the customs territory of the Community for the purpose of studying there and intended for their personal use during the period of their studies. Relief shall be granted at least once per school year.[6]

Free circulation is provided for consignments of negligible value, ie any consignment dispatched to its consignee by letter or parcel post containing goods of a total value not exceeding 10 Ecu,[7] as well as to small consignments of a non-commercial nature,[8] ie any consignments which are of an occasional nature, contain goods exclusively for the personal use of the consignee or his family which do not by their nature or quantity reflect any commercial intent, goods the total value of which, including that of the products referred to in Article 30, does not exceed 30 Ecu, and are sent to the consignee by the consigner free of payment of any kind.

Title VIII[9] concerns capital goods and other equipment belonging to undertakings[10] which definitively cease their activity in a third country and move to the custom territory of the Community in order to carry on a similar activity there. Without prejudice to the measures in force in the Member States with regard to industrial and commercial policy, they shall be admitted free of import duties where they:

(1) except in special cases justified by the circumstances, have actually been used in the undertaking for a minimum of 12 months before the date on which the undertaking ceased to operate in the third country from which it has transferred its activities;
(2) are intended to be used for the same purposes after the transfer; and
(3) are appropriate to the nature and size of the undertaking in question.[11]

---

2 Ibid Title III, Arts 16–19.
3 Ibid Art 18.
4 Ibid Title IV, Arts 20–24.
5 Ibid Art 21.
6 Ibid Arts 25 and 26.
7 Ibid Title VI, Arts 27and 28.
8 Ibid Title VII, Arts 29–31.
9 Ibid Arts 32–38.
10 'Undertaking' means an independent economic unit of production or of service industry. Ibid Art 32(2).
11 Ibid Art 33.

The same provisions apply *mutatis mutandis* to capital goods and other equipment belonging to persons engaged in a liberal profession and to legal persons engaged in a non-profitmaking activity who transfer this activity from a third country into the customs territory of the Community.[12]

Title IX[13] and Title X[14] apply respectively to products received by Community farmers from properties situated outside the Community[15] and to seeds, fertilizers and products for the treatment of soil and crops imported by farmers in third countries for the use in properties situated in the Community but adjoining their properties in third countries.[16]

Goods contained in the personal luggage[17] of travellers coming from a third country are admitted free of import duties, provided such imports are of a non-commercial nature.[18]

Relief is also granted to educational, scientific and cultural materials, scientific instruments and apparatus.[19]

With regard to educational, scientific and cultural materials, Regulation 918/83 distinguishes the goods listed in Annex I, such as books, publications and documents, which are admitted free of import duties whoever the consignee and whatever the intended use of such materials may be,[20] from the goods listed in Annex II, such as visual and auditory materials of an educational, scientific or cultural character, which are admitted free of import duties provided they are intended either for public educational, scientific or cultural establishments or organizations, or for the establishments or organizations in the categories specified opposite each article in column 3 of the said Annex, on condition that they have been approved by the competent authorities of the Member States to receive such articles duty-free.[1]

Scientific instruments and apparatus[2] not included in Article 51 may also be admitted free of import duties when they are imported exclusively for a non-commercial purpose.

---

12 Ibid Art 38.
13 Ibid Arts 39–41. These provisions apply *mutatis mutandis* to the products of fishing or fish-farming activities carried out in the lakes or waterways bordering a Member State and a third country by Community fishermen and to the products of hunting activities carried out on such lakes or waterways by Community sportsmen (cf Art 42 of the Regulation).
14 Ibid Arts 43–44.
15 Relief is limited only to products: (1) which have not undergone any treatment other than that which normally follows their harvest or production (Art 40); (2) brought into the customs territory of the Community by the agricultural producer or on his behalf (Art 41).
16 Member States may make relief conditional upon the granting of reciprocal treatment (cf Art 44(3)).
17 According to Art 45(2)(A), 'personal luggage' means the whole of the luggage which a traveller is in a position to submit to the customs authorities on his arrival in the Community, as well as any luggage submitted to this same authority at a later date, provided that evidence can be produced to prove that it was registered, at the time of the traveller's departure, as accompanied luggage with the company which transported it into the Community from the third country of departure.
18 'Imports of a non-commercial nature' means imports which are of an occasional nature, and consist exclusively of goods for the personal use of the travellers or their families, or of goods intended as presents, the nature and quantity of such goods should not be such as might indicate that they are being imported for commercial reasons (cf Art 45(2)(B)).
19 Ibid Title XII, Arts 50–59.
20 Ibid Art 50.
 1 Ibid Art 51.
 2 A 'scientific instrument or apparatus' means any instrument or apparatus which, by reason of its objective technical characteristics and the results which it makes it possible to obtain, is mainly or exclusively suited to scientific activities. See Art 54.

According to Article 60, relief is granted to laboratory animals and biological or chemical substances which are intended for either:

(1) public establishments principally engaged in education or scientific research and those departments of public establishments which are principally engaged in education or scientific research; or
(2) private establishments principally engaged in education or scientific research and authorized by the competent authorities of the Member States to receive such articles duty-free.

Title XIV[3] relates to therapeutic substances of human origin[4] and blood-grouping[5] and tissue-typing reagents.[6] Relief is limited to products which:

(1) are intended for institutions or laboratories approved by the competent authorities, for use exclusively for non-commercial medical or scientific purposes;
(2) are accompanied by a certificate of conformity issued by a duly authorized body in the third country of departure; and
(3) are in containers bearing a special label identifying them.[7]

Relief from import duties is granted to pharmaceutical products used on occasions of international sport events.[8]

Title XVI[9] is devoted to goods for charitable or philanthropic organizations. Regulation 918/83 sets out three categories:

(1) general purposes: in so far as this does not give rise to abuses or major distortions of competition, goods sent to or imported by organizations the accounting procedure of which enables the competent authorities to supervise their operations and which offers all the guarantees considered necessary;[10]
(2) for the benefit of handicapped persons: it includes articles for the use of the blind[11] and articles for other handicapped persons.[12] The relief for this category is subject to the condition that the provisions in force in the Member States enable the persons concerned to establish their status as blind or handicapped persons entitled to such relief;[13]
(3) for the benefit of disaster victims.[14] The granting of the relief is subject to a decision by the Commission, acting at the request of the Member State or

3 Ibid Arts 61–63.
4 'Therapeutic substances of human origin' means human blood and its derivatives (whole human blood, dried human plasma, human albumin and fixed solutions of human plasmic protein, human immunoglobulin and human fibrinogen. See Art 61(2).
5 'Blood-grouping reagents' means all reagents, whether of human, animal, plant or other origin used for blood-type grouping and for the detection of blood incompatibilities. See Art 61(2).
6 'Tissue-typing reagents' means all reagents whether of human, animal, plant or other origin used for the determination of human tissue-types. See Art 61(2).
7 Ibid Art 62.
8 Ibid Art 64.
9 Ibid Arts 65–85.
10 Ibid Arts 65–69.
11 Ibid Arts 70–71.
12 Ibid Arts 72–74.
13 Ibid Art 75.
14 Ibid Arts 79–85.

States concerned in accordance with an emergency procedure entailing the consultation of the other Member States.[15]

According to Article 86, on production of satisfactory evidence to the competent authorities by the persons concerned, and provided that the operations involved are not in any way of commercial character, honorary decorations or awards are admitted free of import duties.

Regulation 918/83 also applies to presents received in the context of international relations[16] as well as to goods to be used by monarchs or heads of State.[17]

Title XX[18] relates to goods imported for trade promotion purposes which comprises the following categories:

(1) samples of goods[19] of negligible value: they can be used only to solicit orders for goods of the type they represent with a view to their being imported into the customs territory of the Community;
(2) printed matter and advertising material: they must relate to goods for sale or hire, or to transport, commercial insurance or banking services offered by a person established outside the customs territory of the Community;[20]
(3) products used or consumed at a trade fair or similar event.[1]

Goods which are to undergo examination, analysis or tests to determine their composition, quality or other technical characteristics for purposes of information or industrial or commercial research may be admitted free of import duties[2] on condition that the goods to be examined, analyzed or tested are completely used up or destroyed in the course of the examination, analysis or testing[3] and that the quantities are strictly necessary for the purpose for which they are imported.[4]

Under Title XXII and Title XXIII relief is to be granted respectively to consignments sent to organizations protecting copyrights or industrial and commercial patent rights[5] and to tourist information literature.[6]

Finally, under Regulation 918/83 other items may be admitted free of import

---

15 Ibid Art 81.
16 Ibid Arts 87–89.
17 Ibid Art 90.
18 Ibid Arts 91–99.
19 'Sample of goods' means any article representing a type of goods whose manner of presentation and quantity, for goods of the same type of quality, rule out its use for any purpose other than that of seeking orders. See Art 91(3).
20 Ibid Art 92.
 1 According to Art 95(2), 'trade fair or similar event' means: (1) exhibitions, fairs, shows and similar events connected with trade, industry, agriculture or handicrafts; (2) exhibitions and events held mainly for charitable reasons; (3) exhibitions and events held mainly for scientific, technical, handicraft, artistic, educational or cultural, or sporting reasons, for religious reasons or for reasons of worship, trade union activity or tourism, or in order to promote international understanding; (4) meetings of representatives of international organizations or collective bodies; (5) official or commemorative ceremonies and gathering; but not exhibitions staged for private purposes in commercial stores or premises to sell goods of third countries.
 2 Ibid Art 100.
 3 Ibid Art 101.
 4 Ibid Art 103.
 5 Ibid Art 107.
 6 Ibid Art 108.

duties: miscellaneous documents and articles;[7] ancillary materials for the stowage and protection of goods during their transport;[8] litter, fodder and feedingstuff for animals during their transport;[9] fuel and lubricants present in land motor vehicles;[10] materials for the construction, upkeep or ornamentation of memorials to, or cemeteries for, war victims;[11] coffins, funerary urns and ornamental funerary articles.[12]

Relief from export duties is governed by Chapter II of Regulation 918/83, under which relief is granted to consignments of negligible value;[13] domesticated animals exported at the time of transfer of agricultural activities from the Community to a third country;[14] products obtained by agricultural producers farming on properties located in the Community;[15] seeds exported by agricultural producers for use on properties located in third countries;[16] fodder and feedingstuffs accompanying animals during their exportation.[17]

Relief from import duties is given irrespective of whether the goods declared for free circulation come directly from third countries or have been placed in another customs procedure.[18] If relief from import duties is made conditional on the goods being put to a particular use by the recipient, only the competent authorities of the Member State in whom territory the goods are to be put to such a use may grant this relief.[19]

Appropriate measures are to be taken by Member States to ensure that the goods are not put to any other use without the relevant import duties being paid, unless the alternative use is in conformity with the conditions laid down by Regulation 918/83.[20] If the same person simultaneously fulfils the conditions of different provisions granting relief from import or export duties, the provisions in question are to apply concurrently.[1] If provisions of the Regulation make the granting of relief conditional to the fulfillment of certain conditions, the person concerned must prove to the competent authorities that the conditions required are met.[2] In cases in which the duty-free importation or exportation is determined in Ecu, Member States may round off, upwards or downwards, the sum arrived at by converting that amount into the national currency.[3]

Regulation 918/83 does not prevent the granting of relief under a series of international agreements concerning privileges and immunities[4] and does not prevent the preservation of the special status granted either by Greece to Mount Athos or by Spain and France to Andorra.[5]

---

7 Ibid Art 109.
8 Ibid Art 110.
9 Ibid Art 111.
10 Ibid Arts 112–116.
11 Ibid Art 117.
12 Ibid Art 118.
13 Ibid Art 119.
14 Ibid Art 120.
15 Ibid Arts 121–123.
16 Ibid Arts 124–125.
17 Ibid Art 126.
18 Ibid Art 127.
19 Ibid Art 128.
20 Ibid Art 129.
 1 Ibid Art 130.
 2 Ibid Art 131.
 3 Ibid Art 132.
 4 Ibid Art 133(1).
 5 Ibid Art 135.

Until the establishment of Community provisions, Member States are allowed to grant special relief to armed forces which are not serving under their flag[6] stationed on their territory under international agreements and to third-country airlines in pursuance of bilateral agreements based on reciprocity.[7] They may also grant relief to workers returning home after having resided on grounds of their occupation for at least six months outside the Community customs territory.[8] Until the establishment of the Community provisions in the field concerned, Member States may apply special relief granted on imports of instruments and apparatus used in medical research, establishing medical diagnoses or carrying out medical treatment.[9] Regulation 918/83 applies without prejudice to the provisions governing the stores of vessels, aircraft and international trains and without prejudice to rules on relief introduced by other Community acts.[10]

6 Ibid Art 136(1)(a).
7 Ibid Art 136(2).
8 Ibid Art 136(2).
9 Ibid Arts 137–138.
10 Ibid Art 139.

Chapter 7

Export procedures

INTRODUCTION

In 1981 the Council first enacted a Directive to harmonize the national procedures for the export of Community goods,[1] that is, products originating in
Member States or products coming from third countries which are in free
circulation in Member States.[2] Council Directive 81/177 provided for a general procedure and simplified procedures.[3] Implementing rules were set out in
Commission Directive 82/347,[4] and the application of Directive 81/177 was
subject to committee procedures under the general terms of Council Directive
79/695 on the harmonization of procedures for the release of goods for free
circulation.[5]

This legislation has been replaced with the recent codification of EC customs
law by the adoption of the European Community Customs Code[6] and its implementing regulation.[7] As with any codification, the Customs Code, which entered into force on 1 January 1994,[8] has completed, reorganized, and simplified
the pre-existing law; it provides the definitions and general provisions of administrative law pertaining to customs procedures, and the creation of a Customs Code Committee.[9]

---

1 Council Directive 81/177, OJ 30.3.81 L83/40.
2 See Council Directive 81/177, Art 1, first paragraph; EEC Art 9(2).
3 Ibid Arts 2–20.
4 Commission Directive 82/347, OJ 7.6.82 L156/1.
5 See Art 24 of Council Directive 79/695 on the harmonization of procedures for the release of
  goods for free circulation OJ 13.8.1979 L205/19.
6 Council Regulation 2913/92 establishing the Community Customs Code OJ 19.10.92 L302/1.
  Exportation is a customs procedure: ibid Art 4(16)(h). The repealed and amended prior
  Community legislation is listed in ibid Arts 251–252, *European Community Customs Code
  With Anti-Dumping and Countervailing Duties, Annotated* 2 vols (Michie Law Publishers,
  Charlottesville VA, 1994).
7 Commission Regulation 2454/93 laying down provisions for the implementation of Council
  Regulation (EEC) No 2931/92 establishing the Community Customs Code OJ 11.10.1993
  L253/1, as amended. As to VAT exemptions for exports, see B J M Terra *Community Customs
  Law* (Kluwer, The Hague, London, Boston, 1995) pp 841–851.
8 Art 253 of Council Regulation 2931/92, OJ 11.10.1993 L253/1. With exception of Title VIII
  concerning custom appeals procedures for the UK, until 1 January 1995; and the provisions
  concerning re-exportation in Arts 161, 182 and 183, which applied from 1 January 1993.
  Ibid.
9 Ibid Art 247; to replace the Committee on General Customs Rules established by Council
  Directive 79/695, OJ 13.8.1979 L205/19.

THE GENERAL PROCEDURE

Arts 161 and 162 of the Customs Code deal, respectively, with export procedure and export declarations and with release for export. Art 161 entered into force on 1 January 1993, one year before the other provisions of the Customs Code.

The export procedure allows Community goods[10] to leave the Community customs territory.[11] It entails the application of exit formalities including commercial policy measures and, where necessary, export duties.[12] It applies to all Community goods intended for export, with the general exception of goods destined for Helgoland and goods placed under outward processing or transit procedures,[13] and specific exemptions to be determined in accordance with the committee procedure of Art 249 of the Customs Code.

In principle, goods leaving the customs territory of the Community permanently are subject to an export declaration.[14] The declaration is made by means of the Single Administrative Document (SAD)[15] unless this is dispensed with by the customs authorities.[16] Where the export declaration is made on the basis of the Single Administrative Document, copies 1, 2 and 3 are to be used.[17] It must be accompanied by all documents necessary for the correct application of export duties and of the provisions governing the export of the goods in question.[18]

The declaration must be lodged with the customs office responsible for supervising the place of establishment of the exporter or where the goods are prepared for export shipment.[19] Except in specified circumstances, third-party

10 Ibid Art 4(7) defines Community goods as goods wholly obtained or produced in the customs territory of the Community under the conditions referred to in Art 24 (on rules of origin) and not incorporating goods imported from countries or territories not forming part of the Community customs territory; goods imported from countries or territories not forming part of the customs territory of the Community which have been released for free circulation; and goods obtained or produced in the Community customs territory, either from the second category of goods alone or from goods in the first and second categories.

11 Ibid Art 161(1), first paragraph.

12 Ibid Art 161(1), second paragraph. Article 4(11) defines 'export duties' as customs duties and charges having an effect equivalent to customs duties payable on the exportation of goods, and agricultural levies and other export charges laid down under the CAP or under the specific arrangements applicable to certain goods resulting from the processing of agricultural products.

13 Articles 161(2), 161(3), and 163 of Council Regulation 2931/92, OJ 11.10.1993 L253/1.

14 Ibid Art 161(4).

15 Commission Regulation 2454/93 Art 205(1), OJ 11.10.93 L253/1.

16 It may be dispensed with in accordance with ibid Art 207. As to computerized declarations, see Arts 222–224.

17 Ibid Art 792, which also provides that the customs office where the export declaration has been lodged is to stamp box A and, where appropriate, complete box D. On granting release of the goods, it is to retain Copy 1, send Copy 2 to the statistical office of the Member State of the customs office of export, and return Copy 3 to the person concerned. This is without prejudice to Art 207, which provides that the customs administrations may in general dispense with production of one or more copies of the SAD intended for use by that Member State if the information is available in other media.

18 Commission Regulation 2454/93 Art 221(1), OJ 11.10.93 L253/1.

19 Ibid Art 161(5), which also provides that derogations are to be determined according to the committee procedure. For these purposes, the exporter is the person on whose behalf the export declaration is made and who is the owner of the goods or has a similar right of disposal over them at the time when the declaration is accepted: Art 788(1). Where ownership or a

representation for customs purposes is possible.[20] In cases involving sub-contracting, the export declaration may also be lodged at the customs office responsible for the place where the sub-contractor is established.[1] In certain cases the declaration may be lodged with any customs office, in the Member State concerned, which is competent for the operation in question.[2] Where there are duly justified reasons and an export declaration is accepted at another customs office,[3] controls relating to the application of prohibitions and restrictions are to take account of the special situation.[4]

Community goods declared for export are subject to customs supervision[5] from the time of acceptance of the customs declaration until the time they leave the customs territory of the Community or are destroyed or the customs declaration is invalidated.[6]

Release for export shall be granted on the condition that the goods concerned leave the customs territory of the Community in the same condition as when the export declaration was accepted.[7] In respect of presentation of the goods, Copy 3 of the SAD and the goods released for export must be presented to customs at the customs office of exit.[8] The customs office of exit must satisfy itself that the

similar right of disposal over the goods belongs to a person established outside the Community pursuant to the contract on which the export is based, the exporter is considered to be the contracting party established in the Community: Art 788(2).

20 See Council Regulation 2913/92 Art 5, OJ 19.10.92 L302/1.

1 Commission Regulation 2454/93 Art 789, OJ 10.11.93 253/1. In this case the supplementary or replacement declaration may be lodged at the customs office responsible for the place where the exporter is established. Where the sub-contractor is established in a Member State other than where the exporter is established, this possibility only applies on condition that agreements have been concluded between the administrations of the Member States concerned. See ibid Art 281.

2 Ibid Art 790.

3 As to alternatives, see ibid Art 971, first paragraph.

4 Ibid Art 791(1), second paragraph. In these cases, where export formalities are not completed in the exporter's Member State, the customs office where the export declaration was lodged was required until 31 December 1995 to send a copy of the SAD to a designated officer in the exporter's Member State: Art 791(2) and Art 915, as amended by Commission Regulation 3254/94, OJ 31.12.94 L394/1.

5 'Supervision by customs authorities' means action taken in general by those authorities with a view to ensuring that customs rules and, where appropriate, other provisions applicable to goods subject to customs supervision are observed: ibid Art 4(13).

6 Ibid Art 59(2).

7 Ibid Art 162. Goods have left the customs territory of the Community in an unaltered state when the control copy of the export declaration, endorsed by the responsible customs office is received by the national authority concerned: Case 55/74 *Firma Robert Unkel v Hauptzollamt Hamburg-Jonas* [1975] ECR 9. Goods leaving a free zone or customs warehouse may be exported or re-exported from the Community customs territory: Art 177, first paragraph, first indent. The customs authorities must satisfy themselves that the rules governing exportation or re-exportation have been respected where goods are exported or re-exported from a free zone or customs warehouse: Art 181.

8 Ibid Art 793(1). 'Customs office of exit' means the following. In the case of goods exported by rail, post, air or sea, it means the customs office competent for the place where the goods are taken over under a single transport contract for transport to a third country by the railway companies, the postal authorities, the airlines or the shipping companies: Art 793(2)(a). In the case of goods exported by pipeline and of electrical energy, it means the office designated by the Member State where the exporter is established: Art 793(2)(b). In the case of goods exported by other means or in circumstances not covered by the first two cases, it means the last customs office before the goods leave the customs territory of the Community: Art 793(2)(c).

goods presented correspond to those declared and must supervise and certify their physical departure.[9]

The goods may be examined in places designated and hours appointed for that purpose by the customs authorities.[10] However, at the request of the declarant, the customs authorities may authorize the examination of goods in other places or outside normal hours, in which case any costs involved are borne by the declarant.[11] The customs authorities are required to inform the declarant or its representative when they elect to examine goods[12] or when they decide to examine a part of the goods only.[13] The declarant is required to render the customs authorities the assistance required to facilitate their work; the customs authorities may also require the declarant or its representative to be present and, if necessary, they can proceed with the examination of the goods, at the declarant's risk and expense in the absence of the declarant.[14] If the customs authorities wish to take samples, they are required to inform the declarant or its representative.[15] The declarant, or the person designated by the declarant, is required to render the customs authorities all the assistance needed to facilitate the operation.[16] In general, the quantities taken by the customs office as samples cannot be deducted from the quantity declared.[17] However, where an export or outward processing declaration is concerned, the declarant must be authorized, where circumstances permit, to replace the quantities of goods taken as samples by identical goods, in order to make up the consignment.[18]

In the case of split exportation, the endorsement is given only for those goods which are actually exported.[19] Where the customs office establishes that goods are missing, it must note the copy of the declaration presented and inform the customs office of export.[20] Where it establishes that there are goods in excess, it must refuse exit to the goods until the export formalities have been completed.[1] When it establishes a discrepancy in the nature of the goods, it is to

---

9 Ibid Art 793(3), first paragraph, as substituted by Commission Regulation 3254/94, OJ 31.12.94 L346/1, which also provides that this is to be done by an endorsement on the reverse of Copy 3 when the declarant enters 'RET-EXP' in Box 44 or otherwise indicates its wish to have Copy No 3 returned to it. The endorsement must take the form of a stamp showing the name of the office and the date. The customs office of exit must return Copy 3 to the person presenting it or a named intermediary for return to the declarant.

10 Ibid Art 239(1).

11 Ibid Art 239(2).

12 Ibid Art 240(1).

13 Ibid Art 240(2), which also provides that the customs authorities' choice of which goods to examine is final.

14 Ibid Art 241.

15 Ibid Art 242(1). Samples are to be taken by the customs authorities themselves, but they may ask that this be done under their supervision by the declarant or by a person designated by the declarant: Art 242(2), first paragraph.

16 Ibid Art 243(1). If the declarant refuses to be present, to designate a person, or to render all necessary assistance, the provisions of Arts 241(1), (2) and (3) apply: ibid Art 243(2).

17 Ibid Art 245(1).

18 Ibid Art 245(2).

19 Ibid Art 793(3), second paragraph, which also provides that, in the case of split exportation via several different customs offices, the customs office of exit where the original of Copy 3 was presented shall, upon receiving a duly substantiated request, certify a copy of Copy 3 for each part of the goods in question, with a view to it being presented to another office of exit concerned. The original of Copy 3 must be noted accordingly: Art 793(3), second paragraph. Where the entire operation is carried out on the territory of one Member State, that Member State may provide for the non-endorsement of Copy 3, in which case this copy is not to be returned: Art 793(3), third paragraph.

20 Ibid Art 793(4), first paragraph.

1 Ibid Art 793(4), second paragraph.

refuse exit until the export formalities have been completed, and also inform the customs office of export.[2] In the case of goods exported by rail, post, air or sea, the customs office of exit must endorse Copy 3 of the export declaration[3] after making the endorsement 'Export' in red on the transport document and affixing its stamp. The endorsement 'Export' is not required where, in the case of regular shipping lines or direct transport or flights to third country destinations, the operators are able to guarantee the regularity of operations by other means.[4] Where goods sent to a third country or a customs office of exit under a transit procedure are concerned, the office of departure is to endorse Copy 3[5] and return it to the declarant after making the endorsement 'Export', in red, on all copies of the transit document or any other document replacing it.[6] The customs office of exit may ask the exporter to provide evidence that the goods have left the customs territory of the Community.[7]

Goods not subject to prohibition and not exceeding 3000 Ecu in value per consignment and per declarant may be declared at the customs office of exit.[8]

When goods leave the Community customs territory without an export declaration, the declaration must be lodged retrospectively by the exporter at the customs office competent for the place where he is established.[9] Acceptance of the declaration is subject to presentation by the exporter, to the satisfaction of the customs authorities of the customs office concerned, of evidence concerning the nature and quantity of the goods and the circumstances under which they left the Community customs territory. The office must also endorse Copy 3 of the SAD.[10]

Where goods released for export do not leave the Community customs territory, the exporter is required to inform immediately the customs office of export.[11] Where, in specified cases,[12] a change in the transport contract has the effect of terminating inside the Community customs territory a transport operation which should have finished outside it, the companies or authorities in question may only carry out the amended contract with the agreement of the customs office[13] or, in the case of a transit operation, the office of departure.[14]

---

2 Ibid Art 793(4), third paragraph.
3 The endorsement is to be done in accordance with Art 793(3).
4 Ibid Art 793(5). This does not apply where presentation at the office of departure as referred to in Art 419(4) and (7) and Art 434(6) and (9) is dispensed with: Art 793(6), second paragraph. These cases concern certain Community goods which are consigned for transport through an EFTA country and placed under the internal transit procedure and then transported by rail other than through an EFTA country.
5 The endorsement is to be done in accordance with Art 793(3).
6 Ibid Art 793(6), which also provides that the customs office of exit is to control the physical exit of the goods.
7 Ibid Art 793(7).
8 Ibid Art 794(1), first paragraph. Member States may provide that this provision shall not apply when the person making the export declaration is acting as a professional customs agent on behalf of others: Art 794(1), second paragraph.
9 Ibid Art 795, first paragraph, which also provides that Art 790 applies in these circumstances.
10 Ibid Art 795, second paragraph. Retrospective acceptance of the declaration does not however preclude application of the penalties in force or the consequences which may arise as a result of the CAP: Art 795, third paragraph.
11 Ibid Art 796/1), which also provides that Copy 3 of the declaration must be returned to the office.
12 Namely the cases referred to in Art 793(5) (goods exported by rail, post, air or sea) or Art 793(6) (goods sent to a third country or a customs office of exit under a transit procedure).
13 That is, the customs office competent for the place where the goods were taken over under the transport contract: see Art 793(2)(a).
14 Ibid Art 796(2), which also provides that in this case Copy 3 must be returned.

SIMPLIFIED PROCEDURES

The Community Customs Code and its implementing regulation provide for various simplified export procedures.[15]

An oral declaration[16] may be made for the export of goods of a non-commercial nature contained in travellers' personal luggage or sent by private individuals,[17] small quantities of goods of a commercial nature,[18] means of transport registered in the Community customs territory and intended for re-importation,[19] certain other goods,[20] and other goods in cases of negligible economic importance where authorized by the customs authorities.[1]

The simplified declaration procedure allows goods to be entered for export on presentation of a simplified declaration with subsequent presentation of a supplementary declaration which may be of a general, periodic or recapitulative nature.[2] Authorization may be granted on written request.[3] The simplified declaration takes the form of an incomplete SAD containing at least the particulars necessary for identification of the goods.[4]

The procedure for incomplete declaration allows the customs authorities to accept, in justified cases, a declaration which does not contain all the particulars required, or which is not accompanied by all the necessary documents.[5] In order to be acceptable, an export declaration must contain at least certain minimum contents.[6] They include certain particulars referred to in the SAD;[7] all the information required for the proper application of any export duties or measures provided for under the CAP to which the goods are subject;[8] and any further information considered necessary to identify the goods.[9]

The local clearance procedure permits the presentation of goods for export to be carried out at the premises of the person concerned or at other places designated or approved by the customs authorities.[10] Authorization to use this pro-

---

15 See Council Regulation 2913/92 Art 76, OJ 19.10.92 L302/1, as to the procedures and general requirements.

16 Oral declarations can only be made at the customs office of exit: Commission Regulation 2454/93 Art 794(2), OJ 11.10.93 L253/1. Such declarations may be declared inapplicable by the customs authorities when the person clearing the goods is acting as customs agent for another or where the customs authorities are not satisfied that the particulars are accurate or complete: ibid Art 227.

17 Ibid Art 226(a).

18 Ibid Art 226(b), which refers to Art 225(b).

19 Ibid Art 226(c), insofar as it refers to Art 231(b).

20 Ibid Art 226(c), insofar as it refers to Art 231(c), which in turn refers to Council Regulation 918/93, Chapter II, OJ 24.3.83 L105/1, as amended.

1 Ibid Art 226(d).

2 Ibid Art 253(2).

3 Ibid Art 282, which also provides that Arts 261 and 262 are to be applied *mutatis mutandis*. As to the possibility of monitoring compliance and the refusal of authorization, see Art 261. As to the contents of authorization, and therefore the information required to be supplied in any request for authorization, see Art 262.

4 Ibid Art 282(2), which refers to Art 280 in respect of minimum contents of declarations. Where circumstances so permit, the customs authorities may allow this request to be replaced by a global request covering export operations to be carried out over a given period: Art 288(2), second paragraph.

5 Ibid Art 253(1). Arts 255–259 apply *mutatis mutandis* to export declarations: Art 280(4).

6 As to which, see Art 280. This Art also provides that such declarations may be accepted at the declarant's request.

7 As to which, see Art 280(1). As to further items which may be omitted, see Art 280(2).

8 Ibid Art 280(1), first indent.

9 Ibid Art 280(1), second indent.

10 Ibid Art 253(3).

cedure may be granted to any person[11] on written request containing certain particulars.[12] It is to be granted if, first, the applicant's records enable the customs authorities to carry out effective checks, in particular retrospective checks and, second, it is possible to guarantee an effective check on compliance with export prohibitions or restrictions.[13] However, authorization is in principle to be refused where the applicant has committed a serious infringement or repeated infringements of customs rules.[14]

Provision is made for monitoring compliance with the local clearance procedure.[15] Before removal of the goods, the approved exporter must duly notify the customs authorities of the removal in the form and manner specified by them for the purpose of obtaining release of the goods; enter the goods in its records;[16] and make available to the customs authorities any documents the presentation of which may be required for application of the provisions governing export of the goods.[17] In certain circumstances, justified by the nature of the goods and the rapid turnover of export operations, the customs authorities may exempt the approved exporter from the requirement to notify the competent customs office of each removal of goods.[18] To check that the goods have actually left the Community customs territory, Copy No 3 of the SAD is used as evidence of exit.[19]

Another simplified procedure applies in cases involving sub-contracting.[20] The supplementary or replacement declaration may be lodged at the customs office responsible for the place where the exporter is established. However, where the sub-contractor is established in a different Member State, this possibility only applies on condition that agreements have been made between the administrations of the Member States concerned.[1]

In addition, where the whole of an export operation takes place on the territory of a single Member State, that Member State, while ensuring compliance with Community policies, may provide for other simplifications.[2]

Finally, the customs authorities may authorize a declarant to replace all or part of the particulars required under the general procedure by sending to the

---

11 Known as an 'approved exporter'.
12 As to the categories of goods for which authorization may be granted, see Art 263. As to specific rules stipulated in the authorization, see Art 287. In certain circumstance authorization may be given for a global declaration covering export operations over a certain period: Art 288(2), second paragraph.
13 Ibid Art 264(1).
14 Ibid Art 264(2), first indent. Authorization is in principle to be revoked where this case arises: Art 265(2). As to avoidance of revocation, see Art 265(1).
15 See also Art 266, as substituted in part by Commission Regulation 2193/94 Art 1, OJ 9.9.94 L235/6.
16 Entry may be replaced by any other formality offering similar guarantees stipulated by the customs authorities. The entry must indicate the date on which it is made and the particulars necessary for identification of the goods: Art 285(1)(b).
17 Ibid Art 285(1).
18 Provided that the approved exporter supplies the office with all the information it considers necessary to enable it to exercise its right to examine the goods should the need arise: Art 285(2).
19 Ibid Art 286(1), first paragraph. The authorization to use the procedure must stipulate that Copy No 3 be authenticated in advance: Art 286(1), second paragraph. As to procedures for prior authentication, see Art 286(2). As to procedures to be carried out by the exporter before departure of the goods, see Art 286(3). The use of commercial or administrative documents instead of the SAD may be authorized in certain circumstances: see Art 288.
20 That is, when Art 789 applies.
 1 Ibid Art 281, which also provides for relevant procedures.
 2 Ibid Art 289.

customs office designated for that purpose, with a view to their processing by computer, codified data, or data made out in any other form specified by those authorities, corresponding to the particulars required for written declarations.[3]

TEMPORARY EXPORTATION USING AN ATA CARNET

In respect of temporary exportation, an ATA carnet[4] may be used for export on certain conditions.[5] First, the ATA carnet must be issued in a Member State of the Community and endorsed and guaranteed by an association established in the Community forming part of an international guarantee chain.[6] Second, the ATA carnet is applicable only to certain goods. The goods must be Community goods.[7] They must not have been subject on export from the Community customs territory to customs export formalities with a view to the payment of refunds or other export amounts under the CAP.[8] They must not have been granted any other financial benefit under the CAP, coupled with an obligation to export.[9] No request for repayment must have been submitted in respect of the goods.[10] Third, all documents necessary for the correct application of export duties and of the provisions governing the export of the goods in question must be presented,[11] and the customs authorities may require presentation of the transport document.[12] Fourth, the goods must be intended for reimportation.[13]

Where goods covered by an ATA carnet are entered for the purpose of temporary exportation, the customs office of export is to verify the information given in boxes A to G of the exportation voucher against the goods under cover of the carnet.[14] It must also complete, where appropriate, the box on the cover page of the carnet headed 'Certificate by customs authorities'.[15] It must also complete the counterfoil and box H of the exportation voucher,[16] enter its name in box H(b) of the reimportation voucher,[17] and retain the exportation voucher.[18] If the customs office of export is not the office of exit, the customs office of export must carry out these formalities, with the exception of completing box 7 of the exportation counterfoil, which must be done by the customs office of

---

3 Ibid Art 222.
4 That is, the international customs document for temporary importation established by virtue of the ATA Convention or the Istanbul Convention: Commission Regulation 2454/93 Art 1(2), OJ 11.10.93 L25371, as amended by Commission Regulation 1762/95 Art 1, OJ 21.7.95 L171/8, which also adds Art 1(11) defining the Istanbul Convention as the Convention on Temporary Admissions agreed at Istanbul on 26 June 1990.
5 Ibid Art 797(1).
6 Ibid Art 797(1)(a), which also provides that the Commission is to publish a list of the associations.
7 Ibid Art 797(1)(b), first indent. As to the definition of Community goods, see Art 4(7).
8 Ibid Art 797(1), second indent.
9 Ibid Art 797(1), third indent.
10 Ibid Art 797(1), fourth indent.
11 These documents are listed in Art 221.
12 Ibid Art 797/1)(c), which refers to the documents specified in Art 221.
13 Ibid Art 797(1)(d).
14 Ibid Art 797(2)(a).
15 Ibid Art 797(2)(b).
16 Ibid Art 797(2)(c).
17 Ibid Art 797(2)(d).
18 Ibid Art 797(2)(e).

exit.[19] The time limit for reimportation of the goods laid down by the customs authorities in box H(b) of the exportation voucher may not exceed the validity of the carnet.[20]

Where goods which left the Community customs territory under cover of an ATA carnet are no longer intended to be reimported, an export declaration containing certain particulars[1] must be presented to the customs office of export.[2] On presentation of the carnet, the customs office of export is to endorse Copy 3 of the export declaration and invalidate the reimportation voucher and counterfoil.[3]

19 Ibid Art 797(3). However, where the formalities discharging a temporary export operation in respect of Community goods are carried out by a customs office other than the office where the goods enter the Community customs territory, conveyance of the goods from that office to the office where the formalities are carried out does not require any formality: Art 290(3).
20 Ibid Art 797(4).
 1 Specified in Annex 37.
 2 Ibid Art 798, first paragraph.
 3 Ibid Art 798, second paragraph.

Part II

General commercial policy

Chapter 8

Imports

INTRODUCTION

The Treaty establishing the European Communty provides that the common commercial policy shall based on uniform principles.[1] In respect of imports, these uniform principles are expressed in four main regulations and numerous more specific measures. Of the four main regulations, the first is Council Regulation 3285/94 on common rules on imports.[2] It is the general regulation governing imports from third countries, except for textile products and products from non-market economy countries. The second main regulation is Council Regulation 519/94 on common rules for imports from certain third countries.[3] It is the general regulation governing imports from non-market economy countries, except for textile products. The third main regulation is Council Regulation 3030/93 on common rules for imports of certain textile products from third countries.[4] It covers imports of textile products from third countries with which the Community has concluded bilateral agreements, protocols or other arrangements. The fourth main regulation is Council Regulation 517/94 on common rules for imports of textile products from certain third countries not covered by bilateral agreements, protocols or other arrangements, or by other specific Community import rules.[5] It covers imports of textile products from non-market economy countries with which the Community has not concluded specific arrangements. The four main regulations thus distinguish among imports first according to origin, namely whether the product originates in a market economy country or not; second according to the type of product, namely whether the product is a textile product or not; and third, in the case of textile products, according to whether the textile product originates in a country with which the Community has made a specific arrangement or not. Within this broad framework, numerous specific measures govern more detailed aspects of imports into the Community. The basic purposes of the main regulations and more specific measures are to manage trade, to regulate and control the type and volume of imports, and thus within limits to protect Community industry.

---

1 EC Art 113(1).
2 OJ 31.12.94 L349/53, which substituted and repealed Council Regulation 518/94 following the conclusion of the Uruguay Round Agreement on Safeguards.
3 OJ 10.3.94 L67/89, as amended. These third countries are generally known as non-market economy countries or state-trading countries.
4 OJ 8.11.93 L275/1, as amended.
5 OJ 10.3.94 L67/1, as amended.

NON-TEXTILE IMPORTS FROM MARKET ECONOMY COUNTRIES

Imports from market economy countries of products other than textiles are governed by Council Regulation 3285/94 on common rules on imports.[6] This Regulation applies to imports of products originating in third countries,[7] except for textile products covered by Council Regulation 517/94, other than certain products in so far as those products originate in a WTO member country,[8] and products originating in certain third countries.[9] The basic principle is that imports of the products to which Council Regulation 3285/94 applies shall take place freely and without being subject to any quantitative restrictions, though this is without prejudice to safeguard measures.[10]

In order to manage and control the volume of imports, Council Regulation 3285/94 establishes three different procedures: an information and consultation procedure,[11] an investigation procedure,[12] and surveillance.[13] It also provides for safeguard measures.[14] It does not however take precedence over special rules contained in agreements between the Community and third countries.[15] Nor does it preclude the adoption or application by Member States of prohibitions, quantitative restrictions or surveillance on the usual grounds,[16] or of special formalities regarding foreign exchange,[17] or of formalities introduced pursuant to international agreements in accordance with the Treaty.[18] Member States are required however to inform the Commission of any such measures or formalities.[19] This Regulation is also without prejudice to the operation of measures of the common agricultural policy, including those regarding processed agricultural products, and it operates by way of complement to those instruments.[20]

As to the information and consultation procedure, Member States are required to inform the Commission if trends in imports appear to call for surveillance or safeguard measures.[1] Consultations may be held at the request of a

---

6 Council Regulation 3285/94 on common rules for imports and repealing Regulation 518/94, OJ 31.12.94 L349/53.

7 Ibid Art 1(1).

8 Ibid Art 1(1), first indent, which also provides that the relevant products are listed in Annex II.

9 Ibid Art 1(1), second indent, which also provides that these third countries are listed in Council Regulation 519/94 on common rules for imports from certain third countries.

10 Ibid Art 1(2), which refers to the safeguard measures which may be taken under Title V of this Regulation.

11 See ibid Title II, Arts 2–4.

12 See ibid Title III, Arts 5–10.

13 See ibid Title IV, Arts 11–15.

14 See ibid Title V, Arts 16–22.

15 Ibid Art 24(1).

16 Ibid Art 24(2)(a).

17 Ibid Art 24(2)(b).

18 Ibid Art 24(2)(c).

19 Ibid Art 24(2)(b).

20 Ibid Art 25(1). See however ibid Art 25(2), first and second paragraphs, respectively, in respect of such products in respect of which Community rules either require production of a licence or other import document or provide for the application of quantitative import restrictions.

1 Ibid Art 2, which also provides that the information shall contain certain evidence and that the Commission shall pass it on to all Member States forthwith. The criteria for the evidence are established by Art 10, which lists the following factors that must be considered in examining the trend of imports, their conditions, and the serious injury or threat of serious injury to Community producers: the volume of imports, price of imports, and consequent impact on Community producers as indicated by trends in certain listed factors (Art 10(1)). Where a

Member State or on the initiative of the Commission.[2] The consultations take place within an advisory committee.[3] They are to cover the terms and conditions of importation, import trends, and the various aspects of the economic and commercial situation in respect of the product in question,[4] as well as the measures, if any, to be taken.[5]

As to the investigation procedure, except for provisional safeguards,[6] the Community investigation procedure must be implemented before any safeguard measure is applied.[7] The aim of the investigation is to determine whether imports of the product in question are causing or threatening to cause serious injury to the Community producers concerned.[8] Where after consultation it is apparent to the Commission that there is sufficient evidence to justify an investigation, the Commission is to initiate an investigation within one month of receipt of the information[9] and then commence an investigation, acting in co-operation with the Member States.[10] It may seek all information it deems necessary and endeavour to check it.[11] This information, except for internal Community or national documents and confidential information, may be inspected by interested parties.[12] The Commission may hear interested parties, and it must hear those parties which have applied in writing and showed that they are actually likely to be affected by the outcome of the investigation and that there are special reasons for them to be heard orally.[13] At the end of the investigation the Commission must submit a report on the results to the committee.[14] The investigation is to be terminated where, within nine months of its instigation, the Commission considers that no Community surveillance or safeguard measures are necessary.[15] However, if the Commission considers that such measures are

threat of serious injury is alleged, the Commission must also examine whether it is clearly foreseeable that a particular situation is likely to develop into actual injury, taking account of factors such as the rate of increase of exports to the Community, the export capacity of the country of origin or export, and the likelihood that any resulting exports will be to the Community (Art 10(2)).

2 Ibid Art 3, which also provides that consultations must take place within eight working days after the information is received by the Commission and, in any event, before the introduction of any Community surveillance or safeguard measure.

3 Ibid Art 4(1), which provides that the advisory committee is made up of representatives of each Member State and chaired by a representative of the Commission.

4 Ibid Art 4(3), first indent.

5 Ibid Art 4(3), second indent.

6 Pursuant to ibid Art 8.

7 Ibid Art 5(1).

8 Ibid Art 5(2), which also provides that the factors described in Art 10 shall be used as a basis. 'Serious injury' means a significant overall impairment in the position of Community producers. 'Threat of serious injury' means serious injury that is clearly imminent. 'Community producers' means the producers as a whole of the like or directly competing products operating within the territory of the Community, or those whose collective output of the like or directly competing products constitutes a major proportion of the total Community production of those products. See ibid Art 5(3)(a),(b), and (c) respectively.

9 Ibid Art 6(1)(a), which also lays down the requirements for publication of a notice in the OJ.

10 Ibid Art 6(1)(b).

11 Ibid Art 6(2), first paragraph. The second paragraph of this Art provides that the Commission may be assisted in this task by staff of the Member State on whose territory these checks are carried out, provided that this Member State so wishes.

12 Ibid Art 6(2), third paragraph, which also provides that interested parties are those which have made themselves known in accordance with paragraph (1)(a) following publication in the OJ of the notice of investigation.

13 Ibid Art 6(4).

14 Ibid Art 7(1).

15 Ibid Art 7(2).

necessary, it must take the necessary decisions no later than nine months from the initiation of the investigation.[16]

Recourse to investigation does not preclude the use of specified surveillance measures or provisional safeguard measures.[17] Provisional safeguards can be applied in critical circumstances where delay would cause damage which it would be difficult to repair, making immediate action necessary.[18] They can also be applied where a preliminary determination provides clear evidence that increased imports have caused or are threatening to cause serious injury.[19] The maximum duration of such measures is 200 days.[20] They should take the form of an increase in the existing level of customs duty (whether the latter is zero or higher) if such action is likely to prevent or repair the serious injury.[1]

Surveillance may be applied when developments on the Community market in respect of a product originating in a third country threaten to cause injury to Community producers, and where the interests of the Community so require.[2] Importation of the product may be subject to retrospective Community surveillance or prior Community surveillance.[3] Products under prior Community surveillance may be put into free circulation only on production of an import document, endorsed by the competent authority designated by Member States, free of charge and for any quantity requested.[4] The import document is valid throughout the Community, regardless of the Member State of issue.[5] With regard to the product under surveillance, Member States are required to inform the Commission of details of sums of money, quantities of goods, and details of imports for the specified period.[6] Similar provisions apply in respect of surveillance confined to one or more Community regions.[7] Surveillance measures are valid only for a limited period.[8]

Safeguard measures may be taken when a product is imported into the Community in such greatly increased quantities and/or on such terms or conditions as to cause, or threaten to cause, serious injury to Community producers.[9] The

---

16 Ibid Art 7(3), which also provides that such decisions shall be taken in accordance with Titles IV (surveillance) and V (safeguards) and that in exceptional circumstances the time limit may be extended by a further maximum period of two months, subject to the requirement of publication of a notice giving the duration of and reasons for the extension.

17 Ibid Art 8(1),first sub-paragraph, which refers to surveillance measures in accordance with Arts 11–15 and provisional safeguard measures in accordance with Arts 16–18.

18 Ibid Art 8(1), second sub-paragraph, first indent.

19 Ibid Art 8(1), second sub-paragraph, second indent.

20 Ibid Art 8(2).

1 Ibid Art 8(3). If the measures are repealed because no serious injury or threat of serious injury exists, the duties collected as a result of the measures must be automatically refunded as soon as possible: ibid Art 8(5), which also provides for the procedure.

2 Ibid Art 11(1).

3 Ibid Art 11(1). The decision to impose surveillance is to be taken by the Commission (see ibid Art 11(2)), subject to referral by any Member State to the Council (see ibid Art 16(7)), which acting by a qualified majority may confirm, amend or revoke the Commission decision (see ibid Art 16(8), first paragraph). If the Council has taken no decision within three months of the referral, the Commission measure is deemed revoked (see ibid Art 16(8)), second paragraph).

4 Ibid Art 12(1), which provides further procedures. As to the form, see ibid Art 10(2) and the model given in Annex I.

5 Ibid Art 12(3).

6 Ibid Art 15(1).

7 As to which, see ibid Arts 11, 13, 14.

8 Unless otherwise stipulated, they cease to be valid at the end of the second six-month period following the six months in which the measure was introduced: ibid Art 11(3).

9 See ibid Art 16(1), first sub-paragraph.

Commission, acting at the request of a Member State or on its own initiative, may limit the period of validity of import documents[10] or alter the import rules for the product by providing that it may be put into free circulation only on production of an import authorization.[11] As regards WTO members, such measures may only be taken when both preconditions are met.[12] If a quota is allocated among supplier countries, allocation may be agreed with those of them having a substantial interest in supplying the product concerned for import into the Commuity.[13] Otherwise the quota is to be allocated in proportion to the share of imports from each supplier.[14] However, provided its obligation to conduct any consultations within the WTO framework are repected, the Community may depart from this method of allocation in the case of serious injury if imports from one or more supplier countries have increased disproportionately over a previous representative period.[15] Safeguard measures apply to all products put into free circulation after their entry into force,[16] but do not, under specified conditions, prevent the release for free circulation of products already on their way to the Community.[17] In addition to such measures as may be taken by the Commission, the Council[18] may, where the interests of the Community so require, adopt appropriate measures to prevent a product being imported into the Community in such greatly increased quantities and/or on such terms or conditions as to cause, or threaten to cause, serious injury to Community producers of like or directly competing products.[19] However, no safeguard measure may be applied to a product originating in a developing country WTO member as long as that country's share of Community imports of the product do not exceed 3 per cent.[20] Safeguard measures must be limited to the time period necessary to prevent or remedy serious injury and to facilitate adjustment on the part of Community producers. They must not exceed four years, including provisional measures.[1] In specified conditions, however, the period may be extended.[2] The total period of safeguards, including provisional measures, must not exceed eight years.[3] While any surveillance or safeguard measure[4] is in operation, consultations within the committee must be held[5] to examine

---

10 Ibid Art 16(1), first sub-paragraph, (a), which refers to Art 12 for the meaning of import documents.
11 Ibid Art 16(1), first sub-paragraph, (b), which also provides that the granting of the import authorization is to be governed by such provisions and subject to such limits as the Commission shall lay down. The measures under Art 16(1)(a) and (b) take effect immediately: see Art 16(1), second sub-paragraph. The decision-making procedure is the same as that for surveillance: see ibid Art 16(7),(8).
12 Ibid Art 16(2): in other words, both greatly increased quantities and specified terms or conditions.
13 Ibid Art 16(4)(a),first sub-paragraph.
14 Ibid Art 16(4)(a), second sub-paragraph, which also provides further conditions.
15 Ibid Art 16(4)(b).
16 Ibid Art 16(5)(a).
17 See ibid Art 16(5)(b).
18 Acting by a qualified majority on a proposal by the Commission: ibid Art 17, first sub-paragraph.
19 Ibid Art 17.
20 Ibid Art 19, which further provides that this is on condition that developing country members with less than a 3% import share account collectively for not more than 9 per cent of total Community imports of the product concerned.
 1 Ibid Art 20(1).
 2 Ibid Art 20(2).
 3 Ibid Art 20(4). See also Art 22.
 4 That is, measures applied in accordance with Titles IV and V of this Regulation: ibid Art 21(1).
 5 At the request of a Member State or on the initiative of the Commission: ibid Art 21(1).

the effects of the measure[6] and to ascertain whether its application is still necessary.[7]

The Council may similarly adopt appropriate measures to allow the rights and obligations of the Community, or of all of its Member States, to be exercised and fulfilled at international level, in particular those relating to trade in primary products.[8]

NON-TEXTILE IMPORTS FROM NON-MARKET ECONOMY COUNTRIES

Imports from non-market economy countries of products other than textiles are governed by Council Regulation 519/94.[9] This Regulation applies to imports of products[10] originating in certain third countries,[11] except for textile products covered by Council Regulation 517/94.[12] The basic principles underlying Council Regulation 519/94 are two-fold. First, imports into the Community of the products to which the Regulation applies shall take place freely and without being subject to quantitative restrictions,[13] except for safeguard measures[14] or certain quantitative quotas.[15] Second, imports into the Community of certain other products are subject to Community surveillance.[16]

---

6 Ibid Art 21(1)(a).
7 Ibid Art 21(1)(b). As to the procedure for revoking or amending a measure, see ibid Art 21(2).
8 Ibid Art 23.
9 Council Regulation 519/94, OJ 10.3.94 L67/89.
10 This includes not only products covered by the EC Treaty but also ECSC products, without prejudice to any measures implementing an agreement relating specifically to such products: ibid Art 1(1), as amended by Council Regulation 168/96, OJ 1.2.96 L25/2.
11 As provided in ibid Art 1(1), these third countries are listed in Annex I. The original list of countries included Albania, Armenia, Azerbaijan, Belarus, People's Republic of China, Estonia, Georgia, Kazakhstan, North Korea, Kyrgyzstan, Latvia, Lithuania, Moldova, Mongolia, Russia, Tajikistan, Turkmenistan, Ukraine, Uzbekistan, and Vietnam. After they signed Free Trade Agreements with the Community, Estonia, Latvia and Lithuania were removed from Annex I by Council Regulation 839/95, Art 1, OJ 19.4.95 L85/9. As a result of changed economic conditions in China and Russia, the Community recently revised its anti-dumping law in respect of these two countries, but this change in law and practice did not affect the common rules for imports in respect of China and Russia: see Council Regulation 905/98, seventh recital, OJ 30.3.98 L128/18. Consequently, China and Russia remain on the list of third countries in Annex I of Council Regulation 519/94.
12 Ibid Art 1(1).
13 Ibid Art 1(2).
14 Ibid Art 1(2), first indent, which refers to the safeguard measures which may be taken under Title V of this Regulation.
15 Ibid Art 1(2), second indent, which refers to the quotas listed in Annex II. This Annex gives a list of quotas for certain products originating in China. As from 1 January 1998, the list includes footwear; tableware and kitchenware of porcelain or china; ceramic tableware or kitchenware other than of porcelain or china; and toys: see ibid, Annex II, as last amended by Council Regulation 847/97 Art 2 and Annex III, OJ 14.5.97 L122/1. At the request of a Member State or on the initiative of the Commission, Annex II may be the subject of consultations within the advisory committee established by ibid Art 4 and the Commission may then propose appropriate changes to the Council: see ibid Art 1(4).
16 Ibid Art 1(3), which provides that the products in question are listed in Annex III and that Community surveillance is to be conducted in accordance with the detailed rules laid down in Art 10. Annex III gives a list of products originating in the People's Republic of China, subject to Community surveillance. As from 1 January 1998, the list includes ammonium chloride, other olyhydric alcohols, citric acid, tetracyclines and their derivatives, chloramphenicol, basic dyes and preparations based thereon, vat dyes and preparations based thereon,

In order to manage and control imports, Council Regulation 519/94 establishes three different procedures: an information and consultation procedure,[17] an investigation procedure,[18] and surveillance.[19] It also provides for safeguard measures.[20] It does not however take precedence over special rules contained in agreements between the Community and third countries.[1] Nor does it preclude the adoption or application by Member States of prohibitions, quantitative restrictions or surveillance on the usual grounds,[2] or of special formalities regarding foreign exchange,[3] or of formalities introduced pursuant to international agreements in accordance with the Treaty.[4] Member States are required however to inform the Commission of any such measures or formalities.[5] This Regulation is also without prejudice to the operation of measures of the common agricultural policy, including those regarding processed agricultural products, and it operates by way of complement to those instruments.[6]

The provisions in Council Regulation 519/94 in respect of the information and consultation procedure, investigation, surveillance and safeguards are identical to those in Council Regulation 518/94 with certain exceptions, all of which tend to give the Community institutions more power and discretion. These exceptions are as follows. In conducting the investigation, the Commission must take account of the particular economic system of these third countries.[7] Surveillance may be imposed if the Community's interests so require, without any requirement of threat of injury to Community producers of like or directly competing products.[8] Where the Community interest so requires, the Commission may, at the request of a Member State or on its own initiative, limit the period of validity of any required import document.[9] It may also make the issue of this document subject to certain conditions and, as an exceptional measure, subject to insertion of a revocation clause or to the prior information and consultation procedure.[10] The safeguard measures that may be taken by the Commission are limited to altering the import rules for the product by providing

fireworks, signalling flares, rain rockets, fog signals and other pyrotechnic articles, polyvinyl alcohol, gloves, footwear, ornamental ceramic articles of porcelain, glassware, bicycles, toys, puzzles, parts and accessories of toys, playing cards, and articles falling within specified HS/CN codes: see ibid, Annex III, as last amended by Council Regulation 847/97 Art 2 and Annex IV, OJ 14.5.97 L122/1. The procedures for changing Annex III are the same as those for changing Annex II: see ibid Art 1(4).

17 See ibid Title II, Arts 2–4.
18 See ibid Arts 5–8.
19 See ibid Arts 9–14.
20 See ibid Arts 15–18.
 1 Ibid Art 19(1).
 2 Ibid Art 19(2)(a).
 3 Ibid Art 19(2)(b).
 4 Ibid Art 19(2)(c).
 5 Ibid Art 19(2)(b).
 6 Ibid Art 20(1). See however ibid Art 20(2), first and second paragraphs, respectively, in respect of such products which Community rules require either production of a licence or other import document or provide for the application of quantitative import restrictions.
 7 Ibid Art 8(2).
 8 See ibid Art 9(1). There is also no express provision requiring the use of the *contrefilet* committee procedure: compare Council Regulation 518/94 Art 9(2), OJ 10.3.94 L67/77.
 9 Ibid Art 11, first indent.
10 Ibid Art 11, second indent. Note that these powers are even more extensive than those granted to the Commission in respect of safeguard measures by Council Regulation 518/94 Art 14, OJ 10.3.94 L67/77.

that it may be put into free circulation only on production of an import authorization.[11] However, the Council may adopt any appropriate measures.[12]

IMPORTS OF TEXTILE PRODUCTS UNDER BILATERAL AGREEMENTS OR OTHER ARRANGEMENTS

Council Regulation 3030/93 on common rules for imports of certain textile products from third countries[13] applies to imports into the Community of textile products from third countries with which the Community has concluded bilateral agreements, protocols or other arrangements.[14] It also applies to imports of textile products which, so far as the Community is concerned, have not been integrated into GATT 1994 as provided in the World Trade Organisation (WTO) Agreement on Textiles and Clothing (ATC) and which originate in third countries that are WTO members.[15] This Regulation thus provides the framework for the management of the many textile agreements previously concluded by the Community under the Multi-Fibre Arrangement as well as similar arrangements. It provides for quantitative limits, folklore and handloom products, temporary imports, outward processing, prices, flexibility, additional imports, regional concentration, safeguard measures, surveillance, circumvention, consultations, and the functioning of a textile committee.[16]

IMPORTS OF TEXTILE PRODUCTS NOT COVERED BY BILATERAL AGREEMENTS OR OTHER ARRANGEMENTS

Council Regulation 517/94 provides common rules for imports of textile products falling within Section XI of the Combined Nomenclature and of other textile products, originating in third countries and not covered by bilateral agreements, protocols or other arrangements or by other specific Community import rules.[17] It establishes the legal framework for managing and controlling textile imports from countries, particularly non-market economy countries, which are not governed by bilateral arrangements between the Community and the exporting country in question. It provides for a Community information and investigation procedure, surveillance and safeguard measures, the management of Community import restrictions, and decision-making procedures.[18]

---

11 See ibid Art 15(1). In other words, there is no express provision for the Commission to limit the period of validity of import documents, as it may do pursuant to Council Regulation 518/94 Art 14(1)(a), OJ 10.3.94 L67/77.
12 Ibid Art 16(1): compare Council Regulation 518/94 Art 15(1), OJ 10.3.94 L67/77.
13 OJ 8.11.93 L275/1, as amended. The Annexes to this Regulation were substituted in late 1996 by Commission Regulation 2231/96, OJ 28.11.96 L307/1.
14 Ibid Art 1, first indent, as substituted by Council Regulation 824/97 Art 1(1), OJ 8.5.97 L119/1.
15 Ibid Art 1, second indent, as so substituted.
16 This Regulation is discussed in detail in Chapter 18 on Textiles in this book.
17 Council Regulation 517/94 Art 1(1), OJ 10.3.94 L67/1, which further provides that the other textile products are listed in Annex I of the Regulation. Annex IV of this Regulation was substituted most recently by Council Regulation 1325/95, OJ 13.6.95 L128/1. Annexes III(B), IV and VI of this Regulation were substituted most recently by Commission Regulation 1457/97, OJ 26.7.97 L199/6.
18 This Regulation is discussed in detail in Chapter 18 on Textiles in this book.

SPECIFIC MEASURES

The Community has also taken numerous specific measures in respect of imports. Two examples involving systematic treatment of imports are given here.[19]

The first example concerns imports of agricultural products originating in third countries following the accident at the Chernobyl nuclear power station. Council Regulation 737/90[20] covers agricultural products and various processed agricultural products, with the exception of certain products unfit for human consumption and other products which may come to be excluded from the scope of the Regulation.[1] The release for free circulation of the covered products is subject to compliance with certain maximum permitted levels of radioactivity.[2] Member States are required to check compliance with these levels, taking into account contamination levels in the country of origin. This may include the presentation of export certificates. Taking each case individually, or generally for a given product, Member States are to take the necessary measures.[3] In the event of cases of repeated non-compliance with the maximum permitted levels, the necessary measures may be taken.[4] Such measures may include the prohibition of the import of products originating in the third country concerned.[5]

A second example of specific Community measures in respect of imports concerns the import and the export of certain dangerous chemicals, which are governed by Council Regulation 2455/92.[6] In respect of imports,[7] this measure establishes a common system of notification and information for imports from third countries of certain chemicals which are banned[8] or severely restricted[9] on

---

19 As to further details, see the other chapters of this book, most of which, except for Chapter 9 on Exports, deal with specific measures in respect of imports.
20 See Council Regulation 737/90, OJ 29.3.90 L 82/1, the expiry date of which was extended to 31 March 2000 by Council Regulation 686/95, OJ 31.3.95 L71/15. Council Regulation 737/90 replaced and simplified Council Regulation 3955/87, OJ 30.12.87 L371/14, as amended, for which detailed implementing rules were laid down by Commission Regulation 1983/88, OJ 6.7.88 L174/32.
1 See ibid Art 1. The products unfit for human consumption are listed in Annex I. Further products may be excluded pursuant to the procedure set down in ibid Art 7.
2 Ibid Art 2. The maximum permitted levels are laid down in Art 3.
3 Ibid Art 4(1). Member States are required to supply the Commission with all information concerning application of the Regulation, including cases of non-compliance, and the Commission is required to circulate this information to the other Member States: ibid Art 4(2).
4 Ibid Art 5, which further provides that such measures are to be taken accordance to the procedure laid down in Art 7, namely the '*filet*' or 'net' procedure.
5 Ibid Art 5.
6 OJ 29.8.92 L251/13, as amended. It does not apply however to substances or preparations imported or exported for the purposes of analysis or scientific research and development, as defined in ibid Art 2, where the quantities involved are sufficiently small that they are unlikely to affect human health or the environment adversely: ibid Art 1(3).
7 For this purpose, 'import' means the physical introduction into the customs territory of the Community of products which are placed under a customs procedure other than transit procedure: ibid Art 2(6).
8 'Banned chemical' means a chemical which has, for health or environmental reasons, been prohibited for all uses by final governmental regulatory action: ibid Art 2(3).
9 'Severely restricted chemical' means a chemical for which, for health or environmental reasons, virtually all uses have been prohibited by final governmental regulatory action but for which certain specific uses remain authorized: ibid Art 2(4).

account of their effects on human health and the environment.[10] It applies the international notification and 'prior informed consent' (PIC) procedure[11] established by the United Nations Environment Programme (UNEP) and the Food and Agriculture Organization (FAO).[12]

Each Member State is required to designate an authority competent for the procedure and so to inform the Commission.[13] The Commission acts as the common designated authority as far as the participation of the Community in the international PIC procedure is concerned.[14] The Commission is required to notify the competent bodies dealing with the international PIC procedure of the chemicals which are banned or severely restricted in the Community.[15] It must also forward forthwith to the Member States information which it receives regarding chemicals subject to the PIC procedure and the decisions of third countries regarding bans or import conditions. It must evaluate in close co-operation with the Member States the risks posed by these chemicals. After taking any decisions, the Commission must inform the IRPTC[16] whether import into the Community of each of the chemicals is allowed, restricted or prohibited.[17]

The basic principles to be observed by the Commission in making decisions are, first, that, in the case of a substance or preparation banned by Community legislation, import consent for a banned use is to be refused.[18] Second, in the case of a substance or preparation severely restricted by Community legislation, import consent is to be subject to conditions, with the appropriate conditions being decided on a case-by-case basis.[19] Third, in the case of a substance or preparation not banned or severely restricted by Community legislation, import consent shall not normally be refused. However, if the Commission, in consultation with Member States, considers that a proposal shall be made to the Council to ban or severely restrict the substance or preparation not produced in the Community, interim import conditions, set on a case-by-case basis,

---

10 Ibid Art 1(1). As to the international list of banned and severely restricted chemicals subject to the PIC procedure, a list of participating countries, and the decisions of those countries regarding the import of these chemicals, see ibid Art 5(3) and Annex II, as substituted most recently by Commission Regulation 1237/97, OJ 1.7.97 L173/37. As to updating of the Annexes, see ibid Art 11(1). If a Member State applies, with respect to other substances, a national system using similar information procedures, it must so inform the Commission: see ibid Art 10.

11 'Prior informed consent' means the principle that international shipment of a chemical which is banned or severely restricted in order to protect human health or the environment should not proceed without the agreement, where such agreement exists, or contrary to the decision of the designed national authority of the importing country: ibid Art 2(7).

12 Ibid Art 1(1). As to the PIC procedure, see the London Guidelines for the Exchange of Information on Chemicals in International Trade, Decision 14/27 of the Governing Council of UNEP of 17 June 1989 as amended in May 1989; FAO International Code of Conduct on the Distribution and Use of Pesticides, Rome 1986, as amended in November 1989.

13 Ibid Art 3(1).

14 Ibid Art 3(2).

15 Ibid Art 5(1), which also requires the Commission to provide all relevant information and identify and provide reasons for the relevant control actions. It further provides that the chemicals are listed in Annex I, which in 1994 was substituted by Council Regulation 3135/95 OJ 22.12.94 L332/1.

16 International Register of Potentially Toxic Chemicals.

17 Ibid Art 5(2), first sub-paragraph.

18 Ibid Art 5(2), second sub-paragraph, (a). As to the determination of whether regulatory action qualifies as a ban or severe restriction, see ibid Art 11(1), second sub-paragraph.

19 Ibid Art 5(2), second sub-paragraph, (b).

may be imposed until the Council has taken a decision.[20] In addition, in the case of a substance or preparation banned or severely restricted by the legislation of one or more Member States, the Commission must, at the written request of the Member State concerned, prepare its decision on the reply to be made to the IRPTC, taking into consideration the Member State's ban or severe restrictions.[1] The Commission must, whenever practicable, make use of existing Community procedures and it must ensure that its response does not conflict with existing Community legislation.[2]

Exporters are required to comply with the decision of the country of destination participating in the PIC procedure.[3] If a participating importing country does not make a response, or responds with an interim decision which does not address importation, the status quota in respect of imports of the chemical is to continue. This means that the chemical should not be exported without the explicit consent of the importing country, unless it is a pesticide which is registered in the importing country or is a chemical the use or exportation of which has been allowed by other action of the importing country.[4]

Member States are to take action against infringements.[5] In addition, if a Member State authority receives a notification from a competent third country authority concerning the export to the Community of a chemical prohibited or severely restricted under that country's legislation, it is required to send the notification and all relevant information forthwith to the Commission,[6] which is to forward it to the other Member States.[7] Provision is also made for the exchange of information and monitoring by the Member States[8] and the Commission.[9]

---

20 Ibid Art 5(2), second sub-paragraph, (c).
 1 Ibid Art 5(2), third sub-paragraph.
 2 Ibid Art 5(2), fourth sub-paragraph.
 3 Ibid Art 5(5).
 4 Ibid Art 5(5).
 5 Ibid Art 6.
 6 Ibid Art 8(1).
 7 Ibid Art 8(2).
 8 See ibid Art 9(1), (3).
 9 See ibid Art 9(2), (3). Art 9(2) requires the Commission to report regularly to the European Parliament and the Council.

Chapter 9

Exports

COMMON RULES FOR EXPORTS

Basic principles and general matters

The aim of the Common Commercial Policy, as of other trade policies, is to control quantities of imports and maximise the quantity of exports. This aim of maximising exports is reflected in the basic policy which underlies Council Regulation 2603/69[1] establishing common rules for exports.[2]

Regulation 2603/69 establishes common rules for exports from the EC. It is divided into four titles. Title I establishes the basic principle of free exportation.[3] Title II provides for a Community information and consultation procedure on exports.[4] Title III concerns protective measures.[5] Title IV consists of transitional and final provisions,[6] including those on permissible Member State restrictions[7] and exports of basic and processed agricultural products.[8] In the Annexes to the regulation such products as are excluded from the freedom of exports under its Art 10 are listed.[9]

The principle of Community export policy is that exports to third countries

---

1 See Council Regulation 2603/69, preamble, sixth recital, OJ 27.12.69 L324/25, as amended by the 1972 Accession Treaty of Denmark, Ireland and the United Kingdom. The provisions of this regulation are applied to the French overseas departments by Council Regulation 2604/69, OJ 27.12.69 L324/34.
2 Council Regulation 3918/91 of 19 December 1991, preamble, fourth recital, OJ 31.12.91 L372/91, as amended.
3 Council Regulation 2603/69 Art 1.
4 Ibid Arts 2–5.
5 Ibid Arts 6–9.
6 Ibid Arts 10–13.
7 Ibid Art 11.
8 Ibid Art 12.
9 Annex I and Annex II to Council Regulation 2603/69. See Regulation 2603/69 Art 10(1), first indent, concerning Annex I, and Art 10(1), second indent, concerning Annex II (as substituted by Council Regulation 3918/91 Art 1). Both Annexes list the CN headings (previously CTT) and descriptions of the products concerned. Annex I also lists the Member States applying the restriction. Annex II was introduced by Council Regulation 2918/91, and concerns products covered by international commitments entered into by the Community or all its Member States. Products have been removed from Annex I upon their liberalization in the Member States which previously imposed restrictions. See Council Regulation 234/71 of 1 February 1971, OJ 4.2.71 L28/2; Council Regulation 2812/71 of 12 October 1971, OJ 14.10.71 L231/4; Council Regulation 1275/75 of 20 May 1975, OJ 22.5.75 L131/1; Council Regulation 1170/76 of 17 May 1976, OJ 20.5.76 L131/5.

shall be free, that is, they are not to be subject to any quantitative restriction, with the exception of those restrictions which are applied in conformity with the Regulation.[10] This policy is motivated, inter alia, by the consideration that exports are almost completely liberalized in all the Member States.[11] However, quantitative restrictions on grounds of public morality, public policy and public security, the protection of health and life of humans, animals or plants, national cultural treasures and of industrial and commercial property remain the domain of the Member States.[12]

Certain sensitive categories of exports thus are not covered by the common policy.[13] More recently, restrictions flowing from the Common Foreign and Security Policy (and previously European Political Co-operation) and other forms of international co-operation, as well as restrictions formerly under the national public policy exception, have been brought under the Regulation.[14]

Very few quantitative restrictions apply to non-agricultural exports from the Member States. However, Regulation 2603/69, as amended by Regulation 3918/91, provides for certain restrictions.[15]

Until 31 December 1992 the principle of the freedom of export did not apply to two categories of products.[16] The first category consisted of the products listed in Annex I of the Regulation which were subject to quantitative

---

10 Council Regulation 2603/69 Art 1. On the deletion of certain products from the Annexes to Council Regulation 2603/69 establishing common rules for exports, thus liberalizing the export of such products, see Council Regulation 234/71 of 1 February 1971, OJ 4.2.71 L28/2; Council Regulation 2182/71 of 12 October 1971, OJ 14.10.71 L231/4; Council Regulation 1275/75 of 20 May 1975, OJ 22.5.75 L131/1; and Council Regulation 1170/76, OJ 20.5.76 L131/5.

11 Council Regulation 2603/69, preamble, third recital. Paradoxically, however, progress towards a common export policy is lagging behind even the modest gains made concerning imports. See Robert Pouvoyeur and Paul Roosens, 'Reflexions autour du caractère commun de la politique commerciale de l'exportation de la CEE' (1986) 293 *Revue du Marché Commun* 26, and the section on export aids below.

12 Council Regulation 2603/69 Art 11.

13 As a result restrictions on exports warranted by Regulation 2603/69 often apply to agricultural goods, low-tech industrial goods, base metals and scrap, and other products seemingly ill-qualified for such treatment other than by domestic political expediency in one or more Member States. The most important category of goods excepted from the principle of freedom of exports in Council Regulation 2603/69 is that of crude oil and petroleum oils/carbon fuel, although it seems that these could also be covered by the public policy/public security exception of Art 11. See Council Regulation 1934/82 Art 1; Council Regulation 3918/91 Art 2, Annex II. See fn 14, p 167 below on the emergency response measures of the International Energy Agency and the EC.

14 See for example Council Regulation 2219/89, OJ 22.7.1989 L211/4; Council Regulation 3911/92 OJ L395/1; and Council Directive 92/52 OJ 1.7.92 L179/129.

15 Regulation 2603/69 Art 10 (as substituted, with the Annex, by Regulation 1934/82 Arts 1, 2). Both Regulation 3918/91 and 1934/82 dealt primarily with the problem of restricting oil imports in order to secure supply in times of energy crises. Regulation 1934/81 moreover aimed to protect the Greek oil processing industries which were dependent on differences between domestic and world market oil prices.

Article 1 of Council Regulation 1934/82 introduced the exclusion of exports of crude oil and certain oil products directly in Art 10, rather than in the Annex. The principle of freedom of exports did not apply to these products for all the Member States. This was the result of the refusal of France to join the International Energy Agency, which barred the Community from becoming a member, or applying EIA policies directly, obliging it to declare the Member States free to meet their international commitments. See E L M Volker's note on Case 174/84 *Bulk Oil (Zug) AG v Sun International Ltd and Sun Trading Co* (1987) 24 CMLRev 99 at 108–109.

16 Council Regulation 2603/69 Art 10(1), as substituted by Council Regulation 3918/91 Art 1.

restrictions by certain specified Member States.[17] The second category consisted of exports which were then restricted by the Member States pursuant to a decision taken in European Political Co-operation.[18] The export of both of these categories of products was to be free after 31 December 1992; after this date the maintenance by Member States of quantitative restrictions would be incompatible with the single market, which entailed the abolition of goods controls at the Community's internal frontiers.[19]

Member States, acting independently, may adopt quantitative restrictions on exports on grounds of public morality, public policy or public security; the protection of health and life of humans, animals or plants; the protection of national treasures possessing artistic, historic or archaeological value; or the protection of industrial property or commercial property.[20]

The regulation on common rules for exports operates without prejudice to the operation either of the instruments establishing the common organization of agricultural markets or of the special instruments adopted under EC Art 235 for processed agricultural products.[1] However, the provisions relating to protective measures[2] do not apply to those agricultural products in respect of which Community rules on trade with third countries make provisions for the application of quantitative export restrictions.[3] Similarly, the provisions relating to the supply of statistical data by Member States to the Commission and to surveillance by Member States of exports[4] do not apply to those products in respect of which Community rules on trade with third countries require the production of a licence or other export document.[5]

As under other secondary legislation governing the common commercial policy, an advisory committee of representatives from Member States under the chairmanship of a representative of the Commission is set up to carry out the administrative work arising from the operation of the regulation.[6] The work of the committee is particularly concerned with consultation procedures.[7] Consultation may be held at any time, either at the request of a Member State or on the

---

17 Council Regulation 2603/69 Art 10(1), first indent, Annex (as substituted by Council Regulation 3918/91 Art 1, Annex).

18 Council Regulation 2603/69 Art 10(1), second indent, as substituted by Council Regulation 3918/91 Art 1. For example, exports of certain chemical products were subject to the issue by the competent authorities in Member States of a prior export authorization or to equivalent measures: Council Regulation 428/89 Art 1, OJ 22.2.89 L50/1. However, if there was reason to believe that the products under consideration would be used for the development or production of chemical weapons, or that there was a risk of their being delivered directly or indirectly to belligerent countries or to areas of serious international tension, no authorization was to be issued or exportation was to be prohibited by equivalent measures: ibid Art 2. Council Regulation 428/89 was repealed by Council Regulation 3381/94 Art 23, OJ 31.12.94 L367/71. Art 30(5) of the Single European Act determined that the external policies of the European Community and the policies agreed in European Political Co-operation must be consistent. See also the Joint Action on transparency in nuclear-related export controls, OJ 12.5.97 L120/1.

19 Council Regulation 3918/91 preamble, seventh indent.

20 Ibid Art 11.

1 Ibid Art 12(1). The Regulation is intended to operate by way of complement to those instruments: ibid.

2 Ie ibid Arts 6, 7.

3 Ibid Art 12(2).

4 See Council Regulation 2603/69 Art 5.

5 Council Regulation 2603/69 Art 12(2).

6 Ibid Art 4(1). The chairman convenes committee meetings, and provides all the Member States with all relevant information: Art 4(2).

7 Ibid Arts 3,4,9.

Commission's initiative.[8] Consultation procedures may take place following notification to the Commission by a Member State of unusual developments on the market which it considers require protective measures.[9] It is mandatory that consultation procedures take place:

(1) before the introduction of any information procedure[10] or protective measure;[11] and
(2) to examine the effect of any such protective measures[12] or any interim protective measures taken by a Member State,[13] and ascertain whether the conditions for their application are still satisfied.[14]

Before the introduction of any information procedure or protective measures, consultation must in particular cover:

(1) terms and conditions of export, export trends and the various aspects of the economic and commercial situation as regards the product in question; and
(2) the measures, if any, to be adopted.[15]

Such measures may be taken either by the Commission[16] or by the Council.[17]

In order to prevent a critical situation arising on account of a shortage of essential products or to remedy such a situation, and where Community interests call for immediate intervention, the Commission, acting at the re-

8 Ibid Art 3(1).
9 See ibid Arts 2, 3(2). The consultation must take place within four working days: Art 3(2).
10 Ie under ibid Art 5. For the purposes of assessing the economic and commercial situation as regards a particular product the Commission may request Member States to exercise surveillance over exports of the product and to supply statistical data on market trends in the product: see Art 5. See Commission Decision of 22 March 1979 relating to the monitoring within the Community of exports of untreated calf and bovine hides, OJ 5.4.1979 L85/44. This product was included in the categories of products in respect of which the principle of the freedom of export did not apply until 31 December 1992: Council Regulation 2603/69 Art 10(1), first indent, as substituted by Council Regulation 3918/91 Art 1(1).
11 Ibid Art 3(2). Regulation 2603/69 does not however require Member States to provide information or give prior notice of measures concerning products covered by Art 10 (as substituted most recently by Council Regulation 3918/91): Case 174/84 *Bulk Oil (Zug) AG v Sun International Ltd and Sun Oil Trading Co* [1986] ECR 559, paragraph 55. In the latter case the European Court nevertheless found that such an obligation existed even before the end of the transitional period by virtue of the combined provisions of the Council Decisions of 9 October 1961 and 25 September 1962 and Council Decision 69/494. It held however that a Member State which fails to give prior notice, delays doing so or fails to do so in an adequate manner fails to fulfil its Community obligations. It should be noted that such failure does not create individual rights which a national court must protect: ibid, paras 61, 62.
12 Ie any measure taken under ibid Art 6 or Art 7.
13 A Member State could take unilateral interim protective measures where it considered that there existed in its territory a situation such as that described in ibid Art 6(1), Art 8(1). It had first to hear the opinion expressed in the committee or, where urgency precluded such a procedure, to notify the Commission, which had to inform the other Member States: Art 8(2). Art 8 was to apply until the end of 1972, by which time the Council was to decide on adjustments to be made to it: Art 8(4). The application of Art 8 was extended from 31 December 1972 to 31 December 1984 by EC Council Regulation 2747/72 but it then lapsed.
14 Council Regulation 2603/69 Art 9(1). Measures under Art 6 or Art 7 may be revoked or amended: see Art 9(2).
15 Ibid Art 4(3)(a),(b).
16 Under ibid Art 6.
17 Under ibid Art 7.

quest of a Member State[18] or on its own initiative, may make the export of a product subject to the production of an export authorization.[19] Where intervention by the Commission is requested by a Member State, the Commission must take a decision within a maximum of five working days of receipt of the request; if it refuses to give effect to the request, it must communicate its decision to the Council, which, acting by a qualified majority, may decide differently.[20] The Commission must inform the Council and the Member States of the measures, which take effect immediately.[1] The measures may be limited to exports to certain countries or exports from certain Member States but shall not affect products already on their way to the Community frontier.[2] Any Member State may refer the measures taken to the Council, which, again acting by qualified majority, may decide differently.[3] Within 12 working days of a measure taking effect the Commission must propose to the Council appropriate measures.[4] If the Council takes no action within six weeks of the Commission's original measure taking effect, that measure is deemed to be revoked.[5]

Where the interests of the Community so require, the Council may adopt measures

(1) to prevent a critical situation arising owing to a shortage of essential products or to remedy such a situation; or
(2) to allow international undertakings entered into by the Community on exports or all the Member States to be fulfilled, in particular those relating to trade in primary products.[6]

These measures may be limited to exports to certain countries or to exports from certain regions of the Community, but they must not affect products already on their way to the Community frontier.[7] When quantitative restrictions on exports are introduced, account is to be taken, in particular, of the previous normal volume of exports and the need to avoid jeopardizing achievement of the aim pursued in introducing the restrictions.[8]

While such measures are in operation, consultations within the Advisory Committee shall take place, either at the request of a Member State or on the initiative of the Commission. The purpose of the consultations is (1) to examine the effects of the measures and (2) to ascertain whether the conditions for their application are still satisfied.[9] Where the Commission considers that any measure which it has taken or which has been taken by the Council should be re-

---

18 See ibid Art 6(4).
19 Ibid Art 6(1).
20 Ibid Art 6(4).
 1 Ibid Art 6(2).
 2 Ibid Art 6(3).
 3 Ibid Art 6(5).
 4 The measures to be proposed are provided in Art 7, as to which see below.
 5 Ibid Art 6(6).
 6 Ibid Art 7(1). As to examples of temporary restrictions for the first reason, see Council Regulation 3951/88, OJ 30.12.1987 L371/6, extended by Council Regulation 4249/88, OJ 31.12.88 L373/53 (non-ferrous metal waste and scrap).
 7 Ibid Art 7(2).
 8 See ibid Art 7(3).
 9 Ibid Art 9(1).

voked or amended, it must proceed in one of two ways.[10] Where the Council has taken no decision on a measure taken by the Commission, the Commission shall amend or revoke the measure forthwith and immediately deliver a report to the Council.[11] In all other cases, the Commission shall propose to the Council that the measures adopted by the Council be revoked or amended, and the Council shall act by a qualified majority.[12]

Petro-chemical products

With regard to certain petro-chemical products,[13] Member States are authorized to implement, without prejudice to rules adopted by the Community in this field, the emergency sharing system introducing an allocation obligation vis-à-vis third countries provided for in international commitments previously entered into.[14] This restriction on exports applies until the Council adopts appropriate measures pursuant to international commitments entered into by the Community or all its Member States.[15] Member States are required to inform the Commission of measures they intend to adopt, and the Commission must communicate the adopted measures to the Council and the other Member States.[16]

The scope of the restriction on the export of crude oil and the question of the Community's exclusive competence in the field of foreign trade relations were considered by the European Court of Justice in Case 174/84 *Bulk Oil (Zug) AG v Sun International Ltd*.[17] This case was a reference under EEC Art

---

10 Ibid Art 9(2).
11 Ibid Art 9(2)(a).
12 Ibid Art 9(2)(b).
13 See Council Regulation 2603/69 Annex II, as substituted by Council Regulation 3918/91 Art 1(2), Annex II.
14 Regulation 2309/69 Art 10(2), first paragraph, Annex II, as substituted by Council Regulation 3918/91 Art 1, Annex II. This is a reference to the emergency response measures agreed upon by the International Energy Agency (of which all EC Member States, with the exception of France, are members) involving minimum stock obligations, and in time of crisis demand restraint, allocation and rationing powers. Its central feature is the emergency oil-sharing system set out in an emergency management manual adopted by the EIA in 1976 as a collective response against short-term shortages among members. The system is triggered by a fall in supply of at least 7 per cent in one or more Member States, and involves demand restraint, the use of emergency reserves and the joint re-allocation of available supplies. See J C Woodlife 'A New Dimension to International Co-operation: The OECD's International Energy Agreement' (1975) 24 ICLQ 525. IEA emergency measures (co-ordinated with France) were activated at the start of the Gulf War in January 1991.

A parallel EC system consists of Council Directive 68/414 of 20 December 1968, OJ 23.12.68 L308/14, amended by Directive 72/425 (OJ 28.12.72 L291/154), imposing an obligation on Member States to maintain minimum stocks of crude oil and/or petroleum products; Council Directive 73/238, OJ 16.9.73 L228/1 on measures to mitigate the effects of difficulties in the supply of crude oil and petroleum products; Council Decision 77/186, OJ 5.3.77 L61/23 on the exporting of crude oil and petroleum products from one Member State to another in the event of supply difficulties; Council Decision 77/706, OJ 16.11.77 L292/9 on the setting of a Community target for the reduction of primary sources of energy in the event of difficulties in the supply of crude oil and petroleum products. A sharing system for the quantities of petroleum products saved as a result of the joint reduction of consumption is provided for in Decision 77/706, Art 1, sub-paragraph 3.
15 Regulation 2603/69 Art 10(2), first paragraph, as substituted by Council Regulation 3918/91 Art 1.
16 Council Regulation 2603/69 Art 10(2), second paragraph, as substituted by Council Regulation 3918/91 Art 1.
17 [1986] ECR 559.

177 for a preliminary ruling concerning the compatibility with Community law of the policy[18] applied by the UK in 1981 of quantitative restrictions on the export of crude oil to non-member countries, in particular Israel. Sun agreed to sell Bulk substantial quantities of British North Sea crude oil. Consistent with government policy, the contract contained a destination clause prohibiting buyers from exporting the oil to a destination other than Member States and certain other countries. After Sun became aware that Bulk intended to deliver the oil to Israel, British Petroleum, the supplier of the oil, refused to put the oil on board the ship denominated by Bulk, and Sun did likewise. Bulk made a claim against Sun. The dispute was referred to arbitration, and it was subsequently appealed to the High Court and then referred by order of the Commercial Court of the Queen's Bench Division to the European Court of Justice.

The European Court of Justice held, first, that the Agreement of 20 May 1975 between the EEC and Israel did not expressly prohibit quantitative restrictions on exports or measures having equivalent effect.[19] Consequently, it did not deprive Member States of their power to introduce such restrictions.[20] Secondly, the Court held that, since full responsibility for commercial policy was transferred to the Community by EEC Art 113(1), measures of commercial policy of a national character were permissible after the end of the transitional period only by virtue of specific authorization by the Community.[1] Art 10 of Regulation 2603/69 and the Annex to that Regulation constitute such a specific authorization in respect of exports of oil to non-member countries, without making any distinction between previously existing quantitative restrictions and those which were subsequently introduced.[2] Consequently, the Council could, without contravening EEC Art 113, provisionally exclude a product such as oil from the common rules on exports to non-member countries, in view in particular of the international commitments entered into by certain Member States and taking into account the particular characteristics of that product, which is of vital importance for the economy of a state and for the functioning of its institutions and public services.[3] As a result, Regulation 2603/69 does not prohibit a Member State from imposing new quantitative restrictions or measures having equivalent effect on its exports of oil to non-member countries.[4]

---

18 This policy was not incorporated in legislation or any other legal measure but made public on several occasions by government statements: [1986] ECR 559 at 578.
19 Ibid paragraph 15. In this respect the Court followed Case 225/78 *Procureur de la République v Bouhelier* [1979] ECR 3151.
20 Ibid paragraph 17.
 1 Ibid paragraph 31. On this point the Court followed its judgment in Case 41/76 *Donckerwolke v Procureur de la République* [1976] ECR 1921.
 2 Ibid paragraph 33.
 3 Ibid paragraph 36.
 4 [1986] ECR 559 at 588, [1986] 2 CMLR 732 at 761, paragraph 37. But compare the criticism of the Court's broad interpretation of Art 10 of Regulation 2603/69 and consequent broadening of the basis for EC Art 115 measures by Volker (1987) 24 CMLR 99. Note moreover that Regulation 1934/82 Art 1, closed the 'specific authorization gap' for exports by introducing a clear distinction between the products in the Annex, which were excluded from the principle of freedom of export only for those Member States likewise listed in the Annex, and crude and petroleum oils, which were excluded for all the Member States.

SPECIFIC MEASURES

Contaminated foodstuffs and feedingstuffs

The Council has adopted a measure on the special conditions for exporting foodstuffs and feedingstuffs following a nuclear accident or any other case of radiological emergency.[5] Foodstuffs[6] and feedingstuffs[7] in which the level of radioactive contamination exceeds the relevant maximum permitted levels laid down in Arts 2 and 3 of Regulation (Euratom) 3954/87[8] may not be exported.[9] Member States must carry out checks to ensure that the maximum permitted levels are observed.[10] They are required to communicate to the Commission the fullest information on the application of the measure, and in particular on any cases where the maximum permitted levels have been exceeded. The Commission must forward this information to the other Member States.[11]

Cultural goods

Specific measures also apply to the export of cultural goods.[12] The export of cultural goods outside the customs territory of the Community is subject to the presentation of an export licence.[13] A licence is not required for certain categories of goods.[14] A licence may be refused where the cultural goods in question are covered by legislation protecting national treasures of artistic, historical or archaeological value in the Member State concerned.[15] Direct export from the customs territory of the Community of national treasures having artistic, historical or archaeological value which are not cultural goods within the meaning of the Regulation is subject to the national law of the Member State of export.[16] Of special interest is the fact that for implementation purposes, the provisions of EC Council Regulation 1468/81[17] on mutual assistance between the administrative authorities of the Member States and co-operation between the latter and the Commission to ensure the correct application of the law of customs or

---

5 Council Regulation 2219/89, OJ 22.7.1989 L211/4. With respect to the grant of refunds on exports of agricultural products to third countries, Member States have the power to set maximum radioactivity levels for the purpose of determining whether agricultural products intended for such export are 'products of sound and merchantable quality': see Case C-371/92 *Greece v Ellinika Dimitriaka AE* [1994] ECR I-2391.

6 'Foodstuffs' are defined as 'products which are intended for human consumption either immediately or after processing': ibid Art 1(2).

7 'Feedingstuffs' are defined as 'products which are intended only for animal nutrition': ibid Art 1(2).

8 OJ 30.12.1987 L371/11, as amended.

9 Ibid Art 2.

10 Ibid Art 3.

11 Ibid Art 4.

12 Council Regulation 3911/92, OJ 31.12.92 L395/1, Annex I of which was amended by Council Regulation 3911/92. Council Regulation 3911/92 was implemented by Commission Regulation 752/93, OJ 31.3.93 L77/24. Regulation 752/93 sets out the form and use of the standardized export licence required for the export of cultural goods.

13 Ibid Art 2(1). As to the list of cultural goods, see ibid Annex, as amended by Council Regulation 2469/96, OJ 24.12.96 L335/9. This is without prejudice to the power of the Member States under EC Art 36: ibid Art 1.

14 See ibid Art 2(2), second sub-paragraph.

15 Ibid Art 2(2), third sub-paragraph.

16 Ibid Art 2(4).

17 OJ 2.6.81 L144/1.

agricultural matters, will be applied *mutatis mutandis* (in particular the provisions regarding the confidentiality of information).[18]

Dangerous chemicals

Likewise, measures have been adopted regarding the export of dangerous chemicals.[19] The Community has established a common system of notification and information for imports from and exports to third countries in respect of certain banned or severely restricted chemicals.[20] In respect of exports, when a chemical subject to notification is due to be exported from the Community to a third country for the first time following the date as of which it first becomes subject to the Regulation, the exporter must provide the designated authority of the Member State in which the exporter is established with certain information to enable the authority to effect a notification.[1] These requirements may be waived where the export of a chemical relates to an emergency situation in which any delay may endanger public health or the environment in the importing country.[2] The designated authority must notify the Commission, which must inform other Member States and the International Register of Potentially Toxic Chemicals (IRPTC).[3] The Commission assigns to each notification a reference number, which is communicated to the authorities of the Member States and published,[4] and which must accompany subsequent exports of the chemical concerned.[5] Dangerous chemicals intended for export are subject to specific packaging and labelling requirements.[6]

Dual-use goods

An integrated system for the control of exports of dual-use goods[7] was established as from 1 July 1995.[8] Depending on the good in question, an authoriza-

---

18 Ibid Art 6.
19 See Council Regulation 2455/92 OJ 29.8.92 1992 L251/13, as amended. Prior export authorization was previously required for certain chemicals pursuant to Council Regulation 428/89, OJ 22.2.89 L50/1, but this latter regulation was repealed by Council Regulation 3381/84, OJ 31.12.94 L367/71 on dual-use goods.
20 For further discussion, see Chapter 8 on Imports in this book.
 1 Council Regulation 2455/92 Art 4(1), first sub-paragraph, OJ 29.8.92 L251/13. The required information is specified in Annex III. As to confidentiality of data, see Art 4(5).
 2 Ibid Art 4(1), second sub-paragraph.
 3 Ibid Art 4(1), third sub-paragraph.
 4 Ibid Art 4(1), fourth sub-paragraph.
 5 Ibid Art 4(3). See also Art 4(4).
 6 See ibid Art 7.
 7 'Dual-use goods' refers to goods which can be used for both civil and military purposes: Council Regulation 3381/94 Art 2, OJ 31.12.94 L367/1.
 8 Council Regulation 3381/94 setting up a Community regime for the control of dual-use goods (OJ 31.12.94 L367/1), as amended by Council Regulation 837/95 (OJ 21.4.95 L90/1) and Council Decision 96/173 (OJ 1.3.96 L52/1), together with Council Decision 94/942/CFSP on the joint action adopted by the Council on the basis of Article J.3 of the Treaty on European Union concerning the control of exports of dual-use goods (OJ 31.12.94 L367/9), as amended by Council Decision 95/127/CFSP (OJ 21.4.95 L90/2), Council Decision 95/128/CFSP (OJ 21.4.95 L90/3), Council Decision 97/100/CFSP, OJ 4.2.97 L34/1; Council Decision 97/419/CFSP, OJ 7.7.97 L178/1; Council Decision 97/633/CFSP, OJ 29.9.97; and Council Decision 98/106/CFSP, OJ 6.2.98 L32/1. TEU Article J.8(2) provides that the Council shall take the decisions necessary for defining and implementing the common foreign and security policy on the basis of the general guidelines adopted by the European Council. It shall ensure the unity, consistency and effectiveness of action by the Union. Rules restricting exports of

tion must or may be required for export.[9] A Member State may prohibit or make subject to authorization the export of other dual-use goods;[10] it is required to notify the other Member States and the Commission of any such measures.[11] Though in principle an individual authorization is required for each export, Member States may apply simplified formalities.[12] In particular, they may issue a general authorization in respect of a type or category of dual-use goods[13] or a global authorization to a specific exporter in respect of a type or category of dual-use goods which may be valid for exports to one or more specified countries.[14] Export authorization may be subject however to the requirement of a statement of end-use and other conditions concerning the end-use and/or re-export of the goods.[15] In deciding whether or not to grant authorization, the competent authorities shall take into account common guidelines.[16] In exceptional circumstances, where a Member State considers that an

dual-use goods to third countries fall within the scope of EC Art 113 and in such matters the EC has exclusive competence, which excludes the competence of the Member States save where the Community grants them specific authorization: C-83/94 *Leifer, Krauskopf and Holzer* [1995] ECR I-3231. Taken together, the Joint Action and the Council Regulation are intended to help establish a coherent Community system for the control of exports of dual-use goods. The former establishes lists of goods, guidelines and destinations, whereas the latter sets up a system of licences and consultative procedures. See also Emiliou 'Strategic Export Controls, National Security and the Common Commercial Policy' (1996) 1 *European Foreign Affairs Review* 55; Wolfgang and Hoelscher 'The New European Export Controls in an International Perspective', (1996) 20 *World Competition* 79.

9 Council Regulation 3381/94 Art 3(1), (2), OJ 31.12.94 L367/1, as amended by Council Regulation 837/95, OJ 21.4.95 L90/1. The goods for which authorization is required are listed in Council Decision 94/942/CFSP Annex I (OJ 31.12.94 L367/8), as amended by Council Decision 96/173/CFSP (OJ 1.3.96 L52/1), and Council Decision 96/173 (OJ 1.3.96 L52/1). In addition, an authorization is required for the export of other dual-use goods if the exporter has been informed by its authorities that the goods in question are or may be intended, in their entirety or in part, for use in connection with the development, production, handling, operation, maintenance, storage, detection, identification or dissemination of chemical, biological or nuclear weapons or the development, production, maintenance or storage of missiles capable of delivering such weapons, as covered by the corresponding non-proliferation arrangements: ibid Art 4(1).

10 Council Regulation 3381/94 Art 5(1) and Annex IV, OJ 31.12.94 L367/1, as amended in particular by Council Decision 96/173, OJ 1.3.96 L52/1. This includes measures existing at the time of entry into force of the Regulation as well as subsequent measures: ibid Art 5(2).

11 Council Regulation 3381/94 Art 5(3), OJ 31.12.94 L367/1. The European Court of Justice has held that EC Art 113 and in particular Art 11 of Council Regulation 2603/69 establishing common rules for exports do not prevent national provisions under which the export of a product capable of being used for military purposes is subject to the issue of a licence on the ground that this is necessary in order to avoid the risk of a serious disturbance to its foreign relations which may affect the public security of the Member State within the meaning of Art 11 of the Regulation: Case C-70/94 *Fritz Werner Industrie-Ausrüstungen GmbH v Germany* [1995] ECR I-3189. Compare Case C-367/89 *Richardt and 'Les Accessoires Scientifiques'* [1991] ECR I-4621. See also Govaere and Eeckhout 'On Dual Use Goods and Dualist Case Law: The *Aimé Richardt* Judgment on Export Controls' (1992) 29 CMLR 941. Cf also Case C-62/88 *Greece v Council* [1990] ECR I-1527; Case 222/84 *Johnston v Chief Constable of the Royal Ulster Constabulary* [1986] ECR 1651; Case C-120/94 *Commission v Greece* [1996] ECR I-1513.

12 Council Regulation 3381/91 Art 6(1), OJ 31.12.94 L367/1. The export authorization is valid throughout the Community: ibid Art 6(3). Compare Case C-367/89 *Richardt and 'Les Accessoires Scientifiques'* [1991] ECR I-4621.

13 In accordance with Annex II to Decision 94/942/CFSP (OJ 31.12.94 L367/8, as amended): ibid art 6(1)(a).

14 Ibid Art 6(1)(b).

15 Council Regulation 3381/94 Art 6(2), OJ 31.12.94 L367/1.

16 Council Regulation 3381/91 Art 8, OJ 31.12.94 L367/1. The common guidelines are set out in Council Decision 94/942/CFSP, Annex III, OJ 31.12.94 L367/1.

exportation would be contrary to its essential foreign policy or security interests or to the fulfilment of its international obligations or commitments, it may prevent the dual-use goods from leaving the Community via its territory even though the export was duly authorized.[17] A Co-ordinating Group chaired by a representative of the Commission and composed of a representative from each Member State has been established to deal with questions regarding the application of the control system and measures to be taken by Member States to inform exporters of their obligations.[18] This regime does not however resolve all potential conflicts between the exclusive competence of the EC in matters of commercial policy under EC Art 113 and the powers of the Member States on grounds of public security under EC Art 223, in particular because Art 1 of the Export Regulation 2603/69 has been held to have direct effect.[19] In addition, conflicts may arise between the exercise of powers under Community rules and those under the CFSP, for example. TEU Article L places the CFSP outside the jurisdiction of the European Court of Justice.

Other measures

Other measures have been adopted in respect of infant formulae and follow-on formulae intended for export to third countries.[20] Such are indeed the type of exports where restrictions are justified other than by protectionist impulses, as was previously the case for all products covered by the Annex to Regulation 2603/69, later Annex I.

EXPORT AIDS

The system of aids for exports is a sensitive area in which the Common Commercial Policy is incomplete.[1] Export aids, such as export refunds, have of

---

17 Council Regulation 3381/94 Art 10(4), first paragraph, OJ 31.12.94 L367/1. See Joined Cases C-70/94 and C-83/94 *Fritz Werner Industrie-Ausrustungen GmbH v Germany; Leifer, Krauskopf and Holzer* [1995] ECR I-3189. Whether there is a threat to public security is a matter for the national court, and an obligation on the exporter to prove that the goods will be used exclusively for civil purposes or a refusal to issue a licence if the goods can objectively be used for military purposes can be consistent with the principle of proportionality: Case C-83/94 *Leifer, Krauskopf and Holzer* [1995] ECR I-3231.
18 Council Regulation 3188/94 Art 16, OJ 31.12.94 L367/1.
19 Case C-83/94 *Leifer, Krauskopf and Holzer* [1995] ECR I-3231.
20 Council Directive 92/52 of 18 June 1992, OJ 1.7.92 L179/129. Referring to Council Directive 89/389 of 3 May 1989, OJ 30.6.89 L186/27 on the approximation of laws of the Member States relating to foodstuffs for particular nutritional uses in Commission Directive 91/321, OJ 4.7.91 L175/35, Council Directive 92/52 concerns infant formulae and follow-on formulae as defined in Commission Directive 91/321, intended for export to third countries (Art 1). Directive 92/52 aims to ensure that such exports from the Community bear proper labelling regarding their nutritional value (Art 3(1) and 3(3)) and comply with the standards set out in Arts 3, 4, 5, 6 and 7(2) to (6) of Commission Directive 91/321 (Art 3(3)(a) and 3(4)) or the relevant world standards established by the Codex Alimentarius (Art 3(3)(a)) and Council Directive 89/396 of 14 June 1989, OJ 30.6.89 L186/21 (last amended by Directive 91/238, OJ 27.4.91 L107/50) (Art 3(3)(c)). Exports of products which do not comply with Directive 92/52 shall be prohibited by the Member States from 1 June 1994 (Art 4).
 1 See Robert Pourvoyeur and Paul Roosens 'Reflexions autour du caractere commun de la politique commerciale de l'exportation de la CEE' (1986) 293 *Revue du Marché Commun* 26.

course long been part of the Common Agricultural Policy.[2] More generally, however, Art 112 of the EEC Treaty provided that, before the end of the transitional period, Member States were progressively to harmonize the systems whereby they grant aid for exports to third countries, to the extent necessary to ensure that competition between undertakings of the Community is not distorted.[3] On a proposal from the Commission, the Council, acting unanimously, was to issue any necessary directives for this purpose.[4] These provisions did not apply to such drawback of customs duties or charges having equivalent effect, nor to the repayment of indirect taxation, including turnover taxes, export duties and other indirect taxes, as were allowed when goods were exported to a third country in so far as such drawback or repayment did not exceed the amount imposed, directly or indirectly, on the products exported.[5] In so far as Art 112 established uniform principles in export policy, it remains relevant for the purpose of measures adopted under Art 113.[6]

In 1962 the Council adopted a programme of action in matters of Common Commercial Policy.[7] Part B of this programme[8] sets out three principles to be observed in achieving the objective of harmonization of the systems of aid granted by Member States for exports to third countries:

(1) obligations undertaken by Member States within the framework of other international organizations, in particular the General Agreement on Tariffs and Trade, were to remain in force;[9]
(2) systems of aid for exports to third countries must be harmonized to the extent necessary to ensure that competition between undertakings of the Community was not distorted;[10]
(3) drawback of customs duties or repayment of indirect taxation should be excluded from the ambit of the provisions for harmonization.[11]

Recognising that the methods of granting export aids are numerous,[12] the procedure in the programme for action envisaged the compilation during the transitional period of a schedule of the systems of aids for exports in force in the Member States on the basis of which all measures of aid, whether direct or indirect, granted by Member States would be harmonized in accordance with

---

2 See generally Chapter 16 in this book on Agricultural Products. As to export aids generally in the agricultural sector, see S Dumont *Subventions aux exportations agricoles: Contentieux Etats-Unis/CEE* (Presses Universitaires de France, Paris, 1994). With regard to ECSC products, see 'State Aid C57/97 (ex NN 116/96) Spain (97/C329/03), Commission communication pursuant to Art 6(5) of Decision 2496/ECSC of 18 December 1996', OJ 31.10.97 C32974.
3 EEC Treaty Art 112(1), first paragraph. As to the transitional period, see EEC Art 8.
4 Ibid Art 112(1), second paragraph.
5 Ibid Art 112(2).
6 See also Chapters 5 and 7 in this book.
7 See Council Decision of 25 September 1962, Annex, OJ 1962 2353/62.
8 Ibid Part B.
9 See the EEC Treaty Art 112(1), first paragraph.
10 Ibid.
11 See ibid Art 112(2). While a refund of customs duties or indirect taxes is of benefit to exporters, it is generally considered permissible and is sanctioned by the General Agreement on Tariffs and Trade (Geneva, 30 October 1947; 55 UNTS 194; Cmd 7258) Art VI.
12 They may include, among other things, direct government subsidies to exporters, government insurance at a low premium of commercial or political risks, for example against changing foreign exchange rates, and the granting by the state of credits for exports on favourable conditions.

Art 112.[13] The Commission was able to prepare a schedule of measures of aid, but subsequent action upon it was very limited.[14]

Recently, however, the Commission has submitted a proposal for a Council regulation on the implementation by the Commission of actions to promote exports to Japan. Based on EC Art 113, it is intended to formalise pre-existing initiatives aimed at reducing the persistent trade imbalance, in particular by means of seminars and networking, participation in fairs and missions, training programmes and other activities designed to maximimse the ability of European exporters to enter the Japanese market. The proposal provides for financial resources to be approved annually as well as for the establishment of an advisory committee These activities are intended to be complementary to Member State activities.[15]

EXPORT CREDITS

Export credit is of great importance in international trade and is a key instrument of commercial policy.[16] Credit facilities extended to a buyer in a third country may however have a significant influence on competition at the international level. Similarly, preferential credit facilities offered to an exporter by a Member State may be in the nature of a state aid, giving rise to distortions in competition between Community undertakings in markets in third countries. For example, in Joined Cases 6 and 11/69 *EC Commission v France*[17] the European Court of Justice declared that France had failed to fulfil its obligations under the EEC Treaty by the maintenance of the preferential discount rate applied by the Banque de France for short and long-term credits given for exports to Member States.[18]

Rules regarding export credit may also have economic effects even within a single Member State. For example, in Case C-63/89 *Les Assurances du crédit and Compagnie Belge d'assurance crédit SA v Council and Commission*[19] private export credit insurance providers sought damages for harm resulting from an alleged distortion of competition as a result of the exclusion of public export credit operations from the scope of Council Directive 73/239,[20] continued by Council Directive 87/343,[1] which co-ordinated the financial guarantees required of insurance companies. The alleged damages amounted to the financial cost of setting up reserves not obligatory for public export credit operations. The Court of Justice held however that the exclusion was not discriminatory, because the protection of insured persons normally provided by the directives was in this instance provided by the State itself. It should be noted however that the

13 EEC Council Decision of 25 September 1962, Annex, Part B.
14 A directive was adopted regulating subsidies for the shipbuilding industry: see Council Council Directive 69/262, OJ 15.8.69, as subsequently replaced, amended and repealed.
15 Commission of the European Communities, Proposal for a Council Regulation on the implementation by the European Commission of actions to promote exports to Japan (COM(95)188 final, Brussels 25 May 1995).
16 Council Directive 70/509 preamble, third indent, OJ 23.11.70 L154/1; Council Directive 70/510, preamble, third indent, OJ 21.11.70 L254/26; Council Directive 71/86 OJ 13.2.71 L36/14.
17 [1969] ECR 523.
18 See also Case 57/86 *Greece v Commission* [1988] ECR 2855.
19 [1991] ECR I-1799.
20 OJ 16.8.73 L228/3, as amended.
 1 OJ 4.7.87 L185/72.

exclusion applies only to public operations, irrespective of the legal status of the undertaking effecting such operations, and not to public insurance undertakings or undertakings acting on behalf of the State, which remain subject to the requirements laid down in the directive in respect of operations effected for their own account and not guaranteed by the State.[2]

The insurance of the risk of extending such export credit facilities is also significant. In contrast to the harmonization of export aids, where relatively little action has been taken, the Community has made limited progress under EEC Art 113 with respect to export credits and export credit insurance. In 1960 a Policy Co-ordination Group was set up to co-ordinate credit insurance policies, guarantees and financial credits. It consists of a limited number of representatives from each Member State and from the Commission holding positions of responsibility relating specifically to export credit insurance and credit policy towards developing countries. Secretarial services for the Group are provided by the Secretariat of the Council.[3]

The co-ordination of credit insurance policies, guarantees and financial credits is currently governed by Council Decision 73/391.[4] This Decision establishes a procedure for consultation in matters of credit insurance, credit guarantees and financial credits. Consultation is to take place when a state, any other state organization or any body for credit insurance or finance proposes to grant or guarantee, fully or partially, foreign credits (1) linked to exports of goods or services and (2) which depart from specified Community norms or from any other norm adopted by the Member States.[5] The procedure applies whether the credits are supplier credits or financial credits, whether they form the subject matter of individual contracts or global credit arrangements,[6] or whether the credits are purely private or are sponsored fully or partially out of public funds. The Community norms which cannot be departed from without consultation refer to the duration of credits, the percentage of local expenditure and leasing contracts.[7] The duration of any credit granted, whether supplier credit or financial credit, must not exceed five years calculated from specified starting points.[8] In the case of guaranteed private credits, the balance of the local portion payable on credit must not exceed 5 per cent of the contract price, except that consultation is not required in the case of contracts which provide for payment

---

2 [1991] ECR I-1799 at I-1848 (paragraph 22). As the Court of Justice pointed out, private insurers could instead pursue the argument that individual Member States infringe the State aids and competition provisions of the Treaty: ibid at I-1849 (paragraph 24).

3 Council Decision of 27 September 1960 setting up a Policy Co-ordination Group on Credit Insurance, Credit Guarantees and Financial Credits, OJ 27.10.60, 66/1339. For the consultation procedure, see Council Decision 65/53, OJ 5.2.65, 19/255.

4 Council Decision 73/391, OJ 17.12.73 L346/1, amended by Council Decision 76/641, OJ 16.8.76 L223/25 and by the Accession Treaty of Spain and Portugal of 1985.

5 Council Decision 73/791 Art 1. The Community norms are specified in Annex I.

6 'Global credit arrangement' means any understanding or statement, in whatever form, whereby the intention to guarantee supplier or financial credits or to open financial credits, up to a specified or ascertainable ceiling, and in respect of a connected series of transactions, is made known to a third country or to exporters or to financial institutions: ibid Art 3(1), first paragraph. The consultation procedure applies to such global arrangements even where the nature of the transactions has not been specified and no formal commitment has been entered into, without prejudice to the right to decide on each particular contract: ibid Art 3(1), second paragraph. A Member State which has granted a global arrangement is, at a date subsequent thereto and every six months thereafter, required to give notification of the use made of that arrangement: ibid Art 3(3).

7 See ibid Annex I.

8 Ibid Annex I, part A, as substituted by Council Decision 76/641, OJ 16.8.76 L223/25.

of the local portion to be made, at the latest, upon the expiry of a period of three months calculated from the final completion of the works or deliveries.[9] For the purpose of the application of these rules, leasing contracts are to be treated as credits, and where their total duration is not expressly restricted, it is to be regarded as being in excess of five years.[10]

The consultation procedure differs according to whether the proposed credit is to be granted by an individual contract or by a global credit arrangement. In the case of an individual contract, the Member State initiating consultation is required to supply to the Policy Co-ordination Group information concerning the country of destination, location of the transaction, characteristics of the transaction, principal credit terms applied for, credit terms the authorities in the exporting country propose to offer, and the precise grounds for not applying the Community norms.[11] In the case of a global credit arrangement, the required information concerns the country of destination, the ceiling of the global credit arrangement, the purpose of credit, credit terms, and the precise grounds for not applying the Community norms.[12] This information is to be transmitted by telex to recipients designated by each Member State, the Commission and the Council Secretariat respectively.[13] Member States and the Commission may indicate that the proposed terms do not call for any comments, request additional details, make comments and reservations or express an unfavourable opinion, or request a consultative meeting.[14] This procedure must be initiated within a period of seven calendar days from the date of the introductory communication from the consulting Member State;[15] additional details, when requested within this period, must be provided by the consulting Member State within five calendar days at the latest;[16] and participants are allowed a maximum period of three working days following receipt of such additional details within which to express an opinion.[17] Except in certain specified exceptional circumstances,[18] the consulting Member State must suspend its decision until the expiry of these prescribed periods or, where a consultative meeting is due to take place automatically,[19] until such meeting has been held.[20]

In addition to these general procedures, special procedures apply in three instances.[1] The first arises when a Member State asks another Member State whether it has knowledge of a transaction which until then has not been the subject of consultation and, in particular, of the credit terms alleged by an exporter or financial institution and the requested Member State does not reply within seven calendar days.[2] The second is the case of untied credits

---

9 Ibid Annex I, part B.
10 Ibid Annex I, part C.
11 Ibid Art 4.
12 Ibid Art 5.
13 Ibid Art 9.
14 Ibid Art 10(1). Where transactions subject to consultation receive an unfavourable opinion from five Member States, consultative meetings shall take place automatically: ibid Art 10(2).
15 Ibid Art 11, first paragraph.
16 Ibid Art 11, second paragraph.
17 Ibid Art 11, third paragraph. Failure to reply is deemed an absence of comments: ibid Art 12, first paragraph.
18 See ibid Art 13.
19 See ibid Art 10(2).
20 Ibid Art 10(3).
 1 Ibid. Title II Special Procedures.
 2 Ibid Art 16.

departing from the Community norms or any other norm adopted by the Member States within the framework of the Policy Co-ordination Group.[3] The third concerns the conclusion by a Member State with a third country of an agreement which refers to the possible grant of credits without specifying the precise terms thereof.[4]

Consultative meetings are to be held on the occasion of any meeting of the Policy Co-ordination Group or of its subgroups, but special meetings shall also be convened if any Member State so requests.[5] Member States and the Commission are required to communicate to the designated recipients,[6] if possible four days before the consultative meeting, a list of the matters which they intend to submit for discussion.[7] Consultative meetings are held at the Secretariat of the Council.[8] In all cases the final decision in respect of each transaction shall be made known to the other Member States. The notification of the decision must be accompanied by a statement of the reasons for which the consulting Member State was unable to take account of any comments, reservations or unfavourable opinions expressed by the partners consulted.[9] The Policy Co-ordination Group is required to submit half-yearly reports on the application of the general and special consultative procedures and it may also draw up supplementary reports.[10]

In the course of taking measures to implement the principles laid down in the provisions concerning the common commercial policy, the Community is empowered not only to adopt internal rules of Community law but also to conclude agreements with third countries pursuant to Arts 113(2) and 114 of the EEC Treaty.[11]

In 1978 the EEC Council adopted on behalf of the Community the OECD Arrangement on Guidelines for Officially Supported Export Credits.[12] This was an informal arrangement, and the Council deemed its publication to be unwise as it might increase the risk of purchasing countries coming to regard the arrangement terms as the norm, or even as established rights, or try to get their classification under the arrangement altered in their favour.[13] In 1992, however, a consolidated text of the Arrangement was adopted and published, and the 1978 Decision was extended for an indefinite period.[14] The guidelines apply to officially supported export credits with a repayment term of two years or more

---

3 Ibid Art 17.
4 Ibid Art 18.
5 Ibid Art 14, first paragraph.
6 See ibid Art 9.
7 Ibid Art 14, second paragraph.
8 Ibid Art 14, third paragraph.
9 Ibid Art 15.
10 Ibid Art 19.
11 Opinion 1/75 [1975] ECR 1355. The understanding on a local cost standard negotiated under the auspices of the Organisation for Economic Co-operation and Development provided an informal agreement that exporting countries should not provide financing for local expenditure in excess of the amount represented by the cost of the equipment. On the question whether the Community or Member States should enter into the arrangement the European Court of Justice asserted the exclusive Community jurisdiction in the field of export assistance.
12 Council Decision of April 1978; Act of Accession (1985), Art 26, Annex I, Part VII, point 8. See also OECD *The Export Credit Financing Systems in OECD Member Countries* (4th edn, May 1990).
13 Answer to Written Question 1163/80 (OJ 10.12.80, C322/12).
14 Council Decision 93/112 of 14.12.92 extending the Decision of 4 April 1978 on the application of certain guidelines in the field of officially supported export credits, OJ 22.2.93 L44/1.

relating to contracts for sales of goods and/or services or to leases equivalent in effect to such sales. The Arrangement on Guidelines has been applied alongside Council Decision 73/391.[15] In 1996 the OECD announced new rules on tied aid in respect of export credits.[16]

Special guidelines apply to ships, nuclear power plants, power plants other than nuclear power plants and aircraft.[17] Participants must require purchasers of exported goods and services receiving officially supported export credits to make cash payments at or before the starting point equal to a minimum of 15 per cent of the export contract value. Participants must not provide official support for such cash payments other than insurance and guarantees against the usual pre-credit risks.[18] Guidelines are established for prepayment;[19] minimum interest rates;[20] local costs:[1] maximum period of validity of commitments prior commitments and certain aid commitments;[2] trade related concessional or aid credits;[3] special sectors;[4] and procedures.[5] The guidelines are stated to represent the most generous credit terms and conditions that participants may offer when giving official support, and the participants undertake to take the necessary steps to prevent them from being regarded as the normal terms and conditions.[6] To this end, they undertake to continue to respect less generous terms which may be customary in individual industrial branches or industrial sectors.[7] They also undertake to respect certain procedures, to make maximum use of the framework for information exchange, to consider favourably face-to-face transactions if a participant so requests in the case of important transactions[8] and not to derogate with respect to various guidelines.[9]

In 1992 the Commission submitted a proposal for a Council decision on co-ordination and information procedures in matters of officially supported export credits, credit insurance, credit guarantees and financial credits.[10] The proposal aimed to take account of amendments to the OECD Arrangement, to align internal procedures with Arrangement procedures, and to set up a procedure consistent with the 1987 'Comitology' Decision.[11] According to the proposal,

---

15 OJ 17.12.73 L346/1, as amended.
16 See also Dunne 'Export credit guidelines agreed', *Financial Times* 6 December 1996, p 4.
17 Ibid paragraph 1(b); paragraph 9. See also Annex II Understanding on Export Credits for Ships, Annex III Sector Understanding on Export Credits for Nuclear Power Plants and Annex IV Sector Understanding on Export Credits for Civil Aircraft.
18 Ibid paragraph 3.
19 Ibid paragraph 4.
20 Ibid paragraph 5.
 1 Ibid paragraph 6.
 2 Ibid paragraph 7.
 3 Ibid paragraph 8.
 4 Ibid paragraph 9.
 5 Ibid paras. 14–19.
 6 Ibid paragraph 10(a)(1).
 7 Ibid paragraph 10(a)(2).
 8 Ibid paragraph 10(b), (c). On face-to-face consultations in important transactions, see the Protocol among participants to the arrangement on guidelines for officially supported export credits (attached to the Arrangement). On the framework for information exchange (FIE), see Annex VI.
 9 Ibid paragraph 12.
10 Commission of the European Communities, Proposal for a Council Decision on co-ordination and information procedures in matters of officially supported export credits, credit insurance, credit guarantees and financial credits, COM(92)502 final, Brussels 1 December 1992.
11 Council Decision 87/373, OJ 18.7.87 L197/33.87 L197/33.

the Community's position in OECD discussions was to be expressed by the Commission in accordance with a co-ordination (management committee) procedure.[12] Member States were required to provide specified information to other Member States and the Commission. At the request of a Member State or on its own initiative, the Commission was to be entitled to investigate any question relating to a wide range transactions relating to credit insurance, credit guarantees and financial credits. This proposal has not however been adopted.[13]

In 1970 the Council issued two directives on the adoption of common credit insurance policies for medium and long-term transactions. Directive 70/509[14] concerned public buyers, and Directive 70/510[15] concerned private buyers.[16] Both directives provided[17] that Member States were to put into force a common credit insurance policy[18] and the endorsement for extension of the bond guaranteeing satisfactory performance of the contract.[19] Member States were to ensure that credit insurance organizations guaranteeing the account of or with the support of the State insure transactions which are covered by the common policy in accordance with its terms and such specific rules as were adopted by the Council.[20] The common policy was to cover transactions guaranteed under specific policies and which:

(1) include either a credit risk of 24 months or more, or a manufacturing risk of 12 months or more, or a combination of both these risks for a cumulative period of 24 months or more;
(2) involve
   (a), in the case of Directive 70/509, a public buyer or a private buyer whose commitments are guaranteed by a public authority or by a body which is defined as a public body by the directive[1] or
   (b), in the case of Directive 70/510, a private buyer;[2]
(3) are on a supplier credit basis.[3]

In respect of private buyers only, transactions could be guaranteed either solely against political risks or against both political and commercial risks.[4] An Advisory Committee for Export Credit Insurance, consisting of representatives

12 The committee was to be composed of the same members as the Policy Coordination Group for credit insurance, credit guarantees and financial credits, and to be chaired by a representative of the Commission: Art 2(1).
13 The proposed Decision, if adopted, would have repealed Council Decision 73/391, OJ 17.12.73 L346/1, and Council Decision 76/641, OJ 16.8.76 L223/25.
14 OJ 23.11.70 L254/1, amended by Council Directive 73/101, OJ 1.1.73 L2/1 and by the Accession Treaties of Denmark, Ireland and the United Kingdom of 1972, of Greece of 1979, and of Spain and Portugal of 1985 and the Accession Treaties of Austria, Finland and Sweden of 1994.
15 OJ 23.11.70 L254/26, amended by Council Directive 73/101, OJ 1.1.73 L2/1OJ, and by the Accession Treaties of Denmark, Ireland and the United Kingdom of 1972, of Greece of 1979 and of Spain and Portugal of 1985 and the Accession Treaties of Austria, Finland and Sweden of 1994.
16 See also Act of Accession (1985) Art 26, Annex I, Part VII, points 5, 6.
17 Council Directive 70/509 Art 1(1); Council Directive 70/510, Art 1(1).
18 Defined in ibid Annex A, and subject to the provisions of ibid Annex D.
19 See ibid Annexes B and B/l.
20 Directive 70/509 Art 2; Directive 70/510 Art 2.
 1 See Directive 70/509 Art 3(1), second paragraph.
 2 As defined in Directive 70/510, Art 4.
 3 Directive 70/509 Art 3(1); Directive 70/510 Art 3(1).
 4 Directive 70/510 Art 3(2).

of the Member States and chaired by a representative of the Commission, was also established.[5]

As of 1 April 1999 these measures will be repealed and replaced by the recently enacted directive harmonizing the main provisions concerning export credit insurance for transactions with medium and long-term cover.[6] Based on the OECD guidelines, it applies to cover for transactions related to the export of goods and/or services originating in a Member State, in so far as this support is provided directly or indirectly for the account of, or with the support of, one or more Member States, involving a total risk period of two years or more.[7] Member States are required to ensure that insurers cover export transactions in accordance with certain common principles.[8] These principles apply to supplier credit or buyer credit transactions with public or private borrowers.[9] They concern the definition of the risks involved, the status of the debtor, covered risks, extent of cover, percentage of cover, the uninsured percentage, cover for transactions in foreign currency, foreign supplies, effective date of cover, liability of the insurer, decisions of a third country, decisions of the country of the insurer or policyholder, force majeure, general exclusions, settlement of disputes, bilateral intergovernmental debt restructuring agreements, and other matters.[10] The Directive also provides for general principles for setting the premium.[11] Implementing decisions are to be taken by the Commission in conjunction with a regulatory committee.[12]

In 1971 the Council issued a directive designed to harmonize the basic provisions in respect of guarantees, either for public buyers or for private buyers, regarding short-term transactions (political risks).[13] It covered political risks only, as private credit insurance companies operated with respect to other short-term risks.[14]

In 1982 the Council issued a Decision on the rules applicable to certain subcontracts with parties in other Member States or in third countries for export guarantees and finance. It was designed to deal with the problems for exports[15]

---

5 Directive 70/509 Art 4, first paragraph. As to the operation of the committee, see ibid Arts 4,5,6. The committee could also to be consulted with regard to the application of Directive 70/510: Directive 70/510, Art 5.

6 Council Directive 98/29, OJ 19.5.98 L148/22, which provides in Art 7 for such repeal and in Art 8 for transposition by 1 April 1999.

7 Ibid Art 1, which also states that the 'risk period' refers to the repayment period including the manufacturing period. It also provides that the Directive does not apply to cover for bid, advance payment, performance and retention bonds, or to cover for risks relating to construction equipment and material when locally used for the performance of the commercial contract.

8 Ibid Art 2, which refers to the Annex containing the common principles. This Art also provides that the term 'insurers' refers to any institution providing cover directly or indirectly in the form of export credit insurance, guarantees or refinancing for the account of the Member State or with the support of the Member State representing the government itself or controlled by and/or acting under the authority of the government providing cover.

9 Ibid Annex, Chapter 1, section 1, sub-section (1)(a). As to 'supplier credit', see ibid sub-section (2). As to 'buyer credit', see ibid, sub-section (3).

10 See ibid Annex, Chapter 1: Constituents of Cover.

11 Ibid Annex, Chapter II: Premium.

12 Ibid Art 3. As to the committee, see Art 4.

13 Council Directive 71/86, OJ 13.2.71 L36/14, extended by the Accession Treaty of Denmark, Ireland and the United Kingdom of 1972. The harmonized provisions are set out in the Annex.

14 Ibid, preamble, eighth recital.

15 Council Decision 82/854, OJ 18.12.82 L357/20, repealing and replacing EC Council Decision 70/552, OJ 30.12.70 L284/59.

raised by sub-contracting for the provision of export guarantees and finance.[16] The Decision is addressed to all the Member States. It provides for automatic inclusion, in the cover which a Member State may grant to a principal contractor, of sub-contracts with parties in one or more of the Member States where the amount of those sub-contracts is equal to or less than:

(1) 40 per cent for contracts of a value less than 7.5m Ecu;
(2) 3m Ecu for contracts of a value between 7.5m and 10m Ecu;
(3) 30 per cent for contracts of a value over 10m Ecu.[17]

As regards the financing of sub-contracts, equal treatment is to be afforded to export contracts containing a sub-contract element which is equivalent to that set out above, with treatment applicable to export contracts comprising exclusively national supplies.[18] Sub-contracts relating to export transactions concluded on the basis of credits involving any form of financial support from a Member State, however, were excluded.[19] This Decision entered into force on 1 January 1983.

Complementing this Decision, the Council in 1984 issued Directive 84/568 concerning the reciprocal obligations of credit insurance organizations of the Member States in the case of joint guarantees for a contract involving one or more sub-contracts in one or more Member States.[20] Its purpose is to improve the competitiveness of Community exports on third country markets by facilitating co-operation between export undertakings in different Member States. Member States are to ensure that their export credit insurance organizations comply with the provisions of the annexed model export credit agreement as regards reciprocal obligations if deciding to grant, jointly with an organization or public department of another Member State, guarantees relating to a contract involving one or more sub-contracts in one or more Member States.[1] The EC Commission may at any time submit proposals to modify the directive,[2] and within two years after implementation must report on the experience gained from the application of the annexed provisions.[3] The specimen agreement[4] defines the scope of the export contract guarantee,[5] the obligation of the principal insurer, being the sole manager of the risk, including the sub-contracted

---

16 See ibid, preamble, third recital.
17 Council Decision 82/854, Art 1, Annex, Section II. For the meaning of 'sub-contract', see Annex, Section I. This definition assumes, among other things, that the sub-contractor is not a co-signatory to the contract concluded between the principal contractor and the buyer, and that the principal contractor has sole responsibility to the buyer for the performance of the contract and bears all risks which may be guaranteed in relation to it. For detailed rules for the calculation of the percentages referred to in Annex, Section II, see Annex Section V.
18 Ibid Annex, Section III. This requirement is to be applied without prejudice to the customary criteria applied in banking matters.
19 Ibid Art 2.
20 As to Council Directive 84/568, see below.
 1 Council Directive 84/568 Art 1(1). The annexed provisions do not preclude the adoption of additional provisions not affecting the scope of the annexed provisions: Art 1(2). Implementation by Member States was required by June 1985: see Art 3.
 2 Ibid Art 2, second paragraph.
 3 Ibid Art 2, first paragraph.
 4 See ibid Annex. The agreement may be applied by analogy to establish or cover a single buyer credit for the whole of a contract where the credit insurers in the Member States are able to agree that their buyer credit systems are sufficiently compatible to do so: see Annex Art 5.
 5 See ibid Annex Art 1.

element,[6] and that of each of the joint insurers.[7] Any dispute arising out of the agreement is to be resolved by arbitration.[8]

The Council also introduced a credit guarantee for exports of agricultural products and foodstuffs from the Community to the Soviet Union.[9] It was subsequently amended to cover the purchase of agricultural and food products originating also in Bulgaria, Czechoslovakia, Hungary, Poland, Romania, Yugoslavia, Lithuania, Latvia or Estonia.[10] Later it was amended to extend to the purchase and exportation of such products to Russia.[11]

---

6 See ibid Annex Art 2.
7 See ibid Annex Art 3.
8 See ibid Annex Art 6.
9 Council Decision 91/373 on the conclusion by the European Economic Community of an Agreement in the form of an exchange of letters between the European Economic Community and the Union of Soviet Socialist Republics on a credit guarantee for exports of agricultural products and foodstuffs from the Community to the Soviet Union, OJ 25.7.91 L202/39; Council Regulation 599/91, OJ 14.3.91 L67/21, amended first by Council Regulation 1758/91 OJ 22.6.91 L158/4. The conditions under which the credit guarantee agreement shall be concluded with a pool of commercial banks were provided in Commission Regulation 2150/91, OJ 23.7.91 L200/12, as amended. With regard to export refunds on exports of dairy products, see Chapter 16 on Agricultural Products.
10 Council Regulation 3281/91, OJ 12.11.91 L310/1. Implementing rules are laid down in Commission Regulation 33/63/91, OJ 20.11.91 L318/31, and Commission Regulation 3426/91, OJ 27.11.91 L325/7. As to the Agreement with the USSR in respect of this extension, see Agreement in the form of a complementary Exchange of letters, OJ 10.3.92 L64/22.
11 Council Decision 92/152 on the conclusion of an Agreement in the form of a complementary Exchange of Letters between the European Economic Community and the Union of Soviet Socialist Republics on a credit guarantee for exports of agricultural products and foodstuffs to the Soviet Union OJ 10.3.92 L64/22; Council Regulation 599/91, OJ 14.3.91 L67/21.

Chapter 10

Pre-shipment inspection

INTRODUCTION

Pre-shipment inspection (PSI) refers to the employment by governments or other public authorities of specialised private companies to verify shipment details of goods ordered from other countries. PSI agencies check mainly the price, the quantity and the quality of goods. PSI is designed to protect national financial interests against the flight of capital, commercial fraud and the evasion of customs duties, on the one hand, and to compensate for inadequate administrative infrastructure, on the other hand. It is used by numerous developing countries, mostly in Africa, and is carried out on the customs territory of the exporting country prior to shipment.

In the past, however, certain aspects of PSI have led to disagreements between PSI agencies and exporters. The principal matters of concern to exporters included the lack of transparency in respect of the mandate of PSI agencies, lack of information in respect of procedures, methodology and criteria for price verification, the absence of any neutral appeal or arbitration procedure, the protection of the confidential business information, and adverse effects of price verifications, notably delay.[1]

The aims of importing countries, the concerns of exporters and the interests of PSI agencies form the background of the WTO Agreement on Pre-shipment Inspection and thus of current Community legislation.

THE WTO PSI AGREEMENT

A WTO Agreement on Pre-shipment Inspection[2] was adopted as part of the Uruguay Round multilateral trade negotiations. It aimed to provide an agreed international framework of rights and obligations for both users of PSI and exporters, to apply to PSI agencies mandated by governments the principles and obligations of GATT 1994, to provide transparency of PSI operations and relevant laws and regulations, and to establish a speedy, effective and equitable means of settling disputes.[3] It applies to all PSI activities carried out on the territory of WTO

---

1 See the Conclusions of the International Symposium on Pre-Shipment Inspection, organized by the International Chamber of Commerce and ICC United Kingdom, Birmingham, 22 March 1988.
2 Agreement establishing the World Trade Organization, Annex 1A, OJ 23.12.94 L336/290.
3 See ibid preamble.

Members.[4] However, Members are not required to allow government entities of other Members to conduct PSI activities on their territory.[5]

Art 2 of the WTO PSI Agreement lays down the obligations of user Members. User Members are obliged inter alia to ensure that PSI agencies carry out their activities in a non-discriminatory, transparent and timely manner, which avoids conflicts of interest.[6] Detailed guidelines apply to price verification.[7] User Members must ensure that PSI agencies establish an appeals procedure.[8]

Art 3 lays down the obligations of exporter Members. Exporter Members are required inter alia to ensure that their laws and regulations in respect of PSI are applied in a non-discriminatory and transparent manner.[9] They are to offer technical assistance, if requested, to user Members.[10] They are to encourage exporters and PSI agencies to resolve their disputes and must establish independent review procedures for this purpose.[11]

Pursuant to Art 4 of the WTO PSI Agrement, the Independent Entity (IE) was established in December 1995 to settle disputes between exporters and PSI agencies. It came into operation on 1 May 1996. The IE is constituted jointly by the WTO, the International Chamber of Commerce (ICC) representing exporters, and the Internatinal Federation of Inspection Agencies (IFIA) representing PSI agencies. It is established as a subsidiary body of the WTO Council for Trade in Goods, is administered by the WTO and is located in Geneva. If a complaint is filed, the IE appoints either a three-member panel or a single independent trade expert, depending on agreement between the parties. The panel is required to take a decision by majority vote within eight working days of the filing of the complaint. Costs are to be apportioned based on the merits of the case by the panel or the expert.[12]

PSI OF EXPORTS FROM THE COMMUNITY

Following the WTO PSI Agreement, the Community enacted in 1994 a Council regulation on preshipment inspection of exports from the Community.[13] The

---

4 Ibid Art 1(1). 'PSI activities' mean all activities relating to the verification of the quality, the quantity, the price, including currency exchange rate and financial terms, and/or customs classification of goods to be exported to the territory of the user Member: ibid Art 1(3). 'User Member' means a WTO Member of which the government or any government body contracts for or mandates the use of PSI activities: ibid Art 1(2).

5 Ibid Art 1(4), note 1.

6 See ibid Art 2(1), (5)–(19)

7 See ibid Art 2(20).

8 Ibid Art 2(21).

9 Ibid Art 3(1),(2).

10 Ibid Art 3(3).

11 See ibid Art 4.

12 See Decision of 13 December 1995 by the WTO General Council on the Operation of the Independent Entity established under Article 4 of the Agreement on Pre-shipment Inspection, including Annex I Agreement between the World Trade Organization, the International Chamber of Commerce (ICC), and the International Federation of Inspection Agencies (IFIA) with respect to the Implementation of Article 4 of the WTO Agreement on Pre-shipment Inspection; Annex II Structure and Functions of the Independent Entity established by Article 4 of the WTO Agreement on Pre-shipment Inspection; Annex III Rules of Procedure for the Operation of Independent Reviews under Article 4 of the WTO Agreement on Pre-shipment Inspection. The document is available on request from the WTO Secretariat and can be accessed directly in the WTO Internet Web site at http://www.unicc.org/wto.

13 Council Regulation 3287/94, OJ 31.12.94 L349/79. It came into force on 1 January 1995: ibid Art 10.

Community authorities were concerned that PSI could lead to interference with the price mechanism and to other practices which might constitute obstacles to trade.[14] The Community measure was designed to ensure that PSI was carried out according to the provisions of the WTO Agreement,[15] to provide uniform regulation of the activities of PSI entities[16] and to simplify procedures, in particular in respect of the settlement of disputes.[17]

The Regulation applies to preshipment inspection programmes (PSI programmes) carried out on the Community customs territory. More specifically, it applies to activities carried out on the Community customs territory by PSI agencies which, for the account of governments or public entities of third countries, carry out controls on the quality, quantity or price[18] of goods destined for export to the territory of these third countries.[19] The activities of PSI agencies are subject to a prior notification procedure on a generic basis according to specified conditions.[20] PSI agencies are required to communicate to the Commission the provisions (except for remuneration) of contracts agreed with governments or public entities of third countries for the account of which the PSI programmes have been established. In particular, notification must cover the activities in respect of the physical inspection of merchandise before it is exported in order to verify conformity of the shipment (namely quality and quantity) with the contract specifications and the respect of rules and standards of the importing country or recognized at international level.[1] It must also cover activities concerning verification of the price and, where applicable, the currency exchange rate, on the basis of the contract between the exporter and the importer, the pro forma invoice, and, where applicable, the application for import authorization.[2] Any modifications must be notified, and the measures taken to comply with the Regulation must also be indicated.[3]

The Regulation lays down certain conditions to which PSI agencies are subject when carrying out their activities.[4]

First, before any checks are made, the PSI agency must inform the exporter of the details of the inspection and the criteria that will be applied.[5] When requested by the exporter, the PSI agency must also undertake, prior to the date of the physical inspection, a preliminary verification of price, and, where applicable, of the currency exchange rate, on the basis of the contract between exporter and importer, the pro forma invoice, and, where applicable, the application for import authorization. After this preliminary verification has taken place, the PSI agency must immediately inform the exporter in writing either of its acceptance or of its detailed reasons for non-acceptance of the price and/or currency exchange rate.[6]

---

14 Ibid preamble, second recital.
15 Ibid preamble, fourth recital. Consequently the Community Regulation follows almost verbatim the WTO PSI Agreement on many points.
16 Ibid, sixth recital.
17 Ibid preamble, eighth and ninth recitals.
18 Including exchange rate and financial terms.
19 Ibid Art 1.
20 Ibid Art 2(1).
1 Ibid Art 3(a).
2 Ibid Art 3(b).
3 Ibid Art 2(2). The Commission is required to copy all the notifications to the Member States: ibid Art 2(3).
4 Ibid Art 4.
5 Ibid Art 4(a), first sub-paragraph.
6 Ibid Art 4(a), third sub-paragraph.

The checks must be carried out in a time span that avoids unreasonable delays. Within five working days following receipt of the final documents and completion of the inspection, the PSI agency must either issue a Clean Report of Findings or provide a detailed written explanation as to why such a report has not been issued. In the latter case the exporters must be given the opportunity to present their views in writing, and if they so request, a reinspection must be arranged at the earliest mutually convenient date.[7] In order to avoid delays in payment, the PSI agency must send to the exporter, or its designated representative, a Clean Report of Findings as expeditiously as possible.[8]

Secondly, the PSI must be carried out in a non-discriminatory manner, on the basis of objective procedures and criteria which are applied on an equal basis to all exporters affected by the PSI activities.

Thirdly, PSI agencies are not permitted to request exporters to provide certain information regarding:

(1) manufacturing data related to patented, licensed or undisclosed processes, or to processes for which a patent is pending;[9]
(2) unpublished technical data other than data necessary to demonstrate compliance with technical regulations or standards;[10]
(3) internal pricing, including manufacturing costs;[11]
(4) profit levels;[12]
(5) the terms of contracts between exporters and their suppliers, unless it is not otherwise possible for the PSI agency to conduct the inspection.[13]

PSI agencies are required to treat all information provided by exporters as business confidential, to the extent that the information is not already published, generally available to third parties, or otherwise in the public domain. The information is to be shared with the governments contracting or mandating the PSI agency only to the extent that such information is customarily required for letters of credit or other forms of payment or for customs, import licensing or exchange control purposes.[14]

Fourthly, PSI agencies are required to establish procedures to receive, consider and render decisions in respect of grievances raised by exporters.[15] The Regulation lays down guidelines for these procedures. PSI agencies must designate one or more officials who are to be available during normal business hours in each city or port in which they maintain a PSI administrative office to receive, consider and render decisions on exporters' appeals or grievances.[16] Exporters must provide in writing to the designated official(s) a statement of the facts of the specific transaction, the nature of the grievance and a suggested

---

7 Ibid Art 4(a), second sub-paragraph.
8 Ibid Art 4(a), fourth sub-paragraph, which also provides that, in the event of a clerical error in the Report, the PSI entity must correct the error and forward the corrected information to the appropriate parties as expeditiously as possible.
9 Ibid Art 4(c)(i).
10 Ibid Art 4(c)(ii).
11 Ibid Art 4(c)(iii).
12 Ibid Art 4(c)(iv).
13 Ibid Art 4(c)(v), first sub-paragraph, which also provides that in this case the PSI agency is to request only the information necessary for this purpose.
14 Ibid Art 4(c)(v), second sub-paragraph.
15 Ibid Art 4(d).
16 Ibid Art 4(d)(i).

solution.[17] The designated official(s) must afford sympathetic consideration to exporters' grievances and must render a decision as soon as possible after receipt of the required documentation.[18]

The Regulation also lays down certain conditions which PSI agencies must meet when carrying out their activity in respect of price verification.[19]

First, a PSI agency is permitted to reject a contract price agreed between exporter and importer only if it can demonstrate that its findings of an unsatisfactory price are based on a process of verification which conforms to specified criteria.[20]

Secondly, the PSI agency must base its price comparison for checking the export price on the price(s) of identical or similar goods offered for export from the same country of exportation at or about the same time, under competitive and comparable conditions, in conformity with customary commercial practices and net of any applicable standard discounts.[1] The Regulation sets out the specific factors on which such a comparison is to be based.[2] Only prices providing a valid basis of comparison are to be used, taking account of the relevant economic factors pertaining to the country of importation and a country or countries used for price comparison.[3] The PSI agency must not rely upon the price of goods offered for export to different countries of importation to impose arbitrarily the lowest price upon the shipment.[4] The PSI agency must take specific elements into account.[5] At any stage in the process, the PSI agency must give the exporter an opportunity to explain the price.[6]

Thirdly, when checking the price, the PSI agency is required to make appropriate allowances for the terms of the sales contract and generally applicable adjusting factors.[7]

Fourthly, the verification of transportation charges must relate only to the agreed price of the mode of transport in the country of exportation as indicated in the sales contract.

Fifthly, certain elements are not to be used for price verification purposes. They are the selling price in the country of importation of goods produced in that country, the price of goods for export from a country other than the country of exportation, the cost of production, and arbitrary or fictitious prices or values.[8]

The Regulation provides for the settlement of disputes which may arise. If, as a result of its obligations towards the government or a public entity of a third country, the PSI agency does not respect the conditions in respect of its

---

17 Ibid Art 4(d)(ii).
18 That is, the documentation required by the terms of Art 4(d)(ii): ibid Art 4(d)(iii).
19 Ibid Art 5.
20 Ibid Art 5(a), which also provides that the criteria are set out in Art 5(b)–(e) inclusive.
1 Ibid Art 5(b).
2 See ibid Art 5(b)(i)–(iv).
3 Ibid Art 5(b)(i).
4 Ibid Art 5(b)(ii).
5 Ibid Art 5(b)(iii), which refers to the specific elements listed in Art 5(c).
6 Ibid Art 5(b)(iv).
7 Ibid Art 5(c), which further provides that the factors must include but not be limited to the following: the commercial level and quantity of the sale, delivery periods and conditions, price escalation clauses, quality specifications, special design features, special shipping or packing specifications, order size, spot sales, seasonal influences, licence or other intellectual property fees, services rendered as part of the contract if not customarily invoiced separately, and certain elements relating to the exporter's price, such as the contractual relationship between exporter and importer.
8 Ibid Art 5(e).

activities or price verification, or if it does not comply with dispute settlement procedures laid down in the Regulation,[9] or if there is any other reason to believe that the WTO Agreement on PSI is not respected, recourse may be had to any appropriate procedure.[10]

A specific procedure is provided by the Regulation when a dispute cannot be resolved otherwise, and at the earliest two working days after the submission of the grievance to the PSI agency itself.[11] At the request of the exporter or the PSI agency, a three-member panel is established, or if the parties so agree one independent trade expert is selected, by the WTO Independent Entity (IE).[12] The object of the review is to establish whether, during the disputed inspection, the parties have complied with the provisions of the WTO Agreement and thus with the provisions of the Council Regulation. The procedures are to be expeditious and give both parties an opportunity to present their views in writing.[13] The panel is to decide by majority vote within eight working days of the request for independent review. The time limit may be extended by agreement between the parties. The decision must be communicated to the parties. Costs are apportioned by the panel or the expert on the basis of the merits of the case.[14] The panel decision is binding on the PSI agency and the exporter which are parties to the dispute.[15]

Member States are required to take appropriate measures to implement the Regulation, in particular the independent review procedure, and to appoint an official responsible for PSI questions.[16] The Community and Member States may provide user countries with technical assistance related to PSI. Normally this assistance should be aimed at removing the circumstances which have led the user countries to resort to PSI.[17]

---

9 In Art 7.
10 Ibid Art 6, which further provides that this may include the procedure laid down by Council Regulation 2641/84, OJ 20.9.84 L252/1 ('the New Commercial Policy Instrument'). The latter was repealed by Council Regulation 3286/94, OJ 31.12.94 L349/71 ('the Trade Barriers Regulation'), which provides that any references to the repealed Regulation are to be construed as references to the new Regulation: Council Regulation 3286/94 Art 15(2), OJ 31.12.94 L349/71.
11 That is, according to the procedure established by ibid Art 4(d): ibid Art 7.
12 Ibid Art 7(a)-(c).
13 Ibid Art 7(d).
14 Ibid Art 7(e).
15 Ibid Art 7(f).
16 Ibid Art 8, first sub-paragraph.
17 Ibid Art 8, second sub-paragraph.

Chapter 11

Administration of quotas

THE GENERAL PROCEDURE

Introduction

In accordance with the GATT,[1] most products are imported into the Community without any quantitative restrictions. The Community's Customs Code,[2] however, refers to the use of quotas or tariff ceilings, for example in respect of preferential tariff measures or suspensive measures.[3] In addition, quantitative restrictions are used in respect of certain importing countries and sectors.

The current generally applicable Community procedure for the administration of quotas on imports into and exports from the Community was laid down in 1994.[4] It governs the administration of quantitative import and export quotas, whether autonomous or conventional, established by the Community.[5] It provides for general administrative principles, specific rules for different administrative methods, rules governing import or export licences, and other matters. However, it does not apply to Annex II products[6] or to other products that are subject to specific common import or export arrangements laying down special provisions for quota administration.[7]

---

1 GATT Art XI.
2 Council Regulation 2913/92, OJ 19.10.92 L302/1.
3 Ibid Art 20(5).
4 Council Regulation 520/94, OJ 10.3.94 L66/1. This Regulation replaced Council Regulation 1023/70, OJ 8.6.70 L124/1, as amended, which like its predecessor (Council Regulation 2043/68, OJ 18.12.68 L303/39) provided for the allocation of quotas among the Member States. The enactment of the 1994 Regulation was part of the creation of the internal market and the development of a uniform Common Commercial Policy. See Council Regulation 520/94, preamble, fourth and fifth recitals. See also Case 51/87 *Commission v Council* [1988] ECR 5459. As to detailed implementing measures, see Commission Regulation 738/94, OJ 31.3.94 L87/47, as amended by Commission Regulation 1150/95, OJ 23.5.95 L116/3.
5 Council Regulation 520/94 Art 1(1), OJ 10.3.94 L66/1. It applies in respect of quotas established under Council Regulation 519/94 Annex II, OJ 10.3.94. L67/89.
6 That is, agricultural products listed in Annex II to the EC Treaty.
7 Ibid Art 1(2). For example, quotas in respect of non-textile imports from China are governed by Council Regulation 520/94: see Council Regulation 519/94 Art 22, third paragraph. As to textiles, see below.

Administrative principles

Quotas must be allocated among applicants as soon as possible after they have been opened.[8] They may be allocated in tranches.[9] Quotas may, inter alia, be administered by one of the following three methods, or by a combination of them:[10]

(1) a method based on traditional trade flows;[11]
(2) a method based on the order in which applications are submitted ('first come, first served');[12] or
(3) a method allocating quotas in proportion to the quantities requested when the applications are submitted (using the 'simultaneous examination' procedure).[13]

Quantities that are not allocated, assigned or used must be redistributed in time to allow them to be used before the end of the period covered by the quota.[14]

Except where other provisions are adopted when the quota is set, the release for free circulation or export of products subject to quotas is conditional on the presentation of an import or export licence issued by the Member States.[15] Member States are required to designate the administrative authorities competent for carrying out implementing measures for which they are responsible.[16]

The Commission is required to publish a notice announcing the opening of quotas in the *Official Journal of the European Communities*. The notice must set out the allocation method chosen, the conditions to be met by licence

---

8 Ibid Art 2(1).
9 Ibid Art 2(1). As to procedure for deciding that quotas shall be allocated in tranches, see Art 23. Article 23 provides that the Commission proposal for measures is to be submitted to a committee, composed of representatives of the Member States and chaired by a Commission representative. The Commission is to adopt the measure, which shall apply immediately. However, if the measure is not in accordance with the opinion of the Committee, expressed by weighted majority voting, it is to be communicated by the Commission to the Council. In that event the Commission may defer application of the measure for a period of not more than one month. The Council, acting by a qualified majority, may take a different decision within this time limit.
10 Ibid Art 2(2). The allocation method is to be decided following the procedure laid down in Art 23: Art 2(3). If none of the three methods is appropriate to the specific requirements of a quota which has been opened, the Commission is to determine the appropriate method following the procedure laid down in Art 23: Art 2(4).
11 Ibid Art 2(2)(a), which also provides that the specific rules in respect of this method are laid down in Arts 6–11.
12 Ibid Art 2(2)(b), which also provides that the specific rules in respect of this method are laid down in Art 12.
13 Ibid Art 2(2)(c), which also provides that the specific rules in respect of this method are laid down in Art 13.
14 Ibid Art 2(5), as substituted by Council Regulation 138/96, OJ 27.1.96 L21/6. which also provides that the procedure for redistribution is laid down in Art 14. If it is not possible to redistribute the quantities in time to be used during the current quota period, the Commission is to decide, on a case-by-case basis and according to the procedure laid down in Art 23, on their possible redistribution during the following quota period: Art 2(5), second paragraph, as so substituted.
15 Ibid Art 2(6), which also provides that the issue of the licence must be in accordance with this Regulation 520/94.
16 That is, responsible under the Regulation: Art 2(6), which also provides that the Member States are required to so notify the Commission. As to the competent authorities, see Commission Regulation 738/94 Art 2 and Annex I, OJ 31.3.94 L87/47, as substituted by Commission Regulation 1150/95, OJ 23.5.95 L116/3.

applications, time limits for submitting the applications and a list of competent national authorities to which they must be sent.[17]

All Community importers and exporters, no matter where they are established in the Community, may submit a single licence application for each quota or tranche of a quota.[18] The application can be submitted to the competent authority of the Member State of their choice. It must be submitted in the official language or languages of the Member State concerned.[19] Where a quota is limited to one or several regions of the Community, the application must be submitted to the competent authorities in the Member State(s) of the region(s) concerned.[20]

The Commission is assisted by a committee composed of representatives of the Member States and chaired by a Commission representative.[1]

Methods for allocating quotas

Specific rules govern each of the three different administrative methods for allocating quotas.[2]

The first method is based on traditional trade flows. When this method is used, one portion of the quota must be reserved for traditional importers or exporters,[3] while the other is to be set aside for other importers or exporters.[4] The allocation is to be carried out according to certain principles.[5]

When making their application, traditional importers are required to provide specific documents in order to qualify for the allocation of the part of the quota set aside for them and to provide evidence of the imports or exporters carried out during the reference period. They must provide a certified copy of the original of the entry for free cirulation or export declaration made out in the name of the importer or exporter concerned, or, where applicable, that of the operator whose activities they have taken over;[6] or any equivalent evidence as determined by the Commission.[7] Member States are required to inform the Commission of the number, aggregate amount and composition of the applications.[8]

The Commission is required to examine the information provided by the

---

17 Ibid Art 3. For example, see the Notice regarding China, OJ 26.4.97 L130/6.
18 As to application forms for licences or extracts of licences, see ibid Art 17(4). As to the procedure for licence applications, see Commission Regulation 738/94 Art 4, OJ 31.3.94 L87/47.
19 Ibid Art 4, first paragraph. The arrangements for submission of applications are to be determined according to the procedure laid down in Art 23: Art 4(2).
20 Ibid Art 4(1), second paragraph.
1 As to the committee, see ibid Arts 2, 22, 23.
2 As to the protection of confidentiality and the disclosure of information in respect of applications for and the grant of licences, as well as other related matters, see ibid Art 25.
3 Importers or exporters deemed to be 'traditional' are those able to demonstrate that, in the course of a previous period (known as 'the reference period'), they have imported into the Community or exported from it the product or products covered by the quota: Art 6(2).
4 Ibid Art 6(1). The relative portions and the reference period are to be determined according to the procedure laid down in Art 23. Until 31 December 1996 the Commission was required to ensure that the portion set aside for other applicants makes due and fair allowance for the situation created by the existence of national regulations applied under Council Regulation 288/82 on common rules on imports (OJ 9.2.82 L35/1), as amended, and Council Regulation 3420/83 on import arrangements for products originating in State-trading countries, not liberalized at Community level (OJ 8.12.83 L346/6), as amended: Art 6(4).
5 Ibid Art 6(5). For example, see Commission Regulation 1393/97, OJ 19.7.97 L190/24.
6 Ibid Art 7, first indent.
7 Ibid Art 7, second indent, which also provides that the procedure for determining the evidence is laid down in Art 23.
8 Ibid Art 8.

Member States at the same time.[9] It must also establish the quantitative criteria according to whether traditional importers' or exporters' applications are to be met as follows. Where the aggregate applications are equal to or less than the amount set aside for traditional importers or exporters, the applications are to be met in full.[10] However, where aggregate applications exceed the amount set aside for traditional importers or exporters, applications are to be met on a pro rata basis, calculated in accordance with each applicant's share of the total reference imports or exports.[11] Where the use of this quantitative criterion would entail allocating amounts greater than those applied for, the excess quantities are to be reassigned.[12]

The portion of the quota set aside for non-traditional importers or exporters is allocated on a 'first come, first served' basis.[13] Where no applications are received from traditional importers or exporters, the importers or exporters that do apply are to have access to the whole quota or tranche concerned.[14] In this case, the allocation is done on a 'first come, first served' basis.[15]

The second method is based on the order in which applications are submitted ('first come, first served' basis). When this method is used, the Commission is required to determine, in conjunction with the relevant committee,[16] the quantity to which operaters are entitled until the quota is exhausted.[17] The quantity is to be the same for all operators.[18] Licence-holders may submit a new application when they can prove that they have indeed imported or exported the total quantity for which they were issued a licence or a portion to be determined.[19] To ensure equal access to the quota, the Commission is required to specify the dates and times of access to the Community's balance available in the notice opening the quota.[20]

The third method is the allocation of quotas in proportion to the quantities requested. When this method is used, the competent authorities of the Member States are required to inform the Commission of the applications in compliance with certain deadlines and procedures.[1] Within the deadline,[2] the Commission is to examine the information provided by the authorities of the Member States at the same time and to determine the quantity of the quota or of the tranches for which the national authorities are to issue import or export licences.[3] Where

---

9 Ibid Art 9.
10 Ibid Art 9, first indent.
11 Ibid, second indent.
12 Ibid Art 9, third indent, which also provides that the procedure for reassignment is laid down in Art 14.
13 That is, in accordance with Art 12: Art 10.
14 Ibid Art 11, first paragraph.
15 That is, in accordance with the procedure laid down in Art 12: Art 11, second paragraph.
16 That is, the committee established by Art 22.
17 Ibid Art 12(1), first paragraph, which further provides that the procedure laid down in Art 23 is to be used.
18 Ibid Art 12(1), second paragraph, which also provides that, in setting the quantity, allowance is to be made for the need to assign economically significant quantities having regard to the nature of the product concerned. As to the assignment of the quantities, see Art 12(2).
19 Ibid Art 12(3). If a portion is sufficient, it is determined according to the procedure laid down in Art 23. The new applications are processed according to the same procedure as the first applications. This procedure is to be repeated until the quota is exhausted: Art 12(3).
20 Ibid Art 12(4).
1 Ibid Art 13(1), first paragraph, which further provides that these deadlines and procedures are to be established following the procedure laid down in Art 23. The information given by the national authorities to the Commission must specify the number of applicants and the aggregate quantities applied for: Art 13(1), second paragraph.
2 Set following the procedure laid down in Art 23: Art 13(2).
3 Ibid Art 13(2).

applications are equal to or less than the quantity of the quota, the applications are to be met in full.[4] Where they exceed the quota, they are to be met on a pro rata basis, in proportion to the quantities applied for.[5]

Quantities for redistribution are to be determined by the Commission.[6] When the quota was initially allocated on a 'first come, first served' basis, the Commission must immediately add the quantities for redistribution to any amounts still available, or use them to reconstitute the quota if the latter is exhausted.[7] Where the quota was initially allocated using another method, the quantities for redistribution are to be reassigned by the Commission in conjunction with the Committee.[8]

Quotas and import or export licences

When the 'first come, first served' method of allocating quotas is used, Member States are to issue licences immediately on verification of the Community balance available.[9] In other cases the Commission must notify the national authorities, within a specific period,[10] of the quantities for which they issue licences to the various applicants.[11] The national authorities are then to issue licences within ten working days of notification of the Commission decision or within the time limit set by the Commission.[12] They are required to inform the Commission that the licences have been issued.[13] The issue of licences may be made conditional upon the lodging of a security.[14]

The licences authorize the import or export of products which are subject to quotas.[15] They are valid throughout the Community, regardless of the place of import or export mentioned in the application.[16] An exception, however, is a licence granted in respect of a quota which is limited to one or several regions of the Community. In this case the licence is valid only in the Member State(s) of the region(s) in question.[17] Licences are valid for four months, unless a different period is set.[18]

---

4 Ibid Art 13(3).

5 Ibid Art 13(4).

6 Ibid Art 14, which further provides that the determination is to be made on the basis of information provided by the Member States in accordance with Art 20. According to Art 20, national authorities are required to notify the Commission, immediately on being so informed and in any case not less than 20 days after the expiry date of the licences, of the quantities of quotas assigned and not used, with a view to their subsequent redistribution.

7 Ibid Art 14(2).

8 That is, according to the procedure laid down in Art 23: Art 14(3), first paragraph. In this case the Commission must publish an additional notice in the *Official Journal of the European Communities*: Art 14(3), second paragraph. As to recent examples involving China, see Commission Regulations 728/97 (OJ 25.4.97 L108/19) and 1140/97 (OJ 24.6.97 L165/1).

9 Ibid Art 15(1). As to licences generally, see Chapters 8 and 9 on Imports and Exports in this book.

10 To be determined in accordance with the procedure laid down in Art 23.

11 Ibid Art 15(2), first indent, which also provides that the Commission must also so inform the other Member States.

12 Ibid Art 15(2), second indent.

13 Ibid Art 15(2), third indent.

14 Ibid Art 16, which also provides that the procedure to be applied is laid down by Art 23.

15 As to the common forms, see Commission Regulation 738/84, Art 6, Annex IIA (imports), Annex IIB (exports), OJ 31.3.94 L87/47.

16 Ibid Art 17(1), first paragraph.

17 Ibid Art 17(1), second paragraph.

18 Ibid Art 17(2), which also provides that a period different from four months may be set in accordance with the procedure laid down in Art 23.

AGRICULTURAL PRODUCTS

According to the Uruguay Round Agreement on Agriculture, quantitative restrictions on imports of agricultural products must be converted into ordinary customs duties.[19] This does not however exclude the use of quotas.[20] In fact the Agreement on Agriculture provides for a series of tariff quotas under arrangements for current and minimum access.[1] In addition, the obligation to convert quantitative restrictions into ordinary customs duties does not apply to any primary agricultural product and its worked and/or prepared products which meet certain conditions for special treatment.[2] Furthermore, quotas may be imposed on imports of agricultural products from countries not subject to the GATT agreements.[3]

The basic arrangements for the administration of quotas is the same in all agricultural sectors.[4] The cereals sector can therefore serve as an example. Tariff quotas resulting from agreements negotiated within the framework of the Uruguay Round are to be opened and administered as provided in the basic regulation on the common organization of the market in question.[5] Quotas are therefore administered by the Commission in conjunction with a management committee.[6] Quotas may be administered using one of the following methods,

19 Agreement on Agriculture Art 4(2) and note 1, OJ 31.12.94 L336/22. See also Chapter 16 on Agricultural Products in this book.
20 That is, as provided in the Agreement on Agriculture, Art Annex 5: ibid Art 4(2). Nor does it exclude recourse to special safeguard measures as provided in Art 5: Art 4(2). The safeguard measures however are additional customs duties rather than quantitative restrictions. As to the administration of autonomous quotas for certain agricultural and industrial products, see Council Regulation 2631/97, OJ 31.12.97 L356/1. As to certain fishery products, see Council Regulation 730/98. OJ 2.4.98 L102/1.
1 Ibid Art 4(1). As to the quotas for 1995, see Council Regulation 3280/94, OJ 31.12.94 L347/94. For example, see Commission Regulation 2125/95 opening and providing for the administration of tariff quotas for preserved mushrooms of the genus *Agaricus spp.*, OJ 7.9.95 L212/16.
2 Agreement on Agreement Annex V, which sets forth the following conditions for special treatment: (1) imports of the designated products comprise less than 3% of corresponding domestic consumption in the base period 1986–88; (2) no export subsidies have been provided since the beginning of the base period for the designated products; (3) effective production-restricting measures are applied to the primary agricultural product; (4) the products are designated with the symbol 'ST-Annex V' in Section I-B of a Member's Schedule annexed to the Marrakesh Protocol, as being subject to special treatment reflecting factors of non-trade concerns, such as food security and environmental protection; and (5) minimum access opportunities in respect of the designated products correspond, as specified in Section I-B of Part I of the Schedule of the Member concerned, to 4% of base period domestic consumption of the products from the beginning of the first year of the implementation period and, thereafter, are increased by 0.8% per year of corresponding domestic consumption in the base period per year for the remainder of the implementation period: Annex V, paragraph 1. As to the end of special treatment, see Annex V, paragraphs 2, 5, 6.
3 Council Regulation 3290/94 Art 4(2), OJ 31.12.94 L349/105.
4 See Chapter 16 on Agricultural Products in this book.
5 As to cereals, see Council Regulation 1766/92, OJ 1.7.92 L181/21, as amended in particular by Council Regulation 3290/94, OJ 31.12.94 L349/105. See also Council Regulation 3379/94 Art 3, OJ 31.12.94 L366/3, which provides inter alia that the administration of quotas for various agricultural products imported pursuant to the Europe Agreements is to be conducted in accordance with the rules provided in basic regulations on the common organization of the markets concerned. As to detailed rules in respect of tariff quota for milk and milk products under that Regulation, see Commission Regulation 629/95, OJ 24.3.95 L66/6.
6 Ibid Art 12(1), as substituted by Council Regulation 3290/94, OJ 31.12.943 L349/105. As to the management committee procedure, see Art 23.

or a combination of them: the method based on traditional trade flows ('traditional/new arrivals' method), the method based on the order in which the applications are submitted ('first come, first served' method), or the method allocating quotas in proportion to the quantities requested when applications are submitted ('simultaneous arrivals' method).[7] Other appropriate methods may be adopted.[8] The method chosen must however avoid any discrimination between the operators concerned.[9]

The method of administration must, where appropriate, give due weight to the supply requirements of the Community market and the need to safeguard market equilibrium. At the same time it may draw on methods which have been applied in the past to similar quotas, without prejudice to the rights resulting from agreements concluded within the framework of the Uruguay Round negotiations.[10]

Rules are to be adopted according to the management committee procedure to provide for the opening of annual quotas, if necessary phased over the year. They must also determine the method of administration to be applied. In addition, where appropriate, they are to provide for guarantees covering the nature, provenance and origin of the product; recognition of the document used for verifying these guarantees; and the conditions under which import licences are issued and their term of validity.[11]

Consistently with these provisions, the Community has opened and provided for the administration of Community tariff quotas bound in GATT for certain agricultural, industrial and fisheries products.[12] These quotas are administered by the Commission, which is empowered to take all appropriate measures to ensure their effective administration.[13] However, while the Commission in conjunction with the Customs Code Committee is entitled to make technical amendments and certain adjustments to the procedures,[14] it does not, on this basis, have the power to transfer preferential quantities from one quota period to another,[15] change timetables provided for in the agreements or exchanges of letters,[16] open and administer quotas under new agreements,[17] or adopt legislation which affects the administration of quotas subject to import certificates.[18]

When an importer applies for access to the tariff quota, and the application is accepted by the customs authorities, the Member State is, by notifying the Commission, to draw the corresponding amount from the volume of the quota.[19] In so far as the available balance permits, drawings are to be granted by the Commission on a 'first come, first served' basis.[20] However, if requests exceed

---

7 Ibid Art 12(2), first paragraph.
8 Ibid Art 12(2), second paragraph.
9 Ibid Art 12(2), third paragraph.
10 Ibid Art 12(3).
11 Ibid Art 12(3).
12 Council Regulation 1808/95, OJ 27.7.95 L176/1, as amended, which replaced Council Regulation 3280/94, OJ 31.12.94 L347/1. This takes into account the powers of the Commission under Council Regulation 3290/94, OJ 31.12.94 L349/105: see Council Regulation 1808/93, preamble, sixteenth recital. As to the products covered, see Annexes I, II, III, IV and V. Annex II has been amended by Commission Regulation 1340/97, OJ 12.7.97 L184/10.
13 Ibid Art 6(1). The Commission is assisted by a Customs Code Committee: Art 10(1). The Committee acts by the safety-net (*contrefilet*) procedure: see Art 10(2), third paragraph.
14 Ibid Art 9(1).
15 Ibid Art 9(2), first indent.
16 Ibid Art 9(2), second indent.
17 Ibid Art 9(2), third indent.
18 Ibid Art 9(2), fourth indent.
19 Ibid Art 6(2), first paragraph.
20 Ibid Art 6(2), third paragraph.

the available balance of the quota volume, the balance is to be allocated in proportion to the requests.[1] Quantities drawn but not used are to be returned to the relevant quota volume.[2] Each Member State is to guarantee importers equal and continuous access to the quotas in so far as the balance of the quota volumes permits.[3]

TEXTILES

The general procedure

The administration of quotas in respect of textile imports is governed by different rules depending on how the supplying country is classifed under Community law. Council Regulation 3030/93[4] contains specific rules for the administration of Community quantitative limits[5] in respect of two categories of products and supplier countries. The first category consists of imports of certain textile products[6] from countries with which the Community has concluded bilateral agreements, protocols or other arrangements.[7] The second category comprises imports of products which have not been integrated into the WTO and which originate in WTO members.[8] Within the Community the management of quotas is however basically the task of the Commission. National authorities can issue import authorizations only on confirmation by the Commission that there are still quantities available of the total Community quota for the categories of products and for the third countries concerned for which an application has been submitted.[9] Consequently, before issuing the authorization, the national authorities are required to notify[10] the Commission of the amounts of the requests, supported by the original export certificates,[11] which they have received. In order to be valid, a request must establish clearly in each case the supplier third country, the category of textile product concerned, the amounts to be imported, the number of the export licence, the quota year and the Member State in which the products are intended to be put into free circulation.[12]

1 Ibid Art 6(4).
2 Ibid Art 6(3).
3 Ibid Art 8.
4 OJ 8.11.93 L275/1, as amended. Annexes I, II, III, IV, V, VI, VII, VIII, IX and XI have been further amended by Commission Regulation 2231/96, OJ 28.11.96 L307/1. Annex X was further amended by Council Regulation 2315/96, OJ 4.12.96 L314/1. Annex VII was further amended by Commission Regulation 447/97, OJ 8.3.97 L68/16. Annexes III and V were further amended by Commission Regulation 152/97, OJ 29.11.97 L26/8. Most recently (to the date of writing), Annexes I, III, V, and VII were amended and Annexes II, VIII and IX were substituted by Commission Regulation 8567/8, OJ 24.4.98 L122/11. See also Chapter 18 on Textiles in this book.
5 Such limits are provided for in ibid Art 2(1).
6 Listed in ibid Annex I, as amended.
7 Listed in ibid Annex II, as amended.
8 Council Regulation 3030/93 Art 1(1), second indent,as so substituted, which also provides that the relevant textile products are listed in Annex X and that 'integrated into GATT 1994' is within the meaning of Art 2(6) or (8) of the WTO Agreement on Textiles and Clothing (ATC).
9 Ibid Art 2(7).
10 Normally by electronic communication within the integrated network set up for this purpose, unless for imperative technical reasons it is necessary to use other means of communication temporarily: ibid Art 12(3).
11 As to the double-checking system, see ibid Annex III, as amended.
12 Ibid Art 12(2).

The Commission is then to confirm that the requested amount(s) are available on a 'first come, first served' basis. However, in exceptional cases where there is reason to believe that requests exceed the quota, the Commission may limit[13] the amount to be allocated on a 'first come, first served' basis to 90 per cent of the quota in question. As soon as this limit is reached, the allocation of the remainder is to be decided.[14] As far as possible, the Commission must confirm to national authorities the full amount requested for each category of products and each third country concerned. When a request cannot be confirmed because the quota is used up, it is stored by the Commission in chronological order of receipt and then confirmed in the same order when further amounts become available.[15]

To the extent that the availability of the amount has been confirmed by the Commission, the national authorities are required to issue the authorization within five working days of the presentation by the importer of the original of the corresponding export licence.[16] The import licence is valid for six months from the date of issue and may be extended on duly motivated request for another three months and in exceptional circumstances for a further three months.[17]

The authorized imports are charged against the quota for the year in which the products are shipped in the supplier country concerned.[18] Unused quantities are to be notified to the Commission and automatically transferred into the remaining quota amount for the product and country concerned.[19]

State-trading countries

The administration of quotas in respect of textiles from certain third countries not covered by bilateral agreements, protocols or other arrangements is governed by Council Regulation 517/94.[20] Its provisions are generally similar to those of Council Regulation 3030/93.[1] The basic principle of allocation is 'first come, first served'.[2] However, when requests exceed the available quota, the Commission may divide the quantitative limits into tranches or fix maximum amounts per allocation, and it may also reserve a proportion of the quota amount for requests supported by evidence of past import performance.[3] The

---

13 Following the procedure set out in ibid Art 17.

14 Ibid Art 12(1). As to the procedure for allocating the remainder, see Art 17.

15 Ibid Art 12(4), which also provides that if requests notified exceed the quota, the Commission is to contact the supplier country in order to seek clarification and a rapid solution.

16 Ibid Annex III, Art 14(1), which also provides that this presentation must be done not later than 31 March of the year following that in which the goods covered by the licence have been shipped.

17 Ibid Annex III, Art 14(2).

18 Ibid Art 2(3), which also provides that shipment is considered as having taken place on the date when the products were loaded onto the exporting means of transport.

19 Ibid Art 12(5). As to cancellation of export or import licences, see Art 12(7).

20 OJ 10.3.94 L67/1, as amended. The products are listed in Annex I. The countries concerned are State-trading countries as listed in Annex II, as amended: Albania, Armenia, Azerbaijan, Belarus, People's Republic of China, Georgia, Kazakhstan, North Korea, Kyrgyzstan, Moldova, Mongolia, Russia, Tajikistan, Turkmenistan, Ukraine, Uzbekistan and Vietnam.

1 OJ 8.11.93 L275/1, as amended, as to which see above. Note, however, that imports of certain products are permitted only after an annual quantitative limit is established: see Art 3(3), Annex V as amended.

2 Ibid Art 17(2).

3 Ibid Art 17(3). The relevant procedures are laid down in Art 25.

period of validity of import licences is six months but it may be modified where necessary.[4]

In fact requests have exceeded the quota amounts for every year since at least 1994. In 1994 the quotas for specified products and countries were divided into tranches.[5] The first tranche was itself divided into two parts, one reserved for traditional importers and the other for other operators.[6] The quota amount which could be allocated to a traditional operator was limited to the amount actually imported for the same product category and country in the base year.[7] For other operators, allocation was limited by a ceiling.[8] In addition, the duration of validity for import licences was fixed at 90 days from the date of issue.[9] In order to qualify for a licence the operator had to prove the existence of a contract and to certify in writing that it had not already benefited inside the Community from an authorization for the category and country concerned.[10]

The second tranche for 1994 was also divided into two parts, one reserved for traditional importers and the other for other operators.[11] The mechanism of allocation was the same as for the first tranche.[12] However, a traditional importer could receive a new allocation only for quantities for which no import authorization had been issued pursuant to Council Regulation 934/94, and a non-traditional importer could receive a new allocation only if goods had actually been imported before 12 July 1994 under an authorization under Council Regulation 934/94.[13]

In 1995 the quotas were similarly divided into tranches.[14] The first tranche was again divided into two parts, one for traditional importers and the other for other operators.[15] However, the part reserved for non-traditional importers was distributed in proportion to the requested quantities instead of on a 'first come, first served' basis, and the allocation of each importer was limited to a specified ceiling.[16] The second tranche was also divided into two parts, one for traditional importers and the other for other operators.[17] The basic principle

---

4 Ibid Art 21(2), which further provides that the appropriate procedure is laid down in Art 25. As to extension of duration, see Commission Regulation 1855/94, OJ 28.7.94 L192/34.
5 Commission Regulation 934/94 Art 2, OJ 28.4.94 L107/19. The quotas concerned are listed in Annex I. Details as to the first tranche are contained in Annex II.
6 Ibid Art 3, first paragraph. As to the first tranche, see Annex II. Traditional operators referred to those who furnished proof of having imported, during 1992, products falling within the same category and originating in the same country. As to the second tranche, see Annex III.
7 Ibid Art 4, first paragraph, which provides that the base year was 1992; see also Art 3, second paragraph. As to proportional reduction, see Art 4, second paragraph.
8 Ibid Art 5, which also provides that 'first come, first served' refers to the chronological order in which the notification of requests submitted to national authorities are received by the Commission. The maximum quantities by category per operator are set out in Annex III. As to the possible increase in these quantities, see Art 5.
9 Ibid Art 6, first paragraph.
10 Ibid Art 6, second paragraph.
11 Commission Regulation 1664/94 Art 3, first paragraph, OJ 9.7.94 L176/4. As to the products and countries, see Annex I. As to the division of the second tranche, see Annex II. The definition of traditional importer and the base year were the same as in Commission Regulation 934/94: see Art 3, second paragraph, and Art 4.
12 See ibid Arts 4, 5.
13 Ibid Art 6, which specifies that both instances refer to the same category and country in each of the two years.
14 Commission Regulation 2994/94 Art 2, OJ 3.12.94 L310/48.
15 Ibid Art 3, first paragraph.
16 Ibid Art 5. As to the ceilings, see Annex III.
17 Commission Regulation 1473/95 Art 3, OJ 29.6.95 L154/13.

was again 'first come, first served'.[18] As with the first tranche, however, traditional importers were limited to the quantity actually imported in 1992 for the same category and country,[19] and other operators were limited to a predetermined quantity.[20]

For 1996 quotas were again distributed on a 'first come, first served' basis.[1] The two-tranche system was used.[2] Quantitative limits applied to any single traditional importer[3] or other operator.[4] However, if, after this distribution, quantities for a specific product and country remained within the part reserved for one category of importers, the Commission is empowered to transfer these quantities to the part reserved for the other category of importers, and the transferred quantity is to be distributed according to the quantitative criteria applicable to the latter category of operators.[5] In addition, any operator which has used a licence up to at least 50 per cent of the allocated quantity is entitled to apply for a new licence, for the same category and country, and subject to a quantity ceiling, provided that quantities are still available.[6]

OTHER SPECIFIC ARRANGEMENTS

Other specific common import or export arrangements sometimes lay down special provisions for quota administration. Two examples may be given.

The first example is the Agreement between the Community, on the one hand, and Denmark and the Faroe Islands, on the other hand.[7] It provides inter alia that the abolition of customs duties on certain fish and fishery products is subject to Community tariff quotas and ceilings. In 1997 the Community provided for the administration of these quotas and ceilings as from 1 January to 31 December of each year.[8] Customs duties on listed products imported into the Community from the Faroe Islands are suspended at the levels of and within the limits of specified tariff quotas.[9]

When an importer enters a product for free circulation in a Member State, accompanied by a request for preferential treatment and a movement certificate, the Member State concerned is to notify the Commission, thus drawing a quantity from the quota.[10] Drawings are to be granted by the Commission on a first come, first served basis according to the date when the declarations for free

---

18 Ibid Art 2.
19 Ibid Art 4, second paragraph.
20 Ibid Art 2. See also preamble, fifth recital. As to the predetermined limits, see Annex IV.
 1 That is, in chronological order of reception by the Commission of the notifications by the Member States of requests from individual operators: see Commission Regulation 2738/95 Art 2, first paragraph, OJ 29.11.95 L285/5.
 2 Ibid Art 3.
 3 Ibid Art 6(1), first paragraph, which also provides that the base year is 1992. If requests exceed the reserved amount, the allocation is to be reduced proportionately: Art 6(1), second paragraph.
 4 Ibid Art 6(2), which also provides that the limits are set out in Annex III.
 5 Ibid Art 6(3).
 6 Ibid Art 8. The quantity ceilings are set forth in Annex III.
 7 See also the relevant section in Chapter 24 in this book.
 8 Council Regulation 669/97, OJ 18.4.97 L101/1, as amended.
 9 Ibid Art 1. The products and quotas are laid down in Annex I. Certain products are also subject to import ceilings and/or Community surveillance: see Art 4(1), Annex II, Annex III.
10 Ibid Art 3, first paragraph.

circulation were accepted by the national customs authorities, provided quota is available.[11] Unused quantities must be returned to the quota.[12] If requests exceed the available quota, allocation is to be made in proportion to the requests.[13]

The quotas are administered by the Commission, which may take any appropriate administrative measure to ensure efficient operation.[14] The Commission may make certain technical adjustments.[15] However, it is not entitled, on this basis, to carry over preferential quantities from one quota period to another,[16] amend the timetables laid down in the Agreements or protocols,[17] transfer quantities from one quota to another,[18] open and administer quotas resulting from new agreements,[19] or adopt legislation affecting the administration of quotas subject to import certificates.[20]

The second example consists of tariff ceilings for agricultural products imported into the Community under the Additional Protocols to the Agreements between the Community and individual Mediterranean countries.[1] Such imports are subject to tariff ceilings and Community surveillance.[2] Quantities are charged against the ceilings as and when they are entered with customs for free circulation, accompanied by a movement certificate.[3] The extent to which a ceiling is used up is to be determined at Community level.[4] Member States are required to inform the Commission of imports charged under these arrangements.[5] As soon as the ceilings are reached, the Commission may adopt a regulation re-establishing, until the end of the calendar year, the customs duties applicable to third countries.[6] Similar provisions apply to the administration of reference quantities.[7]

The Commission, in conjunction with the Customs Code Committee,[8] is entitled to make certain amendments, adaptations and adjustments to the proce-

---

11 Ibid Art 3, third paragraph. When notifying the Commission of the requests, the Member States are required to indicate the date on which the declarations were accepted. They are also required to send the requests to the Commission forthwith after acceptance. See Art 3, second paragraph.
12 Ibid Art 3, fourth paragraph.
13 Ibid Art 3, fifth paragraph.
14 Ibid Art 2.
15 Ibid Art 5(1), which provides that, in this respect, the Commission is to be assisted by the Customs Code Committee. As to the Committee, see Art 6. The Customs Code Committee was established by Council Regulation 2913/92 (the European Community Customs Code), Art 247.
16 Ibid Art 5(2), first indent.
17 Ibid Art 5(2), second indent.
18 Ibid Art 5(2), third indent.
19 Ibid Art 5(2), fourth indent.
20 Ibid Art 5(2), fifth indent.
 1 See Council Regulation 934/95, OJ 28.4.95 L96/6, as amended most recently in respect of Annex II by Commission Regulation 519/98, OJ 6.3.98 L66/3. The countries concerned are Cyprus, Egypt, Jordan, Israel, Tunisia, Syria, Malta, Morocco and the Occupied Territories. As to the Agreements, see Chapter 26 in this book.
 2 Ibid Art 1.
 3 Ibid Art 1(2), second paragraph.
 4 Ibid Art 1(2), third paragraph.
 5 Ibid Art 1(2), fourth paragraph.
 6 Ibid Art 1(3).
 7 See ibid Art 2.
 8 As to which, see ibid Art 4. The Customs Code Committee was established by Council Regulation 2913/92 (the European Community Customs Code) Art 247 OJ 19.10.92 L302/1.

dures.[9] However, it is not empowered on this basis to carry over preferential quantities from one period to another,[10] amend the timetables laid down in the agreements or protocols,[11] transfer quantities under one ceiling or reference quantity to another,[12] or open and administer ceilings or reference quantities resulting from new agreements.[13]

9 Ibid Art 3(1), which also provides that these powers are subject to the procedure provided in Council Regulation 3448/93 (OJ 20.12.93 L318/18) which lays down trade arrangements applicable to certain goods resulting from the processing of agricultural products.
10 Council Regulation 934/95 Art 3(2), first indent, OJ 28.4.95 L96/6.
11 Ibid Art 3(2), second indent.
12 Ibid Art 3(2), third indent.
13 Ibid Art 3(2), fourth indent.

Chapter 12

Deflection of trade

EC ARTICLE 115: AN OVERVIEW

As a customs union covering all trade in goods, the Community involves the prohibition between Member States of customs duties on imports and exports and of all measures having equivalent effect, as well as the adoption of a common customs tariff in their relations with third countries.[1] The Treaty provisions concerning the elimination of customs duties between Member States,[2] and those concerning the elimination of quantitative restrictions between Member States,[3] apply both to products originating in Member States and to products coming from third countries which are in free circulation in Member States.[4]

Products coming from a third country are considered to be in free circulation in a Member State if two conditions are satisfied: first, the import formalities have been complied with and any customs duties or charges having equivalent effect which are payable have been levied in that Member State; and, second, if the goods have not benefited from a total or partial drawback of such duties or charges.[5] Goods from third countries which are in free circulation in the Community thus benefit, in principle, from the EC Treaty provisions on the free movement of goods.

Assuming certain conditions are satisfied, however, an exception to this principle may be provided by EC Art 115.

EC Art 115 states that, in order to ensure that the execution of measures of commercial policy taken in accordance with the EC Treaty by any Member State is not obstructed by deflection of trade, or where differences between such measures lead to economic difficulties in one or more Member States, the European Commission is to recommend methods of co-operation between Member States.[6] If co-operation is not successful, the Commission may authorize Member States to take necessary protective measures in accordance with conditions and details which it is to determine.[7] Provision is made for cases of urgency.[8] In the selection of measures, priority must be given to those which cause the least disturbance of the functioning of the common market.[9]

1 EC Art 9(1).
2 Title I, Chapter 1, Section 1 of the EC Treaty.
3 Title I, Chapter 2 of the EC Treaty.
4 EC Art 9(2).
5 Ibid Art 10(1).
6 The practice of issuing such recommendations has fallen into disuse.
7 EC Treaty, Art 115(1).
8 See below.
9 EC Art 115(3).

EC Art 115 is designed to prevent deflections of trade due to any differences in Member States' trade policies which may persist in the absence of a real Common Commercial Policy. It provides measures to control indirect imports into one Member State through another Member State of goods originating in a third country. It thus constitutes a safeguard clause regulating the authorization of certain national quantitative restrictions which, together with Art 36, forms the most important exception to EC Arts 30 and 34.[10] In the past it was used very frequently, especially in respect of textiles.

Once the Community's Common Commercial Policy has been completed, however, recourse by a Member State to Art 115 to prevent deflections of trade becomes problematic. Recent legislative reforms have deprived Art 115 of much of its importance. Today it is only of relatively limited practical significance.

The following paragraphs describe Commission implementing measures, the interpretation of EC Art 115 by the European Court of Justice, and finally the role of Art 115 today.

COMMISSION DECISIONS IMPLEMENTING EC ARTICLE 115

The general rules for the application of Art 115, notably concerning surveillance and protective measures, were first set out by the Commission in Decision 71/202.[11] It was replaced and substantially modified by Decision 80/47,[12] which came into force on 1 April 1980. After the Single Act it was in turn replaced and brought up to date by Decision 87/433,[13] which has been in force from 1 October 1987. The Decision applies to imports into a Member State of products originating in a third country which have been put into free circulation in the Community which are not subject to uniform conditions of import in the Member States.[14]

Two kinds of authorization may in principle be granted by the Commission

---

10 See also P Oliver *Free Movement of Goods in the EEC* (2nd edn, 1988) paragraph 9.23.
11 Commission Decision 71/202 EEC, OJ 3.6.71 L121/26 as modified by Commission Decision 73/75 EEC, OJ 1973 L80/22.
12 Decision 71/202 was repealed by EC Commission Decision 80/47 Art 5(2), OJ 22.1.80 L16/14, after criticism in Case 41/76 *Criel v Procureur de la Republique* [1976] ECR 1921. In Decision 71/202 the Commission had issued a blanket authorization to the Member States for the use of import licences to conduct intra-Community surveillance of indirect imports.
13 EC Commission Decision 87/433 OJ 21.8.87 L238/26. This decision revised and modified Decision 80/47 in the light of past experience and the objectives of the single market action programme (compare preamble and Arts 1, 2(2), 2(5)f, 3(2), 3(3), first paragraph (e); 6(2), second paragraph). The preamble of Decision 87/433 stresses that the authorization of Art 115 measures be guided by the principles of necessity and proportionality included in the Treaty. The text of Decision 80/47 was amended, and its scope extended 'to all those cases where disparities exist in commercial policy measures taken by the Member States in compliance with the Treaty, including cases where disparities in tariff-measures are still authorized' (OJ L238, 21.8.87, p 27). The amendments primarily served to restrict the use of Art 115 measures while stressing the Commission's discretionary powers, and introduced the possibility of Commission inquiries to check the information supplied by Member States (providing for the provisional authorization of interim protective measures pending the results of the inquiry).
14 EC Commission Decision 87/433 Art 1, replacing EC Commission Decision 80/47 Art 1 which covered third country imports in free circulation in the Community where (1) the imports were subject to a quota or to a voluntary restraint measure applied by the third country pursuant to a trade agreement, and (2) the imports were likely to be the subject of protective measures under Art 115 of the Treaty.

pursuant to Decision 80/47, namely authorizations for intra-Community sur-veillance and authorizations for protective measures.[15]

A Member State may obtain by request[16] an authorization from the Commission to subject imports of an identified product to a licensing procedure for a specified time when there is a danger that imports of that product will give rise to economic difficulties.[17] In recent years, the Commission has tightened the conditions under which it has been willing to authorize protective measures. This has led to a drastic reduction both in the number of authorizations and in the number of applications for such authorizations by the Member States.[18]

As a general rule the Commission will not give such authorization unless:

(1) there have been significant imports of the product in the calendar year preceding the year in which the application is made; and
(2) import opportunities for the product in question opened by the Community vis-à-vis the third country of origin exceed 1 per cent of the total import opportunities opened by the Community vis-à-vis all third countries subject to similar rules.[19]

The import document is to be issued by the Member State concerned for any quantity requested, free of charge and within a maximum period of five working days from the date of application by the importer, wherever may be its place of business in the Community.[20] The information which may be required for the import document is limited to:

(1) the country of origin and the exporting Member State;
(2) the name of the consignor in the exporting Member State;
(3) the name of the importer;
(4) a description of the product with details of its trade designation, Common Customs Tariff heading and NIMEXE code;
(5) the value and quantity of the product;
(6) scheduled delivery dates; and
(7) evidence to show that it is in free circulation.[1]

By request to the Commission a Member State may obtain authorization to take protective measures against a product otherwise in free circulation in

15 It seems that both must be in the nature of protective measures or that surveillance must be regarded as a preparatory procedure to a protective measure, otherwise it is difficult to see how surveillance is authorized by the provisions of EC Art 115, first paragraph.
16 The request must (1) describe the product; (2) state the rules governing direct imports; (3) give the volume or quantity of imports of the product originating in the third country concerned, originating in all third countries and originating in the Community; and (4) set out the economic difficulties alleged: EC Commission Decision 87/433 Art 2(4), first paragraph (a)–(d). Information under heads (3) and (4) must cover the two preceding years and the current year: Art 2(4), second paragraph. Where the information cannot be supplied accurately or in time, the request must contain the information available: Art 2(4), second paragraph.
17 Ibid Art 2(1). Economic difficulties may be indicated by such factors as consumption of the product and the respective market shares held by national production, the third country concerned and all third countries: Art 2(4), first paragraph (d).
18 P Eeckhout *The European Internal Market and International Trade: A Legal Analysis* (Clarendon, Oxford, 1994) at p 178.
19 Ibid Art 2(2).
20 Ibid Art 2(3).
 1 Ibid Art 2(4); but see Case 41/76 *Criel v Procureur de la Republique* [1976] ECR 1921 at 1938.

order to ensure that the execution of commercial measures taken by a Member State in accordance with the Treaty are not obstructed by deflection of trade or where imports of that product give rise to economic difficulties.[2] Authorization to take protective measures may only be granted for a limited period, and where this is warranted by the gravity of the economic difficulties encountered by the requesting Member State.[3] Although EC Art 115 distinguishes between measures taken to ensure the effectiveness of the Common Commercial Policy against deflections of trade and measures taken to combat economic difficulties, in the practice of the Commission these two facets of the provision tend to be read in conjunction.[4]

The introduction of the request may not prevent the issue of import documents for which application has already been made.[5] The Member State is to inform applicants for import documents under the surveillance procedure of the introduction of a request for protective measures, and a copy of the request

2 Case 1/84R *Ilford SpA v EC Commission* [1984] ECR 423 at 429; Commission Decision 87/433 Art 3(1). The request for authorization must give the information detailed in heads (1) and (2) of fn 16 above, and give particulars of (1) the exporting Member State; (2) the date of application for an import document; (3) the volume or quantity of imports of the product originating in the third country concerned, originating in other third countries with which there are similar import arrangements, originating in all third countries and originating in the Community; (4) where possible the volume or quantity of re-exports of that product; and (5) the alleged economic difficulties as shown by the trend of such factors as production, utilisation of capacity, consumption, respective market shares held by the third country concerned, all third countries and national production, prices (that is to say, depressed prices or prevention of normal price rises), profits or losses, and employment: Art 3(3), first paragraph (a)–(e). The information required under heads (3)–(5) must cover the two preceding years and the current year: Art 3(2), second paragraph Where the information cannot be supplied accurately or in time the request must contain the information available. Where it considers it necessary, the Commission may hold an inquiry to check the validity of the information supplied by the Member States. In that case it may, where a lack of protective measures would result in the danger of material injury to the sector in question, authorize the application of provisional basis, pending the results of the inquiry Art 3(3), second paragraph.
3 Commission Decision Art 3(3).
4 The Commission Decision, implementing EC Art 115, stated that the fact that the Common Commercial Policy has not yet been fully realized means that there will still be disparities among the Member States' commercial policies which are likely to cause deflections of trade, which EC Art 115 is designed to prevent where such deflections lead to economic difficulties in one or more Member States: Commission Decision 80/47, OJ 22.1.80, L16/14, preamble, eighth recital. This Decision was replaced and repealed by Commission Decision 87/433, which refers simply to deflections of trade, which EC Art 115 is designed to prevent: Commission Decision 87/433, preamble, seventh recital, OJ 21.8.87 L238/47. See also P Vogelenzang, 'Two Aspects of Art 115 of the EEC Treaty' (1981) 18 CMLRev 169 at 170, n 3.
5 Ibid Art 3(4). This clause reflects the case law on the admissibility of complaints concerning the application of Art 115 in regard to the direct and individual concern required for Art 173 actions which has been at issue in Case 62/70 *Bock* [1971] ECR 897; Case 29/75 *Kaufhof* [1976] ECR 431; Case 231/82 *Spijker Kwasten BV v EC Commission* [1983] ECR 2559; and Case 1/84R *Ilford SpA v EC Commission* [1984] ECR 423. In Case 62/70, where the authorization under Art 115 had been requested specifically to deal with an import licence which had already been requested, and where the applicant had been notified of the impending rejection of this application contingent upon this authorization, the action was ruled to be admissible under reference to Joined Cases 106 and 107/63 *Toepfer* [1965] ECR 405. The same factual constellation was found in Case 29/75, where the Court implicitly rejected the Commission's argument that the application was inadmissible. In Case 231/82 the Court rejected the action, referring to its judgment in Case 25/62 *Plaumann* [1963] ECR 95, and distinguishing it from Case 62/72 since although the applicant was the only importer of the goods in question, the authorization granted did not concern the pending application for a licence, whereas regarding future applications direct effect could not be argued.
  However, if the volume of pending applications is more than 5% of the possible direct imports from the third country or 1 per cent of the total extra-Community imports during the

is to be sent to the other Member States.[6] The Commission is to decide on the request within five working days of its receipt.[7]

The relevant authorities of the importing Member State may ask an importer to state the origin of products subject to surveillance or protective measures on the customs declaration or on the application for an import document.[8] A serious and well-founded doubt is necessary before additional proof of the origin of such products can be requested, and such a request is not in itself enough to prevent the import of the products.[9]

JUDICIAL INTERPRETATION OF EC ARTICLE 115

During the transitional period,[10] in cases of urgency, Member States were entitled to take protective measures unilaterally and then notify them to the other Member States and to the Commission, which could decide that the Member State concerned should amend or abolish the measures.[11] Failure to notify such measures to the Commission did not render them invalid.[12] After the end of the transitional period on 31 December 1971, however, Member States were not entitled to apply protective measures unilaterally.[13] This point was stated clearly by the European Court of Justice in Case 41/76 *Donckerwolcke*.[14]

The case was a reference for a preliminary ruling under EEC Art 177. The defendants in the main action were merchants established in Belgium who had imported into France cloth of synthetic fibres and packing sacks from the Lebanon and Syria. The goods had been duly put into free circulation in Belgium and subsequently introduced into France under the Community goods movement certificates used by the Belgian authorities. The certificates did not contain any indication of the actual origin of the product. However, French legislation required that, for goods which did not as yet come within the common commercial policy, the importer was obliged to state both the Member State in which the goods were first released to the Community market and also the original source. After the conviction and sentencing of the defendants at first instance, the appellate court referred the case to the European Court of Justice.

The European Court stated that, during the transitional period, when the importation in question occurred, the requirement of an import licence imposed on the importer of goods put into free circulation in another Member

last twelve-month period for which statistical information is available, the maximum period for the issue of import documents is increased to ten working days from the date of the importer's application (Art 3(5)(i)), and the Member State may reject the application for import documents if the Commission's decision authorizes it to do so (Art 3(5)(ii)).

6 Ibid Art 3(6).
7 Ibid Art 3(7). In practice Commission decisions have often been retroactive. Concerning retroactivity see especially Case 1/84R *Ilford SpA v EC Commission* [1984] ECR 423 at 431, where the Court underlined retroactive authorization of interim measures may be legal, but only where the retroactive nature of the decision is made explicit and adequately justified. Exhaustively on import licences and retroactivity, and the development of the Commission's and the Court's position in this context see Vogelenzang, op cit, at 187–195.
8 Ibid Art 4(1).
9 Ibid Art 4(2).
10 See EEC Art 8.
11 EC Art 115, second paragraph.
12 Case 27/78 *Amministrazione delle Finanze dello Stato v Rasham* [1978] ECR 1761 .
13 See EC Art 115, second paragraph.
14 Case 41/76 *Suzanne Criel, née Donckerwolcke and Henri Schou v Procureur de la République* [1976] ECR 1921.

State was, within limits, compatible with Community law at the time.[15] Even then, Member States did not enjoy an absolute discretion and could not introduce any new quantitative restrictions or equivalent measures which made more restrictive the rules applicable on the entry into force of the Treaty.[16] After the end of the transitional period, however, full responsibility in the matter of commercial policy was transferred to the Community by means of EEC Art 113(1). Consequently, measures of commercial policy of a national character were permissible after the end of the transitional period only by virtue of specific authorization of the Community.[17]

The authorization by the Commission is necessary even in an emergency.[18] This is expressly stated in Art 115 as amended by the Treaty on European Union. The second paragraph of the Article enables the Member States requesting authorization to take the necessary measures in case of urgency; in such a case the measures are formulated by the Member States in question. Their application remains subject however to a Commission decision, and the Commission may decide at any time that the Member States concerned shall amend or abolish the measures in question. This clause reflects general practice.[19]

It should be noted that in theory the Commission has the discretion to authorize or refuse the use of Art 115.[20] In practice the Commission's granting of authorization is contingent on a request to that effect by a Member State. This reflects the nature of Art 115 as a pragmatic political compromise. On the one hand, the Commission is able to bring national restrictions under Community control. On the other hand, certain Member States have under this system managed to continue specific restrictive practices for decades. In fact, although the use of Art 115 was to be phased out with the completion of the Common Commercial Policy it passed the 1992 deadline practically unscathed.

The derogations allowed under EC Art 115 must be strictly interpreted and applied.[1] On the one hand, they constitute not only an exception to EC Arts 9 and 30, which are fundamental to the operation of the market. On the other hand, they are also an obstacle to the implementation of the Common Commercial Policy provided for by EC Art 113.

---

15 [1976] ECR 1921 at 1940, paragraph 49.

16 [1976] ECR 1921 at 1940, paragraphs 50, 51.

17 [1976] ECR 1921 at 1937, paragraph 32. See also Case 1/84R *Ilford SpA v EC Commission* [1984] ECR 423 at 430, paragraph 18.

18 Case 179/78 *Procureur de la Republique v Rivoira* [1979] ECR 1147. Compare Commission Decision 87/433 Art 3(3), OJ 21.8.87 L238/26, on interim protective measures.

19 It should be recalled that retroactivity of such authorization is possible under certain conditions. Cf P Eeckhout *The European Internal Market and International Trade: A Legal Analysis* (Clarendon, Oxford, 1994) at pp 179–181.

20 Such authorization must be explicit and also otherwise in accordance with the provisions of Commission Decision 87/433 OJ L238, 21.8.87, p 26. In Case C-29/92 *Asia Motor France v Commission* [1992] ECR I-3935, the applicants failed in their plea that what they claimed had been a failure by the Commission to act under Art 169 against a presumed breach of Art 30 by France constituted an implicit authorization of the contested national measure under Art 115, and that therefore the Commission had exceeded its powers.

1 Case 29/75 *Kaufhof AG v EC Commission* [1976] ECR 431 at 443. See also Case 62/70 *Bock v EC Commission* [1971] ECR 897 at 909, and Case 41/76 *Criel v Procureur de la Republique* [1976] ECR 1921 at 1937. In Case 29/75, above, the Court annulled the Commission's decision to authorize Germany to apply measures under the EEC Treaty Art 115, because it failed to review independently whether the measures were in accordance with the treaty and necessary within the meaning of Art 115. In Case 62/70, above, the Commission's decision was annulled because, in the Court's view, the volume of exports which the measure was intended to cover was so small that the adoption of a measure under Art 115 was not necessary within the meaning of Art 115, first paragraph.

If the Common Commercial Policy were complete in all respects, Art 115 would in theory be redundant.[2] Until recently, however, it has retained its importance. The Common Commercial Policy was incomplete in respect of certain sensitive products, arrangements with regard to quantitative restrictions and voluntary export restraints applicable to those products varied between Member States, and with the accession of new Member States the uniform application of the Common Customs Tariff may take further time to achieve.

The principal use of Art 115 has been in the textiles sector, where the most extensive set of national quotas had been negotiated under the Multi-Fibre Arrangement (MFA).[3] The Court of Justice held that EC Arts 113 EC and 115, taken together, were to be interpreted as meaning that the Commission could still apply Art 115 in relation to international trade in textiles even after the conclusion of the MFA and the adoption of Regulation 3589/82.[4]

The *Tezi Textiel* cases concerned textile products imported from Macao and in free circulation in Italy. The products were subject to a Community quota under the MFA, divided into national subquotas, and also to a Commission authorization under Art 115 of national surveillance by the Benelux countries. The applicant brought an action before the Dutch courts against the refusal of import licences for such products from Italy, which formed the subject of a reference for a preliminary ruling.[5] It also brought a direct action against the Commission for its repeated authorization of exclusion from Community treatment.[6]

Tezi's main argument was that the adoption of measures of Common Commercial Policy under Art 113 foreclosed subsequent recourse to Art 115. The Commission argued that the first paragraph of Art 115 covered measures implemented by the Member States in order to comply with Community obligations as well as those taken for purely national reasons, and that the lack of uniformity in the system introduced by Regulation 3589/82 determined the applicability of Art 115.

The Court found that although Regulation 3589/82 formed 'a step towards a common commercial policy based, in accordance with Art 113(1) of the Treaty,

---

2 Compare COM(85) 310 final *Completing the Internal Market. White Paper from the Commission to the European Council (Milan, 28 and 29 June 1985)* paragraphs 35 and 26. Art 115 is discussed here in the context of removing internal border controls, since under this Article 'National measures stemming from authorization by the Commission necessarily involve formalities at internal frontiers'. The Commission expressed the aim of abolishing the national and regional quotas required for the full application of the common commercial policy before 1992. Art 115 would then no longer be applicable, and import restrictions would have to take place on a Community wide basis. If all individual quotas for the Member States would not have been abolished, alternatives to internal border controls would have to be found. Experience has shown otherwise. The EC Art 115 in the Treaty on European Union in fact largely retains the wording and intent of the previous EEC Art 115.

3 Figures for the application of Art 115 are found in the general reports of the Community. See also A Sapir 'Does 1992 come before or after 1990? On Regional versus Multilateral Integration' CEPR Discussion Paper 313 (London, 1989) at 12–14; C Stevens 'The Impact of 1992 on the Maghreb and Sub-Saharan Africa' (1990) 29 JCMS 217 at 226–227.

4 Case 59/84 *Tezi Textiel BV v EC Commission* [1986] ECR 887; Case 242/84 *Tezi BV v Minister for Economic Affairs* [1986] ECR 933. In Case 52/77 *Cayrol v Rivoira* [1977] ECR 2261, the issue of the application of Art 115 to measures taken under the common commercial policy was first raised. Here under the Trade Agreement between the EEC and Spain (Regulation 1524/70, OJ 1970 L182/1) the Member States had been authorized to impose seasonal national quotas on Spanish table grapes. The Court concluded that Spanish table grapes were not covered by the common commercial policy between 1 July and 31 December, the period for which the seasonal quotas had been authorized.

5 Case 242/84 fn 4 above.

6 Case 59/84 fn 4 above.

on uniform principles', it did not bring about complete uniformity of conditions for imports, and hence Art 115 remained applicable.[7] In following the Commission's argument, the Court seemed to come close to accepting that Community regulation might entail the introduction of new disparities, which would then legitimize the use of Art 115 in order to perpetuate them.[8]

Tezi meant at least that the applicability of Art 115 was not limited to national measures of trade policy otherwise in accordance with the Treaty that had received specific authorization from the Commission. Another important result of this judgment was that Community measures taken under the Common Commercial Policy which entailed the setting of national subquotas were legal. These subquotas in turn constituted a serious obstacle to the free movement of goods. Hence their use was to be seen as an exception, requiring express and specific authorization.[9]

THE ROLE OF EC ARTICLE 115 TODAY

EC Art 115 has only limited practical significance today. In 1994 the Community enacted new legislation on the administration of quotas.[10] It abolished the allocation of quotas among Member States as inconsistent with the completion of the internal market and the development of a uniform Common Commercial Policy.[11] In addition, in 1994 the Community also enacted new common rules on imports.[12] National restrictions on imports were abolished,[13] except for the general, security and balance of payments exceptions permitted under GATT 1994.[14] Since these measures were enacted, EC Art 115 has not been used.

7 Case 59/84 *Tezi Textiel* [1986] ECR 887, at paragraphs 36–38. Compare Art 1 of EC Commission Decision 87/433 OJ 21.8.87 L238/26, which has made the absence of 'uniform conditions of imports in the Member States' the exclusive criterion determining the scope of the implementation of Art 115. The Court distinguished both from Case 41/76 *Donckerwolcke v Procureur de la Republique* [1976] ECR 1921 and Case 218/82 *Commission v Council* [1983] ECR 4063, where it had not considered the legal consequences of non-uniform measures of commercial policy. In Case 218/82, the Court clearly stated that while the division of a Community quota into subquotas may be legal, it cannot be allowed to hinder the free movement of goods imported under these subquotas once the goods have been brought into free circulation in one of the Member States.

8 Compare the contrary Opinion of Advocate General Verloren van Themaat in Case 59/84 and 242/84, delivered on 2 October 1985, [1986] ECR 887. For other critical views of *Tezi* see M Cremona 'The Completion of the Internal Market and the Incomplete Commercial Policy of the European Community' (1990) 15 ELR 283; Oliver, fn 10, p 204 above.

9 Compare Case 51/87 *Commission v Council* ('GSP Case') [1988] ECR 5459. This case concerned the generalised system of preferences for certain imports from developing countries established by Regulation 3294/86 1986 OJ L373/1 (industrial products), and Regulation 3925/86 OJ L373/68 (textiles). For the textiles regulation the Commission proposed a system of establishing a Community reserve and transfer of national subquota shares to replace the traditional rigid national subquotas in this sector. Regarding industrial goods the Commission contested the legality of national subquotas outright. The Court recognized the need for a transfer system, accepted that fixed national shares were incompatible with the Treaty, and declared void the contested regulations. See Cremona, fn 8 above.

10 Council Regulation 520/94, OJ 10.3.94 L66/1, as to which see Chapter 11 on the Administration of Quotas in this book.

11 Ibid preamble, fourth and fifth recitals.

12 Council Regulation 3285/94, OJ 31.12.94 L349/53, as to which see Chapter 8 on Imports in this book.

13 Ibid Arts 1(2), 24(2).

14 This was consistent with the completion of the internal market, and it also stemmed from the requirement to abolish all import restrictions other than those applied in conformity with GATT Article XIX: see WTO Agreement on Safeguards, Art 11(1).

However, EC Art 115 may still be of potential importance in several circumstances.

First, if import quotas were to be applied on a regional basis, a deflection of trade might occur in order to circumvent the restrictions. This could be prevented by recourse to EC Art 115.[15] The likelihood of this is now substantially reduced, however, because most quotas can no longer be applied on a regional basis.

Second, Member States are entitled to institute import prohibitions conforming to the General Exception[16] and the Security Exceptions[17] of GATT 1994.[18] In principle EC Art 115 could be invoked to ensure the effectiveness of such national restrictions.

Art 115 does not apply, however, to another possible source of deflection of trade. Under the WTO Agreement, WTO members are permitted inter alia to institute quantitative restrictions or impose tariff surcharges on imports in order to forestall or remedy a serious balance of payments problem.[19] Currently this applies to all of the Community's Member States.[20] It will continue to apply to those Member States which do not participate in monetary union.[1] It would therefore appear that such Member States may be able unilaterally to introduce national quantitative restrictions or tariff surcharges against imports from third countries in such circumstances.[2] Under EC Art 109h, the Council may allow a Member State inter alia to take measures needed to avoid deflection of trade where the State which is in difficulties maintains or reintroduces quantitative restrictions against third countries.[3] Where a sudden balance of payments crisis occurs and no immediate decision under Art 109h(2) is taken, a Member State may, as a precaution, take necessary protective measures.[4] These measures however lie outside the scope of EC Art 115.

---

15 Note that, under Commission Decision 87/433 Art 2(2), the authorization would be granted under Art 115 only where there were significant imports of the product from other Member States.
16 GATT 1994 Art XX.
17 Ibid Art XXI.
18 See Council Regulation 3285/94 Art 24(2)(1)(i), OJ 31.12.94 L349/53.
19 GATT 1994 Art XII; Understanding on the Balance of Payments Provisions of the GATT 1994 paras 1–4.
20 EC Art 109h.
 1 See EC Art 109k(6).
 2 See also Council Regulation 3290/94 Art 24(2)(a)(i), OJ 31.12.94 L349/105.
 3 EC Art 109h(2)(b). Further measures may be authorized by the Commission: Art 109h(3), first paragraph. They are subject to change or revocation by the Council, acting by a qualified majority: Art 109h(3), second paragraph.
 4 EC Art 109i(1), which also provides that the measures must cause the least possible disturbance in the functioning of the common market and must not be wider in scope than is strictly necessary to remedy the sudden difficulties which have arisen. The Commission and the other Member States must be informed: Art 109i(2). Acting by a qualified majority, the Council may amend, suspend or abolish the protective measures: Art 109i(3).

Chapter 13

Dumping and subsidies

INTRODUCTION

Following the conclusion of the Uruguay Round of GATT,[1] the European Community has adopted new rules on anti-dumping[2] and countervailing duty law.[3] These two new Regulations implement the new GATT Codes on the Interpretation of Article VI[4] and on Subsidies and Countervailing Measures.[5] Thus, for the first time, the Community has established different Regulations for Anti-dumping and Countervailing Duty law. However, the Regulations only diverge with the respect to the respective rules on the calculation of the dumping margin and the countervailable subsidy margin. Injury and procedural issues are regulated in essentially the same way.

Anti-dumping measures and measures countervailing subsidies target different unfair trade practices. Anti-dumping measures are intended to offset the distortive effects which dumping practised by firms established in third countries cause in the Community market. Countervailing measures have the purpose of offsetting the distortive effects in the Community market resulting from unfair foreign government subsidization. The measures may overlap sometimes. Following Article VI of GATT, both Regulations prohibit the imposition of both countervailing and anti-dumping measures on the same product for the purpose of dealing with one and the same situation arising from dumping or from subsidization.[6] In practice, the European Community has basically limited itself to the use of anti-dumping duties.

---

1 The Uruguay Round was launched on 20 September 1986 in Punta del Este, Uruguay. See GATT BISD 33 Supp 11 (1987). It concluded in Geneva on 17 December 1993. Its Final Act was signed in Marrakesh on 15 April 1994. After ratification by most contracting parties it entered into force on 1 January 1995. See 33 ILM 3 (1994); see also 33 ILM 1125 (1994); see also Council Decision 94/800, concerning the conclusion on behalf of the European Community, as regards matters within its competence, of the agreements reached in the Uruguay Round multilateral negotiations (1986–1994), OJ 23.12.94 L336/1.
2 See Council Regulation 384/96, OJ 6.3.96 L56/1, as amended by Council Regulation 2331/96, OJ 6.12.96 L317/1, and Council Regulation 905/98, OJ 30.4.98 L128/18, replacing Council Regulation 3283/94, OJ 31.12.94 L349/1, as amended by Council Regulation 1251/95, OJ 2.6.95 L122/1.
3 See Council Regulation 2026/97, OJ 21.10.97 L288/1, replacing Council Regulation 3284/94, OJ 31.12.94 L349/22, as amended by Council Regulation 1252/95, OJ 2.6.95 L122/2.
4 See *Agreement on the Implementation of Article VI* OJ 23.12.94 L336/103.
5 See *Agreement on Subsidies and Countervailing Measures* OJ 23.12.94 L336/156.
6 Council Regulation 384/96 Art 14(1), OJ 6.3.96 L56/1; see also Council Regulation 2026/97 Art 24(1), OJ 21.10.97 L288/1.

INSTITUTIONAL FRAMEWORK

The institutional framework of the Anti-dumping and Countervailing Duty Regulations reflects the traditional division of powers in trade policy between the different Community authorities.[7] The Community institutions dealing with countervailing and anti-dumping measures are the Commission, the Council and the advisory committees in which representatives of the Member States participate. Legal acts adopted in application of these Regulations may be reviewed by the Court of First Instance and the European Court of Justice.

The Commission plays a preponderant role in the implementation of the Countervailing and Anti-dumping Regulations. Directions C and E of Directorate General I are in charge of the conduct of all investigations, including the determination of dumping or unfair subsidization, injury and Community interest. Furthermore it is for the Commission to initiate, impose provisional duties, accept undertakings, terminate proceedings without measures, order the registration of imports and make proposals for the imposition of definitive duties.

All actions by the Commission must be taken in consultation with an advisory committee. The advisory committee consists of representatives of each Member State, with a representative of the Commission as a chairman.[8] Consultations with the advisory committee must take place when the Regulations require it or at the request of a Member State or the Commission. In exceptional circumstances consultation may be in writing.[9] Matters to be covered in the consultations are, in particular, the existence of dumping or subsidization and the method to establish the dumping margin or rate of subsidization, the existence and extent of injury, the causal link between dumped imports and injury and the determination of the measures which are appropriate.

It is for the Council to decide, acting by simple majority, following a proposal from the Commission, on the imposition of definitive duties.[10] However, when objections have been raised in the advisory committee with regard to a Commission decision, the Council can reverse the Commission's decision only by qualified majority within one month of the Commission's decision.[11] The Council has generally followed the Commission's proposals.[12]

It is for the customs officials of the Member States to collect definitive duties, require a bond for provisional duties or register imported products in the form and at the rate specified and according to criteria laid down in the regulations imposing measures.[13] Member States must co-operate with the Commission in

---

7 See Art 113 of the EC Treaty.
8 Council Regulation 384/96 Art 15, OJ 6.3.96 L56/1; see also Council Regulation 2026/97 Art 25, OJ 21.10.97 L288/1.
9 Council Regulation 384/96 Art 15(3), OJ 6.3.96 L56/1; see also Council Regulation 2026/97 Art 25(3), OJ 21.10.97 L288/1.
10 Council Regulation 384/96 Art 9(4), OJ 6.3.96 L56/1; see also Council Regulation 2026/97 Art 15(1), OJ 21.10.97 L288/1; see also Case 299/85 *Tokyo Juki Industrial Co Ltd v Council and Commission* [1986] ECR 2965; see also Case C-121/86 *Epicheiriseon Metalleftikon Viomichanikon Kai Naftukiakon v Council* [1989] ECR 3919.
11 Council Regulation 384/96 Arts 7(6), 8(5), 9(2), OJ 6.3.96 L56/1; see also Council Regulation 2026/97 Arts 12(5) 13(5) and 14(2), OJ 21.10.97 L288/1.
12 But see *Dead Burned Magnesite from the PRC and North Korea* OJ 19.6.85 L149/2 (where the Council exceptionally did not accept a Commission proposal to impose definitive duties).
13 Council Regulation 384/96 Arts 14(1),14(5) and 14(6), OJ 6.3.96 L56/1; see also Council Regulation 2026/97 Arts 24(1), 24(5) and 24(6), OJ 21.10.97 L288/1.

the investigation of alleged dumping or subsidy practices.[14] The verification visits carried out by the Commission are assisted by officials of those Member States who so request.[15]

The Community authorities have wide discretionary powers in their decisions in connection with proceedings relating to the possible adoption of anti-dumping or countervailing duties.[16]

SUBSTANTIVE ELEMENTS

To take any measures, the Community authorities must make an affirmative determination of three basic elements: the existence of dumping or a countervailable subsidy, the existence of injury resulting from the unfair dumping or subsidizing practice, and an affirmative determination that the Community interest calls for the adoption of measures.[17]

Determination of dumping

The legal definition of dumping is based on the notion of price discrimination on two different markets and not on the notion of an export sale made at a price below cost.[18] A determination of dumping consists in a comparison between the price of the product exported to the Community and the 'normal value' of the identical or closely similar product.[19] To assess whether dumping exists it will be necessary to make three basic calculations: the calculation of normal value and export price and a fair comparison between the export price and the normal value.

Normal value

The methodology used by the Community authorities to establish the normal value varies depending on whether the export country is a market economy or a non-market economy country.[20]

Normal value for market economy countries

In general, normal value is established on the basis of the comparable price actually paid or payable for the like product in the ordinary course of trade by independent customers in the exporting country.[1] The exporting country will

---

14 Art 6(3) of Council Regulation 384/96, OJ 6.3.96 L56/1; see also Council Regulation 2026/97 Art 11(3), OJ 21.10.97 L288/1.
15 Council Regulation 384/96 Art 16(4), OJ 6.3.96 L56/1; see also Art 26(4) of Council Regulation 2026/97, OJ 21.10.97 L288/1.
16 See Case 122/86 *Anonymos Etaireia Epicheiriseon Metalleftikon Viomichanikon kai Naftiliakon AE v Commission and Council* [1989] ECR 3959.
17 Council Regulation 384/96 Arts 1(1), 7(1) and 9(4), OJ 6.3.96 L56/1; see also Council Regulation 2026/97 Arts 1(1), 12(1) and 15(1), OJ 21.10.97 L288/1.
18 See Case 157/87 *Electroimpex v Council* [1990] ECR I-3021.
19 Council Regulation 384/96 Art 1(2) and 1(4), OJ 6.3.96 L56/1.
20 As to the distinction between market and non-market economies see the Opinion of Advocate General van Gerven in Case C-16/90 *Nolle v Hauptzollamt Bremen-Freihafen* [1991] ECR I-5163.
1 Council Regulation 384/96 Art 2(1), OJ 6.3.96 L56/1.

normally be the country of origin but it may also be an intermediate country.[2] If the exporter in the exporting country does not produce or does not sell the like product, the normal value may be established on the basis of the prices of other sellers or producers.[3] The Commission will try to establish a single normal value for the product concerned for each producer for the entire investigation period. The investigation of dumping will cover a period of not less than six months immediately prior to the initiation of the proceedings.[4] In practice, the investigation period is normally of at least one year.[5] Information relating to a period subsequent to the investigation will normally not be taken into account.[6] If a party considers that the investigation period chosen by the Commission is not appropriate, it must submit its objections at the earliest opportunity.[7]

In order to qualify as normal value, the sales in the domestic market of the exporting country in the ordinary course of trade must be at least 5 per cent of the exports to the Community.[8] Domestic sales below cost of production will be excluded for the purposes of calculating whether domestics sales constitute at least 5 per cent of the export sales.[9] However, domestic sales must not be considered only if it is determined that such sales are made within an extended period of time in substantial quantities and are at prices which do not provide for recovery.[10] Thus, domestic sales must not be considered as sales below cost if prices which are below cost at the time of sale are above weighted average costs for the period of investigation;[11] or the sales below costs are not in an extended period of time considered to be of one year but in no case less than six months;[12] or the weighted average selling price is not below the weighted

---

2 Ibid Art 1(3), which also indicates when the use of an intermediate country as the exporting country would not be appropriate.

3 Ibid Art 2(1); see also *Stainless steel fasteners and parts thereof originating in the PRC, India, the Republic of Korea, Malaysia, Taiwan and Thailand* OJ 20.2.98 L50/1.

4 Council Regulation 384/96 Art 6(1), OJ 6.3.96 L56/1.

5 See *Polyester filament yarn from Indonesia and Thailand* OJ 29.5.96 L128/3 (where the investigation of dumping covered the period from 1 July 1993 to 30 June 1994). A period of a calendar year may be chosen where this facilitates the examination of data see *Furfuryl alcohol from the People's Republic of China and Thailand* OJ 7.5.96 L112/18 (investigation period calendar year 1994). A longer time period may be used see *Disodium carbonate from the United States of America* OJ 13.4.95 L83/8 (investigation period of 18 months).

6 Council Regulation 384/96 Art 6(1), OJ 6.3.96 L56/1; see also *Disodium carbonate from the USA* OJ 12.10.95 L244/32; see also *Microwave ovens from the PRC, the Republic of Korea, Thailand and Malaysia* OJ 7.7.95 L156/5; see also Case 204/84 *Toyo Bearing v Council* [1987] ECR 1809.

7 See *Ferro-silico-manganese from Russia, Ukraine, Brazil and South Africa* OJ 14.10.95 L248/1.

8 Art 2(2)Council Regulation 384/96, OJ 6.3.96 L56/1, which also allows the Commission to make some exceptions; see also *Certain magnetic disks from the United States, Mexico and Malaysia* OJ 17.10.95 L249/3 (where the domestic sales price was refused because the producer did not reach the 5% threshold of sales); see also Case C-105/90 *Goldstar Co Ltd v Council* [1992] ECR I-677.

9 See *Dot matrix printers from Japan* OJ 24.11.88 L317/33; see also *Disodium carbonate from the United States of America* OJ 13.4.95 L83/8; see also *Bicycles from Indonesia, Malaysia and Thailand* OJ 14.10.95 L248/12; see also Joined Cases 277 & 300/85 *Canon v Council* [1988] ECR 5731.

10 This applies to both domestic sales and sales in third countries. See Council Regulation 384/96 Art 2(4), OJ 6.3.96 L56/1; but see *Urea from Saudi Arabia, Czechoslovakia, GDR, Kuwait, USSR, Trinidad and Tobago* OJ 7.11.87 L317/1 (following the practice previous to the new rules).

11 Council Regulation 384/96 Art 2(4)(a), OJ 6.3.96 L56/1.

12 Ibid Art 2(4)(b).

average unit cost or the volume of sales below unit cost is less than 20 per cent of sales being used to determine normal value.[13]

Sales in the domestic market between producers or exporters and third parties with which they have association or compensatory agreements will not be used for the purpose of establishing the normal value unless the Community authorities determine that the transaction prices are not affected by such relationships.[14] The Commission will take as the domestic price that charged to the first independent buyer in the domestic market.[15] In cases where the producer sells its products in the domestic market through a related sales organization it will consider as the domestic price that price charged by the related sales organization to the first independent customer. In these cases it will not take into account the related sales subsidiary expenses.[16] The Commission will follow this approach even if the related sales organization is a different legal entity but is still economically controlled by the producer.[17] However, in cases where the sales are to independent distributors the normal value will be established on the sales to the independent distributors instead of those to the unrelated customers.[18]

If there are no sales of the like product in the domestic market of the exporting country or these sales are insufficient or the market does not permit a proper comparison, the normal value must be based on either the constructed value of the like product or the prices of export of the like product to a third country provided that the prices are representative.[19] In practice, the Community authorities have disregarded, for various reasons, the export prices to third countries.[20]

The purpose of constructing the normal value is to determine the selling price of the product as it would be if that product was sold in its country of export or

---

13 Ibid Art 2(4)(b); see also *Personal fax machines from the PRC, Japan, Republic of Korea, Malaysia, Singapore, Taiwan and Thailand* OJ 31.10.97 L297/61.
14 Council Regulation 384/96 Art 2(1)(b), OJ 6.3.96 L56/1.
15 Ibid Art 2(1).
16 See *Electronic Typewriters from Japan* OJ 15.8.85 L163/2; see also *Compact Disc Players from Japan and Korea* OJ 18.7.89 L205/9; see also *Drams from Japan* OJ 25.7.90 L193/1; see also *Dot matrix printers from Japan* OJ L317/33; see also *Electronic Scales from Japan* OJ 16.10.85 275/5; see also Joined Cases 277 & 300/85, *Canon v Council* [1988] ECR 5731(upholding the Commission practice); see also Case 250/85 *Brother Industries v Council* [1988] ECR 5683; see also Case 301/85 *Sharp v Council* [1988] ECR 5813; see also Joined Cases 273/85 & 107/86 *Silver Seiko v Council* [1988] ECR 5927; see also Case C-179/87 *Sharp Corp v Council* [1992] ECR I-1635.
17 This has been upheld by the European Court of Justice. See Joined Cases 273/85 & 107/86, *Silver Seiko v Council* [1988] ECR 5927 (where the Court held: 'The division of production and sales activities within a group made up of legally distinct companies can in no way alter the fact that the group is a single economic entity which carries out in that way activities that are in other cases carried out by what is in legal terms as well a single entity. By taking into consideration the sales' subsidiary's prices it is possible to ensure that costs which manifestly form part of the selling price of a product where the sale is made by an internal sales department of the manufacturing organization are not left out of account where the same selling activity is carried out by a company which, despite being financially controlled by the manufacturer, is a legally distinct entity.')
18 See *Compact disc players from Japan and Korea* OJ 17.1.90 L13/21.
19 Council Regulation 384/96 Art 2(3), OJ 6.3.96 L56/1.
20 See *Ballbearings from Singapore* OJ 23.3.84 L79/8; see also *Bisphenol from the USA* OJ 26.1.83 L23/9; see also *Electronic Typewriters from Japan* OJ 22.6.85 L163/1; see also *Colour television receivers originating in Malaysia, the PRC, the Republic of Korea, Singapore and Thailand* OJ 1.4.95 L73/3. In this sense the new GATT Antidumping Code seems to put a stronger emphasis on the use of the export prices to third countries. See Art 2(2) of the *Agreement on Implementation of Article VI of GATT 1994* OJ 23.12.94 L336/106.

origin.[1] In practice the Commission will always calculate the constructed value in order to check whether the domestic sales have been in the ordinary course of trade. The constructed value will be based on the cost of production including a reasonable amount for selling, general and administrative costs plus a reasonable amount for profits.[2] The cost of production must be calculated on the basis of all costs, fixed and variable, in the country of origin of material and manufacturer plus a reasonable amount for selling administrative and general expenses. In cases where the raw materials are purchased from related suppliers, the Community authorities will normally require evidence that the purchase prices are at arms length or that the purchase price covers the cost of production of the raw materials.[3]

The determination of selling and general administrative expenses must be based on data pertaining to production and sales in the ordinary course of trade of the producer.[4] The selling and administrative expenses to be included in the cost of production are those incurred in the domestic market and not those incurred in the export country.[5] The Commission will include in the cost of production an amount corresponding to the sales and general administrative expenses incurred by the domestic sales organization of the exporter. The Commission will do this even if the exporter has no sales in its domestic market.[6] If the selling and general expenses cannot be determined on the basis of the data relating to the production and sales in the ordinary course of trade of the producer, the Community authorities will establish those amounts on the basis of the weighted average of the actual amounts determined for other exporters or producers subject to investigation in respect of production and sales of the like product in the domestic market of the country of the country of origin;[7] or on the basis of the actual amounts applicable to production and sales, in the ordinary course of trade, of the same category of products for the export or producer in question in the domestic market of the country of origin;[8] or on the basis of any other reasonable method.[9]

The Commission will calculate the costs on the basis of the records kept by

---

1 See Joined Cases 277 & 300/85, *Canon v Council* [1988] ECR 5731; see also Joined Cases 260/85 & 106/86 *Tokyo Electric Co v Council* [1988] ECR 5855; see also Joined Cases 273/85 & 107/86 *Silver Seiko v Council* [1988] ECR 5927
2 Council Regulation 384/96 Art 2(3), OJ 6.3.96 L56/1; see also *Advertising matches from Japan* OJ 17.6.97 L158/9.
3 See *Titanium mill products from Japan and the USA* OJ 26.4.85 L113/30.
4 Council Regulation 384/96 Art 2(6), OJ 6.3.96 L56/1.
5 Ibid Art 2(6); see also *Plain Paper Photocopiers from Japan* OJ 24.12.87 L54/12; see also Case 250/85 *Brother Industries v Council* [1988] ECR 5683; see also Joined Cases 277 & 300/85 *Canon Inc v Council* [1988] ECR 5731; see also Joined Cases 260/85 & 106/86 *TEC v Council* [1988] ECR 5855; see also Joined Cases 273/85 & 107/86 *Silver Seiko v Council* [1988] ECR 5927.
6 See Joined Cases 260/85 & 106/86 *Tokyo Electric Co v Council* [1988] ECR 5855 (upholding this practice).
7 See Council Regulation 384/96 Art 2(6)(a), OJ 6.3.96 L56/1; see also *Disodium Carbonate from the United States of America* OJ 13.4.95 L83/8; see also *Advertising matches from Japan* OJ 17.6.97 L158/9.
8 Council Regulation 384/96 Art 2(6)(b), OJ 6.3.96 L56/1; see also *Colour television receivers from Malaysia, the PRC, the Republic of Korea and Thailand* OJ 1.10.94 L255/50 (provisional); see also *Colour television receivers originating in Malaysia, the PRC, the Republic of Korea, Singapore and Thailand* OJ 1.4.95 L73/3 (definitive); see also Joined Cases 260/85 & 106/86 *Tokyo Electric Co v Council* [1988] ECR 5855 (upholding a restrictive interpretation of the concept 'same category of products').
9 Council Regulation 384/96 Art 2(6)(c), OJ 6.3.96 L56/1; see also *Microwave ovens from the PRC, the Republic of Korea, Thailand and Malaysia* OJ 7.7.95 L156/5.

the party under investigation provided that such records are in accordance with the generally accepted accounting principles of the country concerned and they reasonably reflect the costs associated with the production and sale of the product under consideration.[10] In the allocation of costs the Community authorities will consider the evidence submitted on the proper allocation of costs provided that it is shown that such allocations have been historically used. Otherwise, preference will be given to the allocation of costs on the basis of turnover.[11] In any case, the costs must be adjusted appropriately for those non recurring items of cost which benefit future and or current production.[12]

Following the new Anti-dumping Code, the EC Regulation provides for consideration of start up phases.[13] A start up phase exists where there is a significant investment and new production facilities. This may cover both new products or new factories. When the costs for part of the period for cost recovery are affected by start up operations which take place within and during part of the investigation period, the average costs of the start up period will be those applicable, under the allocation rules at the end of such phase, and must be included at that level, for the period concerned, in the weighted average costs. The length of the start up phase is left open. It is determined in relation to the circumstances of the producer or exporter concerned but will not exceed an appropriate initial portion of the period for cost recovery.[14]

The margin of profit to be added to the cost of production will also be based on the production and sales in the domestic market, in the ordinary course of trade, of the like product by the exporter or producer under investigation.[15] The Commission will normally disregard non profitable sales for the purpose of establishing the profit margin.[16] In the case of a producer with a subsidiary, the Community authorities may use the combined profit margins of the two companies.[17] If such amounts cannot be determined, the profit margin will be based on the weighted average of the actual amounts determined for other exporters or producers subject to investigation in respect of production and sales of the like product in the domestic market of the country of origin;[18] or on the basis of the actual amounts applicable to production sales, in the ordinary course of trade, of the same category of products for the exporter or producer in question in the domestic market of the country of origin;[19] or any other reasonable method provided that the amount of profit does not exceed the profit normally realized by other exporters or producers on sales of products of the same category in the domestic market of the country of origin.[20]

---

10 Council Regulation 384/96 Art 2(5), OJ 6.3.96 L56/1.
11 Ibid.
12 Ibid.
13 See Art 2(2)(1)(1) and fn 6 of the *Agreements on the Implementation of Article VI of GATT 1994*; see also Art 2(5) of Council Regulation 384/96.
14 Council Regulation 384/96 Art 2(5), OJ 6.3.96 L56/1.
15 Ibid Art 2(6).
16 See *Bicycles from Indonesia, Malaysia and Thailand* OJ 14.10.95 L248/12; see also *Stainless steel fasteners and parts thereof originating in the PRC, India, the Republic of Korea, Malaysia, Taiwan and Thailand* OJ 20.2.98 L50/1.
17 See Joined Cases 273/85 & 107/86 *Silver Seiko v Council* [1988] ECR 5927.
18 Council Regulation 384/96 Art 2(6)(a), OJ 6.3.96 L56/1; see also *Disodium Carbonate from the United States of America* OJ 13.4.95 L83/8; see also *Microwave ovens from the PRC, the Republic of Korea, Thailand and Malaysia* OJ 7.7.795 L156/5; see also Joined Cases 260/85 & 106/86 *Tokyo Electric Co v Council* [1988] ECR 5855 (upholding this practice).
19 Council Regulation 384/96 Art 2(6)(b), OJ 6.3.96 L56/1.
20 Ibid Art 2(6)(c).

Normal value for non-market economy countries

If the allegedly dumped products are being exported from non-market economy countries, the Community authorities will try to establish the normal value of such products by reference to a market economy country.[1] The aim of this provision is to prevent account from being taken of prices and costs in non-market economy countries which are not normally the result of market forces.[2] The Community authorities will generally not take into account the circumstances of non-market economy countries in transition to market economy systems. Rather they will look at the non-market economy as a whole and not to the competitiveness of the specific producers under consideration.[3]

The first step in the determination of the normal value for the non-market economy country is the selection of an analogue market economy country. The Community authorities have a wide margin of discretion in the selection of the analogue country.[4] However, this discretion is not absolute and it is subject to the Court's review.[5] Basically the new rules codify previous Commission practice. The selection of the analogue country will be done in a not unreasonable manner taking account of any reliable information made available at the time of the selection and having regard to the time limits.[6] If possible, the Community authorities will use as an analogue country, one which is subject to the same investigation.[7] Only exceptionally will the Community market be used as an analogue country.[8]

In the selection of the analogue market economy country, the Community authorities will not look at the macroeconomic data of that country but rather to its specific market for the like product.[9] The two main factors in the selection

---

1 For these purposes, the list of non-market economies includes Albania, Armenia, Azerbaijan, Belarus, Georgia, Kazakhstan, North Korea, Kyrgyzstan, Moldavia, Mongolia, Tajikistan, Turkmenistan, Ukraine, Uzbekistan and Vietnam. See Council Regulation 384/96 Art 2(7)(a), OJ 6.3.96 L56/1, as amended by Council Regulation 905/98, OJ 30.4.98 L128/18.

2 See Joined Cases 294/86 & 77/87 *Technointorg v Commission and Council* [1988] ECR 6077; see also Joined Cases C-305/86 & C-160/87 *Neotype Techmashexport v Commission and Council* [1990] ECR I-2945; see also Case 157/87 *Electroimpex v Council* [1990] ECR I- 3021; see also Case-16/90 *Detlef Nolle v Hauptzollamt Bremen-Freihafen* [1991] ECR I-5163.

3 See *Video tapes in cassettes from China* OJ 26.4.91 L106/15; see also *Coumarin originating in the PRC* OJ 4.4.96 L86/1.

4 See Joined Cases 305/86 & 160/87 *Neotype Techmashexport v Commission and Council* [1990] ECR I-2945; see also Joined Cases 294/86 & 77/87 *Technointorg v Commission and Council* [1988] ECR 6077; see also Case T-164/94 *Ferchimex SA v Council* [1995] ECR II-2681.

5 See Case C-16/90 *Detlef Nolle v Hauptzollamt Bremen-Freihafen* [1991] ECR I-5163; see also Case C-26/96 *Rotexchemie International Handels GmbH & Co v Hauptzollamt Hamburg-Waltershof* [1997] ECR I-2817.

6 Council Regulation 384/96 Art 2(7)(a), OJ 6.3.96 L56/1, as amended by Council Regulation 905/98, OJ 30.4.98 L128/19.

7 Ibid; see also *Microwave ovens from the PRC, the Republic of Korea, Thailand and Malaysia* OJ 7.7.95 L156/5.

8 Council Regulation 384/96 Art 2(7)(a), OJ 6.3.96 L56/1, as amended by Council Regulation 905/98, OJ 30.4.98 L128/19.

9 See *Unwrought unalloyed magnesium from the PRC* OJ 14.5.98 L142/25 (where the analogue country for the PRC was Norway); see also *Coumarin originating in the PRC* OJ 4.4.96 L86/1 (where the analogue country for the PRC was the USA); see also *Ammonium nitrate from Russia* OJ 23.8.95 L198/1; see also *Powdered activated carbon from the PRC* OJ 15.8.95 L192/14; see also *Refractory Chammottes from the PRC* OJ 29.7.95 L179/56; see also Joined Cases 305/86 & 160/87 *Neotype Techmashexport v Commission and Council* [1990] ECR I-2945, (upholding this practice); see also Case C-323/88 *Sermes v Directeur des Services des Douanes de Strasbourg* [1990] ECR I-3027.

of the analogue country are whether the analogue country's market is competitive, and the similarity of the production volume and methods of the like product. In this sense, 'like product' is to be understood as meaning an identical product, that is, a product similar in all respects to the product under consideration or, in the absence of such a product, another product having characteristics closely resembling those of the production in question.[10] Minor differences between the products will not prevent them from being considered alike but may result in adjustment of the differences. In the analysis of whether the analogue country's market is competitive the Commission will look at different factors such as whether several producers compete,[11] whether the market is not isolated from imports with high trade barriers,[12] whether there is a substantial domestic market for the product concerned,[13] whether prices are affected by governmental regulations,[14] etc. In determining the similarity of the analogue country's market with the exporter's market, the Community authorities will have regard to different factors such as whether the volume of production of the analogue country is similar to that of exports to the Community from the non-market economy country,[15] and will give special emphasis to whether the producers in the analogue country use the same production techniques and have the same access to raw materials as the producers under investigation.[16] In the analysis of the analogue country's market no factor is totally decisive.[17] In practice, the Commission will take into account considerations of administrative convenience. It will first take into consideration those analogue countries suggested by the parties.[18] The Commission will also prefer to choose those

10 See Joined Cases C-304/86 & C-185/87 *Enital SpA v Commission and Council* [1990] ECR I-2939.
11 See *Tube or pipe fittings, of iron or steel, originating in the PRC, Croatia, Thailand, Slovak Republic and Taiwan* OJ 3.10.95 L234/4. However, the mere fact that there is only one producer in the reference country does not in itself preclude the prices there from being the result of genuine competition, since such competition may just as well result, in the absence of price controls, from the presence of significant imports from other countries. See Case C-26/96 *Rotexchemie International Handels GmbH & Co v Hauptzollamt Hamburg-Waltershof* [1997] ECR I-2817.
12 See *Ammonium nitrate from Russia* OJ 23.8.95 L198/1; see also *Unwrought magnesium originating in Russia and Ukraine* OJ 23.12.95 L312/37.
13 See *Unwrought magnesium originating in Russia and Ukraine* OJ 23.12.95 L312/37; see also *Powdered activated carbon from the PRC* OJ 15.8.95 L192/14.
14 See *Polyenthine from the USSR, GDR, Czechoslovakia and Poland* OJ 27.5.83 L138/65.
15 See *Unwrought magnesium originating in Russia and Ukraine* OJ 23.12.95 L312/37; see also *Powdered activated carbon from the PRC* OJ 15.8.95 L192/14; see also *Furfuraldehyde from the PRC* OJ 21.1.95 L15/11.
16 See *Tube or pipe fittings, of iron or steel, originating in the PRC, Croatia, Thailand, Slovak Republic and Taiwan* OJ 3.10.95 L234/4; see also *Coumarin from the PRC* OJ 7.10.95 L239/4; see also *Unwrought unalloyed magnesium from the PRC* OJ 14.5.98 L142/25 (where the Commission used Norway as an analogue country despite the fact its industry used a production technique different to those used in China on the basis that the Norwegian production method was much more effective).
17 See Joined Cases 305/86 & 160/87 *Neotype Techmashexport v Commission and Council* [1990] ECR I-2945; see also Joined Cases C-320/86 & C-188/87 *Stanko France v Commission and Council* [1990] ECR I-3013.
18 See *Ammonium nitrate from Russia* OJ 23.8.95 L198/1; see also *Unwrought magnesium originating in Russia and Ukraine* OJ 23.12.95 L312/37; see also *Refractory Chammottes from the PRC* OJ 29.7.95 L179/56; see also *Microwave ovens from the PRC, the Republic of Korea, Thailand and Malaysia* OJ 7.7.95 L156/5 (where the fact that no other analogue country was suggested was decisive in the selection of another country under investigation).

countries in which the industry is willing to co-operate in the determination of the normal value.[19] If the co-operating firm in the analogue country is related to the complainant the information provided can still be used if it is checked and confirmed by the Commission.[20] The parties to the investigation must be informed shortly after the initiation of the investigation of the envisaged analogue country and must be given ten days to comment.[1]

Once the Community authorities have chosen an analogue country they must determine whether they will use its domestic prices, its export prices to third countries or a constructed value in that analogue country.[2] The Commission will first try to establish the normal value on the domestic price of sales made in the analogue country.[3] The mere fact that the producers in the analogue country have also been accused of dumping does not make the use of the domestic prices in that country unreliable. In order to consider the domestic sales in the analogue country the volume of the profitable sales must be at least 5 per cent of the exports sales from the non-market economy producers to the Community.[4] Otherwise, the Commission must use the export price to third countries, including the Community, or the constructed value in the analogue country. In practice, the Community authorities have very rarely used the export price to a third country. The Community authorities will establish the constructed value on the basis of the information provided by the co-operating industries in the analogue country.[5] No adjustments are made for any comparative advantage that might be claimed by the exporting non-market economy country other than those specifically provided for the comparison of the export price and the normal value.[6]

Special rules for China and Russia

In April 1998, in recognition of the efforts made by the People's Republic of China and the Russian Federation to transform their economies, the Community adopted special rules for these countries regarding the calculation of the normal value.[7]

19 See *Unwrought magnesium originating in Russia and Ukraine* OJ 23.12.95 L312/37; see also *Powdered activated carbon originating in the People's Republic of China* OJ 3.6.96 L134/20; see also *Certain handbags from the PRC* OJ 4.2.97 L33/11.
20 See *Refractory chamottes from the PRC* OJ 27.1.96 L21/1.
 1 Council Regulation 384/96 Art 2(7)(a), OJ 6.3.96 L56/1, as amended by Council Regulation 905/98, OJ 30.4.98 L128/19.
 2 See ibid Art 2(7)(a).
 3 See *Coumarin from the PRC* OJ 7.10.95 L239/4; see also *Powdered activated carbon from the PRC* OJ 15.8.95 L192/14; see also Joined Cases C-320/86 & C-188/87 *Stanko France v Commission and Council* [1990] ECR I-3013; see also Joined Cases 294/86 & 77/87 *Technointorg v Commission and Council* [1988] ECR 6077.
 4 See *Refractory chamottes from the PRC* OJ 19.7.95 L179/56.
 5 The constructed value is established as normal when determining the constructed value for a market economy country. See Council Regulation 384/96 Arts 2(3), 2(4), 2(5) and 2(6), OJ 6.3.96 L56/1; see also *Unwrought magnesium originating in Russia and Ukraine* OJ 23.12.95 L312/37.
 6 See *Caustic-burned natural magnesite from the PRC* OJ 8.3.84 L66/32; see also Joined Cases 294/86 & 77/87 *Technointorg v Commission and Council* [1988] ECR 6077. However, in Case C-16/90 *Detlef Nolle v Hauptzollamt Bremen-Freihafen* [1991] ECR I-5163, the Court held that in anti-dumping investigations account should be taken of the natural comparative advantages enjoyed by producers in non-market economies.
 7 See Council Regulation 905/98, OJ 30.4.98 L128/19; see also *Communication from the Commission to the Council and the European Parliament on the Treatment of Former Non-Market Economies in Anti-Dumping Proceedings and a Proposal for a Council Regulation, Amending Council Regulation 384/96*, Brussels 12.12.1997 COM (97) 677 final. These new rules will apply to investigations initiated after the 1 July 1998. See Council Regulation 905/98 Art 2, OJ 30.4.98 L128/18.

In anti-dumping investigations initiated after 1 July 1998 concerning imports from the Russia Federation and the People's Republic of China, the normal value will be determined in accordance with the rules laid down for imports from market economy countries, if it is shown, on the basis of properly substantiated claims by one or more producers subject to the investigation that market economy conditions prevail for this producer or producers in respect of the manufacture and sale of the like product concerned.[8] The decision as to whether domestic prices and costs should be used will be based on the following criteria. First, the decisions of the firms regarding prices, costs and inputs, including for instance raw materials, costs of technology and labour, output, sales and investment must be made in response to market signals reflecting supply and demand, and without significant State interference in this regard, and the costs of the major inputs must substantially reflect market values. Second, the firms must have one clear set of basic accounting records which are independently audited in line with international accounting standards and are applied for all purposes. Third, the production costs and financial situation of the firms must not be subject to significant distortions carried over from the former non-market economy system, in particular in relation to depreciation of assets, other write offs, barter trade and payment via compensation of debts. Fourth, the firms concerned must be subject to bankruptcy and property laws which guarantee legal certainty and stability for the operation of firms. Fifth, the exchange rate conversions must be carried out at the market rate.[9]

The determination of whether the producer meets such criteria must be made, on the basis of a written claim by the producer or producers, within three months of the initiation of the investigation, after specific consultation of the Anti-Dumping Advisory Committee and after the Community industry has been given an opportunity to comment.[10] Such determination will remain in force throughout the entire investigation.[11]

If the Community authorities consider that the exporting producers do not meet the required criteria, the calculation of the normal value will be based on the general rules applying to imports from non-market economy countries.[12]

Export price

For dumping to exist the export price must be lower than the normal value. The export price is defined as the price actually paid or payable for the product when sold from the exporting country to the Community.[13] Again, the Community authorities have a wide margin of discretion in establishing the export price.[14] The Commission will consider sales that have been concluded even though the products that are subject to the sale have not entered the Community.[15] The export

---

8 Council Regulation 384/96 Art 2(7)(b), OJ 6.3.96 L56/1, as amended by Council Regulation 905/98, OJ 30.4.98 L128/19.
9 Ibid Art 2(7).
10 Ibid.
11 Ibid.
12 Council Regulation 384/96 Art 2(7)(b), OJ 6.3.96 L56/1, as amended by Council Regulation 905/98, OJ 30.4.98 L128/19.
13 Council Regulation 384/96 Art 2(8), OJ 6.3.96 L56/1.
14 See Case 256/84 *Koyo Seiko v Council* [1987] ECR 1899. However, the authorities must state the method used in the calculation of the export price. See Case 258/84 *Nippon Seiko v Council* [1987] ECR 1923.
15 Furthermore, the Commission may use an offer for sale for the purpose of calculating the export price. See *Herbicide from Rumania* OJ 30.1.88 L26/107.

price is the price at which the product leaves the country of exportation, not the price at which it enters the Community market. Thus, the Community will net back the export price to the ex-factory level in the exporting country.[16]

If there is no export price or the export price is unreliable because there is an association or compensatory agreement between the exporter and the importer, the export price will be constructed on the basis of the price at which the imported products are first resold to an independent buyer or, if the products are not resold to an independent buyer or are not resold in the condition in which they were imported, on any reasonable basis.[17] If the exporters do not co-operate in the establishment of the export price but the importers do, the Commission will consider the prices produced by the importers with due adjustments.[18] However, if the exporters do not co-operate and the importers do not provide sufficient information the Commission will establish the export price on the basis of the facts available.[19] In cases where the producer exports to the Community through a related sales subsidiary the Commission will generally construct the export price on the basis of the price at which the imported products are first resold to an independent buyer.[20] However, if the prices to the related party are comparable to those at which the products were sold to independent parties in the Community, the sales to the related party will be used for the establishment of the export price.[1] In cases where all sales are done through selling organizations in third countries, the Commission will construct the export price on the basis of the sales price from the selling organization in the third market to the independent buyer in the Community.[2] If the producer sells its product through an unrelated trading house, the Community authorities will use as the export price the price which the foreign producer charged to the trading house.

In all cases in which the export price must be constructed on the basis of the price paid by the independent buyer or on any other reasonable basis, the Community authorities will make adjustments for all costs plus a reasonable margin for selling and general expenses and profit to establish a reliable export price at the Community frontier level.[3] The costs to be adjusted will be, among others, transport, insurance, handling, loading and ancillary costs, customs duties anti-dumping duties and taxes.[4] These allowances are those inherent in

---

16 See *Ammonium nitrate from Russia* OJ 23.8.95 L198/1.
17 Council Regulation 384/96 Art 2(9), OJ 6.3.96 L56/1.
18 See *Powdered activated carbon from the PRC* OJ 15.8.95 L192/14.
19 See *Refractory Chammottes from the PRC* OJ 29.7.95 L179/56 (where the Commission used the data of EUROSTAT); see also *Certain handbags from the PRC* OJ 4.2.97 L33/11 (where the Commission resorted to the cif import prices of the unrelated importers sampled for purposes of the injury determination in order to establish the export price of the non-co-operating Chinese exporters); see also Case T-161/94 *Sinochem Heilongjiang v Council of the European Union* [1996] ECR II-695.
20 See *Polyester yarn from Mexico, South Korea, Taiwan and Turkey* OJ 17.6.88 L151/39; see also *Certain magnetic disks from the United States, Mexico and Malaysia* OJ 17.10.95 L249/3; see also *Personal fax machines from the PRC, Japan, Republic of Korea, Malaysia, Singapore, Taiwan and Thailand* OJ 31.10.97 L297/61; see also Joined Cases 277 & 300/85, *Canon Inc v Council* [1988] ECR 5731; see also Case C-156/87 *Gestetner v Council* [1990] ECR I-781.
1 See *Tube of pipe fittings, of iron or steel, originating in the PRC, Croatia, Thailand, Slovak Republic and Taiwan* OJ 3.10.95 L234/4.
2 See *Microwave ovens from the PRC, the Republic of Korea, Malaysia and Thailand* OJ 4.1.96 L2/1 (1996).
3 Article 2(9)(b); see also *Stainless steel bars from India* OJ 29.5.98 L155/3; see also *Certain magnetic disks from the United States, Mexico and Malaysia* OJ 17.10.95 L249/3; see also *Powdered activated carbon from the PRC* OJ 15.8.95 L192/14; see also Case 255/84 *Nachi Fujikoshi v Council* [1987] ECR 1861.
4 Council Regulation 384/96 Art 2(9)(b), OJ 6.3.96 L56/1.

the construction of an export price in the commonest cases of an association or compensatory agreement between the exporter and importer or a third party, but it may be possible to include other allowances, when needed, for other reasons.[5] The purpose of the allowances is to establish the export price as if the product had been sold to an independent importer. In the establishment of the selling and general administration expenses incurred by the related distributor the Community authorities have a margin of discretion.[6] The Commission may even calculate such amount by reference to the expenses incurred by a subsidiary company selling products other than the product under investigation.[7] In the determination of the profit margin the Community authorities will use the profits made by independent importers in the same sector and not the actual profit of the related importer.[8]

Comparison

Once the export price and the normal value have been determined the Community authorities must compare both prices. The regulation calls for a fair comparison at the same level of trade and with respect to sales made as nearly as possible at the same time and taking into account differences which may affect the price comparability.[9] For this purpose the regulation establishes an exhaustive list of factors for which adjustments are possible.[10] The adjustments must be claimed and demonstrated by the interested parties.[11] But the Commission has occasionally made adjustments even where the foreign exporters did not claim them. In practice the Commission compares domestic prices or cost with export prices at the ex factory level. The Commission will deduct all expenses incurred as of the moment that the normal product left the factory plus packing. This will produce an ex-factory normal value and an ex-factory export price. The factors for which adjustments are possible are the following:

(1)   Differences in the physical characteristics of the product concerned. The amount of the adjustment must correspond to a reasonable estimate of the market value of the difference.[12]

---

5 See Case C-156/87 *Gestetner v Council* [1990] ECR I-781.
6 See Joined Cases 260/85 & 106/86 *Tokyo Electric Co v Council* [1988] ECR 5855.
7 Council Regulation 384/96 Art 2(9)(b), OJ 6.3.96 L56/1.
8 See *Certain magnetic disks from the United States, Mexico and Malaysia* OJ 17.10.95 L249/3; see also Joined Cases 273/85 & 107/86 *Silver Seiko v Council* [1988] ECR 5927.
9 Council Regulation 384/96 Art 2(10), OJ 6.3.96 L56/1, which also establishes that any duplication when making adjustments must be avoided.
10 Ibid; see also Case 204/84 *Toyo Bearing v Council* [1987] ECR 1809; see also Joined Cases 294/86 & 77/87 *Technointorg v Commission and Council* [1988] ECR 6077.
11 Council Regulation 384/96 Art 2(10), OJ 6.3.96 L56/1; see also Case 260/84 *Minebea v Council* [1987] ECR 1975; see also Joined Cases C-304/86 & C-185/87 *Enital SpA v Commission and Council* [1990] ECR I-2939; see also Joined Cases C-320/86 & C-188/87 *Stanko France v Commission and Council* [1990] ECR I-3013; see also Case 157/87 *Electroimpex v Council* [1990] ECR I- 3021; see also Case C-156/87 *Gestetner Holdings v Council and Commission* [1990] ECR I-781; see also Case 255/84 *Nachi Fujikoshi v Council* [1987] ECR 1861; see also Case 258/84 *Nippon Seiko v Council* [1987] ECR 1923; see also *Microwave ovens from the PRC, the Republic of Korea, Thailand and Malaysia* OJ 7.7.95 L156/5 (where the Commission took only into account those adjustments claimed by the parties).
12 Council Regulation 384/96 Art 2(10)(a), OJ 6.3.96 L56/1; but see *Sensitized paper for color photographs from Japan* OJ 11.5.84 L124/45 (as an example of the previous practice of basing the difference on the cost of production).

(2) An adjustment to the normal value must be made for import charges and indirect taxes borne by the like product and by materials physically incorporated therein, when destined for consumption in the exporting country and not collected or refunded in respect of the product exported to the Community.[13]

(3) Discounts, rebates and quantities if they are properly quantified and directly linked to the sales. Adjustments will also be made for deferred discounts and rebates where the claim is based on consistent practice in prior periods, including compliance with the conditions required to qualify for the discount or rebates.[14]

(4) For differences in levels of trade, including any difference which may arise in Original Equipment Manufacturer (OEM)[15] sales if, in relation to the distribution chain in both markets, it is shown that the export price, including a constructed export price, is at a different level of trade to the normal value and the difference has affected price comparability which is demonstrated by consistent and distinct differences in functions and prices of the seller for the different levels of trade in the domestic market of the exporting country. The amount of the adjustment will be based on the market value of the difference.[16] Two conditions must be met. First, it must be shown that the export price, including the constructed export price, is at a different level of trade than the normal value. Second, the difference must have affected price comparability which is demonstrated by consistent and distinct differences in functions and prices of the seller for the different levels of trade in the domestic market of the exporting country.[17] Thus, the Regulation presupposes that the producer is selling at different levels of trade in its domestic market. However, in those cases where the producer sells in its domestic market through related subsidiaries it will be impossible for it to prove consistent and distinct differences in functions and prices for different levels in trade in its domestic market because in fact there is only one level of trade in sales to unrelated parties

---

13 Council Regulation 384/96 Art 2(10)(b), OJ 6.3.96 L56/1; see also *Stainless steel bars from India* OJ 29.5.98 L155/3.

14 Council Regulation 384/96 Art 2(10)(c), OJ 6.3.96 L56/1.

15 OEMs are companies which sell under their own brand name products which they have bought from other companies.

16 Council Regulation 384/96 Art 2(10)(d)(i), OJ 6.3.96 L56/1, as amended by Council Regulation 2331/96, OJ 6.12.96 L317/1. This adjustment was introduced following the new rules of the new Anti-dumping Code. See Art 2(4) of the *Agreement on Implementation of Article VI of GATT 1994*. The Code does not however call for an adjustment based on the market value.

17 See *Stainless steel fasteners and parts thereof originating in the PRC, India, the Republic of Korea, Malaysia, Taiwan and Thailand* OJ 20.2.98 L50/1 (where the adjustment was granted to two Indian producers on the basis that they had proved sufficient evidence showing that a part of domestic sales was made at a level of sale different to export sales and that this difference affected price comparability demonstrated by consistent and distinct differences in the functions and prices of the two companies for the different levels of trade); see also *Personal fax machines from the PRC, Japan, the Republic of Korea, Malaysia, Singapore, Taiwan and Thailand* OJ 30.4.98 L128/1 (where the Council rejected several claims for adjustment on the basis that the exporters have failed to show that the export price was at a different level of trade from the normal value and that this difference affected price comparability. In this sense, the Council maintained that 'the fact that certain costs may be incurred on the domestic market in selling to distributors which are not incurred in the similar export level is linked to the specific structure or circumstances of the markets under consideration, but could not per se lead to an adjustment when it is clear that prices are made to similar types of consumers, ie distributors'); see also *Advertising matches from Japan* OJ 17.6.97 L158/9.

in the domestic market. Thus, following the *EC–Anti-dumping duties on audio tapes in cassettes originating in Japan*, GATT panel,[18] the Community has introduced an amendment by which in circumstances not evisaged under the previous condition, when an existing difference in level of trade cannot be quantified because of the absence of the relevant levels on the domestic market of the exporting countries, or where certain functions are shown clearly to relate to levels of trade other than the one which is to be used in the comparison, a special adjustment may be granted.[19] This new possibility, however, requires the producer to show that it is performing certain functions which clearly relate to levels of trade other than the one which is used in the comparison.

(5) Transport from the premises of the exporter to an independent buyer if such costs are incurred in the prices charged. The costs will include transport, insurance, handling, loading and ancillary costs.[20]

(6) Differences in the directly related packing costs for the product concerned.[1]

(7) Differences in the costs of any credit granted for sales under consideration. However, this must have been taken into account in the determination of the prices charged.[2]

(8) Differences in the direct costs of providing warranties, guarantees, technical assistance and services, as provided by law or in the sales contract.[3]

(9) Differences in commissions paid in respect of the sales under consideration.[4]

(10) If the price comparison requires a conversion of currencies, such conversion must be made using the rate of exchange at the date of sale. The date of sale will normally be that of the invoice or if more appropriate, the date of the contract, purchase order or order confirmation. Following the new Anti-dumping Code,[5] the new EC rules now allow hedging to be taken into consideration if it is directly linked to the export sale involved. In such cases the rate of exchange in the forward sale will be used.[6] Fluctuations in exchange rates will be ignored and the exporter will be granted

---

18 See *EC Anti-dumping duties on audio tapes in cassettes originating in Japan* ADP 136, unadopted, 28 April 1995.

19 Council Regulation 384/96 Art 2(10)(d)(ii), OJ 6.3.96 L56/1, as amended by Council Regulation 2331/96, OJ 6.12.96 L317/1. This new possibility applies only to proceedings and not to investigations such as reviews, refund investigations, anti-absorption investigations and anti-circumvention investigations, initiated after the date the amendment was published 7 December 1996. See Council Regulation 2331/96 Art 2, OJ 6.12.96 L317/1; see also *Personal fax machines from the PRC, Japan, the Republic of Korea, Malaysia, Singapore, Taiwan and Thailand* OJ 30.4.98 L128/1 (where the Council granted an adjustment for costs incurred by several producers to encourage levels of trade other than the one used in the comparison). Concerning the Community's previous practice See *Electronic Typewriters from Japan* OJ 22.6.85 L163/1; see also Case 204/84 *Toyo Bearing v Council* [1987] ECR 1809; see also Case 258/84 *Nippon Seiko v Council* [1987] ECR 1923; see also Case 260/84 *Minebea v Council* [1987] ECR 1975; see also Case 250/85 *Brother Industries v Council* [1988] ECR 5683; see also Joined Cases 277 & 300/85 *Canon Inc v Council* [1988] ECR 5731; see also Joined Cases 273/85 & 107/86 *Silver Seiko v Council* [1988] ECR 5927.

20 Council Regulation 384/96 Art 2(10)(e), OJ 6.3.96 L56/1.

1 Ibid Art 2(10)(f).

2 Ibid Art 2(10)(g).

3 Only direct costs are taken into account for adjustment purposes. See ibid Art 2(10)(h).

4 Ibid Art 2(10)(i).

5 See Art 2(4)(1) of the *Agreement on Implementation of Article VI of GATT 1994* OJ 23.12.94 L336/106.

6 Council Regulation 384/96 Art 2(10)(j), OJ 6.3.96 L56/1. However, the Commission has traditionally refused to take into account the forward contract price on the basis that contracts were not tied to the invoices relating to the export transactions for the product under consideration. See *Disodium carbonate from the United States* OJ 12.10.95 L244/32.

60 days to reflect a substantial movement in exchange rates during the period of investigation.[7] The Community authorities may take into account the official rates of exchange on the basis of which international commercial transactions are carried out.[8]

(11) Again, as a result of the *EC Anti-dumping duties on audio tapes in cassettes originating in Japan*, GATT panel,[9] the Regulation now provides for an adjustment to be made for differences in other factors not provided for under the previous possibilities if the exporter shows that they affect price comparability, in particular that customers consistently pay different prices on the domestic market because of the differences in such factors.[10]

Once the normal value and the export price are adjusted to the same level of trade, the Community authorities will compare both prices to establish the dumping margin. The dumping margin is the amount by which the normal value exceeds the export price.[11] Following the new Anti-dumping Code,[12] the Regulation establishes new rules on the comparison of the normal value with the export price. The comparison is normally made by comparing the weighted average of the normal values with the weighted average of the export prices or by comparing the normal values on a transaction by transaction basis with the export prices on a transaction by transaction basis.[13] However if there is a pattern of export prices which differs significantly among different purchasers, regions or time periods and the previous methods would not reflect the full degree of dumping,[14] it will be possible to compare the weighted average normal value with the export prices on a transaction by transaction basis.[15] In practice, in most cases it will be easy to prove that there is a case for the exception. Thus, in practice the Commission in most cases will continue to use its previous practice of comparing the average normal value with the export prices on a transaction by transaction basis.[16] When doing this, the Community

7 Council Regulation 384/96 Art 2(10)(j), OJ 6.3.96 L56/1. This provision also follows the new provisions of the Anti-dumping Code. See Art 2(4)(1) of the *Agreement on Implementation of Article VI of GATT 1994* OJ 23.12.94 L336/106.

8 See Case 255/84 *Nachi Fujikoshi v Council* [1987] ECR 1861; see also Joined Cases 305/86 & 160/87 *Neotype Techmashexport v Commission and Council* [1990] ECR I-2945.

9 See *EC Anti-dumping duties on audio tapes in cassettes originating in Japan* ADP 136, unadopted, 8 June 1995.

10 Council Regulation 384/96 Art 2(10)(k), OJ 6.3.96 L56/1, as amended by Council Regulation 2331/96, OJ 6.12.96 L317/1; see also *Personal fax machines from the PRC, Japan, Republic of Korea, Malaysia, Singapore, Taiwan and Thailand* OJ 31.10.97 L297/61 (where the Commission rejected several adjustment claims for other factors such as salesmen's salaries and other related costs or promotion expenses on the basis that the companies did not provide any evidence that such factors affected price comparability). Again this possibility will only apply to proceedings and not investigations, initiated after the publication of the amendment—7 December 1996. See Council Regulation 2331/96 Art 2, OJ 6.12.96 L317/1.

11 Council Regulation 384/96 Art 2(12), OJ 6.3.96 L56/1.

12 See Art 2(4)(2) of the *Agreement on Implementation of Article VI of GATT 1994* OJ 23.12.94 336/106.

13 Council Regulation 384/96 Art 2(11), OJ 6.3.96 L56/1.

14 Thus, the Community authorities must give reasons.

15 Ibid Art 2(11).

16 See *Powdered activated carbon from the PRC* OJ 15.8.95 L192/14; see also *Microwave ovens from the PRC, the Republic of Korea, Malaysia and Thailand* OJ 4.1.96 L2/1; see also *Certain magnetic disks from the United States, Mexico and Malaysia* OJ 17.10.95 L249/3; see also Case 204/84 *Toyo Bearing v Council* [1987] ECR 1809 (upholding this practice on grounds that otherwise it would not be possible to countervail dumping practices); see also Case 255/84 *Nachi Fujikoshi v Council* [1987] ECR 1861; see also Case 256/84 *Koyo Seiko v Council* [1987] ECR 1899.

authorities will only credit those export sales prices above the weighted normal value with a zero margin. Where there is an OEM, the Community authorities may calculate an average dumping margin for both the producer and the OEM.[17] It is general practice of the Community institutions to calculate a dumping margin for products where one firm is a subsidiary and therefore subject to control by another one, on the basis of an average of the data submitted by both producers.[18] In practice the Commission will generally calculate a weighted average dumping margin expressed as a percentage of CIF export price for each producer.[19] However, in the case of non-market economies, the Community authorities will establish a dumping margin for the entire country as a whole and not on an individual firm basis.[20] The Commission will usually not make exceptions for individual industries because of the general political and economic context of the non-market economy country. The Community authorities consider that in non-market economies it is extremely difficult to establish whether a company enjoys independence from the state and in particular whether it has permanent independence where it appears to enjoy independence at a certain point of time. The Commission has even rejected individual treatment for joint ventures on grounds that they were partly controlled in their operation by the non-market economy country's partners and they were not entirely free to determine the destination of their sales.[1] However, in exceptional circumstances, the Community authorities will grant individual treatment if the firm is able to prove that it can act independently, as witnessed by whether the majority of the shares belong to genuinely private companies and no State officials appear on the board or in a key management position (in this sense, the fact that the company concerned is controlled by a foreign investor will be considered a relevant indication of independence); whether the company has full control over its supply of raw materials and inputs in general; whether proof is given that profits can be exported and capital invested can be repatriated (only in case of foreign investment); whether export prices are determined freely (in this sense, the fact that export sales are made to a related party outside the country in question will be a decisive factor); and whether the freedom to carry out business activities is guaranteed.[2]

---

17 See Case C-133/87 & C-150/87 *Nashua Corpn v Commission and Council* [1990] ECR I-719.

18 See *Ferro-silico-magnese from Russia, Ukraine, Brazil and South Africa* OJ 14.10.95 L248/1.

19 Council Regulation 384/96 Art 2(12), OJ 6.3.96 L56/1.

20 See *Colour television receivers originating in Malaysia, the PRC, the Republic of Korea, Singapore and Thailand* OJ 1.4.95 L73/3; see also *Microwave ovens from the PRC, the Republic of Korea, Malaysia and Thailand* OJ 4.1.96 L2/1; see also *Tube or pipe fittings, of iron or steel, originating in the PRC, Croatia, Thailand, Slovak Republic and Taiwan* OJ 3.10.95 L234/4; see also *Bicycles from the PRC* OJ 9.9.93 L228/1.

1 See *Microwave ovens from the PRC, the Republic of Korea, Thailand and Malaysia* OJ 7.7.95 L156/5; see also *Microwave ovens from the PRC, the Republic of Korea, Malaysia and Thailand* OJ 4.1.96 L2/1. Such Community practice has been upheld by the Court in Case T-155/94 *Climax Paper Coverters Ltd v Council of the European Union* [1996] ECR II-873; see also Case T-170/94 *Shanghai Bicycles Corpn v Council of the European Union* (1997) Transcript, 25 September.

2 See *Communication from the Commission to the Council and the European Parliament on the Treatment of Former Non-Market Economies in Anti-Dumping Proceedings and a Proposal for a Council Regulation, Amending Council Regulation 384/96*, Brussels 12.12.1997 COM (97) 677 final, paragraph 6; see also *Certain Ring Binder Mechanisms from Malaysia and the PRC* OJ L22/1; see also *Handbags from the PRC* OJ 4.2.97 L33/11 (1997); see also *Personal fax machines from the PRC, Japan, the Republic of Korea, Malaysia, Singapore, Taiwan and Thailand* OJ 30.4.98 L128/1.

The Regulation establishes a *de minimis* dumping rule. When with respect to individual exports it is determined that their dumping margin, expressed as a percentage of the export price, is below 2 per cent, the investigation must be terminated immediately with respect to those individual exports.[3] However, those exports will remain part of the proceedings and may be reinvestigated in country wide reviews.[4]

Determination of unfair subsidization

For political reasons, the European Community, unlike the US, has very rarely countervailed foreign subsidization practices.[5] Thus, in adopting its new regulation on protection against subsidized measures,[6] the Community has basically restricted itself to reproducing the new GATT Subsidies Code.[7]

Countervailing duties are imposed for the purpose of offsetting any countervailable subsidy granted for the manufacture, production, export or transport of any product whose release for free circulation in the Community causes injury.[8] Thus, the Community authorities must establish whether an imported product benefits from a countervailable subsidy. This determination requires two basic operations. First, the Community authorities must identify the countervailable subsidy. Secondly, they must calculate the amount of the countervailable subsidy.

Identification of the countervailable subsidy

A countervailable subsidy is a subsidy which is specific and not subject to any exceptions as a non-actionable subsidy.[9] A subsidy is deemed to exist if there is a financial contribution by a government or any income or price support within the meaning of Art XVI of GATT, and a benefit is thereby conferred.[10] Thus, the identification of a countervailable subsidy requires the following four determinations. First, it must be determined whether there is a financial contribution or any income or price support within the meaning of Article XVI. Second, it must be determined whether the subsidy is specific. Third, it must be

---

3 Council Regulation 384/96 Art 9(3), OJ 6.3.96 L56/1.
4 Ibid. This provision overrules previous case law considering that producers which obtained a zero margin in the original investigation should not be included in the review. See Case C-216/91 *Rim Electrometalurgia SA v Council* [1993] ECR I-6303.
5 See *Certain seamless tubes of non alloy from Spain* OJ 28.11.80 L322/30; see also *Women's shoes from Brazil* OJ 14.11.81L 327/39; see also *Certain sheets and plates of iron or steel from Brazil* OJ 17.2.83 L45/11; see also *Certain steel plates from Brazil* OJ 29.7.83 L205/29; see also *Tube and pipe fittings of malleable cast iron from Spain* OJ 17.3.84 L74/47 (1984); see also *Ballbearings from Thailand* OJ 16.6.90 L152/59; see also *Polyester fibres and polyester yarns from Turkey* OJ 31.5.91 L137/81. These cases were adopted in accordance with the rules of Council Regulation 2423/88, OJ 209/1, replacing Council Regulation 2176/84, OJ L201/1, which in turn replaced Council Regulation 3017/79, OJ L339/1.
6 See Council Regulation 2026/97, OJ 21.10.97 L288/1, replacing Council Regulation 3284/94 OJ L349/22 as amended by Council Regulation 1252/95 OJ L122/2 (1995). As to cases initiated under this Regulation see *Farmed Atlantic salmon from Norway* OJ 31.8.96 C253/20; see also *Stainless steel bars from India* 30.10.97 C328/16; see also *Cochineal Carmine from Peru* OJ 6.11.97 C335/5.
7 See *Agreement on Subsidies and Countervailing Measures* OJ 23.12.94 L336/156.
8 Council Regulation 2026/97 Arts 1(1) and 1(2), OJ 21.10.97 L288/1.
9 Ibid Arts 1(2), 2 and 3.
10 Ibid Art 2.

established whether the subsidy is subject to any exception as a non actionable subsidy. Fourth, it must be determined whether the practice confers a benefit to the recipient.

Financial contribution by a government

A subsidy is deemed to exist only if there is a financial contribution by a government in the country of origin or export.[11] The financial contribution may be given by the government of both the country of origin of the product or that of export if there is an intermediate country between the country of origin and the Community market.[12] For the purposes of the countervailing duties Regulation, the term 'government' is considered to include any public body within the territory of the country of origin or export.[13] The Regulation lays down the following open list of practices which may be considered to be financial contributions. First, it includes practices which involve direct transfer of funds or potential direct transfer of funds or liabilities.[14] Second, it includes as a financial contribution, the non-collection or forgoing of government revenue that is otherwise due.[15] Third, is the provision of goods or services other than general infrastructure or purchase goods.[16] Fourth, are practices where the government makes payments to a funding mechanism or entrusts or directs a private body to carry out one or more of the previous type of functions which would normally be vested in the government, and the practice in no real sense, differs from practices normally followed by governments.[17] Finally, a subsidy may also be deemed to exist if there is any form of income or price support within the meaning of Article XVI of the GATT 1994.[18]

Identification of the benefit to the recipient

A subsidy is only deemed to exist if it confers a benefit to the recipient.[19] In practice, the identification of the benefit conferred is made together with the measure of the subsidy.

Determination of specificity

Only subsidies which are specific to an enterprise or industry or a group of enterprises or industries within the jurisdiction of the granting authority are countervailable.[20] The subsidy must benefit a specific firm or industry or group of firms or industries.

11 Ibid Art 2(1).
12 Ibid Art 1(3).
13 Ibid.
14 Ibid Art 2(1)(a)(i).
15 Ibid Art 2(1)(a)(ii); see also *Farmed Atlantic salmon from Norway* OJ 30.9.97 L267/19 (where the reduction in, or exemption from employers' social security contributions was considered as a government revenue that is forgone or not collected). However, the exemption of an exported product from duties or taxes borne by the like product when destined for domestic consumption, or the remission of such duties or taxes in an amount not in excess of that which has been accrued, if such exemption is granted in accordance with the provisions of Annexes I to III of the regulation is not deemed to be a subsidy. See ibid Art 2(1)(a)(ii).
16 Ibid Art 2(1)(a) (iii).
17 See ibid Art 2(1)(a) (iv).
18 See ibid Art 2 (1)(b).
19 See ibid Art 2(2).
20 See ibid Arts 3(1) and 3(2).

Following the Subsidies Code,[1] the Regulation establishes certain rules for the purpose of determining whether a subsidy is specific or not. A subsidy can be specific *de iure* or *de facto*. A subsidy is considered to be specific *de iure* in the following cases. First, if the granting authority, or the legislation pursuant to which the granting authority operates, explicitly limits access to the subsidy to certain enterprises.[2] In this sense, a subsidy which is limited to certain enterprises located within a designated geographical region within the jurisdiction of the granting authority will also be considered to be specific.[3] However, if it establishes objective criteria or conditions governing the eligibility for, and the amount of the subsidy, the subsidy will not be considered to be specific as long as such eligibility is automatic and such criteria and conditions are strictly adhered to.[4] Second, all subsidies contingent in law, or in fact, upon export performance, including those illustrated in Annex I to the Regulation are also specific *de iure*.[5] Finally, specific subsidies are also considered to be those contingent upon the use of domestic over imported goods.[6]

However, specific subsidies are also considered to include those which are specific *de facto*. In order to determine whether a subsidy is specific *de facto*, the Community authorities may determine whether the subsidy programme is used by a limited number of certain enterprises, or whether it is used predominantly by certain enterprises, or whether there is a granting of disproportionally large amounts of subsidy to certain enterprises, or the manner in which discretion has been exercised by the granting authority in the decision to grant a subsidy.[7] In all cases, a determination of specificity must be clearly sustained on the basis of positive evidence.[8]

Non-actionable subsidies

For an specific subsidy to be countervailable, it must not be a non-countervailable subsidy within the meaning of the Regulation.[9] The Regulation establishes an exhaustive list of non-actionable subsidies.

First, subsidies which are not specific are not countervailable.[10]

Second, certain research and development subsidies are not considered to be actionable.[11] Subsidies for research activities conducted by firms or by

1 See Art 2 of the *Agreement on Subsidies and Countervailing Measures* OJ 23.12.94 L336/156. In practice the GATT rules on specificity follow the US legislation and practice on such issues. See *Carlise Tire and Rubber Corpn v United States* 564 F Supp 834 (1983); see also *Certain Softwood Products from Canada* 48 Fed Reg 24159 (1983); see also *Anhydrous and Aqua Ammonia from Mexico* 48 Fed Reg 28522(1983).
2 Council Regulation 2026/97 Art 3(2)(a), OJ 21.10.97 L288/1.
3 However, the setting or charge of generally applicable tax rates by all levels of government will not be considered to be a specific subsidy. See ibid Art 3(3).
4 Objective criteria or conditions mean criteria or conditions which are neutral, which do not favour certain enterprises over other, and which are economic in nature and horizontal in application, such as number of employees or size of the enterprise. See ibid Art 3(2)(b).
5 Ibid Art 3(4)(a); see also ibid *Illustrative of Export Subsidies* Annex I; see also *Cochineal Carmine from Peru* OJ 6.1.97 C335/5 (where the alleged unfair subsidies are a simplified drawback of 5% of the fob value of the exported goods, an exemption from all national, provincial and local taxes for exporters located in special treatment and develoment zones, and subsidies granted pursuant to the export promotion programme operated by the Ministry of External Relations).
6 Council Regulation 2026/97 Art 3(4)(b), OJ 21.10.97 L288/1.
7 Ibid Art 3(4)(c).
8 Ibid Art 3(5).
9 Ibid Art 4.
10 Ibid Art 4(1)(a).
11 Ibid Art 4(2).

higher education or research establishments on a contract basis with firms will not be subject to countervailing measures, if the subsidies cover not more than 75 per cent of the costs of industrial research or 50 per cent of the costs of pre-competitive development activity, provided that the subsidies are limited exclusively to certain costs.[12] The term industrial research means planned search or critical investigation aimed at discovery of new knowledge, with the objective that such knowledge may be useful in developing new products, processes or services, or in bringing about a significant improvement to existing products, processes or services.[13] The term pre-competitive development activity is considered to mean the translation of industrial research findings into a plan, blueprint or design for new, modified or improved products, processes, or services whether intended for sale or use, including the creation of a first prototype which would not be capable of commercial use.[14] This exception for research and development subsidies does not apply to civil aircraft projects as defined in the 1979 Agreement on Trade in Civil Aircraft, as amended by later agreements.[15]

Third, certain subsidies to disadvantaged regions are also not considered to be actionable.[16] These subsidies must fulfil certain requirements. First, they must be given pursuant to a general framework of regional development.[17] Second, they must be given to a disadvantaged region.[18] Third, each disadvantaged region receiving the subsidy must be a clearly designated contiguous geographical area with a definable economic and administrative identity.[19]

Fourth, the regulation also exempts as non actionable those subsidies which are given to promote adaptation of existing facilities to new environmental requirements imposed by law and/or regulations which result in greater constraints and financial burdens on firms.[20] The enviromental subsidy must fulfil certain conditions. First, it must be a one-time non-recurring measure.[1] Second, it must be limited to 20 per cent of the cost of adaptation.[2] Third, it must not cover the cost of replacing and operating the subsidized investment, which must be fully borne by the firms.[3] Fourth, it must be directly linked to and proportionate to a firm's planned reduction of nuisances and pollution, and must not cover any manufacturing cost savings which may be achieved.[4] Fifth, it must be available to all firms which can adopt the new equipment and/or reduction processes.[5]

---

12 The costs should be limited to personnel costs; costs of instruments, equipment, land and building used exclusively and permanently for the research activity; costs of consultancy and equivalent services used exclusively for the research activity; additional overheads costs incurred directly as a result of the research activity; other running costs incurred directly as a result of the research activity. See ibid Art 4(2).

13 Ibid Art 4(2).

14 The concept of pre-competitive development may include other activities. See ibid Art 4(2).

15 Ibid Art 4(2).

16 See ibid Art 4(3).

17 As to the concept of general framework of regional development see ibid Art 4(3).

18 As to the criteria to determine whether a certain region is disadvantaged see ibid Art 4(3)(c).

19 Ibid Art 4(3)(a).

20 Existing facilities are those having been in operation for at least two years at the time when new environmental requirements are imposed. See ibid Art 4(4).

 1 Ibid Art 4(4)(a).

 2 Ibid Art 4(4)(b).

 3 Ibid Art 4(4)(c).

 4 Ibid Art 4(4)(d).

 5 Ibid Art 4(4)(e).

Finally, the Regulation exempts, as non-actionable subsidies, the element of subsidy which may exist in any of the government support programmes for agriculture listed in Annex IV to the Regulation.[6]

Calculation of the amount of the countervailable subsidy

The amount of the countervailable subsidy is to be calculated in terms of the benefit conferred to the recipient which is found to exist during the investigation period for subsidization.[7] The basic rule for the identification and calculation of the benefit to the recipient is whether the government action is consistent with commercial considerations. The difference between the government programme and the commercial considerations standard is considered to be the benefit conferred to the recipient. In this sense, the Regulation does not include any distortion test. The Regulation lays down basic principles for the application of the 'consistent with commercial considerations test' with regard to government provision of equity;[8] government loans;[9] government loan guarantees;[10] and the provision of goods or services or purchase of goods by the government.[11]

The amount of the countervailable subsidies must be determined per unit of the subsidized product exported to the Community.[12] If claimed and proven by the interested party, application fees and other costs necessarily incurred in order to qualify for, or to obtain, the subsidy together with export taxes, duties or other charges levied on the export of the product specifically intended to offset the duty will be deducted from the total subsidy.[13] If the subsidy is not granted by reference to the quantities manufactured, produced, exported or transported, the amount of the countervailable subsidy will be determined by allocating the value of the total subsidy over the level of production, sales or exports of the products concerned during the investigation period for subsidization.[14] In cases where the subsidy can be linked to the acquisition or future acquisition of fixed assets, the amount of the countervailable subsidy will be calculated by spreading the subsidy across a period which reflects the

---

6 Ibid Art 4(1)(c).
7 Normally this period will be the most recent accounting year of the beneficiary. See ibid Art 5; see also *Steel plates from Brazil* OJ 29.7.83 L205/29. However, it may be any other period of at least six months prior to the initiation of the investigation for which reliable financial and other relevant data are available. See ibid Art 5; see also *Polyester yarns from Turkey* OJ 31.5.91 L137/8; see also *Tube and pipe fittings of malleable cast iron from Spain* OJ 19.11.83 L322/13; see also *Farmed Atlantic salmon from Norway* OJ 30.9.97 L267/19 (where the Community authorities used as the investigation period the 18 months immediately preceding the initiation of the investigation).
8 Council Regulation 2026/97 Art 6(a), OJ 21.10.97 L288/1.
9 Ibid Art 6(b).
10 Ibid Art 6(c).
11 Ibid Art 6(d).
12 Ibid Art 7(1).
13 Ibid Art 7(1); see also *Pipe fittings of malleable cast iron from Spain* OJ 29.11.83 L323/13; see also *Certain sheets and plates of iron from Brazil* OJ 17.2.83 L45/11; see also *Certain women's shoes from Brazil* OJ 14.11.81 327/39.
14 Council Regulation 2026/97 Art 7(2), OJ 21.10.97 L288/1. See *Farmed Atlantic salmon from Norway* OJ 30.9.97 L267/19 (where the amount of each subsidy was allocated over the total sales). The Commission has usually used the accounting year of the beneficiary as this period. However, this has not always beeen the case. See *Polyester yarns from Turkey* OJ 31.5.91 L137/8.

normal depreciation of such assets in the industry concerned.[15] If the assets are non-depreciating, the subsidy is to be treated as an interest free loan.[16] If the amount of the subsidy cannot be linked to the acquisition of fixed assets it will be allocated to the investigation period unless special circumstances arise which justify attribution over a different period.[17]

As the Anti-dumping Regulation, the Regulation against foreign unfair subsidization establishes a *de minimis* subsidization rule. The amount of the countervailable subsidies will be considered to be *de minimis* if such amount is less than 1 per cent *ad valorem* of the product.[18] Following the Subsidies Code,[19] the Community Regulation establishes special *de minimis* rules for developing countries. Generally, developing countries benefit from a 2 per cent *de minimis* rule.[20] However, those developing countries mentioned in Annex VII of the Subsidies Code,[1] together with those developing countries which have eliminated export subsidization programs including those of Annex I, will benefit from a 3 per cent *de minimis* rule.[2]

Determination of injury

The imposition of an anti-dumping or countervailing duty requires both the existence of dumping or a countervailable subsidy and injury.[3] The determination of injury is also important because it can have an impact on the extent of the relief measure imposed by the Community authorities. The Regulations impose a lesser duty rule. The amount of the duty should be less than the dumping margin or the countervailable subsidy if that lesser duty would be adequate to remove the injury.[4]

The Community authorities have a wide margin of discretion in the determination of injury.[5] A determination of injury involves four basic steps. First, it

15 Council Regulation 2026/97 Art 7(3), OJ 21.10.97 L288/1; see also *Certain sheets and plates of iron or steel from Brazil* OJ 17.2.83 L45/11; see also *Certain steel plates from Brazil* OJ 29.7.83 L205/29. The Commission has usually allocated the subsidy in equal parts over the entire depreciation period. See *Ballbearings from Thailand* OJ 16.6.90 L152/59.
16 Council Regulation 2026/97 Art 7(3), OJ 21.10.97 L288/1.
17 Ibid Art 7(4).
18 Ibid Art 14(5).
19 Arts 27(9) and 27(10) of the *Agreement on Subsidies and Countervailing Measures* OJ 23.12.94 L336/156.
20 Council Regulation 2026/97 Art 14(5)(a), OJ 21.10.97 L288/1.
 1 Ibid Art 14(5)(b); see also Annex VII of the *Agreement on Subsidies and Countervailing Measures* OJ 23.12.94 L336/156. These countries are those least developed countries designated as such by the United Nations which are members of the WTO together with certain other developing countries as long as they do not reach a GNP per capita of $1000 per year.
 2 Council Regulation 2026/97 Art 14(5)(b), OJ 21.10.97 L288/1.
 3 Council Regulation 384/96 Arts 1(1) and 9(4), OJ 6.3.96 L56/1; see also Council Regulation 2026/97 Arts 1(1) and 15(1), OJ 21.10.97 L288/1; see also Case C-129/86 *Greece v Council* [1989] ECR 3963; see also Case C-121/86 *Anonymos Etaireia Epicheiriseon Metalleftikon Viomichanikon kai Naftiliakon v Council* [1989] ECR 3919; see also *Ammonium nitrate originating in Lithuania* OJ 23.8.95 L198/27 (termination because the imported dumped products did not contribute to injury).The rules regarding the determination of injury for both anti-dumping and countervailing measures are basically the same. Thus, from now on, except in the case of differences, all references will be made to the antidumping regulation.
 4 Council Regulation 384/96 Arts 7(2) and 9(4), OJ 6.3.96 L56/1; see also Joined Cases 277 & 300/85 *Canon Inc v Council* [1988] ECR 5731 (requiring the Community authorities to ascertain whether the amount of the duties is necessary in order to remove the injury); see also Case 256/84 *Koyo Seiko v Council* [1987] ECR 1899.
 5 See Case 239/82/ & 157/82 *Allied Corpn v Commission* [1984] ECR 1005.

must be determined whether the product under investigation and the product of the domestic industry are like products. Second, it must be decided whether the domestic producers of the like product constitute a Community industry within the sense of the regulations. Third, the Community authorities must decide whether the Community industry is experiencing injury in the sense of material injury, threat of material injury or material retardation. Finally it must be determined whether there is a causal link between the dumped or subsidized products and the injury.

Like product

The effect of the dumped or unfairly subsidized imports must be determined with regard to the domestic producers of the like product. Like product is defined as a product which is identical, that is, alike in all respects, or in the absence of such a product another product which has characteristics closely resembling those of the product under investigation.[6] The regulation places great emphasis on physical similarity. If two products are different they will not be considered as like products even if they are in competition. There must be a close relationship between the imported product and the domestic product. The Community authorities will consider different factors such as the physical characteristics, the application and use of the products, technical characteristics, their production process, the raw materials used etc. The Commission will place a strong emphasis on interchangeability.[7] It will, however, disregard differences in quality but such differences may qualify for an adjustment in price comparison.[8]

Domestic industry

The domestic industry is normally defined as the Community producers as a whole of the like product or those of them whose collective output constitutes a major proportion of the total Community production.[9] A single producer may be considered as Community industry if its share of Community production is sufficiently large.[10] Producers of only one Member State may also be considered as Community industry if their combined production accounts for a major part of the total Community production.[11]

However, if the Community producers are related to the exporters or importers or are themselves importing the allegedly dumping product, the Community authorities may consider the Community industry as the rest of the producers.[12] Nevertheless, the Community authorities have considered that this provision

6 Council Regulation 384/96 Art 1(4), OJ 6.3.96 L56/1.
7 See *Certain tube of pipe fittings, of iron or steel originating in the People's Republic of China, Croatia and Thailand* OJ 3.4.96 L84/1; see also *Coumarin originating in the PRC* OJ 4.4.96 L86/1; see also *Powdered activated carbon from the PRC* OJ 15.8.95 L192/14; see also *Unwrought magnesium originating in Russia and Ukraine* OJ 23.12.95 L312/37.
8 See *Certain handbags from the PRC* OJ 4.2.97 L33/11; see also *Refractory Chamottes from the PRC* OJ 29.7.95 L179/56; see also *Certain tube or pipe fittings, of iron or steel originating in the People's Republic of China, Croatia and Thailand* OJ 3.4.96 L84/1; see also Joined Cases 294/86 & 77/87 *Technointorg v Commission and Council* [1988] ECR 6077.
9 Council Regulation 384/96 Art 4(1), OJ 6.3.96 L56/1.
10 See *Coumarin from the PRC* OJ 7.10.95 L239/4.
11 See *Chemical Fertilizer from the USA* OJ 19.1.83 L15/1; see also *Furfuraldehyde from the PRC* OJ 21.7.94 L186/11.
12 Council Regulation 384/96 Art 4(1)(a), OJ 6.3.96 L56/1; see also *Electronic scales from Japan* OJ 24.3.84 L80/9.

does not provide for the automatic exclusion of the producers related to the exporters or who are themselves importing the allegedly dumped product, but rather imposes on them the obligation to consider on a case by case basis whether the exclusion of any producer in this situation is warranted.[13] In this sense, the Community authorities will usually not exclude a producer from the concept of Community industry if it has imported the product under investigation in very small quantities or it has done so in order to survive in the market or to fill the gap in the variety of products offered.[14]

Under certain circumstances, the Community market may be divided into two or more competitive markets and the producers within each market regarded as a Community industry for the purpose of making a determination of injury.[15] The producers of such subdivided markets may be considered as Community industry if they sell all or almost all of their production of the product in question in that market and the demand of that market is not to any substantial degree supplied by producers of the product located elsewhere in the Community. In such cases, it will be considered that there is injury to the Community industry only if there is a concentration of the dumped imports under investigation into that market and there is injury to the producers of all or almost all of the production within that subdivided market.[16]

Material injury

The determination of injury implies an assessment of whether the domestic industry is experiencing material injury. The concept of material injury may actually include three different cases: material injury *stricto sensu*, a threat of material injury and the material retardation of the establishment of the Community industry.[17] In all three cases, its determination must be based on positive evidence.[18]

The regulation does not provide a definition of material injury but rather simply states different factors to take into account when assessing its existence. In this sense, the Community authorities have wide discretion when assessing these factors. The list of factors is considered to be merely indicative. No one factor or group of factors can give decisive guidance in the determination of injury.[19]

13 See *Colour television receivers from Malaysia, the PRC, the Republic of Korea and Thailand* OJ 1.10.94 L255/50; see also *Microwave ovens from the PRC, the Republic of Korea, Thailand and Malaysia* OJ 7.7.95 L156/5; see also *Polyester yarn from Mexico, South Korea, Taiwan and Turkey* OJ 17.6.88 L151/39; see also Case C-156/87 *Gestetner Holdings v Council and Commission* [1990] ECR I-781 (upholding this practice); see also Joined Cases 260/85 & 106/86, *Tokyo Electric Co v Council* [1988] ECR 5855; see also Joined Cases 273/85 & 107/86, *Silver Seiko v Council* [1988] ECR 5927; see also Case C-179/87 *Sharp Corpn v Council* [1992] ECR I-1635.
14 See *Colour television receivers originating in Malaysia, the PRC, the Republic of Korea, Singapore and Thailand* OJ 1.4.95 L73/3; see also *Certain handbags from the PRC* OJ 4.2.97 L33/11; see also *Advertising matches from Japan* OJ 17.6.97 L158/9.
15 Council Regulation 384/96 Art 4(1)(b), OJ 6.3.96 L56/1.
16 Ibid; see also *Certain categories of glass from Turkey, Yugoslavia, Romania, Bulgaria, Hungary and Czechoslovakia* OJ 28.2.86 L51/73.
17 Council Regulation 384/96 Art 3(1), OJ 6.3.96 L56/1.
18 Ibid Art 3(2).
19 See Joined Cases 277 & 300/85 *Canon Inc v Council* [1988] ECR 5731; see also Joined Cases 273/85 & 107/86 *Silver Seiko v Council* [1988] ECR 5927; see also Joined Cases C-304/86 & C-185/87 *Enital SpA v Commission and Council* [1990] ECR I-2939; see also Joined Cases C-320/86 & C-188/87 *Stanko France v Commission and Council* [1990] ECR I-3013; see also Joined Cases 305/86 & 160/87 *Neotype Techmashexport v Commission and Council* [1990] ECR I-2945; see also Joined Cases 294/86 & 77/87 *Technointorg v Commission and Council* [1988] ECR 6077.

The Community authorities must first determine the volume of the dumped imports.[20] In this sense, they must analyze whether there has been a significant increase in dumped imports in absolute terms or relative to production or consumption in the Community market. In practice the Commission looks at all imports and not only at those which have been dumped. Sometimes, it has taken into account projected imports as well as actual imports.[1] The increase in dumped imports is analyzed in absolute and relative terms. The Community authorities attach great importance to the increase in imports and increases in the market share. A proof of either will be a strong indicator of injury. But a finding of injury is not necessarily precluded by a relatively small market share or by small increases.[2]

With regard to the volume of imports it is important to note that the regulation has established a *de minimis* injury rule. If the imports of a country represent a market share of the Community market below 1 per cent the proceedings must be terminated unless such countries collectively account for 3 per cent of the Community consumption.[3]

The Community authorities must also analyze the effect of the dumped imports on the prices. The Community authorities will determine whether there has been a significant price undercutting by the dumped imports as compared to the price of the Community produced like product or whether the effect of such imports is to depress prices to a significant degree or prevent, to a significant degree, price increases which otherwise would have occurred.[4] The determination of price undercutting plays in practice a dual role. First, it is essential to determine injury. However, the extent of the price undercutting will be taken into account in determining which relief should be established to remove the injury. The Commission compares the weighted average resale prices of the foreign producers with the prices of exactly similar models or products of the EC producers.[5] If the prices of the EC producers have been surpressed or depressed, the Commission will compare the average resale prices of the foreign

20 See Council Regulation 384/96 Art 3(3), OJ 6.3.96 L56/1.
1 See *Louvre doors from Malaysia and Singapore* OJ 22.5.81 L135/33.
2 See *Mounted piezo-electric quartz crystal units from Japan, South Korea and the USA* OJ 27.6.80 L162/62 (1980).
3 Council Regulation 384/96 Art 5(7), OJ 6.3.96 L56/1. Note that the rates are based on the market share and not on the import share as in the Anti-dumping Code. See Art 5(8) of the *Agreement on Implementation of Article VI of GATT 1994* OJ 23.12.94 L336/103 (where the de minimis rule is established as 3% of the imports of the like product in the importing country unless countries which individually account for less than 3% of the imports of the like product in the importing country collectively account for more than 7% of imports of the like product in the importing country). In general the EC test is more liberal than the Code's test but when in specific cases the import test is more liberal than the market share test, the Community authorities should apply the import test in order to comply with the Anti-dumping Code. See *Unwrought magnesium originating in Russia and Ukraine* OJ 23.12.95 L312/37 (where Kazakhstan was excluded from the investigation because its exports were less than 1% of the Community's market share); see also *Certain magnetic disks from the United States, Mexico and Malaysia* OJ 17.10.95 L249/3; see also *Tube or pipe fittings, of iron or steel, originating in the PRC, Croatia, Thailand, Slovak Republic and Taiwan* OJ 3.10.95 L234/4.
4 Council Regulation 384/96 Art 3(3), OJ 6.3.96 L56/1.
5 In so doing the Commission must make the necessary adjustments on the basis of the information available at the time without imposing the burden of proof on any of the parties. See *European Fertilizer Manufacturers Association v Council of the European Union* (1997) Transcript, 17 December.

producers with target prices covering Community producers' costs of production plus a reasonable amount of profit.[6]

The Community authorities have traditionally cumulated the imports from
different firms of one country and from different countries in order to assess
the effect of the imports on the domestic industry.[7] The new Codes basically
legitimate the Community cumulation practices.[8] The Community authorities
will cumulate imports from different firms from one country.[9] They may also
cumulate imports from different countries under certain conditions.[10] First, the
margin of dumping for each country must be more than *de minimis*.[11] Second,
the volume of imports of each country must not be negligible.[12] Thirdly, the
cumulative assessment of the effects of imports is appropriate in the light of the
conditions of competition between importers and conditions of competition
between imported products and the like Community products. Finally, the imports of a product from more than one country must be simultaneously subject
to the same investigation.[13] In deciding whether to cumulate or not, the Community authorities have analyzed different factors such as the dumping margin,
the volume of imports, conditions of competition between imported products
and between imported products and the like Community product on the basis
of the similarity of the characteristics, interchangeability of end uses, similarity
of the channels of distribution and price, geographical markets where the products were sold, etc.[14] Cumulation is not always automatic.[15]

The imports must have a consequent impact on the Community industry.[16]
The analysis of the impact of the dumped imports on the Community industry
will include an evaluation of all the relevant economic factors.[17] The regulations provide an indicative and non-exhaustive list of factors.[18] The Commu-

---

6 See Case 250/85 *Brother Industries v Council* [1988] ECR 5683 (upholding this practice); see
   also Joined Cases 260/85 & 106/86 *Tokyo Electric Co v Council* [1988] ECR 5855; see also
   Joined Cases 273/85 & 107/86 *Silver Seiko v Council* [1988] ECR 5927; see also *Hydraulic
   excavators from Japan* OJ 6.7.85 L176/1 (1985).
7 See Case 255/84 *Nachi Fujikoshi v Council* [1987] ECR 1861 (upholding this practice); see
   also Joined Cases 294/86 & 77/87 *Technointorg v Commission and Council* [1988] ECR
   6077
8 Article 3(3) of the *Agreement on the Implementation of Article VI of GATT 1994*; OJ 23.12.94
   L336/103; see also Art 15(3) of the *Agreement on Subsidies and Countervailing Measures* OJ
   23.12.94 L336/156.
9 See *Propan-1 oil from the US* OJ 19.4.84 L106/55. This cumulation is not expressly mentioned in the Regulation but it seems to be legitimized by the possibility of cumulating from
   different countries.
10 Council Regulation 384/96 Art 3(4), OJ 6.3.96 L56/1.
11 That is 2% of the export price. See ibid Art 9(3).
12 That is 1% of the Community market unless such countries collectively account for 3% or
   more of the Community consumption. See Art 5(7).
13 This last requirement overrules previous Commission practice of cumulating imports subject
   to different investigations.
14 See *Certain magnetic disks from the United States, Mexico and Malaysia* OJ 17.10.95 L249/3;
   see also *Ammonium nitrate from Russia* OJ 23.8.95 L198/1; see also *Personal fax machines
   from the PRC, Japan, the Republic of Korea, Malaysia, Singapore, Taiwan and Thailand* OJ
   30.4.98 L128/1.
15 See *Cotton yarn from Brazil, Egypt, Turkey and Thailand* OJ 27.9.91 L271/17.
16 Council Regulation 384/96 Art 3(2), OJ 6.3.96 L56/1.
17 Ibid Art 3(5).
18 These factors are the fact that the industry is still in the process of recovering from the effects
   of past dumping or subsidization, the magnitude of the actual margin of dumping, the actual
   or potential decline in sales, profits, output, market share, productivity, return on investments, utilization capacity, factors affecting Community prices, actual or potential negative

nity authorities have paid most attention to production, capacity and capacity utilization, stocks, market share, prices, profits and employment.

In determining whether there is a threat of material injury, the Community authorities must base their analysis on facts and not merely on allegations, conjecture or remote possibility. The change in circumstances which would create a situation in which the dumping would cause injury must be clearly foreseen and imminent.[19] The Community authorities must consider different factors such as a significant increase of dumped imports into the Community market indicating the likelihood of substantial increased imports;[20] the capacity of the exporter to increase the dumped exports to the Community;[1] and whether the imports are entering at prices that would, to a significant degree, depress prices or prevent increases which otherwise would have occurred and would probably increase demand for further imports;[2] and the inventories of the product under investigation.[3]

Causality

A determination of injury is justified only if the dumped or subsidized imports are as a result of dumping or unfair subsidization, causing injury to the Community.[4] It must be demonstrated that the volume and/or price levels identified are responsible for the impact on the Community industry.[5] In this sense the regulations provide for an exhaustive list of other factors which must be analyzed to make sure that the injury caused by these other factors is not attributed to the dumped imports.[6] However, in the assessment of injury it is not necessary to make a comprehensive analysis of the market as a whole but only a finding of whether the dumped imports are causing injury. The fact that other factors have contributed to injury does not exclude the determination of injury.[7] A no injury determination of injury will be warranted only if there is no causal relationship at all between the dumped imports and the injury suffered.[8]

Community interest

A finding of both the existence of dumping or unfair subsidization and injury does not automatically give rise to the imposition of measures. In order for anti-dumping or countervailing duties to be imposed it must be determined that the

---

effects on cash flow, inventories, employment, growth, and ability to raise capital investments. See Art 3(5). However, the Community authorities are not obliged to analyze all those factors. See Joined Cases 277 & 300/85 *Canon Inc v Council* [1988] ECR 5731.
19 Council Regulation 384/96 Art 3(9), OJ 6.3.96 L56/1.
20 Ibid Art 3(9)(1)(a).
 1 Ibid Art 3(9)(1)(b).
 2 Ibid Art 3(9)(1)(c).
 3 Ibid Art 3(9)(1)(d).
 4 Ibid Art 3(6).
 5 Ibid.
 6 Article 3(7).
 7 See Case 250/85 *Brother Industries v Council of the European Community* [1988] ECR 5683; see also *Sinochem National Chemicals Import and Export Corpn v Council of the European Union* (1998) Transcript, 29 January.
 8 See Joined Cases 277 & 300/85 *Canon Inc v Council* [1988] ECR 5731; see also Joined Cases 273/85 & 107/86 *Silver Seiko v Council* [1988] ECR 5927; see also *Disodium Carbonate from the United States* OJ L244/32 (1995)(dumped imports need not be the only cause of injury. It is enough that the injury caused is regarded as material).

interests of the Community call for intervention.[9] Community interests include all the various interests taken as a whole, including the interests of the domestic industry, importers, users and consumers.[10] The Community interest provisions try to highlight the two interests to be taken into account. These are the need on the one hand to eliminate the injurious dumping and restore effective competition and on the other hand to take into account the interests of users and consumers of the imported products. In order to take into account the interests of all domestic parties the regulations provide certain procedural rights to complainants, importers, users, consumers and their organizations.[11] The regulations place a strong emphasis on the opinion of the Advisory Committee. The balance of views expressed in the Committee must be taken into account by the Commission in any proposal to take definitive measures.[12] In practice, the Community authorities have a wide margin of discretion when assessing the interests of the Community.[13] The Commission places great emphasis on the need to eliminate the trade distorting effects arising from unfair commercial practices and to restore effective competition in the Community market for the products concerned.[14] It will usually consider that it is in the interests of consumers and users to eliminate the trade distorting effects of injurious dumping.[15] The fact that the Community producers are facing difficulties due, in part, to causes other than dumping is not considered by the Community authorities to be a reason for depriving them of protection of injurious dumping or unfair subsidization.[16]

Sampling

The Community authorities may use sampling for the calculation of dumping or unfair subsidization margins, injury and the determination of the level of anti-dumping or countervailing duties in cases where the number of complainants, exporters, or importers, types of products or transactions is large.[17] The

---

9 Council Regulation 384/96 Arts 7(1), 9(4) and 21, OJ 6.3.96 L56/1; see also Council Regulation 2026/97 Arts 12(1)(d), 15(1) and 31, OJ 21.10.97 L288/1.

10 Council Regulation 384/96 Art 21(1), OJ 6.3.96 L56/1; see also Council Regulation 2026/97 Art 31(1), OJ 21.10.97 L288/1. See also *Advertising matches from Japan* OJ 17.6.97 L158/9 (where the Commission considered the impact of the possible measures on the Community industry, importers and traders, users and on the competitive environment in the Community market). The rules on Community interest for anti-dumping and countervailing measures are basically the same. Thus from now on only the anti-dumping Regulation provisions will be mentioned.

11 Council Regulation 384/96 Arts 21(2), 21(3) and 21(4), OJ 6.3.96 L56/1.

12 Ibid Art 21(5).

13 See Joined Cases 277 & 300/85 *Canon Inc v Council* [1988] ECR 5731; see Case 250/85 *Brother Industries v Council* [1988] ECR 5683; see also Case C-156/87 *Gestetner v Council* [1990] ECR I-781; see also Case C-179/87 *Sharp Corpn v Council* [1992] ECR I-1635.

14 See *Tube or pipe fittings, of iron or steel, originating in the PRC, Croatia, Thailand, Slovak Republic and Taiwan* OJ 3.10.95 L234/4; see also *Microwave ovens from the PRC, the Republic of Korea, Malaysia and Thailand* OJ 4.1.96 L2/1; see also *Certain magnetic disks from the United States, Mexico and Malaysia* OJ 17.10.95 L249/3.

15 See *Coumarin originating in the PRC* OJ 4.4.96 L86/1.

16 See Joined Cases 277 & 300/85 *Canon Inc v Council* [1988] ECR 5731; see also Case 250/85 *Brother Industries v Council* [1988] ECR 5683.

17 Art 17 Council Regulation 384/96, OJ 6.3.96 L56/1; see also Council Regulation 2026/97 Art 27, OJ 21.10.97 L288/1; see *Certain handbags from the PRC* OJ 4.2.97 L33/11; see also Case 246/87 *Continentale Produkten v Hauptzollamt Munchen-West* [1989] ECR 1151 (upholding this practice); see also Case T-166/94 *Koyo Seiko v Council* [1995] ECR II-2129.

Commission must make the final selection of the parties, types of products or transactions to be used as a sample. However, preference must be given to choosing a sample in consultation with, and with the consent of the parties concerned. For this purpose, the parties must make themselves known and provide sufficient information within three weeks of initiation to enable a representative sample to be chosen.[18]

In cases where the Commission uses sampling methods, any anti-dumping duty applied to importers from exporters or producers which have made themselves known but were not included in the examination must not exceed the weighted average margin of dumping established for the parties in the sample. For this purpose, the Commission will disregard any zero or *de minimis* margins and any margins established as a result of non-co-operation.[19]

However, an individual margin of dumping or subsidization will be calculated for any export or producer not initially selected in the sample who submits the necessary information.[20] The Community authorities will apply individual duties to imports from any exporter or producer who is granted individual treatment.[1] Individual treatment will not be granted if the number of exporters and importers is so large that individual treatment would be too burdensome and prevent a timely completion of the investigation.[2]

If there is no co-operation by some or all of the parties selected and this is likely to materially affect the outcome to the investigation a new sample will be selected. However if non-co-operation persists or there is insufficient time to select a new sample the determination of dumping will be based on the best information available.[3]

PROCEDURAL ISSUES

The rules of procedure of anti-dumping and countervailing determinations are based on three basic principles. First, they aim to safeguard the rights of all parties concerned including complainants, exporters or producers, importers, consumers and users. Secondly, while providing wide powers for the Commission, they establish mechanisms of control by the Council and the Advisory Committees. Finally, they give a sufficient margin of discretion for the Community authorities for administrative convenience purposes.

The rules of procedure can be divided into those referring to the initiation of the proceedings, the investigation, provisional measures, termination, reviews and anti-absorption and anti-circumvention rules.[4]

---

18 Council Regulation 384/96 Art 17(2), OJ 6.3.96 L56/1; see also Council Regulation 2026/97 Art 27(2), OJ 21.10.97 L288/1.
19 Council Regulation 384/96 Art 9(6), OJ 6.3.96 L56/1.
20 See Council Regulation 384/96 Art 17(3), OJ 6.3.96 L56/1; see also Council Regulation 2026/97 Art 27(3), OJ 21.10.97 L288/1.
1 Council Regulation 384/96 Art 9(6), OJ 6.3.96 L56/1; see also Council Regulation 2026/97 Art 15(3), OJ 21.10.97 L288/1.
2 Council Regulation 384/96 Art 17(3), OJ 6.3.96 L56/1; see also Council Regulation 2026/97 Art 27(3), OJ 21.10.97 L288/1.
3 Council Regulation 384/96 Arts 17(4) and 18, OJ 6.3.96 L56/1; see also Council Regulation 2026/97 Arts 27(4) and 28, OJ 21.10.97 L288/1.
4 The rules of procedure are basically the same for anti-dumping and countervailing investigations. Thus only the provisions of the anti-dumping regulation will be mentioned unless those of the countervailing duties regulation differ.

Initiation

An anti-dumping or countervailing duty investigation may be self-initiated by the Commission or at the request of a Member State on the basis of sufficient evidence of dumping or unfair subsidization and injury and a causal link between them.[5]

However, most cases are initiated after a written complaint has been filed by a natural or legal person or any association not having legal personality, acting on behalf of the Community industry.[6] Private complaints may be submitted to the Commission, or to a Member State which must forward them to the Commission.[7] The complaint must contain sufficient evidence of dumping or unfair subsidization, injury and a causal link between them.[8] The complaint must also identify the complainant, the Community industry on whose behalf it is acting, the allegedly dumped or unfairly subsidized product together with the exporting countries and known producers or exporters and importers.[9]

Following the new rules of the Anti-dumping Code[10] and the Subsidies and Countervailing Measures Code,[11] the regulation establishes a requirement of standing for the complainants. The complaint must be made by or on behalf of the Community industry. It will only be considered to be made on behalf of the Community industry if it is supported by those Community producers whose collective output constitutes more than 50% of the total production of the like product produced by those producers expressing either support for or opposition to the complaint and it is expressly supported by those Community producers whose collective output constitutes at least 25% of the total production of the like product produced by the Community industry.[12]

The Commission must examine the complaint and determine whether it justifies the initiation of an investigation. The standard of review will be whether there is sufficient evidence of dumping, unfair subsidization, injury and a causal link between them.[13] The complaint must not be publicized until it has been decided to initiate an investigation.[14] If the complaint is withdrawn it will be considered not to have been filed.[15]

The Commission, after consulting the Advisory Committee, must decide within 45 days of the filling of the complaint whether to initiate the investigation.[16] It is believed that around 50% of all complaints are refused. If the Community authorities refuse to initiate an investigation they must inform the complainants.[17] A refusal to initiate may be subject to judicial review.

If the Community authorities decide to initiate the proceeding they must publish a notice in the Official Journal.[18] The notice of initiation must contain

---

5 Council Regulation 384/96 Arts 5(6) and 5(1)(b), OJ 6.3.96 L56/1.
6 Ibid Art 5(1).
7 Ibid Art 5(1)(a).
8 Ibid Art 5(2).
9 Ibid.
10 See Art 5(4) of the *Agreement on the Implementation of Article VI of GATT 1994* OJ 23.12.94 L336/106.
11 See Art 11(4) of the *Agreement on Subsidies and Countervailing Measure* OJ 23.12.94 L336/156.
12 Council Regulation 384/96 Art 5(4), OJ 6.3.96 L56/1.
13 Ibid Art 5(7).
14 Ibid Art 5(5).
15 Ibid Art 5(8).
16 Ibid Art 5(9).
17 Ibid.
18 Ibid.

a description of the product, an enumeration of the countries under investigation, a summary of the information received and the requirement that all interested parties must provide all relevant information to the Commission within a certain time period.[19] The notice of initiation serves as a notice for all parties. However, the Commission is also required to inform all importers and exporters known to be concerned, as well as their government representatives, of the initiation of the proceeding and the substance of the complaint.[20]

The Regulation on Countervailing Duties provides for the initiation of special investigations to determine whether a subsidy is specific or whether it fulfils the conditions of a non-countervailable subsidy or the requirements of the Agreement on Agriculture for domestic support.[1] In no case will an investigation be initiated when a subsidization programme has been informed to the WTO Committee on Subsidies and Countervailing Measures as a non-countervailable subsidy unless the WTO bodies have determined that the program does not fulfil the requirements for a countervailable subsidy or there has been a violation of Art 8 of the Code.[2]

Investigation

The investigation must simultaneously cover both the existence of dumping or unfair subsidization and injury.[3] The Commission will send questionnaires to the domestic producer, to foreign producers or exporters and to unrelated and related importers. In the case of non-market economy countries, the Commission will also send questionnaires to the producers of the analogue country. The parties have 30 days to respond to the questionnaires from the date of receipt of the questionnaire.[4] Under certain circumstances an extension will be granted.[5] Generally the Commission requires the parties to provide a computerized response to the questionnaires. But the lack of such computerized response is not to be considered to constitute non-co-operation if the interested party shows that to present the response as requested would result in an unreasonable extra burden or cost.[6] All information must be examined for accuracy to the degree possible.[7]

The Commission may require the Member States to provide it with information and to carry out all necessary inspections.[8] The Community authorities may also carry out investigations on the spot to examine the records of importers, exporters, traders, agents, producers, trade associations and organizations and to verify information provided on dumping and injury.[9]

---

19 Art 5(10) Ibid; see also *Handbags from the PRC* OJ C 132/4 (1996); see also *Luggage and travel goods from the PRC* OJ 4.5.96 C 111/4; see also *Synthetic fibre ropes from India* OJ 4.4.96 C 102/16; see also *Unbleached cotton fabrics from PRC, Egypt, India, Indonesia, Pakistan and Turkey* OJ 21.2.96 C 50/3.
20 Council Regulation 384/96 Arts 5(6) and 5(1)(b), OJ 6.3.96 L56/1.
 1 See Council Regulation 2026/97 Arts 10(4), 10(5) and 10(6), OJ 21.10.97 L288/1.
 2 See ibid Art 10(6); see also Arts 8(3), 8(4) and 8(5) of the *Agreement on Subsidies and Countervailing Measures* OJ 23.12.94 L336/156.
 3 Council Regulation 384/96 Art 6(1), OJ 6.3.96 L56/1.
 4 Ibid Art 6(2).
 5 Ibid.
 6 Ibid Art 18(2).
 7 Ibid Art 6(8).
 8 Ibid Arts 6(3) and 6(4).
 9 Ibid Art 16 (1).

Furthermore, they may carry out investigations in third countries if they obtain the agreement of the firms concerned and the foreign country authorities do not object after notification.[10] In practice, firms and foreign governments will not object to such verifications in order to avoid the rules on non-co-operation.[11] If an interested party refuses access to the Community authorities, does not provide the necessary information within the time limits, significantly impedes the investigation or supplies false or misleading information, the findings may be based on the best information available.[12] In practice, the Commission will establish the highest subsidization or dumping margin for non-co-operators.[13] This is generally done on the basis that there is no reason to consider that the non-co-operating firms would dump less than the co-operating firms. However, the Commission must inform the firms of the nature of the information to be verified during the verification visits and make them aware of the consequences of non-co-operation.[14] The Community authorities are under no obligation to draw up a report after each verification in the course of the investigation.[15]

The regulations provide opportunities for both hearings and meetings between the parties. The undertakings concerned must have been offered the opportunity during the investigation to make known their views on the truth and relevance of the facts and circumstances alleged and their observations on any documents used.[16] The Community authorities will hear interested parties which have made themselves known if they have made a written request within the period prescribed in the notice of initiation, they show that they are an interested party likely to be affected by the result of the proceedings and they prove that they have particular reasons to be heard.[17] In practice the parties will use the hearings to explain or amplify the information provided. The Commission will also provide for meetings between the interested parties so that they can present opposing views and offer rebuttal arguments. However, the parties have no obligations whatsoever to attend such meetings.[18]

The Community regulations place a special emphasis upon the rules for disclosure and confidentiality. Following the case law of the Court of Justice they try to establish a balance between the right of disclosure of information and the right of

---

10 Ibid Art 16 (2).
11 See *Aspartame from the USA and Japan* OJ 29.11.90 L330/16.
12 Council Regulation 384/96 Art 18(1), OJ 6.3.96 L56/1. However, the Regulations require the Community authorities to check the best information available before using it as a basis for a determination. See ibid Art 18(5).
13 The regulations explicitly provide for a less favourable result where the parties in question did not co-operate. See Council Regulation 384/96 Art 18(6), OJ 6.3.96 L56/1; see also *Personal fax machines from the PRC, Japan, Republic of Korea, Malaysia, Singapore, Taiwan and Thailand* OJ 31.10.97 L297/61; see also *Advertising matches from Japan* OJ 17.6.97 L158/9; see also *Colour television receivers from Malaysia, the PRC, the Republic of Korea and Thailand* OJ 1.10.94 L255/50; see also *Microwave ovens from the PRC, the Republic of Korea, Thailand and Malaysia* OJ 7.7.95 L156/5.
14 Council Regulation 384/96 Art 16(3) and 18(1), OJ 6.3.96 L56/1.
15 See Case T-171/94 *Descom Scales Manufacturing Corpn v Council* [1995] ECR II-2413.
16 See Case T-161/94 *Sinochem Heilongjiang v Council of the European Union* [1995] ECR II-695; see also 85/76 *Hoffmann-La Roche v Commission* [1979] ECR 461; see also Case C-69/89 *Nakajima v Council* [1993] ECR I-2069; see also T-30/91 *Solvay v Commission* [1995] ECR II-1775; see also T-36/91 *ICI v Commission* [1995] ECR II-1847.
17 Council Regulation 384/96 Art 6(5), OJ 6.3.96 L56/1.
18 Ibid Art 6(6).

confidentiality of the parties.[19] All complainants, importers or exporters which have made themselves known, and the representatives of the exporting country may upon written request, inspect all information made available by any party.[20] 'Any party' must be interpreted to mean not only the parties subject to the investigation but all those whose information has been used.[1] The parties may respond to such information and their comments should be taken into consideration to the extent that they are sufficiently sustained in their response.[2] However internal documents and confidential information will not be disclosed. The Community authorities must treat as confidential all information which is by its nature confidential or which is provided on a confidential basis by the parties.[3] If the Community authorities consider that a request for confidentiality is not warranted and the provider is not willing to provide the information in any other way, the information must be disregarded unless it can be demonstrated from appropriate sources that the information is correct.[4] In any case, except in exceptional circumstances the provider of the confidential information must provide a non confidential summary of such information which can permit a reasonable understanding of the substance of the information submitted in confidence.[5] In no way will the confidential rules prevent the disclosure of the general information on which the Community authorities have made their determination.[6] The parties may request the disclosure of the details on which both the decision to impose both provisional and definitive duties has been made.[7]

Following the new Codes,[8] the regulations establish a deadline for the conclusion of the investigation. Whenever possible the investigations must be concluded within one year. The deadline may be extended to a maximum of 15 months after the initiation of the proceedings.[9] The Community authorities have interpreted this deadline as more of a guide than a mandatory period.[10] In practice the Community authorities will explain the reasons for their delay.[11]

Provisional measures

The Commission may impose provisional measures within nine months from initiation if it has made a provisional affirmative determination of both unfair

---

19 See Case 264/82 *Timex Corpn v Council* [1985] ECR 849; see also Case 236/81 *Celanese v Council and Commission* [1982] ECR 1183; see also Case C-49/88 *Al-Jubail Fertilizer Co v Council* [1991] ECR I-3187.
20 Council Regulation 384/96 Art 6(7), OJ 6.3.96 L56/1.
1 See Case 264/82 *Timex Corpn v Council* [1985] ECR 849.
2 Council Regulation 384/96 Art 6(7), OJ 6.3.96 L56/1.
3 Ibid Art 19(1); see also ibid Art 19(5), which lays down rules of conduct for officials of the EC or Member States.
4 Ibid Art 19(3).
5 Ibid Art 19(2).
6 Ibid Art 19(4).
7 Ibid Art 20.
8 See Art 5(10) of *The Agreement on the Interpretation of Article VI of GATT 1994*; OJ 23.12.94 L336/106; see also Art 11(11) of the *Agreement on Subsidies and Countervailing Measures* OJ 23.12.94 L336/156.
9 Council Regulation 384/96 Art 6(9), OJ 6.3.96 L56/1.
10 See Case C-121/86 *Anonymos Etaireia Epicheiriseon Metalleftikon Viomichanikon kai Naftukiakon v Council* [1989] ECR 3919; see also Case 246/87 *Continentale Produkten v Hauptzollamt Munchen-West* [1991] 1 CMLR 761.
11 See *Advertising matches from Japan* OJ 17.6.97 L158/9; see also *Magnetic Disks originating in Malaysia, Mexico and the United States of America* OJ 13.4.96 L92/1; see also *Microwave ovens from the PRC, the Republic of Korea, Thailand and Malaysia* OJ 7.7.95 L156/5.

subsidization or dumping and injury and it considers that the Community interests require it.[12] The Commission can only take action after consulting or notifying the Advisory Committee.[13] It may also take measures, subject to the same conditions, at the request of any Member States.[14] The Council may, by qualified majority, decide differently and reverse the Commission's decision.[15]

The regulations establish the basic lesser duty rule for the imposition of provisional measures too. The amount of the provisional duty must not exceed the margin of dumping or unfair subsidization as provisionally established. However, the duty should be less than the dumping or subsidization margin if a lesser duty would be adequate to remove the injury to the Community industry.[16] Provisional duties will be imposed by regulation and will take the form of a security.[17] The release of the products concerned for free circulation in the Community will be conditional on the provision of such security. The Regulation establishing the provisional measures will expire after six months. However, provisional measures may also be imposed for nine months or extended by the Council up to another three months if the exporters representing a significant percentage of the trade involved so request or do not object.[18]

Commission Regulations imposing provisional measures may be subject to judicial review. However, when the amounts secured as provisional measures are collected in accordance with the Regulation imposing definitive measures, the importers required to pay the duties may not rely on any legal effect arising out of the Commission regulation. But it will be possible to claim an interest in seeking a declaration that the provisional regulation is void, with a view to a damages claim, in respect of the amounts secured which are discharged because the rate of the definitive duty is lower than the rate of the provisional duty, provided that evidence is adduced in connection with the amounts secured.[19]

Termination

Anti-dumping and countervailing proceedings may be terminated in different ways. First, they may be terminated without the adoption of any measures. They may also be terminated with the acceptance of an undertaking from the producer or exporter or the exporting country. Finally, they may be terminated with the final adoption of definitive duties by the Council.

Termination without measures

The Commission may terminate the proceedings without the imposition of any measures if there is a withdrawal of the complaint or when it considers that the measures are not necessary. If the complaint is withdrawn the proceeding may

12 Council Regulation 384/96 Art 7(1), OJ 6.3.96 L56/1.
13 Ibid Art 7(4).
14 Ibid Art 7(5).
15 Ibid Art 7(6).
16 Ibid Art 7(2).
17 Ibid Art 14(1) and 7(3).
18 Ibid Art 7(7); see also *Bicycles from Indonesia, Malaysia and Thailand* OJ 10.2.96 L32/1; see also *Coumarin from the PRC* OJ 12.4.96 L28/1.
19 See Joined Cases C-320/86 & C-188/87 *Stanko France v Commission and Council* [1990] ECR I-3013; see also Joined Cases C-304/86 & C-185/87 *Enital SpA v Commission and Council* [1990] ECR I-2939.

be terminated only if the Commission does not consider the termination to be against the interests of the Community.[20] In practice, the Commission will terminate the proceedings whenever the complaint is withdrawn.[1]

The Commission may also terminate the proceedings without taking any measures, whenever it considers that these are not necessary because of the absence of dumping or an unfair subsidy or injury or where they would not be in the Community interest.[2] However, the Commission must first consult the Advisory Committee. If the Committee raises any objections the Commission will have to make a proposal to terminate the proceedings without measures to the Council. The proceeding will be terminated if within one month, the Council acting by qualified majority does not decide otherwise.[3] The provisional duties will not be confirmed and the securities will be released.[4] Terminations without measures may be subject to judicial review.

Undertakings

The Commission may also terminate the proceedings with the acceptance of an undertaking whenever there has been a provisional affirmative determination of dumping or unfair subsidization and injury caused by such practice.[5] Undertakings may be offered by the exporters or producer but not by the importers.[6] There must be a satisfactory voluntary undertaking to revise prices or to cease exports of dumped or subsidized products in order to remove the injury.[7] Save in exceptional circumstances, an undertaking offered after the final disclosure before the definitive imposition of duties will not be accepted.[8]

In cases where a regional market has been used to determine injury the exporters or producers or their governments must be given the opportunity to offer an undertaking in respect of the region concerned.[9] In such cases, special account must be taken of the interest of the region.

Undertakings may also be offered by the Commission. However, in no case

---

20 Council Regulation 384/96 Art 9(1), OJ 6.3.96 L56/1.
1 See *Furfuryl alcohol from the People's Republic of China and Thailand* OJ 7.5.96 L112/18; see also *PET video films originating in the Republic of China* OJ 20.7.96 L181/27; see also *Portland cement from Poland, the Czech and Slovak Republics* OJ 18.1.96 L13/27; see also *Parts of gas-fuelled non-refillable pocket lighters from Japan* OJ 7.10.95 L239/30.
2 Council Regulation 384/96 Art 9(2), OJ 6.3.96 L56/1; see also *Unwrought pure magensium from Kazakhstan* OJ 12.7.96 L174/32; see also Case C-129/86 *Greece v Council* [1989] ECR 3963; see also Case C-121/86 *Anonymos Etaireia Epicheiriseon Metalleftikon Viomichanikon kai Naftukiakon v Council* [1989] ECR 3919.
3 Council Regulation 384/96 Art 9(2), OJ 6.3.96 L56/1; see also Case T-212/95 *Asociacion de Fabricantes de Cemento de Espana v Commission of the European Communities* [1998] 1 CMLR 833.
4 Ibid Art 10(3); see also *Furfuryl Alcohol from the PRC and Thailand* OJ 7.5.96 L112/18; see also *Cotton fabric from the PRC, India, Indonesia, Pakistan and Turkey* OJ 20.2.96 L42/16.
5 Council Regulation 384/96 Art 8(2), OJ 6.3.96 L56/1; see also *Farmed Atlantic salmon from Norway* OJ 30.9.97 L267/81.
6 See also Case C-133/87 & C-150/87, *Nashua Corpn v Commission and Council* [1990] ECR I-719; see also Case C-156/87 *Gestetner v Council* [1990] ECR I-781. The Regulation on Countervailing Duties also allows undertakings to be offered by the government representatives of the exporters or producers. See Council Regulation 2026/97 Art 13(1)(a), OJ 21.10.97 L288/1.
7 Council Regulation 384/96 Art 8(1), OJ 6.3.96 L56/1.
8 Ibid Art 8(2).
9 Ibid Art 4(3).

will the exporters be obliged to accept such an offer and the refusal must in no way prejudice the consideration of the case.[10]

The Community authorities have a wide margin of discretion to refuse or accept an offered undertaking.[11] They may refuse the undertaking if acceptance is considered to be impractical.[12] The Commission will refuse undertakings offered in cases such as those where there is no commitment by the government to guarantee the monitoring of the execution of the undertaking,[13] or when previous undertakings offered from those exporters or authorities have been breached,[14] where the minimum prices offered are not sufficient to remove the injury,[15] or especially when the investigation refers to consumer electronic products.[16] However, the Community authorities have the obligation to inform the exporter or government representative and give them an opportunity to comment as well as to state the reasons for the refusal in the final regulation imposing definitive measures.[17] The rejection of an undertaking is not subject to judicial review. The parties may only challenge the regulation imposing final measures.[18]

If the Commission decides to accept an undertaking it must consult the Advisory Committee. If no objections are raised in the Committee the undertaking will be accepted and the proceedings will be terminated. However, if objections are raised the Commission will have to make a proposal to the Council for acceptance of the undertakings and termination of the proceedings. The investigation must be considered terminated if within one month the Council acting by qualified majority has not decided otherwise.[19] Provisional duties may not be collected when undertakings are accepted.[20] Even after the acceptance of the undertaking, the investigation should be completed. If a negative determination of dumping or injury is made, the undertaking will lapse save in cases where such negative determination is due in large part to the existence of an undertaking. If a final affirmative determination of injury and the existence of dumping or unfair subsidization is made, then the undertaking will continue regardless of the margin of dumping or injury.[1]

10 Ibid Art 8(2).
11 See Case 204/84 *Toyo Bearing v Council* [1987] ECR 1809; see also Case 258/84 *Nippon Seiko v Council* [1987] ECR 1923; see also Case 260/84 *Minebea v Council* [1987] ECR 1975; see also Joined Cases 294/86 & 77/87 *Technointorg v Commission and Council* [1988] ECR 6077.
12 Council Regulation 384/96 Art 8(3), OJ 6.3.96 L56/1.
13 See *Powdered activated carbon originating in the People's Republic of China* OJ 3.6.96 L134/20.
14 See *Furfuraldehyde from the PRC* OJ 21.1.95 L15/11 (1995).
15 See *Ferro-silico-magnese from Russia, Ukraine, Brazil and South Africa* OJ 14.10.95 L248/1.
16 See *Colour television receivers originating in Malaysia, the PRC, the Republic of Korea, Singapore and Thailand* OJ 1.4.95 L73/3.
17 Council Regulation 384/96 Art 8(3), OJ 6.3.96 L56/1; see also Case 255/84 *Nachi Fujikoshi v Council* [1987] ECR 1861; see also Case 256/84 *Koyo Seiko v Council* [1987] ECR 1899; see also Case 204/84 *Toyo Bearing Co v Council* [1987] ECR 1809; see also *Sinochem National Chemicals Import and Export Corporation v Council of the European Union* (1998) Transcript, 29 January.
18 See Joined cases C-133/87 & C-150/87, *Nashua Corpn v Commission and Council* [1990] ECR I-719.
19 See Art 8(5); see also *Ferro-silico-magnese from Russia, Georgia, Ukraine, Brazil and South Africa* OJ 14.10.95 L248/56 (acceptance of undertaking).
20 See Case 113/77 *NTN Toyo Bearing Company v Council* [1979] ECR 1185; see also Case 118/77 *Import Standard Officer v Council* [1979] ECR 1277; see also Case 119/77 *Nippon Seiko v Council and Commission* [1979] ECR 1303; see also Case 120/77 *Koyo Seiko v Council and Commission* [1979] ECR 1337; see also Case 121/77 *Nachi Fujikoshi Corpn v Council* [1979] ECR 1363.
1 Ibid Art 8(6).

The Commission will require the exporter to provide regularly information relevant to the fulfilment of the undertaking. The non-compliance of this obligation will be considered a violation of the undertaking.[2] If an undertaking is violated or withdrawn, a definitive duty will be imposed on the basis of the facts established within the context of the previous investigations if the investigations were concluded with a final determination of dumping and injury and the exporter concerned has been given an opportunity to comment.[3] The Commission is not required to conduct any further investigation for the definitive duties to be imposed.[4] However, if there is reason to believe that an undertaking is being violated or in cases of withdrawal or violation of an undertaking the previous investigation had not been concluded, the Commission will impose a provisional duty, after consulting the Advisory Committee, on the basis of the best information available.[5] If the firm does not co-operate in the investigation and there is no other information available, the Commission may base its final determination on the basis of the prices which the firm previously bound itself to observe.[6] In no case, may the change of measures from an undertaking to a duty generate a new five year sunset period.

Termination with definitive duties

It is for the Council to decide whether to impose a definitive duty.[7] The Commission must submit to the Council a proposal after consultation with the Advisory Committee.[8] If the facts as finally established show that there is dumping or unfair subsidization and injury caused thereby and the Community interest calls for intervention, the Council will impose a definitive duty acting by simple majority on the proposal from the Commission.[9] The regulations impose a lesser duty rule for the imposition of any duty. The amount of the duty must not exceed the margin of dumping or unfair subsidization but it should however be less than this margin if the lesser duty would be adequate to remove the injury to the Community industry.[10] However, the Council has wide discretion in deciding the form of the duties.[11] The Council will usually impose the duty in the form of an *ad valorem* duty or a specific duty per quantity of product or on a variable duty based on a minimum price. The purpose of the duty will be to bring about an increase in the price of the product in question in order to counterbalance the dumping or unfair subsidization and protect the Community industry from the injury caused thereby.[12] The duties must be imposed, on

2 Ibid Art 8(7).
3 Ibid Art 8(9).
4 See Joined Cases 239 & 275/82, *Allied Corporation v Commission* [1984] ECR 1005.
5 Council Regulation 384/96 Art 8(10), OJ 6.3.96 L56/1; see also *Farmed Atlantic salmon from Norway* OJ 17.12.97 L346/63.
6 See Case 53/83 *Allied Corporation v Commission* [1985] ECR 1621.
7 See Case 299/85 *Tokyo Juki Industrial Co v Council and Commission* [1986] ECR 2965; see also Case C-121/86 *Anonymos Etaireia Epicheiriseon Metalleftikon Viomichanikon kai Naftukiakon v Council* [1989] ECR 3919.
8 Council Regulation 384/96 Art 9(4), OJ 6.3.96 L56/1.
9 Ibid.
10 Ibid.
11 See Joined Cases C-133/87 & C-150/87, *Nashua Corpn v Commission and Council* [1990] ECR I-719; see also Case C-189/88 *Cartorobica SpA v Ministero delle Finanze dello Stato* [1991] ECR I-1269.
12 See Case C-358/89 *Extramet Industrie SA v Council* [1990] ECR I-431; see also Case 69/89 R *Nakajima All Precision Co v Council* [1989] ECR 1689.

a non discriminatory basis, by a regulation which will be published in the Official Journal and contain the names of the exporters and countries concerned, a description of the product and a summary of the facts and considerations relevant to the dumping and injury determinations.[13]

Where there has been the imposition of provisional duties, the Council must decide when imposing the definitive duties, what portion of the provisional duties is to be definitively collected.[14] In most cases, the Council will decide to collect the provisional duties but generally the provisional duties will be released if there is only a final determination of threat of injury or material retardation.[15] If the definitive duty is higher than the provisional duty, the difference will be disregarded when collecting the provisional duties. If the definitive duty is lower than the provisional duty, the latter will be recalculated.[16]

The duties will only apply to the products and countries specified in the Regulation.[17] A product will not be automatically subject to the anti-dumping duty merely because it is classified under the same tariff heading.[18] Furthermore, the anti-dumping duty will not apply to parts or components of the product unless specified.[19] The duties must be collected by the Member States in the form and rate specific to, and in accordance with the criteria laid down in, the regulation imposing the duties.[20] Thus, the Member States have no margin of discretion when collecting the duties.

In general, provisional and definitive duties must only be applied to products which enter into free circulation after the time when the decision taken to impose them enters into force.[1] However definitive duties may be imposed on products which were entered for consumption up to 90 days prior to the date of the application of provisional duties but not before the initiation of the investigation.[2] However the retroactive imposition of definitive duties is

---

13 Council Regulation 384/96 Arts 9(5), 14(1) and 14(2), OJ 6.3.96 L56/1.
14 Ibid Art 10(2). The Council must give reasons for its decision to collect the provisional duties. See Case 121/77 *Nachi Fujikoshi v Council* [1979] ECR 1363; see also Case 120/77 *Koyo Seiko v Council and Commission* [1979] ECR 1337; see also Case 119/77 *Nippon Seiko v Council and Commission* [1979] ECR 1303; see also Case 118/77 *Import Standard Officer v Council* [1979] ECR 1277; see also Case 113/77 *NTN Toyo Bearing Co v Council* [1979] ECR 1185; see also Case 120/83 R *Raznoimport v Commission* [1983] ECR 2573.
15 Council Regulation 384/96 Art 10(2), OJ 6.3.96 L56/1; see *Magnetic Disks originating in Malaysia, Mexico and the United States of America* OJ 13.4.96 L92/1; see also *Certain tube or pipe fittings, of iron or steel originating in the People's Republic of China, Croatia and Thailand* OJ 3.4.96 L84/1; see also *Disodium Carbonate from the United States* OJ 12.10.95 L244/32; but see *Ferro-silico-magnese from Russia, Ukraine, Brazil and South Africa* OJ 14.10.95 L248/1 (where provisional duties were not definitively collected).
16 Council Regulation 384/96 Art 10(3), OJ 6.3.96 L56/1; see also *Personal fax machines from the PRC, Japan, the Republic of Korea, Malaysia, Singapore, Taiwan and Thailand* OJ 30.4.98 L128/1; see also *Advertising matches from Japan* OJ 16.10.97 L284/57; see also *Colour television receivers originating in Malaysia, the PRC, the Republic of Korea, Singapore and Thailand* OJ 1.4.95 L73/3.
17 In this sense, a change in the name or political organization of the geographical area referred to as the country of origin or of export in the Regulation cannot remove by itself products originating in that area from the duty's field of application. See C-177/96 *Belgian State v Banque Indosuez* [1997] ECR I-5659.
18 See Case C-90/92 *Dr Tretter v Hauptzollamt Stuttgart-Ost* [1993] ECR I-3569.
19 See Case C-99/94 *Robert Birkenbeul GmbH & Co KG v Hauptzollamt Koblenz* [1996] ECR I-1791.
20 Council Regulation 384/96 Art 14(1), OJ 6.3.96 L56/1.
 1 Ibid Art 10(1).
 2 Ibid Art 10(4); see also Case 246/87 *Continentale Produkten v Hauptzollamt Munchen-West* [1989] ECR 1151 (considering that this practice does not infringe the legitimate expectations of the importer).

subject to certain requirements. First, the imports must have been registered in accordance with Art 14(5). Second, the importers must have been provided with an opportunity to comment. Third, there must be, for the product in question, a history of dumping over an extended period of time or the importer was aware or should have been aware of the dumping or unfair subsidization practice. Finally in addition to the level of imports which caused injury during the investigation period there is a further substantial increase in imports which, in the light of its timing and volume, is likely to seriously undermine the remedial effect of the definitive duty to be applied.[3] The imposition of retroactive duties is also possible in cases of violation or withdrawal of undertakings provided that such imports have been registered and that the retroactive assessment does not apply to imports entered before the violation or withdrawal of the undertaking.[4]

The regulation allows the possibility of suspending the measures previously imposed if the market conditions have temporarily changed to an extent that injury would be unlikely to resume as a result of such suspension. The Commission, after consulting the Advisory Committee, may suspend the measures for a period of nine months, after giving the Community industry an opportunity to comment, if it considers that such suspension is in the Community interest.[5] The Council, however, may decide by simple majority on a proposal by the Commission, to extend the suspension for a further period not exceeding one year.[6]

Reviews

Anti-dumping and countervailing duties must apply to all prospective imports from the countries for which they have been imposed as long as they are necessary to counteract the dumping or unfair subsidization which is causing injury.[7] Thus, to ensure that the measures apply only as long as they are necessary, the regulations provide for four types of reviews: an expiry review, an interim review, a newcomers review and a refund review. The reviews are always initiated by the Commission after consultation with the Advisory Committee.[8] Although they are in general conducted following the relevant procedural rules of the two regulations, they must always be concluded within 12 months of their date of initiation.[9] However, the Community authorities have considered that this one year period is only indicative and not mandatory.[10] The amendment, repeal or maintenance of the measures resulting from

---

3 Council Regulation 384/96 Art 10(4), OJ 6.3.96 L56/1.
4 Ibid Art 10(5).
5 Ibid Art 14(4); see also *Certain types of electronic microcircuits known as EPROMs from Japan* OJ 15.7.95 L165/26; see also *Certain types of electronic microcircuits known as DRAMs from Japan and the Republic of Korea* OJ 9.6.95 L126/58.
6 Council Regulation 384/96 Art 14(4), OJ 6.3.96 L56/1; see also *Certain types of electronic microcircuits known as EPROMs from Japan* OJ 13.4.96 L92/4; see also *Certain Types of Electronic Microcircuits known as DRAMS from Japan and the Republic of Korea* OJ 6.3.96 L55/1.
7 Council Regulation 384/96 Art 11(1), OJ 6.3.96 L56/1.
8 Ibid Art 11(6).
9 Ibid Art 11(5).
10 See *Certain large electrolytic aluminium capacitors from Japan* OJ 23.12.97 L351/17 (where owing to the volume and the complexity of the data gathered and examined, the investigation exceeded the normal period of 12 months); see also Joined Cases T-163/94 & T-165/94, *NTN Corpn and Koyo Seiko v Council* [1995] ECR II-1381.

the reviews falls under the competence of the Community institution responsible for the introduction of the original measures.[11]

Expiry review

A definitive duty will expire five years from its imposition or from the conclusion of the most recent review which has covered both dumping or unfair subsidization and injury.[12] However, in order to ensure that the duty is in force as long as it is necessary, the regulations provide for a review in order to determine whether its expiry would be likely to lead to a continuation or recurrence of dumping or unfair subsidization or injury.[13] Hence, the Commission must publish a notice of impending expiry in the Official Journal at an appropriate time in the final fifth year of the duty.[14] The Commission may initiate a review on its own initiative or upon request made by, or on behalf of, the Community producers filed not later than three months before the end of the five year period.[15] The request must contain sufficient evidence that the removal of the measure would be likely to result in a continuation or recurrence of dumping and injury.[16] If the Community authorities decide to initiate the review, the exporters, importers and government representatives will be given an opportunity to comment on the review.[17] The Community authorities must decide on the basis of all relevant and duly supported evidence presented.[18] The duties will remain in force pending the outcome of the review.[19] If the Community authorities decide that the measures should not expire they will be extended for another five years.[20] If they decide that the measures should expire or there is an actual expiry of the measures they must announce it in the Official Journal.[1]

Interim review

For the purpose of guaranteeing that the measures are in force as long as, and to the degree, necessary to countervail the injurious effects caused by dumping or unfair subsidization, the regulations provide for an interim review. The need

11 Council Regulation 384/96 Art 11(6), OJ 6.3.96 L56/1.
12 Ibid Art 11(2).
13 Ibid Art 11(2).
14 Ibid Art 11(2)(c); see also *Oxalic Acid from India* OJ 30.5.96 C155/5; see also *Gas-fuelled, non-refillable pocket flint lighters from Japan and the Republic of Korea* OJ 30.5.96 C155/6; see also *Video tapes in cassettes from the PRC* OJ 24.4.96 C119/3; see also *Ball bearings from Thailand* OJ 3.1.98 C1/12; see also *Certain magnetic disks from Japan, Taiwan and the PRC* OJ 22.4.98 C123/5; see also *Binder and baler twine from Brazil* OJ 9.4.98 C111/3.
15 Council Regulation 384/96 Arts 11(2) and 11(2)(c), OJ 6.3.96 L56/1.
16 Ibid Art 11(2)(a) The regulations provide a non-exhaustive list of factors which may indicate such likelihood. As to the standard of the injury review see *Commission of the European Communities v NTN Corpn* (1998) Transcript, 10 February.
17 Ibid Art 11(2)(b).
18 Ibid; see also *Certain types of electronic microcircuits known as EPROMs from Japan* OJ 16.4.97 L99/16 (where the review was terminated without the measures being extended on the basis of the unlikelihood of recurrence of injury if the measures expired).
19 Council Regulation 384/96 Art 11(2), OJ 6.3.96 L56/1.
20 See *Plain paper photocopiers from Japan* OJ 12.10.95 L244/1.
 1 Council Regulation 384/96 Art 11(2)(c), OJ 6.3.96 L56/1; see also *Welded wire-mesh from the Republic of Yugoslavia, Republic of Bosnia-Herzegovina and Macedonia* OJ 8.5.96 C136/10; see also *Audiotapes in cassettes from Japan and the Republic of Korea* OJ 4.5.96 C132/6 (1996).

for the continued imposition of measures may be reviewed on the initiative of the Commission, at the request of a Member State or following a request by an exporter or importer or Community producer which contains sufficient evidence of the need for such a review and that the measure is no longer necessary or it is not sufficient to counteract the injurious effects caused by the unfair practices.[2] In carrying out the investigations the Commission may decide whether the circumstances with regard to the unfair practices or injury have significantly changed or whether the measures are achieving their intended purposes.[3] Again, an interim review stops the five year expiry period. Measures resulting from the review expire after five years.

Newcomers review

Countervailing and anti-dumping duties are imposed prospectively on all imports of a certain product coming from a certain country.[4] However, a review is also possible for the purpose of determining individual margins of dumping or subsidization for new exporters in the exporting country which have not exported the product during the investigation period on which the measures are based.[5] The newcomer must show that it is not related to any of the exporters or producers in the exporting country which are subject to the duties and that it has actually exported to the Community following the investigation period or that it has entered into an irrevocable contractual obligation to export.[6] The review must be carried out on an accelerated basis by the Commission after the Community producers have been given an opportunity to comment.[7] No duty must apply for newcomers while the review is in process.[8] However imports of the new exporter will be registered in order to ensure that if there is a final positive determination of the unfair practices and injury the duties can be imposed retroactively to the date of the initiation of the review.[9] Measures resulting from a newcomers

---

2 See *Silicon carbide from Ukraine* OJ 7.5.96 C135/4; see also *Hematite pig-iron from Brazil, Poland, Russia, Ukraine and the Czech Republic* OJ 10.4.96 C104/11; but see *Espadrilles from the PRC* OJ 26.9.95 L229/10 (where the initiation of an interim review was refused because of lack of sufficient evidence).

3 Council Regulation 384/96 Art 11(3)(b), OJ 6.3.96 L56/1; see also *Certain large electrolytic aluminium capacitors from Japan* OJ 23.12.97 L351/17 (where the duty was partially reduced on the basis of lower dumping margin); see also *Ball bearings with a greatest external diameter not exceeding 30 mm from Japan* OJ 7.5.97 L117/29 (where the review was terminated without an increase of duties due to the lack of any changes concerning injury).

4 See *Plain paper photocopiers from Japan* OJ 12.10.95 L244/12.

5 Council Regulation 384/96 Art 11(4), OJ 6.3.96 L56/1. In contrast, the Anti-Subsidy Regulation provides for accelerated reviews by which any exporter whose exports are subject to a definitive countervailing duty, but who was not individually investigated during the investigation for reasons other than a refusal to co-operate with the Commission, must be entitled, upon request, to an accelerated review in order that the Commission may promptly establish an individual countervailing duty rate for that exporter. See Council Regulation 2026/97 Art 20, OJ 21.10.97 L288/1.

6 Council Regulation 384/96 Art 11(4)(a), OJ 6.3.96 L56/1; see also *Sacks and bags made of polyethylene or polypropylene from India* OJ 17.4.98 L115/3; see also *Synthetic fibres of polyesters originating in India and the Republic of Korea* OJ 23.5.98 L131/1; see also *Synthetic fibres of polyester from India and the Republic of Korea* OJ 1.11.95 L262/28.

7 Council Regulation 384/96 Art 11(4)(b), OJ 6.3.96 L56/1.

8 Ibid; see also *Sacks and bags made of polyethylene or polypropylene from India* OJ 17.4.98 L115/3.

9 Council Regulation 384/96 Art 11(4)(b), OJ 6.3.96 L56/1. See *Farmed Atlantic salmon from Norway* OJ 24.3.98 L88/31 (where an undertaking was accepted from a new exporter).

review expire after a five year period. Where there has been sampling in the original investigation, there is no possibility for a newcomers review.[10]

Refunds

Anti-dumping and countervailing duties are imposed prospectively for five years. However, if the collection of the duties exceeds the actual dumping or subsidization margin the excess must be reimbursed.[11] The importer must submit an application to the Commission via the Member State of the territory in which the products were released for free circulation within six months of the date on which the amount of the definitive duties was imposed or the date on which a decision was made to collect the amounts secured by way of provisional duties.[12] The request must contain precise information on the amount of the refund of the duties claimed and all customs documentation relating to the calculation and payment of such amount. It must also include evidence on the normal values and export prices to the Community for the exporter to which the duty applies.[13] In this sense, the regulation following the new Anti-dumping Code no longer requires consideration of the anti-dumping duty as a cost.[14] If the exporter increases its prices at the level of the duty, the importer may apply for a refund.[15] The Commission will decide whether, and to what extent, the application should be granted.[16] It may at any time during the refund review decide to initiate an interim review.[17] If the Commission decides that a refund is justified the payment of such will be done by the Member State of the territory through which the importer has applied for a refund.[18] Payment of the authorized refund should normally be made within 90 days of the Commission's decision.

Anti-absorption and anti-circumvention

In order to make sure that both anti-dumping and countervailing duties achieve their purpose, the regulations establish rules to prevent anti-absorption and anti-circumvention practices.

Unlike the Antidumping Code, the Community Regulation imposes on the importers the obligation to absorb the anti-dumping duty.[19] In order to guarantee this rule, the Regulation establishes an investigation procedure which may be opened by the Commission, after consulting the Advisory Committee, upon request of the Community industry.[20] The Community industry must submit information showing that the imposed measures have led to no movement,

10 Council Regulation 384/96 Art 11(4)(c) and 11(4)(b), OJ 6.3.96 L56/1.
11 Ibid Art 11(8); see also Case 312/84 *Continentale Produkten Gesellschaft v Commission* [1987] ECR 841.
12 Ibid Art 11(8)(a).
13 Ibid Art 11(8)(b).
14 See Art 9(3)(3) of the *Agreement on the Implementation of Article VI of GATT* OJ 23.12.94 L336/106.
15 Council Regulation 384/96 Art 11(10), OJ 6.3.96 L56/1. This provision actually applies to all review procedures.
16 Ibid Art 11(8)(c).
17 Ibid.
18 Ibid.
19 Ibid Art 12. There is no such rule in the Anti-Subsidy Regulation.
20 Ibid Art 12(1); see also *Certain television camera systems from Japan* OJ 10.4.96 C 104/9.

or insufficient movement, in resale prices or subsequent selling prices in the Community. The Commission must give an opportunity to exporters, importers and Community producers to clarify the situation with regard to the resale prices and the subsequent selling practices.[1] If it is considered that the measures should have led to a movement of the prices, the export prices will be reassessed and new dumping margins will be calculated taking into account the reassessed export prices.[2] However, it will be possible to take into account changes in the normal values where evidence of this is produced by the exporter.[3] In this sense, anti-dumping duties will not be treated as a cost. If the investigation shows increased dumping, the measures in force will be amended by the Council, by simple majority, on a proposal by the Commission.[4]

Again, unlike both codes, the regulations establish procedures for the purpose of preventing duties being circumvented via third countries' exports or assembly operations in the Community.[5] Circumvention is defined as a change in the pattern of trade between third countries and the European Community which results from a practice, process or work for which there is insufficient due cause or economic justification other than the imposition of the duty, and where there is evidence that the remedial effects of the duty are being undermined in terms of the prices and or quantities of like products and there is evidence of dumping in relation to the normal values previously established for like or similar products.[6] The regulations consider that an assembly operation in the Community or a third country is presumed *iuris et de iure* to circumvent the measures in force if:

(1) the operations started or substantially increased since or just prior to, the initiation of the investigation and the parts concerned are from the country subject to the measures;[7] and

(2) the parts constitute 60% or more of the total value of the parts of the assembled products;[8] and the remedial effects of the duty are being undermined in terms of the prices and/or quantities of the assembled like product and there is evidence of dumping in relation to the normal values previously established for the like or similar products.[9]

The Commission will initiate an investigation, after consulting the advisory committee, upon a request which contains sufficient evidence of

---

1 Council Regulation 384/96 Art 12(2), OJ 6.3.96 L56/1.
2 Ibid.
3 Ibid Art 12(5).
4 Ibid Art 12(3); see also Council Regulation 384/96, OJ 6.3.96 L56/1; see also *Certain electronic weighing scales from Japan* OJ 12.10.95 L244/15 (termination without any new measures).
5 Council Regulation 384/96 Art 13, OJ 6.3.96 L56/1. The legality of these rules in the international trading system is doubtful. The Community has already been criticized in a GATT panel report for these measures. See *EC—Regulation on Imports of Parts and Components* BISD 37S/132 (1991).
6 Ibid Art 13(1).
7 Ibid Art 13(2)(a).
8 However in no case will it be considered to be circumvention where the value added to the parts brought in during the assembly or completion operation is greater than 25% of the manufacturing cost. See ibid Art 13(2)(b); see also *Certain electronic weighing scales from Japan and Singapore* OJ 31.5.98 L141/57 (where the circumvention investigation was terminated without an extension of the duties on the basis that the average value added established during the investigation period was found to be above 25%).
9 Ibid Art 13(2)(c).

circumvention.[10] In its regulation of initiation, the Commission must instruct the customs authorities to register all imports coming from the third countries. However, imports will not be subject to registration if they are accompanied by a customs certificate issued by the Commission declaring that the importation of the goods does not constitute circumvention.[11] The extension of the measures to the third countries will be taken by the Council acting by simple majority on a proposal from the Commission resulting from the investigation.[12]

JUDICIAL REVIEW

There are no special provisions in the Anti-dumping and Countervailing Duty Regulations for judicial review. Thus, the general provisions of the EC Treaty apply.

For an act to be reviewable it must produce legal effects and be a measure definitively laying down the position of the institution on the conclusion of the anti-dumping procedure, and not an intermediate step intended to pave the way for the final decision.[13] Acts taken following anti-dumping and countervailing duty investigations may be challenged through two mechanisms. First, they may be challenged in the national courts of the Member States implementing the measures adopted by the Community institutions. In deciding on these issues, the national courts may or must refer the case to the European Court of Justice for an Art 177 preliminary ruling.[14]

Most cases, however, have been based on Art 173 of the Treaty.[15] In June 1993, following the Treaty of the European Union,[16] the Council extended the jurisdiction of the European Court of First Instance to include all actions brought by non-privileged applicants under Art 173.[17] Thus actions by Member States, the Council or the Commission against anti-dumping and

---

10 Ibid Art 13(3); see also *Certain magnetic disks originating in Canada, Hong Kong, India and Thailand* OJ 20.10.95 L252/9; see also *Television camera systems originating in Japan* OJ 6.6.98 L163/21; see also *Gas-fuelled, non-refillable pocket flint lighters from the PRC* OJ 8.5.98 L135/38.

11 Council Regulation 384/96 Art 13(4), OJ 6.3.96 L56/1.

12 Ibid Art 13(3).

13 See Case 229/86 *Brother Industries v Commission* [1987] ECR 3757; see also Case T-134/95 *Dyssan Magnetics Ltd and Review Magnetics (Macao) Ltd v Commission of the European Communities* [1996] ECR II-181 (where the Court considered a Commission decision to initiate anti-dumping proceedings as not challengeable); see also Case 60/81 *IBM v Commission* [1981] ECR 2639; see also Case T-75/96R *Soktas Pamuk Ve Tarim Urunlerini DeGerlendirme Ticaret Ve Sanayi AS v Commission of the European Communities* [1996] ECR II-859; see also Case T-212/95 *Asociacion de Fabricantes de Cemento de Espana v Commission of the European Communities* [1998] 1 CMLR 833.

14 See Art 177 of the EC Treaty.

15 Art 173 reads:
    The Court of Justice shall review the legality of the acts adopted jointly by the European Parliament and the Council, of acts of the Council, of the Commission and of the ECB, other than recommendations and opinions, and of acts of the European Parliament intended to produce legal effects vis-à-vis third parties.
    ... Any natural or legal person, may under the same conditions, institute proceedings against a decision addressed to that person or against a decision which, although in the form of a regulation or a decision addressed to another person, is of direct and individual concern to the former.'

16 See Art 168a of the EC Treaty.

17 See Dec 93/350 OJ L144/21 (1993).

countervailing measures may still be brought before the Court of Justice.[18] Petitions by private parties challenging anti-dumping and countervailing actions under Art 173 must be brought before the Court of First Instance. Decisions of the Court of First Instance can be appealed against to the European Court of Justice on a point of law.[19]

Private parties must prove legal standing in order to challenge anti-dumping and countervailing actions under Art 173.[20] The basic test is whether the Community action is of direct and individual concern for the petitioner.[1] A private party will be deemed to be directly and individually concerned by the regulation or act resulting from the proceeding if the information provided by it to the Commission has contributed directly to an element in that act that is vital to the operative part of the act. There are three categories of potential non-privileged applicants who may seek to annul an anti-dumping duty or countervailing duty regulation or measure: the producers and exporters of the product, the complainants and the importers of the product.

Acts adopted pursuant to the regulations on protection against dumped or subsidized imports from countries not members of the European Community are liable to be of direct and individual concern, within the meaning of the second paragraph of Art 173 of the Treaty, to those producers and exporters who are able to establish that they were identified in the measures adopted by the Commission or the Council or were concerned in the preliminary investigation.[2] However the measures must have important consequences for the legal position of the exporters or producers.[3] The producers or exporters may only challenge those parts of the measures which are exclusively applicable to them.[4] Exporters or producers who participated in the investigations may challenge regulations imposing definitive measures and ordering the collection of provisional duties, regulations imposing provisional duties, and decisions not to review a duty or an undertaking.[5]

---

18 See Art 172 of the EC Treaty.
19 See Rules of Procedure ECJ, Arts 110–123, OJ L176/28 (1991).
20 The petitioners must have legal personality. An applicant is a legal person if it has acquired legal personality in accordance with the law governing its constitution or if it has been treated as an independent legal entity by the Community institutions. See Case 50/84 *Bensider v Commission* [1984] ECR 3991; see also Case 175/73 *Union Syndicale v Council* [1974] ECR 917; see also Case T-161/94 *Sinochem Heilongjiang v Council* [1996] ECR II-695; see also Case T-170/94 *Shanghai Bicycle Corpn v Council of the European Union* (1997) Transcript, 25 September.
1 See Art 173(4).
2 See Joined Cases 239 & 275/82 *Allied Corpn v Commission* [1984] ECR 1005; see also Case 113/77 *Toyo Bearing v Council* [1979] ECR 1185; see also Case 53/83 *Allied Corpn v Council* [1985] ECR 1621; see also Case 204/84 *Toyo Bearing v Council* [1987] ECR 1809.
3 See Case 229/86 *Brother Industries Ltd v Commission* [1987] ECR 3757. In this sense, the judicial protection afforded to individual undertakings concerned by an anti-dumping duty cannot be affected by the mere fact that the duty in question is a single duty imposed by reference to a State and not to individual undertakings. See Case T-170/94 *Shanghai Bicycle Corpn v Council of the European Union* (1997) Transcript, 25 September.
4 See *Case* 240/84 *Toyo Bearing v Council* [1987] ECR 1809; see also Case C-156/87 *Gestetner v Council* [1990] ECR I-781; see also *Case* C-174/87 *Ricoh v Council* [1992] ECR I-1335; see also Case 255/84 *Nachi Fujikoshi v Council* [1987] ECR 1861; see also Case 256/84 *Koyo Seiko v Council* [1987] ECR 1899; see also Case 258/84 *Nippon Seiko v Council* [1987] ECR 1923.
5 This is still the case even if it was ultimately decided not to accept the information provided by the producer or exporter with regard to the central points at issue. See Case T-161/94 *Sinochem Heilongjiang v Council of the European Union* [1996] ECR II-695.

Complainants may also challenge Community acts adopted following the anti-dumping and countervailing duty regulations.[6] However, the Court will analyze the part played by the applicant in the proceeding in order to determine its legal standing.[7] Complainants may challenge regulations imposing provisional or definitive duties or ordering definitive collection of provisional duties, decisions not to open a proceeding, decisions to terminate a proceeding without protective action or to terminate an investigation because of acceptance of undertakings and decisions not to review an undertaking or duty.

Importers can be divided into two groups with regard to standing. An importer of a product that is subject to anti-dumping or countervailing duty can challenge an anti-dumping or countervailing regulation when it is associated with a producer or exporter of the product and was involved in the Commission's preliminary investigations of the anti-dumping or countervailing duty.[8] This is particularly the case where the export price used in determining the anti-dumping duty was calculated on the basis of the importer's selling price of the goods on the Community market.[9] Traditionally, however, unrelated importers have not been granted legal standing.[10] The Court has denied standing to exclusive unrelated importers even where they had a *de facto* dependency to the exporters or producer.[11] The Court will, however, grant standing to those unrelated importers who were involved in the investigations establishing the duty and were identified explicitly or implicitly by the measure in question.[12]

The Court grants a wide discretion to the Community authorities in the implementation of the anti-dumping and countervailing duty regulations.[13] However, even if discretionary powers are conferred on the Community institutions by Community rules for protection against dumped or subsidized imports from non-member countries, the Court will verify whether those institutions have observed the procedural guarantees afforded by those rules and whether or not they have committed manifest errors in their assessment of the facts, have omitted to take any essential matters into consideration or have based the reasons of their decision on considerations amounting to a misuse of powers.[14]

---

6 See Case 191/82 *Fediol v Commission* [1983] ECR 2913.

7 See Case 264/82 *Timex Corpn v Council* [1985] ECR 849.

8 See Case 113/77 *NTN Toyo Bearing v Council* [1979] ECR 1185; see also Joined Cases 305/86 & 160/87 *Neotype Techmashexport v Commission and Council* [1990] ECR I-2945; see also Case C-133/87 & C-150/87 *Nashua Corpn v Commission and Council* [1990] ECR I-719.

9 See Joined Cases 277 & 300/85 *Canon v Council* [1988] ECR 5731.

10 See Case 307/81 *Alusuisse v Council* [1982] ECR 3463.

11 See Case 205/87 *Nuova Ceam Srl v Commission* [1987] ECR 4427.

12 See Case C-358/89 *Extramet Industrie SA v Commission* [1991] ECR I-2501. However, when the amounts secured by way of the provisional anti-dumping duty have been collected in their entirety under the regulation imposing a definitive anti-dumping duty an importer who has paid those duties may place no reliance on any legal effect arising out of the provisional regulation. See Case C-304/86 and C-185/87 *Enital v Commission and Council* [1990] ECR I-2939; see also Case T-208/95 *Miwon Co Ltd v Commission of the European Communities* [1996] ECR II-635.

13 See Case 53/83 *Allied Corpn v Commission of the European Communities* [1985] ECR 1621; see also Case 191/82 *FEDIOL v Commission of the European Communities* [1983] ECR 2913; see also Case T-162/94 *NMB France SARL v Commission of the European Communities* [1997] ECR II-427.

14 See Case 187/85 *Fediol v Commission* [1988] ECR 4155; see also Case C-129/86 *Greece v Council* [1989] ECR 3963; see also Case 260/84 *Minebea v Council* [1987] ECR 1975; see also Case 42/84 *Remia v Commission* [1985] ECR 2545; see also Case C-121/86 *Anonymos Etaireia Epicheiriseon Metalleftikon Viomichanikon kai Naftukiakon v Council* [1989] ECR 3919; see also Case C-156/87 *Gestetner Holdings v Council and Commission* [1990] ECR I-782.

Chapter 14

Foreign obstacles to trade: the Trade Barriers Regulation

INTRODUCTION

As part of the legislation implementing the Uruguay Round, on December 1994, the European Community enacted Council Regulation (EC) 3286/94,[1] laying down Community procedures in the field of the common commercial policy in order to ensure the exercise of the Community rights under international trade rules, in particular those established under the auspices of the World Trade Organization.[2]

SUBSTANTIVE ELEMENTS AND TRACKS

The new Trade Barriers Regulation aims to tackle foreign obstacles to trade against which the Community may have a right of action under international trade rules.[3] International trade rules are primarily those established under the auspices of the WTO and laid down in the Annexes of the WTO Agreement, but they can also be those laid down in any other agreement to which the

---

1 Council Regulation 3286/94, OJ 31.12.96 L349/71, as amended by Council Regulation 356/95, OJ 23.2.95 L41/3; see also European Commission *What is the Community's Trade Barriers Regulation? Opening New Trade Opportunities for European Business*, Office for Official Publications of the European Communities (1996). This Regulation, usually referred as the Trade Barriers Regulation, takes the place of Regulation No 2641/84, the so called 'New Commercial Policy Instrument'. See Council Regulation No 2641/84, OJ 1.11.84 L252/1, as amended by Council Regulation No 522/94, OJ 10.3.94 L 66/10. Cases initiated under Regulation No 2641/84 were: *Unauthorized Sound Recordings in Indonesia* OJ 21.5.87 C 136 /21; *Exclusion from the US Market of Certain Aramid Fibres* OJ 5.2.86 C25/2; see also *Port Charges in Japan on Cargoes and Shipping Companies* OJ 16.2.91 C40/18; see also *Pirate Sound Recordings in Thailand* OJ 20.7.91 C189/26; see also *Fund Levy and Customs Duty in Turkey* OJ 31.8.93 C235/4. Known rejected complaints were *Deprivation of Patent Protection by Jordan for a New Polymorphus Substance* OJ 1.2.89 L30/67; see also Case 70/87 *FEDIOL v Commission* [1989] ECR 1781.
2 Council Regulation 3286/94 Art 1, OJ 31.12.96 L349/71, as amended by Council Regulation 356/95, OJ 23.2.95 L41/3. The TBR does not apply in cases covered by other existing rules in the common commercial policy field. It operates by way of complement to the rules establishing the common organization of agricultural markets and their implementing provisions and the specific rules adopted pursuant to Art 235 of the Treaty, applicable to goods processed from agricultural products. Furthermore, the application of the TBR is without prejudice to other measures which may be adopted pursuant to Art 113 of the Treaty, as well as to Community procedures dealing with matters concerning obstacles to trade raised by Member States in the committee established by Art 113 of the Treaty. See ibid Art 15.
3 Ibid Art 2.

Community is a party and which sets out rules applicable to trade between the Community and third countries.[4]

Obstacles to trade are any trade practices adopted or maintained by a third country in respect of which international trade rules establish a right of action.[5] The concept 'obstacles to trade' has been interpreted as encompassing those practices which are actually taking place but also the existence of laws or regulations which may result in the imposition of illegal obstacles to trade.[6] Furthermore, the Commission has considered that the concept of obstacles to trade may encompass both obstacles to the import into or export from the foreign country.[7] As the Regulation is based only on Art 113 of the Treaty, the obstacles to trade may affect all trade in goods but only trade in services to a limited extent. A right of action only exists against obstacles to trade in services in respect of which international agreements can be concluded by the Community on the basis of Art 113.[8] Concerning the protection of intellectual property rights, however, the Commission has been able to adopt a broad interpretation which allows it to tackle, at least partially, foreign trade obstacles affecting IPRs.[9]

The Trade Barriers Regulation strongly limits any action to the rule of international law by requiring that there must be a right of action deriving from international trade rules. However, such right of action exists when international trade rules either prohibit a practice outright, or give another party affected by the practice a right to seek the elimination of the effects of the practice

---

4 Ibid Art 2 (2).

5 Ibid Art 2(1) The trade obstacle must be created by a trade practice of the country in question. There must be some sort of government relation. However, the Commission has considered as obstacles to trade trading practices adopted by foreign enterprises which are due to the lack of adequate laws or enforcement of such laws by the foreign government public authorities. See *Protection of Sound Recordings in Thailand* OJ 16.1.96 L11/7 (where the alleged practice was the lack of adequate enforcement of laws protecting intellectual property rights); see also *Trade Barriers to the Leather Sector in Japan* OJ 9.4.97 C110/2 (where one of the alleged practices was the toleration by the Japanese government of restrictive business practices in the leather sector).

6 See *United States Anti-dumping Act of 1916* OJ 25.2.97C58/14; see also *United States Anti-dumping Act of 1916* OJ 28.4.98 L126/38 (where the alleged trade practice was the existence of the United States Anti-dumping Act of 1916 which if applied would impose treble damages against foreign firms). In this sense, the Commission's interpretation seems to be fully supported by previous GATT precedent. See *United States—Definition of Industry Concerning Wine and Grape Products* SCM/71 (24 March 1986) adopted by the Committee on Subsidies and Countervailing Measures on 28 April 1992 BISD 39S/436, paragraph 4.1; see also Article XVI (4)of the Agreement of WTO which reads: 'Each Member shall ensure the conformity of its laws, regulations and administrative procedures with its obligations as provided in the annexed Agreements.'

7 See *Trade Obstacles to Leather in Argentina* OJ 26.2.97 C59/6 (where one of the alleged obstacles was Argentina's practices restricting exports of hides).

8 Council Regulation 3286/94 Art 2(8), OJ 31.12.96 L349/71, as amended by Council Regulation 356/95, OJ 23.2.95 L41/3.

9 As from a strictly legal point of view the TBR is simply a domestic procedural regulation, the Commission has considered that for the purposes of Art 113 what is important is whether or not the foreign trade practice is an obstacle to the trade of goods and services which fall under its scope. Whether the protection of intellectual property rights fall within the scope of Art 113 is of no relevance. Rather what is important is whether the foreign violation of intellectual property rights affects the trade of goods or services which are supposed to be protected by such rights. The division of powers between the Member States and the Community and the scope of Art 113 will only be of relevance if after a whole investigation has been followed it is considered necessary to go to the WTO, or to take retaliatory measures or enter into an agreement. See *Trade Obstacles to Cognac in Brazil* OJ 2.4.97 C103/3; see also *Music Licensing Practices in the United States* OJ 11.6.97 C177/2.

in question.[10] Thus, the TBR may be used against practices which violate international agreements or which simply nullify or impair the benefits arising from such agreements.[11]

With this purpose, the TBR establishes three tracks. First, the Regulation maintains a residual defensive action and allows for complaints to be brought on behalf of the Community industry which contain sufficient evidence of injury as a result of obstacles to trade in third countries that have an affect on the market of the Community.[12] The characteristic feature of this track is that the foreign obstacle must have an effect on the Community domestic market and result in injury to the domestic industry of the Community.[13]

Second, the main improvement of the Regulation is to require the Community institutions to act when receiving complaints from Community enterprises or any association, having or not legal personality, acting on behalf of Community enterprises which contain sufficient evidence of adverse trade effects as a result of obstacles to trade that have an effect in the market of a third country and which result in a material impact on the Community market.[14] Action on behalf of Community enterprises requires a right of action which is based on international trade rules contained in multilateral or plurilateral trade agreements.[15] Bilateral agreements and all agreements which are not exclusive trade agreements should not be considered as multilateral or plurilateral trade agreements.

A complaint on behalf of a Community enterprise must contain sufficient evidence of adverse effects together with a material impact on the market of the Community or a region of the Community or on a sector of economic activity therein as a result of the foreign obstacle to trade.[16] Adverse effects could include the halt of export, the loss of foreign world market share, increased competition in the Community market as a result of loss of foreign market share, increased

10 Council Regulation 3286/94 Art 2(1), OJ 31.12.96 L349/71, as amended by Council Regulation 356/95, OJ 23.2.95 L41/3.
11 See *Trade Barriers to the Leather Sector in Japan* OJ 9.4.97 C110/2 (9 April 1997)(where it was alleged that restrictive business practices nullified or impaired the benefits of GATT).
12 Council Regulation 3286/94 Art 1(a), OJ 31.12.96 L349/71, as amended by Council Regulation 356/95, OJ 23.2.95 L41/3.
13 Ibid Art 3(1) As to the concept of injury see ibid Art 3(1); see also ibid Art 10 (1); see also ibid Art 10(2); see also ibid Art 10(3). As to the concept of domestic industry see ibid Art 2(5).
14 Article 1(b); see also ibid Art 4. As to the concept of Community enterprise see Art 2(6). In practice, it seems that most of the complaints received under the TBR have been filed not by individual enterprises but rather by association of enterprises. See *United States Anti-dumping Act of 1916* OJ 25.2.97 C58/14 (where the complaint was filed by EUROFER); see also *Trade Obstacles to Leather in Argentina* OJ 26.2.97 C59/6 (where the complaint was filed by COTANCE); see also *Trade Obstacles to Cognac in Brazil* OJ 2.4.97 C103/3 (where the complaint was filed by BNIC); see also *Trade Obstacles to Copper Scrap in Korea and India* OJ 22.5.96 C148 (where the complaint was filed by EUROMETAUX); see also *Trade Barriers to the Leather Sector in Japan* OJ 9.4.97 C110/2 (where the complaint was filed by COTANCE); see also *Rules of Origin for Textiles in the United States* OJ 4.3.97 L62/43(where the complaint was filed by FEDERTESSILE); see also *Protection of Sound Recordings in Thailand* OJ 16.1.96 L11/7 (where the complaint, under the old NCPI, was filed by IFPI); see also *Music Licensing Practices in the United States* OJ 11.6.97 C177/2 (where the complaint was filed by IMRO); see also *Brazilian Import Licensing regime for Steel Plates* OJ 27.6.97 C197/2 (where the complaint was filed by EUROFER); see also *Brazilian Import Licensing Regime for Textile Products* OJ 27.2.98 C/63/2 (where the complaint was filed by FEBELTEX).
15 Council Regulation 3286/94 Art 4(1), OJ 31.12.96 L349/71, as amended by Council Regulation 356/95, OJ 23.2.95 L41/3.
16 Ibid Art 4(2). As to the definition of adverse effects see ibid Art 2(4); see also ibid Art 10 (4); see also ibid Art 10(5); see also ibid Art 10(6).

costs, disruption of market distribution activities, etc.[17] The Commission has interpreted adverse effects to include even the loss of image of the European enterprise.[18] Yet, in order to weed out any frivolous complaints, the Community enterprises must allege the existence of a material impact on the Community market or of a region of the Community, or on a sector of economic activity.[19]

Finally, the TBR allows Member States to request the Commission to start a procedure against obstacles to trade that have an effect on the markets of the Community with a view to removing the injury resulting therefrom, and to respond to obstacles to trade which have an effect on the market of a third country, with a view to removing the adverse effects resulting therefrom.[20] Member States may ask for action to tackle obstacles to trade against which the Community has a right of action arising from any international agreement to which the Community is a party. Thus, Member States can ask the Community institutions to take action under bilateral agreements.

PROCEDURE

A written complaint must be submitted to the Commission, which shall send a copy thereof to the Member States.[1] The complaint may be withdrawn, in which case the procedure may be terminated unless such termination would not be in the interests of the Community.[2]

Within 45 days from the filing of the complaint, the Commission must decide whether or not to initiate an investigation procedure.[3] Within such period, the Commission must make a determination of whether there is prima facie evidence of the facts alleged in the complaint and whether an examination procedure is in the interest of the Community.[4] Before deciding on the initiation of a

17 See *United States Antidumping Act of 1916* OJ C 28.4.98 L126/36 (where the Commission has considered important legal costs resulting from the alleged trade barrier as an adverse effect).

18 See *Rules of Origin for Textiles in the United States* OJ 4.3.97 L62/43 (where it was considered that the changes of rules of origin in the United States which considered that products which had traditionally been labelled as Made in Italy should be labelled as Made in China resulted in a loss of image for the Community enterprises trading with the products).

19 Council Regulation 3286/94 Art 2(4), OJ 31.12.96 L349/71, as amended by Council Regulation 356/95, OJ 23.2.95 L41/3. In this sense, the Commission will give great relevance to the loss of jobs in a Community economic sector or region. See *Rules of Origin for Textiles in the United States* OJ 22.11.96 C351/6 (1996); see also *Rules of Origin for Textiles in the United States* OJ L62/43 (4 March 1997) (where the Commission considered as material impact the fact that the US trade barrier strongly affected enterprises located in Italian regions whose economy and jobs are highly dependent on the textile industry); see also *Brazilian Import Licensing Regime for Textile Products* OJ 27.2.98 C/63/2 (where the Commission considered as material impact the great importance of exports for the Community's textile sector as well as for the economy of the Community and several of its regions).

20 Council Regulation 3286/94 Art 6, OJ 31.12.96 L349/71, as amended by Council Regulation 356/95, OJ 23.2.95 L41/3. In practice, no case has been initiated under the TBR at the request of Member States. The latter have preferred to use the general system of Art 113 of the Treaty. See European Commission *The Global Challenge of International Trade: A Market Access Strategy for the European Union* (Office for Official Publications of the European Communities, 1996).

1 Ibid Art 5 (1). As to the rules on confidentiality see ibid Art 9.

2 Ibid Art 5(2).

3 Ibid Art 5(4); see also ibid Art 6(5).

4 Art 8(1). Unlike the Anti-dumping Regulation, the TBR leaves as undefined the concept of Community interest. However, the Commission has interpreted the concept of Community interest in a broad way. It has generally considered that simply ensuring that third countries

procedure the Commission must consult the Member States as represented in the TBR advisory committee.[5]

Where it becomes apparent after consultation that the complaint does not provide sufficient evidence to justify initiating an investigation, the complainant must be informed.[6] If, however, it is apparent to the Commission that there is sufficient evidence to justify initiating an examination procedure and that it is necessary in the interest of the Community, it shall announce the initiation of an examination procedure in the Official Journal of the European Communities.[7]

It is the Commission, acting in co-operation with the Member States, who must conduct all investigations and negotiations.[8] It must decide within five months from the initiation of the procedure whether any actions should be taken.[9] During such period, the Commission must determine whether there is a right of action for the Community under international trade agreements and there are adverse effects or injury resulting from the foreign obstacles to trade. If necessary, the Commission shall seek all the information it deems necessary and attempt to check this information with the importers and organizations, provided that the undertakings or organizations concerned give their consent.[10] Furthermore, where necessary, the Commission shall carry out investigations in the territory of third countries, provided that the governments of the countries have been officially notified and raise no objection within a reasonable period.[11]

When it is found as a result of the examination procedure that the interests of the Community do not require any action to be taken, the procedure must be terminated.[12]

If, after an examination procedure, the third country or countries concerned

---

fully comply with their commitments under the WTO Agreements is a priority for the European Community. See *United States Anti-dumping Act of 1916* OJ 25.2.97 C58/14; see also *Trade Obstacles to Leather in Argentina* OJ 26.2.97 C59/6 (where the Commission considered it to be in the Community interest to prevent other South American countries adopting the alleged Argentinean practice); see also *Brazilian Import Licensing Regime for Textile Products* OJ 27.2.98 C63/2 (where the Commission considered the interest of the Community exports to lie in open access to third countries). The Commission in practice will decide for the initiation of the procedure even though it has doubts as to whether the Community may resort to the WTO Dispute Settlement Mechanism or it has a clear right of action under any other trade agreement. See *United States Anti-dumping Act of 1916* OJ 25.2.97 C58/14. The TBR, however, allows for action to be taken without a prior investigation procedure in clear cut cases. See Council Regulation 3286/94 Art 12(1), OJ 31.12.96 L349/71, as amended by Council Regulation 356/95, OJ 23.2.95 L41/3.

5 Ibid Art 8 (1) On the consultation procedure and the TBR advisory committee see ibid Art 7. The committee procedure to be followed in this consultation for the initiation of the investigation is the advisory committee procedure and thus the Committee's decision is not binding on the Commission. In order to secure the coherence of the Community's trade policy, the Regulation requires also the Commission to inform the Art 113 committee of any events which take place under the TBR. See ibid Art 7(2).

6 Ibid Art 5(3).

7 Art 8(1)(a) (describing also the contents of such announcement). The Commission must also inform the representatives of the country or countries which are the subject of the procedure, with whom, where appropriate, consultation may be held. See ibid Art 8(1)(b).

8 Ibid Art 8(1)(c).

9 In complex cases, the period may be extended to seven months. See ibid Art 8(8).

10 Ibid Art 8(2)(a) The Commission shall be assisted in its investigation by officials of the Member State in whose territory the checks are carried out, provided that the Member State in question so requests. See ibid Art 8(2)(c).

11 Ibid Art 8(2)(b) Concerning further particulars of the investigation procedure see ibid Art 8(4); see also Art 8(5); see also Art 8(6); see also Art 8(7).

12 Ibid Art 11 (1); see also *Mass Housing Levy in Turkey* OJ 17.12.96 L326/71 (such case was initiated under the NCPI but it was terminated in accordance with the TBR).

take measures which are considered satisfactory and therefore no action by the Community is required, the procedure may be suspended.[13]

Where following an investigation procedure, it is found that the Community's international obligations require the prior discharge of an international procedure for consultation of for the dispute settlement of disputes, no Community measures must be taken until that procedure has been terminated, and taking account of the results of the procedure.[14]

If after the examination procedure, it appears that the most appropriate means to resolve a dispute arising from an obstacle to trade is the conclusion of an agreement with the third country or countries concerned, which may change the substantive rights of the Community and of the third country or countries concerned, the procedure shall be suspended and negotiations shall be carried out according to the provisions of Art 113 of the Treaty.[15]

In all such cases, the safeguard committee procedure shall apply.[16] Thus, the Commission representative must submit to the TBR advisory committee a draft of the decision to be taken.[17] The Commission will adopt a decision which it must communicate to the Member States and which will apply after a period of ten days if during this period no Member State has referred the matter to the Council which acting by qualified majority can revise the Commission's decision.[18] However, the Commission's decision shall apply after a period of 30 days, if the Council has not given a ruling within this period, calculated from the day on which the matter was referred to the Council.[19]

Where it is found that action is necessary in the interests of the Community in order to ensure the exercise of the Community's rights under international trade rules, with a view to removing the injury or the adverse trade effects resulting from obstacles to trade adopted or maintained by third countries and after following dispute settlement procedures, if required, measures of commercial policy may be adopted by the Council by qualified majority not later than 30 working days after receiving a proposal from the Commission.[20]

All commercial policy measures to be taken must be compatible with existing international obligations and procedures.[1] In this sense, the Community may

---

13 Council Regulation 3286/94 Art 11(2)(a), OJ 31.12.96 L349/71, as amended by Council Regulation 356/95, OJ 23.2.95 L41/3. As to the procedure to be followed after the suspension of the investigation procedure see ibid Art 11(2)(b); see also ibid Art 11(2)(c); see also *Piracy of Sound Recordings in Thailand* OJ 16.1.96 L11/7.

14 See Art 12 (2); see also *Rules of Origin for Textiles in the United States* OJ 4.3.97 L62/43 (where the Community decided to follow the Dispute Settlement Procedure of the WTO); see also *United States Anti-dumping Act of 1916* OJ 28.4.98 L126/36.

15 Council Regulation 3286/94 Art 11(3), OJ 31.12.96 L349/71, as amended by Council Regulation 356/95, OJ 23.2.95 L41/3. In this sense see Case C-327/91 *France v Commission* [1994] ECR I-3641 (where the Court made clear that the Commission may conclude international agreements on its own in very limited and exceptional cases only).

16 Council Regulation 3286/94 Art 11, OJ 31.12.96 L349/71, as amended by Council Regulation 356/95, OJ 23.2.95 L41/3; see also ibid Art 13(1); see also ibid Art 13 (2).

17 The Committee will discuss the matter within a period to be fixed by the chairman, depending on the urgency of the matter. See ibid Art 14(2).

18 Ibid Art 14(3); see also ibid Art 14(4).

19 Ibid Art 14 (5).

20 Ibid Art 12(1); see also ibid Art 13(3).

1 Ibid Art 12(3) Furthermore, where the Community has requested an international dispute settlement body to indicate and authorize the measures which are appropriate for the implementation of the results of an international dispute settlement procedure, the Community commercial policy measures which may be needed in consequence of such authorization must be in accordance with the recommendation of such international dispute settlement body. See ibid Art 12(2).

adopt inter alia the suspension or withdrawal of any concession resulting from commercial policy negotiations;[2] the raising of existing customs duties or the introduction of any other charge on imports;[3] or the introduction of quantitative restrictions or any other measures modifying import or export conditions or otherwise affecting trade with the third country concerned.[4]

2 Ibid Art 12(3)(a).
3 Ibid Art 12(3)(b).
4 Ibid Art 12(3)(c).

Chapter 15

Counterfeit and pirated goods

BACKGROUND

Community legislation in respect of counterfeit goods can be traced to the mid-1980s. These measures may be classified into two categories. The first category consists of measures concerned with the assertion of Community interests on the markets of third countries ('offensive measures'). The second category consists of measures concerned with the protection of the Community market, typically in respect of imports but sometimes also in respect of exports ('defensive measures'). This chapter deals mainly with the second category.[1] By way of background, however, it is useful to sketch briefly certain measures of the first category, which were the first to be enacted. The two types of measures are interrelated by virtue of the interpenetration of markets in international trade. Not surprisingly, they embody some of the same concerns in respect of economic and trade policy. In addition, the prior, 'offensive' measures provided guidance to some extent in the drafting of the subsequent, 'defensive' legislation.

The first Community measure to be adopted in respect of counterfeit goods was concerned with the protection of Community interests against counterfeit goods in third country markets.[2] In the wake of the failure of the Tokyo Round tariff negotiations to adopt a counterfeiting and piracy code,[3] Council Regulation 2641/84 was adopted to strengthen the common commercial policy with regard in particular to protection against illicit commercial practices.[4] Known as the 'New Commercial Policy Instrument', it was intended to complement existing anti-dumping legislation. Its aim was two-fold: first, to provide the Community with procedures enabling it to respond to any illicit commercial practice with a view to removing the injury resulting from it; and, secondly, to ensure full exercise of the Community's rights with regard to the commercial practices of third countries.[5]

In the terms of the Regulation, illicit commercial practices were defined as any international trade practices attributable to third countries which are

---

1 As to the first category of measures, see Chapter 14 on the Trade Barriers Regulation.
2 Note that 'counterfeit goods' were defined in terms of Community law or the law of the Community's Member States, not in terms of the law of the relevant third country.
3 Nor was adequate protection provided by the Paris Convention for the protection of industrial property, Arts 9(1),(5),(6), signed in Paris on 20 March 1883, as last amended in Stockholm on 14 July 1967.
4 OJ 20.9.84 L252/1. As to implementing legislation, see Commission Regulation 3077/87, OJ 15.10.87 L291/19.
5 Ibid Art 1.

incompatible with international law or with the generally accepted rules.[6] The Regulation provided for a formal complaint on behalf of Community industry, a consultation procedure, and a Community examination procedure.[7] When action was deemed necessary, any commercial policy measures could be taken which were compatible with the Community's existing international obligations and procedures.[8] Such measures included suspension or withdrawal of any concession resulting from commercial policy negotiations;[9] the raising of existing customs duties or the introduction of any other charge on imports;[10] or the introduction of quantitative restrictions or any other measures modifying import or export conditions or otherwise affecting trade with the third country concerned.[11]

The 'New Commercial Policy Instrument' was used by the Community in respect of alleged counterfeit goods in two instances.[12]

The first instance concerned the unauthorized reproduction of sound recordings in Indonesia.[13] The complaint was submitted in 1987 by the association of members of the International Federation of Phonogram and Videogram Producers (IFPI) on behalf of European producers said to represent virtually the whole Community sound recording industry. The complainants alleged that Indonesia failed to provide the Community industry with effective protection against unauthorized reproduction of sound recordings, thus breaching certain Articles of the Paris Convention for the Protection of Intellectual Property, of which Indonesia was a member. It also alleged that Indonesia was in breach of the Berne Convention for the Protection of Literary and Artistic Works and the Paris text of the Universal Copyright Convention, to neither of which Indonesia was a party but which were to be regarded as generally accepted rules. According to the complainant, unauthorized reproduction and the distribution of 'pirated' copies deprived Community producers of sales on the Indonesia market and also on the markets of other countries, notably in the Middle East. The procedure was suspended, however, after the Indonesia Government gave an undertaking that it would change its copyright law.[14] The procedure was terminated in 1988.[15]

---

6 Ibid Art 2(1).
7 See ibid Arts 3–9.
8 Ibid Art 10(3).
9 Ibid Art 10(3)(a).
10 Ibid Art 10(3)(b).
11 Ibid Art 10(3)(c).
12 It also was invoked in other instances. Case 70/87 *Fédération de l'Industrie de l'Huilerie de la CEE (Fediol) v Commission* [1989] ECR 1781 concerned a complaint requesting the Commission to initiate the examination procedure in respect of certain commercial practices of Argentina regarding the export of soya cake to the Community. Secondly, Commission Decision 82/251 initiated an international consultation and disputes settlement procedure concerning the United States measure excluding imports of certain aramid fibres into the United States (OJ 5.5.87 L117/18). The matter was the AKZO case against the USA for alleged infringement of GATT Article III:4. It led eventually to a GATT Panel decision of 7 November 1989, which found that s 337 of the US Tariff Act of 1930 as applied to patent-based imported products was inconsistent with Article III:4 of GATT and could not be justified on the basis of Article XX(d) of GATT: see 'United States Section 337 of the Tariff Act of 1930, Report by the Panel adopted on 7 November 1989 (L/6439)', BISD, 1990, 36th Supplement. See also p 259, n 1 above.
13 Notice of initiation of an 'illicit commercial practice' procedure concerning the unauthorized reproduction of sound recordings in Indonesia, OJ 21.5.87 C136/3.
14 See Commission Decision 87/533, OJ 25.11.87 L355/22.
15 See Commission Decision 88/827 terminating the examination procedure, OJ 17.5.88 L123/51.

The second instance concerned the alleged duplication of Community sound recordings on a massive scale ('piracy') in Thailand.[16] The complaint was lodged in 1991 by the International Federation of the Phonographic Industry (IFPI), European office, representing virtually all producers of sound recordings in the Community. It alleged the unauthorized duplication of original phonograms distributed to the public with labels, artwork, trademarks and packaging different from, although similar to, those of the original legitimate phonograms. According to the complainant, Thailand was thus in breach of the Berne Convention for the Protection of Literary and Artistic Works, as amended. This action was alleged to have reduced the sales of Community producers in Thailand and also restricted Community producers' access and sales to third countries. However, Thailand refused to comply with the Community complaint and threatened to take retaliatory measures.[17] In 1996 the procedure was suspended by the Commission on the grounds that Thailand had made efforts to reduce the level of piracy, in particular by adopting legislation, even though the effects of the legislation were not yet clear.[18]

The approach followed in 'the New Commercial Policy Instrument' was not very effective. In 1994 it was replaced by Council Regulation 3286/94, the 'Trade Barriers Regulation'.[19] The latter is concerned with 'obstacles to trade', which it defines as any trade practice adopted or maintained by a third country in respect of which international trade rules establish a right of action.[20] In respect of counterfeit goods, it is oriented, like its predecessor, toward practices in third country markets. Since 1986 these 'offensive' commercial policy measures have been complemented by 'defensive' measures concerned expressly with imports of counterfeit goods into the Community market.

THE FIRST COUNTERFEIT GOODS REGULATION

The first Community measure that focussed specifically on the import of counterfeit goods into the Community was adopted on the bases of EEC Arts 113 and 235 in 1986.[1] It defined 'counterfeit goods' as any goods bearing without authorization a trade mark which is identical to a trade mark validly registered in respect of such goods in or for the Member State in which the goods are entered for free circulation, or which cannot be distinguished in its essential aspects from such a trade mark, and which thereby infringes the rights of the owner of the trade mark in question under the law of that Member State.[2] The

---

16 *Piracy of Community sound recordings in Thailand*, OJ 20.7.91 C189/26.
17 See *Agence Europe*, No 5782 (ns), Thursday 30 July 1992, p 7.
18 See *Agence Europe*, No 6649 (ns), Saturday 20 January 1996, p 10.
19 Council Regulation 3286/94 laying down Community procedures in the field of the common commercial policy in order to ensure the exercise of the Community's rights under international trade rules, in particular those established under the auspices of the World Trade Organization, OJ 31.12.94 L349/71, as to which see Chapter 14 in this book.
20 Ibid Art 2(1).
 1 Council Regulation 3842/86, OJ 18.12.86 L357/1. Art 235 was used as an additional legal basis because the Community was considered to lack competence to take all the necessary measures to which goods found to be counterfeit needed to be subjected: ibid Preamble, ninth recital. Implementing provisions were laid down by Commission Regulation 2077/87, OJ 15.10.87 L191/19.
 2 Ibid Art 1(2)(a).

Regulation laid down, first, the conditions under which customs authorities were to intervene in case of goods entered for free circulation where they were suspected of being counterfeit, and, secondly, the measures to be taken by the competent authorities with regard to those goods when it was established that they were indeed counterfeit.[3] It did not apply to goods which bore a trade mark with the consent of the owner of that trade mark but which were entered for free circulation without the owner's consent ('parallel imports').[4]

The release for free circulation of goods found to be counterfeit was prohibited.[5] In each Member State, a trade mark owner was entitled to apply in writing to the competent authority for suspension by the customs authorities of the release of goods which it had valid grounds for suspecting to be counterfeit.[6] The authority was required to take a decision on the application and to notify the applicant in writing of the decision.[7] When the application was granted, it was to specify for what period the customs authorities could take action.[8] The decision granting the application by the trade mark holder was to be forwarded immediately to the customs offices of the Member State which were liable to be concerned with the imports of the counterfeit goods.[9]

When the customs office was satisfied that goods entered for free circulation corresponded to the description of the counterfeit goods, it was to take interim measures by suspending release of the goods. It was required to inform the person making the entry, the authority which decided on the application and the applicant. The customs office was entitled to take samples to expedite the procedure.[10] If within ten working days of the suspension of the release, the customs office had not been informed that the matter had been referred to the authority competent to take a substantive decision, or that the authority had taken interim measures, the goods were to be released.[11]

Without prejudice to any other rights of action open to a trade mark owner, the Member States were to adopt measures necessary to allow the competent authorities to take definitive measures by destroying goods found to be counterfeit, or disposing of them outside commercial channels, without compensation of any sort,[12] or taking any other deterrent measures which met certain

---

3 Council Regulation 3842/86, Art 1(a),(b), OJ 18.12.86 L357/1.
4 Ibid Art 1(3), first sub-paragraph. Nor did it apply to goods entered for free circulation which bore a trade mark under conditions other than those agreed with the owner of that trade mark: Art 1(3), second sub-paragraph. It also did not apply to goods contained in travellers' personal luggage or sent in small consignments of a non-commercial nature within certain specified limits: ibid Art 9.
5 Ibid Art 2. As to the procedure, see ibid Art 5.
6 Ibid Art 3(1). As to the application, see Art 3(2). The Member States were entitled to appoint the customs authorities themselves as the competent authorities to decide on the application: Art 3(4).
7 Ibid Art 3(3), first sub-paragraph.
8 Ibid Art 3(3), second sub-paragraph, which also provided that, upon application by the trade mark owner, the period could be extended by the authority which took the initial decision.
9 Ibid Art 4.
10 Ibid Art 5(1). The law in force in the Member State in whose territory the goods were declared for release for free circulation were to apply to effect the referral to the competent authority for a substantive decision and the arriving at the decision to be taken by that authority: Art 5(2)(a),(b).
11 Provided that all import formalities had been complied with: ibid Art 6(1).
12 Ibid Art 7(1)(a).

conditions.[13] The counterfeit goods could be handed over to the Public Exchequer.[14] Unless contrary to national law, the customs office or competent authority was to inform the trade mark owner, upon request, of the names and addresses of the consignor, importer and consignee of the goods and of the quantity of goods in question.[15]

Except as otherwise provided by national law, the acceptance of an application did not entitle the trade mark owner to compensation where counterfeit goods were not detected by a customs office and their release was therefore not suspended.[16] Nor, except as otherwise provided by national law, did the exercise by a customs office or other authority of its powers render it liable to the importer or any other person in the effect of loss or damage as a result of their action.[17]

The Committee on General Customs Rules[18] was entitled to examine any question regarding the application of the Regulation.[19] Member States were required to communicate all relevant information on the application of the Regulation to the Commission,[20] which in turn was to communicate it to the other Member States.[1]

TRIPS AND ITS IMPACT

Both the Community's first counterfeit goods regulation[2] and the Commission's initial proposal for its revision[3] preceded the conclusion of the Uruguay Round of multilateral trade negotiations, in particular the Agreement on Trade-Related Aspects of Intellectual Property Rights (TRIPS).[4] Before the Commission submitted its initial proposal to the Council, the TRIPS Agreement was available in draft form,[5] and the TRIPS Agreement was concluded before the Commission submitted an amended proposal.[6] Consequently, the sections of the TRIPS Agreement dealing with border safeguards follow closely the original

13 In particular, having the effect of effectively depriving those responsibile for importation of the economic benefits of the transaction and constituting an effective deterrent to further transactions of the same kind: ibid Art 7(1)(b), first sub-paragraph. The following were not regarded as having such effect: re-exporting the counterfeit goods in an unaltered state; other than in exceptional cases, simply removing the trade marks; or subjecting the goods to a different customs procedure: Art 7(1)(b), second sub-paragraph.
14 Ibid Art 7(2).
15 Ibid Art 7(3).
16 Ibid Art 8(1).
17 Ibid Art 8(2).
18 Provided for in Council Directive 79/695 Art 24, OJ 13.8.79 L205/19.
19 Ibid Art 11(1).
20 Ibid Art 11(2), first sub-paragraph. The relevant information and the procedure for exchanging the information are laid down in Commission Regulation 3077/87, OJ 15.10.87 L291/19.
 1 Ibid Art 11(3), second sub-paragraph.
 2 Council Regulation 3842/86, OJ 18.12.86 L357/1.
 3 Commission of the European Communities, Proposal for a Council Regulation (EEC) laying down measures to prohibit the release for free circulation, export or transit of counterfeit and pirated goods (presented by the Commission), COM(93) 329 final, Brussels, 13 July 1993.
 4 Agreement establishing the World Trade Organization, Annex 1C, OJ 23.12.94 L336/213.
 5 Ibid at 2 (Explanatory Memorandum).
 6 Commission of the European Communities, Amended proposal for a Council Regulation (EC) laying down measures to prohibit the release for free circulation, export, re-export or placing under a suspensive procedure of counterfeit and pirated goods (Amendment to the proposal for a Council Regulation (EEC) laying down measures to prohibit the release for free circulation, export or transit of counterfeit and pirated goods) (presented by the Commission pursuant to Art 189a(2) of the EC Treaty), COM(94) 43 final, Brussels, 18.2.94.

Community regulation. They also provided a model for the Community's current regulation.[7]

In the TRIPS Agreement, Section 4 on Special Requirements Related to Border Measures (Arts 51–60) and Section 5 on Criminal Procedures (Art 61) concern counterfeit and pirated goods. Article 51 requires Members to adopt procedures[8] enabling intellectual property right holders to apply to competent authorities for the suspension of the release into free circulation of goods suspected of being counterfeit trademark or pirated copyright goods.[9] It also provides that Members may apply the same provisions to exports.

The right holder must provide adequate evidence to satisfy the competent authority that, under the law of the country of importation, there is a prima facie infringement of the holder's intellectual property right. It must also supply a sufficiently detailed description of the goods to make them readily recognizable by the customs authorities. The competent authorities are required to inform the applicant within a reasonable period whether they have accepted the application and, where determined by the competent authorities, the period for which the customs authorities will take action.[10]

The competent authority is entitled to require an applicant to provide security or equivalent assurance sufficient to protect the defendant and the competent authority and to prevent abuse of the procedure.[11] However, if the owner, importer or consignee of the goods posts security with the customs authority sufficient to protect the right holder for any infringement, the goods must be released into free circulation, provided that all other conditions of importation have been complied with.[12]

If the competent authority suspends the release of the goods, it must notify the applicant and the importer promptly.[13] Suspension is to last for ten days, but it may be extended for a further ten days if the customs authorities have been informed that proceedings leading to a decision on the merits have been initiated by a party other than the defendant, or that a duly empowered authority has taken provisional measures prolonging the suspension. If proceedings leading to a decision on the merits have been initiated, there must be a review, including a right to be heard, at the request of the defendant with a view to deciding whether the measures are to be modified, revoked or confirmed.[14]

---

7 Council Regulation 3295/94 laying down measures to prohibit the release for free circulation, export, re-export or entry for a suspensive procedure of counterfeit and pirated goods, OJ 31.12.94 L341/8.

8 It is understood that there is no obligation to apply such procedures to imports of goods put on the market in another country by or with the consent of the right holder, or to goods in transit: ibid Art 51, n 13.

9 For this purpose, 'counterfeit trademark goods' means any goods, including packaging, bearing without authorization a trademark which is identical to the trademark validly registered in respect of such goods, or which cannot be distinguished in its essential aspects from such a trademark, and which thereby infringes the rights of the owner of the trademark in question under the law of the country of importation. 'Pirated copyright goods' means any goods which are copies made without the consent of the right holder or person duly authorized by the right holder in the country of production and which are made directly or indirectly from an article where the making of that copy would have constituted an infringement of a copyright or a related right under the law of the country of importation. See ibid Art 51, n 14.

10 Ibid Art 52.

11 Ibid Art 53(1), which also provides that such security or equivalent assurance shall not unreasonably deter recourse to these procedures.

12 Ibid Art 53(2), which further provides that the payment of such security does not prejudice any other remedy available to the right holder.

13 Ibid Art 54.

14 Ibid Art 55.

Relevant authorities have the authority to order the applicant to compensate the importer, consignee and owner of the goods for any injury caused to them by wrongful detention of goods or by detention of goods released after a period of suspension.[15]

Both the applicant and the importer have the right to inspect the goods, subject to the protection of confidential information. Where a positive determination has been made on the merits, the competent authorities may inform the right holder of the names and addresses of the consignor, importer and consignee and the quantity of goods in question.[16]

Where, under the applicable national law, the competent authority is able to suspend release on its own initiative, it may at any time seek information from the right holder which may help them to exercise their powers. It must also notify the importer and the right holder promptly of any suspension. Public authorities and officials are exempt from appropriate remedial measures only where their actions are taken or intended in good faith.[17]

Without prejudice to other rights of action open to a right holder, and subject to judicial review, the competent authority may order the destruction or disposal of infringing goods.[18] Except in exceptional circumstances, the re-exportation of counterfeit trademark goods in an unaltered state or subjecting them to a different customs procedure is not to be allowed.[19]

A *de minimis* rule excludes quantities of goods of a non-commercial nature contained in travellers' personal luggage or sent in small consignments.[20]

Criminal procedures and penalities are to be applied at least in cases of wilful trademark counterfeiting or copyright piracy on a commercial scale.[1]

These TRIPS provisions provided both the framework and a model for the current Community measure, Council Regulation 3295/94.[2] In addition, it is possible that they can be invoked in order to help interpret this Regulation, because the latter states that it takes into account the terms of the TRIPS Agreement, including on trade in counterfeit goods, in particular the measures to be taken at the frontier.[3]

THE CURRENT COMMUNITY REGULATION

Council Regulation 3295/94 came into effect as of 1 July 1995.[4] It was based on EC Art 113.[5] It lays down, first, the conditions under which customs authorites are to take action where goods suspected of being counterfeit or pirated are

---

15 Ibid Art 56.
16 Ibid Art 57.
17 Ibid Art 58.
18 This is subject to the principles set out in ibid Art 46, which includes avoidance of harm to the right holder, consistency with constitutional principles, proportionality, and taking account of the interests of third parties.
19 Ibid Art 59.
20 Ibid Art 60.
 1 Ibid Art 61, which also provides for available remedies.
 2 Council Regulation 3295/94, OJ 31.12.94 L341/8.
 3 Ibid, Preamble, sixth recital. See Case 70/87 *Fédération de l'Industrie de l'Huilerie de la CEE (FEDIOL) v Commission* [1989] ECR 1781.
 4 Council Regulation 3295/94 Art 17, second sub-paragraph, OJ 30.12.94 L341/8. It repealed Council Regulation 3842/86. Implementing rules were laid down by Commission Regulation 1367/95, OJ 17.6.95 L133/2, which repealed Commission Regulation 3077/87, the previous implementing regulation, and came into effect as of 1 July 1995.
 5 In its Opinion 1/94 *World Trade Organization* [1994] ECR I-5267 the European Court of

entered for free circulation, export or re-export, found when checks are made on goods placed under a suspensive customs procedure,[6] or re-exported subject to notification.[7] Its scope is thus much broader than that of its predecessor, which covered only goods entered for free circulation. Secondly, the Regulation lays down the measures to be taken by the competent authorities with regard to those goods where it has been established that the goods are indeed counterfeit or pirated. In this respect its coverage is also wider than that of its predecessor, which did not cover pirated goods.[8] As with its predecessor, the Regulation provides an additional remedy, which complements but does not replace existing national rules. In addition, the investigations to determine if goods are counterfeit or pirated are carried out by Member States authorities, not Community authorities, and many of the substantive rules are national law, not Community law.[9]

The Regulation encompasses both counterfeit and pirated goods. It defines three categories of 'counterfeit goods'. The first category includes goods, including their packaging, which bear without authorization a trade mark which is identical to the trade mark validly registered in respect of the same type of goods, or which cannot be distinguished in its essential aspects from such trade mark, and which thereby infringe the rights of the holder of the trade mark in question under Community law or the law of the Member State in which the application for action by the customs authorities is made'.[10] The second category refers to any trade mark symbol (logo, label, sticker, brochure, instructions for use or guarantee document) whether presented separately or not, in the same circumstances.[11] The third category includes packaging materials bearing the trade marks of counterfeit goods, presented separately in the same circumstances.[12] 'Pirated goods' are defined as goods which are or embody copies without the consent of the holder of the copyright or neighbouring rights,[13] or the holder of a design right,[14] whether registered under national law or not, or

Justice stated that external measures in respect of counterfeit goods were within the exclusive competence of the Community. This Opinion provided the basis for the extension of the 1986 Regulation to other types of intellectual property rights in 1994.

6 Within the meaning of Council Regulation 2913/92 establishing the Community Customs Code Art 84(1)(a), OJ 19.10.92 L302/1.

7 Council Regulation 3295/94 art 1(1)(a), OJ 30.12.94 L341/8.

8 As compared to its predecessor, Council Regulation 3295/94 thus had two purposes. The first purpose was to extend protective measures to other types of intellectual property rights, namely copyright, neighbouring rights and design rights. The second purpose was to remedy certain operational problems, in particular by making it easier for trademark holders to ask customs authorities to intervene. See Commission of the European Communities, Proposal for a Council Regulation (EEC) laying down measures to prohibit the release for free circulation, export or transit of counterfeit and pirated goods (presented by the Commission), COM(93) 329 final, Brussels, 13 July 1993, at 2.

9 Hence the possibility of variation and distortion of trade among Member States.

10 Ibid Art 1(2)(a), first indent. Note that trade marks registered under national law and Community trade marks registered under Council Regulation 40/94, OJ 14.1.94 L11/1 are both covered. In both cases, however, the definition of infringement is governed by national law: see Council Regulation 40/94 Art 14.

11 Ibid Art 1(2)(a), second indent.

12 Ibid Art 1(2)(a), third indent.

13 As to the meaning of 'copyright or neighbouring rights', see the international conventions referred to in the TRIPS Agreement Art 1(3), in particular the Berne Convention on the protection of literary and artistic works, signed on 9 September 1886, revised at Paris on 24 July 1971, and the International Convention for the Protection of Performers, Producers of Phonograms and Broadcasting Organizations, adopted at Rome on 26 October 1961.

14 It is open to question, however, whether this term covers semi-conductor topography designs: see also Council Directive 87/54, OJ 27.1.87 L24/36.

of a person duly authorized by the holder in the country of production, where the making of those copies infringes the right in question under Community law or the law of the Member State in which the application for action by the customs authorities is made.[15] Also covered is any mould or matrix which is specifically designed or adapted for the manufacture of a counterfeit trade mark or of goods bearing such a trade mark or of pirated goods, provided that the use of the moulds or matrices infringes the rights of the holder of a right under Community law or the law of the Member State in which the application for action by the customs authorities is made.[16]

In other words, the Regulation protects trade marks, copyright and design rights. Infringements of trade marks are classified as counterfeit goods. Infringements of copyright and design right are classified as pirated goods.

The Regulation does not apply, however, to goods which bear a trade mark with the consent of the trade mark holder, or which are protected by a copyright or neighbouring right or a design right and which have been manufactured with the consent of the right holder but placed in one of the covered situations[17] without the right holder's consent.[18] Nor does it apply to such goods which have been manufactured or bear a trade mark under conditions other than those agreed with the right holder.[19]

The release for free circulation, export, re-export or placing under a suspensive procedure of goods found[20] to be counterfeit or pirated is prohibited.[1] As was the case with its predecessor, Council Regulation 3295/94 does not require proof of injury.

In each Member State a right holder[2] may now apply in writing directly to the competent service of the customs authority for action.[3] The application must include a sufficiently detailed description of the goods to enable the customs authorities to recognize them as well as proof that the applicant is the holder of the right for the goods.[4] The applicant must also provide all other pertinent information available to it to enable the competent customs service to take a

---

15 Ibid Art 1(2)(b).
16 This is to be treated as counterfeit or pirated goods, as appropriate: ibid Art 1(3).
17 That is, the situations referred to in Art 1(1)(a): entry for free circulation, export or re-export; placed under the suspensive procedure; re-exported subject to notification.
18 Ibid Art 1(4), first sub-paragraph.
19 Ibid Art 1(4), second sub-paragraph.
20 On completion of the procedure provided for in ibid Art 6.
 1 Ibid Art 2.
 2 'The holder of a right' means the holder of a trade mark, as referred to in Art 1(2)(a), and/or one of the rights referred to in Art 1(2)(b), or any other person authorized to use the trade mark and/or rights, or their representative: ibid Art 1(2)(c). The holder may be represented by a natural or legal person, including a collecting society which has as its sole or principal purpose the management or administration of copyrights or neighbouring rights: Commission Regulation 1367/95 Art 1, OJ 17.6.95 L133/2.
 3 Council Regulation 3295/94 Art 3(1), OJ 30.12.94 L341/8. Each Member State is required to design the service within the customs authority competent to receive and deal with applications: ibid Art 3(8). Under the previous Regulation Member States were entitled to designate the customs authority as the 'competent authority' but not required to do so, with the result that different Member States designated different authorities, such as customs authorities, courts or ministries.
 4 When the right holder itself applies, the proof must be as follows: in the case of a right that is registered or for which an application has been lodged, proof of registration with the relevant office or lodging of the application; in the case of a copyright, neighbouring right or design right that is unregistered or for which an application has not been lodged, any proof of authorship or of its status as original holder. This proof is also required where the application is made by any other person authorized to use the right, who must provide in addition the document by virtue of which that person is authorized to use the right. The two preceding

decision.[5] The application must also specify the length of the period during which the customs authorities are requested to take action.[6]

The competent customs service is to deal with the application and must notify the applicant in writing of its decision.[7] If the application is granted, it must specify the period during which action will be taken.[8] The decision granting the application must be forwarded immediately to the customs offices of the Member State which is liable to be concerned with the goods.[9] If the application is refused, reasons must be given, and they may form the subject of an appeal.[10] Member States may require the holder of a right to provide security to cover its liability and to ensure payment of relevant costs.[11] The right holder is required to inform the customs service if the right ceases to be validly registered or expires.[12]

Under the current Regulation, customs authorities may also act on their own initiative in order to give the right holder time to apply for action. If, in the course of checks made under specified customs procedures, it appears evident to the customs authorities that goods are counterfeit or pirated, the authorities may notify the holder of the right, where known, of a possible infringement. Notification must take place in accordance with the national law of the Member State in question. The customs authority may suspend release of the goods or detain them for three working days to enable the holder of the right to apply for action.[13]

Regulation 3295/94, as its predecessor, provides both interim measures and definitive measures.

Interim measures are to be taken when a customs office to which a decision granting a right holder's application has been forwarded is satisfied that the goods correspond to the description of the counterfeit or pirated goods described in the decision. In this case it must suspend release of the goods or detain them.[14] It must immediately inform the service that dealt with the application, and either the customs office or the relevant service must inform the applicant and the declarant. In accordance with national laws in respect of confidentiality, they must also notify the right holder, at its request, of the name

proofs are required where a representative of the holder or any other person authorized to use the rights applies, and this person must also provide proof of authorization to act. See Commission Regulation 1367/95 Art 2(a), (b), (c), respectively, OJ 17.6.95 L133/2.

5 However, the information is not a condition of admissibility of the application: Council Regulation 3295/94 Art 3(2), second sub-paragraph, OJ 30.12.94 L341/10. Contrary to its predecessor, the current Regulation gives an indicative list of the relevant information as follows: the place where the goods are situated or the intended destination, particulars identifying the consignment or packages, the scheduled date of arrival or departure of the goods, the means of transport used, and the identity of the importer, exporter or holder: ibid Art 3(2), third sub-paragraph. Also to be included are particulars of the goods, including value and packing, plus any information that could help distinguish them from goods for which there is a protected right. The information should be as detailed as possible to enable the customs authorities, using risk analysis, to identify suspect consignments accurately and without excessive effort. See Commission Regulation 1367/95 Art 3, OJ 17.6.95 L133/2.

6 Council Regulation 3295/94 Art 3(3), OJ 30.12.94 L341/8.

7 Ibid Art 3(5), first sub-paragraph.

8 Ibid Art 3(5), second sub-paragraph, which also provides that, on application by the holder of the right, the period may be extended by the service which took the initial decision.

9 Ibid Art 5.

10 Ibid Art 3(5), third sub-paragraph.

11 Ibid Art 3(6).

12 Ibid Art 3(7).

13 Ibid Art 4.

14 Ibid Art 6(1), first sub-paragraph.

and address of the declarant and, if known, those of the consignee as to enable the right holder to ask the competent authorities to take a substantive decision. The applicant and the persons involved in the relevant operations[15] are entitled to inspect the goods.[16]

The law of the Member State in the territory of which the goods are placed in one of the relevant situations[17] is to apply as regards:

(1) referral to the competent authority for a decision on the merits and immediate notification of the customs service or office;[18] and
(2) reaching a decision taken by that authority.[19]

In the absence of Community rules, the criteria to be used in reaching a decision are to be the same as those used to determine whether goods produced in the Member State infringe the rights of the holder. The competent authority must give reasons for its decision.[20]

If within ten working days of notification of suspension of release or detention, the customs office has not been informed that the matter has been referred for a decision on the merits, or that interim measures have been adopted, the goods are to be released, provided that all customs formalities have been complied with and the detention order has been revoked.[1] However, in the case of goods suspected of infringing design rights, the owner, importer or consignee is entitled to have the goods released, or their detention revoked, against provision of a security, provided certain conditions are satisifed.[2] The security must be sufficient to protect the interests of the right holder, and its payment is without prejudice to other remedies.[3] National law applies in respect of the conditions governing storage of the goods during the period of suspension of release or detention.[4]

Definitive measures are to be taken if the goods are found to be counterfeit or pirated goods.[5] As a general rule, the goods are to be destroyed or disposed of outside commercial channels. This is to be done in accordance with the relevant provisions of national law, in such a way as to preclude injury to the right holder, and without compensation of any sort and at no cost to the exchequer.[6]

---

15 That is, the operations specified in ibid Art 1(1)(a): entry for free circulation, export, or re-export, placing under a suspensive procedure, or re-export subject to notification.
16 Ibid Art 6(1), second sub-paragraph.
17 That is, the situations specified in ibid Art 1(1)(a): entry for free circulation, export, or re-export, found when checks are made on goods placed under a suspensive procedure, or re-exported subject to notification.
18 Ibid Art 6(2)(a).
19 Ibid Art 6(2)(b).
20 Ibid Art 6(2)(a).
 1 Ibid Art 7(1), first sub-paragraph. The period may be extended by a maximum of ten working days in appropriate cases: ibid, art 7(1), second sub-paragraph. The time limit is to be counted from the day of receipt of the request for action in the case of an application under Art 4 (application lodged following notification by the customs authorities that they have acted on their own initiative) which is lodged before the expiry of three working days: Commission Regulation 1367/95 Art 4, OJ 17.6.95 L133/2.
 2 Council Regulation 3295/94 Art 7(2), first sub-paragraph, OJ 30.12.94 L341/8, which sets out the following conditions: the customs office has been informed that the matter has been referred to a competent authority for a decision on the merits; the authority has not yet imposed interim measures; and all customs formalities have been completed.
 3 Ibid Art 7(2), second sub-paragraph.
 4 Ibid Art 7(3).
 5 Ibid Art 8(1).
 6 Ibid Art 8(1)(a).

Alternatively, any other measures may be taken which effectively deprive the persons concerned of the economic benefits of the transaction.[7] The Regulation states expressly that certain measures are not to be regarded as having this effect. These measures include re-exporting the goods in the unaltered state; other than in exceptional cases, simply removing the trade marks which were affixed without authorization; and placing the goods under a different customs procedure.[8] The goods may also be handed over to the exchequer.[9] The customs office or other competent service is to inform the right holder, upon request, of the names and addresses of the consignor, importer, exporter, and manufacturer of the goods and of the quantities of the goods in question.[10]

The current Regulation does not contain any provision analogous to that in its predecessor stating that the measures should serve as an effective deterrent to further transactions of the same kind.[11] However, it does require each Member State to introduce penalties to apply in the event of infringements of the prohibition in Article 2 of the release for free circulation, export, re-export or placing under a suspensive procedure of goods found to be counterfeit or pirated. These penalties must be sufficiently severe to encourage compliance with the relevant provisions.[12]

The Regulation does not apply to goods of a non-commercial nature contained in travellers' personal luggage within the limits laid down in respect of relief from customs duty.[13]

In implementing the Regulation, the Commission is to be assisted by the Customs Code Committee.[14] The Committee acts as a regulatory committee.[15]

Member States are required to communicate all relevant information on the application of the Regulation to the Commission, which is to communicate the information to the other Member States.[16] On the basis of this information, the Commission was required to report to the European Parliament and the Council on the operation of the system, and to propose any amendments or additions, before 1 July 1997.[17]

---

7 Ibid Art 8(1)(b).
8 Ibid Art 8(1), second sub-paragraph.
9 Ibid Art 8(2), which further provides that, in this event, the conditions laid down in Art 8(1)(a) are to apply.
10 Ibid Art 8(3), which also provides that this is in addition to the information given pursuant to the second sub-paragraph of Art 6(1) and under the conditions laid down therein.
11 Council Regulation 3842/86, Art 7(1)(b), OJ 18.12.86 L357/1.
12 Council Regulation 3295/94 Art 11, OJ 30.12.94 L341/8.
13 Ibid Art 10. This is stricter than the previous *de minimis* rule, which also excluded goods of a commercial nature in travellers' personal luggage and goods sent in small consignments of a non-commercial nature: see Council Regulation 3842/86 Art 9, OJ 18.12.86 L357/1.
14 Established by the Community Customs Code, Council Regulation 2913/92 Art 247, OJ 19.10.92 L302/1: ibid Art 13(1).
15 See ibid Art 14(4). This is variant III(a) under Council Decision 87/373, OJ 18.7.87 L197/33.
16 Ibid Art 14. The required information is laid down by Commission Regulation 1367/95, Art 5, OJ 17.6.95 L133/2.
17 Ibid Art 15. Recently the Commission proposed to extend the scope of the Regulation to cover some patents, to extend customs authorities' scope for action to cover free zones, free warehouses, and all suspect goods from the time that they come under customs supervision; and simplifying the Regulation to take account of the Community trade mark through the introduction of a single system for applying for protection which is valid in a number of Member States. See Commission of the European Communities 'Report from the Commission on the implementation of Council Regulation (EC) No 3295 of 22 December 1994 as regards border controls on trade in goods which may be counterfeit or pirated; Proposal for a Council Regulation (EC) amending Regulation (EC) No. 3295/94 laying down measures to prohibit the release for free circulation, export, re-export or entry for a suspensive procedure of counterfeit and pirated goods' (presented by the Commission) (COM(1998) 25 final, Brussels, 28.1.98).

Part III

Specific sectors

Chapter 16

Agricultural products

THE COMMON AGRICULTURAL POLICY

Nature and scope

The EC Treaty provides that the activities of the European Community must include the adoption of a common policy in the sphere of agriculture.[1] It treats agriculture as one of the main Community policies.[2] The common market is required to extend to agriculture and trade in agricultural products.[3] In turn, the operation and development of the common market must be accompanied by the establishment of a common agricultural policy.[4]

The Treaty does not give a precise definition of 'agriculture'[5] or even of 'agricultural holding'.[6] It is, however, clear from the scope of the Treaty that 'agriculture' includes horticulture,[7] sylviculture,[8] viticulture[9] and apiculture.[10] By contrast, 'agricultural products' are defined in the Treaty as the products of the soil, of stockfarming and of fisheries and products of first-stage processing directly related to these products.[11] These products are listed in Annex II to the Treaty.[12] The rules for agricultural products are to some extent an exception to the general

---

1 EC Art 3(d).
2 TEU, Part Three, 'Community Policies'. This would appear to denote a lesser emphasis than was previously given to agriculture, however, because in the pre-Maastricht EEC Treaty Arts 38–47 concerning agriculture formed Title II, 'Agriculture', of Part II, 'Foundations of the Community'.
3 EC Art 38(1).
4 Ibid Art 38(4).
5 Member States retain some freedom to determine the scope of application of Community rules: see Case 139/77 *Denkavit Futtermittel GmbH v Finanzamt Warendorf* [1978] ECR 1317. See also Case 23/75 *Rey Soda* [1975] ECR 1279.
6 It is for the Community institutions to work out an appropriate definition: see Case 85/77 *Societé Santa Anna Azienda Avicola v INPS* [1978] ECR 527.
7 EC Annex II.
8 Ibid Annex II. In addition to live trees, this category includes 'other plants, bulbs, roots and the like, cut flowers and ornamental foliage'.
9 Ibid Annex II.
10 Ibid Annex II.
11 Ibid Art 38(2). The European Court of Justice has given a broad interpretation of 'products of first stage processing directly related to these products', requiring only a clear economic interdependence between basic products and products resulting therefrom irrespective of the number of processes involved: see Case 185/73 *Hauptzollamt Bielefeld v Konig* [1974] ECR 607.
12 The description of products in the list, with the chapter number in the Brussels Nomenclature, is as follows: (c.1) Live animals; (c.2) Meat and edible meat offals; (c.3) Fish, crustaceans and molluscs; (c.4) Dairy produce; birds' eggs; natural honey; (c.5) 05.04, Guts, bladders and

rules laid down for the establishment of the common market.[13] As such, they are to be interpreted[14] and implemented[15] restrictively. When they apply,[16] however, these special rules concerning the common agricultural policy take precedence over the general rules for the establishment of the common market.[17]

Objectives and principles

The objectives of the common agricultural policy *stricto sensu* are stated in Title II, 'Agriculture', of the EEC Treaty. It is important to note, however,

stomachs of animals (other than fish), whole and pieces thereof; 05.15, Animal products not elsewhere listed or included; dead animals of c.1 or c.3, unfit for human consumption; (c.6) Live trees and other plants; bulbs, roots and the like; cut flowers and ornamental foliage; (c.7) Edible vegetables and certain roots and tubers; (c.8) Edible fruits and nuts; peel of melons or citrus fruit; (c.9) Coffee, tea and spices, excluding mate (heading 09.3); (c.10) Cereals; (c.11) Products of the milling industry; malt and starches; gluten; insulin; (c.12) Oil seeds and oleaginous fruit; Miscellaneous grains, seeds and fruit; industrial and medical plants; straw and fodder; (c.12) ex 13.03, Pectin; (c.15) 15.01, Lard and other rendered pig fat; rendered poultry fat; 15.02 Unrendered fats of bovine cattle, sheep or goats; tallow (including 'premier jus') produced from those fats; 15.03, Lard stearin, oleostearin and tallow stearin; lard oil, oleo-oil and tallow oil, not emulsified or mixed or prepared in any way; 15.04, Fats and oil, of fish and marine mammals, whether or not refined; 15.07, Fixed vegetable oils, fluid or solid, crude, refined or purified; 15.12, Animal or vegetable fats and oils, hydrogenated, whether or not refined, but not further prepared; 15.13, Margarine, imitation lard and other prepared edible fats; 15.17, Residues resulting from the treatment of fatty substances or animal or vegetable waxes; (c.16) Preparations of meat, of fish, of crustaceans or molluscs; (c.17) 17.01, Beet sugar and cane sugar, solid; 17.02, Other sugars; sugar syrups; artificial honey (whether or not mixed with natural honey); caramel; 17.03, Molasses, whether or not decolourized; 17.05, Flavoured or coloured sugars, syrups and molasses, but not including fruit juices containing added sugar in any proportion; (c.18) 18.01, Cocoa beans, whole or broken, raw or roasted; 18.02, Cocoa shells, husks, skins and waste; (c.20) Preparations of vegetables, fruit or other parts of plants; (c.22) 22.04, Grape must, in fermentation or with fermentation arrested other than by the addition of alcohol; 22.05, Wine of fresh grapes; grape must with fermentation arrested by the addition of alcohol; 22.07, Other fermented beverages (eg cider, perry and mead); ex 22.08, 22.09, Ethyl alcohol or neutral spirits, whether or not denatured, of any strength, obtained from agricultural products here listed, excluding liqueurs and other spirituous beverages and compound alcoholic preparations (known as 'concentrated extracts') for the manufacture of beverages; 22.10, Vinegar and substitutes for vinegar; (c.23), Residues and wastes from the food industries; prepared animal fodder; (c.24) 24.01, Unmanufactured tobacco; tobacco refuse; (c.45) 45.01, Natural cork, unworked, crushed, granulated or ground; waste cork; (c.54) 54.01, Flax, raw or processed but not spun; flaw tow and waste (including pulled or garnetted rags); and (c.57) True hemp *(Cannabis sativa)*, raw or processed but not spun; tow and waste of true hemp (including pulled or garnetted rags or ropes).

Headings 17.05, 22.08–22.10 were added to Annex II by Council Regulation 7a/59 pursuant to EC Art 38(3). As to the validity of that regulation, see Case 185/73 *Hauptzollamt Bielefeld v Konig* [1974] ECR 607.

As Annex II adopts word for word certain headings of the Common Customs Tariff, it is appropriate to refer to established interpretations and methods of interpretation relating to the tariff in interpreting Annex II: Case 77/83 *Srl CILFIT and Lanificio di Gavardo SpA v Ministero della Sanita* [1984] ECR 1257.

13 EC Art 38(2). The exceptions are laid down in ibid Arts 39–46.
14 See Joined Cases 2, 3/62 *EEC Commission v Luxembourg and Belgium* [1962] ECR 425.
15 See Case 16/69 *EC Commission v Italy* [1969] ECR 377.
16 Ie, to the products listed in EC Annex II; see Joined Cases 2, 3 *EEC Commission v Luxembourg and Belgium* [1962] ECR 425. The rules of the common agricultural policy do not apply therefore to products not listed in EC Annex II.
17 Case 83/78 *Pigs Marketing Board v Redmond* [1978] ECR 2347; Case 177/78 *Pigs and Bacon Commission v McCarren & Co Ltd* [1979] ECR 2161; Case 68/86 *United Kingdom v Council* [1988] ECR 855; Case 131/86 *United Kingdom v Council* [1988] ECR 905; Case 131/87 *Re Trade in Animal Glands: Commission v Council* [1989] ECR 3743; Case C-331/88 *R v Minister for Agriculture, Fisheries and Food, ex p FEDESA* [1991] ECR I-4023.

that the Single European Act added to the EEC Treaty new titles concerning economic and social cohesion[18] and the environment.[19] Each of these new Titles contains objectives which affect agriculture and trade in agricultural products.

The objectives of the common agricultural policy *stricto sensu* are:

(1) to increase agricultural productivity by promoting technical progress and by ensuring the rational development of agricultural production[20] and the optimum utilization of the factors of production, in particular labour;[1]
(2) thus[2] to ensure a fair standard of living for the agricultural community, in particular by increasing the individual earnings of persons engaged in agriculture;[3]
(3) to stabilize markets;[4]
(4) to assure the availability of supplies;[5]
(5) to ensure that supplies reach consumers at reasonable prices.[6]

In working out the policy and its application so as to achieve these objectives, three factors must be taken into account:

(1) the particular nature of agricultural activity, which results from the social structure of agriculture and from structural and natural disparities between the various agricultural regions;[7]
(2) the need to effect the appropriate adjustments by degrees;[8] and
(3) the fact that in the Member States agriculture constitutes a sector closely linked with the economy as a whole.[9]

As these objectives are disparate and potentially conflicting, they may not all be simultaneously and fully attained.[10] Consequently, the Community institutions may give any one of them temporary priority in light of economic factors or conditions.[11] In doing so, however, they may not discriminate between

18 EC Title V, 'Economic and social cohesion' Arts 130a–130e.
19 EC Title VII, 'Environment' Arts 130r–130t.
20 As to this factor, see Case 34/62 *Germany v Commission* [1963] ECR 131 at 162, per Advocate General Roemer.
1 EC Art 39(1)(a).
2 Any mandatory link between Arts 39(1)(a) and 39(1)(b) was rejected, however, by Advocate-General Capotorti in Case 114/76 *Bela-Muhle Josef Bergmann KG v Grows-Farm GmbH and Co KG* [1977] ECR 1211 at 1229–1230.
3 EC Art 39(1)(b).
4 Ibid Art 39(1)(c). This objective does not extend to the maintenance of positions established under previous market conditions: Joined Cases 63–69/72 *Werhahn v EC Council* [1973] ECR 1229.
5 EC Art 39(1)(d).
6 Ibid Art 39(1)(e). 'Reasonable' does not mean the lowest possible prices but prices which are reasonable in the light of the common agricultural policy: Case 34/62 *Germany v Commission* [1963] ECR 131.
7 EC Art 39(2)(a).
8 Ibid Art 39(2)(b); cf also EC Art 40(1).
9 Ibid Art 39(2)(c).
10 See Case 5/67 *W Beus GmbH & Co v Hauptzollamt Munchen* [1968] ECR 83 at 98.
11 Case 5/73 *Balkan-Import-Export GmbH v Hauptzollamt Berlin-Packhof* [1973] ECR 1091. See also Joined Cases 63–69 *Wilhelm Werhahn Hansamuhle v Council* [1973] ECR 1229.

producers or consumers within the Community.[12] They must also, where necessary, take account, in favour of farmers, of the principle of Community preference.[13]

The EC Treaty provides that, in order to attain the objectives of the common agricultural policy, a common organization of agricultural markets must be established.[14] Depending on the product, this organization may take one of the following forms:

(1) common rules on competition;
(2) compulsory co-ordination of the various national market organizations; or
(3) a European market organization.[15]

In practice the third form has invariably been adopted. A Community-wide market organization for each product has been established for the majority of temperate zone agricultural products.[16] These common market organizations replace the different national market organizations which previously existed. Once a common market organization has been established, the Member States are obliged to abstain from all measures which would derogate from it.[17] In the case of products for which no common market organization has been established, agricultural marketing has been subject, since the end of the transitional period, to the Treaty provisions concerning the free movement of goods. Any national market organizations which still exist may not derogate from these provisions.[18]

The common market organizations may include all measures required to attain the objectives of the common agricultural policy.[19] These measures may include, in particular, the regulation of prices, aids for the production and marketing of the various products, storage and carryover arrangements and common machinery for stabilizing imports or exports.[20] Any common price policy must be based on common criteria and uniform methods of calculation.[1] Member States are not permitted to adopt unilateral measures which conflict with such a policy.[2] The objectives of the common organizations of the markets are limited, however, to the objectives of the common agricultural policy.[3]

---

12 EC Art 40(3), paragraph 2. This phrase has been interpreted to refer only to discrimination between producers or between consumers: Case 5/73 *Balkan-Import-Export GmbH v Hauptzollamt Berlin-Packhof* [1973] ECR 1091.
13 Case 5/67 *W Beus GmbH v Hauptzollamt Munchen* [1968] ECR 83; see also Case 72/69 *Hauptzollamt Bremen-Freihafen v Bremer Handelsgesellschaft* [1970] ECR 427.
14 EC Art 40(2), first paragraph.
15 EC Art 40(2)(a)–(c).
16 The exceptions are alcohol, honey, potatoes, wood and wool.
17 Case 51/74 *P J Van der Hulst's Zonen v Produktschap voor Siergewassen* [1975] ECR 79; Case 111/76 *Officier van Justitie v Van den Hazel* [1977] ECR 901; Case 83/78 *Pigs Marketing Board v Redmond* [1978] ECR 2347; Case 177/78 *Pigs and Bacon Commission v McCarren & Co Ltd* [1979] ECR 2161.
18 Case 48/74 *Charmasson v Minister for Economic Affairs and Finance (Paris)* [1974] ECR 1383.
19 EC Art 40(3), first paragraph.
20 Ibid Art 40(3), first paragraph.
 1 Ibid Art 40(3), third paragraph.
 2 Case 31/74 *Galli* [1975] ECR 47.
 3 EC Art 40(3), second paragraph.

The common organizations must not discriminate between producers or consumers.[4] The aim of this provision is to guarantee equality of treatment as between producers and as between consumers,[5] since equal treatment is a fundamental principle of the Community.[6] Consequently, similar situations affecting either producers or consumers may not be treated differently unless the differentiation can be justified objectively.[7] Conversely, it is not discriminatory to accord different treatment to situations which are not identical.[8] The principle of equal treatment does not however apply in all respects to third countries[9] with which the Community has external relations.

THE URUGUAY ROUND AND THE AGREEMENT ON AGRICULTURE

The Uruguay Round of multilateral trade negotiations began at Punta del Este on 20 September 1986. It concluded with the signature of the Final Act embodying the results of the negotiations and the Agreement establishing the World Trade Organization in Marrakesh on 15 April 1994. That portion of the agreements which falls within EC competence has been approved on behalf of the European Community.[10] This, as held by the European Court of Justice,[11] includes the Agreement on Agriculture[12] and the Agreement on the Application of Sanitary and Phytosanitary Measures.[13] Consequently, subject to ratification by all signatories, the Final Act and the WTO Agreement may be expected to lead to substantial changes in the customs and commercial policy aspects of the CAP.

---

4 Ibid Art 40(3), second paragraph.
5 Case 5/73 *Balkan-Import-Export GmbH v Hauptzollamt Berlin-Packhof* 1973 ECR 1091.
6 Joined Cases 117/76 and 16/77 *Albert Ruckdeschel & Co v Hauptzollamt Hamburg-St Annen* [1977] ECR 1753. The rule against such discrimination applies not only to Community measures but also to implementation by Member States: Cases 201, 202/85 *Klensch v Secretaire d'Etat a l'Agriculture et a la Viticulture* [1986] ECR 3477.
7 See, eg, Case 222/78 *ICAP v Beneventi* [1979] ECR 1163; Case 51/74 *P J Van der Hulst's Zonen v Produktschap voor Siergewassen* [1975] ECR 79; Case 114/76 *Bela-Muhle Josef Bergmann KG v Grows-Farm GmbH and Co KG* [1977] ECR 1211; Case 8/82 *Kommanditgesellschaftt in der Firma Hans-Otto Wagner GmbH Agrarhandel v Bundesanstalt fur Landwirtschaftliche Marktordnung* [1983] ECR 371.
8 See, eg, Joined Cases 279, 280, 285, 286/84 *Walter Rau Lebensmittelwerke v EEC* [1987] ECR 1069; Case 15/83 *Denkavit Nederland BV v Hoofproduktschap voor Akkerbouwprodukten* [1984] ECR 2171.
9 Case 245/81 *Edeka Zentrale AG v Germany* [1982] ECR 2745.
10 Council Decision (EC) No 94/800 of 22 December 1994 concerning the conclusion on behalf of the European Community, as regards matters within its competence, of the agreements reached in the Uruguay Round multilateral negotiations (1986–1994), OJ 23.12.94 L336/1, Art 1. See also Council Regulation (EC) No 3286/94 of 22 December 1994 laying down Community procedures in the field of the common commercial policy in order to ensure the exercise of the Community's rights under international trade rules, in particular those established under the auspices of the World Trade Organization, OJ 31.12.94 L349/71, as amended by Council Regulation 356/95, OJ 23.2.95 L41/3.
11 Opinion 1/94 *World Trade Organization* [1994] ECR I-5267.
12 Agreement establishing the World Trade Organization, Annex IA, OJ 23.12.94 L336/22. On the negotiations, see John M Breen *Agriculture* in *The GATT Uruguay Round: A Negotiating History (1986–1992)*, General Editor: Terence P Stewart (Kluwer, Deventer and Boston, 1993).
13 Agreement establishing the World Trade Organization, Annex IA, OJ 23.12.94 L336/40.

The same may be said of the International Dairy Arrangement[14] and of the Arrangement regarding Bovine Meat negotiated bilaterally with Uruguay.[15] Both of these trade agreements have been approved on behalf of the European Community with regard to matters falling within its competence.[16] They are part of the WTO Agreement for those Members that have accepted them and the agreements are binding on those Members; however, they do not create either rights or obligations for Members that have not accepted them.[17]

The Agreement on Agriculture aims to establish 'a fair and market-oriented agricultural trading system', to initiate a reform process 'through the negotiation of commitments on support and protection and through the establishment of strengthened and more operationally effective GATT rules and disciplines', and 'to provide for substantial progressive reductions in agricultural support and protection sustained over an agreed period of time, resulting in correcting and preventing restrictions and distortions in world agricultural markets'.[18] It expresses the commitment of Members to achieving specific binding commitments in regard to market access, domestic support,[19] export competition and reaching an agreement on sanitary and phytosanitary issues.[20] It applies to agricultural products.[1] The Agreement lays down a six-year timetable[2] for the extension of access to the Community market for agricultural products from third countries on the one hand and the gradual reduction in support granted by the Community on exports of agricultural products on the other hand.

With regard to imports, the general principle is that all measures restricting imports of agricultural products should be converted into customs duties (tarification) and the application of such measures is to be prohibited in the future.[3] Subject to special safeguard provisions[4] and other limited exceptions,[5] Members have undertaken specific market access concessions.[6] In particular,

---

14 Agreement establishing the World Trade Organization, Annex 4, OJ 23.12.94 L336/290. See also Case C-61/94 *Commission v Germany* [1996] ECR I-3989
15 Agreement establishing the World Trade Organization, Annex 4, OJ 23.12.94 L336/10.
16 Council Decision 94/800, OJ 23.12.94 L336/1, Art 2(1) (International Dairy Arrangement), Art 3(1) (Arrangement regarding Bovine Meat).
17 Agreement establishing the World Trade Organization, Art 2(3), OJ 23.12.94 L336/3.
18 Agreement on Agriculture, OJ 23.12.94 L336/22, preamble, recitals 2, 3.
19 Domestic support commitments are specified in the Agreement on Agriculture, Arts 6 and 7, Annexes 2, 3, 4. The basic principle is that domestic support measures must be reduced unless they have no, or at most minimal, trade-distorting effects or effects on production: Art 6(1), Annex 2, paragraph 1.
20 Ibid preamble, recital 4.
1 Ibid Art 2, Annex I: HS Chapters 1–24 less fish and fish products, and HS Codes 2905 43 (mannitol), 2905 44 (sorbitol), 3301 (essential oils), 3501–3505 (albuminoidal substances, modified starches, glues), 3809 10 (finishing agents), 3823 60 (sorbitol n.e.p.), 4101–4103 (hides and skins), 4301 (raw furskins), 5001–5002 (raw silk and silk waste), 5101–5103 (wool and animal hair), 5201–5203 (raw cotton, waste and cotton carded or combed), 5301 (raw flax) and 5302 (raw hemp); the product descriptions in round brackets are not necessarily exhaustive. This list does not limit the product coverage of the Agreement on the Application of Sanitary and Phytosanitary Measures.
2 Agreement on Agriculture Art 1(f).
3 Ibid Arts 4, 6, 7 and Annexes 2, 3, 4, 5 and attachment to Annex 5, OJ 23.12.94 L336/22. As to tarification, see Council Regulation 3290/94, OJ 31.12.94 L349/105. As to specific products, see also the relevant sections in this chapter. These measures do not apply to fish and fishery products.
4 Agreement on Agriculture, Art 5, OJ 23.12.94 L336/22.
5 Ibid Annex 5.
6 Ibid Art 4(1).

they must not maintain, resort to, or revert to any measures of the kind which have been required to be converted into ordinary customs duties.[7] These measures include, inter alia, quantitative import restrictions, variable import levies, minimum import prices, discretionary import licensing, non-tariff measures maintained through State-trading enterprises, voluntary export restraints, and similar border measures other than ordinary customs duties.[8]

Notwithstanding these provisions, special safeguard measures in the form of an additional import duty, or surcharge, may be taken in respect of designated agricultural products in either of two circumstances:[9] first, if the volume of such imports exceeds a certain level (the 'trigger level'),[10] and, second, if the import price of the product falls below a certain price (the 'trigger price').[11] In the first case the duty may not exceed more than one-third of the ordinary customs duty in effect in the year in which the action is taken, and it can be maintained only until the end of the year in which it is imposed.[12] In the second case the duty is set according to a sliding scale based on the difference between the cif import price and the trigger price.[13] The operation of the special safeguard is to be carried out in a transparent manner.[14] In the first case the Member taking action must give notice in writing, including relevant data, to the Committee on Agriculture as far in advance as may be practicable and in any event within ten days of the implementation of the action.[15] In the second case the Member taking action must give notice in writing, including relevant data, to the Committee on Agriculture within ten days of implementation of the first such action or, for perishable and seasonal products, for the first action in any period.[16] In either case a Member taking action must afford any interested Members the opportunity to consult with it in respect of the conditions of application of the action.[17]

In addition, general safeguard measures may be taken as provided under the common organization of the market for specific products.[18]

With regard to exports, each Member undertakes not to provide export subsidies otherwise than in conformity with the Agreement and with the commit-

---

7 Ibid Art 4(2).
8 Ibid Art 4(2), n 1.
9 Ibid Art 5(1), which also provides that the products are those to which tarification applies and which are designed in the Member's Schedule with the symbol 'SSG'. As to the products in respect of which special safeguard measures may be taken by the Community, see the discussion of specific products below, where such measures are referred to as 'special safeguard measures'.
10 Ibid Art 5(1)(a).
11 Ibid Art 5(1)(b), which also provides that the price is to be determined on the basis of the cif import price of the shipment concerned expressed in terms of the importing Member's domestic currency.
12 Ibid Art 4, which also provides for the setting of the trigger level.
13 Ibid Art 5. No additional duty is to be imposed if the difference between the cif import price and the trigger price is less than or equal to 10% of the trigger price: ibid Art 5(a).
14 Ibid Art 5(7).
15 Ibid, which also provides for the case in which changes in consumption volumes must be allocated to individual tariff lines and for consultation.
16 Ibid.
17 Ibid. In addition, when special safeguard measures are taken, Members undertake not to have recourse, in respect of such measures, to the provisions of paragraphs 1(a) and 3 of GATT 1994 Art XIX or paragraph 2 of Art 8 of the Agreement on Safeguards: ibid Art 5(8).
18 As to specific products, see below, where such measures are referred to as general safeguard measures.

ments specified in that Member's Schedule.[19] Subject to certain limited exceptions,[20] Members agree not to provide specified export subsidies in excess of specified budget outlay and quantity commitment levels for specified agricultural products and not to provide any such subsidies for other agricultural products.[1] The export subsidies which are subject to reduction commitments include:

(1) the provision by government or their agencies of direct subsidies, including payments-in-kind, to a firm, an industry, producers of an agricultural product, a co-operative or other association of such producers, or a marketing board, contingent on export performance;

(2) the sale or disposal for export by governments or their agencies of non-commercial stocks of agricultural products at a price lower than the comparable price charged for the like product to buyers in the domestic market;

(3) payments on the export of an agricultural product that are financed by virtue of governmental action, whether or not a charge on the public account is involved, including payments that are financed from the proceeds of a levy imposed on the agricultural product concerned or on an agricultural product from which the exported product is derived;

(4) the provision of subsidies to reduce the costs of marketing exports of agricultural products (other than widely available export promotion and advisory services) including handling, up-grading and other processing costs, and the costs of international transport and freight;

(5) internal transport and freight charges on export shipments, provided or mandated by governments, on terms more favourable than for domestic shipments; and

(6) subsidies on agricultural products contingent on their incorporation in exported products.[2]

Other export subsidies must not be applied in a manner which results in, or which threatens to lead to, circumvention of export subsidy commitments, and non-commercial transactions must not be used to circumvent such commitments.[3] The per-unit subsidy on an incorporated agricultural primary product must not exceed the per-unit subsidy that would be payable on exports of the primary product as such.[4] During the implementation period, export subsidies that conform to these provisions are to be subject to countervailing duties only upon a determination of injury or threat thereof based on volume, effect on prices, or consequent impact in accordance with Article VI of GATT 1994 and Part V of the Agreement on Subsidies and Countervailing Measures,[5] and due restraint must be shown in initiating any countervailing duty investigations.[6]

---

19 Agreement on Agriculture Art 8, OJ 23.12.94 L336/22. 'Export subsidies' refers to subsidies contingent upon export performance, including export subsidies listed in Art 9 of the Agreement: ibid Art 1(e), OJ 23.12.94 L336/22.

20 Ibid Arts 3(3), 9(2b), 9(4).

1 Ibid Art 3(3). On definition of terms, see Art 1. The prohibited types of export subsidies are listed in ibid Art 9(1). The specified agricultural products and the budgetary outlay and quantity commitment levels are listed in Section II of Part IV of each member's Schedule.

2 Ibid Art 9(1).

3 Ibid Art 10(1).

4 Ibid Art 11.

5 OJ 23.12.94 L336/94.

6 Agreement on Agriculture Art 13(c)(i), OJ 23.12.94 L336/22.

Such subsidies are also exempt from actions based on Article XVI of GATT 1994 or Arts 3, 5 and 6 of the Subsidies Agreement.[7]

Members agree to work toward the development of internationally agreed disciplines concerning export credits, export credit guarantees or insurance programmes and, after agreement on such disciplines, to provide export credits, export credit guarantees or insurance programmes only in conformity therewith.[8]

With regard to food aid, Member donors undertake to ensure that the provision of international food aid is not tied directly or indirectly to commercial exports of agricultural products to recipient countries.[9] International food aid transactions, including bilateral food aid which is monetized, is to be carried out in accordance with the FAO 'Principles of Surplus Disposal and Consultative Obligations', including, where appropriate, the system of Usual Marketing Requirements.[10] Aid is to be provided to the extent possible in fully grant form or on terms no less concessional than those provided for in Article IV of the Food Aid Convention 1986.[11]

Specific provisions govern the institution of any new export prohibition or restriction on foodstuffs.[12]

The Uruguay Round agreements have already had a fundamental effect on the Common Agricultural Policy. In particular, the commitment to tarification as expressed in the Agreement on Agriculture requires the abolition of variable import levies and of numerous other measures and charges previously provided for under the common organizations of agricultural markets. It will also lead to many other changes in EC agricultural trade legislation.[13] This will be seen in the following paragraphs, which first consider certain common or 'horizontal' rules concerning import and export licences and advance fixing certificates,[14] securities,[15] export refunds,[16] and advance payment of export refunds.[17] Rules concerning specific products and specific countries or areas can then be examined.[18]

---

7 Ibid Art 13(c)(ii).
8 Ibid Art 10(2).
9 Ibid Art 10(4)(a).
10 Ibid Art 10(4)(b).
11 Ibid Art 10(4)(c); Food Aid Convention 1986, OJ 1986 L195/1.
12 Agreement on Agriculture Art 12, OJ 23.12.94 L336/22.
13 See Council Regulation 3290/94 on the adjustments and transitional arrangements required in the agricultural sector in order to implement the agreements concluded during the Uruguay Round of multilateral trade negotiations, OJ 31.12.94 L349/105.
14 Commission Regulation 3719/88 laying down common detailed rules for the application of the system of import and export licences and advance fixing certificates for agricultural products, OJ 2.12.88 L331/1, as amended.
15 Commission Regulation 2220/85 laying down common detailed rules for the application of the system of securities for agricultural products, OJ 3.8.85 L205/5, as amended.
16 Commission Regulation 3665/87 laying down common detailed rules for the application of the system of export refunds on agricultural products, OJ 14.12.87 L351/1, as amended.
17 Commission Regulation 565/80 on the advance payment of export refunds in respect of agricultural products, OJ 7.3.80 L62/5, as amended. Measures regarding the common organization of the market for a specific product are discussed in the section relating to the specific product. Measures regarding a specific country or group of countries are discussed in the section relating to that country or group of countries.
18 In order to enable the reader easily to ascertain the relevant law in respect of each product, the provisions of the Agreement on Agriculture, such as special safeguards, together with standard provisions of the common organizations, are reiterated as necessary in respect of each product.

IMPORT AND EXPORT LICENCES AND ADVANCE FIXING CERTIFICATES

Scope and application

Import and export licences or certificates are generally required in respect of all imports to and all exports from the Community.[19] The common rules apply[20] in particular to such trade in bananas,[1] beef and veal,[2] cereals,[3] eggs,[4] fruit and vegetables,[5] live plants and cut flowers,[6] milk and milk products,[7] oils and fats,[8] ovalbumin and lactalbumin,[9] pigmeat,[10] poultrymeat,[11] rice,[12] seeds,[13] sheepmeat and goatmeat,[14] sugar, isoglucose and insulin syrup,[15] products processed from fruit and vegetables,[16] wine[17] and agricultural products exported in the form of goods not covered by Annex II of the EEC Treaty.[18]

The general requirement for these licences and certificates is, however, subject to exceptions. Certain specific exceptions are provided in the Community rules which apply to particular agricultural products.[19] More generally, licences and certificates are not required in respect of products:

(1) where the amount of the export refund per export declaration does not exceed Ecu 60;[20]
(2) which are not placed in free circulation in the Community;[1]
(3) in respect of which export is effected under procedures and arrangements which are free of customs duties, charges having equivalent effect or export duties;[2]
(4) which are placed in free circulation under provisions governing the treatment of returned goods;[3]

19 Commission Regulation 3719/88 Art 1, OJ 2.12.88 L331/1. This regulation has been amended many times.
20 Commission Regulation 3183/80 Art 1.
 1 Council Regulation 404/93 Art 17, OJ 25.2.93 L47/1.
 2 See Council Regulation 805/68 Art 9, OJ 28.6.68 L148/24.
 3 See Council Regulation 1766/92 Art 9, OJ 1.7.92 L181/21.
 4 See Council Regulation 2771/75 Art 3, OJ 1.11.75 L282/49.
 5 Council Regulation 2200/96 Art 31, OJ 21.11.96 L297/1.
 6 Council Regulation 234/68 Art 8, OJ 2.3.68 L55/1.
 7 See Council Regulation 804/68 Art 13, OJ 28.6.68 L148/13.
 8 See Council Regulation 136/66 Art 2, OJ 30.9.66 L172, p 3025/66.
 9 Council Regulation 2783/75 Art 2, OJ 1.11.75 L282/104.
10 See Council Regulation 2759/75 Art 8, OJ 1.11.75 L282/1.
11 See Council Regulation 2777/75 Art 3. OJ 1.11.75 L282/77.
12 See Council Regulation 3072/95 Art 9, OJ 30.12.95 L329/18.
13 See Council Regulation 2358/71 Art 4, OJ 5.11.71 L246/1.
14 See Council Regulation 3013/89 Art 9, OJ 7.10.89 L289/1.
15 Council Regulation 1785/81 Art 13, OJ 1.7.81 L177/4.
16 Council Regulation 2201/96 Art 11, OJ 21.11.96 L297/29.
17 See Council Regulation 822/87 Art 52, OJ 27.3.87 L84/1.
18 See Council Regulation 1222/94 Art 6, OJ 31.5.94 L136/5.
19 See the regulations cited in notes accompanying the preceding paragraph.
20 Council Regulation 3667/87 Art 2a, first indent, OJ 14.12.87 L351/1, as inserted by Council Regulation 1384/95, OJ 20.6.95 L134/4. Where an export declaration includes several separate codes of the refunds nomenclature or the combined nomenclature, the entries to each of the codes are regarded as constituting a separate transaction: ibid.
 1 Commission Regulation 3719/88 Art 2(1)(a), OJ 2.12.88 L331/1.
 2 Ibid Art 2(1)(b), OJ 2.12.88 L331/1, as amended by Commission Regulation 1199/95 Art 1, OJ 30.5.95 L119/5.
 3 Commission Regulation 3719/88 Arts 6, 39, OJ 2.12.88 L331/1. See also Council Regulation 2137/95 OJ 8.9.95 L214/25.

(5) for re-export in respect of which the exporter provides proof of a favourable decision for the repayment or remission of import duties.[4]

In cases in which advance fixing of a refund is not requested, a licence is not required for the purpose of operations:

(1) for the victualling within the Community of seagoing vessels or aircraft, to international organizations established within the Community, or to armed forces stationed within the territory of, but not subject to the flag of, a Member State;[5]
(2) of a non-commercial nature;[6]
(3) in respect of goods on which duties have been recovered or remitted;[7] and
(4) relating to products in small quantities.[8]

Previously, in respect of trade in such goods, the amount of any levy to be charged or refund to be received could be fixed in advance of a transaction by advance fixing certificates.[9] Pursuant to the Uruguay Round agreements, variable levies previously charged on imports have now been abolished.[10] However, in order to facilitate monitoring of compliance with the limits on export subsidies in terms of value, the granting of export refunds is subject as a general rule to the requirement of an export licence, and export refunds must be fixed in advance.[11]

Applications and issue

Applications for import and export licences and advance fixing certificates for agricultural products may be made to the competent agencies of the Member States[12] either on authorized forms[13] or, provided all the information which would have appeared on the form, had it been used, is included, by written telecommunications.[14] Applications for licences with advance fixing of the

4 Commission Regulation 3719/88 Art 7, OJ 2.12.88 L331/1. See also Council Regulation 918/83, OJ 23.4.83 L405/1.
5 Commission Regulation 3719/88 Art 5(1), first indent, OJ 2.12.88 L331/1.
6 Ibid Art 5(1), second indent, OJ 2.12.88 L331/1. 'Operations of a non-commercial character' means imports and exports by private individuals: Art 5(2).
7 Ibid Art 5(1), third indent, OJ 2.12.88 L331/1; see also Council Regulation 918/83, OJ 23.4.83 L105/1.
8 Ibid Art 5(1), fourth indent.
9 Commission Regulation 3719/88 Art 1, OJ 2.12.88 L331/1.
10 Commission Regulation 3719/88 Art 2, OJ 2.12.88 L331/1, as amended by Commission Regulation 1199/95 Art 1 OJ 30.5.95 L119/4.
11 Commission Regulation 1199/95 amending Regulation (EEC) No 3719/88 laying down common detailed rules for the application of the system of import and export licences and advance-fixing certificates for agricultural products, to take account of the adjustments necessary for implementing the Agreement on Agriculture resulting from the Uruguay Round, preamble, fourth and fifth recitals, OJ 30.5.95 L119/4. See also Council Regulation 3290/94 preamble, recitals 14 and 15, 31.12.94 L349/105.
12 For a complete list of national agencies, see OJ C207, 15.8.81, p.2 (amended by OJ C302, 21.11.81, p. 2).
13 Commission Regulation 3719/88 Art 13(1), first paragraph, Art 16, Annex I, OJ 2.12.88 L331/1.
14 Ibid Art 13(1), second paragraph. Member States may also require such an application to be followed by submission of a form, but such a requirement will not affect the validity of the application by written telecommunication: Art 13(1), second paragraph.

refund, and the licences themselves, must indicate the eleven-digit product code taken from the nomenclature of agricultural products for use with export re-funds.[15] Where the rate of refund is differentiated according to destination, the country of destination or, as relevant, the area of destination must be indicated on both the application and the licences themselves.[16] Applications which contain conditions other than those sanctioned by Community law will be rejected.[17]

No application will be accepted unless security has been given in favour of, or proof that security has been given is furnished to, the competent national agency.[18] At the applicant's option, the security may consist of either a cash deposit or a guarantee issued by an authorized institution.[19] Applications, in-cluding the lodging of security, and cancellations of applications for licences or certificates[20] are subject to date and time requirements.[1] Licences and certifi-cates must be issued in at least two copies: a holder's copy issued to the appli-cant and an issuing agency's copy retained by the issuing agency.[2]

Upon applicant by the titular holder of a licence or certificate, or by the transferee,[3] to the competent agencies of the Member States, a licence or certifi-cate, within the limit of the total quantity authorized, may be divided into extracts.[4] Such an extract must be drawn up in at least two copies, as above,[5] and specify the quantity for which it has been issued.[6]

Unless a licence or certificate states that it becomes valid on the day of its issue,[7] it must be considered to have been issued and become valid on the day on which the application was lodged.[8] In both cases the day on which a licence or certficate becomes valid will be included in the calculation of its period of validity.[9]

15 Ibid Art 13a, first paragraph, OJ 2.12.88 L331/1, as inserted by Commission Regulation 1199/95 Art 1, OJ 30.5.95 L119/4.
16 Ibid Art 13a, third paragraph, OJ 2.12.88 L331/1, as inserted by Commission Regulation 1199/95 Art 1, OJ 30.5.95 L1119/4.
17 Ibid Art 14(1).
18 Ibid Art 14(2). No security is required in respect of specified small amounts or where a licence has been made out in the name of an intervention agency: Art 14(3). Nor is security required in the case of export licences or certificates not involving advance fixing which are issued in respect of exports to third countries in connection with approved non-Community food-aid operations: Art 14(4). As to the legality of the requirement of securities, see Case 11/70 *Internationale Handelsgesellschaft mbH v Einfuhr-und Vorratsstelle fur Getreide und Futtermittel* [1970] ECR 1125. See also R Barents *The Agricultural Law of the EC: An Inquiry into the Administrative Law of the European Community in the Field of Agriculture* (Kluwer, Deventer, 1994) pp 277 ff. With regard to special wording required in applications for licences in connection with a food-aid operation, see ibid Art 14a, as inserted by Commission Regula-tion 1199/95 Art 1, OJ 30.5.95 L119/5.
19 Commission Regulation 2220/85 laying down common detailed rules for the application of the system of securities for agricultural products, Arts 8, 16, OJ 3.8.85 L205/5, as amended.
20 Applications may be cancelled only by letter or written telecommunication: ibid Art 13(2).
1 Ibid Art 13(1), second paragraph, Arts 14(2), 15(1),(2). All time limits are expressed in Belgian local time: Art 15(3).
2 Ibid Art 19. As to sets of forms, see Art 16(2). As to the obligation of the national agencies to ensure delivery of the documents, see Case 61/72 *Mij PPW International NV v Hoofdproduktschap voor Akkerbouwprodukten* [1973] ECR 301.
3 As to the transfers of licences and certificates, see below.
4 Commission Regulation 3719/88 Art 20(1), first paragraph, OJ 2.12.88 L331/1.
5 Ibid Art 20(1), second paragraph.
6 Ibid Art 20(1), third paragraph. No further extract may be made from an extract of a licence or certificate: Art 20(2).
7 Ibid Art 21(2).
8 Ibid Art 21(1). For the meaning of 'the day on which the application was lodged', see Art 15(1).
9 Ibid Art 21.

Rights and obligations

The issue of an import or export licence not only authorizes the import or export of a specified quantity of an agricultural product; it also imposes an obligation to import or export that quantity during the period of the licence's validity.[10] The issue of an advance fixing certificate equally gives rise to such an obligation.[11] Where the quantity actually imported or exported is greater or less by not more than 5 per cent of the quantity indicated in the licence or certificate, it is nevertheless considered to come within the terms of the licence or certificate.[12]

Obligations deriving from licences and certificates are not transferable,[13] but rights arising therefrom may be transferred by the titular holder during the relevant period of validity.[14] Transfers of rights in relation to each licence, certificate or extract from it[15] may only be made to single transferees.[16] Transferees may not themselves further transfer their rights nor may they transfer them back to the titular holder.[17] Transfers take effect from the date of the indorsement of licences, certificates or extracts.[18] Extracts have the same legal effect as the licences and certificates from which they have been extracted within the limits of the quantity in respect of which they have been issued.[19]

The obligation to import or to export under the terms of a licence or a certificate is considered to have been fulfilled on the day on which the appropriate customs formalities have been completed.[20] Securities lodged in respect of licences or certificates will be released on production of proof that those formalities have been completed,[1] generally by production of a holder's copy of a licence or certificate indorsed to that effect.[2] Where the obligation to import or export has not been fulfilled, the security will in the absence of force majeure become forfeit in proportion to the quantity of product actually not imported or exported.[3] The security will also become forfeit in whole or in part, as appropriate, save in case of force majeure, when proof of the completion of customs

---

10 Commission Regulation 3719/88 Art 8(1), OJ 2.12.88 L331/1.
11 Ibid Art 8(2). In certain cases the import or export must be made from or to a particular country or group of countries: see Arts 8(3), 44.
12 Ibid Art 8(4),(5).
13 Ibid Art 9(1), first paragraph.
14 Ibid.
15 As to extracts from licences and certificates, see above.
16 Commission Regulation 3719/88 Art 9(1), OJ 2.12.88 L331/1.
17 Ibid Art 9(4).
18 Ibid Art 9(3). As to the indorsement procedure, see Art 9(2). As to the application of the principle of proportionality, see Case 181/84 *R v Intervention Board for Agricultural Produce, ex p ED & F Man (Sugar)* [1985] ECR 2889.
19 Ibid Art 10. As to the legal effects in other Member States, see Art 11.
20 Ibid Art 29, OJ 2.12.88 L331/1. As to customs formalities, see Art 22 and Art 23, as amended by Commission Regulation 1199/95 Art 1, OJ 30.5.95 L119/4. As to the meaning of 'the day on which customs formalities are completed', see Art 32.
 1 Ibid Arts 30, 33(1),(2), as amended by Commission Regulation 1199/95, OJ 30.5.95 L119/4.
 2 Ibid Art 31(1). In some cases additional supporting documents are also required: see Art 31(2)–(4) (amended by EC Commission Regulation 2646/81 and 3392/81). See also Case 186/73 *Norddeutsches Vieh-und Fleischkonter GmbH v Einfuhr- und Vorratsstelle fur Schlachtvieh, Fleisch und Fleischerzeugnisse* [1974] ECR 533.
 3 Commission Regulation 3719/88 Art 33(2), OJ 2.12.88 L331/1; see also Commission Regulation 2220/85 Arts 20–25, OJ 3.8.85 L205/5, as amended. The principle that 'the penalty must be made commensurate with the degree of failure to implement the contractual obligations or with the seriousness of the breach of these obligations' is known as the *Atalanta* rule, because it was formulated by the European Court of Justice in Case 240/78 *Atalanta Amsterdam BV v Produktschap voor Vee en Vlees* [1979] ECR 2137.

formalities has not been furnished within specified periods of the expiry of a licence or certificate.[4]

However, the Uruguay Round reforms introduced a new system to encourage operators to return quickly to the issuing body any export licences which they do not intend to use. With regard to export licences with advance fixing of the refund, where the licence is returned to the issuing body within a period corresponding to the initial two-thirds of its terms of validity, the amount of security to be forfeited is reduced by 40 per cent.[5] Where the licence is returned within a period corresponding to the last third of its term or during the month following the expiry date, the amount of the security to be forfeited is reduced by 25 per cent.[6]

Authentication, loss and force majeure

Any doubts concerning the authenticity of an import or export licence, advance fixing certificate or extract, or entries or indorsements thereon, are to be resolved by returning the questionable document (or a photocopy) to the authorities concerned for checking.[7] Random checks of photocopies of documents are also authorized.[8] Provisions have been laid down concerning the issue of duplicate documents when a licence, certificate or extract has been lost.[9] When a duplicate is issued, it may not be used to carry out import or export transactions. However, a duplicate will replace a lost holder's copy for the purpose of providing the proof required for the release of a security.[10] Loss in this context includes the theft of a licence or certificate either before or after the performance of an import or export transaction.[11] The loss of a licence or certificate does not, however, automatically result in the lapse of the obligation created by its issue.[12]

Where an import or export cannot be performed during the period of validity of a licence or certificate as a result of force majeure, the titular holder may apply to the issuing agency and request either that the period of validity be extended or that the licence or certificate be cancelled.[13] Such a request must be received not more than 30 days after the period of validity has expired,[14] and proof of the circumstances which are alleged to constitute force majeure must be supplied.[15] The concept of force majeure is interpreted by reference to the

4 Commission Regulation 3719/88 Art 33(3), OJ 2.12.88 L331/1; see also Commission Regulation 2220/85 Arts 20–28, OJ 3.8.85 L205/5, as amended.
5 Commission Regulation 3718/88 Art 33, paragraph 2, last sub-paragraph, first indent, OJ 2.12.88 L331/1, as inserted by Commission Regulation 1199/95 Art 1, OJ 30.5.95 L119/4.
6 Ibid Art 33, paragraph 2, last sub-paragraph, second indent, OJ 2.12.88 L331/1, as inserted by Commission Regulation 1199/85 Art 1, OJ 30.5.95 L119/4.
7 Ibid Art 27(1). Member States must inform each other and the EC Commission of irregularities and infringements concerning licences, certificates and extracts: Art 28(1),(2).
8 Ibid Art 27(1), second paragraph.
9 Ibid Art 34.
10 Ibid Art 35(5).
11 Case 808/79 *Pardini SpA* [1980] ECR 2103.
12 Case 158/73 *Kampffmeyer v Einfuhr- und Vorratsstelle fur Getreide und Futtermittel* [1974] ECR 101.
13 Commission Regulation 3719/88 Art 36(1), OJ 2.12.88 L331/1.
14 Ibid Art 36(2).
15 Ibid Art 36(2).

particular legal context in which it operates.[16] In the present context it is not confined to absolute impossibility but includes abnormal circumstances, outside the control of the titular holder, and which arise in spite of the fact that it has taken all the precautions which could reasonably be expected of a prudent and diligent trader.[17] In that sense, the loss of a licence or certificate may constitute a case of force majeure[18]. It is for the issuing agency to decide whether the circumstances involved constitute force majeure and, if it so decides, whether the licence or certificate, as the case may be, is extended by an appropriate period or cancelled and the security released.[19]

EXPORT REFUNDS AND LEVIES

Export refunds and levies have long been part of the Common Agricultural Policy. Art 40(4) of the EEC Treaty authorized the setting up of one or more agricultural guidance and guarantee funds in order to enable the common organization of agricultural markets to attain its objectives.[20] In 1962 the Council exercised its power[1] to set up a single European Agricultural Guidance and Guarantee Fund.[2] One of the purposes of the Guarantee Section of the EAGGF is to finance refunds on exports of agricultural products to third countries.[3]

Refunds on exports to third countries are granted in accordance with the rules of Community law within the framework of the common organization of agricultural markets.[4] Entitlement to a refund therefore arises in the context of a particular common organization when the Community price for the relevant agricultural product is higher than its price on the world market. The exporter will sell at the world market price and recover the difference between that price and the Community price as an export refund. The Council determines the procedure for financing such refunds where necessary.[5] The regulations adopted by the Council establishing the common organizations of the markets in agricultural products confer powers on the Commission,[6] acting by the management committee procedure, to adopt rules for the application of the system of

---

16 Case 158/73 *Kampffmeyer v Einfuhr- und Vorratsstelle fur Getreide und Futtermittel* [1974] ECR 101, ECJ. See also R Barents *The Agricultural Law of the EC: An Inquiry into the Administrative Law of the European Community in the Field of Agriculture* (Kluwer, Deventer, 1994) pp 293 ff.
17 Case 186/73 *Norddeutsches Vieh- und Fleischkontor GmbH v Einfuhr- und Vorratsstelle fur Schlachtvieh, Fleisch and Fleischerzeugnisse* [1974] ECR 533.
18 Case 158/73 *Kampffmeyer v Einfuhr- und Vorratsstelle fur Getreide und Futtermittel* [1974] ECR 101.
19 Commission Regulation 3719/88 Arts 36(4), 37, OJ 2.12.88 L331/1.
20 See EC Art 40(4). As to the organization see ibid Art 40(2). As to the objectives see EC Art 39.
 1 By virtue of EC Art 43(2).
 2 Council Regulation 25 of 4 April 1962, OJ 20.4.62 L30/991.
 3 Council Regulation 729/70 Art 1(2)(a), OJ 28.4.79 L94/13. This Regulation repealed and replaced Council Regulation 17/64, OJ Sp. Ed. 27.2.64 586/103.
 4 Council Regulation 729/70 Art 2(1), OJ 28.4.70 L30/991. Export refunds are based on the regulations establishing common organizations of markets in various agricultural products, not on the export procedure based on the Community customs code: Case C-334/95 *Krüger GmbH v Hauptzollamt Hamburg-Jonas* [1998] 1 CMLR 520. See also Court of Auditors Special Report on the system for the payment of refunds on agricultural exports (85/C 215/01) and Court of Auditors Special Report No 2/90 on the management and control of export refunds accompanied by the replies of the Commission (90/ C 133/01).
 5 Ibid Art 2(2). The Council acts by a qualified majority on a proposal from the Commission.
 6 By virtue of EC Art 155.

export refunds. The Commission has laid down a code of common detailed rules for this purpose.[7] Without prejudice to any derogations contained in the Community rules for particular agricultural products, entitlement to an export refund generally arises after the completion of customs export formalities and on proof that the product has reached its destination or has left the geographical territory of the Community.[8] Payment is made to the exporter by the Member State in whose territory the custom export formalities were completed.[9] The same procedure is adopted in the case of expenditure incurred in the supply of agricultural products as food aid to third countries.[10] The payment of export refunds for live animals is subject to compliance with the provisions established in Community legislation concerning animal welfare.[11]

Export refunds have been introduced in respect of the following agricultural products:[12] beef and veal;[13] cereals;[14] eggs;[15] fruit and vegetables;[16] milk and milk products;[17] oils and fats;[18] pigmeat;[19] poultrymeat;[20] products processed from fruit and vegetables;[1] rice;[2] sugar, isoglucose and insulin syrup;[3] and wine.[4] Refunds are granted in respect of such products which come within the terms of

7 The original Commission Regulation 2730/79 (as amended) has been repealed and replaced by Commission Regulation 3665/87 which lays down common detailed rules for the application of the system of export refunds on agricultural products, OJ 14.12.87 L351/1, as amended (as regards the adjustments necessary for the implementation of the Uruguay Round Agreement on Agriculture) by Commission Regulation 1384/95, OJ 20.6.95 L134/14 and most recently by Commission Regulation 2114/97, OJ 29.10.97 L295/2 and Commission Regulation 604/98, OJ 18.3.98 L80/19. All references to Regulation 2730/79 in Community provisions are to be deemed to refer to Regulation 3665/87 acording to the table of equivalence in the latter: see Art 50(2), second paragraph (as amended by Commission Regulation 3993/88 Art 1(5), OJ 22.12.88 L354/22), Annex I. The application of Community provisions on export refunds is, however, a matter for the national bodies appointed for that purpose, and the interpretation by the Commission of Community rules has no binding force as regards either Member States or individuals: Case C-371/92 *Elliniko Dimosio (Greek State) v Ellinika Dimitriaka AE* [1994] ECR I-2391. Commission Regulation 3846/87, as rectified and amended, introduces for use in connection with export refunds on agricultural products a nomenclature, the 'refund nomenclature', based on the Combined Nomenclature (CN). The Annex to this Regulation, which gives the current nomenclature, was recently amended by Commission Regulation 409/98, OJ 25.2.98 L55/1.
8 See ibid Arts 9–12. See also Case 276/84 *Gebruder Metelmann GmbH & Co KG v Hauptzollamt Hamburg-Jonas* [1985] ECR 4057.
9 See ibid Arts 25–31. As to former GDR before German reunification, see Case C-223/95 *Firma A Moksel AG v Hauptzollamt Hamburg-Jonas* [1997] ECR I-2379.
10 Under the terms of Council Regulation 2681/74 Art 2, OJ 25.10.894 L288/1. See also Case 13/72 *Netherlands v Commission* [1973] ECR 27.
11 Council Regulation 805/68 Art 13(9), OJ 28.6.68 L148/24, as amended. See also Council Directive 91/628, OJ 11.12.91 L340/17, as amended.
12 Commission Regulation 3665/87 Art 1, OJ 14.12.87 L351/1, as amended by Commission Regulation 1384/95 Art 1, OJ 20.6.95 L134/14. As to the agricultural product nomenclature for export refunds, see Commission Regulation 3846/87, OJ 24.12.87 L366/1, as amended. As to specific products, see below.
13 Council Regulation 805/68 Art 13, OJ 28.6.68 L148/24.
14 Council Regulation 1766/92 Art 13, OJ 1.7.92 L181/21.
15 Council Regulation 2771/75 Art 8, OJ 1.11.75 L282/49.
16 Council Regulation 1035/72 Art 26, OJ 20.5.72 L118/1.
17 Council Regulation 804/68 Art 17, OJ 28.6.68 L148/13.
18 Council Regulation 136/66 Art 3, OJ 30.9.66 L172, p 3025/66.
19 Council Regulation 2759/75 Art 13, OJ 1.11.75 L282/1.
20 Council Regulation 2777/75 Art 8, OJ 1.11.75 L282/77.
 1 Council Regulation 426/86 Arts 13, 14 and 14a, OJ 27.2.76 L49/1.
 2 Council Regulation 1418/76 Art 14, OJ 25.6.76 L166/1.
 3 Council Regulation 1785/81 Art 17, OJ 1.7.81 L177/4.
 4 Council Regulation 822/87 Arts 55 and 56, OJ 27.3.87 L84/1.

Art 9(2) of the EC Treaty,[5] even if the packaging does not come within those terms.[6] Provision is made for refunds on compound products.[7] No refund may be granted on products which are not of sound and fair marketable quality, or on products intended for human consumption whose characteristics or conditions exclude or substantially impair their use for that purpose.[8] Refunds cannot be granted on exports subject to an export levy or other export charge fixed in advance or by tender.[9]

Provision has always been made for advance fixing of export refunds.[10] For most processed products and goods obtained from basic products, an amount equal to the export refund is paid, at the request of the party concerned, as soon as the basic products are placed under customs control, ensuring that the processed products or the goods will be exported within a set time limit.[11] For products and goods intended for export without further processing when the products or goods are of a kind that can be stored, an amount equal to the export refund is paid, at the request of the party concerned, as soon as the products or goods have been brought under the customs warehousing or free zone procedure with a view to their being exported within a set time limit.[12] The benefit of these arrangements is subject to the lodgment of a security guaranteeing reimbursement of an amount equal to the amount paid, plus an additional amount.[13]

As a result of the Uruguay Round agreements, however, advance fixing is the general rule. The grant of an export refund is subject to the requirement of an export licence comprising advance fixing of the refund.[14] The requirement does not apply to exports of non-Annex II products or to exports relating to food aid within the meaning of Art 10(4) of the Uruguay Round Agreement on Agriculture.[15]

The date of acceptance of the export declaration for the product determines the rate of the refund where the refund is fixed in advance and any adjustment to be made to the rate of the refund where it is so fixed.[16] It is also used to establish the quantity, nature and characteristics of the product exported.[17]

Refunds are to be paid only upon proof that the products for which an export declaration has been accepted have, within 60 days of the date of the acceptance, left the customs territory of the Community in an unaltered state.[18] Compliance with this condition is not prejudiced by freezing of the products or by repackaging,

---

5 EC Art 9(2), refers to products originating in Member States and to products coming from third countries which are in free circulation in Member States.
6 Council Regulation 3665/87 Art 8(1), first paragraph, OJ 14.12.87 L351/1.
7 See ibid Art 8(2),(3).
8 Ibid Art 13.
9 Ibid Art 14.
10 Ibid Arts 22, 23. For further rules, see Council Regulation 565/80, OJ 7.3.80 L62/5, as amended, and Commission Regulation 1618/81, OJ 18.6.81 L160/17.
11 Council Regulation 565/80 Art 4, OJ 7.3.80 L62/5, as amended.
12 Ibid Art 5, as amended.
13 Ibid Art 6.
14 Commission Regulation 3665/87 Art 2a, first paragraph, OJ 14.12.87 L351/1, as inserted by Commission Regulation 1384/95 Art 1, OJ 20.6.95 L134/14.
15 Ibid Art 2a, first paragraph, OJ 14.12.87 L351/1, as inserted by Commission Regulation 1384/95 Art 1, OJ 20.6.95 L134/14.
16 Ibid Art 3(2). Ibid Art 3(1) defines the 'day of export' as the date on which the customs authority accepts the export declaration in which it is stated that a refund will be applied for.
17 Ibid Art 3(4). As to the information which must be contained in the document used for export, see ibid Art 3(5).
18 Ibid Art 4(1). When a trader has received advance payment of export refunds and the product actually exported corresponds to that mentioned in the payment declaration but differs in characteristics (*in casu* ash content of flour), the provisions limiting the amount of the sums to

provided that the repackaging does not result either in a change in tariff nomenclature or in the subheading of the nomenclature used for refunds or other amounts applicable to exports.[19] In specified circumstances,[20] payment of the refund is also conditional on the product having been imported into a non-member country and, where appropriate, into a specific non-member country within 12 months following the date of acceptance of the export declaration.[1] If, after leaving the Community customs territory, the product perishes in transit as a result of force majeure, the amount of the refund is to be paid in part if the refund varies according to destination[2] or in total if the refund does not so vary.[3]

The Uruguay Round Agreement on Agriculture led to the introduction of a system of penalties for changing the destination where the actual rate of refund is less than the rate for the destination fixed in advance. The previous rule was that, where there was a change of destination, the refund applicable to the actual destination was payable, subject to a ceiling of the level of the amount applicable to the destination fixed in advance.[4] This opened the possibility of abuse whereby destinations with the highest rates of refund were selected systematically, and it is this abuse which the new system is intended to prevent.[5] Now, if the rate of refund corresponding to the actual destination is equal to or greater than the rate for the destination indicated in the application, the rate of refund for the indicated destination applies.[6] However, if the rate of refund for the actual destination is less than the rate for the indicated destination, the refund to be paid is to be that resulting from the application of the rate corresponding to the actual destination, reduced, except in the case of force majeure, by 20 per cent of the difference between the refund for the indicated destination and the refund for the actual destination.[7]

The refund is paid only on written application by the exporter and is paid by the Member State in whose territory the export declaration was accepted.[8] Provision is made for the period of submission[9] of a claim for the refund and the documents required.[10]

be repaid to the unjustified credit from which the trader has benefited must be applied, and not those which penalize failure by the trader to comply with the time limits laid down. Hence the refund to which the trader is entitled is that which would have been applicable if the product had been correctly described in the payment declaration: Joined Cases C-5/90 and C-206/90 *Bremer Rolandmuhle Erling & Co v Hauptzollamt Hamburg-Jonas* [1992] ECR I-1157.

19 Ibid Art 4(3), second paragraph.
20 Ibid Art 5(1), first paragraph, (a),(b).
1 Ibid Art 5(1). This provision is subject to the doctrine of force majeure, as to which see above.
2 Ibid Art 5(3), first indent. As to the conditions of partial payment, see ibid Art 20.
3 Ibid Art 5(3), second indent. But see Case C-109/95 *Astir AE v Greece* [1997] ECR I-1385.
4 Commission Regulation 3665/87 Art 20, OJ 14.12.87 L351/1. For detailed rules regarding the recovery of amounts unduly paid and sanctions, see Commission Regulation 3665/87 Art 11, OJ 14.12.87 L351/1, as substituted by Commission Regulation 2945/94 Art 1, OJ 3.12.94 L310/57.
5 Commission Regulation 1384/95, preamble, recital 5, OJ 20.6.95 L134/14.
6 Commission Regulation 3665/87 Art 20(3)(a), OJ 14.12.87 L351/1, as substituted by Commission Regulation 1384/95 Art 1, OJ 20.6.95 L134/14. As to re-imports of previously exported products, see Commission Regulation 313/97, OJ 21.2.97 L51/31.
7 Commission Regulation 3665/87 Art 20(3)(b), OJ 14.12.87 L351/1, as substituted by Commission Regulation 1384/95 Art 1, OJ 20.6.95 L134/14.
8 Ibid Art 47 (1), as amended by Commission Regulation 1829/94, OJ 27.7.94 L191/5. As to the meaning of 'export declaration' see Case C-49/94 *Ireland v Commission* [1995] ECR I-2683.
9 Ibid Art 47(2), (6).
10 Ibid Art 47. Member States may prescribe a special form: ibid Art 47(1); and may require translation into the official language or one of the official languages of the Member State: ibid Art 47(7).

The converse of export refunds, export levies are intended to discourage Community producers and traders from exporting products for which demand exceeds supply within the Community in circumstances in which world market prices exceed Community prices. Export levies and charges have been introduced at various times in respect of the following agricultural products:[11] cereals;[12] oils and fats;[13] sugar;[14] rice;[15] and certain products processed from fruit and vegetables and containing added sugar.[16]

Save as otherwise provided,[17] levies are chargeable on all exports from the geographical territory of the Community of all such products which come within the terms of Art 9(2) of the EC Treaty,[18] irrespective of the legal position with regard to their packaging.[19] Levies are also chargeable on exports of products which do not come within the scope of that Article provided that one of the components of such a product does come within its terms.[20] Levies are not chargeable on exports in respect of which a refund has either been fixed in advance[1] or determined by a tendering procedure.[2] Nor are levies chargeable for certain other products which include those for victualling seagoing vessels or aircraft serving international routes,[3] those for the armed forces of a Member State who are stationed outside the Community,[4] small quantities of a non-commercial nature,[5] and goods contained in travellers' personal luggage.[6]

Unless a levy is fixed in advance, it is chargeable at the rate applicable on the day when the competent customs authority accepts the document expressing the intention to export subject to a levy.[7] The Member State in the territory of which these customs export formalities are completed is required to collect the levy.[8] Where the rate of levy varies according to the destination of the product, a security is required of the exporter,[9] who, subject to force majeure, is required

---

11 Commission Regulation 120/89 Art 1, OJ 20.1.89 L16/19, as amended by Commission Regulation 1431/93, OJ 10.6.93 L140/27. As to specific products, see below.
12 They were originally introduced by Council Regulation 2742/75 Art 6(2), OJ 1.11.75 L281/57 and Council Regulation 2747/75 Art 2(1), first indent, OJ 1.11.75 L281/82. Neither measure is currently in force.
13 See Council Regulation 136/66 Art 20(1), second indent, OJ 30.9.66 L172/3025, as substituted by Council Regulation 1562/78, OJ 7.7.78 L185/1.
14 See Council Regulation 1785/81 Art 18(1),(4), OJ 1.7.81 L177/4.
15 They were originally introduced by Council Regulation 1603/74 Art 1(1), OJ 27.6.74 L172/9. This measure is no longer in force.
16 They were originally introduced by Council Regulation 520/77 Art 1(1), OJ 21.3.77 L73/26. This measure is no longer in force.
17 Ie in Commission Regulation 120/89, OJ 20.1.89 L16/19, as amended by Commission Regulation 1431/93, OJ 10.6.93 L140/27.
18 EC Art 9(2) refers to products originating in Member States and to products coming from third countries which are in free circulation in Member States.
19 Commission Regulation 120/89 Art 2(1), OJ 20.1.89 L16/19, as amended by Commission Regulation 1431/93, OJ 10.6.93 L140/27.
20 Ibid Art 2(2). As to the movement within the Community of products subject to a levy, see Art 8.
1 Ibid Art 3(1).
2 Ibid Art 3(1).
3 Ibid Art 3(2)(a).
4 Ibid Art 3(2)(b).
5 Ibid Art 3(2)(c).
6 Ibid Art 3(2)(d). See also Art 3(2)(e), and Commission Regulation 565/80 Arts 4, 5, OJ 7.3.80 L62/5, as amended by Commission Regulation 2026/83, OJ 22.7.83 L199/2.
7 Commission Regulation 120/89 Art 4, OJ 20.1.89 L16/19.
8 Ibid Art 5(1).
9 Ibid Art 5(2)(a). The security may be either a cash deposit or an approved guarantee: Art 5(2)(f).

to furnish proof within six months of the completion of customs export formalities that the product has reached a destination.[10] When such proof is furnished the security will be released in whole or in part according to the destination reached and the resulting amount of levy.[11] When such proof is not furnished, subject to force majeure, the product will be deemed to have reached a destination in which the highest rate of levy is chargeable and the security will be forfeit and treated as a levy.[12] If, by reason of force majeure, the time limit is not observed, the competent national authorities may, upon request, extend the time limit for such period as is considered necessary in view of the circumstances.[13] Special rules are laid down in respect of products which re-enter the Community[14] and products with a station of destination within the Community,[15] and in respect of inward processing.[16] Where a levy greater than zero is chargeable on a product, the party concerned may, subject to certain conditions,[17] request the cancellation of an export licence or withdraw an application for an export licence for the product[18] with the consequence that the relevant security will be released.[19] Special rules govern the supply of agricultural products to certain areas such as the smaller Aegean islands.[20]

SPECIFIC PRODUCTS

Bananas

Until 1993 banana imports into the Community were governed by a variety of national market organizations or special measures. In 1957 the Community concluded, on the basis of EEC Art 136, an Implementing Convention on the Association of Overseas Countries and Territories.[1] Annexed to the Convention was a Procotol on the tariff quota for imports of bananas (the so-called 'German banana Protocol'). It permitted Germany to import free of duty an agreed annual amount of bananas ('dollar bananas') from Latin American countries. Other banana imports were governed by national measures. Subsequently, however, the third Lome Convention, in particular its Fourth Protocol, provided for banana imports from ACP countries.[2] This provision was reaffirmed by the fourth Lome Convention, the Fifth Protocol of which supplemented the Lome III provisions by recording the agreement of the parties to protect the position of 'traditional suppliers'.[3] At the same time, however, a declaration annexed to

---

10 Ibid Art 5(2)(b), OJ 20.1.89 L16/19.
11 Ibid Art 5(2)(d),(e).
12 Ibid Art 5(2)(c).
13 Ibid Art 5(3).
14 Ibid Art 7.
15 Ibid Art 8.
16 Ibid Art 9.
17 See ibid Art 12(1)(a)–(c).
18 Ibid Art 12(1).
19 Ibid Art 12, second paragraph.
20 See Council Regulation 2019/93, OJ 27.7.93 L184/1, as amended, and, in respect of implementing measures, Commission Regulation 2958/93, OJ 28.10.93 L267/4, as amended. Cereals are an example: see Commission Regulation 3175/94, OJ 23.12.94 L335/54, as amended.
 1 See Annex IV of the Treaty of Rome.
 2 As to the Lome Convention, see Chapter 28 below on the African, Caribbean and Pacific countries in Part III on Preferential Arrangements and Bilateral Agreements.
 3 Fourth ACP-EC Convention of Lome as revised by the Agreement signed in Mauritius on 4 November 1995, preamble and Protocol No 5, Art 1 (1996) 155 *The Courier* (January-

the Fifth Protocol provided that the Protocol would not prevent the Community from establishing common rules for bananas, so long as the traditional ACP suppliers were not placed, with regard to access to the Community market, in a position less favourable than in the past or at the present.[4]

In 1993 the Community replaced the various national measures by a common organization of the market in bananas.[5] Designed to help achieve the single market, it was intended to create 'a balanced and flexible' regime to permit the free movement of bananas within the Community and the implementation of common arrangements with third countries.[6] The common organization consists of common quality and marketing standards, assistance to producers, and provisions concerning trade with third countries. Unless otherwise provided, it applies to fresh, dried, preserved or frozen bananas; powder and flakes of bananas; homogenized preparations of bananas; jams, jellies,

February). See also Joined Cases C-228/90 to C-234/90, C-339/90 and C-353/90 *Simba SpA v Ministero delle Finanze (Dogane di Savona e della Spezia)* [1992] ECR I-3713; and Case C-469/93 *Amministrazione delle Finanze dello Stato v Chiquita Italia SpA* [1995] ECR I-4533.

4 Lome IV, Annex LXXIV, added a Declaration regarding Protocol No 5. Neither the Declaration nor the Protocol applied to Haiti or the Dominican Republic, which were considered to be new signatories of the Lome Convention and thus excluded from the category of traditional suppliers: see Lome IV, Annex LXXV, Declaration of the Community regarding Protocol No 5.

5 Council Regulation 404/93, OJ 25.2.93 L47/1. The Regulation provoked very substantial litigation. Germany brought an ultimately unsuccessful action to annul Title IV on trade with third countries, as well as Art 21(2) discontinuing the tariff quota laid down in the 'German banana protocol': Case C-280/93 *Germany v Council* [1994] ECR I-4973. A German action *ex* EC Art 186 for interim measures was rejected: Case C-280/93R *Germany v Council* [1993] ECR I-3667. A number of banana importers brought actions *ex* EC Art 173 to annul certain provisions of the Regulation. In the following cases, the European Court of Justice declared a suit inadmissible for want of direct and individual concern, while at the same time preserving the action insofar as they sought an order requiring the Community to make good any damage caused by the adoption of the Regulation if the action by Germany should lead to the annulment of the regime: Case C-256/93 *Pacific Fruit Co NV and Pacific Fruit Co BV v Council and Commission*, 21.6.93, OJ 10.8.93 C215/10; Case C-257/93 *Leon Van Parijs v Council and Commission* [1993] ECR I-3335; Case C-262/93 *Anton Durbeck GmbH v Council and Commission*, 21.6.93, OJ 10.8.93 C215/11; Case C-282/93 *Comafrica SpA v Council and Commission*, 21.6.93, OJ 10.8.93 C215/12; Case C-283/93 *Pacific Fruit Co Italy SpA v Council and Commission*, 21.6.93, OJ 10.8.93 C215/13; Case C-286/93 *Atlanta AG v Council and Commission*, 21.6.93, OJ 10.8.93 C215/13. Several cases for annulment only were dismissed: Case C-276/93 *Chiquita Banana Co BV v Council* [1993] ECR I-3345; Case C-287/93 *Simba SpA v Council*, 21.6.93, OJ 10.8.93 C215/14. Two applications for interim measures were also dismissed: Case C-282/93R *Comafrica SpA v Council and Commission* (6 July 1993, unreported) English transcript; Case C-276/93 *Chiquita Banana Company BV v Council* [1993] ECR I-3345. In Case C-465/93 *Atlanta Fruchthandelsgesellschaft mbH v Bundesamt für Ernahrung und Forstwirtschaft* [1995] ECR 3761, the European Court of Justice held, in effect, that a German banana importer was entitled to an order granting additional import licences for third-country bananas for the second half of 1993, over and above the quantities already allocated, until the Court of Justice decided the question of validity. It stated that EC Art 189 is to be interpreted as not precluding national courts from granting interim relief to settle or regulate the disputed legal positions or relationships with reference to a national administrative measure based on a Community regulation which is the subject of a reference for a preliminary ruling on its validity. On the same day the European Court of Justice held *ex* Art 177 that the import regime provided in the common market organization in bananas was compatible with Commuity law: Case C-466/93 *Atlanta Fruchthandelsgesellschaft mbH v Bundesamt für Ernahrung und Forstwirtschaft* [1995] ECR I-3799. See also Joined Cases C-71/95, C-155/95 and C-271/95 *Belgium v Commission* [1997] ECR I-687 and Case C-369/95 *Somalfruit SpA and Camar SpA v Ministero delle Finanze and Ministero del Commercio con l'Estero* [1997] ECR I-6619.

6 See Council Regulation 404/93, Preamble, seventh recital OJ 25.2.93 L47/1.

marmalades, purees and pastes of bananas; bananas otherwise prepared: mixtures of bananas, and banana juice.[7] However, the most important provisions concerning trade with third countries apply only to fresh products falling within CN code ex 0803, excluding plantains.[8] In 1997 the Dispute Settlement Body of the World Trade Organization declared numerous aspects of the common organization of the banana market to be incompatible with GATT 1994.[9] The EU must bring its rules into compliance with WTO rules by 1 January 1999 at the latest.[10] The following paragraphs describe the market organization that was originally enacted and that is currently being revised.[11]

Quality standards apply to all banana imports. They are to be laid down for bananas intended to be supplied fresh to the consumer.[12] Marketing standards may also be laid down for processed products made from bananas.[13] Unless the Commission decides otherwise,[14] products for which common standards have been laid down may be marketed in the Community only if they comply with those standards.[15]

Compensation for loss of income is available to Community producers who are members of a recognized producers' organization which is marketing in the Community bananas complying with the common standards laid down.[16] Individual producers are eligible for compensation in specified instances.[17] The producer regions in the Community are the Canary Islands, Guadeloupe, Martinique, Madeira, the Azores and the Algarve, and Crete and Lakonia.[18]

With regard to import duties, unless otherwise provided, the rates of duty in the CCT apply to producers covered by the common organization.[19]

An importation of bananas into the Community is subject to the submission of an import licence.[20] The licence is issued by a Member State at the request of any party concerned.[1] It is valid throughout the Community and is subject to the provision of security.[2]

Imports of bananas into the Community are classified into three categories: traditional imports from ACP States, non-traditional imports from ACP States,

---

7 Ibid Art 1(2), as adjusted by Commission Regulation 3518/93, OJ 22.12.93 L320/15.
8 Ibid Art 15a, as substituted by Council Regulation 3290/94 Annex XV, OJ 31.12.94 L349/105.
9 See 'European Communities—Regime for the Importation, Sale and Distribution of Bananas' (WT//DS527/AB/R), (1997) 2 ITLR 528 (Appellate Body Report).
10 By agreement of the contending parties, within the framework of the 1994 WTO Dispute Settlement Understanding, Art 21.3.
11 See *Agence Europe* No 7160 (n.s.), Saturday, 14 February 1998; No 7199 (n.s.), Friday, 10 April 1998, p 9.
12 Ibid Art 2(1).
13 Ibid Art 2(2).
14 According to the management committee procedure: ibid Arts 3(1), 27.
15 Ibid Art 3(1). Checks for this purpose may be carried out by the bodies designated by the Member States: ibid Art 3(2).
16 Ibid Art 12(1). Detailed rules as regards the aid scheme to compensate for loss of income are laid down in Commission Regulation 1858/93, OJ 13.7.93 L170/5.
17 Ibid.
18 Council Regulation 404/93 Art 12(2), OJ 25.2.93 L47/1.
19 Ibid Art 15, as substituted by Council Regulation 3290/94 Annex XV, 31.12.94 L349/105. However, a derogation is provided for imports of so-called 'non-traditional ACP bananas': ibid Art 18(2), as so substituted. The general rules for the interpretation of the combined nomenclature and the special rules for its application apply to the classification of products covered by the common organization, and the tariff nomenclature resulting from the Regulation is incorporated in the CCT: ibid Art 22, as so substituted.
20 Council Regulation 404/93 Art 17, first paragraph, OJ 25.2.93 L47/1.
 1 Ibid Art 17, first paragraph.
 2 Ibid Art 17, second paragraph.

and imports from non-ACP third countries.[3] This classification is the basis for determining any applicable quotas, any applicable duty and the allocation of import licences.

Traditional ACP bananas up to specified amounts may be imported into the Community free of duty.[4]

For imports of non-traditional ACP bananas and third country bananas a tariff quota of 2.2 million tonnes (net weight) is opened each year.[5] The quota is divided into specific shares allocated to specified countries or groups of countries,[6] largely as a result of the Framework Agreement on Bananas concluded within the Uruguay Round.[7] Provision is made for an increase in the allocated quantities when the tariff quota is increased.[8] Limited provision is also made for the possibility of reallocation of unused quota within a group and from one group to another, though quota cannot be reallocated within or towards non-traditional ACP quantites.[9]

Within the framework of the quota, imports of non-traditional ACP bananas are subject to a zero duty, and imports of third country bananas are subject to a levy of Ecu 75 per tonne.[10] Outside the framework of the tariff quota, imports of non-traditional ACP bananas are subject to a customs duty per tonne equal to the rate of duty in the CCT, less Ecu 100,[11] while imports of third country

3 Ibid Art 15a, second paragraph, as added by Council Regulation 3290/94, OJ 31.12.94 L349/105. This paragraph defines the categories as follows. 'Traditional imports from ACP States' ('traditional ACP bananas') means the quantities of bananas set out in the Annex to the Regulation exported by each ACP State which has traditionally exported bananas to the Community. 'Non-traditional imports from ACP States' ('non-traditional bananas') means the quantities of bananas exported by the ACP States which exceed the quantity set out in the Annex. 'Imports from non-ACP third countries' means quantities exported by other third countries. The first two categories are based on the criteria of supplier and quantity, whereas the third category is based on the criteria of supplier only.

4 The specified amounts (in tonnes/net weight) for each country are as follows: Ivory Coast 155,000; Cameroon 155,000; Surinam 38,000; Somalia 60,000; Jamaica 105,000; St Lucia 127,000; St Vincent and the Grenadine 82,000; Dominica 71,000; Belize 40,000; Cape Verde 4,800; Grenada 14,000; Madagascar 5,900: Regulation 404/93, Annex, OJ 25.2.93 L47/1.

5 Ibid Art 18(1), first paragraph, as substituted by Council Regulation, 3290/94, OJ 31,.12.94 L349/105. Re-exported bananas, whether non-traditional or third country, are not charged to the tariff quota: ibid Art 18(3), as so substituted.

6 Commission Regulation 478/95 Art 1(1), Annex I, OJ 4.3.95 L49/13. The groups and shares are: Table 1: Colombia 21.0%, Costa Rica 23.4%, Nicaragua 3.0%, Venezuela 2.0%; Table 2 (non-traditional ACP quantities): Dominican Republic 55,000 tonnes, Belize 15,000 tonnes, Ivory Coast 7,500 tonnes, Cameroon 7,500 tonnes, other ACP countries 5,000 tonnes; Table 3: Others: 50.6%—90,000 tonnes.

7 See Commission Regulation 3224/94, OJ 24.12.94 L337/72. The Agreement was necessary because the tariff import arrangements provided in the common organization of the market for bananas replaced the 20% duty on banana imports which was previously consolidated in GATT. It was concluded with Colombia, Costa Rica, Nicaragua and Venezuela. The Agreement was challenged by Germany, but the European Court of Justice held that it was not necessary to give an opinion because before the case was heard the Agreement had already been concluded: Opinion 3/84, GATT-WTO-Framework Agreement on Bananas [1995] ECR I-4577. However, the European Court of Justice has annulled part of this Agreement in so far as it exempts certain categories of operators from its export-licensing system: see Case C-122/95 *Germany v Council*, (10 March 1998, unreported).

8 Commission Regulation 478/95 Art 1(2),(3) OJ 24.12.94 L337/72.

9 Ibid Art 2. See also Joined Cases C-9, 23 and 156/95 *Belgium and France v Commission* [1997] 3 CMLR 511.

10 Ibid Art 18(1), second paragraph, as so substituted. Provision is also made for the volume of the quota to be increased when Community demand in relation to supply increases: see ibid Art 18(1), fourth paragraph, as so substituted.

11 Ibid Art 18(2), as so substituted.

bananas remain subject to the CCT rate.[12] The tariff quota laid down in the 1957 'German banana protocol' is discontinued.[13]

With regard to the allocation of import licences, the tariff quota is distributed as follows: 66.5 per cent to the category of operators who marketed third country and/or non-traditional ACP bananas; 30 per cent to the category of operators who marketed Community and/or traditional ACP bananas, and 3.5 per cent to the category of operators established in the Community who started marketing bananas other than Community and/or traditional ACP bananas from 1992.[14] Access to the quota for the first two categories is restricted to operators established in the Community who marketed on their own account a minimum quantity of bananas of the respective origins.[15] Import licences are to be allocated on the basis of the average quantities of bananas sold by the operator in the three most recent years for which figures are available.[16]

Except as otherwise provided by the common organization, it is forbidden to levy any charge having an effect equivalent to a customs duty, or apply any quantitative measure or measure having equivalent effect.[17]

In respect of bananas, two types of safeguard measures are provided.

First, special safeguard measures in the form of an additional import duty may be imposed if the conditions set out in Art 5 of the Uruguay Round Agreement on Agriculture are fulfilled, unless the imports are unlikely to disturb the Community market or where the effects would be disproportionate to the intended objective.[18]

Second, general safeguard measures may be taken if, by reason of imports or exports, the Community market is affected by, or is threatened with, serious disturbance likely to jeopardize the objectives of the Common

---

12 Ibid Art 15(1).

13 Ibid Art 21(2).

14 Council Regulation 404/93 Art 19(1), first paragraph, OJ 25.2.93 L47/6. The Commission has proposed that the allocation by volume and the administration of the tariff quota should be based on the criterion of effective importation, instead of marketing, and that these provisions be amended accordingly: see OJ 3.6.95 C136/18.

15 Ibid Art 19(1), second paragraph. Supplementary criteria are to be laid down, and Member States are to draw up a list of importers: ibid Art 19(1), third paragraph. As to detailed rules for the application of these import arrangements, see Commission Regulation 1442/93, OJ 12.6.93 L142/7. With regard to 'Category C operators', the Court of Justice has held that (1) the expression has the same meaning in Council Regulation 404/93 Art 19(1)(c) and in Commission Regulation 1442/93 Art 2(c); (2) when applying for registration under Category C, an operator must not have already developed an activity aimed at marketing bananas; (3) an operator may apply for registration under Category C even if he intends to transfer the import licence to a third party; (4) economic operators who entered into business prior to 1992 with a view to importing the bananas specified in Regulation 1442/93 Art 2(c) and who imported those bananas in 1992 or later can be registered as Category C operators; and (5) Regulation 1442/93 Art 3(2), which provides that wholesalers and retailers are not to be regarded as operators, is not applicable to the concept of operator within the meaning of Art 2(c) of that Regulation: Case C-389/93 *Anton Durbeck GmbH v Bundesamt für Ernahrung und Forstwirtschaft* [1995] ECR I-1309. As to the validity of the fixing of a uniform reduction coefficient for determining the quantities of bananas to be allocated to each operator in certain categories in the context of the tariff quota, see Case C-478/93 *Netherlands v Commission* [1995] ECR I-3081.

16 Council Regulation 404/93 Art 19(2), first paragraph, OJ 25.2.93 L47/6 which also establishes which categories of sales are to be taken into account. As to cases of hardship, see Case C-68/95 *T Port GmbH & Co v Bundesanstalt* [1996] ECR I-6065. This case led to the creation of a special reserve within the tariff quota: see Commission Regulation 1154/97, OJ 26.6.97 L168/65.

17 Ibid Art 21(1).

18 Ibid Art 15(2), as so substituted. As to the trigger prices and trigger volumes, see ibid Art 15(3).

Agricultural Policy.[19] Such measures are to be decided by the Commission, either at the request of a Member State or on its own initiative. They are immediately applicable, but must be notified to the Member States.[20] Within three working days of the notification a Member State may refer the measures to the Council. Acting by a qualified majority, the Council may amend or annul the measure in question.[1]

Beef and veal

The common organization of the market in beef and veal takes the form of a single price system within the Community and a single trading system at the Community's external frontiers.[2] It applies to domestic bovine animal[3] products and extends to live animals; fresh, chilled, frozen and prepared or preserved meat and edible offals; fats of bovine cattle; and other prepared or preserved meat products which contain bovine meat or offal.[4]

A system of import and export licences is applied to trade in beef and veal products.[5] Licences are required to import into the Community a range of such products.[6] In other cases imports and exports may be made conditional on the production of an appropriate licence.[7]

Imports of all products which are subject to the common organization of the market in beef and veal are subject to the relevant rates of duty laid down by the Common Customs Tariff.[8] The tariff classification of those products is subject to the general rules for the interpretation of and the special rules for the application of the Common Customs Tariff and is incorporated in it.[9] In the absence of specific derogations,[10] the levying of any other charge which is equivalent in its effect to a customs duty and the application of any quantita-

---

19 That is, as set down in EC Art 39: ibid Art 23, as so substituted. Such measures may be taken only until the disturbance or threat of disturbance has ceased: ibid.
20 Ibid Art 23(2).
 1 Ibid Art 23(3).
 2 The common organization of the market in beef and veal was established by Council Regulation 805/68, OJ 28.6.68 L148/24, as amended.
 3 'Bovine animals' means live animals of the domestic bovine species other than pure-bred breeding animals, falling within subheadings 0102.90.10 and 0102.90.37 of the Common Customs Tariff: Council Regulation 805/68 Art 1(2)(a), OJ 28.6.68 L148/24, as substituted by Council Regulation 3905/87, OJ 30.12.87 L370/7. Wild buffalo are included: Case 309/81 *HP Klughardt oHG v Hauptzollamt Hamburg-St Annen* [1982] ECR 4291.
 4 Council Regulation 805/68 Art 1(1), as substituted.
 5 Ibid Art 9, as substituted by Council Regulation 3290/94 Arts 1, 2, Annex VIII, OJ 31.12.94 L349/105. For special detailed rules concerning import and export licences for beef and veal, see Commission Regulation 1445/95, OJ 27.6.95 L143/35 as amended. As to management measures on imports, see Commission Regulation 3076/94, OJ 17.12.94 L325/8. As to certain transitional measures regarding export licences, see Commission Regulation 1182/95, OJ 25.5.95 L118/45.
 6 EC Council Regulation 805/68 Art 9(1), first paragraph, as substituted by Council Regulation 3290/94, OJ 31.12.94 L349/105.
 7 Ibid Art 9(1), second paragraph, as substituted by Council Regulation 3290/94, OJ 31.12.94 L349/105.
 8 Ibid Art 10, OJ 28.6.68 L148/24, as substituted by Council Regulation 3290/94 Arts 1, 2, Annex VIII, OJ 31.12.94 L349/105.
 9 Ibid Art 15(1), as substituted by Council Regulation 3290/94 Arts 1, 2, Annex VIII, OJ 31.12.94 L349/105.
10 See also Case 70/77 *Simmenthal SpA v Amministrazione delle Finanze dello Stato* [1978] ECR 1453.

tive restriction or a measure having equivalent effect are prohibited in trade with third countries.[11] Charges which are levied in respect of public and veterinary health inspections of products imported from third countries which are determined according to their own particular criteria, and which are not comparable to the criteria used as a basis for charges which might be levied on similar Community products, will be regarded as charges which are equivalent to customs duties.[12]

In addition to being subject to the CCT, certain categories of imports are subject to import tariffs or fixed duties.[13] These fixed duties replaced the previous system of variable import levies and are to be progressively reduced.

Special concessionary import schemes were agreed under the GATT and were continued in similar terms under the WTO Agreement. They apply to various categories of products: frozen beef and veal;[14] specified mountain breeds and Alpine cattle;[15] high quality cuts and frozen Buffalo meat;[16] and frozen thin skirt.[17]

Special provisions are laid down for imports of pure-bred animals for breeding.[18] Quotas are also set for the import at nil or reduced levy, but subject to customs duty, of manufacturing grade beef[19] or of young male cattle for fattening.[20]

Under the Lome Convention special arrangements apply to annual import quota for beef from six African ACP countries: Botswana, Kenya, Madagascar, Swaziland, Zimbabwe and Namibia.[1]

---

11 Council Regulation 805/68 Art 15(2), as substituted by Council Regulation 3290/94 Arts 1, 2, Annex VIII, OJ 31.12.94 L349/105.
12 Case 21/75 *I Schroeder KG v Oberstadtdirektor der Koln* [1975] ECR 905.
13 Council Regulation 805/68 Art 11, as substituted. The relevant products include, for example, fresh, chilled and frozen beef and veal: see Commission Regulation 139/81, OJ 17.1.81 L15/74, corrected by Commission Regulation 1652/87, OJ 13.6.87 L153/33, and amended by Commission Regulation 3988/87, OJ 31.12.87 L376/31, and Commission Regulation 1476/92, OJ 6.6.92 L155/28.
14 See Commission Regulation 1042/97, OJ 11.6.97 L152/2. As to frozen beef intended for processing, see Commission Regulation 1006/97, OJ 5.6.97 L145/10.
15 Commission Regulation 935/97, OJ 28.5.97 L137/3.
16 Commission Regulation 936/97, OJ 28.5.97 L137/10; Commission Regulation 1323/97, OJ 10.7.97 L182/12.
17 Commission Regulation 996/97, OJ 4.6.97 L144/6.
18 Commission Regulation 2342/92, OJ 11.8.92 L227/12, amended by Commission Regulation 3224/92, OJ 5.11.92 L320/30, Commission Regulation 3661/92, OJ 19.12.92 L370/16, and Commission Regulation 286/93, OJ 10.2.93 L34/7.
19 See Commission Regulation 1136/79, OJ 9.6.79 L141/10, corrected by Commission Regulation 3584/81, OJ 15.12.81 L359/12, and amended by the following Commission Regulations: 410/84, OJ 18.2.84 L48/11, 2036/84, OJ 17.7.84 L189/14, 1121/87, OJ 24.4.87 L109/12, 3988/87, OJ 31.12.87 L376/31, 817/89, OJ 31.3.89 L86/37, and 3661/92, OJ 19.12.92 L370/16. See also Commission Regulation 3172/94, OJ 23.12.94 L335/50, amended by Commission Regulation 844/95, OJ 19.4.95 L85/20; and Commission Regulation 757/95, OJ 4.4.95 L75/10. Requirements for this purpose are estimated at six-month intervals: see Council Estimate 94/792 for the period 1 January to 30 June 1995, OJ 16.12.94 L323/48.
20 See Commission Regulation 612/77, OJ 25.3.77 L77/18, amended by Commission Regulation 1384/77, OJ 28.6.77 L157/16, Commission Regulation 411/84, OJ 18.2.84 L48/12, and Commission Regulation 1121/87, OJ 24.4.87 L109/12. See also Commission Regulation 692/95, OJ 31.3.95 L71/48. Requirements are estimated at six-month intervals: see Council Estimate 94/791, OJ 16.12.94 L323/46.
1 See Council Regulation 715/90, OJ 30.3.90 L84/85, as temporarily adapted (until 30 June 1996) with a view to the implementation of the Uruguay Round Agreement on Agriculture by Commission Regulation 1636/95, OJ 6.7.95 L155/25. See also Commission Decision 95/182, OJ 30.5.95 L119/35. As to the Lome Convention, see also Chapter 28 on the African, Caribbean and Pacific countries in this book.

Tariff quotas resulting from agreements concluded within the framework of the Uruguay Round are to be opened and administered according to detailed rules to be adopted by the management committee procedure.[2] The quotas are to be administered according to the 'first come, first served' principle, the 'simultaneous examination' method, the 'traditional/new arrivals' method, a combination of these, or other appropriate methods.[3]

A Supplementary Trade Mechanism (STM) was previously introduced on the accession of Spain and Portugal to monitor trade between these countries and the rest of the Community.[4] It set indicative ceilings which at this time apply only to third country imports into Spain.[5]

Special arrangements[6] apply under Association Agreements with regard to imports from Poland,[7] Hungary,[8] the Czech Republic,[9] the Slovak Republic,[10]

2 Council Regulation 805/68 Art 12(1), as substituted by Council Regulation 3290/94 Arts 1, 2, Annex VIII, OJ 31.12.94 L349/105.

3 Ibid Art 12(2), as substituted. The method of administration of quotas must, where appropriate, give due weight to the supply requirements of the Community market and the need to safeguard the equilibrium of that market, whilst at the same time possibly drawing on methods which have been applied in the past to similar quotas, without prejudice to the rights resulting from agreements concluded as part of the Uruguay Round negotiations: see ibid Art 12(3).

4 See Commission Regulation 887/88, OJ 1.7.88 L166/26; Commission Regulation 3913/89, OJ 23.12.89 L375/28; Commission Regulation 3270/90, OJ 14.11.90 L314/5; Commission Regulation 1871/91, OJ 29.6.91 L168/59; Commission Regulation 3059/91, OJ 19.10.91 L289/22; Commission Regulation 3718/91, OJ 20.12.91 L351/25; Commission Regulation 1038/92, OJ 28.4.92 L110/41; Commission Regulation 2148/92, OJ 29.7.92 L214/25; Commission Regulation 3832/92, OJ 31.12.92 L387/49; Commission Regulation 1112/93, OJ 7.5.93 L113/10, as derogated from by Commission Regulation 3520/93, OJ 22.12.93 L320/18 and amended by Commission Regulation 936/94, OJ 28.4.94 L107/27 and Commission Regulation 3083/94, OJ 17.12.94 L325/42.

5 See Commission Regulation 1870/86, OJ 18.6.86 L162/16; Commission Regulation 3060/94, OJ 16.12.94 L323/18.

6 See generally Council Regulation 3066/95, OJ 30.12.95 L328/31, as amended. As to tariff quotas for the first half of 1998, see Commission Regulation 2542/97, OJ 18.12.97 L347/17, and Commission Regulation 2524/97, OJ 17.12.97 L346/48. Preferential treatment goes hand-in-hand, however, with acceptance of Community measures to manage the relevant import market if necessary: see Commission Regulation 1566/95, OJ 1.7.95 L150/95.

7 Council Regulation 3492/93, OJ 21.12.93 L319/4. See also Commission Regulation 1390/94, OJ 18.6.94 L152/20, amended by Commission Regulation 468/95, OJ 3.3.95 L48/4; Commission Regulation 3170/94, OJ 23.12.94 L335/43, amended by Commission Regulation 844/95, OJ 19.4.95 L85/20. See also Commission Decision 92/323 (animal health conditions and veterinary certificates), OJ 30.6.92 L177/18.

8 Council Regulation 3491/93, OJ 21.12.93 L319/1. See also Commission Regulation 1390/94, OJ 18.6.94 L152/20, amended by Commission Regulation 468/95, OJ 3.3.95 L48/4; Commission Regulation 3170/94, OJ 23.12.94 L335/43, amended by Commission Regulation 844/95, OJ 19.4.95 L85/20.

9 Council Regulation 3296/94, OJ 30.12.94 L341/14. Exchange of letters between the European Economic Community and the Czech Republic concerning certain arrangements for live bovine animals, OJ 31.12.94 L360/211, implemented by Council Decision 910/94 OJ 31.12.94 L360/1. See also Commission Regulation 1390/94, OJ 18.6.94 L152/20, amended by Commission Regulation 468/95, OJ 3.3.95 L48/4; Commission Regulation 3170/94, OJ 23.12.94 L335/43, amended by Commission Regulation 844/95, OJ 19.4.95 L85/20.

10 Council Regulation 3297/94, OJ 30.12.94 L341/17. See also Exchange of letters between the European Economic Community and the Slovak Republic concerning certain arrangements for live bovine animals, OJ 31.12.94 L359/211, implemented by Council Decision 909/94 OJ 31.12.94 L359/1. See also Commission Regulation 1390/94, OJ 18.6.94 L152/20, amended by Commission Regulation 468/95, OJ 3.3.95 L48/4; Commission Regulation 3170/94, OJ 23.12.94 L335/43, amended by Commission Regulation 844/95, OJ 19.4.95 L85/20.

Bulgaria,[11] and Romania,[12] and under other agreements with regard to imports from Latvia,[13] Lithuania[14] Estonia[15] and Slovenia.[16] Importation of beef at a reduced levy is also permitted from certain parts of ex-Yugoslavia.[17]

Specific animal health measures apply with regard to imports from particular countries[18] and the export of bovine embryos into the Community.[19]

In order to enable beef and veal products to be exported from the Community on the basis of prices or quotations on the world market, the difference between those prices or quotations and prices within the Community may covered by a scheme of export refunds.[20] The refund payable will be the same for the whole Community, but it may be varied according to the destination of the products exported. Export refunds are fixed by the Commission[1] at least every three months,[2] and are in principle the amount applicable on the day of application.[3] Specific rules have been laid down for export

11 Council Regulation 3383/94, OJ 31.12.94 L368/5. See also Agreement in the form of an exchange of letters between the European Community and Bulgaria concerning certain arrangements for live bovine animals, OJ 31.12.94, implemented by Council Decision 908/94 OJ 31.12.94 L358/1. See also Commission Regulation 1389/94, OJ 18.6.94 L152/16, amended by Commission Regulation 1850/94, OJ 28.7.94 L192/24.

12 Council Regulation 3382/94, OJ 31.12.94 L368/1. See also Agreement in the form of an exchange of letters between the European Community and Romania concerning certain arrangements for live bovine animals, OJ 31.12.94 L357/186, implemented by Council Decision 907/94 OJ 31.12.94 L357/1. See also Commission Regulation 1389/94, OJ 18.6.94 L152/16, amended by Commission Regulation 1850/94, OJ 28.7.94 L192/24.

13 Council Regulation 1276/95, OJ 7.6.95 L124/2.

14 Council Regulation 1277/95, OJ 7.6.95 L124/3.

15 Council Regulation 1275/95, OJ 7.6.95 L124/1.

16 Commission Regulation 481/97, OJ 15.3.97 L75/24.

17 See Council Regulation 70/97, OJ 18.1.97 L16/1, as amended. As to detailed implementing rules for 1998, see Commission Regulation 262/98, OJ 31.1.98 L25/50 and Commission Regulation 546/98, OJ 11.3.98 L72/8, as amended. On adaptation to the Uruguay Round decisions, see Commission Regulation 1424/95, OJ 24.6.95 L141/19.

18 See Commission Decision 92/460 (imports from Switzerland), OJ 7.9.92 L261/1, amended by Commission Decision 92/518, OJ 11.11.92 L325/23 and Commission Decision 94/667, OJ 8.10.94 L260/32; Commission Decision 92/463, OJ 7.9.92 L261/50 (imports from Iceland); Commission Decision 93/491, OJ 10.9.93 L229/18 (imports from new Zealand). See also Commission Decision 91/189 establishing the protocols for the standardization of materials and procedures for veterinary tests and the conditions for the approval of markets in connection with imports, OJ 17.4.91 L96/1.

19 Commission Decision 92/452 establishing lists of embryo collection teams approved in third countries, OJ 92/452, OJ 29.8.92 L250/40, amended by Commission Decision 94/678, OJ 20.10.94 L269/40, Commission Decision 94/737, OJ 15.11.94 L294/37, and Commission Decision 95/93, OJ 1.4.95 L73/86.

20 EC Council Regulation 805/68 Art 13(1), as substituted by Council Regulation 3290/94 Arts 1, 2, Annex VIII, OJ 31.12.94 L349/105. This is only possible however within the limits resulting from agreements concluded in accordance with EC Art 228: ibid see also Commission Regulation 2655/89, OJ 1.9.89 L255/64.

1 This is done by the management committee procedure: ibid Art 13(3), first paragraph. The factors to be taken into account when fixing refunds are set out in ibid Art 13(4), as substituted. See also Commission Regulation 3794/89, OJ 16.12.89 L367/56; Commission Regulation 2715/90, OJ 22.9.90 L258/26; Commission Regulation 704/92, OJ 21.3.92 L75/18; Commission Regulation 811/92, OJ 1.4.92 L86/65; Commission Regulation 1457/93, OJ 12.6.93 L142/55.

2 Ibid Art 13(3), second paragraph, as substituted.

3 Ibid Art 13(7), first paragraph, as substituted. That is, advance fixing of the refund is compulsory. In the case of a differentiated refund, the refund is that applicable on the same day (1) for the destination indicated on the licence, or (2) for the actual destination if it differs from the destination indicated on the licence, in which case the amount applicable may not exceed the amount applicable for the destination indicated on the licence: ibid. As to advance fixing, see Commission Regulation 2721/81, OJ 19.8.71 L2655/17. As to the differentation of ex-

refund arrangements in respect of the welfare of live bovine animals during transport.[4]

Numerous provisions provide for the export of beef products from intervention stocks,[5] in particular to parts of the former Soviet Union.[6] There are also specific measures for supplying the Canary Islands with beef and veal products[7] and with live animals;[8] the Azores and Madeira with beef and veal products[9] and with live animals;[10] and the French overseas departments with live animals[11] and breeding horses.[12]

The use of inward or outward processing arrangements may, in special cases, be prohibited by the Council to the extent necessary for the proper working of the common organization of the market.[13] By way of derogation, however, if a

port refunds for beef from male animals and female animals respectively, see Commission Regulation 32/82, OJ 8.1.82 L4/11, amended by Commission Regulations 752/82, OJ 1.4.82 L86/50, 2304/82, OJ 21.8.82 L246/9, 631/85, OJ 13.3.85 L72/24, 2688/85, OJ 26.9.85 L255/11, and 3169/87, OJ 24.10.87 L301/21. The conditions for granting special export refunds on certain cuts of boned meat were laid down in Commission Regulation 1964/82, OJ 21.7.82 L212/48, amended most recently by Commission Regulation 2469/97, OJ 12.12.97 L341/8. As to certain preserved beef and veal products, see Commission Regulation 2388/84, OJ 18.8.84 L221/28, amended by Commission Regulation 1032/86, OJ 10.4.86 L95/17, Commission Regulation 3425/86, OJ 11.11.86 L316/9, Commission Regulation 3988/87, OJ 31.12.87 L376/31, and Commission Regulation 3661/92, OJ 19.12.92 L370/16. As to the collection of samples in connection with physical checks of boneless beef, see Commission Regulation 2457/97, OJ 11.12.97 L340/29.

4 See Commission Regulation 615/98, OJ 19.3.98 L82/19.

5 See Commission Regulation 2824/85, OJ 10.10.85 L268/14; Commission Regulation 3815/87, OJ 19.12.87 L357/24, as amended; Commission Regulation 910/91, OJ 12.4.91 L91/45, amended by Commission Regulation 2345/91, OJ 2.8.91 L214/29, and Commission Regulation 2891/91, OJ 2.10.91 L275/5; Commission Regulation 1428/92, OJ 2.6.92 L150/11; Commission Regulation 2873/93, OJ 21.10.93 L262/36; Commission Regulation 3208/93, OJ 24.11.93 L289/13; Commission Regulation 3335/93, OJ 4.12.93 L299/15: Commission Regulation 3554/93, OJ 24.12.93 L324/31; Commission Regulation 2178/94, OJ 7.9.94 L233/9; Commission Regulation 2783/94, OJ 17.11.94 L296/8; Commission Regulation 561/95, OJ 15.3.95 L57/55, amended by Commission Regulation 1181/95, OJ 25.5.95 L118/40.

6 With respect specifically to the Soviet Union, see Commission Regulation 1512/91, OJ 5.6.91 L141/21; Commission Regulation 1513/91, OJ 5.6.91 L141/24; Commission Regulation 1582/91, OJ 12.6.91 L147/20, amended by Commission Regulation 2546/91, OJ 28.8.91 L239/5, and Commission Regulation 3061/91, OJ 19.10.91 L289/25; Commission Regulation 2742/91, OJ 19.9.91 L262/13, amended by Commission Regulation 386/92, OJ 19.2.92 L43/14; Commission Regulation 2892/91, OJ 2.10.91 L275/6. See also Commission Regulation 847/92, OJ 3.4.92 L88/49, amended by Commission Regulation 899/92, OJ 9.4.92 L95/48 (Russia); Commission Regulation 3045/92, OJ 23.10.92 L307/24 (Georgia); Commission Regulation 2755/94, OJ 12.11.94 L292/10 (city of Moscow).

7 Commission Regulation 1912/92, OJ 11.7.92 L192/31, as amended. See also Commission Regulation 230/95, OJ 4.2.95 L27/5, and Commission Regulation 882/98, OJ 25.4.98 L124/27.

8 Commission Regulation 2254/92, OJ 4.8.92 L219/34, amended by Commission Regulation 3661/92, OJ 19.12.92 L370/16, Commission Regulation 1736/93, OJ 1.7.93 L160/39, Commission Regulation 3022/94, OJ 14.12.94 L321/4, and Commission Regulation 798/95, OJ 8.4.95 L80/21.

9 Commission Regulation 1913/92, OJ 11.7.92 L192/35, amended by Commission Regulation 2660/92, OJ 15.9.92 L270/5, Commission Regulation 3661/92, OJ 19.12.92 L370/16, Commission Regulation 2139/93, OJ 31.7.93 L191/96, Commission Regulation 577/94, OJ 17.3.94 L74/19, Commission Regulation 2490/94, OJ 15.10.94 L265/19, and Commission Regulation 798/95, OJ 8.4.95 L80/21.

10 Commission Regulation 2255/92, OJ 4.8.92 L219/37, as amended.

11 Commission Regulation 2312/92, OJ 7.8.92 L222/32, as amended, most recently by Commission Regulation 2517/97, OJ 17.12.97 L346/17.

12 Commission Regulation 1148/93, OJ 12.5.93 L116/15, amended most recently by Commission Regulation 2517/97, OJ 17.12.97 L346/17.

13 Council Regulation 804/68 Art 14(1), OJ 28.6.68 L148/24, as substituted.

situation of exceptional urgency arises and the Community market is disturbed or is liable to be disturbed by the inward or outward processing arrangements, the Commission shall, at the request of a Member State or on its own initiative, decide upon the necessary measures.[14] It must inform the Council and the Member States, and the measures can be valid for a maximum of six months. The measures may be referred to the Council by any Member State, and the Council, acting by a qualified majority, may confirm, amend or repeal the Commission decision. If the Council has not acted within three months, the Commission decision is deemed to have been repealed.[15]

In respect of beef and veal, two types of safeguard measures are provided.

First, special safeguard measures in the form of an additional duty are to be applied if the conditions set out in Art 5 of the Agreement on Agriculture[16] are fulfilled. This duty may not be imposed, however, if the imports are unlikely to disturb the Community market, or where the effects would be disproportionate to the intended objective.[17]

Second, if by reason of imports or exports the Community market in any beef or veal products is affected by, or is threatened with, serious disturbances likely to jeopardize the achievement of the objectives of the common agricultural policy, general safeguard measures may be taken in trade with third countries until such disturbances or threat of disturbances have come to an end.[18]

Cereals

The common organization of the market in cereals takes the form of a single price system for cereals within the Community and a single trading system at its external frontiers.[19] The common organization applies to the following cereals: common wheat and meslin; rye; barley; oats; maize and other cereals; durum wheat; wheat or wheat flour; rye flour; cereal groats and cereal meal; and a range of other products such as manioc and processed products including starches, glucose and residues.[20]

A system of import and export licences is applied to cereal products so as to enable trade movements to be monitored in order to assess market trends and to ensure the application of the rules concerning the common organization of the market.[1] Imports into the Community, or exports from it, of any of the cereal products covered by the market organization are subject to the submis-

---

14 Ibid Art 14(2), as substituted.

15 Ibid Art 14(3), as substituted.

16 Council Decision 94/800, Annex Ia, Agreement on Agriculture, Art 5, OJ 23.12.94 L336/22, as to which see above.

17 Council Regulation 805/68 Art 11, as substituted by Council Regulation 3290/94 Arts 1, 2, Annex VIII, OJ 31.12.94 L349/105.

18 Council Regulation 805/68 Art 16(1), as substituted by Council Regulation 3290/94 Arts 1, 2, Annex VIII, OJ 31.12.94 L349/105. The prohibition, in whole or in part, of the use of inward or outward processing arrangements in respect of beef and veal is also authorized to the extent necessary for the proper working of the common organization of the market: Art 14, as substituted.

19 The common organization of the market in cereals is currently laid down in Council Regulation 1766/92, OJ 1.7.92 L181/21, as amended. Annex B of Council Regulation 1766/92 has been replaced by Annex B of Commission Regulation 2193/93, OJ 5.8.93 L196/22.

20 Ibid Art 1, Annex A.

1 Ibid Art 9, as substituted by Council Regulation 3290/94 Annex I, OJ 31.12.94 L349/105. Special detailed rules for the application of the system of licences are provided by Commission Regulation 1162/95, OJ 23.5.95 L117/2 as amended.

sion of a licence.[2] Import and export licences are to be issued by the Member States to any applicant irrespective of the place of its establishment within the Community.[3] They are valid throughout the Community.[4] Applicants must lodge a security[5] which, except in cases of force majeure, will be forfeited in whole or in part if the permitted import or export transaction is not completed during the period of validity of the licence.[6]

Imports of all products covered by the common organization of the market in cereals are subject to the relevant rates of duty laid down in the Common Customs Tariff.[7] The general use of this instrument results from the policy of 'tarification', as agreed during the Uruguay Round. However, as a result of subsequent agreement between the EU and the USA (the so-called 'Blair House II'), a minimum price system is to operate whereby cereals imports should not enter the EU at prices below 155 per cent of the EU intervention price.[8] With regard to the CCT, the general rules for the interpretation of the combined nomenclature and the special rules for its application apply to the tariff classification of cereals products.[9] The levying of any charge having an effect equivalent to a customs duty, or the application of any quantitative restriction or measure having equivalent effect, is prohibited in trade with third countries.[10]

Pursuant to the Uruguay Round agreements, the system of variable import levies which previously operated in the cereals sector has in principle been replaced by tariffs.[11] Tariff quotas may be administered on a 'first come, first served' basis, using the 'simultaneous examination' method or using the 'traditional/new arrivals' method, or any other appropriate method, so long as they avoid any discrimination between the operators concerned.[12] In addition, special arrangements have been adopted with regard to imports of cereals substitutes and processed cereal and rice products from ACP States or the OCT in

2 Ibid Art 9(1), first paragraph. as substituted.
3 Ibid Art 9(1), first paragraph, as substituted. The issue of licences is without prejudice to any measures taken with regard to the application of tariff quotas or export refunds: ibid.
4 Ibid Art 9(1), third paragraph, as substituted.
5 As to rates, see Commission Regulation 1162/95, OJ 24.5.95 L117/2.
6 Ibid Art 9(1), third paragraph, as substituted. As to the Commission's powers concerning the period of validity of licences, see Case 808/79 *Pardini SpA* [1980] ECR 2103.
7 Ibid Art 10(1), as substituted. As to import duties on cereals, see Commission Regulation 898/98, OJ 28.4.98 L126/23.
8 Ibid Art 10(2), as substituted. The products are those products covered by CN codes ex 1001 other than merlin, 1002, 1003, ex 1005 other than hybrid seed, and ex 1007 other than hybrid for sowing. The charge is equal to the intervention price valid for such products on importation and increased by 55%, minus the cif import price applicable to the consignment in question; the duty may not exceed the rate of duty in the CCT: ibid. The method of calculation is laid down in ibid Art 10(3). On detailed rules for the application of these provisions, see ibid Art 10(4). As to import duties on cereals, see Commission Regulation 1249/96, OJ 29.6.96 L161/125, as amended; Commission Regulation 1081/97, OJ 14.6.97 L157/3.
9 Ibid Art 15(1).
10 Ibid Art 15(2).
11 Ibid Art 12(1), as substituted. This is subject to the exception set out in 'Blair House II', above. Detailed rules for administering the quotas are to be adopted according to the management committee procedure: ibid Art 12(1), Art 23. As to the content of these detailed rules, including import quotas for Spain and Portugal, see ibid Art 12(4). As to tariff quotas, see eg Commission Regulation 529/97, OJ 22.3.97 L82/44 (quality wheat).
12 Ibid Art 12(2). The method of administration shall, where appropriate, give due weight to the supply requirements of the Community market and the need to safeguard the equilibrium of that market, whilst at the same time possibly drawing on methods which may have been applied in the past to corresponding quotas, without prejudice to the rights resulting from agreements concluded in the framework of the Uruguay Round negotiations: ibid Art 12(3), as substituted.

order to apply to customs duties the exemption from the fixed component of the levy previously granted to these countries, as well as to replace the concession covering the variable component of the levy by a flat-rate reduction in the import duty in whole or in part.[13]

In order to enable cereal products[14] to be exported from the Community on the basis of prices or quotations on the world market, the difference between those prices or quotations and the price within the Community is covered by a scheme of export refunds.[15] The refund payable will be the same for the whole Community, but it may be varied according to the destination of the product exported.[16] Export refunds are fixed by the Commission at regular intervals or by invitation to tender.[17] For cereals products exported without further processing, they are granted only on application and on presentation of the relevant export licence.[18] The general rule is that refunds must be fixed in advance. They are in principle the amount applicable on the day of application for the licence, or, in the case of a differentiated refund, that applicable on the same day (1) for the destination indicated on the licence or, (2) where appropriate, for the real destination, if it is not the same as that indicated on the licence.[19] The Commission may also fix corrective amounts.[20] Compliance with volume limits pursuant to international agreements thus is to be ensured on the basis of export certificates, but with regard to compliance with the obligations arising under the Agreement on Agriculture the ending of a reference period does not affect the validity of export licences.[1]

To the extent necessary for the proper working of the common organization

---

13 Commission Regulation 2023/95, OJ 23.8.95 L198/15.
14 Either products covered by the common organization (listed in ibid Art 1) or processed products listed in ibid Annex B: ibid Art 13(1).
15 Ibid Art 13(1). Under the Uruguay Round agreement, the EU is committed to reducing its expenditure on export refunds for cereals by 36% between 1995 and 2001. The volume of exports in receipt of export refunds must fall by 21% during the same period. As to provisions to take account of the features of production peculiar to certain spirituous beverages obtained from cereals, see ibid Art 13(9). Detailed rules for the application of the system of export refunds are provided by Commission Regulation 1501/95, OJ 30.6.95 L147/7, as amended. As to the fixing and granting of adjusted refunds in respect of cereals exported in the form of certain spirit drinks, see Commission Regulation 2825/93, OJ 16.10.93 L258/6. See also: Commission Regulation 821/88, OJ 29.6.68 L149/46; Commission Regulation 1680/78, OJ 18.7.78 L193/10; Commission Regulation 1842/82, OJ 4.7.81 L183/10; Commission Regulation 2723/87, OJ 11.9.87 L261/11; Commission Regulation 1349/92, OJ 27.5.92 L145/40; Commission Regulation 2145/92, OJ 30.7.92 L214/20; Commission Regulation 1256/93, OJ 26.5.93 L128/6; Commission Regulation 1501/95, OJ 30.6.95 L147/7; and Commission Regulation 2078/95, OJ 31.8.95 L205/36, all as amended.
16 Ibid Art 13(3), first paragraph. As to monthly adjustments and corrective amounts, see ibid Art 13(8). As to destination zones, see EC Commission Regulation 3817/85, OJ 31.12.85 L368/16. As to the classification of cereals for the purpose of export refunds, see Case 3/81 *Ludwig Wunsche & Co v Bundesanstalt fur landwirtschaftliche Marktordnung* [1982] ECR 2319; Case 145/81 *Hauptzollamt Hamburg-Jonas v Ludwig Wunsche & Co* [1982] ECR 2493.
17 Ibid Art 13(3).
18 Ibid Art 13(4). As to other products, see ibid Art 13(6). As to cereals exported in the form of certain spirit drinks, see Commission Regulation 2825/93, OJ 16.10.93 L258/6.
19 Ibid Art 13(5), first paragraph. If the real destination is not the same as that indicated on the licence, the amount applicable shall not exceed the amount applicable for the destination on the licence: ibid Art 13(5)8b). These provisions concerning granting and amount of refunds may also apply to processed products, that is, those listed in ibid Annex B: see ibid Art 13(6). They may be waived, however, in the case of food-aid products: ibid Art 13(7).
20 Ibid Art 13(8), second paragraph.
 1 Ibid Art 13(10).

of the cereals market, the Council may prohibit, in whole or in part, the use of inward processing arrangements for specified products.[2]

In respect of cereals, three types of safeguard measures are provided.

First, special safeguard measures in the form of an additional import duty may be imposed in order to prevent or counteract adverse effects on the Community market caused by imports if the conditions set out in special safeguard provisions of the Agreement on Agriculture[3] are fulfilled.[4] This additional duty may not be imposed, however, if the imports are unlikely to disturb the Community market, or where the effects would be disproportionate to the intended objective.[5]

Second, general safeguard provisions authorize the taking of appropriate measures necessitated by world prices reaching the level of Community prices and where that situation is likely to continue and to deteriorate, thereby disturbing or threatening to disturb the Community market.[6]

Third, if, by reason of an increase in imports or exports, the Community market in one or more of the products covered by the common organization is affected by, or is threatened with, serious disturbance likely to jeopardize the achievement of the objectives set out in EC Art 39, general safeguard measures may be applied in trade until the disturbance or threat of disturbance has ceased.[7]

The Community has been a party to the International Wheat Agreement of 1986, comprising the Wheat Trade Convention of 1986 and the Food Aid Convention of 1986, as extended, which expired on 30 June 1995.[8] In May 1995 the Commission submitted to the Council a proposal for a Council Decision concerning the approval by the EU of the Cereals Trade Convention and the Food Aid Convention, two distinct legal instruments which together constitute the International Cereals Agreement of 1995.[9]

Dried fodder

The common organization of the market in dried fodder takes the form of a system of aid for the production of dried fodder within the Community and a

2 Ibid Art 14(1). Council measures may be taken only on a proposal by the Commission and after consulting the European Parliament: ibid. A rapid procedure is provided in cases of exceptional urgency and if the Community market is disturbed or likely to be disturbed by inward processing arrangements: ibid Art 14(2), (3). As to the relevant products, see ibid Art 14(1), Art 1 and Annex B.

3 Council Decision 94/800, Annex Ia, Agreement on Agriculture, Art 5, OJ 23.12.94 L336/22, as to which see above.

4 Ibid Art 11(1), as substituted.

5 Ibid. As to trigger prices and trigger quantities, see ibid Art 11(2). As to the determination of the relevant import prices, see ibid Art 11(3). As to the adoption of detailed implementing rules, see ibid Art 11(4).

6 Ibid Art 16. For detailed rules, see Commission Regulation 1501/95, OJ 30.6.95 L147/7 as last amended by Commission Regulation 95/96, OJ 24.1.96 L18/10. As to an export tax on cereals products, see Commission Regulation 965/97, OJ 15.5.97 L123/23.

7 Ibid Art 17(1), first paragraph. General implementing rules are to be adopted by the Council, acting on the basis of EC Art 43, and these are to determine the cases and limits within which Member States may take protective measures: ibid Art 17(1), second paragraph. The measures themselves are to be decided by the Commission, at the request of a Member State or on its own initiative: ibid Art 17(2). However, the Council may on referral by a Member State, and acting by a qualified majority, amend or annul the measure in question: ibid Art 17(3).

8 OJ 17.7.86 L195/2.

9 As to cereals food aid, see Council Regulation 1292/96, OJ 5.7.96 L166/1; Commission Regulation 2200/87, OJ 25.7.87 L204/1; Commission Regulation 538/97, OJ 25.3.97 L83/8.

single trading system at the Community's external frontiers.[10] It applies to various forms of dried fodder produced from lucerne and similar products, protein concentrates obtained from lucerne and grass juices, and dehydrated products obtained from solid residue and juice resulting from the preparation of such concentrates.[11]

The Common Customs Tariff applies to imports of dried fodder from third countries.[12] The general and special rules for the interpretation and application of the tariff apply to the products subject to this common organization of the market and the tariff nomenclature resulting from the application of Community provisions is incorporated in the tariff.[13] In the absence of specific derogating provisions, the levying of any charge equivalent to a customs duty and the application of any quantitative restriction or measure having equivalent effect is prohibited in trade in dried fodder with third countries.[14]

There are no special safeguard measures in respect of dried fodder. However, general safeguard measures apply. If, by reason of imports or exports, the Community market in these products is affected by, or is threatened with, serious disturbance likely to jeopardize the achievement of the objectives of the common agricultural policy, appropriate measures may be taken in trade with third countries until the disturbance or threat of disturbance has ceased.[15] These measures must be applied in compliance with the international obligations of the Community.[16]

Eggs and poultrymeat

The common organizations of the market in eggs and poultrymeat are formally separate in that each has its own enabling regulation.[17] In practice, because of their natural relationship, the arrangements in respect of each particular are almost identical.[18] Their shared dependence on the price of cereal feedingstuffs is also a unifying factor.

The common organization of the market in eggs applies to fresh, preserved or

10 Council Regulation 603/95, 21.3.95 L63/1. As to detailed implementing rules, particularly with regard to aids, see Commission Regulation 787/95, OJ 7.4.95 L79/5.
11 Ibid Art 1. As to certain tariff quotas for the second half of 1995, see Commission Regulation 1440/95, OJ 27.6.95 L143/17.
12 Ibid Art 13.
13 Ibid Art 14(1).
14 Ibid Art 14(2).
15 Ibid Art 15(1). As to the adoption of general implementing rules and the procedures for deciding on, notifying and challenging such measures, see ibid Art 15(2), (3), (4).
16 Ibid Art 15(4). Specific arrangements apply in respect of the supply of dried fodder to the smaller Aegean islands: see Council Regulation 2019/93, OJ 27.7.93 L184/1, as amended, and for detailed rules, see Commission Regulation 2958/93, OJ 28.10.93 L267/4, as amended.
17 As to eggs, see Council Regulation 2771/75, OJ 1.11.75 L282/49, as amended in the light of the Uruguay Round by Council Regulation 1574/93, OJ 24.6.93 L152/1, Council Regulation 3290/94, OJ 31.12.94 L349/105, Council Regulation 1474/95, OJ 29.6.95 L145/19, and Council Regulation 1475/95, OJ 29.6.95 L145/25. As to poultrymeat, see Council Regulation 2777/75, OJ 1.11.75 L282/77, as amended in the light of the Uruguay Round by Council Regulation 1574/93, OJ 24.6.93 L152/1, Council Regulation 3290/94, OJ 31.12.94 L349/105, Council Regulation 1514/95 OJ 30.6.95 L147/45, and Council Regulation 2000/95, OJ 18.8.95 L195/12. Analogous rules apply to ovalbumin and lactalbumin, as to the basic regulation of which see Council Regulation 2783/75, OJ 1.11.75 L282/104, as amended in particular by Council Regulation 3290/94, OJ 31.12.94 L349/105.
18 A single management committee has been established for the two common organizations: ibid Art 16(1) (same Art in the two basic regulations).

cooked poultry eggs in shell[19] and other eggs, not in shell, and other egg yolks suitable for human consumption.[20] The common organization of the market in poultrymeat applies to live chickens, ducks, geese, turkeys and guinea-fowl of domesticated species;[1] fresh, chilled or frozen edible offals thereof;[2] fresh, chilled, frozen or salted poultry liver;[3] types of poultry fat;[4] and other prepared or preserved goose or duck liver, poultrymeat or poultry offal.[5] While providing for marketing standards and action by trade associations, these common organizations largely consist of single trading systems at the external frontiers of the Community.

The Common Customs Tariff of the Community applies to trade in both eggs[6] and poultrymeat.[7] The tariff nomenclature of the products covered by these two market organizations forms part of the Common Customs Tariff and is subject to the general and special rules for its interpretation and application.[8] Unless otherwise provided, the levying of any other customs duty or charge having an equivalent effect and the application of any quantitative restriction or measure having an equivalent effect are prohibited in trade with third countries.[9] In respect of such trade in fresh poultrymeat, charges to cover the cost of public health inspections upon importation are permitted derogations from this general prohibition.[10]

Pursuant to the Uruguay Round agreements, the system of variable levies previously in force in this sector was replaced as of 1 July 1995 by a system of import licences, duties and tariff quotas.[11] Imports or exports may be subject to presentation of licence, issued by the Member States to any applicant, subject to the lodging of a security and valid throughout the Community.[12]

Tariff quotas have been opened as agreed in the Uruguay Round.[13]

19 Council Regulation 2771/75 Art 1, as amended by Council Regulation 1574/94 Art 1, OJ 24.6.93 L152/1. 'Eggs in shell' means poultry eggs in shell, fresh or preserved, other than eggs for hatching: Art 1(2)(a).
20 Ibid Art 1(1).
1 Council Regulation 2775/75, OJ 1.1.75 L282/77 Art 1(1)(a), as amended by Council Regulation 1574/93 Art 2, OJ 24.6.93 L152/1. 'Live poultry' means live fowls, ducks, geese, turkeys and guinea-fowl each weighing more than 185g: Art 1(2)(a).
2 Ibid Art 1(1)(b), as amended.
3 Ibid Art 1(1)(c), as amended.
4 Ibid Art 1(1)(d), (e), as amended.
5 Ibid Art 1(1)(f), as amended.
6 Council Regulation 2771/75 Art 4, as substituted by Council Regulation 3290/94 Annex XI, OJ 31.12.94 L349/105.
7 Council Regulation 2777/75 Art 4, as substituted by Council Regulation 3290/94 Annex XII, OJ 31.12.94 L349/105.
8 Council Regulation 2771/75 Art 10, as so substitued; Council Regulation 2775/75 Art 10, as so substituted.
9 Council Regulation 2771/75 Art 10(2), as so substituted; Council Regulation 2777/75 Art 10(2), as so substituted.
10 See Case 30/79 *Berlin Land v Wigei, Wild-Geflugel-Eier-Import GmbH & Co KG* [1980] ECR 151.
11 Council Regulation 2771/75 Arts 3–6, as substituted by Council Regulation 3290/94 Annex XII, OJ 31.12.94 L349/105; Council Regulation 2777/75 Arts 3–6, as substituted by Council Regulation 3290/94 Annex XI, OJ 31.12.94 L349/105.
12 Ibid Art 3(1), as so substituted.
13 Ibid Art 6(1), as so substituted. As to methods of administering the quotas and the factors to be taken into account in administering them, see ibid Art 6(3),(4), as so substituted. As to such quotas, see Council Regulation 774/94, OJ 8.4.94 L91/1, as amended; Commission Regulation 1431/94, OJ 23.6.94 L156/91, as amended; Commission Regulation 1474/95, OJ 29.6.95 L145/47, as amended; Commission Regulation 1251/96, OJ 29.6.96 L161/136, as amended. As to the administration of quotas in the egg sector and for egg albumin, see Commission Regulation 1474/95, OJ 29.6.95 L145/19, as amended. As to arrrangements with Slovenia, see Commission Regulation 509/97, OJ 21.3.97 L80/3.

To the extent necessary to enable eggs and poultrymeat to be exported from the Community on the basis of the prices for those products on the world market, and within the limits resulting from international agreements, particularly the Uruguay Round, export refunds may be available to cover the difference between those prices and the prices within the Community.[14] Refunds are the same for the whole Community, although they may vary according to destination, where the world market situation or the specific requirements of certain markets make this necessary.[15] The list of products on which an export refund is granted and the amount of the refund is fixed at least once every three months, though the amount of the refund may remain at the same level for a longer period or be adjusted in the interim by the Commission at the request of a Member State or on its own initiative.[16] Refunds are granted only on application and on presentation of the relevant export licence, except in the case of day-old chicks or eggs for hatching for which a licence may be granted *ex post*.[17] In principle, the amount of the refund is that applicable on the date of application for the licence.[18] Refunds are paid upon proof that the products have been exported from the Community, that the products are of Community origin (except for inward processing) and, in the case of a differentiated refund, that the products have reached the destination indicated on the licence or another destination for which a destination was fixed.[19]

There are three types of safeguard measures in respect of eggs and poultrymeat.

First, special safeguard measures in the form of an additional import duty may be taken if necessary to prevent or counteract adverse effects on the Community market resulting from imports and if the conditions set out in Art 5 of the Uruguay Round Agreement on Agriculture are fulfilled, unless the imports are unlikely to disturb the Community market or where the effects would be disproportionate to the intended objective.[20]

Second, general safeguard measures may be taken where prices on the Community market rise significantly and where that situation is likely to continue, thereby disturbing or threatening to disturb that market.[1]

Third, to the extent necessary for the proper working of the common organization of the market, the Council may, in special cases, prohibit in whole or in part the use of inward or outward processing arrangements.[2] If such a situation arises with exceptional urgency and the Community market is disturbed or likely to be disturbed by the inward or outward processing arrangements, the Commission is to decide on the necessary measures, either at the request of a Member State or on its own initiative.[3]

---

14 Ibid Art 8(1), as so substituted. As to derogations in the poultrymeat sector from the common detailed rules regarding export refunds, import and export licences and advance-fixing certificates, see Commission Regulation 437/95, OJ 1.3.95 L45/30, as amended, and Commission Regulation 2000/95, OJ 18.8.95 L195/12.
15 Ibid Art 8(3), as so substituted. As to the factors which are to be taken into account in fixing export refunds, see ibid Art 8(4).
16 Ibid Art 8(3), fourth paragraph, as so substituted.
17 Ibid Art 8(6), as so substituted. As to export licences, see Commission Regulation 1372/95, OJ 17.6.95 L133/26, as amended.
18 Ibid Art 8(7), which also provides for differentiated refunds.
19 Ibid Art 8(9).
20 Ibid Art 5(1). As to the trigger prices, trigger volumes and import prices, see ibid Art 5(2), (3).
 1 Ibid Art 7, first paragraph, as so substituted. General rules for application of this provision are to be adopted by Council on the basis of EC Art 43: ibid second paragraph, as so substituted.
 2 Ibid Art 9(1). The voting procedure is provided in EC Art 43: ibid.
 3 Ibid Art 9(2), as so substituted. As to procedures, see ibid Art 9(2),(3).

Flax and hemp

The common organization of the market in flax and hemp consists of measures directed towards both Community production and trade with third countries.[4] It applies to raw or processed (but not spun) flax and true hemp and both tow and waste of flax and true hemp.[5]

Imports are subject to the Common Customs Tariff. Apart from the duties imposed thereunder, there is a general prohibition in trade with third countries on the levying of any charge which has an effect equivalent to a customs duty[6] and on applying any quantitative restriction or any measure which has an equivalent effect.[7]

In addition, without prejudice to any more restricted measures adopted by Member States, there are conditions for imports of raw true hemp and seed or hemp varieties.[8] Imports are subject to checks to ensure that these conditions are complied with.[9] All imports by natural or legal persons of hemp seed falling within CN code 1207 99 91 is subject to a system of control which shall apply until the seeds are used for a purpose other than sowing.[10] Member States are required to communicate to the Commmission the provisions adopted by them to ensure such controls, and if these provisions do not enable an effective control the amendments which the Member State is to make to them are to be decided by a management committee procedure.[11]

There are no special safeguard measures in respect of flax and hemp. However, general safeguard measures may be applied if, by reason of imports or exports, the Community market is affected by, or is threatened with, serious disturbance likely to jeopardize the achievement of the objectives of the Common Agricultural Policy.[12]

Fruit and vegetables

The common organization of the market in fruit and vegetables lays down common quality standards for the relevant products; involves producers' organizations in the improvement of market structures and in intervention measures; provides a prices and intervention system for internal trade; and establishes a single trading system at the external frontiers of the Community.[13] It applies

---

4 Council Regulation 1308/70, OJ 4.7.70 L146/1, as amended.
5 Ibid Art 1(1), as amended by Council Regulation 3995/87 OJ 31.12.87 L377/34. True hemp includes pulled or garneted rags and hempen ropes: Art 1(1), as so amended.
6 Council Regulation 1308/70 Art 7, first indent, as substituted by Council Regulation 3290/94 Annex VI, OJ 31.12.94 L349/105.
7 Ibid Art 7, second indent, as so substituted.
8 Ibid Art 8(2), (3), as so substituted. For example, the conditions include a limit on the tetrahydrocannabinol content of raw true hemp: ibid Art 8(2). Hemp seed falling within CN code 1207 99 91 may be imported only by research organizations and institutes or natural or legal persons who can provide proof of a sufficient level of activity in the sector concerned: ibid Art 8(5).
9 Ibid Art 8(4), first paragraph. Importing Member States are required to issue a certificate indicating compliance: ibid Art 8(4), second paragraph.
10 Ibid Art 8(6).
11 Ibid Art 8(7). As to the management committee procedure, see ibid Art 12.
12 Ibid Art 8a(1), first paragraph, as so substituted. As to the duration of and the procedures for adopting such measures, see ibid Art 8a(1), second paragraph, (2), (3), (4).
13 Council Regulation 2200/96, OJ 21.11.96 L297/1, which replaced and repealed Council Regulation 1035/72, OJ 20.5.72 L118/1, as amended.

to most fresh fruits and vegetables,[14] with the principal exception of potatoes. With regard to imports, it provides for customs duty, licences, tariff quotas, safeguards and export refunds.

Except as otherwise provided in the basic Regulation,[15] imports are subject to the rates of duty in the Common Customs Tariff.[16] The general rules for the interpretation of the combined nomenclature and the special rules for its application apply to the classification of products, and the tariff nomenclature resulting from the application of the basic Regulation are incorporated in the CCT.[17]

Imports to or exports from the Community of the products covered by the common organization require the presentation of a licence.[18] Import and export licences are issued by the Member States to any applicant, are subject to the lodging of a security, and are valid throughout the Community.[19]

Tariff quotas are to be opened pursuant to the agreements concluded in the framework of the Uruguay Round.[20] They may be administered on a 'first come, first served' basis, by the 'simultaneous examination' method, by the 'traditional/new arrivals' method' or by any other appropriate method.[1] They must however avoid discrimination between the operators concerned.[2]

In addition, products covered by quality standards are accepted for importation from third countries only if they conform to the quality standards or to standards at least equivalent to them. Products covered by quality standards are accepted for export to third countries only if they conform to those standards.[3]

After completion of import formalities, imports of products covered by quality standards are subject to further requirements.[4] The standards apply to fruit and vegetable products to be delivered fresh to the consumer.[5]

Standards have been established by product or group of products and for products for industrial processing.[6] Quality standards have so far been estab-

---

14 Ibid Art 1(2).
15 Eg by ibid Art 33, as to which see below.
16 Ibid Art 32(1). As to the method of determining the entry price, see ibid Art 32(2), (3), (4).
17 Ibid Art 36(2). The Combined Nomenclature codes for fruit and vegetables were amended by Commission Regulation 997/95, OJ 4.5.94 L101/16. As to tomatoes and table grapes, see Commission Regulation 2087/97, OJ 14.11.97 L297/1, and Commission Regulation 2520/97 adapting Council Regulation 2200/96 as regards the combined nomenclature codes for tomatoes and table grapes, OJ 17.12.97 L346/1. As to certain other fruit and vegetables, see Commission Regulation 2086/97, OJ 14.11.97 L312/1, and Commission Regulation 3846/87, OJ 24.12.87 L366/1, as amended most recently by Commission Regulation 2541/97, OJ 18.12.97 L347/14.
18 Ibid Art 31(1).
19 Ibid Art 31(1), second and third paragraphs.
20 Ibid Art 34(1).
1 Ibid Art 34(2), first and second paragraphs. As to factors to be taken into account in the management of tariff quotas, see ibid Art 34(3),(4).
2 Ibid Art 34(2), second paragraph.
3 Ibid Art 9(1), first paragraph. However, derogations may be granted by a management committee procedure to suit the requirements of the intended markets: Art 9(1), second paragraph. Nonetheless, products for export to third countries are subject to a check for compliance with quality standards before they leave the Community customs territory: Art 9(2).
4 Ibid Art 8(2).
5 Ibid Art 2(1). As to the products, see Annex I. Standards for these products are adopted by the management committee procedure, but account is to be taken of the UN/ECE standards recommended by the Economic Commission for Europe's Working Party on perishable product standardization and quality: Art 2(2), first paragraph. Until new standards are adopted, the standards drawn up pursuant to Council Regulation 1035/72 Art 2, continue to apply: Art 2(2), second paragraph. The Commission, by the management committee procedure, may add other products to the covered list: Art 2(3).
6 Ibid Art 2(1), first and third paragraphs.

lished for the following fruit: apricots;[7] cherries and strawberries;[8] and table grapes.[9] Quality standards have also been established for the following vegetables: cauliflower, lettuce, curled-leaved and broad-leaved (Batavian) endives, onions, tomatoes, apricots, peaches and plums;[10] asparagus and cucumbers;[11] garlic;[12] cabbages, brussels sprouts and ribbed celery;[13] leeks, aubergines and courgettes;[14] tomatoes;[15] onions and witloof chicory;[16] sweet peppers;[17] leeks;[18] and various other products.[19]

Three quality classifications for fruit and vegetables are generally specified: 'Extra' Class, Class I, and Class II. However, a Class III classification is permitted when it can be justified by reference to both the economic benefits which the producers derive from the particular product and the need to satisfy the requirements of consumers.[20] In circumstances in which the supply of products which conform to the quality standards is insufficient to meet consumer demand, measures in derogation of the standards may be temporarily applied.[1] In the converse situation, measures may be adopted altering the quality or minimum size requirements for products marketed within the Community.[2]

Products for which quality standards have been laid down will only be accepted for importation from third countries if they conform to the standards for the 'Extra' Class, Class I or Class II or their equivalent[3] and satisfy marking requirements so as to indicate the variety, the country of origin and the quality class.[4] Products to which quality standards apply are similarly not acceptable for export to third countries unless they conform to the 'Extra' Class, Class I or Class II or their equivalent.[5]

General compliance with the quality standards is ensured by a system of checks by sampling at all marketing stages and during transport.[6] The Member

7 Commission Regulation 1108/91, OJ 1.5.91 L110/67.
8 Commission Regulation 899/87, OJ 31.3.87 L88/17.
9 Commission Regulation 1730/87, OJ 23.6.87 L113/25.
10 Council Regulation 23 of 4 April 1962, Annex II. As to plums, see also Commission Regulation 1591/87, OJ 6.6.87 L146/36. As to lettuces, curled-leaved endives and broad-leaved (Batavian) endives, see also Commission Regulation 79/88, OJ 14.1.88 L10/88, as amended.
11 Council Regulation 1677/88, OJ 16.6.88 L150/21.
12 Council Regulation 10/65, OJ 5.2.65 L19/246 (amended by Council Regulation 918/78, OJ 3.5.78 L119/15).
13 Council Regulation 1591/87, OJ 6.6.87 L146/36.
14 Commission Regulation 1292/81, OJ 15.5.81 L129/38 (amended by Commission Regulation 1076/89, OJ 27.4.89 L114/14).
15 Commission Regulation 778/83, OJ 31.3.83 L86/14, as amended.
16 Commission Regulation 2213/83, OJ 4.8.83 L213/13, as amended.
17 Commission Regulation 79/88, OJ 14.1.88 L10/8, as amended.
18 Commission Regulation 1076/89, OJ 27.4.89 L114/14.
19 See Commission Regulation 58, OJ 20.4.62 L30/965, as amended.
20 Council Regulation 1035/72, OJ 20.5.71 L118/1, Art 2(1), second paragraph, Art 4 and 5 (amended by Council Regulation 1117/88, OJ 14.1.88 L10/88). A supplementary class has been added in respect of certain products: see Council Regulation 211/66, OJ 20.12.66 L233/3939, as amended.
1 Council Regulation 1035/72 Art 5(1), OJ 20.5.72 L118/1.
2 Ibid Art 5(2) (amended by Council Regulation 1117/88, OJ 14.1.88 L10/88).
3 Ibid Art 11.
4 Ibid Art 9, second to fourth paragraphs.
5 Council Regulation 1035/72 Art 12, OJ 20.5.72 L118/1.
6 See ibid Title III. As to the consequences of a failure to implement this system, see Case 322/82 *EC Commission v Italy* [1983] ECR 3689. For imports, this may include approval of the official inspection agencies of the exporting country: see ibid Art 10, second paragraph. Exports are subject to a check before leaving the Community customs territory: ibid Art 9(2).

States are under a duty to inform each other and the Commission of the measures which they have taken to implement these provisions.[7]

In order to enable fruit and vegetable products to be exported from the Community in economically significant quantities on the basis of prices on the world market and within the limits resulting from the the Community's international agreements, the difference between those prices and prices within the Community may be covered by a scheme of export refunds.[8] The refund payable will be the same for the whole Community, but it may be varied according to the destination of the product exported.[9] Export refunds are fixed at regular intervals by the management committee procedure and may be adjusted in the intervening period by the Commission, at the request of a Member State or on its own initiative.[10] Refunds are granted on application and presentation of the relevant export licence.[11] The refund payable is that applicable on the day of application for the licence.[12] The refund is paid upon proof that the products have been exported from the Community, that the products are of Community origin, and, in the case of a differentiated refund, that they have reached the destination indicated on the licence or another destination for which a refund is fixed.[13]

Export certificates are to be issued for specific reference periods to ensure compliance with the limits on volumes arising from international agreements. With regard to compliance with the obligations arising under the Agreement on Agriculture, the ending of a reference period does not affect the validity of export licences.[14]

Safeguard measures are of two types.

First, in order to prevent or counteract adverse effects on the Community market which may result from imports, special safeguard measures in the form of an additional import duty may be taken if the conditions set out in Art 5 of the Uruguay Round Agreement on Agriculture are fulfilled, unless the imports are unlikely to disturb the Community market, or where the effects would be disproportionate to the intended objective.[15]

Second, general safeguard measures may be taken when trading with third countries if, by reason of imports or exports, the Community market is affected by, or is threatened with, serious disturbance likely to jeopardize the achievement of the objectives of the Common Agricultural Policy.[16] Such measures

---

7 See ibid Arts 38(1), 44.
8 Ibid Art 35(1).
9 Ibid Art 35(3), first and second paragraphs.
10 Ibid Art 35(3), third and fourth paragraphs. As to the factors to be taken into account in fixing refunds, see ibid Art 35(4).
11 Ibid Art 35(6).
12 Ibid Art 35(7), which also provides for differentiated refunds.
13 Ibid Art 35(9).
14 Ibid Art 35(10).
15 Ibid Art 33(1). As to trigger prices, trigger volumes and the determination of import prices, see ibid Art 33(2),(3). As to rules of application, see Commission Regulation 1555/96, OJ 3.8.96 L193/1, as amended. As to the fundamental importance of the actual import price for the functioning of the protective system, see Joined Cases C-351/93, C-352/93 and C-353/93 *H A van der Linde and Tracotex Holland BV v Minister van Landbouw, Natuurbeheer en Visserij* [1995] ECR I-85.
16 Ibid Art 37(1), first paragraph. In respect of dessert apples from Chile, the European Court of Justice has held that a regulation suspending the issue of import licences is of direct and individual concern to importers whose goods were in transit to the Community at the time of its entry into force, and also that the adoption of the measure without invoking any overriding public interest may give rise to non-contractual liability on the part of the Community: see Case C-152/88 *Sofrimport SARL v Commission* [1990] ECR I-2477. However, in respect

may be applied only until, depending on the case, the disturbance or threat of disturbance has ceased or the quantities withdrawn or bought in have diminished appreciably.[17] The necessary measures are decided by the Commission, at the request of a Member State or on its own initiative.[18] They are immediately applicable but must be notified to the Member States.[19] The latter may refer the measure to the Council, which, acting by a qualified majority, may amend or annul the measure.[20]

Hops

The common organization of the market in hops[1] applies to dried hops[2] and products prepared from hops[3] and, in respect of marketing and trade with third countries, to the largely interchangeable products of hop saps and extracts.[4] It is concerned with regulating marketing by means of a certification procedure; establishing quality standards; requiring the registration of supply contracts; providing for the recognition of producer groups; granting aid both to support the market and to encourage structural improvements; and establishing a system of trade with third countries.

A certification procedure applies to all hops which are harvested within the Community and to products prepared either from such hops or from hops which have been imported from third countries.[5] In order to qualify for the certificate the hops or their derivatives must satisfy the minimum quality standards which are appropriate to a specific stage of marketing.[6] The certificates must testify, at least, to the place of production, the year of harvesting, and the variety.[7] Hops and their derivatives subject to this procedure may only be marketed or exported if a certificate has been issued in respect of them.[8] That

of the same products it subsequently held that a regulation introducing a countervailing charge was neither of direct and individual concern to an importer who had goods in transit nor a breach of the principle of legitimate expectations: Case T-489/93 *Unifruit Hellas EPE v Commission* [1994] ECR II-1201.

17 Ibid Art 37(1), second paragraph. For examples, see Commission Regulation 763/97, OJ 29.4.97 L112/1, as amended, and 1216/97, OJ 28.6.97 L170/48 (fresh sour cherries from Bosnia-Herzegovina, Croatia and FYRM); Commission Regulation 544/97, OJ 26.3.97 L84/8, and 903/97, OJ 22.5.97 L130/6 (garlic from China).

18 Ibid Art37(2). If the Commission receives a request from a Member State, it must take a decision within three working days following receipt of the request: ibid.

19 Ibid Art 37(2).

20 Ibid Art 37(3).

1 The enabling regulation is Council Regulation 1696/71, OJ 4.8.71 L175/1, as amended, and in particular as substituted by Council Regulation 3290/94, OJ 31.12.94 L349/105.

2 Ibid Art 1(1), (3)(a).

3 Ibid Art 2(1), as substituted by Council Regulation 1170/77, OJ 3.6.77 L137/7.

4 Ibid Art 1(2), as substituted by Council Regulation 3998/87, 31.12.87 L377/40. These products are not among the agricultural products listed in the EC Treaty, Annex II. This marketing organization was extended to them under the authority of EC Arts 113 and 235.

5 Ibid Art 2(1), as substituted by Council Regulation 1170/77, OJ 3.6.77 L137/7. For further provisions concerning certification, see Council Regulation 1784/77, OJ 8.8.77 L200/1 as amended and Commission Regulation 890/78, OJ 29.4.78 L117/23 as amended.

6 Ibid Art 2(2), as substituted by Council Regulation 1170/77, OJ 3.6.77 L137/7.

7 Ibid Art 2(3), as substituted by Council Regulation 1170/77, OJ 3.6.77 L137/7.

8 Ibid Art 3(1), as amended by Council Regulation 1170/77, OJ 3.6.77 L137/7. The Community has recognized the equivalence with Community certificates of attestations accompanying hops imported from certain third countries and issued by specified agencies: see Commission Regulation 3077/78, OJ 28.12.78 L367/28, as last amended by Commission Regulation 539/98, OJ 10.3.98 L70/3.

requirement may, however, be waived either in order to satisfy the trade requirements of third countries[9] or in respect of products intended for special
uses[10] provided two conditions are satisfied:

(1) that the normal marketing of certificated products is not prejudiced;[11] and
(2) that there are guarantees intended to obviate confusion with such products.[12]

In a similar way, hops and their derivatives may only be imported into the
Community if they satisfy quality standards which are at least equivalent to
the minimum standards applicable to the marketing of comparable products
which have been harvested within the Community.[13] This requirement may be
satisfied by the imports being accompanied by an attestation issued by the
authorities of the country of origin and recognized as equivalent to the certificate issued by the Community's own certification procedure.[14]

The Common Customs Tariff applies unless otherwise provided to all imports of hops and hop products.[15] The general rules for the interpretation of the
combined nomenclature and the special rules for its application apply to the
classification of these products.[16] In the absence of express provisions to the
contrary, there is a general prohibition in trade with third countries on levying
any charge which has an effect equivalent to a customs duty and on applying
any quantitative restriction or measure which has an equivalent effect.[17]

There are no special safeguards in respect of hops. However, in the event that
the Community market in hops and hop products, by reason of imports and
exports, is affected by, or is threatened with, serious disturbances which may
jeopardize the attainment of the objectives of the common agricultural policy,
general safeguard measures may be applied in trade with third countries until the
disturbance or threat ceases.[18] The necessary measures may be taken by the Commission either on its own initiative or at the request of a Member State.[19] Such
measures are subject to a procedure of referral to and review by the Council.[20]

Live grasses and cut flowers

The common organization of the market in live trees and other plants, bulbs,
roots and the like, cut flowers and ornamental foliage,[1] covers a range of

---

9 Council Regulation 1696/71 Art 3(2), first paragraph (a), OJ 4.8.71 L175/1.
10 Ibid Art 3(2), first paragraph (b).
11 Ibid Art 3(2), second paragraph, first indent.
12 Ibid Art 3(2), second paragraph, second indent.
13 Ibid Art 5(1). For further rules on the importation of hops from third countries, see Commission Regulation 3076/78, OJ 28.12.78 L367/17 as amended.
14 Council Regulation 1696/71 Art 5(2), OJ 4.8.71 L175/1, as substituted with amendments by
   Council Regulations 1170/77, OJ 3.6.77 L137/7 and 235/79, OJ 9.2.79 L34/4. For further
   rules on the equivalence with Community certificates of attestations accompanying imported
   hops, see Commission Regulation 3077/78, OJ 28.12.78 L367/28 as amended.
15 Council Regulation 1696/71, OJ 4.8.71 L175/1, as substituted by Council Regulation 3290/94,
   OJ 31.12.94 L349/105.
16 Ibid Art 15(1).
17 Ibid Art 15(2), as so substituted.
18 Ibid Art 15a(1), first paragraph, as so substituted.
19 Ibid Art 15a(2), as so substituted.
20 Ibid Art 15a(3), as so substituted.
1 The enabling regulation is Council Regulation 234/68, OJ 2.3.68 L55/1, as amended, and in
   particular as substituted by Council Regulation 3290/94, OJ 31.12.94 L349/105.

products known collectively as 'live plants'.[2] It is concerned with promoting their rational marketing and ensuring stable market conditions.[3] To those ends, quality standards are laid down; provision is made for the improvement of the organization of production and marketing; and a system of trade with third countries is established.[4]

Imports may be subject to an import licence, which is to be issued by the Member States to any applicant.[5] They are issued subject to the lodging of a security and are valid throughout the Community.[6]

The Common Customs Tariff applies to imports of live plant products from third countries.[7] The general rules for the interpretation of the combined nomenclature and the special rules for its application apply to the classification of these products, and the tariff nomenclature resulting from the application of the basic Regulation are incorporated in the CCT.[8] Except as otherwise provided by the basic Regulation, the levying of any charge having equivalent effect to a customs duty or the application of any quantitative restriction or measure having equivalent effect is expressly prohibited in trade with third countries.[9] An internal levy is charged by a Member State which falls more heavily on export sales than on home sales, or which is designed to finance activities which make the home market more profitable than exports, or which in any other way places the product for the home market at an advantage in comparison with the product for export, has an effect equivalent to that of a customs duty and is accordingly contrary to Community law.[10]

The importation of live plant products from or originating in third countries is subject to standard procedures in respect of treatment.[11]

For the purpose of stabilizing prices in respect of the economically significant trade in flowering bulbs, corms and tubers,[12] minimum export prices for those products are fixed annually.[13] Those products may only be exported to third countries at or above the applicable minimum price.[14]

The quality standards which have been fixed for live plant products apply,

---

2 See ibid Art 1, which defines 'live plants' by reference to Chapter 6 of the Common Customs Tariff. Chicory plants and roots in customs heading 0601 20 10 are excluded from the common organization: ibid.

3 Ibid, preamble, second recital.

4 See generally Commission of the European Communities, 'European Union Strategy for Trade in Live Plants and Floricultural Products (CN Code 0602)' (Communication from the Commission to the Council), COM (97) 36 final, Brussels, 17.2.97. As to a specific measure to increase the consumption of Community live plants and floricultural products within the Community and abroad, see Council Regulation 2275/96, OJ 29.11.96 L308/7, and, as to detailed implementing rules, Commission Regulation 803/98, OJ 17.4.98 L115/5.

5 Council Regulation 234/68, OJ 2.3.68 L55/1, Art 8(1), as substituted by Council Regulation 3290/94, OJ 31.12.94 L349/104.

6 Ibid Art 8(2), as so substituted.

7 Ibid, OJ 2.3.68 L55/1, Art 9, as substituted by Council Regulation 3290/94, OJ 31.12.94 L349/105, Annex XIX.

8 Ibid Art 10(1).

9 Ibid Art 10(2).

10 See Case 51/74 *P J Van der Hulst's Zonen v Produktschap voor Siergewassen* [1975] ECR 79.

11 See Council Regulation 3279/75, OJ 18.12.75 L326/1.

12 Council Regulation 234/68, OJ 2.3.68 L55/1, preamble, fifth recital.

13 Ibid Art 7(1), first paragraph, as amended by Council Regulation 3991/87, OJ 31.12.87 L362/19.

14 Council Regulation 234/68 Art 7(1), second paragraph, as amended by Council Regulation 3991/87, OJ 31.12.87 L362/19.

subject to certain derogations, to exports to third countries.[15] The adoption of standards relating to quality grading, wrapping, presentation and marking is authorized for live plant products or groups of such products produced in the Community.[16] The Council has established such standards in relation to flowering bulbs, corms and tubers[17] on the one hand, and fresh cut flowers and fresh ornamental foliage[18] on the other. Products in respect of which quality standards have been adopted may not be displayed or offered for sale, sold, delivered or otherwise marketed except in accordance with the relevant standards.[19] In such cases, all offers made to the public, whether by way of advertisements, catalogues or price lists, must if the price is quoted state the nature of the product and its size grading.[20] Products to which quality standards apply are subject to quality inspection controls administered by the Member States[1] in a co-ordinated and uniform manner.[2]

There are no special safeguards in respect of live grasses and cut flowers. However, if by reason of imports or exports, the Community market is affected by, or is threatened with, serious disturbance likely to jeopardize the achievement of the objectives of the Common Agricultural Policy, general safeguard measures may be applied in trade with third countries until the disturbance or threat of disturbance has ceased.[3] The measures are decided by the Commission, either at the request of a Member State or on its own initiative. They are immediately applicable and must be notified to the Member States.[4] Within three working days of the day of notification, a Member State may refer the matter to the Council, which, acting by a qualified majority, may amend or annul the measure in question.[5]

Milk and milk products

The common organization of the market in milk and milk products takes the form of a single price system, a system of production and user aids and means of supply control within the Community and a single trading system at the Community's external frontiers.[6] It applies to milk and milk products, and extends to fresh, preserved, concentrated or sweetened milk and cream; butter, cheese and curd; lactose and lactose syrup and other preparations used in animal feeding.[7]

---

15 As to flowering bulbs, corms and tubers, see Commission Regulation 537/70, OJ 24.3.70 L67/10 (amended by Commission Regulations 1793/73, OJ 4.7.73 L181/12 and 2971/76, OJ 8.12.76 L339/77). As to fresh cut flowers, see Commission Regulation 801/71, 20.4.71 L88/7.
16 Council Regulation 234/68 Art 3, first paragraph, OJ 2.3.68 L55/1.
17 See Council Regulation 315/68, OJ 21.3.68 L71/1, as amended.
18 See Council Regulation 316/68, OJ 21.3.68 L71/8, as amended.
19 Council Regulation 234/68 Art 3, second paragraph. Adjustments to quality standards to take account of production requirements and marketing techniques are authorized by Art 4.
20 Ibid Art 6.
 1 Ibid Art 5(1).
 2 Ibid Art 5(2).
 3 Ibid Art 10a(1), as so substituted. General rules in this respect are to be adopted by the Council: ibid.
 4 Ibid Art 10a(2), which also provides that if the Commission receives a request from a Member State, it must take a decision within three working days following receipt of the request.
 5 Ibid Art 10a(3).
 6 See Council Regulation 804/68, OJ 28.6.68 L148/13, as amended, and in particular Title III as substituted by Council Regulation 3290/94, OJ 31.12.94 L349/105.
 7 Ibid Art 1, as amended by Council Regulation 3904/87, OJ 30.12.87 L370/1.

Imports require an import licence, and exports may be made subject to an export licence.[8] Licences are to be issued by Member States to any applicant.[9] They are issued subject to the lodging of a security which will become forfeit, in whole or in part, if the authorized transaction is not fully effected during the period of validity of the licence, and they are valid throughout the Community.[10] The relevant date for determining the period of validity of a licence is the date when the application was lodged, even when that date may differ from the date on which the application was actually granted or when the licence was physically delivered to the applicant.[11]

Imports of products covered by the common organization of the market in milk and milk products are subject to the relevant rates of duty laid down by the Common Customs Tariff.[12] The general rules for the interpretation and the special rules for the application of the tariff apply to those products and the resulting tariff nomenclature is incorporated in the CCT.[13] In the absence of specific derogations, the levying of any other charge which is equivalent in its effect to a customs duty, and the application of any quantitative restriction or measure which has an equivalent effect, are prohibited in trade with third countries.[14]

Tariff quotas are to be opened as a result of the Uruguay Round agreements. They may be administered by any of the following methods or a combination of them: 'first come, first served'; the 'simultaneous examination' method; the 'traditional/new arrivals' method; or any other appropriate method as long as the method of administration avoids any discrimination between the operators concerned.[15]

Imported butter must generally satisfy the quality standards which are applicable to Community-produced butter.[16]

Various special trade arrangements also apply to dairy products. In respect of butter imported from New Zealand into the UK, arrangements in the form of reduced-levy quotas have been renewed periodically since the end of the UK accession transitional period.[17] Analogous arrangements apply to imports of Commonwealth cheese.[18] The Europe Agreements provide for the import of certain dairy products from Eastern and Central European countries at a reduced levy.[19] Quotas provided in the EEA Agreement continue to apply to cheese

---

8 Ibid Art 13(1), as so substituted.

9 Ibid Art 13(2), first paragraph, as so substituted.

10 Ibid Art 13(2), second paragraph, as so substituted. As to special rules implementing the system of import and export licences and advance fixing of refunds, see Commission Regulation 1466/95, OJ 28.6.95 L144/22, as amended.

11 See Case 109/82 *Interagra SA v Fonds d'Orientation et de Regularisation des Marches Agricoles* [1983] ECR 127.

12 Ibid Art 14, as so substituted.

13 Ibid Art 19(1), as so substituted.

14 Ibid Art 19(2), as so substituted. See also Case 199/82 *Amministrazione delle Finanze dello Stato v San Georgio SpA* [1983] ECR 3595.

15 Ibid Art 16(2), as so substituted. As to the factors to be taken into account, see ibid Art 16(3), as so substituted. As to detailed rules on import arrangements, see Commission Regulation 1600/95, OJ 17.9.95 L151/12, as amended most recently by Commission Regulation 2432/97, OJ 9.12.97 L337/9.

16 EC Council Regulation 804/68, OJ 28.6.68 L148/13 as amended, Art 16.

17 For the original accession arrangements, see the Act of Accession (1972), Protocol 18.

18 For example, see agreements with Australia (OJ 27.11.84 L308/55) and New Zealand (OJ 27.11.84 L308/60). See also Council Regulation 3340/84, OJ 30.11.84 L312/5.

19 Europe Agreements: Hungary, OJ 31.12.93 L347/2 (as amended and supplemented); Bulgaria, OJ 31.12.94 L358/2 (as amended and supplemented); Czech Republic, OJ 31.12.94 L360/2 (as amended and supplemented); Romania, OJ 31.12.94 L357/2; Slovak Republic, OJ 31.12.94 L359/2. These arrangements apply to Poland (4,100 tonnes of powder, 1,400

imports from Norway.[20] The GATT Agreements led to the opening of an additional quota for cheese to be exported to the US.[1]

The use of inward processing arrangements may be prohibited, in whole or in part, by the Council to the extent necessary for the proper working of the common organization of the market.[2] By way of derogation, however, if such a situation arises with exceptional urgency and the Community market is disturbed or is liable to be disturbed by the inward processing arrangements, the Commission shall, at the request of a Member State or on its own initiative, decide on the necessary measures.[3] The measures are to be notified to the Member States and are immediately applicable and valid for no more than six months.[4] Within a week of the day on which they were notified, they may be referred by any Member State to the Council, which, acting by a qualified majority, may confirm, amend or repeal the Commission decision. If the Council has not acted within three months, the Commission decision is deemed to have been repealed.[5]

In order to enable milk and milk products to be exported, the difference between world market prices and the prices within the Community may be covered by a scheme of export refunds.[6] The refund payable is to be the same for the whole Community, but it may be varied according to the destination of the particular product where the world market situation or the specific requirements of certain markets make this necessary.[7] Export refunds are fixed by the Commission at regular intervals or by invitation to tender for products for which that procedure was made available in the past.[8] Refunds are granted upon application and on presentation of the relevant export licence.[9] The amount of refund is that applicable on the day of application[10] and, in the case of a differentiated refund, that applicable on the same day for (1) the destination indicated on the licence or, (2) where appropriate, the actual destination if it differs from the destination indicated on the licence.[11] Refunds become payable upon proof that the products are of Community origin,[12] the products have

tonnes of butter and 2,800 tonnes of cheese), Hungary (1,400 tonnes of cheese), Czech Republic (1,400 tonnes of cheese), Slovak Republic (1,400 tonnes of cheese), Romania (1,500 tonnes of cheese) and Bulgaria (2,200 tonnes of cheese). As to detailed rules, see Commission Regulation 2508/97, OJ 16.12.97 L345/31.

20 OJ 3.1.94 L1/3.
 1 See Commission Regulation 1466/95 Art 9a, OJ 28.6.95 L144/22, as amended; Commission Regulation 1876/97, OJ 27.9.97 L265/28; and Commission Regulation 2178/97, OJ 1.11.97 L298/65.
 2 Ibid Art 18(1), which also provides for the required procedures.
 3 Ibid Art 18(2), as so substituted.
 4 Ibid Art 18(2).
 5 Ibid Art 18(3), as so substituted.
 6 Ibid Art 17(1), as so substituted. Export refunds apply not only to the products listed in Art 1, but also to a range of other goods listed in the Annex. As to the method for allocating the quantities which may be exported with a refund, see ibid Art 17(2), as so substituted. As to special detailed implementing rules, see Commission Regulation 1466/95, OJ 28.6.96 L144/22, as amended and corrected.
 7 Ibid Art 17(3), first and second paragraphs, as so substituted.
 8 Ibid Art 17(3), third paragraph, as so substituted. As to the factors to be taken into account in fixing refunds, see ibid Art 17(4), as so substituted. As to the determination of Community prices and world market prices, see ibid Art 17(5), as so substituted.
 9 Ibid Art 17(6), as so substituted.
10 EC Council Regulation 876/68 Art 5(2).
11 Ibid Art 17(7), first paragraph, as so substituted.
12 Except that no export refund is granted on products which are imported from third countries and re-exported to third countries, unless the exporter proves that the product to be exported and the product previously imported are one and the same, and that all import duties were collected on importation: ibid Art 17(11), as so substituted. See also Case 89/83 *Hauptzollamt*

been exported from the Community, and, in the case of a differentiated refund, the products have reached the destination indicated on the licence or another destination for which a refund was fixed.[13]

Export certificates providing for a reference period are used to ensure compliance with the limits on volumes arising from the Uruguay Round agreements, but the ending of a reference period stated on the certificate does not affect the validity of export licences.[14]

Both special and general safeguard measures may taken in the dairy sector.

First, in order to prevent or counteract adverse effects on the Community market resulting from imports, special safeguard measures in the form of an additional import duty may be taken if the conditions set out in Article 5 of the Uruguay Round Agreement on Agriculture have been fulfilled, unless the imports are unlikely to disturb the Community market, or where the effects would be disproportionate to the intended objective.[15]

Second, certain general measures may be taken when the free-at-frontier price[16] significantly exceeds the level of Community prices, and where that situation is likely to continue, thereby disturbing or threatening to disturb the Community market.[17] The measures include total or partial suspension of levies and/or collection of export charges.[18]

Third, if, by reason of imports or exports, the Community market is affected by, or is threatened with, serious disturbance likely to jeopardize the achievement of the objectives of the Common Agricultural Policy, appropriate measures may be applied in trade with third countries until the disturbance or threat of disturbance has ceased.[19] The necessary measures are to be decided by the Commission, at the request of a Member State or on its own initiative. The measures are immediately applicable and must be notified to

---

Hamburg-Jonas v Dimex Nahrungsmittel Im- und Export GmbH & Co KG [1984] ECR 2815. As to the applicability of these provisions to the export of goods listed in the Annex, see ibid Art 17(12).

13 Ibid Art 17(10). In the last case the amount applicable may not exceed the amount applicable for the destination indicated on the licence: ibid Art 17(7)(b).

14 Ibid Art 17(13).

15 Ibid Art 15(1). As to trigger prices, trigger volumes, and the determination of import prices, see ibid Art 15(2), (3).

16 The free-at-frontier price is determined for each pilot product on the basis of the most favourable purchasing opportunities in international trade for the relevant products: ibid Art 14(4), first paragraph. Account is taken of possible future differences between the pilot product and specific prodcts in so far as marketing may be affected: ibid Art 14(4), second paragraph.

17 Ibid Art 20(1), as so substituted. A significant excess within the meaning of paragraph 1 exists when the free-at-frontier price exceeds the intervention price fixed for the product in question, increased by 15%, or, as regards products for which there is no intervention price, a price derived from the intervention price, to be determined according to the management committee procedure, taking account of the nature and composition of the product in question: ibid Art 20(2), as so substituted. The situation is deemed to be likely to continue when an imbalance exists between supply and demand and that imbalance is likely to continue, in view of foreseeable trends in production and market prices: ibid Art 20(3). The Community market is deemed to be disturbed or under threat of disturbance when the high level of prices in international trade hinders imports of milk products into the Community, or causes milk products to leave the Community, so that security of supply is no longer ensured or threatens to be no longer ensured in the Community: ibid Art 20(4).

18 Ibid Art 20(5), as last amended by Council Regulation 3290/94, OJ 31.12.94 L349/105.

19 Ibid Art 21(1), first paragraph, as so substituted. The measures must be applied having regard to the obligations arising under agreements concluded in accordance with EC Art 228(2): ibid Art 21(4), as so substituted. General implementing rules are to be laid down by the Council: ibid Art 21(1), second paragraph, as so substituted.

the Member States.[20] Within three working days of the day on which they were notified, a Member State may refer the measures to the Council, which shall meet without delay and, acting by a qualified majority, may amend or annul the measure in question.[1]

Oils and fats

The common organization of the market in oils and fats[2] applies to oil seeds, oleaginous fruit, vegetable oils and fats, and oils and fats of fish and marine mammals.[3] It takes the form of intra-Community price systems for olive oil on the one hand and for other vegetable oils and oil seeds on the other. In addition, in respect of olive oil, provision is made for production and consumption aids and for the establishment of a buffer stock to counteract the effect of variable annual olive yields. In trade with third countries the Common Customs Tariff applies,[4] while the system of variable levies which previously applied have been replaced by other mechanisms as a result of the Uruguay Round.[5] Except as otherwise provided, the levying of any charge having equivalent effect to a customs duty or the application of any quantitative restriction or measure having equivalent effect is prohibited in trade with third countries.[6]

For the purposes of both intra-Community trade and trade with third countries (with the exception of exports), the Member States are required to adopt a standard set of descriptions and definitions in respect of olive oil.[7]

Imports of olive oil[8] or of certain other products[9] are subject to the presentation of an import licence.[10] Exports of olive oil are subject to the presentation of an export licence.[11] Exports of other products covered by the regime may be subject to presentation of export licences.[12] Licences are issued by the Member States to any applicant.[13] They are issued subject to the lodging of a security and are valid throughout the Community.[14]

Provision is also made for export refunds. To the extent necessary to enable the olive oil and rape seed harvested in the Community to be exported on the basis of

20 Ibid Art 21(2), as so substituted.
 1 Ibid Art 21(3), as so substituted.
 2 Council Regulation 136/66, OJ 1.10.66 L172/3025, as amended and partly substituted in particular by Council Regulation 3290/94 Annex IV, OJ 31.12.94 L349/105. As to the aims and methods of the regime, see Case 26/69 *EC Commission v France* [1970] ECR 565. See also Case 232/81 *Agricola Commerciale Olio Srl v EC Commission* [1984] ECR 3881.
 3 Ibid Art 1, as amended by Council Regulation 3994/87, OJ 31.12.87 L377/31. The list of products may be changed and special derogations may be made by the Council acting under powers given: ibid Art 36.
 4 Ibid Art 2a, as so substituted. The general rules for the interpretation of the Combined Nomenclature and the special rules for its application apply to the tariff classification of these products, and the tariff nomenclature resulting from the application of the regime are incorporated in the CCT: ibid Art 3a(1), as so substituted.
 5 See ibid Title I, as substituted by Council Regulation 3290/94, OJ 31.12.94 L349/105.
 6 Ibid Art 3a(2), as so substituted.
 7 Ibid Art 35, Annex. This provision is without prejudice to the harmonization of legislation on olive oil for human consumption.
 8 That is, products listed in ibid Art 1(2)(c).
 9 That is, products falling within CN codes 0709 90 39, 0711 20 90, 2306 90 19, 1522 00 31, 1522 00 39.
10 Ibid Art 2(1), first paragraph, as so substituted.
11 Ibid Art 2(1), second paragraph, as so substituted.
12 Ibid Art 2(1), third paragraph, as so substituted.
13 Ibid Art 2(1), fourth paragraph, as so substituted.
14 Ibid Art 2(1), fifth paragraph, as so substituted.

quotations or prices for those products on the world market, and within limits resulting from the Community's international obligations, the difference between those quotations or prices and Community prices may be covered by export refunds.[15] Refunds are the same for the whole Community.[16] However, they may vary according to destination when the situation on the world market or the specific requirements of certain markets make this necessary. Where olive oil is concerned, the refund may also be fixed at different levels according to quality and presentation where the situation on the world market or the specified requirements of certain markets make this necessary.[17] For olive oil, refunds may be fixed at regular intervals or by tender, and the latter may be restricted to certain countries of destination, certain quantities and qualities and presentations.[18] Refunds are granted only on request and on presentation of the relevant export licence.[19] The refund to be paid is that applicable on the day of application for the licence, and in the case of a differentiated refund, that applicable on the same day for the destination indicated on the licence, or, if appropriate, for the actual destination if it differs from that indicated on the licence.[20]

Export levies may be charged to cover the difference in prices when olive oil is exported to third countries and world prices are higher than Community prices.[1] The levy is fixed by the Commission.[2]

Special and general safeguard measures apply in respect of oils and fats.

First, in order to prevent or counteract adverse effects on the Community market which may result from imports, such imports may be subject to special safeguard measures in the form of an additional duty[3] if the conditions set out in Art 5 of the Uruguay Round Agreement on Agriculture are fulfilled, unless the imports are unlikely to disturb the Community market or where the effects would be disproportionate to the intended objective.[4]

Second, if, by reason of imports or exports, the Community market in these products is affected by, or threatened with, serious disturbance likely to jeopardize the achievement of the objectives of the Common Agricultural Policy, general safeguard measures may be taken in trade with third countries until the disturbance or threat of disturbance has ceased.[5] Measures are decided by the Commission, at the request of a Member State or on its own initiative. The measures are immediately applicable, and the Member States are notified.[6] Any Member State may, within three working days of the day on which it is notified,

---

15 Ibid Art 3(1), as so substituted. As to the determination of the method of allocating quantities which may be exported with refunds, see ibid Art 3(2), as so substituted. As to special detailed implementing rules, see Commission Regulation 2543/95, OJ 31.10.95 L260/33, as amended.
16 Ibid Art 3(3), first paragraph, as so substituted.
17 Ibid Art 3(3), second paragraph, as so substituted. As to the factors to be taken into account in fixing export refunds, see ibid Art 3(4) (olive oil) and Art 3(5) (colza and rape seed).
18 Ibid Art 3(3), third paragraph, as so substituted.
19 Ibid Art 3(6), as so substituted. Such requirements may be waived in the case of food-aid operations: ibid Art 3(8).
20 Ibid Art 3(7), first paragraph. In the latter case the amount applicable may not exceed the amount applicable to destination indicated on the licence: ibid. These conditions may be waived in the case of food-aid operations: ibid Art 3(8), as so substituted.
1 Ibid Art 20, as so substituted. As to the amount of the levy, see ibid Art 20(2), first paragraph (unrefined olive oil) and Art 20(2), second paragraph (refined olive oil).
2 Ibid Art 20(3).
3 That is, additional to the rate of duty applied under the CCT: ibid Art 2a, as so substituted.
4 Ibid Art 2b(1), as so substituted. As to trigger prices, trigger volumes, and determination of import prices, see ibid Art 2b(2), (3), (4).
5 Ibid Art 3b(1), first paragraph, as so substituted.
6 Ibid Art 3b(1), second paragraph, as so substituted.

refer the measures to the Council, which shall meet without delay and, acting by a qualified majority, may amend or annul the measure.[7]

Pigmeat

The common organization of the market in pigmeat[8] applies to live swine of domestic species (excluding pure-bred breeding animals[9]); pigmeat, offals and fats, whether fresh, chilled, frozen, salted, in brine, dried or smoked; lard and other rendered and solvent-extracted pig fats; sausages and other preserved or prepared pigmeat or offal.[10] It shares many features of the common organizations of the markets in eggs and poultrymeat. In common with eggs and poultrymeat, the production of pigmeat is closely affected by the price of cereal feedingstuffs.[11] The market in pigmeat therefore makes similar provision to involve trade organizations in action to facilitate the adjustment of supply to demand and also establishes a single trading system at the external frontiers of the Community. In addition, in the case of pigmeat, there is a system of price support and intervention in respect of the market within the Community.

Imports or exports may be subject to the presentation of a licence.[12] Licences are issued by the Member States to any applicant.[13] They are issued subject to the lodging of a security and are valid throughout the Community.[14]

The Common Customs Tariff of the Community applies to trade in pigmeat.[15] The general rules for the interpretation of the combined nomenclature and the special rules for its application apply to these products, and the tariff nomenclature resulting from the application of the basic Regulation is incorporated in the CCT.[16]

Tariff quotas are to be opened for pigmeat imports.[17] They may be administered by a 'first come, first served' method, the 'simultaneous examination' method, the 'traditional/new arrivals' method, or a combination of these, or by other appropriate methods, but must avoid any discrimination between the operators involved.[18] The quotas are annual quotas, suitably phased over the year if necessary.[19]

Where prices on the Community market rise significantly and where that

---

7 Ibid Art 3b(3), as so substituted.
8 Council Regulation 2759/75, OJ 1.11.754 L282/1, as amended in particular by Council Regulation 3290/94 Annex X, OJ 31.12.94 L349/105.
9 Ibid Art 1(1)(a), as amended by Council Regulation 3906/87, OJ 30.12.87 L370/11.
10 Ibid Art 1(1), as so amended.
11 Ibid preamble, fourth recital.
12 Council Regulation 2759/75, OJ 1.11.75 L282/1, Art 8(1), first paragraph, as substituted by Council Regulation 3290/94, OJ 31.12.94 L349/105. As to detailed implementing rules, see Commission Regulation 1370/95, OJ 17.6.95 L133/9, as amended. As to the example of imports from Slovenia, see Commission Regulation 571/97, OJ 27.3.97 L85/56.
13 Ibid Art 8(1), second paragraph, as so substituted.
14 Ibid Art 8(1), third paragraph, as so substituted.
15 Ibid Art 9, as substituted by Council Regulation 3290/94, OJ 31.12.94 L349/105.
16 Ibid Art 15(1), as so substituted.
17 Ibid Art 11(1), as so substituted.
18 Ibid Art 11(2), as so substituted. See Commission Regualtion 1486/95, OJ 29.6.95 L145/58, as amended.
19 Ibid Art 11(4), as so substituted. As to the factors to be considered in the administration of quotas, see ibid Art 11(3), as so substituted.

situation is likely to continue, thereby disturbing or threatening to disturb that market,[20] import duties may be totally or partially suspended.[1]

To the extent necessary for the proper working of the common organization of the market, the Council, acting by a qualified majority on a proposal from the Commission, may, in special cases, prohibit in whole or in part the use of inward processing arrangements.[2] However, if this situation arises with exceptional urgency and the Community market is disturbed or likely to be disturbed by inward or outward processing arrangements, the Commission is to decide on the necessary measures, either at the request of a Member State or on its own initiative. Such measures are immediately applicable, valid for no more than six months, and are to be notifed to the Council and the Member States.[3] The measures may be referred to the Council by any Member State within a week of the day on which they were notified. The Council, acting by a qualified majority, may confirm, amend or repeal the Commision decision. If the Council has not acted within three months, the Commission decision is deemed to have been repealed.[4]

Except as otherwise provided in or pursuant to the Regulation, the levying of any charge having equivalent effect to a customs duty, or the application of any quantitative restriction or measure having equivalent effect, is prohibited in trade with third countries.[5] A charge which has an effect equivalent to a customs duty on imports into the Community includes any monetary charge levied on or because of importation, which is imposed exclusively on the imported product and which has the same restrictive effect on the free movement of goods as a customs duty.[6] Accordingly, a monetary charge levied for the public and veterinary health inspection of imported products which is fixed by reference to factors distinct from those used to fix any monetary charges which might be levied on similar Community products is a charge which has an effect equivalent to a customs duty.[7]

Export refunds may be available to cover the difference between Community prices and world market prices to the extent necessary to allow pigmeat products to be exported on the basis of quotations or prices for those products on the world market, and within the limits resulting from international agreements concluded by the Community.[8] Refunds are the same for the whole Community but may vary according to destination where the world market situation or the specific requirements of certain markets make this necessary.[9]

---

20 Ibid Art 12(1), as so substituted. As to the meaning of 'a significant rise in prices', see ibid Art 12(2), as so substituted. As to the meaning of 'likely to continue', see ibid Art 12(3), as so substituted.

1 Ibid Art 12(4), as so substituted. Such measures are to be decided according to the management committee procedure: ibid Art 12(4) as so substituted, Art 24.

2 Ibid Art 14(1), as so substituted.

3 Ibid Art 14(2), as so substituted.

4 Ibid Art 14(3), as so substituted.

5 Ibid Art 15(2), as so substituted.

6 See Case 21/75 *I Schroeder KG v Oberstadtdirektor der Koln* [1975] ECR 905.

7 See Case 21/75 *I Schroeder KG v Oberstadtdirektor der Koln* [1975] ECR 905. See also Case 132/78 *Denkavit Loire Sarl v France* [1979] ECR 1923 and Case 214/88 *Amministrazione delle finanze dello Stato v Societa Politi & Co Srl* [1989] ECR 2785.

8 Ibid Art 13(1), as so substituted. As to the allocation of quantities which may be exported with a refund, see ibid Art 13(2), as so substituted. As to the agricultural product nomenclature for export refunds in the pigmeat sector, see Commission Regulation 3846/87, OJ 24.12.87 L366/1, as amended. As to special conditions for granting export refunds in the pigmeat sector, see Commission Regulation 2331/97, OJ 26.11.97 L323/19.

9 Ibid Art 13(3), first paragraph, as so substituted.

The list of products on which an export refund is granted and the amount of the refund are fixed at least once every three months. However, the amount of the refund may remain at the same level for more than three months and may, where necessary, be adjusted in the intervening period by the Commission at the request of a Member State or on its own initiative.[10] Refunds are granted only on application and on presentation of the relevant export licence.[11] The refund to be paid is that applicable on the day of application for the licence and, in the case of a differentiated refund, that applicable on the same day for the destination indicated on the licence or, where appropriate, for the actual destination if it differs from the destination indicated on the licence.[12] Refunds are paid on proof that the products have been exported from the Community, that the products are of Community origin,[13] and that in the case of a differentiated refund the products have reached the destination indicated on the licence or another destination for which the refund was fixed.[14] Compliance with volume limits agreed under the Uruguay Round, for example, is ensured on the basis of export certificates issued for specified reference periods, but the ending of a reference period does not affect the validity of export licences.[15]

Special and general safeguard measures apply in respect of pigmeat.

First, in order to prevent or counteract adverse effects on the Community market which may result from imports, special safeguard measures in the form of an additional import duty may be imposed if the conditions set out in Art 5 of the Agreement on Agriculture are fulfilled, unless the imports are unlikely to disturb the Community market, or where the effects would be disproportionate to the intended objective.[16]

Second, if, by reason of imports or exports, the Community market is affected by, or is threatened with, serious disturbances likely to jeopardize the achievement of the objectives of the Common Agricultural Policy, general safeguard measures may be applied in trade with third countries until the disturbance or threat of disturbance has ceased.[17] The Commission is to decide upon the necessary measures, either at the request of a Member State or on its own initiative. The measures are immediately applicable and must be notified to the Member States.[18] They may be referred to the Council by any Member State within three working days of the day on which they were notified. The Council is to meet without delay and, acting by a qualified majority, may amend or annul the measure in question.[19]

---

10 Ibid Art 13(3), third paragraph, as so substituted. As to the factors to be taken into account when refunds are being fixed, see ibid Art 13(4), as so substituted. As to the establishment of the Community price and the world market price, see ibid Art 13(5), as so substituted.
11 Ibid Art 13(6), as so substituted. This requirement may be waived in the case of food-aid products: ibid Art 13(8), as so substituted.
12 Ibid Art 13(7), as so substituted. In the latter case the amount applicable may not exceed the amount applicable for the destination indicated on the licence. These requirements may be waived in the case of food-aid products: ibid Art 13(8), as so substituted.
13 Except in the case of inward processing: ibid Art 13(9), second indent, as so substituted. As to inward processing, see ibid Art 13(10), as so substituted.
14 Ibid Art 13(9), as so substituted.
15 Ibid Art 13(11), as so substituted.
16 Ibid Art 10(1), as so substituted. As to trigger prices, trigger volumes and import prices, see ibid Art 10(2).
17 Ibid Art 16(1), first paragraph, as so substituted.
18 Ibid Art 16(2), as so substituted.
19 Ibid Art 16(3), as so substituted.

Products processed from fruit and vegetables

The common organization of the market in products processed from fruit and vegetables[20] applies to a very wide range of preserved fruits and vegetables, preserved parts of fruits and plants, pectic substances, jams and other cooked fruit preserves, and fruit juices.[1] It is largely concerned with making Community products more competitive with similar products originating in non-member producing countries.[2] Its most important features are therefore a system of production aids together with the establishment of a single trading system at the external frontiers of the Community; there is no general price support system for products produced and marketing within the Community.

Imports or exports are subject to the presentation of an import or export licence.[3] The licence is issued by the Member States to any applicant, irrespective of its place of establishment in the Community.[4] The licence is valid throughout the Community and is subject to the lodging of a security.[5]

Unless otherwise specified, the rates of duty in the Common Customs Tariff apply to these products.[6] The general rules for the interpretation of the combined nomenclature and the special rules for its application apply to their tariff classification, and the tariff nomenclature resulting from the application of the regime are incorporated in the CCT.[7] Unless otherwise provided, the levying of any customs duty or charge which has an equivalent effect and the application of any quantitative restriction or measure which has an equivalent effect are prohibited in trade with third countries.[8]

A minimum import price for the marketing years 1995 through 1999 is fixed for certain products.[9] Where the minimum import price is not observed, a countervailing charge in addition to customs duty is to be imposed, based on the prices of the main supplier countries.[10]

Tariff quotas are to be opened.[11] They are to be administered on a 'first come, first served' basis, by the 'simultaneous examination' method, by the 'traditional/new arrivals' method, or a combination of these, or by another

20 Council Regulation 2201/96, OJ 21.11.96, OJ L297/29, which repealed and replaced Council Regulation 426/86, OJ 27.2.86 L49/1, as amended.
1 Ibid Art 1.
2 Ibid preamble, sixth recital.
3 Ibid Art 11(1), first sub-paragraph.
4 Ibid Art 11(1), second sub-paragraph.
5 Ibid Art 11(1), third sub-paragraph.
6 Ibid Art 12(1).
7 Ibid Art 21(1).
8 Ibid Art 21(2).
9 That is, the products listed in Annex II: ibid Art 13(1), first sub-paragraph. The factors to be taken into account in determining the minimum import price include the free-at-frontier prices on import into the Community, the world market prices, the situation on the internal Community market, and the trend of trade with third countries: ibid. As to the fixing of minimum import prices for dried grapes, currants, processed cherries, and sour cherries, see ibid Art 13(2)–(5). As to verification of compliance and information requirements, see eg Commission Regulation 2479/96, OJ 24.12.96 L335/18; Commission Regulation 2480/96, OJ 24.12.96 L335/28, as amended (Central and Eastern European Countries and Baltic States).
10 Ibid Art 13(1), second sub-paragraph. As to the fixing of a countervailing charge for dried grapes, sour cherries and processed cherries, see ibid Art 13(6), (7). The countervailing charge may not exceed the difference between the minimum import price and the actual import price: Joined Cases C-351/93, C-352/93 and C-353/93 *H A van der Linde and Tracotex Holland BV v Minister van Landbouw, Natuurbeheer en Visserij* [1995] ECR I-85.
11 Ibid Art 15(1).

appropriate method, but must avoid any discrimination between the operators involved.[12] The quotas are to be annual, suitably phased over the year.[13]

Export refunds to cover the difference between the Community price and the world market price may be granted to enable export of two categories of products.[14] The first category consists of economically significant quantities of dried or preserved products without added sugar.[15] The second category consists of specified sweeteners used in pectic substances and pectinates or prepared or preserved vegetables or fruit or fruit juices.[16]

Refunds are the same for the whole Community but may vary according to destination where the situation in international trade or the specific requirements of certain markets make this necessary.[17] They are granted only on application and on presentation of the relevant export licence.[18] The applicable refund is that of the day of application for the licence and, in the case of a differentiated refund, that applicable on the same day for the destination indicated on the licence or for the actual destination if it differs from the destination indicated on the licence.[19]

For products in the first category, the refund is to be paid upon proof that the products have been exported from the Community, that the products are of Community origin, and in the case of a differentiated refund that the products have reached the destination indicated on the licence or another destination for which the refund was fixed.[20] For products in the second category, the refund is to be paid upon proof that the products either are of Community origin or have been imported from third countries and import duties have been paid;[1] that the products have been exported from the Community; in the case of a differentiated refund that the products have reached the destination indicated on the licence or another destination for which the refund was fixed.[2] In addition, in order for products in the second category to benefit from the refund, the processed products must be accompanied, upon export, by a declaration from the applicant stating the quantities of raw and white sugar and beet and cane syrups, isoglucose, glucose and glucose syrup used in manufacture.[3]

---

12 Ibid Art 15(2). As to the factors to be taken into account in the administration of quotas, see ibid Art 15(3).

13 Ibid Art 15(4).

14 Ibid Art 16(1). As to the method for the allocation of quantities which may be exported with a refund, see ibid Art 16(2). .

15 Ibid Art16(1)(a). As to the factors to be taken into account when fixing refunds and the determination of prices, see ibid Art 17(1), (2), (3), (5).

16 Ibid Art 16(1)(b). The specified sweeteners are white and raw sugar falling within CN code 1701, glucose and glucose syrup falling within CN codes 1702 30 51, 1702 30 59, 1702 30 91, 1702 30 99 and 1702 40 90, isoglucose falling within CN codes 1702 30 10, 1702 40 10, 1702 60 10 and 1702 90 30, and beet and cane syrups falling within CN code 1702 90 90: ibid. As to the amount of the refund for these products, see ibid Art 18(1), (2), (4).

17 Ibid Art 16(3).

18 Ibid Art 16(4). This requirement may be waived in the case of food-aid operations: ibid Art 16(6).

19 Ibid Art 16(5). In the latter case, the amount applicable may not exceed the amount applicable for the destination indicated on the licence. These requirements may be waived in the case of food-aid operations: ibid Art16(6).

20 Ibid Art 17(4).

1 Provided that the exporter proves that the product to be exported and the product previously imported are one and the same, and also that import duties were collected on importation: ibid Art 18(5).

2 Ibid Art 18(6).

3 Ibid Art 18(3), first sub-paragraph. The accuracy of this declaration is subject to checking by the competent authorities of the Member States concerned: ibid Art 18(3), second sub-paragraph.

Compliance with volume limits arising from the Uruguay Round agreements is ensured by export certificates issued for specified reference periods, but the ending of a reference period does not affect the validity of export licences.[4]

To the extent necessary for the proper working of the common organization of the market in cereals, sugar and fruit and vegetables, the Council, acting by a qualified majority on a proposal from the Commission, may in particular cases prohibit in whole or in part the use of certain inward processing arrangements.[5] However, by way of derogation, if this situation arises with exceptional urgency and the Community market is disturbed or is liable to be disturbed by the inward processing arrangements, the Commission shall decide on the necessary measures, at the request of a Member State or on its own initiative. The measures are immediately applicable, are valid for no more than six months, and must be notified to Council and the Member States.[6] The Commission's decision may be referred to the Council by any Member State within a week of the day on which it was notified. The Council, acting by a qualified majority, may confirm, amend or repeal the Commission's decision. If the Council has not acted within three months, the Commission's decision is deemed to have been repealed.[7]

Provision is also made for the imposition of a charge on exports of specified products containing a minimum of 35 per cent added sugar.[8]

Both special and general safeguard measures apply in respect of products processed from fruit and vegetables.

First, in order to prevent or counteract adverse effects on the Community market which may result from imports of certain products, special safeguard measures in the form of an additional import duty may be imposed if the conditions set out in Art 5 of the Agreement on Agriculture have been fulfilled, unless the imports are unlikely to disturb the Community market or where the effects would be disproportionate to the intended objective.[9]

Second, if, by reason of imports or exports, the Community market is affected by, or is threatened with, serious disturbance likely to jeopardize the achievement of the objectives of the Common Agricultural Policy, general safeguard measures may be applied in trade with third countries until the disturbance or threat of disturbance has ceased.[10] The measures are decided by the Commission, either at the request of a Member State or on its own initiative. They are immediately applicable and must be notified to the Member States.[11] They may be referred to the Council by any Member State within three working days of the day on which they were notified. The Council is to meet without delay and, acting by a qualified majority, may amend or annul the measure in question.[12]

---

4 Ibid Art 16(7).
5 Ibid Art 19(1). The arrangements in question concern the sweeteners specified in ibid Art 16(1)(b), on the one hand, and fruit and vegetables, on the other hand, intended for the manufacture of products covered by this common organization of the market: ibid Art 19(1).
6 Ibid Art 19(2).
7 Ibid Art 19(3).
8 Ibid Art 20(1). Such a charge may be imposed where pursuant to Council Regulation 1785/81, OJ 1.7.81 L177/4, a levy exceeding Ecu 5 per 100 kilograms is charged on exports of white sugar: ibid. As to the fixing of the charge, see ibid Art 20(2), (3).
9 Ibid Art 14(1). As to trigger prices and trigger volumes, see ibid Art 14(2). As to the determination of import prices, see ibid Art 14(3). As to the adoption by the Commission of detailed implementing rules, see ibid Art 14(4).
10 Ibid Art 22(1).
11 Ibid Art 22(2).
12 Ibid Art 22(4).

Rice

The common organization of the market in rice,[13] which shares many features with that for cereals, takes the form of a price system within the Community and a trading system with third countries. It applies to paddy, husked and milled rice,[14] broken rice,[15] flaked rice and rice flour, groats, meal, pellets and starch.[16]

Imports into or exports from the Community of any of the products which are within the common organization of the market in rice are subject to the submission of a licence.[17] Import and export licences may be issued by the Member States to any applicant irrespective of its place of establishment in the Community.[18] They are issued subject to the lodging of a security and are valid throughout the Community.[19]

Unless otherwise provided, the rates of duty in the CCT apply to these products.[20] However, a special import duty, which may not be more than the CCT rate, applies to husked indica and japonica rice covered by CN code 1006 20 and to wholly milled rice covered by CN code 1006 30.[1] No duty is charged on imports of products covered by CN codes 1006 10, 1006 20 or 1006 40 00 into the French overseas department of Reunion and intended for consumption there.[2] The duty to be charged on imports of products covered by CN code 1006 30 into Reunion and intended for consumption there is to be multiplied by a coefficient of 0,30.[3]

A subsidy may be fixed for consignments to the French overseas department of Reunion, intended for consumption there, of products falling within CN code 1006 (excluding code 1006 10 10) which come from the Member States or which come from a third country and are in free circulation in the Community.[4] The subsidy is granted on application and may be fixed, where appropriate, by a tendering procedure.[5]

To the extent necessary to enable these products to be exported without further processing or in the form of certain processed goods,[6] the difference between world market prices and the Community price may be covered by an

---

13 Council Regulation 3072/95, OJ 30.12.95 L329/18.
14 'Milled rice' means semi-milled or wholly milled rice: Council Regulation 1418/76 Art 1, as amended by Council Regulations 3877/87, OJ 20.12.87 L361/1 and 1806/89, OJ 24.6.89 L177/1; Annex A, point 1(c),(d), as amended by Council Regulation 3877/87.
15 As to broken rice, see Case C-159/88 *C M Van Sillevoldt v Hoofproduktschap foor Akkerbouwprodukten* [1990] ECR I-2215.
16 Council Regulation 3072/95, OJ 30.12.95 L329/18 Art 1(1), Annex A.
17 Ibid Art 9(1), first paragraph. As to special detailed rules for the application of the system of import and export licences, see Commission Regulation 1162/95, OJ 24.5.95 L117/2. As to tariff quotas, see Commission Regulation 1522/96, OJ 31.7.96 L190/1.
18 Ibid Art 9(1), second paragraph.
19 Ibid Art 9(1), third paragraph.
20 Ibid Art 11(1).
 1 Ibid Art 11(2), which also provides for the calculation of this duty. See also Commission Regulation 1252/97, OJ 1.7.97 L173/96.
 2 Ibid Art 11(3)(a).
 3 Ibid Art 11(3)(b).
 4 Ibid Art 10(1), first paragraph. As to the factors to be taken into account in fixing the subsidy, see ibid Art 10(1), second paragraph. See Commission Regulation 2692/89, OJ 7.9.89 L261/8.
 5 Ibid Art 10(1), third paragraph. It is fixed according to the management committee procedure but where the need arises it may be altered in the interval by the Commission at the request of a Member State or on its own initiative: ibid Art 10(1), fourth paragraph. As to such a procedure, see Commission Regulation 531/97, OJ 22.3.97 L82/50.
 6 Listed in ibid Annex B.

export refund.[7] Refunds shall be the same for the whole Community but may vary according to destination, where the world market situation or the specific requirements of certain markets make this necessary.[8] Refunds may be fixed at regular intervals or by invitation to tender; in the former case they may be adjusted in the intervening period by the Commission at the request of a Member State or on its own initiative.[9] Refunds on products exported without further processing are granted only on application and on presentation of the relevant export licence.[10] The refund on such products is that applicable on the date of application for the licence and, in the case of a differentiated refund, that applicable on the same day for the destination indicated on the licence or the actual destination if it differs from the destination indicated on the licence.[11] These provisions may be applied to products which are exported in processed form.[12] The refund may be increased by an additional compensatory amount for paddy rice harvested within the Community and husked rice obtained therefrom which is exported without further processing in the form of wholly milled or semi-milled rice during certain periods and subject to certain conditions.[13] The refund is paid upon proof that the products, in the case of paddy rice and husked rice, are of Community origin,[14] that the products have been exported from the Community and, in the case of a differentiated refund, that the products have reached the destination indicated on the licence or another destination for which a refund was fixed.[15] Compliance on volume limits agreed in the Uruguay Round is ensured on the basis of export certificates issued for specified reference periods, but the ending of a reference period does not affect the validity of the licences.[16]

To the extent necessary to ensure the proper working of the common organization of the market in rice, the Council, by a qualified majority and on a proposal from the Commission, may in special cases prohibit in whole or in part the use of inward or outward processing arrangements.[17] By way of derogation, if this situation arises with exceptional urgency and the Community market is disturbed or is liable to be disturbed by inward or outward processing arrangements, the Commission is to decide on the necessary measures, at the request of a Member State or on its own initiative. Such measures are immediately applicable, are valid for no more than six months and must be notified to the Council and the Member States.[18] The Commission decision may be referred to the Council by any Member State within a week of the day on which

---

7 Ibid Art 13(1). Exports are subject to limits resulting from the Community's international agreements: ibid. As to factors to be taken into account in allocating quantities which may be exported with a refund, see ibid Art 13(2).
8 Ibid Art 13(3).
9 Ibid Art 13(3), second and third paragraph. As to the factors to be taken into account in fixing refunds, see ibid Art 13(4).
10 Ibid Art 13(7). This may be waived in the case of food-aid operations: ibid Art 13(10).
11 Ibid Art 13(8). In the latter case the amount applicable may not exceed the amount applicable for the destination indicated on the licence: ibid. These provisions may be waived in the case of food-aid operations: ibid Art 13(10).
12 Ibid Art 13(9).
13 Ibid Art 13(12), first paragraph. As to the calculation of the compensatory amount, see ibid Art 13(11), second and third paragraphs.
14 Except in the case of inward processing and when the levy was collected on importation: see ibid Art 13(13).
15 Ibid Art 13(12).
16 Ibid Art 13(14).
17 Ibid Art 14(1).
18 Ibid Art 14(2).

it was notified. The Council, acting by a qualified majority, may confirm, amend or repeal the Commission decision. If the Council has not acted within three months, the Commission decision is deemed to have been repealed.[19]

Both special and general safeguard measures apply in respect of imports of rice.

First, in order to prevent or counteract adverse effects on the Community market which may result from imports, such imports may be subject to special safeguard measures in the form of an additional import duty if the conditions set out in Art 5 of the Uruguay Round Agreement on Agriculture have been fulfilled, unless the imports are unlikely to disturb the Community market, or where the effects would be disproportionate to the intended objective.[20]

Second, if, by reason of imports or exports, the Community market is affected by, or threatened with, serious disturbance likely to jeopardize the achievement of the objectives of the Common Agricultural Policy, general safeguard measures may be applied in trade with third countries until the disturbance or threat of disturbance has ceased.[1] The measures are decided by the Commission, at the request of a Member State or on its own initiative. They are immediately applicable and must be notified to the Member States.[2] The measures may be referred to the Council by any Member State within three working days of the day on which they were notified. The Council is to meet without delay and, acting by a qualified majority, may amend or annul the measure in question.[3]

Safeguard measures in respect of exports may be taken where the quotations or prices on the world market for these products reach the level of Community prices, and where that situation is likely to continue and to deteriorate, thereby disturbing or threatening to disturb the Community market.[4] The measures which may be taken are application of an export levy, fixing of a time limit for the issue of export licences, total or partial suspension of the issue of export licences, and total or partial rejection of outstanding applications for the issue of export licences.[5] The levy to be charged is that applicable on the day of export, unless the applicant for an export licence requests at the time of requesting the licence that the levy applicable on the day of lodgment of the licence application is to be applied.[6] In urgent cases the Commission may suspend export licences totally or partially or reject outstanding applications for the issue of export licences totally or partially. Such decision must be notified to the Member States and published on the notice boards at Commission head-

---

19 Ibid Art 14(3).
20 Ibid Art 12(1). As to trigger prices, trigger volumes and the determination of import prices, see ibid Art 12(2) and (3).
1 Ibid Art 17(1), first paragraph. As with all agricultural products, the measures regarding rice must be applied having regard to the obligations arising from the Community's international agreements: ibid Art 17(4).
2 Ibid Art 17(2).
3 Ibid Art 17(3).
4 Ibid Art 16(1). A recent example concerns imports for the OCTs: see Commission Regulations 21/97, OJ 9.1.97 L5/24, and 304/97, OJ 21.2.97 L51/1. As to when world market quotations or prices are regarded as as having reached the level of Community prices, see ibid Art 16(2). As to when the situation is regarded as likely to persist or deteriorate, see ibid Art 17(3), as so substituted. As to when the Community market is regarded as being disturbed or threatened with disturbances, see ibid Art 16(4).
5 Ibid Art 16(5), first paragraph. The measures must be repealed at the latest when it is found that, for a period of three weeks, the world market quotations or prices are above Community prices: ibid Art 16(5), second paragraph. As to the factors to be taken into account in fixing the export levy, see ibid Art 16(6),(7).
6 Ibid Art 16(9).

quarters. Total or partial suspension of export licences may be applicable for a maximum of seven days.[7]

Seeds

The marketing organization for seeds[8] applies to the following seeds for sowing or of a kind used for sowing dried seeds of leguminous vegetables: spelt;[9] hybrid maize; rice; oil seeds and oleaginous fruit; and other seeds, fruit and spores.[10] In addition to regulating the Community market mainly by means of production aids, it establishes a single system of trading at the Community's external frontiers.[11]

Imports of all products which come within the market organization for seeds are subject to the relevant rates of duty of the Common Customs Tariff.[12] The tariff classification of those products is subject to the general rules for the interpretation of the combined nomenclature and the special rules for its application, and the tariff nomenclature resulting from the basic Regulation is incorporated in the CCT.[13] In the absence of specific derogations, the levying of any charge which is equivalent in its effect to a customs duty and the application of any quantitative restriction or measure having an equivalent effect are prohibited in trade with third countries.[14]

A system of import licences is applied to trade in seeds.[15] Imports into the Community of any of the products which are subject to this marketing organization may be made conditional on the submission of an import licence.[16] These licences are to be issued by the Member States to any applicant irrespective of the place of its establishment in the Community.[17] With the exception of imports which are carried out under the terms of registered contracts for growing in third countries, the issue of a licence is conditional upon the lodging of a deposit to guarantee that importation in full takes place during the period of validity of the licence.[18]

Special safeguard measures do not apply in respect of seeds. However, if, by reason of imports or exports, the Community market in any of the products which are subject to this marketing organization experiences or is threatened by serious disturbances which may endanger the objectives of the Common Agricultural Policy, general safeguard measures may be taken in trade with third countries until the disturbances or threat of disturbances have ceased.[19]

---

7 Ibid Art 16(12).
8 Council Regulation 2358/71, OJ 5.11.71 L246/1, as amended and as substituted in particular by Council Regulation 3290/94, Annex XX, OJ 31.12.94 L349/105.
9 This is a species of grain related to wheat.
10 Council Regulation 2358/71 Art 1, OJ 5.11.71 L246/71, as amended by Council Regulation 3997/87, OJ 31.12.87 L377/37. As to the amendment of the code numbers of certain products, see Commission Regulation 3375/93, OJ 10.12.93 L303/9.
11 Council Regulation 2358/71, OJ 5.11.71 L246/1, as amended and as substituted in particular by Council Regulation 3290/94, OJ 31.12.94 L349/105.
12 Ibid Art 5(1), as so substituted.
13 Ibid Art 5(2), as so substituted.
14 Ibid Art 6, as so substituted.
15 Ibid Art 4.
16 Ibid Art 4(1), first paragraph. As to the products which require an import licence, see Commission Regulation 1119/79, OJ 7.6.79 L139/13, as amended.
17 Council Regulation 2358/71 Art 4(1), first paragraph, OJ 5.11.71 L246/1.
18 Ibid Art 4(1), third paragraph. For special provisions for the implementation of this system of import licences, see Commission Regulation 1119/79, OJ 7.6.79 L139/13, as amended.
19 Ibid Art 7(1), as so substituted.

The necessary measures are to be decided by the Commission, at the request of a Member State or on its own initiative.[20] They are immediately applicable and must be notified to the Member States.[1] Measures may be referred to the Council by any Member State within three working days of the date on which they were notified. The Council is to meet without delay and, acting by qualified majority, may amend or annul the measure in question.[2]

Sheepmeat and goatmeat

The common organization of the market in sheepmeat and goatmeat[3] applies to the following products: live sheep and goats;[4] sheepmeat and goatmeat and their edible offals, whether fresh, chilled, frozen, salted, in brine, dried or smoked; fats of sheep and goats both unrendered and rendered; and other prepared or preserved meat or offals of sheep and goats other than those for the manufacture of pharmaceutrical products.[5] It takes the form of a price, premium and intervention system within the Community and a single trading system at the external frontiers of the Community.

Imports or exports may be subject to the presentation of a licence.[6] Licences are issued by the Member States to any applicant irrespective of its place of establishment within the Community.[7] They are issued subject to the lodging of a security and are valid throughout the Community.[8]

Unless otherwise provided, the CCT rates of duty apply to these products.[9] The general rules for the interpretation of the combined nomenclature and the detailed rules for its application apply to the tariff classification of these products, and the tariff nomenclature resulting from the application of the Regulation are incorporated into the CCT.[10] Unless otherwise provided, the levying of any charge having equivalent effect to a customs duty, and the application of any quantitative restriction or measure having equivalent effect, are prohibited in trade with third countries.[11]

Pursuant to the Uruguay Round agreements, tariff quotas are to be opened.[12] They are to be administered by the 'first-come, first-served' method, the 'simultaneous examination' method or the 'traditional/new arrivals' method or a combination of these, or another appropriate method, but must avoid any discrimination between the operators concerned.[13] Country-specific tariff quotas

---

20 Ibid Art 7(2), as so substituted.
 1 Ibid Art 7(2), as so substituted.
 2 Ibid Art 7(4), as so substituted.
 3 Council Regulation 3013/89, OJ 7.10.89 L289/1, as amended and as substituted in particular by Council Regulation 3290/94 Annex IX, OJ 31.12.94 L349/105.
 4 Pure-bred breeding animals are included: Council Regulation 3013/89 Art 1(b), OJ 7.10.89 L289/1, as amended.
 5 Ibid Art 1. As to the amendment of certain CN codes, see Commission Regulation 1096/94, OJ 12.5.94 L121/9.
 6 Ibid Art 9(1), first paragraph, as so substituted.
 7 Ibid Art 9(1), second paragraph, as so substituted.
 8 Ibid Art 9(1), third paragraph, as so substituted.
 9 Ibid Art 10, as so substituted.
10 Ibid Art 14(1), as so substituted.
11 Ibid Art 14(2), as so substituted.
12 Ibid Art 12(1), as so substituted. They are to be established on an annual basis, suitably phased over the year if necessary: ibid Art 12(4), as so substituted.
13 Ibid Art 12(2), as so substituted. As to the factors to be taken into account in administering the tariff quotas, see ibid Art 12(3), as so substituted.

have superseded the voluntary restraint agreements previously concluded by the Community with numerous supplying countries. The following counties are covered by these arrangements: Argentina, Australia, Bosnia Herzegovina, Bulgaria, Chile, Croatia, Hungary, Iceland, Macedonia, Poland, New Zealand, Romania, Slovenia, Uruguay.[14] In addition, imports of live animals and meat from Bulgaria, Czech Republic, Hungary, Poland, Romania, Slovakia, Estonia and Lithuania are subject to tariff quotas as agreed under various Association Agreements.[15] Similar arrangements apply to live animals from the former Yugoslav Republic of Macedonia.[16]

Special and general safeguard measures are provided in respect of sheepmeat and goatmeat.

First, in order to prevent or counteract adverse effects on the Community market which may result from imports, such imports may be subject to special safeguard measures in the form of an additional import duty if the conditions set out in Art 5 of the Uruguay Round Agreement on Agriculture are fulfilled, unless the imports are unlikely to disturb the Community market or where the effects would be disproportionate to the intended objective.[17]

Second, if, by reason of an increase in imports or exports, the Community market is affected by, or is threatened with, serious disturbance likely to jeopardize the achievement of the objectives of the Common Agricultural Policy, general safeguard measures may be applied in trade with third countries until the disturbance or threat of disturbance has ceased.[18] The Commission is to decide on the necessary measures, at the request of a Member State or on its own initiative. The measures are immediately applicable and must be notified to the Member States.[19] They may be referred to the Council by any Member State within three working days of the day on which they were notified. The Council is to meet without delay. Acting by a qualified majority, it may amend or annul the measure in question.[20]

In addition, to the extent necessary for the proper working of the common organization of the market, the Council, acting by a qualified majority on a proposal from the Commission, may, in special cases, prohibit in whole or in part the use of inward processing arrangements.[1] However, by way of derogation, if this situation arises with exceptional urgency and the Community market is disturbed or is liable to be disturbed by the inward or outward processing arrangements, the Commission is to decide on the necessary measures, on its own initiative or at the request of a Member State. Such measures are immediately applicable, are valid for no more than six months and must be notified to the Member States.[2] The measures may be referred to the Council by any Member State within a week of the day on which they were notified. The Council,

---

14 Commission Regulation 1440/95 Art 2, first indent, Annex I, OJ 27.6.95 L143/17. With regard to Australia and New Zealand, see also Council Decision 95/327 amending the Agreements in the form of exchanges of letters adjusting the quantities provided for in the voluntary restraint agreements concluded by the European Community with Australia and New Zealand respectively on trade in sheepmeat and goatmeat as a result of the enlargement of the Community, OJ 12.8.95 L191/29, to which the respective Agreements are attached.
15 Commission Regulation 1440/95 Art 2, second indent, Annex II, OJ 27.6.95 L143/17.
16 Ibid Art 2, third indent, Annex III, OJ 27.6.95 L143/17.
17 Ibid Art 11(1), as so substituted. As to trigger prices, trigger volumes, and the determination of import prices, see ibid Art 11(2),(3), as so substituted.
18 Ibid Art 15(1), first paragraph, as so substituted.
19 Ibid Art 15(2), as so substituted.
20 Ibid Art 15(3), as so substituted.
 1 Ibid Art 13(1), as so substituted.
 2 Ibid Art 13(2), as so substituted.

acting by a qualified majority, may confirm, amend or repeal the Commission decision. If the Council has not acted within three months, the Commission decision is deemed to have been repealed.[3]

Sugar, isoglucose and insulin syrup

The common organization of the markets in the sugar sector[4] applies, in particular, to beet and cane sugar or chemically pure sucrose in solid form; sugar beet and sugar cane; molasses, liquid sugars and syrups; artificial honey and caramel; beet pulp and the waste products of sugar manufacture; isoglucose; isoglucose syrups; and insulin syrup.[5] Isoglucose is a direct substitute for liquid sugar derived from sugar beet and sugar cane, so there is a close link between the markets in these two products. The situation in the Community concerning sweeteners is also characterised by structural surpluses, hence any Community action in respect of one of the products will have repercussions on the other. Consequently the present common organization embraces both sugar and isoglucose, thus enabling appropriate action to be taken with regard to both products.[6]

Imports into, or exports from, the Community of all products subject to the marketing organization in the sugar sector with the exception of beet pulp and waste products from the manufacture of sugar are subject to the presentation of an import or export licence.[7] All such licences are issued by the Member States to any applicant irrespective of the place of its establishment within the Community.[8] They are valid throughout the Community.[9] The issue of licences is conditional upon the lodging of a deposit which will become forfeit, in whole or in part, if the authorized transaction is not fully effected during the period of validity of the licence.[10]

Import of products in the sugar sector are subject to the relevant rates of duty laid down by the Commmon Customs Tariff of the Community.[11] However, to ensure that the Community market is adequately supplied with raw sugar for refining falling within CN codes 1701 11 10 and 1701 12 10 and with molasses by means of imports from third countries, the Commission may, following the management committee procedure, suspend in whole or in part the application of import duties on these products and establish the arrangements for any such suspension.[12] Suspension may apply for the period in

---

3 Ibid Art 13(3), as so substituted.
4 Council Regulation 1785/81, OJ 1.7.81 L177/4, as amended and as substituted in particular by Council Regulation 3290/94 Annex IV, OJ 31.12.94 L349/105.
5 Ibid Art 1(1), as substituted by EC Council Regulation 3993/87, OJ 31.12.87 L377/24 and Council Regulation 133/94, OJ 27.1.94 L22/7. As to amendment of the Combined Nomenclature code for certain products, see Commission Regulation 283/95, OJ 14.2.93 L34/3.
6 Ibid, preamble, 2nd recital.
7 Council Regulation 1785/81 Art 13(1), first paragraph, as substituted by Council Regulation 3290/94 Annex IV, OJ 31.12.94 L3349/105. Provision is made to extend the licence system to the exempted products: ibid Art 13(2)(a).
8 Ibid Art 13(1), second paragraph, as so substituted.
9 Ibid Art 13(1), third paragraph, as so substituted.
10 Ibid Art 13(1), third paragraph, as so substituted. Forfeiture of the entire security cannot however be prescribed as a penalty for failure to comply with the time limit imposed for the submission of applications for export licences: Case 181/84 *R v Intervention Board for Agricultural Produce (IBAP), ex p E D & F Man (Sugar)* [1985] ECR 2889.
11 Ibid Art 14(1), as so substituted.
12 Ibid Art 14(2), first paragraph, as so substituted.

which the world market price plus the CCT import duty, in the case of raw sugar, exceeds the intervention price of the product or, in the case of molasses, exceeds a specified price level.[13]

The general rules for the interpretation of the combined nomenclature and the special rules for its application apply to the tariff classification of these products, and the tariff nomenclature resulting from the application of the basic Regulation is incorporated in the CCT.[14] In the absence of specific derogations, the levying of any other customs duty or charge which has an equivalent effect, and the application of any quantitative restriction or measure which has an equivalent effect, are prohibited in trade with third countries.[15]

As a result of the Uruguay Round, tariff quotas replacing the previous system of variable import levies were to be opened.[16] The quotas are to be administered by the 'first come, first served' method, the 'simultaneous examination' method, the 'traditional/new arrivals' method, a combination of these, or any other appropriate method, provided that they avoid any discrimination between the operators concerned.[17]

A special regime applies to the importation into the Community of raw or white cane sugar which originates in any of a number of states, countries and territories.[18] This system of preferential imports is established under the terms of the Convention of Lome with the African, Caribbean and Pacific states[19] and has been extended to the overseas countries and territories of the Member States[20] and to India.[1] The imports of sugar under these provisions are preferential in that the Community import levy does not apply to them.[2] The prohibitions on the levying of any customs duty and the application of any quantitative restriction, and charges and measures which have equivalent effects, must not

---

13 Ibid Art 14(2), second paragraph, as so substituted. The relevant price level for molassses is that corresponding to the price of molasses used as a basis, for the sugar marketing year under consideration, for determining revenue from sales of molasses pursuant to the provisions of ibid Art 4(2): ibid Art 14(2), second paragraph, second indent. The world market price applies to standard quality: ibid Art 15a, as so substituted.
14 Ibid Art 19(1), as so substituted.
15 Ibid Art 19(2), as so substituted.
16 Ibid Art 16(1), as so substituted.
17 Ibid Art 16(2), as so substituted. As to the factors to be taken into account in adminstration of quotas, see ibid Art 16(3).
18 See Council Regulation 1785/81 Art 33, Annex II, OJ 1.7.81 L177/4.
19 ACP-EEC Convention of Lome (Lome, 28th February 1975; TS 105 (1979); Cmnd 7751; OJ L25, 30.1.76, p 2), Protocol 3; Second ACP-EEC Convention of Lome (Lome, 31 October 1979; T 3 (1983); Cmnd 8761; OJ L347, 22.10.83, p 2), Protocol 7; Third ACP-EEC Convention of Lome (Lome, 8 December 1984; EC 19 (1985); Cmnd 9511; *The Courier* Jan–Feb 1985; Fourth ACP-EEC Convention of Lome (Lome, 15th December 1989, OJ 17.8.91 L229/3); Lome IV Convention as revised by the agreement signed in Mauritius, 4 November 1995, *The Courier*, no 155, January–February 1996. See also Council Regulation 1255/82, OJ 26.5.82 L147/1 (accession of Zimbabwe to the Lome Convention); Council Regulation 1764/84, OJ 26.6.84 L166/5 (giving Ivory Coast an ACP quota); Council Regulation 1763/84, OJ 26.6.84 L166/1 (giving full ACP membership to St Christopher and Nevis); Council Regulation 1256/82, OJ 26.5.82 L147/4 (giving full ACP membership to Belize); Council Decision 95/85, OJ 31.5.95 L120/37 (allocating quota to Zambia).
20 Council Decision 80/1186, OJ 3.12.80 L361/1 as amended. See also Joined Cases 250/86 and 11/87 *RAR Refinarias de Acucar Reunidas SA v EC Council and EC Commission* [1989] ECR 2045.
 1 Council Decision 75/456, OJ 23.7.75 L190/35 and the Agreement between the European Economic Community and India on Cane Sugar, OJ 23.7.75 L190/35. See also Council Regulation 1243/84, OJ 5.5.84 L120/1.
 2 Council Regulation 1785/81 Art 35(1), OJ 1.7.81 L177/4.

in any circumstances be derogated from in respect of preferential sugar.[3] Where the quality of imported preferential sugar deviates from the standard quality which has been adopted by the Community,[4] the prices will be adjusted by means of increases or reductions, as the situation requires.[5]

Extra raw sugar, known as Special Preferential Sugar, is imported from ACP States at reduced duty in order to meet the needs of Community refiners.[6]

Export refunds may be available to cover the difference between the Community price and the world market price in order to permit exports of solid beet sugar and cane sugar, molasses, liquid sugars and syrups and artificial honey and caramel in either unprocessed or processed form.[7] Provision may also be made for export refunds for other products.[8] Refunds are the same for the whole Community but may vary according to destination, where the world market situation or the specific requirements of certain markets make this necessary.[9] Refunds may be fixed at regular intervals or in certain cases by invitation to tender.[10] Refunds are granted on application and on presentation of the relevant export licence.[11] The refund is that applicable on the day of application of the licence and, in the case of a differentiated refund, that applicable on the same day for the destination indicated on the licence or for the actual destination if it differs from the destination indicated on the licence.[12] The refund is paid upon proof that the products have been exported from the Community and that, in the case of a differentiated refund, the products have reached the destination indicated on the licence or another destination for which a refund was fixed.[13]

---

3 Ibid Art 35(2).
4 As to this quality, see Council Regulation 431/68 (raw sugar), OJ 10.4.68 L89/3 and Council Regulation 793/72 (white sugar), OJ 21.4.72 L94/1.
5 Council Regulation 1785/81 Art 34, OJ 1.7.81 L177/4. For further rules on the importation of preferential sugar, see Commission Regulation 2782/76, OJ 18.11.76 L318/13, as amended.
6 Ibid Art 37, as amended and implemented. The first 75,000 tonnes are allocated to Ivory Coast, Swaziland, Malawi and Zimbabwe, the traditional suppliers of Portugal; the rest is divided among ACP States pro rata with ACP Preferential Quotas. This sugar is not included in the category of ACP preferential sugar under the Lome Convention, and the price paid for it is not the guaranteed price paid for ACP Preferential Sugar. The Community sugar refining industry is limited to the United Kingdom, France, Portugal and Finland.
7 Ibid Art 17(1), as so substituted. The refund for raw sugar may not exceed that for white sugar: ibid Art 17(1), second paragraph. The refund for processed products may not be greater than that for products exported without further processing: ibid Art 17(3), as so substituted.
8 Ibid Art 17(2), first paragraph.
9 Ibid Art 17(5), first paragraph, as so substituted. This may be waived in the case of food-aid operations: ibid Art 17(10), as so substituted. As to the factors to be taken into account in determining the amount of the refund, see ibid Art 17(2), second paragraph, and Art 17(6), as so substituted; see also Art 17(10), as so substituted. As to the method to be adopted for the allocation of quantities export with a refund, see ibid Art 17(4), as so substituted.
10 Ibid Art 17(5), second paragraph. Refunds fixed at regular intervals may, where necessary, be adjusted in the intervening period by the Commission at the request of a Member State or on its own initiative: ibid Art 17(5), third sub-paragraph, as so substituted.
11 Ibid Art 17(7), as so substituted.
12 Ibid Art 8, first paragraph, as so substituted. In the latter case the amount applicable may not exceed the amount applicable for the destination indicated on the licence: ibid.
13 Ibid Art 17(11).

Specific conditions govern the granting of refunds on exports in the natural state of certain non-denatured products.[14]

Special and general safeguard measures are available in respect of imports of sugar.

First, in addition to the appropriate CCT duty, in order to prevent or counteract adverse effects on the Community market which may result from imports, such imports may be subject to special safeguard measures in the form of payment of an additional import duty if the conditions set out in Art 5 of the Uruguay Round Agreement on Agriculture are fulfilled unless the imports are unlikely to disturb the Community market, or where the effects would be disproportionate to the intended objective.[15]

Second, if, by reason of imports or exports, the Community market is affected by, or threatened with, serious disturbance likely to jeopardize the achievement of the objectives of the Common Agricultural Policy, appropriate measures may be applied in trade with third countries until the disturbance or threat of disturbance has ceased.[16] At the request of a Member State or on its own initiative the Commission is to decide on the necessary measures. The measures are immediately applicable and must be notified to the Member States.[17] They may be referred to the Council by any Member State within three working days of the day on which they were notified. The Council is to meet without delay and, acting by a qualified majority, may amend or annul the measure in question.[18]

In addition, to the extent necessary for the proper working of the common organization of the markets in the sugar sector, the Council, acting by qualified majority on a Commission proposal, may prohibit in whole or in part the use of inward processing arrangements.[19] If this situation arises with exceptional urgency, and the Community market is disturbed or is liable to be disturbed by inward or outward processing arrangements, the Commission is to decide on the necessary measures, either at the request of a Member State or on its own initiative.[20] Such measures are immediately applicable, are valid for no more than six months, and must be notified to the Council and the Member States.[1] They may be referred to the Council by any Member State within a week of the day on which they were notified. Acting by a qualified majority, the Council may confirm, amend or repeal the Commission decision. If the Council has not acted within three weeks, the Commission decision is deemed to have been repealed.[2]

Provision may also be made for an export levy when the world market price for sugar exceeds the intervention price. The levy must be applied when the cif price of white sugar or raw sugar is greater than the intervention price plus an amount equal to the sum of 10 per cent of the intervention price and the storage

---

14 See ibid Art 17(12), (13), Art 17a, 17b, 17c, as so substituted.
15 Ibid Art 15(1), as so substituted. As to trigger prices, trigger volumes and the determination of import prices, see ibid Art 15(2),(3), as so substituted.
16 Ibid Art 21(1), as so substituted.
17 Ibid Art 21(2).
18 Ibid Art 21(3), as so substituted.
19 Ibid Art 18(1). As to arrangements, see Case C-103/96 *Directeur Général des Douanes et Droits Indirects v Eridania Beghin-Say* [1997] ECR I-1453.
20 Ibid Art 18(2), as so substituted.
 1 Ibid Art 18(2), as so substituted.
 2 Ibid Art 18(3).

levy applicable during the marketing year concerned.[3] In these circumstances, provision may also be made for import subsidies.[4]

Tobacco

The common organization of the market in raw tobacco[5] applies to raw or unmanufactured tobacco and tobacco refuse falling with CN heading 2401.[6] It comprises a premium system, measures to orient and limit production, and arrangements for trade with third countries.[7]

Imports of these products from third countries are subject to the relevant rates of duty laid down by the Common Customs Tariff.[8] The general rules for the interpretation of the combined nomenclature and the special rules for its application apply to the classification of these products.[9] In the absence of specific derogations, the levying of any other charge which has an effect equivalent to a customs duty and the application of any quantitative restriction or measure having an equivalent effect are prohibited in trade with third countries.[10]

There are no export refunds for tobacco.

Special safeguard measures are not applicable in respect of tobacco. However, if, by reason of imports or exports, the Community market experiences or is threatened by serious disturbances likely to jeopardize the achievement of the objectives of the Common Agricultural Policy, appropriate general safeguard measures may be taken in trade with third countries until the disturbances or threats of disturbance have ceased.[11] If this situation arises, the Commission is to decide on the necessary measures, at the request of a Member State or on its own initiative. The measures are immediately applicable and the Member States must be notified.[12] The measures may be referred to the Council by any Member State within three working days of the day on which they were notified. The Council is to meet without delay, and acting by a qualified majority it may amend or annul the measure in question.[13]

Wine

The common organization of the market in wine[14] applies to grape juice, grape must, wine of fresh grapes, fresh grapes (other than table grapes), wine vinegar, piquette, wine lees and grape marc.[15] It consists of rules governing production

---

3 Ibid Art 20(1), as so substituted.
4 Ibid Art 20(2), first paragraph. As to the decision-making procedure, see ibid Art 20(2), third paragraph, as so substituted.
5 Council Regulation 2075/92, OJ 230.7.92 L215/70, as amended and in particular as substituted by Council Regulation 3290/94, OJ 31.12.94 L349/105.
6 Ibid Art 1, second paragraph.
7 Ibid Art 1, first paragraph.
8 Ibid Art 15, as so substituted.
9 Ibid Art 16(1), as so substituted.
10 Ibid Art 16(2), as so substituted.
11 Ibid Art 16a(1), first paragraph, as so substituted.
12 Ibid Art 16a(2), as so substituted.
13 Ibid Art 16a(3), as so substituted.
14 Council Regulation 822/87, OJ 27.3.87 L84/1, as amended and in particular as substituted by Council Regulation 3290/94 Annex XVI, OJ 31.12.94 L349/105.
15 Ibid Art 1(2), as amended. 'Grape juice' means unfermented but fermentable grape must which has undergone the appropriate treatment rendering it fit for consumption as it is and which has an actual alcoholic strength by volume of not more than 1% vol; 'grape must'

and control of the development of wine-growing potential, rules governing oenological practices and processes, a price system and rules governing intervention and other measures to improve market conditions, arrangements for trade with third countries, and rules governing circulation and release to the market.[16] The Council has also enacted rules governing the preparation and marketing of liqueur wines[17] and the definition, description and presentation of spirit drinks.[18]

Imports into the Community of grape juice, grape musts and wine of fresh grapes are conditional on the production of an import licence.[19] Imports of any other products covered by the common organization of the market in wine, as well as exports of all products within the scope of the wine marketing organization, may also be made conditional on the production of a licence.[20] Licences are issued by the Member States, upon request, to any applicant irrespective of its place of establishment in the Community.[1] Licences are valid throughout the Community.[2] A licence is issued subject to the provision of a security which is liable to forfeiture, in whole or in part, if the authorized import or export transaction is not fully executed during the period of validity of the licence.[3]

Imports of products which are within the scope of this marketing organization are subject to the relevant rates of duty laid down by the Common Customs Tariff.[4] For musts falling within CN code 2204 30 for which application of the CCT duties depends on the import price of the imported product, the accuracy of that price is to be checked by means of a flat-rate import value calculated by the Commission, depending on the origin and product on the

means the liquid product obtained naturally or by physical processes from fresh grapes with an actual alcoholic strength by volume of not more than 1%; 'wine' means the product obtained exclusively from the total or partial alcoholic fermentation of fresh grapes, whether or not crushed, or of grape musts; 'fresh grapes' means the fruit of the vine used in making wine, ripe or even slightly raisined, which may be crushed or pressed by normal wine-cellar means and which may spontaneously produce alcoholic fermentation; 'wine vinegar' means vinegar which is obtained exclusively by acetous fermentation of wine, and has a total acidity of not less than 60 g/l expressed in acetic acid; 'piquette' means the product obtained by the fermentation of untreated grape marc macerated in water, or by leaching fermented grape marc with water; 'wine lees' means the muddy residue accumulating in wine vessels after fermentation or during the storage of wine, dried or not; and 'grape must' means the residue from the pressing of fresh grapes, whether or not fermented: Art 1(4)(a), Annex I, amended by Council Regulations 2253/88, OJ 26.7.88 L198/35 and 4250/88, OJ 31.12.88 L373/35.

16 Council Regulation 822/87 Art 1(1).
17 See Council Regulation 4252/88, OJ 31.12.88 L373/79. As to the definition of 'liqueur wines', see Council Regulation 822/87 Art 1(4)(a), second indent, Annex I (14), OJ 27.3.87 L84/1, as inserted by Council Regulation 4250/88, OJ 31.12.88 L373/55.
18 See Council Regulation 1576/89, which was enacted pursuant to Council Regulation 822/87 Art 72(1).
19 Council Regulation 822/87 Art 52(1), as substituted by Council Regulation 3290/94, OJ 31.12.94 L349/105. As to general rules for the import of wines, grape juice and grape must, see Council Regulation 2390/89 OJ 9.8.89 L232/1, as amended. As to special detailed rules in respect of import and export licences in the wine sector, see Commission Regulation 3388/81, OJ 28.11.81 L341/19, as amended.
20 Ibid Art 52(1), as so substituted. As to derogations in respect of certain oenological practices not allowed by Community rules, see Council Regulation 1873/84, OJ 3.7.84 L176/6, as amended; and as extended to 31 December 1998 by Council Regulation 2612/97, OJ 24.12.97 L353/2.
1 Ibid Art 52(2), first paragraph, as so substituted.
2 Ibid Art 52(2), second paragraph, as so substituted.
3 Ibid Art 52(2), third paragraph, as so substituted.
4 Ibid Art 53(1), as so substituted.

basis of the weighted average prices for the product on Member States' representative import markets or on other markets where applicable.[5] The general and special rules for the interpretation and application of the tariff apply to the tariff classification of those products and the resulting tariff nomenclature is incorporated in the Common Customs Tariff.[6] Save as otherwise provided, the levying of any other charge equivalent to a customs duty and the application of any quantitative restriction or measure which has an equivalent effect is prohibited in trade with third countries.[7]

Imports of products to which alcohol has been added are prohibited, with the exception of those products equivalent to products originating in the Community in respect of which such an admixture is permitted.[8]

Imported wine intended for direct human consumption and described with the aid of a geographical ascription may be eligible, with regard to its marketing in the Community and with the proviso that reciprocity exists, for control and protection arrangements provided by Community legislation regarding quality wines produced in specified regions.[9]

Member States are required, however, to take all necessary measures to enable interested parties to prevent[10] the use in the Community of a geographical indication attached to grape must and wine of fresh grapes for products not originating in the indicated place. This applies even where the true origin of the goods is indicated or the geographical indication is used in translation or is accompanied by expressions such as 'kind', 'type', 'style', 'imitation' or the like.[11]

Reduced duties apply to certain wines from Bulgaria, Hungary, and Romania.[12]

Export refunds may be available for certain products to the extent necessary to enable these products to be exported on the basis of world market prices and within the limits of the Community's international obligations.[13] The relevant products fall into two groups: first, grape juice, grape must, wine of fresh grapes, grape must with fermentation arrested by the addition of

---

5 Ibid Art 53(2), first paragraph, as so substituted. In certain circumstances the lodging of a security is required: see ibid Art 53(2), third paragraph, as so substituted.
6 Ibid Art 58(1), as so substituted.
7 Ibid Art 58(2), as so substituted.
8 Ibid Art 59(1), as so substituted.
9 Ibid Art 61(1), as so substituted. The relevant Community legislation is Council Regulation 823/87, OJ 27.3.87 L84/59, as amended. This provision is to be implemented by means of agreements with third countries on the basis of EC Art 113: ibid Art 61(2), as so substituted.
10 On the terms stipulated in Arts 23 and 24 of the Agreement on Trade-Related Aspects of Intellectual Property Rights.
11 Ibid Art 72a(1), first paragraph, as so substituted. For these purposes, 'geographical indications' mean indications which identify a product as originating in the territory of a third country which is a member of the WTO, or in a region or locality within that territory, in cases where a certain quality, reputation, or other given characteristic of the product may be attributed essentially to that geographical place of origin: ibid Art 72a(1), second paragraph, as so substituted. These provisions apply notwithstanding other specific provisions in Community legislation laying down rules for the designation and presentation of the relevant products: ibid Art 72a(2), as so substituted.
12 Council Regulation 933/95, OJ 28.4.95 L96/1. As to Slovenia, see Council Regulation 70/97, OJ 18.1.97 L16/1.
13 Council Regulation 822/87 Art 55(1), as so substituted. As to the factors to be taken into account in the allocation of quantities which may be exported with refunds, see ibid Art 55(2), as so substituted. As to product nomenclature, see Commission Regulation 3846/87 OJ 24.12.87 L336/1, as amended by Commission Regulation 1297/97, OJ 4.4.97 L176/30.

alcohol, fresh grapes other than table grapes and wine vinegar;[14] and, secondly, sugars falling within CN code 1701, glucose and glucose syrup falling within CN codes 17092 30 91, 1702 30 99, 1702 40 90 and 1702 90 50, including in the form of products falling within CN codes 1702 30 51 and 1702 30 59, incorporated into products falling within CN codes 2009 60 11, 2009 60 71, 2009 60 79 and 2204 30 99.[15]

Refunds are the same for the whole Community but may vary according to destination where the situation on the international market or the specific requirements of certain markets make this necessary.[16] They are fixed at regular intervals by the management committee procedure,[17] but may be adjusted in the intervening period by the Commission at the request of a Member State or on its own initiative.[18] They are granted only on application and on presentation of the relevant export licence.[19] The refund is that applicable on the day of application for the licence and, in the case of a differentiated refund, that applicable on the same day for the destination indicated on the licence or, if appropriate, for the actual destination if it differs from that indicated on the licence.[20] The refund is to be paid upon proof that the products are of Community origin,[1] have been exported from the Community and, in the case of a differentiated refund, have reached the destination indicated on the licence or another destination for which the refund was fixed.[2]

Compliance with export volume limits agreed during the Uruguay Round is ensured on the basis of export certificates issued for specific periods, but the ending of a reference period does not affect the validity of export licences.[3]

To the extent necessary for the proper working of the common organization of the market, the Council may, in particular cases and by qualified majority vote on a Commission proposal, prohibit wholly or in part the use of inward processing arrangements.[4] If this situation occurs with particular urgency, and if the Community market is or is likely to be disturbed by outward or inward processing arrangements, the Commission is to decide on the necessary measures, at the request of a Member State or on its own initiative. The measures apply immediately, their period of validity may not exceed six months,

---

14 Ibid Art 55(1)(a).
15 Ibid Art 55(1)(b), as so substituted. As to the amount of refund on these products, see ibid Art 56(2), first paragraph, as so substituted.
16 Ibid Art 55(3), first paragraph, as so substituted.
17 Ibid Art 55(3), second paragraph, as so substituted. As to the procedure, see ibid Art 83. As to factors to be taken into account when fixing refunds, see ibid Art 56(3), as so substituted.
18 Ibid Art 55(3), third paragraph, as so substituted. The intervals at which the list of products is to be fixed and the amount of the refund are determined by the management committee procedure: ibid Art 56(5), as so substituted.
19 Ibid Art 55(4), as so substituted. This may be waived in the case of food-aid operations: ibid Art 55(6), as so substituted.
20 Ibid Art 55(5), first paragraph, as so substituted, which also provides that, in the latter case, the amount applicable may not exceed the amount applicable to the destination indicated on the licence. These provisons may be waived in the case of food-aid operations: ibid Art 55(6), as so substituted.
1 Except in the case of products imported for inward processing and for which import duties have been collected on importation: ibid Art 56(7).
2 Ibid Art 56(6), as so substituted. To qualify for the refund, processed products must, on export, be accompanied by a declaration from the applicant indicating the amounts of raw sugar, white sugar, glucose and glucose syrup used in their manufacture: Art 56(2), second paragraph, as so substituted.
3 Ibid Art 55(7), as so substituted.
4 Ibid Art 57(1), as so substituted.

and the Council and the Member States must be notified.[5] Any Member State may refer the Commission's decision to the Council within one week of the day on which it was notified. Acting by a qualified majority, the Council may confirm, amend or annul the Commission's decision. If the Council has not reached a decision within three months, the Commission's decision is deemed to have been repealed.[6]

Special and general safeguard measures are applicable in respect of wine.

First, in order to prevent or counteract adverse effects on the Community market which may result from imports, such imports are subject to special safeguard measures in the form of an additional import duty if the conditions set out in Art 5 of the Agreement on Agriculture are fulfilled, unless the imports are unlikely to disturb the Community market, or where the effects would be disproportionate to the intended objective.[7]

Second, if, by reason of imports or exports, the Community market in one or more products is affected by, or is threatened with, serious disturbance likely to jeopardize the achievement of the objectives of the Common Agricultural Policy, appropriate general safeguard measures may be applied in trade with third countries until the disturbance has ceased.[8] If this situation arises, the Commission, at the request of a Member State or on its own initiative, is to decide upon the necessary measures. The measures are immediately applicable, and the Member States must be notified.[9] Any Member State may refer the Commission's measures to the Council within three working days of the day on which they were notified. The Council is to meet without delay, and acting by a qualified majority may amend or annul the measure in question.[10]

Other Annex II products

The products which are subject to the Common Agricultural Policy of the Community are set out in Annex II to the EEC Treaty.[11] A special common organization of the market applies to products in respect of which no special, individual market organization has been established.[12] It applies to a wide range of animal and vegetable products[13] which fall into the following categories: pure-bred breeding animals and other live animals such as asses, mules and hinnies; meat and edible offals from such animals and other edible prod-

---

5 Ibid Art 57(2), as so substituted.
6 Ibid Art 57(3), as so substituted.
7 Ibid Art 54(1), as so substituted. As to trigger prices, trigger volumes and the determination of import prices, see ibid Art 54(2), (3), as so substituted.
8 Ibid Art 60(1), first paragraph, as so substituted. In order to justify whether measures are justified, the following in particular must be taken into account: the quantities in respect of which import licences have been issued or applied for and the figures given in the forecast supply balance; and, where appropriate, the scale of intervention: ibid Art 60(1), second paragraph, as so substituted.
9 Ibid Art 60(2), as so substituted.
10 Ibid Art 60(3), as so substituted.
11 EEC Treaty, Annex II, as amended by Council Regulation 7a, OJ 31.1.61 L7/71/61; OJ Sp Ed 1959–62, 68.
12 Council Regulation 827/68, OJ 30.6.68 L151/16, as amended and in particular as substituted by Council Regulation 3290/94 Annex XXI, OJ 31.12.94 L349/105. As to organic products, see Council Regulation 2092/91, OJ 22.7.91 L198/1, as amended, and Commission Regulation 94/92, OJ 17.1.92 L11/14, as amended.
13 See ibid Art 1, Annex (as replaced by EC Council Regulation 3911/87, OJ 30.12.87 L387/36).

ucts of animal origin; other animal products unfit for unfit for human consumption;[14] dried leguminous and other vegetables; dates, bananas, coconuts and other nuts; coffee; tea; spices; vegetable and fruit flours; starches; vegetable products used in perfumery and pharmacy or for insecticidal, fungicidal and similar purposes; chicory, locust beans and the stones and kernels of fruits; cereal straw and husks; mangolds, swedes, fodder roots and other fodder products; animal fats for industrial uses; lard; meat and fish extracts; cocoa beans and shells; fermented beverages such as cider, perry and mead; meat and fish flours and meals; brans and other milling residues; wastes and residues from sugar manufacture; wine lees; vegetable products used for animal feed, such as acorns and sweet chestnuts; sweetened forage derived from marine sources.

The aim of this marketing organization is to establish a single market for all such products.[15] No system of prices or system of trade is established for these products. The substantive provisions of the enabling regulation are limited to basic rules concerning customs duties, quantitative restrictions, free movement and protective measures.

Imports into the Community of goods which are within this residual marketing organization are subject to the appropriate duties laid down by the Common Customs Tariff.[16] The general rules for the interpretation of the combined nomenclature and the special rules for its application apply to the classification of these products, and the tariff nomenclature resulting from the application of the basic Regulation is incorporated into the CCT.[17] Save as otherwise provided, and subject to obligations arising under international agreements relating to the products subject to this marketing organization,[18] the levying of any charge which has an effect equivalent to a customs duty and the application of any quantitative restriction or measure which has an equivalent effect are prohibited in trade with third countries.[19]

Special safeguard measures do not apply in respect of these products. However, if, by reason of imports or exports, the Community market in any of the products which are subject to this marketing organization experiences, or is threatened by, serious disturbances which may jeopardize the objectives of the Common Agricultural Policy, appropriate general safeguard measures may be taken in trade with third countries until such disturbances or the threat of disturbances has come to an end.[20] If the situation arises, the Commission is to take the necessary measures, at the request of a Member State or on its own initiative. The measure is immediately applicable and the Member States must be notified.[1] The Commission measures may be referred to the Council by any Member State within three working days of the day on which they were noti-

---

14 This does not include wool: see Case 77/83 *CILFIT Srl v Ministero della Sanita* [1984] ECR 1257, ECJ.

15 Council Regulation 827/68, preamble, fourth recital, OJ 30.6.68 L151/16.

16 Council Regulation 827/68, art 2(1), OJ 30.6.68 L151/16, as substituted by Council Regulation 3290/94, OJ 31.12.94 L349/105.

17 Ibid Art 2(2), as so substituted.

18 See the International Cocoa Agreements 1980 (Geneva, 19 November 1980; Misc 10 (1981), Cmnd 8226, OJ 31.10.81 L313/3); 1986 (OJ 12.3.87 L69/26); and 1993 (OJ 23.2.94 L52/26) and the International Coffee Agreement 1994, OJ 26.8.94 L222/4.

19 Ibid Art 2(3), as so substituted.

20 Ibid Art 3(1), as so substituted.

 1 Ibid Art 3(2), as so substituted.

fied. The Council is to meet without delay, and by a qualified majority it may amend or annul the measure in question.[2]

Non-Annex II products

The CAP led to increased prices of basic agricultural products used as raw material by the Community's food industry. Consequently a special trading system was adopted in 1966 to cover trade in goods processed from these basic products.[3] This system in revised form still governs these so-called 'non-Annex II products'.[4]

The regulation distinguishes among three categories of products: agricultural products,[5] basic products,[6] and goods.[7] It may also apply to certain products in the framework of preferential trade.[8]

Goods[9] are subject to a charge on importation into the Community.[10] For processed products,[11] the charge previously consisted in the past of a fixed component and a variable component. The fixed component took the form of

2 Ibid Art 3(3), as so substituted.
3 Council Regulation 160/66, OJ 1.9.66 L195/3361.
4 The current regulation is Council Regulation 3448/93, OJ 20.12.93 L318/18. Implementing measures are laid down by Commission Regulation 1294/94, OJ 4.6.94 L141/12, as amended. As to detailed rules for implementing certain preferential trade arrangements, see Commission Regulation 1460/96, OJ 26.7.96 L187/18. As to methods of analysis and other technical provisions necessary for the application of the import procedures for such products containing milk fats, see Commission Regulation 4154/87, OJ 31.12.87 L392/19, as amended.
5 That is, products covered by Annex II to the Treaty: Council Regulation 3448/93 Art 1(2), first paragraph, first indent. OJ 20.12.93 L318/18. These products are included within the CAP.
6 That is, certain agricultural products listed in Annex A of Council Regulation 3448/93, or assimilated to those products, or resulting from their processing, for which differences are established between prices on the Community market and prices on the world market: Council Regulation 3448/93 Art 1(2), first paragraph, second indent, OJ 20.12.93 L318/18. There are certain exceptions in respect of products covered by preferential agreements: see Art 1(2), first paragraph, second indent, (i), (ii). The products listed in Annex A by CN code are: 0401 unconcentrated and unsweetened milk and cream; 0402 concentrated or sweetened milk and cream; ex 0403 buttermilk, curdled milk and cream, yoghurt, kephir and other fermented or acidified milk and cream; 0404 whey and products consisting of natural milk constituents not elsewhere specified or included; 0405 butter and other fats and oils derived from milk; 0709 90 60 fresh or chilled sweet corn; 0712 90 19 dried sweet corn, other than hybrids for sowing; Chapter 10 cereals; 1701 cane or beet sugar and chemically pure sucrose, in solid form; 1703 molasses resulting from the extraction or refining of sugar.
7 That is, products not covered by Annex II to the Treaty and listed in Annex B to the Regulation, obtained wholly or partly from agricultural products: ibid Art 1(2), third indent. These goods, which contain too many products to be listed here, are currently divided into two categories: processed products on which variable and fixed imported charges are levied, and goods on which there is no variable import levy.
8 Ibid Art 1(3), first paragraph. In this case the list of products covered is to be established by the agreement concerned: ibid Art 1(3), second paragraph.
9 That is, goods listed in Annex B of the Regulation.
10 Ibid Art 2(1), which also provides that the charge is to take account, first, of the production and marketing conditions of the goods and, second, of the difference between the prices of the Community market of agricultural products used in their production and the prices of imports from third countries where the total cost of the basic products in question is higher in the Community or, if provided by a preferential agreement, the prices of the agricultural products in certain third countries.
11 Listed in Table 1 of Annex B of the Regulation. This Table may be amended by the Council in accordance with the procedure laid down in EC Art 113: ibid Art 12(1).

an *ad valorem* duty to take account of the production and marketing conditions of the goods, while the variable 'agricultural component' was designed to offset the difference in prices on the Community market and the lower price of imports.[12] However, under the Uruguay Round Agreement the fixed component will be reduced over a period of six years, and the 'agricultural component' will be replaced by fixed amounts, which will then be progressively reduced.[13] For other goods[14] the agricultural component consists of a duty or specific amount established per measurement unit.[15] With the exception of safeguard measures,[16] the levying of any customs duty or charge having equivalent effect other than this charge is prohibited.[17]

Special rules govern imports within the framework of preferential arrangements.[18]

Export refunds may be available for these products.[19] However, no export refund may be granted on agricultural products incorporated into goods not covered by a common organization of the market providing for export refunds on products exported in the form of such goods.[20] When levies, charges or other measures are applied to exports of basic products,[1] appropriate measures in respect of related goods may be decided, taking due account of the specified interests of the processing industry.[2]

Safeguard measures are also provided. Where there is a danger that a reduction in the agricultural component applicable to goods under a preferential arrangement could disturb the agricultural market(s) in the goods concerned, the safeguard clauses applicable to imports of the agricultural products shall also apply to goods.[3]

12 Ibid Art 2. As to the determination of the variable component, see ibid Art 3. As to the establishment of the agricultural component, see ibid Art 13.

13 As to the calculation of the variable component after import levies on basic products are replaced by fixed amounts, see ibid Art 5. As to the determination of the agricultural component in the case of trade in the framework of preferential agreements, see ibid Art 6.

14 Listed in Table 2 of Annex B of the Regulation. This Table may be amended in accordance with the safety net (*contrefilet*) procedure, which is provided in ibid Art 16: ibid Art 12(2). As to the establishment of the committee, see ibid Art 15.

15 Ibid Art 2(3). This charge may not exceed the maximum charge laid down by the CCT: ibid Art 4(1). As to the calculation of any additional duty on various kinds of sugar, see ibid Art 4(2).

16 As provided in ibid Art 10.

17 Ibid Art 2(4).

18 See ibid Art 7. For example, see Council Regulation 339/97, OJ 27.2.97 L58/1 (Europe Agreements).

19 Ibid Art 8(1). As to the fixing of refunds, see ibid Art 8(2)–(4). As to detailed rules for granting and fixing export refunds, see Commission Regulation 1222/94, OJ 31.5.94 L136/5, as amended. As to detailed rules for advance-fixing certificates for exports, see Commission Regulation 1223/94, OJ 31.5.94 L136/33, as amended. As to certain transitional measures for the issue of advance fixing certificates before the entry into force of the Uruguay Round, see Commission Regulation 2668/95, OJ 3.6.95 L123/5, as amended by Commission Regulation 2306/95, OJ 30.9.95 L233/50. As to spirituous beverages, see Commission Regulation 1014/90, OJ 25.4.90 L105/9, as amended. Export refunds in respect of certain types of whiskey are governed by the cereals regime, as to which see above.

20 Ibid Art 8(2).

1 Listed in Annex A.

2 Ibid Art 9.

3 That is, to the goods listed in Annex B: ibid Art 10, first paragraph.

Outermost regions

Special provisions apply to certain geographically peripheral Community regions,[4] namely the French overseas departments,[5] the Azores and Madeira,[6] and the Canary Islands.[7]

For example, the CCT import duties do not apply to direct imports into the French overseas departments of quantities of the following products up to specified annual supply requirements: cereals for animal feed originating in developing countries, cereals for human consumption originating in the overseas countries and territories or in the ACP States, and, in certain circumstances, cereals for animal feed originating in other third countries and cereals for human consumption originating in developing countries.[8] No export refunds are paid on exports of cereals or cereal-based products from the French overseas departments.[9]

Customs duties do not apply to direct imports from third countries into the Azores and Madeira of certain products covered by specific supply arrangements for products used as inputs for everyday consumption or manufacture of certain essential foodstuffs.[10] The products covered by specific supply arrangements may not be re-exported to third countries or redispatched to the rest of the Community, with the exception of traditional exports or shipments to the rest of the Community of products processed in the Azores and Madeira.[11] No export refunds are paid on these products.[12]

Customs duties do not apply to direct imports from third countries into the Canary Islands of products covered by specific supply arrangements within

4 See EC Art 227(2), as substituted by the Amsterdam Treaty.
5 See Council Regulation 3763/91, OJ 24.12.91 L356/1, as amended and in particular as substituted by Council Regulation 3290/94 Annex XXII, OJ 31.12.94 L349/105.
6 See Council Regulation 1600/92, OJ 27.6.92 L171/1, as amended and in particular as substituted by Council Regulation 3290/94 Annex XXII, OJ 31.12.94 L349/105.
7 See Council Regulation 1601/92, OJ 27.6.92 L173/13, as amended and in particular as substituted by Council Regulation 3290/94 Annex XXII, OJ 31.12.94 L349/105.
8 Council Regulation 3763/91 Art 2(1),(2), OJ 24.12.91 L356/1, amended by Council Regulation 3290/94 Annex XXII, OJ 31.12.94 L349/105. As to detailed rules, see Commission Regulation 388/92, OJ 19.2.92 L43/16, as amended most recently by Commission Regulation 2521/97, OJ 17.12.97 L346/42.
9 Ibid Art 2(5).
10 Council Regulation 1600/92 Art 3(1), OJ 27.6.92 L173/1, as amended by Council Regulation 3290/94 Annex XXII, OJ 31.12.94 L349/105. For the Azores the products originally concerned were cereals, rice and raw sugarbeet: ibid Annex I. For Madeira the products were cereals, hops, rice, vegetable oils, beef and veal, pigmeat, milk products and for 1992–93 to 1995–96 seed potatoes: ibid Annex II. As to current arrangements for specific products, see Commission Regulation 1913/92, OJ 11.7.92 L192/35, as amended (beef and veal for Azores and Madeira); Commission Regulation 1273/97, OJ 2.7.97 L174/43, as amended (cereal products for Azores and Madeira); Commission Regulation 1262/97, OJ 2.7.97 L174/17, as amended (eggs and poultrymeat for Azores and Madeira); Commission Regulation 1725/92, OJ 27.6.92 L73/1, as amended (pigmeat for Azores and Madeira); Commission Regulation 1324/96, OJ 10.7.96 L171/3, as amended (rice products for Azores and Madeira); Commission Regulation 26/98, OJ 8.1.98 L4/53 (sheepmeat and goatmeat for Azores and Madeira); Commission Regulation 2177/92, OJ 31.7.92 L217/71, as amended, and its Annex as replaced by Commission Regulation 2431/97, OJ 9.12.97 L337/7 (sugar for Azores and Madeira); Commission Regulation 2219/92, OJ 1.8.92 L218/75, as amended (dairy products for Madeira); Commission Regulation 2026/92, OJ 23.7.92 L207/18, as amended (olive oil for Madeira); Commission Regulation 2999/92, OJ 17.10.92 L310/7, as amended (processed fruit and vegetables for Madeira).
11 Ibid Art 8.
12 Ibid Art 9.

certain quantitative limits.[13] Nor do customs duties apply to direct imports of specified categories of raw and semi-manufactured tobacco.[14] The products covered by specific supply arrangements may not be re-exported to third countries or redispatched to the rest of the Community, with the exception of traditional exports or shipments to the Community of products processed in the Islands.[15] No export refunds are paid on these products.[16]

13 Council Regulation 1601/92 Art 3(1), OJ 27.6.92 L173/13, as amended by Council Regulation 3290/94, OJ 31.12.94 L349/105. The products covered by specific supply arrangements included cereals, hops, rice, vegetable oils, sugar, concentrated fruit juice, beef and veal, frozen pigmeat, frozen poultrymeat, dried eggs, table wines, seed potatoes, milk products and, for the 1992–93 to 1995–96 marketing years, fresh or chilled pigmeat and processed meat products: ibid Annex.
14 Ibid Art 6(1).
15 Ibid Art 8.
16 Ibid Art 9.

Chapter 17

Health measures in the agricultural sector

THE WTO AGREEMENT ON THE APPLICATION OF SANITARY AND PHYTOSANITARY MEASURES

The WTO Agreement on the Application of Sanitary and Phytosanitary Measures[1] resulted from the Uruguay Round. Its purpose is to elaborate rules for the application of the rules of GATT 1994 which relate to the use of sanitary or phytosanitary measures, in particular the provisions of GATT Article XX(b).[2] In other words, it is designed to establish a multilateral framework of rules and disciplines to guide the development, adoption and enforcement of such measures in order to minimise their negative effects on trade.[3] This framework is to be based on the use of international standards, guidelines and recommendations, without requiring Members to change their appropriate level of protection of human, animal or plant life or health.[4] It recognizes that developing country Members may encounter special difficulties of compliance with measures of importing Members, hence of access to markets, and also in the formulation and implementation of such measures in their own territories.[5]

The Agreement applies to all sanitary and phytosanitary measures which may, directly or indirectly, affect international trade.[6] Such measures must be developed and applied in accordance with the provisions of the Agreement.

---

1 OJ 23.12.94 L336/40. The Agreement is part of Annex IA of the Agreement establishing the World Trade Organization, OJ 23.12.94 L336/3.
2 Ibid preamble, eighth recital. GATT Article XX(b) states that, subject to the requirement that such measures are not applied in a manner which would constitute a means of arbitrary or unjustifiable discrimination between countries where the same conditions prevail, or a disguised restriction on international trade, nothing in this Agreement shall be construed to prevent the adoption or enforcement by any contracting party of measures necessary to protect human, animal or plant life or health.
3 Ibid preamble, fourth recital.
4 Ibid preamble, sixth recital.
5 Ibid preamble, seventh recital.
6 Ibid Art 1(1). A sanitary or phytosanitary measure is any measure (1) to protect animal or plant life or health within the territory of the Member from risks arising from the entry, establishment or spread of pests, diseases, disease-carrying organisms or disease-causing organisms; (2) to protect human or animal life or health within the territory of the Member from risks arising from additives, contaminants, toxins or disease-causing organisms in foods, beverages or foodstuffs; (3) to protect human life or health within the territory of the Member from risks arising from diseases carried by animals, plants or products thereof, or from the entry, establishment or spread of pests; or (4) to prevent or limit other damage within the territory of the Member from the entry, establishment or spread of pests: ibid Annex A, Art 1, first paragraph. Such measures include not only formal legal measures, but also procedures; end product criteria; processes and production methods; testing, inspection and approval procedures; quarantine treatments; pro-

356

Members have the right to take such measures necessary for the protection of human, animal or plant life or health, provided that they are not inconsistent with the provisions of the Agreement.[7] They must ensure that any measure is applied only to the extent necessary to protect life or health, is based on scientific principles and is not maintained without sufficient scientific evidence, except for provisional measures adopted in cases where relevant scientific evidence is insufficient.[8] They must ensure that such measures do not discriminate arbitrarily or unjustifiably between Members and are not applied in a manner which would constitute a disguised restriction on international trade.[9] Measures conforming to the Agreement are presumed to be in accordance with GATT 1994 obligations.[10]

In order to harmonize measures on as wide a basis as possible, Members are to base their measures on international standards, guidelines or recommendations, with certain exceptions.[11] The most important exception is that Members may introduce or maintain measures resulting in higher standards, if there is a scientific justification or as a consequence of the level of protection a Member determines to be appropriate in accordance with its assessment of risks according to specified criteria.[12] A Committee on Sanitary and Phytosanitary Measures is to monitor the process of international harmonization and co-ordinate efforts with relevant international organizations.[13]

Members are required to accept the sanitary or phytosanitary measures of other Members as equivalent, even if they differ from their own or from those used by other Members trading in the same product, if the exporting Member demonstrates objectively to the importing Member that its measures achieve the importing Member's appropriate level of sanitary or phytosanitary protection.[14]

Members are also required to ensure that their measures are adapted to the sanitary or phytosanitary characteristics of the area from the product originated and to which the product is destined.[15] In particular, they are required to recognize the concepts of pest-free or disease-free areas and areas of low pest or disease prevalence.[16]

Members are further required to notify changes in their measures in order to ensure transparency,[17] to observe certain control, inspection and approval procedures,[18] to facilitate technical assistance especially to developing country

---

visions on statistical methods; sampling and risk assessment; and packaging and labelling requirements directly related to food safety: ibid Annex A, Art 1, second paragraph. The Annexes are an integral part of the Agreement: ibid Art 1(3).

7 Ibid Art 2(1).
8 Ibid Art 2(2). The exception is provided in ibid Art 5(7).
9 Ibid Art 2(3).
10 Ibid Art 2(4).
11 Ibid Art 3(1).
12 Ibid Art 3(3). The required criteria are laid down in ibid Art 5(1)–(8). They include both scientific evidence and economic factors, together with the principles of non-discrimination and proportionality, in particular in respect of effects on trade.
13 Ibid Art 3(5). As to establishment and role of this Committee, see ibid Art 12.
14 Ibid Art 4(1), which also provides that, for this purpose, reasonable access is to be given, upon request, to the importer Member for inspection, testing and other relevant procedures. Upon request, Members are to enter into consultations with the aim of achieving agreement on recognition of equivalence: ibid Art 4(2).
15 Ibid Art 6(1).
16 Ibid Art 6(2), which also provides the criteria for the determination of such areas.
17 Ibid Art 7. Publication, entry points and notification procedures are provided in Annex B.
18 Ibid Art 8. The procedures are laid down in Annex C.

Members[19] and to allow special and differential treatment in certain circumstances to developing country Members.[20]

Provision is made for consultation and dispute settlement, in particular according to the GATT 1994 Dispute Settlement Understanding.[1]

ANIMAL FEEDINGSTUFFS

General principles

The Community's legislation concerning animal feedingstuffs is intended mainly to regulate the placing of these products on the Community market. It therefore applies to all products that are marketed in the Community, that is, not only to products of Community origin but also to imported products. Conversely, however, this legislation is not normally concerned with products which are marketed in other countries. In other words, it does not usually apply to Community products that are intended for export. In respect of trade, the following paragraphs thus are concerned mainly with imports into the Community. Consequently they will be of most interest to third country exporters, Community importers and distributors, and their legal advisers.

For the purpose of laying down Community standards for animal feedingstuffs and securing compliance by the Member States, the Council has issued directives for the approximation of the relevant national laws and administrative provisions.[2] By these means three types of control are exercised over animal feedingstuffs: sampling and analysis; composition; and marketing. Co-operation between the Community and the Member States in the implementation of these measures is achieved through the Standing Committee for Feedingstuffs, which consists of representatives of the Member States and is chaired by a representative of the Commission.[3] The Commission may also consult the Advisory Committee on Feedingstuffs in respect of any problems concerning the production, marketing or consumption of animal feedingstuffs.[4]

Control by sampling and analysis

With regard to control by sampling and analysis, the Commission is authorized to issue directives laying down Community rules establishing uniform methods for sampling and analysing animal feedingstuffs.[5] The Member States are required to take all measures[6] to ensure that official controls of feedingstuffs

---

19 Ibid Art 9.
20 Ibid Art 10.
 1 Ibid Art 11.
 2 Ie under EC Arts 43(2),(2) and 100.
 3 Council Directive 70/372 Art 1, OJ 3.7.70 L171/1.
 4 Commission Decision 87/76 Art 3(1), OJ 14.2.87 L45/19. Within this Committee there is a Special Section on the Approximation of Laws which deals with any problems concerning the approximation of national laws on animal feedingstuffs: see Commission Decision 87/87 Art 2(1), OJ 14.2.87 L45/22.
 5 Council Directive 70/373 Art 2, OJ 3.8.70 L170/2, as amended by Council Directive 72/275, OJ 29.7.72 L275/39, Council Decision 101/73, OJ 1.1.73 L2/1, and Council Regulation 3768/85, OJ 31.12.85 L362/8. These measures are to be taken in the light of current scientific and technical knowledge and of proven methods: ibid Art 2.
 6 The Commission must be notified of all measures taken: Council Directive 70/373 Art 5, OJ 3.8.70 L170/2.

concerning their quality and composition are carried out in accordance with the terms of the Commission directives.[7] The Commission exercises this authority in consultation with the Standing Committee on Feedingstuffs by means of a management committee procedure.

Control of composition

With regard to control of composition, a first type of control concerns additives.[8] The basic principle is that additives may only be contained in feedingstuffs[9] intended for animals[10] in accordance with uniform Community rules.[11] It is not, however, the purpose of those rules to subject the marketing of livestock products to any restrictions.[12] Nor do these rules apply to animal feedingstuffs which are intended for export to third countries.[13]

The directive lists the authorized substances and specifies the quantities which are permitted as additives.[14] The lists are subject to amendment in the light of scientific and technical developments.[15] An additional substance may be added only if it satisfies five conditions:

(1) it has a favourable effect on feedingstuffs or livestock production;
(2) at the permitted level it does not endanger animal or human health or harm the consumer by altering the characteristics of livestock products;
(3) its presence can be controlled;

7 Ibid Art 1.
8 Additives are substances added to feedingstuffs which are likely to affect the characteristics of the feedingstuffs or animal production: Council Directive 70/524 Art 2, OJ 14.12.70 L270/1. Substances inevitably present in feedingstuffs either in the natural state or as residues from previous processing are not additives for this purpose: Case 5/77 *Tedeschi v Denkavit Commerciale srl* [1977] ECR 1555. See also Case C-316/96 *Commission v Italy* [1997] ECR I-7231.
9 'Feedingstuffs' means the following products which are intended for oral animal feeding: products of vegetable or animal origin, in their natural state, fresh or preserved; products resulting from the industrial processing of these products; and organic or inorganic substances, used singly or in mixtures, whether or not containing additives: Council Directive 70/524 Art 2, OJ 14.12.70 L270/1. Member States may apply the rules in the directive to supplementary feedingstuffs: ibid Art 12, as substituted by Council Directive 84/587, OJ 8.12.84 L319/13. 'Supplementary feedingstuffs' means mixtures of feedingstuffs which have a high content of certain substances only if they are used in combination with other feedingstuffs; and 'daily ration' means the average total quantity of feedingstuffs, calculated on a moisture content of 12%, required daily by an animal of a given species, age, category and yield, to satisfy all its needs: ibid Art 2. 'Complete feedingstuffs' means mixtures of feedingstuffs which, by reason of their composition, are sufficient for a daily ration; and 'premixtures' means additive concentrates intended for the industrial manufacture of animal feedingstuffs: ibid Art 2.
10 'Animals' means animals belonging to species normally nourished or kept or consumed by human beings: ibid Art 2 as amended.
11 See Council Directive 70/524 Art 3. Council Directive is intended to harmonize all material conditions for marketing animal feedingstuffs as regards their presence or absence of additives and their marketing, including quality criteria. Member States therefore ceased to have any autonomous powers to legislative or even to apply Art 36 of the EEC Treaty to such matters: Case 29/87 *Dansk Denkavit v Landbrugsministeriet* [1990] 1 CMLR 203, ECJ.
12 Ibid Art 20. As to the interpretation of this principle, see Case 28/84 *Commission v Germany* [1985] ECR 3097 and Case 196/84 *Denkavit Futtermittel GmbH v Land Nordrhein-Westfalen* [1985] ECR 3181.
13 Ibid Art 22.
14 The principal list is set out in ibid Annex I as amended. Art 4 as amended authorizes the use of additional substances which are listed in Annex II as amended provided certain minimum conditions are satisfied.
15 Ibid Art 7(1).

(4) at the permitted level it does not exclude the treatment or prevention of animal disease; and
(5) its use for serious reasons of animal or human health must not be restricted to veterinary or medical purposes.[16]

Conversely, an authorized substance may be deleted if it fails to satisfy any of these conditions.[17] Decisions to add or to delete substances are taken by the Commission, in consultation with the Standing Committee for Feedingstuffs, acting through a management committee procedure.[18] If a Member State considers that the use of any of the authorized additives might nevertheless endanger animal or human health it may temporarily suspend its use or reduce the maximum permitted level, immediately informing the Commission and the other Member States and giving the reasons for its action.[19] In such circumstances it is the duty of the Commission to consider whether the list of authorized substances should be amended.[20]

Feedingstuffs which contain authorized additives[1] may only be placed on the market if the additives are specified on the packaging, the recipient or by means of a label giving prescribed particulars.[2] The Member States are expected to take steps to verify compliance with the conditions laid down by the directive.[3]

Control of undesirable substances

A second type of control of composition concerns the control of the presence of undesirable substances.[4] These are substances which are either found naturally in feedingstuffs or their constituents, or are present as residues from processing which, if present in excessive quantities, can endanger animal or human health.[5] The directive identifies such substances and specifies their maximum permitted levels in particular feedingstuffs.[6] The Member States

16 Ibid Art 7(2)A(a)–(e) in respect of Annex I. Substances may be added to Annex II if conditions (2), (3) and (5) are satisfied and it can be assumed that the other conditions are also satisfied: Art 7(2)C.
17 Ibid Art 6(2)B in respect of Annex I. As an alternative such a substance may be temporarily transferred to Annex II provided it satisfies conditions (2) and (5): Art 7(2)B.
18 Council Directive 70/254 (as amended) Art 7(1). and Art 23.
19 Ibid Art 11(1).
20 Ibid Art 7(2),(3). In such cases an expedited form of management committee procedure is prescribed by Council Directive 70/524 Art 24. In the event of a decision to amend, the national measures may be maintained until the entry into force of the amendments: Art 11(3).
1 These include trace elements, growth stimulators, certain vitamins and similar active substances: Council Directive 70/524 Art 14(1)B.
2 Ibid Art 14(1). Member States may provide that, in specified conditions, other information may be provided on the packaging, the receptacle or the label: ibid Art 14(4). An appropriate document is authorized in respect of feedingstuffs in bulk: ibid Art 16(7). As to the packaging requirements for supplementary feedingstuffs which contain additives in excess of the maximum permitted for complete feedingstuffs, see Art 17.
3 Ibid Art 21, which specifies check sampling as a minimum control.
4 Council Directive 74/63, OJ 11.2.74 L38/31, as amended. Council Directive 74/63 is without prejudice to the other provisions of Community law concerning additives in animal feedingstuffs, marketing of animal feedingstuffs, the establishment of maximum levels of pesticides residues on and in products intended for animal feed, micro-organisms in animal feedingstuffs, and certain products used in animal feedingstuffs: Art 1(2).
5 See Case 5/77 *Tedeschi v Denkavit Commerciale srl* [1977] ECR 1555.
6 Council Directive 74/63 Art 1(1), Annex, OJ 11.2.74 L38/31. In the absence of special provisions, complementary feedingstuffs are also subject to the terms of the directive: ibid Art 4. As to the definition of the various categories of feedingstuffs, see ibid Art 2.

are required to prescribe the observance of the terms of the directive[7] and to provide a means for exercising national control.[8] The maximum permitted levels of undesirable substances may, however, be exceeded in certain exceptional cases, including animal feedingstuffs and raw materials intended for export to third countries.[9]

Amendments to the listed substances and products, a periodic codification of the annexes and definitions of criteria of acceptability of tested raw materials are authorized in the light of scientific and technological developments.[10] Decisions in this respect are made by the Commission, in consultation with the Standing Committee for Feedingstuffs, through a management committee procedure.

In derogation from the principal provisions of the directive, the Member States may provisionally reduce or set the maximum permitted content of undesirable substances in feedingstuffs or raw materials, or forbid the use of feedingstuffs or raw materials which contain certain substances, in each case on the grounds that either animal or human health or the environment is endangered.[11] The other Member States and the Commission must be notified without delay of any such measures and the reasons for them.[12] In general, the Member States are under a duty to ensure that feedingstuffs which conform to the directive are not subject to any other marketing restrictions in respect of the presence of undesirable substances,[13] although where a Member State is validly exercising its provisional authority to derogate from the directive it may prohibit the marketing of products which have been found to infringe its temporary national provisions and the importation of such products from other Member States.[14] The Commission is under a duty to decide, without delay, whether the terms of the directive should be modified in such circumstances.[15]

Specific rules lay down animal health requirements and veterinary certification for the importation of petfood from third countries.[16]

---

7 Ibid Art 3(1). The EC Commission must be informed of the measures taken: Art 12.
8 Ibid Art 8(1), which specifies random sampling as a minimum control.
9 Ibid Art 11. The other two exceptions refer to (1) fodder produced and used on the same agricultural holding where particular local reasons justify its use and provided neither animal nor human health is threatened thereby, and (2) feedingstuffs intended for delivery to recognized manufacturers where specified information is provided on an accompanying document.
10 Ibid Art 6.
11 Ibid Art 5(1). When exercising this authority a Member State must ensure that the measures it has taken apply in identical terms both to national products and to those imported from other Member States: see Case 5/77 *Tedeschi v Denkavit Commerciale srl* [1977] ECR 1555.
12 Ibid Art 5(1).
13 Council Directive 74/63 Art 7. As to the interpretation of this directive, see Case 28/84 *EC Commission v Germany* [1985] ECR 3097; Case 195/84 *Denkavit Futtermittel GmbH v Land Nordrhein-Westfalen* [1985] ECR 3181.
14 Case 5/77 *Tedeschi v Denkavit Commerciale srl* [1977] ECR 1555.
15 Council Directive 74/63 Art 5(2). In such cases an expedited management committee procedure is prescribed: see Art 10. The national measures may be maintained until a decision is taken by either the Council or the Commission: Art 5(2). In other specified instances Member States are also permitted to maintain national measures until a Community decision, which is subject to a time limit, has been taken: see Art 6bis.
16 Commission Decision 94/309, OJ 1.6.94 L137/62, as amended.

Control of protein sources

A third type of control of composition concerns the control of manufactured protein sources[17] which are used as or as constituents of animal feedingstuffs.[18] The Member States are required to prescribe that feedingstuffs which belong to certain product groups or which contain certain products are only to be marketed if they are sanctioned by the directive and satisfy the conditions laid down in it.[19] It should be noted, however, that the directive does not apply to products intended for export to third countries.[20]

The products which are covered by the directive are subject to amendment in the light of scientific or technical developments.[1] A product may be added subject to three conditions:

(1) if it has nutritional value for animals;
(2) if, used sensibly, it has no detrimental effect on human or animal health or on the environment and does not harm consumers by impairing the distinctive features of animal products; and
(3) if its presence in feedingstuffs can be monitored.[2]

A product may be deleted if it fails to satisfy any of those conditions.[3]

In addition, the directive requires that criteria concerning composition, purity and physico-chemical and biological properties be established in the light of prevailing scientific and technical knowledge.[4] Decisions on these matters are made by the Commission, in consultation with the Standing Committee for Feedingstuffs,[5] through a management committee procedure.

Where, in spite of satisfying the terms of the directive, new data or the re-evaluation of existing data reveals that a product endangers human or animal health, a Member State may temporarily restrict or suspend its use.[6] The other Member States and the Commission must be informed of any such action and the reasons for it.[7] In such cases the Commission, in consultation with the Standing Committee for Feedingstuffs, is under a duty to examine without delay the reasons for the action of the Member State and to take appropriate measures.[8]

In relation to marketing, the Member States are required to ensure that the products covered by the directive are only subject to marketing restrictions as

---

17 Council Directive 82/471, OJ 21.7.82 L213/8, as amended.
18 Feedingstuffs are defined with reference to Council Directive 70/524 Art 2, OJ 14.12.70 L270/1: EC Council Directive 82/471 Art 2.
19 Ibid Art 3(1), Annex. Derogations may be granted by Member States for the purpose of practical tests or scientific objectives if sufficient official controls are provided: ibid Art 3(2).
20 Ibid Art 16.
 1 Ibid Art 6(1).
 2 Ibid Art 6(2)A.
 3 Ibid Art 6(2)B.
 4 Ibid Art 6(3).
 5 In certain cases the Scientific Committee for Animal Nutrition, established by Commission Decision 76/791, OJ 9.10.76 L279/35, as amended, must also be consulted: see Council Directive 82/471 Art 6(1).
 6 Ibid Art 8(1).
 7 Ibid Art 8(1).
 8 Ibid Art 8(2). Such measures may include proposals to amend the directive, in which case an expedited management committee procedure is prescribed: see Arts 8(3), 14. National safeguard measures may be maintained until an amending measure, if adopted, enters into force: Art 8(3).

prescribed by the directive, in particular regarding labelling.[9] Prescribed particulars must appear on packages or containers or on labels attached to them.[10] Animal products must not be subjected to marketing restrictions as a result of the directive.[11] The Member States are expected to monitor compliance with the directive in the course of marketing.[12]

Specific rules lay down the animal health requirements and veterinary certification for imports of processed animal protein from third countries. Different processing and certification requirements are established for processed animal protein derived from high-risk material, processed animal protein derived from low-risk material, and fishmeal and meal derived from other sea animals.[13]

Control of marketing

With regard to control of marketing, the Council has enacted directives concerning, respectively, straight feedingstuffs,[14] compound feedingstuffs,[15] and medicated feedingstuffs[16] marketed within the Community. These directives lay down common Community rules on the presentation, packaging and labelling subject to which these types of feedingstuffs may be marketed. The first two directives apply the general principle that these feedingstuffs may only be marketed if they are wholesome, unadulterated, of merchantable quality, do not endanger animal or human health, and are not presented or marketed in a

---

9 Ibid Art 10.
10 Ibid Art 5(1). Where the products are marketed in other Member States, those particulars must be given in at least one of the official languages of the countries of destination: ibid Art 9.
11 Ibid Art 11.
12 Ibid Art 12, which specifies sampling as a minimum control.
13 See Commission Decision 94/344, OJ 21.6.94 L154/45, the Annexes of which set out the form for health certificates. High-risk material and low-risk material were defined in Council Directive 90/667, OJ 27.12.90 L363/51, as amended. The three types of products must be processed in a registered and approved plant in accordance with ibid. The list of third countries from which Member States authorized importation of processed animal protein, except for fishmeal and similar products, was established by Commission Decision 94/278, OJ 11.5.94 L120/44.
14 Council Directive 77/101, OJ 3.2.77 L32/1, as amended. 'Straight feedingstuffs' is defined for this purpose according to Council Directive 70/524 Art 2, OJ 14.12.70 /270/1, means the various vegetable and animal products in their natural state, fresh or preserved, and their derivates after industrial processing, as well as the various organic and inorganic substances intended, as such, for oral animal feeding. This directive is without prejudice to the Community rules concerning additives, undesirable substances, maximum pesticide residues, marketing of simple or compound feedingstuffs or pathogenic micro-organisms in animal feedingstuffs: Art 1(2).
15 Council Directive 79/373, OJ 6.4.79 L86/30, as amended, in particular by Council Directive 90/44, OJ 31.1.90 L27/35. 'Compound feedingstuffs' means organic or inorganic substances in mixtures, whether or not containing additives, for oral animal feeding in the form of complete feedinstuffs or complementary feedingstuffs: ibid Art 2(b). 'Feedingstuffs', 'daily ration', 'complete feedingstuffs' and 'animals' are defined in Art 2(a),(c),(d),(h) in the same terms as in Council Directive 70/524, cf above. 'Complementary feedingstuffs' is defined in Art 2(c) in the same terms as 'supplementary feedingstuffs' in Council Directive 70/524, cf above. The directive is without prejudice to Community rules concerning straight feedingstuffs, additives, undesirable substances, the organization of the markets in agricultural products, certain products used in animal feedingstuffs or the approximation of the laws of the Member States relating to the making up, by mass or by volume, of certain prepackaged products: Art 1(2), as amended.
16 Council Directive 90/167, OJ 7.4.90 L92/42, as amended.

manner which is likely to mislead.[17] They also rely on the Member States to take steps to ensure compliance by means of official inspection in the course of marketing.[18]

In respect of straight feedingstuffs, the Member States are placed under a duty to apply the general provisions set out in the directive, including the names and descriptions under which they may be marketed.[19] The directive specifies the particulars which producers, manufacturerers, packers, importers, sellers or distributors, established within the Community, must ensure are set out on the packages or containers, or on labels attached to them, in which the feedingstuffs are marketed.[20] A limited number of additional particulars are also permitted,[1] but beyond that any other information must be communicated separately.[2]

The directive does not permit any marketing restrictions other than those which it authorizes,[3] but in other respects considerable discretion is left with the Member States. Thus

(1) they may prescribe that certain feedingstuffs may only be marketed in sealed packages or containers which cannot be used again;[4]
(2) they may apply provisions similar to those laid down in the directive to feedingstuffs which are not subject to it;[5]
(3) they may prescribe that feedingstuffs marketed in their territories must comply with the composition requirements set out in the directive;[6]
(4) they may recommend quality criteria;[7] and, perhaps most important for the present purposes,
(5) they may refrain from applying the terms of the directive to straight feedingstuffs which are intended for export to third countries.[8]

Amendments to the detailed provisions contained in the Annex to the directive may be made by the Commission, in consultation with the Standing Committee for Feedingstuffs, acting through a management committee procedure.[9]

In respect of compound feedingstuffs, the directive requires them to be marketed in sealed packages or containers which cannot be used again.[10] Producers, packers, importers, sellers or distributors, established within the Community,

---

17 Council Directive 77/101 Art 3, OJ 3.2.77 L32/1; Council Directive 79/373 Art 3, OJ 6.4.79 L86/30.
18 Council Directive 77/101 Art 12; EC Council Directive 79/373 Art 12.
19 Council Directive 77/101 Arts 4, 5. For the general provisions and the names and descriptions, see Annex, as amended by Commission Directive 82/937, OJ 31.12.82 L383/11 (as amended).
20 Council Directive 77/101 Art 7(1). The necessary particulars may be stated in an accompanying document when either the feedingstuffs are marketed in bulk or a common sign is used on both the document and on the individual package or container in order to identify the consignment: ibid Art 7(2), (3). In respect of trade between the Member States, these particulars must be in at least one of the official languages of the country of destination: ibid Art 11.
1 Ibid Art 7(5).
2 Ibid Art 7(7).
3 Ibid Art 9.
4 Ibid Art 6.
5 Ibid Arts 7(6), 14(a).
6 Ibid Art 8.
7 Ibid Art 14(b).
8 Ibid Art 14(c).
9 Ibid Arts 10, 13.
10 Council Directive 79/373 Art 4(1), OJ 6.4.79 L86/30. Exceptions are authorized in certain cases: see ibid Art 4(2) and Commission Directive 80/511, OJ 21.5.80 L126/14, as amended.

must ensure that certain specified particulars, such as ingredients,[11] are visibly, legibly and indelibly set out on packages or containers or on attached labels.[12] Some further particulars are also permitted.[13] The directive forbids all other marketing restrictions on compound feedingstuffs.[14] The rights of the Member States are not affected, however, in the following respects:

(1) to recommend types of compound feedingstuff with certain analytical characteristics;[15]
(2) to refrain from applying the terms of the directive to compound feedingstuffs which are intended for export to third countries;[16]
(3) to refrain from applying the terms of the directive to compound feedingstuffs which are specially labelled to show that they are intended for animals which are kept for scientific or experimental purposes.[17]

Amendments to the Annex to this directive may also be made by the Commission with the same consultation and through the same management committee procedure.[18]

In respect of medicated feedingstuffs, the directive lays down requirements regarding ingredients, manufacture, packaging, labelling, method of supply, and safeguards in the case of treatment of animals whose meat, flesh, offal or products are intended for human consumption.[19] Pending the implementation of Community measures relating to imports of medicated feedingstuffs from third countries, Member States are required to apply to those imports measures which are at least equivalent to those of the directive.[20]

Substances having a hormonal action or a thyrostatic action

On the grounds that residues may be dangerous for consumers and may affect the quality of meat,[1] the Community has prohibited, except for therapeutic

---

11 As to the listing of ingredients, see Art 5c, as so substituted. Ingredients may be listed by category: ibid Art 5c(3); as to the categories, see Commission Directive 91/357, OJ 17.7.91 L193/34, as amended. As to the main ingredients normally used and marketed for the preparation of compound feedingstuffs intended for animals other than pets, see Commission Decision 87/92, OJ 4.11.92 L319/19. As to the ingredients whose use is prohibited in compound feedingstuffs, see Commission Decision 91/516, OJ 9.10.91 L281/23, as amended by Commission Decision 92/508, OJ 29.10.92 L312/36, and Commission Decision 95/274, OJ 18.7.95 L167/24.
12 Council Directive 79/373 Art 5(1), OJ 6.4.79 L86/30, as substituted by Council Directive 90/44, OJ 31.1.90 L27/35. In respect of feedingstuffs either exempted under Art 4(2) or marketed in bulk, the required particulars may be stated on an accompanying document: ibid Art 5(2), as so substituted. See also Art 5(3),(4) (as so substituted) and the particulars in Annex (as so substituted).
13 Ibid Art 5(5), (6), as so substituted. As to requirements regarding additional information, see ibid Art 5e, as so substituted.
14 Ibid Art 9.
15 Ibid Art 14(a).
16 Ibid Art 14(b).
17 Ibid Art 14(c).
18 See ibid Arts 10, 13.
19 See Council Directive 90/167, OJ 7.4.90 L92/42, as supplemented by Annexes, OJ 3.1.94 L1/220.
20 Ibid Art 14.
 1 Council Directive 81/602, preamble, first recital, OJ 7.8.81 L222/32.

purposes,[2] the administration to farm animals[3] of substances having a hormonal action or a thryostatic action.[4] In addition, the marketing of animals containing such substances is limited.

Member States must not:

(1) administer to any farm animal any substance having a thyrostatic action or an oestrogenic, androgenic or gestagenic action;[5]
(2) permit the marketing or the slaughter of any animal to which any such substance has been administered;[6]
(3) permit the marketing of the meat of any such animal;[7] and
(4) permit the processing of the meat of any such animal and the marketing of a meat product made from or with such meat.[8]

Member States must prohibit the marketing of stilbenes, their derivatives, their salts or esters, as well as of substances having a thyrostatic action, for the purpose of their administration to animals of any kind.[9]

It should be noted that, within the Community, the use in livestock farming of certain substances having a hormonal action is prohibited.[10] Until 1988, as an exception to the principle of the prohibition on the administration of such substances, Member States could authorize the administration to farm animals of substances having an esterogenous, androgenous or gastagenous effect in certain limited circumstances and subject to specified conditions.[11] Since then, however, such derogations from the principle of prohibition of such substances are not permitted, except that the administration to farm animals for therapeutic purposes of oestradiol-17-B, testosterone and progesterone and those derivatives which readily yield the parent compound on hydrolisis after absorption at the site of application may be authorized.[12] Therapeutic treatment[13] is prohibited for animals intended for fattening.[14]

Trade of meat from animals which have had administered to them in any way whatsoever substances with a thyrostatic, oestrogenic, androgenic or gestagenic action is prohibited.[15] Imports of such meat from third countries were until recently similarly prohibited except for specified derogations.[16] The specified

---

2 'Therapeutic purpose' is defined in ibid Art 1(2), second indent.
3 'Animals' and 'meat products' for this purpose are defined according to Council Directive 64/433 (OJ 29.7.64 L121/2012), Council Directive 71/118 (OJ 8.3.71 L55/23) and Council Directive 77/99 (OJ 31.1.77 L26/85): ibid Art 1(1). 'Farm animals' are defined in ibid Art 1(2), first indent.
4 Ibid supplemented by Council Directive 85/358, OJ 23.7.85 L191/46.
5 Ibid Art 2(1)(a).
6 Ibid Art 2(1)(b).
7 Ibid Art 2(1)(c).
8 Ibid Art 2(1)(d).
9 Ibid Art 3.
10 See Council Directive 88/146, OJ 16.3.88 L70/16.
11 Ibid Art 4(1),(2).
12 Ibid Art 2.
13 As defined in ibid Art 1.
14 Ibid Art 1.
15 Ibid Art 5, first paragraph.
16 Ibid Art 6(1). On 13 February 1998 the WTO Dispute Settlement Body adopted the Appellate Body report and the Panel report, as modified by the Appellate Body, finding that the EC import prohibition was inconsistent with Arts 3.3 and 5.1 of the WTO Sanitary and Phytosanitary Agreement. Subsequently the Arbitrator found that a reasonable time for implementation by the Community was fifteen months from the date of adoption. See European Communities—

derogations concern animals intended for breeding or breeding animals at the end of their breeding life which have previously had specified treatment, or meat from such animals which meets specified conditions.[17] With regard to similar specified substances, national legislation remains applicable in the absence of Community measures adopted unanimously by the Council acting on a proposal by the Commission.[18] Member States may not however authorize the use of new similar substances.[19] Pending the enactment of Community measures, Member States are required to ensure that their national legislation applicable to products imported from third countries is not more favourable than those applicable to such products in intra-Community trade.[20]

Member States are required to establish methods of control, such as sampling, and to take other measures to ensure the effective implementation of these provisions.[1] Such methods and measures must be communicated at least once each year to the Commission,[2] which reports to the Standing Veterinary Committee.[3] In addition, provision is made for methods to be used for detecting residues of substances having a hormonal action and of substances having a thyrostatic action.[4]

ANIMAL HEALTH

General principles

As a logical extension of its regulation of the markets in animals and meat, the Community exercises control over the health standards of animals and the conditions of meat. Within the framework of the Common Agricultural Policy, three principal issues arise:

(1) the need to safeguard health, both animal and human;
(2) the need to obviate the obstacles to intra-Community trade which would result from differences between the health requirements of the Member States; and
(3) the need to ensure that imports of animals, meat and related products from third countries satisfy Community standards.

In the interests of resolving those issues and thereby promoting the objectives of the Common Agricultural Policy, Community standards have been laid down

Measures Affecting Meat and Meat Products (Hormones) (WT/DS26) (complaint by the United States); European Communities—Measures Affecting Meat and Meat Products (Hormones) (WT/DS48) (complaint by Canada); see (1998) 2 ITLR 1109.
17 See Council Directive 88/299, OJ 21.5.88 L128/36.
18 Council Directive 88/146 Art 5, 1st and second paragraphs, OJ 16.3.88 L70/16. A Community procedure for the establishment of maximum residue limits of veterinary medicinal products in foodstuffs of animal origin was established by Council Directive 90/2377, OJ 18.8.90 L224/1, as amended.
19 Ibid Art 5, third paragraph.
20 Ibid Art 6.
 1 See Council Directive 85/358, OJ 23.7.85 L191/46.
 2 Ibid Art 9(1).
 3 Ibid Art 9(2); see also Arts 10, 11.
 4 Commission Decision 93/256, OJ 14.5.93 L118/64. As to the examination of animals and fresh meat for the presence of residues, see Council Directive 86/469. OJ 26.9.86 L275/36. As to reference methods and laboratories, see Commission Decision 93/257, OJ 14.5.93 L118/75.

by the Council using its authority to issue directives for the approximation of the relevant national laws and administrative provisions of the Member States.[5] By these means numerous measures have been taken in respect of intra-Community trade and of trade with third countries.

Council directives have been enacted in respect of the identification and registration of animals,[6] intra-Community trade in bovine animals and swine,[7] intra-Community trade in ovines and caprines,[8] intra-Community trade in certain live animals and products,[9] zootechnical and genealogical conditions concerning intra-Community trade in equidae,[10] protection of animals during transport,[11] veterinary checks in intra-Community trade,[12] organization of inspections in respect of animal nutrition,[13] intra-Community trade in fresh meat,[14] trade in fresh poultrymeat,[15] intra-Community trade in meat products,[16] and the control of specified diseases.[17]

5 Ie under EC Arts 43(2) and 100.

6 Council Directive 92/102, OJ 5.12.92 L355/32, as amended.

7 Council Directive 64/432, OJ 29.7.64 L121/1977, as amended.

8 Council Directive 91/68, OJ 19.2.91 L46/19, as amended.

9 Council Directive 90/425, OJ 18.8.90 L224/29, as amended.

10 Council Decision 90/427, OJ 18.8.90 L224/55, as amended; see also Council Decision 90/429, as amended. Equidae means wild or domesticated animals of the equine (including zebras) or asinine species or the offspring of crossings of those species: Council Directive 90/426 Art 2(b), OJ 18.8.90 L224/42.

11 See Council Directive 91/628, OJ 11.12.91 L340/17. See also Council Directive 91/629, OJ 11.12.91 L340/28 and Council Directive 91/630, OJ 11.12.91 L340/33.

12 Council Decision 89/662, OJ 31.12.89 L395/13, as amended.

13 Council Directive 95/454, OJ 8.11.95 L265/17.

14 Council Directive 64/433, OJ 29.7.64 L121/2012, as amended; Council Directive 72/461, OJ 31.12.72 L302/24, as amended.

15 Council Directive 71/118, OJ 8.3.71 L55/23, as amended.

16 Council Directive 77/99, OJ 31.1.77 L26/85; Council Directive 80/215, OJ 21.2.80 L47/4.

17 As to the notification of animal diseases within the Community, see Council Directive 82/894, OJ 31.12.82 L378/58, as amended; Commission Decision 84/90, OJ 21.2.84, as amended; Commission Decision 90/442, OJ 21.8.90 L227/39, as amended. As to certain general measures, as well as specific measures in respect to swine vesicular disease, see Council Directive 91/119, OJ 15.3.91 L62/69. As to the control of classical swine fever, see Council Directive 80/217, OJ 21.2.80 L47/11, as amended; Council Directive 80/1095, OJ 1.12.80 L325/1, as amended; Commission Decision 81/400, OJ 11.6.81 L152/37, as amended; Commission Decision 92/1, OJ 4.1.92 L1/20. As to the control of foot-and-mouth disease, see Council Directive 85/511, OJ 26.11.85 L315/11; see also Commission Decision 93/242, OJ 4.5.93 L110/36, as amended. As to enzootic bovine leukosis, see Commission Decision 85/445, OJ 2.10.85 L260/18. As to bovine spongiform encephalopathy (BSE), see Commission Decision 91/89, OJ 22.2.91 L49/31; Commission Decision 92/290, OJ 4.6.92 L152/37, as modified; Commission Decision 94/381, OJ 7.7.94 L172/23, as amended by Commission Decision 95/60, OJ 11.3.95 L55/43; Commission Decision 94/382, OJ 7.7.94 L172/25, as amended by Commission Decision 95/29, OJ 18.2.95 L38/17; Commission Decision 94/474, OJ 29.7.94 L194/96, as amended by Commission Decision 98/272, OJ 24.4.98 L122/59, which also established a system of epidemio-surveillance for BSE, and by Council Decision 98/256. Council Regulation 820/97, OJ 7.5.97 L117/1, established a system of identification and registration of bovine animals ('animal passports') and labelling of beef and beef products. It requires imported animals to have an eartag, unless the holding of destination is a slaughterhouse in a Member State where checks are carried out and the animal is slaughtered within 20 days of undergoing the checks: ibid Art 4(3). In the case of animals exported to third countries, the passport must be surrendered by the last keeper to the competent authority at the place where the animal is exported: ibid Art 6(5). As to labelling of beef produced, in full or in part, in a third country, see ibid Art 15. Commission Decision 98/272, OJ 24.4.98 L122/59 established a system of epidemio-surveillance for BSE. Council Decision 98/256, OJ 15.4.98 L113/32, prohibited the export from the UK to other Member States or to third countries of live bovine animals and bovine embryos, meat meal, bone meal, and meat-and-bone meal of mammalian origin, and animal feed and fertilisers containing such material: see Art 1; as to the exception

The standards set by Community law concerning health and hygiene for intra-Community trade in animals, meat and related products necessitate equivalent provisions concerning their importation from third countries.[18] Given the sensitive and often controversial nature of the subject, it is not surprising that the basic legal framework[19] for such imports is provided by a large number of Council directives. They establish the basic principles in respect of veterinary checks, health standards, countries from which imports are authorized, inspections, control of specific diseases and marketing of specific products.[20] These measures are supplemented by Council decisions and implemented mainly by Commission directives.

Co-operation between the Community and the Member States in the implementation of these measures is achieved through the Standing Veterinary Committee[1] and the Standing Committee on Zootechnics,[2] each of which consists of representatives of the Member States and is chaired by a representative of the Commission. In addition to carrying out the tasks imposed on them by the relevant Council directives, these committees may also consider any other question arising under such instruments. The Commission may also consult the Scientific Veterinary Committee,[3] which consists of experts in animal health, veterinary measures related to public health and the protection of animals. It may also seek opinions from the Advisory Veterinary Committee, composed of representatives of organizations concerned with agriculture, industry, commerce, workers, consumers and the Veterinary Federation of the European Community.[4] There is also a computerized network linking veterinary authorities (Animo).[5]

for certain pet food, see Art 2. It also prohibited the export from the UK to other Member States or third countries of meat, products liable to enter the human food chain or animal food chain, and materials destined for use in cosmetics or medical or pharmaceutical products derived from bovine animals slaughtered in the UK (see Art 3) and specified materials derived from bovine animals not slaughtered in the UK (see Art 8). See also Case C-157/96 *R v MAFF, ex p National Farmers Union* [1998] 2 CMLR 1125.

18 For this purpose, a third country is one in which Council Directive 64/432, OJ 29.7.64 L121/1977, as amended, and Council Directive 64/433, OJ 29.7.64 L121/2012, as amended, do not apply: Council Directive 72/462 Art 2(c), as substituted by Council Directive 83/91, OJ 5.3.83 L59/34. In relation to imports from third countries, public health and veterinary inspections are necessary to ensure non-discriminatory treatment of traders who, on the one hand, put fresh meat on the market in intra-Community trade and those who, on the other hand, import from third countries: Case 70/77 *Simmenthal SpA v Amministrazione delle Finanze dello Stato* [1978] ECR 1453; see also Case 1/83 *IFG Intercontinentale Fleischhandelgesellschaft mbH & Co KG v Freistaat Bayern* [1984] ECR 349. As to the Shift project database in respect of the Community's import requirements, see Commission Decision 92/563, OJ 10.12.92 L361/45. As to Community financial assistance to improve checks at the external borders of Finland, see Commission Decision 95/100, OJ 5.4.95 L76/19.

19 That is, in addition to the EC Treaty.

20 For example, as to the imports of agricultural products originating in third countries following the accident at the Chernobyl nuclear power station, see Commission Recommendation 86/156, OJ 7.5.86 L118/28; Council Regulation 3994/87, OJ 11.7.87, L192/49, as amended; and Commission Regulation 1983/88, OJ 6.7.88 L174/32. See also Case C-62/88 *Greece v Council* [1990] ECR I-1527 and Case C-371/92 *Greece v Ellinika Dimitriaka AE* [1994] ECR I-2391.

1 Established by Council Decision 68/361, OJ 18.10.68 L255/23.

2 Established by Council Decision 77/505, OJ 12.8.77 L206/11.

3 Established by Commission Decision 81/651; OJ 19.8.81 L233/32, as amended.

4 See Commission Decision 87/89, OJ 14.2.87 L45/56. The Committee was originally established by Commission Decision 76/559, OJ 30.6.76 L171/37.

5 Commission Decision 91/398, OJ 9.8.91 L221/30, as amended. As to implementing rules, see Commission Decision 91/539, OJ 25.10.91 L294/47. As to implementation, see Commission Decision 94/34, OJ 26.1.94 L21/22. As to the Community's financial contribution, see Commission Decision 91/426, OJ 23.8.91 L234/27, as amended; Commission Decision 93/28, OJ 25.1.93 L16/28; Commission Decision 94/990, OJ 31.12.94 L378/67 (Austria); Commission

Veterinary checks on imports

The basic legislation in respect of veterinary and zootechnical checks in intra-Community trade[6] provided that general principles in respect of similar checks on imports entering the Community from third countries should be laid down before 31 December 1990.[7] This was done in two Council directives, one concerning animals[8] and the other concerning products other than animals.[9] Within the framework of these directives, the Council has laid down animal health measures applicable to specific products.[10] In addition, it has laid down animal health and public health requirements governing trade in and imports into the Community of animals and products not yet covered by specific rules harmonized at Community level.[11] This section is concerned mainly with the two principal general directives.

With regard to imports of animals,[12] Member States are required to ensure that importers are obliged to give one working day's notice of the number, nature and estimated arrival time of the animals, that the animals are conveyed directly, under official supervision, to the relevant border inspection post or quarantine

Decision 94/966, OJ 31.12.94 L371/32 (Finland); Commission Decision 95/85, OJ 28.3.95 L68/29 (Sweden). As to the designation of a common host centre, see Commission Decision 91/638, OJ 13.12.91 L343/48, and Commission Decision 92/373, OJ 14.7.92 L195/31. As to the list and identity of the units in the network, see Commission Decision 92/175, OJ 25.3.92 L80/1, as amended. As to computer retrieval of local units, see Commission Decision 92/341, OJ 8.7.92 L188/37, as amended. As to co-operation between the Animo host centre and the Member States, see Commission Decision 92/486, OJ 7.10.92 L291/20. As to the minimal configuration of certain equipment, see Commission Decision 91/585, OJ 15.11.91 L314/54, as amended. As to the model for messages, see Commission Decision 91/637, OJ 13.12.91 L343/46, and Commission Decision 93/70, OJ 2.2.93 L25/34. As to maps for use for the network, see Commission Decision 92/176, OJ 25.3.92 L80/33. As to the provisional setting-up of the network in Italy, see Commission Decision 93/227, OJ 23.4.93 L97/31.

6 That is, Council Directive 89/662 Art 19, OJ 31.12.89 L395/13, as amended, and Council Directive 90/425 Art 23, OJ 18.8.90 L224/29. As to animals, semen, ova and embryos not subject to specific Community rules referred to in the latter Directive, see Council Directive 92/65, OJ 14.9.92 L268/54.

7 As to the computerization of veterinary import procedures, see Council Decision 92/438, OJ 25.8.92 L24/727, as amended.

8 Council Directive 91/496, OJ 24.9.91 L268/56, as amended. As to detailed implementing rules in respect of veterinary checks on live animals, see Commission Decision 97/794, OJ 26.11.97 L323/31.

9 Council Directive 90/675, OJ 31.12.90 31.12.90 L373/1, as amended. This Directive will be repealed with effect as of 30 June 1999, though acts adopted on the basis of it will remain in force until provisions intended to replace them are adopted on the basis of the Directive that replaces Council Directive 90/675: see Art 33 of the new Directive, Council Directive 97/78, OJ 30.1.98 L24/9, which according to its Art 34 will come into effect as of 1 July 1999. As to consequent amendments of other legislation, see Council Directive 97/79, OJ 30.1.98 L24/31. The new Directive will establish harmonized conditions for all products of animal origin imported from third countries into the Community. The following paragraphs are concerned with the Directive currently in force.

10 See below.

11 Council Directive 92/65, OJ 14.9.92 L268/54, as amended, covers animals, semen, ova and embryos. Council Directive 92/118, OJ 15.3.93 L62/49, as amended, covers products of animal origin.

12 The Directive does not apply to family pets accompanying travellers for non-commercial purposes, other than *equidae*: Council Directive 91/496 Art 1(2), OJ 24.9.91 L268/56. Transitional measures in respect of veterinary checks on live animals entering new Member States from third countries are provided in Commission Decision 94/957, OJ 31.12.94 L371/19, as amended (Finland) and Commission Decision 94/970, OJ 31.12.94 L371/41 (Austria). As to protection measures in respect of foot-and-mouth disease in Russia, see Commission Decision 95/301, OJ 3.8.95 L184/59, as amended.

centre, that the animals may not leave the post or centre until proof has been supplied that veterinary checks have been carried out and paid for, and that the customs authority does not authorize release for free circulation until such proof has been provided.[13] Each consignment of animals from a third country must be subjected to a documentary check[14] and an identity check[15] at one of the border inspection posts in order to verify their origin, their subsequent destination and that the particulars on the certificates or documents afford the guarantees required by Community rules or any relevant national rules.[16] An official veterinarian must carry out a physical check on animals presented at the border inspection post.[17] All expenditure incurred for these purposes is chargeable to the consignor, the consignee or their agent, without reimbursement by the Member State.[18]

Entry is prohibited where the checks show that animals of species in respect of which import rules have been harmonized at Community level come from a territory or part of a territory of a third country not included in Community lists or from which imports are prohibited;[19] animals do not comply with relevant national rules;[20] animals are suffering from, suspected to be suffering from, or infected by a contagious disease or a disease presenting a risk for public health or animal health;[1] the exporting third country has not complied with Community requirements;[2] animals are not in a fit state to continue their journey;[3] or the veterinary certificate or document does not meet the conditions set down by Community rules or relevant national rules.[4]

Where it is suspected that veterinary legislation has not been complied with or there is doubt about the identity of the animal, the official veterinarian or competent authority shall carry out any veterinary checks deemed appropriate.[5] Member States are to take the appropriate administrative or penal measures to penalize any infringement of veterinary legislation by national or legal persons where it is found that Community rules have been infringed, in particular where it is found that the certificates or documents drawn up do not correspond to the actual state of the animals, that the identification marks do not comply with those rules, that the animals were not presented for inspection or that the animals have not been sent to the destination originally intended.[6]

Where checks show that an animal does not meet Community or relevant national requirements, the competent authority, after consultation with the

---

13 Council Directive 91/496 Art 3(1), OJ 24.9.91 L268/56. As to the list of border inspection posts and detailed rules concerning checks see Commission Decision 97/778, OJ 19.11.97 L315/15, as amended.

14 'Documentary check' means verification of the veterinary certificates or documents accompanying an animal: ibid Art 2(2)(a).

15 'Identity check' means verification, by visual inspection only, for consistency between the documents or certificates and the animals and for the presence and conformity of the marks which must appear on the animal: ibid Art 2(2)(b). As to certain detailed rules, see Commission Directive 92/424, OJ 14.8.92 L232/34.

16 Ibid Art 4(1). As to the requirements in respect of border inspection posts, see ibid Art 6.

17 Ibid Art 2, which also specifies the nature of the check. As to animals of species not covered by Annex A of Directive 90/425, OJ18.8.90 L224/28, see ibid Art 8. As to certain derogations, see Commission Decision 92/432, OJ 29.8.92 L237/29.

18 Ibid Art 4(4).

19 Ibid Art 5(a), which does not apply to specified *equidae*.

20 Ibid Art 5(b).

1 Ibid Art 5(c).

2 Ibid Art 5(d).

3 Ibid Art 5(e).

4 Ibid Art 5(f). In specified instances animals may be placed in quarantine: see ibid Art 10.

5 Ibid Art 11(1).

6 Ibid Art 11(2).

importer or its representative, must decide to shelter, feed, water and if necessary treat the animals; to place them in quarantine or isolate the consignment; or to re-dispatch them.[7] If re-dispatch is impossible, in particular for reasons of animal welfare, the official veterinarian may in specified conditions authorize slaughter of the animals for human consumption, slaughter of the animals for purposes other than human consumption, or deduction of the carcases.[8]

Less frequent identity checks and/or physical checks may on a reciprocal basis be authorized under certain conditions.[9]

Safeguard measures are also provided.[10] If specified diseases or other risks in the territory of a third country so warrant in the light of the finding of its veterinary experts, the Commission may adopt specified measures on its own initiative or at the request of a Member State. They are to be adopted without delay and depending on the gravity of the situation.[11] The measures include, first, the suspension of imports coming from part or all of the third country concerned[12] and where appropriate from the transit third country or, second, to set special conditions in respect of such imports.[13] If veterinary checks indicate that a consignment is likely to constitute a danger for animal or human health, the veterinary authority is required to seize and destroy the consignment and immediately inform the other border inspection posts and the Commission of the findings and of the origin of the product.[14]

With regard to imports of products other than animals,[15] Member States are required to ensure that customs authorities do not authorize entry for home use unless proof has been supplied that veterinary checks have been carried out and paid for.[16] Each consignment of products from a third country is subject to a documentary check[17] and an identity check[18] on entry[19] to verify the origin,

7 Ibid Art 12(1), first pararaph.
8 Ibid Art 12(1), second paragraph.
9 Ibid Art 16, which also sets out the conditions for this derogation.
10 Ibid Art 18.
11 Ibid Art 18(1). In certain cases the Commission may also take provisional protective measures: ibid Art 18(3). In respect of products the rules on imports of which have not yet been harmonized, a Member State may, after informing the Commission of the need for measures and in certain conditions, take interim protective measures: ibid Art 18(5). As to protective measures in respect of live birds from Hong Kong and China, see Commission Decision 98/85, OJ 21.1.98 L15/45.
12 Ibid Art 18(1), first indent.
13 Ibid Art 18(1), second indent.
14 Ibid Art 18(2).
15 That is, animal products or products of animal origin or, in certain circumstances, fresh fish landed immediately from fishing vessels, certain plant products, and by-products of animal origin not covered by Annex II to the EC Treaty: Council Directive 90/675 Art 2(a), OJ 31.12.90 L373/1. Transitional measures in respect of products entering new Member States from third countries are provided in Commission Directive 94/958, OJ 31.12.94 L371/21, as amended, (Finland) and Commission Decision 94/971, OJ 31.12.94 L371/44 (Austria). As of 30 June 1999 Council Directive 90/675 will be repealed and replaced by Council Directive 97/78, OJ 30.1.98 L24/9, Art 33 of which provides that legislation adopted under the former directive remains in force until replaced by legislation adopted under the latter.
16 Ibid Art 3.
17 'Documentary check' means verification of the veterinary certificates or documents accompanying a product: ibid Art 2(2)b).
18 'Identity check' means verification, by visual inspection only, for consistency between the documents or certificates and the products and for the presence of the stamps and marks which must appear on the products in accordance with Community rules or in the case of products trade in which has not been harmonized at Community level, in accordance with the relevant national legislation: ibid Art 2(2)(c).
19 As specified in ibid Art 4(2). As to the requirements to be satisfied by border inspection posts, see ibid Art 9.

destination and that the specified particulars afford the guarantees required by Community rules or the relevant national legislation.[20] Entry is prohibited when the checks show that the products come from a territory or part of a territory of a third country which does not meet specified health conditions.[1] The Member States must ensure that importers are obliged to give prior notice to the veterinary staff of the inspection post where the products are to be submitted specifying the amount, nature and estimated time of arrival of the products.[2] All expenditure incurred for the purpose of checks is chargeable to the consignor, the consignee or their agent, without reimbursement by the Member State.[3] For admission to a free zone or free warehouse[4] products must undergo a documentary check and verification by simple visual inspection, and, if necessary, where there are grounds for suspicion, an identity check and a physical check.[5] Products to be stored under the customs warehousing procedure[6] or the temporary storage of goods procedure[7] must undergo an identity check as well as veterinary checks.[8]

Products for which the veterinary requirements concerning trade have been harmonized at Community level and which have been presented at a point of entry must undergo certain checks.[9] The official veterinarian must carry out a physical check on each consignment on the basis of a representative sample, perform laboratory tests which have to be carried out on the spot, and take official samples to be examined for residues or pathogens and have them analysed as soon as possible.[10] The Commission may however determine that checks are to be less frequent with respect to certain third countries or third country establishments offering satisfactory guarantees as regards checks at the point of origin.[11]

Products for which trade rules have not yet been harmonized at Community level must satisfy analogous conditions.[12]

Where it is suspected that veterinary legislation has not been complied with or there is doubt about the identity of the animal, the official veterinarian or competent authority shall carry out any veterinary checks deemed appropriate.[13]

---

20 Ibid Art 4(1). As to the list of border inspection posts, see Commission Decision 95/357, OJ 6.9.95 L211/43. As to requirements for approval of such posts, see Commission Decision 92/525, OJ 17.11.92 L331/16, as amended. As to the procedures for veterinary checks at border inspection posts for third country products, see Commission Decision 93/13, OJ 15.1.93 L9/33, as amended. As to procedures for checks on such products in free zones, free warehouses, customs warehouses and during transport from one third country to another, see Commission Decision 93/14, OJ 15.1.93 L9/42.
1 Ibid Art 4(3). As to the exception for products to be stored in a free zone, see ibid Art 7.
2 Ibid Art 4(4).
3 Ibid Art 4(7).
4 As defined in Council Regulation 2504/88 Art 1(4)(a),(b), OJ 15.8.88 L225/1.
5 Ibid Art 5(1).
6 As defined in Council Regulation 2504/88, OJ 15.8.88 L225/1.
7 As defined in Council Regulation 4151/88, OJ 31.12.88 L367/1.
8 Ibid Art 6(1). Costs are to be borne by the operator seeking customs warehousing or temporary storage and must be paid before the products enter the warehouse: ibid Art 6(4).
9 Ibid Art 8(1). As to products not to be entered for home use in the territory of the Member State which carried out the checks, see ibid Art 10. As to the form of certificate for the latter products, see Commission Decision 92/527, OJ 18.11.92 L332/22.
10 Ibid Art 8(2), first paragraph.
11 Ibid Art 9(3), second paragraph. As to the criteria to be taken into account in granting such derogations, see ibid Art 9(3), third paragraph. As to the reduced frequency of certain checks, see Commission Decision 94/360, OJ 25.6.94 L158/41, as amended.
12 See ibid Art 11. As to situations in which products do not meet the conditions, see ibid Art 16.
13 Ibid Art 11(1).

Safeguards are provided.[14] If specified diseases or other risks in the territory of a third country so warrant in the light of the finding of its veterinary experts, the Commission may adopt specified measures on its own initiative or at the request of a Member State. They are to be adopted without delay and depending on the gravity of the situation.[15] The measures include, first, the suspension of imports coming from part or all of the third country concerned[16] and where appropriate from the transit third country or, second, to set special conditions in respect of such imports.[17] If veterinary checks indicate that a consignment is likely to constitute a danger for animal or human health, the veterinary authority is required to seize and destroy the consignment and immediately inform the other border inspection posts and the Commission of the findings and of the origin of the product.[18]

Trade in animals, meat and related products

One set of measures in respect of imports concerns animals, fresh meat, meat products, and certain related matters. The Community has also regulated exports of certain live animals and related products.

A basic directive concerns the importation of bovine animals, swine and fresh meat from third countries.[19] Within this framework general provisions authorize the Council, acting on a proposal from the Commission, to designate those third countries or parts of them from which the Member States may authorize imports.[20] Those provisions apply to the importation of domestic bovine animals and swine for breeding, production or slaughter and to fresh meat from domestic bovine animals, swine, sheep, goats and solipeds.[1] The decision whether all or part of a particular third country is to be thus designated is taken in the light of six factors:

14 See ibid Art 19.
15 Ibid Art 19(1). In certain cases the Commission may also take provisional protective measures: ibid Art 19(3). In respect of products the rules on imports of which have not yet been harmonized, a Member State may, after informing the Commission of the need for measures and in certain conditions, take interim protective measures: ibid Art 19(5).
16 Ibid Art 19(1), first indent.
17 Ibid Art 19(1), second indent.
18 Ibid Art 19(2).
19 Council Directive 72/462, OJ 31.12.82 L302/28, as amended. As to animal health conditions in ovines and caprines, see Council Decision 91/68, OJ 19.2.91 L46/19, as amended. As to the organization of veterinary checks, see Council Directive 91/496, OJ 24.9.91 L268/56, as amended. As to the form of certification, see Commission Decision 93/198, OJ 6.4.93 L86/34.
20 Council Directive 72/462 Art 3(1), as amended. The list of approved countries is published in the Official Journal: ibid Art 3(3), as amended. Provision is also made for the supplementing and amendment of the list: see Art 3(1), as so substituted, and Art 30. As to the list of third countries from which Member States may authorize imports of bovine animals, swine and fresh meat, see Council Decision 79/542, OJ 14.6.79 L146/15, as amended. As to animal health conditions and veterinary certification, see Commission Decision 97/221, OJ 4.4.97 L89/32, as amended. As to the list of third countries authorized to use the specimen animal health certificate, see Commission Decision 97/222, OJ 4.4.97 L89/39, as amended; and Commission Decision 98/10, OJ 7.1.98 L3/14.
1 Ibid Art 1(1), as so substituted. Fresh meat from cloven-hoofed wild animals and wild solipeds is also included: Art 1(10), as so substituted. For exemptions, see Art 1(2), as so substituted. For this purpose 'meat' includes all parts of the relevant animals which are suitable for human consumption, and 'fresh meat' means meat which has not undergone any treatment other than cold treatment to ensure preservation: Council Directive 64/433 Art 2(a), (b), OJ 29.7.64 L121/2012, as substituted by Council Directive 83/90, OJ 5.3.83 L59/10. A soliped is an animal with uncloven hoofs.

(1) the general state of animal health in the country, particularly with reference to exotic animal diseases and the environmental health situation which might endanger public and animal health in the Member States;[2]

(2) the regularity and rapidity of information from that country concerning the existence of infections or contagious animal diseases in its territory;[3]

(3) the country's rules on the prevention and control of animal diseases;[4]

(4) the structure and powers of its veterinary services;[5]

(5) the organization and implementation of measures to prevent and control infectious or contagious animal diseases;[6] and

(6) the country's legislation concerning the use of substances which are harmful or which are likely to render the consumption of the meat harmful or dangerous to human health.[7]

It is specifically provided in relation to bovine animals that the Member States are only to authorize imports from a designated third country if it has also been free from diseases to which such animals are susceptible and the animals have not been vaccinated during prescribed periods.[8] Animals may only be imported if they have remained continuously in a designated third country either from birth or for prescribed minimum periods on the day of loading for dispatch.[9] The animals must also satisfy any relevant health requirements according to their species or destination.[10] They must be accompanied by an official health certificate in approved form drawn up by the competent authority of the exporting third country.[11] Upon their arrival in the territory of the Community the animals must be subjected immediately to an official animal health inspection to ensure compliance with Community requirements,[12] and if this reveals that those requirements have not been satisfied the Member States, whether of transit[13] or destination, are authorized (as appropriate) to prohibit the movement,[14] place in quarantine,[15] return,[16] slaughter or destroy[17] the animals concerned. Animals which are imported for slaughter must, immediately

---

2 Ibid Art 3(2), as so substituted.

3 Ibid Art 3(2)(b), as so substituted.

4 Ibid Art 3(2)(c), as so substituted.

5 Ibid Art 3(2)(d), as so substituted.

6 Ibid Art 3(2)(e), as so substituted.

7 Ibid Art 3(2)(f), as substituted by Council Directive 86/469, OJ 26.9.86 L275/36.

8 Ibid Art 6, as so substituted. Derogations from Art 6 are permitted under Art 7 (as so substituted) and Art 29. Without prejudice to Art 6, the Member States may prohibit the importation of animals from a designated third country in which there is an outbreak of an infectious or contagious animal disease likely to endanger the health of livestock in the Member States: Art 28(1), (3), (4) (as so substituted) and Art 30. A Member State must prohibit the introduction of certain animals from a country whose foot-and-mouth disease vaccines are deficient: Art 9, as so substituted.

9 Ibid Art 10, as so substituted. See also Council Directive 77/96, OJ 31.1.77 L26/67, as amended.

10 Ibid Art 11, as so substituted.

11 Ibid Art 11, as so substituted. As to the protocols for the standardization of materials and procedures for veterinary tests and the conditions for the approval of markets, see Commission Decision 91/189, OJ 17.4.91 L96/1.

12 Ibid Art 12(1), as so substituted. As to veterinary checks on imports generally, see below.

13 Ibid Art 12(5), (6), as so substituted.

14 Ibid Art 12(2), as so substituted.

15 Ibid Art 12(3)(a), as so substituted.

16 Ibid Art 12(3)(b), as so substituted.

17 Ibid Art 12(3)(c), as so substituted.

upon their arrival in the Member State of destination, be taken to a slaughter-house and slaughtered within three days.[18]

Specific rules have been laid down for the importation of live animals from Bosnia-Herzegovina,[19] Bulgaria,[20] Canada,[1] Croatia,[2] Czechoslovakia,[3] Estonia,[4] Hungary,[5] Iceland,[6] Latvia,[7] Lithuania,[8] New Zealand,[9] Poland,[10] Romania,[11] Slovenia,[12] Switzerland[13] and Uruguay.[14]

Other special rules concern equidae.[15] In order to be imported, such animals must come from a listed third country or part of a third country, be free from specified diseases, comply with other animal health requirements, and be identified by means of specified documents and be accompanied by a certificate drawn up by an official veterinarian of the exporting third country.[16] Specific provisions govern the import of registered horses.[17] Imports of such animals for

18 Ibid Art 13, as so substituted.
19 Commission Decision 92/271, OJ 21.5.92 L138/39.
20 Commission Decision 92/325, OJ 30.6.92 L177/52, as amended.
 1 Commission Decision 83/494, OJ 6.10.83 L272/37
 2 Commission Decision 94/321, OJ 8.6.94 L143/11.
 3 Commission Decision 92/244, OJ 9.5.92 L124/40; Commission Decision 92/324, OJ 30.6.92 L177/35.
 4 Commission Decision 93/184, OJ 31.3.93 L78/31.
 5 Commission Decision 92/322, OJ 30.6.92 L177/1, as amended.
 6 Commission Decision 92/463, OJ 7.9.92 L261/50, as amended.
 7 Commission Decision 93/181, OJ 31.3.93 L78/1.
 8 Commission Decision 93/183, OJ 31.3.93 L78/21.
 9 Commission Decision 93/491, OJ 10.9.93 L229/18.
10 Commission Decision 92/323, OJ 30.6.92 L177/18.
11 Commission Decision 92/402, OJ 8.8.92 L224/18.
12 Commission Decision 93/182, OJ 31.3.93 L78/11.
13 Commission Decision 92/460, OJ 7.9.92 L261/1, as amended.
14 As to importation of sheep and goats from Uruguay, see Commission Decision 98/146, OJ 17.2.98 L46/8.
15 As to the movement and imports of equidae, see Council Directive 90/426, OJ 18.8.90, as amended in particular by Council Directive 92/36, OJ 10.6.92 L157/28.
16 Council Directive 90/426 Arts 11–16, OJ 18.8.90 L224/42; as to amendments with regard to African horse sickness, see Council Directive 92/36, OJ 10.6.92 L157/28. As to the regionalization of certain third countries for such imports, see Commission Decision 92/160, OJ 18.3.92 L71/27, as amended, for example, with regard to Morocco by Commission Decision 95/322, OJ 11.8.95 L190/9; with regard to Quatar by Commission Decision 93/344, OJ 90.6.93 L138/11; and with regard to Russia by Commission Decision 97/685, OJ 21.10.97 L287/54. As to health guarantees for the transport of equidae from one third country to another, see Commission Decision 94/467, OJ 26.7.94 L190/28. As to control rules and measures to combat African horse sickness, see Council Directive 92/35, OJ 10.6.92 L157/19. As to Community financial contribution towards eradication of African horse sickness in Morocco, see Commission Decision 92/581, OJ 31.12.92 L390/127. As to Community financial contributions for control of foot-and-mouth disease in Morocco, see Commission Decision 93/85, OJ 12.2.93 L36/43 (supply of vaccine); Commission Decision 93/89, OJ 12.2.93 L36/51 (epidemiological studies). As to protection measures in respect of Venezuelan equine encephalomyelitis in Venezuela and Colombia, see Commission Decision 95/461, OJ 8.11.95 L265/40. As to imports for breeding and production, see below.
17 As to animal health conditions and veterinary certification for temporary admission of registered horses, see Commission Decision 92/360, OJ 15.5.92 L130/67, as amended. As to imports of registered horses from specific countries, see Commission Decision 94/561, OJ 19.8.94 L214/17 (Macau, Peninsula Malaysia, Singapore); Commission Decision 95/322, OJ 11.8.95 L190/9 (Morocco); Commission Decision 95/323, OJ 11.8.95 L190/11 (Syria); Commission Decision 97/160, OJ 4.3.97 L62/39 (Lebanon). As to health conditions and veterinary certification for entry of registered horses for racing and similar events after temporary export, see Commission Decision 93/195, OJ 6.4.93 L86/1, as amended.

slaughter is authorized subject to specified health conditions.[18] The importation of serum from equidae from third countries is also regulated.[19]

In respect of the designated countries[20] lists of approved slaughterhouses, cutting plants and stores are drawn up from which the Member States may authorize the importation of fresh meat.[1] Such establishments may not be listed unless they are situated in a designated third country the competent authorities of which have officially approved them for the purpose of exports to the Community.[2] The decision at Community level whether such an establishment is to be approved is taken in the light of four factors:

(1) the guarantees by the third country of compliance with the requirements of the Community;[3]
(2) its regulations regarding the use of substances which might affect the wholesomeness of the meat;[4]
(3) compliance with Community requirements or the provision of similar guarantees which meet Community health conditions;[5] and
(4) the organization, powers and supervision of that country's meat inspection service.[6]

In order to verify compliance with these provisions, approved establishments are subject to on-the-spot veterinary inspection by experts of the Member States and of the Commission.[7] If such an inspection should reveal serious facts about an approved establishment, approval may be withdrawn under the authority of the Commission acting in consultation with the Standing Veterinary Committee.[8]

Establishments for the purpose of importing fresh meat into the Community have been approved in Argentina,[9] Australia,[10] Botswana,[11] Brazil,[12] Bulgaria,[13]

18 See Commission Decision 93/196, OJ 6.4.87 L86/7.
19 Commission Decision 94/143, OJ 5.3.94 L62/41, as amended.
20 That is, designated under Council Directive 72/462 Art 3(1), as amended.
 1 Ibid Art 4(1), as substituted by Council Directive 89/227, OJ 6.4.89 L93/25. Provision is also made for amending and supplementing the lists: see ibid Art 4(1), as so substituted, and Art 30. Amendments or supplements to the list are proposed by the Commission and notified to the Member States, which within one week may make observations, which are to be taken into account by the Commission before adopting any decision; difficulties are referred to the Standing Veterinary Committee: Commission Decision 90/13, OJ 11.1.90 L8/70. The lists are published in the Official Journal: ibid Art 4(4), as so substituted.
 2 Ibid Art 4(3), as so substituted, which also requires compliance with Council Directive 64/433, Annex I, OJ 29.7.64 L121/2012, and constant veterinary supervision in the third country.
 3 Council Directive 72/462 Art 4(2)(a), OJ 31.12.72 l302/28, as so substituted.
 4 Ibid Art 4(2)(b), as so substituted.
 5 Ibid Art 4(2)(c), as so substituted.
 6 Ibid Art 4(2)(d), as so substituted.
 7 Ibid Art 5, as so substituted, which specifies that the costs of such inspections are to be borne by the Community. As to such inspections, see Commission Decision 86/474, OJ 30.9.86 L279/55.
 8 Ibid Art 5, as so substituted, and Art 30.
 9 Commission Decision 81/91, OJ 5.3.81 L58/91, as amended by Commission Decision 86/349 (OJ 29.7.86 L205/41) and Commission Decision 86/392 (OJ 14.8.86 L228/44), see also Amendment 90/0223(03), OJ 23.2.90 C43/4.
10 Commission Decision 83/384, OJ 13.8.83 L222/36, as amended by Commission Decision 83/532 (OJ 29.10.83 L297/45) and Commission Decision 86/389 (OJ 14.8.86 L228/34); see also Amendment 90/0315(02), OJ 15.3.90 C65/3.
11 Commission Decision 83/243, OJ 19.5.83 L129/70, as amended by Commission Decision 86/243 (OJ 19.6.86 L163/43).
12 Commission Decision 81/713, OJ 10.9.81 L257/28, as amended by Commission Decision 86/391 (OJ 14.8.86 L228/41) and Commission Decision 89/282 (OJ 21.4.89 L110/54); see also Amendment 90/0315(03), OJ 15.3.90 C65/4.
13 Council Decision 82/735, OJ 8.11.82 L311/16.

Chile,[14] Czechoslovakia,[15] Greenland,[16] Guatemala,[17] Hungary,[18] Iceland,[19] Madagascar,[20] Malta,[1] Mexico,[2] Morocco,[3] Namibia,[4] New Zealand,[5] Paraguay,[6] Poland,[7] Romania,[8] South Africa,[9] Swaziland,[10] Switzerland,[11] Turkey,[12] United States of America,[13] Uruguay,[14] the Federal Republic of Yugoslavia,[15] and the former Yugoslav Republic of Macedonia.[16]

Imported fresh meat must come from animals which have remained in a designated third country for specified minimum periods before slaughter.[17] That country during the previous 12 months must also have been free of those diseases to which the animals from which the meat has come are susceptible,[18] and must not have carried out any vaccinations against such diseases.[19] The meat, which must also satisfy the relevant health requirements,[20] may be imported either as whole or as part carcases provided, in the latter case, that it is possible to reconstruct the entire carcase of each animal therefrom.[1] Imports of fresh meat must also satisfy slaughtering and hygiene conditions,[2] must undergo both

14 Commission Decision 87/124, OJ 2.2.87 L51/41.
15 See OJ 15.3.90 C65/9.
16 Commission Decision 85/539, OJ 12.12.85 L334/25.
17 Commission Decision 82/923, OJ 31.12.82 L381/40.
18 Council Decision 82/733, OJ 8.11.82 L311/10, as amended by Council Decision 86/245 (OJ 18.6.86 L163/49). As to live pigs, pigmeat, meat products, and porcine embryos, see Commission Decision 94/668, OJ 8.10.94 L260/34.
19 Commission Decision 84/24, OJ 25.1.84 L20/21.
20 Commission Decision 90/165, OJ 6.4.90 L91/34.
 1 Commission Decision 87/548, OJ 18.11.87 L327/28.
 2 Ie United Mexican States: Commission Decision 87/424, OJ 15.8.87 L228/43.
 3 Commission Decision 86/65, OJ 15.3.86 L72/40.
 4 Commission Decision 82/913, OJ 31.12.82 L381/28; Commission Decision 90/432, OJ 18.8.90 L223/19.
 5 Commission Decision 83/402, OJ 24.8.83 L233/24, as amended by Commission Decision 86/432 (OJ 5.9.86 L253/28).
 6 Commission Decision 83/423, OJ 27.8.83 L283/39, as amended by Commission Decision 86/390 (OJ 14.8.86 L228/39).
 7 Commission Decision 84/28, OJ 26.1.84 L21/42, as amended by Commission Decision 86/252 (OJ 21.6.86 L165/43).
 8 Commission Decision 83/218, OJ 7.5.83 L121/23.
 9 Commission Decision 82/913, OJ 31.12.82 L381/28.
10 Commission Decision 82/814, OJ 4.12.82 L343/24.
11 Council Decision 82/734, OJ 8.11.92 L311/13, as amended by Council Decision 82/960 (OJ 31.12.82 L386/48), Council Decision 85/468 (OJ 11.10.85 L269/59) and Council Decision 92/2 (OJ 4.1.92 L1/22).
12 Commission Decision 83/234, OJ 17.5.83 L127/20.
13 Commission Decision 87/257, OJ 9.5.87 L121/46, last amended by Commission Decision 98/113, OJ 6.2.98 L31/8.
14 Commission Decision 81/92, OJ 5.3.81 L58/43, as amended by Commission Decision 86/485 (OJ 3.10.86 L282/31); see also Amendment 90/0223(04), OJ 23.2.90 C43/4.
15 Commission Decision 98/8, OJ 6.1.98 L2/12.
16 Commission Decision 95/45, OJ 8.3.95 L51/13.
17 Ibid Art 14(1), as so substituted.
18 Ibid Art 14(2)(a), as so substituted. Without prejudice to this provision, the Member States may prohibit the importation of fresh meat from a designated third country in which there is an outbreak of an infectious or contagious disease which can be carried by fresh meat and which is likely to endanger public health or the health of livestock in the Member States: ibid Art 28(2)–(4), as so substituted.
19 Ibid Art 14(2)(b), as so substituted. Derogations from this provision may be permitted under Art 15 (as so substituted) and Art 29.
20 Ibid Art 16, as so substituted.
 1 Ibid Art 17(1), as so substituted. Derogations from this provision may be permitted under Art 18 (as so substituted) and Art 29.
 2 Ibid Art 17(2)(a), (c), (f), (g), as so substituted.

ante-mortem and post-mortem veterinary inspections[3] and bear the appropriate health mark.[4] The Member States must prohibit the importation of fresh meat from certain types of animals,[5] types of fresh meat[6] and meat which has been subjected to certain forms of treatment[7] or certain types of infection.[8]

All imports of fresh meat from designated third countries must be accompanied by official animal health and public health certificates drawn up in the exporting country.[9] Specific rules have been laid down regarding animal health conditions and veterinary certification for the import of fresh meat[10] from Albania,[11] Argentina,[12] Australia,[13] Belize,[14] Botswana,[15] Brazil,[16] Bulgaria,[17] Canada,[18] Chile,[19] Colombia,[20] Costa Rica,[1] Croatia,[2] Cuba,[3] Cyprus,[4] Czech Republic,[5] the Federal Republic of Yugoslavia,[6] Greenland,[7] Guatemala,[8] Honduras,[9] Hungary,[10] Iceland,[11] Israel,[12] Madagascar,[13]

3 Ibid Art 17(2)(b), (d), as so substituted.
4 Ibid Art 17(2)(e), as so substituted. The provisions of Arts 17 and 18 do not apply to fresh meat imported for uses other than for human consumption, for exhibition, study or analysis, or intended exclusively for the supply of international organizations: Art 19 (as so substituted). As to the conditions of importation from third countries of fresh meat for purposes other than human consumption, see Commission Decision 89/18, OJ 11.1.89 L8/17.
5 Ibid Art 20(a), (b) (i), (f), as so substituted.
6 Ibid Art 20(b)(iii), (g)–(k), as so substituted.
7 Ibid Art 20(c), (d), as so substituted.
8 Ibid Art 20(e), as so substituted. See also Art 21, as so substituted.
9 Ibid Art 22, Annex A, as so substituted. As to such certificates, see Commission Decision 93/198, OJ 6.4.93 L86/34, as amended (domestic ovines and caprines).
10 Although El Salvador appears on the list of third countries from which Member States may authorize the importation of bovine animals, swine and fresh meat (Council Decision 79/452, OJ 14.6.79 L146/15, as amended), Member States may not authorize the importation of fresh meat from El Salvador: Commission Decision 91/446, OJ 28.8.91 L239/18.
11 Commission Decision 89/197, OJ 17.3.89 L73/53.
12 Commission Decision 93/402, OJ 22.7.93 L179/11, as amended most recently by Commission Decision 98/16, OJ 10.1.98 L6/40. As to health protection measures which have been taken in respect of such imports under the previously applicable Commission Decision 84/414, OJ 28.8.85 L229/22, see Commission Decision 89/179, OJ 8.3.89 L64/19.
13 Commission Decision 80/801, OJ 5.9.80 L234/41, as amended.
14 Commission Decision 84/292, OJ 30.5.84 L144/10.
15 Commission Decision 92/22, OJ 16.1.92 L10/34.
16 Commission Decision 93/402, OJ 22.7.93 L179/11, as amended by Commission Decision 95/349, OJ 26.8.95 L202/10. As to health protection measures which have been taken in respect of such imports within the framework of the previously applicable Commission Decision 84/414 (OJ 28.8.85 L229/22), see Commission Decision 89/3, OJ 7.1.89 L5/32, as amended.
17 Commission Decision 92/222, OJ 25.4.92 L108/38.
18 Commission Decision 80/804, OJ 9.8.80 L236/25, as amended most recently by Commission Decision 98/91, OJ 23.1.98 L18/27.
19 Commission Decision 93/402, OJ 22.7.93 L179/11.
20 Commission Decision 93/402, OJ 22.7.93 L179/11.
 1 Commission Decision 81/887, OJ 12.11.81 L324/25.
 2 Commission Decision 92/390, OJ 23.7.92 L207/53, as amended by Commission Decision 93/234, OJ 30.6.93 L106/16.
 3 Commission Decision 86/72, OJ 21.3.86 L76/47.
 4 Commission Decision 86/463, OJ 23.9.86 L271/23.
 5 Commission Decision 94/845, OJ 31.12.94 L352/38.
 6 Commission Decision 97/737, OJ 29.10.97 L295/39.
 7 Commission Decision 86/117, OJ 15,4,86 L99/26.
 8 Commission Decision 82/414, OJ 26.6.82 L182/27.
 9 Commission Decision 89/221, OJ 5,4,89 L92/16.
10 Commission Decision 82/8, OJ 13.1.82 L8/9, as amended.
11 Commission Decision 83/84, OJ 3.3.83 L56/26.
12 Commission Decision 91/445, OJ 28.8.91 L239/17.
13 Commission Decision 90/156, OJ 4.4.90 L89/13.

Malta,[14] Mexico,[15] Morocco,[16] Namibia,[17] New Zealand,[18] Nicaragua,[19] Panama,[20] Paraguay,[1] Poland,[2] the State of Rio Grande do Sul in Brazil,[3] Romania,[4] Slovak Republic,[5] Slovenia,[6] South Africa,[7] Swaziland,[8] Switzerland,[9] Turkey,[10] United States of America,[11] Uruguay,[12] and Zimbabwe.[13]

Upon its arrival in the territory of the Community, the Member States must ensure that the meat is subjected to an animal health inspection without delay;[14] and the importation of meat which does not pass such an inspection is prohibited.[15] Before a consignment of imported meat is released for consumption in the territory of the Community it must satisfy an official public health examination carried out by random sampling.[16] Meat which is released as a result of this procedure must be accompanied by an appropriate certificate.[17] Meat which does not pass the inspection may not be marketed in the Community;[18] it must either be returned or be destroyed in the light of animal and public health considerations.[19]

As far as the Member States are concerned, they are required to draw up and communicate to the Commission lists of approved frontier inspection posts for the importation of animals and inspection posts for the importation of fresh meat.[20] In order to be approved, these inspection posts must have certain specified facilities and accommodation.[1] Compliance with these conditions is verified by independent veterinary experts.[2]

14 Commission Decision 84/294, OJ 30.5.84 L144/17.
15 Commission Decision 83/380, OJ 13.8.83 L222/27.
16 Commission Decision 84/295, OJ 30.5.84 L144/21.
17 Commission Decision 92/24, OJ 16.1.92 L10/46.
18 Commission Decision 80/805, OJ 9.9.80 L236/28, as amended.
19 Commission Decision 92/280, OJ 26.5.92 L144/21.
20 Commission Decision 86/63, OJ 15.3.86 L73/36.
 1 Commission Decision 93/402, OJ 22.7.93 L179/11.
 2 Commission Decision 82/9, OJ 13.1.82 L8/15.
 3 Commission Decision 80/1300, OJ 31.12.80 L377/51.
 4 Commission Decision 82/132, OJ 3.3.82 L60/16, as amended.
 5 Commission Decision 94/846, OJ 31.12.94 L352/48.
 6 Commission Decision 92/377, OJ 16.7.92 L197/75, amended by Commission Decision 93/234, OJ 30.4.93 L106/16.
 7 Commission Decision 91/121, OJ 16.1.92 L10/28.
 8 Commission Decision 92/23, OJ 16.1.92 L10/40.
 9 Commission Decision 81/526, OJ 18.7.81 L196/19. As to fresh pigmeat, see Commission Decision 94/667, OJ 8.10.94 L260/32.
10 Commission Decision 90/445, OJ 22.8.90 L228/28.
11 Commission Decision 82/186, OJ 30.6.82 L186/54, as amended.
12 Commission Decision 93/402, OJ 22.7.93 L179/11, as amended by Commission Decision 94/334, OJ 15.6.94 L148/12, and Commission Decision 95/443, OJ 28.10.95 L258/65.
13 Commission Decision 92/25, OJ 16.1.92 L10/52, as amended.
14 Ibid Art 23(1), as so substituted. Specific provision is made for the examination of fresh pigmeat imports for trichinae: Council Directive 77/96, OJ 31.1.77 L26/67.
15 Ibid Art 23(2), as so substituted. Fresh meat may be transported through a Member State from one third country to another under Art 23(3) (as so substituted).
16 Ibid Art 24(1)–(3), as so substituted.
17 Ibid Art 25, Annex B, as so substituted.
18 Ibid Art 24(5), as so substituted.
19 Ibid Art 24(5), as so substituted.
20 Ibid Art 27(1), as so substituted.
 1 See ibid Art 27(2), (3), as so substituted. As to the guidelines for the approval of frontier inspection posts for the importation of bovine animals and swine from third countries, see Commission Decision 84/390, OJ 8.8.84 L211/20.
 2 Ibid Art 27(5), as so substituted, which also stipulates that the experts must be nationals of a Member State other than the one in which the post to be checked is located. The costs of this verification procedure are to be borne by the Community: Art 27(6), as so substituted.

With regard to fresh poultrymeat, animal health conditions for imports are laid down in a Council directive.[3] Fresh poultrymeat may be imported if it comes from a listed third country or part of a third country,[4] comes from a third country in which avian influenza and Newcastle disease are legally notifiable diseases throughout the country in accordance with international standards and which is free from avian influenza and Newcastle disease,[5] satisfies certain health requirements, comes from flocks which prior to consignment have, without interruption been held in the third country or part thereof for a specified period, and is accompanied by a certificate drawn up by an official veterinarian of the exporting third country.[6] Inspections are carried out to ensure that these provisions are effectively applied.[7]

Community law permits a Member State when importing fresh poultrymeat from a third country to levy a charge to cover the costs of inspecting such imports. This is so even when the law of the importing Member State allows such imports only if a public health inspection which satisfies Community standards has been carried out in the exporting country and in respect of which that country has already levied charges. Public health inspections of such imports at the external frontiers of the Community may be systematic and designed to verify whether the consignments bear the required markings and whether the meat is fit for human consumption.[8] This is, in effect, a permitted derogation from the general prohibition on the levying of customs duties and charges having equivalent effect on trade in poultrymeat.[9]

Subject to Community rules applying specifically to the import of fresh poultrymeat from third countries, national provisions relating to such imports must be at least equivalent to those applied to intra-Community trade.[10]

Community rules also specify health conditions which must be also satisfied by imports from third countries of poultry and hatching eggs.[11]

The Council has enacted directives concerning the marketing of milk and

---

3 Council Directive 91/494, OJ 24.9.91 L268/35, as amended and updated in particular in respect of intra-Community trade by Council Directive 92/116, OJ 15.3.93 L62/1. As to certain third countries, see Commission Decision 94/984, OJ 31.12.94 L378/11, as amended.

4 As to the provisional list of authorized third countries, see Commission Decision 94/85, OJ 17.2.94 L44/31, as amended; Commission Decision 97/4, OJ 4.1.97 L2/6.

5 Or, though not free from such diseases, apply measures to control them which are at least equivalent to those laid down in Council Directives 92/40 and 92/66: Council Directive 91/494 Art 1, OJ 24.98.94 L268/35, as amended by Council Directive 93/121, OJ 31.12.93 L340/9. As to the classification of third countries with regard to avian influenza and Newcastle disease, see Commission Decision 93/342, OJ 8.6.93 L137/24, as amended in particular in respect of criteria for classification by Commission Decision 94/438, OJ 15.7.94 L181/35.

6 Council Directive 91/494 Arts 9–12, OJ 24.9.91 L268/35, as so amended.

7 Ibid Art 13.

8 Case 30/79 *Berlin Land v Wigei, Wild-Geflugel-Eier-Import GmbH & Co KG* [1980] ECR 151.

9 See Council Regulation 2777/75 Art 10(2), OJ 1.11.75 L282/77, as substituted by Council Regulation 3290/94, OJ 31.12.94 L349/105. The derogation applies from the date of the notification of the enabling directive to the Member State in question, whether or not that Member State has already adopted the necessary measures to comply with it: Case 88/82 *Amministrazione delle Finanze v Armando and Leonelli* [1983] ECR 1061.

10 Council Directive 71/118 Art 15, OJ 8.3.71 L55/23, as substituted by Council Directive 75/431, OJ 24.7.75 L192/6.

11 Council Directive 90/539, OJ 31.10.90 L303/6, as amended. As to marketing of egg products, see Council Directive 89/437, OJ 22.7.89 L212/87, as amended.

milk-based products.[12] Measures have also been enacted in respect of the importation of apiculture products,[13] rabbit meat and farmed-game meat,[14] and wild-game meat.[15] The list system for authorizing importing countries is used for milk and milk products,[16] rabbit meat and farmed game meat,[17] wild-game meat,[18] certain products of animal origin, fishery products and live bivalve molluscs.[19] Measures have been laid down in respect of aquaculture animals and products,[20] *Crassostrea gigas*,[1] and fishery products.[2] Special conditions are laid down in respect of the import of fishery products from Argentina,[3] Chile,[4] Morocco,[5] and Turkey.[6] Special conditions are also laid down in respect

12 Council Directive 92/46, OJ 14.9.92 L268/1, as amended. As to temporary and limited derogations, see Council Directive 92/47, OJ 14.9.91 L268/33, as amended. As to health conditions and veterinary certificates for imports not intended for human consumption, see Commission Decision 95/341, OJ 24.8.95 L200/42. As to treatment of products for human consumption from countries or areas where there is a risk of foot-and-mouth disease, see Commission Decision 95/342, OJ 24.8.95 L200/50. As to the specimen health certificate for imports, see Commission Decision 95/343, OJ 24.8.95 L200/52.
13 Commission Decision 94/860, OJ 31.12.94 L352/69.
14 Commission Decision 97/467, OJ 26.7.97 L199/57, as amended.
15 Council Directive 92/45, OJ 14.9.92 L268/35, as amended. As to animals not covered by specific rules, see Council Directive 92/65, OJ 14.9.82 L268/54. As to the list of authorized establishments, see Commission Decision 97/468, OJ 26.7.97 L199/62.
16 Commission Decision 95/340, OJ 24.8.95 L200/38, as amended. See also Case C-147/96 *Netherlands v Commission*, OJ 6.7.96 C197/9, not yet decided, in respect of a challenge by the Netherlands to a Commission decision not to include the Dutch Antilles in the list of third countries entitled under Council Directive 92/46 to export dairy products to the Community.
17 Commission Decision 97/467, OJ 26.7.97 L199/576, as amended.
18 Commission Decision 94/86, OJ 17.2.94 L44/33; Commission Decision 97/218, OJ 3.4.97 L88/25; Commission Decision 97/220, OJ 3.4.97 L88/70; Commission Decision 97/217, OJ 3.4.97 L88/20.
19 Council Decision 95/408, OJ 11.10.95 L243/17. See also Commission Decision 97/296, OJ 14.5.97 L122/21, as amended. As to the provisional list of permitted establishments, see 98/71, OJ 17.1.98 L11/39, as last amended by Commission Decision 97/666, OJ 15.10.97 L283/1.
20 Council Directive 91/67, OJ 19.2.91 L46/1, as amended.
 1 The main oyster species farmed in the Community: see Commission Decision 95/352, OJ 30.8.95 L204/13.
 2 Council Directive 91/493, OJ 24.9.91 L268/15, as amended. Certain third countries are covered by specific decisions: see below. As to health certificates for fishery products from other countries, see Commission Decision 95/328, OJ 12.8.95 L191/32. As to detailed rules in respect of visual inspection for detecting parasites in fishery products, see Commission Decision 93/140, OJ 9.3.93 L56/42. As to minimum hygiene rules in respect of fishery products caught on board certain vessels, see Council Directive 92/48, OJ 7.7.92 L187/41. As to live bivalve molluscs, see Council Directive 91/492, OJ 24.9.91 L268/1, as amended; Commission Decision 92/92, OJ 11.2.92 L34/34; Commission Decision 93/25, OJ 25.1.93 L16/22. As to cooked crustaceans and molluscan shellfish, see Commission Decision 93/51, OJ 21.1.93 L13/11. As to protective measures in respect of scallops from Japan, see Commission Directive 92/91, OJ 8.2.92 L32/37. As to sampling and limits for mercury, see Commission Decision 93/351, OJ 16.6.93 L144/23. As to derogation from approval conditions for border inspection posts, see Commission Decision 93/352, OJ 16.6.93 L144/25. As to certain measures in respect of Albania, see Commission Decision 94/621, OJ 21.9.94 L246/25, as amended. As to certain measures in respect of Japan, see Commission Decision 95/119, OJ 8.4.95 L80/56. As to special conditions in respect of Madagascar, see Commission Decision 97/757, OJ 12.11.97 L307/33. As to measures in respect of certain fishery products from China until 28 February 1998, see Commission Decision 97/620, OJ 17.9.97 L254/17.
3 See Commission Decision 93/437, OJ 12.8.93 L202/42, as amended.
4 See Commission Decision 93/436, OJ 12.8.93 L202/31, as amended.
5 Commission Decision 95/30, OJ 24.2.95 L42/32, as amended in respect of Annex B by Commission Decision 95/298, OJ 3.8.95 L184/48.
6 Commission Decision 94/777, OJ 6.12.94 L312/35 (live products); Commission Decision 84/778, OJ 6.12.94 L312/40 (frozen products).

of the import of fishery and aquaculture products from Albania,[7] Gambia,[8] India,[9] Korea,[10] Madagascar,[11]Peru,[12] the Philippines,[13] New Zealand,[14] Senegal,[15] Taiwan,[16] and Thailand.[17]

All expenditure incurred in the Member States in connection with the inspection of animals and fresh meat, the slaughter or destruction of animals and the storage and destruction of meat are chargeable to the consignor, the consignee or their representative, without compensation by the Member State involved.[18] Such health inspections and the resulting charges are permitted derogations from the prohibition on the levying of charges having an effect equivalent to customs duties.[19] But such derogations only become effective after the Member States have been given the opportunity to organize the prescribed inspections.[20] The derogations cannot, however, be applied by analogy to the importation of other products, such as game, from third countries.[1]

Subject to Community rules relating specifically to the import of fresh meat from third countries, national provisions relating to such imports may not be more favourable than those for intra-Community trade.[2]

With the framework of general directives regarding health and veterinary inspections[3] and country of origin,[4] the Community has laid down animal health conditions and certificates for imports of meat products.[5]

7 Commission Decision 95/90, OJ 30.3.95 L70/27, as amended.
8 Commission Decision 96/356, OJ 8.6.96 L137/31
9 Commission Decision 97/876, OJ 31.12.97 L356/57.
10 Commission Decision 95/454, OJ 7.11.95 L264/37; Commission Decision 95/453, OJ 7.11.95 L264/35.
11 Commission Decision 97/757, OJ 12.11.97 L307/33.
12 Commission Decision 95/173, OJ 23.5.95 L116/41, as amended. As to live bivalve molluscs and related products from Peru, see Commission Decision 95/174, OJ 23.5.95 L116/47.
13 Commission Decision 95/190, OJ 3.6.95 L123/20.
14 Commission Decision 94/448, OJ 20.7.94 L184/16, as amended.
15 Commission Decision 96/355, OJ 8.6.96 L137/24.
16 Commission Decision 94/766, OJ 30.11.94 L305/31.
17 See Commission Decision 94/325, OJ 10.6.94 L145/30, as substituted in respect of Annex B by Commission Decision 95/178, OJ 24.5.95 L117/35.
18 Council Directive 72/462 Arts 12(8), 23(4), 26, as so substituted. As to the harmonization of rules in respect of financing of inspections and controls of fresh meat and poultrymeat, see Council Directive 85/73, OJ 5.2.85 L32/14, as amended.
19 See Council Regulation 425/77, OJ 5.3.77 L61/1; and Case 35/76 *Simmenthal SpA v Italian Minister for Finance* [1976] ECR 1871.
20 Case 70/77 *Simmenthal Spa v Amministrazione delle Finanze dello Stato* [1978] ECR 1453.
1 Case 137/77 *Frankfurt-am-Main City v Neumann* [1978] ECR 1623; Case 138/77 *Ludwig v Hamburg City* [1978] ECR 1645.
2 Council Directive 64/433 Art 14, OJ 29.7.64 L121/2012, as substituted by Council Directive 83/90, OJ 5.3.83 L59/10; Council Directive 72/461 Art 11, OJ 31.12.72 L302/24, as renumbered by corrigendum OJ 20.7.73 L200/42.
3 Council Directive 72/462, OJ 31.12.72 L302/28, as amended.
4 Council Decision 79/542, OJ 14.6.79 L146/15, as amended.
5 Commission Decision 91/449, OJ 29.8.91, as amended. Meat products consist, for this purpose, of products prepared wholly or partly from meat, which has undergone treatment to ensure a certain degree of preservation. 'Meat' means meat as defined by Council Directive 64/433 Art 2(a) (OJ 29.7.64 L121/2012), Council Directive 71/118 Art 1 (OJ 8.3.71 L55/23), Council Directive 72/461 Art 1 (OJ 31.12.72 L302/24), and Council Directive 72/462 Art 2 (OJ 31.12.72 L302/28): Council Directive 77/99 Art 2(1)(b) (OJ 31.1.77 L26/85), as amended. 'Treatment' means the treatment of fresh meat, whether or not combined with other foodstuffs, by heating, salting or drying, or a combination of these processes: Council Directive 77/99 Art 2(1)(d), OJ 31.1.77 L26/85, as substituted by Council Decision 88/658, OJ 31.12.88 L382/15. As to checks on the effectiveness of treatment, see Annex A, chapter V, as substituted by Council Decison 88/658, OJ 31.12.88 L382/15. Meat which has merely been chilled or frozen is not regarded as a meat product, and the directive does not cover meat extracts,

Community approval has been given for the importation of meat products into the Community from establishments[6] in Argentina,[7] Bahrain,[8] Botswana,[9] Brazil,[10] Czech Republic,[11] Namibia,[12] Tunisia,[13] Uruguay,[14] and Zimbabwe[15] as well as Bulgaria, Poland, Romania, Slovenia, the Yugoslav Republics of Serbia, Montenegro and Macedonia[16] and Chile, Croatia and Slovakia.[17]

With regard to meat products, in the absence of relevant provisions of Community law, national provisions applicable to the import of meat products from third countries may not be more favourable than those applicable to intra-Community trade.[18]

Animal products not subject to specific harmonized Community rules are governed by a separate directive.[19] The rules, principles and safeguard measures which it lays down are the same as those governing products, other than animals, which are imported from third countries.[20]

More specific conditions have also been laid down for the import of petfood and related products;[1] processed animal protein intended for animal consumption;[2] pig bristles;[3] bones, horns, hooves and related products, excluding meals, for further processing not intended for human or animal consumption;[4] and of certain raw materials, such as glands and organs, including blood, for the pharmaceutical processing industry.[5]

Rules have been laid down in respect of veterinary checks on products imported in certain Greek islands from third countries.[6] Specific measures have been taken to adjust Community rules to the European Economic Area (EEA)

---

meat consomme and stock, meat sauces and similar products not containing fragments of meat; bones, peptones, animal gelatine, meat powder, blood plasma, dried blood, bone extracts, etc; fats melted down from animal tissues; and stomachs, bladders and intestines: Council Directive 77/99 Art 2(1)(a), as so substituted.

6 As to the list of certain products, see Commission Decision 97/365, OJ 12.6.97 L154/51.

7 Commission Decision 86/414, OJ 23.8.86 L237/36, as amended by Commission Decision 94/463 (OJ 26.7.94 L190/21); and Commission Decision 97/397, OJ 24.6.97 L165/3. As to the model for the public health certificate in respect of meat products from Argentina, Brazil and Uruguay, see Commission Decision 87/221, OJ 7.4.87 L93/11.

8 Commission Decision 94/59, OJ 1.2.94 L27/53.

9 Commission Decision 94/465, OJ 26.7.94 L190/25.

10 Commission Decision 87/119, OJ 18.2.87 L49/37, as amended by Commission Decision 95/236 (OJ 7.7.95 L156/84).

11 Commission Decision 97/299, OJ 16.5.97 L124/50.

12 Commission Decision 95/427, OJ 24.10.95 L254/28.

13 Commission Decision 92/245, OJ 9.5.92 L124/42.

14 Commission Decision 86/473, OJ 30.9.86 L279/53, as amended by Commission Decision 94/464 (OJ 26.7.94 L190/23).

15 Commission Decision 94/40, OJ 27.1.94 L22/50.

16 See Commission Decision 92/447, OJ 28.8.92 L248/69, which lays down specimen animal health certificates.

17 See Commission Decision 97/569, OJ 19.3.98 L82/47. As to Croatia, see also Commission Decision 98/10, OJ 7.1.98 L3/14.

18 Council Directive 80/215 Art 12, OJ 21.2.80 L47/4.

19 Council Directive 92/118, OJ 15.3.93 L62/49, as amended.

20 That is, those laid down by Council Directive 90/675, OJ 31.12.90 L373/1, as to which see above.

1 Commission Decision 94/309, OJ 1.6.94 L137/62, as amended.

2 Commission Decision 94/344, OJ 21.6.94 L154/45, as amended.

3 Commission Decision 94/383, OJ 8.7.94 L174/33.

4 Commission Decision 94/446, OJ 19.7.94 L183/46, as amended.

5 As to products and countries appearing on the list established by Council Decision 97/542, see Commission Decision 92/183, OJ 31.3.92 L85/33. As to other products or countries, see Commission Decision 92/187, OJ 2.4.92 L87/20.

6 Commission Decision 94/361, OJ 23.9.94 L248/26.

Agreement.[7] There are also specific measures in respect of the French overseas departments[8] and the Canary Islands.[9]

The Community has also regulated exports. Veterinary checks are required on animals and related products intended for export to a third country through the territory of one or more Member States other than that of origin.[10] The Member State of origin must ensure that each consignment of animals is accompanied by health certificates, which contain, where necessary, the additional guarantees provided for by Community legislation for animals intended for slaughter.[11] Where incidents occur during transport or the consignee third country refuses a consignment, the Member State of transit may take measures in respect of the animals, including the dispatch of the animals for slaughter.[12] The Member State of origin is also required to ensure that each consignment is accompanied by veterinary certificates or documents meeting the veterinary requirements of the third country of destination.[13] However, where the competent authorities of the originating Member State do not have the requisite information, particularly where there is no bilateral agreement between the originating Member State and the destination country, the competent authority must complete a specified certificate.[14] In addition, the Animo message[15] must specify the third country of destination.[16]

Trade in breeding animals, semen and embryos

Specific measures govern the importation of breeding animals into the Community.[17] The importation into the Community of animal semen and embryos from third countries is also limited.

The Community has adopted provisions relating to the approval of purebred bovines for breeding,[18] performance monitoring methods and methods for assessing cattle's genetic value for pure bred bovine animals,[19] the criteria for

7 See, eg, Commission Decision 94/453, OJ 22.7.94 L187/11.
8 Council Directive 91/3763, OJ 24.12.91 L356/1.
9 Council Directive 92/1601, OJ 27.6.92 L173/13, as amended in particular by Council Regulation 3290/94, OJ 31.12.94 L349/105.
10 Council Directive 90/425 Art 3(1)(g), OJ 18.8.90 L224/29, as amended.
11 Ibid Art 2(1).
12 Ibid Art 2(2).
13 Ibid Art 3(1).
14 Ibid Art 3(2). The certificate must be drawn up in one of the languages of the Member State of origin and (with regard to Community destination countries) at least one of the languages of the Member State of destination; indicate, as consignee, the natural or legal person carrying out exit formalities; and indicate, as place of destination, the exit point from the territory, eg border inspection post or other exit point: ibid Art 4.
15 As provided in Commission Decision 91/637, OJ 13.12.91 L343/48, as amended. As to the computerized network Animo, see above.
16 Ibid Art 5(1), which also provides that this must be specified under the heading 'Observations'. The Animo message must be addressed to the competent authority of the place of destination, that is, the border inspection post of exit or the local authority in which the point of exit is situated, and the central authorities of the place of destination and of the Member State(s) of transit: ibid Art 5(2).
17 See Commission Regulation 2342/92, OJ 11.8.92 L227/12, as amended. As to general principles regarding zootechnical and genealogical conditions applicable to such imports, see Council Directive 94/28, OJ 12.7.94 L178/66. As to zootechnical and pedigree requirements for marketing of purebred animals, see Council Directive 91/174, OJ 5.4.91 L85/37.
18 See Council Directive 87/328, OJ 26.8.87 L167/54 and Council Directive 94/28, OJ 12.7.94 L178/66, modifying Council Directive 77/504 Art 3, OJ 12.8.77 L206/8.
19 See Commission Decision 86/130, OJ 17.4.86 L101/37, as amended.

the recognition of breeders' organizations and associations which maintain or establish herd-books,[20] the criteria for the creation of herd-books[1] and the criteria for entering cattle in herd-books.[2] Officially recognized breeders' organizations may not oppose entry into their herd books of pure-bred bovines for breeding which satisfy these specified particulars and criteria.[3] In intra-Community trade, Member States may require a pedigree certificate.[4] In the absence of Community rules on the subject, the conditions applicable to imports of pure-bred breeding bovines from third countries must not be more favourable than those governing intra-Community trade.[5]

A directive lays down animal health requirements applicable to intra-Community trade in and importation from listed third countries of bovine semen.[6]

A further directive provides for animal health conditions governing intra-Community trade in and importation from third countries of bovine embryos.[7] Such embryos may be imported only from listed countries or parts of countries,[8] must be collected by a listed embryo collection team, are subject to specified health conditions, require the submission of an animal health certificate drawn up and signed by the official veterinarian of the third country of collection, are subject to control before being put into free circulation or placed under customs procedure, and may be prohibited in whole or in part under specified safeguard measures.[9]

Analogous provisions apply to pigs for breeding,[10] to sheep and goats,[11] and to poultry and hatching eggs.[12]

20 See Commission Decision 84/247, OJ 12.5.84 L125/58, as amended.
1 See Commission Decision 84/247, OJ 12.5.84 L125/58, as amended.
2 See Commission Decision 84/419, OJ 5.9.84 L237/11, as amended; see also Commission Decision 86/130, OJ 17.4.86 L101/37, as amended.
3 Council Directive 77/504 Arts 4, 6, OJ 12.8.77 L206/8.
4 Ibid Art 5; as to the pedigree certificate, see Commission Decision 86/404, OJ 20.8.86 L233/19.
5 Ibid Art 7.
6 Council Directive 88/407, OJ 22.7.88 L194/10, as amended. As to animal health conditions and certification, see Commission Decision 94/577, OJ 26.8.94 L221/26. Commission Decision 90/14, Annex, OJ 11.1.90 L8/71, as substituted by Commission Decision 91/276 (OJ 30.5.91 L135/58), lists the countries as Australia, Austria, Canada, Czechoslovakia, Finland, Hungary, Israel, New Zealand, Norway, Poland, Romania, Sweden, Switzerland, United States of America, and Yugoslavia. Austria, Finland, Norway and Sweden were deleted by Commission Decision 94/453 22.7.94 L187/11. As to health protection measures in respect of imports from Israel, see Commission Decision 91/227, OJ 30.5.91 L135/60. As to the list of authorized semen collection centres, see Commission Decision 93/693, OJ 22.12.93 L320/35, as amended.
7 Council Directive 89/556, OJ 19.10.89 L302/1, as amended. As to health conditions and certification, see Commission Decision 94/471, OJ 15.9.92 L270/27, as amended.
8 As to the list of third countries, see Commission Decision 91/270, OJ 29.5.91 L134/56.
9 Ibid Arts 7–14, as amended. As to the list of approved collection teams, see Commission Decision 92/452, OJ 29.8.92 L250/40, as amended.
10 See also Council Directive 88/66, OJ 31.12.88 L382/36, as to the zootechnical standards applicable to breeding animals of the porcine species. As to the acceptance of pure-bred pigs for breeding, see Council Directive 90/118, OJ 17.3.90 L71/34, as amended. As to hybrid pigs for breeding, see Council Directive 90/119, OJ 17.3.90 L71/36, as amended.
11 As to pure-bred breeding sheep and goats, see Council Directive 89/361, OJ 6.6.89 L153/30. As to the criteria for approval of breeders' organizations for pure-bred breeding sheep and goats, see Commission Decision 90/254, OJ 8.6.90 L145/30, as amended. As to the criteria for approval governing entry in flock-books, see Commission Decision 90/255, OJ 8.6.90 L145/32, as amended. As to methods for assessing the genetic value of animals, see Commission Decision 90/256, OJ 8.6.90 L145/35, as amended. As to the criteria for acceptance for breeding purposes of pure-bred breeding sheep and goats and the use of their semen, ova or embryos, see Commission Decision 90/257, OJ 8.6.90 L145/38, as amended. As to zootechnical certificates, see Commission Decision 90/258, OJ 8.6.90 L145/39, as amended.
12 Council Directive 90/539, OJ 321.10.90 L303/6, as amended.

Animal health requirements govern the intra-Community trade in and imports from listed countries of porcine semen.[13] Imports of semen, ova and embryos of the ovine, caprine and equine species and ova and embryos of the porcine species are authorized from listed countries.[14]

With regard to equidae, special rules concern country of origin, health conditions and veterinary certification of imports of equidae for breeding and production[15] and trade in equine semen,[16] ova and embryos.[17]

The Community has also enacted measures in respect of trade and imports of animals, semen, ova and embryos not subject to specific rules.[18]

PLANT HEALTH

Protective measures against diseases of plants and pesticide residues

For further promotion of agricultural productivity and health, the Council has exercised its authority to harmonize the laws and practices of the Member States by laying down common standards for the protection of plants from diseases and the progressive eradication of such diseases. Both general and specific measures have been taken.[19]

Pursuant to the completion of the Community's internal market as an area without internal frontiers, specific categories of producers, collective warehouses, dispatching centres, and importers are required to be listed in an official register.[20] They are required to keep an updated plan of the premises on which plants and related objects are stored, to keep records for example of plants stored or

13 Council Directive 90/429, OJ 18.8.90 L224/62, as amended; Commission Decision 93/199, OJ 6.4.93 L86/43, as amended. As to veterinary checks, see Council Directive 90/675, OJ 31.12.90 L373/1, as amended. As to health conditions and veterinary certification, see Commission Decision 93/199, OJ 6.4.93 L86/43. The importation of porcine semen is authorized from Canada, New Zealand, Norway, Switzerland, and the United States of America: Commission Decision 93/160, OJ 19.3.93 L67/27, as amended in particular by Commission Decision 94/453, OJ 22.7.94 L187/11. As to semen collection centres approved for export to the Community of porcine animals from certain third countries, see Commission Decision 95/94, OJ 1.4.95 L73/87

14 As to a provisional list, see Commission Decision 94/63, OJ 2.2.94 L28/47. As to the specimen health certificate for intra-Community trade in pig ova and embryos, see Commission Decision 95/483, OJ 18.11.95 L275/30.

15 See Commission Decision 93/197, OJ 6.4.93 L86/16, as amended. As to the identification document (passport) for registered equidae, see Commission Decision 93/623, OJ 3.12.93 L298/45. As to criteria for approval or recognition of organizations maintaining studbooks, see Commission Decision 92/353, OJ 11.7.92 L192/63. As to co-ordination between such organizations, see Commission Decision 92/354, OJ 11.6.92 L192/66. As to imports of registered equidae, see above.

16 As to the specimen animal health certificate for trade in equine semen, see Commission Decision 95/307, OJ 4.8.95 L185/58.

17 As to the specimen health certificate for trade in equine ova and embryos, see Commission Decision 95/294, OJ 2.8.95 L182/27.

18 Council Directive 92/65, OJ 23.10.92 L264/62, as amended.

19 The Community also provides financing for programmes for the control of organisms harmful to plants or plant products in the French overseas departments, the Azores and Madeira: see Commission Decision 93/522, OJ 8.10.93 L251/35. As to the 1995 programmes, see Commission Decision 95/382, OJ 28.9.95 L231/36 (French overseas departments); Commission Decision 95/383, OJ 28.9.95 L231/43 (Madeira); and Commission Decision 95/384, OJ 28.9.95 L231/50 (Azores).

20 See Commission Directive 92/90, OJ 26.11.92 L344/38.

dispatched and to keep related documents for at least one year, to designate a person to liaise with official bodies, and to meet certain other obligations.[1]

By a directive issued in 1977,[2] Member States are required to ban or regulate the introduction, not only from other Member States but also from third countries,[3] of specified organisms[4] which are harmful to plants[5] or to plant products.[6] Plants, plant products, their packaging and the vehicles in which they are transported must be subjected to meticulous official examination[7] before being allowed to enter the territory of a Member State so as to ensure that they are not contaminated by any prohibited organism[8] and that any relevant special requirements have been complied with.[9] When, in the light of such examination, the provisions of the directive are considered to be satisfied, a phytosanitary certificate is to be issued on the authority of which the plants or plant products may be introduced into another Member State.[10] In principle, plants and plant products to which such a certificate applies may not be prohibited or restricted from entry on the territory of a Member State on grounds of plant health.[11]

However, in respect of plants and plant products which come from a third country, special provisions for examination and certification are laid down.[12] Member States must require a meticulous official examination, in totality or by representative sample of the plants or plant products and, if necessary, of the vehicle in which they were transported to ensure that they are not contaminated by specified organisms and that certain products meet specified health conditions.[13] The products must also be accompanied by specific certificates,

---

1 Ibid Art 2(2).
2 Council Directive 77/93, OJ 31.1.77 L26/20, as amended.
3 The directive does not apply to the French overseas departments, the Canary Islands, Ceuta or Melilla: ibid Art 1(2), as amended. As to derogations, see Commission Decision 97/89, OJ 30.1.97 L27/45 (seed potatoes from Canada); Commission Decision 98/92, OJ 23.1.98 L18/30 (seed potatoes from Canada); Commission Decision 98/86, OJ 22.1.98 L17/25 (plants of *Vitis* L, other than fruits, from Croatia); Commission Decision 98/187 (plants of *Vitis* L, other than fruits, from Latvia); Commission Decision 98/201, OJ 13.3.98 L76/39 (plants of *Vitis* L, other than fruits, from Hungary or Romania); Commission Decision 98/112, OJ 4.2.98 L28/43 (potatoes other than potatoes intended for planting from Slovenia).
4 'Harmful organisms' means pests of plants or plant products, which belong to the animal or plant kingdoms, or which are viruses, mycoplasms or other pathogens: ibid Art 2(1)(e), as amended. They are listed specifically under ibid Arts 3–5, as amended; in Annex I, as amended; Annex II. Amendments to the Annexes may be made by the Council under ibid Arts 13 (as amended) and 16 (as amended).
5 'Plants' means living plants and living parts of plants, including fresh fruit and vegetables, cut flowers etc, and seeds: ibid Art 2(1)(a) (as first substituted by Council Directive 85/574).
6 Ibid Art 1(1). 'Plant products' means products of plant origin, unprocessed or having undergone simple preparation, in so far as these are not plants: Art 2(1)(b). Certain harmful organisms, plants, plant products and other objects may however be introduced into or moved within the Community for trial or scientific purposes and for work on varietal selections: see Commission Directive 95/44, OJ 3.8.95 L184/34.
7 See ibid Art 6, as amended by Council Directive 85/574, OJ 31.12.85 L372/25. Examination may be by representative sample: ibid Art 6. As to the interpretation and effect of Council Directive 77/93, see Case 37/83 *Rewe-Zentral Finanz AG v Direktor der Landwirtschaftskammer Rheinland* [1984] ECR 1229.
8 Ibid Art 6(1)(a),(b).
9 Ibid Art 6(1)(c), Annex IV, Part A, as amended.
10 Ibid Art 7, as substituted by Council Directive 85/574, OJ 31.12.85 L372/25. For the forms of certificate, see Annex VII, as amended.
11 Council Directive 79/93 Arts 8(1), 11, and Art 9, OJ 31.1.77 L26/20, as amended.
12 Council Directive 77/93 Art 12, as amended. As to minimum conditions for plant health checks, see Commission Directive 98/22, OJ 28.4.98 L126/26.
13 Ibid Art 12(1),(a), as amended.

including a phytosanitary certificate dated not more than 14 days before the date on which the product left the exporting country.[14]

Further, in circumstances in which a Member State considers that it is in imminent danger of the introduction or spread of harmful organisms[15] it may take additional temporary protective measures.[16] The measures taken and the reasons for them must be notified immediately to the other Member States and to the EC Commission.[17] A decision whether to amend or rescind such measures may be taken by the Commission, in consultation with the Standing Committee on Plant Health,[18] acting through a management committee procedure.[19] Member States may or must ban the introduction into their territory of certain plants or plant products either completely[20] or unless certain requirements are met.[1] The general provisions of this directive do not derogate from any specific provisions of Community law relating to plant health except where it lays down more exacting standards.[2]

Derogations have been authorized to allow the import of strawberry plants intended for planting, other than seeds, originating in Australia;[3] growing medium originating in third countries;[4] plants of *Chamaecyparis Spach*, *Juniperus L* and *Pinus L*, respectively, originating in Japan;[5] oak logs with bark attached originating in Canada or the USA;[6] oak wood from Canada;[7] and sawn wood of conifers from Canada.[8]

Directives have been issued which lay down minimum measures to be taken by the Member States to control and prevent the spreading of the following particular plant diseases: potato wart disease,[9] potato cyst eelworm,[10] San Jose scale,[11] carnation leaf-rollers,[12] and potato ring rot.[13]

Directives have also been issued to fix maximum levels for pesticide residues

---

14 Ibid Art 12(1)(b).
15 This includes those not listed in ibid Annexes I, II.
16 Ibid Art 15(1).
17 Ibid Art 15(1). As to the procedure for the notification of interception of a consignment or a harmful organism from third countries and presenting an imminent phytosanitary danger, see Commission Directive 94/3, OJ 5.2.94 L32/37.
18 This committee was established by Council Decision 76/894 Art 1, OJ 9.12.25 L340/25. It consists of representatives of the Member States and is chaired by a Commission representative: ibid Art 1. Its functions are delegated to it by Council measures on plant health, and it may examine other matters within the scope of those measures raised by the chair on its own initiative or at the request of a Member State: ibid Art 2.
19 Council Directive 77/93 Arts 15(2), 17, OJ 31.1.77 L26/36. The national measures may be maintained pending such a decision: ibid Art 15(2).
20 Ibid Art 4, Annex III, as amended.
 1 Ibid Art 5, Annex IV, as amended.
 2 Ibid Art 18.
 3 Commission Decision 93/411, OJ 24.7.93 L182/63, as amended and as extended to 31.12.98 by Commission Decision 97/353, OJ 10.6.97 L151/40.
 4 Commission Decision 93/447, OJ 20.8.93 L209/32, as amended.
 5 Commission Decision 93/452, OJ 21.8.93 L210/29, as amended.
 6 Commission Decision 93/467, OJ 27.8.93 L217/49, as amended.
 7 Commission Decision 85/634, OJ 31.12.85 L379/45, as amended.
 8 Commission Decision 90/505, OJ 13.10.90 L282/63, as amended.
 9 Council Directive 69/464, OJ 24.12.69 L323/1, as amended.
10 Council Directive 69/465, OJ 24.12.69 L323/3, as amended.
11 Council Directive 69/466, OJ 24.12.69 L323/5. Phytosanitary inspection of imported products is justified under this directive in order to prevent the spreading of harmful organisms: Case 4/75 *Rewe-Zentralfinanz GmbH v Landwirtschaftskammer* [1975] ECR 843.
12 Council Directive 74/647, OJ 28.12.74 L352/41.
13 Council Directive 93/85, OJ 18.10.93 L259/1.

in and on fruit and vegetables[14] and in and on cereals,[15] to prohibit the placing on the market and use of plant protection products containing certain active substances,[16] and to establish Community methods of sampling for the official control of pesticide residues in and on fruit and vegetables.[17] Maximum levels have also been fixed for pesticide residues in and on foodstuffs of animal origin.[18] These various maximum levels do not apply however to products intended for export to third countries.[19] As a result of reported cases of cholera, special measures have been imposed on imports of certain fruit and vegetables originating in or consigned to Uganda, Kenya, Tanzania and Mozambique.[20]

Marketing of seeds and propagating material for agriculture, horticulture and forestry

With regard to the marketing of seeds and propagating material, the Council has adopted a series of directives to restrict the marketing of such seeds and materials so as to allow only those which satisfy common Community standards.[1]

A basically uniform approach is adopted by a series of directives concerned with beet seed,[2] fodder plant seed,[3] cereal seed,[4] seed potatoes,[5] the seed of oil and fibre plants,[6] and vegetable seed.[7] The directives apply to the marketing of

---

14 Council Directive 76/895, OJ 9.12.76 L340/26, as amended. See also Council Directive 90/642, OJ 14.12.90 L350/71, as amended.

15 Council Directive 86/362, OJ 7.8.86 L221/37, as amended.

16 Council Directive 91/414, OJ 19.8.91 L230/1. See also Commission Decision 98/242, OJ 28.3.98 L96/45. The previous legislation was Council Directive 79/117, OJ 8.2.79 L33/36, as amended. As to the interpretation of this directive, see Case 125/88 *Officier van Justitie v Nijman* [1989] ECR 3533.

17 Commission Directive 79/700, OJ 15.8.79 L207/26.

18 See Council Directive 86/363, OJ 7.8.86 L221/43. See also Recommendation of the EFTA Surveillance Authority, No 167/97/COL, OJ 6.11.97 L303/26.

19 Council Directive 76/895 Art 9, OJ 9.12.76 L340/26; Council Directive 86/362 Art 14(a), OJ 7.8.86 L221/37; Council Directive 79/117 Art 5(b), OJ 8.2.79 L33/36; Council Directive 86/363 Art 14, OJ 7.8.86 L221/43.

20 Commission Decision 98/116, OJ 6.2.98 L31/28, which is to be reviewed before 30 September 1998. Imports of pistachios from Iran were suspended for health reasons until 15 December 1997 (Commission Decision 97/613, OJ 11.9.97 L248/33).

1 In 1981 a Special Section on the Approximation of Laws was created within the Advisory Committee on Seeds: Commission Decision 81/195, OJ 2.4.81 L88/42, as amended.

2 Council Directive 66/400, OJ 11.7.66 L125/2290, as amended. The Community has also recognized the equivalence of checks on practices for the maintenance of varieties carried out in specified third countries: Council Decision 97/788, OJ 25.11.97 L322/39.

3 Council Directive 66/401, OJ 11.7.66 L125/2298, as amended, in particular in respect to the Annexes, by Commission Directive 78/386, OJ 25.4.78 L113/1, as amended, and by Commission Directive 82/287, OJ 13.5.82 L131/24, as amended.

4 Council Directive 66/402, OJ 11.7.66 L125/2309, as amended in particular by Commission Directive 86/320, OJ 23.7.86 L200/38, as amended.

5 Council Directive 66/403, OJ 11.7.66 L125/2320. As to more stringent measures against certain diseases, see Commission Decision 93/231, OJ 30.4.913 L106/11. As to Community grades of seed potatoes, see Commission Directive 93/5017, OJ 30.4.93 L106/7.

6 Council Directive 69/208, OJ 10.7.69 L169/3, as amended, in particular in respect of the Annexes by Commission Directive 78/388, OJ 25.4.78 L113/20, as amended, and by Commission Directive 82/287, OJ 13.5.82 L131/24. The marketing of seed of certain species is limited to 'basic seed' and 'certified seed': Commission Directive 86/109, OJ 8.4.86 L93/21, as amended.

7 Council Directive 70/458, OJ 12.10.70 L225/7, as amended. See also Commission Directive 89/14, OJ 11.1.89 L8/9; Commission Decision 90/209, OJ 28.4.90 L108/104, as amended.

those seeds within the Community.[8] Definitions of basic seed and certified seed, the former bred to be the progenitor of the latter, are laid down at the outset.[9] The Member States are under a duty not to place seed on the market unless it has been certified in accordance with the conditions specified in the directives.[10] Seed must be examined officially by any relevant international methods which are currently in force.[11] Certain derogations from these requirements are, however, permitted in respect of the breeding, development and scientific testing of seed and of seed which is marketed for processing.[12] The criteria laid down by these directives are regarded as minima in that individual Member States may impose additional or more stringent requirements for the certification of seed in their own territory.[13] Requests by breeders that the descriptions of the genealogical components of seeds be treated as confidential must be granted by the Member States.[14] Seeds which are marketed under the terms of the directives must be packaged, sealed, labelled and marked in specific ways,[15] and packages and labels must note whether the seed has undergone any chemical treatment.[16]

Subject to certain exemptions, seed which satisfies the prescribed criteria must not be subject to any other marketing restrictions.[17] Seed which is produced directly from basic seed which was certified in one Member State and is harvested in another Member State or in a third country may be certified in the Member State which produced the basic seed, subject to a satisfactory field inspection and official examination.[18] Any temporary difficulties in the general

8 Council Directive 66/400 Art 1; Council Directive 66/401 Art 1; Council Directive 66/402 Art 1; Council Directive 66/403 Art 1; Council Directive 69/208 Art 1; Council Directive 70/458 Art 1.

9 Council Directive 66/400 Art 2, as amended; Council Directive 66/401 Art 2, as amended; Council Directive 66/402 Art 2, as amended; Council Directive 66/403 Art 2, as amended; Council Directive 69/208 Art 2, as amended; Council Directive 70/458 Art 2, as amended.

10 Council Directive 66/400 Art 3(1), Annex I(B); Council Directive 66/401 Art 3(1)-(3), Annex III; Council Directive 66/402 Art 3(1), Annex II; Council Directive 66/403 Art 3(1), Annexes I, II; Council Directive 69/208 Art 3(1)-(3), Annex II; Council Directive 70/458 Art 3, 20(2), Annex II.

11 Council Directive 66/400 Art 3(2); Council Directive 66/401 Art 3(4); Council Directive 66/402 Art 3(3); Council Directive 69/208 Art 3(4); Council Directive 70/458 Art 20(3). As to the examination of seed potatoes, see Council Directive 66/403 Arts 5–7.

12 Council Directive 66/400 Arts 3(4), 4; Council Directive 66/401 Arts 3(5), 4; Council Directive 66/402 Arts 3(4), 4; Council Directive 66/403 Art 3(2)(B); Council Directive 69/208 Arts 3(5), 4; Council Directive 70/458 Arts 20(4), 21. As to a temporary derogation to meet market demand, see Commission Decision 97/406, OJ 27.6.97 L169/89.

13 Council Directive 66/400 Art 5; Council Directive 66/401 Art 5; Council Directive 66/402 Art 5; Council Directive 66/403 Art 3(3); Council Directive 69/208 Art 5; Council Directive 70/458 Art 22.

14 Council Directive 66/400 Art 6; Council Directive 66/401 Art 6; Council Directive 66/402 Art 6; Council Directive 69/208 Art 6. There are no comparable provisions in respect of seed potatoes and vegetable seed.

15 Council Directive 66/400 Arts 9–12, Annex III, as amended; Council Directive 66/401 Arts 8–11, 13, Annex IV, as amended; Council Directive 66/402 Arts 8–11, 12, Annex IV, as amended; Council Directive 66/403 Arts 8–11, Annex III, as amended; Council Directive 69/208 Arts 8–11, Annex IV, as amended; Council Directive 70/458 Arts 24–28, Annex IV, as amended.

16 Council Directive 66/400 Art 13; Council Directive 66/401 Art 12; Council Directive 66/402 Art 12; Council Directive 66/403 Art 12; Council Directive 69/208 Art 12; Council Directive 70/458 Art 29.

17 Council Directive 66/400 Art 14; Council Directive 66/401 Art 14; Council Directive 66/402 Art 14; Council Directive 66/403 Art 13; Council Directive 69/208 Art 13; Council Directive 70/458 Art 30.

18 Council Directive 66/400 Arts 15, 16; Council Directive 66/401 Arts 15, 26; Council Directive 66/402 Arts 15, 16; Council Directive 66/403 Arts 14, 15; Council Directive 69/208 Arts 14, 15; Council Directive 70/458 Arts 31, 32.

supply of either basic or certified seed may be overcome by the Commission in consultation with the Standing Committee on Seeds and Propagating Material for Agriculture, Horticulture and Forestry,[19] and by a management committee procedure, permitting the Member States affected to market seed and seed varieties which would not normally satisfy the Community requirements.[20]

Compliance with the terms of the directives during marketing must be officially controlled by the Member States.[1] In the interests of uniformity Community comparative tests are also carried out and the results are communicated to the Standing Committee on Seeds and Propagating Material for Agriculture, Horticulture and Forestry.[2] Each directive expressly provides that it is without prejudice to the laws of the Member States justified on grounds of the protection of human, animal and plant life or the protection of industrial and commercial property.[3]

A directive incorporating comparable provisions, with variations in the light of the nature of the subject matter, has been issued in respect of the marketing within the Community of material for the vegetative propagation of the vine.[4] In addition, Member States may provide for the marketing of propagative material produced in third countries.[5]

A further directive provides that a common catalogue of varietes of agricultural plant species be compiled based on the national catalogues of the Member States.[6] This directive establishes criteria for inclusion in the common catalogue of those varieties of beet, fodder plant, cereal, potato, and oil and fibre plant the marketing of the seeds of which are subject to the directives described above.[7]

Though relevant to imports, the directives concerning seeds and propagating material do not apply to seeds and material which are intended for export to third countries.[8]

---

19 This committee was established by Council Decision 66/399 Art 1, OJ 11.7.66 L125/2289. It comprises representatives of the Member States and is chaired by a Commission representative: ibid Art 1. It carries out duties devolved upon it by the directives on the marketing of seeds and propagating material, and considers questions arising under those directives and referred by the chair on its own initiative or at the rquest of representatives of Member States: ibid Art 2.

20 Council Directive 66/400 Arts 17, 21; Council Directive 66/401 Arts 17, 21; Council Directive 66/402 Arts 17, 21; Council Directive 66/403 Arts 16, 19; Council Directive 69/208 Arts 16, 20; Council Directive 70/458 Arts 33, 40.

 1 Council Directive 66/400 Art 19; Council Directive 66/401 Art 19; Council Directive 66/402 Art 19; Council Directive 66/403 Art 18; Council Directive 69/208 Art 18; Council Directive 70/458 Art 35.

 2 Council Directive 66/400 Art 20; Council Directive 66/401 Art 20; Council Directive 66/402 Art 20; Council Directive 69/208 Art 19; Council Directive 70/458 Arts 36–39. There is no comparable provision in respect of seed potatoes.

 3 Council Directive 66/400 Art 22; Council Directive 66/401 Art 22; Council Directive 66/402 Art 22; Council Directive 66/403 Art 20; Council Directive 69/208 Art 21; Council Directive 70/458 Art 41.

 4 Council Directive 68/193, OJ 17.4.68 L93/15, as amended.

 5 Council Directive 74/649, OJ 28.12.74 L352/45.

 6 Council Directive 70/457, OJ 12.10.70 L225/1.

 7 Ibid Art 1.

 8 Council Directive 66/400 Art 18; Council Directive 66/401 Art 18; Council Directive 66/402 Art 18; Council Directive 66/403 Art 17; Council Directive 66/404 Art 16; Council Directive 68/193 Art 15; Council Directive 69/208 Art 17; Council Directive 70/457 Art 22; Council Directive 70/458 Art 34.

Another series of directives was adopted as part of the completion of the internal market. They concern ornamental plant propagating material and ornamental plants,[9] vegetable propagating material other than seed,[10] and fruit plant propagating material and fruit plants intended for fruit production.[11]

Propagating material[12] or ornamental plants[13] may not be placed on the market[14] except by accredited suppliers[15] and unless they meet certain requirements.[16] Such material must be marketed with a reference either to the variety or the group of plants to which they belong.[17] Member States must not impose more stringent conditions or marketing restrictions than those laid down in schedules to be established for each genus or species.[18] A procedure is laid down[19] for deciding whether such propagating material and ornamental plants produced in a third country and affording the same guarantees as regards obligations on the supplier, identity, characteristics, plant health, growing medium, packaging, inspection arrangements, marking and sealing, are equivalent in all respects to such material and plants produced in the Community and complying with Community requirements.[20] Following this decision, such products imported by a Member State in accordance with these provisions are not to be subject to any marketing restrictions as regards these matters in other Member States.[1] However, until 31 December 1998,[2] Member States may apply to the import of propagating material and ornamental plants from third countries conditions equivalent to those applicable to the production and marketing of products obtained in the Community.[3]

---

9 The framework measure is Council Directive 91/682, OJ 31.12.91 L376/21, as amended.

10 The framework measure is Council Directive 92/33, OJ 10.6.92 L157/1, as amended.

11 The framework measure is Council Directive 92/34, OJ 10.6.92 L157/10.

12 That is, seeds, parts of plants and all plant material intended for the propagation of ornamental plants and other plants for ornamental purposes: Council Directive 91/682 Art 3(a), OJ 31.12.91 L376/21.

13 That is, plants intended, after marketing, to be planted or replanted: ibid Art 3(b).

14 'Placing on the market' means the holding available in stock, displaying or offering for sale, selling and/or delivering to another person, in whatever form, of propagating material or ornamental plants: ibid Art 3(d).

15 A supplier is any natural or legal person carrying out professionally at least one of the following activities with regard to propagating material or ornamental plants: reproducing, producing, preserving and/or treating and placing on the market: ibid Art 3(c). As to accreditation, see ibid Art 6; see also Art 3(2). As to implementing measures concerning supervision and monitoring of suppliers and establishments, see Commission Directive 93/63, OJ 7.10.93 L250/31.

16 Ibid Art 8(1), first paragraph, OJ 31.12.91 L376/21. This does not apply to material or plants intended for trials or scientific purposes or selection work: ibid Art 8(2), second paragraph.

17 Ibid Art 9(1). As to the varieties, see ibid Art 9(2). As to additional implementing provisions in respect of lists of varieties, see Commission Directive 93/78, OJ 14.10.93 L256/19.

18 Ibid Art 15. As to genus or species, see ibid Annex. As to the establishment of schedules, see ibid Art 4. As to conditions to be met, see Commission Directive 93/49, OJ 7.10.93 L250/9, as amended.

19 Ibid Art 21, which provides for the creation of the Standing Committee for Propagating Material and Ornamental Plants and taking of decisions by the 'net' (*filet*) procedure.

20 Ibid Art 16(1). As to transitional measures, see ibid Art 16(2), first and second paragraphs.

1 Ibid Art 16(2), third paragraph.

2 Commission Decision 95/19 Art 1, OJ 7.2.95 L28/10 set the deadline of 31.12.96. The deadline for decision has been extended to 31.12.98 by Commission Decision 97/108, OJ 8.2.97 L39/20.

3 Council Directive 91/682 Art 16(2), OJ 31.12.91 L376/21.

Analogous provisions apply to vegetable propagating and planting material other than seeds,[4] on the one hand, and to fruit plant propagating material and fruit plants intended for fruit production,[5] on the other hand.

None of these measures apply to propagating material or plants intended for export to third countries, provided that the products are properly identified as such and kept sufficiently isolated.[6]

4 Council Directive 92/33, OJ 10.6.92 L157/1. As to conditions to be met, see Commission Directive 93/61, OJ 7.10.93 L250/19. As to implementing measures, see Commission Directive 93/62, OJ 7.10l.93 L250/29. As to deferral of the date until 31 December 1996, see Commission Decision 95/25, OJ 16.2.95 L36/34.
5 Council Directive 92/34, OJ 10.6.92 L157/10. As to conditions to be met, see Commission Directive 93/48, OJ 7.10.93 L250/1. As to implementing measures, see Commission Directive 93/64, OJ 7.10.93 L250/33. As to lists of varieties, see Commission Decision 93/79, OJ 14.10.93 L256/25. As to deferral of the date to 31 December 1996, see Commission Decision 95/26, OJ 16.2.95 L36/36.
6 Council Directive 91/682 Art 2, first paragraph, OJ 31.12.91 L376/21; Council Directive 92/33 Art 2, first paragraph, OJ 10.6.92 L157/1; Council Directive 92/34 Art 2, first paragraph, OJ 10.6.92 L157/1.

Chapter 18

Textiles

THE URUGUAY ROUND AND THE AGREEMENT ON TEXTILES AND CLOTHING

The Uruguay Round of multilateral trade negotiations resulted in a fundamental reform of the legal framework for the international trade in textile products, including trade between the European Union and its trading partners.[1] Prior to the Uruguay Round the international trade in textiles was governed by the Arrangement regarding international trade in textiles, or Multi-Fibre Arrangement (MFA).[2] The MFA, which succeeded a more limited agreement,[3] entered into force in 1974. Subsequently it was amended, enlarged and periodically extended until 31 December 1994.[4] The negotiations on textiles during the

1 See Council Decision 94/800 concerning the conclusion on behalf of the European Community, as regards matters within its competence, of the agreements reached in the Uruguay Round multilateral negotiations (1986–1994), OJ 23.12.94 L336/1. The agreements reached in the Uruguay Round multilateral negotiations included the Agreement on Textiles and Clothing, annexed as Annex 1A to the Agreement establishing the World Trade Organization: see OJ 23.12.94 L336/50. On the previous system, see Nicolaas Max Blokker *International Regulation of World Trade in Textiles* (Nijhoff, Dordrecht, 1989).
2 930 UNTS 166. Council Decision 74/214 concluding the Arrangement regarding International Trade in Textiles, OJ 30.4.74 L118/1, and Annex: Arrangement regarding International Trade in Textiles, OJ 30.4.74 L118/2. As of MFA IV the Members included: Argentina 27.9.91, Austria 8.4.92, Bangladesh 5.8.91, Brazil 11.9.91, Canada 4.12.91, PRC 10.10.91, Colombia 15.11.91, Costa Rica 9.8.91, Czechoslovakia 1.6.92, Dominican Republic 28.10.91, Egypt 15.10.91, El Salvador 2.8.91, EEC 18.12.91, Fiji 1.12.92, Finland 20.8.91, Guatemala 6.4.92, Haiti, Hong Kong 29.8.91, Honduras 20.11.92, Hungary 1.8.91, India 29.11.91, Indonesia 11.12.91, Jamaica 2.8.91, Japan 23.8.91, Republic of Korea (South Korea) 28.1.92, Macau 5.8.91, Malaysia 10.3.92, Maldives, Mexico 6.7.92, Norway 14.10.91, Pakistan 23.12.91, Panama 7.1.92, Peru 4.9.91, Philippines 15.10.91, Poland 12.10.92, Romania 30.8.91, Singapore 19.9.91, Sri Lanka 15.8.91, Switzerland 16.4.91, Thailand 14.9.91, Turkey 16.9.91, USA 2.8.91, Uruguay 14.4.92, Yugoslavia 14.10.91.
3 GATT: Basic Instruments and Selected Documents (BISD), 10th Supplement, 1962, p 18.
4 Council Decision 77/806 concerning the conclusion of the Protocol extending the Arrangement regarding the international trade in textiles, OJ 30.12.77 L348/58, and the Protocol, OJ 30.12.77 L348/60; Council Decision 86/590 concerning the conclusion of the Protocol extending the Arrangement regarding international trade in textiles, OJ 4.12.86 L341/33, and the Protocol, OJ 4.12.86 L341/34; Council Decision 93/97 on the conclusion of the Protocol maintaining in force the Arrangement regarding international trade in textiles (MFA), OJ 16.2.93 L38/33, and the Protocol, OJ 16.2.94 L38/34; Council Decision concerning the conclusion of the Protocol maintaining in force the Arrangement regarding international trade in textiles (MFA), OJ 18.5.94 L124/11, and the Protocol, OJ 18.5.94 L124/12.

Uruguay Round, however, resulted in an agreement to phase out the MFA during a period of ten years.[5]

An Agreement on Textiles and Clothing (ATC)[6] is annexed to the Agreement establishing the World Trade Organization.[7] It has been approved on behalf of the European Community with regard to matters within the Community's competence;[8] such matters include the entire ATC.[9] As an integral part of the WTO Agreement, the ATC is legally binding on all WTO Members,[10] including former MFA signatories and also those countries which previously were not parties to the MFA. However, neither the WTO Agreement nor the ATC is in principle susceptible of being directly invoked in Community or Member State courts.[11]

The ATC provides rules for the transition period leading to the integration of the textiles and clothing sector into GATT 1994.[12] Members are to allow for continuous industrial adjustment and increased competition in their markets.[13] In doing so, they are to take account of the special situation of small suppliers and new entrants,[14] the situation of those Members not formerly parties to the MFA,[15] and the particular interests of cotton-producing exporting Members.[16]

All existing[17] quantitative restrictions within bilateral agreements maintained[18] or notified[19] under the MFA must, within 60 days of the entry into force of the WTO Agreement,[20] be notified in detail to the new Textiles Monitoring Body (TMB).[1] No new restrictions may be introduced except under the ATC provisions or relevant GATT 1994 provisions.[2] Existing restrictions are to be phased out in three stages over a ten-year period.[3] At the beginning of each stage Mem-

---

5 See Bagchi 'The Integration of the Textile Trade into GATT' (1994) 28 JWT 31; Blokker and Deelstra 'Towards a Termination of the Multi-Fibre Arrangement?' (1994) 28 JWT 97; Smeets 'Main Features of the Uruguay Round Agreement on Textiles and Clothing, and Implications for the Trading System' (1995) 29 JWT 97.

6 Annex 1A, OJ 23.12.94 L336/50.

7 OJ 23.12.94 L336/3.

8 Council Decision 94/800 Art 1(1), OJ 23.12.94 L336/1.

9 Opinion 1/94 *World Trade Organization* [1994] ECR I-5267.

10 Agreement establishing the World Trade Organization Art 2(1), OJ 23.12.94 L336/3. However, it is not binding on countries which are not Members of WTO, including (as of August 1998) China.

11 Council Decision 94/800 preamble, fifteenth recital, OJ 23.12.94 L336/1.

12 Ibid Art 1(1). The products covered are set out in the Annex: ibid Art 1(7). Note that the ATC cannot be extended: ibid Art 9.

13 Ibid Art 1(5). See also ibid Art 7(1). See also Commission of the European Communities, 'Report from the Commission to the Council on the respect of market access commitments by WTO Members in the textiles and clothing sectors', COM(97)219, Brussels, 15.5.97.

14 Ibid Art 1(2).

15 Ibid Art 1(3).

16 Ibid Art 1(4).

17 That is, in force on the day before the entry into force of the WTO Agreement: ibid Art 2(1).

18 Under MFA Art 4.

19 Under MFA Arts 7 or 8.

20 Members have agreed that as of the date of the entry into force of the WTO Agreement, all such restrictions maintained between GATT 1947 contracting parties, and in place on the day before such entry into force, are governed by the provisions of the ATC: ibid Art 2(1).

1 Ibid Art 2(1). The TMB is set up by Art 8. Any unilateral measure taken under MFA Art 3 prior to the date of entry into force of the WTO Agreement may remain in effect for the duration specified in the measure, but not exceeding 12 months, if it has been reviewed by the Textiles Surveillance Body (TSB) established under the MFA. If the measure has not been reviewed by the TSB, it shall be reviewed by the TMB. See ibid Art 2(5).

2 Ibid Art 2(4).

3 Ibid Arts 2(6), 2(8), 9. Thus the ATC carries over existing MFA restrictions until the relevant products are integrated. There is however one exception: bilateral restrictions applied under

bers must integrate into GATT 1994 a specified proportion of the total volume of their 1990 imports of textile products.[4] At each phase the products to be integrated must encompass products from each of four groups: tops and yarns, fabrics, made-up textile products, and clothing.[5] Members are required to notify their integration programme to the TMB at least 12 months before it comes into effect and the TMB is to circulate it to all Members.[6]

In conjunction with phased integration, the level of each restriction in force is to be increased annually by not less than the growth rate established for the respective restrictions increased by a certain percentage. During the first stage[7] existing restrictions are to be increased by the growth rate increased by 16 per cent.[8] During the second stage[9] the increase is to be the growth rate for the respective restrictions during the first stage, increased by 25 per cent.[10] During the third stage[11] the increase is to be the growth rate for the respective restrictions during the second stage, increased by 27 per cent.[12] Flexibility provisions[13] are to be the same as those provided for in the MFA bilateral agreements for the 12-month period prior to the entry into force of the WTO Agreement.[14] No quantitative limits are to be placed or maintained on the combined use of swing, carryover and carry forward.[15]

Similarly, within the same period, Members must notify to the TMB[16] any other non-MFA restrictions, whether consistent with GATT or not.[17] Except for restrictions justified under a GATT 1994 provision, all restrictions must be either (1) brought into conformity with GATT 1994 within one year following the entry into force of the WTO Agreement,[18] or (2) phased out progressively

the MFA by WTO Members to non-Members who were signatories to the MFA will be discontinued: see Smeets 'Main Features of the Uruguay Round Agreement on Textiles and Clothing, and Implications for the Trading System' (1995) 29 JWT 97 at 98.

4 Ibid Art 2(6). The products are set out in the Annex in terms of HS lines or categories. Not less than 16% by volume must be integrated on the date of entry into force of the WTO Agreement: ibid Art 2(6). Of the remaining products, not less than 17% must be integrated by the end of the third year of the WTO Agreement: ibid Art 2(8)(a). Not less than 18% by volume of the remaining products must be integrated by the end of the seventh year of the WTO Agreement: ibid Art 2(8)(b). All remaining products are to be integrated by the end of the ten-year period: ibid Art 2(8)(c).

5 Ibid Art 2(6), 2(8)(a),(b),(c).

6 Ibid Art 2(11). As to the products integrated by the Community into GATT 1994 on 1 January 1998, see Council Regulation 2315/96, OJ 4.12.96 L314/1.

7 That is, from the date of entry into force of the WTO Agreement until the 36th month that it is in effect, inclusive: ibid Art 2(13).

8 Ibid Art 2(13).

9 That is, from the 37th to the 84th month that the WTO Agreement is in effect, inclusive: ibid Art 2(14)(a).

10 Ibid Art 2(14)(a).

11 That is, from the 85th to the 120th month that the WTO Agreement is in effect: ibid Art 2(14)(b).

12 Ibid Art 2(14)(b). 'The most important question to be answered is whether the quotas for the most sensitive products will grow sufficiently to make the integration of these products into GATT 1994 not too big a step': Blokker and Deelstra, 'Towards a Termination of the Multi-Fibre Arrangement?' (1994) 28 JWT 97 at 108.

13 That is, swing, carryover and carry forward: ibid Art 2(16).

14 Ibid.

15 Ibid.

16 Or provide the TMB with notifications submitted regarding the restrictions to any other WTO body: ibid Art 3(1).

17 Ibid Art 3(1). 'Restrictions' means all unilateral quantitative restrictions, bilateral arrangements and other measures having a similar effect: ibid Art 3(1), n 1.

18 Ibid Art 3(2)(a). This action must be notified to the TMB: ibid.

according to a programme presented by the Member to the TMB not later than six months following the entry into force of the WTO Agreement.[19]

Any restrictions which were initially adopted under the MFA are, for the period of their duration under the ATC, to be administered by the exporting Members.[20] Importing Members are not obliged to accept shipments in excess of the restrictions.[1] Members agree that the introduction of any changes[2] in the implementation or administration of restrictions should not upset the balance of rights and obligations under the ATC, nor adversely affect the access available to a Member, nor impede the full utilization or such access, nor disrupt trade under the ATC.[3] Where changes are necessary, however, Members agree that the initiator will inform and, wherever possible, initiate consultations with the affected Member prior to implementing the changes, with a view to reaching a mutually acceptable solution regarding appropriate and equitable adjustment. Where consultation prior to implementation is not feasible, it must take place, at the request of the affected Member, within 60 days if possible. If a mutually satisfactory solution cannot be reached, any Member involved may refer the matter to the TMB.[4]

It is agreed that circumvention frustrates the implementation of the Agreement.[5] The ATC provides that Members should establish the necessary legal provisions and/or administrative procedures to address and take action against such circumvention.[6] The Members agree that, consistent with their domestic laws and procedures, they will co-operate fully to address problems arising from circumvention.[7] A Member which believes that circumvention is occurring, and that no or inadequate measures are being taken, should consult with the Member or Members concerned with a view to seeking a mutually satisfactory solution. Consultations should be held promptly, and within 30 days when possible. Failing achievement of a satisfactory solution, the matter may be referred by any Member involved to the TMB.[8]

Members agree to take necessary action, consistent with their domestic laws and procedures, to prevent, to investigate and, where appropriate, to take legal and/or administrative action against circumvention practices within their territory.[9] They also agree to co-operate fully, consistent with their domestic laws and procedures, in instances of circumvention or alleged circumvention to establish the relevant facts in the places of import, export and where applicable transshipment.[10] Where investigation shows that there is sufficient evidence that cir-

---

19 Ibid Art 3(2)(b). The programme must provide for all restrictions to be phased out within a period not exceeding the duration of the ATC: ibid.
20 Ibid Art 4(1).
 1 Ibid.
 2 For example, changes in practices, rules, procedures and categorization of textile and clothing products, including those changes relating to the Harmonized System: ibid Art 4(2).
 3 Ibid Art 4(2).
 4 Ibid Art 4(4).
 5 By transhipment, re-routing, false declaration concerning country or place of origin, or falsification of official documents: ibid Art 5(1).
 6 Ibid Art 5(1).
 7 Ibid Art 5(1).
 8 Ibid Art 5(2).
 9 Ibid Art 5(3).
10 Ibid Art 5(3). It is agreed that such co-operation, consistent with domestic laws and practices, will include investigation of circumvention practices which increase restrained exports to the Member maintaining such restraints; exchange of documents, correspondence, reports and other relevant information to the extent available; and facilitation of plant visits and contacts, upon request and on a case-by-case basis: ibid Art 5(3).

cumvention has occurred,[11] Members agree that appropriate action[12] should be taken. Any such action may be taken after consultation, and any agreement must be notified to the TMB. If a mutually satisfactory solution is not reached, any Member concerned may refer the matter to the TMB for prompt review and recommendations.[13] Similar provisions apply with regard to false declarations.[14]

The ATC provides for a safeguard mechanism during the transitional period.[15] It may be applied by any Member to products covered by the ATC,[16] except those integrated into GATT 1994 pursuant to the ATC.[17] Members not maintaining former MFA restrictions now covered by the ATC must notify the TMB within 60 days of the entry into force of the WTO Agreement as to whether or not they wish to retain the right to use safeguards.[18] Members which have not accepted the Protocols extending the MFA since 1986 must make this notification within six months.

Safeguard action may be taken when, on the basis of a determination[19] by a Member,[20] it is demonstrated that a particular product is being imported into its territory in such increased quantities as to cause serious damage, or actual threat thereof,[1] to the domestic industry producing like and/or directly competitive products.[2] To be taken only following consultation,[3] such action consists of restraint on exports of a particular product from a Member or Members, with the level of the restraint to be fixed at a level not lower than the actual level of exports or imports

11 For example, where evidence is available concerning the country or place of true origin, and the circumstances of the circumvention: ibid Art 5(4).

12 This means action to the extent necessary to address the problem. It may include the denial of entry of goods, or, where the goods have entered, having due regard to the actual circumstances and the involvement of the country or place of true origin, the adjustmnent of charges to restrain levels to reflect the true country or place of origin. Where there is evidence of the involvement of the territories of the Members through which the goods have been transhipped, the action may also include the introduction of restraints with regard to these Members. See ibid Art 5(4). However, this may generally exclude Members through whose territories shipments have transitted with no change or alteration made to the goods contained in the shipment in the place of transit: ibid Art 5(5).

13 Ibid Art 5(4).

14 Ibid Art 5(6).

15 Ibid Art 6.

16 Listed in the Annex: ibid Art 1(7).

17 Ibid Art 6(1). Safeguard measures should be applied as sparingly as possible, consistently with the provisions of ibid Art 6, and the effective implementation of the integration process under the ATC: ibid.

18 Ibid.

19 In making a determination of serious damage, or actual threat thereof, the Member must examine the effect of those imports on the state of the particular industry, as reflected in changes in such relevant economic variables as output, productivity, utilization of capacity, inventories, market share, exports, wages, employment, domestic prices, profits and investment. However, none of these, either alone or combined with other factors, can necessarily give decisive guidance. See ibid Art 6(3). The period of validity of a determination cannot exceed 90 days from the date of initial notification by the Member affected to the Member(s) which would be affected: ibid Art 6(5).

20 A customs union may apply a safeguard measure as a single unit on behalf of a Member State. When a customs union applies a safeguard measure as a single unit, all the requirements for the determination of serious damage or actual threat thereof must be based on conditions existing in the customs union as a whole. When a safeguard measure is applied on behalf of a Member State, all the requirements for the determination of serious damage, or actual threat thereof, must be based on the conditions existing in that Member State and the measure shall be limited to that Member State. See ibid Art 6(2), n 1.

1 Serious damage or actual threat thereof must demonstrably be caused by such increased quantities in total imports of that product and not by such other factors as technological changes or changes in consumer preference: ibid Art 6(2).

2 Ibid Art 6(2).

3 See below.

from the Member or Members concerned during the 12-month period terminating two months preceding the month in which the request for consultation was made.[4] Any safeguard measures are to be applied on a Member-by-Member basis.[5] They must not however be applied to the exports of any Member whose exports of the particular product are already under restraint under the ATC.[6]

Certain types of interests must be given special consideration in applying safeguard measures. They include least-developed country Members, which are to be accorded the most favourable treatment;[7] small-volume exporters;[8] wool-producing developing country Members with respect to wool products;[9] and re-imports, when coming from a Member for which this type of trade represents a significant proportion of its total exports of textiles and clothing.[10]

A Member proposing to take safeguard action must request consultation with the potentially affected Member(s).[11] It must also communicate the request, including all relevant factual data, to the chairman of the TMB, who must inform the members of the TMB. Consultations are to be held without delay and normally be completed within 60 days of the date on which the request was received.[12] Details of the agreed restraint measure must be communicated to the TMB within 60 days of the conclusion of the agreement, and the TMB must determine whether the agreement is justified.[13] However, if the parties cannot reach agreement within 60 days, the Member proposing to take safeguard action may apply the restraint by date of import or date of export within 30 days following the end of the 60-day consultation period, and at the same time refer the matter to the TMB, which is to examine the matter and make appropriate recommendations.[14] In highly unusual and critical circumstances, where delay would cause damage difficult to repair, safeguard action may be taken provisionally, subject to the condition that the request for consultations and the request to the TMB be effected no more than five working days after taking the action.[15]

---

4 See ibid Art 6(8).
5 Ibid Art 6(4). The Member(s) to whom serious damage or actual threat thereof is attributed are to be determined on the basis of a sharp and substantial increase in imports, actual or imminent (and measurable), from such a Member or Members individually, and on the basis of the level of imports as compared with imports from other sources, market share, and import and domestic prices at a comparable stage of commercial transaction. However, none of these factors, either alone or combined with other factors, can necessarily give decisive guidance. See ibid.
6 Ibid Art 6(4).
7 Ibid Art 6(6)(a).
8 Ibid Art 6(6)(b).
9 Ibid Art 6(6)(c).
10 Ibid Art 6(6)(d).
11 The request must be accompanied by specific and relevant factual information, as up-to-date as possible. It must deal, in particular, with (1) the factors (see ibid Art 6(3)) on which the invoking Member has based its determination of the existence of serious damage or actual threat thereof, and (2) the factors (see ibid Art 6(4)) on the basis of which it proposes to invoke safeguard action in respect to the Member(s) concerned. The information must be related, as closely as possible, to identifiable segments of production and to the relevant reference period (see ibid Art 6(8)). The invoking Member must also indicate the specific level at which imports of the product from the Member(s) concerned are proposed to be restrained, which must not be lower that the actual level of exports or imports from the Member concerned during the 12-month period terminating two months preceding the month in which the request for consultation was made (see ibid Art 6(8)). See ibid Art 6(7).
12 Ibid Art 6(7).
13 That is, justified in accordance with ibid Art 6: ibid Art 6(9).
14 Ibid Art 6(10). Either Member may refer the matter to the TMB before the expiry of the 60-day period: ibid.
15 Ibid Art 6(11). Again, the TMB may examine the matter if consultations do not result in agreement. The TMB must make recommendations if the parties do not reach agreement, and it may do so if they have already reached agreement. See ibid.

These safeguard measures may be maintained for up to three years without extension, or until the product is integrated into GATT 1994, whichever comes first.[16] However, the level of the restraint is to be increased each year by a specified growth rate.[17]

The ATC establishes a Textiles Monitoring Body (TMB) consisting of a chairman and ten members. The membership is to be balanced and broadly representative of the Members, and it is to provide for rotation of its members at regular intervals.[18] The ACT expressly provides that consensus within the TMB does not require the assent or concurrence of members appointed by Members involved in an unresolved issue under review by the TMB.[19] If a mutually agreed solution to disputes cannot be reached by bilateral consultation, the TMB may make recommendations at the request of either Member and following consideration of the matter.[20] The Members are required to endeavour to accept in full the TMB recommendations,[1] but if they are unable to do so, they must provide the TMB with reasons for their action within one month after receiving the recommendations.[2] The TMB must then issue any further recommendations it considers appropriate.[3] If, after these further recommendations, the matter remains unresolved, either Member may bring the matter before the Dispute Settlement Body.[4]

BILATERAL AGREEMENTS AND THEIR MANAGEMENT

During the existence of the MFA the European Community concluded bilateral agreements regarding textile imports with numerous countries, both within the framework of the MFA and outside it.[5] These agreements continue to govern imports into the Community of textiles originating in these countries,

---

16 Ibid Art 6(12).
17 After the first year, the level is that of the first year increased by not less than 6% per year, unless otherwise justified to the TMB. The restraint level may be exceeded in either year of any of two subsequent years by carry forward and/or carryover of 10% of which carry forward shall not represent more than 5%. No quantitative limits shall be placed on the combined use of carryover, carry forward and specific provisions (set down in ibid Art 6(14)) concerning cumulation of levels of restraint. See ibid Art 6(13).
18 Ibid Art 8(1). The TMB closely resembles the Textiles Surveillance Body under the MFA.
19 Ibid Art 8(2).
20 Ibid Art 8(5).
 1 Ibid Art 8(9).
 2 Ibid Art 8(10).
 3 Ibid.
 4 Ibid, which further provides that the Member may invoke paragraph 2 of GATT 1994 Art XXIII and the relevant provisions of the Dispute Settlement Understanding.
 5 Council Decision 92/184 on the conclusion of agreements between the European Economic Community and certain third countries on international trade in textiles, OJ 4.4.92 L90/1; Council Decision 92/625 on the provisional application of agreements between the European Economic Community and certain third countries on international trade in textiles, OJ 31.12.92 L410/1; Council Decision 94/216 on the conclusion of agreements between the European Community and certain third countries on international trade in textiles, OJ 30.4.94 L110/1; Council Decision 94/277 on the provisional application of certain Agreements and Protocols between the European Economic Community and certain third countries on trade in textile products, OJ 17.5.94 L123/37; amended to take account of the accession of Austria, Finland and Sweden and applied on a provisional basis as from 1 January 1995, pending their formal conclusion, subject to a reciprocal application by the partner countries, by Council Decision 95/131 on the provisional application of certain Agreements between the European Community and certain third countries on trade in textile products, OJ 26.4.95 L94/1. As to specific countries, see below.

pending integration into GATT 1994 or phasing out pursuant to the ATC. Agreements under the MFA were concluded by the Community[6] with Argentina,[7] Armenia,[8] Azerbaijan,[9] Bangladesh,[10] Belarus,[11] Brazil,[12] People's Republic of China,[13] Colombia,[14] Georgia,[15] Hong Kong,[16] Guatemala,[17]

6 As of the entry into force of MFA IV on 1 August 1986, the MFA comprised 41 parties, including the European Community, Austria, Canada, Finland, Norway, Sweden and the USA plus 34 other countries. Some of the latter concluded bilateral agreements with the Community, and it is these agreements with which this paragraph is concerned.

7 Agreement between the European Economic Commuity and the Republic of Argentina on trade in textile products, OJ 16.06.87 L156/2. Amended by: Agreement in the form of an exchange of letters, OJ 31.12.92 L410/125 (implemented by Council Decision 92/625, OJ 31.12.92 L410/1; and by Council Decision 94/216, OJ 30.04.94 L110/1); and Agreement in the form of an exchange of letters OJ 26.4.95 L94/3 (implemented by Council Decision 95/131, OJ 26.4.95 94/1).

8 Agreement between the European Economic Community and the Republic of Armenia on trade in textile products, OJ 17.5.94 L123/64 (implemented by Council Decision 94/277, OJ 17.5.94 L123/1).

9 Agreement between the European Economic Community and the Republic of Azerbaijan on trade in textile products, OJ 17.5.94 L123/92 (implemented by Council Decision 94/277, OJ 17.5.94 L123/1).

10 Agreement between the European Economic Community and the Republic of Bangladesh on trade in textile products, OJ 19.8.87. L233/2. Amended by: Agreement in the form of an exchange of letters, OJ 31.12.92 L410/137 (implemented by Council Decision 92/625, OJ 31.12.92 L410/1; and by Council Decision 94/216, OJ 30.4.94 L110/1); and Agreement in the form of an exchange of letters, OJ 26.4.95 L38/24 (implemented by Council Decision 95/131, OJ 26.4.95 L94/1).

11 Agreement between the European Economic Community and the Republic of Belarus on trade in textile products, OJ 17.5.94 L123/120 (implemented by Council Decision 94/277, OJ 17.4.94 L123/1). Amended by: Agreement in the form of an exchange of letters, OJ 26.4.95 L94/44 (implemented by Council Decision 95/131, OJ 26.4.95 L94/1).

12 Agreement between the European Economic Community and the Federative Republic of Brazil on trade in textile products, OJ 14.9.87 L263/2. Amended by: Agreement in the form of an exchange of letters, OJ 31.12.92 L410/152 (implemented by Council Decision 92/625, OJ 31.12.92 L410/15; and by Council Decision 94/216, OJ 30.4.94 L110/1); and Agreement in the form of an exchange of letters, OJ 26.4.95 L94/67 (implemented by Council Decision 95/131, OJ 26.4.95 L94/1).

13 Agreement between the European Economic Community and the People's Republic of China on trade in textile products, OJ 31.12.88 L380/2 (implemented by Council Decision 90/647, OJ 15.12.90 L352/1). Amended by: Agreement in the form of an exchange of letters, OJ 31.12.92 L410/103 (implemented by Council Decision 92/625, OJ 31.12.92 L410/1; and by Council Decision 94/216, OJ 30.4.94 L110/1); Agreement in the form of an exchange of letters, OJ 26.4.95 L94/107 (implemented by Council Decision 95/131, OJ 26.4.95 L94/1); and Agreement on the modification of certain provisions of the 1988 bilateral agreement, OJ 31.10.95 L261/2 (implemented by Council Decision 95/440, OJ 31.10.95 L261/1).

14 Agreement in the form of an exchange of letters between the European Economic Community and the Republic of Colombia on trade in textile products, OJ 15.10.87 L292/2. Amended by: Agreement in the form of an exchange of letters, OJ 31.12.92 L410/89 (implemented by Council Decision 92/625, OJ 31.12.92 L410/15; and by Council Decision 94/216, OJ 30.4.94 L110/1).

15 Agreement between the European Economic Community and the Republic of Georgia on trade in textile products, OJ 17.5.94 L123/250 (implemented by Council Decision 94/277, OJ 17.5.94 L123/1).

16 Agreement between the European Economic Community and Hong Kong on trade in textile products, OJ 14.4.88 L97/2. Amended by: Agreed Minute, OJ 29.9.88 L269/57; Agreed Minute, OJ 31.12.88 L382/44; Agreed Minute, OJ 4.10.89 L286/21; Agreement in the form of an exchange of letters OJ 31.12.92 L410/2 (implemented by Council Decision 92/625, OJ 31.12.92 L410/1; and by Council Decision 94/216, OJ 30.4.94 L110/1); and Agreement in the form of an exchange of letters, OJ 26.4.95 L94/155 (implemented by Council Decision 95/131, OJ 26.4.95 L94/1).

17 Agreement in the form of an exchange of letters between the European Economic Community and the Republic of Guatemala on trade in textile products, OJ 15.10.87 L292/26. Amended by: Agreement in the form of an exchange of letters, OJ 31.12.92 L410/178 (implemented by Council Decision 92/625, OJ 31.12.92 L410/1; and by Council Decision 94/216, OJ 30.4.94 L110/1).

India,[18] Indonesia,[19] Kazakhstan,[20] Kyrgyz Republic,[1] Macao,[2] Malaysia,[3] Mexico,[4] Moldova,[5] Mongolia,[6] Pakistan,[7] Peru,[8] Philippines,[9]

18 Agreement between the European Economic Community and the Republic of India on trade in textile products, OJ 27.9.88 L267/2 (implemented by Council Decision 88/495, OJ 27.9.88 L267/1). Amended by: Agreement in the form of an exchange of letters, OJ 31.12.92 L410/180 (implemented by Council Decision 92/625, OJ 31.12.92 L410/1; and by Council Decision 94/216, OJ 30.4.94 L110/1); and Agreement in the form of an exchange of letters, OJ 26.4.95 L94/191 (implemented by Council Decision 95/131, OJ 26.4.95 L94/1).
19 Agreement between the European Economic Community and Indonesia on trade in textile products, OJ 19.8.87 L233/39. Amended by: Agreement in the form of an exchange of letters, OJ 31.12.92 L410/65 (implemented by Council Decision 92/625, OJ 31.12.92 L410/1; and by Council Decision 94/216, OJ 30.4.94 L110/1); and Agreement in the form of an exchange of letters, OJ 26.4.95 L94/214 (implemented by Council Decision 95/131, OJ 26.4.95 L94/1).
20 Agreement between the European Economic Community and the Republic of Kazakhstan on trade in textile products, OJ 17.5.94 L123/278 (implemented by Council Decision 94/277, OJ 123 17.5.94 L123/1).
1 Agreement between the European Economic Community and the Kyrgyz Republic on trade in textile products, OJ 17.5.94 L123/306 (implemented by Council Decision 94/277, OJ 123 17.5.94 L123/1).
2 Agreement between the European Economic Community and Macao on trade in textile products, OJ 16.10.86 L293/186. Amended by; Agreement in the form of an exchange of letters, OJ 31.12.92 L410/53 (implemented by Council Decision 92/625, OJ 31.12.92 L410/1; and by Council Decision 94/216, OJ 30.4.94 L110/1); and Agreement in the form of an exchange of letters, OJ 26.4.95 L94/237 (implemented by Council Decision 95/131, OJ 26.4.95 L94/1).
3 Agreement between the European Economic Community and Malaysia on trade in textile products, OJ 19.8.87 L233/83. Amended by: Agreement in the form of an exchange of letters, OJ 31.12.92 L410/194; Agreement in the form of an exchange of letters (implemented by Council Decision 92/625, OJ 31.12.92 L410/1; and by Council Decision 94/216, OJ 30.4.94 L110/1); and Agreement in the form of an exchange of letters, OJ 26.4.95 L94/262 (implemented by Council Decision 95/131, OJ 26.4.95 L94/1).
4 Agreement in the form of an exchange of letters between the European Economic Community and the United Mexican States on trade in textile products, OJ 15.10.87 L292/74. Amended by: Agreement in the form of an exchange of letters, OJ 31.12.92 L410/206 (implemented by Council Decision 92/625, OJ 31.12.92 L410/1; and by Council Decision 94/216, OJ 30.4.94 L110/1).
5 Agreement between the European Economic Community and the Republic of Moldova on trade in textile products, OJ 17.5.94 L123/390 (implemented by Council Decision 94/277, OJ 17.5.94 L123/1).
6 Accord entre la Communauté économique européenne et la Mongolie relatif au commerce de produits textiles, OJ 17.5.94 L123/418 (implemented by Council Decision 94/277, OJ 17.5.94 L123/1; and by Council Decision 95/441, OJ 31.10.95 L261/14). Amended by: Agreement in the form of an exchange of letters, OJ 26.4.95 L94/285 (implemented by Council Decision 95/131, OJ 26.4.95 L94/1).
7 Agreement between the European Economic Community and the Islamic Republic of Pakistan on trade in textile products, OJ 5.9.87 L255/2. Amended by: Agreement in the form of an exchange of letters, OJ 31.12.92 L410/208 (implemented by Council Decision 92/625, OJ 31.12.92 L410/1; and by Council Decision 94/216, OJ 30.4.94 L110/1); and Agreement in the form of an exchange of letters, OJ 26.4.95 L94/306 (implemented by Council Decision 95/131, OJ 26.4.95 L94/1).
8 Agreement between the European Economic Community and the Republic of Peru on trade in textile products, OJ 14.9.87 L263/82. Amended by: Agreement in the form of an exchange of letters, OJ 31.12.92 L410/91 (implemented by Council Decision 92/625, OJ 31.12.92 L410/1; and by Council Decision 94/216, OJ 30.4.94 L110/1); and Agreement in the form of an exchange of letters, OJ 26.4.95 L38/332 (implemented by Council Decision 95/131, OJ 26.4.95 L94/1).
9 Agreement between the European Economic Community and the Republic of Philippines on trade in textile products, OJ 5.9.87 L255/44. Amended by: Agreement in the form of an exchange of letters, OJ 31.12.92 L410/77 (implemented by Council Decision 92/625, OJ 31.12.92 L410/1; and by Council Decision 94/216, OJ 30.4.94 L110/1); and Agreement in the form of an exchange of letters, OJ 26.4.95 L94/348 (implemented by Council Decision 95/131, OJ 26.4.95 L94/1).

Russia,[10] Singapore,[11] Slovenia,[12] South Korea,[13] Sri Lanka,[14] Tajikistan,[15] Thailand,[16] Turkmenistan,[17] Ukraine,[18] Uruguay,[19] Uzbekistan,[20] and Vietnam.[1] Commitments similar to the MFA have been undertaken with the Community by Albania,[2] Estonia,[3] Latvia,[4] and Lithuania.[5] Other bilateral agreements have been concluded with certain other non-MFA countries, in particular from

10 Agreement between the European Economic Community and the Russian Federation on trade in textile products, OJ 17.5.94 L123/528 (implemented by Council Decision 94/277, OJ 17.5.94 L123/1.
11 Agreement between the European Economic Community and the Republic of Singapore on trade in textile products, OJ 16.6.87 L156/88. Amended by: Agreement in the force of an exchange of letters, OJ 31.12.94 L410/14 (implemented by Council Decision 92/625, OJ 31.12.92 L410/1; and by Council Decision 94/216, OJ 30.4.94 L110/1); and Agreement in the form of an exchange of letters, OJ 26.4.95 L38/415 (implemented by Council Decision 95/131, OJ 26.4.95 L94/1).
12 Agreement between the European Economic Community and the Republic of Slovenia on trade in textile products, OJ 17.5.94 L123/608 (implemented by Council Decision 94/277, OJ 17.5.94 L123/1).
13 Agreement between the European Economic Community and the Republic of Korea on trade in textile products, OJ 14.9.87 L263/38. Amended by: Agreement in the form of an exchange of letters, OJ 31.12.92 L410/164 (implemented by Council Decision 92/625, OJ 31.12.92 L410/1; and by Council Decision 94/216, OJ 30.4.94 L110/1); and Agreement in the form of an exchange of letters, OJ 26.4.95 L94/459 (implemented by Council Decision 95/131, OJ 26.4.95 L94/1).
14 Agreement between the European Economic Community and the Democratic Socialist Republic of Sri Lanka on trade in textile products, OJ 5.9.87 L255/86. Amended by: Agreement in the form of an exchange of letters, OJ 31.12.92 L410/220 (implemented by Council Decision 92/625, OJ 31.12.92 L410/1; and by Council Decision 94/216, OJ 30.4.94 L110/1); and Agreement in the form of an exchange of letters, OJ 26.4.95 L94/483 (implemented by Council Decision 95/131, OJ 26.4.95 L94/1).
15 Agreement between the European Economic Community and the Republic of Tajikistan on trade in textile products, OJ 17.5.94 L123/663 (implemented by Council Decision 94/277, OJ 17.5.94 L123/1).
16 Agreement between the European Economic Community and the Kingdom of Thailand on trade in textile products, OJ 5.9.87 L255/127. Amended by: Agreement in the form of an exchange of letters, OJ 31.12.92 L410/232 (implemented by Council Decision 92/625, OJ 31.12.92 L410/1; and by Council Decision 94/216, OJ 30.4.94 L110/1).
17 Agreement between the European Economic Community and Turkmenistan on trade in textile products, OJ 17.5.94 L123/690 (implemented by Council Decision 94/277, OJ 17.5.94 L123/1).
18 Agreement between the European Economic Community and Ukraine on trade in textile products, OJ 17.5.94 L123/718 (implemented by Council Decision 94/277, OJ 17.5.94 L123/1). Amended by: Agreement in the form of an exchange of letters, OJ 26.4.95 L94/508 (implemented by Council Decision 95/131, OJ 26.4.95 L94/1).
19 Agreement between the European Economic Community and the Eastern Republic of Uruguay on trade in textile products, OJ 14.9.87 L263/121. Amended by Agreement in the form of an exchange of letters, OJ 31.12.92 L410/271 (implemented by Council Decision 92/625, OJ 31.12.92 L410/1; and by Council Decision 94/216, OJ 30.4.94 L110/1); and Agreement in the form of an exchange of letters, OJ 26.4.95 L94/531 (implemented by Council Decision 95/131, OJ 26.4.95 L94/1).
20 Agreement between the European Economic Community and Uzbekistan on trade in textile products, OJ 17.5.94 L123/745 (implemented by Council Decision 94/277, OJ 17.5.94 L123/1).
1 Accord entre la Communauté économique européenne et la République socialiste du Viêtnam relatif au commerce de produits textiles et d'habillement, OJ 31.12.92 L410/279 (implemented by Council Decision 92/625, OJ 31.12.92 L410/1). Amended by: Agreement in the form of an exchange of letters, OJ 26.4.95 L94/550 (implemented by Council Decision 94/277, OJ 17.5.94 L123/1).
2 Agreement between the European Economic Community and the Republic of Albania on trade in textile products, OJ 17.5.94 L123/3 (implemented by Council Decision 94/277, OJ 17.5.94 L123/1).
3 Agreement on free trade and trade-related matters between the Republic of Estonia and the European Community, OJ 31.12.94 L373/2 (implemented by Council Decision 94/974, OJ 31.12.94 L373/1; and by Council Decision 94/975, OJ 31.12.94 L373/166) Protocol 1 on trade in textile and clothing products. Amended by: Agreement in the form of an exchange of letters, OJ 26.4.95 L94/151 (implemented by Council Decision 94/277, OJ 17.5.94 L123/1).

Eastern and Central Europe, including Bulgaria,[6] the Czech Republic,[7] Hungary,[8] Poland,[9] Romania,[10] and Slovakia.[11]

An autonomous regime governs the imports of textile products from the Republic of China (Taiwan).[12]

4 Agreement between the European Economic Community and the Republic of Latvia on trade in textile products, OJ 17.5.94 L123/334 (implemented by Council Decision 94/277, OJ 17.5.94 L123/1).

5 Agreement between the European Economic Community and the Republic of Lithuania on trade in textile products, OJ 17.5.94 L123/362 (implemented by Council Decision 94/277, OJ 17.5.94 L123/1).

6 Agreed Minute amending the Agreement between the European Economic Community and the Republic of Bulgaria on trade in textile products, OJ 27.2.91 L53/19 (implemented by Council Decision 91/95, OJ 27.2.91 L53/18). Additional Protocol to the Europe Agreement on trade in textile products between the European Economic Community and the Republic of Bulgaria, OJ 17.5.94 L123/147 (implemented by Council Decision 94/277, OJ 17.5.94 L123/1). Amended by: Agreement in the form of an exchange of letters, OJ 26.4.95 L94/84 (implemented by Council Decision 95/131, OJ 26.4.95 L94/1).

7 Agreed Minute amending the Agreement between the European Economic Community and the Czech and Slovak Federal Republic on trade in textile products, OJ 18.1.91 L13/18. Agreed Minute, OJ 27.1.91. L53/35 (implemented by Council Decision 91/99, OJ 27.2.91 L53/34). Additional Protocol to the Europe Agreement on trade in textile products between the European Economic Community and the Czech and Slovak Federal Republic, OJ 31.12.92 L410/485 (implemented by Council Decision 92/625, 31.12.92 L410/1). Additional Protocol to the Europe Agreement on trade in textile products between the European Economic Community and the Czech Republic, OJ 17.5.94 L123/198 (implemented by Council Decision 94/277, OJ 17.5.94 L123/1). Amended by: Agreement in the form of an exchange of letters, OJ 26.4.95 L94/368 (implemented by Council Decision 95/131, OJ 26.4.95 L94/1).

8 Agreed Minute amending the Agreement between the European Economic Community and the Republic of Hungary on trade in textile products, OJ 27.2.91 L53/23 (implemented by Council Decision 91/96, OJ 27.2.91 L53/22). Additional Protocol to the Europe Agreement on trade in textile products between the European Economic Community and the Republic of Hungary, OJ 31.12.92 L410/391 (implemented by Council Decision 92/625, 31.12.92 L410/1). Amended by: Agreement in the form of an exchange of letters, OJ 26.4.95 L94/166 (implemented by Council Decision 95/131, OJ 26.4.95 L94/1).

9 Agreed Minute amending the Agreement between the European Economic Community and the Republic of Poland on trade in textile products, OJ 27.2.91 L53/27 (implemented by Council Decision 91/97, OJ 27.2.91 L53/26). Additional Protocol to the Europe Agreement on trade in textile products between the European Economic Community and the Republic of Poland, OJ 31.12.92 L410/391 (implemented by Council Decision 92/625, 31.12.92 L410/1). Amended by: Agreement in the form of an exchange of letters, OJ 26.4.95 L94/368 (implemented by Council Decision 95/131, OJ 26.4.95 L94/1).

10 Agreed Minute amending the Agreement between the European Economic Community and the Republic of Romania on trade in textile products, OJ 27.2.91 L53/31 (implemented by Council Decision 91/98, OJ 27.2.91 L53/30). Additional Protocol to the Europe Agreement on trade in textile products between the European Economic Community and Romania on trade in textile products, OJ 17.5.94 L123/476 (implemented by Council Decision 94/277, OJ 17.5.94 L123/1). Amended by: Agreement in the form of an exchange of letters, OJ 26.4.95 L94/391 (implemented by Council Decision 95/131, OJ 26.4.95 L94/1).

11 Agreed Minute amending the Agreement between the European Economic Community and the Czech and Slovak Federal Republic on trade in textile products OJ 18.1.91 L13/18. Agreed Minute, OJ 27.1.91. L53/35 (implemented by Council Decision 91/99, OJ 27.2.91 L53/34). Additional Protocol to the Europe Agreement on trade in textile products between the European Economic Community and the Czech and Slovak Federal Republic, OJ 31.12.92 L410/485 (implemented by Council Decision 92/625, 31.12.92 L410/1). Additional Protocol to the Europe Agreement on trade in textile products between the European Economic Community and the Slovak Republic, OJ 17.5.94 L123/556 (implemented by Council Decision 94/277, OJ 17.5.94 L123/1). Amended by: Agreement in the form of an exchange of letters, OJ 26.4.95 L94/368 (implemented by Council Decision 95/131, OJ 26.4.95 L94/1).

12 Council Regulation 3951/92 on the arrangements for imports of certain textile products originating in Taiwan, OJ 31.1292 L405/6, as amended, applied until 31 December 1995. From 1 January 1996 until 31 December 1998 imports into the Community of textile products from Taiwan are governed by Council Regulation 3060/95, OJ 30.12.95 L326/25.

A system of monitoring applies with regard to textile imports from certain Mediterranean countries, such as Egypt, Malta[13] and Turkey.[14] In respect of trade in textile products, the Community and Egypt have concluded a Memorandum of Understanding, which applies on a provisional basis, subject to reciprocal provisional application by Egypt, as from 1 January 1998.[15]

The management of these bilateral agreements is currently governed by common rules for imports of textile products from third countries.[16] These rules apply to textile imports from certain countries with which the Community has concluded bilateral agreements, protocols or other arrangements.[17] They also apply to imports of textile products which, so far as the Community is concerned, have not been integrated in GATT 1994 and which originate in third countries which are WTO Members.[18] This Regulation does not however derogate in any way from bilateral agreements, protocols or arrangements on textile trade concluded by the Community, and the latter prevail in all cases of conflict.[19] As already noted, provision has recently been made for the integration of imports of textile products into WTO rules and disciplines in three stages in accordance with the Uruguay Round Agreement on Textiles and Clothing.[20]

13 Agreement establishing an Association between the European Economic Community and Malta, OJ 14.3.771 L61/2, as supplemented by the Additional Protocol, OJ 29.11.77 304/2, by the Supplementary Protocol to the Agreement, OJ 23.3.89 L81/2, and the Protocol extending the first stage of the Agreement, OJ 9.5.91 L116/67. See also Council Regulation 578/93 establishing ceilings and Community surveillance for imports of certain products originating in Malta (1993), OJ 13.3.93 L61/8; Council Regulation 3383/93 establishing ceilings and Community surveillance for imports of certain products originating in Malta (1994), OJ 13.12.93 L306/3.

14 These arrangements were initiated by Commission Regulation 2819/79 making the importation of certain textile products originating in certain third countries subject to Community surveillance, OJ 15.12.79 L320/9, which then applied to Egypt, Greece, Portugal, Spain, Turkey and Malta. This regulation was amended by Commission Regulations 3044/79, OJ 31.12.79 L343/8; Commission Regulation 1782/80, OJ 9.7.80 L174/16; Commission Regulation 4121/88, OJ 29.12.88 L361/28: Commission Regulation 4033/89, OJ 30.12.89 L382/72; Commission Regulation 3788/90, OJ 24.12.91 L356/67; Commission Regulation 3789/91, OJ 24.12.91 L356/69.

15 OJ 13.2.98 L41/2, approved by Council Decision 98/135, OJ 13.2.98 L41/1.

16 Council Regulation 3030/93, OJ 8.11.93 L275/1, as amended. Annexes I, II, III, IV, V, VI, VII, VIII, IX and XI have been amended by Commission Regulation 2231/96, OJ 28.11.96 L307/1. Annex X was further amended by Council Regulation 2315/86, OJ 4.12.96 L314/1. Annex VII was further amended by Commission Regulation 447/97, OJ 8.23.97 L68/16. Annexes III and V were further amended by Commission Regulation 152/97, OJ 29.1.97 L26/8. Most recently (to the date of writing), Annexes I, III, V, VII were amended and Annexes II, VIII and IX were substituted by Commission Regulation 856/98, OJ 24.4.98 L122/11. See also Council Regulation 3313/94 establishing a transitional regime applicable to the importation into Austria, Finland and Sweden of certain textile products falling under Regulations (EEC) No 3951/92, (EEC) No 3030/93 and (EC) No 517/94, OJ 31.12.94 L350/6, as amended by Council Regulation 1209/95, OJ 31.5.95 L120/1.

17 Ibid Art 1(1), first indent, as substituted by Council Regulation 824/97, OJ 8.5.97 L119/1, which also provides that the relevant textile products are listed in Annex I and the relevant third countries are listed in Annex II.

18 Ibid Art 1(1), second indent, as so substituted, which also provides that the relevant textile products are listed in Annex X and that 'integrated into GATT 1994' is within the meaning of Art 2(6) or (8) of the WTO Agreement on Textile and Clothing (ATC).

19 Ibid Art 20. These provisions were re-emphasized by the Commission in December 1996: see Notice to Operators (96/C387/04), Agreement between the European Community and the People's Republic of China on trade in textile products not covered by the MFA bilateral agreement on textile products, OJ 21.12.96 L387/4. The Notice also reiterated that, in accordance with Art 19 of the Regulation, the Commission reserves the right to amend Appendix C to Annex V of the Regulation.

20 Ibid Art 1(1), second indent, and Art 1(7), as substituted and added by Council Regulation 3289/94, OJ 31.12.94 L349/85. As to the list of products integrated on 1 January 1998, see Council Regulation 2315/96, OJ 4.12.96 L314/1.

Subject to the provisions of these common rules, imports of the textile products listed in Annex I,[1] originating in the supplier countries listed in Annex II,[2] are liberalized and thus are not subject to quantitative restrictions or measures having equivalent effect.[3] However, where imports of these products into the Community are effected at abnormally low prices, the Commission on its own initiative or at the request of a Member State may request consultations with the authorities of the supplier country, in accordance with the provisions of any bilateral arrangement with the supplier country concerned and in accordance with the common Community rules.[4] In addition, these products originating in specified supplier countries are subject to a system of safeguard measures.[5]

Imports of certain other textile products[6] originating in listed supplier countries,[7] are subject to annual Community quotas.[8] Release for free circulation of such imports is subject to the presentation of an import authorization issued by the Member States' authorities.[9] The authorized imports are charged against

1 Ibid Art 1(1). These products are listed in Annex I, as substituted by Commission Regulation 2231/96 Art 1, OJ 28.11.96 L307/1 in 161 categories, divided into five groups. Group I, containing the most sensitive products, is sub-divided into Group IA (textiles, comprising three categories) and Group IB (clothing, comprising five categories). This classification is based on the Combined Nomenclature (CN): ibid Art 1(3). The procedures for the application of the classification are set out in ibid Annex III, as substituted by Commission Regulation 2231/96 Art 1, OJ 28.11.96 L307/1 and as amended by Commission Regulation 856/98, OJ 24.4.98 L122/11.

2 Ibid Art 1(1). The supplier countries listed in Annex II, as substituted by Commission Regulation 856/98, OJ 24.4.98 L122/11 are Albania, Argentina, Armenia, Azerbaijan, Bangladesh, Belarus, Brazil, Bulgaria, China, Czech Republic, Egypt, Estonia, Georgia, Hong Kong, Hungary, India, Indonesia, Kazakhstan, Kyrgyzstan, Latvia, Lithuania, Macao, Malaysia, Malta, Moldova, Mongolia, Morocco, Pakistan, Peru, Philippines, Poland, Romania, the Russian Federation, Singapore, Slovakia, Slovenia, South Korea, Sri Lanka, Taiwan, Tajikistan, Thailand, Tunisia, Turkey, Turkmenistan, Ukraine, United Arab Emirates, Uzbekistan, and Vietnam.

3 Ibid Art 1(4).

4 Ibid Art 6(1). The procedure for consultations is laid down in ibid Art 16.

5 Ibid Art 10(1). The relevant countries are listed in Annex IX, as substituted by Commission Regulation 856/98, OJ 24.4.98 L122/11. The measures are discussed below.

6 These products are listed in Annex V, as substituted by Commission Regulation 2231/96 Art 1, OJ 28.11.96 L307/1 and as amended by Commission Regulation 856/98, OJ 24.4.98 L122/11. In tabular form, it contains the following information: the third country of origin; category number of the product; unit of the quantitative limits, eg tonnes or number of pieces; and, where applicable, the annual Community quota ceiling for each of the years 1993 to 1995 inclusive, arranged opposite the name of the supplying country to which it applies.

7 The countries are listed in Annex V, as substituted by Commission Regulation 2231/96, OJ 28.11.96 L307/1 and as amended by Commission Regulation 856/98, OJ 24.4.98 L122/11. They are Argentina, Belarus, Brazil, Bulgaria, China, Czech Republic, Hong Kong, Hungary, India, Indonesia, Macao, Malaysia, Mongolia,Pakistan, Peru, Philippines, Poland, Romania, Russian Federation, Singapore, Slovak Republic, South Korea, Sri Lanka, Taiwan, Thailand, Ukraine, Uzbekistan, and Vietnam.

8 Ibid Art 2(1), as substituted by Council Regulation 3289/94, OJ 31.12.94 L349/85. As to the example of Community quantitative limits for non-MFA textiles from China in 1997 see Commission Regulation 152/97, OJ 29.1.97 L26/8.

9 Ibid Art 2(2), which also provides that the authorization is issued in accordance with ibid Art 12. The procedure for authorization is set out in Annex III, as substituted: ibid Art 12(6). The authorization may be issued by the competent authorities of any Member State, irrespective of the Member State of destination indicated on the export licence, to the extent the Commission has confirmed the availability of the amount requested within the quantitative limit in question: ibid Annex III, Art 14, second sub-paragraph, as substituted by Commission Regulation 2231/96, OJ 28.11.96 L307/1. The information to be provided by the importer, as well as the common form of the Community import licence, are set out in Annex III, as so substituted. Annex III, Part II (Arts 11–17) deals with the double-checking system for administering quantitative limits. The double-checking system requires the presentation of an export licence

the quota for the year in which the products are shipped in the supplier country concerned.[10] Where under particular circumstances additional imports are required, however, the Commission may open up additional amounts during a given quota year.[11]

The quotas do not apply to specific cottage industry and folklore products,[12] with the exception of products from Brazil, Hong Kong and Macao[13] and subject to specified limits in the case of products from China.[14] Nor do the quotas apply to products placed in a free zone or imported under the arrangements governing customs warehouses, temporary importation or inward processing.[15] In addition, they do not apply to re-imports into the Community of textile products from specified countries effected in accordance with regulations on outward processing.[16]

Providing they notify the Commission in advance, specified supplier countries[17] may benefit from flexibility provisions. They may on certain conditions effect transfers between different categories of imports subject to quantitative limits for:

(1) advance utilization in the current year of an amount established for the following year;
(2) carry-over of amounts not utilised; or
(3) transfers between product categories up to specified maximum percentages.[18]

The cumulative application may not result in the increase in any Community quantitative limit for a given year beyond a specified maximum.[19]

---

issued by the authorities of the supplier country in order to obtain a licence for importation into the Community. The burden of the system rests mainly on the supplier countries, in the sense that the allocation among individual suppliers of export authorizations within the quota limits is an onerous task.

10 Ibid Art 2(3).
11 Ibid Art 8, first paragraph. Such measures are to be taken in accordance with the procedure laid down in Art 17: ibid Art 8, third paragraph. For example, see Commission Regulation 283/98, OJ 4.2.98 L28/9 (quotas for 1998 trade fairs).
12 Ibid Art 3(1). The products are specified in Annexes VI and VIa. Such imports must be accompanied by a certificate issued by the competent authorities of the country of origin in accordance with the provisions of Annexes VI and VIa and must fulfil the other conditions laid down therein: ibid Art 2(1).
13 Ibid Art 3(3).
14 Ibid Art 3(4).
15 Ibid Art 4(1), first paragraph. However, an import authorization is required for category 33 products from China: ibid Art 4(1), first paragraph, n 1, and Appendix A to Annex V.
16 Ibid Art 5. Such re-imports are subject however to conditions on outward processing traffic laid down in Annex VII, as substituted by Commission Regulation 2231/96, OJ 28.11.96 L307/1. Annex VII was previously amended in 1995 by Commission Regulation 1616/95, OJ 5.7.94 L154/3, to take account of the provisions of Council Regulation 3036/94 establishing economic outward processing arrangements applicable to certain textiles and clothing products reimported into the Community after working or processing in certain third countries, which came into force on 1 January 1995. Annex VII also lists the supplier countries. As to re-imports from China, see Commission Regulation 447/97, OJ 8.3.97 L68/16, and Commission Regulation 1445/97, OJ 25.7.97 L198/1.
17 Flexibility provisions may not be used by Colombia, Egypt, Guatemala, Malta, Mexico, Morocco, Tunisia and Turkey: ibid Art 7, Annexes V and VIII, as so substituted.
18 Ibid Art 7. The relevant quota amounts are listed in Annex V, as so substituted and amended. The conditions are stipulated in Annex VIII, as substituted by Commission Regulation 856/98, OJ 24.4.98 L122/11.
19 Ibid. Annex VIII, col 8, as so substituted.

Provision is made for action in the event of a sudden regional concentration of direct imports.[20] The Commission is to seek a solution in conjunction with the Textile Committee[1] and also by conducting consultations with the supplier country.[2]

Provision is also made for surveillance and safeguard measures. The common rules lay down the procedures and formalities concerning single and double checking, economic outward processing, classification and certification of origin where, in accordance with the relevant provisions of an agreement, protocol or other arrangement between the Community and a supplier country, a system of surveillance is introduced on a category of products not subject to quantitative limits.[3]

When imports into the Community from specified countries[4] of a category of any liberalized product exceed the previous year's total imports into the Community of products in the same categorty by a specified percentage, they may under a 'surge clause' and after consultation[5] be made subject to quantitative limits.[6] With regard to products not yet integrated into WTO disciplines and originating from a WTO member country, safeguard action may be taken after consultation with the supplier country,[7] and only where it is demonstrated that

---

20 Ibid Art 9.
1 Ibid Art 9(1), Art 17. The Textile Committee is composed of representatives of the Member States and chaired by a non-voting Commission representative ibid Art 17(1). The chair submits draft measures to the committee, which delivers an opinion on them acting by a qualified majority ibid Art 17(4), first paragraph. Where a proposed measure conforms with the committee's opinion, the Commission may adopt it: ibid Art 17(4), second paragraph. If the committee does not give an opinion or the proposed measure is not in conformity with it, the Commission must submit to the Council a proposal for the measures to be taken, on which the Council must act by a qualified majority: ibid Art 17(4), third paragraph. If the Council fails to take a decision within one month, the Commission is to adopt the proposed measures: ibid Art 17(4), fourth paragraph. The chair may consult the committee on any other matter relating to the operation of Regulation 3030/93: ibid Art 17(5).
2 Ibid Art 9(2). The procedure for consultations is laid down in Art 16.
3 Ibid Art 13(1). These procedures and formalities are contained in Annexes III and IX. The categories of products and third countries currently subject to surveillance are listed in the tables in Annex III: ibid Art 13(2).
4 Listed in Annex IX.
5 Ibid Art 10(3), as substituted by Council Regulation 3289/94 Art 1, OJ 31.12.94 L349/85.
6 Ibid Art 10(1). The percentages are indicated in Annex IX. Annex IX provides for the so-called 'basket extractor mechanism' or system of 'basket exit thresholds'. Quantitative limits have been imposed in a number of instances. For example, with regard to imports from the People's Republic of China, see Commission Regulation 2797/94 establishing provisional quantitative limits on imports into the Commuity of certain textile products originating in the People's Republic of China (category 14, category 17), in the Republic of Indonesia (category 23) and in the Republic of India (category 23, category 24), OJ 18.11.94 L287/3; Commission Regulation 469/94 establishing a provisional quantitative limit on imports into the Community of certain textile products (category 97) originating in the People's Republic of China, OJ 3.3.94 L59/3; Commission Regulation 1135/94 establishing a provisional quantitative limit on imports into the Community of certain textile products (category 28) originating in the People's Republic of China, OJ 19.5.94 L127/10; Commission Regulation 1136/94 establishing a provisional quantitative limit on imports into the Community of certain textile products (category 68) originating in the People's Republic of China, OJ 19.5.94 L127/12; the last three provisional restrictions were made definitive until 31 December 1995 by Commission Regulation 1167/94 on arrangements for imports into the Community of certain textile products (categories 28, 68 and 97) originating in the People's Republic of China, OJ 25.5.94 L130/18; Commission Regulation 810/95 imposing definitive quantitative limits on imports into the Community of certain textile products (categories 14, 17 and 29) originating in the People's Republic of China, OJ 12.4.95 L82/2.
7 Ibid Art 10(6)(a), as substituted by Council Regulation 3289/94 Art 1, OJ 31.12.94 L349/85.

a particular product is being imported into the Community in such increased quantities as to cause serious damage, or actual threat thereof, to the domestic industry producing like and/or directly competitive products.[8] Regional safeguard measures may also be taken,[9] but such measures shall be exceptional, temporary and disturb the operation of the internal market as little as possible and shall only be adopted after alternative solutions have been examined.[10]

Where the Commission has proof[11] that products from an Annex V supplier country[12] and subject to quota[13] have been transhipped, re-routed or otherwise imported so as to circumvent quantitative limits, it shall ask for consultations with the supplier country with a view to agreeing adjustments up to the corresponding quantitative limits.[14] If, with a maximum period of two months,[15] the Commission and the supplier country fail to reach an agreement, and if the Commission notes that there is clear evidence of circumvention, it may deduct an equivalent volume of products originating in the supplier country concerned from the quantitative limits.[16]

For the purposes of the surge clause,[17] introducing or increasing quotas,[18] or taking action where the Commission finds that goods have been transhipped, re-routed or otherwise imported to circumvent quantitative limits,[19]

---

8 Ibid Art 10(5)(a), as substituted by Council Regulation 3289/94 Art 1, OJ 31.12.94 L349/85. Serious damage or actual threat thereof must demonstrably be caused by such increased quantities in total imports of that product and not by such other factors as technological changes or changes in consumer preference: ibid. As to criteria for determining serious damage, see ibid Art 10(5)(b), (c), as so substituted. In highly unusual and critical circumstances where delay would cause damage which would be difficult to repair, the Commission may impose a provisional quantitative limit on imports, subject to the condition that a request for consultation be effected not more than five working days after taking action. The provisional limit shall not be lower than the actual level from the supplier country during the 12-month period terminating two months preceding the month in which the request for consultation is made. See ibid Art 10(6)(b), as substituted by Council Regulation 3289/94 Art 1, OJ 31.12.94 L349/85. Such measures may remain in place (1) for up to three years without extension; or (2) until the product is integrated into GATT 1994, whichever comes first: ibid Art 10(12), as so substituted.
9 Ibid Art 11(1). Measures are to be taken in accordance with the procedure laid down in Art 17: ibid Art 11(3).
10 Ibid Art 11(2).
11 Such proof must be based on enquiries carried out in accordance with the procedures established in Annex IV: ibid Art 15(1). Annex IV provides rules for administrative co-operation with supplier countries with regard, among other things, to verification of declarations of origin or export licences.
12 See ibid Annex V, as substituted by Commission Regulation 3305/95 Art 1, OJ 30.12.95 L323/1.
13 This may be either annual quantitative limits referred to in Art 2 and laid down in Annex V, or regional quotas introduced on the basis of Art 9: ibid Art 15(1).
14 Ibid Art 15(1).
15 Ibid Art 15(3), 16. The two months' period applies to all supplier countries except Hong Kong, for which the maximum period is one month: ibid Art 16(2).
16 Ibid Art 15(3). The procedure to be followed is established in Art 17.
17 Ibid Art 10(1), as substituted by Council Regulation 3289/94 Art 1, OJ 31.12.94 L349/85. The Community insisted on the introduction of this controversial mechanism during the negotiations for the second extension of the Multi-Fibre Arrangement. The aim was to guard against harmful effects stemming from sudden growth in the use of a previously under-utilized quota. The clause is to be found in the Conclusions of the Textile Committee of GATT, annexed to the Protocol extending (for the second time) the Arrangement regarding International Trade in Textiles (Geneva, 22.12.81), OJ 29.3.82 L83/9 (implemented by Council Decision 82/179, OJ 3.29.82 L83/8). The significant extent of the opposition to this mechanism can be gauged from the vague way in which it is framed in paragraph 10 of the Conclusions.
18 As to increasing quotas, see ibid Art 8. As to the introduction of quotas, see Arts 9 and 10.
19 Ibid Art 15.

the Commission is to conduct consultations with the appropriate supplier country.[20]

Consultations with Hong Kong are to be initiated within 15 days of notification of the request for consultation.[1] The request by the Commission must be accompanied by a statement setting out the reasons and circumstances which, in the Community's opinion, justify the submission of the request.[2] A further 15 days are allowed in which to reach agreement on a mutually acceptable conclusion.[3]

In all other cases the Commission must notify the supplier country of the request for consultation,[4] which must be followed within a reasonable period (and in any case not later than 15 days following the notification) by a statement setting out the reasons and circumstances which, in the Community's opinion, justify the submission of the request.[5] The Commission must initiate consultations within one month of the notification with a view to reaching agreement on a mutually acceptable conclusion within a further month.[6]

COMMON RULES FOR IMPORTS EXCEPT FROM STATE-TRADING COUNTRIES

Other textile imports[7] with certain exceptions[8] are covered by various general rules. These rules are intended to eliminate exceptions and derogations resulting from remaining national commercial policy measures, and thus complete the common commercial policy as it pertains to imports as a necessary complement to the completion of the internal market.[9] They have

---

20 See ibid Arts 8, second paragraph, 9(2), 10(3)(a), 10(6)(a), 15(1), 15(5) as added by Council Regulation 3289/94 Art 1, OJ 31.12.94 L349/85, and, as to Art 15(5), as substituted by Council Regulation 824/97 Art 1(6), OJ 8.5.97 L119/1.
1 Ibid Art 16(2), second indent.
2 Ibid Art 16(2), first indent.
3 Ibid Art 16(2), second indent. For the purposes of the surge clause, it would be possible to extend this time limit to a maximum of 60 days following the request: see Art 10(9), as substituted by Council Regulation 3289/94, OJ 31.12.94 L349/85.
4 Ibid Art 16(1), first indent.
5 Ibid Art 16(1), second indent.
6 Ibid Art 16(1), third indent. A period of 60 days following the request for consultation applies with regard to the surge clause: ibid Art 10(9), as substituted by Council Regulation 3289/94, OJ 31.12.94 L349/85.
7 That is, those not covered by bilateral agreements, protocols or other arrangements.
8 See the following section.
9 See Council Regulation 517/94 on common rules for imports of textile products from certain third countries not covered by bilateral agreements, protocols or other arrangements, or by other specific Community rules, preamble, fifth and sixth recitals, OJ 10.3.94 L67/1; Council Regulation 518/94 on common rules for imports and repealing Regulation No 288/82, preamble, sixth and seventh recitals, OJ 10.3.94 L67/77, now repealed by Council Regulation 3285/94 on the common rules for imports and repealing Regulation No 518/94, OJ 31.12.94 L349/53; Council Regulation 519/94 on common rules for imports from certain third countries and repealing Regulations Nos 1765/82, 1766/92 and 3420/83, preamble, sixth and seventh recitals, OJ 10.3.94 L67/89. The relevant changes consisted, first, of the abolition of the subdivision of Community quotas into regional subquotas and the abolition of regional-specific quotas and, second, of the abolition of national quotas and their replacement by Community quotas. Cf also Commission of the European Communities 'Implications of the Internal Market for Commercial Policy in the Textile and Clothing Sectors' Commission Communication to the Council, SEC(92)896, 27 May 1992; Council Resolution of 17 June 1992 on the textile and clothing industries, OJ 15.7.92 L178/3. See also Case 59/84 *Tezi Textiel BV v Commission* [1986] ECR 887; Case 242/84 *Tezi BV v Minister for Economic Affairs* [1986] ECR 933.

also recently been revised as necessary to take account of the results of the Uruguay Round.[10]

The general regulation on common rules for imports applies to imports of all products, including textile products, except for two categories of imports.[11] The first excluded category consists of textile products from certain third countries not covered by bilateral agreements, protocols or other arrangements or by other specific Community rules.[12] The second excluded category refers to products originating in certain third countries listed in Regulation 519/94 on common rules for imports from certain third countries; this category does not include textiles and is not considered further here.[13]

The general principle underlying the common rules for imports is that imports shall take place freely and shall not be subject to any quantitative restrictions.[14] Provision is made however for a Community information and consultation procedure,[15] a Community investigation procedure,[16] surveillance[17] and safeguard measures.[18] The investigation procedure must be implemented before any safeguard measure is applied.[19] The investigation must seek to determine whether imports of the product in question are causing or threatening to cause serious injury to the Community producers concerned.[20] The investigation procedure does not preclude surveillance or provisional safeguard measures.[1] When a product is imported into the Community in such greatly increased quantities and/or on such terms or conditions as to cause, or threaten to cause, serious injury to Community producers,[2] safeguard measures may be taken by the Commission on its own initiative or at the request

10 Council Regulation 517/94 preamble, eighth recital, OJ 10.3.94 L67/1; Council Regulation 3285/94 preamble, eleventh recital, OJ 31.12.94 L349/53.
11 Council Regulation 3285/94 on the common rules for imports and repealing Regulation (EC) No 518/94 Art 1(1), OJ 31.12.94 L349/53.
12 That is, products covered by Council Regulation 517/94, OJ 10.3.94 L67/1: ibid Art 1(1), first indent. Following the accession of Austria, Finland and Sweden, Council Regulation 517/94 was amended by Council Regulation 1325/95, OJ 13.6.95 L128/1. Following the initialling of an agreement on trade in textiles with the Former Yugoslav Republic of Macedonia (FYROM), the FYROM was excluded from the scope of application of this Regulation: see Commission Regulation 1457/97, OJ 26.7.97 L199/6.
13 Council Regulation 519/94, OJ 10.3.94 L67/89: ibid Art 1(1), second indent. This Regulation specifically excludes textiles products covered by Council Regulation 517/94: ibid Art 1(1). Nor are textiles listed in the annexes: cf ibid Annexes II, III.
14 Council Regulation 3285/94 Art 1(2), OJ 31.12.94 L349/53.
15 Ibid Arts 2–4.
16 Ibid Arts 5–10.
17 Ibid Arts 11–15.
18 Ibid Arts 16–22.
19 Ibid Art 5(1).
20 Ibid Art 5(2). 'Serious injury' means a significant overall impairment in the position of Community producers: ibid Art 5(3)(a). 'Threat of serious injury' means serious injury that is clearly imminent: ibid Art 5(3)(b). 'Community producers' means the producers as a whole of the like or directly competing producers operating within the territory of the Community, or those whose collective output of the like or directly competing products constitutes a major proportion of the total Community production of those products: ibid Art 5(3)(c).
1 Ibid Art 8(1), first paragraph. Provisional safeguard measures are to be applied (1) in critical circumstances where delay would cause damage which it would be difficult to repair, making immediate action necessary, and (2) where a preliminary determination provides clear evidence that increased imports have caused or are threatening to cause serious injury: ibid Art 8(1), second paragraph. The maximum duration of such measures is 200 days: ibid Art 8(2). They must take the form of an increase in the existing level of customs duty (whether the latter is zero or higher) if such action is likely to prevent or repair the serious injury: ibid Art 8(3).
2 As regards WTO members, safeguard measures may be taken only if both conditions are met: ibid Art 16(2).

of any Member State.[3] They may include limitation of the period of validity of import documents, requirement of an import authorization before the product may be put in free circulation or the imposition of a quota.[4] Surveillance or safeguard measures limited to one or more specific regions may be authorized in exceptional circumstances.[5]

These common rules on imports operate by way of complement and without prejudice to the operation of the instruments establishing the common organization of agricultural markets, or of national administrative provisions derived therefrom, or of the specific instruments applicable to goods resulting from the processing of agricultural products.[6]

COMMON RULES FOR IMPORTS FROM STATE-TRADING COUNTRIES

The general regulation does not cover textile imports from certain third countries, particularly State-trading countries, which are not covered by bilateral agreements, protocols or other arrangements, or by other specific Community rules. Such imports are governed instead by Council Regulation 517/94, which with regard to these suppliers applies to imports of textile products falling within Section XI of the Combined Nomenclature and of other listed textile products.[7]

---

3 Ibid Art 16(1).
4 Ibid Art 16(1(a), (b), (3). Any quota must not be set lower than the average level of imports over the last three representative years for which statistics are available unless a different level is necessary to prevent or remedy injury: ibid Art 16(3(b). When a quota is allocated among supplier countries, allocation may be agreed with those having a substantial interest in supplying the product for import: ibid Art 16(4)(a), first paragraph. Failing this, the quota is to be allocated among supplier countries in proportion to their share of imports into the Community of the product concerned during a previous representative period, due account being taken of any specific factors which may have affected or may be affecting the trade in the product: ibid Art 16(4)(b). In case of serious injury, however, the Community may depart from this method of allocation if imports originating in one or more supplier countries have increased in disproportionate percentage in relation to the total increase of imports of the product concerned over a previous representative period, provided that its obligation to see that consultations are conducted under the auspices of the WTO Committee on Safeguards is not disregarded: ibid Art 16(4)(b). The total period of application of a safeguard measure, including the period of application of any provisional measures, the initial period of application and any prorogation, may not exceed eight years: ibid Art 20(5); cf also Art 22. Textiles thus fall under these quota rules or quota rules established by other specific instruments, and as a result they are excluded from the scope of Council Regulation 520/94 establishing a Community procedure for administrative quantitative quotas: see Council Regulation 520/94 preamble, eleventh recital, and Art 1(1), OJ 10.3.94 L66/1.
5 Ibid Art 18. See also Arts 13, 14, 15 (surveillance) and art 16(5)(a) (safeguards).
6 Ibid Art 25(1). Certain provisions of the common rules do not apply however to such products: ibid Art 25(2), (3).
7 Council Regulation 517/94 Art 1(1), OJ 10.3.94 L67/1, Art 1(1), first indent. Ibid Art 1(2). Products covered are listed in Annex I: ibid They are classified into categories as described in Art 1(2). With regard to textile products, this Regulation repeals Council Regulations 288/82, 1765/82, 1766/82 and 3429/83: ibid Art 27(1). Following the accession of Austria, Finland and Sweden, a transitional regime for imports into these countries was established by Council Regulation 3313/94 establishing a transitional regime applicable to the importers into Austria, Finland and Sweden of certain textile products falling under Regulations No 3851/92, No 3030/93 and No 517/94, OJ 31.12.94 L350/6, amended by Council Regulation 1209/95, OJ 31.5.95 L120/1. Then Council Regulation 517/94 was amended by Council Regulation 1325/95, OJ 13.6.95 L128/1. As to the Community import licence, see Commission Regulation 3168/94, OJ 23.12.94 L335/23. As to the management and distribution of quotas for 1998, see Commission Regulation 2458/97, OJ 11.12.97 L340/31.

Textile imports are classified into groups, either according to originating country or according to product and originating country, and different principles are applied to each group.

First, with regard to all textile products except those originating in specifed third countries, mainly State-trading countries,[8] the general principle is that imports shall be free and not subject to any quantitative restriction.[9] This is without prejudice however to surveillance and safeguard measures,[10] measures taken under specific common import rules for the duration of those rules,[11] and specified annual quotas.[12]

Second, specified textile products originating in the People's Republic of China or North Korea are subject to annual quotas,[13] and their release into free circulation is subject to the presentation of an import authorization or equivalent document issued on a 'first come, first served' basis by the Member States following notification to and confirmation by the Commission.[14]

Third, other specified textile products originating in China or North Korea may be imported into the Community provided an annual quota has been established.[15]

---

8 The countries listed in the Regulation are Albania, Armenia, Azerbaijan, Belarus, People's Republic of China, Estonia, Georgia, Kazakhstan, North Korea, Kyrgyzstan, Latvia, Lithuania, Moldova, Mongolia, The Russian Federation, Tajikistan, Turkmenistan, Ukraine, Uzbekistan, Vietnam: ibid Annex II. Trade in textiles between the Community and the countries in transition in Central and Eastern Europe and the former USSR are now governed mainly however by bilateral agreements. As to these agreements, see the chapter in this book on preferential arrangements and bilateral agreements. However, pending conclusion of a new agreement, special arrangements apply to certain textiles from Russia: see Commission Regulation 1025/97, OJ 7.6.97 L150/20.
9 Council Regulation 517/94 Art 2(1), OJ 10.3.94 L67/1.
10 Ibid Art 2(1), first indent, Arts 11–16.
11 Ibid Art 2(1), second indent.
12 Ibid Art 2(1), third indent and Annex IIIA (list of annual quantitative restrictions), Annex I (list of products), Annex II (excluded countries); Art 2(1), fourth indent and Annex IIIB (list of annual quantitative restrictions and list of included countries). Annex IIIB has been amended and substituted numerous times, most recently substituted by Commission Regulation 1457/97, OJ 26.7.97 L199/6. The former group of quantitative restrictions is suspended however until the products in question are integrated into normal WTO rules and disciplines in accordance with the Textiles and Clothing Agreement: ibid Art 2(2).
13 Ibid Art 3(1) and Annex IV, as substituted most recently by Commission Regulation 1457/97, OJ 26.7.97 L199/6. At the request of a Member State or on the Commission's initiative, Annexes III to VII may be revised: ibid Art 5. As to Annex IIIB (Annual Community quantitative limits referred to in Art 2(1), four indent) Annex IV (Annual Community quantitative limits referred to in Art 3(1) and Annex VI (Outward processing traffic: Annual Community limits referred to in Art 4), the most recent revisions as of the date of writing are contained in Commission Regulation 1457/97, OJ 26.7.97 L199/6. As to Annex V (referred to in Art 3(3), the most recent revision is Commission Regulation 1476/96, OJ 27.7.96 L188/4.
14 Ibid Arts 3(2), 17–24.
15 Ibid Art 3(3). The quota is to be established according to the 'safety net' (*contrefilet*) procedure: ibid Art 25(4); cf also Council Decision 87/373 Art 2 (procedure 3b), OJ 18.7.1987 L197/33. For examples, see Commission Regulation 1470/94 opening quantitative import quotas for textile products in category 169 from the People's Republic of China and amending Annexes IV and V of Council Regulation No 517/94, OJ 28.6.94 L159/14; Commission Regulation 2612/94 opening quantitative import quotas for textile products in categories 127B and 145 from the People's Republic of China and amending Annexes IV and V of Council Regulation No 517/94, OJ 28.10.94 L297/7; Commission Regulation 2980/94 opening quantitative import quotas for textile products in categories 146A and 146B from the People's Republic of China and amending Annexes IV and V of Regulation No 517/94, OJ 8.12.94.87 L315/2.

Fourth, all other textile products[16] originating in specified third countries[17] shall be free, subject to any surveillance or safeguard measures and any measures taken under specific common import rules.[18]

Re-imports into the Community of textile products after processing, except from the specified State-trading countries, are not subject to quotas.[19] However, re-imports of specified textile products after processing in the Republics of Bosnia-Herzegovina, Croatia and the former Yugoslav Republic of Macedonia are exempt from specified annual Community quotas distributed among Member States only if they are effected in accordance with Community rules on economic outward processing and up to specified Community-wide limits.[20]

Provision is made for a Community information and investigation procedure[1] and surveillance and safeguard measures.[2] Surveillance measures may be taken by the Commission, on its own initiative or at the request of a Member State, where imports of textile products threaten to cause injury to Community production of like or directly competitive products.[3] In relation to products liberalized at Community level and originating in the specified State-trading countries,[4] however, surveillance may also be introduced where the economic interests of the Community so require.[5] Similar provisions apply in the case of a surge of imports.[6] Products subject to prior Community surveillance or safeguard measures may be put into free circulation only on production of an import document.[7]

All Community importers may submit applications for import authorization to the competent authority of the Member State of their choice.[8] Member States' authorities are required to notify the Commission of the amount of requests.[9] The availability of the requested amounts is to be confirmed by the Commission on a 'first come, first served' basis[10] and normally by electronic means.[11] Where there is reason to believe that anticipated requests may exceed quotas,

---

16 That is, other than those referred to in ibid Art 3(1) and Annex IV, on the one hand, and Art 3(3) and Annex V, on the other hand.
17 That is, the State-trading countries listed in ibid Annex II: ibid Art 3(4).
18 Ibid Art 4. On surveillance and safeguard rules, see ibid Arts 11–16.
19 Ibid Art 4(1), Annex II (list of countries).
20 Ibid Art 4(2) and Annex VI (list of products and countries), Annex IIIB (Community quotas, distributed among Member States, from which these imports are exempted), Annex VI (Community-wide quotas to which these imports are subject).
1 Ibid Arts 6–10.
2 Ibid Arts 11–16.
3 Ibid Art 11(1), (2). For examples, see Commission Regulation 2635/95 introducing a prior surveillance of imports of certain textile products originating in the United Arab Emirates, OJ 14.11.95 L271/1.
4 Listed in ibid Annex II.
5 Ibid Art 11(2). The procedure is set out in ibid Art 25(5).
6 Ibid Art 12.
7 Ibid Art 14(1); see also Art 15.
8 Ibid Art 18(1). The form for applications is to be established in accordance with the procedure set down in ibid Art 25(3): ibid Art 21(3). For details required in the application, see ibid Art 18(1), as amended by Commission Regulation 3168/94 establishing in the field of application of Council Regulation (EC) No 517/94 a Community import licence and amending certain provisions of the Regulation Art 1, OJ 23.12.94 L335/23. The application must, where necessary, be accompanied by documentary evidence of previous imports for each category and each third country concerned: ibid Art 18.
9 Ibid Art 17(1).
10 Ibid Art 17(2).
11 Ibid Art 17(4).

the Commission may divide the quota into tranches or fixed maximum amounts per allocation; it may also reserve a proportion of a specific quota for requests supported by evidence of past import performance.[12]

National authorities are required to issue import authorizations within five working days of notification of the Commission decision or within the time limit set by the Commission, and they must inform the Commission of the issue of authorization within ten days of the issue.[13] The authorization may be made conditional upon the lodging of a security.[14] The authorization refers to the import of products which are subject to quantitative limits and are valid throughout the territory of application of the EC Treaty, regardless of the place of import mentioned in the application.[15] The period of validity is six months, subject to modification.[16] Subject to change in legislation, an import authorization may not be loaned or transferred, whether for consideration or free of charge, by the person in whose name it is issued.[17] Authorizations which are wholly or partly unused must be returned to the authorities of the Member State of issue within 15 days of their expiry, except in cases of force majeure.[18] Member States' authorities are required to inform the Commission, within 30 days following the end of each month, of the quantities of products subject to quotas which have been imported during the preceding month.[19]

Unused allocations are to be notifed to the Commission by national authorities and automatically transferred into the remaining Community quota.[20]

12 Ibid Art 17(3). This provision has recently been frequently invoked. For example, see Commission Regulation 934/94 establishing rules for management and distribution with regard to certain textile quotas established under Regulation No 517/94, OJ 28.4.94 L107/91; Commission Regulation 1664/94 introducing specific rules for the amendment and distribution of the second tranche of certain textile quotas established under Council Regulation No 517/94, OJ 9.7.94 L176/4; Commission Regulation 2944/94 establishing rules for management and distribution with regard to textile quotas established for 1995 under Council Regulation 517/94, OJ 3.12.94 L310/48; Commission Regulation 1473/95 establishing rules for management and distribution of the second tranche of textile quotas established under Council Regulation No 517/94, OJ 29.6.95 L145/13. This last measure did not apply to quotas applicable to products originating in China, since the bilateral agreement on textile products not covered by the MFA bilateral agreement of 1988, initialled on 18 January 1995 and put into provisional application by Council Decision 95/155 (OJ 6.5.95 L104/1) foresees that these quantities will be export managed by the People's Republic of China: ibid preamble, fourth recital.
13 Ibid Art 19. The issue of authorizations is to be made according to the conditions and detailed rules laid down in ibid Art 19(1) and Annex VIII, as substituted and added by Commission Regulation 3168/94 establishing in the field of application of Council Regulation No 517/94 a Community import licence and amending certain provisions of the Regulation, OJ 23.1294 L335/23.
14 Ibid Art 20.
15 Ibid Art 21(1).
16 Ibid Art 21(2). The procedure for modification of the period of validity is set down in ibid Art 25(3). For example, see Commission Regulation 1855/94 authorizing the competent authorities of the Member States to extend, on specific conditions, the period of validity of import authorizations issued on the basis of Regulation No 934/94, OJ 28.7.94 L192/34.
17 Ibid Art 22.
18 Ibid Art 23(1). Any security lodged will be forfeited if this time limit is not complied with, except in cases of force majeure: ibid Art 23(2).
19 Ibid Art 24.
20 Ibid Art 17(5).

GENERALIZED SCHEME OF PREFERENCES CONCERNING TEXTILE PRODUCTS

Within the framework of the United Nations Conference on Trade and Development (UNCTAD) the European Economic Community in 1971 opened a scheme of generalized tariff preferences, notably in respect of finished and semi-finished industrial products, textile products and some agricultural products from developing countries. It is an exception to the most-favoured nation clause under the GATT. With regard to textiles, it has been limited since 1980 to products originating in countries having signed bilateral agreements with the Community within the framework of the MFA[1] or to such products originating in countries or territories undertaking similar commitments.[2] This scheme, as modified and periodically extended, is still in force.[3]

OUTWARD PROCESSING AND REIMPORTATION

The arrangements for importation into the Community include specific measures applicable to products resulting from outward processing arrangements (OPT, outward processing traffic).[4] This refers to the procedure whereby textile products are temporarily exported from the Community in order to be worked or processed in a third country, and then after working or processing are reimported into the Community.[5]

Only natural or legal persons established in the Community may benefit from these arrangements.[6]

Several additional conditions must be fulfilled.[7] The potential beneficiary must manufacture, in the Community, products which are similar to and at the same stage of manufacturing as the compensating products in respect of which the application for the arrangement is made.[8] It must also perform, in

---

1 Preference was originally granted in the form of duty-free ceilings only to those beneficiaries under the generalized preference scheme which were signatories to the Long-Term Arrangement regarding International Trade in Cotton Textiles (LTA), or which undertook similar commitments. The LTA was replaced from 1980 onwards by the MFA.

2 Albania, Estonia, Latvia and Lithuania were added by Council Regulation 3917/92, OJ 31.12.92 L396/1. Belarus, Ukraine, Moldova, Uzbekistan, Russia, Tajikistan, Armenia, Azerbaijan, Turkmenistan, Kazakhstan, Kyrgyzstan and Georgia were added by Council Regulation 3667/93 supplementing Regulation No 3917/92, OJ 31.12.93 L338/1.

3 As to the GSP, see Chapter 22 in this book on the Generalized Scheme of Preferences.

4 Council Regulation 3036/94 establishing economic outward processing arrangements applicable to certain textile and clothing products reimported into the Community after working or processing in certain third countries, OJ 13.12.94 L322/1, which repealed Council Regulation 636/82, OJ 20.3.82 L76/1, with effect from 31 December 1994. It applies to textile and clothing products listed in Chapters 50–63 of the Combined Nomenclature and resulting from outward processing operations: ibid Art 1(1). A regulatory committee on economic outward processing arrangements for textiles is set up; it operates according to the 'net' (*filet*) procedure: ibid Art 12.

5 Outward processing operations, as defined in ibid Art 1(2). The products resulting from such operations are known as compensating products: ibid Art 1(4)(a).

6 Ibid Art 2(1).

7 Entitlement under the scheme may be refused if the competent authorities are unable to obtain all the necessary guarantees to enable them to exercise effective control over the fulfilment of these conditions: ibid Art 5(2).

8 Ibid Art 2(2)(a), first indent. Member States may derogate from this condition in certain circumstances: see ibid Art 3.

its own factory, within the Community, the main production processes on those products, at least sewing and assembly, or knitting in the case of fully fashioned garments obtained from yarn.[9] Allocation is subject to quantity limits and other conditions.[10] The goods must be in free circulation and of Community origin, subject to a derogation of not more than 14 per cent of the total value of the goods except in exceptional and economically justified circumstances.[11] The processing operations carried out in third countries may be less extensive but must not be more extensive than those stipulated for each product.[12]

The annual quantities which may be authorized are to be established at Community level.[13] They are allocated by the competent authorities among potential beneficiaries on the basis of applications and only upon confirmation by the Commission that there are still quantities available within the overall Community quota for the entire category and the third country concerned.[14] Past beneficiaries are given precedence,[15] and the remainder is distributed by the Commission on the basis of notifications received by the Member States and on a first come, first served basis.[16] Consistent with the objective of maintaining the industrial activity of the beneficiary in the Community,[17] allocations are to be granted only to those manufacturers who can prove that in the preceding year they maintained production in the Community, and each manufacturer may apply for a total quantity of compensating products with a value of outward processing no higher than 50 per cent of the value of its Community production.[18] Unused allocations are to be re-credited to the Community quota.[19]

Authorization for OPT may be granted only where it is possible for the competent authorities to identify temporarily exported goods in the reimported

---

9 Ibid Art 2(2)(a), second indent. Member States may derogate from this condition in certain circumstances: see ibid Art 3.

10 Ibid Art 2(2)(b), which also refers to further conditions set out in ibid Art 3.

11 Ibid Art 2(2)(c). However, past beneficiaries who benefited in 1994 from a percentage higher than 14% may continue to do so for the same quantities for a period of three years on the basis of a list to be established by the Commission. Thereafter, such exceptions may be renewed on the basis of a decision taken in accordance with the procedure laid down in Art 12. See ibid Art 2(2)(c), second paragraph.

12 Ibid Art 2(2)(d), and Annex II.

13 Ibid Art 3(1). For example, see Council Regulation 1385/94 opening and providing for the administration of Community tariff quotas for frozen hake fillets and for processing work in respect of certain textile products under Community outward processing arrangements, OJ 18.6.94 L152/4.

14 Ibid Art 3(2).

15 See ibid Art 3(4). See also ibid Art 3(5), fifth and sixth paragraphs. The allocation may be reduced however if it is established that the level of employment in the applicant's firm has been significantly reduced due to outward processing operations carried out in the previous year: ibid Art 5(4). These 'grandfather clause' rights were subsequently specified to mean that a past beneficiary obtains, for each category and third country, an amount equal to the whole quantity for which he carried out outward processing operations. These operations carried out are those for which compensating products of a specific category and country have been reimported under the economic outward processing arrangements during the course of the year 1993 or 1994, the choice being left to the applicant: Commission Regulation 1836/95 laying down certain provisions for the implementation of Council Regulation No 3036/94, OJ 27.7.95 L175/21.

16 Ibid Art 3(5), first paragraph.

17 See ibid Art 3(3).

18 Ibid Art 3(5), second paragraph.

19 Ibid Art 3(6). 'Unused quantities' are those quantities for which prior authorizations have been issued but not used within a time limit of six months or nine months in case of extension of the original time limit by the competent authorities: ibid Art 3(6), third paragraph.

compensating products.[20] Conditions are to be laid down regarding the quantities of goods, procedures for identifying the temporarily exported goods in the compensating products and the time limit for reimportation.[1] Providing that such conditions are complied with and other required customs formalities are observed, the reimportation of the compensating products cannot be refused.[2]

20 Ibid Art 5(1).
1 Ibid Art 5(3). An extension of the time limit for reimportation may be granted where it is justified by the circumstances: ibid Art 9, first paragraph.
2 Ibid Art 8(1).

Chapter 19

European Coal and Steel Community products

INTRODUCTION

The European Coal and Steel Community (ECSC) Treaty applies to coal and coke fuels, iron and steel.[1] In respect of commercial policy, however, the Treaty provides that it does not affect the powers of the Member States, except as otherwise provided in it.[2] Consequently, even though the ECSC has legal personality and specific capacity to act in international relations,[3] trade matters in respect of ECSC products were regarded until recently as falling outside the competence of the ECSC or the EC. In international trade agreements the only parties on the Community side were the ECSC Member States. In 1991–92, however, recourse was had to ECSC Art 95 in order to facilitate implementation of the Europe Agreements with Central and Eastern European countries.[4] Subsequently, the European Court of Justice held that ECSC Art 71 refers only to international agreements relating specifically to ECSC products. As a result the EC is now recognized to have sole competence *ex* EC Art 113 to conclude external agreements of a general nature, encompassing all types of goods, even where those goods include ECSC products.[5] Only when an agreement concerns exclusively ECSC products do the ECSC Member States have sole competence. However, Member States are required to inform the Commission of proposed commercial arrangements or similar arrangements.[6] In addition, in respect of mutual assistance among Member States with re-

---

1 As to the products covered by the expressions 'coal' and 'steel', see ECSC Treaty Annex I. As to scrap, see ibid Annex II. As to special steels, see ibid Annex III. Other products are outside the ECSC Treaty and, in respect of commercial policy, fall within the competence of the EC *ex* Art 113.
2 Ibid Art 71, first paragraph.
3 See ibid Art 6. See also Arts 3(a),(f). In respect of commercial policy, see also Arts 72–75.
4 ECSC Art 95, which is analogous to EC Art 235, provides that, in all cases not provided for in the Treaty, where it is apparent that a decision or recommendation of the High Authority is necessary to attain one of the objectives of the Community, the decision may be taken or the recommendation may be made with the unanimous consent of the Council and after the Consultative Committee has been consulted. After recourse to ECSC Art 95, there persisted a disagreement between the Council and most of the Member States, on the one hand, and the Commission, on the other hand, as to whether ECSC Art 71 reserved competence in trade matters in respect of ECSC products to the Member States, or whether these matters were covered by EC Art 113. As to the change of practice and this debate, see I Macleod, I D Hendry and S. Hyett, *The External Relations of the European Communities* (Clarendon Press, Oxford, 1996) pp 401–402.
5 Opinion 1/94 *World Trade Organization* [1994] ECR I-5267.
6 ECSC Art 75.

gard to the implementation of measures, the Commission has the power to propose to Member States the methods by which this mutual assistance may be provided.[7]

AUTONOMOUS MEASURES

The Community Customs Code applies to ECSC products.[8] However, the ECSC Treaty provides that, subject to minimum and maximum rates of duty which may be set by the Community,[9] each Member State fixes its own tariffs on ECSC products according to its national procedures.[10]

There is no special import or export regime for ECSC products. Council Regulation 3285/94 on common rules for imports[11] applies to ECSC products.[12] This Regulation does not however apply to imports from State-trading countries.[13] Imports of ECSC products from State-trading countries are subject to the common rules for imports from certain third countries.[14] ECSC products are included within the GSP.[15]

The ECSC Treaty provides that the administration of import and export licences for trade with third countries is a matter for the Government in whose territory the place of destination for imports or the place of origin for exports is situated.[16] Decisions have been taken by the Representatives of the Member States meeting within the Council, for example in respect of imports of ECSC

---

7 ECSC Art 71, third paragraph. For example, see Commission Decision 92/406 (OJ 7.8.92 L222/71), which provided that import quotas were to be used solely to supply the needs of industries in importing countries and that re-export of the products in an unaltered state to other Member States would be prevented. The Commission has authorized Member States to suspend customs duties on certain products in short supply in the Community: see Commission Decision 813/97, OJ 6.5.97 L116/16; Commission Decision 563/98, OJ 13.3.98 L76/7.
8 Council Regulation 2913/92 Art1, second indent, OJ 19.10.92 L302/1.
9 ECSC Art 72, first paragraph.
10 ECSC Treaty Art 72, second paragraph, which also provides that the High Authority (now the Commission) may, on its own initiative or at the request of a Member State, deliver an opinion suggesting amendment of the tariffs of the State. In practice the rates for ECSC products are included in the CCT for information. See also Decision 86/98 of the Representatives of the Member States meeting in the Council on the uniform application of the customs nomenclature in respect of ECSC products (OJ 26.3.86 L81/29).
11 OJ 31.12.94 L349/53.
12 This includes safeguard measures, subject to the provisions of agreements concerning specifically ECSC products. However, since ECSC products were previously subject to national measures, it also provides that residual national restrictions relating to ECSC products must be progressively dismantled in accordance with the provisions of the WTO: ibid Art 26. As to the progressive dismantling of Spanish restrictions on certain coal imports, see Council Decision 95/251, OJ 11.7.95 L159/17.
13 That is, the imports from certain third countries listed in Council Regulation 519/94 (OJ 10.3.94 L67/89), as amended in particular by Council Regulation 847/97, OJ 14.5.97 L122/1.
14 This includes safeguard measures: see Commission Regulation 2604/97, OJ 23.12.97 L351/28. During 1997 the Community introduced surveillance measures on certain imports from countries other than EFTA or EEA countries: see Commission Regulation 2412/96, OJ 19.12.96 L329/11. But see previously I Macleod, I D Hendry and S Hyett *The External Relations of the European Communities* (Clarendon Press, Oxford, 1996) pp 294–295.
15 See Council Regulation 3281/94 Annex II, OJ 31.12.94 L348/1.
16 Ibid Art 73, first paragraph. The High Authority (now the Commission) is empowered however to supervise the administration and verification of these licences with respect to coal and steel: Art 73, second paragraph.

products from the twelve Republics of the former USSR[17] and most recently from Kazakhstan[18] and from the Russian Federation and Ukraine.[19]

However, on the basis of ECSC Art 74 the High Authority (now the Commission) may take certain safeguard or anti-dumping measures.[20] Consequently, while recognizing that the issue of import documents (subject to standard conditions) is the responsibility of national authorities, the ECSC has adopted *ex* ECSC Art 74 a Community recommendation[1] on prior Community surveillance of imports of certain iron and steel products.[2] Similarly, the Commission has adopted anti-dumping measures *ex* ECSC Art 74 which apply EC principles by analogy to ECSC products.[3]

BILATERAL AGREEMENTS

EFTA countries

Bilateral agreements have been concluded between the ECSC Member States and Switzerland,[4] between the ECSC Member States and Iceland,[5] and between the ECSC and its Member States and Norway.[6] The Agreement with Switzerland may be taken as an example.[7] It contained a standstill provisions in respect of customs duties[8] and equivalent charges.[9] Customs duties on imports[10] and customs duties of a fiscal nature[11] were to be progressively abolished. Charges equivalent to customs duties on imports introduced on or after 1 January 1972 were to be abolished on entry into force of the Agreement.[12]

17 Decision 92/585 of the Representatives of the Governments of the Member States meeting within the Council, OJ 31.12.92 L396/48.
18 Decision 95/110 of the Representatives of the Member States meeting within the Council, OJ 8.4.95 L80/40.
19 Decision 95/130 of the Representatives of the Member States meeting within the Council, OJ 19.4.95 L85/44.
20 Ibid Art 74.
 1 ECSC recommendations are analogous to directives under the EC Treaty: see ECSC Art 14, EC Art 189.
 2 Commission Recommendation 3118/94/ECSC, OJ 21.12.94 L330/6, as amended by Commission Recommendation 73/95 (OJ 19.1.95 L13/1) and Commission Recommendation 393/95 (OJ 25.2.95 L43/23). But compare Commission Regulation 2604/97, OJ 23.12.97 L351/28, which refers only to 'the Treaty establishing the European Community'.
 3 See, eg, Commission Decision 1775/92, OJ 2.7.92 L182/23; Commission Decision 2297/92, OJ 6.8.92 L221/36. As to the possible application of the EC Trade Barriers Regulation (Council Regulation 3286/94, OJ 23.12.94 L349/71) to ECSC products, see I Macleod, I D Hendry and S Hyett *The External Relations of the European Communities* (Clarendon Press, Oxford, 1996) p 295; the argument follows the logic of the European Court of Justice in Opinion 1/94 *World Trade Organization* [1994] ECR I-5267 in respect of ECSC competence in external relations.
 4 OJ 19.12.73 L350/13. See also Additional Agreement concerning the validity of this Agreement for Liechtenstein, OJ 19.12.73 L350/29. As to international railway tariffs for the carriage of coal and steel through Swiss territory, see Agreement (OJ 29.5.57 L17/223), Supplementary Protocol (OJ 18.1.79 L12/15), Second Supplementary Protocol (OJ 12.8.81 L227/11).
 5 OJ 19.12.73 L350/2.
 6 OJ 27.12.74 L348/17.
 7 As to the products covered, see Agreement Art 1 and Annex, OJ 19.12.73 L350/13. It was stated in the Agreement that it did not modify the provisions of the ECSC Treaty or the powers and jurisdictions deriving from them: Agreement Art 11.
 8 Agreement Art 2(1).
 9 Ibid Art 5(1).
10 Ibid Art 2(2).
11 Ibid Art 3(1).
12 Ibid Art 5(2).

Other charges equivalent to customs duties were to be abolished progressively.[13] New customs duties on exports, and equivalent charges, were prohibited,[14] and those in force were to be abolished not later than 1 January 1974.[15] Analogous provisions applied to quantitative restrictions on imports and equivalent measures.[16] Products imported from Switerzerland were not to enjoy more favourable treatment than that applied by the Member States among themselves.[17] The Agreement contains a non-discrimination clause.[18] It also provides for the free movement of payments relating to trade in goods and the transfer of such payments.[19] The standard exceptions to free movement apply.[20] There is a duty of loyal co-operation.[1] Provision is made for safeguard measures[2] and anti-dumping measures.[3] A Joint Committee was established to oversee the implementation of the Agreement.[4]

Mediterranean countries

An Agreement on ECSC products was also concluded in 1970 with Turkey.[5] It provided for the progressive abolition of customs duties, equivalent charges, quantitative restrictions and equivalent measures.[6] These trade barriers were to be abolished in accordance with a timetable adopted by mutual agreement.[7] The treatment accorded to Turkey was not to be more favourable than that extended by the ECSC Member States to each other.[8] Provision was made for consultations at the request of either party.[9]

The ECSC Member States concluded Agreements with the Maghreb and Mashrak countries when the EC concluded Association Agreements with the same countries.[10] These Agreements remain in force until they are gradually replaced by the recently concluded Euro-Mediterranean Agreements. The Agreement with Tunisia[11] may serve as an example. It provides for trade co-operation and certain institutional matters. In respect of trade co-operation, the object of the Agreement is to promote trade between the parties, taking account of their

13 Ibid Art 5(3).
14 Ibid Art 6, first paragraph.
15 Ibid Art 6, second paragraph.
16 As to the standstill clause, see ibid Art 9(1). As to abolition of measures in force, see Art 9(2).
17 Ibid Art 10.
18 Ibid Art 13.
19 Ibid Art 14.
20 See ibid Arts 12, 15, 16.
 1 Ibid Art 17.
 2 See ibid Arts 19, 20. As to procedures, see Art 23. As to balance of payments problems, see Art 24.
 3 Ibid Art 21. As to procedures, see Art 23.
 4 Ibid Art 25. See also Arts 26, 27.
 5 OJ 29.12.72 L293/63, amended by Supplementary Protocol (OJ 31.12.77 L361/187 which also reprints the original Agreement).
 6 Ibid Art 1.
 7 Ibid Art 2(1). The parties were also to determine conditions for any preferential treatment: Art 2(2).
 8 Ibid Art 3.
 9 Ibid Art 4.
10 The ECSC concluded agreements with Algeria (OJ 27.09.78 L263/119), Morocco (OJ 27.09.78 L264/119), Tunisia (OJ 27.09.78 L265/119), Egypt (OJ 12.12.79 L316/2), Jordan (OJ 12.12.79 L316/13), Lebanon (OJ 12.12.79 L316/24), Syria (OJ 12.12.79 L316/35) and Israel (OJ 28.6.75 L165/62).
11 OJ 27.9.78 L265/119. As to the products covered, see Art 1 and the Annex. This Agreement will be gradually replaced by the Euro-Mediterranean Agreement. See Chapter 26 in this book on Mediterranean Countries.

respective levels of development and of the need to ensure a better balance in their trade. In particular, the Agreement is intended to increase the rate of growth of Tunisia's trade and to improve its conditions of access to the Community market.[12] Tunisian products are to be imported into the Community free of customs duties, equivalent charges, quantitative restrictions and equivalent measures.[13] Tunisia is required to grant at least MFN treatment.[14] Provision is made for certain derogations on the part of Tunisia and for safeguard measures.[15] If the offers made by Tunisian undertakings are likely to be detrimental to the functioning of the common market, and if the detriment is attributable to a difference in prices, Member States may take appropriate measures.[16] A Joint Committee is established to oversee the implementation of the Agreement.[17] The standard exceptions to free movement of goods apply, and provision is also made for the settlement of disputes.[18]

Countries in transition

Several sets of measures have been concluded with Central and Eastern European Countries, including the former USSR, in respect of ECSC products.[19]

First, the ECSC and its Member States, together with the European (Economic) Community, are parties to the Europe Agreements concluded with countries of Central and Eastern Europe.[20] The Agreement with Hungary[1] may serve as

12 Ibid Art 2.

13 Ibid Art 3(1).

14 Ibid Art 4, and Co-operation Agreement between the European Economic Community and Tunisia Art 26(1), OJ 27.9.78 L265/1.

15 See Agreement Art 4, which refers to Arts 25–38 of the Co-operation Agreement.

16 Agreement Art 5(1). As to procedures, including possible withdrawal of tariff concessions, see Art 5(2),(3).

17 Ibid Art 7(1). See also Arts 7(2)-9.

18 See ibid Art 10, which provides that Arts 48–56 of the Co-operation Agreement apply *mutatis mutandis*.

19 See also Council Regulation 190/98, OJ 27.1.98 L20/1 (double-checking in respect of certain ECSC and EC steel products from the former Yugoslav Republic of Macedonia under the EC-FYROM Co-operation Agreement).

20 These relevant Agreements, which were initially brought into force in respect of ECSC products by means of Interim Agreements, are as follows: Poland (OJ 31.12.93 L348/2, as amended), Hungary (OJ 31.12.93 L347/2, as amended), Romania (OJ 31.12.94 L357/2, as amended), Bulgaria (OJ 31.12.94 L358/3, as amended), Czech Republic (OJ 31.12.94 L360/2, as amended), Slovak Republic (OJ 31.12.94 L359/2, as amended). As to the Baltic countries, see Chapter 25 in this book on Countries in Transition. See also Decision 1/93 of the EC-Czech Republic and Slovak Republic Joint Committee (OJ 29.6.93 L157/59: exports from Slovak Republic; OJ 29.6.93 L157/67: exports from Czech Republic, as amended). As to steel imports from central and eastern Europe, see also ECSC Consultative Committee Resolution 93/C121/04 concerning 'External measures' – steel imports from countries of central and eastern Europe (PECO), OJ 1.5.93 L121/4. As to the double-checking of certain products, see Council Regulation 3054/95, OJ 31.12.95 L325/1 (Bulgaria, Romania, Slovak Republic). As to renewal of the double-checking system for 1998, see Decision 3/97 of the EC-Bulgaria Association Council, OJ 19.1.98 L13/85 (Bulgaria); Council Regulation 84/98, OJ 19.1.98 L13/1 (Romania); Council Regulation 85/98, OJ 19.1.98 L13/15 (Slovakia); Decision 3/97 of the EC-Slovakia Association Council, OJ 19.1.98 L13/71 (Slovakia). See also Decision 4/96 of the EC-Poland Association Council, OJ 5.3.97 L64/13; Decision 3/97 of the EC-Czech Association Council, OJ 19.1.98 L13/99, and Council Regulation 87/98, OJ 19.1.98 L13/43. As to the implementation of competition provisions to ECSC products, see eg Decision 2/97 of the EC-Bulgaria Association Council, OJ 21.1.98 L15/37. References to the EC in these instances includes both EC and the Member States.

1 OJ 31.12.93 L347/1.

an example. Provisions in respect of ECSC products are laid down in a Protocol to the Agreement.[2]

In respect of ECSC steel products, customs duties on imports from Hungary into the Community are to be abolished progressively over a period of six years following the entry into force of the Agreement.[3] For imports from the Community into Hungary, customs duties were progressively abolished by 1 January 1994 for certain products[4] and will be by 1 January 2001 for other products.[5] Quantitative restrictions on Hungarian imports into the Community are to be abolished as of the entry into force of the Agreement.[6] Quantitative restrictions and equivalent measures on Community imports into Hungary are to be abolished as of the entry into force of the Agreement.[7]

In respect of ECSC coal products, customs duties on imports from Hungary into the Community were progressively abolished before 31 December 1995.[8] Customs duties on imports from the Community into Hungary are to be progressively abolished by 1 January 2001.[9] Quantitative restrictions on imports from Hungary into the Community are to be abolished at the latest by one year after entry into force of the Agreement, except for certain listed products in respect of which a further three years is permitted.[10] Quantitative restrictions and equivalent measures on imports from the Community to Hungary are to be abolished progressively between 1 January 1995 and 31 December 2000.[11] The Agreement includes provisions in respect of competition.[12] During the first five years of the Agreement, Hungary is entitled exceptionally to derogate from the Agreement by granting state aids for restructuring purposes.[13]

In respect of all ECSC products, the above provisions in respect of customs duties also apply to customs duties of a fiscal nature.[14] Charges equivalent to customs duties on imports from Hungary into the Community are to be abolished upon entry into force of the Agreement.[15] Charges equivalent to customs duties on imports from the Community into Hungary were progressively abolished before 1 January 1997.[16] Similarly, customs duties on exports, equivalent charges, quantitative restrictions on exports, and equivalent charges on trade

---

2 Ibid Art 16, which refers to Protocol 2. As to procedures in respect of safeguard measures, see Commission Decision 264/94, OJ 5.2.94 L32/3.
3 Ibid Art 2.
4 Ibid Art 3(2), which refers to products listed in Annex I to the Protocol and to the timetable set out in Art 10(1) of the Agreement.
5 Ibid Art 3(1), which refers to the products not listed in Annex I to the Protocol and to the timetable set out in Art 10(3) of the Agreement.
6 Ibid Art 4(1).
7 Ibid Art 4(2).
8 Ibid Art 5.
9 Ibid Art 6, which refers to timetable set out in Art 10(3) of the Agreement.
10 Ibid Art 7(1). The products with a longer period for abolition of restrictions are listed in Annex II. As to Community tariff quotas *ex* ECSC Art 95 in respect of steel products from the Czech Republic and the Slovak Republic until 31 December 1995, see Commission Decision 1970/93, OJ 23.7.93 L180/10, as amended.
11 Ibid Art 7(2), which refers to the timetable laid down by Art 10(4) of the Agreement.
12 Ibid Art 8.
13 Ibid Art 8(4), which also provides that the amount and intensity of the aid must be strictly limited to what is absolutely necessary in order to reach the stated goals and that it must be progressively reduced. See also Art 8(5),(6).
14 See ibid Art 9, which refers to Art 11 of the Agreement.
15 Ibid Art 9, which refers to Art 12 of the Agreement; this requirement is set out in Art 12, first paragraph.
16 Ibid Art 9, which refers to Art 12 of the Agreement; this requirement is set out in Art 12, second paragraph.

between the parties are to be abolished at the latest by the end of the fifth year after entry into force of the Agreement.[17]

A contract group is to be established by the Association Council to discuss implementation of the Protocol.[18]

Second, pending the entry into force of the relevant Europe Agreements, the Baltic States' relations with the Community in respect of ECSC products are governed by Free Trade Agreements. The FTA between the Community and Estonia[19] may serve as an example. ECSC products are subject to the general rules of the FTA.[20]

Third, ECSC products are included in the Parternship and Co-operation Agreements concluded with most other countries of the former USSR.[1] The development of relations between the EU and the Russian Federation may serve as an example.[2] Pending the entry into force of the PCA signed in 1994, trade in ECSC products was regulated by an Interim Agreement.[3] ECSC products were governed by the basic provisions on trade in goods (with the exception that the prohibition on quantitative restrictions did not apply to ECSC products),[4] together with the provisions of the Agreement between the ECSC and Russia on trade in certain steel products.[5] Analogous provisions applied under the PCA.[6] ECSC products were governed by the basic provisions in respect of trade in goods (except that the prohibition on quantitative restrictions on products from Russia imported into the Community did not apply),[7] together with the provisions of an agreement to be concluded concerning exchanges of ECSC steel products.[8] An Agreement between the ECSC and the Russian Federation on trade in certain steel products was signed on

---

17 Ibid Art 9, which refers to Art 13 of the Agreement. An exception are those measures that might be required for the administration of international obligations: Agreement Art 13.

18 Ibid Art 10.

19 OJ 31.12.94 L373/2. See also Decision 2/97 of the Estonia-EC Joint Committee, OJ 12.9.97 L249/23.

20 Ibid Arts 3(1), 9, 10, 17. As to the FTA generally, see Chapter 25 in this book on Countries in Transition.

1 As to the contents and legal status of these Agreements, see Chapter 25 in this book on Countries in Transition. As to the interim agreements, including ECSC products, see Interim Agreement with Armenia, OJ 24.9.97 L262/5, approved on behalf of the Community by Commission Decision 97/629, OJ 24.9.97 L262/5; Interim Agreement with Georgia, OJ 24.9.97 L262/7, approved on behalf of the Community by Commission Decision 97/630, OJ 24.9.97 L262/6; Interim Agreement with Kyrgyz Republic, OJ 26.11.97 L323/39, approved on behalf of the Community by Commission Decision 97/796; Interim Agreement with Uzbekistan, OJ 14.2.98 L43/1, approved on behalf of the Community by Council Decision 98/138. As to Kazakstan, see Decision 97/862 of the Representatives of the Governments of the Member States meeting within the Council, OJ 23.12.97 L351/60.

2 Agreement on Partnership and Co-operation, signed in Corfu on 24 June 1994 by the European Union and the Russian Federation.

3 OJ 13.10.95 L247/2. See generally the relevant section in Chapter 25 in this book on Countries in Transition.

4 Ibid Art 14(1), first indent, which excludes the application of Art 8 on quantitative restrictions.

5 Ibid Art 14(1), second indent.

6 Agreement on Partnership and Co-operation, signed in Corfu on 24 June 1994 by the European Union and the Russian Federation.

7 PCA Russia Art 21(1), first indent, which states that the provisions of Art 15 of the PCA do not apply.

8 Ibid Art 21(1), second indent. As to this agreement, see the Exchange of letters on ECSC steel products outside the Agreement (appended to the Agreement). It states inter alia that the agreement should be concluded as rapidly as possible and that it should include a system of double licensing together with control of origin.

7 December 1995.[9] It provided for quantitative limits and export licences. In 1997 the ECSC and the Russian Federation concluded an Agreement concerning trade in certain steel products.[10] It establishes quantitative limits for the entry into free circulation into the Community of certain steel products from Russia for the 1997–2001 period, but also provides a framework of progressive liberalization and the development of competition which could lead eventually to the removal of all quantitative restrictions.[11]

Fourth, an Agreement was concluded in 1993 between the ECSC and its Member States, on the one hand, and the Republic of Slovenia, on the other hand.[12] Respect of democratic principles and human rights constitute an essential element of the Agreement.[13] The objective of the Agreement is to promote trade between the parties, taking account of their respective levels of development and the need to ensure a better balance in their trade, with a view to improving Slovenian access to the Community market.[14]

Products from Slovenia, with some exceptions,[15] are to be imported into the Community free of customs duties, equivalent charges, quantitative restrictions and equivalent measures.[16] This is subject, however, to the establishment by the Community of conditions and tariff ceilings for imports of certain products.[17] In addition, the Community has reserved the right to call on the Joint Committee[18] to determine special conditions for certain sensitive products.[19] Slovenia is required to grant the Community at least MFN status.[20] Slovenia is entitled to derogate from the Agreement by introducing new customs duties, equivalent charges, quantitative restrictions or equivalent measures, or increasing those already applied, if necessary for its industrialization and development.[1]

9 OJ 8.1.96 L5/25. It was subsequently extended to 30 June 1997: Council Assent 24/94 (OJ 7.1.97 C3/15); Commission Decision 97/120 (OJ 15.2.97 L45/40) and the attached Agreement. A separate Agreement on trade in certain steel products was concluded between the EC and Ukraine (OJ 5.8.96 L5/48) and then extended (Council Assent 23/96, OJ 7.1.97 C3/15). As to the administration of this Agreement, see Commission Decision 140/97, OJ 22.7.97 L193/12. As to the administration of the import restrictions under the two Agreements, see Commission Decision 3/96, OJ 8.1.96 L5/1, as amended. As to the Agreement with Uzbekistan, see the Interim Agreement, OJ 27.5.98 L153/18, approved on behalf of the ECSC and the EAEC by Commission Decision 98/343, OJ 27.5.98 L153/17. New agreements between the Community and Russia and between the Community and Ukraine were concluded in 1997: see below.
10 OJ 4.11.97 L300/51, approved on behalf of the ECSC by Commission Decision 97/742, OJ 4.11.97 L300/51. As to the similar Agreement between the ECSC and the Ukraine, see OJ 4.8.97 L210/32, approved by Commission Decision 97/482/ECSC, OJ 4.8.97 L210/31.
11 As to transitional measures, see Decision 97/636/ECSC of the Representatives of the Member States, meeting within the Council, OJ 1.10.97 L268/31. As to the administration of restrictions, see Commission Decision 2136/97, OJ 4.11.97 L300/15. As to the establishment of a double-checking system without quantitative limits, see Agreement in the Form of an Exchange of Letters, OJ 4.11.97 L300/37, and Council Regulation 2135/97, OJ 4.11.97 L300/1.
12 OJ 22.11.94 L287/2. The products covered are listed in Annex I: Agreement Art 1, second paragraph.
13 Ibid Art 1, first paragraph.
14 Ibid Art 2.
15 See ibid Art 3(2). See also Art 3(3).
16 Ibid Art 3(1).
17 Ibid Art 3(2). The products are listed in Annex II.
18 As to which, see ibid Arts 8, 9, 10.
19 Ibid Art 3(3), first paragraph, which also provides for specific procedures and guidelines. See also Art 3(3), second and third paragraphs.
20 See ibid Art 4, which provides that Arts 19–34 of the Co-operation Agreement (OJ 22.11.93 L287/2) shall apply; Art 20 of the Agreement is the MFN clause.
 1 Co-operation Agreement Art 22(2), as applied to ECSC products by Art 4 of the ECSC Agreement.

Provision is also made for safeguard measures[2] and anti-dumping measures.[3] A Joint Committee is established to administer the Agreement.[4]

India

A Protocol concerning economic and commercial co-operation was agreed in 1981 between the ECSC and India.[5] It applies to ECSC products certain provisions of the Agreement for Commercial and Economic Co-operation between the EEC and India of 23 June 1981.[6] According to these provisions, the parties are to accord each other MFN treatment in accordance with the GATT.[7] They are also to grant each other the highest degree of liberalization of imports and exports which they generally apply to third countries, as well as to undertake to discuss ways and means of providing maximum facilities compatible with their respective policies and obligations.[8] Provision is also made for consultations and exchanges of information in the industrial field[9] as well as for various forms of economic co-operation.[10]

North America

The Community and Canada have also concluded an agreement in respect of ECSC products.[11] It provides that the basic provisions of the 1976 Framework Agreement for commercial and economic co-operation between the Community and Canada are to apply to ECSC products.[12] These provisions include MFN treatment in accordance with the GATT, commercial co-operation, economic co-operation and the establishment of a Joint Co-operation Committee.

MULTILATERAL AGREEMENTS

European Economic Area Agreement

The Agreement on the European Economic Area[13] contains a Protocol on Trade in Coal and Steel Products.[14] Quantitative restrictions on exports, equivalent

2 ECSC Agreement Art 6; Co-operation Agreement Art 30, as applied to ECSC products by Art 4 of the ECSC Agreement.

3 Co-operation Agreement Art 29, as applied to ECSC products by the ECSC Agreement Art 4.

4 ECSC Agreement Art 8.

5 OJ 8.12.81 L352/28.

6 Ibid Art 1. The 1981 Agreement for commercial and economic co-operation between the Community and India has been replaced by the Co-operation Agreement between the Community and concluded in 1994, as to which see Chapter 32 in this book on Asia.

7 Agreement for commercial and economic co-operation between the European Economic Community and India, Art 2, OJ 16.11.81 L328/7.

8 Ibid Art 3.

9 Ibid Art 4.

10 Ibid Art 5.

11 Protocol, OJ 24.9.76 L60/28.

12 Ibid Art 1. As to the Framework Agreement, see OJ 24.9.76 L260/2. See also Chapter 30 in this book on North America.

13 OJ 3.1.94 L1/3, as amended by Protocol (OJ 3.1.94 L1/572), as to which generally see Chapter 23 in this book on EFTA Countries.

14 Ibid, Protocol 14. Unless otherwise provided, it does not affect the Free Trade Agreements. When the Free Trade Agreements do not apply, the provisions of Protocol 14 apply. However,

measures, customs duties, and equivalent charges are to be abolished.[15] There is a standstill on restrictions or administrative and technical regulations which would impede free movement of products.[16] Provision is made for exchange of information on markets.[17]

Fourth Lome Convention

Protocol 9 of the Fourth Lome Convention provides that ECSC products originating in the ACP States are to be admitted into the Community free of customs duties and equivalent charges.[18]

However, if offers made by ACP firms are likely to be detrimental to the functioning of the common market, and if any such detriment is attributable to a difference in the conditions of competition as regards prices, the Community may take safeguard measures.[19] ECSC products originating in the Community and imported in the ACP States are treated in the way as other products.[20] Provision is made for consultations at the request of either party.[1]

when the substantive provisions of the Free Trade Agreements apply, their institutional provisions also apply. See Protocol 14 Art 2(1). As to competition rules, see ibid Art 4 and Protocol 25 and, in respect of secondary legislation, Protocol 21 and Annex XIV.

15 Ibid Art 2(2).
16 Ibid Art 3.
17 See ibid Art 6(1),(3).
18 Fourth Lome Convention, Protocol 9, Art 1, (1996) 155 *The Courier* (January-February). As to rules of origin, see Protocol 9, Art 5.
19 Ibid Art 3, which refers specially to the withdrawal of the concessions referred to in Art 1.
20 Ibid Art 2. As to this treatment, see the Fourth Lome Convention, Part Three, Title 1, Chapter 1. See also the section on the Fourth Lome Convention in Chapter 28 in this book on African, Caribbean and Pacific Countries.
 1 Fourth Lome Convention, Protocol 9, Art 4.

Chapter 20

Euratom products

INTRODUCTION

The European Atomic Energy Community (Euratom) Treaty provides for the setting up by the Euratom Member States of a common customs tariff.[1] It also provides that the EAEC may conclude international agreements.[2] It does not however contain any provisions that refer specifically to trade. Consequently, there is nothing to prevent agreements concluded pursuant to Art 113 of the EC Treaty from extending to international trade in Euratom products.[3]

AUTONOMOUS MEASURES

On the basis of EC Art 113, specific measures have been enacted to prevent trade (including trade in Euratom products) between the Community and Iraq.[4]

BILATERAL AGREEMENTS

Countries in transition

The Europe Agreements[5] concluded between the Community and the Member States, on the one hand, and the countries of Central and Eastern Europe, on the other hand, provide for Euratom products. The Europe Agreement with

---

1 EAEC Art 94. As to the goods and products covered, see Annex IV EAEC.
2 EAEC Art 101. As to the exclusive powers of EAEC, see Ruling 1/78 *Re the Draft Convention on the Physical Protection of Nuclear Materials* [1978] ECR 2151.
3 See Opinion 1/94 *World Trade Organization* [1994] ECR I-5267 at I-5396 (paragraph 24). Certain action has also been based on TEU Art 3.3: see Joint Action on the EU contribution to the promotion of transparency in nuclear-related export controls, OJ 12.5.97 L120/1.
4 Council Regulation 2340/90, OJ 9.8.90 L213/1, as amended. The original Regulation applied from 7 August 1990 to both Iraq and Kuwait: Art 1. The restrictions in respect of Kuwait were lifted as of 2 March 1991: Council Regulation 542/91 Art 1, OJ 7.3.91 L60/5. See also Commission Communication pursuant to Art 6 of Council Regulation 2465/96 regarding the interruption of economic and financial relations between the EC and Iraq, OJ 20.3.97 L90/11.
5 As to which, see Chapter 25 in this book on Countries in Transition.

Hungary[6] may serve as an example. It provides for co-operation in the field of energy[7] and nuclear safety.[8]

More elaborate provisions are contained in the agreements with Russia. According to the Interim Agreement,[9] trade in nuclear materials is governed by three sets of provisions. The first set consists of the basic provisions[10] of the Interim Agreement, with the exceptions that the prohibition on quantitative restrictions[11] and certain safeguard provisions[12] do not apply to nuclear materials.[13] The second set consists of certain provisions of the 1990 Agreement on trade and commercial and economic co-operation,[14] in particular in respect of co-operation, consultations and safeguard measures. The third set consists of an Exchange of Letters attached to the Interim Agreement.[15] This Exchange of Letters expresses the understanding of the parties to the effect that Russia intends to act as a stable, reliable and long-term supplier of nuclear materials to the Community, that the Community considers Russia as a source of supply which is separate and distinct from other suppliers, that consultations are to be held regularly or on request on developments in the parties' trade of nuclear materials, and that the parties have agreed to facilitate by all practicable means the process of nuclear disarmament.[16] The parties also agreed to take all necessary steps to arrive at an arrangement covering trade in nuclear materials by 1 January 1997.[17] In addition, steps are to be taken to conclude an agreement regarding nuclear safeguards, physical protection and administrative co-operation. Until the agreement is reached, the respective legislation and international non-proliferation obligations of the parties apply as regards the transfer of nuclear materials.[18]

The same provisions are reiterated in the 1994 Agreement on Partnership and Co-operation between the European Union and Russia.[19]

ACP countries

The Fourth Lomé Convention gives special emphasis to the control of international movements of hazardous waste and radioactive waste.[20] The Community is required to prohibit all direct or indirect export of such waste to the ACP

---

6 OJ 31.12.93 L347/1.
7 Ibid Art 77.
8 Ibid Art 78.
9 OJ 13.10.95 L247/2.
10 Including the human rights and democracy clause in Art 1.
11 Ibid Art 8.
12 Ibid Art 10(1)-(5), (7).
13 Ibid Art 15(1), first indent.
14 OJ 15.3.90 L68/3. The Interim Agreement, in Art 15(1), second indent, refers to the 1989 Agreement, but this appears to be a typographical error. The 1989 Agreement refers only to textiles, whereas the 1990 Agreement has a broader scope. In addition, the cross-references specified in the Interim Agreement Art 15(5), do not make sense with reference to the 1989 Agreement and appear to refer to the 1990 Agreement.
15 Interim Agreement Art 15(1), third indent.
16 See Exchange of Letters in relation to Art 15, OJ 3.10.95 L247/25.
17 Agreement Art 15(2). Unless the arrangement is reached, the provisions of Art 15 of the Agreement continue to apply: ibid Art 15(3).
18 Ibid Art 15(4).
19 Agreement on Partnership and Co-operation signed in Corfu on 24 June 1994 by the European Union and the Russian Federation, Art 22. See also Joint Declaration in relation to Art 22(1), second indent.
20 See Fourth Lomé Convention, Part Two, Title I, Art 39. 'Hazardous waste' covers the categories of products listed in Annexes 1 and 2 to the Basle Convention on the Control of Transboundary

States, while at the same time the ACP States are required to prohibit the direct or indirect import into their territory of such waste from the Community or from any other country.[1] This does not however prevent a Member State to which an ACP State has chosen to export waste for processing from returning the processed waste to the ACP State of origin.[2] The prohibition measures are to be strictly monitored.[3]

North America

In 1958 Euratom and the US signed an Agreement on the peaceful use of nuclear energy.[4] It provides, inter alia, that the Commission will take all action available under the EAEC Treaty to minimize the impact of customs duties on goods and products imported under the joint programme.[5] The Community guarantees that no material transferred under the Agreement will be used for atomic weapons, research on or development of atomic weapons, or any other military purpose.[6] This also applies to source and special nuclear material utilized in, recovered from, or produced as a result of the use of materials, equipment or devices transferred pursuant to the Agreement.[7] Nor will material, including equipment and devices, be transferred to unauthorized persons or beyond the control of the Community, except with agreement of the USA and under other conditions.[8] Provision is made for safeguards.[9]

An Additional Agreement between Euratom and the USA was concluded in 1960.[10] As amended, it provides for the transfers of special nuclear material, as well as the performance of services with respect to special nuclear material. Special nuclear material produced through the use of material transferred to the Community, or to authorized persons within the Community, under the Agreement may be transferred to any nation outside the Community or any other groups of nations, provided that the transferee has an appropriate agreement for co-operation with the USA or guarantees the use of such material for peaceful purposes under safeguards acceptable to the parties.[11] Special provisions

---

Movements of Hazardous Wastes and their Disposal: Art 39(3), first paragraph. As to radioactive waste, the applicable definitions and thresholds are those laid down in the framework of the International Atomic Energy Agency: Art 39(3), second paragraph.

1 Ibid Art 39(1), second paragraph, which also provides that these obligations are without prejudice to specific international undertakings by the parties now or in the future. Provision is made for the adoption of necessary internal legislation and administrative regulations and for related consultations: Art 39(1), fourth paragraph.
2 Ibid Art 39(1), third paragraph.
3 Ibid Art 39(2), which also provides for consultations.
4 JO 19.3.59 L17/309. See also Agreement for the Co-operation between the EAEC and the US Department of Energy in the field of controlled thermonuclear fusion, OJ 14.2.87 L46/50.
5 Ibid Art X.
6 Ibid Art XI(1).
7 Ibid Art XI(3). 'Source material' means (1) uranium, thorium or any other material which is determined by either party to be source material; or (2) ores containing one or more of the foregoing materials, in such concentration as either party may determine from time to time: Art XV(c). 'Special nuclear material' means (1) plutonium, uranium enriched in the isotope 233 or in the isotope 235, and any other material which either party determines to be special nuclear material; or (2) any material artificially enriched by any of the foregoing: Art XV(b).
8 Ibid Art XI(2).
9 Ibid Arts XI(4), XII.
10 JO 29.4.61 No 31, pp 668/61, as amended (JO No 72, 8.8.62, pp 2043/62; JO 21.10.64 pp 2586/64; OJ 22.5.74 L139/24).
11 Additional Agreement Art I bis (D).

apply to special nuclear material of non-United States origin which was exported from the Community to the USA and then is re-exported from the USA to the Community. Such material is not to be charged against the quantity authorized for transfer to the Community, and if it has not been improved in the USA it is exempt from the safeguards required under the Agreement.[12] The net amounts of special nuclear material other than U-235 in enriched uranium which may be transferred by the US Atomic Energy Commission[13] is not to exceed the quantities authorized for transfer by US law.[14]

In 1959 an Agreement was concluded between Euratom and Canada for co-operation in the peaceful uses of atomic energy.[15] It was amended in 1978 to require more stringent safeguards in respect of sales abroad of Canadian material, equipment and information.[16] Material subject to the 1959 Agreement is not to be used for the manufacture of any nuclear weapon, for other military uses of nuclear energy, or for the manufacture of any other nuclear explosive device. In addition, equipment or material transferred between Canada and the Community after the Amended Agreement came into force is subject to the 1959 Agreement only if the supplying party so informs the other party in writing prior to the transfer. In the case of transfer of equipment from the Community to Canada, notification may also be given by an EAEC Member State.

The EAEC and Canada have concluded agreements in respect of fusion research and development[17] and controlled nuclear fusion.[18] They provide, inter alia, for exchange and provision of equipment, instruments, materials, and, in the latter case, of fuels and spare parts. In respect of exchange of equipment, instruments, materials, fuels and spare parts under the 1995 Agreement, the receiving party must notify customs authorities that the items provided by the sending party are for carrying out agreed activities of a scientific character, and not of a commercial character.[19] Transfers of tritium and tritium-related equipment are governed by the 1959 Agreement on Co-operation in the Peaceful Uses of Atomic Energy.[20]

The EAEC and Canada have also concluded an Agreement on the management of atomic waste.[1]

12 Ibid Art I bis (E).
13 Under ibid Art I(F).
14 Ibid Art II bis (B), added by Amendment to the Additional Agreement for Co-operation Art IV, OJ 22.5.74 L139/24.
15 OJ 24.11.59 60/1165 as amended. See also Implementing Agreement on the involvement of Canada in the EAEC contribution to the engineering design activities (EDA) for the International Thermonuclear Experimental Reactor (ITER), OJ 6.9.95 L211/40.
16 See Amendment in the form of exchange of letters, OJ 8.3.78 L65/16.
17 Memorandum of Understanding concerning co-operation in the field of fusion research and development, OJ 11.2.86 L35/10.
18 Memorandum of Understanding for co-operation in the field of controlled nuclear fusion, OJ 6.9.95 L211/31.
19 Ibid Annex II, Art V(3)(b)(B.2), first paragraph (f).
20 As amended by the Amendment of 15 July 1991: ibid Annex II, Art V(3)b)(B.2), second paragraph.
 1 The Agreement was concluded between Atomic Energy of Canada Ltd and Euratom in 1980 and then renewed in 1985 and 1990, unpublished (see SEC(90)1986 24 Oct 1990; SEC(90)1986/2).

Oceania

An Agreement between Euratom and Australia concerning transfers of nuclear material from Australia to the Euratom was concluded in 1982 for a period of 30 years.[2] It applies to transfers[3] of four types of nuclear material.[4]

The first type is nuclear material transferred from Australia to the Community for peaceful purposes, either directly or through a third country, provided that Australia has so informed Euratom in writing before or at the time of the transfer.[5] The second type comprises all forms of nuclear material prepared by chemical or physical processes or isotopic separation.[6] The third type consists of all generations of nuclear material produced by neutron irradiation.[7] The fourth type, if so provided in a bilateral agreement between Australia and a Euratom Member State, is nuclear material produced, processed or used in equipment which the Member State, or Australia in consultation with the Member State, has designated to the Community as equipment of Australian origin, or as equipment derived from equipment or technology of Australian origin, and which is within the jurisdiction of the Member State at the time of designation and use.[8]

This material must not be used or, or diverted to, the manufacture of nuclear weapons or other nuclear explosive devices, research on or development of nuclear weapons or other nuclear explosive devices, or be used for any military purpose.[9] Compliance with this prohibition is to be ensured by a system of safeguards applied by Euratom and the International Atomic Energy Agency pursuant to the Euratom Treaty and various safeguards agreements.[10] Material covered by the Agreement must also be subject at all times to adequate levels of physical protection.[11] Measures of physical protection are to be applied by the Member States.[12] Nuclear material transferred to the Community is not to be transferred beyond the Community to any other country without the prior

---

2 Agreement 4.10.81 L281/8. As to the duration, see Art XX(1).

3 Material is transferred pursuant to the Agreement only to a natural or legal person authorized to receive the items: ibid Art II.

4 Nuclear material means any source material or special fissionable material as those terms are defined in Art XX of the Statute of the International Atomic Energy Agency: ibid Art I(c). The nuclear material covered by the Agreement remains subject to its provisions until it is determined that the material is no longer usable, or that it is practically irrecoverable for processing into a form in which it is usable for any nuclear activity relevant from the point of view of safeguards, or until it has been transferred beyond the Community in accordance with the provisions of Art IX of the Agreement: ibid Art III.

5 Ibid Art II(1)(a), which also provided for material previously transferred between Australia and the EAEC Member States pursuant to bilateral agreements.

6 Provided that the quantity of nuclear material so prepared is only regarded as falling within the scope of the Agreement in the same proportion as the quantity of nuclear material used in its preparation, and which is subject to the Agreement, bears to the total quantity of nuclear material so used: ibid Art II(1)(b).

7 Provided that the quantity of nuclear material so produced is only regarded as falling within the scope of the Agreement in the same proportion as the quantity of nuclear material which is subject to the Agreement and which, used in its production, contributes to this production: Art II(1)(c).

8 Ibid Art II(1)(d).

9 Ibid Art IV.

10 See ibid Art V. See also Arts VI, VII.

11 Ibid Art VIII(1). As to the criteria, see Annex B to International Atomic Energy Agency document INFCIR C/254.

12 Ibid Art VIII(2), which also provides guidelines.

consent of Australia.[13] It is only to be enriched beyond 20 per cent in the isotope uranium 235 according to certain conditions.[14] It can only be reprocessed according to certain conditions.[15] Provision is made for consultations, the preservation of confidentiality, and eventual suspension or cancellation of further transfers of nuclear material by Australia and eventual corrective steps.[16] Disputes are to be settled by negotiation or, at the request of either party, by a three-member arbitral tribunal.[17]

MULTILATERAL AGREEMENTS

In 1978 the ECSC and seven ECSC Member States[18] concluded with the International Atomic Energy Agency (IAEA) an Agreement in implementation of the Treaty on the Non-Proliferation of Nuclear Weapons.[19] In so far as the Agreement concerns trade, the Member States agree to accept safeguards on all source or special fissionable material in all peaceful nuclear activities within their territories, under their jurisdiction or carried out under their control anywhere, for the exclusive purpose of verifying that the material is not directed to nuclear weapons or other nuclear explosive devices.[20] The Agency has the right and the obligation to ensure that safeguards are applied,[1] and the Community undertook to co-operate with the Agency.[2] The safeguards are to be implemented in a manner designed, inter alia, to avoid hampering international exchange of nuclear material[3] or undue interference in the peaceful nuclear activities of the Community.[4] The Community is required to notify the Agency of transfers of nuclear material subject to safeguards out of the States.[5]

In 1978 Euratom and the UK concluded with the IAEA a Co-operation Agreement in respect of non-military materials and equipment.[6] In 1981 Euratom, France and the IAEA concluded a similar agreement.[7]

---

13 Ibid Art IX. As to Australia's consent, see Art XII.
14 Ibid Art X, which also provides that the conditions must be agreed upon in writing between the parties, as set out in Annex B. As to Australia's consent, see Art XII.
15 Ibid Art XI, which also provides that the conditions must be agreed upon in writing between the parties, as set out in Annex C. As to Australia's consent, see Art XII.
16 Ibid Art XV, which also provides that these provisions would apply in the event of detonation of a nuclear explosive device by a non-nuclear-weapon State member of the Community.
17 Ibid Art XVI.
18 Belgium, Denmark, Germany, Ireland, Italy, Luxembourg and the Netherlands.
19 OJ 22.2.78 L51/1.
20 Ibid Art 1. As to the procedures for implementing safeguards, see Arts 27–38. Note that they apply to nuclear material received, produced, shipped, lost or otherwise removed from inventory: Art 32(a). See also the Protocol.
1 Ibid Art 2.
2 Ibid Art 3(a).
3 Ibid Art 5(a).
4 Ibid Art 5(b). As to the non-application of safeguards to nuclear material used in non-peaceful activities, see Art 14.
5 Ibid Art 12, which also provides that the safeguards terminate when the recipient State has assumed responsibility for the material. The Agency must keep records indicating each transfer and, where applicable, the re-application of safeguards to the transferred nuclear material. As to more specific provisions in respect of transfers into or out of the States, see Arts 91–97.
6 *Collection of Agreements concluded by the European Communities*, viii, (II), 3381.
7 *Collection of Agreements concluded by the European Communities*, xi, (II), 2497.

The EAEC and its Member States are parties to the International Convention on the Physical Protection of Nuclear Materials.[8] The Convention applies to nuclear material[9] used for peaceful purposes while inter alia in international nuclear transport.[10] The parties to the Convention are not permitted to export or authorize the export,[11] or to import or authorize the import,[12] of nuclear material unless they have received assurances that the material will be protected during international nuclear transport at prescribed levels.[13] The same prohibition applies to transit, including through airports or seaports,[14] and to transport from part of a State to another part of the same State through international waters or airspace.[15] The responsibility for receiving assurances may be transferred, by mutual agreement, to the State Party involved in the transport as the importing State.[16] Specific forms of co-operation and assistance are provided in case of theft, robbery or any other unlawful taking of nuclear material.[17]

8 Misc 27 (1980), Cmnd 8112, 18 ILM 1419.
9 As to the products covered, see Art 1(a), Annex II.
10 Ibid Art 2(1).
11 Ibid Art 4(1).
12 Ibid Art 4(2).
13 As to the levels of protection, see Annex I.
14 Ibid Art 4(3).
15 Ibid Art 4(4).
16 Ibid Art 4(6).
17 See ibid Art 5(2). See also Art 7.

Chapter 21

Services

INTRODUCTION

Trade in services is an increasingly important part of international trade. As of 1996 services constituted approximately 20 per cent of all international trade. So far as the European Union is concerned, trade in services, both intra-EC and foreign trade, comprised in the same year about 18 per cent of all imports and 20 per cent of all exports.[1]

It is surprising, therefore, that there is no single legal (or indeed economic) definition of what constitutes a 'service'. In terms of European Community law, services is a residual category. Services are considered to be 'services' within the meaning of the EC Treaty where they are normally provided for remuneration, in so far as they are not covered by the provisions relating to freedom of movement for goods, capital and persons.[2] The EC Treaty also states that 'services' shall in particular include:

(1) activities of an industrial character;
(2) activities of a commercial character;
(3) activities of craftsmen; and
(4) activities of the professions.[3]

Nor is there a definition of 'services' in the Uruguay Round General Agreement on Trade in Services (GATS),[4] though the concept of a 'service' is wider in GATS than in the EC Treaty.[5]

---

1 Calculated from the *IMF Balance of Payments Statistics Yearbook 1997*. It refers to the 15 EC Member States.
2 EC Art 60, first sub-paragraph.
3 Ibid second sub-paragraph.
4 Virtually the same may be said of the GATT in respect of goods, but the GATT Preamble refers to goods, and tariff concessions are according to Art II GATT to be granted on a product-by-product basis.
5 See Leivo *The Need for an Exclusive External Competence of the European Community with regard to International Trade in Services*, College of Europe Working Papers, No 17, Series: Law (European Interuniversity Press, Brussels, 1996) at pp 42–43. As to a comparison between GATS and EC regulation of trade in services, see Footer 'Global and Regional Approaches to the Regulation of Trade in Services' (1994) 43 *International and Comparative Law Quarterly* 661; Kennett 'The European Community and the General Agreement on Trade in Services' in N Emiliou and D O'Keeffe (eds) *The European Union and World Trade Law after the GATT Uruguay Round* (John Wiley & Sons, Chichester, 1996) pp 136–148; Eeckhout 'The General Agreement on Trade in Services and Community Law' in S.V. Konstadinidis (ed) *The Legal Regulation of the European Community's External Relations after the*

This chapter is based on the broad conception of services used in GATS. This conception consists, not of a definition, but of an indicative list, including business services, communication services, construction and related engineering services, distribution services, educational services, environmental services, financial services, health-related services, tourism, travel, transport services, and other services not included elsewhere.[6] Not all of these services, however, are discussed here. Instead, after analysing the powers and competence of the European Union in respect of trade in services, the chapter concentrates on those services which are likely to be of most importance to most readers and in respect of which the Community has already taken measures.[7] The main focus is on autonomous Community measures, though various bilateral and multilateral agreements are also discussed.[8]

POWERS AND COMPETENCE

Art 113 is the legal basis of the EC's common commercial policy (CCP). It enumerates matters covered by the CCP,[9] but it does not refer expressly to trade in services.[10] The extent of the Community's legal powers in respect of trade in services has therefore been the subject of interpretation by the European Court of Justice. In an early Opinion *ex* Art 228(1),[11] the European Court of Justice recognized the exclusive competence of the Community in respect of a local cost standard, without drawing a distinction between goods and services.[12] Subsequently, it emphasised that the enumeration in EC Art 113 of the matters covered by the CCP, and thus within the EC's exclusive powers, was not

---

Completion of the Internal Market (Dartmouth Publishers, Aldershot, 1996) pp 107–122. As to the interaction of these two regulatory regimes, see Ehlermann and Campogrande 'Rules on Services in the EEC: A Model for Negotiating World-Wide Rules' in E U Petermann and M Hilf (eds) *The New GATT Round of Multilateral Trade Negotiations—Legal and Economic Problems* (Kluwer, Deventer, 1998) pp 481–498; Messerlin 'Services' in Commission of the European Communities *The European Community as a World Trade Partner* (European Economy, No 52) (Office of Official Publications of the European Communities, Luxembourg, 1993) pp 129–156.

6 See Annex: Indicative list of service industries used in GATS offers, in Messerlin 'Services' in Commission of the European Communities *The European Community as a World Trade Partner* (European Economy, No 52) (Office of Official Publications of the European Communities, Luxembourg, 1993) pp 129–156. Maritime and air transport however are not included in GATS.

7 The chapter does not discuss international agreements concluded by the EU Member States themselves.

8 For further discussion of the provisions in respect of trade in services contained in bilateral agreements, see the chapters in Part IV of this book.

9 Article 113(1) states that the common commercial policy shall be based on uniform principles, particularly in regard to changes in tariff rates, the conclusion of tariff and trade agreements, the achievement of uniformity in measures of liberalization, export policy and measures to protect trade such as those to be taken in the event of dumping and subsidies.

10 Consequently some authors concluded that Art 113 referred only to goods: see eg Perreau de Pinninck 'Les compétences communautaires dans les négociations sur le commerce des services' (1991) 27 *Cahiers de Droit Européen* 390 at 402; for a different view, see Vigneron and Smith 'Le fondement de la compétence communautaire en matière de commerce international des services' (1992) 28 *Cahiers de Droit Européen* 515 at 535. These articles give a good survey of Community law and practice in respect of trade in services. As to the relation between the internal market and external relations in respect of services, see the annual report by the European Commission on the Community single market.

11 Now Art 228/6.

12 Opinion 1/75 *Local Cost Standard* [1975] ECR 1355.

exhaustive, thus giving a broad interpretation of the CCP.[13] These cases concerned the express powers of the EC in the field of external relations. In addition, since the early 1970s the European Court of Justice has developed the principle that, in respect of external relations, the Community enjoys certain implied powers.[14] As is well-known, the underlying idea was the theory of parallelism.[15] Stated simply, this meant that the Community's exclusive competence could flow, not merely from express powers conferred by EC Art 113, but also 'from the provisions of the Treaty establishing its internal competence, or from the existence of legislative acts of the institutions giving effect to that internal competence, or else from the need to enter into international commitments with a view to achieving an internal Community objective'.[16]

Against this background, the European Court of Justice laid down in November 1994 the basic principles which now define the legal powers of the Community in respect of trade in services. On the one hand, as stated by the Court, 'it follows from the open nature of the common commercial policy, within the meaning of the Treaty, that trade in services cannot immediately, and as a matter of principle, be excluded from the scope of Art 113'.[17] On the other hand, the European Court of Justice held that the powers of the EC in respect of trade in services are not necessarily exclusive. Instead, the legal power to act in respect of trade in services may be either exclusive or shared with the Member States, depending on how the services are supplied.

Following the definition of trade in services in the Uruguay Round's General Agreement on Trade in Services (GATS),[18] the European Court of Justice distinguished four modes of supply of services:

(1) cross-frontier supplies not involving any movement of persons;
(2) consumption abroad, entailing the movement of the consumer into the territory of the WTO member country in which the supplier is established;
(3) commercial presence, that is, the presence of a subsidiary or branch in the territory of the WTO member country in which the service is to be rendered; and
(4) the presence of natural persons from a WTO member country, enabling a supplier from one member country to supply services within the territory of any other member country.[19]

Having regard to the provisions of the EC Treaty,[20] it concluded that the cross-

---

13 See Opinion 1/78 *International Agreement on Natural Rubber* [1979] ECR 2871; Case 45/86 *Commission v Council* [1987] ECR 5459.
14 Case 22/70 *Commission v Council (ERTA)* [1971] ECR 263.
15 As to the development of the Community's implied powers in the field of external relations, see also Mauna, 'The Implied External Competence of the European Community after the ECJ Opinion 1/94 – Towards Coherence or Diversity?' (1995) 2 LIEI 115.
16 As argued by the Commission in Opinion 1/94 *World Trade Organization* [1994] ECR I-5267 at I-5409 and I-5410 (paragraph 72). This broad interpretation of the *ERTA* case co-existed with a narrower interpretation until Opinion 1/94, in which the European Court of Justice confirmed the latter interpretation.
17 Ibid at I-5401 (paragraph 41).
18 Marrakesh Agreement establishing the World Trade Organization, Annex 1B: General Agreement on Trade in Services, Art I:2, in World Trade Organization *The Results of the Uruguay Round of Multilateral Trade Negotiations: The Legal Texts* (1995) at p 328.
19 Opinion 1/94 *World Trade Organization* [1994] ECR I-5267 at I-5401 (paragraph 43).
20 In particular, first, the distinction between 'a common commercial policy' and 'measures concerning the entry and movement of persons' in Art 3(b) and 3(d), respectively; and, second,

frontier supply of services, not involving any movement of persons, was part of the common commercial policy.[1] In such matters, the Community has express powers and exclusive competence.

However, the other three modes of supplying services, namely consumption abroad, commercial presence, and presence of natural persons, fall outside the common commercial policy.[2] The same is true of international agreements regarding transport.[3] In these matters the Community thus has no express powers; any powers it may have in these areas must be implied. In dealing with these issues, the European Court of Justice did not always distinguish very clearly between express or implied powers, on the one hand, and exclusive or shared competence, on the other hand. Nonetheless, it laid down two preconditions for the recognition of implied powers. First, it pointed out that '[o]nly in so far as common rules have been established at internal level does the external competence of the Community become exclusive'.[4] Second, it stated:

'[w]henever the Community has included in its internal legislative acts provisions relating to the treatment of nationals of non-member countries or expressly conferred on its institutions powers to negotiate with non-member countries, it acquires exclusive external competence in the spheres covered by those acts.'[5]

In the absence of either precondition, however, the Community may have implied powers, but such powers can only be shared with the Member States. Moreover, an internal power to harmonize *ex* EC Art 100a which has not been exercised in a specific field cannot confer implied exclusive competence in that field on the Community.[6] Nor can Art 235 in itself vest exclusive competence in the Community in external relations.[7] Consequently, in respect of services supplied by consumption abroad, commercial presence, and presence of natural persons, the Community has implied powers, but both the Community and the Member States have concurrent competence.[8]

---

the existence in the Treaty of specific chapters on the free movement of natural and legal persons, distinct from the provisions on the common commercial policy: see ibid at I-5402 (paragraph 46).

1 Ibid at I-5401 (paragraph 44).
2 Ibid at I-5402 (paragraph 47).
3 Ibid, at I-5404 (paragraph 53).
4 Ibid at I-5411 (paragraph 77).
5 Ibid at I-5416 (paragraph 95).
6 Ibid at I-5414 (paragraph 88).
7 Ibid at I-5414 (paragraph 89), in which the European Court of Justice further stated that the principle according to which internal competence can give rise to exclusive external competence only if it is exercised, except where internal powers can only be effectively exercised at the same time as external powers, applies a fortiori to Art 235.
8 As to the conclusion by the EC, as regards matters within its competence, of the results of the WTO negotiations on financial services and on the movement of natural persons, see Council Decision 96/412, OJ 6.7.96 L167/23. As to the argument that the same arguments in favour of an exclusive commercial policy in respect of goods also apply to services, see P. Runge Nielsen *Services and Establishment in Community Banking Law: A Study of its Legal Approach and Implications* (DJOEF Publishing Company, Copenhagen, 1994) at 267–278, 338; Leivo *The Need for an Exclusive External Competence of the European Community with regard to International Trade in Services*, College of Europe Working Papers, No 17, Series: Law (European Interuniversity Press, Brussels, 1996);Vereecken 'La competenza della Comunità a concludere accordi internazionali in materia di servizi' (1996) 35 *Diritto Comunitario e degli Scambi Internazionali* 87. As to earlier, contrary views, see eg Timmermans 'Common Commercial Policy (Art 113 EEC) and International Trade in Services', in F Capotorti *et al* (eds) (Nomos, Baden-Baden, 1987); Mengozzi 'Trade in Services and Commercial Policy' in M Marescau (ed) *The European Community's Commercial Policy after 1992: The Legal Dimension* (Kluwer, Dordrecht, 1993) pp 223–247.

These arrangements can potentially be modified pursuant to the Amsterdam Treaty, which was agreed in June 1997 and signed on 2 October 1997 but which at the time of writing has not yet been ratified. The Amsterdam Treaty provides for the potential extension of Community powers in respect of trade in services. The Council, acting unanimously on a proposal from the Commission and after consulting the European Parliament, may extend the application of Art 113 to international negotiations and agreements on services and intellectual property in so far as they are not covered by it.[9]

In 1996 the Council approved the conclusion, on behalf of the Community, as regards matters within its competence, of the results of the WTO negotiations on financial services and on the movement of natural persons.[10]

AUDIOVISUAL SERVICES

The principal Community measure affecting trade in audiovisual services is the so-called 'Television without Frontiers' Directive.[11] Adopted in the light of the European Convention on Transfrontier Television,[12] it lays down certain general provisions and more specific rules in respect of inter alia the promotion of distribution and production of television programmes.

Member States are required to ensure that the law applicable to broadcasts intended for the public in that Member State is respected by two categories of broadcasters.[13] The first category consists of broadcasters under its jurisdiction.[14] The second category is comprised of broadcasters who, while not being under the jurisdiction of any Member State, make use of a frequency or a satellite capacity granted by, or a satellite up-link situated in, that Member State.[15] Member States are also required to ensure freedom of reception and, except for specified reasons, not to restrict retransmission on their territory of broadcasts from other Member States.[16] The Directive does not apply to broadcasts intended exclusively for reception in States other than Member States and which are not received, directly or indirectly, in one or more Member States.[17]

---

9 Amsterdam Treaty Art 113, fifth subparagraph.
10 Council Decision 96/412, ON 6.7.96 L167/23. The Second Protocol to the GATS concerning financial services and the Third Protocol to the GATS concerning movement of natural persons, the schedules of specific commitments, the list of the exemptions of the Community and the Member States, and related documents are attached to this Decision.
11 Council Directive 89/552, OJ 17.10.89 L298/23CRISP, No 1525–1526, 1996. As to a general survey of EU audiovisual policy, see A Lange and J-L Renaud *The Future of the European Audiovisual Industry* (1989). See also the F Dehousse 'La politique européenne de l'audiovisuel' Centre de recherche et d'information socio-politiques (CRISP), *Courrier hebdomadaire*, No 1525–1526, 1996. As to television broadcasting as a service, see Case 155/73 *Italy v Sacchi* [1974] ECR 409 at 427; Case 52/79 *Procureur du Roi v Debauve* [1980] ECR 833; Case 352/85 *Bond Van Adverteerders v Netherlands* [1988] ECR 2085. As to international aspects of TV broadcasting, see (1990) 16 *Droit et Pratique du Commerce International* 326.
12 Adopted by the Council of Europe, Strasbourg, 5.5.89, European Treaty Series, No 132, 1989.
13 Council Directive 89/522 Art 1, OJ 17.10.89 L298/23.
14 Ibid Art 1, first indent.
15 Ibid Art 1, second indent.
16 Ibid Art 2(2).
17 Ibid Art 2(3).

The Directive also requires Member States to reserve a specified proportion of transmission time to European works.[18] This 'cultural quota' has two main aspects.[19]

First, Member States must ensure, where practicable and by appropriate means, that broadcasters reserve for European works a majority proportion of their transmission time, excluding the time appointed to news, sports events, games, advertising, and teletext services. This proportion is to be achieved progressively, on the basis of suitable criteria, having regard to the broadcaster's informational, educational, cultural and entertainment responsibilities to its viewing public.[20] If this proportion cannot be attained, it must not be lower than the average for 1988 in the Member State concerned,[1] except that for Greece and Portugal the base year is 1990.[2]

Second, Member States are required to ensure, where practicable and by appropriate means, that broadcasters reserve at least 10 per cent of their transmission time, excluding the time appointed to news, sports events, games, advertising, and teletext services, for European works created by producers who are independent of broadcasters. Alternatively, at their own discretion, they may reserve at least 10 per cent of their programming budget for the same purpose. As with the first requirement, this proportion is to be achieved progressively, on the basis of suitable criteria, having regard to the broadcasters' informational, educational, cultural, and entertainment responsibilities. Unlike the first requirement, however, it must be achieved by earmarking an adequate proportion for recent works, that is to say works transmitted within five years of their production.[3]

The same definition of 'European works' applies for the purpose of both requirements.[4] For these purposes, 'European works' means works which fall into any one of three different categories.

The first category consists of works originating from Member States of the Community and, as regards television broadcasts falling within the jurisdiction of Germany, works from German territories where the Basic Law does not apply and which fulfil certain other conditions.[5] These other conditions are that the works are works mainly made with authors and workers residing in one or more Member States (or, where pertinent, German territories where the Basic Law does not apply), provided that the works comply with one of the three following conditions:[6]

(1) they are made by one or more producers established in one or more of those States;[7]

---

18 Ibid Art 4. Articles 4–8 do not apply to local television broadcasts not forming part of a national network: ibid Art 9.
19 As to this controversy, including the US complaint under GATT, see, eg, Wallace and Goldberg 'The EEC Directive on Television Broadcasting' (1989) 9 *Yearbook of European Law* 175; Lupinacci 'The Pursuit of Television Broadcasting in the European Community: Cultural Preservation or Economic Protectionism?' (1991) 24 *Vanderbilt Journal of International Law* 113; Salvatore 'Quotas on TV Programmes and EEC Law' (1992) 29 *Common Market Law Review* 967.
20 Council Directive 89/522 Art 4(1).
1 Ibid Art 4(2), first sub-paragraph.
2 Ibid Art 4(2), second sub-paragraph.
3 Ibid Art 5.
4 See ibid Arts 4(1), 5.
5 Ibid Art 6(1)(a).
6 Ibid Art 6(2).
7 Ibid Art 6(2)(a).

(2) production of the works is supervised and actually controlled by one or more producers established in one or more of those States;[8] or

(3) the contribution of co-producers of those States to the total co-production is preponderant and the co-production is not controlled by one or more producers established outside those States.[9]

The second category consists of works originating from European third states party to the European Convention on Transfrontier Television and fulfilling the same other conditions.[10]

The third category consists of works from other European third countries which fulfil certain further conditions.[11] These further conditions are that the works must be made exclusively or in co-production with producers established in one or Member States or by producers established in one or more European third countries within which the Community will conclude agreements, if those works are mainly made with authors and workers residing in one or more European States.[12]

In addition, however, works which are not European works because they do not fulfil any of these conditions, but which are made mainly with authors and workers residing in one or more Member States, are to be considered as European works to an extent corresponding to the proportion of the contribution of Community co-producers to the total production costs.[13]

When they consider it necessary for purposes of language policy, the Member States may lay down more detailed or stricter rules, in particular on the basis of language criteria, as regards some or all programmes of television broadcasters under their jurisdiction.[14]

Starting from 3 October 1991, Member States were required to report to the Commission every two years on the application of these provisions.[15] The Commission is required to inform the other Member States and the European Parliament.[16] The Council is required to review the application on these provisions, together with any proposals by the Commission for revision of these measures not later than the end of the fifth year after the adoption of the Directive.[17]

These 'cultural quota' provisions have been extremely controversial and were the subject of discussion and negotiation between the US and the European Community within the framework of the GATT.[18] As a result, the audiovisual

8 Ibid Art 6(2)(b).
9 Ibid Art 6(2)(c).
10 Ibid Art 6(1)(b).
11 Ibid Art 6(1)(c).
12 Ibid Art 6(3). With regard to EFTA States, the works referred to in ibid Art 6(1)(c) are also works made, as described in Art 6(3), by and with producers established in European third countries with which the EFTA State concerned has agreements to this effect: see Council of the European Communities and Commission of the European Communities *Agreement on the European Economic Area* Art 36(2) and Annex X, paragraph 1(a).
13 Council Directive 89/522 Art 6(4).
14 Ibid Art 8, which also provides that, in doing so, Member States are obliged to observe Community law.
15 Ibid Art 4(3), first and second sub-paragraphs.
16 Ibid Art 4(3), third sub-paragraph.
17 Ibid Art 4(4).
18 See, eg, Filipek 'Culture Quotas: The Trade Controversy over the European Community's Broadcasting Directive' (1992) 28 *Stanford Journal of International Law* 323; Kessler 'Protecting Free Trade in Audiovisual Entertainment: A Proposal for Counteracting the European Union's Trade Barriers to the US Entertainment Industry's Exports' (1995) 26 *Law and Policy in International Business* 563.

sector was included within the GATS, but the European Union did not make any specific undertakings in respect of the opening of its audiovisual market.[19]

In addition, the Television without Frontiers Directive also prohibits the television broadcast of any cinematographic work until two years after it was first shown in cinemas in one of the Member States, unless otherwise agreed between its rights holders and the broadcaster. The period is reduced to one year in the case of works co-produced by the broadcaster.[20] The Directive also includes requirements in respect of advertising,[1] sponsorship,[2] and protection of minors.[3]

CAPITAL MOVEMENTS

Prior to 1 January 1994, the Council had the power to enact directives in respect the movement of capital between Member States and third countries. It was to endeavour to attain the highest possible degree of liberalization. Such measures were to be enacted by a qualified majority, except that unanimity is required for measures which constituted a step back as regards the liberalization of capital movements.[4] A Member State could, however, take steps to prevent its residents from using free transfer facilities within the Community to take advantage of more liberal rules in other Member States in respect of transfers to or from third countries.[5]

Under the Third Capital Movements Directive,[6] Member States were required, in respect of movements of capital to or from third countries, to endeavour to attain the same degree of liberalization as that which applies to operations with residents of other Member States.[7] This did not, however, prejudice the application to third countries of domestic rules or Community law, particularly any reciprocal conditions, concerning operations involving establishment, the provisions of financial services, and the admission of securities to capital markets.[8] Where large-scale short-term capital movements to or from third countries seriously disturbed the domestic or external monetary or financial situation of

---

19 See also Waregne 'Le GATT et l'audiovisuel' Centre de recherche et d'information socio-politiques (CRISP) *Courrier hebdomadaire* No 1449–1450, 1994, at 48–56; Endelman 'Regulating Culture: The Audiovisual Controversy in the GATT Accord' (1995) 18 *Boston College International and Comparative Law Review* 443; F Dehousse 'La politique européenne de l'audiovisuel' Centre de recherche et d'information socio-politiques (CRISP) *Courrier hebdomadaire* No 1525–1526, 1996, at 47–48. This solution is, however, only temporary. The matter will be included in the next round of GATS negotiations, which according to GATS Art XIX(1) are to commence five years at the latest from the date of coming into force of GATS, thus in principle beginning on 1 January 2000. In addition, the Community obtained under GATS Art II(2) an exemption from the MFN clause, but this exemption is subject to the restrictions that the exemption would be re-examined five years after the coming into force of GATS and, in any event, would last a maximum of ten years: see GATS, Annex on Article II Exemptions, paragraphs 3, 6.
20 Council Directive 89/522 Art 7.
1 See ibid Arts 10–16, 18–21, Art 13 of which prohibits all forms of television advertising for cigarettes and other tobacco products.
2 See ibid Art 17, 21.
3 See ibid Art 22.
4 EC Art 70(1).
5 Ibid Art 70(2).
6 Council Directive 88/361, OJ 8.7.88 L178/5.
7 Ibid Art 7(1), first sub-paragraph.
8 Ibid Art 7(1), second sub-paragraph.

the Member States, or of a number of them, or caused serious strains in exchange relations within the Community or between the Community and third countries, Member States were required to consult with each other on any measure to be taken to counteract the difficulties.[9]

As from 1 January 1994, these and other related EC Treaty provisions were replaced by new provisions of the Maastricht Treaty.[10] All restrictions on the movement of capital between Member States and between Member States and third countries are prohibited.[11] All restrictions on payments between Member States and between Member States are also prohibited.[12] These general principles are subject however to several qualifications or exceptions.

First, these prohibitions are without prejudice to the application to third countries of any restrictions which existed on 31 December 1993 under national or Community law adopted in respect of the movement of capital to or from third countries involving direct investment, including in real estate, establishment, the provision of financial services, or the admission of securities to capital markets.[13] This provision thus grandfathers any restrictions legitimately adopted before 1 January 1994 while prohibiting restrictions since then.

Second, the Council may, after 1 January 1994, adopt measures on the movement of capital to or from third countries involving direct investment including investment in real estate, establishment, the provision of financial services, or the admission of securities to capital markets. Such measures are to be adopted by a qualified majority on a proposal from the Commission, except that unanimity is required for measures which constitute a step back in Community law as regards liberalization of the movement of capital to or from third countries.[14]

Third, the general prohibitions on restrictions are without prejudice to the right of Member States to apply relevant provisions of their tax law which distinguish between tax-payers who are not in the same situation with regard to their place of residence, or with regard to the place where their capital is invested.[15] Measures taken by Member States must not, however, constitute a means of arbitrary discrimination or a disguised restriction on the free movement of capital and payments between Member States or between Member States and third countries.[16]

Fourth, they are also without prejudice to the right of Member States to take all requisite measures to prevent infringements of national law and regulations, in particular in the field of taxation and the prudential supervision of financial

---

9 Ibid Art 7(2), which also provides that the consultation is to take place within the Committee of Governors of the Central Banks (now the European Monetary Institute) and the Monetary Committee on the initiative of the Commission or of any Member State.

10 See EC Art 73a.

11 Ibid Art 73b(1), which also provides that this prohibition operates within the framework of the provisions set out in this Chapter, that is, EC Treaty Chapter 4 on Capital and Payments.

12 EC Art 73b(2), which also provides that this prohibition operates within the framework of the provisions set out in this Chapter, that is, EC Treaty Chapter 4 on Capital and Payments.

13 EC Art 73c(1).

14 Ibid Art 73c(2).

15 Ibid Art 73d(1)(a).

16 Ibid Art 73d(3). However, these limitations need not be interpreted in the same way in respect of capital movements to and from third countries as they are interpreted in respect of movements between Member States. This follows from the case law of the European Court of Justice, eg, Case 270/80 *Polydor v Harlequin* [1982] ECR 329. See also J A Usher *The Law of Money and Financial Services in the European Community* (1994) at 182.

institutions, or to lay down procedures for the declaration of capital movements for purposes of administrative or statistical information, or to take measures which are justified on grounds of public policy or public security.[17] Measures taken by Member States must not, however, constitute a means of arbitrary discrimination or a disguised restriction on the free movement of capital and payments between Member States or between Member States and third countries.[18]

Fifth, Member States which, as of 31 December 1993, enjoyed a derogation on the basis of existing Community law were entitled to maintain existing authorized restrictions until 31 December 1995 at the latest.[19]

Sixth, all the provisions of Chapter 4 on Capital and Payments of the EC Treaty, including the prohibitions on capital movement restrictions, are without prejudice to the applicability of restrictions on the right of establishment which are compatible with the Treaty.[20]

Safeguard measures are also possible. Where, in exceptional circumstances, movements of capital to or from third countries cause, or threaten to cause, serious difficulties for the operation of economic and monetary union, the Council may take safeguard measures with regard to third countries. Such measures are to be taken only if they are strictly necessary. They are limited to a period not exceeding six months.[1]

Moreover, in certain cases in the context of the common foreign and security policy (CFSP), the Council may take the necessary urgent measures on the movement of capital and payments as regards the third country concerned.[2] The cases are those in which, in a common position or in a joint action adopted under the CFSP, it is provided for an action by the Community to interrupt or to reduce, in part or completely, economic relations with one or more third countries.[3]

Furthermore, so long as the Council has not taken monetary measures in such cases under the CFSP, a Member State may, for serious political reasons and on grounds of urgency, take unilateral measures against a third country in respect of capital movements and payments.[4]

Capital movements to and from third countries may also be affected by economic and monetary union (EMU). The Council has the power to conclude formal agreements on an exchange rate system for the single currency in relation to non-Community currencies.[5] It also has the power to adopt, adjust or

---

17 EC Art 73d(1)(b).
18 EC Art 73d(3).
19 EC Art 73e.
20 EC Art 73d(2).
1 EC Art 73f, which also provides that any such measures are to be taken by the Council acting by a qualified majority on a proposal from the Commission and after consulting the European Central Bank. Prior to the third stage of EMU, it is likely that the consultative role of the ECB can be exercised by the European Monetary Institute, and also that such measures may be taken in case of difficulties for the introduction of EMU. See J A Usher *The Law of Money and Financial Services in the European Community* (1994) at 183.
2 Ibid Art 73g(1), which further provides that the cases are those set out in Art 228a EC and that procedure for taking measures is that provided for in Art 228a EC.
3 Ibid Art 228a.
4 EC Art 73g(2), first sub-paragraph, which further provides that the Commission and the other Member States must be informed of such measures by the date of their entry into force at the latest. Acting by a qualified majority on a Commission proposal, the Council may decide that the Member State concerned shall amend or abolish the measures. The President of the Council is required to inform the European Parliament of any such decision taken by the Council. See Art 73g(2), second sub-paragraph.
5 Ibid Art 109(1), which further provides that, in this respect, the Council must act unanimously on a recommendation from the ECB or the Commission and must consult the ECB and the European Parliament.

abandon the central rates of the single currency within the exchange rate system.[6] In the absence of an exchange rate system in relation to one or more non-Community currencies, the Council may formulate general orientations for exchange rate policy in relation to these currencies.[7] Where agreements concerning monetary or foreign exchange regime matters need to be negotiated by the Community with one or more States or international organizations, the Council has the power to decide the arrangements for the negotiations and for the conclusion of such agreements.[8] The Council has the power to decide on the position of the Community at international level as regards issues of particular relevance to EMU.[9] However, without prejudice to Community competence and Community agreements as regards EMU, Member States may negotiate in international bodies and conclude international agreements.[10] Acting by qualified majority on a proposal from the Commission, the Council may decide that the Member State must amend or abolish such measures.[11]

Capital movements are also dealt with in certain bilateral agreements concluded between the Community and third countries. The Agreement on the European Economic Area is based on the principles of free movement of capital and non-discrimination based on nationality, or on place of residence of the parties, or place where such capital is invested.[12] Provision is made for appropriate measures and safeguard measures to prevent evasion of legal rules or market disturbances.[13]

The Europe Agreements, as exemplified by the agreement with Hungary, provide for current payments and movement of capital.[14] Liberalization of current payments, in freely convertible currency, is to proceed to the extent to which the underlying transactions in respect of movements of goods, services or persons have been liberalized.[15] Capital account transactions are to benefit from free movement if they relate to direct investments, other investments, and the liquidation or repatriation of these investments or related profits.[16] No new

6 Ibid Art 109(1), which further provides that, in this respect, the Council is to act by a qualified majority on a recommendation from the ECB or the Commission and must consult the ECB, and that the President of the Council must inform the European Parliament of the adoption, adjustment or abandonment of the central rates for the single currency.

7 Ibid Art 198(2), which further provides that the Council is to act by a qualified majority, either on a recommendation from the Commission and after consulting the ECB, or on a recommendation from the ECB, and that these general orientations shall be without prejudice to the primary objective of the ECB to maintain price stability.

8 Ibid Art 109(3), first sub-paragraph, which also provides that the Council is to act by a qualified majority on a recommendation from the Commission and after consulting the ECB, that the arrangements must ensure that the Community expresses a single position, and that the Commission is to be fully associated with the negotiations. Such agreements are binding on the institutions of the Community, the ECB, and the Member States: Art 109(3), second sub-paragraph.

9 Ibid Art 109(4), which further provides that the Council is to act by a qualified majority, on a proposal from the Commission, and after consulting the ECB, and that this is subject to Art 109(1).

10 Ibid Art 109(5).

11 Ibid Art 70(2), second sub-paragraph.

12 Council of the European Communities and Commission of the European Communities *Agreement on the European Economic Area* Art 40(1) and Annex XII (1992).

13 Ibid Art 43(2).

14 Europe Agreement establishing an association between the European Communities and their Member States, of the one part, and the Republic of Hungary, of the other part, Title V, Chapter I, OJ 31.12.93 L347/2, approved by Council and Commission Decision 93/742, OJ 31.12.93 L347/1.

15 Ibid Art 59.

16 Ibid Art 60(1).

foreign exchange restrictions are to be introduced as from the start of the second stage of the association, and existing restrictions are not to be made more restrictive.[17] However, Hungary is not barred from applying restrictions on outward investments by Hungarian nationals and companies.[18] Measures are to be taken to permit the creation of the necessary conditions for the gradual application of Community rules on the free movement of capital and, subsequently, for these rules to be applied in full.[19]

The Lomé Convention contains specific provisions in respect of current payments and capital movements.[20] With regard to capital movements linked with investments and to current payments, the parties are to refrain from taking action in the field of foreign exchange transactions which would be incompatible with their obligations under the Convention resulting from provisions relating to trade in goods and services, establishment and industrial co-operation. This does not, however, prevent the Parties from adopting protective measures justified by reasons relating to economic difficulties or severe balance-of-payments problems.[1] In respect of foreign exchange transactions linked with investments and current payments, the ACP States, on the one hand, and the Member States, on the other hand, are to avoid, as far as possible, taking discriminatory measures vis-à-vis each other, or according more favourable treatment to third States, taking full account of the evolving nature of the international monetary system, the existence of specific monetary arrangements, and balance-of-payments problems.[2] However, to the extent that such measures or treatment are unavoidable, they must be maintained or introduced in accordance with accepted international monetary rules, and every effort must be made to minimise any adverse effects on the parties affected.[3]

The EC Member States which are Member countries of the OECD are also covered by the OECD Code of Liberalization of Current Invisible Operations and the OECD Code of Liberalization of Capital Movements.[4]

COMPUTER SOFTWARE

Member States are required to protect computer programmes, by copyright, as literary works within the meaning of the Berne Convention for the Protection of Literary and Artistic Works.[5] This protection applies to the expression in any form of a computer programme, but ideas and principles which underlie any element of a computer programme, including those which underlie its interfaces, are not protected by copyright under the Directive.[6] A computer programme is protected if it is original in the sense that it is the author's own

---

17 Ibid Art 60(2).
18 Ibid Art 60(3).
19 See ibid Art 61.
20 See Lomé IV Convention as revised by the agreement signed in Mauritius on 4 November 1995, Art 273, (1996) 155 *The Courier*.
1 Ibid Art 273(1).
2 Ibid Art 273(2), first sub-paragraph.
3 Ibid Art 273(2), second sub-paragraph.
4 These codes were updated and strengthened in 1989. See generally OECD *Liberalization of Capital Movements and Financial Markets in the OECD Area* (1990).
5 Council Directive 91/250 on the legal protection of computer programmes, Art 1(1), OJ 17.5.91 L122/42, which also provides that the term 'computer programmes' shall include their preparatory design material. As to the Berne Convention, see 168 CTS 185; 3/4 Peaslee 513.
6 Ibid Art 1(2).

intellectual creation, and no other criteria are to be applied to determine its eligibility for protection.[7] Protection is granted to certain restricted acts,[8] with specified exceptions.[9] Member States are required to provide appropriate remedies in respect of particular acts.[10]

The term of protection is for the life of the author plus 70 years after the author's death or after the death of the last surviving author.[11] Where the origin of the work, within the meaning of the Berne Convention, is a third country, and the author of the work is not a Community national, the term of protection granted by the Member States expires on the date of expiry of the protection granted in the country of origin of the work, but may not exceed 70 years.[12] In respect of certain related rights, these terms also apply to rightholders who are not Community nationals, provided Member States give them protection. However, without prejudice to the international obligations of the Member States, the term of protection granted by Member States to these related rights is to expire no later than the date of expiry of the protection granted in the country of which the rightholder is a national and may not exceed 50 years after the date of first performance or other specified event.[13] Member States which, in particular pursuant to their international obligations, granted a longer term of protection may maintain this period until the conclusion of international agreements on the term of protection by copyright or related rights.[14]

In addition to incorporating provisions in respect of intellectual property in bilateral trade agreements,[15] the Community has concluded agreements for scientific and technological co-operation. For example, such an agreement was concluded between the Community and Australia in 1994[16] and between the Community and Canada in 1996. These agreements provide for participation in joint research, shared use of research facilities, visits and exchange, exchange of information, and other activities.[17] They make special detailed provision for the dissemination and utilization of information and management, allocation and exercise of intellectual property rights.[18]

FINANCIAL SERVICES

Introduction

The financial services sector includes banking, securities and insurance. However, Community law does not currently govern international trade in these

---

7 Ibid Art 1(3). As to the meaning of 'author', see ibid Art 2.
8 See ibid Art 4.
9 See ibid Art 5. As to decompilation, see ibid Art 6.
10 See ibid Art 7.
11 See Council Directive 93/98 harmonizing the term of protection of copyright and certain related rights, Art 1, OJ 24.11.93 L290/9.
12 Ibid Art 7(1). See also Art 1.
13 Ibid Art 7(2). See also Art 3.
14 Ibid Art 7(3).
15 As to which, see Part IV of this book.
16 Agreement concerning scientific and technical co-operation between the European Community and Australia, OJ 22.7.94 L188/18, approved by Council Decision 94/457, OJ 22.7.94 L188/17. Agreement for Scientific and Technological Co-operation between the European Community and Canada, OJ 22.3.96 L74/26, approved by Council Decision 96/219, OJ 22.3.96 L74/25.
17 EC–Australia Agreement Art 4; EC–Canada Agreement Art 5.
18 See the Annex to these Agreements.

services. As the European Commission has recognized, '[t]hird-country access [to the EU market] by way of the provision of cross-border financial services ... is at present not regulated in the Community'.[19]

To take the example of banking, the basic Community legal instruments which affect third-country banks or other credit institutions[20] are concerned almost entirely with establishment or the provision of services within the EC, not with international trade in services.[1] Consequently, one author recently concluded that the provision of banking services within the Community by undertakings established solely outside the Community was 'virtually non-existent'.[2] In his view, 'banking services performed by undertakings established outside the Community are not governed by Community law, nor are they subjected to the requirements on reciprocity in the Second Banking Directive'.[3] Moreover, even though there are no applicable Community rules, the Member States are prohibited from entering into agreements with third countries as to trade in banking services, because the Community has exclusive competence in the matter.[4] Consequently, the relevant law regarding trade in services *stricto sensu* is to be found in GATS, which lies outside the scope of this book, or in bilateral or other multilateral agreements, examples of which are dealt with later in this chapter.

It is therefore necessary to take a broader view of Community law which might affect trade in services. In particular, one must focus on Community rules which might constitute barriers affecting trade in services,[5] and most notably on Community law in respect of the establishment in the Community of third-country providers of financial services. The basic concept underlying these provisions is that of reciprocity.[6]

Banking

In respect of banking by credit institutions having their head office outside the Community, separate provisions apply to the establishment of branches within the Community, on the one hand, and the establishment of subsidiaries within

---

19 'First European Commission Report to the Council on EEC Relations with Third Countries in the Banking and Insurance Sectors (1)', *Europe Documents*, No 1800, 3 October 1992, at 7.

20 Council Directive 77/80, OJ 17.12.77 L322/30; Council Directive 89/646, OJ 30.12.89 L386/1.

1 See P Runge Nielsen *Services and Establishment in European Community Banking Law: A Study of its Legal Approach and Implications* (DJOEF Publishing, Copenhagen, 1994) at pp 280–339; P Metzger *GATS and the European Union: Free Trade in Banking?* (College of Europe Working Papers, No 14) (European Interuniversity Press, Brussels, 1995).

2 P Runge Nielsen *Services and Establishment in European Community Banking Law: A Study of its Legal Approach and Implications* (DJOEF Publishing, Copenhagen, 1994) at p 315.

3 Op cit at p 315. Third-country undertakings which do not have a subsidiary within the EU do not meet the requirements of the EC Treaty in respect of establishment or services. Nor are they covered by the rules in the First Banking Directive in respect of strict reciprocal treatment, which apply to undertakings intending to set up a branch within a Member State.

4 Op cit at pp 315–316.

5 For a similar view, see M J Trebilcock and R Howse *The Regulation of International Trade* (1995) at pp 218–221.

6 See P Eeckhout *The European Internal Market and International Trade: A Legal Analysis* (1994) at 47–84; P Runge Nielsen *Services and Establishment in Community Banking Law: A Study of its Legal Approach and Implications* (DJOEF Publishing Company, Copenhagen, 1994) at pp 285–296.

the Community or the acquisition of EC credit institutions by third-country credit institutions, on the other hand.[7]

The First Banking Directive concerns the establishment of branches.[8] Member States must not apply to branches of credit institutions[9] having their head office outside the Community, when commencing or carrying on their business in the Community, provisions which result in more favourable treatment than that accorded to branches of credit institutions which have their head office in the Community.[10] However, through agreements concluded with third countries, the Community may agree to apply provisions which, on the basis of the principle of reciprocity, accord to branches of a credit institution having its head office outside the Community identical treatment through the territory of the Community.[11] The competent authorities of the Member State in which such a branch is established are required to notify the Commission and the Advisory Committee[12] of all authorizations for branches granted to credit institutions heading their head office outside the Community.[13]

The Second Banking Directive concerns the establishment of subsidiaries and the acquisition of EC credit institutions.[14] The competent authorities of the Member States are required to inform the Commission:

(1) of any authorization of a direct or indirect subsidiary one or more parent undertakings of which are governed by the laws of a third country;[15] or
(2) whenever such a parent undertaking acquires a holding in a Community credit institution such that the latter would become its subsidiary.[16]

In both instances, the Commission is required to inform the Banking Advisory Committee.[17]

In specified circumstances, the Commission is also entitled to request Member States to inform it:

---

7 As to a different categorization of credit institutions for the purpose of solvency ratios, see Council Directive 89/647, OJ 30.12.89 L386/14.
8 Council Directive 77/780 on the co-ordination of laws, regulations, and administrative provisions relating to the taking up and pursuit of business of credit institutions (First Banking Directive), OJ 17.12.77 L322/31. Ibid Art 1, third indent, provides that a 'branch' means 'a place of business which forms a legally dependent part of a credit institution and which conducts directly all or some of the operations inherent in the business of credit institutions; any number of branches set up in the same Member State by a credit institution having its head office in another Member State shall be regarded as a single branch'.
9 A 'credit institution' means 'an undertaking whose business is to receive deposits or other repayable funds from the public and to grant credits for its own account': ibid Art 1, first indent.
10 Ibid Art 9(1), OJ 17.12.77 L322/31.
11 Ibid Art 9(3).
12 As to which, see ibid Art 11.
13 Ibid Art 9(2).
14 Council Directive 89/646 on the co-ordination of laws, regulations and administrative provisions relating to the taking up and pursuit of the business of credit institutions and amending Directive 77/780/EEC, OJ 30.12.89 L386/1 (Second Banking Directive). Ibid Art 1(13) provides that 'subsidiary' shall mean 'a subsidiary undertaking as defined in Arts 1 and 2 of Directive 83/249/EEC; any subsidiary of a subsidiary undertaking shall also be regarded as a subsidiary of the parent undertaking which is at the head of those undertakings'. As to grandfathered rights of third-country credit institutions, see ibid Art 23.
15 Ibid Art 8, first paragraph, first indent.
16 Ibid Art 8, first paragraph, second indent.
17 Ibid Art 8 first paragraph, first and second indents, respectively.

(1) of any request for the authorization of a direct or indirect subsidiary by a third-country parent undertaking;[18] or
(2) whenever the Member States are informed[19] that a third-country undertaking proposes to acquire a holding in a Community credit institution such that the latter would become its subsidiary.[20]

The specified circumstances are two-fold.[1] The first arises when it appears to the Commission, on the basis of reports[2] or other information, that a third country is not granting Community credit institutions effective market access comparable to that granted by the Community to credit institutions from the third country. In these circumstances, the Commission may submit proposals to the Council for a negotiating mandate with a view to obtaining comparable competitive opportunities for Community credit institutions.[3] The second arises when it appears to the Commission, on similar bases, that Community credit institutions already established in a third country do not receive national treatment offering the same competitive opportunities as are available to domestic credit institutions and that the conditions of effective market access are not fulfilled. In these circumstances, the Commission may initiate negotiations in order to remedy the situation.[4] In addition, it may be decided[5] that Member States' authorities must limit or suspend their decisions regarding pending or future requests for authorizations and the acquisition of holdings by direct or indirect parent undertakings governed by the laws of the third country in question.[6] Such limitations or suspension may not apply to the setting up of subsidiaries by credit institutions or their subsidiaries duly authorized in the Community, or to the acquisition of holdings in Community credit institutions by such institutions or subsidiaries.[7] All such measures must be consistent with the Community's international agreements regarding the taking-up and pursuit of the business of credit institutions.[8]

The supervision of every credit institution which has a credit institution or a financial institution in the Community as a subsidiary, or which holds a participation in such institutions, is subject to supervision on the basis of its consolidated financial situation.[9] Similar provisions apply in respect of any credit institution the parent undertaking of which is a financial holding company.[10] However, if the undertaking that should be included is situated in a third country where there are legal impediments to the transfer of the necessary information, the Member States or other competent authority[11] responsible for exercising supervision on a consolidated basis may decide that a credit institution, finan-

---

18 Ibid Art 9(5)(a).
19 Pursuant to ibid Art 11.
20 Ibid Art 9(5)(b).
1 Ibid Art 5, first sub-paragraph. As to the lapse of the obligation to inform, see ibid Art 5, second sub-paragraph.
2 As to which, see ibid Art 9(2).
3 Ibid Art 9(3.
4 Ibid Art 9(4), first sub-paragraph.
5 By a regulatory committee acting according to the *contrefilet* procedure: see ibid Art 22(2).
6 Ibid Art 9(4), second sub-paragraph, which also provides that the duration of the measures must not be more than three months. The measures may, however, be continued by the Council, acting on a Commission proposal, before the end of the three-month period and in light of the results of the negotiations: ibid Art 9(4), third sub-paragraph.
7 Ibid Art 9(4), fourth sub-paragraph.
8 Ibid Art 9(6).
9 Council Directive 92/30 Art 3(1), OJ 28.4.92 L110/52.
10 Ibid Art 3(2).
11 As to which, see ibid Art 4.

cial institution, or auxiliary banking services undertaking which is a subsidiary, or in which a participation is held, need not be included in the consolidation.[12] In this case, the competent authorities of the Member State in which the credit institution subsidiary is situated may ask the parent undertaking for information which may facilitate their supervision of that credit institution.[13]

Provision is also made for the negotiation of international agreements to deal with such situations. At the request of a Member State or on its own initiative, the Commission may submit proposals to the Council for the negotiation of agreements with one or more third countries regarding the means of exercising supervision on a consolidated basis over credit institutions the parent undertakings of which have their head offices situated in a third country.[14] The Commission and the Advisory Committee set up pursuant to the First Banking Directive are to examine the outcome of these negotiations.[15]

Investment services

In respect of investment services, the competent authorities of the Member States are required to inform the Commission of the authorization of any firm which is a direct or indirect subsidiary of a parent undertaking governed by the law of a third country.[16] They are also required to inform the Commission whenever such a parent undertaking acquires a holding in a Community investment firm such that the latter would become its subsidiary.[17] Whenever authorization is granted to any firm which is the direct or indirect subsidiary of a parent undertaking governed by the law of a third country, the competent authorities must specify the structure of the group in their notification to the Commission.[18] Member States are also to inform the Commission of any general difficulties which their investment firms encounter in establishing themselves or providing services in any third country.[19]

Substantially the same provisions regarding comparable market access and national treatment apply to investment firms as in the banking sector. Whenever it appears to the Commission, either on the basis of reports[20] or from other information, that a third country does not grant Community investment firms effective market access comparable to that granted by the Community to investment firms from that third country, the Commission may submit proposals to the Council for an appropriate negotiating mandate with a view to obtain comparable competitive opportunities for Community investment firms.[1] Whenever

12 Ibid Art 3, first indent.
13 Ibid Art 3(4).
14 Ibid Art 8(1), first indent. Analogous provisions apply to credit institutions situated in third countries the parent undertakings of which, whether credit institutions or financial holding companies, have their head offices in the Community: ibid Art 8(1), second indent. As to the purposes of such agreements, see ibid Art 8(2).
15 Ibid Art 8(3). As to the Advisory Committee, see Council Directive 77/80 Art 11, OJ 17.12.77 L322/30.
16 Council Directive 93/22 on investment services in the securities field, Art 7(1)(a), OJ 11.6.93 L141/27.
17 Ibid Art 7(1)(b).
18 Ibid Art 7(1), third sub-paragraph.
19 Ibid Art 7(2).
20 As to which, see ibid Art 7(3).
 1 Ibid Art 7(4), which also provides that the Council shall act by a qualified majority. As to the requirement that, in this case, Member States inform the Commission of applications, see ibid Art 7(6), first sub-paragraph, (a), and second sub-paragraph.

it appears to the Commission, on the same bases, that Community investment firms in a third country are not granted national treatment affording the same competitive opportunities as are available to domestic investment firms, and that the conditions for effective market access are not fulfilled, the Commission may initiate negotiations to remedy the situation.[2] In this instance, it may also be decided that the competent authorities of the Member States must limit or suspend their decisions regarding pending or future requests for authorization by direct or indirect parent undertakings governed by the law of the third country in question.[3] Such limitations or suspensions may not be applied to the setting up of subsidiaries by investment firms duly authorized in the Community, or by their subsidiaries, or to the acquisition of holdings in Community investment firms by such firms or subsidiaries.[4] Any measures taken under these provisions must comply with the Community's obligations under any international agreements, bilateral or multilateral, governing the taking up or pursuit of the business of investment firms.[5]

Insurance

In respect of insurance services, a distinction must be made between direct insurance other than life insurance ('non-life insurance'), life insurance and motor vehicle insurance.

In respect of non-life insurance, specific rules apply to agencies or branches established within the Community and belonging to undertakings whose head offices are outside the Community.[6] Access to the market of a Member State by means of establishment by any undertaking whose head office is outside the Community is subject to an official authorization.[7] The authorization may be granted if the undertaking fulfils specified conditions.[8] Special rules apply in respect of technical reserves[9] and the requirement of a specific solvency

---

2 Ibid Art 7(5), first sub-paragraph. As to the requirement that, in this case, Member States inform the Commission of proposed acquisitions, see ibid Art 7(6), first sub-paragraph, (b), and second sub-paragraph.

3 Ibid Art 7(5), second sub-paragraph, which also provides that the duration of the measures may not exceed three months. However, the Council may, acting on a Commission proposal, decide by a qualified majority whether the measures are to be continued: see ibid Art 7(5), third sub-paragraph.

4 Ibid Art 7(5), fourth sub-paragraph.

5 Ibid Art 7(7).

6 Council Directive 73/239 on the co-ordination of laws, regulations and administrative provisions relating to the taking-up and pursuit of the business of direct insurance other than life insurance (the First Non-Life Directive), Title III, OJ 16.8.73 L228/3, as amended. Any permanent presence of an undertaking in the territory of a Member State is treated in the same way as an agency or branch, even if that presence does not take the form of a branch or agency, but consists merely of an office managed by the undertaking's own staff or by a person who is independent but has permanent authority to act for the undertaking as an agency would: Council Directive 88/357 (Second Non-Life Directive) Art 3, OJ 4.7.88 L172/1. As to provisions peculiar to the freedom to provide services, see the Second Non-Life Directive, Title III, and Council Directive 92/49 (Third Non-Life Directive), Title IV, OJ 11.8.92 L228/1. These services provisions apply to any establishment situated in a Member State which wishes to provide services in another Member State. They are not specific to branches belonging to undertakings whose head offices are outside the Community.

7 Ibid Art 23(1).

8 As to which, see ibid Art 23(2).

9 Ibid Art 24.

margin.[10] By means of international agreements, the Community may agree to the application of different provisions for the purposes of ensuring, under conditions of reciprocity, adequate protection for insured persons in the Member States.[11] The Community has concluded an agreement in respect of non-life insurance with Switzerland.[12]

In respect of life insurance, specific rules apply to agencies or branches established within the Community and belonging to undertakings whose head offices are outside the Community.[13] In addition, specific rules apply to subsidiaries of parent undertakings governed by the laws of a third country and to acquisitions of holdings by such parent undertakings.[14] Member States are required to notify the Commission of authorization of establishment or acquisition.[15] When authorization is granted to the direct or indirect subsidiary of one or more parent undertakings governed by the law of third countries, the structure of the group must be specified in the notification which the competent authorities address to the Commission.[16] In respect of Community undertakings in third countries, provisions regarding comparable effective market access and national treatment, including potential limitations or suspensions of requests for authorization or acquisition, apply in the same terms as those which apply in the banking sector.[17] Similarly, measures taken under these provisions must comply with the Community's obligations under any international agreements governing the taking-up and pursuit of the business of insurance undertakings.[18]

In respect of motor vehicle insurance, provisions regarding comparable effective market access and national treatment, including potential limitations or suspensions of requests for authorization or acquisition,[19]apply in the same terms as those which apply in respect of life insurance[20] and in the banking sector.[1]

Bilateral agreements

Several bilateral agreements contain provisions which apply to different types of financial services without distinguishing between them. The Agreement on

10 Ibid Art 25. As to specific advantages open to an undertaking which, having obtained an authorization from one Member State, obtains an authorization from one or more other Member States to establish other agencies or branches, see ibid Art 26, as substituted by Council Directive 84/641 Art 12, OJ 27.12.84 L339/21.

11 Ibid Art 29.

12 See Council Decision 91/370, OJ 27.7.91 L205/21, and the attached Agreement, OJ 27.7.91 L205/3. The basic principle of the Agreement is reciprocity: see the Agreement Art 1.

13 See Council Directive 79/267 (the First Life Directive), Title III, OJ 13.3.79 L63/1, as amended by Council Directive 90/619 (the Second Life Directive) Art 8(1), OJ 29.11.90 L330/50. These provisions are substantially the same as those which apply to non-life insurance, as to which see above. As to special provisions in respect of services, see the First Life Directive, as amended and substituted by Council Directive 92/96 (the Third Life Directive) Arts 32–44, OJ 9.12.92 L360/1.

14 First Life Directive, as amended by Second Life Directive Art 8(2) and Art 9.

15 First Life Directive Art 32a, first sub-paragraph, as substituted by Second Life Directive Art 9.

16 First Life Directive Art 32a, second sub-paragraph, as substituted by Second Life Directive Art 9.

17 Ibid Art 32b, as so substituted. As to the banking sector, see above in respect of the Second Banking Directive.

18 Ibid Art 32b(7), as so substituted.

19 See Council Directive 73/239 (First Non-Life Directive), Title IIIA and Title IIIB, OJ 16.8.73, as substituted by Council Directive 90/618 Art 3, OJ 29.11.90 L330/44.

20 As to which, see above.

 1 As to the banking sector, see above in respect of the Second Banking Directive.

the European Economic Area provides that, within the framework of its provisions, there shall be no restrictions on freedom to provide services within the territory of the Contracting Parties in respect of nationals of EC Member States and EFTA States who are established in an EC Member State or an EFTA State other than that of the person for whom the services are intended.[2] Specific provisions apply to different types of financial services.[3]

In respect of the Europe Agreements, the Agreement between the Community and Hungary may serve as an example.[4] The parties undertake to take the necessary steps to allow progressively the supply of services between them, taking into account the development of their respective services sectors.[5] The basic principles in respect of trade in financial services[6] are, first, the possibility of accelerating the granting of national treatment,[7] and, second, the right of each party to adopt non-discriminatory measures necessary for the conduct of monetary policy, prudential supervision, or integrity and stability of the financial system.[8]

PROFESSIONAL SERVICES

Legal services provide a useful example of trade in professional services.

In respect of lawyers established in the Community, the basic Community measure concerns the mutual recognition of higher-education diplomas.[9] However, it applies only to nationals of Member States, who wish to pursue a regulated profession in another Member State in a self-employed capacity or as an employed person.[10] In respect of nationals of Member States who hold a diploma, certificates, or other evidence of formal qualifications awarded in a third country,[11] the Council has recommended that the Governments of the Member States should allow such persons to take up and pursue regulated professions within the Community by recognizing these diplomas, certificates, and other evidence of formal qualifications in their territories.[12] Neither of these measures applies to nationals of third countries.

In respect of the provision of legal services, the basic Community measure is Council Directive 77/249.[13] It applies, however, only to nationals of Member

2 Council of the European Communities and Commission of the European Communities *Agreement on the European Economic Area* Art 36(1) (1992).
3 Ibid Art 36(2), Annex IX, as amended.
4 Europe Agreement establishing an association between the European Communities and their Member States, of the one part, and the Republic of Hungary, of the other part, OJ 31.12.93 L347/2, approved by Council and Commission Decision 93/742, OJ 31.12.93 L347/1.
5 Ibid Art 55(1).
6 Listed in ibid Annex XIIa: see ibid Art 49.
7 Ibid Art 44(6), first sub-paragraph.
8 Ibid Art 45(2).
9 See Council Directive 89/48 on a general system for the recognition of higher-education diplomas awarded on completion of professional education and training of at least three years' duration, OJ 24.1.89 L19/16 (the HED Directive).
10 Ibid Art 2, first sub-paragraph.
11 And who thus are in a position comparable to those described in ibid Art 3: see Council Recommendation 89/49, Preamble, third recital, OJ 24.1.89 L19/24.
12 Council Recommendation 89/49 concerning nationals of Member States who hold a diploma conferred in a third state, OJ 24.1.89 L19/24. A recommendation is not legally binding: see EC Art 189.
13 Council Directive 77/249 to facilitate the effective exercise by lawyers of freedom to provide services, OJ 26.3.77 L78/17 (the Lawyers' Services Directive).

States.[14] It does not apply to third-country nationals. Moreover, it applies only to designated categories of persons.[15] These categories represent the designations used by Member States for persons entitled to perform certain professional activities. The Directive does not include any analogous designations used by third countries. It would seem therefore that it does not apply to nationals of Member States who have obtained their professional qualifications in a third country.

In 1998 the Community enacted a directive to facilitate practice of the profession of lawyer on a permanent basis in a self-employed or salaried capacity in a Member State other than that in which the professional qualification was obtained.[16] It applies, however, only to nationals of a Member State who are authorized to pursue a professional activity under a professional title granted by a Member State,[17] and who wish to practise law on a permanent basis in a Member State other than that in which the professional qualification was obtained.[18] By its terms, it does not cover the provision of services, which is stated to be covered by the Lawyers' Services Directive.[19]

Matters not covered by Community law remain governed by the laws of the Member States,[20] including any international agreements entered into by the Member States. For example, US law firms have relied mainly on bilateral treaties on friendship, commerce and navigation in establishing a presence in Community Member States. In addition, because such a law firm would not benefit from Community rules in respect of the freedom of establishment and freedom to provide services, it would have to establish such a presence in each Member State in which it wishes to practise. Legal services are not (yet) included within the scope of the GATS.[1]

PUBLIC PROCUREMENT

The general legal framework for Community public procurement law is supplied by the multilateral Uruguay Round Government Procurement Agreement,

---

14 The Directive is based on EC Arts 57 and 66, which refer only to nationals of the Member States in respect of the freedom of establishment and the freedom to provide services, respectively. See also Case 65/77 *Razanatsimba* [1977] ECR 2229.

15 Ibid Arts 1, 2.

16 Directive 98/5 of the European Parliament and the Council, OJ 14.3.98 L77/36. See also Proposal 95/C128/06 for a European Parliament and Council Directive, COM(94) 572 final—94/0299(COD), submitted by the Commission on 30 March 1995, OJ 24.5.95 C128/6. See also Lonbay 'Lawyers bounding over the borders: the Draft Directive on lawyer's establishment' (1996) 21 *European Law Review* 50; 'Directive on Lawyers' Freedom of Establishment' (1995) 1 *Columbia Journal of European Law* 556–558.

17 See ibid Art 2, first and second paragraphs, and Art 3. Article 1(2)(b) provides that 'home Member State' means the Member State in which the lawyer acquired the right to use one of the professional titles before practising the profession of lawyer in another Member State. See also Arts 8 (salaried practice), 10 (like treatment as a lawyer of the host Member State), and 11 (joint practice).

18 See ibid Art 1(1).

19 Ibid Art 1(4).

20 See also Joined Cases 35–36/82 *Morson v Netherlands and Head of the Plaatselijke Politie; Jhanjan v Netherlands* [1982] ECR 3723.

1 See further Barsade 'The Effect of EC Regulations upon the Ability of US Lawyers to Establish a Pan-European Practice', (1994) 28 *The International Lawyer* 313.

which came into force on 1 January 1996.[2] The new GPA is based on the principles of non-discrimination and national treatment. It applies to works, supplies, and services, including certain utilities. It includes central government, sub-federal units and local governments. It also introduces improved legal remedies.[3]

Except for this framework, however, the Community lacks a real common commercial policy in respect of public procurement.[4] The keynotes of Community public procurement policy in respect of third countries have therefore been two-fold. On the one hand, the basic Community measures on public procurement apply only to firms established in the Community. On the other hand, Community agreements with third countries in respect of public procurement have been based on the principles of reciprocity and balanced concessions.[5]

Until recently the principal Community measure in respect of the award of contracts for public works did not contain any specific provisions regarding third countries.[6] The same was true of the principal measures on public service contracts[7] and on the definition and use of compatible technical specifications for the procurement of air-traffic management equipment and systems.[8] Now, however, in respect of contracts for works or services, Member States are required, for the purposes of the award of public contracts by contracting authorities, to apply in their relations conditions as favourable as those which they grant to third countries in implementation of the GPA.[9] The principal

2 See Council Decision 94/800, OJ 22.12.94 L336/1, and the attached Agreement, OJ 23.12.94, L336/3. The relevant Community directives were amended by European Parliament and Council Directive 97/5052, OJ 28.11.97 L328/1, Art 4(1) which provides that Member States must bring into force the laws, regulations and administrative provisions necessary to comply with the Directive by 13 October 1998. See also Trepte 'The GATT GPA and the Community Procurement Rules: Realignment and Modification' (1995) 4 *Public Procurement Law Review* CS42. As to consequent changes in EC procurement rules, see Economic and Social Committee, Opinion 95/C256/02 on the proposal for a European Parliament and Council Directive amending Directive 92/50, Directive 93/36, and Directive 93/37, and the proposal for a European Parliament and Council Directive amending Directive 93/38, OJ 2.10.95 C256/4.
3 See further de Graaf and King 'Towards a More Global Government Procurement Market: The Expansion of the GATT Government Procurement Agreement in the Context of the Uruguay Round' (1995) 29 *The International Lawyer* 435.
4 See Commission of the European Communities 'Public Procurement in the European Union: Exploring the Way Forward' (Green Paper presented by the Commission) COM(96) 583 final, Brussels, 27.11.96, especially 45–49. See also Arrowsmith *Remedies for Enforcing Public Procurement Rules* (1993); Bovis 'The European Public Procurement Rules and their Interplay with International Trade' (1997) 31 *Journal of World Trade* 63; Footer 'Public Procurement and EC External Relations: A Legal Framework' in N Emiliou and D O'Keeffe (eds) *The European Union and World Trade Law after the GATT Uruguay Round* (1996) 293–309.
5 See Council Resolution of 21 December 1976 concerning access to Community public supply contracts for products originating in non-member countries, OJ 15.1.77 C11/1, and the attached Commission Statement concerning Art 115 of the Treaty, OJ 15.1.77 C11/2.
6 Council Directive 93/37 concerning the co-ordination of procedures for the award of public works contracts, OJ 9.8.93 L199/54 (Works Directive).
7 Council Directive 92/50 (the Services Directive), OJ 24.7.92 L209/1.
8 Council Directive 93/65, OJ 29.7.93 L187/52.
9 In respect of works, see Council Directive 93/37, Art 33a, as inserted by European Parliament and Council Directive 97/52 Art 3(6), OJ 28.11.97 L328/1. In respect of services, see Council Directive 92/50 Art 38a, as inserted by European Parliament and Council Directive 97/52 Art 1(7), OJ 28.11.97 L328/1, which further provides that to this end Member States shall consult each other within the Advisory Committee on public contracts on the measures to be taken pursuant to the GPA.

measure on supplies contracts already required that Member States apply in their relations with each other conditions as favourable as those which they grant to third countries in implementation of the GATT on the restricted procedure, information and review.[10]

In respect of the water, energy, transport and telecommunications sectors, Member States are also required, for the purposes of the award of contracts by the contracting entities, to apply in their relations with each other conditions as favourable as those which they grant to third countries in implementation of the GPA.[11] However, specific provisions apply to tenders comprising products originating in third countries with which the Community has not concluded, multilaterally or bilaterally, an agreement ensuring comparable and effective access for Community undertakings to the markets of those third countries.[12] Any tender made for the award of a supply contract may be rejected when the proportion of the products originating in third countries[13] exceeds 50 per cent of the total value of the products constituting the tender.[14] There is an exception to the rule for third countries with which the Community or Member States have concluded an agreement.[15] Except in specified conditions,[16] where two or more tenders are equivalent in the light of the award criteria,[17] preference must be given to the tenders which may not be rejected on the basis of the criterion of origin.[18]

In addition, in the same sectors, Member States are required to inform the Commission of any general difficulties encountered, in fact or in law, by their undertakings in securing the award of service contracts in third countries.[19] The Commission is required to submit periodic reports to the Council on market

---

10 Council Directive 93/36 (the Supplies Directive) Art 28, OJ 9.8.93 L199/1, which refers in particular to GATT Arts V and VI.

11 Council Directive 93/38 (the Utilities Directive) Art 42a, as inserted by Directive 98/4 of the European Parliament and the Council, Art 1(13), OJ 1.4.98 L101/1.

12 Council Directive 93/38 Art 36(1), OJ 9.8.93 L199/84, which also provides that this is without prejudice to the obligations of the Community or its Member States in respect of third countries. The Commission is required to submit an annual report to the Council on progress made in multilateral or bilateral negotiations regarding access for Community undertakings to the markets of third countries in fields covered by the Directive, on any result which such negotiations achieve, and on the implementation in practice of all concluded agreements: ibid Art 36(6). These provisions were also contained in the first Utilities Directive, Council Directive 90/531 Art 29, OJ 29.10.90 L297/1. Council Directive 93/38 was amended by Directive 98/4 of the European Parliament and the Council, OJ 1.4.98 L101/1, in order to render it compatible with the GPA.

13 Originally as determined in accordance with Council Regulation 802/68, OJ 28.6.68 L148/1, as amended, and now in accordance with Community rules of origin, as to which see Chapter 2 in this book on Origin of Goods.

14 Ibid Art 36(2), first sub-paragraph. This are the so-called 'preference and exclusion rules'. For this purpose, software used in telecommunications network equipment are to be considered as products: ibid Art 36(2), second sub-paragraph.

15 Ibid Arts 36(1), 36(5). As to a specific conflict, see Grimes 'Conflicts between EC Law and International Treaty Obligations: A Case Study of the German Telecommunications Dispute' (1994) *35 Harvard International Law Journal* 535.

16 Namely, a tender shall not be preferred to another where its acceptance would oblige the contracting entity to acquire material having technical characteristics different from those of existing material, resulting in incompatibility or technical difficulties in operation and maintenance or disproportionate costs: ibid Art 36(4).

17 Defined in ibid Art 34.

18 Ibid Art 36(3), which also provides that the prices of these tenders shall be considered as equivalent for this purpose if the price difference does not exceed 3%.

19 Ibid Art 37(1).

access.[20] It may approach the third country concerned to try to remedy the situation when it establishes any of three situations.[1] The first situation occurs whenever, in respect of the award of service contracts, a third country does not grant Community undertakings effective access comparable to that granted by the Community to undertakings from that country.[2] The second situation occurs whenever, in respect of such contracts, a third country does not grant Community undertakings national treatment or the same competitive opportunities as are available to national undertakings.[3] The third situation occurs whenever, in respect of such contracts, a third country grants undertakings from other third countries more favourable access than Community undertakings.[4]

In addition, if it is informed by the Member States of any general difficulties encountered, in law or in fact, by their undertakings in securing the award of service contracts in third countries, the Commission may at any time propose that the Council suspend or restrict the award of service contracts to any of three specified categories of undertakings.[5] The first category consists of undertakings governed by the law of the third country in question.[6] The second category consists of undertakings affiliated to undertakings in the first category and having their registered office in the Community but having no direct and effective link with the economy of a Member State.[7] The third category consists of undertakings submitting tenders which have as their object services originating in the third country in question.[8] The Commission may propose these measures on its own initiative or at the request of a Member State.[9]

In 1987 the Community established a Community programme in the field of trade electronic data exchange systems.[10] Subsequently it was amended to enable firms in third countries with which the Community has concluded agreements associating those countries with the Tedis programme to take part in the programme.[11] Undertakings, including small and medium-sized enterprises, research institutes and other bodies established in that country may tender for and carry out contracts under the Tedis programme under the same terms and conditions as those applicable to undertakings, research institutes, and other bodies established within the Community. Such agreements have been concluded thus far with Iceland,[12] Norway,[13] and Switzerland.[14]

---

20 Ibid Art 37(2). See for example Commission of the European Communities, 'Report from the Commission concerning negotiations regarding access to third countries' markets in the fields covered by Directive 93/38/EC (the Utilities Directive), COM(94)342 final, Brussels, 7.9.94.
1 Ibid Art 37(3).
2 Ibid Art 37(3)(a).
3 Ibid Art 37(3)(b).
4 Ibid Art 37(3)(c).
5 Ibid Art 37(4), which also provides that the period is to be determined in the decision, and that the Council is to act by a qualified majority as soon as possible.
6 Ibid Art 37(4)(a).
7 Ibid Art 37(4)(b).
8 Ibid Art 37(4)(c).
9 Ibid Art 37(4), second sub-paragraph. These provisions are without prejudice to the obligations of the Community in relation to third countries: ibid Art 37(5).
10 Council Decision 87/499, OJ 8.10.87 L285/55.
11 Council Decision 89/241, OJ 11.4.89 L97/46.
12 OJ 30.12.89 L400/12, approved by Council Decision 89/891, OJ 10.12.89 L11.
13 OJ 30.12.89 L400/17, approved by Council Decision 89/692, OJ 30.12.89 L400/16. An agreement was also concluded with Sweden before its accession to the EU: OJ 30.12.89 L400/22, approved by Council Decision 89/693, OJ 30.12.89 L400/21.
14 OJ 30.12.89 L400/27, approved by Council Decision 89/694, OJ 30.12.89 L400/26.

Common rules govern the conditions for granting and using authorization for the prospection, exploration and production of hydrocarbons.[15] However, Member States may refuse, on grounds of national security, to allow access to and exercise of these activities to any entity which is effectively controlled by third countries or third country nationals.[16] In addition, Member States are required to inform the Commission of any general difficulty encountered, *de jure* or *de facto*, by entities in access to or exercise of the activities of prospecting, exploring for and producing hydrocarbons in third countries, which have been brought to their attention.[17] When the Commission establishes that a third country is not granting Community entities comparable treatment to that which the Community grants entities from that third country, it may submit proposals to the Council for a mandate to negotiate with a view to obtaining comparable competitive opportunities.[18] On its own initiative or at the request of a Member State,[19] the Commission may also propose that the Council authorize one or more Member States to refuse an authorization to an entity which is effectively controlled by the third country concerned and/or nationals of that third country.[20] Any such measures are without prejudice to the Community's obligations under any international agreement governing access to an exercise of the activities of prospecting, exploring for and producing hydrocarbons.[1]

In respect of bilateral agreements, the most significant have been those with the US. On 25 May 1993 the Community and the US concluded an Agreement in the form of a Memorandum of Understanding (MOU) on Government Procurement.[2] Its purpose was to provide a framework of balanced rights and obligations to open up parts of their respective procurement markets with a view to achieving liberalization and expansion of trade. The Community undertook to ensure comparable and effective access for Community undertakings to United States markets as regards the award of supplies and works contracts by its entities in the electrical power sector, and consequently it extended the benefit of the provisions of Directive 90/531 to tenders comprising US-originating products made for the award of a supply contract by specified contracting entities.[3]

---

15 Directive 94/22 of the European Parliament and of the Council, OJ 30.6.94 L164/3.
16 Ibid Art 2(2), second sub-paragraph.
17 Ibid Art 8(1), which also provides that Member States and the Commission are required to ensure that commercial confidentiality is protected. The Commission is required to report periodically to the European Parliament and the Council on the situation of entities in third countries and on any negotiations: ibid Art 8(3).
18 Ibid Art 8(3), which also provides that the Council is to act by a qualified majority.
19 Ibid Art 8(4), second sub-paragraph.
20 Ibid Art 8(4), first sub-paragraph. The Council is to act by a qualified majority as soon as possible: ibid Art 8(4), third sub-paragraph.
 1 Ibid Art 8(5).
 2 OJ 20.5.93 L125/2, approved by Council Decision 93/323 OJ 20.5.93 L125/1. The legal basis of this Council Decision was challenged successfully by the European Parliament: see Case C-360/93 *European Parliament v Council* [1996] ECR I-1195. As to this case, see also Footer 'External Aspects of the Community's Public Procurement Policy in the Utilities Sectors' (1994) 3 *Public Procurement Law Review* 187.
 3 See Council Decision 93/324, OJ 20.5.93 L125/54, Annex 3 of which lists the contracting entities. Thus the MOU disapplied the exclusion and preference rules in respect of such products. Subsequently, however, the US imposed sanctions under Title VII of the 1988 Trade Act, thus preventing Community tenderers from competing for US Federal Government procurement contracts not covered by the Agreement. The Community then restricted access for US tenderers in respect of certain contracts for supplies, services or works awarded by certain public authorities in the EC. See Council Regulation 1461/93, OJ 17.6.93 L146/1. The public authorities are listed in Annex I, as completed by Council Regulation 1836/95, OJ 2.8.95 L183/4. The services to which the restrictions apply are listed in Annex II.

This Agreement was replaced in 1995 when the Community and the US concluded another Agreement on government procurement.[4] It extended the 1993 Agreement until the entry into force of the Marrakesh Government Procurement Agreement (GPA).[5] Under the extended Agreement, the US was to grant EC suppliers of goods and services, including construction services, treatment no less favourable than for specified out-of-state or out-of-city suppliers.[6] The US and the EC were to co-operate and take all necessary steps to improve substantially the transparency of the notices of intended procurement in order to ensure that contracts covered by the Government Procurement Agreement can be clearly identified as such.[7] The US was to implement its obligations in respect of the Rural Electrification Administration[8] as soon as possible after entry into force of the Agreement, but no later than entry into force of the WTO Agreement.[9]

The EEA Agreement contains specific provisions in respect of public procurement, the basic principles of which are the same as those of the Community directives.[10]

The Europe Agreements, to take the agreement with Hungary as an example, do not contain specific provisions in respect of trade in services in public procurement.[11] Instead, the treatment of such services is linked together with the treatment of establishment and operation of works contracts.[12] The Parties consider the opening up of the award of public contracts on the basis of non-discrimination and reciprocity, in particular in the GATT context, to be a desirable objective.[13] Provision is made for the introduction of national treatment on the basis of graduated reciprocity.[14] The Association Council may take measures to implement progressively the liberalization of trade in services.

Agreements on procurement by telecommunications operators and government procurement have been concluded between the Community and Israel.[15] The first Agreement aims to secure a reciprocal, transport and non-discriminatory access of the Parties' suppliers and services producers to purchases of products and services, including construction services, by

---

4 Agreement in the form of an exchange of letters between the European Community and the US on government procurement, OJ 20.6.95 L134/26, approved by Council Decision 95/215, OJ 20.6.95 L134/25. The Parties agreed to amend their respective Appendix I of the Uruguay Round Government Procurement Agreement.
5 Agreement in the form of an exchange of letters, ibid point 4.
6 Ibid point 2.
7 Ibid point 3.
8 Contained in Annex 3 of its Appendix I, attached to the Agreement.
9 Ibid point 5.
10 Council of the European Communities and Commission of the European Communities *Agreement on the European Economic Area* Art 65(1) and Annex XVI (1992). See also F Weiss *Public Procurement in European Community Law* (1993) 156–159.
11 Europe Agreement establishing an association between the European Communities and their Member States, of the one part, and the Republic of Hungary, of the other part, Art 66, OJ 31.12.94 L347/2, approved by Council and Commission Decision 93/742, OJ 31.12.94 L347/1.
12 See ibid Art 66(3).
13 Ibid Art 66(1).
14 See ibid Art 66(2).
15 Agreement between the European Community and the State of Israel on procurement by telecommunications operators, OJ 30.7.97 L202/74, and Agreement between the European Community and the State of Israel on government procurement, OJ 30.7.97 L202/85, both approved by Council Decision 97/474, OJ 30.7.97 L202/72. In view of the fact that the services in question were not merely transfrontier, the Agreements were concluded on the bases of Arts 113, 66, 57(2), in conjunction with EC Art 228(3),(4).

telecommunications operators of both Parties.[16] It establishes a general binding principle of non-discrimination;[17] provides for procurement procedures based on the principles of non-discrimination, transparency and fairness;[18] and provides for challenge procedures,[19] exchange of information,[20] dispute settlement[1] and safeguards.[2] The second Agreement complements and broadens the scope of the Parties' commitments under the GPA *vis-à-vis* each other.[3]

In 1997 an analogous Agreement was concluded between the Community and the Republic of Korea.[4]

TECHNICAL STANDARDS

The Uruguay Round of multilateral trade negotiations resulted, inter alia, in the Agreement on Technical Barriers to Trade (TBT).[5] One of the purposes of the TBT Agreement is to ensure that technical regulations and standards, including packaging, marking and labelling requirements, and procedures for assessment of conformity with technical regulations and standards do not create unnecessary obstacles to international trade.[6] It encouraged WTO members to enter into negotiations for the conclusion of agreements for the mutual recognition of each other's conformity assessment.[7]

Such agreements are also promoted by Community law. Council Resolution 90/C 10/01 of 21 December 1989 provides that, in its relations with third countries, the Community will endeavour to promote international trade in regulated products, in particular by concluding mutual recognition agreements on the basis of EC Art 113.[8] It opened the way for the Community's participation in a global approach to conformity assessment.[9]

The European Union has initialled such mutual recognition agreements (MRAs) with Canada on 30 May 1997 and the US on 20 June 1997.[10] For example, the

16 Agreement between the European Community and the State of Israel on procurement by telecommunications operators, Art 1(1), OJ 30.7.97 L202/74. As to the scope of the Agreement, see ibid Art 1(3), (4) and Annexes I and II.
17 See ibid Art 2.
18 See ibid Art 3.
19 See ibid Art 4 and Annex III.
20 See ibid Art 5.
 1 See ibid Art 6.
 2 See ibid Art 7. As to consultations, see ibid Art 8.
 3 Agreement between the European Community and the State of Israel on government procurement, Art 1 (obligations of the EC), Art 2 (obligations of Israel), OJ 30.7.97 L202/85.
 4 Agreement on telecommunications procurement between the European Community and the Republic of Korea, OJ 22.11.97 L321/32, and Agreement in the form of a memorandum concerning the procurement of private telecommunications operators between the European Community and the Republic of Korea, OJ 22.11.97 L321/41, both approved on behalf of the Community by Council Decision 97/784, OJ 22.11.97 L321/30.
 5 Included in Annex 1A of the Marrakesh Agreement establishing the World Trade Organization. See World Trade Organization *The Results of the Uruguay Round of Multilateral Trade Negotiations* (1994) pp 138–162.
 6 Ibid preamble, fifth recital.
 7 See ibid.
 8 Council Resolution 90/C 10/01, OJ 16.1.90 C10/1. The different approach of the adoption of uniform standards is illustrated by the EEA Agreement, Annex II (Technical standards, testing and certification), as amended by Decision 14/97 of the EEA Joint Committee (OJ 10.7.97 L182/46) and Decision 51/97 of the EEA Joint Committee (OJ 20.11.97 L316/12).
 9 See also S Farr *Harmonisation of Technical Standards in the EC* (2nd edn, 1996) pp 97–105.
10 See the Internet at http://europa.ue.it/en/comm/dg01/mra02.html (USA) and mra04.html (Canada). See also Chapter 30 in this book.

MRA between the US and the Community specifies the conditions by which each party will accept or recognize results of conformity assessment procedures, produced by the other party's conformity assessment bodies or authorities, in assessing conformity to the importing party's requirements, as specified on a sector-specific basis, and provides for other related co-operative activities.[11] It covers conformity assessment of telecommunications equipment, electromagnetic compatibility (EMC), electrical safety, recreational craft, pharmaceutical good manufacturing practice (HMP), and medical devices.[12] The objective of the Agreement is to provide effective market access throughout the territories of the parties, with regard to conformity assessment for all covered products, and, if disputes arise, to provide for prompt settlement if possible.[13] Though it may take some time before the MRAs enter into force, the Parties may be willing to undertake some certain activities before the formal procedures are completed.[14] The EU has concluded similar agreements with Australia and New Zealand.[15]

TELECOMMUNICATIONS

Since the mid-1980s, Community law has developed rapidly in respect of telecommunications.[16] Trade in telecommunications services is affected today by a wide range of Community policies, legislation and bilateral agreements, as well as Member States' laws, GATT/WTO law,[17] and other international commitments.[18] The last three topics lie outside the scope of this book. The

11 Agreement on Mutual Recognition between the United States of America and the European Community Art 2, as to which see European Commission, Directorate General I Home Page on the Internet: http://www.europa.eu.int/en/comm/dg01/mra01.htm. See also the website of the TransAtlantic Business Dialogue at http://www.mac.doc.gov/tabd/tabd.html.

12 See ibid Sectoral Annexes.

13 Ibid Art 2.

14 To take the EU–USA MRA as an example, the Agreement will enter into force on the first day of the second month following the date on which the parties have exchanged letters confirming the completion of their respective procedures for its entry into force (see Art 21 of the MRA). In addition to the formal adoption procedures, however, the Conformity Assessment Bodies which are to participate in the MRA must be identified and listed in the annexes. The transition periods provided for in the sectoral annexes begin upon entry into force of the MRA.

15 See Commission of the European Communities, Proposal for a Council Decision on the conclusion of the Agreement on Mutual Recognition in relation to Conformity Assessment, Certificates and Markings between the European Community and Australia, and Proposal for a Council Decision on the conclusion of the Agreement on Mutual Recognition in relation to Conformity Assessment between the European Community and New Zealand, COM(1998) final (98/0126(ACC), 98/0127(ACC), Brussels, 24.3.1998.

16 See (as of 1994) Malanczuk 'Ten Years of European Telecommunications Law and Policy—A Review of the Past and of Recent Developments' (1994) 1 *Telecommunications and Space Journal* 27; and, more recently, A Blandin-Obernesser *Le régime juridique communautaire des services de télécommunications* (1996), especially pp 43–50 in respect of Community competence.

17 As to GATT/WTO law, see Malanczuk and de Vlaam 'International Trade in Telecommunications Services and the Results of the Uruguay Round of GATT' in C Scott and O Audéound (eds) *The Future of EC Telecommunications Law* (Series of Publications by the Academy of European Law in Trier, vol 19) (1996) 153–167; Bronckers and Larouche 'Telecommunications Services and the World Trade Organization' (1997) 31 *Journal of World Trade* 5.

18 As to the relationship in the telecommunications sector between Community tariff regulation and commitments in the International Telecommunications Union (ITU), see the early article by Kohnstamm 'Conflicts between International and European Network Regulation: An Analysis of Third Parties' Rights in European Community Law' (1990) 2 *Legal Issues of European Integration* 45. As to analogous issues in respect of telecommunications procurement, see Grimes 'Conflicts between EC Law and International Treaty Obligations: A Case Study of the German Telecommunications Dispute' (1994) 35 *Harvard International Law Journal* 535.

following discussion concentrates on Community legislation and bilateral agreements.[19]

The Commission's 1995 Green Paper outlined a common approach for the provision of telecommunications infrastructure. It contained a substantial discussion of the external aspects of EU telecommunications policy.[20] The main issues concern services, market access, procurement and technical standards.[1]

Two basic principles govern EC law and policy in respect of trade in telecommunications services.[2] The first is the principle of reciprocity. It has been stated in respect of open network provision,[3] terminal equipment,[4] satellite earth station equipment,[5] satellite communications[6] and mobile and personal communications.[7] The second principle is the use of multilateral and bilateral agreements, with a preference for the former. It has been stated in respect of open network provision,[8] terminal equipment,[9] and satellite earth station equipment.[10]

19 As to the general context, see, eg, Richardson 'International Trade Aspects of Telecommunications Services' (1986) 23 *Common Market Law Review* 385; Robinson, 'Globalization, Telecommunications and Trade', (1991) *Futures* (October) 801.
20 See Commission of the European Communities 'Green Paper on the Liberalization of Telecommunications Infrastructure and Cable Television Networks: Part II—A Common Approach to the Provision of Infrastructure for Telecommunications in the European Union' COM(94) 682 final, Brussels, 25.1.95, at 95–103. See also Commission of the European Communities 'External Aspects of Telecommunications' ISEC/B31/89, 29 November 1989.
1 The following paragraphs deal with services and market access. Procurement is discussed earlier in this chapter. Technical barriers to trade (standards) are discussed in relation to specific bilateral agreements.
2 See also Commission of the European Communities 'The Consultation on the Green Paper on the Liberalization of Telecommunications Infrastructure and Cable Television Networks' (Communication from the Commission to the Council and the European Parliament) COM(95) 158 final, Brussels, 3.5.95.
3 Council Directive 90/387 on the establishment of the internal market for telecommunications services through the implementation of open network provision, Preamble, twentieth recital, OJ 24.7.90 L192/1, refers to 'the increased participation of Community service producers in third country markets' and 'with a view to reaching a situation where the progressive realization of the internal market for telecommunications services will, where appropriate, be accompanied by reciprocal market opening in other countries'. As to the application of ONP to voice telephony and on universal service, see European Parliament and Council Directive 98/10, OJ 1.4.98 L101/24.
4 Council Directive 91/263 on the approximation of the laws of the Member States concerning telecommunications terminal equipment, including the mutual recognition of their conformity, Preamble, sixth recital, OJ 23.5.91 L128/1, refers to creating 'the conditions for an open and unified market', while the seventh recital refers to 'real, comparable access to third country markets for European manufacturers'. As to telecommunications terminal equipment and satellite earth station equipment, including mutual recognition of their conformity, see European Parliament and Council Directive 98/13, OJ 12.3.98 L74/1.
5 Council Directive 93/97 supplementing Directive 91/263 in respect of satellite earth station equipment, Preamble, twenty-seventh recital, refers to 'real, comparable access to third country markets, in particular the United States of America and Japan, for European manufacturers'.
6 Commission Directive 94/47 amending Directive 88/301 and Directive 90/388 in particular with regard to satellite communications, Preamble, eighteenth recital, states, with more ambiguity, that the Directive refers to ensuring that 'nationals of Member States are afforded equivalent treatment in third countries'.
7 Commission Directive 96/2 amending Directive 90/388 with regard to mobile and personal communications, Preamble, twentieth recital, OJ 26.1.96 L20/59, refers to ensuring that 'nationals of Member States are afforded equivalent treatment in third countries'.
8 Council Directive 90/387, Preamble, twenty-first recital, OJ 24.7.90 L192/1, states that this result should be achieved preferably through multilateral negotiations in the framework of GATT, it being understood that bilateral discussions between the Community and third countries may also contribute to this process.
9 Council Directive 91/263 Preamble, seventh recital, OJ 23.5.91 L128/1, uses virtually the same language as the Open Network Provision Directive.
10 Council Directive 93/97, Preamble, twenty-seventh recital, OJ 24.11.93 L290/1 also uses

Perhaps the most complete legislative expression of these principles is contained in a 1996 Commission Directive with regard to the implementation of full competition in telecommunications markets.[11] According to its terms,[12] Directive 90/388 on competition in the markets for telecommunications services does not prevent measures regarding undertakings not established in the Community from being adopted so as to ensure that nationals of Member States are afforded comparable and effective treatment in third countries.[13] Community undertakings should benefit from effective and comparable access to third country markets and enjoy a similar treatment in a third country as is offered by the Community framework to undertakings owned, or effectively controlled, by nationals of the third country concerned. World Trade Organisation telecommunications negotiations should result in a balanced and multilateral agreement, ensuring effective and comparable access for Community operators in third countries.

The EU has also begun to formulate policy guidelines regarding electronic commerce and governance of the Internet.[14]

The EU and the US have established bilateral consultations in respect of procurement and effective market access in the field of telecommunications equipment.[15] Since 1987 the Commission has conducted High Level Meetings with Japan to discuss telecommunications questions of mutual interest. The Community also has close links with the EFTA countries, which are full members of ETSI and CEN-CENELEC.[16] In the view of the Commission, telecommunications will also be an important factor in the integration of the Central and Eastern European countries.[17]

The EEA Agreement provides for the freedom to provide telecommunications services.[18] The Fourth Lomé Convention provides for co-operation in the field of communications, including satellite communications.[19]

---

virtually the same language as the Open Network Provision Directive.

11 Commission Directive 96/19 amending Directive 90/388, OJ 22.3.96 L74/13. This principle was not stated in Commission Directive 90/388 on competition in markets for telecommunications services, OJ 24.7.90 L192/10.

12 Ibid Preamble, twenty-eighth recital, second sub-paragraph.

13 Such measures must be adopted in accordance with Community law and existing international obligations: ibid.

14 See Commission of the European Communities, 'Globalization and the Information Society: The Need for Strengthened International Co-ordination' (Communication from the Commission to the Council, the European Parliament, the Economic and Social Committee, and the Committee of the Regions), COM(1998)50 final, Brussels, 4.2.1998; Commission of the European Communities, 'International Policy Issues related to Internet Governance' (Communication from the Commission to the Council), COM(1998)111 final, Brussels, 20.2.1998.

15 See Marc ' "Fortress Europe" in the Telecommunications Sector as a Consequence of "Europe 1992": Reality or Imagination' (1993) 6 *The Transnational Lawyer* 111. As to EC–USA relations in respect of satellite communications, see Malanczuk 'Ten Years of European Telecommunications Law and Policy—A Review of the Past and of Recent Developments' (1994) 1 *Telecommunications and Space Journal* 27 at 45 and sources cited there.

16 See Commission of the European Communities 'External Aspects of Telecommunications' ISEC/B31/89, 29 November 1989, at 5.

17 For an early view, see Commission of the European Communities, 'The Community's Relations with the Countries of Central and Eastern Europe: The Role of Telecommunications' (Communication from the Commission to the Council and the European Parliament), COM(90) 258 final, Brussels, 14 June 1990.

18 Council of the European Community and Commission of the European Community *Agreement on the European Economic Area* Art 36 and Annex XI (1992), as amended.

19 Lomé IV Convention as revised by the agreement signed in Mauritius on 4 November 1995, Arts 132–133, (1996) 155 *The Courier*.

It may also be noted that the European Commission has launched a project to reinforce co-operation between European and Chinese private businesses in the computer software sector. Under the aegis of this initiative, the European Software Institute and the China Software Industry Association recently signed the first Euro-Chinese Agreement in the software field.[20]

The Commission has submitted a proposal for a Council decision approving the results of the Uruguay Round in respect of trade in telecommunications services.[1] These results are the Fourth Protocol to the GATS, together with the schedule of specific commitments of the Community and the Member States, the Decision of the Council for Trade in Services on Commitments on Telecommunications Services, and the 15 February 1997 Report of the Group on Basic Telecommunications to the Council on Trade in Services.[2] They are designed to guarantee on an MFN basis the full liberalization, with certain limited exceptions, of the Community telecommunications market by 1 January 1998.[3]

TRANSPORT

Introduction

According to the EC Treaty, the activities of the Community are to include a common policy in the field of transport.[4] The basic principle is that the objectives of the Treaty shall, in matters governed the Treaty Title IV on transport, be pursued by the Member States within the framework of a common transport policy.[5] This Title applies to transport by rail, road and inland waterway.[6] However, the Council may, acting by a qualified majority, decide whether, to what extent, and by what procedure appropriate provisions may be laid down for sea and air transport.[7] Clarifying these provisions, the European Court of Justice has held that sea and air transport remain subject to the general rules of the Treaty.[8] It has also held that the competition rules apply to the transport sector.[9] However, the extent to which the Community has competence in respect of air transport, particularly regarding third countries,

---

20 See the China-Europe Software Initiative, at Internet address http://www.esi.es/Projects/chinesi.html. See also EU–CHIP (Euro Chinese Information Point) at Internet address http://www.esi.es/EU-CHIP/presentation.html. EU–CHIP is sponsored by the DG III of the European Commission and made in partnership between ERCIM (European Research Consortium for Informatics and Mathematics and ESI (European Software Institute).
1 Commission of the European Communities 'Proposal for a Council Decision concerning the conclusion on behalf of the European Community, as regards matters within its competence, of the results of the WTO negotiations on basic telecommunications services' (presented by the Commission), COM(97) 368 final, Brussels, 15.7.97.
2 See ibid Art 1.
3 See European Commission, Directorate General XIII 'Status Report on European Union Telecommunications Policy' Part V. The World Wide Dimension, Brussels, 7 May 1997, at Internet address http://www.ispo.cec.be/inforsoc/telecompolicy/en/tcstatus.htm#E10E27.
4 EC Art 3(f).
5 Ibid Art 74.
6 Ibid Art 84(1).
7 Ibid Art 84(2).
8 Case 167/73 *Commission v France* [1974] ECR 359.
9 Joined Cases 209–213/84 *Ministère public v Lucas Asjes* [1986] ECR 1425.

remains very controversial.[10] The following paragraphs discuss rail transport, road transport, inland waters, maritime transport, and air transport.

Rail

Building on earlier Community measures,[11] the Commission recommended in 1982 that national railway undertakings of the Community should co-ordinate their effects with those of interested railway undertakings from third countries in order to define a high-quality international passenger transport system.[12] Subsequently the Council invited the railway companies of the Member States to develop an active policy of co-operation, with a view to promoting international transport by rail, and in particular to consult the railway companies of relevant third countries in order to ensure co-ordinated implementation of Council guidelines.[13] In its Resolution on the development of a European high-speed rail network, the Council requested the Commission to consider how the development of the Community's relations with the EFTA countries and the Central and Eastern European countries will affect the network.[14] However the basic Council Directive on the development of the Community's railways makes no specific provision for third countries.[15] The same is true of the recent Council Resolution on the development of rail transport and combined transport.[16]

Road transport

In respect of road transport generally, general rules have been laid down regarding admission to the occupation of road haulage operation and road passenger transport operator and mutual recognition of qualifications.[17] In addition, the AETR Agreement provides for conditions to be filled by drivers, rest and

---

10 See, eg, Close 'External Relations in the Air Transport Sector: Air Transport Policy or the Common Commercial Policy' (1990) 27 *Common Market Law Review* 107; P Eeckhout *The European Internal Market and International Trade: A Legal Analysis* (1994) at 84–118; J Goh *European Air Transport: Law and Competition* (1997); Balfour 'Air Transport—A Community Success Story?' (1994) 31 CMLRev 1025 at 1041–1042; Lewis 'EC Air Transport Policy: Third Package Proposals for Liberalization' (1992) 2 *EIU* (Economist Intelligence Unit) *European Trends*, 42 at 49. See also Commission of the European Communities 'Air Transport Relations with Third Countries' (Communication from the Commission to the Council), COM(92)434 final, Brussels, 21 October 1992.

11 See Council Regulation 1017/68, OJ 23.7.68 L175/1 (competition rules); Council Regulation 1191/69, OJ 28.6.69 L156/1 (obligations inherent in the concept of public service); Council Regulation 2183/78, OJ 21.9.78 L258/1 (uniform costing principles); Council Decision 82/529, OJ 9.8.82 L234/5 (fixing of rates); Council Decision 83/418, OJ 26.8.83 L237/33 (commercial independence of railways in management of international passenger and luggage traffic).

12 Commission Recommendation 82/922 Annex, paragraph 5, OJ 31.12.82 L381/38.

13 Council Recommendation 84/646 Art 6, OJ 21.12.84 L333/63.

14 Council Resolution 91/C33/01, OJ 8.2.91 C33/1.

15 Council Directive 91/440, OJ 24.8.91 L237/25; Corrigendum, OJ 6.11.91 L305/22. Article 1, fourth indent, of this Directive provides that an aim of the Directive is to facilitate the adoption of the Community railways to the needs of the Single Market and to increase their efficiency by ensuring access to the networks of Member States for international groupings of railway undertakings and for railway undertakings engaged in the international combined transport of goods. However, Art 3, fourth indent, defines 'international groupings' as meaning any association of at least two railway undertakings established in different Member States for the purpose of providing international transport services between Member States.

16 Council Resolution 95/C169/91, OJ 5.7.95 L169/1.

17 Council Directive 96/26, OJ 23.5.96 L124/1.

driving periods, and staffing.[18] It applies to international road transport operations to and/or from third countries which are contracting parties to the Agreement, or in transit from such countries, for the whole of the journey where such operations are effected by vehicles registered in a Member State or in one of these third countries.[19] It also applies, with regard to any journey made within the Community, to transport operations to and/or from a third country effected by vehicles registered in a third country which is not a contracting party to the Agreement.[20]

In respect of road transport of passengers, non-resident carriers, established in a Member State and authorized in that State to perform the occupation of road passenger transport operator in international transport operations, are entitled temporarily to perform certain cabotage operations in another Member State without being required to have a registered office or other establishment in the latter State.[1] They must be authorized by the home Member State.[2] They are subject to certain safety regulations of the host Member State.[3] Safeguard measures may be adopted by the Commission on referral by a Member State in the event of serious disturbance of the internal transport market in a given geographical area due to or aggravated by cabotage.[4]

The Community has adopted common rules for the international carriage of passengers by coach or bus.[5] Provision is made for the requirement of a Community licence.[6] Authorization for access to the market is required except for occasional services, special regular services, and own-account transport operations.[7] These rules apply to carriage within the Community territory by carriers for hire or reward or own-account carriers established in a Member State, using vehicles registered in a Member State, and suitable for and intended to carry more than nine persons, including the driver.[8] In the event of carriage from a Member State to a third country and vice versa, they apply to the part of the journey on the territory of the Member State of picking up or setting down,

---

18 European Agreement concerning the work of crews of vehicles engaged in international road transport (AETR), OJ 8.4.78 L95/1.
19 Council Regulation 2829/77 on the bringing into force of the AETR Agreement Art 1(2), first indent, OJ 24.12.77 L334/11.
20 Ibid Art 1(2), second indent.
1 Council Regulation 2454/92 Arts 1, 2, 3, OJ 29.8.92 L251/1.
2 Ibid Art 5.
3 Ibid Art 4.
4 Ibid Art 8(1). As to the relevant procedure, see ibid Art 8(3)–(5). As to the Advisory Committee, see ibid Art 9.
5 Council Regulation 684/92, OJ 20.3.92 L74/1, as amended recently by Council Regulation 11/98, OJ 8.1.98 L4/1. As to determination of the taxable amount for VAT purposes in respect of transport services supplied in the context of cross-frontier motor-coach package tours, albeit among the Member States, the European Court of Justice has held that, in the case of the supply of cross-frontier passenger transport on an all-inclusive basis, the total consideration for the final service must, for the purposes of determining the part of the transport operation taxable in each of the Member States concerned, be allocated on a pro rata basis, having regard to the distances covered in each such State: Case C-116/96 *Reisebüro Binder GmbH v Finanzamt Stuttgart-Körperschaften* [1997] ECR I-6103.
6 Ibid Art 3a, as inserted by Council Regulation 11/98 Art 1(3), OJ 8.1.98 L4/1. The latter Regulation, Art 2, requires Member States to adopt the necessary implementing measures before 11 December 1998.
7 Ibid Art 4, as substituted by Council Regulation 11/98 Art 1(4), OJ 8.1.98 L4/1. As to definitions, see ibid Art 2(3.1) (occasional services), Art 2(1.2) (special regular services), and Art 2(3.4) (own-account transport operations).
8 Ibid Art 1(1), first sub-paragraph.

after conclusion of the necessary agreement between the Community and the third country concerned.[9] Pending the conclusion of such agreements, the rules do not affect provisions relating to such carriage contained in bilateral agreements concluded by Member States with those third countries. However, Member States are required to endeavour to adapt those agreements to ensure compliance with the principle of non-discrimination between Community carriers.[10]

The Agreement on the International Carriage of Passengers by Road by means of Occasional Coach and Bus Services (ASOR) lays down certain documentary requirements in respect of occasional coach and bus services, such as closed-door tours, between the territories of two contracting parties, or starting and finishing in the territory of the same contracting party, and in transit through the territory of another contracting party or through the territory of a non-contracting State.[11]

In respect of road haulage, any carrier established in a Member State and entitled to carry out road haulage operations in that State is permitted, under certain conditions, to carry out cabotage operations of the same kind or cabotage operations with vehicles in the same category.[12] From 1 January 1994 to 30 June 1998, these operations were to be carried out within Community cabotage quotas,[13] allocated among the Member States.[14] Cabotage authorizations are distributed by the Commission to the Member States of establishment and issued to carriers applying for them by the competent authorities of the Member State of establishment.[15] The performance of operations is subject, on a national treatment basis,[16] to host State provisions regarding rates and conditions of the transport contract, weights and dimensions of vehicles, requirements relating to carriage of certain categories of goods, driving and rest time, and value-added tax on transport services.[17] Safeguard measures may be taken in the event of serious disturbance of the national transport market in a given geographical area due to or aggravated by cabotage.[18] In addition, the Council of the EU has announced its intention gradually to develop transport relations between the Community and third countries, provided that an adequate level of harmonization of conditions of competition is being achieved between the parties involved.[19]

The Community has concluded agreements in respect of transit with Hungary[20] and with the Czech and Slovak Federal Republic,[1] agreements in the

9 Ibid Art 1(2).
10 Ibid Art 1(3).
11 Agreement on the International Carriage of Passengers by Road by means of Occasional Coach and Bus Services (ASOR), OJ 5.8.82 L230/39, concluded by Council Decision 82/505, OJ 5.8.82 L230/38. The original contracting parties were the EEC, Austria, Spain, Finland, Norway, Portugal, Sweden, Switzerland, and Turkey. As to implementation, see Council Decision 56/83, OJ 13.1.83 L10/1, and Council Decision 87/286, OJ 3.6.87 L143/32.
12 Council Regulation 3118/93 Art 1(2), OJ 12.11.93 L279/1.
13 Ibid Art 2(1), as amended by Council Regulation 3315/94 Art 1, OJ 31.12.94 L350/9.
14 As to the allocation, see ibid Art 2(3), as so amended.
15 Ibid Art 3(2).
16 Ibid Art 6(3).
17 Ibid Art 6(1).
18 Ibid Art 7.
19 See Council Resolution 94/C309/03 on road freight transport in the Single European Market, OJ 5.11.94 C309/4.
20 See Council Decision 92/609, OJ 31.12.92 L407/47 and the attached Agreement, OJ 31.12.94 L407/49. The Europe Agreement with Hungary provides for the negotiation of special transport agreements in respect of air transport and inland transport: Europe Agreement with Hungary Art 57(3).
1 See Council Decision 92/610, OJ 31.12.92 L407/56, and the attached Agreement, OJ 31.12.92 L407/57.

field of transport with Slovenia,[2] and the former Yugoslav Republic of Macedonia,[3] an agreement on the carriage of goods by road and rail with Switzerland,[4] and an agreement on transit traffic with Switzerland.[5]

The Europe Agreements, as exemplified by the agreement with Hungary, provide for the Parties to undertake to apply effectively the principle of unrestricted access to the market and traffic on a commercial basis in respect of international maritime transport.[6]

Inland waterways

Without prejudice to its obligations under the Revised Convention on the Navigation of the Rhine,[7] the Community has laid down technical requirements for inland waterway vessels.[8] Pending the conclusion of agreements on the mutual recognition of navigability certificates between the Community and third countries, Member States may recognize the navigability certificates of vessels from third countries and, where appropriate, issue Community certificates or supplementary Community certificates to vessels from third countries.[9] Common rules have been laid down in respect of occupation of carrier of goods by waterway and on mutual recognition of qualifications.[10]

Maritime transport

The Member States, though not the Community, are parties to numerous international conventions in respect of shipping, notably the 1974 United Nations Convention on a Code of Conduct for Liner Conferences.[11] In 1979 a Council

2 See Council Decision 93/409, and the attached Agreement, OJ 29.7.93 L189/161. An Additional Protocol to the Agreement was concluded in 1997: OJ 23.12.97 L351/63, approved on behalf of the Community by Council Decision 97/863, OJ 23.12.97 L351/62.

3 OJ 18.12.97 L348/169, approved on behalf of the Community by Council Decision 97/832, OJ 18.12.97 L348/169.

4 See Council Decision 92/578, OJ 21.12.92 L373/26, and the attached Agreement, OJ 21.12.92 L373/28.

5 Agreement between the European Economic Community and the Swiss Confederation on the Carriage of Goods by Road and Rail, OJ 21.12.92 L373/29, approved by Council Decision 92/578, OJ 21.12.92 L373/26. As to administrative arrangements, see Commission Decision 93/117, OJ 25.2.93 L47/27.

6 Europe Agreement establishing an association between the European Communities and their Member States, of the one part, and the Republic of Hungary, of the other part, Art 56, OJ 31.12.93 L347/2, approved by Council and Commission Decision 93/742, OJ 31.12.93 L347/2. This Article also provides for more specific obligations.

7 Convention for Rhine Navigation, concluded 17 October 1868, Mannheim,138 CTS, 59 BFSP, 5 Peaslee 151, and Additional Protocols. As to access of EC Member States, see Council Regulation 2919/85, OJ 22.10.85 L280/4. See also Opinion 1/76 *Laying-Up Fund* [1977] ECR 741.

8 Council Directive 82/714, OJ 28.10.82 L301/1.

9 Ibid Art 18, which also provides that the Community certificates must be issued in accordance with this Directive.

10 Council Regulation 87/540, OJ 12.11.87 L322/20.

11 UN Doc TD/Code 11/Rev 1 and Corr 1; 13 ILM 917. As to other conventions, see Council Recommendation 77/584, OJ 19.7.78, OJ 194/17 (various conventions on safety in shipping); Council Regulation 79/114, OJ 8.2.79 L33/31 (1978 International Convention on standards of training, certification and watchkeeping for seafarers); Council Recommendation 79/487, OJ 22.5.79 L125/18 (International Convention for Safe Containers (CSC)); Council Recommendation 83/419, OJ 26.8.83 L237/34 (1979 International Convention on Maritime Search and Rescue (SAR)). As to the implications of these conventions for the

Regulation laid down the principles which were to govern Member States becoming parties to this Code.[12] It provided, inter alia, that the Code was not to be applied among Member States and, subject to reciprocity, between Member States and other OECD countries.[13] Other countries were to participate subject to reciprocity defined at governmental or shipowners' level.[14]

In the late 1970s the Community established a consultation procedure in respect of relations between Member States and third countries in the field of cargo shipping.[15] Provision was subsequently made for the possibility of countermeasures, forming part of national legislation, to be applied jointly by the Member States in relation with a third country or group of third countries.[16] Member States were required, following consultation, to endeavour to concert any countermeasures they may take,[17] and the Council, acting unanimously, could decide on the joint application by Member States of appropriate countermeasures forming part of their national legislation,[18] but Member States remained free to apply national countermeasures unilaterally.[19]

A package of measures was enacted in late 1986.[20] The principle of freedom to provide services was applied to maritime transport between Member States and between Member States and third countries.[1] It provided, inter alia, for the prohibition of cargo-sharing in future agreements with third countries, save in exceptional circumstances,[2] and for the possibility of Community action when a Member State's nationals or shipping companies were experiencing, or were threatened by, a situation where they did not have an effective opportunity to ply for trade to and from a particular third country.[3]

---

transfer of ships from one register to another within the Community, see Council Regulation 613/91, OJ 15.3.91 L68/1. As to relations between the Member States and the International Association of Lighthouse Authorities, see Council Decision 92/143, OJ 4.3.92 L59/17. As to implementation of IMO Resolution A.747(18) on application of tonnage measurement of ballast spaces in segregated ballast oil tankers, see Council Regulation 2978/94, OJ 12.12.94 L319/1. As to application of the International Safety Management (ISM) Code to roll-on/roll-off passenger ferries, see Council Regulation 3051/95, OJ 30.12.95 L320/14. As to uniform application of international legal instruments in respect of marine equipment, see Council Directive 96/98, OJ 17.2.97 L46/25. As to general background, see Cafruny 'The Political Economy of International Shipping: Europe versus America' (1985) 39 *International Organization* 79.

12 Council Regulation 954/79, OJ 17.5.79 L121/1. See also Commission Opinion 81/326, OJ 15.5.81 L129/68 (Netherlands); Commission Opinion 82/24, OJ 15.1.82 L10/29 (Germany); Commission Opinion 82/154, OJ 9.3.82 L65/28 (Denmark); Commission Opinion 82/210, OJ 15.4.82 L99/39 (Belgium); Commission Opinion 82/508, OJ 5.8.82 L229/28 (UK).

13 Ibid Art 4(4).

14 Ibid Art 4(1).

15 Council Decision 77/587, OJ 17.9.77 L239/23.

16 Council Decision 78/774 Art 4, OJ 21.9.78 L258/35.

17 Council Decision 83/573 Art 2(1), OJ 28.11.93 L332/37.

18 Ibid Art 2(2).

19 Ibid Art 4.

20 As to the implications of this package for other organizations in the maritime transport sector, see Fournasier 'External Competence of the Community in Maritime Transport' (1989) 91 *Diritto Marittimo* 31.

1 Council Regulation 4055/86, OJ 31.12.86 L378/1, as amended.

2 Ibid Art 5. As to such an arrangement, see Council Decision 87/475 relating to maritime transport between Italy and Algeria, OJ 25.9.87 L272/37, and Case 355/87 *Commission v Council* [1989] ECR 1517. See also Charles-Le Bihan and Lebullenger 'Common Maritime Transport Policy: Bilateral Agreements and Freedom to Provide Services' (1989) 9 *Yearbook of European Law* 209.

3 Ibid Art 6. In certain circumstances, such action could include the negotiation and conclusion of cargo-sharing arrangements.

A second measure laid down rules for the application of EC Arts 85 and 86 to maritime transport.[4] Assuming certain conditions are satisfied, technical agreements,[5] agreements between carriers concerning the operation of scheduled maritime transport services,[6] and agreements between transport users and conferences concerning the use of scheduled maritime transport services[7] are exempted from the application of Art 85(1). In cases of certain conflicts between these provisions and laws, regulations or administrative action of third countries, the Commission has the power to undertake consultations[8] and, if necessary, to make recommendations to the Council for a mandate to open negotiations.[9]

A third measure established a procedure to be used when action by a third country or its agents restricts, or threatens to restrict, free access by shipping companies of Member States, or by ships registered in Member States, to the transport of liner cargoes, bulk cargoes, passengers, or persons or goods to or between offshore installations.[10] Co-ordinated action may be requested by a Member State[11] to the Commission, which in turn makes a recommendation to the Council for specific co-ordinated action.[12] The Council is required to take into account external trade policy considerations, as well as the port interests and shipping policy considerations of the Member States concerned.[13] Co-ordinated action may consist of diplomatic representations or specified countermeasures, including the obligation to obtain a permit, the imposition of a quota, and the imposition of taxes or duties.[14] If the Council does not act within a specified time, the Member States may take national measures.[15] In cases of urgency, such national measures may be taken on a provisional basis.[16] The procedure may also be applied when action by a third country or its agents restricts, or threatens to restrict, the access of shipping companies of another OCED country where, on a basis of reciprocity, it has been agreed between that country and the Community to resort to co-ordinated resistance in the case of restriction of access to cargo.[17]

Community shipowners also enjoy the freedom to provide maritime transport services within a Member State (maritime cabotage), on condition that the ships are registered in, and fly the flag of, a Member State and comply with all

---

4 Council Regulation 4056/86, OJ 31.12.86 L378/4.
5 Ibid Art 2.
6 Ibid Art 3.
7 Ibid Art 6.
8 Ibid Art 9(1).
9 Ibid Art 9(2), first sub-paragraph. The Commission is to conduct these negotiations in consultation with an Advisory Committee: ibid Art 9(2), second sub-paragraph.
10 Council Regulation 4058/86, OJ 31.12.86 L378/21.
11 Ibid Art 3, first sub-paragraph.
12 Ibid Art 3, second sub-paragraph. As to voting procedure in the Council, see ibid Art 3, third sub-paragraph.
13 Ibid Art 3, fourth sub-paragraph.
14 Ibid Art 4(1). Diplomatic representations must be made before countermeasrues are taken: ibid Art 4(2), first paragraph. Countermeasures are without prejudice to the international legal obligations of the EC and the Member States, must take into consideration all the interests concerned, and shall neither directly nor indirectly lead to deflection of trade within the Community: ibid Art 4(2), second sub-paragraph. As to the factors which must be specified by the Council when deciding on countermeasures, see ibid Art 5.
15 Ibid Art 6(1).
16 Ibid Art 6(2). Any national measures must be notified to the Commission and the other Member States: ibid Art 6(3).
17 Ibid Art 8.

the conditions for carrying cabotage within that Member State.[18] For this purpose, 'Community shipowner' is not restricted to nationals of a Member State, established in a Member State in accordance with the legislation of that Member State and pursuing shipping activities.[19] It also includes two other categories. The first category consists of shipping companies established in accordance with the legislation of a Member State and whose principal place of business is situated, and effective control exercised, in a Member State.[20] The second category consists of nationals of a Member State establishing outside the Community, or shipping companies established outside the Community and controlled by nationals of a Member State, if their ships are registered in and fly the flag of a Member State in accordance with its legislation.[1]

The Community has also adopted certain common safety and environmental standards. Minimum safety requirements apply, with certain exceptions, to all vessels bound for or leaving Community ports and carrying dangerous or polluting goods.[2] Common criteria and harmonized procedures on inspection and detention, based on the principle of port State control, have been adopted in respect of vessels using Community ports and sailing in the waters under the jurisdiction of the Member States, in order to ensure more effective enforcement of international standards for ship safety, pollution prevention, and shipboard living and working conditions.[3]

Common rules and standards also apply for ship inspection and survey organizations and for relevant activities of maritime organizations in order to ensure compliance with international conventions on safety at sea and prevention of maritime pollution, while furthering the objective of freedom to provide services.[4] In order for a Member State to accept that an organization located in a third country is to carry out inspection and survey of ships or issue of certificates and exemption certificates, it may request that the third country grant a reciprocal recognition for those recognized inspection organizations which are located in the Community.[5] In exercising their inspection rights and obligations as port states, Member States must ensure that ships flying a third country flag are not treated more favourably than ships entitled to fly the flag of a Member State.[6]

Minimum standards apply to the level of training of seafarers.[7] Member States are required to ensure that on board all ships flying the flag of a Member State, and on all passenger ships starting and/or finishing a voyage in a Member State port, there are at any time means in place for effective oral communication related to safety, as well as adequate means of communication

---

18 Council Regulation 3577/92 Art 1, OJ 12.12.92 L364/7. As to the 1993 request for Spain for safeguard measures, see Commission Decision 93/125, OJ 27.2.93 L49/88 and Commission Decision 93/396, OJ 16.7.93 L173/33.
19 Ibid Art 2(2)(a).
20 Ibid Art 2(2)(b).
 1 Ibid Art 2(2)(c).
 2 Council Directive 93/75, OJ 5.10.93 L247/19, as amended by Commission Directive 96/39, OJ 7.8.96 L196/7.
 3 Council Directive 95/21, OJ 7.7.95 L157/1. As to a common model for an identity card for inspectors, see Commission Directive 96/40, OJ 7.8.96 L196/8.
 4 Council Directive 94/57, OJ 12.12.94 L319/20, in particular Art 1.
 5 Ibid Art 5(3).
 6 Ibid Art 12(1)(a).
 7 Council Directive 94/58, OJ 12.12.94 L319/28. Warships, fishing vessels, pleasure yachts not engaged in trade, and wooden ships of primitive build are exempted: see ibid Art 1. These requirements apply in conjunction with the 1978 IMO Convention on Standards of Training, Certification and Watchkeeping for Seafarers (STCW Convention): ibid Art 2.

between ship and shore, either in a common language or in the language of the shore-based authorities.[8] They are also required to ensure that on board passenger ships, nominated personnel to assist passengers in cases of emergency are readily identifiable and have sufficient communication skills, taking into account an appropriate and adequate combination of any of several criteria.[9] The criteria include inter alia the language or languages appropriate to the principal nationalities of passengers carried on a particular route;[10] the likelihood that an ability to use elementary English vocabulary for basic instructions can provide a means of communicating with a passenger in need of assistance whether or not the passenger and crew member share a common language;[11] the extent to which complete safety instructions have been provided to passengers in their native language or languages;[12] and the languages in which emergency announcements may be broadcast.[13]

Special provisions apply to the surveillance and control of transfrontier traffic in hazardous waste.[14]

Air transport

Civil air transport between the Community and third countries is governed mainly by the Convention on International Civil Aviation (the Chicago Convention) and bilateral agreements between Member States and third countries. In 1979 the Community established a consultation procedure on relations between Member States and third countries in the field of air transport and on action relating to such matters within international organizations.[15]

The Community has however enacted rules in respect of licensing of air carriers which apply to all carriers established in the Community.[16] Similarly, common rules on access for Community air carriers to intra-Community routes for scheduled and non-scheduled air services apply to any air carrier with a valid operating licence granted by a Member State.[17] This category is more narrow than it appears, however, because the licence is to be granted in accordance with Council Regulation 2407/92, OJ 24.8.92 L240/1.[18] The latter Regulation provides that no undertaking shall be granted an operating licence by a Member State unless, inter alia, its principal place of business and, if any, its registered office are located in that Member State.[19] In addition, the undertaking must be owned and continue to be owned directly or through majority ownership by Member States and/or nationals of Member States, and must at all times be effectively controlled by such States or such nationals.[20] Alternatively,

---

8 Ibid Art 8(1). See also ibid Art 8(3) for analogous requirements regarding oil, chemical and liquified gas tankers.
9 Ibid Art 8(2).
10 Ibid Art 8(2)(a).
11 Ibid Art 8(2)(b).
12 Ibid Art 8(2)(d).
13 Ibid Art 8(2)(e).
14 See Council Directive 84/631, OJ 12.12.84 L326/31, as amended. See also Mensbrugghe 'Les frontières maritime de la CEE (Observations à propos de la Directive 84/361 sur les transferts transfrontaliers de déchets dangereux) (1989) 328 *Revue du Marché Commun* 360.
15 Council Decision 80/50, OJ 24.1.80 L18/24. The Decision was taken on 20 December 1979.
16 Council Regulation 2407/92, OJ 24.8.92 L240/1.
17 Council Regulation 2408/92 Art 2(b), OJ 24.8.92 L240/7.
18 Ibid.
19 Council Regulation 2407/92 Art 4(1), OJ 24.8.92 L240/1.
20 Ibid Art 4(2). See also Commission Decision 95/404 (Swissair/Sabena), OJ 7.10.95 L239/19.

a licence may be granted to an air carrier which, at the time of adoption of the Regulation, did not meet these conditions but met either one of two other conditions.[1] The first was to have its central administration and place of business in the Community and have been providing scheduled or non-scheduled air services in the Community during the 12 months prior to adoption of the Regulation.[2] The second was to have been providing scheduled air services between Member States on the basis of third and fourth-freedom traffic rights during the 12 months prior to adoption of the Regulation.[3] The same conditions apply in respect of the setting of fares and rates[4] and the operation of air cargo services between Member States.[5]

The same definition of a 'Community air carrier' applies in respect of access to the allocation of slots in third countries.[6] Appropriate action, including the suspension wholly or partially of certain obligations, may be taken whenever it appears that a third country, with respect to the allocation of slots, does not grant Community air carriers treatment comparable to that granted by Member States to carriers from that country,[7] or does not grant Community air carriers *de facto* national treatment,[8] or grants air carriers from third countries more favourable treatment than Community air carriers.[9] Member States are to inform the Commission of any serious difficulties encountered, in law or in fact, by Community air carriers in obtaining slots at airports in third countries.[10]

Reciprocity provisions also apply in respect of access to the groundhandling market at Community airports. A Member State may suspend wholly or partially certain obligations, including access to airport installations, in respect of suppliers of groundhandling services and airport users from a third country, in any of three situations.[11] The first situation occurs whenever it appears that a third country, with respect to access to the groundhandling[12] or self-handling market,[13] does not, *de jure* or *de facto*, grant suppliers of groundhandling services and self-handling airport users from a Member State treatment comparable to that granted by Member States to suppliers of groundhandling services and

---

1 See Council Regulation 2408/92 Art 15, OJ 24.8.92 L240/8, and Council Regulation 2343/90 Art 2(e)(ii), OJ 11.8.90 L217/8.
2 Council Regulation 2343/90 Art 2(e)(ii)(1), OJ 11.8.90 L217/8.
3 Ibid Art 2(e)(ii)(2).
4 See Council Regulation 2409/92, OJ 24.8.92 L240/15, in particular Arts 1, 2(h).
5 See Council Regulation 294/91, OJ 8.2.91 L36/1, in particular Arts 1, 2(b). This Regulation cannot however prevent Member States from concluding between themselves certain more flexible arrangements. Nor can be it be used to make existing rights and arrangements in respect of market access, implementing capacity, and operating flexibility more restrictive. See ibid Art 10(1) and (2), respectively.
6 See Council Regulation 95/93, OJ 22.1.93 L14/1, in particular Art 2(e).
7 Ibid Art 12(1)(a).
8 Ibid Art 12(1)(b).
9 Ibid Art 12(1)(c).
10 Ibid Art 12(2).
11 Council Directive 96/67 Art 20, OJ 25.10.96 L272/36. These provisions are without prejudice to the international obligations of the Community: ibid Art 20(1). Any action must also be taken in accordance with Community law: ibid Art 20(2).
12 'Groundhandling' means certain services provided to airport users at airpots: ibid Art 2(e). As to the services, see ibid Annex.
13 'Self-handling' means a situation in which an airport user directly provides for itself one or more categories of groundhandling services and concludes no contract of any description with a third party for the provision of such services. Among themselves, airport users are not deemed to be third parties where one holds a majority holding in the other, or a single body has a majority holding in each: ibid Art 2(f).

self-handling airport users from that country.[14] The second situation occurs whenever it appears that the third country does not, *de jure* or *de facto*, grant suppliers of groundhandling services and self-handling airport users from a Member State national treatment.[15] The third situation occurs whenever it appears that a third country grants suppliers of groundhandling services and self-handling airport users from other third countries more favourable treatment than suppliers of groundhandling services and self-handling airport users from a Member State.[16] The Member State concerned is required to inform the Commission of any withdrawal or suspension of rights or obligations.[17]

Obligations of reciprocity are also part of Community rules in respect of computerized reservations systems (CRS).[18] For example, the obligation of a system vendor to provide the opportunity to participate in distribution facilities on an equal and non-discriminatory basis does not apply in respect of a parent carrier of a third country to the extent that its CRS does not conform to the Community Regulation or does not offer Community air carriers equivalent treatment to that provided under the Community Regulation.[19] Similar provisions apply in respect of the obligations of parent and participating carriers to avoid linking the use of a specific CRS with the receipt of a commission or other incentive.[20] Respect for analogous provisions regarding reciprocity is required in order for agreements between undertakings in respect of CRS to qualify for the bloc exemption from Art 85(1)EC.[1]

A directive has been enacted on mutual acceptance among Member States of personnel licences issued by Member States for the exercise of functions in civil aviation.[2] However, when a Member State, for reasons of equivalence, issues a licence on the basis of a licence issued by a third country, together with the privileges and certificates pertaining thereto, this must be recorded in the licence, and other Member States are not obliged to accept such a licence.[3]

Certain developing countries are exempt from Community restrictions on the operation of subsonic jet aeroplanes operating from airports in the Community.[4]

Recently the Commission submitted a proposal to the Council for a directive establishing a safety assessment of third countries' aircraft using Community airports.[5] It would require Member States to collect certain information[6] and to proceed to ramp inspections of aircraft suspected of non-compliance with

14 Ibid Art 20(1)(a).
15 Ibid Art 20(1)(b).
16 Ibid Art 20(1)(c).
17 Ibid Art 20(2).
18 Council Regulation 2299/89 Art 7, OJ 29.7.89 L220/1.
19 Ibid Art 7(1).
20 Ibid Art 7(2).
 1 See Council Regulation 3976/87 Art 2(2), fifth indent, OJ 31.12.87 L374/9; Commission Regulation 3652/93 Art 9, OJ 31.12.93 L333/37.
 2 Council Directive 91/670, OJ 31.12.91 L373/21.
 3 Ibid Art 6.
 4 Council Directive 92/14, OJ 23.3.92 L76/21, as amended by Council Directive 98/20, OJ 7.4.98 L107/4. The exemption applies to certain listed airplanes which were on the register of certain listed developing countries in the reference year and continue to be operated by natural or legal persons established in those countries. As to the aeroplanes and countries, see ibid Annex.
 5 Commission of the European Communities, Proposal for a Council Directive establishing a safety assessment of third countries aircraft using Community airports, COM(97) 55 final, 97/0039 (SYN), Brussels, 17.2.1997.
 6 See ibid Art 4.

international safety standards.[7] Member States would be required to ground dangerous aircraft,[8] subject to certain procedural guarantees.[9] The proposed directive is not to affect Member States' right, with due regard to Community law, to carry out inspection of any aircraft landing at its airports.[10]

In 1992 the Community concluded an agreement on trade in large civil aircraft with the USA.[11] It has also concluded an agreement on civil aviation with Norway.[12]

Bilateral agreements

Certain bilateral agreements contain provisions applying to several modes of transport. The EEA Agreement covers rail, road and inland waterway transport.[13] It contains specific provisions on various modes of transport, including maritime transport.[14] In respect of modes of transport not covered by these specific provisions, the general principle is that legal provisions of an EC Member State or an EFTA State shall not be made less favourable in their direct or indirect effect on carriers of other States as compared with carriers which are nationals or that State.[15] In addition, in the case of carriage within the territory of the Contracting Parties, there shall be no discrimination which takes the form of carriers charging different rates and imposing different conditions for the carriage of the same goods over the same transport links on grounds of country of origin or of destination of the goods in question.[16]

The Fourth Lomé Convention provides for co-operation aimed at the development of road transport, railways, port installations and shipping, transport by domestic waterways, and air transport.[17] Its aims include greater complementarity of transport systems at national, regional, and international level.[18] In respect of air transport in particular, the objectives are to promote, inter alia, the implementation of the International Civil Aviation Organization air navigation plan and the application of international operating standards.[19] In respect of shipping, the objective of co-operation is to ensure harmonious development of efficient and reliable shipping services on economically

7 See ibid Art 5.
8 Ibid Art 8(1).
9 See ibid Arts 7, 8(5).
10 Ibid Art 2, third sub-paragraph.
11 Agreement between the European Economic Community and the Government of the United States of America concerning the application of the GATT Agreement on Trade in Civil Aircraft on trade in large civil aircraft, OJ 17.10.92 L301/32. As it concerns subsidies and trade in goods, it is discussed in Chapter 30 in this book.
12 See the Agreement between the EEC, Norway and Sweden, concluded prior to Swedish accession: Council Decision 92/384, OJ 18.7.92 L200/20, and the attached agreement, OJ 18.7.92 L200/21; as amended by Decision of the Joint Committee, OJ 23.8.93 L212/19, which was approved by Council Decision 93/453, OJ 23.8.93 L212/17.
13 Council of the European Communities and Commission of the European Communities *Agreement on the European Economic Area* Art 47(1).
14 Ibid Art 47(2), Annex XIII (1992).
15 Ibid Art 48(1). Deviations must be notified to the EFTA Joint Committee, and Contracting Parties not accepting the deviation are entitled to take corresponding countermeasures: ibid Art 48(2).
16 Ibid Art 50(1).
17 Lomé IV Convention as revised by the agreement signed in Mauritius on 4 November 1995, Art 123(1), (1996) 155 *The Courier*.
18 Ibid Art 123(2)(c).
19 Ibid Art 125(2).

satisfactory terms by facilitating the active participation of all parties according to the principle of unrestricted access to the trade on a commercial basis.[20] The Parties underline the importance of the UN Convention on a Code of Conduct for Liner Conferences[1] and its ratification instruments.[2] Consequently, they agree, when ratifying the Code, on taking prompt measures for its implementation at national level, in conformity with its scope and provisions.[3] The parties are not to prevent non-Conference lines from operating in competition with a Conference line as long as they comply with the principle of fair competition on a commercial basis.[4] Attention is to be given to encouraging the efficient shipment of cargoes at economically and commercially meaningful rates and to the aspirations of ACP States for greater participation in such international shipping services, notably bulk cargo shipping, and the parties agree that competitive access to the trade shall not be impaired.[5]

THE LOMÉ CONVENTION

The Fourth Lomé Convention[6] is treated separately because, in addition to its specific provisions on capital movements and transport,[7] it contains a number of general provisions in respect of trade in services. It recognizes the importance of services generally in the formulation of development policies and the need to increase co-operation between the Community and the ACP States in this sphere.[8] Particular attention is to be paid to services that support economic development, tourism, and transport, communications and information technology,[9] in particular those aspects oriented towards trade.[10] In respect of trade in services in particular, the parties recognize its importance[11] and also that the long-term aim in this area is a progressive liberalization, with due respect for national policy objectives, and taking due account of the level of development of ACP States.[12] In respect of qualification and treatment of business entities with regard to establishment and services, the parties have agreed to the principle of non-discrimination.[13] However, if such treatment cannot be provided by a Member State or an ACP State for a given activity, the ACP State or the Member State, as the case may be, shall not be bound to accord such treatment to the activity to the nationals and companies or firms of the State concerned.[14]

20 Ibid Art 126(2).
1 UN Doc TD/Code 11/Rev 1 and Corr 1; 13 ILM 917.
2 Lomé IV Convention as revised by the agreement signed in Mauritius on 4 November 1995, Art 127(1), (1996) 155 *The Courier*.
3 Ibid Art 127(2), which also provides that the Community shall assist ACP States to apply the relevant provisions of the Code.
4 Ibid Art 127(3).
5 Ibid Art 128. As to financial and technical assistance for shipping, see ibid Art 129.
6 Lomé IV Convention, as revised by the agreement signed in Mauritius on 4 November 1995, (1996) 155 *The Courier*.
7 As to which, see above.
8 Lomé IV Convention, as revised by the agreement signed in Mauritius on 4 November 1995, Art 114(1), (1996) 155 *The Courier*.
9 Ibid Art 115(1).
10 See ibid Art 117, first indent, Art 118, Art 120(1),(2), Art 121, Art 123, Arts 127–129, and Arts 135–138.
11 See ibid Art 185(1).
12 Ibid Art 185(2). Future negotiations are to build on the results of the Uruguay Round multilateral trade talks: see ibid Art 185(3), (4), (5).
13 Ibid Art 274(1).
14 Ibid Art 274(1).

Part IV

Preferential Arrangements and
Bilateral Agreements

Chapter 22

Generalized Scheme of Preferences (GSP)

INTRODUCTION

This chapter and the remaining chapters in Part IV consider two different types of trading arrangements: the Generalized Scheme of Preferences (GSP), on the one hand, and bilateral trade-related agreements, on the other hand. By way of introduction, however, two general points need to be made.

First, the legal framework of the Community's trade relations with any specific country is usually composed of autonomous measures[1] and conventional measures.[2] The GSP is an example of an autonomous measure, while the bilateral agreements are conventional measures. Most of Part IV is devoted to bilateral agreements. However, the reader should keep in mind that they are only part of the legal framework of trade between the Community and any specific country. In order to understand the entire spectrum of legal relations between the Community and any single country, it is necessary to consider these conventional measures together with autonomous measures of the Common Commercial Policy and other related acts.[3]

Second, a bilateral agreement between the Community and a specific country often forms part of a broader pattern of Community policy in respect of a given

---

1 That is, measures taken by the Community which apply to one or more, sometimes all, of its trading partners, subject to any exceptions, derogations, preferences, etc, granted by agreements, whether bilateral or multilateral. Such measures include the basic customs and commercial policy regulations and the Generalized Scheme of Preferences. The autonomous measures which apply to many or all of the Community's trading partners are dealt with in Parts I–III of this book.

2 That is, based on agreements, of which bilateral agreements are a subset in a set that also includes multilateral agreements. For the purposes of co-ordination of Community policy, and also from the standpoint of any third country, account must also be taken of treaties and trade agreements concluded by the EU Member States. Such agreements lie outside the scope of this book. However, the provisions governing matters covered by the Common Commercial Policy contained in friendship, trade and navigation treaties, and trade agreements concluded between Member States and third countries, may be automatically renewed or maintained in force up to 30 April 2001, as regards those areas not covered by agreements between the Community and the third countries concerned and in so far as the provisions are compatible with common policies: see Council Decision 97/351, OJ 10.6.97 L151/24.

3 The most important autonomous measure is the Community Customs Code, as to which see Chapters 1–7 in this book. Also important are relevant international commodity agreements or other international legal instruments, in particular those concerning the WTO and GATT. However, within the Community system bilateral agreements take precedence over autonomous measures. For an example in respect of textiles, see Council Regulation 3030/93 on common rules for imports of certain textile products from third countries, Art 20, OJ 8.11.93 L275/1.

economic sector or geo-political region.[4] For example, agreements in respect of textiles have usually been concluded by the Community with a number of countries at the same time.[5] This is true also of other sectors and other types of acts. This chronological, often geo-political development of Community policy is difficult to grasp if one concentrates on relations between the Community and a particular country, but it should be kept in mind. Nevertheless this section focuses on specific regions or countries, because such an approach is likely to be more useful to the legal adviser who is usually confronted with country-specific or region-specific problems.

EVOLUTION OF THE GENERALIZED SCHEME OF PREFERENCES (GSP)

Originally sponsored by the United Nations Conference on Trade and Development (UNCTAD), the GSP has been implemented by the Community since 1971.[6] It extends unilateral tariff preferences to developing countries.[7] Between 1971 and 1994 the Community renewed the GSP on an annual basis. It carried out a comprehensive ten-year review of the GSP in 1980[8] and a more limited mid-term review in 1985.[9] A second ten-year review, originally scheduled for 1990, was postponed pending conclusion of the Uruguay Round. Following the completion of this review, a new GSP was adopted on 19 December 1994.[10] It entered into force on 1 January 1995.[11] It applies for a period of four years in the case of industrial products.[12] For agricultural products, the GSP previously in force was extended for one year in 1995[13] and again until June 1996[14] when

---

4 As well as policies of the third country concerned.
5 For example, see Council Decision 92/625, OJ 31.12.92 L410/1, which provided for the provisional application of Community agreements on trade in textiles with 26 countries. The same pattern in respect of other agreements is clearly revealed by a glance at the *Directory of Community Legislation in Force and Other Acts of the Community Institutions*, of which the most recent edition at the time of writing was the 31st edn (volume as at 1 June 1998).
6 The GSP falls within the Community's Common Commercial Policy: Case 45/86 *Commission v Council* [1987] ECR 1493.
7 The GSP consists essentially in the suspension of the customs duties set out in the CCT: Case 51/87 *Commission v Council* [1988] ECR 5459.
8 See Council Regulation 3322/80, OJ 29.12.80 L354/114.
9 See Council Regulation 3599/85, OJ 30.12.85 L352/1.
10 As to industrial products including textiles, see Council Regulation 3281/94, OJ 31.12.94 L348/1; as to agricultural products, see Council Regulation 3283/94, OJ 31.12.94 L348/57. As to background, main provisions and comparison with the previous GSP, see Waer and Driessen 'The New European Union Generalized System of Preferences: A Workable Compromise in the EU—but a Better Deal for the Developing Countries?' (1995) 29 JWT 97. The GSP was adopted on the basis of EC Art 113 alone, rather than jointly on Arts 113 and 130u; the latter basis would have necessitated use of the co-decision procedure provided by EC Art 189c. As to the obligation to consult the European Parliament, see Case C-65/93 *European Parliament v Council* [1995] ECR I-643. As to rules of origin, see Commission Regulation 2454/93, Part I, Title IV, Chapter 2, Section I (OJ 11.10.93 L253/1), as substituted by Commission Regulation 3254/94 Art 1, OJ 31.12.94 L346/1.
11 The Regulation was published on 17 January 1995 but the OJ was antedated. As to the compatibility of such antedated publication with Community law, see Waer and Driessen op cit at 121. In respect of a similar problem concerning the 1993 GSP Regulation, see Case C-65/93 *European Parliament v Council* [1995] ECR I-643, paragraph 29.
12 That is, until 31 December 1998: Council Regulation 3281/94 Arts 1(2), 21, OJ 31.12.94 L348/1.
13 Council Regulation 3085/95, OJ 30.12.95 L326/10.
14 Council Regulation 3085/95, OJ 30.12.95 L326/10.

a multiannual scheme was established for the period from 1 July 1996 to 30 June 1999.[15]

The GSP system is managed by the Commission in conjunction with the Committee for the Management of Generalized Preferences.[16]

INDUSTRIAL PRODUCTS

The GSP for industrial products applies to products falling within Chapters 25 to 97 of the CCT, with the exception of specified products,[17] originating in certain beneficiary countries.[18] The preferential duties for these imports are established according to the principle of tariff modulation.[19] Imported products are divided into four categories: non-sensitive,[20] semi-sensitive,[1] sensitive,[2] and very sensitive.[3] Different preferential duties apply to each product category. CCT duties are suspended for non-sensitive products;[4] 35 per cent of the CCT duty is applied to semi-sensitive products;[5] 70 per cent of the CCT duty is applied to sensitive products;[6] and 85 per cent of the CCT duty is applied to very sensitive products.[7] These modulated preferential duties apply to all beneficiary countries, with the exception of the least developed countries[8] and specified Latin American countries conducting a campaign to combat drugs.[9]

The principle of tariff modulation is complemented by a graduation mechanism, by which certain sectors in certain countries may be excluded from preferences.[10] It applies to specified combinations of countries and sectors which meet

15 Council Regulation 1256/96, OJ 29.6.96 L160/1, as adapted by Commission Regulation 380/98, OJ 19.2.98 L48/20. Although this regulation came into force on 1 July 1996, it applies only from 1 January 1997, and the previous scheme remains in force for the period from 1 July to 31 December 1996: see ibid Art 19. As to a long-term strategy, see Commission of the European Communities, 'Improving Market Access for Least Developed Countries' (Communication from the Commission), COM(97)156 final, Brussels, 16.4.97.
16 As to the Committee, see Council Regulation 3281/94 Arts 17–19, OJ 31.12.94 L348/1.
17 Council Regulation 3281/94 Art 1(2), OJ 31.12.94 L348/1. The included products are listed in Annex I, as adapted by Commission Regulation 380/98, OJ 19.2.98 L48/20. The excluded products are listed in Annex IX. Note that ferro-alloys have been removed from the list of excluded products and added to the list of very sensitive included products in Annex I, Part 1.
18 Listed in Annex III: ibid Art 1(3). As to the rules of origin, see ibid Art 1(4).
19 This replaces the former system of duty-free access within tariff ceilings and fixed duty-free amounts for sensitive products.
20 Listed in Council Regulation 3281/94 Annex I, Part 4, OJ 31.1294 L348/1, as adapted by Commission Regulation 380/98, OJ 19.2.98 L48/20.
 1 Listed in ibid Annex I, Part 3, as adapted.
 2 Listed in ibid Annex I, Part 2, as adapted. These products include chemicals, shoes, electronics, cars and brushes.
 3 Listed in ibid Annex I, Part 1, as adapted. These products are basically textiles and ferro-alloys.
 4 Ibid Art 2(4).
 5 Ibid Art 2(3).
 6 Ibid Art 2(2).
 7 Ibid Art 2(1).
 8 Listed in Annex IV: ibid Art 3(1).
 9 Namely Colombia, Venezuela, Ecuador, Peru and Bolivia, as listed in Annex V, and subject to procedures laid down in Art 18(3): ibid Art 3(2).
10 Ibid Art 4(1). The previous GSP used individual quotas or exclusion of certain countries to take account of different degrees of competitiveness of different countries in relation to specific products. In contrast, the graduation mechanism is based on the principle that the giving of preferences should be a transitional measure, to be used at need and phased out when the need is considered no longer to exist. The graduation mechanism can thus be used to transfer preferential margins gradually from advanced to less developed countries. See ibid Preamble, tenth and thirteen recitals.

certain criteria in respect of industrial development and specialization of imports into the Community.[11] As a result of this mechanism, the preferential margin was reduced by 50 per cent from 1 April 1995 and abolished from 1 January 1996 in respect of specific sectors in Hong Kong, Singapore, South Korea, Saudi Arabia, Oman, Brunei, Qatar, United Arab Emirates, Kuwait, Bahrain, Libya and Naura.[12] In respect of other countries and sectors,[13] it was reduced by 50 per cent from 1 January 1997 and abolished from 1 January 1998.[14]

The graduation mechanism also applies to countries whose exports to the Community in a given sector of products covered by the GSP exceed 25 per cent of beneficiary countries' exports to the Community in that sector.[15] The preferential margin for these countries and sectors was abolished as of 1 January 1996.[16] Certain other countries and sectors are excluded from the GSP if the new GSP would result in higher preferences than those which prevailed in 1993.[17] In addition, the most advanced beneficiary countries were excluded from entitlement to preferences as from 1 January 1998.[18] The graduation mechanism does not apply however to countries whose exports to the Community in a given sector of products covered by the scheme do not exceed 2 per cent of beneficiary countries' exports to the Community in that sector.[19]

The new GSP provides two types of special incentive arrangements. First, additional preferences may be granted to beneficiary countries which actually apply International Labour Organization Conventions Nos 87 and 98 concerning freedom of association and protection of the right to organize and to bargain collectively and Convention No 138 concerning child labour.[20] Second, additional preferences may be granted to beneficiary countries which actually apply ITTO (International Tropical Timber Organization) standards relating to the sustainable management of forests.[1]

---

11 Ibid Art 4(2). The sector/country combinations, that is, the sectors affected by the graduation mechanism in each country, are listed in Annex II, Part 1. The industrial development criteria are integrated into a development index, based on a formula which combines per capita income with the level of manufactured exports. The sectoral specialization index is derived from the relationship between a country's share of Community imports in a specific sector and its share of Community imports as a whole. As to these indices, see Annex II, Part 2.

12 Ibid Art 4(3), first indent. These countries, which have an annual per capita income of more than $6000, are listed in Annex VII.

13 That is, those listed in Annex II, Part 1, as adapted, but not in Annex VII. As to this abolition of preferential margin as of 1 January 1998, see Commission communication 97/C384/05, OJ 18.12.97 C384/5.

14 Ibid Art 4(3), second indent. ECSC products remain excluded from GSP in the case of countries which did not qualify in 1994: ibid Art 4(4). As to the application of this graduation mechanism as of 1 January 1998, see Commission communication 97/C384/05, OJ 18.12.97 C384/5.

15 Ibid Art 5(1). This is the so-called 'lion's share clause' or 'solidarity mechanism'. It appears to be directed mainly against Chinese imports, according to Waer and Driessen, op cit at 111.

16 Ibid Art 5(1).

17 Ibid Art 5(3). The countries and sectors are listed in Annex VI.

18 Ibid Art 6(1), which also provides that the Commission is to submit proposals in this respect before 1 January 1997. Hong Kong, Singapore and South Korea have been withdrawn from the GSP list as from 1 May 1998: Council Regulation 2623/97, OJ 30.12.97 L354/9.

19 Ibid Art 5(2). The specific countries are not listed in the Regulation.

20 Ibid Art 7(1), which also provides that the country concerned must request the additional preferences in writing and provide proof that it has adopted and actually applies the Conventions in question. As to procedures for implementing these arrangements, see ibid Art 7(2),(3). As to application of these incentive arrangements, see Council Regulation 1154/98, OJ 4.6.98 L160/1.

1 Ibid Art 8(1), which also provides that the country concerned must request the additional preferences in writing and provide proof that it has adopted and actually applies the standards in question. As to implementation procedures, see Art 8(2),(3).

The GSP may be withdrawn temporarily, in whole or in part, in specified circumstances.[2] The circumstances are the practice of forced labour,[3] export of goods made by prison labour,[4] manifest shortcomings in customs controls on export or transit of drugs or failure to comply with international conventions on money laundering,[5] fraud or failure to provide administrative co-operation as required for verification of certificates of origin,[6] and manifest cases of unfair trading practices, including discrimination against the Community and failure to comply with obligations under the Uruguay Round to meet agreed market-access objectives.[7] Withdrawal is decided by the Council, following a Commission proposal after Commission consultations, investigation and hearings, and acting by a qualified majority.[8]

Provision is made in respect of the concurrence of anti-dumping duties and GSP benefits.[9]

The GSP is subject to a safeguard clause, according to which CCT duties may be reintroduced, at the request of a Member State or on the Commission's own initiative, and after investigation, when a product is imported on terms which cause, or threaten to cause, serious difficulties to a Community producer of like or directly competing products.[10] In addition, any strictly necessary preventive measures may be taken by the Commission, after informing the Member States, where exceptional circumstances requiring immediate action make either notification or examination impossible.[11]

The Community has also opened supplementary generalized tariff preferences for certain industrial products originating in beneficiary countries and sold at the Berlin 'Partners in Progress' trade fair.[12]

AGRICULTURAL PRODUCTS

A new multiannual GSP for agricultural products was adopted in June 1996.[13] It entered into force on 1 July 1996.[14] According to its terms, however, the previous scheme applied *mutatis mutandis* until 1 January 1997.[15] Consequently the new scheme applies only for the period from 1 January 1997 until 30 June 1999.[16]

---

2 Ibid Art 9(1).
3 As defined in the Geneva Conventions of 25 September 1926 and 7 September 1956 and International Labour Organization Conventions Nos 29 and 105: ibid Art 9(1), first indent. As to the temporary withdrawal of access to GSP from Myanmar, see Council Regulation 552/97, OJ 27.3.97 L85/8.
4 Ibid Art 9(1), second indent.
5 Ibid Art 9(1), third indent.
6 Ibid Art 9(1), fourth indent.
7 Ibid Art 9(1), fifth indent.
8 Ibid Arts 9(2) and 12(3). As to the procedure which must be followed, see Arts 10–12.
9 Ibid Art 13.
10 Ibid Art 14(1). As to the investigation procedure, see Art 14(2)–(5).
11 Ibid Art 14(6). The GSP provisions do not however affect the application of safeguard clauses adopted as part of the CAP, or as part of the common commercial policy, or any other safeguard clauses which may be applied: Art 14(7).
12 Council Regulation 2142/86, OJ 20.7.86 L188/1; Council Regulation 1004/91, OJ 25.4.91 105/1; Council Regulation 1250/92, OJ 16.5.92 L131/1; Council Regulation 1290/94, OJ 4.6.94 L141/1.
13 Council Regulation 1256/96 Art 1(1), OJ 29.6.94 L160/1.
14 Ibid Art 19(1).
15 Ibid Art 19(2). This scheme is based on Council Regulation 3058/95, OJ 30.12.95 L326/10.
16 Ibid Art 19(3).

The GSP in force until 1 January 1997 for agricultural products thus consisted temporarily of the renewal of the previous scheme.[17] It provided for the partial suspension of CCT duties for certain products within the framework of global fixed reduced-duty amounts,[18] a partial or total suspension of CCT duties for other products,[19] and a total suspension of CCT duties for other products.[20] These arrangements applied only to imports from certain countries.[1] The fixed reduced-duty amounts were administered by the Commission.[2] With regard to imports of products imported without quantitative restrictions,[3] the Commission was entitled to take protective measures in specified circumstances. Where the Commission found that such products were imported into the Community in quantities or at prices which placed or were likely to place Community producers of similar or directly competitive products at a serious disadvantage, the levying of customs duties applied within the Community could be reintroduced in whole or in part on imports of the products in question from the country or countries or territory or territories which were the cause of this disadvantage. Such measures could also be taken in the event of actual or potential serious disadvantage which was confined to a single region of the Community.[4] These measures were without prejudice to the application of any safeguard clauses under the common agricultural policy, the common commercial policy or other safeguard clauses.[5]

From 1 January 1997 there is a new GSP for agricultural products.[6] It applies to specified products falling within Chapters 1–24 of the CCT[7] and, on certain conditions,[8] to other specified products.[9] These arrangements apply only to

17 Council Regulation 3282/94 Art 1, OJ 31.12.94 L348/57, provided for the extension until 31 December 1995 of three previously applicable regulations: Council Regulation 3833/90 (OJ 31.12.90 L370/87), as amended, the basic GSP regulation for agricultural products; Council Regulation 3835/90 (OJ 31.12.90 L370/126), as amended, which amended the basic Regulation in respect of certain products from Bolivia, Colombia, Ecuador and Peru; and Council Regulation 3900/91 (OJ 31.12.91 L368/11), as amended, which amended the basic Regulation in respect of certain products from Costa Rica, El Salvador, Guatemala, Honduras, Nicaragua and Panama.
18 Council Regulation 3833/90 Art 1(1), first indent, OJ 31.1290 L370/86. The products are listed in Annex I. The reduction does not apply for imports of unmanufactured tobacco from China: Art 1(3), second paragraph.
19 Ibid Art 1(1), second indent. The products are listed in Annex II.
20 Ibid Art 1(1), third indent. The products are listed in Annex IV.
1 Ibid Art 1(2). As regards the products in Annexes I and II, the countries are listed in Annex III: Art 1(2), first indent. As regards the products in Annex IV, the countries are listed in Annex V: Art 1(2), second indent. Preferences are suspended for Korea: Art 1(3), first paragraph.
2 Ibid Art 3, first paragraph.
3 That is, the products listed in Annex II originating in the countries listed in Annex III or the products listed in Annex IV originating in the countries listed in Annex V: see ibid Art 6.
4 Ibid Art 7. The Commission may, by means of a regulation, introduce the levying of customs duties for a specified period: ibid Art 8(1). Where action by the Commission is requested by a Member State, the Commission must give its decision within a period of not more than ten working days from the date of the receipt of the request and must inform the Member State of its decision: ibid Art 8(2). Each Member State may refer the measure taken by the Commission to the Council within a period of ten working days following the date on which it was notified. The referral to the Council does not cause the measure to be suspended. The Council is to meet immediately, and it may, acting by a qualified majority, amend or rescind the measure in question: ibid Art 8(3).
5 Ibid Art 9.
6 Council Regulation 1256/96, OJ 29.6.94 L160/1.
7 These products are listed in ibid Annex I: ibid Art 1(2). As to the adaptation of Annex I as from 1 January 1998, see Commission Regulation 381/98, OJ 19.2.98 L48/25.
8 Laid down in ibid Art 3: ibid Art 1(2).
9 These products are listed in ibid Annex VI: ibid Art 1(2). As to adaptation of Annex VI as from 1 January 1998, see Commission Regulation 381/98, OJ 19.2.98 L48/25.

specified countries and territories.[10] The new agricultural GSP scheme embodies the same principles and mechanisms as the GSP for industrial products.

The preferential duties for agricultural imports, as for industrial products, are established according to the principle of tariff modulation.[11] Imported products are divided into four categories: non-sensitive,[12] semi-sensitive,[13] sensitive,[14] and very sensitive.[15] Different preferential duties apply to each product category. CCT duties are suspended for non-sensitive products;[16] 35 per cent of the CCT duty is applied to semi-sensitive products;[17] 70 per cent of the CCT duty is applied to sensitive products;[18] and 85 per cent of the CCT duty is applied to very sensitive products.[19] These modulated duties apply to all beneficiary countries, except for the least developed countries,[20] and specified Latin American countries conducting a campaign to combat drugs.[1]

As with industrial products, the principle of tariff modulation in respect of agricultural products is complemented by a graduation mechanism, by which certain sectors in certain countries may be excluded from preferences.[2] It applies to specified combinations of countries and sectors which meet certain criteria in respect of industrial development and specialization of agricultural imports into the Community.[3] The preferential margin for these country/sector combinations are to be reduced by 50 per cent on 1 January 1997 and abolished as from 1 January 1999.[4]

The graduation mechanism also applies to countries whose exports to the Community of products covered by the GSP in a given sector exceeds 25 per cent of beneficiary countries' exports to the Community in that sector.[5] The preferential margin for these countries and sectors is to be abolished as of 1 January 1997.[6] However, the graduation mechanism does not apply to countries whose exports to the Community of products covered by the scheme in a given sector does not exceed 2 per cent of beneficiary countries'

10 Ibid Art 1(3), which provides that these countries and territories are listed in Annex III. The products must also comply with a definition of origin adopted in accordance with the procedure laid down in Council Regulation 2913/92 Art 249, OJ 19.10.92 L302/1: ibid Art 1(4).
11 This replaces the previous system of partial suspension of CCT duties for certain products within tariff ceilings, partial or total suspension of CCT duties for other products, and total suspension of CCT duties for other products: see Council Regulation 3383/90 Art 1, OJ 31.12.90 L370/86.
12 Listed in ibid Annex I, Part 4, as adapted.
13 Listed in ibid Annex I, Part 3, as adapted.
14 Listed in ibid Annex I, Part 2, as adapted
15 Listed in ibid Annex I, Part 1, as adapted.
16 Ibid Art 2(4).
17 Ibid Art 2(2).
18 Ibid Art 2(2).
19 Ibid Art 2(1).
20 Ibid Art 3(1). The relevant products are listed in Annex I and Annex VI (both as adapted) and the relevant countries are listed in Annex IV.
 1 Ibid Art 3(2). The relevant countries are listed in Annex VI, as adapted. The relevant products are listed in Annex VI, as adapted except for those marked with an asterisk. This is without prejudice to the procedure laid down in ibid Art 17(3), which provides for the possible suspension, in whole or in part, of this exemption.
 2 Ibid Art 4(1). This is based on the principle that preferences should be seen as a transitional measure, to be used at need and phased out when the need is considered no longer to exist: ibid preamble, fourth recital, fifth paragraph.
 3 Ibid Art 4(2). The sector/country combinations are listed in Annex II, Part 1. The criteria are listed in Annex II, Part 2.
 4 Ibid Art 4(3).
 5 Ibid Art 5(1).
 6 Ibid.

exports to the Community in that sector.[7] In addition, the most advanced beneficiary countries are to be excluded from entitlement to preferences as from 1 January 1998.[8]

The new GSP for agricultural products, as for industrial products, provides two types of special incentive arrangements. First, as from 1 January 1998 additional preferences may be granted to beneficiary countries which actually apply International Labour Conventions Nos 87 and 98 concerning the right to organize and ILO Convention No 138 concerning child labour.[9] Second, also as from 1 January 1998 additional preferences may be granted to beneficiary countries which actually apply domestic legal provisions incorporating the substance of international environmental standards for agriculture.[10]

The GSP may be temporarily withdrawn, in whole or in part, in specified circumstances.[11] The circumstances are the practice of forced labour,[12] export of goods made by prison labour,[13] manifest shortcomings in customs controls on export or transit of drugs or failure to comply with international conventions on money laundering,[14] fraud or failure to provide administrative co-operation as required for the verification of certificates of origin,[15] manifest cases of unfair trading practices,[16] and manifest cases of infringement of objectives of international conventions, such as NAFO, NEAFC, ICCAT, NASCO concerning the conservation and management of fishery resources.[17] Withdrawal is to be decided by the Council, following a Commission proposal after Commission consultations, investigation and hearings, and acting by a qualified majority.[18]

Provision is made in respect of concurrence of anti-dumping duties and GSP benefits.[19]

---

7 Ibid Art 5(2).

8 Ibid Art 6, which also provides that the Commission is to submit proposals in this respect before 1 January 1997. Hong Kong, Singapore and South Korea have been withdrawn from the list as of 1 May 1998: Council Regulation 2623/97, OJ 30.12.97 L354/9.

9 Council Regulation 1256/96 Art 7(1), OJ 29.6.94 L160/1, which also provides that the country concerned must request the additional preferences in writing and provide proof that it has adopted and actually applies the Conventions in question. As to procedures for implementing these arrangements, see ibid Art 7(2), (3). As to the application of these incentive arrangements, see Council Regulation 1154/98, OJ 4.6.98 L160/1.

10 Ibid Art 8(1), which also provides that the country concerned must request the additional preferences in writing and provide proof that it has adopted and actually applies the domestic legal provisions in question. As to implementation procedures, see Art 8(2), (3).

11 Ibid Art 9(1).

12 As defined in the Geneva Conventions of 25 September 1926 and 7 September 1958 and International Labour Organization Conventions Nos 29 and 105: ibid Art 9(1), first indent. As to the temporary withdrawal of access to GSP from Myanmar, see Council Regulation 552/97, OJ 27.3.97 L85/8.

13 Ibid Art 9(1), second indent.

14 Ibid Art 8)1), third indent.

15 Ibid Art 9(1), fourth indent.

16 Ibid Art 9(1), fifth indent, which also provides that this includes discrimination against the Community and failure to comply with obligations under the Uruguay Round to meet agreed market-access objectives.

17 Ibid Art 9(1), sixth indent. See Northwestern Atlantic Fisheries Organization (NAFO), MISC 9 (1979), Cmnd 7569; Northeast Atlantic Fisheries Commission (NEAFC), MISC 2 (1980), Cmnd 8474; International Convention for the Conservation of Atlantic (ICAAT), 673 UNTS 63, 6 ILM 293, 20 UST 2887; North Atlantic Salmon Convention (NASCO), MISC 7 (1983), Cmnd 8830.

18 Ibid Arts 9(2) and 12(3). As to the procedure which must be followed, see Arts 10–12.

19 Ibid Art 13.

As with industrial products, the GSP is subject to a safeguard clause, according to which CCT duties may be reintroduced, at the request of a Member State or on the Commission's own initiative, and after investigation, when a product is imported on terms which cause, or threaten to cause, serious difficulties to a Community producer of like or directly competing products.[20] In addition, any strictly necessary preventive measures may be taken by the Commission, after informing the Member States, where exceptional circumstances requiring immediate action make either notification or examination impossible.[1]

20 Ibid Art 14(1). As to the investigation procedure, see Art 14(2)–(5).
1 Ibid Art 14(6). The GSP provisions do not however affect the application of safeguard clauses adopted as part of the CAP, as part of the common commercial policy, or any other safeguard clauses which may be applied: ibid Art 14(7),

Chapter 23

EFTA countries

INTRODUCTION

The Community, its Member States and the then members[1] of the European Free Trade Association (EFTA) concluded the Agreement on the European Economic Area (EEA) in Oporto on 2 May 1992.[2] Since then, however, the ranks of the EEA have been depleted by the accessions to the Community as of 1 January 1995 of Austria, Finland and Sweden, as well as by the rejection of the EEC Agreement by referendum in Switzerland.[3] This section examines the legal framework of trade between the Community and the remaining EFTA countries, namely Iceland, Liechtenstein, and Norway as part of the EEA on the one hand and Switzerland on the other hand.

EEA MEMBER COUNTRIES

The EEA now consists of Iceland, Norway and Liechtenstein.[4] The EEA Agreement entails the application, as between the EEA members and the Community,[5] of inter alia EC Treaty provisions and secondary legislation in respect of the free movement of goods, persons, services and capital.[6] It also involves the establishment of a system based on EC Arts 85 and 86 to ensure that competition is not distorted.[7] Provision is also made for an EEA Council, an EEA Joint Committee, an EEA Joint Parliamentary Committee, an EEA Consultative

---

1 That is, Austria, Finland, Iceland, Liechtenstein, Norway, Sweden, and Switzerland.
2 OJ 3.1.94 L1/3, as adjusted by Protocol (OJ 3.1.94 L1/572). All references hereinafter to the EEA Agreement are to the Agreement as thus adjusted. See also Opinion 1/91 *Re the Draft Treaty on a European Economic Area* [1991] ECR I-6079; Opinion 1/92 *Re the Draft Treaty on a European Economic Area (No 2)* [1992] ECR I-2821.
3 However, the EEA may form a transitional step to full accession for the countries of Central and Eastern Europe which seek Community membership. For a comparison of the EEA and the Europe Agreements, see Peers 'An Ever Closer Waiting Room: The Case for Eastern European Accession to the European Economic Area' (1995) 32 CMLRev 187.
4 As to special provisions for Liechtenstein, see Decision 1/95 of the EEA Council, OJ 20.4.95 L86/58.
5 It includes trade between the EFTA states and Ceuta and Melilla: Protocol 49.
6 EEA Arts 1(2)(a)–(d). For more specific provisions, see EEA Arts 8–27 (free movement of goods), Arts 28–35 (persons), EEA Arts 36–39 (services) and Arts 40–45 (capital). As to intellectual property, see EEA Art 65(2), Protocol 28 and Annex XVII, as amended by Decision of the EEA Joint Committee 10/95 (OJ 2.3.95 L47/30).
7 EEA Art 1(2)(e).

Committee, an EFTA Surveillance Authority for competition matters, and an EFTA Court.[8]

In respect of the products covered by the EEA Agreement, two points in particular deserve to be noted. The basic free movement and trade provisions apply only to products originating in the contracting parties.[9] In addition, the EEA Agreement applies only however to two groups of products: first, products falling within Chapters 25 to 97 of the Harmonized System, excluding the products listed in Protocol 2;[10] and, second, products specified in Protocol 3, subject to the specific arrangements set out in that Protocol.[11]

Customs duties on imports or exports, equivalent charges, and customs duties of a fiscal nature are prohibited between the parties.[12] The same prohibition applies to quantitative restrictions on imports and equivalent measures[13] as well as to quantitative restrictions on exports and equivalent measures.[14] The standard exceptions apply.[15] The imposition of internal taxation in excess of that imposed directly or indirectly on domestic products, or of internal taxation of such a nature as to afford indirect production to other products, is prohibited.[16] When products are exported, any repayment of internal taxation must not exceed the internal taxation imposed on them directly or indirectly.[17]

Specific arrangements apply to agricultural and fishery products.[18] In respect of veterinary and phytosanitary matters, specific provisions are laid down.[19] Leaving aside detailed provisions, the general principles are, first, that the parties may not apply more favourable rules on imports from third countries than

---

8 See the institutional provisions in EEA Arts 89–113. See also Agreement between the EFTA States on the establishment of a surveillance authority and a Court of Justice, OJ 31.12.94 L344/68. As to Community arrangements for implementing the EEA Agreement, see Council Regulation 2894/94, OJ 30.11.94 L305/6.

9 EEA Art 8(2). See also Protocol 4, in particular as amended by Art 3 of Decision 1/95 of the EEA Council (OJ 20.4.95 L86/58), which provides that Liechtenstein is excluded from the territory of the EEA for the purpose of determining the origin of specified products until the year 2000.

10 EEA Art 8(3)(a). The products listed in Protocol 2 are: HS heading No 35.01 casein, caseinates and other casein derivatives, casein glues; 35.02 albumins, albuminates and other albumin derivates—10 egg albumin,—ex 10—other than unfit, or to be rendered unfit, for human consumption,—90 other: ex 90 milk albumin (lactalbumin), other than unfit, or to be rendered unfit, for human consumption; 35.05 destrins and other modified starches; glues based on starches, or on dextrines or other modified starches; 10 dextrins and other modified starches: ex 10 starches, exterified or etherified. These processed agricultural products are covered by a separate agreement, as to which see Council Decision 96/753, OJ 31.12.96 L345/78, and the attached document.

11 EEA Art 8(3)(b).

12 Ibid Art 10. As to customs duties of a fiscal nature, however, see Protocol 5.

13 Ibid Art 11. However, Iceland is permitted to retain certain quantitative restrictions on imports: see Protocol 7.

14 Ibid Art 12.

15 Ibid Art 13.

16 Ibid Art 14.

17 Ibid Art 15.

18 EEA See Arts 17–20. See also Protocol 42, which provides for the entry into force of certain bilateral arrangements concerning specific agricultural products. See also EEC–Norway Agreements in the form of exchange of letters concerning agriculture and fisheries, OJ 22.11.86 L328/77. As to certain arrangements in agriculture, see Agreements with Iceland (OJ 1.5.93 L1099/32; OJ 1.5.93 L109/36) and Norway (OJ 1.5.93 L109/43; OJ 1.5.93 L105/47). See also Council Regulation 1108/93, OJ 7.5.93 L113/1.

19 EEA Art 17. The specific provisions are laid down in Annex I, as amended by Decisions of the EEA Joint Committee 2/95 (OJ 2.3.95 L47/22), 3/95 (OJ 2.3.95 L47/23) and 4/95 (OJ 2.3.95 L47/24).

those resulting from the Agreement, but the EFTA States may maintain their national legislation on imports from third countries regarding substances having a hormonal or thyrostatic action.[20] Second, in trade between EFTA States or between an EFTA State and the Community, animals and products coming from third countries, or partially or totally derived therefrom, must comply with the rules of the importing party.[1]

Provisions in respect of border controls, animal welfare and financial arrangements in numerous relevant Community acts do not apply.[2] Special provision is made for the provisional application of the legislation of the EFTA States in respect of BSE[3] and other matters.[4] Provision is also made for the taking of interim safeguard measures on serious public or animal health grounds.[5] Basic principles are laid down in respect of on-the-spot inspections.[6] The parties are required to ensure that these provisions, as well as those in respect of technical regulations, standards and certification,[7] are not compromised by other technical barriers to trade.[8] The standard exceptions to free movement apply to these products.[9] Special provisions are laid down in respect of fish and other marine products.[10]

Provision is made for customs co-operation and trade facilitation.[11] A party considering the reduction of the effective level of its duties or equivalent charges applicable to third countries benefiting from MFN treatment is required, so far as practicable, to notify the EEA Joint Committee.[12] In April 1997 the EU and Norway signed a customs co-operation agreement.[13]

Special provision is made for the abolition of technical barriers to trade in wine.[14] The Community and Norway have concluded an Agreement on reciprocal trade in cheese.[15]

20 Annex I, Sectoral Adaptation, I Veterinary Issues, paragraph (1)(a), first indent.
1 Ibid paragraph 1(a), second indent.
2 Ibid I Veterinary Issues, paragraph 2. The acts are listed following the basic provisions.
3 Ibid I Veterinary Issues, paragraph 5.
4 See paragraphs 6, 7, 8.
5 Ibid paragraph 9(1)(a), first sub-paragraph. Such measures must be notified to each contracting party and to both the European Commission and the EFTA Surveillance Authority (second sub-paragraph), and consultations must also be held (paragraph 9(1)(b), first sub-paragraph). See also paragraphs 9(2),(3).
6 Paragraph 10. As to the designation of common reference laboratories, see paragraph 11.
7 As laid down in Protocol 12 and Annex II: EEA Art 23(a). Annex II has been amended by the following Decisions of the EEA Joint Committee: 5/95 (OJ 2.3.95 L47/25), 6/95 (OJ 2.3.95 L47/26), 7/95 (OJ 2.3.95 L47/27), 8/95 (OJ 2.3.95 L47/28), 9/95 (OJ 2.3.95 L47/29), 11/95 (OJ 13.4.95 L83/41), 12/95 (OJ 13.4.95 L83/42), 13/94 (OJ 13.4.95), 14/95 (OJ 13.4.95 L83/45), 15/95 (OJ 13.4.95 L83/46), 16/95 (OJ 13.4.95 L83/47), 17/95 (OJ 13.4.95 L83/48), 60/97 (OJ 5.2.98 L30/30).
8 EEA Art 18.
9 Ibid Art 18. As to the protection of intellectual property in connection with the development and manufacture of flavouring substances, however, see Commission Recommendation 98/282, OJ 29.4.98 L127/32.
10 EEA Art 20 and Protocol 9.
11 See ibid Art 21 and Protocols 10 and 11. As to the Agreement on customs co-operation, see Council Decision 97/269, OJ 23.4.97 L105/13.
12 EEA Art 22. As to the Joint Committee, see ibid Arts 92–95.
13 See OJ 23.4.97 L105/15 (exchange of letters) and OJ 23.4.97 L105/17 (Agreement): see also *Agence Europe*, No 6953 (n.s.), Saturday 12 April 1997.
14 Art 23(b) and Protocol 47 as amended by Decision of the EEA Joint Committee 1/95 (OJ 2.3.95 L47/19) and by Decision of the EEA Joint Committee 39/97, OJ 23.10978 L290/24, and also as amended, in respect of Liechtenstein, by Art 4 of Decision 1/95 of the EEA Council (OJ 20.4.95 L86/58).
15 Agreement on reciprocal trade in cheese, amended in 1986 (OJ 17.7.87 L196/78, as amended), adapted in 1992 (OJ 20.2.92 L44/39) and 1993 (OJ 25.3.93 L72/27).

There are also specific provisions in respect of energy[16] and ECSC products.[17]

Safeguard measures are permitted in respect of the free movement of goods when certain problems result from the removal of customs duties on imports or exports, or equivalent charges, or quantitative restrictions on exports or equivalent measures.[18] Such measures may be taken when two conditions are satisfied. The first condition is that the result of the removal of the measure is either re-exported towards a third country against which the party maintains, for the product concerned, quantitative export restrictions or other export measures, or a serious shortage or threat of a shortage of a product essential to the exporting party.[19] The second condition is that the situation gives rise to, or is likely to give rise to, major difficulties for the exporting party.[20] Anti-dumping measures, countervailing duties and measures against illicit commercial practices attributable to third countries cannot be applied between the parties.[1]

Subject to specific provisions,[2] there are no restrictions on the freedom to provide services.[3]

SWITZERLAND

Switzerland and the Community concluded an Agreement in 1972 which, with numerous amendments and derogations, is still in force.[4] It applies to products listed in Chapters 25 to 99 of the Harmonized System, except for certain specified products,[5] and to also certain other products.[6]

Customs duties on imports are subject to a standstill clause[7] and those in force were to be progressively abolished by 1 July 1977,[8] as are customs duties of a fiscal nature.[9] A standstill clause also applies to taxes equivalent to customs duties,[10] and those in force were to be progressively abolished by 1 July 1977.[11]

16 EEA Art 24 and Annex IV.
17 Ibid Art 27 and Protocols 14 and 25.
18 Ibid Art 25. As to procedures, see ibid Art 113. As to arbitration procedures, see Protocol 33.
19 Ibid Art 25(a).
20 Ibid Art 25(b).
1 Unless otherwise specified in the Agreement: ibid Art 26. See also Protocol 13.
2 Annexes IX to XI contain specific provisions on services: ibid Art 36(2).
3 Ibid Art 36(1). As to the meaning of services, see ibid Art 37.
4 OJ 31.12.72 L300/189, as amended. As to rules of origin, see Art 11 and Protocol No 3, which also deals with methods of administrative co-operation. Protocol No 3 was amended by Decisions 1/75 and 2/75 (OJ 31.12.75 L338/73) and Decision 1/77 (OJ 29.12.77 L342/27) of the EEC–Switzerland Joint Committee. See also Council Regulation 4282/88, OJ 31.12.88 L381/35, in respect of the safeguard measure laid down in Art 2 of Decision 5/88 of the EEC–Switzerland Joint Committee amending Protocol No 3. Protocol No 3 was then consolidated and modified by Agreement in the form of exchange of letters in 1984 (OJ 11.12.84 L323/312); further amended in 1988 in respect of Spain, Canary Islands, Ceuta and Melilla (OJ 19.4.88 L100/13); and further amended by Decision 1/94 of the Joint Committee (OJ 6.8.94 L204/150). Documentation in respect of origin was simplified by Decision 2/87 of the Joint Committee (OJ 31.12.87 L388/38) and Decision 1/96 of the Joint Committee (OJ 23.7.97 L185/1). As to the Protocol on mutual assistance in customs matters, see Council Decision 97/403, OJ 27.6.97 L169.76.
5 Listed in Annex I. The annexes and protocols are an integral part of the Agreement: ibid Art 33.
6 Ibid Art 2. These other products are listed in Protocol No 2, as amended by Agreements in the form of exchange of letters (OJ 28.10.76 L298/43; OJ 26.11.76 L328/57; OJ 2.12.83 L337/1).
7 Ibid Art 3(1).
8 Ibid Art 3(2).
9 Ibid Art 4(19).
10 Ibid Art 6(1).
11 Ibid Art 6(3).

Customs duties on exports and equivalent measures are prohibited.[12] Quantitative restrictions and equivalent measures on imports are subject to a standstill clause,[13] and those in force were to be phased out.[14] Changes in the customs tariff or equivalent taxes by one party in respect of third countries must be notified to the other party in advance.[15]

Certain products were subject to a special customs regime.[16] Special customs rules also applied to processed agricultural products.[17] Special provision was also made for possible modification of the regime for petroleum products.[18] In respect of agricultural products not covered by the Agreement, the parties declared their readiness to promote the harmonious development of agricultural trade while respecting their own agricultural policies.[19] As from 1 January 1977, imports into the Community from Switzerland could not be accorded more favourable treatment than that accorded among Member States.[20]

The Agreement includes an exception for customs unions, free trade areas and border trade to the extent that they do not modify the trade provisions of the Agreement, in particular the rules of origin.[1] It also includes the standard exceptions to the free movement of goods.[2] There is also an exception in respect of information contrary to essential security interests,[3] the arms trade and related research and development activities,[4] and national security.[5]

The Agreement also includes a 'loyalty clause'[6] in terms similar to those of EC Art 5. It also includes provisions in respect of competition, including state aids.[7] Safeguard measures are provided in the event that an increase in imports causes, or threatens to cause, serious harm to the producers in the territory of the importing party and if the increase in imports is imputable to the operation of the Agreement.[8] Provision is also made for anti-dumping measures[9] and

---

12 Ibid Art 7(1). In respect of certain products, customs duties on exports and equivalent charges were to be abolished by 1 January 1993: Art 7(2) and Annex III, as substituted by Supplementary Protocol (OJ 13.10.89 L295/29).
13 Ibid Art 13(1).
14 Ibid Art 13(2) and Arts 13a, 13b, 24a as inserted by Supplementary Protocol (OJ 13.10.89 L295/29).
15 Ibid Art 12.
16 Ibid Art 8. The products and provisions are set out in Protocol No 1, as amended by Agreement in the form of exchange of letters (OJ 28.10.78 L303/25).
17 Ibid Art 9. The products and provisions are set out in Protocol No 2. Provision is made for modification of the Agreement in case of changes in the agricultural policy of either party: Art 10. The Protocol was adjusted to take account of the Uruguay Round results by Council Regulation 1863/97, OJ 27.9.97 L265/1.
18 Ibid Art 14.
19 Ibid Art 15.
20 Ibid Art 16.
1 Ibid Art 17.
2 Ibid Art 20.
3 Ibid Art 21(a).
4 Ibid Art 21(b).
5 Ibid Art 21(c).
6 Ibid Art 22(1), (2). Article 22(3) provides for the taking of appropriate measures if one party considers that the other party has failed to fulfil its obligations under the Agreement. The procedures are set out in Art 27.
7 See ibid Art 23. As to procedures, see Art 27, as substituted by Supplementary Protocol (OJ 13.10.89 L295/30).
8 Ibid Art 24. As to procedures, see Art 27, as so substituted. As to all safeguard measures, including interim measures, provided by the Agreement, see Council Regulation 2841/72, OJ 31.12.72 L300/284, as amended.
9 Ibid Art 25. As to procedures, see Art 27, as so substituted.

safeguard measures in the event of regional economic problems[10] and problems caused by re-exports towards third countries.[11]

A Joint Committee is established to oversee the operation of the Agreement.[12]

In June 1997 the Community and Switzerland signed a Mutual Assistance Protocol in customs matters.[13] The Community and Switzerland have also concluded agreements in respect of certain cheeses,[14] inward and outward processing of textiles,[15] and products of the clock and watch industry.[16] In 1985 an Agreement was concluded on trade arrangements for soups, sauces and condiments.[17] It provided for the renunciation by Switzerland of the right to levy certain customs duties on certain sauces and condiments, and conversely for the abolition by the Community of customs duties on certain soups and sauces.[18]

An Agreement has also been concluded between the Member States of the ECSC and Switzerland in respect of ECSC products.[19]

The Community and Switzerland have also concluded on Agreement on trade electronic data interchange systems (the Tedis programme).[20]

10 Ibid Art 26. As to procedures, see Art 27, as so substituted.
11 Ibid Art 24a, as inserted by Supplementary Protocol (OJ 13.10.89 L295/29). As to procedures, see Art 27, as so substituted.
12 Ibid Arts 29–32.
13 OJ 27.6.97 L169/77. The Protocol is annexed to the 1972 Free Trade Agreement. It is intended to enable customs services and administrations to exchange information and pursue infringements against customs legislation.
14 Tariff agreement, negotiated under GATT Article XXVIII, OJ 13.10.69 L257/5, as amended by Agreement in the form of exchange of letters, OJ 13.10.87 L289/33.
15 Arrangement, OJ 24.9.69 L240/5.
16 Agreement, as supplemented, OJ 30.4.74 L118/12, and as amended (OJ 18.9.84 L251/1; OJ 7.4.87 C94/1).
17 Agreement in the form of exchange of letters, OJ 21.11.85 L309/22.
18 Switzerland had previously abolished customs duties on certain other relevant products as of 1 July 1977: see Agreement, Letter No 1, second paragraph.
19 Agreement, OJ 19.12.73 L350/13.
20 OJ 30.12.89 L400/27. In late January 1998 the Commission and Switzerland reached agreement on a future bilateral agreement on land transport, which remains to be concluded by the Council: see *Agence Europe*, No 7146 (n.s.), Monday/Tuesday, 26/27 January 1998, p 8.

Chapter 24

Other European countries
and territories

INTRODUCTION

There are numerous territories, regions or countries which have a special relationship with the Community.[1] Excluding the French overseas departments,[2] many have trade agreements or other arrangements with the Community. They include autonomous or semi-autonomous regions with special relationships with a Member State, namely the Aland Islands, Ceuta and Melilla, the Canary Islands, Channel Islands, Isle of Man, and the Faroe Islands.[3] They also include independent countries within EC boundaries, namely Andorra, Monaco and San Marino. These regions and countries are discussed in this chapter. The Overseas Countries and Territories, which is another group of countries and territories that has a special relationship with the Community, are discussed in a separate chapter.

ALAND ISLANDS

The Aland Islands are an archipelago in the Baltic Sea, equidistant from the Swedish and Finnish mainlands. They constitute a politically autonomous part of Finland.[4] The special status of the Aland Islands was recognized when Fin-

---

1 See Commission of the European Communities 'Background Report: The European Community's Relations to French Overseas Departments, European Autonomous Regions, Independent Countries within EC Boundaries, and Overseas Countries and Territories' ISEC/B20/93, 28 June 1993.

2 Reunion, Guadeloupe, Guiana and Martinique, which are an integral part of the Community and are regions of France. The EC Treaty applies to the Member States: Art 227(1). It also applies to the European territories for whose external relations a Member State is responsible: Art 227(4). The provisions of the Treaty apply to the French overseas departments, the Azores, Madeira and the Canary Islands: Art 227(2), as substituted by the Amsterdam Treaty. As to the special agricultural provisions regarding these areas, see Chapter 16 on Agricultural Products.

3 Though part of this general category, the Azores and Madeira belong to the Community as a result of the 1985 Portuguese Act of Accession. Gibraltar also belongs to this category but has no special bilateral trade agreement with the Community. By virtue of the 1972 Act of Accession, Art 28, OJ 27.3.72 L72/194, the EC Treaties apply to Gibraltar, with important exceptions. In particular Gibraltar is outside the Community customs territory and is treated as a third country for the purposes of measures in respect of imports and exports. See Written EPQ 1823/84, OJ 31.12.85 C341/1.

4 The Community Treaties apply to the Aland Islands only in accordance with Protocol No 2 of the 1994 Act of Accession: EC Art 227(5)(d). See N Fagerlund 'The Special Status of the Aland Islands in the European Union' in L Hannikainen and Frank Horn (eds) *The Aland Islands in International Law: The Autonomous and Demilitarized Region in a Changing European and International Legal Context* (Kluwer, Dordrecht, 1996).

498

land acceded to the Community.[5] In respect of trade, the provisions of the EC Treaty do not preclude the application of existing provisions in force as of 1 January 1994 on the Aland Islands on restrictions, on a non-discriminatory basis, on the right of establishment and the right to provide services by natural persons who do not enjoy regional citizenship in Aland, or by legal persons without permission by the competent authorities of the Aland Islands.[6] In addition, the Aland Islands are excluded from the territorial application of EC provisions in the fields of harmonization of laws of the Member States on turnover taxes and on excise duties and other forms of indirect taxation.[7] This derogation, which concerns duty-free shopping, is aimed at maintaining a viable local economy in the islands and is not to have any negative effects on the interests of the Union or its common policies.[8]

ANDORRA

An Agreement between the Community and the Principality of Andorra[9] was concluded in 1990 for an unlimited duration.[10] It provides for the establishment of a customs union between the parties in respect of products covered by Chapters 25 to 97 of the Harmonized System.[11] It applies to goods produced or in free circulation[12] in the Community or in Andorra.[13] It also applies to goods obtained in the Community or in Andorra, in the manufacture of which were used products from third countries and not in free circulation in the Community or Andorra, so long as the exporting contracting party has levied relevant customs duties.[14] Special provisions preserve duty-free limits for imports by travellers coming into the Community from Andorra.[15]

The parties were to refrain from introducing new customs duties or equivalent charges or increasing those applied as of 1 January 1989.[16] Customs duties and equivalent charges were to be abolished.[17] This did not apply however in respect of the variable component of the duty on processed agricultural products.[18] Quantitative restrictions on imports or exports, and equivalent measures, were prohibited as from 1 January 1991.[19] For products covered by the customs union Andorra adopted, as from 1 January 1991, the Community provisions on import formalities in respect of third countries and the relevant laws, regulations and administrative provisions applicable to customs matters in the Community.[20]

5 Protocol No 2 on the Alands Islands.
6 Protocol No 2 Art 1, second indent.
7 Ibid Art 2(a).
8 Ibid Art 2(b), which also provides for procedures in case the derogation is not longer justified.
9 OJ 31.12.90 L374/16.
10 Ibid Art 20.
11 Ibid Art 2.
12 As to entry for free circulation in Andorra, see ibid Art 8.
13 Ibid Art 3.
14 Ibid Art 4.
15 Ibid Art 13(1). The exemptions are set out in Art 13(2)–(4).
16 Ibid Art 5.
17 Ibid Art 6.
18 Ibid Art 63(c). As a result of tarification following the Uruguay Round agreements, the variable component was converted into a tariff and is to be gradually removed. See Chapter 16 on Agricultural Products.
19 Ibid Art 9.
20 Ibid Art 7(1). Andorra has undertaken to apply most Community veterinary rules: see the Protocol on veterinary matters, see Council Decision 97/345, OJ 6.6.97 L148/15.

Products covered by Chapters 1 to 24 of the Harmonized System are not covered by the customs union. Such products originating in Andorra are exempt from customs duties when imported into the Community.[1] Goods from the Community imported into Andorra are not to be treated less favourably than goods imported into Andorra from third countries.[2]

In addition to the standard exemptions from free trade rules,[3] safeguard measures are provided. If commercial policy measures threaten to deflect trade or to cause economic difficulties, the matter may be brought to a Joint Committee.[4] However, if immediate action is necessary, the party may take the necessary surveillance or protection measures and notify the Joint Committee without delay.[5] Preference in the selection of measures must be given to those which least disturb the operation of the customs union and, in particular, the normal development of trade.[6]

CANARY ISLANDS, CEUTA AND MELILLA

Until 1991 trade between the Community and the Canary Islands, Ceuta and Melilla was governed by the Act of Accession of Spain and Portugal and Protocol 2 annexed to this Act and subsequent regulations adjusting these arrangements.[7] The Community Treaties and acts of the institutions applied to the Canary Islands, subject to certain derogations.[8] These arrangements however were modified in 1991 in order to integrate the Canary Islands into the Community's customs territory.[9]

The CAP applies to the Canary Islands on the terms laid down for mainland Spain, subject to specific supply arrangements[10] and certain exceptions. The

1 Ibid Art 11(1). Rules of origin are set out in the Appendix: ibid Art 11(2).
2 Ibid Art 12(2).
3 Ibid Art 16.
4 Ibid Art 10(1). As to the Joint Committee, see Arts 17, 18.
5 Ibid Art 10(2).
6 Ibid Art 10(3).
7 Council Regulation 1391/87, OJ 22.5.87 L133/5. As to rules of origin and methods of administrative co-operation, see Council Regulation 1135/88, OJ 2.5.88 L114/1, as amended. As to current rules of origin in respect of Ceuta and Melilla, see Council Regulation 2454/93 Arts 139–140, OJ 11.10.93 L253/1. As to tariff quotas for certain fishery products originating in Ceuta, see Council Regulation 2622/97, OJ 30.12.97 L354/7.
8 See Act of Accession, Arts 25 and 155 and Protocol 2 (OJ 15.11.85 L302/1). Certain adjustments to these arrangements were made by Council Regulation 1391/87, OJ 22.5.87 L133/5. As to co-operation in trade, see Council Regulation 1135/88, OJ 2.5.88 L114/1, as amended. Detailed rules for quantitative restrictions on imports of certain agricultural products into Portugal were made by Council Regulation 502/86, OJ 1.3.86 L54/49. As to trade with Spain, see Council Regulation 3734/90, OJ 27.12.90 L363/28. As to fishery quotas for 1990, see Council Regulation 3735/90, OJ 27.12.90 L363/39.
9 See Council Regulation 1911/91, OJ 29.6.91 L171/1. However the Canary Islands remain outside the application of the common VAT system: Art 4(1). These arrangements were not modified by the Decision 1/95 of the EC–Turkey Association Council on implementing the final phase of the Customs Union: see Agreement in the form of exchange of letters concerning the Canary Islands, OJ 13.2.96 L35747. On Spanish request, the Council may allow derogations from the applicable CCP provisions. As to the example of textile and clothing products and certain quota products from China, see Council Regulation 1087/97 OJ 17.6.97 L158/1.
10 Council Regulation 1911/91 Art 2(2), OJ 29.6.91 L171/1. These arrangements were to enter into force not later than 1 January 1992: see Art 10(2). As to such arrangements generally, see Council Regulation 1601/92 (OJ 27.6.92 L173/13) and Commission Regulation 2790/94 (OJ 17.11.94 L296/23). As to forecast supply balances, see eg Commission Regulation 1248/97,

exceptions are two-fold. First, the supplementary trade mechanism provided for in the Act of Accession does not apply to the entry into the Canary Islands of the products in question.[11] Second, the rules in force for mainland Spain apply to products originating in the Canary Islands and sent to other parts of the Community.[12] Similarly, the common fisheries policy applies to the Canary Islands on the terms laid down for mainland Spain.[13]

Certain processed products obtained from raw materials entering the Canary Islands under the specific supply arrangements may be re-exported or re-dispatched within the limits of traditional exports and consignments.[14]

For a transitional period, not extending beyond 31 December 2000, Spain is authorized to impose a tax on production and imports (APIM) on all products entering or produced in the Canary Islands.[15] Exemptions from the tax may however be authorized for local products up to 31 December 1995.[16]

For a transitional period, not extending beyond 31 December 1996, the CCT was to be progressively introduced.[17] When this leads to a deflection of trade, however,the Commission is entitled to decide that the difference in customs duties could be levied on goods in free circulation in the Canary Islands when these are introduced into other parts of Community customs territory.[18] More generally, the Commission is to adopt appropriate measures to prevent speculative movements or deflection of trade from the amendment of these trading arrangements.[19]

The charge known as the 'arbitrio insular—tarifa especial' of the Canary Islands was to be applied to products supplied by other parts of the Community,[20] at first up to 31 December 1992 and then, on a case-by-case basis and at Spain's request, to certain sensitive products until 31 December 2000 at the

OJ 1.7.97 L173/88 (processed fruit and vegetables); Commission Regulation 1269/97, OJ 2.7.97 L174/35 (dairy products); Commission Regulation 1261/97, OJ 2.7.97 L174/15 (breeding rabbits); Commission Regulation 1260/97, OJ 2.7.97 L174/12 (eggs and poultrymeat); Commission Regulation 1355/97, OJ 16.7.97 L186/11 (rice); Commission Regulation 1366/97, OJ 17.7.97 L188/8 (wine); Commission Regulation 2137/97, OJ 31.10.97 L297/1 (olive oil). As to detailed rules for specific products, see eg Commission Regulation 2224/92, OJ 28.6.97 L170/22, as amended (hops); Commission Regulation 1487/95, OJ 29.6.95 L145/63, as amended (pigmeat). As to the sale of intervention beef to supply the Canary Islands, see Commission Regulation 1827/97, OJ 23.9.97 L260/12, and Commission Regulation 2552/97, OJ 19.12.97 L349/18. Similar measures apply to the Azores and Madeira, though they belong to the Community. As to amendments to the CAP, see Council Regulation 284/92, OJ 7.2.92 L31/6.

11 Council Regulation 1911/91 Art 2(1), first indent, OJ 29.6.91 L171/1. As to the partial exemption of processed agricultural products from customs duties, see Case C-300/94 *Tirma SA V Administracion General del Estado* [1996] ECR I-989.

12 Ibid Art 2(1), second indent.

13 Ibid Art 3, which also provides that application of the CFP is to be accompanied by special measures in respect of the Canary Islands.

14 See Commission Regulation 2790/94, OJ 17.11.94 L296/23, as amended.

15 Council Regulation 1911/91 Art 5(1), OJ 29.6.91 L171/1, which also provides that, in respect of agricultural products, this may not be implemented until the entry into force of specific supply arrangements ex Art 2(2). As to phased reduction of the tax rate, see Art 5(2). As to rates, see Art 5(3).

16 Ibid Art 5(4).

17 Ibid Art 6(1), which also lays down the timetable. In respect of agricultural products, however, application of the CCT and other duties is suspended until entry into force of the specific supply arrangements ex Art 2(2): Art 6(2). The introduction of the CCT is without prejudice to specific tariff measures or derogations from the common commercial policy in respet of sensitive products: Art 6(3).

18 Ibid Art 6(5).

19 Ibid Art 8.

20 On terms laid down in the Act of Accession, Protocol 2, Art 6(3).

latest. It was to be phased out from 1 January 1996 so as to be completely eliminated by 31 December 2000.[1]

Without prejudice to these specific measures,[2] the commercial policy applies to the Canary Islands on the terms laid down for Spain in the Act of Accession.[3]

A programme of options specific to the remote and insular nature of the Canary Islands was to be adopted by the Council.[4]

The provisions of Protocol 2 to the Act of Accession relating to bananas continued to apply[5] until adoption of the Community's common organization of the market in bananas.

Provision is also made for the application of safeguard measures until 31 December 1999.[6]

CHANNEL ISLANDS

Special arrangements apply to the Channel Islands[7] in respect of trade in agricultural products.[8] The Community rules applicable to the UK for trade in agricultural products and processed agricultural products apply to the Channel Islands, with the exception of rules on refunds and on compensatory amounts.[9] For this purpose the UK and the Channel Islands are treated as a single Member State.[10] However, no refund or compensatory amount may be granted for these products, originating in the Channel Islands and in respect of which customs formalities are completed in a Member State.[11] When these products are exported from the Channel Islands to third countries or to Member States, the Channel Islands may not grant aid in excess of the refunds or compensatory amounts which may be granted by the UK in the same situation.[12] The Community rules in respect of veterinary legislation, zootechnic legislation, plant health legislation, marketing of seeds and propagating material, food legislation, feedingstuffs legislation, and quality and marketing standards apply to these products imported into the Channel Islands or exported from the Channel

---

1 Ibid Art 6(4). Recently, however, the European Court of Justice has interpreted the relevant Treaty and legislative provisions as precluding the levying of a charge which, though having the appearance of internal taxation, is such as to be levied upon imported products or certain categories of those products, to the exclusion of local products in the same category: Case C-45/94 *Camara de Comercio, Industria y Navegacion, Ceuta v Munipality of Ceuta* [1995] ECR I-4385.

2 That is, those laid down in ibid Arts 2(2), 6(3) and 10(3).

3 Ibid Art 7.

4 Ibid Art 9. This programme (Poseican)was set up by Council Decision 91/314, OJ 29.6.91 L171/5. As to analogous measures in respect of Madeira and the Azores (Poseima), see Council Decision 91/315, OJ 29.6.91 L171/10.

5 Ibid Art 10(3).

6 Ibid Art 11, which also provides that the measures are provided in the Act of Accession, Art 379, and that they are to apply, in the circumstances provided by that Art, to any sector affected by the new arrangements integrating the Canary Islands into the Community.

7 The Community Treaties apply to the Channel Islands only to the extent necessary to ensure the implementation of the arrangements set out in the Accession Treaty (that is, Protocol No 3 of the 1972 Act of Accession): EC Art 227(5)(c).

8 Council Regulation 706/73, OJ 13.3.73 L68/1, as amended. See also the 1972 Act of Accession, Protocol No 3, Art 1(2) (OJ 27.3.72 L73/5).

9 Council Regulation 706/73 Art 1(1) OJ 13.3.73 L68/1.

10 Ibid Art 1(2).

11 Ibid Art 1(3).

12 Ibid Art 1(4) (exports to third countries), Art 1(5) (exports to Member States).

Islands to the Community under the same conditions as in the UK.[13] However, in respect of trade in live animals, fresh meat and meat-related products, the Channel Islands is entitled to retain its specific provisions applicable to imports in relation to foot-and-mouth disease.[14]

FAROE ISLANDS

An Agreement between the Community and Denmark, on the one hand, and the Faroe Islands,[15] a self-governing integral part of Denmark, on the other hand, was concluded in 1991.[16] It was replaced by a new Agreement as of 1 January 1997.[17] Its aims are inter alia to develop economic relations through reciprocal trade and provide fair conditions of competition for trade between the two parties.[18] It applies to products originating in the Community or the Faroe Islands which fall within Chapters 25 to 97 of the Harmonized System[19] and also to certain specified products.[20] It excludes agricultural products listed in Annex II of the EEC Treaty[1] and certain listed products.[2] Customs duties on imports[3] and equivalent charges,[4] import duties of a fiscal nature,[5] customs duties on exports and equivalent charges[6] and quantitative restrictions on imports and equivalent measures[7] are to be abolished. Special provisions are laid down for fish and fishery products,[8] processed agricultural products,[9] and certain petroleum products.[10] The standard exceptions to free trade apply,[11] and

13 Ibid Art 3, first paragraph, as corrected by Corrigendum, OJ 16.6.73 L159/55.
14 Ibid Art 3, second paragraph, as substituted by Council Regulation 1174/86, OJ 24.4.86 L107/1.
15 The Community Treaties do not apply to the Faroe Islands: EC Art 227(5)(a).
16 OJ 31.12.91 L371/2, as amended by Agreement in the form of exchange of letters in 1995 (see OJ 10.3.95 L54/26). As to the Community customs procedure applicable to products from the Faroe Islands, see Council Regulation 2051/74, OJ 2.8.74 L212/33, as amended.
17 Agreement between the European Community, of the one part, and the government of Denmark and the home government of the Faroe Islands, of the other part, OJ 22.2.97 L53/2, approved on behalf of the European Community by Council Decision 97/126, OJ 22.2.97 L53/1.
18 Agreement Art 1.
19 Ibid Art 2(i).
20 Ibid Art 2(ii). The products are specified in Protocols 1, 2 and 4 to the Agreement.
 1 As to other agricultural products, see ibid Art 15. Protocol 4 lays down special provisions applicable to imports of certain agricultural products (other than fish or fishery products): Art 17. It provides tariff quotas for sheepmeat, goatmeat and related products; certain milk products; and fish feed.
 2 Ibid Art 2(i). The excluded products, other than Annex II products, are listed in Annex I of the Agreement.
 3 Ibid Arts 3, 4.
 4 Ibid Art 6.
 5 Ibid Art 5, which also provides for the possibility of certain compensatory measures by the Faroe Islands.
 6 Ibid Art 7.
 7 Ibid Art 13.
 8 Ibid Art 8, Protocol 1. As to tariff quotas, ceilings and surveillance for certain fish and fishery products, see Council Regulation 1983/95, OJ 15.8.95 L192/1. As to detailed rules for fish food, see Commission Regulation 955/97, OJ 30.5.97 L139/8, corrected by Commission Regulation 1295/97, OJ 4.7.97 L176/27. The list of Faroese fishery products subject to tariff concessions has recently been extended by Decision 1/98 of the EC/Denmark-Faroe Islands Joint Committee, OJ 25.3.98 L90/40.
 9 Ibid Art 9, Protocol 2.
10 Ibid Art 14.
11 Ibid Art 21. See also Art 22.

limited safeguards are provided.[12] A Joint Committee is established to administer the Agreement.[13]

ISLE OF MAN

The same special arrangements which apply to the Channel Islands in respect of trade in agricultural products also apply to the Isle of Man.[14] The Community rules applicable to the UK for trade in agricultural products and processed agricultural products apply to the Isle of Man, with the exception of rules on refunds and on compensatory amounts.[15] For this purpose the UK and the Isle of Man are treated as a single Member State.[16] However, no refund or compensatory amount may be granted for these products, originating in the Isle of Man and in respect of which customs formalities are completed in a Member State.[17] When these products are exported from the Isle of Man to third countries or to Member States, the Isle of Man may not grant aid in excess of the refunds or compensatory amounts which may be granted by the UK in the same situation.[18] The Community rules in respect of veterinary legislation, zootechnic legislation, plant health legislation, marketing of seeds and propagating material, food legislation, feedingstuffs legislation, and quality and marketing standards apply to these products imported into the Isle of Man or exported from the Isle of Man to the Community under the same conditions as in the UK.[19] However, in respect of trade in live animals, fresh meat and meat-related products, the Isle of Man is entitled to retain its specific provisions applicable to imports in relation to foot-and-mouth disease.[20]

Since 1982 the Isle of Man has been permitted to apply a system of special import licences for sheepmeat, beef and veal originating in Member States or in third countries.[1] This permission has recently been extended until 31 December 2000.[2]

SAN MARINO

A roughly similar agreement was concluded in 1992 with San Marino.[3] It establishes a customs union for products covered by Chapters 1 to 97 of the

---

12 Ibid Arts 27, 28, 29.
13 Ibid Art 30(1); see also Arts 30(2)-32.
14 Council Regulation 706/73, OJ 13.3.73 L68/1, as amended. See also the 1972 Act of Accession, Protocol No 3, Art 1(2) (OJ 27.3.72 L73/5). The Community Treaty applies to the Isle of Man only to the extent necessary to ensure the implementation of the arrangements set out in the Accession Treaty (that is, Protocol No 3 of the 1972 Act of Accession): EC Art 227(5)(c).
15 Council Regulation 706/73 Art 1(1), OJ 13.3.73 L68/1.
16 Ibid Art 1(2).
17 Ibid Art 1(3).
18 Ibid Art 1(4) (exports to third countries), Art 1(5) (exports to Member States).
19 Ibid Art 3, first paragraph, as corrected by Corrigendum, OJ 16.6.73 L159/55.
20 Ibid Art 3, second paragraph, as substituted by Council Regulation 1174/86, OJ 24.4.86 L107/1, which also provides that these provisions must not be any more restrictive than those in force on 30 September 1985.
 1 Council Decision 82/350, OJ 9.8.92 L234/7, as amended, and as corrected by Corrigendum, OJ 30.8.84 L232/26. This was extended until 31 December 1995 by Council Decision 92/153 (OJ 11.3.92 L65/33) and until 31 January 1996 by Council Decision 95/589 (OJ 31.12.95 L329/37).
 2 Council Decision 96/90 Art 1, OJ 27.1.96 L21/67.
 3 OJ 9.12.92 L359/14. San Marino and Monaco are part of the Community customs territory. The Community has no trade agreement with Monaco.

Harmonized System, except for ECSC products.[4] Customs duties and equivalent charges are prohibited,[5] as are quantitative restrictions and equivalent charges.[6] The standard exceptions apply.[7] In respect of imports from the Community, charges having effect equivalent to customs duties were to be abolished by San Marino as from 1 January 1996.[8] With regard to agricultural products, San Marino undertook to adopt Community veterinary, plant health and quality regulations where necessary for the proper functioning of the Agreement.[9] In respect of third countries, San Marino is to apply relevant Community measures in respect of customs tariff,[10] common commercial policy, agricultural trade, and, where necessary, Community veterinary, plant health and quality regulations.[11] Provision is made for safeguard measures.[12] A Co-operation Committee was established to administer the Agreement.[13]

4 Ibid Art 1.
5 Ibid Art 5(1).
6 Ibid Art 8.
7 Ibid Art 9.
8 Ibid Art 5(2). For this purpose San Marino undertook, within six months of entry into force of the Agreement, to introduce on domestic products intended for home consumption a supplementary tax corresponding to that then levied on imported goods and calculated on the added value of domestic products: see Art 5(2).
9 Ibid Art 5(4).
10 Except for a derogation in respect of publications, works of art, scientific or teaching materials, medicinal preparations and medical equipment offered to the government of San Marino, insignias, medals, stamps, printed matter and other similar objects or paper destined for use by the government, which are exempt from customs duties: ibid Art 6(3).
11 Ibid Art 6.
12 Ibid Art 11.
13 Ibid Art 13. As to decision-making procedures, see also Art 14.

Chapter 25

Countries in transition

THE EUROPE AGREEMENTS

Introduction

The countries in transition comprise the countries of Central and Eastern Europe together with the countries that formerly belonged to the Union of Soviet Socialist Republics (USSR). With countries in the former group plus the Baltic States, the Community has signed bilateral Europe Agreements (EAs). With countries in the latter group, except for the Baltic States, the Community has signed bilateral Agreements on Partnership and Co-operation (PCAs). The PCAs themselves may be divided into two categories: those with Russia, Ukraine, Moldava and Belarus, on the one hand, and those with the non-European former USSR Republics, on the other. These three-tier legal arrangements reflect the EU's geopolitical strategy.[1] In addition, trade in energy products is governed by the Energy Charter Treaty.[2] The Treaty expressed in legally binding terms a political commitment first established by the European Energy Charter in 1991. Its signatories include 44 countries, including the European Community, the USA, Canada, Japan and most of the countries in transition except Hungary.[3]

The EAs are association agreements based on EC Art 238 and are intended as a channel for eventual accession to the Community. EAs[4] came into effect

---

1 Maresceau and Montaguti 'The Relations between the European Union and Central and Eastern Europe: A Legal Appraisal' (1995) 32 CMLRev 1327 at 1328, *passim*, which provides an excellent survey as of April 1995. More recent information may be found in Marc Maresceau (ed) *Enlarging the European Union: Relations between the EU and Central and Eastern Europe* (1997).

2 International Energy Agency *The Energy Charter Treaty: A Description of its Provisions* (OECD IEA, 1994).

3 See Bull EU 12–1991, pt 1.2.114, Bull EU 12–1994 pt 1.2.110. The Treaty is of special importance to Russia, a producer rather than simply a transit country: see Maresceau and Montaguti, 'The Relations between the European Union and Central and Eastern Europe: A Legal Appraisal' (1995) 32 CMLRev 1327 at 1366.

4 The EAs are mixed agreements and needed to be ratified by the Community's Member States. In view of the consequent time required for the EAs' entry into force, the Communty negotiated bilateral Interim Agreements in respect of the EAs' trade and trade-related provisions, concerning which the Community has exclusive competence. These Interim Agreements have now been replaced by the EAs. For examples of the Interim Agreements, see OJ 30.4.92 L114/2, as amended, Additional Protocol, OJ 4.8.93 L195/45, Additional Protocol, OJ 29.1.94 L25/2, Extension, OJ 31.12.94 L408/5 (Poland); OJ 30.4.92 L116/2, as amended, and Addi-

on 1 February 1994 with Poland[5] and Hungary[6] and on 1 February 1995 with Bulgaria,[7] the Czech Republic,[8] Romania,[9] and the Slovak Republic.[10] In June 1995 EAs were signed with the Baltic States,[11] namely Estonia,[12] Latvia[13] and Lithuania.[14] Until the latter group of EAs entered into force, trade relations between the Community and the Baltic States remained governed by free-trade agreements.[15] Agreements with the former Yugoslavia were denounced in 1991,[16] and separate measures have been taken in respect of each new

tional Protocol, OJ 29.1.94 L25/7 (Hungary); Additional Protocol, OJ 4.8.93 L195/47 (Czech and Slovak Federal Republic); Additional Protocol, OJ 29.1.94 L25/22 (Romania); Additional Protocol, OJ 29.1.94 L25/27 (Bulgaria).
5 OJ 31.12.93 L348/2, as amended; Additional Protocol, OJ 31.12.92 L410/461, as amended (OJ 26.4.95 L94/368); Second Additional Protocol, OJ 20.5.97 L127/140.
6 OJ 31.12.93 L347/2, as amended; Additional Protocol, OJ 31.12.92 L410/391, as amended (OJ 26.4.95 L94/166); Second Additional Protocol, OJ 20.5.97 L127/59.
7 OJ 31.12.94 L358/3, as amended; Additional Protocol, OJ 17.5.94 L123/147, as amended (OJ 26.4.95 L94/84); Second Additional Protocol, OJ 31.12.94 L366/22.
8 OJ 31.12.94 L360/2, as amended; Additional Protocol, OJ 17.5.94 L123/198, as amended (OJ 26.4.95 L94/128); Second Additional Protocol, OJ 20.5.97 L127/310. This EA resulted from the renegotiation with the Czech Republic of the earlier EA agreement with the Czech and Slovak Federal Republic after the Federal Republic was dissolved.
9 OJ 31.12.94 L357/2, as amended; Additional Protocol, OJ 17.5.94 L123/476, as amended (OJ 26.4.95 L94/391); Second Additional Protocol, OJ 31.12.94 L366/25.
10 OJ 31.12.94 L359/2, as amended; Additional Protocol, OJ 17.5.94 L123/556, as amended (OJ 26.4.95 L94/436); Second Additional Protocol, OJ 20.5.97 L127/312. This EA resulted from the renegotiation with the Slovak Republic of the earlier EA agreement with the Czech and Slovak Federal Republic after the Federal Republic was dissolved.
11 See *Agence Europe*, no. 6499 (n.s.) 12–13 June 1995.
12 As to the previous legal framework, see the 1994 Free Trade Agreement (OJ 31.12.94 L373/2), as amended, which replaced the 1992 Agreement on Trade and Economic Co-operation (OJ 31.12.92 L403/2), as amended.
13 As to the previous legal framework, see the 1994 Free Trade Agreement and accompanying Agreement on textile products (OJ 31.12.94 L374/2), which replaced the 1992 Agreement on Trade and Economic Co-operation (OJ 31.12.92 L403/11), as amended.
14 As to the previous legal framework, see the 1994 Free Trade Agreement and accompanying Agreement on textile products (OJ 31.12.94 L375/2), which replaced the 1992 Agreement on Trade and Economic Co-operation (OJ 31.12.92 L403/20) as amended.
15 As to Estonia, see the Agreement on free trade and trade-related matters (OJ 31.12.94 L373/2), as amended in particular in respect of textile products (OJ 26.4.95 L94/151). In respect of procedures for application, see Council Regulation 1275/95, OJ 7.6.95 L124/1. There are related agreements with Estonia on maritime transport (OJ 31.12.94 L373/163) and animal health (OJ 31.12.94 L373/164). As to Latvia, see the Agreement on free-trade and trade-related matters (OJ 31.12.94 L374/2), which also provides an Agreement on trade in textile products. In respect of procedures for application, see Council Regulation 1276/95, OJ 7.6.95 L124/2. There are related agreements with Latvia on maritime transport (OJ 31.12.94 L374/216) and animal health (OJ 31.12.94 L374/217). As to Lithuania, see the Agreement on free-trade and trade-related matters (OJ 31.12.94 L375/2), which similarly provides an Agreement on trade in textile products. In respect of certain procedures for application, see Council Regulation 1277/95, OJ 7.6.95 L124/3. There are related agreements on maritime transport (OJ 31.12.94 L375/204) and animal health (OJ 31.12.94 L375/205).
16 The Co-operation Agreement between the EEC and Yugoslavia (OJ 14.2.81 L41/2) was denounced by Council Decision 91/602 (OJ 27.11.91 L325/23). Trade concessions were suspended by Council Regulation 3300/91 (OJ 15.11.91 L315/1), as to which see Case C-162/96 *A Racke GmbH & Co v Hauptzollamt Mainz* [1998] 3 CMLR 219. The application of the Agreements between the EC, its Member States and Yugoslavia was suspended by Decision 91/586 of the Council and the Representatives of the Governments of the Member States (OJ 15.11.91 L315/47). Similar actions were taken in respect of ECSC products: see Decision 91/587, OJ 15.11.91 L315/48, and Decision 91/588, OJ 15.11.91 L315/49, both of the Representatives of the governments of the Member States. See also *Bosphorus Hava Yollari*

country.[17] An EA was initialled with Slovenia, and pending its entry into force an Interim Agreement on trade matters has applied since 1 January 1997.[18]

Building on the EAs, the key feature of the Community's enhanced pre-accession strategy consists of the Accession Partnerships, which provide a single framework for the applicant States comprising priorities in the preparation for accession and financial resources to implement these priorities.[19] Accession Partnerships have been established for Hungary,[20] Poland,[1] Romania,[2] the Slovak Republic,[3] Latvia,[4] Estonia,[5] Lithuania,[6] Bulgaria,[7] Czech Republic,[8] and Slovenia.[9]

Turizm Ve Ticaret Anonim Sirketi v Minister for Transport, Energy and Communications [1994] 3 CMLR 464. See also I Macleod, I D Hendry and S Hyett *The External Relations of the European Communities* (Clarendon Press, Oxford, 1996) pp 361–364. As to the interpretation of the word 'Yugoslavia' after the secession of FYROM, see Case C-177/96 *Belgium v Banque Indosuez* [1997] ECR I-5659.

17 In 1993 a Co-operation Agreement (OJ 29.7.93 L189/2) and an Agreement on ECSC products (OJ 22.1.93 L287/2) were signed with Slovenia. An agreement with Slovenia on textile products (OJ 17.5.94 L123/608) was signed in 1994. In 1997 the EC and the Former Yugoslav Republic of Macedonia concluded a Co-operation Agreement: see OJ 18.12.97 L348/2, approved by Council Decision 97/831, OJ 18.12.97 L348/1. The Agreement entered into force on 1 January 1998. As to its application, see Council Regulation 77/98, OJ 14.1.98 L8/1. An EC-FYROM Transport Agreement came into effect on 28 November 1997: OJ 18.1297 L348/XX. As to Community tariff quotas and ceilings and Community surveillance for certain FYROM products, see Commission Regulation 273/98, OJ 3.2.98 L27/6. As to earlier trade between the Community and the Federal Republic of Yugoslavia (Serbia and Montenegro), see Council Regulation 990/93, OJ 28.4.93 L102/14, as amended. As to the Greek referral to the ECJ for the embargo on the FYROM, see Case C-120/94R *Commission v Greece* [1994] ECR I-3037 and Case C-120/94 *Commission v Greece* [1996] ECR I-1513. See also C Stefanou and H Xanthaki, *A Legal and Political Interpretation of Articles 224 and 225 of the Treaty of Rome: The Former Yugoslav Republic of Macedonia Cases* (1977). Certain elements of the embargo were suspended by Council Regulation 2472/94, OJ 15.10.94 L266/8, as amended. In respect of ECSC products, see Decision 93/235 of the Representatives of the Member States meeting in the Council, OJ 28.4.93 L102/17. As to the arrangement for imports from Bosnia-Herzegovina, Croatia, Slovenia and the former Yugoslav Republic of Macedonia, see Council Regulation 70/97 OJ 18.1.97 L16/1. As to rules of origin, see Chapter 2 in this book.

18 See 'Proposal for a Decision of the Council and Commission on the conclusion of the Europe Agreement between the European Communities and their Member States, of the one part, and the Republic of Slovenia, of the other part', COM(95) 341 final, 12.7.95. See also the European Parliament Resolution on the proposed Europe Agreement with Slovenia, OJ 18.12.95 C339/64. As to the Interim Agreement, see Council Regulation 410/97, OJ 4.3.97 L62/5. As to the administration of tariff quotas and ceilings, see Commission Regulation 428/97, OJ 6.3.97 L65/28. As to beef and veal, see Commission Regulation 2527/97, OJ 17.12.97 L346/56.

19 See Council Regulation 622/98, OJ 20.3.98 L85/1.

20 See Council Decision 98/259, OJ 23.4.98 L121/1, and the Annex.

1 See Council Decision 98/260, OJ 23.4.98 L121/6, and the Annex.

2 See Council Decision 98/261, OJ 23.4.98 L121/11, and the Annex.

3 See Council Decision 98/262, OJ 23.4.98 L121/16, and the Annex.

4 See Council Decision 98/263, OJ 23.4.98 L121/21, and the Annex.

5 See Council Decision 98/264, OJ 23.4.98 L121/26, and the Annex.

6 See Council Decision 98/265, OJ 23.4.98 L121/31, and the Annex.

7 See Council Decision 98/266, OJ 23.4.98 L121/36, and the Annex.

8 See Council Decision 99/267, OJ 23.4.98 L121/41, and the Annex.

9 See Council Decision 98/268, OJ 23.4.98 L121/46, and the Annex.

An example: the EC–Hungary agreement

The trade provisions of the EAs are identical. As an example, we may consider the EA between the Community and Hungary.[10] Its aims are to provide a framework for political dialogue; to establish gradually a free trade area between the Community and Hungary; to make progress towards realizing other economic freedoms; to establish new rules, policies and practices as a basis for Hungary's integration into the Community; to promote economic, financial and cultural co-operation;[11] to support Hungary's efforts to develop its economy and complete its conversion into a market economy; and to set up institutions to make the association effective.[12] These aims are to be achieved during a transition period of a maximum of ten years, divided into two five-year periods.[13]

It should be noted that, in contrast to the EAs with Hungary and Poland, the more recent EAs contain a human rights clause. The general principles of these EAs include respect for the democratic principles and human rights established by the Helsinki Final Act and the Charter of Paris for a new Europe. Together with the principles of market economy, this is stated to inspire the domestic and external policies of the parties and to constitute an essential element of the Association.[14]

During the transitional period the Community and Hungary are to establish a free trade area.[15] The combined nomenclature applies to the classification of goods imported into the Community, while the Hungarian customs tariff applies to the classification of goods imported into Hungary.[16] No new customs duties on imports or exports or charges having equivalent effect are to be introduced, and those applied are not to be increased.[17] Analogous provisions apply to quantitative restrictions.[18] Agriculture is an exception, however, in that these provisions are not to restrict the pursuance by the parties of their respective agricultural policies or the taking of any measures under these policies.[19] The EA does not preclude prohibitions on restrictions of imports, exports of goods in transit justified on grounds of public morality, public policy or public security; the protection of human, animal or plant life and health; the protection of national treasures of artistic, historic or archaeological value; the protection of

---

10 Hereinafter EA Hungary, OJ 31.12.93 L347/2, approved on behalf of the ECSC, EC and EAEC by Decision 93/742 of the Council and the Commission, OJ 31.12.93 L347/1; and amended by Additional Protocol (OJ 29.1.94 L25/7), Agreement (OJ 16.11.94 L295/18), Decision 1/95 of the Association Council (OJ 25.8.95 L201/39).

11 See for example Decision 1/97 of the Association Council between the European Communities and their Member States, of the one part, and the Hungarian Republic, of the other part, OJ 23.9.97 L260/23 (participation of Hungary in EC programmes on training, youth and education). Analogous decisions of the respective Association Councils apply to the Czech Republic (Decision 2/97 of the Association Council, OJ 10.1.097 L277/26), the Slovak Republic (Decision 1/98 of the Association Council, OJ 24.3.98 L88/49) and Poland (Decision 1/98 of the Association Council, OJ 13.3.98 L76/33).

12 Ibid Art 1.

13 Ibid Art 6(1).

14 EA Bulgaria Art 6 (OJ 31.12.94 L358/3); EA Czech Republic Art 6 (OJ 31.12.94 L360/2); EA Slovak Republic Art 6 (OJ 31.12.94 L359/2); EA Romania Art 6 (OJ 31.12.94 L357/2).

15 Ibid Art 7(1).

16 Ibid Art 7(2).

17 Ibid Art 25(1). However, exceptional measures of limited duration may be taken by Hungary in the form of increased customs duties in respect of infant industries or certain sectors undergoing restructuring or facing serious difficulties, particularly where these difficulties produce important social problems: ibid Art 28. As to procedures in this respect, see Commission Decision 264/94, OJ 5.2.94 L3274.

18 Ibid Art 25(2). As to safeguard measures in specified circumstances, see ibid Art 31.

19 Ibid Art 25(3).

intellectual, industrial and commercial property; or rules relating to gold and silver. These measures may not, however, constitute a means of arbitrary discrimination or a disguised restriction on trade between the parties.

In respect of industrial products, customs duties on imports applicable in the Community for goods originating in Hungary are to be abolished immediately or progressively depending on the product and at the latest by the end of the fifth year after the entry into force of the Agreement.[20] Quantitative restrictions on imports to the Community and measures having equivalent effect are to be abolished on the date of the EA's entry into force.[1] Conversely, Hungarian customs duties on products originating in the Community are to be reduced progressively to zero by 1 January 2001 at the latest.[2] Quantitative restrictions and equivalent measures in respect of certain listed imports are to be progressively abolished between 1 January 1995 and 31 December 2000, while for all other products such restrictions are to be abolished on the entry into force of the Agreement.[3] Charges having an effect equivalent to a customs duty are to be abolished by the Community on entry into force, whereas Hungary is required to abolish such charges according to a specified timetable.[4] Any customs duty of exports, charges having equivalent effect, quantitative restrictions on exports and measures having equivalent effect are to be abolished by the two parties at the latest by the end of the fifth year after entry into force of the Agreement.[5] These provisions do not apply to textile products or ECSC products.[6] Nor do they preclude the retention by the Community or the introduction by Hungary of an agricultural component in the duties applicable to certain listed products.[7]

In respect of agricultural products,[8] quantitative restrictions on imports are to be abolished by the Community at the date when the EA enters into force.[9] Specified tariff concessions are agreed for processed agricultural products not covered by Annex II EC,[10] in particular that the agricultural component of the

20 Ibid Art 9(1), (2), (3).
 1 Ibid Art 9(4).
 2 Ibid Art 10(1), (2), (3).
 3 Ibid Art 10(4).
 4 Ibid Art 12.
 5 Ibid Art 13, which excepts those that might be required for the administration of international obligations. As to safeguard measures in specified circumstances, see ibid Art 31.
 6 Ibid Art 8(2). These products are governed by special rules. As to textile products, see ibid Art 15, Protocol 1, amended to take account of the accession of new Member States by Agreement (OJ 26.4.95 L94/166). See generally Chapter 18. As to ECSC products, see ibid Art 16, Protocol 2. See generally Chapter 19 in this book on ECSC Products.
 7 Ibid Art 17(1) (Community), 17(2) (Hungary). As to the listed products, see Annex VII. As to transitional measures pending application of Protocol 3 following the Uruguay Round, see Council Regulation 339/97, OJ 27.2.97 (Poland, Hungary, Slovakia, Czech Republic, Romania, Bulgaria).
 8 That is, the products listed in Chapters 1–24 of the combined nomenclature and of the Hungarian customs tariff and the products listed in Annex I of the EA, but excluding fishery products as defined by Council Regulation 3687/91 (now replaced by Council Regulation 3759/92, OJ 31.12.92 L388/1, as amended): ibid Art 18(2). Fishery products are subject *mutatis mutandis* to ibid Art 23, which provides for the possibility of reciprocal concessions. As to agriculture and accession to the EU, see Commission of the European Communities, 'Study on alternative strategies for the development of relations in the field of agriculture between the EU and the associated countries with a view to future accession of these countries' (Agricultural Strategy Paper), CSE(95)607.
 9 Ibid Art 20(1). As to the adoption of implementing (including safeguard) measures, see Council Regulation 3491/93 Art 1, OJ 21.12.93 L319/1.
10 Ibid Art 19, Protocol 3. As to new autonomous and transitional measures in certain processed agricultural products, see Council Regulation 656/98, OJ 25.3.98 L90/1 (Poland, Hungary, Slovakia, Czech Republic, Romania, Bulgaria).

levy on imports into the Community was to be eliminated by 1 January 1998 at the latest.[11] Various listed agricultural products originating in Hungary benefit, as from the entry into force of the Agreement, from the reduction of levies within the limit of Community quotas or from the reduction of customs duties on specified conditions.[12] Listed agricultural products originating in the Community may be imported into Hungary free of quantitative restrictions[13] or free of such restrictions up to specified quantities.[14] For other listed products the parties are to grant each other reciprocal concessions.[15] The possibility of further concessions is to be examined in the Association Council on a product-by-product and orderly and reciprocal basis.[16] Processed agricultural products originating in the Community and subject to quantitative restrictions in Hungary are to enjoy conditions not less favourable than any most favoured third country with regard to import licences.[17]

11 See ibid Protocol 3, Art 4.
12 Ibid Art 20(2), Annex VIIIa, Annex VIIIb. As to certain agricultural concessions provided in the Uruguay Round and granted for the period 1 January 1996 to 30 June 2001, see Commission Regulation 3066/95, OJ 30.12.95 L328/31, as amended. As to the suspension of certain concessions in respect of the Czech Republic, see Council Regulation 703/98, OJ 31.3.98 L98/1. As to detailed rules in respect of the poultrymeat and egg sectors, see Commission Regulation 2699/93, OJ 1.10.93 L245/88, as amended (Poland, Hungary, Czech Republic, Slovak Republic) and Commission Regulation 1559/94, OJ 1.7.94 L166/62, as amended (Bulgaria, Romania). See also Joined Cases C-15/91 and C-108/91 *Josef Buckl & Sohne OHG v Commission* [1992] ECR I-6061. As to tariff quotas in respect of milk and milk products, see Commission Regulation 629/95, OJ 24.3.95 L66/6, as amended (Hungary, Bulgaria). As to detailed rules in respect of pigmeat, see Commission Regulation 2698/93, OJ 1.10.93 L245/80, as amended (Poland, Hungary, Czech Republic, Slovak Republic); Commission Regulation 1590/94, OJ 1.7.94 L167/16 (Bulgaria, Romania); Commission Regulation 95/386, OJ 30.9.95 L233/45 (Estonia, Latvia, Lithuania). As to certain cereals sector products, see Commission Regulation 1218/96, OJ 29.6.96 L161/51, as amended (Poland, Hungary, Czech Republic, Slovak Republic, Bulgaria, Romania).
13 Ibid Art 20(3), Annex IXa.
14 Ibid Art 20(3), Annex IXb.
15 Ibid Art 20(4), Annexes Xa, Xb, Sc, XIa, XIb, XIc and XId. As to live sheep or goats, sheepmeat and goatmeat, see ibid Annex Xb as well as the 1981 Agreement (OJ 6.6.81 L150/7), extended in 1984 (OJ 9.6.84 L154741, as amended), rectified in 1985 (OJ 23.7.85 L191/51). As to certain concessions, see Council Regulation 95/375, OJ 20.9.95 L223/29. As to analogous arrangements with other EA countries, see in respect of Romania: Agreement (OJ 23.5.81 L137/21), consultations (OJ 23.5.81 L137/21), and extensions (OJ 23.5.81 L137/28, OJ 3.4.85 L96/31); in respect of the Czech Republic: Agreement (OJ 12.7.82 L204/30), extensions (OJ 12.7.82 L204/35, OJ 9.6.84 L154/47), consultations (OJ 12.7.82 L204/37); in respect of Bulgaria: Agreement (OJ 15.2.82 L43/13), extension (OJ 9.6.84 L154/39); in respect of Poland: Agreement (OJ 23.5.81 L137/13), extension (OJ 9.6.84 L154/45). As to wines, see the Agreement in the form of an Exchange of Letters on the reciprocal establishment of tariff quotas between the EC and Romania, OJ 31.12.93 L337/172, amended and extended until 31 December 1998 by a further Agreement in the form of an Exchange of Letters, OJ 18.4.98 L116/3, approved on behalf of the Community by Council Regulation 813/98, OJ 18.4.98 L116/1. As to analogous Agreement between the EC and Bulgaria, see OJ 31.12.93 L337/1, amended and extended until 31 December 1998, as to which see OJ 20.3.98 L96/1.
16 Ibid Art 20(8). As to the Association Council, see ibid Arts 104–107.
17 Ibid Protocol 3, Art 6. Article 4 of Protocol 3 of the Europe Agreement with the Czech Republic provides that the Czech Republic is to determine the agricultural component of the levy, and that the elimination of the non-agricultural component must be completed by 1 January 1998 at the latest. As to the proposed timetable for the reduction of the non-agricultural component, see Commission Proposal for a Council Decision concerning the Community's position with respect to the duties applied by the Czech Republic to imports of processed agricultural goods originating in the Community, COM(96)30 final (Brussels 31.1.96). As to duties applicable from 1996–2000 and after, see Decision 1/97 of the EC–Czech Republic Association Council, OJ 12.4.97 L97/4.

Trade in textile and clothing products was previously subject to separate regulation.[18] An Additional Protocol to the EA[19] provided for the gradual elimination of quantitative restrictions and equivalent measures,[20] Hungarian agreement to restrain its exports of specified products,[1] and the exception from quantitative restrictions of textiles reimported after outward processing.[2] Protocol 1 to the EA provides for the gradual elimination of customs duties on textile imports within six years from the EA's entry into force,[3] the elimination of customs duties on reimports into the Community of textile products after outward processing in Hungary,[4] and the renegotiation of a new Protocol on quantitative arrangements with any such restrictions to be eliminated in accordance with the Uruguay Round agreements.[5]

In addition to anti-dumping provisions,[6] safeguard measures may be taken in specified cases.[7] Such measures may be taken where any product is being im-

---

18 See Council Decision 87/548 in respect of the Agreement initialled on 1 July 1986 (OJ 21.11.87 L331/1), amended by Additional Protocol (OJ 27.12.86 L366/2) and Agreed Minute (OJ 27.2.91 L53/23). As to provisions still in force in respect of analogous agreements (including the EAs) with other EA countries, see in respect of Bulgaria: Agreed Minute (OJ 27.2.91 L53/19), Additional Protocol to the EA (OJ 17.5.94 L123/147), Agreement amending Additional Protocol (OJ 26.4.95 L94/84); in respect of Poland: Agreed Minute (OJ 27.2.91 L53/27), Additional Protocol to the EA (OJ 31.12.92 L410/461), as amended; in respect of Romania: Agreed Minute (OJ 27.2.91 L53/31), Additional Protocol to the EA (OJ 17.5.94 L123/476), Agreement amending Additional Protocol to the EA (OJ 26.4.95 L94/391); in respect of the Czech Republic: Additional Protocol to the EA (OJ 17.5.94 L123/198), Agreement amending Additional Protocol (OJ 26.4.95 L94/128); in respect of Poland: Additional Protocol to the EA (OJ 17.5.94 L123/198, as amended), Agreement amending Additional Protocol (OJ 26.4.95 L94/368); in respect of the Slovak Republic: Additional Protocol to the EA (OJ 17.5.94 L123/556, as amended), Agreement amending Additional Protocol to the EA (OJ 26.4.95 L94/436).
19 OJ 31.12.92 L410/391, as amended, Art 15(5) of which provides that the Additional Protocol, including the Annexes, Appendices, Agreed Minutes and joint memoranda attached to it, is an integral part of the EA.
20 Ibid Art 1(2).
1 Ibid Art 3(1), Annex II.
2 Ibid Art 5(1).
3 EA Hungary, Protocol 1, Art 2(1), (2), OJ 31.12.93 L347/152.
4 Ibid Art 2(3).
5 See ibid Art 3. See the Additional Protocol to the European Agreement on trade in textile products between the European Community and Hungary, OJ 20.5.97 L127/59. As to analogous Additional Protocols with other Europe Agreement countries, see OJ 20.5.97 L127/255 (Czech Republic), OJ 20.5.97 L127/2 (Bulgaria), and OJ 20.5.97 L127/140 (Poland). All were approved by Council Decision 97/295, OJ 20.5.97 L127/1. As to the Uruguay Round agreement, see Chapter 18 on Textiles.
6 Ibid Art 29. As to procedures, see ibid Art 33(2),(3)(b) and Council Regulation 3491/93 Art 4, OJ 21.12.93 L319/1. This Regulation incorporated the same provisions as Council Regulation 519/92, as amended, in respect of the Interim Agreement (OJ 29.2.92 L56/6). The analogous regulations in respect of other EA countries are: Bulgaria: EA Art 30, OJ 31.12.94 L358/3 and Council Regulation 3641/93 (OJ 31.12.93 L333/16); Czech Republic: EA Art 30, OJ 31.12.94 L360/2 and Council Regulation 3296/94, OJ 30.12.94 L341/14; Poland: EA Art 29, OJ 31.12.93 L348/2 and Council Regulation 3492/93 (OJ 21.12.93 L319/4); Romania: EA Art 30, OJ 31.12.94 L357/2, and Council Regulation 3382/94, OJ 31.12.94 L368/1; Slovak Republic: EA Art 30, OJ 31.12.94 L359/2, and Council Regulation 3297/94, OJ 30.12.94 L341/17.
7 Ibid Arts 30, 31. As to agricultural products, see above. As to procedures, see ibid Art 33, and Council Regulation 3491/93 Arts 5–7, OJ 21.12.93 L319/1. For analogous provisions in respect of other EAs, see Council Regulation 3492/93, OJ 21.12.93 L319/4 (Poland); Council Regulation 3641/93, OJ 31.12.93 L333/16 (Bulgaria); Council Regulation 3642/93, OJ 31.12.93 L333/17 (Romania). As to safeguards in respect of ECSC products, see Commission Decision 264/94, OJ 5.2.94 L32/3. For analogous provisions in respect of other EAs, see Council Regulation 3383/94, OJ 31.12.94 L368/5 (Bulgaria); Council Regulation 3296/94, OJ 30.12.94

ported in such increased quantities and under such conditions as to cause, or threaten to cause, either serious disturbances to domestic products of like or directly competitive products, or serious disturbances in any sector of the economy or difficulties which could bring about serious deterioration in the economic situation of a region.[8] Before measures are taken, however, the party proposing to take measures must supply the Association Council with all relevant information with a view to seeking an acceptable solution.[9] The Association Council may take any decision needed to put an end to the difficulties.[10] Such decisions must be taken unanimously, that is by agreement between the parties,[11] and are binding on the parties.[12] If no decision or other satisfactory solution is reached within 30 days of the matter being referred, the importing party may adopt appropriate measures.[13] The measures must not exceed the scope of what is necessary to remedy the difficulties,[14] and in the selection of measures, priority must be given to those which least disturb the functioning of the Agreement.[15] The other party must be notified when imports are subject to an administrative procedure,[16] and the Association Council must be notified immediately of the measures with a view to periodic consultations and eventual abolition of the measures.[17] However, where exceptional circumstances requiring immediate action make prior information or examination impossible, the party may apply immediately the precautionary measures strictly necessary to deal with the situation.[18]

These procedures do not apply to textiles.[19] These products are subject to specific safeguards, such as quantitative limits or surveillance.[20]

In addition, special safeguard measures are provided with regard to agricultural products. If agricultural imports originating in one party cause serious disturbance to the markets of the other party, the parties are to enter into consultations immediately to find an appropriate solution. Pending such a solution, the party concerned may take the measures it deems necessary.[1]

Rules of origin are also laid down.[2] The basic criteria for products other than

---

L341/14 (Czech Republic); Commission Decision 265/94, OJ 5.2.94 L32/6 (Poland); Council Regulation 3382/94, OJ 31.12.94 L368/1 (Romania); Council Regulation 3297/94, OJ 30.12.94 L341/17 (Slovak Republic).

8 Ibid Art 30.
9 Ibid Art 33(2), first paragraph.
10 Ibid Art 33(3)(a), first paragraph.
11 Ibid Art 106, second paragraph.
12 Ibid Art 106, first paragraph.
13 Ibid Art 33(3)(a), second paragraph. As to the procedure on the Community side, see Council Regulation 3491/93 Art 5, OJ 21.12.93 L319/1.
14 Ibid Art 33(3)(a), second paragraph.
15 Ibid Art 33(2), second paragraph.
16 Ibid Art 33(1).
17 Ibid Art 33(2), third paragraph.
18 Ibid Art 33(3)(d). See also Council Regulation 3491/93 Art 6, OJ 21.12.93 L319/1.
19 Council Regulation 3491/93 Art 7, OJ 21.12.93 L319/1.
20 Additional Protocol to the EA Hungary, Arts 7, 8, OJ 31.12.94 L410/391. As to prior surveillance in respect of certain textile products from Albania, Estonia, Latvia and Lithuania, see Council Regulation 601/92, OJ 11.3.92 L65/1.
1 Ibid Art 21. See also Council Regulation 3491/93 Art 1, OJ 21.12.93 L319/1.
2 Ibid Art 34 and Protocol No 4, as amended by Decision 3/96 of the Association Council, OJ 7.4.97 L92/1. As to detailed rules for the application regarding milk and milk products of these arrangements, see Commission Regulation 584/92 (OJ 7.3.92 L62/34), as amended by Commission Regulation 993/97 (OJ 3.6.97 L143/6) (Poland, Hungary, Czech Republic, Slovak Republic) and Commission Regulation 1436/97 (OJ 24.7.97 L196/60) (Poland, Hungary, Czech Republic, Slovak Republic). See also Commission Regulation 1588/94 (OJ 1.7.94 L167/8), as amended by Commission Regulation 1430/97 (OJ 24.7.97 L196/42) (Bulgaria, Romania) and Commission Regulation 579/97 (OJ 2.4.97 L87/8) (Bulgaria, Romania).

wholly obtained products is 'sufficient working or processing',[3] which is defined as change of tariff heading[4] or, for specified products, the performance of specified operations[5] combined in certain cases with a percentage criterion test.[6] Bilateral cumulation is permitted between the Community and Hungary,[7] and limited cumulation is permitted between Hungary and Poland, the Czech Republic and the Slovak Republic.[8]

The EA also makes provision for movement of workers,[9] establishment,[10] and supply of services.[11] It lays down rules in respect of current payments and movement of capital,[12] competition and other economic provisions[13] and approximation of laws.[14] It also provides for economic,[15] cultural[16] and financial co-operation.[17]

In addition to the EA, the Community and Hungary have signed agreements in respect of transit,[18] the reciprocal establishment of tariff quotas for certain wines,[19] the reciprocal protection and control of wine names,[20] and the pig and poultry sectors.[1]

Measures have also been taken concerning the export of certain steel products to the Community from the Slovak Republic[2] and the Czech Republic;[3]

---

3 Ibid Protocol 4, Art 1(1)(b), 1(2)(b).
4 Ibid Protocol 4, Art 4(1).
5 Ibid Art 4(2), Annex II.
6 Ibid Art 4(2)(a),(b).
7 Ibid Art 2, as so substituted.
8 Ibid Protocol 4, Art 3 as so substituted.
9 Ibid Arts 37–43.
10 Ibid Arts 44–54.
11 Ibid Art 55–57.
12 Ibid Art 59–61.
13 Ibid Arts 62–66.
14 Ibid Art 67–69.
15 Ibid Art 70–96. See also Protocol 6 on mutual assistance in customs matters.
16 Ibid Art 97.
17 Ibid Arts 98–103. As to the Protocol concerning sanitary, phytosanitary and animal welfare measures between the Community and its Member States, on one hand, and the Czech Republic, on the other, see OJ 6.4.98 L106/3, approved on behalf of the European Community by Council Decision 98/250, OJ 6.4.98 L106/1.
18 OJ 31.12.93 L347/269. Analogous agreements have been signed by the Community with the Czech and Slovak Republics (OJ 31.12.92 L407/57), as subsequently implemented in two separate Council Decisions 94/909, OJ 31.12.94 L359/1, and 94/910, OJ 31.12.94 L360/1); Romania (OJ 31.12.94 L357/183); and Bulgaria (OJ 31.12.94 L358/214).
19 OJ 31.12.93 L337/84.
20 OJ 31.12.93 L337/94; OJ 31.12.93 L337/167; OJ 31.12.93 L337/169. There are analogous agreements between the Community and Bulgaria (tariff quotas: OJ 31.12.93 L337/3, names: OJ 31.12.93 L337/12) and the Community and Romania (tariff quotas: OJ 31.12.93 L337/173, names: OJ 31.12.93 L337/178).
1 OJ 31.12.93 L347/268. As to analogous arrangements with other EA countries, see OJ 31.12.93 L348/181 (Poland); OJ 31.12.94 L358/219 (Bulgaria).
2 Decision 1/93 of the EC–Czech Republic and Slovak Republic Joint Committee (OJ 29.6.93 L157/59), as amended, and as modified by Decision 1/94 (OJ 16.9.94 L241/20) and Decision 2/94 (OJ 17.12.94 L325/58) of the Joint Committee. See also Decision 4/96 of the EC–Czech Association Council, OJ 5.3.97 L64/13.
3 Decision 1/93 of the EC–Czech Republic and Slovak Republic Joint Committee (OJ 29.6.93 L157/67), as amended, and as modified by Decision 1/94 (OJ 16.9.94 L241/21) and by Decision 2/94 (OJ 17.12.94 L325/58) of the Joint Committee. Dual import controls, without quantitative limits, apply to the import into the EC of certain steel products originating in the Czech Republic, Bulgaria, Romania, or Slovenia: see *Agence Europe*, No 7124 (n.s.), 18 December 1997, p 11; *Agence Europe*, No 7128 (n.s.), Wednesday 24 December 1997.

with Poland in respect of certain oilseeds[4] and potato starch;[5] and with Poland[6] and Romania[7] in respect of certain industrial products. Measures have also been taken with the Czech Republic[8] and the Slovak Republic[9] in respect of fish; with Bulgaria in respect of certain animal feed preparations;[10] with Bulgaria and Romania in respect of milk and milk products;[11] and with Bulgaria,[12] the Czech Republic,[13] Romania,[14] and the Slovak Republic[15] in respect of live bovine animals. For the importation of fresh meat into the Community, establishments have been approved in the Czech Republic,[16] Croatia,[17] the Slovak Republic,[18] and Slovenia.[19]

The Community has also signed an agreement with Albania on trade and economic co-operation[20] and trade in textiles.[1] In 1997 the Community and Albania signed a Memorandum of Understanding (MOU) on customs co-operation.[2]

The Baltic States—an example—the EC–Estonia Free Trade Agreement

Trade between the Community and the Baltic States will be governed by similar arrangements once the relevant EAs enter into force. In the meantime, however, the trade provisions of these Europe Agreements have since 1 January 1995 been applied by means of free trade agreements (FTA). The FTA between the Community and Estonia[3] provides an example. The entire Europe Agreement between the EC and its Member States, of the one hand, and Estonia, on the other hand, entered into force on 1 February 1998.[4]

The FTA between the Community and Estonia provides for the establishment of a free trade area.[5] Respect for human rights and the principles of market

4 Agreement, OJ 18.2.94 L47/19.
5 Commission Regulation 1995/92, OJ 18.7.92 L199/14, as amended.
6 Agreement, OJ 14.10.94 L264/29.
7 See Council Regulation 3419/83, OJ 8.12.83 L346/1, as amended.
8 Agreement, OJ 22.10.94 L272/50.
9 Agreement, OJ 15.11.94 L294/27.
10 Commission Regulation 1550/94, OJ 1.7.94 L166/43, as amended.
11 Commission Regulation 1588/94, OJ 1.7.94 L167/8, as amended.
12 Agreement, OJ 31.12.94 L358/217.
13 Exchange of letters, OJ 21.12.94 L360/211.
14 Agreement, OJ 31.12.94 L357/186.
15 Exchange of letters, OJ 31.12.94 L359/211.
16 Commission Decision 93/546, OJ 27.10.93 L266/31.
17 Commission Decision 93/26, OJ 25.1.93 L16/24.
18 Commission Decision 93/547, OJ 27.10.93 L266/33.
19 Commission Decision 93/27, OJ 25.1.93 L16/26.
20 OJ 25.11.92 L343/2.
 1 OJ 17.5.94 L123/3.
 2 Memorandum of Understanding on the European Commission Customs Assistance Mission to Albania. See also *Agence Europe*, No 7097 (n.s.), Monday/Tuesday 10/11 November 1997, p 9.
 3 OJ 31.12.94 L373/2. As to procedures for applying these trade provisions, see Council Regulation 595/98, OJ 17.3.98 L79/5. Analogous provisions apply to Latvia and Lithuania. See Council Regulation 596/98, OJ 17.3.98 L79/9 (Latvia) and Council Regulation 594/98, OJ 17.3.98 L79/1 (Lithuania).
 4 The Europe Agreements with Latvia and Lithuania entered into force on the same date. See also Decision 1/98 of the Association Council adopting its rules of procedure, OJ 12.3.98 L73/17. Analogous provisions apply to Latvia and Lithuania: see Decision 1/98 of the EC-Latvia Association Council, OJ 12.3.98 L73/31; Decision 1/98 of the EC-Lithuania Association Council, OJ 12.3.98 L73/24:
 5 Ibid Art 2(1). As to rules of origin, see Protocol 3, as amended by Decision 1/97 of the EC–Estonia Joint Committee, OJ 28.4.97 L111/1.

economy constitute essential elements of the Agreement.[6] The FTA covers goods, payments, competition and other economic provisions, and institutional matters.[7] The combined nomenclature of goods applies to trade between the parties.[8] Successive reductions are to be applied to the basic duty for each product, which is that actually applied *erga omnes* on 1 January 1994.[9] Customs duties and quantitative restrictions, and equivalent measures, in respect of imports are to be abolished as between the parties.[10] Similar obligations apply to customs duties on exports and equivalent charges[11] and to quantitative restrictions on exports and equivalent measures.[12] Special provisions apply to textiles.[13] These provisions do not preclude an agricultural component in duties applicable to Annex II products.[14]

The FTA lays down specific provisions in respect of agriculture[15] and fisheries.[16] A standstill clause applies to customs duties, equivalent charges, quantitative restrictions and equivalent measures.[17] For a period of two years, however, Estonia was permitted, on certain conditions, to introduce duties on a limited number of agricultural products originating in the Community.[18] No quantitative restrictions apply to imports into the Community of agricultural products originating in the Community.[19] Other agricultural products may be imported into the Community within the framework of specified concessions,[20] which are subject to revision by agreement.[1] Separate arrangements are made for processed agricultural products.[2] Specified tariff concessions are to be granted by the Community to processed agricultural products originating in Estonia,[3]

---

6 Ibid Art 1(1).
7 Trade in EAEC products is governed in accordance with the EAEC Treaty: Art 3(2).
8 Ibid Art 2(2).
9 Ibid Art 2(3). If however tariff reductions result from for example the Uruguay Round, the reduced duties replace these basic duties: Art 3(4).
10 As to imports into the Community, see ibid Art 4. As to imports into Estonia, see ibid Art 5. This includes customs duties of a fiscal nature: ibid Art 6. The parties are expressly obliged to abolish charges equivalent to customs duties on import: Art 7.
11 Ibid Art 8(1).
12 Ibid Art 8(2). Standstill provisions are provided in Art 18.
13 Ibid Art 9, Protocol 1.
14 Ibid Art 10.
15 The expression 'agricultural products' means the products listed in Chapters 1–24 of the combined nomenclature and the products listed in Annex I of the FTA, but excluding fishery products as defined by Council Regulation 3759/92: ibid Art 11(2). The FTA is not intended however to affect in any way the pursuance by the parties of their respective agricultural policies or the taking of any measures under these policies: Art 18(2).
16 'Fishery products' means products covered by Council Regulation 3759/92: ibid Art 15.
17 Ibid Art 18(1).
18 Ibid Art 18(3).
19 Ibid Art 13(1).
20 Ibid Art 13(2). As to the concessions, see Annexes III (specified duties), IV (minimum import prices for soft fruit for processing) and V (global tariff quotas for live bovine animals, bovine meat, sheep and goatmeat). As to detailed rules for soft fruit, see Commission Regulation 2449/96, OJ 14.12.96 L335/25, as amended. As to post-Uruguay Round concessions, see Council Regulation 1926/96 (OJ 8.10.96 L254/1) and, as to dairy products, Commission Regulation 1713/95 (OJ 14.7.95 L163/5), as amended. As to tariff quotas for beef from 1 July 1997 to 30 June 1998, see Commission Regulation 995/97, OJ 4.6.97 L144/2.
1 Ibid Art 13(3). The possibility of further concessions is to be examined in the Joint Committee product-by-product and on an orderly and reciprocal basis: Art 13(4).
2 Ibid Art 12 and Protocol 2. Pending the entry into force of the 'interim' protocols, concessions previously granted on a provisional and autonomous basis have been extended until 31 December 1998 by Council Regulation 2621/97, OJ 30.12.97 L354/1 (Lithuania, Latvia, Estonia).
3 Protocol 2, Art 1 and Annex 1.

but in respect of certain listed products these reductions are subject to quantitative limits.[4] If imports cause serious disturbance to markets, the parties are to enter into consultations immediately, but pending a solution the party concerned may take the measures it deems necessary.[5]

The same provisions apply, *mutatis mutandis*, to fishery products,[6] for which similar concessions are provided.[7]

Provision is also made for the introduction by Estonia of increased customs duties as an exceptional measure of limited duration in specified circumstances,[8] anti-dumping measures in accordance with the GATT,[9] and safeguard measures.[10] In addition, the standard exceptions to free trade apply.[11]

A Joint Committee is established to settle disputes and perform other functions.[12]

Prior to the signature of the recent EAs with the Baltic States, the Community concluded agreements on fisheries relations with Estonia,[13] Latvia[14] and Lithuania;[15] on textile products with Latvia[16] and Lithuania,[17] now both replaced by free trade provisions;[18] and on maritime transport with Estonia,[19] Latvia,[20] and Lithuania.[1]

AGREEMENTS ON PARTNERSHIP AND CO-OPERATION

Introduction

Partership and Co-operation Agreements (PCAs) have been signed or are foreseen between the Community and most of the countries (except for the Baltic States) that formerly belonged to the USSR.[2] All of these bilateral agreements are mixed agreements. In respect of matters within EC competence, they are based on EC Arts 113 and 235. The enactment of the trade and trade-related chapters of the PCAs, as with the EAs, is planned or underway by means of interim agreements. All PCAs, as the recent EAs, contain a human rights clause.[3] The PCAs

4 Protocol 2, Art 1 and Annex II.
5 Ibid Art 14.
6 Ibid Art 16(2).
7 Ibid Art 16(1), Annex VI.
8 Ibid Art 21.
9 Ibid Art 22.
10 Ibid Arts 23, 24. In respect of procedure, see Art 26.
11 Ibid Arts 28, 41.
12 Ibid Arts 37–39.
13 OJ 9.3.93 L56/2.
14 OJ 9.3.93 L56/6.
15 OJ 9.3.93 L56/10.
16 OJ 17.5.94 L123/334.
17 OJ 17.5.94 L123/362.
18 See Council Decision on the provisional application of certain Additional Protocols to the Free Trade and Europe Agreements with the Republic of Lithuania and the Republic of Latvia, OJ 13.2.98 L41/81, and the attached Protocols.
19 OJ 31.12.94 L373/163.
20 OJ 31.12.94 L374/216.
 1 OJ 31.12.94 L375/204.
 2 For a summary as of April 1995 but still very useful, see Maresceau and Montaguti 'The Relations between the European Union and Central and Eastern Europe: A Legal Appraisal' (1995) 32 CMLRev 1327 at 1349. See also Commission of the European Communities 'Towards a European Union Strategy for Relations with the Transcaucasian Republics' (Communication from the Commission, Brussels, 31 May 1995), COM(95)205 final.
 3 For example, PCA Russia Art 1, OJ 13.10.95 L247/2.

may be divided into two categories: those with Russia, Ukraine, Moldova and Belarus, on the one hand, and those with the non-European former USSR Republics, on the other hand. The PCA with Russia serves an example of the former group, while the PCA with the Kyrgyz Republic is an example of the latter group.

Russia

An example of the first group is the PCA with Russia,[4] which was signed on 24 June 1994. It entered into force on 1 December 1997 for an initial period of ten years. It replaced the previous framework for trade between the Community and Russia, which was provided by the Interim Agreement signed on 17 July 1995.[5] This in turn had replaced a 1989 Trade and Economic Co-operation Agreement[6] in respect of the trade and trade-related provisions. However, with regard to certain other matters such as textiles[7] and matters covered by the Euratom Treaty,[8] relations between the Community and the former members of the USSR, including Russia, remained governed by the previous Community measures. More generally, the 1989 Trade and Co-operation Agreement continued to govern relations between the Community and other former USSR countries until the respective interim agreements entered into force.[9]

The PCA has numerous aims: to provide a framework for political dialogue, to promote trade and investment and harmonious economic relations between the Parties based on the principles of market economy, to strengthen political and economic freedoms, to support Russian efforts to consolidate its democracy and market economy, to provide a basis for co-operation in many fields, to promote activities of joint interest, to provide an appropriate framework for

---

4 Partnership and Co-operation Agreement between the European Communities and their Member States, of the one part, and the Russian Federation, of the other part, OJ 28.11.97 L327/3, approved on behalf of the European Communities by Council and Commission Decision 97/800, OJ 28.11.97 L327/1. See also Rules of Procedure of the Co-operation Council (98/228/ EC), OJ 21.3.98 L87/17. See also Commission of the European Communities 'The European Union and Russia: The Future Relationship' (Communication from the Commission, Brussels, 31 May 1995), COM(95)223 final. Together with other PCAs, it replaced the 1989 Agreement on Trade and Economic Co-operation between the EEC and the EAEC and the USSR (OJ 15.3.90 L68/3); see also Council Decision 90/116, OJ 15.3.90 L68/1.
5 OJ 13.10.95 L247/1.
6 OJ 15.3.90 L68/3. The Russia Federation was considered to be the successor state of the USSR after the latter was dissolved.
7 Agreements concerning textiles have been signed with Armenia (OJ 17.5.94 L123/64), Azerbaijan (OJ 17.5.95 L123/92), Belarus (OJ 17.5.94 L123/120, as amended), Georgia (OJ 17.5.94 L123/250), Moldova (OJ 17.5.94 L123/390), Russia (OJ 17.5.94 L123/528) and Ukraine (OJ 17.5.94 L123/718, as amended).
8 As to such products, see Commission Decision 90/117/Euratom, OJ 15.3.90 L68/2.
9 PCAs were signed with Ukraine on 14 June 1994 (COM (94) 226 final), Council and Commission Decision 98/149, OJ 19.2. L49/1, Moldova on 28 November 1994 (COM(94) 477 final), and Belarus on 6 March 1995 (COM (95) 44 final). Interim agreements were signed with Ukraine on 1 June 1995 and initialled with Moldova on 7 April 1995 and with Belarus on 7 April 1995. Pending their entry into force, the continuation of the 1989 Agreement has been done by means of exchanges of letters. The PCA between the EC and Ukraine entered into force on 1 March 1998: see the Agreement, OJ 19.2.98 L49/1, approved by Council and Commission Decision 98/149, OJ 19.2.98 L49/1. PCAs were signed with Armenia, Azerbaijan and Georgia on 22 April 1996. See 'Accordi di partenariato e di cooperazione tra le Comunità europee e gli Stati membri, da un lato, e l'Armenia, l'Azerbaigian e la Georgia, dall'altro, Lussemburgo, 22 Aprile 1996', Press Release PRES/96/97 of 22.4.96. As to Georgia, see Council Decision 97/301, OJ 21.5.97 L129/22, and the Attached Agreement.

the gradual integration of Russia and a wider area of co-operation in Europe, and to create the necessary conditions for the future establishment of a free trade area between the Community and Russia.[10] Respect for democratic principles and human rights, as defined in particular in the Helsinki Final Act and the Charter of Paris for a New Europe, constitutes an essential element of partnership and of the Agreement.[11]

The parties agree to consider development of relevant titles of the Agreement, in particular Title III and Art 53, as circumstances allow, with a view to the establishment of a free trade area between them.[12]

In respect of trade in goods, the Agreement provides for a most-favoured-nation clause,[13] with certain exceptions.[14] Imports are to be granted national treatment by each party in respect of internal taxes and other internal charges and no less favourable treatment with regard to marketing.[15] Freedom of transit is expressed as a fundamental condition of attaining the objectives of the Agreement,[16] and accordingly each party is to provide freedom of transit through its territory for goods originating in or destined for the customs territory of the other party.[17]

Goods originating in the territory of one party may be imported into the territory of the other party free of quantitative restrictions, and vice versa.[18] This provision does not however apply to textiles,[19] ECSC products,[20] or nuclear materials.[1] Until Russia joins the WTO, the parties are to hold consultations in the Co-operation Committee[2] on their import tariff policies, in particular prior to the increase of tariff protection.[3] The absence of automatic tariff reductions is mitigated in part, however, because the EC GSP system covers relevant products from the former USSR.[4] Provision is made for exemption from import charges and duties of goods imported temporarily.[5]

---

10 Agreement on Partnership and Co-operation establishing a partnership between the European Communities and their Member States, of one part, and the Russian Federation, of the other part, Art 1, OJ 28.11.97 L327/3, approved on behalf of the European Communities by Council and Commission Decision 97/800, OJ 28.11.97 L327/1.
11 Ibid Art 2. See also Art 107(2), the Joint Declaration in relation to Art 107(2), and the Joint Declaration in relation to Arts 2 and 107.
12 Ibid Art 3, which also sets down relevant procedures.
13 Ibid Art 10(1), which refers to the MFN treatment described in Article I, paragraph 1 of the GATT.
14 Ibid Art 10(2). In addition, the MFN treatment granted by Russia does not apply during a five-year transitional period in relation to certain advantages (see Annex I) granted by Russia to other countries of the former USSR. This period may be extended where appropriate for specific sectors by mutual consent. See ibid Art 5(1). However, in relation to MFN treatment granted under Title III, the transitional period expires after three years following the entry into force of the Agreement, or when Russia accedes to the GATT/WTO, whichever is earlier: see ibid Art 5(2).
15 Ibid Art 11(2).
16 Ibid Art 12(1), first paragraph.
17 Ibid Art 12(1), second paragraph.
18 Ibid Art 15. As to derogations allowed to Russia, see ibid Art (15(2) and Annex II.
19 See ibid Art 21. As to the relevant products, see Commission Regulation 1025/97, OJ 7.6.97 L150/20. See also Chapter 18 on Textiles in this book.
20 See ibid Art 21. As to the establishment of a contact group on coal and steel matters, see ibid Art 21(2) and Protocol 1.
1 Ibid Art 15(1), first indent.
2 As to which, see ibid Art 92. As to institutional matters generally, see ibid Arts 90–102.
3 Ibid Art 16.
4 As to the GSP, see Chapter 22 in this book. The basic legislation consists of Council Regulation 3281/94, OJ 19.12.94 L348/1 (industrial products), as corrected in OJ 12.4.95 L82/29, and Council Regulation 3282/94, OJ 19.12.94 L348/57 (agricultural products).
5 Ibid Art 14.

In addition to the standard exceptions as regards restrictions on imports, exports or goods in transit,[6] the Agreement provides for safeguard measures. When goods are imported in such increased quantities and under such conditions as to cause, or threaten to cause, substantial injury to domestic products of like or directly competitive products, a party may take appropriate measures.[7] Before taking any measures, however, the party must supply the Joint Committee with all relevant information with a view to seeking a solution.[8] If no agreement is reached within 30 days of the referral, the party requesting consultations is free to restrict imports of the products concerned or to adopt other appropriate measures to the extent and for such time as is necessary to prevent or remedy the injury.[9] In critical circumstances, where delay would cause damage difficult to repair, the parties may take measures before consultations on the condition that consultations be offered immediately after taking the action.[10] In the selection of measures, priority must be given to those which cause least disturbance to the achievement of the aims of the Agreement.[11] Where a safeguard measure is taken by one party, the other party is free to deviate from its obligations towards the other party in respect of substantially similar trade.[12] However, this right of deviation cannot be exercised for the first three years that a safeguard measure is in effect, provided that it was taken as a result of an absolute increase in imports, for a maximum of four years, and in conformity with the Agreement.[13]

The Agreement also provides for anti-dumping measures, following the GATT or related internal legislation.[14]

Special provisions apply to trade in nuclear materials.[15]

The Agreement also provides for business and investment,[16] the establishment of companies,[17] cross-border supply of services,[18] general matters,[19] payments and capital,[20] competition,[1] intellectual property[2] and legislative co-operation,[3] economic co-operation,[4] co-operation on prevention of illegal activities,[5] cultural co-operation,[6] and financial co-operation.[7]

6 Ibid Art 19.
7 Ibid Art 17(1).
8 Ibid Art 17(2).
9 Ibid Art 17(3).
10 Ibid Art 17(4).
11 Ibid Art 17(5).
12 Ibid Art 17(6), first paragraph. Such action must not be taken before consultations have been offered by the second party, or if agreement is reached within 45 days of the offer: ibid Art 17(6), second paragraph.
13 Ibid Art 17(7).
14 Ibid Art 18, first pararaph. For this purpose Russia has recently been removed from the list of non-market economy countries: see Council Regulation 905/98, OJ 30.4.98 L128/18. As to anti-dumping, see Chapter 13.
15 Ibid Art 22. As to EAEC products, see Chapter 20 in this book.
16 See ibid Arts 23–27.
17 See ibid Arts 28–35.
18 See ibid Arts 36–43. For sectors listed in Annex 5, MFN treatment is the rule (Art 36), but the parties may be subject to certain conditions regulating cross-border supply of services (see Art 38(1)).
19 See ibid Arts 44–51.
20 See ibid Art 52.
1 See ibid Art 53.
2 See ibid Art 54.
3 See ibid Art 55.
4 See ibid Arts 56–83.
5 See ibid Art 84.
6 See ibid Art 85.
7 See ibid Art 86.

The Agreement contains provisions on mutual administrative assistance for the correct application of customs legislation.[8]

Imports of textiles between the Community and Russia are governed by a separate agreement.[9] Trade in specified textile products is liberalized under specified conditions.[10] In relation to these products the Community undertakes to suspend the application of quantitative restrictions,[11] and measures having equivalent effect are prohibited.[12] Russian exports of cottage-industry fabrics are also not subject to quantitative restrictions provided certain conditions are met.[13] Goods imported into the Community for inward processing are not subject to quantitative limits.[14] Specific arrangements are made for re-imports into the Community of goods outward processed in Russia.[15]

Russia is to respect specified quantitative limits on exports, which in addition are subject to a double-checking system.[16] In particular, upon request by the Community a specified proportion of the quantitative limits is to be reserved to the Community textile industry by means of contracts.[17] Provision is made for advance use, carry-over and transfers.[18] Exports of textile products not specifically listed in the Agreement may be made subject to quantitative limits following specified procedures.[19] Any quantitative limits on imports into the Community of textile products from Russia are not to be broken down by the Community into regional shares.[20]

In addition to procedures to prevent circumvention,[1] the Agreement also provides for safeguard measures by the Community.[2] If the Community considers that a textile product is being imported from Russia at a price abnormally lower than the normal competitive level, and is for this reason causing or threatening to cause serious injury to Community producers of like or directly competing products, it may request consultations.[3] If following consultations it is acknowledged by common accord that the relevant conditions exist, Russia is required to take,

---

8 Ibid Protocol 2.
9 OJ 17.5.94 L123/528, which replaced the earlier agreement with the USSR (OJ 30.12.89 L197/2). The Agreement applied until 31 December 1994, was extended automatically for one more year (Agreement Art 19(1)) and since then has been continued by agreement until 30 April 1998: see most recently Commission Regulation 729/98, OJ 1.4.98 L100/52. A new textile agreement initialled on 28 March 1998 provides for the elimination of any quantitative restriction in trade of textile products between the Parties as of 1 May 1998. The text describes the position up to that time. Russia is not a member of the WTO and thus trade in textiles between the Community and Russia is not governed by the Uruguay Round Agreement on Textiles and Clothing.
10 Ibid Art 1(1).
11 Ibid Art 1(2).
12 Ibid Art 1(3).
13 Ibid Art 9. The conditions are laid down in Protocol B.
14 Ibid Art 3(1).
15 Ibid Art 3(3), Annex II.
16 Ibid Art 2(1). The quantitative limits are laid down in Annex II. As to the double-checking system, see Protocol A, Title III.
17 Ibid Art 2(2).
18 Ibid Art 4.
19 Ibid Art 5.
20 Ibid Art 7(1). Procedures are specified, however, to deal with regional concentration or sudden changes in imports: ibid Art 7(2),(3),(4).
 1 Ibid Art 6. The origin of products covered by the Agreement is to be determined by the rules in force in the Community: ibid Art 11(2), first paragraph. The procedures for control of origin of these products are laid down in Protocol A, Title II: ibid Art 11(2), third paragraph.
 2 Ibid Art 10.
 3 Ibid Art 10(1). The procedure for consultations is laid down in Art 15.

within the limits of its powers, the necessary steps, in particular in respect of prices, to remedy the situation.[4] If consultations fail, the Community can temporarily refuse consignments.[5] In totally exceptional and critical circumstances, the Community may temporarily suspend imports pending agreement on a solution by consultations, which are to be opened immediately.[6]

Russia is obliged to create favourable conditions for imports of specified textile products originating in the Community, for example by according them non-discriminatory treatment as regards quantitative restrictions, equivalent measures and import licences.[7]

A new Textile Agreement initialled on 28 March 1998 provides for the elimination of any quantitative restriction in trade on textile products between the parties as of 1 May 1998.[8]

The Community, Canada and Russia in 1998 concluded an Agreement on International Humane Trapping Standards.[9] Intended to harmonize standards in respect of the use of leghold traps, it lays down animal welfare standards in respect of listed animals.[10] A party may continue to prohibit the use, in its territory, of traps that had been prohibited for use at the date of entry into force of the Agreement.[11] Each party must recognize the trapping methods of any other party as equivalent if the other party's trapping methods meet the Standards.[12] No party may impose trade restrictive measures on fur and fur products originating from any other party.[13]

A Community measure provides for the free supply of beef, butter and flour to the ex-USSR.[14]

The non-European former USSR—an example—Kyrgyz

A second group of PCAs links the Community with the non-European former USSR Republics. The proposed PCA with the Kyrgyz Republic[15] provides an example. A mixed agreement to be concluded for an initial period of ten years,

4 Ibid Art 10(2). As to determination of price level, see ibid Art 10(3).
5 Ibid Art 10(4).
6 Ibid Art 10(5).
7 Ibid Art 13(1). The relevant products are listed in Annex I.
8 As to the provisional application of this Agreement, see Council Decision 98/379, OJ 15.6.98 L169/1.
9 Agreement on international humane trapping standards between the European Community, Canada and the Russian Federation, OJ 14.2.98 L42/43, approved on behalf of the Community by Council Decision 98/142, OJ 14.2.98 L42/41.
10 Ibid Art 3 and Annex I.
11 Ibid Art 5.
12 Ibid Art 12(2).
13 Ibid Art 13, which further provides that this is without prejudice to the dispute settlement procedures laid down in Art 15 of the Agreement, or the entitlement to request an appropriate certificate of origin, or the relevant provisions of the Convention on International Trade in Endangered Species of Wild Fauna and Flora (CITES).
14 Council Regulation 598/91, OJ 14.3.91 L67/19, for which detailed rules were initially laid down by Commission Regulation 1251/94, OJ 1.6.94 L137/36. See also Joined Cases T-121/96 and T-151/96 *Mutual Aid Administration Services NV (MAAS) v Commission* (1997) Transcript, 18 September.
15 Proposal for a Council and Commission Decision on the conclusion of the Partnership and Co-operation Agreement between the European Communities and their Member States of the one part, and the Kyrgyz Republic, of the other part (presented to the Council by the Commission), COM(94)412 final. A PCA between the Community and Uzbekistan was concluded on 29 April 1996 (Press Release IP/96/475: Conclusion de l'Accord de Parténariat et de Coopération entre les Communautés européennes, leurs Etats membres et la République

it contains a human rights clause.[16] The Agreement establishes a political dialogue.[17] It also covers trade in goods, labour conditions, establishment and operation of companies, cross-border supply of services, payments and capital, competition, intellectual, industrial and commercial property protection, and co-operation in the legislative, economic, cultural and financial domains. It also sets out an institutional framework, including a Co-operation Council,[18] a Co-operation Committee[19] and a Parliamentary Co-operation Committee.[20] Customs co-operation is covered by a separate protocol.[1]

In respect of trade in goods, the parties engage to accord one another MFN treatment in a range of areas,[2] with specified exceptions.[3] Goods imported temporarily are free from import charges and duties within specified conditions.[4] Such imports are also free of quantitative restrictions and equivalent measures.[5] The standard exceptions to free trade apply.[6] Goods are to be traded between the parties at market-related prices.[7] Safeguard measures are provided subject to prior consultations.[8] Separate agreements apply to textile products,[9] ECSC products,[10] and nuclear materials.[11]

Agreements in respect of trade in textile products have been concluded between the Community and Kazakstan,[12] the Kyrgyz Republic,[13] Tajikistan,[14] Turkmenistan,[15] and Uzbekistan.[16] As the agreements are the same, we may take the Agreement between the Community and Kazakstan as an example.[17]

---

d'Ouzbekistan). An Interim Agreement between the Community and Uzbekistan was concluded in January 1998: see Interim Agreement, OJ 14.2.98 L43/2, approved on behalf of the Community by Council Decision 98/138, OJ 14.2.98 L43/1 and on behalf of the ECSC and the EAEC by Commission Decision 98/343, OJ 27.5.98 L153/17.

16 PCA Kyrgyz Art 2.
17 Ibid Arts 4–7.
18 Ibid Arts 75–76, 78–79. As to the role of the Co-operation Council in settling disputes, see Art 86.
19 Ibid Art 77.
20 Ibid Arts 80–82.
 1 Ibid Art 66, Protocol No 1.
 2 Ibid Art 1.
 3 Ibid Art 8(2),(3). Article 8(2) refers to advantages granted with the aim of creating a customs union or free trade area or pursuant to the creation of such a union or area, advantages granted to particular countries in accordance with the GATT and other international arrangements in favour of developing countries, and advantages accorded to adjacent countries to facilitate frontier traffic. Article 8(3) excepts certain advantages (defined in Annex I) granted by the Kyrgyz Republic to other former USSR states; this exception applies during a transitional period expiring when the Kyrgyz Republic accedes to GATT or on 31 December 1998, whichever is the earlier.
 4 Ibid Art 10.
 5 Ibid Art 11, which excepts (in Art 11(1)) certain provisions of the Acts of Accession of Spain and Portugal.
 6 Ibid Art 15.
 7 Ibid Art 12.
 8 Ibid Art 13.
 9 Ibid Art 16.
10 Ibid Art 17, Title III. See also Chapter 19 in this book on ECSC Products.
11 Ibid Art 18.
12 OJ 17.5.94 L123/278.
13 OJ 17.5.94 L123/306.
14 OJ 17.5.94 L123/663.
15 OJ 17.5.94 L123/690.
16 OJ 17.5.94 L123/745.
17 Agreement between the European Economic Community and the Republic of Kazakstan on trade in textile products, OJ 17.5.94 L123/278. The Agreement entered into force with effect from 1 January 1993 for one year, with automatic extension for a period of one more year up to 31 December 1995 in the absence of six months notice by either party: Art 20.

Trade in specified textile products between the parties is liberalized subject to certain conditions.[18] Quantitative limits may however be reintroduced by the Community under certain conditions.[19] In this case, a double-checking system applies.[20] Inward processing,[1] outward processing,[2] and handicraft products[3] are not subject to the quantitative limits. Provision is made for advance use, carry-over and transfers,[4] as well as for anti-circumvention measures.[5] Exports of certain products not subject to quantitative limits are however always subject to double-checking,[6] and other products may be made subject to this system.[7]

On request from the Community, Kazakstan is to reserve at least 50 per cent of the quantitative limits for five months each year to the Community textile industry.[8] It is also required to create favourable conditions for imports of certain textile products from the Community.[9]

There is a safeguard provision in case of imports into the Community from Kazakstan at prices abnormally lower than the normal competitive level and which cause or threaten to cause serious injury to Community producers of like or directly competing products.[10] The Agreement provides for consultations if problems arise in respect of intellectual property.[11]

18 Ibid Art 1. The products are listed in Annex I.
19 Ibid Art 2(1). As to the conditions, see Art 5. The quantitative limits are not to be broken down into regional shares, but measures are foreseen to deal with sudden regional concentration: see Art 7.
20 Ibid Art 2(2) and Protocol A.
 1 Ibid Art 3(1), first paragraph. However, the release of such products for home use in the Community is subject to a Kazakstan export licence and proof of origin in accordance with Protocol A: Art 3(1), second paragraph.
 2 Ibid Art 3(3), first paragraph. As to conditions, see Protocol C.
 3 Ibid Art 9.
 4 Ibid Art 4.
 5 Ibid Art 6.
 6 Ibid Art 2(3). The products are listed in Annex II.
 7 Ibid Art 2(4).
 8 Ibid Art 2(5). As to implementation, see Art 2(6).
 9 Ibid Art 13(1). The products are listed in Annex I.
10 Ibid Art 10(1). As to procedures, see Art 10(2)-(6). As to consultations, see Art 15.
11 Ibid Art 18.

Chapter 26

Mediterranean countries

MEDITERRANEAN POLICY IN GENERAL

The Mediterranean countries, enhanced by geographical proximity, have long been of great political, economic, social, cultural and strategic importance to the Community. Among the first agreements concluded by the Community were those with Mediterranean countries. Today in fact these countries have assumed an increasing significance in Community policy.[1]

During the 1960s and 1970s the Community concluded a series of agreements with countries bordering on the Mediterranean, including Association Agreements with Cyprus, Malta, Turkey, Algeria, Morocco and Tunisia. For some countries, these were replaced in the late 1970s with Co-operation Agreements[2] containing more or less identical provisions on trade, economic, technical and financial affairs. The countries concerned were Algeria, Egypt, Jordan, Lebanon, Morocco, Syria and Tunisia.[3] The agreements were signed by both the Community and the Member States, and the implementing regulations referred specifically to Art 238 of the EEC Treaty.

In late 1989 the Community adopted a new Mediterranean policy,[4] based on

---

1 Even though the precise boundaries of the region vary according to the purpose of the classification. This book follows current Community policy in including Cyprus, Malta, Turkey, the Maghreb, the Mashrak, Israel, the West Bank and the Gaza Strip as Mediterranean countries.
2 See eg the Co-operation Agreement between the European Economic Community and Tunisia (OJ 27.9.78 L265/2); Additional Protocol (OJ 21.10.87 L297/36). Similar agreements were made with Algeria (OJ 27.9.78 L263/2; Additional Protocol, OJ 21.10.87 L297/2), Morocco (OJ 27.9.78 L264/2; Additional Protocol OJ 13.8.88 L224/18), Egypt (OJ 27.9.78 L266/2; Additional Protocol, OJ 21.10.87 l297/11), Lebanon (OJ 27.9.78 L267/2; Additional Protocol, 21.10.87 l297/29), Jordan (OJ 27.9.78 L268/2; Additional Protocol, 21.10.87 L297/19) and Syria (OJ 27.9.78 L269/2; Additional Protocol, OJ 30.11.88 L327/58).
3 An agreement concluded with Israel in 1975 was amended at this time to bring it in line with the others by adding protocols dealing with industrial, technical and financial co-operation; see above.
4 See Bull EC 11–1989, pt 2.2.29; Bull EC 12–1990, pt 1.4.15; Bull EC 6–1992, pt 1.4.16. As to implementation of the protocols on financial and technical co-operation, see Council Regulation 1762/92, OJ 1.7.92 L181/1. As to financial co-operation for the period 1992–96, see Council Regulation 1763/92, OJ 1.7.92 L181/5. As of 1 January 1997 Council Regulations 1762/92 and 1763/92 were replaced by Council Regulation 1488/96, OJ 30.7.96 L189/1. They are no longer in force except that Council Regulation 1762/92 applies in respect of financial protocols still applicable as of that date and for the commitment of funds remaining under the expired financial protocols.

improved financing and new forms of co-operation.[5] It preserved the previous general pattern but added new elements.

In particular, it involved an improvement in trade arrangements, in particular more rapid dismantling of Community tariffs in respect of agricultural products; an increase in tariff quotas and reference quantities except for the most sensitive products; greater emphasis on respect for human rights and the promotion of democratic values; specific attention to the problem of the transport of hazardous waste; and more extensive financial co-operation.

In respect of trade, the main objective of the new Mediterranean policy is the long-term establishment of an open economic area among the parties. For this purpose, the arrangements under existing Protocols to Association or Co-operation Agreements for imports into the Community of agricultural products from Mediterranean non-member countries have been amended.[6] The countries concerned are Algeria, Cyprus, Egypt, Israel, Jordan, Lebanon, Malta, Morocco, Syria and Tunisia. As part of these changes, the Commission proposed the new concept of Euro-Maghreb partnership, based partly on existing legal instruments but also involving new bilateral agreements with Algeria, Morocco and Tunisia and closer co-operation with the Arab Maghreb Union.[7]

On 27–28 November 1995 the Euro-Mediterranean Conference adopted the Barcelona Declaration.[8] The participants, in addition to the European Union and its Member States, included Algeria, Cyprus, Egypt, Israel, Jordan, Lebanon, Malta, Morocco, Syria, Tunisia, Turkey and the Palestinian Authority. The Declaration expressed their agreement to establish a comprehensive partnership in creating a Euro-Mediterranean area of peace, stability and prosperity. In respect of trade, it confirmed their intention to establish a free trade area by 2010. This will be done through new Euro-Mediterranean agreements and free trade agreements.

These agreements have been or are now being negotiated. As a result, free trade between the Community and Turkey came into effect by 1 January 1996. The same date applies to trade under the Euro-Mediterranean Association Agreement between the Community and Israel. The Community has also concluded Euro-Mediterranean Association Agreements with Tunisia and with Morocco.[9] These Agreements were to enter into force on 1 January 1997. A

---

5 See Protocol on Financial and Technical Co-operation (Tunisia), OJ 25.1.92 L18/35. Analogous measures have been concluded with Cyprus (OJ 21.11.95 L278/22), Malta (OJ 21.11.95 L278/14), Algeria (Council Decision 92/206, OJ 8.4.92 L94/13), Egypt (OJ 8.4.92 L94/22), Jordan (OJ 8.4.92 L94/30), Lebanon (OJ 8.4.92 L94/38), Morocco (Council Decision 92/548, OJ 2.12.92 L352/13), and Syria (OJ 5.2.94 L32/45). As to the implementation of the Protocols, see Council Regulation 1762/92, OJ 1.7.92 L181/1. As to financial co-operation for all Mediterranean non-member countries, see Council Regulation 1763/92, OJ 1.7.92 L181/5. In respect of the Maghreb countries, see F Martines *The Co-operation Agreements with Maghreb Countries* (European University Institute, Florence, 1994).

6 See Council Regulation 1764/92, OJ 1.7.92 L181/9.

7 Bull EC 4–1992, p 1.4.6. See also Economic and Social Committee, Opinion on the Euro-Mediterranean Partnership, OJ 13.11.95 C301/45.

8 As to the text of the Barcelona Declaration, see (1996) 1 *European Foreign Affairs Review* 125.

9 As to the Free Trade Agreement between the EU and Tunisia, signed 17 July 1966, see Commission Proposal for a Decision of the Council and the Commission on the conclusion of a Euro-Mediterranean Agreement establishing an association between the European Communities and their Member States, of the one part, and the Republic of Tunisia, of the other part, COM(95) 235 final, Brussels, 31 May 1995. As to the Free Trade Agreement between the EU and Morocco, signed 26 February 1996, see Commission Proposal for a Decision of the Council and the Commission on the conclusion of a Euro-Mediterranean Agreement establishing an association between the European Communities and their Member States, of the one part, and the Kingdom of Morocco, of the other part, COM(95) 740 final, Brussels, 20 December 1995.

Euro-Mediterranean Interim Association Agreement on trade and co-operation was concluded in February 1997 with the Palestine Liberation Organization (PLO) for the benefit of the Palestinian Authority of the West Bank and the Gaza Strip.[10] Since then, a Euro-Mediterranean Association Agreement between the Community and Jordan has been initialled, negotiations with Egypt and Lebanon were nearly completed, negotiations were due to open with Algeria, and exploratory talks were in progress with Syria.[11] These measures are intended ultimately to create a Euro-Mediterranean free trade area.

The reform of economic and social structures in the framework of the Euro-Mediterranean partnership is underpinned by new financial and technical measures.[12] Their purpose is to contribute to initiatives of joint interest in the three sectors of Euro-Mediterranean partnership: the reinforcement of political stability and democracy, the creation of a Euro-Mediterranean free-trade area, and the development of economic and social co-operation, taking due account of the human and cultural dimension.[13] The potential beneficiary countries are Algeria, Cyprus, Egypt, Israel, Jordan, Lebanon, Malta, Morocco, Syria, Tunisia, Turkey and Gaza and the West Bank.[14] The beneficiaries of support measures include not only States and regions but also a wide variety of public and other organizations.[15] Financing is to be given for selected measures under three-year indicative programmes established at national and regional level in liaison with the European Investment Bank.[16] Community financing is to take the form mainly of grants or risk capital, or, in respect of environmental co-operation measures, of interest rate subsidies.[17] According to its terms, the underlying Regulation is based on respect for democratic principles and the rule of law and also for human rights and fundamental freedoms: these constitute an essential element of the Regulation, and a violation of them will justify the adoption of appropriate measures.[18] Such measures are to be decided by the Council, acting by a qualified majority on a proposal from the Commission.[19]

Consequently, the Community's Mediterranean policy as it has evolved since the early 1970s may be seen as having three tiers. First, all countries in the

---

10 See Council Decision 97/430, OJ 16.7.97 L187/1 and the attached Interim Agreement.
11 See Commission of the European Communities 'Progress Report on the Euro-Mediterranean Partnership and Preparations for the Second Conference of Foreign Affairs Ministers' (Communication from the Commission to the Council and the European Parliament), COM(97)68 final, 19.2.97, p 6. See also *Agence Europe*, No 6957 (n.s.), Friday 18 April 1997, p 7. Recently the Community and Egypt agreed a Memorandum of Understanding (MOU) on trade in textile products: OJ 13.2.98 L41/2; as to its provisional application, pending reciprocal provisional ratification by Egypt, see Council Decision 98/135, OJ 13.2.98 L41/1.
12 Council Regulation 1488/96, OJ 30.7.96 L189/1. The Regulation was adopted on the basis of EC Art 235, because the measures that it provides go beyond the framework of development assistance and are intended to apply to countries only in part classifiable as developing countries: see preamble, eighteenth recital. See also Commission of the European Communities, Commission Report to the Council and the European Parliament on Co-operation with the Mediterranean Partners 1995, COM(97)371 final, Brussels, 18.7.97.
13 Ibid Art 2(1).
14 Ibid Art 1(1), Annex I.
15 Ibid Art 1(2).
16 Ibid Art 5(2); see also preamble, fourteenth recital. As to main objectives of, guidelines for and priority sectors of Community support, see ibid Art 5(2), second paragraph, and Annex II, Section II.
17 Ibid Art 6(1).
18 Ibid Art 3.
19 Council Regulation 1488/96 Art 16, OJ 30.7.96 L189/1, as amended by Council Regulation 780/98 Art 1, OJ 15.4.98 L113/3.

region, with the exception of Libya,[20] have had preferential trade benefits and Community finance: these links are gradually being transformed into Euro-Mediterranean or similar agreements leading to the creation of a Euro-Mediterranean free trade area. Second, countries with close historical ties to individual Member States have agreements which extend to other spheres, such as equality of treatment for nationals. Third, there are especially comprehensive agreements with countries which are (or have been at some time) envisaged as potential members of the Community. This includes in particular Cyprus and Malta, with which the Community undertook to start accession procedures within six months of the conclusion of the 1996 Intergovernmental Conference to revise the Maastricht Treaty on European Union.[1]

CYPRUS

The Community and Cyprus concluded an Association Agreement in 1972.[2] Its aim was progressively to eliminate obstacles in respect of the main body of trade between the parties.[3] It provided for two successive stages: a first stage ending on 30 June 1977, and a second stage of a duration, in principle, of five years.[4] In the event, however, following the nominal end of the first stage, recourse was had to yearly interim arrangements[5] and then unilateral provision by the Community until 1987.[6] In addition, the agreement was modified on a number of occasions.[7] It was originally confined to trade, but a section dealing with co-operation was introduced in 1977. Protocols on financial and technical co-operation were concluded in 1979,[8] 1984,[9] and 1990.[10] In 1995 a new Pro-

---

20 See Council Regulation 3274/93 preventing the supply of certain goods and services to Libya, OJ 30.11.93 L295/1; Council Decision 93/614/CFSP on the common position defined on the basis of TEU Article J.2 with regard to the reduction of economic relations with Libya, OJ 30.11.93 L295/7. See also Council Regulation 3275/93, OJ 30.11.93 L295/4. See also I Macleod, I D Hendry and S Hyett *The External Relations of the European Communities* (Clarendon Press, Oxford, 1996) pp 360–361.

1 See also J Redmond *The Next Mediterranean Enlargement: Turkey, Cyprus and Malta?* (Dartmouth, Aldershot, 1993).

2 Agreement establishing an Association between the European Economic Community and Cyprus, OJ 21.5.73 L133/2, as amended. See also Protocol laying down certain Provisions relating to the Agreement establishing an Association between the European Economic Community and Cyprus, consequent on the Accession of New Member States to the Community, OJ 21.5.73 L133/87.

3 Ibid Art 2(1).

4 Ibid Art 2(2). The Agreement was signed on 1 December 1972 and entered into force on 1 June 1973.

5 See Council Regulation 3498/83 and the attached Protocol concerning the arrangements to be applied during 1983, in the framework of the Decision adopted by the EEC–Cyprus Association Council on 24 November 1980 establishing the process into the second stage of the Association Agreement between the European Economic Community and Cyprus, OJ 15.12.83 L353/1.

6 Council Regulation 3700/83, OJ 30.12.83 L369/1, amended by Council Regulation 3682/85, OJ 28.12.85 L351/9. As to the period from 1973–84, see Tsardanidis, 'The EC–Cyprus Assocation Agreement: Ten Years of a Troubled Relationship' (1984) 22 JCMS 351.

7 Additional Protocol, OJ 28.12.77 L339/2; Supplementary Protocol, OJ 28.6.78 L172/2; Protocol consequent on the Accession of the Hellenic Republic to the Community, OJ 30.6.81 L174/2; Protocol consequent on the accession of Spain and Portugal to the Community, OJ 31.12.87 L393/37.

8 Financial Protocol, OJ 29.11.78 L332/2.

9 Protocol on Financial and Technical Co-operation between the European Economic Community and Cyprus, OJ 28.3.84 L85/37.

10 Protocol on Financial and Technical Co-operation between the European Economic Community and Cyprus, OJ 29.3.90 L82/33.

tocol on financial and technical co-operation was concluded.[11] It provided loans, grants and contribution to risk capital until 31 December 1998 for various activities, including diversification and promotion of Cypriot exports, support for policies and reforms to help the economy become more fully integrated with that of the Community, and the organization of business contacts.[12]

A Protocol laying down conditions and procedures for the second stage of the Agreement was agreed in 1987.[13] The second stage was divided into two phases, one beginning when the Protocol entered into force and terminating ten years later, and the second of a duration of five years, reducible to four years by decision of the Association Council.[14] The customs union was to be fully achieved at the end of the second phase of the second stage.[15]

The 1973 Agreement provided for the reduction by the Community of its customs duties on imports from Cyprus, except for agricultural products and certain other specified products.[16] For certain textile products, tariff reductions were provided within annual tariff quotas.[17] Charges equivalent to customs duties were prohibited for both groups of products.[18] The fixed component of the levy was to be reduced on macaroni and pastry.[19] The duty on citrus fruits was considerably reduced, but (except for grapefruit) in those parts of the year when the Community is applying reference prices a minimum price system is applied.[20] Cyprus was obliged to apply certain specific tariff reductions, and a general reduction of 35 per cent on all products.[1] The Agreement prohibited discrimination in fiscal matters,[2] and an MFN rule was established in respect of export duties.[3] The usual provisions were included in respect of exceptions to the free movement of goods[4] and in respect of dumping and subsidies,[5] and safeguard measures were provided.[6]

The Protocol in respect of the movement to the second stage provided that,

---

11 OJ 21.11.95 L278/23.
12 Ibid Art 3(2), third indent. As part of the pre-accession strategy, Cyprus participates in Community programmes on education, training and youth: see Council Decision 97/739, OJ 4.11.97 L229/21.
13 OJ 31.12.87 L393/1.
14 Ibid Art 1(2). As to the Association Council, see the Agreement Arts 12–14, OJ 21.5.73 L133/2.
15 Cyprus Protocol Art 31. As to arrangements for the passage from the first phase to the second phase of the second stage, see ibid Art 30. As to rules of origin, see the Protocol concerning the definition of the concept of originating products and methods of administrative co-operation annexed to the Additional Protocol, OJ 28.12.77 L339/2, as amended and, in particular, as derogated from by Decision 1/94 of the EC–Cyprus Association Council, OJ 24.2.94 L53/19. As to the interpretation of the rules of origin and methods of administrative co-operation, see Case C-50/90 *Sunzest (Europe) BV and Sunzest (Netherlands) BV v Commission* [1991] ECR I-2917; Case C-432/92 *R v Minister for Agriculture, Fisheries and Food, ex p SP Anastasiou (Pissouri) Ltd* [1994] ECR I-3087.
16 Cyprus Agreement Art 1. The excluded products, in addition to agricultural products, were given in Lists A and B.
17 Ibid Annex 1, Art 2.
18 Ibid Annex 1, Art 3.
19 Ibid Annex 1, Art 4(1).
20 Ibid Art 5.
 1 See Cyprus Agreement Art 3(2) and Annex 2.
 2 Ibid Art 4.
 3 Ibid Art 6.
 4 Ibid Art 11.
 5 Ibid Art 8.
 6 Ibid Art 10.

except for agricultural goods[7] and for some goods (such as casein and petroleum products) for which specific provision is made, Community tariffs on
imports from Cyprus are reduced progressively to zero.[8] Equivalent charges
were prohibited.[9] The ceilings above which normal duties previously applied to
certain sensitive textile products have now been abolished.[10] In respect of imports of Community goods into Cyprus, except for certain specified products,[11]
customs duties and equivalent charges were to be abolished gradually over a
ten-year period.[12] Cyprus was also to abolish quantitative restrictions and equivalent
measures, except for certain listed products.[13] Nevertheless, Cyprus was entitled to impose import licences on imports for home consumption of certain
products.[14] The fixed component of the levy normally imposed by the Community on certain processed agricultural products[15] was abolished.[16] In respect of
agricultural products, residual customs duties and equivalent charges for specific agricultural products covered by reciprocal concessions[17] are to be progressively abolished by both parties.[18] The tariff preference granted to the
Community for certain listed agricultural products is to be maintained.[19] Cyprus is required progressively to abolish residual customs duties and equivalent
charges in respect of sugar originating in the Community.[20] Tariff quotas and
calendars are provided for specified agricultural products, including new potatoes,[1] fresh table grapes,[2] dried grapes,[3] wine of fresh grapes[4] and liqueur wines.[5]
Applicable customs duties are to be phased out for specified products imported
into the Community from Cyprus.[6] Except for specified wines, applicable tariff

7 Protocol laying down the conditions and procedures for the implementation of the second
  stage of the Agreement establishing an Association between the Republic of Cyprus and the
  EEC and adapting certain provisions of the Agreement (hereinafter Cyprus Protocol), Art 3,
  OJ 31.12.87 L393/2.
8 Cyprus Protocol Art 5.
9 Cyprus Agreement, Annex 1, Art 3.
10 Cyprus Protocol Art 4.
11 Listed in ibid Annex 1, and in the Agreement Annex I, List B.
12 Ibid Arts 5(1), 6(1). During the first phase of the second stage, the rate of tariff dismantling
   may be adapted as necessary by the Association Council: ibid Art 7(1).
13 Ibid Art 10. The exceptions are listed in the Agreement, Annex I, List B.
14 Ibid Arts 11(1), 12(1). The products are listed in Annexes 1 and 3.
15 Eg macaroni and pastry.
16 Cyprus Protocol Art 14.
17 The products are listed in Annex IV.
18 Ibid Art 16(1). The products are listed in Annex IV. For certain products, however, Cyprus
   tariffs applied during the first phase of the second stage: Art 16(2). Cyprus is progressively to
   apply the CCT to such products according to the timetable laid down for industrial products
   in Art 8: Art 17(1). For certain agricultural products listed in Annex 5 (fruit salads, grapefruit
   segments, orange or grapefruit juice, grape juice, liqueur wines, and wine), however, Cyprus
   is not to align its customs duties with the CCT during the first phase of the second stage: Art
   17(2).
19 Ibid Art 16(3).
20 Ibid Art 16(3).
1 Ibid Art 18(1), which also provides that the tariff quota applies from 16 May to 30 June.
  Cyprus has undertaken to channel such imports principally towards its main traditional
  markets: Exchange of Letters as regards new potatoes, OJ 31.12.87 L393/31.
2 Ibid Art 18(2), which also provides that the tariff quota applies from 8 June to 4 August.
3 Ibid Art 18(3).
4 Ibid Art 18(5), first paragraph. As to the gradual phasing out of the fixed amount added to
  the price of wine in containers holding two litres or less, see Art 21(1).
5 Ibid Art 18(5), second paragraph.
6 Ibid Art 19(1). The products are cut flowers and buds; certain fresh or chilled vegetables,
  including cabbages, salad vegetables, asparagus, artichokes, courgettes; dried, dehydrated or
  evaporated peppers; avocados and mangoes; passion fruit; kiwi fruit; pimento: certain spices;

quotas on imports into the Community are to be increased.[7] For the purpose of eliminating customs duties, reference quantities are to be established for artichokes and kiwi fruit imported into the Community.[8] The levy on imports of kaskaval cheese imports from Cyprus into the Community is to be reduced.[9] A post-Uruguay Round agreement on oranges has been concluded.[10] Cyprus is to abolish quantitative restrictions and equivalent measures in respect of agricultural products.[11]

The free movement of agricultural products is conditional, however, on agreement on the introduction by Cyprus of Community quality standards, the application by Cyprus internally of domestic price constraints, and the application by Cyprus at the Cyprus frontier of Community measures for these products.[12]

Safeguard measures for Cyprus are provided in specified circumstances[13] and for the Community in respect of specified agricultural products.[14]

The Cypriot Customs Tariff, with specified exceptions,[15] is to be progressively aligned on the CCT.[16]

An Association Council is responsible for the administration of the Agreement, including supervising its proper implementation.[17] A Trade and Economic Co-operation Committee has been established to improve the working of the institutional mechanisms of the Agreement.[18]

MALTA

An Association Agreement[19] was concluded with Malta in 1971. It envisaged a two-stage development in relations with the Community, and set out details for trade liberalization in the first five-year stage. The first stage was twice extended by agreement.[20] After 1980 the trade provisions were continued in force

certain plants; fruit juices; and wine: Art 19(5). As to cut flowers and buds, see also Exchange of Letters, OJ 31.12.87 L393/32. As to preferential duties on certain flowers, see Council Regulation 4088/87, OJ 31.12.87 L382/22, as amended (Cyprus, Israel, Jordan and Morocco). As to prices within this framework, see Commission Regulation 700/88, OJ 18.3.88 L72/16, as amended. As to post-Uruguay Round transitional measures in respect of imports of grape juice and must from Cyprus, see Commission Regulation 1960/95 (OJ 10.8.95 L189/16), as amended, and Commission Regulation 2309/95 (OJ 30.9.95 L233/54), as amended. Both were extended to 30 June 1998 by Commission Regulation 1289/97 (OJ 3.7.97 L175/25).

7 Ibid Art 19(3).
8 Ibid Art 19(4), first paragraph. See also Council Regulation 934/95, OJ 28.4.95 L96/6, as amended most recently by Council Regulation 519/98, OJ 6.3.98 L66/4.
9 Ibid Art 19(6). See also Exchange of Letters, 31.12.87 L393/34.
10 See Council Regulation 592/97, OJ 4.4.97 L89/1, and the attached Agreement in the form of an exchange of letters.
11 Ibid Art 22. As to the use of an import licensing system until the end of the first phase of the second stage, see Art 23.
12 Ibid Art 26(1).
13 Ibid Art 7(3).
14 Ibid Art 19(4), second paragraph; Art 19(5).
15 Namely, the products listed in the Cyprus Protocol, Annex 1, and in the Agreement, List B, Annex I.
16 Ibid Arts 8 and 9, which also lay down the rules for alignment.
17 Agreement Art 12.
18 Protocol Art 32.
19 Agreement establishing an Association between the European Economic Community and Malta, OJ 14.3.71 L61/2.
20 Agreement extending the Provisions governing the First Stage of the Agreement establishing an Association between the European Economic Community and Malta, OJ 27.3.76 L81/2; Additional Protocol, OJ 29.11.77 L304/2.

by the unilateral action of the Community,[1] then by a Supplementary Protocol,[2] then by the unilateral action of the Community[3] and finally by Protocol.[4] Amendments were made in 1976 to cover co-operation and to introduce a financial protocol,[5] and further changes were made in 1977,[6] 1986[7] and 1989.[8] Following the general elections in October 1996, Malta decided not to pursue actively Malta's application for EU membership.[9] In February 1998 the Commission adopted a Communication on deepening of EU–Malta relations.[10]

In 1995 a Protocol on financial and technical co-operation was concluded between the Community and Malta.[11] It provided loans, grants, and contributions to risk capital until 31 October 1998 for various operations,[12] including the diversification and promotion of Maltese exports, support for reforms of commercial, customs and tax policies with a view to integration into the Community, and the organization of business contacts between Malta and the Union.[13]

The trade provisions and those dealing with discrimination, export duties and safeguard measures are similar to those contained in the Cyprus Association Agreement.[14] Duties on imports from Malta into the Community have been totally or partially suspended for numerous products, including certain meat products, fish and fishery products, cut flowers and buds, certain vegetables, sweets, certain food preparations and prepared foods, cereal products, bread, preserved fruits and fruit products, and fruit juices.[15] During 1994 a Community tariff quota was opened for beer made from malt originating in Malta.[16] During the same tariff ceilings and surveillance were imposed on a number of textile products.[17]

TURKEY

In 1964 an Association Agreement[18] was signed between the European Economic Community and Turkey. Known as the Ankara Agreement, it envisaged the even-

---

1 Eg Council Regulation 3508/80, OJ 31.12.80 L367/86; Council Regulation 3704/90, OJ 21.12.90 L358/3.
2 Supplementary Protocol, OJ 23.3.89 L81/2.
3 Council Regulation 3704/90, OJ 21.12.90 L358/3.
4 Protocol extending the first stage of the Agreement, OJ 9.5.91 L116/67.
5 Protocol laying down certain Provisions relating to the Agreement establishing an Association between the European Economic Community and Malta, and Protocol concerning the Definition of the Concept of Originating Products and Methods of Administration Co-operation, and Financial Protocol, OJ 28.4.76 L111/1.
6 Additional Protocol to the Agreement establishing an Association between the European Economic Community and Malta, OJ 29.11.77 L304/2.
7 Protocol on financial and technical co-operation, OJ 5.8.86 L216/2.
8 Protocol on financial and technical co-operation, OJ 27.6.89 L180/47.
9 As a result, Malta no longer participates in the pre-accession strategy or structured dialogue.
10 See 'EU to deepen relations with Malta', Brussels, 5.2.98, http://www.europa.eu.int/search97. See also *Agence Europe*, No 7194 (n.s.), Friday, 3 April 1998, p 5; No 7212 (n.s.), Friday, 1 May 1998, p 6.
11 OJ 21.11.95 L278/14.
12 Ibid Art 2.
13 Ibid Art 3(2), third indent.
14 As to the Association Agreements with Cyprus, see above.
15 Council Regulation 3638/93, OJ 31.12.93 L333/1.
16 Council Regulation 3382/93, OJ 11.12.93 L306/1. See also Exchange of Letters as regards trade in malt beer, OJ 23.3.89 L81/8.
17 Council Regulation 3383/93, OJ 11.12.93 L306/2.
18 Agreement establishing an Association between the European Economic Community and Turkey, OJ 29.12.64 L217/3687. See also Interim Agreement, OJ 3.10.73 L277/2; Agreement extending the Interim Agreement, OJ 25.7.72 L167/8.

tual entrance of Turkey into the Community.[19] The process was to consist of a preparatory stage of about five years, a transitional stage of 12 years leading to a customs union, and a final stage.[20] Successive financial protocols made Community loans and grants available to Turkey,[1] but political considerations prevented the renewal of these arrangements from 1981 until 1986.[2] An agreement with Turkey was also concluded in respect of coal and steel products[3] which provided for the progressive abolition of customs duties and quantitative restrictions in accordance with a timetable to be adopted by mutual agreement.

In 1995 the EC–Turkey Association Council took a decision on implementing the final phase of the Customs Union.[4] The Agreement on the Customs Union between the Community and Turkey was approved by the European Parliament.[5] It provides for the free movement of goods and commercial policy, agricultural products, customs provisions, approximation of laws,[6] institutional matters, and certain general matters. It entered into force on 31 December 1995.[7]

19 See Bourrinet, 'La CEE confrontée à la demande d'adhésion de la Turquie', (1989) 324 RMC 78.
20 Additional Protocol and Financial Protocol, OJ 29.12.72 L293/68; Agreement in the form of an Exchange of Letters amending Art 7 of Annex 6 to the Additional Protocol to the Agreement, OJ 7.2.74 L34/8; Supplementary Protocol to the Agreement consequent on the Accession of New Member States to the Community, OJ 31.12.77 L361/2; Supplementary Protocol to the Agreement, OJ 27.2.88 L53/91. See also Decision 5/72 of the Association Council on methods of administrative co-operation for implementation of Arts 2 and 3 of the Additional Protocol, OJ 5.3.73 L59/74, amended by Decision 2/94 of the EC–Turkey Association Council (OJ 31.12.94 L356/24) and Decision 4/95 of the EC–Turkey Association Council (OJ 13.2.95 L35/48); Exchange of letters concerning Art 3(3) of Decision 1/80 of the Association Council, OJ 11.3.81 L65/36; Decision 1/94 of the EC–Turkey Association Council concerning the application of Art 3 of the Additional Protocol, OJ 31.12.94 L356/23, amended by Decision 3/95, OJ 9.8.95 L188/10.
1 Agreement on the Financial Protocol, OJ 29.12.64 L217/3705; Internal Agreement relating to the Financial Protocol, OJ 12.72 L293/74; Additional Protocol and Financial Protocol, OJ 29.12.72 L293/68; Supplementary Internal Financial Agreement concerning the Supplementary Protocol, OJ 31.12.77 L361/217.
2 See Case 204/86 *Greece v Council* [1988] ECR 5323 and Case 30/88 *Greece v Commission* [1989] ECR 3711.
3 Agreement on Products within the Province of the European Coal and Steel Community, OJ 29.12.72 L293/63, with Supplementary Protocol, OJ 31.12.77 L361/187.
4 Decision 1/95 of the EC–Turkey Association Council (including appended Statements), OJ 13.2.96 L35/1. As to detailed rules of application, see Decision 1/96 of the EC–Turkey Customs Co-operation Committee (OJ 9.8.96 L200/4), as amended by Decision 1/97 of the EC–Turkey Customs Co-operation Committee (OJ 25.6.97 L166/7) and Decision 2/97 of the EC–Turkey Customs Co-operation Committee (OJ 12.9.97 L249/18). The rules laid down in Decision 1/95 are without prejudice to the provisions of the Ankara Agreement and its Additional and Supplementary Protocols: Decision 1/95 Art 1. The list of committees referred to in Annex 9 of Decision 1/95 was extended by Decision 6/95 of the EC–Turkey Association Council, OJ 13.2.96 L35/50; Decision 5/95 of the EC–Turkey Association Council on the arrangements for involving Turkish experts in the work of certain technical committees, OJ 13.2.96 L35/49.
5 Resolution on the draft agreement on the conclusion of a customs union between the EU and Turkey, OJ 6.3.95 C56/99.
6 Including protection of intellectual, industrial and commercial property; competition; trade defence instruments; government procurement; direct taxation; and indirect taxation: see Arts 31–51.
7 Ibid Art 65(1). See also Peers 'Living in Sin: Legal Integration Under the EC–Turkey Customs Union' (1996) 7 *European Journal of International Law* 411. As to future EC–Turkey relations following the December 1997 European Council decision including Turkey among those countries with a vocation to join the EU, but not among the candidates for accession, see European Commission 'Guidelines and Proposals for Future Relations between the European Union and Turkey' Part I, *Europe Documents*, No 2083, 22 April 1998; Part II, *Europe Documents*, No 2084, 24 April 1998.

The custom union comprises the customs territory of the Community[8] and the customs territory of Turkey.[9] The provisions on free movement of goods apply to goods produced in the Community or in Turkey[10] or coming from third countries and in free circulation in the Community or Turkey.[11] It also applies to goods obtained in the Community or in Turkey,[12] in the manufacture of which products coming from third countries and not in free circulation either in the Community or in Turkey were used, provided that import formalities have been complied with and any customs duties or equivalent charges payable have been levied in the exporting state.[13]

Import or export customs duties and equivalent charges are to be wholly abolished between the parties.[14] There is a standstill clause on such duties and charges and on customs duties of a fiscal nature.[15] Quantitative restrictions and equivalent measures are also prohibited on imports[16] or exports.[17] The usual exceptions apply.[18] Within five years of the entry into force of the Customs Union, Turkey is required to incorporate into its internal legal order the Community instruments relating to the removal of technical barriers to trade.[19] In the meantime Turkey is required to refrain from impeding the placing on the market, or taking into service on its territory, of products from the Community which are attested to conform with the relevant Community directives.[20]

With regard to countries which are not members of the Community, Turkey is required to apply provisions and implementing measures which are substantially similar to those of the Community's commercial policy.[1] It must also apply sub-

---

8 As defined in Art 3 of Council Regulation 2913/92 establishing the Community Customs Code, OJ 19.10.92 L302/1, as amended.

9 Decision 1/95 Art 3(3).

10 Decision 1/95 Art 1(1), first indent. This includes goods wholly or partially obtained or produced from products coming from third countries which are in free circulation in the Community or in Turkey.

11 Decision 1/95 Art 3(1), second indent. Products from third countries are considered to be in free circulation in the Community or in Turkey if the import formalities have been complied with and any customs duties or equivalent charges which are payable have been levied, and if they have not benefited from a total or partial reimbursement of these duties or charges: Art 3(2).

12 Ibid Art 3(4), first paragraph.

13 Ibid Art 3(4), second paragraph.

14 Ibid Art 4.

15 Ibid Art 4. See also Additional Protocol Arts 7, 8, 10. See also *Mass Housing Fund Levy in Turkey*, OJ 17.12.96 L326/71.

16 Ibid Art 5.

17 Ibid Art 6.

18 Ibid Art 7.

19 Ibid Art 8(1). The list of these instruments and conditions and detailed arrangements for implementation by Turkey is to be laid down by the Association Council within one year of the entry into force of the Decision: Art 8(2). This does not however preclude the immediate application by Turkey of Community instruments deemed to be of particular importance: Art 8(3). In the interim the Community is required, given certain conditions, to accept the results of Turkish procedures for assessing the conformity of industrial products with Community law: Art 11. As to the list of these instruments, see Decision 2/95 of the EC–Turkey Association Council, OJ 21.7.97 L191/11.

20 Ibid Art 10(1). As to permitted derogations, see Art 10(2). As to procedures in respect of such derogations, see Art 10(3).

1 Ibid Art 12(1), which also lists the relevant Community measures as Council Regulation 3285/84, OJ 31.12.94 L349/53 (common rules for imports); Council Regulation 519/94, OJ 10.3.94 L67/89 (common rules for imports from certain third countries); Council Regulation 520/94, OJ 10.3.94 L66/1 (Community procedure for administering quantitative quotas) and the implementing provisions laid down by Commission Regulation 738/94, OJ 31.3.94 L87/1, as last amended by Commission Regulation 1150/95, OJ 23.5.95 L116/3; Council Regulation 3283/94,

stantially the same commercial policy as the Community in the textile sector.[2] The Decision is not to constitute a hindrance to the implementation by the Community and Japan of their Arrangement relating to trade in motor vehicles.[3]

Turkey is required to align itself on the CCT.[4] By way of derogation, however, Turkey may retain until 1 January 2001 higher duties than the CCT in respect of third countries for products agreed by the Association Council.[5] Turkey is also required to align itself progressively with the Community's preferential customs regime within five years.[6]

In respect of processed agricultural products, however, Turkey may apply an agricultural component on imports of certain goods from third countries.[7] In addition, in respect of the same goods Turkey and the Community may apply an agricultural component in their trade with each other.[8] However, for certain goods a derogation regime is foreseen, in which Turkish import charges are to be reduced in three steps over a period of one year for some goods and three years for others.[9] If imports covered by the derogation regime cause, or threaten to cause, serious disturbances in Turkey which may endanger the objectives of the Customs Union for processed agricultural products, the parties are to hold consultations within the Customs Union Joint Committee with a view to finding a mutually acceptable solution.[10] Annual quotas have been established for

OJ 31.12.94 L349/1, as last amended by Council Regulation 1251/95, OJ 2.6.95 L122/1, and Council Regulation 3284/94, OJ 31.12.94 L349/22, as last amended by Council Regulation 1252/95, OJ 2.6.95 L122/2 (protection against dumped and subsidised imports); Council Regulation 3286/94, OJ 31.12.94 L349/71, as last amended by Council Regulation 356/95, OJ 23.2.95 L41/3 (Community procedures in the field of the common commercial policy); Council Regulation 2603/69, OJ 27.12.69 L324/25, as last amended by Council Regulation 3918/91, OJ 31.12.91 L372/31 (common rules for exports); Council Decision 93/112, OJ 22.2.93 L44/1 (officially supported export credits); Council Regulation 3036/94, OJ 15.12.94 L322/1 (outward processing arrangements for textiles and clothing); Council Regulation 3093/93, OJ 8.121.93 L275/1, as last amended by Council Regulation 1616/95, OJ 5.7.95 L154/3 (textile imports under common rules); Council Regulation 517/94, OJ 10.3.94 L67/1, as last amended by Council Regulation 1325/95, OJ 13.6.95 L128/1 (textile imports under autonomous arrangements); Council Regulation 3951/92, OJ 31.12.92 L405/6, as last amended by Council Regulation 3312/94, OJ 31.12.94 L350/3 (textile imports from Taiwan).

2 Ibid Art 12(2). As to transitional arrangements, see Art 12(3).
3 Ibid Art 12(4). As to this Arrangement, see the Annex to the Agreement on Safeguards attached to the Agreement setting up the World Trade Organization, OJ 23.12.94 L336/184.
4 Ibid Art 13(1). As to adjustment, exceptions or suspension, see Art 13(2), 14(2) and 14(3), respectively.
5 Ibid Art 15.
6 Ibid Art 16(1), which also provides that this includes both the autonomous regimes and preferential agreements with third countries. However, the granting of tariff preferences is conditional on compliance with origin rules identical to those used in the granting of such preferences by the Community: Art 16(2). In certain cases a compensatory levy is due on goods imported into Turkey: Art 16(3).
7 Ibid Art 18. The goods are listed in Annex 1. As to the procedures for establishing the agricultural component, see Art 19.
8 Ibid Art 20(1). Again, the goods are listed in Annex 1: Art 20(2). The Community is to apply to Turkey the same specific duties that represent the agricultural component applicable to third countries: Art 20(3). The agricultural component to be applied by Turkey to goods from the Community is to be calculated according to Art 19: Art 20(4). However, where the duty applicable to a basic agricultural product is reduced, the relevant agricultural component is to be reduced proportionately: Art 22(1). As to reductions within quota limits, see Art 22(2).
9 Ibid Art 21. The goods are listed in Annex 6/Table 1 (reduction over three years) and Annex 6/Table 2 (reduction over one year).
10 Ibid Art 23, first paragraph. As to the Joint Committee, see Arts 52–53. If a mutually satisfactory solution cannot be found, the Joint Committee may recommend appropriate ways of maintaining the proper functioning of the Customs Union, without prejudice to safeguard measures under Art 63: Art 23, second paragraph.

imports of certain pasta products from Turkey into the Community and for certain processed agricultural products from the Community.[11]

Special provisions apply to agricultural products. The common objective was reaffirmed to move towards the free movement of agricultural products.[12] To achieve this aim an additional period was recognized to be necessary.[13] In the meantime, Turkey was to adjust its policy so as to adopt the Common Agricultural Policy measures required to establish freedom of movement of agricultural products.[14] The Community was to take account, as far as possible, of Turkish agriculture's interests when developing its agricultural policy and to notify Turkey of relevant Commission proposals and related decisions.[15] Consultations could be held within the Association Council on the measures proposed or taken by either side.[16] In addition, the Community and Turkey were progressively to improve, on a mutually advantageous basis, the preferential arrangements which they grant each other for their trade in agricultural products.[17] Once it was established that Turkey had adopted the Common Agricultural Policy measures[18] the Association Council was to adopt the provisions necessary to achieve free movement of agricultural products.[19]

In 1998 a new trade regime for agricultural products was adopted.[20] Quantitative restrictions and all equivalent measures on imports and exports of agricultural products are prohibited.[1] A preferential regime for imports into the Community of agricultural products originating in Turkey is established,[2] as is a preferential regime for imports into Turkey of products originating in the Community.[3] Imports of products other than listed products are exempt from *ad valorem* duties.[4] For listed products,[5] the *ad valorem* duties are to be reduced or eliminated during specified periods and according to specified conditions.[6] For certain products, specific duties may, or must, be either reduced or eliminated.[7] A co-operation scheme is established for hazelnuts.[8] A tariff quota is opened for prepared toma-

---

11 See Decision 1/97 of the EC–Turkey Association Council, OJ 17.5.97 L126/6. As to quotas for 1998, see Commission Regulation 2490/97, OJ 13.12.97 L343/10.

12 Decision 1/95 Art 24(1), which reiterates that the objective is provided in the Additional Protocol.

13 Ibid Art 24(2).

14 Ibid Art 25(1), which also provides that any such decisions are to be communicated to the Commission.

15 Ibid Art 25(2).

16 Ibid Art 25(3).

17 Ibid Art 26. Such improvements are to be examined regularly by the Association Council: ibid.

18 That is, those referred to in Art 25(1).

19 Ibid Art 27.

20 See Decision 1/98 of the EC–Turkey Association Council, OJ 20.3.98 L86/1. It applies from 1 January 1998, except that import arrangements for hazelnuts (CN 0802 21 00 and 0802 22 00) laid down in Annex 1 to Protocol 1 apply from 1 January 1999. See ibid Art 8, second paragraph. As to the procedure for adopting implementing rules, see Council Regulation 779/98 Art 1, OJ 15.4.98 L113/1.

1 Ibid Art 1(1). This does not however restrict in any way the pursuance of the parties' respective agricultural policies or the taking of any measures under such policies: ibid Art 1(2).

2 Ibid Art 2, and Protocol 1.

3 Ibid Art 3, and Protocol 2.

4 Ibid Protocol 1, Art 2(1). The products to which *ad valorem* duties apply are listed in Annex 1.

5 That is, those listed in Annex 1.

6 Ibid Protocol 1, Art 2(2). As to the periods and conditions, see ibid Art 2(3)-(4) and the Annexes to Protocol 1.

7 See ibid Protocol 1, Art 3 and Annex 1. As to imports of rye directly into the Community from Turkey, see Protocol 1, Art 3(4).

8 Ibid Protocol 1, Art 4, and Annex 2. It provides for annual consultations between European and Turkish organizations regarding the market situation and for safeguards.

toes.[9] The new regime includes rules of origin.[10] When either the quantities or prices of imported products from either party in respect of which a preferential regime has been granted causes, or threatens to cause, disturbance of the Community or Turkish markets, consultations must be held as soon as possible within the Association Council. This does not however preclude the application, in an emergency, of measures provided for under Community or Turkish rules.[11]

In respect of customs provisions, Turkey is required to adopt provisions based on Community law in various customs fields.[12]

Provision is made for safeguard measures and the settlement of disputes. The mechanism and modalities of previous safeguard measures[13] remain valid.[14] However, if a safeguard or protection measure creates an imbalance between rights and obligations under Decision 1/95, the other party may take rebalancing measures, for which priority must be given to measures as will least disturb the functioning of the Customs Union.[15] Dispute settlement functions are given to the Association Council, but if it fails to settle a dispute relating to the scope or duration of protection measures,[16] safeguard measures,[17] or rebalancing measures[18] within six months of the initiation of the procedure, either party may refer the dispute to binding arbitration.[19]

MAGHREB AND MASHRAK

The EU has concluded with Tunisia and Morocco separate Euro-Mediterranean Agreements of Association which only recently entered into force.[20] They will gradually supplant the previous Co-operation Agreements as well as related agreements concerning ECSC products. However, many provisions of these previous agreements remain in force in the short term. Consequently, the following paragraphs first describe the Co-operation Agreements and then the Euro-Mediterranean Agreements. The Agreements between the Community and Tunisia provide an example.[1]

Under the terms of the Co-operation Agreement, Tunisia undertook, on the one hand, simply to grant the Community MFN treatment.[2] On the other hand,

9 Ibid Protocol 1, Art 4, and Annex 3.
10 See ibid Art 4, and Protocol 4.
11 Ibid Art 5.
12 See ibid Art 28.
13 That is, as provided in the Additional Protocol Art 60.
14 Decision 1/95 Art 63.
15 Ibid Art 64(1).
16 Taken in accordance with Art 58(2).
17 Taken in accordance with Art 63.
18 Taken in accordance with Art 64.
19 Ibid Art 61. As to the arbitration procedure, see Art 62.
20 As to the similar Agreement concluded between the Community and Israel, see below.
 1 As to the Co-operation Agreement, see OJ 27.9.78 L265/1, as amended. As to the Euro-Mediterranean Agreement, see Euro-Mediterranean Agreement establishing an association between the European Communities and their Member States, of the one part, and the Republic of Tunisia, of the other part, OJ 30.3.98 L87/1, approved on behalf of the Community by Council Decision 98/238, OJ 30.3.98 L97/1. Signed on 17 July 1995, it came into effect on 1 March 1998: see *Agence Europe*, No 7173 (n.s.), Thursday, 5 March 1998, p 7.
 2 Co-operation Agreement Art 26(1). This is subject to an exception in respect of customs unions or free trade areas (Art 26(2)) and to a potential derogation in respect of measures regarding Maghreb economic integration or measures benefiting developing countries (Art 26(3)). However, Tunisia is entitled, in certain circumstances, to introduce new customs duties, equivalent charges, quantitative restrictions or equivalent measures: Art 27(2). It must treat the Community as a unity if it imposes quantitative restrictions: Art 28.

products originating in Tunisia, other than Annex II products, may with certain exceptions be imported into the Community free of customs duties, equivalent charges, quantitative restrictions or equivalent measures.[3] The exceptions[4] are petroleum products[5] and processed agricultural products.[6] As regards Annex II (that is, agricultural) products, customs duties on imports were to be reduced by specified amounts.[7]

Special arrangements were made for imports of untreated olive oil from Tunisia, whereby (subject to a maximum) the Common Agricultural Policy import levy was reduced in so far as a corresponding export charge was imposed by the exporting country.[8] Imports of refined olive oil, wholly obtained in Tunisia and transported direct from there to the Community, were exempt from the fixed component of the levy.[9] A similar arrangement concerned bran and sharps from Algeria, Morocco, Tunisia and Egypt.[10] On some products, such as sardines, duties are removed on condition that minimum prices are observed;[11] on others, such as tomato concentrate and fruit salad from the same countries and Israel, the benefit is conferred only at certain times of the year.[12] There were also detailed provisions regarding duty reductions on wine.[13] Egypt was accorded a quota for rice exports at a reduced levy provided a corresponding export charge is imposed.[14]

Following the new Mediterranean policy, these arrangements were amended for certain agricultural products.[15] Customs duties[16] on agricultural products[17] originating in the Mediterranean non-member countries[18] were to be abolished

3 Ibid Art 9(1). In the case of customs duties comprising a protective element and a fiscal element, this prohibition applies to the protective element: Art 10(1).

4 As provided in Art 9(1).

5 For which annual ceilings above which the reintroduction of customs duties actually applied in respect of third countries was permitted: Art 12(1). The ceilings were to be abolished by 31 December 1979 at the latest: Art 12(5).

6 For which import duties were to be reduced by specified percentages: ibid Art 14. The basic products are listed in Annex A. The percentage reductions are specified in Art 9.

7 Ibid Art 15(1), which also sets forth the rates of reduction. Preferential duties have been applied to certain flowers from Cyprus, Israel and Jordan (Commission Regulation 4088/87, OJ 31.12.87 L382/22, as amended; Commission Regulation 700/88, OJ 18.3.88 L72/16, as amended) and to large-flowered roses from Morocco (Commission Regulation 358/89, OJ 14.2.89 L42/19).

8 Ibid Art 16. See now Council Regulation 906/98, OJ 30.4.98 L128/20 and, as to detailed rules, Commission Regulation 150/98, OJ 23.1.98 L18/5. For analogous detailed rules in respect of Algeria, Morocco and Lebanon, see Commission Regulation 148/98, OJ 23.1.98 L18/3 (Algeria); Commission Regulation 152/98, OJ 23.1.98 L18/7 (Morocco); and Commission Regulation 149/98, OJ 23.1.98 L18/4 (Lebanon).

9 Ibid Art 17.

10 Ibid Art 22. As to implementing rules, see Agreement in the form of an exchange of letters, OJ 28.6.76 L169/20. As to analogous agreements with other countries, see OJ 28.6.76 L169/38 (Algeria), OJ 28.6.76 L169/54 (Morocco), OJ 14.6.77 L146/12 (Egypt).

11 Ibid Art 18. Similar provisions apply to Algeria and Morocco.

12 Ibid Art 19. As to analogous agreements, see: tomato concentrates from Algeria (OJ 27.12.88 L358/14); preserved fruit salads from Algeria (OJ 27.12.88 L358/17); preserved fruit salads from Israel (OJ 27.12.88 L358/20); preserved fruit salads from Morocco (OJ 27.12.88 L358/23).

13 Ibid Art 20. See the Agreement in the form of an Exchange of Letters between the European Economic Community and Tunisia concerning Certain Wines originating in Tunisia and entitled to a Designation of Origin (OJ 21.10.78 L296/2). As to tariff quotas, see Council Regulation 3619/87, OJ 2.12.87 L340/29.

14 Co-operation Agreement (Egypt) Art 19, OJ 27.9.78 L266/1.

15 Council Regulation 1764/92, OJ 1.7.92 L181/9.

16 That is, customs duties applicable on 31 December 1991 in the Community as constituted on 31 December 1985.

17 That is, Annex II products.

18 Algeria, Cyprus, Egypt, Israel, Jordan, Lebanon, Malta, Morocco, Syria, Tunisia.

in two equal stages, from 1 January 1992 and from 1 January 1993.[19] This was to apply within the limits, if any, of the tariff quotas and timetables laid down in the relevant Protocols, and taking into account any special provisions.[20] Tariff quotas and reference quantities for agricultural products were to be increased in four equal stages of 5 per cent per year from 1992 to 1995,[1] except for certain listed products for which the increase was to be only 3 per cent per year.[2] Once imports reach the tariff quota level, they may be subject to statistical surveillance.[3]

The Community reserves the right to alter the dispositions on agricultural imports in the event of changes in the Common Agricultural Policy,[4] but undertakes to accord its partners advantages comparable to those in the agreements.[5]

Regarding agricultural products not specifically covered by the agreements, there is a joint declaration of a readiness to foster the harmonious development of trade, and an undertaking not to apply veterinary, health and plant health matters in a discriminatory fashion nor to introduce any new measures unduly obstructing trade.[6]

By letters annexed to the relevant agreements France is authorized to continue granting special treatment to certain imports from Algeria, Morocco and Tunisia.[7]

An Agreement in respect of sea fisheries has been concluded with Morocco.[8]

In addition to the standard exceptions to the free movement of goods,[9] action against dumping and subsidies is permitted in accordance with the rules of the GATT.[10] Subject to following certain procedures,[11] safeguard action may be taken in the event of serious disturbances in any sector of the economy or of difficulties which might bring about serious deterioration in the economic situation of a region.[12] Similarly, action may be taken in the event of serious

---

19 Ibid Art 1(1).
20 Ibid Art 1(2). However, customs duties were to be suspended in full when they reached a level of 2 per cent or less: Art 1(3).
1 Ibid Art 2(1).
2 Ibid Art 2(1), second paragraph. The products are listed in Annex II: fresh cut flowers, fresh or chilled new potatoes, fresh or chilled tomatoes, fresh oranges, mandarines or clementines, finely ground oranges, peeled tomatoes, orange juice, and wine. The increase was to be applied to Cyprus only if an increase was not already provided in the relevant Protocol: Art 2(2).
3 Council Regulation 451/89, OJ 24.2.89 L52/7. For an example, see Council Regulation 316/93, OJ 13.2.93 L37/4.
4 Agreement with Tunisia Art 24(1), first paragraph, in which case the Community is required to take appropriate account of the interests of Tunisia: Art 24(2), second paragraph.
5 Ibid Art 24(2).
6 Joint Declaration 7 on Agricultural Products, appended to the Agreement as part of the Final Act.
7 See Exchange of letterts on goods originating in and coming from certain countries and enjoying special treatment when imported into a Member State, OJ 27.7.78 L265/116.
8 OJ 16.4.88 L99/49.
9 Ibid Art 34.
10 Ibid Art 35.
11 See Art 37. For detailed rules in respect of safeguard measures, see Council Regulation 1664/77, OJ 26.7.77 L186/13. For analogous measures, see respectively Council Regulation 1663/77 (OJ 26.7.77 L186/11) (Algeria); Council Regulation 1658/77, OJ 26.7.77 L186/1 (Egypt); Council Regulation 1659/77, OJ 26.7.77 L186/3 (Jordan); Council Regulation 1661/77, OJ 26.7.77 L186/7 (Lebanon); Council Regulation 1662/77 (OJ 26.7.77 L186/9) (Morocco); Council Regulation 1660/77, OJ 26.7.77 L186/5 (Syria).
12 Ibid Art 36. As to surveillance under a system of tariff quotas, see Case C-46(89 *Société d'initiatives et de coopération agricoles and Société d'interêt professionnel des producteurs et expéditeurs de fruits, légumes, bulbes et fleurs d'Ille-et-Vilaine v Commission* [1990] ECR I-3621.

balance of payments difficulties.[13] In both these cases the action adopted should be that which least disturbs the functioning of the agreements.[14]

A Co-operation Council is established to take decisions in order to achieve the purposes of the Agreement.[15] It is the principal body for settling disputes,[16] but matters may also be referred to arbitration.[17]

A separate series of agreements was concluded with the Mediterranean countries by the Member States of the European Coal and Steel Community.[18]

The Co-operation Agreement between the Community and Tunisia will be gradually supplanted by the new Euro-Mediterranean Agreement, which was signed on 17 July 1996 and entered into force on 1 March 1998.[19] The aims of the new Agreement are to provide an appropriate framework for political dialogue; establish the conditions for the gradual liberalization of trade in goods, services and capital; promote trade and the expansion of harmonious economic and social relations between the parties, notably through dialogue and co-operation, so as to foster the development and prosperity of Tunisia and its people; encourage integration of the Maghreb countries by promoting trade and co-operation between Tunisia and other countries of the region; and promote economic, social, cultural and financial co-operation.[20] Relations between the parties, as well as all provisions of the Agreement, are to be based on the respect for human rights and the democratic principles which guide their domestic and international policies and constitute an essential element of the Agreement.[1] The Agreement provides for political dialogue; the free movement of goods; the right of establishment and services; payments, capital, competition and other economic provisions; economic co-operation; co-operation in social and cultural matters; financial co-operation; and institutional and general matters. The Agreement is concluded for an unlimited period.[2]

In respect of trade in goods, the Agreement provides that the Community and Tunisia shall gradually establish a free trade area over a transitional period lasting a maximum of 12 years.[3] Different provisions govern industrial products, on the one hand, and agricultural and fishery products, on the other hand.

For industrial products, a standstill clause applies to customs duties on imports and charges having equivalent effect in trade between the parties.[4] Products originating in Tunisia are to be imported into the Community free of customs duties and equivalent charges and without quantitative restrictions or equiva-

---

13 Ibid Art 38.

14 Ibid Art 37(2), second paragraph; Art 38.

15 Ibid Art 43(1). As to its composition, role and procedures, see Arts 43–51.

16 Ibid Art 51(1).

17 See Art 51(2).

18 See eg the Agreement between the Member States of the European Coal and Steel Community and Tunisia (OJ 27.9.78 L265/119). Similar agreements were made with Algeria (OJ 27.9.78 L263/119), Egypt (OJ 12.12.79 L316/2), Israel (OJ 28.6.75 L165/62), Jordan (OJ 12.12.79 L316/13), Lebanon (OJ 12.12.79 316/24), Morocco (OJ 27.9.78 L264/119), and Syria (OJ 12.12.79 L316/35). See also Chapter 19 on ECSC Products in this book.

19 Euro-Mediterranean Agreement establishing an association between the European Communities and their Member States, of the one part, and the Republic of Tunisia, of the other part, OJ 30.3.98 L97/2, approved on behalf of the Community by Council Decision 98/238, OJ 30.3.98 L97/1. A similar substitution will be effected in respect of Morocco.

20 Ibid Art 1(2).

1 Ibid Art 2.

2 Ibid Art 93, first sub-paragraph.

3 Ibid Art 6.

4 Ibid Art 8. All provisions in respect of the abolition of customs duties on imports also apply to customs duties of a fiscal nature: ibid Art 13.

lent measures.[5] Customs duties and equivalent charges on specified products originating in the Community imported into Tunisia are to be abolished on the entry into force of the Agreement.[6] Customs duties and equivalent charges on imports of other products originating in the Community and imported into Tunisia are to be abolished gradually according to a fixed schedule.[7] The scheduled reductions do not apply to specified products, for which the arrangements are to be re-examined four years after the Agreement enters into force.[8]

Exceptional derogating measures of limited duration may be taken by Tunisia in the form of an increase or reintroduction of customs duties to protect infant industries, or certain sectors undergoing restructuring or facing serious difficulties, particularly where these difficulties produce major social problems.[9] These duties may not however exceed 25 per cent *ad valorem* and must maintain an element of preference for Community products, and the total value of imports subject to such measures must not exceed 15 per cent of total imports of industrial products from the Community during the last year for which statistics are available.[10] The measures are limited to five years unless a longer duration is authorized by the Association Committee, and in any event they are to cease to apply at the end of the 12-year transitional period.[11] No such measures can be introduced in respect of a product if more than three years have elapsed since the elimination of all duties and quantitative restrictions or charges or equivalent measures concerning that product.[12] Before implementing any exceptional measures, Tunisia is required to inform the Association Committee, and the Community is entitled to request consultations. When taking such measures Tunisia is required to provide the Committee with a schedule for the elimination of the newly introduced duties.[13]

Special provisions apply to processed agricultural products. The Community is entitled to retain an agricultural component on imports from Tunisia of certain listed goods.[14] Similarly, Tunisia is entitled to specify an agricultural component in import duties in force on certain products originating in the Community.[15] For specified products originating in the Community, Tunisia is entitled to apply import duties and equivalent charges subject to certain limits.[16] For other

---

5 Ibid Art 9.
6 Ibid Art 11(1), which also provides that the relevant products are listed in Annexes 3–6.
7 Ibid Art 11(2) and Annex 3; Art 11(3) and Annexes 4 and 5. These schedules may be reviewed by the Association Committee but cannot be extended for a given product beyond the maximum transitional period of 12 years: see Art 11(4). If the Association Committee has not taken a decision within thirty days of its application to review the schedule, Tunisia may suspend the schedule provisionally for a period not exceeding one year: ibid Art 11(4).
8 Ibid Art 12, which refers to the products listed in Annex 6.
9 Ibid Art 14(1).
10 Ibid Art 14(1), third sub-paragraph.
11 Ibid Art 14(1), fourth sub-paragraph. However, in respect of infant industries the Association Council may exceptionally authorize Tunisia to maintain the measures for a maximum period of three years beyond the end of the transitional period: ibid Art 14(2).
12 Ibid Art 14(1), fifth sub-paragraph.
13 Ibid Art 14(1), sixth sub-paragraph, which also provides that the phasing-out must start at the latest two years after the introduction of the duties, though the Association Committee may decide on a different schedule.
14 Ibid Art 10(1), first paragraph, which also provides that the relevant goods are listed in Annex I. As to the purpose and form of the agricultural component, see ibid Art 10(1), second paragraph.
15 Ibid Art 10(2), first paragraph, which also provides that the relevant products are listed in Annex II as well as for the form of the agricultural component.
16 Ibid Art 10(3).

products Tunisia is required to eliminate the industrial component of the duties in accordance with a specified schedule.[17] The agricultural components may be reduced where, in trade between the parties, the charge applicable to a basic agricultural product is reduced or where such reductions are the result of mutual concessions relating to processed agricultural products.[18]

In respect of agricultural and fishery products, the Community and Tunisia are gradually to implement greater liberalization of their trade.[19] Detailed provisions for the import of such products are laid down in Protocols.[20] After 1 January 2000 the parties are to assess the situation with a view to adopting liberalization measures with effect from 1 January 2001.[1] They are also required to examine regularly, in the Association Council, on a product by product and on a reciprocal basis, the possibilities of granting each other further concessions.[2] However, either party may modify the arrangements in respect of agricultural products if specific rules are introduced as a result of the implementation of their agricultural policies, or modification of existing rules, or if the provisions on the implementation of their agricultural policies are modified or developed.[3] If the arrangements made by the Agreement are modified in this way, the modifying Party is required to accord imports originating in the other party an advantage comparable to that provided for in the Agreement.[4]

No new quantitative restrictions on imports, or equivalent measures, are to be introduced in trade between the parties.[5] Quantitative restrictions and equivalent measures in trade between the parties are to be abolished on entry into force of the Agreement.[6] Neither the Community nor Tunisia is to apply to the other's exports customs duties, equivalent charges, quantitative restrictions or equivalent measures.[7]

Products originating in Tunisia must not enjoy more favourable treatment when imported into the Community than that applied by Member States among themselves.[8] The two parties are to refrain from any measure or practice of an internal fiscal nature which discriminates, directly or indirectly, between their respective products.[9] The Agreement does not preclude the maintenance or establishment of customs unions, free trade areas or arrangements for frontier trade except in so far as they alter the trade arrangements

---

17 Ibid Art 10(4).

18 Ibid Art 10(5); as to procedures, see Art 10(6).

19 Ibid Art 16.

20 As to products originating in Tunisia and imported into the Community, see ibid Art 17(1) and Protocols 1 and 2. As to products originating in the Community and imported into Tunisia, see ibid Art 17(2) and Protocol 3.

1 Ibid Art 18(1).

2 Ibid Art 18(2).

3 Ibid Art 20(1), first sub-paragraph. The modifying Party is required to inform the Association Committee, which at the request of the other party must meet to take appropriate account of that Party's interests: Art 20(1), second sub-paragraph. Any modification of the Agreement is to be the subject, at the request of the other party, of consultations within the Association Council: Art 20(3).

4 Ibid Art 21(2).

5 Ibid Art 19(a).

6 Ibid Art 19(b).

7 Ibid Art 19(c). As to relevant safeguards, see Art 26. As to procedures, see Art 27(2),(3)(c),(d).

8 Ibid Art 21.

9 Ibid Art 22(1). In addition, products exported to the territory of the other party may not benefit from repayment of internal taxation in excess of the amount of direct or indirect taxation imposed on them: Art 22(2).

provided for the in the Agreement.[10] The standard exceptions to the free movement of goods apply.[11]

Provision is made for anti-dumping measures[12] and safeguard measures.[13] In respect of the latter, appropriate measures may be taken where any product is imported in such increased quantities and under such conditions as to cause, or threaten to cause, either serious injury to domestic producers or like or directly competitive products or serious disturbances in any sector of the economy or difficulties which could bring about serious deterioration in the economic situation of a region.[14] Priority in the selection of measures must be given to those which least disturb the functioning of the Agreement.[15] In exceptional circumstances, a party may take the precautionary measures strictly necessary to deal with the situation and must inform the other party immediately.[16] In all cases provision is made for informing the other party,[17] supplying information to the Association Committee,[18] notification to the Association Committee of any measures taken, and periodic consultations with a view to the abolition of such measures.[19]

In respect of trade in services, the parties agree to widen the scope of the Agreement to cover inter alia the liberalization of the provision of services by one party's firms to consumers of services in the other.[20] Each party reaffirms its obligations under the GATS, particularly the obligation to grant reciprocal most-favoured-nation treatment in the service sectors covered by that obligation.[1]

In respect of intellectual property, the parties are to provide suitable and effective protection of intellectual, industrial and commercial property rights, in line with the highest international standards.[2] Implementation of this provision is to be regularly assessed by the parties, and if any difficulties arise, either party may request urgent consultations to find mutually satisfactory solutions.[3]

The institutional framework for the Agreement consists of an Association Council and an Association Committee. The Association Council consists of the members of the Council of the European Union and members of the European Commission, on the one hand, and of members of the Government of the Republic of Tunisia, on the other hand.[4] Its role is to examine any major issues arising within the framework of the Agreement and any other bilateral or international issues of mutual interest.[5] It has the power to take decisions and recommendations by agreement between the two parties.[6] Its decisions are binding on the parties, which are to take the measures necessary to implement them.[7]

---

10 Ibid Art 23(1). As to provision for consultations, in particular in the event of a third country acceding to the Community, see Art 23(2).
11 Ibid Art 28.
12 Ibid Art 24. As to procedures, see Art 27(3)(a).
13 See ibid Arts 25, 26.
14 Ibid Art 25. As to conditions and procedures, see Art 27.
15 Ibid Art 27(2), second sub-paragraph.
16 Ibid Art 27(3)(d).
17 Ibid Art 27(1).
18 Ibid Art 27(1), first sub-paragraph.
19 Ibid Art 27(2), third sub-paragraph.
20 Ibid Art 31(1). As to procedures for achieving this objective, see Art 33(2), (3).
 1 Ibid Art 32(1).
 2 Ibid Art 39(1), which also provides that this shall encompass effective means of enforcing such rights.
 3 Ibid Art 39(2).
 4 Ibid Art 79(1).
 5 Ibid Art 78, second sub-paragraph.
 6 Ibid Art 80, third sub-paragraph.
 7 Ibid Art 80, second sub-paragraph.

The Association Committee, which is to meet at the level of officials, consists of representatives of members of the Council of the European Union and of members of the European Commission, on the one hand, and of representatives of the Government of the Republic of Tunisia, on the other hand.[8] It has the power to take decisions for the management of the Agreement as well as in those areas in which the Council has delegated its powers to it.[9] Its decisions are to be drawn up by agreement between the parties and are binding on the parties, which are to take the necessary implementing measures.[10] Provision is also made for facilitating co-operation and contacts between the European Parliament and the Chamber of Deputies of the Republic of Tunisia, and between the Economic and Social Committee of the Community and the Economic and Social Council of the Republic of Tunisia.[11]

In respect of the settlement of disputes, either party may refer to the Association Council any dispute relating to the application or interpretation of the Agreement.[12] The Association Council may settle the dispute by means of a decision.[13] Each party is then bound to take the measures involved in carrying out the decision.[14] If the dispute cannot be settled by the Association Council, provision is made for recourse to arbitration.[15]

ISRAEL

The Community concluded a trade and co-operation agreement with Israel in 1975.[16] The Community also concluded an agreement with Israel in respect of products covered by the ECSC Treaty.[17] In 1995, however, the Community and its Member States, on the one hand, and Israel, on the other hand, concluded a Euro-Mediterranean Association Agreement.[18] This Agreement replaced the two pre-existing agreements as of 1 January 1996.[19] Pending its

---

8 Ibid Art 82(1).
9 Ibid Art 83(1). The Association Council may delegate to the Association Committee, in full or in part, any of its powers: Art 81(2).
10 Ibid Art 83(2).
11 Ibid Art 85.
12 Ibid Art 86(1).
13 Ibid Art 86(2).
14 Ibid Art 86(3).
15 Ibid Art 86(4). Note that, for the application of this procedure, the Community and the Member States are deemed to be a single Party: Art 86(4), first sub-paragraph.
16 OJ 28.5.75 L136/3, as amended; originally concluded by Council Regulation 1274/75, OJ 28.5.75 L136/1. The trade agreement is complemented by an Additional Protocol (on Co-operation) (OJ 27.9.78 L270/2); a Protocol on Financial Co-operation (OJ 27.9.78 L270/9); a Third Additional Protocol (OJ 20.12.84 L332/1); and a Fourth Additional Protocol (OJ 30.11.88 L327/35). Together these documents form an integrated legal instrument: see Additional Protocol Arts 1, 14, and Financial Protocol Art 11; Third Additional Protocol Art 4; Fourth Additional Protocol Art 7. For analysis of the original trade agreement, see T Einhorn *The Role of the Free Trade Agreement between Israel and the EEC: The Legal Framework for Trading with Israel between Theory and Practice* (Nomos, Baden-Baden, 1994); Kapeliuk-Klinger 'A Legal Analysis of the Free Trade Agreement between the European Community and the State of Israel' (1993) 27 *Israel Law Review* 415.
17 OJ 28.6.75 L165/62. As to these products, see Chapter 19 in this book on ECSC Products.
18 Euro-Mediterranean Agreement establishing an Association between the European Communities and their Member States of the one part and the State of Israel of the other part. See also Hirsch 'The 1995 Trade Agreement between the European Communities and Israel: Three Unresolved Issues' (1996) 1 *European Foreign Affairs Review* 87.
19 Ibid Art 85, third paragraph.

ratification by the EC Member States, its trade policy provisions are being applied pursuant to an Interim Agreement.[20]

The Euro-Mediterranean Agreement establishes an Association between the parties.[1] It has four aims.[2] The first aim is to provide an appropriate framework for political dialogue.[3] The second aim is to promote the harmonious development of economic relations between the parties and thus to foster in them the advance of economic activity, the improvement of living and employment conditions, and increased productivity and financial stability; this aim is to be achieved by the expansion inter alia of the right of establishment, the further progressive liberalization of public procurement, the free movement of capital and the intensification of co-operation in science and technology.[4] The third aim of the Agreement is to encourage regional co-operation with a view to the consolidation of peaceful coexistence and economic and political stability.[5] Fourth, the Agreement is intended to promote co-operation in other areas of reciprocal interest.[6] Respect for human rights and democratic principles is an essential element of the Agreement.[7]

In respect of trade, the Agreement is intended to reinforce the free trade area between the Community and Israel.[8] The Combined Nomenclature and the Israeli customs tariff is to be used for the classification of goods.[9] Separate chapters of the Agreement deal with common provisions, industrial products and agricultural products.

The common provisions prohibit quantitative restrictions on imports and measures having equivalent effet,[10] as well as quantitative restrictions on exports and measures having equivalent effect.[11] However, products originating in Israel are not on importation into the Community to be accorded a treatment more favourable than that which the Member States apply among themselves.[12]

20 An Interim Agreement signed on 18 December 1995 brought its trade provisions into effect as of 1 January 1996: see OJ 20.3.96 L71/2. As of the date of writing, the Agreement remains to be ratified by Belgium and France. As to this issue, and the Commission communications regarding the Interim Agreement, see *Agence Europe*, No 7220 (n.s.), Wednesday, 13 March 1998, p 8.

1 Euro-Mediterranean Agreement Art 1(1). The Agreement is concluded for an unlimited period: Art 82, first paragraph. Either Party may denounce it by giving notice to the other, and the Agreement will cease to apply six months after the date of the notification: Art 82, second paragraph.

2 Ibid Art 2.

3 Ibid Art 1(2), first indent. See also Arts 3–5.

4 Ibid Art 1(2), second indent. In 1996 the Community and Israel concluded an Agreement on Scientific and Technical Co-operation, OJ 19.8.96 L209/23, approved on behalf of the Community by Council Decision 96/505, OJ 19.8.96 L209/22.

5 Ibid Art 1(2), third indent.

6 Ibid Art 1(2), fourth indent.

7 Ibid Art 2.

8 Ibid Art 6(1), which further states that this is to be done according to the modalities set out in the Agreement and in conformity with the provisions of the GATT 1994 and of other multilateral agreements on trade in goods annexed to the WTO Agreement. As to rules of origin and methods of administrative co-operation, see ibid Protocol No 4: ibid Art 28. The EC and Israel have also concluded agreements on procurement by telecommunications operators and government procurement: see Council Decision 97/474, OJ 30.7.97 L202/72 and the attached agreements.

9 Ibid Art 6(2). As to rules of origin, see ibid Art 28 and Protocol No 4.

10 Ibid Art 16.

11 Ibid Art 17. As to safeguard measures when this obligation causes specified difficulties, see Art 24.

12 Ibid Art 18(1). Application of the Agreement is without prejudice to Council Regulation 1911/91 on the application of the provisions of Community law to the Canary Islands: ibid Art 18(2).

Direct or indirect discrimination of an internal fiscal nature with regard to like products is prohibited.[13] Exported products may not benefit from repayment of indirect internal taxation in excess of the amount of indirect taxation imposed on them directly or indirectly.[14] The arrangements may be amended if necessary as a result of the establishment, alteration or extension of rules relating to the implementation of either party's agricultural policy.[15] The Agreement does not preclude the maintenance or establishment of customs unions, free trade areas or arrangements for frontier trade, except insofar as they alter the free trade provisions of the Agreement.[16] The standard exceptions to the free movement of goods apply.[17] In addition, the Agreement does not prevent either party from taking any measures which it considers necessary to prevent the disclosure of information contrary to its essential security interests,[18] which relate to production of or trade in military materials or related activities,[19] or which it considers essential for its internal security.[20]

Anti-dumping measures may be taken in accordance with the Agreement on the implementation of GATT 1994 Article VI and its relevant internal legislation.[1]

Safeguard measures may be taken[2] when any product is imported in such increased quantities and under such conditions as to cause, or threaten to cause, serious injury to domestic producers of like or directly competitive products in the territory of either party,[3] serious disturbances in any sector of the economy,[4] or difficulties which could bring about serious deterioration in the economic situation of a region.[5] Appropriate measures may also be taken when the prohibition on quantitative restrictions on exports and equivalent measures[6] leads to specified situations[7] which give rise, or are likely to give rise, to major difficulties for the exporting party.[8] Depending on which safeguard measures are to be taken, the party taking the measures is required to inform the other party

13 Ibid Art 19(1).
14 Ibid Art 19(2).
15 Ibid Art 20(1). In such cases the party in question is required to take due account of the interest of the other party, for example by means of consultation within the Association Council: ibid Art 20(2).
16 Ibid Art 21(1). As to consultation, see ibid Art 21(2). In the event of a third country acceding to the Community, consultation must take place in order to ensure that account can be taken of the mutual interests of the Community and Israel.
17 Ibid Art 27.
18 Ibid Art 76(a).
19 Ibid Art 76(b), which also contains the proviso that such measures must not impair the conditions of competition in respect of products not intended for specifically military purposes.
20 Ibid Art 76(c).
1 Ibid Art 22, which also provides that such measures are to be taken under the conditions and in accordance with the procedures laid down in Art 25 of the Agreement. See in particular Art 25(2), 3(a), 3(d).
2 Ibid Art 23. As to conditions and procedures, see Art 25, in particular Art 25(2), 3(b), 3(d).
3 Ibid Art 23, first indent.
4 Ibid Art 23, second indent.
5 Ibid Art 23, third indent.
6 See ibid Art 17.
7 Namely, (1) re-export towards a third country against which the exporting party maintains, for the product concerned, quantitative export restrictions, export duties or equivalent measures (ibid Art 24(i)) or (2) a serious shortage or threat thereof of a product essential to the exporting party (ibid Art 24(ii)).
8 Ibid Art 24. As to procedures, see Art 25, in particular Art 25(2), 3(c), 3(d). The measures must be non-discriminatory and must be eliminated when conditions no longer justify their existence: ibid Art 24.

and/or to supply relevant information to the Association Committee before adopting the measures.[9] In the selection of measures, priority must be given to those which least disturb the functioning of the Agreement.[10] Measures must be notified to the Association Committee and periodical consultations must be held with a view to abolishing the measures as soon as circumstances permit.[11] However, where exceptional circumstances requiring immediate action make prior information or examination impossible, a party may take such precautionary measures as are strictly necessary to remedy the situation and immediately inform the other party.[12]

Restrictive measures of a limited duration and scope may also be taken in the event of serious balance of payments difficulties.[13]

In respect of industrial products,[14] customs duties on imports and exports, charges having equivalent effect, and customs duties of a fiscal nature are prohibited.[15] However, either party is entitled to retain customs duties on the agricultural component of certain goods originating in the other party.[16] Such duties may be reduced either when the charge applicable to the basic agricultural product is reduced or as a result of mutual concessions for processed agricultural products.[17]

In respect of agricultural products,[18] the aim of the Agreement is to establish progressively a greater liberalization of trade in agricultural products of interest to both parties. From 1 January 2000 the situation is to be reviewed in order to determine the measures to be applied from that date in accordance with this objective.[19] The arrangements for particular products are set out in the Protocols.[20]

For agricultural products originating in Israel and imported into the Community,[1] customs duties are either eliminated or reduced for certain products;[2] customs duties are eliminated within the limit of tariff quotas for certain other products;[3] certain products exempt from customs duties are subject to

---

9 See ibid Art 25(1), (2).
10 Ibid Art 25(2), second paragraph.
11 Ibid Art 25(2), third paragraph.
12 Ibid Art 25(3)(d).
13 Ibid Art 26.
14 That is, products originating in the Community or in Israel, other than those listed in Annex II EC and, as far as products originating in Israel are concerned, other than those listed in Annex I of the Agreement: ibid Art 7.
15 Ibid Art 8. As to a derogation in respect of the agricultural component, see Art 9(3).
16 As to the retention of such duties by the Community, see ibid Art 9(1). The relevant products are listed in Annex II of the Agreement with the exception of the products listed in Annex III. As to the calculation of the agricultural component, see Art 9(1)(b). As to the retention of such duties by Israel, see ibid Art 92(). The relevant products are listed in Annex IV with the exception of the products listed in Annex V. As to the calculation of the agricultural component, see Art 9(2)(b). Israel may enlarge its list under the conditions set down in Art 9(2)(c).
17 Ibid Art 9(4). As to procedures, see Art 9(5).
18 That is, products originating in the Community or Israel and listed in Annex II EC: ibid Art 10.
19 Ibid Art 11.
20 As to agricultural products originating in Israel, see Art 12 and Protocols No 1 and No 3. As to agricultural products originating in the Community, see Art 13 and Protocols No 2 and 3.
1 See ibid Protocol No 1.
2 Ibid Protocol No 1, paragraph 2 and column A of Annex.
3 Ibid Protocol No 1, paragraph 3 and column B of Annex. If imports exceed the tariff quota, the CCT duties may be applied in full or reduced, as indicated in column C. As to imports into the Community of fresh cut flowers and flower buds falling within subheading 0603 10 of the CCT, see the Agreement in the Form of an Exchange of Letters between the Community and Israel relating to Protocol 1 (attached to the main Agreement). As to poultrymeat, see Commission Regulation 2497/96, OJ 28.12.96 L338/48. As to oranges, see the Agreement in the form of an exchange of letters, attached to Council Decision 2397/96, OJ 18.12.96 L327/1.

reference quantities;[4] certain other products are subject to gradually increasing tariff quotas;[5] and certain other products may be subject to a reference quantity if imports threaten to cause difficulties of the Community market.[6]

For agricultural products originating in the Community and imported into Israel[7] import duties on certain products are to be either eliminated or reduced to specified levels within the limit of tariff quotas and subject to specified conditions.[8] Reference quantities are fixed for certain other products for which no tariff quota is established.[9] For other products in respect of which neither a tariff quota nor a reference quantity is established, Israel may fix a reference quantity if the volume of imports threatens to cause difficulties on the Israeli market.[10] For cheeese and curds the tariff quota is to be increased by four equal instalments, each corresponding to 10 per cent of the amount, between 1 January 1997 and 1 January 2000.[11]

The possibility of further concessions is to be examined in the Association Council, product by product and on an orderly and reciprocal basis, taking account of the volume of trade and its sensitivity.[12] At the latest three years after the entry into force of the Agreement, the parties are to examine the possibility of granting each other, on the basis of reciprocity and mutual interest, concessions in trade in fisheries products.[13]

Adequate and effective protection of intellectual property rights is to be granted and ensured in accordance with the highest international standards, including effective means of enforcing such rights.[14] Consultations must be undertaken if problems arise affecting trading conditions.[15]

Special provision is made for plant protection matters.[16] The requirement for phytosanitary certification is limited to specified products and purposes.[17] The introduction of new measures is subject to consultations with the other party.[18]

An Association Council is established to examine any major issues arising under the Agreement and any other bilateral or international issues of mutual interest.[19] It is composed of members of the Council of the European Union and

---

4 Ibid paragraph 4 and column D of Annex. If imports of one of the products exceed the reference quantity, the Community may make such imports subject to a tariff quota: Art 4, second paragraph.

5 Ibid paragraph 5 and column E of Annex.

6 Ibid paragraph 6 and column E of Annex.

7 See ibid Protocol No 2.

8 Ibid Protocol No 2, paragraph 2. The level of duty is indicated in column A of the Annex. The tariff quotas are listed in column B of the Annex. Specific provisions for certain products are laid down in column C of the Annex. For quantities imported in excess of the tariff quotas, the general customs duties applied to third countries will apply: Protocol No 2, paragraph 3.

9 Ibid Protocol No 2, paragraph 4 and column C of Annex. If imports exceed the reference quantity, Israel may subject the product to a tariff quota: Protocol No 2, paragraph 4, second sub-paragraph.

10 Ibid Protocol No 2, paragraph 5.

11 Ibid Protocol No 2, paragraph 6.

12 Ibid Art 14.

13 Ibid Art 15.

14 Ibid Art 39(1). See also Annex VII.

15 Ibid Art 39(2).

16 Ibid Protocol No 3. This is without prejudice to the provisions of the Agreement on the Application of Sanitary and Phytosanitary Measures annexed to the WTO Agreement. As to the latter Agreement, see Chapter 17 in this book on Health Measures in the Agricultural Sector.

17 See ibid Protocol No 3, paragraphs (a), (b).

18 Ibid Protocol No 3, paragraph (c).

19 Ibid Art 67.

members of the European Commission together with members of the Government of Israel.[20] For the purposes of attaining the objectives of the Agreement it has the power to take decisions binding on the parties.[1] These decisions are to be drawn up by agreement between the parties.[2] The implementation of the Agreement is the responsibility of an Association Committee,[3] to which the Association Council may delegate any of its powers.[4] It consists of representatives of the EU Council and the European Commission, on the one hand, and representatives of the Government of Israel, on the other hand.[5] It has the power to take decisions for the management of the Agreement as well as in those areas in which the Association Council has delegated its powers to it.[6] The decisions are to be drawn up by agreement between the parties[7] and are binding on the parties.[8] Provision is also made for parliamentary co-operation.[9]

Disputes relating to the application or interpretation may be referred to the Association Council.[10] The latter may settle the dispute by means of a decision.[11] If this is not possible, arbitration is to be used.[12]

WEST BANK AND GAZA STRIP

A Euro-Mediterranean Interim Association Agreement on trade and co-operation was concluded recently between the Community and the Palestine Liberation Organization (PLO) for the benefit of the Palestinian Authority of the West Bank and the Gaza Strip.[13] Its six objectives are to provide an appropriate framework for a comprehensive dialogue between the parties; to establish the conditions for a progressive liberalization of trade; to foster the development of balanced economic and social relations between the parties; to contribute to the social and economic development of the West Bank and the Gaza Strip; to encourage regional co-operation; and to promote co-operation in other areas of reciprocal interest.[14] The Agreement provides for free movement of goods,[15] payments, capital, competition, intellectual property, and public procurement;[16] economic co-operation and social develop-

---

20 Ibid Art 68(1). As to procedures, see Art 68(2)–(4).
 1 Ibid Art 69(1).
 2 Ibid Art 69(2).
 3 Ibid Art 70(1).
 4 Ibid Art 70(2).
 5 Ibid Art 71(1). As to procedures, see Art 71(2), (3).
 6 Ibid Art 72(1), first paragraph.
 7 Ibid Art 72(2).
 8 Ibid Art 72(1), second paragraph.
 9 Ibid Art 74.
10 Ibid Art 75(1).
11 Ibid Art 75(2). See also Art 75(3).
12 Ibid Art 75(4).
13 See the Agreement, attached to Council Decision 97/430, OJ 16.7.97 L187/1. No later than 4 May 1999 negotiations are to begin with a view to concluding an Association Agreement: ibid Art 75(2). The Interim Agreement may be denounced by notification by either party: Art 75(3).
14 Euro-Mediterranean Interim Association Agreement on trade and co-operation between the European Community, of the one part, and the Palestine Liberation Organization (PLO) for the benefit of the Palestinian Authority of the West Bank and the Gaza Strip, of the other part, Art 1(2), OJ 16.7.97 L187/3.
15 Ibid Title I, Arts 3–26.
16 Ibid Title II, Arts 27–34. As to intellectual property in particular, see Art 33. In respect of public procurement, the parties agree on the objective of reciprocal and gradual liberalization of contracts: Art 34(1).

ment;[17] co-operation on audiovisual and cultural matters, information and communication;[18] financial co-operation;[19] and institutional and general matters.[20] Relations between the parties, as well as all the provisions of the Agreement itself, are to be based on respect of democratic principles and fundamental human rights, which constitute an essential element of the Agreement.[1]

A free trade area between the parties is to be established progressively over a transitional period, not extending beyond 31 December 2001.[2]

In respect of industrial products,[3] a standstill clause applies to customs duties on imports and equivalent charges.[4] Imports into the Community of products from the West Bank and the Gaza Strip are free of customs duties, equivalent charges, quantitative restrictions, equivalent measures[5] and customs duties of a fiscal nature.[6] This does not however preclude the Community from retaining an agricultural component in respect of certain goods.[7] Customs duties and equivalent charges on imports from the Community, as well as customs duties of a fiscal nature,[8] are to be abolished, with specified exceptions.[9] The Palestinian Authority is entitled to retain, for the duration of the Agreement, customs duties and equivalent charges at a specified level of customs duties in relation to certain products.[10] For other specific products, it may levy a fiscal charge, to be gradually abolished according to a prescribed schedule.[11]

In respect of agricultural and fishery products,[12] the parties are to establish progressively a greater liberalization of their trade.[13] Certain products are subject to reduction or elimination of import duty or customs duty or to reference quantities.[14]

17 Ibid Title III, Arts 35–55.
18 Ibid Title IV, Arts 56–60.
19 Ibid Title IV, Arts 61–62.
20 Ibid Title VI, Arts 63–75.
 1 Ibid Art 2, which also states that the human rights in question are as set out in the universal declaration on human rights.
 2 Ibid Art 3, which also provides that it is to be established according to the modalities set out in Title I of the Agreement and in conformity with the provisions of GATT 1994 and other multilateral agreements on trade in goods annexed to the WTO Agreement.
 3 That is, products originating in the Community and in the West Bank and the Gaza Strip other than those in Annex II of the EC Treaty: ibid Art 4. As to rules of origin, see ibid Art 25 and Protocol 3.
 4 Ibid Art 5. As to certain derogations for infant industries, restructuring or serious problems, however, see ibid Art 10.
 5 Ibid Art 6.
 6 Ibid Art 9.
 7 Ibid Art 7(1), first sub-paragraph. The goods are listed in Annex 1. The provisions on agricultural and fishery products in Chapter 2 of the Agreement apply, *mutatis mutandis*, to the agricultural component: ibid Art 7(1), second sub-paragraph.
 8 Ibid Art 9.
 9 Ibid Art 8(1), which also provides that the specified exceptions are listed in Annex 2 and 3. As to derogations for infant industries, restructuring, or serious difficulties, see ibid Art 10.
10 Ibid Art 7(2), first sub-paragraph. The goods are listed in Annex 2. The level is to be not higher than that in force on 1 July 1996. However, the Joint Committee may decide on further concessions granted on a mutual basis: ibid Art 7(3).
11 Ibid Art 8(2), which provides that these products are listed in Annex 3 and also sets out the schedule for abolition of charges. In the event of serious difficulties, the schedule may be reviewed and, on specified conditions, provisionally suspended: ibid Art 8(3).
12 Namely, products listed in Annex II to the EC Treaty: ibid Art 11.
13 Ibid Art 12. Either party is entitled however to amend the arrangements if required by its own agricultural policy: see ibid Art 17, which also sets out procedures.
14 As to agricultural products from West Bank and the Gaza Strip, see ibid Art 13(1) and Protocol 2. As to agricultural products form the Community, see ibid Art 13(2) and Protocol 2. As to further concessions, see ibid Art 14.

There is a standstill on quantitative restrictions on imports and equivalent measures,[15] and those in effect are to be abolished.[16] No customs duties, equivalent charges, quantitative restrictions, or equivalent measures are to be applied to exports.[17] Fiscal discriminatory measures are prohibited.[18] Safeguard measures are provided.[19] There are also the usual exceptions to free trade.[20]

The Agreement also provides for the promotion of the use of Community technical regulations and European standards and conformity assessment procedures.[1] An objective of economic co-operation is to approximate Palestinian Council legislation to that of the Community, in areas covered by the Agreement.[2] Provision is also made for customs co-operation.[3] A joint committee is established to manage the Agreement.[4]

---

15 Ibid Art 15(1).
16 Ibid Art 15(2).
17 Ibid Art 15(3).
18 See ibid Art 18.
19 See ibid Arts 20–23.
20 Ibid Art 24.
 1 Ibid Art 40, second sub-paragraph, first indent.
 2 Ibid Art 41.
 3 Ibid Art 52.
 4 Ibid Art 63.

Chapter 27

Middle East

GULF STATES

The Community and the countries parties to the Charter of the Co-operation Council for the Arab States of the Gulf[1] signed a Co-operation Agreement in 1989.[2] Its aims are inter alia to broaden and consolidate co-operation in trade, taking account of the differences in levels of development of the parties.[3] In respect of trade,[4] its specific objective is to promote the development and diversification of reciprocal commercial exchanges to the highest possible level, inter alia by studying ways and means of overcoming trade barriers to market access.[5] The conclusion of a trade agreement is foreseen.[6] Pending its conclusions, the parties are to accord each other MFN treatment.[7] A Joint Council is established to take decisions in order to attain the objectives of the Agreement.[8] The agreement is concluded for an unlimited period.[9]

On the basis of EC Art 113, specific measures have been enacted to prevent trade (including trade in Euratom products) between the Community and

1 The so-called GCC countries include the State of the United Arab Emirates, the State of Bahrain, the Kingdom of Saudia Arabia, the Sultanate of Oman, the State of Quatar and the State of Kuwait.
2 OJ 25.2.89 L54/3. In 1982 the Communities had concluded a Co-operation Agreement with the Council of Arab Economic Unity (CAEU): OJ 28.10.82 L300/23.
3 Ibid Art 1(b).
4 As to economic co-operation, see ibid Arts 2–10.
5 Ibid Art 11(1).
6 Ibid Art 11(2). As to which, see the appended Joint Declaration concerning Art 11(2), which expresses in its second paragraph the readiness of the European Community to examine the possibility of negotiating this agreement, provided inter alia that the contracting parties find solutions enabling the following conditions to be met: full conformity with the relevant GATT provisions; the adoption of measures ensuring that the agreement does not undermine efforts to restructure the Community's oil refining and petrochemical industries and to maintain a production capacity in those industries; the adoption of measures enabling the worries of the GCC countries concerning sensitive sectors, in particular infant industries, to be resolved; and an undertaking on the part of the Community to maintain non-discriminatory conditions of market access for GCC petroleum products. With regard to the GATT, see paragraph 4 of the Joint Declaration and the Declaration of the EEC concerning this paragraph, appended to the Agreement.
7 Ibid Art 11(3). The nature of this treatment is specified in the appended Exchange of Letters concerning Art 11(3).
8 Ibid Art 12(1). The role, structure, powers of the Joint Council are laid down in Arts 12–14. The Joint Council is assisted by a Joint Co-operation Committee, as to which see Art 15.
9 Ibid Art 23, first paragraph.

Iraq.[10] The prohibition does not apply to products intended for strictly medical purposes, foodstuffs and approved materials and supplies for essential civilian needs.[11]

YEMEN

In 1985 the Community and the Yemen Arab Republic signed a Co-operation Agreement.[12] It was amended and adapted in 1995 following the unification in 1990 of the Yemen Arab Republic and the People's Democratic Republic of Yemen to form the Republic of Yemen.[13] In respect of trade,[14] the Agreement provides that the parties are to grant each other MFN treatment with regard to imports or exports.[15] A Joint Committee was established to review activities under the Agreement and make recommendations.[16] The Agreement applies for an initial period of five years and thereafter for periods of two years subject to right of termination by either party.[17]

A new Co-operation Agreement was concluded in 1997.[18] Respect of democratic principles and human rights are stated to constitute an essential element of the Agreement.[19] The principal objective of the Agreement is to enhance and develop, under a concept of dialogue, various aspects of co-operation, including trade and economic co-operation.[20] Within the limits of its respective competence, the Community is to conduct trade in accordance with the WTO Agreement, and Yemen is to seek to conduct trade accordingly.[1] MFN treatment applies, with the exception of preferences accorded by either party under any arrangement establishing a customs union, a free trade area, or a preferential treatment area.[2] The Agreement provides for various types of trade co-operation.[3] A Joint Co-operation Committee is established to oversee the overall implementation of the Agreement.[4]

10 Council Regulation 2340/90, OJ 9.8.90 L213/1, as amended. The original Regulation applied from 7 August 1990 to both Iraq and Kuwait: Art 1. The restrictions in respect of Kuwait were lifted as of 2 March 1991: Council Regulation 542/91 Art 1, OJ 7.3.91 L60/5. See also *Re Trade with Iraq* (Case 1 0 446/90) [26 February 1992, Landgericht Bonn] [1993] 1 CMLR 66. As to Iraq, see Council Regulation 2465/96 regarding the interruption of economic and financial relations between the EC and Iraq, OJ 27.12.96 L337/1, and Commission Communication pursuant to Art 6 of this regulation, OJ 20.3.97 L90/11.
11 Council Regulation 2340/90, Annex (OJ 9.8.90 L213/1), as amended by Council Regulation 1194/91 Art 1 (OJ 8.5.91 L115/37.
12 OJ 31.1.85 L26/2.
13 Exchange of Letters, OJ 15.3.95 L57/78.
14 The Agreement also provides for commercial, economic and technical co-operation: see ibid Arts 2–4.
15 Ibid Art 1(1). This does not apply however to advantages granted to neighbouring countries to facilitate frontier-zone traffic, advantages granted with the object of establishing a customs union or free trade area, advantages granted to particular countries in conformity with the GATT, or advantages granted by Yemen to certain countries in accordance with the GATT Protocol on Trade Negotiations among Developing Countries: Art 1(2).
16 Ibid Art 5(1).
17 Ibid Art 7(1).
18 Co-operation Agreement between the European Community and the Republic of Yemen, OJ 11.3.98 L72/18, approved by Council Decision 98/189, OJ 11.3.98 L72/17.
19 Ibid Art 1.
20 Ibid Art 2.
 1 Ibid Art 3(a).
 2 Ibid Art 3(b).
 3 See ibid Art 3(d).
 4 Ibid Art 15.

Chapter 28

African, Caribbean and Pacific (ACP) countries

INTRODUCTION

The present ACP–EC Convention of Lomé[1] is the fourth in a series of agreements[2] between the Community and a large group of African, Caribbean and Pacific countries. Beginning in 1975, the agreements were a conscious attempt to establish a new image of equality and partnership for a relationship which, under the preceding Yaounde Conventions,[3] had come to be seen by some as bearing too many resemblances to the state of affairs which obtained during the colonial period.[4]

The Fourth Lomé Convention has 71 ACP parties.[5] It was signed on 15

1 Fourth ACP–EC Convention of Lomé as revised by the Agreement signed in Mauritius on 4 November 1995, (1996) 155 *The Courier* (January–February). References to the Fourth Lomé Convention hereinafter always refer to this revised Convention unless otherwise indicated.

2 ACP–EEC Convention of Lome and Agreement on Products within the Province of the European Coal and Steel Community (Lome, 28 February 1975; TS 105 (1979); Cmnd 7751; OJ 30.1.76 L25/2); Second ACP–EEC Convention of Lome and Agreement on Products within the Province of the European Coal and Steel Community (Lome, 31 October 1979; TS 3 (1983); Cmnd 8761; OJ 22.10.80 L347/2); Third ACP–EEC Convention of Lomé (Lomé, 8 December 1984; EC 19 (1985); Cmnd 9511; *The Courier*, January–February 1985).

3 Convention of Association between the European Economic Community and the African and Malagasy States associated with that Community (Yaounde, 20 July 1963; OJ 1964, p 1430); Convention of Association between the European Economic Community and the African and Malagasy States associated with that Community (Yaounde, 29 July 1969; OJ 28.12.70 L282/2).

4 As to certain recurring legal problems in these Conventions, see Addo, 'A Critical Analysis of the Perennial International Economic Law Problems of the EEC–ACP Relationship' (1990) 33 *German Yearbook of International Law* 37.

5 Currently there are 48 states from Africa, fifteen from the Caribbean and eight from the Pacific. The ACP States are Angola, Antigua and Barbuda, Bahamas, Barbados, Belize, Benin, Botswana, Burkina Faso, Burundi, Cameroon, Cape Verde, Central African Republic, Chad, Comoros, Congo, Djibouti, Dominica, Dominican Republic, Equatorial Guinea, Eritrea, Ethiopia, Fiji, Gabon, Gambia, Ghana, Grenada, Guinea, Guinea Bissau, Guyana, Haiti, Ivory Coast, Jamaica, Kenya, Kiribati, Lesotho, Liberia, Madagascar, Malawi, Mali, Mauritania, Mauritius, Mozambique, Namibia, Niger, Nigeria, Papua New Guinea, Rwanda, St Christopher and Nevis, St Lucia, St Vincent and the Grenadines, Sao Tome and Principe, Senegal, Seychelles, Sierra Leone, Solomon Islands, Somalia, South Africa (qualified membership), Sudan, Surinam, Swaziland, Tanzania, Togo, Tongo, Trinidad and Tobago, Tuvalu, Uganda, western Samoa, Vanuatu, Zaire, Zambia, and Zimbabwe. The Community concluded a Co-operation Agreement with South Africa in 1994: OJ 30.12.94 L341/61. The Community and South Africa have also concluded an Agreement on Scientific and Technological Co-operation: OJ 15.11.97 L314/25, approved on behalf of the Community by Council Decision 97/763, OJ 15.11.97 L313/25. As to sanctions against Haiti and Angola, see I Macleod, I D Hendry and S Hyett *The External Relations of the European Communities* (Clarendon Press, Oxford, 1996) pp 365–366 and p 366, respectively.

December 1989, came into force in 1990 for a period of ten years, and completed a Mid-Term Review in June 1995. It contains 369 articles, ten protocols and 84 annexes covering a wide range of topics. The overriding objectives are co-operation and development, particularly in economic matters. Respect for human rights, democratic principles and the rule of law constitutes an essential element of the Convention.[6] Detailed provision is made for co-operation in the fields of the environment, agricultural co-operation, food security and rural development, development of fisheries,[7] commodities, industrial development, manufacturing and processing, mining, energy, enterprise development, services, trade, social and cultural co-operation, and regional co-operation. The following paragraphs are concerned mainly with the regulation of trade between the ACP States and the Community.[8]

OBJECTIVES, PRINCIPLES AND INSTITUTIONS OF TRADE CO-OPERATION

The basic principles of co-operation under Lomé IV recognize the fundamental importance of trade in the development process. The parties agreed to give high priority to the development of trade, with a view to accelerating the growth of the ACP states' economies and integrating them into the world economy in a

6 Fourth Lomé Convention Art 5(1), third paragraph.
7 The Fourth Lomé Convention Art 65, states the intention of the parties to enter into bilateral agreements on fishing. Bilateral agreements have been concluded with Angola (OJ 19.8.87 L268/86, as amended), Cape Verde (OJ 9.8.90 L212/3, as amended), Comoros, Dominica, Equatorial Guinea (OJ 16.7.84 L188/2, as amended), Gambia (OJ 6.6.87 L146/3, as amended), Guinea (OJ 27.4.83 L111/2, as amended), Guinea Bissau (OJ 28.8.80 L226/34, as amended), Ivory Coast, Madagascar (OJ 18.3.86 L73/26, as amended), Mauritania (OJ 24.10.87 L302/26, as amended), Mauritius (OJ 10.6.89 L159/2, as amended), Mozambique (OJ 10.4.87 L98/12, as amended), Sao Tomé and Principe (OJ 25.2.84 L54/2, as amended), Senegal (OJ 29.8.80 L226/17, as amended), Seychelles (OJ 23.3.84 L79/34, as amended; OJ 7.5.87 L119/26, as amended), Sierra Leone (OJ 15.5.90 L125/28, as amended), and Tanzania (OJ 31.12.90 L379/25).
8 The volume of trade, as distinguished from the regulation of trade, is of course influenced by other aspects of the Lomé Convention, such as export earnings stabilization schemes for agricultural commodities (Stabex: see Arts 186–212) and minerals (Sysmin: see Arts 214–219), financial aid (see Arts 220–257) and investment (see Arts 258–274). As to the operation of Stabex, see Court of Auditors, Special Report 2/95 concerning the Stabex fund in the context of the first financial Protocol of the Fourth Lomé Convention together with the Commission's replies (95/C167/01), OJ 3.7.95 L167/1; Commission of the European Communities, 'Commission Report on the operation in 1996 of the export earnings stabilisation scheme under the fourth ACP–EC Convention as revised by the Agreement signed in Mauritius', COM(97)374 final, Brussels, 18.7.97. The Fourth Lomé Convention also included, as part of the seventh European Development Fund (EDF), machinery for structural adjustment support, particularly import programmes and the distribution of counterpart funds: see Arts 243–250. For an analysis of similar operations under the the sixth EDF, see Court of Auditors, Special Report No 2/94 on the import programmes carried out under the sixth EDF, together with the Commission's replies (94/C97/01), OJ 6.4.94 C97/1. Annex XX of the Fourth Lomé Convention calls for greater emphasis on the development of trade and services in the context of Community aid, as to which see in particular European Commission, ACP-EEC Trade Development Project, doc. VIII/249/94 (Brussels, March 1994). As to debt relief, see Commission of the European Communities, 'Support for Structural Adjustment and Debt Relief in Heavily Indebted ACP States: A Community Response to the HIPC Debt Initiative, Proposal for a Council Decision concerning Exceptional Assistance for the Heavily Indebted ACP Countries' (Communication from the Commission), COM(97)129 final, Brussels, 25.3.97.

harmonious and gradual manner. They also agreed that adequate resources should be devoted to the expansion of ACP trade.[9]

Trade development is to be aimed at developing, diversifying and increasing the ACP States' trade and improving their competitiveness in their domestic markets, the regional and intra-ACP market, and the Community and international markets. The parties undertook to use all means available under the Convention, including trade co-operation and those on financial and technical co-operation, for the achievement of this objective. They also agreed to implement the provisions of the Convention in a coherent and co-ordinated manner.[10]

The importance of trade is reflected in the principles governing the instruments of co-operation. The parties agreed on general trade provisions, special arrangements for Community import of certain ACP products, arrangements to promote the development of ACP trade and services including tourism, and a system of reciprocal information and consultation designed to help apply the trade provisions of the Convention effectively.[11]

The aim of the trade arrangements, based on the parties' international obligations, is to provide a foundation for trade co-operation.[12] These arrangements are to be based on the principle of free access to the Community market for products originating in the ACP States,[13] with special provisions for agricultural products and a safeguard clause.[14] On the ACP side, the arrangements do not include any element of reciprocity as regards market access.[15] However, the arrangements are also to be based on the principle of non-discrimination by the ACP States between the Member States and on according to the Community a treatment no less favourable than MFN treatment.[16]

The basic institutions of the Convention are the Council of Ministers, the Committee of Ambassadors and the Joint Assembly.[17] A Commodities Committee is established to examine general problems, recommend measures, and exchange information regarding trade in commodities.[18]

CO-OPERATION IN TRADE DEVELOPMENT

In order to achieve the trade objectives of the Convention, the parties undertook to give a high priority to trade development programmes in the context of

---

9 Fourth Lomé Convention Art 6a. Note that this Article was added in 1995 as a result of the Mid-Term Review.
10 Fourth Lomé Convention Art 15a. This Article was also added at the Mid-Term Review.
11 Fourth Lomé Convention Art 24.
12 Fourth Lomé Convention Art 25, first paragraph.
13 As to rules of origin, see Fourth Lomé Convention Art 176 and Protocol 1 Concerning the definition of the concept of 'originating products' and methods of administrative co-operation. For sufficiently processed products, the CTH system is used: Protocol 1 Art 3(1). For the purpose of determining ACP origin, cumulation is permitted among the ACP States as a whole, the Community, the overseas countries and territories (OCT) to which Part Four of the EC Treaty applies, and, in specified conditions, neighbouring developing countries belonging to a coherent geographical entity: Protocol 1 Art 6.
14 Fourth Lomé Convention Art 25, second paragraph.
15 Fourth Lomé Convention Art 25, third paragraph. See also Art 174(1).
16 Fourth Lomé Convention Art 25, fourth paragraph. See also Art 174(2((b).
17 Fourth Lomé Convention Art 29. As to their composition, role and functions, see Arts 30 (Council of Ministers), 31 (Committee of Ambassadors) and 32 (Joint Assembly).
18 Fourth Lomé Convention Art 75.

establishing national and regional programmes.[19] Special attention is to be given in particular to international trade.[20]

At the request of the ACP States and ACP regions, operations are to be undertaken in particular for support for the definition of appropriate macro-economic strategies necessary for trade development, support for the creation or reform of appropriate legal and regulatory frameworks as well as reform of administrative procedures, establishment of current trade strategies, support for strengthening trade infrastructure, development in the processing, marketing, distribution and transport sectors for the Community, regional and international markets, support for ACP actions aimed at encouraging private investment and joint ventures, special provisions of the least-developed,[1] landlocked[2] and island States,[3] support for ACP efforts to penetrate third country markets more effectively, and other activities.[4] Technical assistance is also to be given for the establishment and development of insurance and credit institutions in connection with trade and development.[5]

GENERAL TRADE ARRANGEMENTS

The general rule established by the Convention is that products originating in the ACP States are imported into the Community free of customs duties and equivalent charges.[6] Subject to import arrangements for Annex II products covered by a common organization of the market,[7] the Community may not subject imports from the ACP to quantitative restrictions or equivalent measures.[8] The treatment applied to ACP imports may not however be more favourable than that applied to trade among the Member States.[9] The standard exceptions

---

19 Fourth Lomé Convention Art 135, third paragraph. Such programmes are provided for in particular by Art 281.
20 Fourth Lomé Convention Art 136(1). As to safeguarding the interests of ACP States affected by trade liberalization, see Annex XXIX Joint declaration on trade liberalization.
 1 See generally Fourth Lomé Convention Title IV. As to the least-developed States, see Arts 329–331. For the purposes of the Convention, the following are considered the least-developed ACP States: Antiguia and Barbuda, Belize, Benin, Botswana, Burkina Faso, Burundi, Cape Verde, Central African Republic, Chad, Comoros, Djibouti, Dominica, Equatorial Guinea, Ethiopia, Gambia, Grenada, Guinea, Guinea-Bissau, Haiti, Kiribati, Lesotho, Malawi, Mali, Mauritania, Mozambique, Niger, Rwanda, Saint Kitts and Nevis, Saint Lucia, Saint Vincent and the Grenadines, Sao Tome and Principe, Seychelles, Sierra Leone, Solomon Islands, Somalia, Swaziland, Tanzania, Togo, Tonga, Tuvalu, Uganda, Vanuatu, and Western Samoa: Art 330(1). As to future strategy, see Commission of the European Communities, 'Improving Market Access for Least Developed Countries' (Communication from the Commission), COM(97)156 final, Brussels, 16.4.97.
 2 See Arts 332–334. The landlocked ACP States are: Botswana, Burkina Faso, Burundi, Central African Republic, Chad, Lesotho, Malawi, Mali, Niger, Rwanda, Swaziland, Uganda, Zambia, and Zimbabwe: Art 333(1).
 3 See Arts 335–337. The Island ACP States are: Antigua and Barbuda, Bahamas, Barbados, Cape Verde, Comoros, Dominican Republic, Fiji, Grenada, Haiti, Jamaica, Kiribati, Madagascar, Mauritius, Papua New Guinea, Saint Kitts and Nevis, Saint Lucia, Saint Vincent and the Grenadines, Sao Tome and Principe, Seychelles, Tonga, Trinidad and Tobago, Tuvalu, Vanuatu, and Western Samoa: Art 336(1).
 4 Fourth Lomé Convention Art 136(2).
 5 Fourth Lomé Convention Art 137.
 6 Fourth Lomé Convention Art 168(1). This includes ECSC products: Protocol 9 Art 1.
 7 Ibid Art 169(2), first paragraph.
 8 Ibid Art 169(1).
 9 Ibid Art 171. In respect of agricultural products, see also Joined Cases 194 and 241/85 *Commission v Greece* [1988] ECR 1037.

to the free movement of goods apply.[10] However, where such measures affect the interests of the ACP States, the latter are entitled to request consultations.[11]

Special rules apply to agricultural products, either those Annex II products covered by a common organization of the market or those subject to specific rules introduced as a result of the implementation of the CAP.[12] Agricultural products for which Community provisions do not provide for the application of any measures apart from customs duties are to be imported duty-free.[13] For other agricultural products, the Community is to take the necessary measures to ensure more favourable treatment than that granted to third countries benefiting from MFN treatment for the same products.[14] These special rules apply notwithstanding general arrangements applied in respect of third countries.[15]

Detailed rules are laid down for certain agricultural products and processed agricultural products originating in the ACP States or the overseas countries and territories (OCT).[16] Beef and veal is admitted into the Community free of customs duties,[17] but most categories of live animals and meat are subject to reimposition of duty if yearly growth rate is more than 7 per cent.[18] Most of these products also benefited formerly from a 90 per cent reduction in the CAP levy provided a corresponding sum was charged by the ACP State on export;[19] the reduction was subject to maximum tonnages in the case of the largest exporters.[20] After variable levies were replaced by tariff quotas as a result of the

10 Ibid Art 170(1).
11 Ibid Art 170(2), second paragraph.
12 Ibid Art 168(2)(a). See also Annex XXXIV Joint declaration on the arrangements governing access to the markets of the French overseas departments for products originating in the ACP States referred to in Art 168(2); Annex XXXV Joint declaration on products covered by the Common Agricultural Policy; Annex XXXIX ACP declaration on Art 168.
13 Ibid Art 168(2)(a)(i). As to special measures, see below. The Community is required to examine, in consultation with the ACP States, requests by ACP States for specific arrangements for new lines of agricultural production or agricultural products: Art 168(2)(b). It must also examine, on a case-by-case basis, ACP requests for preferential access for agricultural products to the Community market, with a decision if possible within four months and in any case not more than six months after the date of submission: Art 168(2)(c), first paragraph.
14 Ibid Art 168(2)(a)(ii). In this respect the Community is to take decisions in particular with reference to concessions granted to developing third countries, taking account of the possibilities offered by the off-season market: Art 168(c), second paragraph. See also Annex XL Joint declaration concerning agricultural products referred to in Art 168(2)(a)(ii). See also Agreement in the form of an exchange of letters between the Community and the ACP States concerning Annex XL, OJ 21.10.97 L287/31, approved on behalf of the Community by Council Decision 97/683, OJ 21.1097 L287/30.
15 Ibid Art 168(2)(a).
16 The basic regulation is Council Regulation 715/90, OJ 30.3.90 L84/85, as amended. The ACP States are listed in Annex I and the OCT in Annex II. Annex I was amended by Council Regulation 297/91, OJ 8.2.91 L36/9, and Council Regulation 235/94, OJ 3.2.94 L30/12. These arrangements have been extended until 29 February 2000: Council Regulation 444/92 Art 1, OJ 27.2.92 L52/7. As to the derogation from the definition of 'originating products' to take account of the special situation of Fiji and Papua New Guinea regarding the production of canned tuna (HS heading ex 16.04), see Decision 2/97 of the ACP–EC Customs Co-operation Committee, 8.10.97 L275/5. As to detailed implementing rules for imports of rice originating in the ACP or the OCT, see Commission Regulation 2603/97, OJ 23.12.97 L351/22. As to rules of origin generally, see Chapter 2 in this book. Following the Uruguay Round, all levies have been converted into tariff quotas.
17 Ibid Art 2, first paragraph.
18 Ibid Art 2, second paragraph.
19 Ibid Art 3.
20 Ibid Art 4. As to 1995 imports, see Commission Regulation 2449/95, OJ 20.10.95 L252/1.

Uruguay Round agreements, tariff quotas were opened for beef and veal, import licences were issued, and CCT duties were reduced.[1]

Live sheep and goats, sheepmeat and goatmeat are also imported free of customs duty;[2] such products were also exempt from levy,[3] with the exception of sheepmeat which was subject to reduced levy within a fixed tariff quota.[4] Poultrymeat,[5] milk products,[6] and pigmeat[7] were subject to reduced levy up to a fixed quota. Customs duties are reduced to zero on imports of various products, most importantly fish,[8] most types of oils and fats[9] (but not olive oil), various fruits and vegetables,[10] tobacco,[11] flax and hemp, hops, plants and bulbs etc, seed and dried fodder.[12] The duty on other fruits and vegetables was originally reduced but has now been suspended within certain tariff quotas.[13] Subject to a maximum price and a quota, the levy on maize, millet, grain sorghum and rice is reduced,[14] as was the then applicable variable component of the levy on products produced from cereals and rice.[15] The fixed component of the duty applicable to a number of processed products, including chocolate and spaghetti, is removed, as well as in some cases the variable component.[16] Some processed fruits, vegetables and fruit juices are admissible duty or levy free.[17] Specific rules apply to direct imports into the French overseas departments for use and release on the market there.[18] As a result of the Uruguay Round, levies have been converted into tariff quotas.[19]

1 Commission Regulation 1636/95, OJ 6.7.95 L155/25.
2 Ibid Art 5(1).
3 Ibid Art 5(2).
4 Ibid Art 5(3).
5 Ibid Art 6. As to detailed rules, see Commission Regulation 903/90, OJ 10.4.90 L93/20, as amended.
6 Ibid Art 7. As to detailed rules, see Commission Regulation 1150/90, OJ 5.5.90 L114/21, as amended, and Commission Regulation 1220/96, OJ 29.6.96 L161/57, which provides for post-Uruguay Round transitional measures.
7 Ibid Art 8. See Commission Regulation 904/90, OJ 10.4.90 L93/23, as amended.
8 Ibid Art 9.
9 Ibid Art 10.
10 Ibid Art 15(1), adapted by Council Regulation 234/94, OJ 3.2.94 L30/11.
11 Ibid Art 20.
12 Ibid Art 23.
13 Ibid Arts 15(2), 16. Article 16 was amended to include seedless table grapes by Council Regulation 2484/94, OJ 15.10.94 L265/3. As to reference quantities and statistical surveillance for certain products (cabbages, iceberg lettuce, globe artichokes, apricots, cherries, peaches, plums), see Commission Regulation 1280/94, OJ 3.6.94 L140/10, as partly substituted by Commission Regulation 3147/94, OJ 22.12.94 L332/26, which itself was replaced by Commission Regulation 895/95, OJ 25.4.95 L92/10. As to suspension of duty within tariff quotas for other products (tomatoes, cherry tomatoes, figs, strawberries), see Commission Regulation 2763/94, OJ 15.11.94 L294/6, as partly substituted by Commission Regulation 3147/94, OJ 22.12.94 L332/26. As to reduced duty within tariff quota for other products (apples, pears, seedless table grapes), see Commission Regulation 3144/94, OJ 22.12.94 L332/17, as partly substituted by Commission Regulation 894/95, OJ 25.4.95 L92/7.
14 Ibid Art 11. As to special arrangements for imports of grain sorghum and millet, see Council Regulation 865/90, OJ 5.4.90 L90/16, as amended.
15 Ibid Art 14.
16 Ibid Art 22.
17 Ibid Art 18.
18 Ibid Art 24. See for example Council Regulation 3763/91, OJ 24.12.91 L356/1, as amended (various measures) and Commission Regulation 980/82, OJ 22.4.92 L104/31, as amended (marketing in Martinique and Guadeloupe of rice produced in French Guiana).
19 See Council Regulation 3290/94, OJ 31.12.94 L349/105. See also Chapter 16 in this book on Agricultural Products.

However, the Community reserves the right to adapt the import treatment of ACP products, following consultations within the Council of Ministers, if it subjects such products to common organization of the market or to specific rules under the Common Agricultural Policy.[20] In addition, if the Community modifies the common organization of the market for a product, or the specific rules in respect of it within the framework of the CAP, it reserves the right to modify import arrangements, following consultation within the Council of Ministers.[1] If the Community intends to conclude a preferential arrangement with third States, it must inform the ACP States, which are entitled to request consultations in order to safeguard their interests.[2] Information or consultation is also required where existing or new Community measures for the harmonization of laws to facilitate the free movement of goods area are likely to affect ACP interests.[3]

The ACP States are not required to undertake reciprocal obligations.[4] However, they may not discriminate among EC Member States and are required to grant the Community not less than MFN treatment.[5] Conversely, the Community is required not to discriminate among ACP States in respect of trade.[6]

Safeguard measures for non-agricultural products[7] are provided for the Community if the Convention results in serious disturbances in a sector of the economy of the Community, or of one or more Member States, or jeopardizes their external financial stability, or if difficulties arise which may result in a deterioration thereof.[8] Such measures must be notified immediately to the Council of Ministers.[9] In addition, prior consultations must take place, both when the measures are first adopted and when they are extended.[10] Both parties undertake not to use other means for protectionist purposes or to hamper structural development, and the Community is required to refrain from using safeguard measures having the same effect.[11] Safeguard measures are restricted to those which would least disturb trade and must not exceed what is strictly necessary to remedy the

---

20 Fourth Lomé Convention Art 168(2)(d), second paragraph, first indent, which also provides that, in this case, Art 168(2)(a) applies.
 1 Fourth Lomé Convention Art 168(d), second paragraph, second indent, which also provides that, in this case, the Community is to undertake to ensure that ACP products continue to enjoy an advantage comparable to that previously enjoyed in relation to products originating in third countries benefiting from the MFN clause.
 2 Ibid Art 168(e).
 3 Ibid Arts 172, 173. The latter provides that this includes the interpretation, application or administration of existing rules or regulations.
 4 Ibid Art 174(1).
 5 Ibid Art 174(2)(a). This MFN clauses does not apply however in respect of trade or economic relations between ACP States or between one or more ACP States and other developing countries: Art 174(2)(c).
 6 Ibid Art 174(2)(b).
 7 As to agricultural products, see below.
 8 Ibid Art 177(1). As to Community procedures, see Council Regulation 3705/90, OJ 21.12.90 L358/4.
 9 Ibid. At the request of any party, the Council of Ministers must consider the economic and social effects of the application of the safeguard clause: Art 179.
10 Ibid Art 178(1). Such consultations do not prevent any immediate decisions by the Community where special factors necessitate such decisions: Art 178(3). A mechanism is to be instituted for the statistical surveillance of certain ACP exports to the Community: Art 178(4). As to the implementation of the safeguard clause, see Protocol 4.
11 Fourth Lomé Convention Art 177(2).

difficulties.[12] Provision is made for consultation in respect of a range of other matters concerning trade and customs co-operation.[13]

With regard to agricultural products, the safeguard clauses provided in the various common organizations of agricultural markets apply, together with any specific rules introduced as a result of the implementation of the CAP.[14]

General provision is also made for co-operation in respect of trade in services.[15]

In December 1997 the Community adopted economic sanctions against Sierra Leone, but this measure has since been repealed.[16]

SPECIFIC IMPORTANT PRODUCTS

Bananas,[17] beef and veal,[18] rum,[19] and sugar[20] are of special interest to the ACP States and are dealt with in individual protocols.[1] Separate provision is also made for ECSC products.[2]

In respect of bananas,[3] the parties have agreed to the objectives of improving the conditions under which ACP bananas are produced and marketed and of

---

12 Ibid Art 177(4). Particular attention is to be paid to the interests of the least-developed, landlocked and island ACP States when safeguard measures are being taken, modified or removed: Art 180.
13 Ibid Art 181. See also Annex XXX Joint declaration on Art 181.
14 Council Regulation 715/90 Art 30, OJ 30.3.90 L84/85; see also Council Regulation 3705/90 Art 3, OJ 21.12.90 L358/4. The parties to the Lomé Convention have jointly recognized that the safeguard provisions of the Convention apply to products covered by the Common Agricultural Policy only insofar as they are consistent with the specific nature of the specific rules and regulations applicable to CAP products: Fourth Lomé Convention, Annex XXXV Joint declaration on products covered by the Common Agricultural Policy. As to the safeguard measures in the agricultural sector, see Chapter 16 on Agricultural Products in this book. As to recent examples of protective measures for health reasons, see Commission Decision 97/878, OJ 31.12.97 L356/64 (fishery products originating in Uganda, Kenya, Tanzania, Mozambique) and Commission Decision 87/147, OJ 17.2.98 L46/13 (fishery and acquaculture products originating in Bangladesh).
15 Ibid Art 185. See also Part II, Title IX Development of Services and Annex XX Joint declaration on the improved use of the trade and services development provisions.
16 See Common Position 97/826/CFSP of the Council on the basis of TEU Article J.2, OJ 15.12.97 L344/3, and Council Regulation 2465/97, OJ 15.12.97 L344/1. Article 7 of the latter Regulation provided that the Regulation applied within the territory of the EC, including its air space, to any aircraft or any vessel under the jurisdiction of a Member State, to any person elsewhere who is a national of a Member State, and to any body which is incorporated or constituted under the law of a Member State. This measure was repealed by Council Regulation 941/98, OJ 8.5.98 L136/1.
17 Ibid Art 183, Protocol 5 on bananas.
18 Protocol 7 on beef and veal.
19 Ibid Art 182, Protocol 6 on rum.
20 Protocol 8 containing the text of Protocol 3 on ACP sugar appearing in the ACP–EC Convention of Lomé signed on 28 February 1975 and the corresponding declarations annexed to that Convention.
1 The Protocols form an integral part of the Convention: Art 368. The special undertakings on rum and bananas and Protocols 5 and 6 do not apply in relations between the ACP States and the French overseas departments: Art 184. Nor do the special undertakings on sugar and Protocol 3: Art 213(7).
2 Fourth Lomé Convention Protocol 9 concerning products within the province of the European Coal and Steel Community.
3 Fourth Lomé Convention Protocol 5 on bananas. Following the enactment of a common organization on the market in bananas, a special system was established to assist traditional ACP suppliers (Belize, Cameroon, Cape Verde, Dominica, Grenada, Ivory Coast, Jamaica, Madagascar, Saint Lucia, Saint Vincent and the Grenadines, Somalia, Suriname): Council Regulation 2686/94, OJ 5.11.94 L286/1. See also Chapter 16 on Agricultural Products in this book.

continuing the advantages enjoyed by traditional suppliers.[4] In respect of banana exports to the Community, no ACP State is to be placed, as regards access to its traditional markets and its advantages on those markets, in a less favourable situation than in the past or at present.[5] The parties agree to confer to determine measures to improve the conditions of production and marketing of bananas.[6] A permanent joint group is established to review specific problems.[7] The Community has pledged to support any joint organization which may be established by the banana-producing ACP States to achieve the objectives of the Protocol.[8]

In respect of beef and veal,[9] special measures are taken to enable ACP States which are traditional suppliers to maintain their position on the Community market.[10] The traditional suppliers are assigned reference quantities of boneless meat per calendar year and per country.[11] Within these reference quantities a reduction of 92 per cent in import duties other than customs duties is to apply.[12] Provision is made for consideration of appropriate measures to ensure deliveries in the event of actual or foreseeable drop in exports due to disasters, such as drought, cyclones or animal diseases.[13] If, in the course of a given year, an ACP State is not in a position to supply its fixed quantity but does not wish to benefit from such measures, the Community can share out the shortfall amount among other ACP States concerned.[14] If the Lomé Convention safeguard clause[15] is

---

4 Fourth Lomé Convention Protocol 5, first paragraph. Not being exporters to the Community, Haiti and Dominican Republic are not considered traditional suppliers: Annex LXXV Community declaration relating to Protocol 5.

5 Ibid Art 1. The parties have agreed that this Article does not prevent the Community from establishing common rules for bananas, in full consultation with the ACP, so long as no ACP State, traditional supplier to the Community, is placed in a less favourable situation than in the past or at present as regards access to, and advantages in, the Community: Annex LXXIV Joint declaration relating to Protocol 5. In respect of these provisions, the European Court of Justice has held that the Community's only obligation is to maintain the advantages, with respect to access of ACP bananas to the Community market, which the ACP States had before the Fourth Lomé Convention. Therefore Council Regulation 404/93 establishing a new common organization of the market in bananas was able, without being in breach of Art 168(1) of the Fourth Lomé Convention, to impose a levy on imports of non-traditional ACP bananas exceeding a specified tonnage: Case C-280/93 *Germany v Council* [1994] ECR I-4973. As to licences for traditional imports in the fourth quarter of 1995, see Commission Regulation 2326/95, OJ 4.10.95 L235/2, and Commission Regulation 2500/95, OJ 27.10.95 L257/25.

6 Ibid Art 2, which also lays down guidelines for these measures.

7 Ibid Protocol 5, Art 3.

8 Ibid Protocol 5, Art 4. As to the scope of the Community's obligations under these and related provisions, see the Report of the WTO Appellate Body, European Communities—Regime for the Importation, Sale and Distribution of Bananas (WT/DS27/AB/R), [1997] 2 ITLR 528.

9 Fourth Lomé Convention Protocol 7 on beef and veal. See also the section on beef and veal in Chapter 16 on Agricultural Products in this book. The Protocol is to be implemented in accordance with the common market organization, but the latter is not to affect the obligations entered into by the Community under the Protocol: Protocol 7, Art 5. See also Annex LXXVI Joint declaration relating to Protocol 7; Annex LXXVII Community declaration relating to Protocol 7. As to customs duties, see above. See also Case 124/84 *H Spitta und Co v Hautzollamt Frankfurt am Main-Ost* [1985] ECR 1923.

10 Fourth Lomé Convention Protocol 7, first paragraph.

11 Ibid Art 2, which provides for the following traditional suppliers and reference quantities: Botswana 18,916,000 tonnes, Kenya 142,000 tonnes, Madagascar 7,579,000 tonnes, Swaziland 3,363,000 tonnes, Zimbabwe 9,100,000 tonnes, and Namibia 13,000,000 tonnes. As to the allocation of import licences starting January 1998, see Commission Decision 98/69, OJ 16.1.98 L10/42.

12 Ibid Art 1.

13 Ibid Art 3, which provides for delivery in the preceding year or the following year.

14 Ibid Art 4, which also sets out the procedure.

15 Provided in Art 177(1).

applied in the beef and veal sector, the Community must take the necessary measures to maintain the volume of exports from the ACP States to the Community at a level compatible with its obligations under the Protocol.[16]

In respect of rum,[17] rum, arrack and taffia[18] are to be imported into the Community duty free under conditions such as to permit the development of traditional trade flows between the ACP States and the Community and between the Member States.[19] Until 31 December 1995 the Community was permitted to limit the quantities which could be imported free of customs duties.[20] However, as from 1996 the Community is to establish modalities for the projected abolition of this tariff quota.[1] Provision is made for a joint working party to examine specific problems[2] and also for Community assistance to promote and expand ACP sales on the Community market.[3]

In respect of sugar,[4] in the First Lomé Convention the Community undertook, for an indefinite period, to purchase and import, at guaranteed prices, specific quantities of raw or white cane sugar, originating in the ACP States producing and exporting cane sugar and which those States undertook to deliver to it.[5] The general safeguard measures provided in the Convention[6] do not apply to these imports.[7] An agreed annual quantity is assigned to each exporting country.[8] Except in specified circumstances,[9] the quantities cannot be reduced without the

---

16 Ibid Art 6.
17 Fourth Lomé Convention Protocol 6 on rum.
18 That is, products of codes 2208 40 10, 2208 40 90, 2208 90 11 and 2208 90 19 of the Combined Nomenclature.
19 Protocol 6 Art 1. As to the requirement of consultation if the Community introduces a common organization of the market in alcohol, see Joint declaration relating to Protocol 6 Annex LXXVI.
20 Ibid Art 2(a). The limitation was a temporary derogation from Art 168(1) of the Convention.
 1 Ibid Art 2(b). Provision is also made for re-examination of the rate of increase, consultations and other measures: ibid Art 2(c)–(f).
 2 Ibid Art 3.
 3 Ibid Art 4.
 4 Fourth Lomé Convention Protocol 8. As to procedures for changing the Protocol, see Protocol 8, Art 2. As to sugar imports, see also Council Regulation 1785/81 Art 37/3, OJ 1.7.81 L177/4, as amended, the common organization of the market for sugar. This provision states that, if there is a shortfall in sugar imports to fill the maximum needs of Community refineries, the requirement is to be met by importing special preferential sugar at a special rate of duty under ACP States and other States. As to such an agreement, see Council Decision 95/284, OJ 1.8.95 L181/22. As to import quotas for the period 1 July 1997 to 28 February 1998, see Commission Regulation 1314/97, OJ 9.7.97 L180/12. As to allocation by country of origin, see Commission Regulation 1250/97, OJ 1.7.97 L173/92.
 5 First Lomé Convention Art 25, Protocol 3. This obligation is reiterated in the Fourth Lomé Convention Art 213(1) and in Protocol 8, Art 1(1).
 6 That is, as laid down in Art 177.
 7 Ibid Art 213(2); Protocol 8, Art 1(2). The latter also provides that the operation of the common organization of the market in sugar shall not prejudice the commitment of the Community in this respect.
 8 Fourth Lomé Convention Protocol 8, Art 3(1), which also provides for the following agreed quantities of cane sugar, expressed in metric tonnes of white sugar: Barbados 49,300 tonnes, Fiji 163,600 tonnes, Guyana 157,700 tonnes, Jamaica 118,300 tonnes, Kenya 5,000 tonnes, Madagascar 10,000 tonnes, Malawi 20,000 tonnes, Mauritius 487,200 tonnes, Republic of Congo 10,000 tonnes, Swaziland 116,400 tonnes, Tanzania 10,000 tonnes, Trinidad and Tobago 69,000 tonnes, and Uganda 5,000 tonnes. Lower quantities prevailed until 30 June 1975: Art 3(3). As to the Agreements in the form of an exchange of letters on guaranteed prices for the 1996/97 delivery period, see OJ 13.1.98 L7/34 (India) and OJ 13.1.98 L7/28 (other countries), both approved on behalf of the Community by Council Decision 98/17, OJ 13.1.98 L7/27.
 9 Set out in Protocol 8, Art 7.

consent of the individual States concerned.[10] The delivery period is 1 July to 30 June.[11] Prices are to be freely negotiated between buyers and sellers,[12] but the Community undertakes to purchase, at the guaranteed price, quantities of sugar within the agreed quantities which cannot be marketed in the Community at a price equivalent to or in excess of the guaranteed price.[13]

If an exporting ACP State fails to deliver its agreed quantity in full for reasons of force majeure, the Commission must allow the necessary additional delivery period if the ACP State so requests.[14] However, if during the delivery period the ACP State informs the Commission of the shortfall and does not wish to have the additional period, the Commission is entitled to reallocate the shortfall, after consultation with the States concerned, for delivery during the period.[15] But if an exporting State fails to deliver its agreed quantity in full for reasons other than force majeure, that quantity can be reduced in respect of each subsequent delivery by the undelivered quantity.[16] In respect of these subsequent delivery periods, this shortfall may be reallocated between other States in consultation with the States concerned.[17] The life of the Protocol is not limited to that of the Convention.[18]

In respect of coal and steel products, such products originating in the ACP States are admitted into the Community free of customs duties and equivalent charges.[19] The ACP States are required to grant to such products originating in the Community a treatment no less favourable than MFN treatment.[20]

If offers made by ACP firms are likely to be detrimental to the functioning of the Community market because of a difference in the conditions of competition as regards prices, the Member States may take appropriate measures, such as withdrawing the right to duty-free entry.[1] Provision is also made for consultations.[2]

---

10 Ibid Art 3(2).

11 Ibid Art 4(1).

12 Ibid Art 5(1).

13 Ibid Art 5(3). As to determination of the guaranteed price, see Art 5(4). Purchase is to be done through the medium of intervention agencies or other agents: Art 6.

14 Ibid Art 7(1).

15 Ibid Art 7(2).

16 Ibid Art 7(3).

17 Ibid Art 7(4).

18 Ibid Arts 10, 8(2). Given specified conditions, the Protocol may be denounced by the parties subject to two years' notice: Art 10. However, the Community has declared that this provision is for purposes of juridical security only and does not represent any qualification or limitation of the principles of the Protocol: Declaration by the Community on Art 10 of Protocol 3.

19 Fourth Lomé Convention Protocol 9, Art 1.

20 Fourth Lomé Convention Protocol 9, Art 2; Fourth Lomé Convention Art 174(2)(a).

1 Fourth Lomé Convention Protocol 9, Art 3.

2 Fourth Lomé Convention Protocol 9, Art 4.

Chapter 29

Overseas countries and territories

The Overseas Countries and Territories (OCT)[1] consist of certain territorial collectivities, territories and countries outside of the Community but for which certain Community Member States have special responsibility.[2] They include the territorial collectivities of the French Republic, namely Mayotte and Saint Pierre and Miquelon; the French overseas territories, namely New Caledonia and Dependencies, French Polynesia, French Southern and Antarctic Territories, and Wallis and Futuna Islands; the overseas territories of the Netherlands, namely Aruba, Netherlands Antilles, Bonaire, Curacao, Saba, Sint Eustatius and Sint Maarten; the overseas countries and territories of the UK, namely Anguilla, Cayman Islands, Falkland Islands, South Sandwich Islands and Dependencies, Montserrat, Pitcairn, Saint Helena and Dependencies, British Antarctic Territory, British Indian Ocean Territory, Turks and Caicos Islands, and British Virgin Islands; and the country having special relations with Denmark, namely Greenland.[3]

Relations between the Community and the OCT are currently governed not only by Part Four of the EC Treaty but also by a 1992 Council Decision in

---

1 In French, *Pays et territoires d'outre-mer (PTOM)*.
2 The OCT were part of the group of non-European countries and territories which had (and have) special relations with certain Community Member States: see EC Art 131. Part IV of the EEC Treaty made special arrangements for the association of these countries and territories with the Community. In respect of trade, Member States were to apply to the OCT the same treatment as they accord to each other: EC Art 132(1). Each OCT was to apply to the Member States and with the other OCT the same treatment which it applied to the European State with which it had special relations: EC Art 132(2). Customs duties on imports were to be abolished: EC Art 133(1),(2). A partial exception was made for customs duties levied for development, industrialization or budgetary purposes: EC Art 133(3). Provision was also made to deal with deflections of trade (EC Art 134) and the free movement of workers (EC Art 135). These special arrangements applied to the overseas countries and territories were listed in Annex IV to the Treaty and now after the Amsterdam Treaty are listed in Annex II: EC Art 227(3), as amended by the Amsterdam Treaty. Some of these countries and territories have of course become independent, and the provisions of Part Four no longer apply to them. Their trade relations with the Community are governed instead by the Fourth Lomé Convention, as to which see Chapter 28 in this book. OCT which become independent are entitled to request accession to the Lomé Convention: see Fourth Lome Convention Art 362.
3 Council Decision 91/482, Annex I, OJ 19.9.91 L263/1.

recently revised form.[4] The latter provides for co-operation in a wide range of areas in a form generally analogous to the provisions of the Fourth Lomé Convention.[5] In a Declaration attached to the Amsterdam Treaty, the Intergovernmental Conference invited the Council to review the association agreements by February 2000.[6]

In respect of trade, the object of the 1992 Council Decision is to promote trade between the OCT and the Community and also between the OCT themselves.[7] Provision is made for numerous trade-related measures.[8]

Products originating in the OCT enter the Community free of import duty.[9] Similarly, products not originating in the OCT but which are in free circulation in the OCT and are re-exported to the Community enter the Community free of customs duty and equivalent taxes on three conditions:[10] they have paid, in the OCT concerned, customs duty or equivalent charges at a level equal to, or higher than, the applicable Community customs duty on the same products originating in third countries eligible for the MFN clause;[11] they have not been the subject of an exemption from, or refund of, in whole or in part, customs duties or equivalent taxes;[12] and they are accompanied by an export certificate.[13] This does not however apply to Annex II products or processed agricultural products,[14] products subject on import into the Community to quantitative restrictions or limitations,[15] or products subject on import into the Community to anti-dumping duties.[16]

---

4 Council Decision 91/482, OJ 19.9.91 L263/1, as amended at midterm by Council Decision 97/803, OJ 29.11.97 L329/50. It was originally applicable for ten years starting on 1 March 1996: Art 240(1). It replaced Council Decision 86/283, OJ 1.7.86 L175/1. The Decision applies to Greenland, subject to specific provisions set out in the Protocol on special arrangements for Greenland, annexed to the Treaty amending, with regard to Greenland, the EEC Treaty (OJ 1.2.85 L29/1). This Protocol provides that the treatment on import into the Community of products subject to the common organization of the market in fishery products, originating in Greenland, shall, while complying with the mechanisms of the common organization, involve exemption from customs duties, equivalent charges, quantitative restrictions and equivalent measures if the possibilities for access to Greenland fishing zones, pursuant to an agreement between the Community and the authority responsible for Greenland, are satisfactory to the Community: Protocol Art 1(1).
5 See ibid preamble, *passim*. The human rights clause (Art 3) is however weaker than the analogous provision (Art 5(1), third paragraph) in the Fourth Lomé Convention.
6 Declaration 36, Declaration on the Overseas Countries and Territories, attached to the 1997 Amsterdam Treaty.
7 Council Decision 91/482 Art 100(1), OJ 19.9.91 L263/1, as amended.
8 See ibid Art 85(2).
9 Ibid Art 101(1), as amended. See also however Art 101(4), (5). As to special derogation in respect of connections and contact elements for wire and cables from Montserrat until 31 October 1999, see Commission Decision 95/375, OJ 20.9.95 L222/16. As to time limits in respect of decisions on requests for derogation from the origin rules, see Case C-430/92 *Netherlands v Commission* [1994] ECR I-5197. As to the relative responsibilities of importer and exporter concerning post-clearance recovery of customs duties, see Case C-97/95 *Pascoal and Filhos Lda v Fazenda Publica* [1997] ECR I-4209.
10 Ibid Art 101(2).
11 Ibid Art 101(2), first indent. See also Case C-310/95 *Road Air B V v Inspecteur der Invoerrechten en Accijnzen* [1997] ECR I-2229.
12 Ibid Art 101(2), second indent.
13 Ibid Art 101(2), third indent.
14 Ibid Art 101(3), first indent, as amended. As to such products, see below.
15 Ibid Art 101(3), second indent.
16 Ibid Art 101(3), third indent.

OCT products imported into the Community are also free of quantitative restrictions or equivalent measures.[17] The usual exceptions apply.[18]

The OCT, however, may introduce customs duties or quantitative restrictions that they consider necessary in respect of Community products or products from other OCT.[19] The OCT must not discriminate between Community Member States or be less favourable than MFN treatment.[20] However, this does not preclude a country or territory from granting certain other OCT or other developing countries more favourable treatment than that accorded to the Community.[1] The Community must not discriminate between the OCT in the field of trade.[2]

Provision is made for safeguard measures.[3] Priority is to be given to measures which least disturb the functioning of the association and the Community, and measures must not exceed what is strictly necessary to remedy the difficulties.[4] Particular attention is to be paid to the interests of the least-developed OCT.[5]

Special undertakings are given in respect of rum.[6]

The importance of trade in services for the OCT is recognized,[7] and the long-term aim of the parties is a progressive liberalization of trade in services, on certain conditions.[8]

---

17 Ibid Art 102, as amended, which also provides that this is without prejudice to Arts 108a and 108b which limit the import of rice and sugar of ACP/OCT cumulated origin to specific annual ceilings. The latter Articles were introduced as a result of a massive deflection of trade, in which rice essentially from Surinam, an ACP country, transited through the Dutch West Indies, an OCT, became of OCT origin, and benefited from complete access to the EC market. See *Agence Europe*, No 6910 (n.s.), Saturday 8 February 1997, p 8. See also Case T-41/97R *Antillean Rice Mills v Council* [1997] ECR II-447; Case T-26/97 *Antillean Rice Mills NV v Commission* [1997] ECR II-1347; Case T-41/97 *Antillean Rice Mills NV v Council* OJ 10.5.97 C142/23. The issue was resolved by the enactment of Council Regulation 2603/97 L23.12.97 L351/22. As to rules for issuing import licences for sugar, see Commission Regulation 2553/97, OJ 19.12.97 L349/26. See also Case C-147/96 *Netherlands v Commission* OJ 6.7.96 C197/9 not yet decided (challenge to Commission decision not to include Dutch Antilles in list of third countries approved under Council Directive 92/46 to export dairy products to the Community).

18 Ibid Art 103. Special provisions govern the movement of hazardous and radioactive waste: see Art 103(3) and Part Two, Title I. As to imports of fresh meat from Greenland, see Commission Decision 86/117, OJ 15.4.86 L99/26. As to the addition of Greenland to the list of third countries from which Member States may authorize imports of bovine animals, swine and fresh meat, see Commission Decision 85/488, OJ 5.11.85 L293/17.

19 Ibid Art 106(1).

20 Ibid Art 106(2)(a).

1 Ibid Art 106(2)(b).

2 Ibid Art 106(2)(c).

3 See ibid Art 109(1). As to procedure, see Annex IV. See also Case C-260/90 *Leplat v French Polynesia* [1992] ECR I-643. Safeguard measures in respect of rice have been in force since 1 January 1997: see Council Regulation 10367, OJ 10.6.97 L151/8.

4 Ibid Art 109(2). As to this proportionality test, see Joined Cases T-480/93 and T-483/93 *Antillean Rice Mills NV v Commission* [1995] ECR II-2305.

5 Ibid Art 110.

6 Ibid Art 111, Annex V. This does not apply to relations between the OCT and the French overseas departments: Art 112. Annex V provides, inter alia, that specified quantities of rum may be imported into the Community free of customs duties until 31 December 1995 and that the Council is to establish the arrangements applicable from 1996, taking into account the situation and prospects on the Community rum market and of the exports from the OCT and ACP States.

7 Ibid Art 113(1).

8 Ibid Art 113(2). The conditions are due respect for the OCT's local policy objectives, and taking due account of the level of development of the OCT.

Provision is also made for the stabilization of export earnings from agricultural commodities (Stabex)[9] and a special financing facility for mineral products (Sysmin).[10]

Certain other provisions also directly concern trade. The Community is to prohibit all direct or indirect export of hazardous waste and radioactive waste from the Community to the OCT, and the OCT is to prohibit such imports.[11] However, these provisions do not prevent a Member State to which an OCT has chosen to export waste for processing from returning the processed waste to the OCT of origin.[12] Provision is made for the fixing of export refunds on available agricultural products to be fixed further in advance.[13] Co-operation in the field of commodities is to aim at diversification and improvement of the competitiveness of OCT products on world markets.[14] Emphasis is also given to supporting trade in goods and services between OCT and between OCT and ACP States.[15]

Detailed rules are laid down separately for certain agricultural products and processed agricultural products originating in the ACP States or the overseas countries and territories (OCT).[16] Beef and veal is admitted into the Community free of customs duties,[17] but most categories of live animals and meat are subject to reimposition of duty if the yearly growth rate is more than 7 per cent.[18] Most of these products also benefited formerly from a 90 per cent reduction in the CAP levy provided a corresponding sum was charged by the ACP State on export;[19] the reduction was subject to maximum tonnages in the case of the largest exporters.[20] After variable levies were replaced by tariff quotas as a result of the Uruguay Round agreements, tariff quotas were opened for beef and veal, import licences were issued, and CCT duties were reduced.[1]

Live sheep and goats, sheepmeat and goatmeat are also imported free of customs duty;[2] such products were also exempt from levy,[3] with the exception of sheepmeat which was subject to reduced levy within a fixed tariff quota.[4]

---

9 See ibid Arts 114–136, as amended.
10 Ibid Arts 137–142.
11 Ibid Art 16(1), second paragraph.
12 Ibid Art 16(1), third paragraph.
13 Ibid Art 27, first paragraph. As to advance fixing, see Chapter 16 on Agricultural Products in this book.
14 Ibid Art 35.
15 See ibid Art 72.
16 The basic regulation is Council Regulation 715/90, OJ 30.3.90 L84/85, as amended. The ACP States are listed in Annex I and the OCT in Annex II. Annex I was amended by Council Regulation 297/91, OJ 8.2.91 L36/9, and Council Regulation 235/94, OJ 3.2.94 L30/12. These arrangements have been extended until 29 February 2000: Council Regulation 444/92 Art 1, OJ 27.2.92 L52/7. As to rules of origin, see Chapter 2 in this book. See also Council Regulation 2603/97, OJ 23.12.97 L351/22 and Council Decision 91/482, Annex II, OJ 19.9.91 L263/1, as amended by Council Decision 97/803, OJ 29.11.97 L329/50. Following the Uruguay Round, all levies have been converted into tariff quotas.
17 Council Regulation 715/90 Art 2, first paragraph, OJ 30.3.90 L84/85.
18 Ibid Art 2, second paragraph.
19 Ibid Art 3.
20 Ibid Art 4. As to 1995 imports, see Commission Regulation 2449/95, OJ 20.10.95 L252/1.
 1 Commission Regulation 1636/95, OJ 6.7.95 L155/25.
 2 Ibid Art 5(1).
 3 Ibid Art 5(2).
 4 Ibid Art 5(3).

Poultrymeat,[5] milk products,[6] and pigmeat[7] were subject to reduced levy up to a fixed quota. Customs duties are reduced to zero on imports of various products, most importantly fish,[8] most types of oils and fats[9] (but not olive oil), various fruits and vegetables,[10] tobacco,[11] flax and hemp, hops, plants and bulbs etc, seed and dried fodder.[12] The duty on other fruits and vegetables was originally reduced but has now been suspended within certain tariff quotas.[13] Subject to a maxium price and a quota, the levy on maize, millet, grain sorghum and rice is reduced,[14] as was the then applicable variable component of the levy on products produced from cereals and rice.[15] The fixed component of the duty applicable to a number of processed products, including chocolate and spaghetti, is removed, as well as in some cases the variable component.[16] Some processed fruits, vegetables and fruit juices are admissible duty or levy free.[17] Specific rules apply to direct imports into the French overseas departments for use and release on the market there.[18] As a result of the Uruguay Round, levies have been converted into tariff quotas.[19]

In respect of ECSC products, customs duties and equivalent charges on OCT imports into the Community are suspended.[20] Imports into the OCT of such products from the Community are to be treated in terms similar to those applying to other non-agricultural products.[1] Provision is made for consultation[2] and eventual safeguard measures.[3]

---

5 Ibid Art 6. See also Commission Regulation 903/90, OJ 10.4.90 L93/20, as amended.
6 Ibid Art 7. As to detailed rules, see Commission Regulation 1150/90, OJ 5.5.90 L114/21, as amended.
7 Ibid Art 8.
8 Ibid Art 9.
9 Ibid Art 10.
10 Ibid Art 15(1), adapted by Council Regulation 234/94, OJ 3.2.94 L30/11.
11 Ibid Art 20.
12 Ibid Art 23.
13 Ibid Arts 15(2), 16. Article 16 was amended to include seedless table grapes by Council Regulation 2484/94, OJ 15.10.94 L265/3. As to reference quantities and statistical surveillance for certain products products (cabbages, iceberg lettuce, globe artichokes, apricots, cherries, peaches, plums), see Commission Regulation 1280/94, OJ 3.6.94 L140/10, as partly substituted by Commission Regulation 3147/94, OJ 22.12.94 L332/26, which itself was replaced by Commission Regulation 895/95, OJ 25.4.95 L92/10. As to suspension of duty within tariff quotas for other products (tomatoes, cherry tomatoes, figs, strawberries), see Commission Regulation 2763/94, OJ 15.11.94 L294/6, as partly substituted by Commission Regulation 3147/94, OJ 22.12.94 L332/26. As to reduced duty within tariff quota for other products (apples, pears, seedless table grapes), see Commission Regulation 3144/94, OJ 22.12.94 L332/17, as partly substituted by Commission Regulation 894/95, OJ 25.4.95 L92/7.
14 Ibid Art 11.
15 Ibid Art 14.
16 Ibid Art 22.
17 Ibid Art 18.
18 Ibid Art 24.
19 See Chapter 16 in this book.
20 Decision 91/483 of the Representatives of the Governments of the Member States, meeting within the Council, Art 1, OJ 19.9.91 L263/145.
1 Ibid Art 2.
2 Ibid Art 3.
3 Ibid Art 5.

Chapter 30

North America

NORTH AMERICA FREE TRADE AGREEMENT (NAFTA)

The North American Free Trade Agreement (NAFTA) was concluded by Canada, Mexico and the US in 1992.[1] At present the Community has no formal legal relations with NAFTA.[2] In the view of the Commission, NAFTA is unlikely to have a significant effect on the Community's trade and investment relations with the US and Canada, and it is likely to permit a greater expansion of trade between the Community and Mexico.[3] However, the Community of course has numerous trade relations with Canada, Mexico and the US separately.

CANADA

A Framework Agreement for commercial and economic co-operation was concluded in 1976 between the Community and Canada.[4] The parties undertake to accord each other MFN treatment, on an equal and reciprocal basis, in accordance with the GATT.[5] The Agreement provides for commercial and economic co-operation and for the establishment of a Joint Co-operation Committee.[6] In respect of commercial co-operation, the parties undertake to promote the development and diversification of their reciprocal commercial exchanges to the highest possible level.[7] To this end, they are to co-operate internationally and bilaterally in the solution of commercial problems of common interest, use their

---

1 North American Free Trade Agreement between the Government of Canada, the Government of the United Mexican States and the Government of the US, 1992, 32 ILM 605 (1993). See also James R Holbein and Donald J Murch *NAFTA, Final Text, Summary, Legislative History and Implementation Directory* (Oceana Publications, New York, 1994).
2 Links between the Community and the US however have intensified recently; see below.
3 See European Commission, Information Note—North American Free Trade Agreement (NAFTA), COM(93) 188 final, 12.5.93. See also European Parliament, Resolution on the Free Trade Agreement between the US, Canada and Mexico (NAFTA), Resolution A3–0378/92, OJ 25.1.92 C21/77; Written Question No 614/92 by Karla Peijs to the Commission of the European Communities, 23.3.92, and Answer given by Mr Andriessen on behalf of the Commission, 16.7.92 C274/42; Written Question E-4081/93 by Enrique Sapena Granell and José Vázquez Fouz, and Answer given by Sir Leon Brittan on behalf of the Commission, 25.2.84, OJ 31.10.94 C306/15; Written Question E-202/94 by Sotiris Kostopoulos to the Commission, 22.2.94, OJ 31.10.94 C306/15 (see Answer by Sir Leon Brittan to Written Question No E-4081/93).
4 OJ 24.9.76 L260/2.
5 Ibid Art I.
6 As to the Joint Co-operation Committee, see Art IV.
7 Ibid Art II(1), first paragraph.

best efforts to grant each other the widest facilities for commercial transactions, and take fully into account their respective interests and needs regarding access to and further processing of resources.[8] They are also to use their best endeavours to discourage, in conformity with their legislation, restrictions of competition by enterprises of their respective industries, including pricing practices distorting competition.[9]

In 1989 the Community and Canada concluded an Agreement concerning trade and commerce in alcoholic beverages.[10] In respect of distilled spirits, the Agreement provides for national treatment by the Canadian authorities of Community products as regards measures affecting listing, delisting, distribution and mark-up.[11] However, the Ontario authorities were allowed to accord a preference to Ontario brandy as regards mark-up until 1993.[12] Sales by a distillery on its premises may also be limited to distilled spirits produced there.[13] In respect of beer, Canada is required to accord national treatment to Community-produced beer as regards listing or delisting.[14] No increase of mark-up differentiations existing on 1 December 1998 is permitted as between Canadian and Community beers.[15] In respect of wine, national treatment is to be accorded by Canada to Community wines as regards listing, delisting, and distribution.[16] However, sales by a winery on its premises may be limited to wines produced there.[17] Private wine store outlets in Ontario may be required to sell only Canadian-produced wine.[18] The competent Canadian authorities may also require that wine sold in grocery stores in Quebec be bottled in Quebec, provided that alternative outlets are provided in Quebec for Community wine, whether or not such wine is bottled in Quebec.[19] The mark-up differentiation in Canada between Community wine and Canadian wine was to be eliminated progressively up to 1995 or 1998, depending on the product.[20] Canadian measures in respect of listing or delisting of Community products are required to be non-discriminatory, based on normal commercial considerations, transparent, and published and made available to interested persons.[1]

In 1994 the Community and Canada also reached an Agreement in respect of the modification or withdrawal of tariff concessions.[2] The Community also has a tariff quota bound in GATT for newsprint coming from Canada.[3]

A Political Declaration and Action Plan between Canada and the EU was signed on 17 December 1997. Building on the similar text between the EU and

8 Ibid Art II(1), second paragraph.
9 Ibid Art II(3).
10 OJ 15.3.89 L71/42. The preamble refers to the findings and conclusions of the GATT Panel on Import, Distribution and Sale of Alcoholic Drinks by Canadian Provincial Marketing Agencies, and also to the parties' desire to resolve their differences over trade in the sector and to ensure respect for international legal obligations while acknowledging the temporary need for structural adjustment. As to monitoring and consultations, see ibid Art 6.
11 Ibid Art 2(2).
12 Ibid Art 2(2)(a), Annex D.
13 Ibid Art 2(2)(b).
14 Ibid Art 3(a).
15 Ibid Art 3(b).
16 Ibid Art 4(1).
17 Ibid Art 4(2)(a).
18 Ibid Art 4(2)(b).
19 Ibid Art 4(2)(c).
20 Ibid Art 4(3), Annexes A, B, C.
1 Ibid Art 5(1). As to Canadian procedures in respect of applications for listing or delisting, see Art 5(2).
2 Agreed Minutes, OJ 18.2.94 L47/14.
3 In respect of the 1997 year, see Commission Regulation 2177/97, OJ 1.11.97 L298/64.

the US of December 1995, it sets out guidelines and areas of future co-operation, including trade and economic relations, foreign and security policy, organized crime, and other areas.[4] Subsequently negotiations were completed on equivalency agreements in respect of veterinary matters, still to be finalized; an agreement on competition, still to be finalized; and an agreement on mutual recognition; and an agreement on customs co-operation.[5]

In 1997 the European Union and Canada initialled a Mutual Recognition Agreement (MRA). It generally allows for the recognition by the EU of product assessments, such as testing, inspection, and certification, performed in Canada, and vice versa, in specified sectors.[6]

In 1998 the Community and Canada concluded an Agreement on Customs Co-operation and Mutual Assistance in Customs Matters.[7] It provides for co-operation in all matters relating to the application of customs legislation.[8] The parties agree to strive for simplification and harmonization of their customs procedures, taking in account the work done in this connection by international organizations.[9] Provision is also made for co-operation in respect of technical assistance to third countries[10] and computerization of customs procedures and formalities.[11] The Agreement also provides for mutual assistance in ensuring the proper application of customs legislation and the prevention, investigation and combating of any breach of customs legislation.[12] This includes information on methods, trends and operations;[13] the provision of information on request;[14] and spontaneous assistance.[15] Assistance may be refused or made subject to conditions if it would infringe upon the sovereignty of an EC Member State or Canada, or prejudice security, public policy or other essential interest,[16] or involve a violation of industrial, commercial or professional secrecy, or be inconsistent with its

---

4 For further details, see *Agence Europe*, No 6883 (n.s.), Monday/Tuesday, 30/31 December 1996, pp 8–9.

5 See Agence Europe, No 7001 (n.s.), Monday/Tuesday 23/24 June 1997, p 7.

6 European Commission, Directorate General I, Home page at http://www.europa.eu.int.en/comm/dg01/mrao1.htm. This MRA is essentially the same as that between the EU and the US, which see for further details.

7 Agreement between the European Community and Canada on customs co-operation and mutual assistance in customs matters, OJ 13.1.98 L7/38, approved on behalf of the European Community by Council Decision 98/18, OJ 13.1.98 L7/37.

8 Ibid Art 2.

9 Ibid Art 4, which also provides that they agree to examine ways and means to resolve any customs-related difficulties that might arise between them.

10 Ibid Art 3.

11 Ibid Art 6.

12 Ibid Art 7(1). Such assistance is to be performed by each Contracting Party in accordance with its relevant laws, rules and other legal instruments, and within the limits of its customs authority's competence and available resources: ibid Art 7(2). It is intended solely for the mutual administrative assistance between the parties, and does not give rise to a right on the part of any private person to obtain information, to obtain, suppress or exclude any evidence, or to impede the execution of a request: ibid Art 7(3). These provisions do not prejudice the rules governing mutual assistance in criminal matters, nor do they apply to information obtained under powers exercised at the request of a judicial authority, except where communication of such information has the prior authorization of the judicial authority consulted for this purpose on a case-by-case basis: ibid Art 7(4).

13 Ibid Art 8.

14 Ibid Art 9.

15 Ibid Art 10.

16 Such as that referred to in ibid Art 16(4), which provides that personal data may be exchanged only where the Contracting Party which will receive the data undertakes to protect the data in a way which is at least equivalent to the protection applicable to that particular case in the Contracting Party which may supply the data. See ibid Art 17(1).

legislation.[17] Management of the Agreement is entrusted to the competent services of the Commission and, where appropriate, to the customs authorities of the EC Member States and to the customs authority of Canada.[18] A Joint Customs Co-operation Committee, consisting of representatives of the customs authorities of the Contracting Parties, is to see to the proper functioning of the Agreement and examine all issues arising from its application.[19]

The Community and Canada have also concluded agreements in respect of fisheries,[20] the peaceful uses of atomic energy[1] and ECSC products.[2] In 1998 the Community also concluded an Agreement with Canada and the Russian Federation on international humane trapping standards.[3] The last Agreement is intended, first, to lay down harmonized technical standards offering a sufficient level of protection to animal welfare and governing the production and use of traps. It is also designed, second, to facilitate trade in traps, pelts and products manufactured from species covered by the Agreement between the Community, in which the use of leghold traps is prohibited, and third countries that have not prohibited the use of leghold traps.[4]

MEXICO

A Framework Agreement for co-operation between the Community and the United Mexican States was concluded in 1991.[5] Its objective was stated to be to impart renewed vigour to relations between the parties, including by means of the promotion of the development of co-operation relating to trade.[6] It

---

17 Ibid Art 17(1).
18 Ibid Art 19(1).
19 Ibid Art 20.
20 Agreement, OJ 31.12.81 L379/54; Agreement in the form of exchanges of letters, OJ 31.12.93 L340/3.
 1 Agreement, OJ 24.11.59 L60/1165, amended by Agreements in the form of exchange of letters in 1978 (OJ 8.3.78 L65/16) and in 1985 (OJ 31.7.85 L191/3, see also the attached Agreed Minute). See also Agreement in the form of exchange of letters intended to replace the Interim Arrangement concerning enrichment, reprocessing and subsequent storage of nuclear material constituting Annex C of the 1978 Agreement (OJ 4.2.82 L27/25); Memorandum of understanding concerning co-operation in the field of fusion research and development, OJ 11.2.86 L35/10; Memorandum of understanding for co-operation in the field of controlled nuclear fusion, OJ 6.9.95 L211/31; Implementing Agreement in respect of the International Thermonuclear Experimental Reactor, OJ 6.9.95 L211/40.
 2 Protocol, OJ 24.9.76 L60/28.
 3 Agreement on international humane trapping standards between the European Community, Canada and the Russian Federation and Agreed Minute between Canada and the European Community concerning the signing of the Agreement, OJ 14.2.98 L42/42, approved by Council Decision 98/142, OJ 14.2.98 L42/40.
 4 Council Regulation 3254/91, OJ 9.11.91 L308/1, prohibits the use of leghold traps in the Community and the introduction into the Community of pelts and manufactured goods of certain wild animal species originating in countries which catch them by means of leghold traps or other methods which, in the terms of the Regulation, do not meet international humane trapping standards.
 5 OJ 11.12.91 L340/2. This replaced an earlier Agreement concluded in 1975 (OJ 23.9.75 L247/11). See also Opinion of the Economic and Social Committee on Relations between the European Union and Mexico, OJ 19.3.96 C82/68.
 6 Ibid Art 1. The Agreement does not contain a human rights and democracy clause. In October 1996 the two parties began formal talks in respect of an economic and commercial co-operation agreement intended to lead to reciprocal trade liberalization. See *Agence Europe*, No 6830 (n.s.), Friday 11 October 1996, p 8; *Agence Europe*, No 6874 (n.s.), Saturday 14 December 1996, p 15.

provides for economic co-operation, financial co-operation, industrial co-operation, investment, technological development and intellectual property matters, co-operation concerning standards, trade co-operation, co-operation in science and technology, co-operation in many other fields, and the establishment of a Joint Committee to oversee the Agreement.[7] The Agreement is concluded for a period of five years, tacitly renewable on a yearly basis unless it is denounced by either party in writing six months before its expiry.[8]

In respect of trade, the Agreement provides for MFN status in accordance with the GATT.[9] The parties undertake to promote, within the framework of their current legislation, the expansion and diversification of trade between them.[10] Provision is made for the interchange of information and consultations on trade matters.[11] Provision is also made for consultation on disputes between the parties,[12] in particular in respect of allegations of dumping or subsidies.[13] In addition to promoting contacts,[14] the parties undertake to consider tax and duty exemption for goods imported temporarily into their territory.[15]

On 8 December 1997 the Community and Mexico signed interim and global Economic Partnership, Political Co-ordination and Co-operation Agreements.[16] They provide a framework for the liberalization of trade and for strengthening relations between the parties on the basis of reciprocity and mutual interest. As of the date of writing, these Agreements have not yet entered into force.[17]

An Agreement on trade in textiles has also been concluded between the Community and Mexico.[18] Its provisions are essentially the same as those of the analogous Agreement between the Community and Brazil.[19]

In 1997 an Agreement was concluded between the Community and Mexico on mutual recognition and protection of designations for spirit drinks.[20]

In accordance with the Community's measures to discourage the illicit manufacture of narcotic drugs and psychotropic substances,[1] the EC and Mexico have also concluded an Agreement on precursors and chemical substances.[2]

---

7 As to the Joint Committee, see ibid Art 39.
8 Ibid Art 43.
9 Ibid Art 11, first paragraph.
10 Ibid Art 12, first paragraph.
11 Ibid Art 13.
12 Ibid Art 14.
13 Ibid Art 15.
14 See ibid Arts 16, 17.
15 Ibid Art 18.
16 As to the global agreement, see Economic Partnership, Political Co-ordination and Co-operation Agreement between the European Community and its Member States of the one part, and the United Mexican States of the other part, OJ 19.11.97 C350/7, and Commission Proposal 97/C350/03 for a Council Decision, COM(97)527 final—97/0289(AVC), OJ 19.11.97 C250/6. As to the interim agreement, see Interim Agreement on trade and trade-related matters between the European Community, of the one part, and the United Mexican States, of the other part, OJ 22.11.97 C356/29, and Commission Proposal 97/C356/10 for a Council Decision, COM(97)525 final—97/0281(AVC), OJ 22.11.97 C356/28.
17 See also *Agence Europe*, No 71782 (n.s.), Wednesday 4 March 1998, p 7.
18 OJ 15.10.87 L292/74.
19 As to which, see above.
20 See Council Decision 97/361, OJ 11.6.97 L152/15, and the attached Agreement and Exchange of Letters. See also Commission Regulation 1434/97, OJ 24.7.97 L196/56.
1 See Council Regulation 3677/90, OJ 20.12.90 L357/1, as amended; and Commission Regulation 3769/92, OJ 29.12.92 L383/17, as amended.
2 OJ 19.2.97 L77/24.

UNITED STATES OF AMERICA

Trade relations between the Community and the US (like those between the Community and Canada) have usually been managed within the GATT. In recent years, however, the two trading partners have agreed several important joint political instruments. A Transatlantic Declaration on EU–US Relations was issued in November 1990.[3] This was complemented on 3 December 1995 by the adoption of the New Transatlantic Action Plan and a comprehensive Joint EU–US Action Plan.[4] In respect of trade, the two parties agreed to work to strengthen the multilateral trading system while at the same time creating a New Transatlantic Marketplace involving co-operation in numerous areas. In early 1998 the European Commission proposed the creation of a New Trans-atlantic Market between the EU and the US.[5]

In addition, the Community and the US have concluded a number of bilateral agreements. In fact, these agreements have sometimes resulted from the settle-ment of disputes arising within the framework of GATT.

In 1987 the Community and the US concluded an Agreement[6] to resolve the long-standing dispute over the effects of the Community's preferential agree-ments[7] in the Mediterranean region in respect of access to the Community market for citrus.[8] This was linked to a dispute over Community export refunds for pasta, which was the subject of a separate agreement in 1987.[9]

In 1992 the Community and the US concluded an Agreement concerning the application of the GATT Agreement on Trade in Civil Aircraft to trade in large civil aircraft.[10] While dealing mainly with subsidies and related measures, it contains provisions in respect of the avoidance of trade conflicts and litiga-tion.[11] The parties agree to seek to avoid any trade conflict on matters covered by the Agreement.[12] Except in case of abrogation of the Agreement on grounds of non-compliance by the other party, they also agree not to initiate action under their national trade laws in respect of government support granted in conformity with the Agreement while the Agreement is in force.[13] Private

---

3 *Agence Europe*, No 1622 (n.s.), 23 November 1990, Europe Documents p 1, reprinted in P Coffrey *The EC and the US* (London, Pinter, 1993) pp 264.

4 'Documents signed at the Last Transatlantic Summit between the European Union and the US (I)' *Agence Europe*, Europe Documents, No 1970, Atlantic Document No 93, 12 January 1996; ... (II)' *Agence Europe*, Europe Documents, No 1971, Atlantic Document No 94, 13 January 1996. The New Transatlantic Action Plan is also known as the New Transatlantic Agenda: see Krenzler and Schomaker 'A New Transatlantic Agenda' (1996) 1 *European Foreign Affairs Review* 9.

5 See European Commission 'New Transatlantic Market' (Commission Communication to the Council, the European Parliament, and the Economic and Social Committee), *Europe Docu-ments*, No 2080–81, 23 March 1998. See also *Agence Europe*, No 7178 (n.s.), 12 March 1998, p 6.

6 Agreement in the form of exchange of letters, OJ 5.3.87 L62/23.

7 That is, with Algeria, Cyprus, Egypt, Israel, Jordan, Lebanon, Malta, Morocco, Syria, Tuni-sia, Turkey and the then Yugoslavia.

8 That is, fresh sweet oranges, fresh lemons, fresh grapefruit, fresh tangerines, orange juice, lemon juice, grapefruit juice, grapefruit segments, dry pectin.

9 Settlement in the form of an exchange of letters, OJ 29.9.87 L275/37.

10 OJ 17.10.92 L301/32.

11 Ibid Art 10.

12 Ibid Art 10.1. This refers to trade actions relating to direct and indirect government support as defined by the Agreement, but does not include actions relating to dumping, intellectual property protection, or anti-trust or competition laws: Art 10.1, n 3.

13 Ibid Art 10.2.

parties are to be encouraged to use the consultation procedures provided by the Agreement[14] in order to resolve disputes.[15]

An Agreement was concluded in 1993 on the application of Council Directive 72/462 on health and veterinary inspection problems on importation of bovine animals, swine and fresh meat from third countries, and the corresponding US regulatory requirements.[16] The parties concluded that both systems provided basically equivalent safeguards against public health risks[17] but there were some differences in requirements which precluded recognition of equivalence and were to be modified as soon as possible.[18] They accepted the desirability of following a mutually agreed approach,[19] including the principle of regionalization for control of animal diseases.[20] The US recognized the need to apply uniform principles to the Community Member States in the context of the completion of the Single European Market.[1] In this respect the US undertook to continue to recognize the freedom of individual Member States from specified animal diseases, without the application of additional safeguards, after implementation of the single market strategy.[2] It also undertook to amend its import policy regulations and legislation in respect of specified diseases.[3] Provision was made for further co-operative measures.[4]

In 1993 a Memorandum of Understanding on oil seeds was agreed following a US complaint under GATT in respect of Community agricultural subsidies.[5] According to the Agreement, the Community is not to finance any market support for specified oilseeds except as provided.[6] It is also required to introduce a system of separate base areas for products benefiting from the crop-specific oilseeds payment system.[7] The Community must also grant a tariff-rate quota for imports of 500,000 metric tons of corn into Portugal, beginning in the 1993–94 marketing year, and the within quota tariff rate must be bound at such levels so as to ensure that the quota will be filled.[8] In addition, it must incorporate the commitments in the Agreement in its schedule of domestic support commitments to be annexed to the Uruguay Round Protocol to the GATT.[9] For its part, the US agreed to forgo any further compensation claim for impairment of GATT bindings.[10]

In 1995 an Agreement was concluded between the Community and the US

---

14 See Art 11.
15 Ibid Art 10.3, which also provides that the other party is to be informed in the event of a request for legal action and an offer must be made to enter into consultations.
16 Agreement in the form of exchange of letters, OJ 19.3.93 L68/3.
17 Ibid first paragraph.
18 Ibid second paragraph.
19 Ibid fourth paragraph, first sub-paragraph.
20 Ibid sixth paragraph, first sub-paragraph.
 1 Ibid fourth paragraph, second sub-paragraph.
 2 Ibid sixth paragraph, second sub-paragraph.
 3 Ibid sixth paragraph, third sub-paragraph.
 4 See ibid paragraphs 7–10.
 5 OJ 18.6.93 L147/26. The Community legislation in question was Council Regulation 1765/92 establishing a support system for producers of certain arable crops (OJ 1.7.92 L181/12).
 6 That is, by Council Regulation 1765/92. See the Memorandum, paragraph 3(a).
 7 Memorandum, fourth paragraph. As to components of the system, see the fifth paragraph and Annex. As to additional discipline, see the sixth paragraph.
 8 Ibid eighth paragraph.
 9 Ibid ninth paragraph.
10 Ibid tenth paragraph.

regarding the application of their competition laws.[11] Its purpose is to promote co-operation and co-ordination between the parties and lessen the probability or impact of differences in their application of their competition laws.[12] To this end it provided for the notification of measures, exchange of information, co-ordination of enforcement activities, positive comity,[13] traditional comity[14] and reciprocal consultation procedures.

On 20 May 1997 the EU and the US initialled a Mutual Recognition Agreement (MRA).[15] Its objective is to facilitate trade and improve market access with regard to assessment of conformity to standards for specified products. The MRA consists of a framework agreement and six sectoral annexes. The Agreement specifies the conditions by which each party will accept or recognize results of conformity assessment procedures, produced by the other party's conformity assessment bodies or authorities, in assessing conformity to the other party's requirements. The mutual recognition requirements are specified on a sector-by-sector basis.[16] Certain provisions are intended to guarantee the autonomy of each party's regulatory agencies. Such agencies retain authority to keep products off the market for reasons of health, safety or environmental protection.[17] A party is entitled to refuse to accept the results of its counterpart's body or organization that is not performing the appropriate assessment procedures correctly.[18] A party can suspend its obligations under a sectoral annex if it suffers loss of market access because the other party is not fulfilling its obligations or fails to maintain the legal and regulatory authorities necessary to implement the Agreement.[19] A party can terminate a sectoral annex.[20] Prompt consultations are to be held if obstacles to access arise. In the absence of a satisfactory outcome of the consultations, the party alleging denial of its market access may, within 90 days of the consultation, invoke its right to terminate the Agreement.[1] A joint committee is established to be responsible for the functioning of the Agreement.[2] Sectoral committees may be established if necessary.

---

11 OJ 27.4.95 L95/47. The Agreement was initially concluded by the European Commission, but in an action brought against the Commission by France the European Court of Justice held that the Commission lacked competence to conclude the Agreement: Case C-327/91 *France v Commission* [1994] ECR I-3641. Subsequently the Agreement was concluded by the Council: OJ 18.6.98 L173/28.
12 Agreement Art I(1).
13 That is, co-operation regarding anti-competitive activities in the territory of one party that adversely affect important interests of the other: Art V.
14 That is, each party is to seek to take into account the important interests of the other when deciding on enforcement measures: Art VI.
15 Agreement on Mutual Recognition between the US and the European Community, as to which see European Commission, Directorate General I Home Page on the Internet: http://www.europa.eu.int/en/comm/dg01/mra01.htm. See also the website of the Transatlantic Business Dialogue at http://www.mac.doc.gov/tabd/tabd.html. See also Commission of the European Communities, Proposal for a Council Decision on the conclusion of an Agreement on Mutual Recognition in relation to Conformity Assessments, between the European Community and the US (presented by the Commission), COM(1998)180 final, Brussels, 30.3.98.
16 The sectoral annexes deal, respectively, with telecommunication equipment, electromagnetic compatibility (EMC), electrical safety, recreational craft, pharmaceutical good manufacturing practice, and medical devices.
17 Ibid Art 15.
18 Ibid Art 9.
19 Ibid Art 16.
20 Ibid Art 21(3).
 1 Ibid Art 2.
 2 Ibid Art 14(1).

In 1997 the EC and the US concluded an Agreement to promote co-operation in science and technology.[3] It includes co-ordinated research projects, joint symposia, training of scientists and technical experts, exchange or sharing of equipment and materials, visits and exchanges of personnel, and exchanges of information.

The EC and the US recently concluded an Agreement on sanitary measures to protect public and animal health in trade in live animals and animal products.[4] The Agreement is designed to put into practice the provisions of the WTO Agreement on the application of sanitary and phytosanitary measures. Its objective is to facilitate trade by establishing a mechanism for the recognition of equivalence of sanitary measures maintained by a party consistent with the protection of public and animal health, and to improve communications and co-operation on sanitary measures.[5] It is initially limited to sanitary measures applied by either party to certain listed animals and animal products, with specified exceptions.[6] It does not apply however to sanitary measures related to food additives, processing aids, flavours, colour additives, sanitary stamps, irradiation (ionisation), contaminants (including pesticides, chemical residues, mycotoxins, natural toxins, physical contaminants and animal drug residues), chemicals originating from the migration of substances from packaging materials, labelling of foodstuffs (including nutritional labelling), feed additives, animal feedingstuffs, medicated feeds and premixes.[7] Each party is required to recognize for trade the health status of regions, as determined by the exporting party, with respect to specified animal and aquaculture diseases.[8] The importing party is also required to recognize regionalization decisions taken by the exporting party in accordance with specified criteria as the basis for trade from a party where an area is affected by one or more listed diseases.[9] The Agreement establishes a consultative process for the determination of equivalence[10] and provides for the status of consultations.[11] It also provides for verification, including the principle that the determination of the nature and frequency of checks to be applied to live animals and animal products at external frontiers rests solely with the importing party.[12] It also provides for exchange of information[13] and for notification of any serious or significant health risk,[14] of the presence or evolution of certain diseases;[15] and of certain other changes or

---

3 See *Agence Europe*, No 7113 (n.s.), Thursday 4 December 1997, p 14; *Agence Europe*, No 7115 (n.s.), Saturday 6 December 1997. See also Commission of the European Communities, Proposal for a Council Decision concluding the Agreement for Scientific and Technological Co-operation between the European Community and the US (presented by the Commission), COM(1998) 137 final, Brussels, 10.3.1998.

4 Agreement between the European Community and the US on sanitary measures to protect public and animal health in trade in live animals and animal products, OJ 21.4.98 L118/3, approved on behalf of the European Community by Council Decision 98/258, OJ 21.4.98 L118/1.

5 Ibid Art 1.

6 Ibid Art 3(1).

7 Ibid Art 3(2).

8 Ibid Art 6(1).The diseases are listed in Annex III.

9 Ibid Art 6(1). The criteria are provided in Annex IV. The diseases are listed in Annex III.

10 See ibid Art 7.

11 See ibid Art 8.

12 See ibid Art 9, in particular Art 9(1).

13 See ibid Art 10.

14 See ibid Art 11(1)(a).

15 See ibid Art 11(1)(b).

measures.[16] Each party may take provisional safeguard measures necessary for the protection of public or animal health. Such measures must be notified to the other party within 24 hours and, on request, consultations must be held within 14 days. The parties are required to endeavour to avoid unnecessary disruption in trade, taking advantage where possible of consultations and other considerations.[17] A Joint Management Committee is established to guide the activities carried out under the Agreement.[18]

An Agreement has also been concluded between the EAEC and the US concerning government procurement.[19]

Provision has been made for the allocation of export licences under the additional quota for cheese to be exported to the US under the GATT Agreements.[20]

---

16 See ibid Art 11(1)(c).
17 See ibid Art 12, which refers also to the consultations and other considerations set down in Art 11(3). The principles of the Agreement are to be applied to address certain outstanding issues listed in Annex VIII: ibid Art 13.
18 Ibid Art 14.
19 Agreement in the form of a Memorandum of Understanding, OJ 20.5.93 L125/2, as amended; Agreement in the form of exchange of letters, OJ 20.6.95 L134/26. See also Council Regulation 1461/93 concerning access to public contracts for tenderers from the US, OJ 17.6.93 L146/1, as amended.
20 As to opening of the procedure for the allocation of licences for 1996, see Commission Regulation 2454/94, OJ 20.10.95 L252/16. As to the allocation of licences, see Commission Regulation 2650/95, OJ 15.11.95 L272/14.

Chapter 31

Central and Latin America

CARTAGENA AGREEMENT (ANDEAN PACT)

The Cartagena Agreement, better known as the Andean Pact, is a subregional integration organization composed of Bolivia, Colombia, Ecuador, Peru and Venezuela.[1] A Co-operation Agreement was concluded between the Community and the Cartagena Agreement and its member countries in 1983.[2] The Agreement entered into force on 1 February 1987.[3] A new Framework Agreement for Co-operation between the Community and the Andean Pact was signed in 1993.[4] It entered into effect on 1 May 1998.[5]

The 1998 Framework Agreement states that the co-operation ties between the parties are based on respect for democratic principles and human rights,

1 Cartagena Agreement: Agreement on Subregional Andean Integration, 8 ILM 910 (1969); modified by the Act of Trujillo: Protocole modifiant le Protocole de Carthagène et créant la Communauté andine (Trujillo, 10 mars 1996), *Documents d'Actualité Internationale*, 12, 1996, 475–477. See also Cartagena Agreement, (1997) 10 Newsletter of Committee C (Antitrust and Trade Law), of the International Bar Association Section on Business Law 16.

2 OJ 8.6.84 L153/2. It was concluded for a period of five years and thereafter for periods of two years, subject to termination by written notice by either party six months prior to the date of expiry of any period: Art 10(2).

3 See European Parliament Resolution on economic and commercial relations between the European Community and the Andean Pact, OJ 19.12.88 C326/324. See also Written Question No 1840/87 by Ludivina García Arias, 30.11.87, and Answer by Mr Cheysson, 17.2.88, OJ 10.5.88 C123/22.

4 See Framework Agreement for Co-operation between the European Economic Community and the Cartagena Agreement and its member countries, namely Bolivia, Colombia, Ecuador, Peru and Venezuela, OJ 28.1.93 C25/32, and Commission Proposal for a Council Decision concerning the conclusion of a framework Co-operation Agreement, OJ 28.1.93 C25/31. As to rules of origin in respect of regional groupings, see Commission Regulation 2454/93, OJ 11.10.93 L253/1, as amended by Commission Regulation 3254/94, OJ 31.12.94 L346/1. As to EU relations with Latin America generally, see Commission of the European Communities, 'The European Union and Latin America: The Present Situation and Prospects for Closer Partnership 1996–2000', Communication from the Commission to the Council and the European Parliament, COM(95)495 final, Brussels, 23.10.95. See also Parlement européen, Rapport de la Commission des relations économiques extérieures sur les relations économiques et commerciales entre l'Union européenne et l'Amérique latine (Rapporteur: Mme Ana Miranda de Lage), Doc. A3–0140/94, PE 204.810/déf, 15.3.94. Council Decision 97/723 (OJ 19.12.96 L329/45) grants a Community guarantee to the European Investment Bank against losses under loans for projects of mutual interest in Latin American and Asian countries with which the community has concluded co-operation agreements.

5 See the Framework Agreement on Co-operation, Information concerning the entry into force (attached to the Agreement at OJ 29.4.98 L127/25), OJ 29.4.98 L127/11, approved on behalf of the Community by Council Decision 98/278, OJ 29.4.98 L127/10).

which constitute an essential component of the Agreement.[6] The parties undertake to intensify their co-operation, in particular in respect inter alia of trade, taking account of the Andean countries' special status as developing countries, and to promote the intensification and consolidation of Andean integration.[7] The parties acknowledge the value, in the light of the aims of the Agreement, of consulting each other on international issues of mutual interest.[8] The Framework Agreement provides for economic co-operation,[9] MFN treatment,[10] trade co-operation, and co-operation in respect of industry, investment, financial institutions, science and technology, standards, technological development and intellectual and industrial property, mining, energy, transport, information technology and communications, tourism, the environment, biological diversity, development, agriculture, forestry and rural areas, health, social development, combating drug abuse, regional integration, government, information, communication and culture, fisheries, training, and institutional matters.[11]

In respect of trade co-operation, the parties undertake to develop and diversify trade to the highest possible degree, taking into account their respective economic situations and facilitating trade transactions between them as far as possible.[12] To this end they are to endeavour to find methods of reducing and eliminating obstacles hindering the development of trade, especially non-tariff and para-tariff barriers, taking into account the work already accomplished by international organizations.[13] They are, where appropriate, to assess the possibility of setting up mutual consultation procedures.[14]

The Agreement provides various means to achieve co-operation in trade.[15] The parties are to take measures aimed at promoting meetings and contacts between entrepreneurs, with the aim of identifying goods suitable for sale on the market of the other party;[16] facilitating co-operation between customs services, in particular as regards vocational training, the simplification of procedures and the detection of customs offences;[17] encouraging trade-promotion activities;[18] providing support for their own organization and firms;[19] taking into account each other's interest with regard to market access for commodities, semi-finished goods and manufactured goods and with regard to the stabilization of world commodity markets;[20] and examining ways and means of facilitating trade and eliminating trade barriers.[1]

---

6 Ibid Art 1.
7 Ibid Art 2(1).
8 Ibid Art 2(2).
9 The aims of such co-operation include encouraging the expansion of trade with a view to promoting diversification and the opening-up of markets, as well as encouraging the flow of investment, technology transfer and greater protection of investment: ibid Art 3(1)(c), (d).
10 In accordance with the GATT: ibid Art 4, first paragraph.
11 By mutual consent, the fields of co-operation may be widened or the level of co-operation may be enhanced: see ibid Art 39.
12 Ibid Art 5(1).
13 Ibid Art 5(2), which thus implicitly refers to the GATT/WTO.
14 Ibid Art 5(3). Compare the unilateral declaration by the Andean Pact expressed in ibid Art 2(2).
15 Ibid Art 6.
16 Ibid Art 6, first indent.
17 Ibid Art 6, second indent.
18 Ibid Art 6, third indent.
19 Ibid Art 6, fourth indent.
20 Ibid Art 6, fifth indent.
 1 Ibid Art 6, sixth indent.

In respect of temporary admission of goods, the parties undertake to grant each other tax and duty exemption for temporary import of goods into their territories, in accordance with their respective laws and taking account, wherever possible, of existing international agreements in the field.[2]

In respect of standards, the parties are to take steps to reduce differences in respect of weights and measures, standardization and certification by promoting the use of compatible systems of standards and certification.[3]

In respect of intellectual property the parties undertake, inter alia, to ensure, so far as their laws, regulations and policies allow, that suitable and effective protection is provided for intellectual and industrial property rights, including geographical designations and appellations of origin, reinforcing this protection where desirable. They also undertake, wherever possible and so far as their laws, regulations and policies allow, to facilitate access to databases and databanks in this field.[4]

The parties are to take steps to encourage the integration of the Andean countries. Priority is to be given inter alia to the promotion of subregional, regional and international trade.[5]

A Joint Committee was established by the 1983 Co-operation Agreement.[6] The 1998 Framework Agreement states that the parties agree to retain the Joint Committee, together with inter alia the Subcommittee on Trade Co-operation.[7]

Neither the Framework Agreement nor any action taken under it is to affect in any way the powers of the Community's Member States to undertake bilateral activities with the Andean Pact countries in the field of economic co-operation or to conclude new economic co-operation agreements with the Andean Pact countries.[8]

Provision is made for the conclusion of a separate protocol between the ECSC and its Member States, on the one hand, and the Cartagena Agreement and its Member States, on the other hand.[9]

The Agreement, once entered into force, has a duration of five years and is to be renewed tacitly on a yearly basis unless one of the contracting parties denounces it in writing six months before the date of expiry.[10]

The Community and the Andean Pact Countries have also concluded an Agreement on precursors and chemical substances.[11] This is designed to complement Community policies to discourage the illicit manufacture of narcotic drugs and psychotropic substances.[12]

---

2 Ibid Art 7.
3 Ibid Art 12.
4 Ibid Art 13, which also provides for the facilitation of access to relevant databases and databanks.
5 Ibid Art 26.
6 Art 5, OJ 8.6.84 L153/2.
7 1992 Framework Agreement Art 32(1).
8 Ibid Art 33(1).
9 Ibid Art 34.
10 Ibid Art 37.
11 OJ 30.12.95 L324/3, L324/11, L324/19, L324/24, L324/35.
12 See Council Regulation 3677/90, OJ 20.12.90 L357/1, as amended; and Commission Regulation 3769/92, OJ 29.12.92 L383/17, as amended.

CENTRAL AMERICAN ECONOMIC INTEGRATION (CAEI) TREATY

In 1986 a Co-operation Agreement was concluded between the Community and the countries parties to the General Treaty on Central American Economic Integration.[13] Its aims included, inter alia, to broaden and consolidate trade relations on the basis of equity and mutual respect and advantage, taking account of the relatively less developed situation of the Central American Isthmus;[14] and to help revitalize, restructure and strengthen the process of economic integration of the Central American countries.[15] It provided for economic co-operation, trade co-operation, MFN treatment, development co-operation and institutional matters. The trade provisions were broadly similar to those of the Co-operation Agreement with the Andean Pact countries.[16]

A new Framework Co-operation Agreement between the Community and the CAEI countries plus Panama was agreed in 1993.[17] Its trade provisions are almost exactly the same as those of the Agreement between the Community and the Andean Pact.[18] The major exception concerns intellectual and industrial property. In this respect the parties undertake, in line with their respective legislation, regulations and policies, to provide suitable and effective protection for intellectual and industrial property rights, including geographical designations and marks of origin, and upgrading that protection where appropriate.[19] The Central American countries shall, in so far as they are able, subscribe to the international conventions on intellectual and industrial property.[20] The Joint Committee established by the 1985 Co-operation Agreement[1] is retained.[2]

SOUTHERN CONE COMMON MARKET (MERCOSUR)

The Southern Cone Common Market (*Mercado Común del Sur*, better known as Mercosur), began in 1990 under the Latin American Free Trade Association and was officially founded in 1991.[3] It consists of Argentina, Brazil, Paraguay and Uruguay.

13 OJ 30.6.86 L172/2. Known as the 'countries of the Central American Isthmus' or 'Central American Isthmus', the countries are Costa Rica, El Salvador, Guatemala, Honduras and Nicaragua: see Art 1. The Agreement was concluded for a period of five years with automatic renewal for two-year periods, subject to termination by written notice six months before the end of any period: Art 11(2).

14 Ibid Art 1(a).

15 Ibid Art 1(d).

16 As to which, see above. This includes the Community's Declaration concerning the GSP: Annex I.

17 Framework Co-operation Agreement between the European Economic Community and the Republics of Costa Rica, El Salvador, Guatemala, Hondoras, Nicaragua and Panama, OJ 18.3.93 C77/31; cf also the Commission Proposal for a Council Decision concerning the conclusion of the Agreement, OJ 18.3.93 C77/30.

18 As to which, see above. The new Framework Agreement also includes unilateral declarations by the Community and by Central America in respect of special concessions in the context of the GSP: see OJ 18.3.93 C77/42.

19 Framework Agreement Art 12(1), OJ 18.3.93 C77/31.

20 Ibid Art 12(2).

1 1986 Agreement Art 7, OJ 30.6.86 L172/2.

2 Ibid Art 33(1).

3 The institutional structure of Mercosur was established, and international legal personality was granted to Mercosur, by the 1994 Protocol of Ouro Preto: see 'Argentina—Brazil—Paraguay—

In December 1995 the European Community and its Member States, on the one hand, and Mercosur and its Party States, on the other hand, signed an Interregional Framework Co-operation Agreement.[4] The Agreement presaged the formation of an interregional framework for co-operation between the Community and its Member States, on the one hand, and Mercosur and its member countries, on the other hand.[5] It is intended to be a non-preferential agreement, to be followed later by reciprocal liberalization of trade and political dialogue.[6] Its provisions concern trade, economic co-operation, encouragement of integration, inter-institutional co-operation, and other areas of co-operation.

In respect of trade, the objectives of the Agreement are to forge closer relations between the parties, with the aim of encouraging the increase and diversification of trade, preparing for subsequent gradual and reciprocal liberalization of trade and promoting conditions which are conducive to the establishment of the Interregional Association, taking into account, in conformity with WTO rules, the sensitivity of certain goods.[7] For these purposes the parties are to agree, through periodic dialogue,[8] on the scope of co-operation in trade matters, without excluding any sector.[9] Co-operation is to focus mainly on market access, trade liberalization and trade discipline; the parties' trade relations with non-member countries; the compatibility of trade liberalization with GATT and WTO rules; the identification of goods which the parties consider to be sensitive or of priority importance; and co-operation and exchanges of information on services, within the parties' respective spheres of competence.[10] The parties are also to co-operate in promoting the approximation of agri-food and

---

Uruguay: Additional Protocol to the Treaty of Asunción on the Institutional Structure of Mercosur ('Protocol of Ouro Preto'), done at Ouro Preto, Brazil, 17 December 1994, in (1995) 34 ILM 1244. This Protocol entered into force on 15 December 1995. For recent surveys, see Ferrere 'MERCOSUR and Other Trade Blocks: A Trend for the Coming Decade' (1996) *International Business Lawyer* (June) 256; 'Survey: Mercosur' *The Economist*, 12 October 1996.

4 Interregional Framework Co-operation Agreement between the European Community and its Member States, on the one hand, and the Southern Common Market and its Party States, on the other hand, OJ 19.3.96 L69/2. See also Commission of the European Communities, 'The European Community and Mercosur: An Enhanced Policy' (Communication from the Commission to the Council and the European Parliament), COM(94)428 final (Brussels, 19.10.94); Solemn Joint Declaration between the Council of the European Union and the European Commission, on the one hand, and the Mercosur Member States on the other, OJ 31.12.94 C377/1; and Economic and Social Committee, Opinion on the communication, OJ 22.1.96 C18/135.

5 See Proposal for a Council Decision concerning the provisional application of certain provisions of the interregional framework co-operation agreement, OJ 19.1.96 C14/17. See also European Parliament, Committee on External Economic Relations, Report on the proposal for a Council Decision concerning the conclusion of the interregional framework co-operation Agreement between the European Community and its Member States, of the one part, and the Southern Cone Common Market and its member countries, of the other part (COM(95)0504 -C4-0130/96-95/0261(CNS) (Rapporteur: Mr Jaime Valdivielso de Cué), Doc. A4-0118/96, PE 216.550/fin, 23.4.96.

6 See Written Question E-2228/95 by Iñigo Méndez de Vigo, 31.7.95, and Answer by Mr Marín, 16.10.95, OJ 6.12.95 C326/34; Written Question E-1855/95 by José Happart, 3.7.95, and Answer by Mr Marín, 25.7.95, OJ 16.10.94 C270/61; Written Question E-2583/94 by Iñigo Méndez de Vigo, 5.12.94, and Answer by Mr Marín, 16.1.95, OJ 3.4.95 C81/47.

7 Interregional Framework Co-operation Agreement between the European Community and its Member States, on the one hand, and the Southern Common Market and its Party States, on the other hand, Art 4, OJ 19.3.96 L69/96.

8 Ibid Art 5(2).

9 Ibid Art 5(1).

10 Ibid Art 5(3). The Agreement is a mixed agreement, the EC and Mercosur and their respective Member States or Party States being signatories.

industrial standards and certification.[11] Provision is also made for co-operation in customs matters,[12] in statistical matters,[13] and regarding intellectual property.[14] In respect of intellectual property, the parties have agreed to co-operate in order to encourage investment, the transfer of technology, trade and all associated economic activity, and to prevent distortions of trade.[15] Within the bounds of their respective laws, regulations and policies, and in line with the undertakings made within the TRIPs Agreement, they are to ensure that there is suitable and genuine protection of intellectual property rights, if necessary by arranging for such protection to be stepped up.[16]

The Agreement also establishes a tripartite institutional framework. First, there is a Co-operation Council composed of members of the Council of the European Union and members of the European Commission, on the one hand, and members of the Mercosur Common Market Council and members of the Mercosur Common Market Group, on the other hand.[17] It has general responsibility for the implementation of the Agreement.[18] Second, it is assisted by a Joint Co-operation Committee, composed of members of the Council of the European Union, on the one hand, and representatives of Mercosur, on the other hand.[19] The Joint Co-operation Council may make proposals to the Co-operation Council, either with the aim of stimulating preparations for the liberalization of trade and of intensifying co-operation[20] or, in more general terms, which contribute to achieving the ultimate aim of EU-Mercosur interregional association.[1] Third, there is a Joint Subcommittee on Trade composed of members of the Council of the European Union and of members of the European Commission, on the one hand, and representatives of Mercosur, on the other hand.[2] Its tasks are to ensure that the trade-related objectives of the Agreement are fulfilled and to conduct preparatory work for the subsequent liberalization of trade.[3]

ARGENTINA

Argentina is a member of Mercosur.[4]

A Framework Agreement for trade and economic co-operation was concluded between the Community and the Argentine Republic in 1990.[5] It states that co-operation ties and the Agreement are based on respect for the democratic principles and human rights which inspire the domestic and external

11 Ibid Art 6.
12 Ibid Art 7. This includes the potential conclusion of a Customs Co-operation Protocol: see Art 7(3).
13 Ibid Art 8. A co-operation programme in the field of statistics was established in mid-1997: see *Agence Europe*, No 6971 (n.s.), Friday/Saturday, 9–10 May 1997, p 10.
14 Ibid Art 9.
15 Ibid Art 9(1).
16 Ibid Art 9(2). For these purposes, intellectual property matters shall encompass copyright and similar rights, trademarks or brands, geographical terms and descriptions of origin, industrial designs and utility models, patents and integrated circuit topography: ibid Art 9(3).
17 Ibid Art 26(1).
18 Ibid Art 25(1).
19 Ibid Art 27(1).
20 Ibid Art 27(5)(c).
 1 Ibid Art 27(5)(d).
 2 Ibid Art 29(2).
 3 Ibid Art 29(1).
 4 As to Mercosur, see above.
 5 OJ 26.10.90 L295/67. The Agreement is concluded for five years, with tacit annual renewal absent denunciation six months before the date of expiry: Art 11(2).

policies of the Community and Argentina.[6] The basic principles of the Agreement are the strengthening of democracy and regional integration.[7] The Agreement provides for MFN treatment, trade co-operation, economic co-operation, agricultural co-operation, industrial co-operation and institutional matters.

MFN treatment is granted by the parties to each other in accordance with the GATT.[8] The parties also undertake to consider granting, each in accordance with its own legislation, relief from duties, taxes and other charges in respect of goods temporarily in their territories for re-export, either unaltered or after inward processing.[9] In matters of trade co-operation, they also undertake to promote the development and diversification of their trade to the highest possible level consistent with their respective economic situations.[10] Various forms of trade co-operation are envisaged.[11]

A Joint Co-operation Committee is established to oversee the operation of the Agreement.[12] As with other Agreements, this Agreement does not affect the powers of the Community Member States to undertake bilateral activities in the field of economic co-operation.[13]

Separate agreements between the Community and Argentina have been concluded in respect of trade in mutton and lamb,[14] textiles,[15] fisheries[16] and oilseeds.[17]

BRAZIL

Brazil is a member of Mercosur.[18]

A Framework Agreement for co-operation was concluded between the Community and Brazil in 1992.[19] It contains a human rights and democracy clause to the effect that co-operation ties and the Agreement are based on respect for the democratic principles and human rights which inspire the domestic and international policies of the parties and which constitute an essential component of the Agreement.[20] It provides for the strengthening of co-operation in respect of economic matters, trade, industry, investment, science and technology, standards, technological development and intellectual property,

---

6 Ibid Art 1(1). Compare the stronger human rights and democracy clause in the Agreement with Brazil, below.
7 Ibid Art 1(2).
8 Ibid Art 2(1).
9 Ibid Art 2(2).
10 Ibid Art 3(1). This includes studying ways and means to eliminate trade barriers: Art 3(2).
11 See Art 3(3).
12 Ibid Art 7.
13 Ibid Art 8(1). The Agreement replaces identical or incompatible provisions of existing bilateral agreements between the Community Member States and Argentina: Art 8(2).
14 See Arrangement in the form of exchange of letters, OJ 18.10.80 L275/14; Agreement in the form of exchange of letters, OJ 18.10.80 L275/37.
15 See Agreement, OJ 16.6.87 L156/2, as amended by Agreements in the form of exchange of letters in 1992 (OJ 31.12.92 L410/125) and 1995 (OJ 26.4.95 L94/3).
16 See Agreement, and Protocol I, OJ 20.12.93 L318/2.
17 Agreement in the form of agreed minutes pursuant to GATT Article XXVIII, OJ 18.2.94 L47/2.
18 As to Mercosur, see above.
19 OJ 1.11.95 L262/54. The Agreement was signed on 29 June 1992, the procedures necessary for entry into force were completed on 30 October 1995, and the Agreement entered into force on 1 November 1995: Annex to Agreement. The Agreement was concluded for a period of five years, with tacit annual renewal absent denunciation in writing six months before expiry: Agreement Art 33. It succeeded a previous Framework Agreement which entered into force in 1982 (OJ 4.10.82 L281/2, as amended).
20 Agreement Art 1.

mining, energy, transport, the use of space technology in the fields of information technology and telecommunications, tourism, the environment, agriculture, forestry and rural areas, public health, social development, the fight against drugs, regional integration and co-operation, public administration, information and culture, fisheries and training.[1] A Joint Committee is established to oversee the operation of the Agreement.[2]

In respect of trade, the Agreement provides for MFN status in accordance with GATT.[3] Provisions in respect of interchange of information and consultations on trade disputes have now been replaced by Uruguay Round instruments.[4] Other provisions concern means of achieving co-operation in trade.[5] The parties undertake to consider tax and duty exemption for temporary import of goods into their territory.[6] They also agree to take steps to promote the use of compatible systems of standards and certification, in particular for example by means of mutual recognition and holding consultations to ensure that standards do not constitute a barrier to trade.[7] With regard to intellectual property, the parties undertake to ensure, so far as their laws, regulations and policies allow, that suitable and effective protection is provided for intellectual property rights.[8] These forms of co-operation may extend to compatible action undertaken within the context of co-operation or integration agreements with countries in the same region,[9] including the promotion of inter-regional trade.[10]

A separate Agreement has been concluded between the Community and Brazil on trade in textile products.[11] Its provisions are similar to those in the analogous agreement with Hong Kong.[12] In addition, special emphasis is given to maintaining the traditional commercial practices and trade flows between the parties.[13]

Separate agreements have also been concluded between the Community and Brazil in respect of manioc[14] and oilseeds.[15]

CHILE

A Framework Agreement between the Community and Chile was concluded in 1990.[16] It contains a human rights and democracy clause that is virtually identi-

---

1 The Agreement replaces identical or incompatible provisions of previous bilateral agreements between the Community's Member States and Brazil (Art 30(2)), but it does not affect the powers of the Member States to undertake bilateral activities in the field of economic co-operation (Art 30(1)).
2 As to the Joint Committee, see Art 29.
3 Ibid Art 4.
4 See ibid Art 5(3),(4),(5),(6).
5 See ibid Art 6.
6 Ibid Art 7.
7 Ibid Art 11.
8 Ibid Art 12(2).
9 Ibid Art 23(1).
10 Ibid Art 23(2), second indent.
11 OJ 14.9.87 L263/2, as amended by Agreements in the form of exchange of letters in 1992 (OJ 31.1292 L410/152) and 1995 (OJ 26.4.95 L94/67).
12 As to which, see Chapter 32 in this book.
13 See ibid Art 14(2). As to consultations, see Art 14(3).
14 Agreement in the form of exchange of letters, OJ 28.7.82 L219/59.
15 Agreement in the form of agreed minutes, OJ 18.2.94 L47/8.
16 OJ 26.3.91 L79/2. As to relations between the EU and Chile, see Parlement européen, Commission des relations économiques extérieures, Rapport sur la communication de la Commission au Conseil et au Parlement européen relative au renforcement des relations entre l'Union européene et le Chile (SEC(95)0563-C4-0153/85 et COM(95)0232-C4-0219/95), Rapporteur: Mme Ana Miranda de Lage, Doc. A4-0329/95, PE 215.382/def, 20.12.95.

cal to that in the Agreement between the Community and Argentina.[17] It was replaced in 1996 by a new EU–Chile Framework Co-operation Agreement.[18] Respect for democratic principles and fundamental human rights are stated to be essential elements of the Agreement.[19] In respect of trade, the Agreement provides for economic and commercial dialogue, co-operation in respect of standardization, customs co-operation, temporary importation of goods, and co-operation in respect of statistics, intellectual property, and public procurement. A Joint Council is established to oversee the implementation of the Agreement.[20] The trade provisions will come into effect only after ratification by the EC Member States, though the co-operation provisions came into effect upon signature as a result of the contemporaneous exchange of letters.[1]

The Community and Chile have also concluded an Agreement on imports of apples and pears from Chile into the Community.[2] It was concluded after a complaint to the GATT by Chile in respect of Community restrictions on imports of apples from Chile.[3] According to the Agreement, the Community undertakes to apply certain provisions in respect of entry prices and countervailing charges, and also to reduce the *ad valorem* duties on imported apples and pears during specific periods of the year.

COLOMBIA

Colombia is a member country of the Cartagena Agreement.[4]

An Agreement on trade in textiles has also been concluded between the Community and Colombia.[5] Its provisions are essentially the same as those of the analogous Agreement between the Community and Brazil.[6]

GUATEMALA

An Agreement on trade in textiles has been concluded between the Community and Guatemala.[7] Its provisions are essentially the same as those of the analogous Agreement between the Community and Brazil.[8]

---

17 As to which, see above.
18 OJ 19.8.96 L209/5, approved on behalf of the European Community by Council Decision 96/504, OJ 19.8.96 L209/1.
19 Ibid Art 1.
20 Ibid Art 33.
 1 OJ 19.8.92 L209/2. See also *Agence Europe*, No 6814 (n.s.), Thursday 19 September 1996, p 10.
 2 Agreement in the form of exchange of letters, OJ 25.5.94 L130/36; Council Decision 94/294, OJ 25.5.94 L130/35. See also Agreement of 30 June 1969, OJ 9.3.70 L54/7.
 3 There were two earlier GATT panel procedures against the Community regime on the importation of dessert apples from Chile: see BISD 27S, p 98, and BISD 36S, p 93; as to the latter, see also *Re Restrictions on Imports of Dessert Applies: Chile v European Economic Community* (Case L/6491) [1992] 2 CMLR 161. The importation into the Community of dessert apples from Chile has also been the subject of litigation in the European Court of Justice: see Case C-152/88 *Sofrimport SARL v Commission* [1990] ECR I-2477; Case T-489/93 *Unifruit Hellas EPE v Commission* [1994] ECR II-1201.
 4 As to which, see above.
 5 Agreement in the form of exchange of letters (OJ 15.10.87 L292/2), as amended by Agreements in the form of exchange of letters in 1992 (OJ 31.12.92 L410/89).
 6 As to which, see above.
 7 Agreement in the form of exchange of letters, OJ 15.10.85 L292/26.
 8 As to which, see above.

PARAGUAY

Paraguay is a member of Mercosur.[9]

A Framework Agreement for co-operation between the Community and the Republic of Paraguay was concluded in 1992.[10] It contains a human rights and democracy clause similar to that in the Agreement between the Community and Argentina.[11] Its other provisions are essentially the same as those of the analogous Agreement with Mexico.[12]

PERU

Peru is a member country of the Cartagena Agreement.[13]

An Agreement on trade in textiles has been concluded between the Community and Peru.[14] Its provisions are essentially the same as those of the analogous Agreement between the Community and Brazil.[15]

URUGUAY

Uruguay is a member of Mercosur.[16]

A Framework Agreement for co-operation has been concluded between the Community and the Eastern Republic of Uruguay.[17] It contains a human rights and democracy clause similar to that in the analogous Agreement between the Community and Brazil.[18]

Its other provisions are essentially the same as those of the analogous Agreement between the Community and Mexico.[19]

An Agreement on trade in textiles has also been concluded between the Community and Uruguay.[20] Its provisions are essentially the same as those of the analogous Agreement between the Community and Brazil.[1]

The Community and Uruguay have also concluded agreements in respect of lamb[2] and oilseeds.[3]

---

9 As to Mercosur, see above.
10 OJ 30.10.92 L313/72.
11 As to which, see above.
12 As to which, see Chapter 30 on North America.
13 As to which, see above.
14 OJ 14.9.87 L263/82, as amended by Agreement in the form of exchange of letters in 1992 (OJ 31.12.92 L410/91) and in 1995 (OJ 26.4.95 L94/332).
15 As to which, see above.
16 As to Mercosur, see above.
17 OJ 8.4.92 L94/2.
18 As to which, see above.
19 As to which, see Chapter 30 on North America.
20 OJ 14.9.87 L263/121, as amended by Agreement in the form of exchange of letters in 1992 (OJ 31.12.92 L410/271) and in 1995 (26.4.95 L94/531).
1 As to which, see above.
2 OJ 18.10.80 L275/37.
3 OJ 18.2.94 L47/29.

Chapter 32

Asia

INTRODUCTION

Numerous bilateral agreements have been concluded between the Community and Asian countries. The following paragraphs consider the agreements between the Community and the following countries or group of countries: Association of South East Asian Nations (ASEAN), South Asian Association for Regional Co-operation (SAARC), Bangladesh, Cambodia, People's Republic of China, Hong Kong, India, Indonesia, Japan, Korea, Laos, Macao, Malaysia, Mongolia, Nepal, Pakistan, Philippines, Singapore, Sri Lanka, Taiwan, Thailand, and Vietnam.[1] The Republics of Kazakstan, Kyrgyz, Turkmenistan and Uzbekistan are considered in the chapter on Countries in Transition.

ASSOCIATION FOR SOUTH-EAST ASIAN NATIONS (ASEAN)

A Co-operation Agreement was signed in 1980 between the Community and the ASEAN member countries.[2] It was intended to strengthen regional integration[3]

---

1 The Community has no diplomatic relations with North Korea or Taiwan. As to North Korea, see European Parliament, Resolution on the Community's Trade Relations with North Korea, OJ 17.2.86 C36/203; Written Question No 442/91 by Michael Hindley, 11.3.91, and Answer given by Mr Andriessen on behalf of the Commission, 18.4.91, OJ 27.6.91 C168/25; Written Question E-552/94 by Sotiris Kostopoulos, 15.3.94, and Answer given by Mr Van den Broek on behalf of the Commission, 4.5.94 OJ 19.12.94 C362/36. As to textile quotas, see Commission Regulation 1457/97, OJ 26.7.97 L199/6.
2 OJ 10.6.80 L1444/2. The ASEAN member countries then were Indonesia, Malaysia, the Philippines, Singapore, and Thailand. In 1985 a Protocol extended the Co-operation Agreement to Brunei-Darussalam: OJ 23.3.85 L81/2. As to the future of relations between the Community and ASEAN, see Commission of the European Communities, 'Creating a New Dynamic in EU-ASEAN Relations' (Communication from the Commission to the Council, the European Parliament, and the Economic and Social Committee), COM(96)0314, Brussels, 3.7.96. The Community also participates in the ASEM process, the informal political dialogue which began in March 1996 between the ASEAN, China, Japan, the Republic of Korea, and the EU. As to the Commission 1997 working paper on the future of the ASEM process, see *Agence Europe* No 7040 (n.s.), Thursday 21 August 1997, p 4. As to rules of origin in respect of regional groupings, see Commission Regulation 2454/93 Art 70, OJ 11.10.93 L253/1, as amended by Commission Regulation 3254/94, OJ 21.12.94 L346/1. Council Decision 96/723 (OJ 19.12.96 L329/45) grants a Community guarantee to the European Investment Bank against losses under loans for projects of mutual interest in Latin American and Asian countries with which the Community has concluded co-operation agreements.
3 Ibid Preamble, second recital.

and consolidate and diversify commercial and economic relations.[4] The parties were conscious that the co-operation was between equal partners but would necessarily take account of the level of development of the ASEAN member countries and the emergence of ASEAN as a viable and cohesive grouping.[5] The Agreement provided for MFN treatment, commercial co-operation, economic co-operation, development co-operation, and the establishment of a Joint Co-operation Committee.[6] It also provided that the provisions of the Agreement shall be substituted for provisions of Agreements concluded between Member States of the Community and the individual ASEAN member countries to the extent to which the latter are either incompatible with or identical to the former.[7]

The parties are to accord each other MFN treatment in accordance with the provisions of the GATT, without prejudice however to the Protocol attached to the Agreement.[8] According to the Protocol, any party which is not a GATT member is bound by the MFN obligations.[9] These obligations do not apply, however, to advantages granted in respect of border trade with neighbouring countries, advantages within the framework of customs unions or free trade areas, advantages granted to particular countries in conformity with the GATT, advantages which ASEAN countries grant to certain countries in accordance with the Protocol on Trade Negotiations among Developing Countries in the context of the GATT, and advantages granted or to be granted within the framework of ASEAN provided they do not exceed those that are granted or may be granted within the framework of ASEAN by ASEAN member countries which are parties to the GATT.[10]

In respect of trade the parties agree to study ways and means of overcoming trade barriers, in particular non-tariff and quasi-tariff barriers.[11] A number of other forms of co-operation are provided. They include the use of best endeavours to grant each other the widest facilities for commercial transactions,[12] bringing together economic operators in the two regions with the aim of creating new trade patterns,[13] and studying and recommending trade promotion measures likely to encourage the expansion of imports and exports.[14]

In respect of economic co-operation, among other measures the parties undertake to improve the existing favourable investment climate inter alia through encouraging the extension, by and to all Community Member States and by and to all ASEA member countries, of investment promotion and protection arrangements which endeavour to apply the principle of non-discrimination, aim to ensure fair and equitable treatment, and reflect the principle of reciprocity.[15]

---

4 Ibid Preamble, third recital.
5 Ibid Preamble, fifth recital.
6 As to the Joint Co-operation Committee, see the Agreement Art 5.
7 Ibid Art 6. This does not however affect the powers of any of the Community's Member States to undertake bilateral activities within any ASEAN member countries in the field of economic co-operation and to conclude, where necessary, new economic co-operation agreements with those countries: Art 3(3).
8 Ibid Art 1.
9 Protocol concerning Art 1 of the Agreement, paragraph 1.
10 Ibid, paragraph 2.
11 Ibid Art 2(2).
12 Ibid Art 2(3)(b).
13 Ibid Art 2(3)d).
14 Ibid Art 2(3)(e).
15 Ibid Art 3(2), second paragraph.

SOUTH ASIAN ASSOCIATION FOR REGIONAL CO-OPERATION (SAARC)

The South Asian Association for Regional Co-operation (SAARC) consists of Bangladesh, Bhutan, India, the Maldives, Nepal, Pakistan, and Sri Lanka. An administrative co-operation agreement in the form of a Memorandum of Understanding (MOU) was signed between the European Commission and the SARC in July 1996. It provides for the exchange of information, institutional support and training, and technical assistance.[16]

BANGLADESH

A Commercial Co-operation Agreement was signed in 1976 between the Community and the People's Republic of Bangladesh.[17] It provided for MFN treatment in accordance with the GATT.[18] Each party was to grant the other the highest degree of liberalization of imports and exports which it applied to third countries in general.[19] In addition, the Community declared its willingness to bind unilaterally the tariff-free status of certain products, including certain freshwater fish, tea,[20] and specified types of leather.[1] Provision was made for trade promotion, the development of economic co-operation, and an increase in co-operation in commercial and related matters in third countries.[2] The Agreement included a substitution clause.[3] A Joint Commission was established to ensure the proper functioning of the Agreement.[4]

In 1986 the Community and Bangladesh signed an Agreement on trade in textile products.[5] Textile products of cotton, wool and man-made fibres[6] originating in Bangladesh and imported into the Community were to be free from quantitative limits, which could however be introduced.[7] If such limits were introduced, a double-checking system was to apply.[8] These limits did not apply to inward processing,[9] outward processing[10] or cottage-industry or handicraft

---

16 Memorandum of Understanding on Administrative Co-operation between the European Commission and the South Asian Association for Regional Co-operation, signed in Brussels on 10 July 1996. See also *Agence Europe*, No 6769 (n.s.), Friday 12 July 1996, p 8.
17 OJ 19.11.76 L319/2.
18 Ibid Art 2.
19 Ibid Art 3.
20 Other than in packages of a net capacity not exceeding 3 kg, which was proposed to be bound at 5%.
 1 Ibid. Annex II.
 2 See ibid Arts 4–7.
 3 Ibid Art 12.
 4 See ibid Arts 8–11 and Annex I.
 5 OJ 19.8.87, amended by Exchange of Letters in 1992 (OJ 31.12.92 L405/45) and in 1995 (OJ 26.4.95 L94/24). This Agreement and the other bilateral agreements between the Community and specific countries in respect of trade in textiles were concluded within the framework of the Multi-Fibre Arrangement (MFA). As to the MFA and general rules in respect of textiles, see Chapter 18 on Textiles in this book.
 6 Listed in the Annex.
 7 Ibid Art 3(1). As to the conditions for the introduction of quantitative limits, see Art 8. As to the establishment of such limits on a regional basis, see Art 8(6) and Protocol C. As to annual growth rates, see Art 8(7) and Protocol D.
 8 Ibid Art 3(2). As to obligations in respect of information in this case, see Art 9. For part of 1992 a double-checking system was introduced for certain products in order to prevent fraud and circumvention: see Agreement in the form of Exchange of Letters, OJ 31.12.95 L405/45.
 9 Ibid Art 6.
10 Ibid Art 4.

products.[11] Provision was also made for advance use, carryover and transfers.[12] A circumvention clause[13] and an anti-concentration clause[14] were included. Provision was also made for a consultation procedure.[15]

CAMBODIA

A Framework Co-operation Agreement between the Community and Cambodia was signed on 29 April 1997.[16] Respect for the democratic principles and fundamental human rights established by the Universal Declaration of Human Rights constitutes an essential element of the Agreement.[17] The main objective of the Agreement is to provide a framework for enhanced co-operation,[18] aiming inter alia at according MFN treatment on trade in goods in all areas specifically covered by the Agreement[19] and promoting and intensifying trade between the parties.[20] The Agreement provides for co-operation in numerous fields, including trade. In respect of trade, MFN treatment is to apply in all matters regarding customs duties and all charges;[1] customs clearance, transit, warehousing and transhipment;[2] taxes and other internal charges levied directly or indirectly on imports or exports;[3] and administrative formalities for the issue of import or export licences.[4] The parties are to seek ways of establishing co-operation in the field of maritime transport[5] and of improving customs co-operation.[6] Cambodia shall improve conditions for the adequate and effective protection and enforcement of intellectual property rights in conformity with the highest international standards.[7] A Joint Committee is established to oversee the operation of the Agreement.[8]

---

11 Ibid Art 5, provided the products meet the conditions laid down in Protocol B.
12 Ibid Art 7
13 Ibid Art 11.
14 Ibid Art 12.
15 Ibid Art 16.
16 Co-operation Agreement between the European Community and Cambodia, OJ 5.4.97 C107/7; see also Proposal for a Council Decision concerning the conclusion of the Co-operation Agreement between the European Community and the Kingdom of Cambodia (97/C104/04), COM(97)78 final—97/0060(CNS) (Submitted by the Commission on 4 March 1997), OJ 5.4.97 C107/6. The Agreement is valid for five years, following which it is renewed automatically from year to year unless denounced by a party six months before its expiry date: ibid Art 21(2).
17 Ibid Art 1. Violation of this provision constitutes a material breach of the Agreement, in which case a party may take appropriate measures without being obliged beforehand to supply the Joint Committee with all relevant information required for a thorough examination of the situation with a view to seeking a solution acceptable to the parties. In this case the other party may avail itself of the procedure relating to the settlement of disputes: see ibid Art 19, and Annex I: Declaration on Art 19—Non-execution of the Agreement. The Annexes form an integral part of the Agreement: ibid Art 20.
18 Ibid Art 2.
19 Ibid Art 2(a), which also sets out the exceptions.
20 Ibid Art 2(b).
1 Ibid Art 4(2)(a).
2 Ibid Art 4(2)(b).
3 Ibid Art 4(2)(c).
4 Ibid Art 4(2)(d).
5 Ibid Art 4(3)(a).
6 Ibid Art 4(3)(b).
7 Ibid Art 4(5), which also provides that, to this end, Cambodia is to accede to the relevant international conventions to which it is not a party. See also Annex II: Joint Declaration on intellectual, industrial and commercial property.
8 Ibid Art 14.

PEOPLE'S REPUBLIC OF CHINA

An Agreement on Trade and Economic Co-operation was concluded between the Community and China in 1985.[9] It provided for co-operation in trade and economic matters and the establishment of a Joint Committee to oversee the operation of the Agreement.[10] The Agreement was concluded for a period of five years, with tacit renewal from year to year unless it was denounced by either party six months before the date of expiry.[11]

In respect of trade, the Agreement includes an MFN clause.[12] This is subject to exceptions in respect of customs unions or free trade areas, border trade with neighbouring countries, and measures taken to meet obligations under international commodity agreements.[13] A balance of trade clause provides that the parties will make every effort to help, each by its own means, to attain a balance in their reciprocal trade.[14] China is to give favourable consideration to imports from the Community.[15] The Community is to strive for an increasing liberalization of imports from China.[16] Trade in goods and the provision of services is to be effected at market-related prices and rates.[17] Payments for transactions are to be made, in accordance with existing laws and regulations, in currencies of the Community's Member States, Renminbi or any convertible currency accepted by the two parties concerned in the transactions.[18]

The parties are to exchange information on any problems which may arise and to open friendly consultations, with the intention of promoting trade, in order to seek mutually satisfactory solutions. Each of the parties is to ensure that no action is taken before consultations are held.[19] In an exceptional case, however, where the situation does not admit any delay, either party may take measures but must endeavour so far as possible to hold friendly consultations before doing so.[20]

---

9 OJ 19.9.85 L250/1. This Agreement replaced the 1978 Trade Agreement (OJ 11.5.78 L123/1): see 1985 Agreement Art 17. As to Community policy toward China, see Commission of the European Communities 'A Long-Term Policy for China-Europe Relations' (Communication from the Commission, Brussels, 5.7.95), COM(95)279 final; Commission of the European Communities, 'Building a Comprehensive Partnership with China' (Communication from the Commission) (COM(1998)181 final, Brussels 25.3.98). For a recent survey of relevant Community law, see Snyder 'Legal Aspects of Trade between the European Union and China: Preliminary Reflections' in N Emiliou and D O'Keeffe (eds) *The European Union and World Trade Law after the GATT Uruguay Round* (Wiley, 1996), pp 363–377.

10 Ibid Arts 2–9 (trade co-operation), 10–14 (economic co-operation), 15 (joint committee).

11 Ibid Art 18.

12 Ibid Art 3(1).

13 Ibid Art 3(2).

14 Ibid Art 4, first paragraph. If an obvious imbalance arises, the matter must be examined within the Joint Committee: Art 4, second paragraph.

15 Ibid Art 5(1), which also provide that, to this end, the competent Chinese authorities will ensure that Community exporters have the possibility of participating fully in opportunities for trade with China.

16 Ibid Art 5(2), which also provides that, to this end, the Community will endeavour progressively to introduce measures extending the list of products for which imports from China have been liberalized and to increase the amounts of quotas. The Joint Committee is to examine the procedure for implementation.

17 Ibid Art 8.

18 Ibid Art 9.

19 Ibid Art 6(1).

20 Ibid Art 6(2). When such measures are taken, the parties are required to ensure that the general objectives of the Agreement are not prejudiced: Art 6(3).

Provision is also made for the promotion of visits, exchanges and contracts in respect of trade and industry.[1]

The Agreement also provides that it does not affect the powers of the EC Member States to undertake bilateral activities with China in the field of economic co-operation and to conclude, where appropriate, new economic co-operation agreements with China.[2]

In addition to this general Agreement, a number of more specific Community rules govern trade between the Community and China, at least so far as Community law is concerned. Imports into the Community from China are governed by a single regulation,[3] with the exception of textiles to which special rules apply.[4] This Regulation applies to all countries considered by the Community to be State-trading countries.[5]

As to textiles, a bilateral Agreement on trade in textile products was concluded within the MFA between the Community and China in 1988.[6] As

---

1 Ibid Art 7.
2 Ibid Art 14.
3 Council Regulation 519/94 on common rules for imports from certain third countries, OJ 10.3.94 L67/89. As to this Regulation, see Chapter 8 on Imports in this book. As to quota administration, see Chapter 11 on Administration of Quotas in this book. As to the operation of quotas and surveillance measures on such imports from China, see most recently Commission of the European Communities '3rd Report from the Commission on the quantitative quotas and surveillance measures applicable to certain non-textile products originating in the People's Republic of China' COM(1998)128 final, Brussels, 9.3.98. As of 1 January 1998, the quota on certain glass tableware from China is abolished, parts and accessories of toys are henceforth excluded from quota, and surveillance measures on a range of products are removed: see Council Regulation 847/97, OJ 14.5.97 L122/1. As to the redistribution of used portions of the 1996 quotas for certain products, see Commission Regulation 728/97, OJ 25.4.97 L108/19. As to administrative procedures for 1998 quotas for certain products, see Commission Regulation 1393/97, OJ 19.7.97 L190/24. As to agricultural products, see Chapter 16 on Agricultural Products in this book. As to garlic from China, imports are limited as to quantity and a licence was required from 1 June 1996 to 31 May 1997: see Commission Regulation 885/96, OJ 16.5.96 L119/12. As to quotas in respect of footware, tableware, cereamics, and toys, see Commission Regulation 2012/97, OJ 16.10.97 L284/42 (1998 quotas) and Commission Regulation 786/98, OJ 15.4.98 L113/17 (redistribution of unused portion of 1997 quotas). As to the administration of this unused portion, see 'Note to Community importers of certain products originating in the People's Republic of China subject to quantitative quotas' (98/C116/07), OJ 16.4.98 C116/5. As to protective measures in respect of certain fishery products, see Commission Decision 97/620, OJ 17.9.97 L254/17.
4 As to textiles, see below.
5 Ibid Art 1. The countries originally listed in Annex I were as follows: Albania, Armenia, Azerbaijan, Belarus, People's Republic of China, Estonia, Georgia, Kazakhstan, North Korea, Krygyzstan, Lavtia, Lithuania, Moldova, Mongolia, Russia, Tajikstan, Turkmenistan, Ukraine, Uzbekistan, and Vietnam. Estonia, Latvia, and Lithuania have since been removed from the list: Council Regulation 839/95, OJ 19.4.95 L85/9. China and Russia remain on the list of these certain third countries for the purpose of the common rules on imports. The list is not affected by the recent revision of Community anti-dumping practice in respect of China and Russia as expressed in Council Regulation 905/98, OJ 30.4.98 L128/18, which amends only the basic anti-dumping Council Regulation 384/96, OJ 6.3.96 L56/1, as amended. As to quantitative quotas for all products except Annex II products and other products, such as textiles, that are subject to specific common import or export arrangements laying down special provisions for quota adminstration, see Council Regulation 520/94, OJ 10.3.94 L66/1. This Regulation is discussed in Chapter 11 on the Adminstration of Quotas. As to quota-free imports into the Canary Islands of textile and clothing products and certain other products from China, see Commission Regulation 1087/97, OJ 17.6.97 L158/1.
6 OJ 31.12.88 L380/2, attached to Council Decision 88/656 (OJ 31.12.88 L380/1) which provided that the Agreement should be applied on a provisional basis. As to definitive approval of the Agreement, see Council Decision 90/647, OJ 15.12.90 L352/1 (with Agreement attached, OJ 15.12.90 L352/2). The Agreement was amended by Agreements in the form of exchange of

recently amended, it applies until the end of 1998.[7] In respect of certain textile products trade between the parties is liberalized subject to certain conditions.[8] As to these products, Community quantitative restrictions then in force are suspended,[9] a standstill clause applies,[10] and measures equivalent to quantitative restrictions are prohibited.[11] However, in respect of specified products China agrees to establish and maintain quantitative limits for its exports to the Community.[12] Within these limits, China undertakes to reserve a specified proportion of its textile exports for use by Community industry.[13] The quantitative limits do not apply to inward processing,[14] outward processing[15] or handicraft

letters in 1992 (OJ 31.1293 L410/103), in 1995 (OJ 26.4.95 L94/107), and in 1996 (OJ 30.3.96 L81/318); and certain provisions, notably in respect of growth rates for quantitative limits and flexibility rates, were modified by Agreement in 1995 and again in 1996 in view of China's eventual accession to the WTO (OJ 31.10.95 L261/2; OJ 30.3.96 L81/318). The 1995 modifying Agreement provided that the modified rates would be the basis of all notifications to the WTO (see paragraph b), that these modified rates would remain suspended until China's accession to GATT/WTO (see paragraph c), and that, should China's accession to GATT/WTO not be completed during the first nine months of 1995, consultations would be held to discuss the terms of a new bilateral textiles agreement for 1996 and subsequent years (see paragraph d). The 1996 Agreement provided that, if China became a member of the WTO before expiry of the Agreement, the restrictions in force would be phased out within the framework of the WTO (paragraph 3). China is not yet (at the time of writing) a member of the WTO, so it must be presumed that the trade in textiles between the Community and China remains governed by the 1988 Agreement, as amended and modified.

7 The 1988 Agreement replaced the 1979 Textile Agreement (OJ 31.12.86 L389/2) and the 1984 Supplementary Protocol (OJ 31.12.86 L389/60). It was originally stated to apply until 31 December 1992 (see Art 20) and then continued to be applied on a provisional basis pending the formal conclusion of a subsequent agreement: see Council Decision 92/625, OJ 31.12.92 L410/1. In 1992 an Agreement in the form of exchange of letters (OJ 31.12.92 L410/103) provided that the 1988 Agreement would be automatically extended until 31 December 1995. It also provided that, if the Uruguay Round Agreement on Textiles and Clothing (ATC) were concluded and entered into force earlier, the 1998 Agreement would be automatically terminated as of the date for the ATC's entry into force (see also 1996 Agreement in the form of exchange of letters amending the 1988 Agreement, OJ 30.3.96 L81/318). The 1996 Agreement in the form of exchange of letters extended the 1988 Agreement from 1 January 1996 until 31 December 1998 (1988 Agreement Art 20, first paragraph, as substituted by 1996 Agreement Art 2(3), OJ 30.3.96 L81/318).

8 1988 Agreement Art 2(1). The products are listed in Annex I, as substituted in 1996 by Appendix 1 to the Agreement in the form of exchange of letters, OJ 30.3.96 L81/319. They are mainly products made exclusively of wool, fine hair, cotton or man-made fibres: see 1996 Agreement, Annex I, first paragraph. Certain other textile products, which are listed in Annex II, are covered by the Agreement only for the purposes of application of the provisions making explicit reference to that Annex: Art 2(2). Imports of these latter products are currently regulated by the 1995 Agreement on trade in textile products not covered by the MFA bilateral agreement on trade in textile products (OJ 6.5.95 L104/2), as to which see below.

9 Ibid Art 2(3).

10 Ibid Art 2(3).

11 Ibid Art 2(4).

12 Ibid Art 3(1). The products and limits are set out in Annex III. Such exports are subject to a double-checking system, specified in Protocol A.

13 Ibid Art 3(2). As to the procedure, see Art 3(3).

14 Ibid Art 4(1), first paragraph, which also provides for certain conditions. However, release for home use in the Community is subject to the production of an export licence issued by China and to proof of origin in accordance with Protocol A: Art 4(1), second paragraph.

15 Ibid Art 4(4), which also provides for certain conditions, including the arrangements laid down in Protocol E. See also Commission Regulation 1280/95, OJ 7.6.95 L124/27, which re-established quantitative limits for certain products after outward processing. As to quantitative limits in 1997 and 1998 for certain textiles for outward processing, see Commission Regulation 1445(97), PJ 25.7.97 L198/1.

products.[16] Provision is made for advance use, carryover, and transfers.[17] Other textile products may be subject to quantitative limits.[18] Provision is made for anti-circumvention measures.[19] Consultation may be requested in the event of a sudden and prejudicial change in traditional trade flows.[20] China undertook to ensure that the supply of raw materials to Community industry was at conditions not less favourable than to Chinese domestic users.[1] It also undertook to take such measures as are required to make possible the export of minimum annual quantities of silk, angora and cashmere.[2]

With regard to imports into China, in return for increased opportunities to export into the Community China is to encourage and facilitate the importation on its market of certain Community textile products.[3] The parties also agree, within the framework of their respective laws, rules and policies, to promote and encourage greater and mutually beneficial foreign investment.[4] In addition, they undertake to improve the investment climate, in particular by encouraging the extension of investment promotion and protection arrangements based on the principles of equity and reciprocity.[5]

The Agreement includes a provision in respect of intellectual property rights. Pending the entry into force of Chinese legislation, consultations are to be held at the request of either party for the purpose of finding an equitable solution in any dispute relating to the protection of marks, designs or models of articles of apparel and textile products.[6]

16 Ibid Art 4(3), which also provides for certain conditions laid down in Protocol B.

17 See Art 5, as substituted in 1996 by Agreement in the form of exchange of letters (OJ 30.3.96 L81/318).

18 Ibid Art 6(1). The products are those listed in Annex I (that is, covered by the Agreement: see Art 2(1)), but not listed in Annex III (which remain subject to annual quantitative restrictions: see Art 3(1)). As to conditions and procedures, see Art 6(2)–(11). For example, a provisional quota was imposed on nets and netting from China in 1994: see Commission Regulation 469/94, OJ 3.3.94 L59/3. Nets and netting are included in Annex I of the Agreement but not in Annex III. These safeguard measures were adopted on the basis of Art 10 of Council Regulation 3030/93 on common rules for imports of certain textile products from third countries (OJ 8.11.93 L275/1). Until 1992 quantitative limits could be established by the Community on a regional basis in accordance with Protocol C (see Art 6(6)) and unused quantities could be reallocated between regions (see Art 10). In the 1992 amending Agreement (OJ 31.1292 L410/103) this was replaced by co-operation to avoid sudden changes in trade flows, monitoring and consultations, and the use of best endeavours to avoid seasonal concentration. The annual growth for quantitative limits is to be determined in accordance with Protocol D: Art 6(7). In 1997 the quota on reimports of certain textile products from China was increased, and Annex VII to Regulation 3030/93 was amended accordingly: see Commission Regulation 1445/97, OJ 25.7.97 L198/1.

19 See Art 7. See also Commission Regulation 560/95, OJ 15.3.95 L57/53.

20 Ibid Art 8(3), as substituted by Agreement in the form of exchange of letters in 1992 (OJ 31.12.92 L410/103).

1 Ibid Art 11, as substituted in 1996 by Agreement in the form of exchange of letters (OJ 30.3.96 L81/318).

2 Ibid Art 11(1), as substituted in 1966 by Agreement in the form of exchange of letters (OJ 30.3.96 L81/318). The products and quantities are listed in Annex IV. As to procedures, see Art 11 as so substituted.

3 Ibid Art 12(1). The products are listed in Annexes I and II. In particular, China is to take the measures necessary to avoid exacerbating and, if possible, to reduce the disequilibrium in its trade balance with the Community: Art 12(1)). In addition, where a need for additional supplies arises on the Chinese market, preference is to be given to Community imports meeting certain conditions: Art 12(2). As to consultations in this respect, see Art 13(2).

4 Ibid Art 12(1).

5 Ibid Art 12(2).

6 Ibid Art 18. As to the procedure, see Art 16.

A Textile Committee is set up to deal with matters arising under the Agreement.[7]

This 1988 bilateral Agreement, however, does not cover trade in certain other textiles.[8] Until January 1995 these products were governed instead by common rules enacted by the Community in 1994.[9] They were subject to annual quotas.[10] The entry of these products into free circulation in the Community was subject to an import authorization.[11] Provision was made for information and investigation procedures[12] and surveillance and safeguard measures.[13] Recently, however, a new Agreement was concluded between the Community and China with regard to these other products, in particular silk and linen.[14] Taken together, the 1988 bilateral Agreement and the new Agreement cover all trade in textiles between the Community and China.

The new Agreement applied from 1 January 1995 for a period of two years, with automatic extension for successive periods of one year unless either party gives notice at least six months in advance that it does not agree with the extension.[15] In respect of these products, the Community is to suspend

7 Ibid Art 16.
8 1988 Agreement Art 2(2), which states that the 1988 Agreement does not cover imports of textile products listed in Annex II to the Agreement.
9 Council Regulation 517/94, OJ 10.3.94 94 L67/1. The products are listed in Annex I. In respect of textiles this Regulation replaced Council Regulation 288/82 on common rules for imports (OJ 9.2.82 L35/1, as amended), Council Regulation 1765/82 on common rules for imports from State-trading countries (OJ 5.7.82 L195/1, as amended) (which did not however apply to China), Council Regulation 1766/82 on common rules for imports from the People's Republic of China (OJ 5.7.82 L195/21, as amended) and Council Regulation 3420/83 on import arrangements for products originating in State-trading countries, not liberalized at Community level (OJ 8.12.83 L346/6, as amended): Art 27(1). Tariff quotas have been opened, and Annexes IV and V of Council Regulation 517/94 have been amended, by Commission Regulation 1756/94 (OJ 19.7.94 L183/9), Commission Regulation 2612/94 (OJ 29.10.94 L279/7) and Commission Regulation 2980/94 (OJ 8.12.94 L315/2). Other provisions were amended, and a Community import licence established, by Commission Regulation 3168/94, OJ 23.12.94 L335/23, as amended. See generally Chapter 18 on Textiles in this book.
10 Ibid Art 2(1), third and fourth indents; Art 3. As to decision-making procedures, see Arts 3(3), 25, Annex IV. For an example, see Commission Regulation 2980/94, OJ 8.12.94 L315/2. As to the management and distribution of 1996 quotas, see Commission Regulation 2738/95, OJ 29.11.95 L285/5.
11 As to the management of Community import restrictions, see ibid Arts 17–24.
12 Ibid Arts 6–19.
13 Ibid Arts 11–16.
14 Agreement on trade in textile products not covered by the MFA bilateral Agreement, OJ 6.5.95 L104/2, as applied provisionally by Council Decision 95/155, OJ 6.5.95 L104/1. The products covered are the textile raw materials and textile products listed in Annex I: Art 1(1). They include textile raw materials (categories 128 and 154), textile products other than those of wool and fine animal hair, cotton and man-made fibres, as well as man-made fibres and filaments and yarns of categories 124, 125A, 125B, 126, 127A and 127B: Agreement, Annex I, Art 1. The basic provisions of the Agreement are similar to those in the Agreement between the Community and Hong Kong, as to which see below. The origin of the products is to be determined in accordance with the rules in force in the Community, and the procedures for the control of origin are laid down in Protocol A: Art 2(2). In December 1996 the Commission issued a Notice to Operators emphasising the provisions of Art 20 of Council Regulation 3030/93 on common rules for imports of certain textile products from third countries. (OJ 8.11.93 L275/1). This Article provides that Council Regulation 3030/90 does not constitute in any way a derogation from the provisions of bilateral agreements, protocols or arrangements on textile trade which the Community has concluded with third countries and which prevail in all cases of conflict. See Notice to Operators (96/C387/04), Agreement between the European Community and the People's Republic of China on trade in textile products not covered by the MFA bilateral Agreement on trade in textile products, OJ 21.12.96 L387/4.
15 Ibid Art 17(1). In addition, the restrictions are to be phased out if China becomes a member of the WTO: Art 17(2).

quantitative restrictions in force and not introduce others, except as provided in the Agreement.[16] Measures having an effect equivalent to quantitative restrictions are prohibited in respect of imports into the Community.[17]

China is to establish and maintain annual quantitative limits on specified products, exports of which are subject to double-checking.[18] In administering these limits, China is to ensure that the Community textile industry benefits from the use of these limits.[19] In particular, 23 per cent of the quantitative limit for specified products for 90 days each year is to be reserved for users belonging to the Community textile industry.[20] China is also required to ensure that the supply to the Community industry of raw materials[1] is made at conditions not less favourable than to Chinese domestic users.[2] The quantitative limits do not apply to products declared to be for re-export[3] or to products re-imported after outward processing in China.[4] Provision is made for consultations, at the Community's request, in the event of a sudden and prejudicial change in traditional trade flows.[5] Provision is also made to try to ensure that Chinese textile exports are evenly spaced over the year.[6] Certain requirements as to the provision of information in respect of export licences, import authorizations and import statistics have been agreed by the parties.[7]

Chinese exports of other textile products[8] may be made subject to quantitative limits in specified circumstances,[9] in particular if such exports reach a predetermined proportion of the total Community imports from all sources of products in that category.[10] In this event the Community is entitled to request consultations[11]

---

16 Ibid Art 1(2). As to quantitative limits for 1997, see Commission Regulation 152/97, OJ 29.1.97 L26/8.
17 Ibid Art 1(3), which further states that this is without prejudice to anti-dumping and countervailing measures.
18 Ibid Art 34(1). The products and quantitative limits are set out in Annex II, which in turn refers to the produce descriptions set out in Annex I. The double-checking system is specified in Protocol A.
19 Ibid Art 3(2), first paragraph.
20 Ibid Art 3(2), second paragraph. As to implementation of these provisions, see Art 3(2), third paragraph.
1 The CN codes and the descriptions of the products are as follows:5002 00 raw silk; 5003 10 and 5003 90 silk waste; 5004 00 silk yarn; 5005 00 yarn spun from silk waste; 5007 20 11, 5007 20 21 and 5007 20 51 silk fabrics, containing at least 85% silk; and 5007 90 10 other fabrics: Annex to the Protocol of Understanding concerning the Implementation of Art 12 of the Agreement.
2 Ibid Art 12. It is understood by both parties that, if exports of such raw materials are made subject to specific measures, practices or policies (such as licences, guidances, fiscal, custom or others), these measures, practices or policies must not have for consequence that the conditions applying to the Community users become less favourable than those applied to users in China notably in terms of actual access or prices. Consequently China is to abstain from any such measures, practices or policies that may result in double pricing. If problems arise, consultations are to be held without delay: Protocol of Understanding concerning the Implementation of Art 12 of the Agreement.
3 Ibid Art 4(1), first paragraph. As to conditions for this exemption, see Art 4(1), second paragraph. As to compensation for re-exported products set off against a quantitative limit, see Art 4(2).
4 Ibid Art 11.
5 Ibid Art 5(1).
6 Ibid Art 5(2).
7 See ibid Art 6.
8 That is, those covered by the Agreement but not included in Annex II (and therefore not automatically subject to quantitative limits *ex* Art 3(1) of the Agreement).
9 Ibid Art 7(1).
10 See ibid Art 7(2), first paragraph.
11 The procedure is laid down in Art 14.

with a view to reaching agreement on an appropriate restraint level.[12] China has undertaken to limit exports of the product for a provisional period of three months pending a mutually satisfactory solution.[13] If the parties cannot reach such a solution within approximately two months,[14] the Community has the right to introduce a definitive quantitative limit.[15]

The Agreement also provides for advance use, carryover and transfers,[16] as well as for anti-circumvention measures.[17]

In respect of intellectual property, the Agreement provides that China will ensure the respect of intellectual property rights on marks, designs and models belonging to Community exports.[18]

HONG KONG

The Basic Law of the Hong Kong Special Administrative Region of the People's Republic of China took effect as of 1 July 1997.[19] It provides, inter alia, that the Hong Kong Special Administrative Region (SAR) will be a separate customs territory.[20] Using the name 'Hong Kong, China', it may participate in relevant international organizations and international trade agreements (including preferential trade agreements), such as the GATT and arrangements regarding international trade in textiles.[1] Export quotas, tariff preferences and other similar arrangements, which are obtained or made by the Hong Kong SAR, or which were obtained or made and remain valid, are to be enjoyed exclusively by the Region.[2] The Hong Kong SAR may issue its own certificates of origin in accordance with prevailing rules of origin.[3] The application to the Hong Kong SAR of international agreements to which China is a party will be decided by the Central People's Government.[4] However, international agreements to which China is not a party but which are implemented in Hong Kong may continue to be implemented in the Hong Kong SAR.[5] Pending any future changes, therefore, the following paragraphs describe the current trade relations between the Community and Hong Kong.

An Agreement on trade in textile products was signed in 1986 between the

---

12 Ibid Art 7(2), first paragraph.
13 Ibid Art 7(3).
14 The time period is laid down in Art 14(1).
15 Ibid Art 7(4), first paragraph, which also provides for the level of the limit. The level may be revised upwards after consultations: Art 7(4), second paragraph. As to the level of the limit, see further Art 7(5),(6).
16 See ibid Art 8.
17 Ibid Art 9.
18 Ibid Art 13, which also provides that if problems arise, consultations are to be held, at the request of either party, for the purpose of finding an equitable solution to any dispute relating to the protection of intellectual property rights on products covered by the Agreement.
19 See 'People's Republic of China: The Basic Law of the Hong Kong Special Administrative Region of the People's Republic of China' (1990) 29 ILM 1551. As to EU policy, see Commission of the European Communities 'The European Union and Hong Kong: Beyond 1997' (Communication from the Commission to the Council) COM(97)171 final, Brussels, 23.4.97.
20 Basic Law Art 116, first paragraph.
 1 Ibid Art 116, second paragraph.
 2 Ibid Art 116, third paragraph.
 3 Ibid Art 117.
 4 Ibid Art 153, first paragraph.
 5 Ibid Art 153, second paragraph.

Community and Hong Kong.[6] Hong Kong agreed to restrain its exports of specified products,[7] which were also subject to a double-checking system.[8] The limits did not apply to inward processing[9] or outward processing.[10] Provision is made for advance use, carryover and transfers.[11] Exports of textile products which are not subject to quantitative limits are subject to the issue of export authorizations,[12] but the Community was entitled to request consultations with a view to establishing a quantitative limit.[13] Provision is made for anti-circumvention measures[14] and anti-concentration measures.[15]

Following the accession of Austria, Finland and Sweden to the Community, and with a view to the application of the Uruguay Round Agreement on Textiles and Clothing, the parties agreed in 1995 on the notional quantitative restrictions to be considered for the purposes of notification to the Textiles Surveillance Body.[16]

INDIA

A Co-operation Agreement between the Community and India was concluded in 1994.[17] Its principal objective is to enhance and develop various aspects of co-operation between the parties.[18] The Agreement states that respect for human rights and democratic principles is the basis for this co-operation and the Agreement, and that such respect is an essential element of the Agreement.[19] It contains provisions in respect of MFN treatment,[20] trade and commercial co-operation, economic co-operation, industry and services, the private sector, energy, telecommunications, electronics and information and satellite technologies, standards,

6 OJ 14.4.88 L97/2, as amended by Agreed Minute in 1988 (OJ 29.9.88 L269/57) and by Exchange of Letters in 1992 (OJ 31.12.92 L410/2), 1993 (OJ 30.4.94 L110/2) and in 1995 (OJ 26.4.95 L94/155). As to the products covered, see Annex I. This Agreement replaced an earlier Agreement (OJ 31.12.86 L388/2) which applied from 1 January 1983 to 31 December 1986. See also Commission Regulation 152/97 Art 1, OJ 29.1.97 L26/8.

7 Ibid Art 3, first paragraph. As to products and limits, see Annex II, as modified by Agreed Minutes in 1988 (OJ 28.9.88 L269/57; OJ 31.12.88 L382/45) and 1989 (OJ 4.19,89 L286/21). Regional shares were previously allowed (see Art 12(1)) but are now prohibited by Agreement in the form of Exchange of Letters in 1992 (OJ 31.12.92 L410/2).

8 Ibid Art 3, second paragraph. As to the double-checking system, see Protocol A.

9 Ibid Art 5, which also establishes the conditions for this exemption.

10 Ibid Art 4.

11 Ibid Art 6.

12 See Art 7. These products are those included in Annex I but not in Annex II.

13 Ibid Art 7(3). As to the procedure, see Art 14(1). As to the conditions for invoking consultations, see Art 7(8),(9). As to information requirements for textiles subject to quantitative limits established under the Agreement, see Art 8.

14 Ibid Art 10.

15 Ibid Art 11.

16 Agreement in the form of Exchange of Letters, OJ 26.4.95 L155. As to the ATC, see Chapter 18 on Textiles in this book.

17 OJ 27.8.94 L223/24. This Agreement was signed on 20 December 1993 and the exchange of instruments took place on 26 July 1994. It entered into force on 1 August 1994. It built upon and replaced the first Agreement between India and the Community signed on 17 December 1973 (OJ 23.3.74 L82/2) and the Agreement on Commercial and Economic Co-operation signed on 23 June 1981 (OJ 27.3.74 L82/2): see Art 29, first paragraph. As to a challenge to the use of EC Art 130y as the legal basis for this Agreement, see Case C-268/94 *Portugal v Council* [1996] ECR I-6177.

18 Agreement Art 1(2).

19 Ibid Art 1(1).

20 Ibid Art 2.

intellectual property, investment, agriculture and fisheries, tourism, science and technology, information and culture, development co-operation, the environment, human resource development, drug abuse control, north-south and regional co-operation, and financial and institutional matters. The Joint Commission set up under the 1981 Agreement is retained.[1] The Agreement was concluded for a period of five years, with automatic renewal on a yearly basis unless denounced six months before its expiry date.[2]

In respect of trade, the Agreement provides that the parties shall grant each other MFN treatment in accordance with the GATT.[3] The parties undertake to develop and diversify their exchanges and improve market access.[4] They are to grant each other the highest degree of liberalization of imports and exports which they generally apply to third countries.[5] They agree to promote exchange of information[6] and co-operation in customs matters.[7] They also undertake to give consideration, each in accordance with its own laws, to exempting from duty, tax and other charges, goods admitted temporarily to their territories for subsequent re-export unaltered or for goods which re-enter their territories after processing in the other party which is not sufficient for the goods to be treated as originating from the territory of that other part.[8]

Provision is made for consultation in the event of disputes in respect of trade between the parties.[9] In respect of anti-dumping or subsidies investigations, each party agrees to examine submissions by the other and to inform interested parties of the essential facts and considerations on which a decision is to be based. The parties are required to do their utmost to reach a constructive solution before imposing definite anti-dumping or countervailing duties.[10]

In respect of intellectual property, the parties have undertaken to ensure, as far as their laws, regulations and policies allow, that suitable and effective protection is provided for intellectual property rights, while reinforcing this protection where desirable.[11]

In addition to this recent Agreement, Agreements between the Community and India were concluded in 1969 on trade in coir products,[12] in 1970 on trade in handicraft products,[13] and in 1975 on preferential imports of cane

---

1 As to the Joint Commission, see Art 22. As to consultations between meetings of the Joint Commission, see Art 23.

2 Agreement Art 29, second paragraph.

3 Ibid Art 2.

4 Ibid Art 3(1).

5 Ibid Art 3(2), which also provides for the examination of ways and means of eliminating barriers, especially non-tariff barriers.

6 Ibid Art 3(3).

7 Ibid Art 3(4).

8 Ibid Art 3(5).

9 Ibid Art 4(6.1).

10 Ibid Art 3(6.2). It is expressly stated that GATT provisions prevail in the event of any inconsistency: Art 3(6.3).

11 Ibid Art 10, which states that intellectual property rights include patents, trade or service marks, copyright and similar rights, industrial designs and integrated circuit topographics. The parties also undertake, whenever possible, to facilitate access to the data bases of intellectual property organizations.

12 Council Decision 69/303, OJ 24.9.69 L240/1.

13 Council Decision 70/386, OJ 10.8.70 L176/1. The Agreement extended to a number of handicraft products the tariff quota opened on 1 September 1969 by Council Regulation 1491/69 (OJ 31.7.69 L187/1): see Annex.

sugar.[14] In respect of sugar, the Community has recently opened a special tariff quota for the import at reduced duty of raw cane sugar for refining for the period of 1 July 1995 to 30 June 2001.[15]

A Protocol on commercial and economic co-operation in respect of ECSC products was concluded with India in 1981.[16]

In 1986 the Community and India signed an Agreement on trade in textile products.[17] Its provisions are essentially the same as those in the analogous agreement with Hong Kong.[18]

INDONESIA

Indonesia is a member country of ASEAN and thus within the Co-operation Agreement between the Commuity and ASEAN.[19] Otherwise the Community and Indonesia have concluded only product-specific agreements. A Co-operation Agreement in respect of manioc was signed in 1982.[20] An Agreement on textile products was concluded in 1986.[1] Its provisions are essentially the same as those in the analogous agreement with Hong Kong.[2]

JAPAN

Community law in respect of trade with Japan consists mainly of autonomous measures.[3] A notable exemption (though not legally binding) is the 31 July 1991 EC–Japan Arrangement concerning the motor vehicle sector.[4] According

---

14 OJ 23.7.75 L190/36. The Community undertook for an indefinite period to purchase and import, at guaranteed prices, a specific quantity (at first 22,000 and then 25,000 metric tonnes) originating in India and which India undertook to deliver: see Arts 1, 3(1), 4(1), 5(3). After an interval of suspension, the quantity was restored at the level of 10,000 tonnes by Agreement in the form of exchange of letters in 1984, OJ 5.5.84 L120/2.

15 Agreement, OJ 1.8.95 L181/28.

16 OJ 8.12.81 L352/28.

17 OJ 27.9.88 L267/2, as amended in 1992 by Agreement in the form of exchange of letters (OJ 31.12.92 L410/180) and in 1995 as a result of EU enlargement and the Uruguay Round negotiations (OJ 26.4.95 L267/1). See also Council Decision 88/495 on the provisional application of the Agreement, OJ 27.9.88 L267/1.

18 See above. As to provisional quantitative limits on certain products during part of 1992, see Commission Regulation 3044/92, OJ 23.10.92 L307/22. As to definitive quantitative limits imposed on certain products in 1995, see Commission Regulation 507/95, OJ 8.3.95 L51/2.

19 See above.

20 OJ 28.7.82 L219/57. This was a voluntary restraint agreement. It was extended by agreement in 1982 (OJ 10.6.86 L155/9) and in 1990 (OJ 12.12.90 L347/24). As to the Community's policy in respect of manioc imports, see the section on Thailand, below. As to tariff quotas for certain manioc products for 1998, see Commission Regulation 2330/97, OJ 26.11.97 L323/13.

1 OJ 19.8.87 L233/39. The Agreement was amended by Exchange of letters in 1992 (OJ 31.12.92 L410/65) and in 1995 (OJ 26.4.95 L94/214).

2 See above. Provisional quantitative limitations were imposed on certain products in 1992, and definitive quantitative limits were imposed on certain products in 1994 and in 1995. As to 1992, see Commission Regulation 2544/92, OJ 1.9.92 L254/62; Commission Regulation 3245/92, OJ 10.11.92 L324/5; Commission Regulation 3431/92, OJ 28.11.92. As to 1994, see Commission Regulation 1629/94, OJ 6.7.94 L171/17. As to 1995, see Commission Regulation 507/95, OJ 8.3.95 L51/2.

3 As to which, see Parts I–III in this book.

4 Known as 'Elements of Consensus', the text has not been published. See *Agence Europe*, No 5447 (n.s.), 2 August 1991, pp 6–7. As to background and contents of the Arrangement and the related question of Japanese 'transplants', see P Eeckhout *The European Internal Market*

to the Arrangement, the Community undertakes to cease authorizing the use of EC Art 115 in respect of Japanese cars, to abolish then existing quantitative restrictions and to achieve full Community acceptance of type approval by the end of 1992. There will be no restrictions on Japanese investment or on the free circulation of Japanese products in the Community. Japan undertakes to monitor its car exports to the Community until the end of 1999. In addition, Japan undertakes to convey to its car manufacturers the Commission concern in respect of excessive concentration of sales of Japanese cars produced in Europe which might cause disruption in specific national markets. Provision is made for biannual consultations and notification to the GATT.[5] Under the WTO Agreement on Safeguards[6] the Community has maintained restraints on car imports from Japan until 31 December 1999.[7]

The Community and Japan have also concluded an Agreement for co-operation in the field of controlled thermonuclear fusion.[8]

REPUBLIC OF KOREA

An Agreement on trade in textiles was concluded between the Community and the Republic of Korea in 1986.[9] Its provisions are essentially the same as those in the analogous agreement with Hong Kong.[10]

An Agreement on co-operation and mutual administrative assistance in customs matters was concluded between the two parties in 1997.[11] The parties, through their customs authorities, are to endeavour to co-operate in respect of customs procedures and training,[12] and also to strive for simplication, harmonization and computerization in customs procedures.[13] Provision is made for mutual assistance in customs matters.[14] A Joint Customs Co-operation Committee is established to ensure the proper functioning of the Agreement.[15]

Since 1996 the Community has participated in the Korean Peninsula Energy Development Organization (KEDO).[16]

---

and International Trade: A Legal Analysis (Clarendon Press, Oxford, 1994) at pp 197–225, on which pp 201–202 the remainder of this paragraph is mainly based. See also Case T-7/92 *Asia Motors France v Commission* [1993] ECR II-669.

5 See also Written Question E-2049/93 by André Sainjon to the Commission, 23 July 1993, Renegotiation of the Agreement on European Imports of Japanese Cars, OJ 24.10.94 C296/29; Written Question E-2205/93 by Cristiana Muscardini to the Commission, 29 July 1993, OJ 24.10.94 C296/29; Written Question E-2236/93 by Mauro Chiabrando, Rinaldo Bontempi and Giuseppe Mottola to the Commission, 30 July 1993, OJ 24.10.94 C296/29; Joint Answer to Written Questions E-2049/93, E-2205/93, E-2236/93 and E-2318/93 given by Mr Bangemann on behalf of the Commission, 19 January 1994, OJ 24.10.94 C296/30.

6 OJ 23.12.94 L336/184, Art 11(2).

7 WTO Agreement on Safeguards, Annex.

8 OJ 28.2.89 L57/63.

9 OJ 14.9.87 L263/38, amended by Exchange of letters in 1992 (OJ 31.12.92) and 1995 (OJ 26.4.95 L94/459).

10 As to which, see above.

11 Agreement between the European Community and the Republic of Korea on co-operation and mutual administrative assistance in customs matters, OJ 13.5.97 L121/14, approved on behalf of the Community by Council Decision 97/291, OJ 13.5.97 L121/3.

12 Ibid Art 3(1)(a).

13 Ibid Art 3(1)(b).

14 See ibid Arts 4–14.

15 See ibid Art 15.

16 See Joint Action 96/195/CFSP of 5.3.96, OJ 13.3.96 L63/1.

In 1997 the Community and Korea concluded an Agreement on telecommunications procurement and an Agreement on procurement of private telecommunications operators.[17]

LAOS

A Co-operation Agreement between the Community and Laos was signed in 1997.[18] Respect for the democratic principles and fundamental human rights established by the Universal Declaration on Human Rights constitutes an essential element of the Agreement.[19] The objective of the Agreement is to provide a framework for enhanced co-operation on numerous matters, including trade.[20] The trade provisions of the Agreement are virtually identical to those of the Agreement between the Community and Cambodia.[1] A Joint Committee is established to oversee the Agreement.[2]

MACAO

In 1992 the Community and Macao concluded an Agreement on trade and co-operation.[3] Its purpose was to strengthen their relations and to promote co-operation, taking account of Macao's special situation and level of development.[4] Co-operation between the parties and the implementation of the Agreement was stated to be based on respect for the democratic principles and human rights which inspire the policies of both the Community and Macao.[5] MFN treatment was provided, with the usual exceptions for customs unions or free trade areas and other advantages accorded under the GATT.[6] The parties undertook to promote trade between them in the greatest possible degree, taking

17 Agreement on telecommunications procurement between the European Community and the Republic of Korea, OJ 22.11.97 L321/32, and Agreement in the form of a memorandum concerning the procurement of private telecommunications operators between the European Community and the Republic of Korea, OJ 22.11.97 L321/41, both approved on behalf of the Community by Council Decision 97/784, OJ 22.11.97 L321/30. As to these Agreements, see Chapter 21 on Services.

18 Co-operation Agreement between the European Community and the Lao People's Democratic Republic, OJ 8.4.97 C109/9; see also Proposal for a Council Decision concerning the conclusion of the Co-operation Agreement between European Community and the Lao People's Democratic Republic (97/C109/06), COM(97)79 final—97/0062(CNS) (submitted by the Commission on 4 March 1997), OJ 8.4.97 C109/8.The Agreement is valid for five years, following which it is renewed automatically from year to year unless denounced by a party six months before its expiry date: ibid Art 21(2).

19 Ibid Art 1. Violation of this provision constitutes a material breach of the Agreement, in which case a party may take appropriate measures without beforehand supplying the Joint Committee with all relevant information required for a thorough examination of the situation with a view to seeking a solution acceptable to the parties. In this case the other party may avail itself of the procedure relating to the settlement of disputes: see ibid Art 19 and Annex I: Joint Declaration on Art 19—Non-execution of the Agreement.

20 Ibid Art 2.

1 See ibid Art 4. As to the EC-Cambodia Agreement, see above.

2 Ibid Art 14.

3 OJ 31.12.92 L404/27. The Agreement was concluded for a period of five years, with tacit annual renewal until denounced in writing six months before the date of expiry: Agreement Art 19(2).

4 Ibid Art 1, first paragraph.

5 Ibid Art 1, second paragraph.

6 Ibid Art 2.

account of their respective economic situations and granting each other the widest possible opportunities.[7] Provision was also made for co-operation in the fields of industry, investment, science and technology, information, communication and culture, training, the environment, social development, the fight against drugs, and tourism.[8] A Joint Committee was established to promote co-operation and oversee the operation of the Agreement.[9]

An Agreement on trade in textiles was concluded between the Community and Macao in 1986.[10] Its provisions are essentially the same as those in the analogous agreement with Hong Kong.[11]

As to 20 December 1999 the Basic Law of the Macao Special Administrative Region of the People's Republic of China will take effect.[12] In terms similar to those of the Basic Law of the Hong Kong SAR, it provides that the Macao Special Administrative Region will be a separate customs territory.[13] Using the name 'Macao, China', it may participate in relevant international organizations and international trade agreements (including preferential trade agreements), such as the GATT and arrangements concerning international trade in textiles.[14] Similarly, on the same conditions, it may maintain and develop relations, and conclude and implement agreements, with foreign states and regions and relevant international organizations in various fields, including trade.[15] Export quotas, tariff preferences and other similar arrangements, which are obtained or made by the Macao SAR, or which were obtained or made but remain valid, are to be enjoyed exclusively by the Region.[16] The Macao SAR may issue its own certificates of origin for products in accordance with the prevailing rules of origin.[17] The application to the Macao SAR of international agreements to which the People's Republic of China is a member or becomes a party shall be decided by the Central People's Government, in accordance with the circumstances and needs of the Region, and after seeking the views of the government of the Region.[18] International agreements to which the People's Republic of China is not a party but which are implemented in Macao may continue to be implemented in the Macao SAR.[19]

7 Ibid Art 3.
8 See ibid Arts 4–14.
9 See Art 16.
10 OJ 16.10.86 L293/187, amended by Agreement in the form of Exchange of letters in 1992 (OJ 31.12.92 L410/53) and in 1995 (OJ 26.4.95 L94/237).
11 As to which, see above.
12 See The Basic Law of the Macao Special Administrative Region of the People's Republic of China (adopted by the Eighth National People's Congress at its First Session on 31 March 1993), published by the Consultative Committee for the Basic Law of the Macao Special Administrative Region of the People's Republic of China, April 1993. The Basic Law is promulgated by Decree No 3 of the President of the People's Republic of China, 31 March 1993, which is included in this text.
13 Ibid Art 112, first paragraph.
14 Ibid Art 112, second paragraph.
15 Ibid Art 136.
16 Ibid Art 112, third paragraph.
17 Ibid Art 113.
18 Ibid Art 138, first paragraph.
19 Ibid Art 138, second paragraph, which also provides that the Central People's Government shall, as necessary, authorize or assist the government of the Region to make appropriate arrangements for the application to the Region of other relevant international agreements.

MALAYSIA

Malaysia is an ASEAN member country and thus within the Agreement between the Community and ASEAN.[20]

An Agreement on trade in textiles was concluded between the Community and Malaysia in 1986.[1] Its provisions are essentially the same as those in the analogous agreement with Hong Kong.[2]

MONGOLIA

An Agreement on trade and economic co-operation was concluded between the Community and Mongolia in 1992.[3] It is stated to be based on respect for the democratic principles and human rights which inspire the domestic and external policies of the Community and Mongolia.[4] It applies to all products except for ECSC products.[5] The parties agree to endeavour to develop and expand trade and economic co-operation, within the framework of their respective existing laws and regulations, and in accordance with the principles of equality and mutual advantage.[6] MFN treatment is provided, with the usual exceptions in respect of customs unions or free trade areas, border trade with neighbouring countries, and advantages accorded to particular countries in accordance with the GATT.[7] The parties undertake to take appropriate measures to promote trade development and diversification.[8]

In addition, Mongolia is to ensure that, in matters that depend on the decision of its government, government agencies or state enterprises, Community exporters or suppliers of goods or services will have the possibility of participating, on an equitable and non-discriminatory basis, in opportunities for trade with Mongolia.[9] The Community is to strive for a progressive liberalization of imports from Mongolia. In particular, it undertakes to abolish quantitative restrictions on imports of specified products from Mongolia.[10] Provision is made for the exchange of information in respect of any problems,[11] though in

20 See above.
1 OJ 19.8.87 L233/83, as amended by Agreement in the form of exchange of letters in 1992 (OJ 31.1292 L410/194) and in 1995 (OJ 26.4.95 L94/262).
2 As to which, see above. As to the imposition of provisional quantitative limits during part of 1992, see Commission Regulation 3058/92, OJ 24.10.92 L308/5.
3 OJ 18.2.93 L41/46. The Agreement was concluded for a period of five years from the date of its entry into force and is tacitly renewed from year to year until denounced in writing with six months' notice: Agreement Art 15.
4 Ibid Art 1.
5 Ibid Art 2(1).
6 Ibid Art 2(2).
7 Ibid Art 3.
8 Ibid Art 4(1).
9 Ibid Art 5(1), which also provides that this specifically concerns the issuing of import licences and the provision of convertible currencies for imports of Community origin.
10 Ibid Art 5(2), which also provides that the products in question are those set out, in respect of Mongolia, in Council Regulation 3420/83, Annex III (OJ 8.12.83 L346/6), now replaced by Council Regulation 519/94, OJ 10.3.94 L67/89, as last amended, with two exceptions. The first exception comprises textile products of Section XI of the Combined Nomenclature. The second exception consists of those restrictions which are listed in Council Regulation 288/82, Annex 1 (OJ 9.2.82 L35/1) (common rules for imports), now replaced by Council Regulation 518/94, OJ 7.3.94 L67/77, as last amended, for the regions of the Community to which such restrictions apply.
11 Ibid Art 6(1).

an exceptional case a party may take immediate measures but must endeavour, as far as possible, to hold friendly consultations before doing so.[12]

Trade in goods and the provision of services is to be effected at market-related prices and rates.[13] Payments for transactions are to be made, in accordance with the parties' respective laws and regulations, in convertible currencies.[14]

Provision is also made for economic co-operation.[15]

A Joint Committee is established to oversee the operation of the Agreement.[16]

An Agreement on trade in textile products was concluded between the Community and Mongolia in 1993.[17] Its provisions are essentially the same as those in the analogous agreement with Hong Kong.[18]

NEPAL

A Co-operation Agreement between the Community and Nepal was signed on 20 November 1995.[19] Respect for human rights and democratic principles constitutes an essential element of the Agreement.[20] The parties are to grant each other MFN treatment with respect of tariffs.[1] They undertake to develop and diversify their commercial exchanges and improve market access.[2] Provision is also made for exchange of information and customs co-operation. They undertake to give consideration, each in accordance with its laws, to exempting from duty, tax and other charges, goods admitted temporarily to their territories for subsequent re-export unaltered or for goods which re-enter their territories after processing in their other party which is not sufficient for the goods to be treated as originating from the other party.[3] The parties will aim to improve conditions for adequate and effective protection and reinforcement of intellectual property rights in conformity with the highest international standards and co-operate to secure these objectives.[4] They are to avoid discriminatory treatment in relation to such rights

---

12 Ibid Art 6(2). The parties are required to ensure that the general objectives of the Agreement are not prejudiced when such measures are taken: Art 6(3).
13 Ibid Art 7.
14 Ibid Art 8.
15 See Arts 9–12.
16 Ibid Art 13.
17 OJ 17.5.94 L123/418. As to its provisional application, see Council Decision 94/277, OJ 17.5.94 L123/1. The Agreement was amended by Agreement in the form of exchange of letters in 1995 (OJ 26.4.95 L94/285).
18 As to which, see above.
19 Co-operation Ageement between the European Community and Nepal, OJ 8.6.96 L137/15, approved on behalf of the Community by Council Decision 96/354, OJ 8.6.96 L137/14. The Agreement is concluded for five years, with subsequent automatic renewals on a yearly basis unless denounced by one party six months before its expiry date: ibid Art 22(2).
20 Ibid Art 1. Violation of this provision is a material breach of the Agreement, in which case a party is entitled to take appropriate measures without beforehand supplying the other party with all relevant information required for a thorough examination of the situation with a view to seeking a solution acceptable to the parties. In this case the other party may request consultations on the measures: see ibid Art 18, and Annex: Joint Declaration (2) of the European Community and His Majesty's Government of Nepal.
1 Ibid Art 3(1), first paragraph. These provisions do not apply to preferences accorded under any arrangement establishing a customs union, a free trade area or a preferential treatment area: ibid Art 3(1), second paragraph.
2 Ibid Art 3(2). See also Art 3(3).
3 Ibid Art 3(6).
4 Ibid Art 4(1).

and to engage in consultations if problems arise.[5] A Joint Commission is established to oversee the operation of the Agreement.[6]

PAKISTAN

An Agreement on trade in handicraft products was concluded between the Community and Pakistan in 1970.[7] It was followed in 1976 by a Commercial Co-operation Agreement.[8] A decade later the Community and Pakistan concluded in 1986 their current Agreement for commercial, economic and development co-operation.[9] A new Co-operation Agreement was initialled on 22 April 1998. It includes a human rights clause and will cover trade and economic matters, development, science and technology, social issues, and intellectual property.[10] As this Agreement has not yet entered into force, the following paragraphs focus on the currently applicable 1986 Agreement.

As provided in the current Agreement,[11] the parties are to accord each other MFN treatment.[12] They agree to grant each other the highest degree of liberalization of imports and exports which they generally apply to third countries.[13] In accordance with their legislation and in the conduct of their policies, they are inter alia to use their endeavours to maintain and strengthen an open and equitable international trading system and respect their GATT obligations, intensify exchanges of information regarding markets, industries and trends, promote visits, and bring together economic operators to identify sectors and products in which exports could be developed and support market development programmes.[14] Provision is also made for economic co-operation,[15] development co-operation,[16] and co-operation with third countries.[17] As in other similar agreements, the Agreement does not affect the powers of the Community's Member States to undertake bilateral activities in the field of economic co-operation or to conclude new economic co-operation agreements.[18] A Joint Commission is established to ensure proper functioning of the Agreement and to help achieve its objectives.[19]

In addition, the Community and Pakistan concluded an Agreement on trade in textiles in 1986.[20] Its provisions are essentially the same as those in the analogous agreement with Hong Kong.[1]

---

5 Ibid Art 4(2).
6 Ibid Art 15.
7 OJ 10.8.70 L176/1. The Agreement extended to certain further products the tariff quota opened in 1969 by Council Regulation 1491/69, OJ 31.7.69 L187/1.
8 OJ 28.6.76 L168/2.
9 OJ 25.4.86 L108/2.
10 See *Agence Europe*, No 7206 (n.s.), Thursday, 23 April 1998, p 6.
11 The Agreement is concluded for a period of five years, with automatic extension from year to year if neither party denounces it six months before the date of expiry: Art 10.
12 Ibid Art 1.
13 Ibid Art 2(2).
14 See ibid Art 2(3)(b),(c),(d),f).
15 Ibid Art 3.
16 Ibid Art 4.
17 Ibid Art 5.
18 Ibid Art 6.
19 Ibid Art 7.
20 OJ 5.9.87 L255/2. It was amended by Agreement in the form of exchange of letters in 1992 (OJ 31.12.92 L410/208) and in 1995 (OJ 24.6.95 L94/306).
1 As to which, see above.

THE PHILIPPINES

The Philippines is a member country of ASEAN.[2] In addition, an Agreement on trade in textiles was concluded between the Community and the Philippines in 1986.[3] Its provisions are essentially the same as those in the analogous agreement with Hong Kong.[4]

SINGAPORE

Singapore is a member country of ASEAN.[5] In addition, an Agreement on trade in textiles was concluded between the Community and Singapore in 1986.[6] Its provisions are essentially the same as those in the analogous agreement with Hong Kong.[7]

SRI LANKA

An Agreement on partnership and development was concluded between the Community and the Democratic Socialist Republic of Sri Lanka in 1995.[8] Its provisions are essentially the same as those in the analogous agreement with India.[9]

An Agreement on trade in textiles was concluded between the Community and Sri Lanka in 1986.[10] Its provisions are essentially the same as those in the analogous agreement with Hong Kong.[11]

TAIWAN

There are no diplomatic relations between EC and Taiwan. Consequently there is no bilateral agreement between the Community and Taiwan.

However, on the basis of EC Art 113, the Community has taken an autonomous measure in respect of imports of certain textile products in Taiwan.[12] The measure applied from 1 January 1995 to 31 December 1995.[13] Its provisions are generally similar to those of the analogous agreement with Hong Kong.[14]

---

2 As to the Agreement between the Community and ASEAN, see above.
3 OJ 5.9.87 L255/44. It was amended by Agreements in the form of exchange of letters in 1992 (OJ 31.12.92 L410/77) and in 1995 (OJ 26.4.95 L94/348).
4 As to which, see above.
5 As to the Agreement between the Community and ASEAN, see above.
6 OJ 16.6.87 L156/88. The Agreement was amended by Agreement in the form of exchange of letters in 1992 (OJ 31.12.92 L410/14) and in 1995 (OJ 26.4.95 L94/415).
7 As to which, see above.
8 OJ 19.4.95 L85/33.
9 As to which, see above.
10 OJ 5.9.87 L255/86. The Agreement was modified by Agreements in the form of exchange of letters in 1992 (OJ 31.12.92 L410/220) and in 1995 (OJ 26.4.95 L94/483).
11 As to which, see above.
12 Council Regulation 3951/92, OJ 31.12.92 L405/6.
13 Ibid Art 1(1), Art 11, second paragraph.
14 As to which, see above.

In addition, within the framework of the common organization of the market in fruit and vegetables[15] and implementing legislation,[16] the Community has taken protective measures in respect of garlic imports from Taiwan.[17]

THAILAND

Thailand is a member country of ASEAN.[18] Other relations between the Community and Thailand have centred on trade in manioc and textiles.

In 1982 the two parties concluded, for a period of four years, a Co-operation Agreement on manioc[19] production, marketing and trade.[20] It was subsequently extended for a further four-year period,[1] and then renewed for a second time in 1990,[2] this time with automatic renewal for subsequent four-year periods unless denounced by either party at least one year before the period expired. The Agreement provided for the limitation by Thailand of its manioc exports to the Community,[3] the agreement by the Community to limit its import levy for the agreed quantity to a maximum of 6 per cent *ad valorem*, and Community assistance for crop diversification in Thailand.[4] A permanent joint working group was established to oversee the application of the Agreement.

An Agreement on trade in textiles was concluded between the Community and Thailand in 1987.[5] Its provisions are essentially the same as those in the analogous agreement with Hong Kong.[6]

VIETNAM

A Co-operation Agreement between the Community and Vietnam was concluded in May 1996.[7] Respect for human rights and democratic principles

15 Then Council Regulation 1035/72, OJ 20.5.72 L118/1.

16 Commission Regulation 1859/93 on the application of the system of import licences for garlic imported from third countries, OJ 31.12.94 L349/105.

17 Import licences were suspended until 31 May 1995 (Commission Regulation 2091/94, OJ 25.8.94 L220/8). Currently, import licences have been restored and a certificate of origin is required (Commission Regulation 1084/95, OJ 16.5.95 L109/1).

18 As to the Agreement between the Community and ASEAN, see above.

19 As to the legal meaning of 'manioc flour', see Case 72/69 *Hauptzollamt Bremen-Freihafen v Bremer Handesgesellschaft* [1970] ECR 427; Case 74/69 *Hauptzollamt Bremen-Freihafen v Waren-Import-Gesellschaft Krohn and Co* [1970] ECR 451.

20 OJ 28.7.82 L219/53. See generally Snyder 'European Community Law and International Economic Relations: The Saga of Thai Manioc' in R St J Macdonald (ed) *Essays in Honour of Wang Tieya* (1993) pp 753–769.

1 Protocol renewing the Co-operation Agreement, OJ 10.6.86 L155/9.

2 Protocol renewing the Co-operation Agreement, OJ 12.12.90 L347/24.

3 For the period from 1 January 1991 to 31 Deember 1994 and each subsequent four-year period, the total export quantity was to be 21 million tonnes of manioc for each period, but not exceeding 5,750,000 tonnes in any one year.

4 As to the operation of the Agreement, see Case 165/84 *John Friedrich Krohn (GmbH & Co KG) v Bundesanstalt für Landwirtschaftliche Marktordnung* [1985] ECR 3997; Case 175/84 *Krohn & Co Import-Export (GmbH & Co KG) v Commission* [1986] ECR 753.

5 OJ 5.9.87 L255/127. The Agreement was amended by Agreements in the form of exchange of letters in 1992 (OJ 31.12.92 L410/232).

6 As to which, see above. As to quantitative limits for part of 1992, see Commission Regulation 3775/92, OJ 29.12.92 L383/61.

7 See Council Decision 96/351 concerning the conclusion of the Co-operation Agreement between the European Community and the Socialist Republic of Vietnam, OJ 7.6.96 L136/28.

constitute an essential element of the Agreement.[8] The objectives of the Agreement are, inter alia, to secure the conditions of and promote an increase and development of bilateral trade.[9] The Agreement provides for most-favoured nation treatment in conformity with GATT.[10] The other trade provisions[11] include an undertaking to develop and diversify commercial exchanges and improve market access,[12] as well as different types of co-operation in trade and commercial matters,[13] including an agreement of consultation as to any dispute which may arise in connection with trade or trade-related matters.[14] In relation to intellectual property, the parties are to aim to improve the conditions for adequate and effective protection and reinforcement of such rights[15] and to co-operate to ensure these objectives, including by technical assistance.[16] They are to avoid discriminatory treatment in relation to intellectual property rights and, if necessary, engage in consultations if problems affecting trade relations arise.[17] Neither the Agreement nor any action taken under it is to affect in any way the powers of the EU Member States to undertake bilateral activities with Vietnam in the framework of economic co-operation or to conclude, where appropriate, new economic co-operation agreements with Vietnam.[18] The Agreement is concluded for a five-year period, with automatic annual renewal unless denounced by a party six months before the expiry date.[19]

An Agreement on trade in textiles was concluded between the Community and the Socialist Republic of Vietnam in 1992.[20] It was roughly similar to the analo-

8 Ibid Art 1.
9 Ibid Art 2(1). Among the other objectives is support for environmental protection and sustainable management of natural resources: Art 2(4).
10 Ibid Art 3, first paragraph.
11 Provision is also made for investments, economic co-operation, science and technology, development co-operation, regional co-operation, environmental co-operation, information and communication, and drug abuse control.
12 Ibid Art 4(1). The Community confirms that Vietnam has access to its GSP and states its willingness to organize workshops in Vietnam for public and private users of GSP with a view to ensuring maximum use of it: see ibid Annex I, Declaration of the European Community concerning tariff adjustments.
13 Ibid Art 4(2)-(5). The standard exceptions to free trade apply: see ibid Art 4(3).
14 Ibid Art 4(6).
15 Ibid Art 6(1)(a). For the purpose of the Agreement, 'intellectual, industrial and commercial property' includes in particular protection of copyright (including computer software) and related rights; trade and service marks; geographical indications, including indications of origin; industrial designs; patents; layout designs of integrated circuits as well as protection of undisclosed information and protection against unfair competition: see ibid Annex II, Joint Declaration of the European Community and of the government of Vietnam.
16 Ibid Art 6(1)(b).
17 Ibid Art 6(2).
18 Ibid Art 16. Annex I includes a Declaration of the European Community to the effect that, in the course of the negotiations, the Community declared that, subject to the provisions of Art 16 of the Agreement, the provisions of the Agreement shall replace provisions of agreements concluded between Member States of the European Union and Vietnam where such agreements are either incompatible with or identical to the provisions of the Agreement.
19 Ibid Art 20(2).
20 OJ 1.12.92 L410/279. It was amended by Agreement in form of exchange of letters in 1995 (OJ 26.4.95 L94/550). It was further amended in 1998 by a new bilateral Agreement between the EC and Vietnam on Trade in Textile Products: see Commission of the European Communities 'Proposal for a Council Decision on the Conclusion of a Bilateral Agreement between the European Community and the Socialist Republic of Vietnam on Trade in Textile Products' (presented by the Commission), COM(1998)156 final, Brussels, 25.3.98. Pending its formal conclusion, it has been applied on a provisional basis as from 1 January 1998 pursuant to Council Decision 98/136, OJ 13.2.98 L41/12. See also Commission of the European Communities 'Proposal for a Council Decision on the Provisional Application of the Agreement in the Form of an Exchange of Letters amending the Agreement between the European Community

gous agreement with Hong Kong.[1] However, it also provides that Vietnam is to reserve to Community textile enterprises a specified share of Vietnamese exports by means of contract between Community and Vietnamese enterprises.[2] In this respect Vietnam is required to follow a quota allocation policy which avoids discrimination against companies fully or partially owned by Community investors operating in Vietnam.[3] The Agreement also contains an intellectual property clause, to the effect that the parties will take all necessary measures to protect trademarks, designs and models and, if necessary, enter into consultations to find an equitable solution to any problems.[4] There is also provision for specific safeguard measures in the event of Vietnamese imports into the Community at prices lower than normal competitive prices and which cause, or threaten to cause, serious injury to Community producers of like products.[5]

As amended in 1997,[6] the Agreement also provides that Vietnam shall ensure that the supply of raw silk and silk waste to Community industry is made at conditions not less favourable than to Vietnamese domestic users.[7] Consultations may be requested by the Community if the level of imports of products in given categories exceeds the preceding year's total volume of imports into the Community from all sources of products in that category by specified percentages.[8]

---

and the Socialist Republic of Vietnam on Trade in Textile and Clothing Products' (presented by the Commission), COM(97)650 final, Brussels 2.12.97. The Agreement applies until 31 December 2000, and then is automatically extended for one year, unless either party notifies the other by 30 June 2000 at the latest that it does not agree with the extension: Art 19(1) as substituted.

1 As to which, see above.
2 See ibid Art 3(3),(4), as amended. Additional quantities may be made available to European industry: see Commission Regulation 2407/97, OJ 4.12.97 L332/38.
3 Ibid. Annex G, Agreed Minute, which also provides that, in order to increase transparency of the quota allocation policy, the government of Vietnam will provide the Commission with the texts of all relevant regulations and general administrative acts as promptly as they have been adopted. The Vietnamese government also undertakes to provide the Commission with statistics regarding quota allocation. The parties are to decide on the content and format of this allocation. At the request of either party, consultation may be held on specific matters related to quota allocation.
4 Ibid Art 5. As to the procedure, see Art 17.
5 Ibid Art 6(1). As to the measures which may be taken, see Art 6(2)-(4). As to the determination of prices, see Art 6(5). As to consultation procedures, see Art 17.
6 See Commission of the European Communities 'Proposal for a Council Decision on the Conclusion of a Bilateral Agreement between the European Community and the Socialist Republic of Vietnam on Trade in Textile Products' (presented by the Commission), COM(1998)156 final, Brussels, 25.3.98. 13.2.98 L41/12.
7 Ibid Art 7, as substituted.
8 Ibid Art 10(2), as substituted.

Chapter 33

Oceania

AUSTRALIA

In 1980, when the Community's first common organization of the market for sheepmeat and goatmeat[1] was agreed, the Community and Australia concluded an Agreement on trade in mutton, lamb and goatmeat.[2] It was a voluntary restraint agreement, according to which Australia agreed to limit its exports of fresh and frozen meat[3] to the Community to specified quantities[4] and, pending consultations, to the traditional pattern of presentation.[5] It contained a safeguard clause[6] and sanctions for exceeding the limit.[7] In return, the Community undertook to limit the applicable duty.[8] A Consultative Committee was established.[9] As a result of the Uruguay Round, the quantitative limit provided by the Agreement has been converted into a tariff quota.[10]

An Agreement was concluded in 1984 between the Community and Australia concerning cheese.[11] It followed an Arrangement between the parties concerning cheese reached within the GATT.

In 1982 an Agreement between the Community and the EACE was concluded concerning transfers of nuclear material.[12]

An Agreement on trade in wine was concluded between the Community and Australia in 1994.[13] The parties agreed to facilitate trade in wine[14] on the basis of non-discrimination and reciprocity.[15] Unless otherwise provided, importation and marketing is to be conducted in compliance with the laws and regulations applying in the territory of the contracting party.[16] The parties are required

---

1 Council Regulation 1837/80, OJ 16.7.80 L183/1.
2 OJ 18.10.80 L275/13.
3 Ibid clause 1.
4 Ibid clause 2, first paragraph.
5 Ibid clause 2, second paragraph.
6 Ibid Art 3.
7 Ibid clause 4.
8 Ibid clause 5.
9 Ibid clause 10.
10 See Chapter 16 on Agricultural Products in this book.
11 Exchange of letters, OJ 27.11.84 L308/55.
12 OJ 4.10.82 L281/8. See Chapter 20 on EAEC Products in this book.
13 OJ 31.3.94 L86/3. See also Lundy and Alexiadis 'The Agreement between Australia and the European Community on Trade in Wine, and Protocol' manuscript 1997.
14 That is, wines falling under HS heading 22.04: Art 2(1).
15 Ibid Art 1.
16 Ibid Art 3(1).

to take all general and specific measures necessary to ensure fulfilment of their obligations under the Agreement.[17] The Community is to authorize importation and marketing of Australian wines produced in accordance with specified oenological practices or processes and compositional and other requirements.[18] A similar obligation applies to Australia.[19] Provision is made for requests for authorization of other oenological practices or processes.[20]

The Agreement also contains provisions in respect of the reciprocal protection of wine names and related provisions on description and presentation. The parties are to take all measures necessary, in accordance with the Agreement, for the reciprocal protection of specified names.[1] In particular, each party must provide the legal means for interested parties to prevent use of a traditional expression or a geographical indication identifying wines for wines not originating in the place indicated by the geographical indication in question.[2] This protection also applies to names even where the true origin of the wine is indicated or the geographical indication or traditional expression is used in translation or accompanied by various expressions.[3] In addition, the registration of a trade mark for wines which contains or consists of a geographical indication, or a traditional identifying expression, must be refused or invalidated on request in respect of wines not originating in the place indicated by the geographical indication or traditional expression.[4] Provision is made for homonymous geographical indications.[5] The protection also applies to wines exported and marketed outside the territories of the contracting parties.[6]

However, the Agreement does not in any way prejudice the right of any person to use, in the course of trade, their name or the name of their predecessor in business, except where the name is used in such a way as to mislead customers.[7] Nor does the Agreement oblige a party to protect a geographical indication or traditional expression of the other party which is not, or ceases to be, protected in its country of origin, or which has fallen into disuse in that country.[8]

In addition, the protection of names does not prevent the use of certain names to describe and present a wine in Australia, and in other countries where the laws and regulations so permit, during certain transitional periods.[9] Special provision is made for the use of the name of a vine variety or a synonym to

---

17 Ibid Art 3(2).
18 Ibid Art 4(1). The oenological practices or processes are listed in Annex I, first paragraph. The compositional and other requirements are provided in the Protocol.
19 Ibid Art 4(2). The oenological practices or processses are listed in Annex I, second paragraph. The compositional and other requirements are provided in the Protocol.
20 Ibid Art 5.
1 Listed in Art 7. As to the wines covered by the Agreement, see Annex II.
2 Ibid Art 6(1). As to measures and proceedings, see Art 13.
3 Ibid Art 6(2).
4 Ibid Art 6(4).
5 Ibid Art 6(5).
6 Ibid Art 7(4).
7 Ibid Art 6(6).
8 Ibid Art 6(7).
9 Ibid Art 8(1). The transitional period ended on 31 December 1993 for the following names: Beaujolais, Cava, Frascati, Sancerre, Saint-Emilion/St Emilion, Vinho Verde/Vino Verde, White Bordeaux: Art 8(1)(a). As to Beaujolais, see also Art 8(3). For the following names the transitional period ends on 31 December 1997: Chianti, Frontigan, Hock, Madeira, Malaga: Art 8(1)(b). For the following names the transitional period remains to be determined: Burgundy, Chablis, Champagne, Claret, Graves, Marsala, Moselle, Port, Sauternes, Sherry, White Burgundy: Art 8(1)(c). As to the third category, see also Art 8(2). As to determination of this period, see Art 9.

describe and present a wine.[10] Provision is made also for the use of geographical indications to describe and present wines originating in Australia.[11]

The Community is to authorize, without any time limit, the import of wines from Australia, provided certain conditions are satisfied in respect of certification and information.[12]

In order to implement the Agreement, the parties agree to maintain direct contact,[13] and a Joint Committee is established.[14] Provision is also made for mutual assistance between control authorities.[15]

In 1996 the Community and Australia initialled a Mutual Recognition Agreement (MRA). As with similar agreements between the Community, and Canada, the US and New Zealand, the MRA was undertaken under the aegis of the 1994 Uruguay Round Agreement on Technical Barriers to Trade. It provides for automatic recognition of conformity assessment procedures carried out by authorized bodies and in respect of specified sectors. On 24 March 1998 the Commission submitted a proposal for a Council Decision concluding the Agreement.[16]

A non-binding Joint Declaration between the EU and Australia, which replaced the non-preferential Framework Agreement for Trade and Co-operation between the Community and Australia originally planned, was signed on 26 June 1997. It covers numerous fields including trade and economic co-operation.[17]

NEW ZEALAND

In 1980, when the Community's first common organization of the market in sheepmeat and goatmeat was enacted,[18] the Community and New Zealand concluded an Agreement in respect of trade in these products.[19] As with the analogous agreement with Australia,[20] the Agreement between the Community and New Zealand was a voluntary restraint agreement. It too has been converted into a tariff quota following the Uruguay Round agreements.

An Agreement, analogous to the Agreement between the Community and Australia, was concluded in 1984 between the Community and New Zealand concerning cheese.[1] It also followed an Arrangement between the parties concerning cheese reached within the GATT.

---

10 Ibid Art 11. As to the name 'Hermitage' as a synonym for the vine variety 'Shiraz', see Art 11(2). As to the names 'Lambrusco' and 'Riesling', see Art 11(3).

11 Ibid Art 12.

12 See ibid Arts 15, 16.

13 Ibid Art 17(1). As to procedures, see Art 17(2).

14 Ibid Art 18.

15 Ibid Arts 19–20.

16 Commission of the European Communities, Proposal for a Council Decision on the conclusion of the Agreement on Mutual Recognition in relation to Conformity Assessment, Certificates and Markings between the European Community and Australia, and Proposal for a Council Decision on the conclusion of the Agreement on Mutual Recognition in relation to Conformity Assessment between the European Community and New Zealand, COM(1998) 179 final (98/0126(ACC), 98/0127(ACC), Brussels, 24.3.1998.

17 See *Agence Europe*, No 7004(n.s.), Friday 27.6.97, p 6. The Joint Declaration may be found in *Agence Europe*, No 6999 (n.s.), Friday 20.6.97, pp 8–9.

18 Council Regulation 1837/80, OJ 16.7.80 L183/1.

19 OJ 18.10.80 L275/28 and Council Decision 80/982, OJ 18.10.80 L275/13. As to the interconnection between the sheepmeat regime and the voluntary restraint agreement, see F Snyder *New Directions in European Community Law* (Weidenfeld & Nicolson, London, 1990) pp 63–99.

20 As to which, see above.

1 Exchange of letters, OJ 27.11.84 L308/55.

Member States of the Community are authorized to provide for derogations from certain prohibitions regarding imports of potatoes, other than potatoes for planting, originating in New Zealand.[2]

In 1996 the Community and New Zealand concluded an Agreement on sanitary measures applicable to trade in live animals and animal products.[3] It was undertaken to put into practice the provisions of the WTO Agreement on the Application of Sanitary and Phytosanitary Measures as regards animal health measures.[4] Its objective is to facilitate trade by establishing a mechanism for the recognition of equivalence of sanitary measures and to improve communication and co-operation on sanitary measures.[5] It is initially limited to sanitary measures applied by either party to listed live animals and animal products.[6] It provides for regionalization,[7] the recognition of equivalence,[8] the recognition of sanitary measures,[9] verification,[10] frontier checks and inspection fees,[11] notification,[12] safeguards,[13] and the exchange of information.[14] A joint management committee is established to deal with all matters in relation to the Agreement and its implementation.[15] The Agreement may be denounced by either party on six months' notice in writing.[16]

In 1996 the Community and New Zealand initialled a Mutual Recognition Agreement (MRA). Inspired by the 1994 Uruguay Round Agreement on Technical Barriers to Trade, it provides for mutual recognition of conformity assessment procedures by designated bodies with respect to products in specified sectors. It is expected to enter into force in 1998.[17]

---

2 See Commission Decision 98/81, OJ 20.1.98 L14/29, which sets down the conditions for such derogations.
3 See Council Decision 97/132, OJ 26.2.97 L57/4 and the attached Agreement.
4 Ibid preamble, second recital.
5 Agreement between the European Community and New Zealand on sanitary measures applicable to trade in live animals and animal products, Art 1.
6 Ibid Art 4(1). The animals and products are listed in Annex I. The Agreement does not apply however to sanitary measures related to food additives, sanitary stamps, processing aids, flavours, irradiation, contaminants, transport, chemicals originating from the migration of substances from packaging materials, labelling of foodstuffs, nutritional labelling, medicated foods, and premixes: ibid Art 4(2).
7 See ibid Art 6, Annexes III and V.
8 See ibid Art 7. As to the determination of equivalence, see Art 8.
9 See ibid Art 9. The sectors, or parts of sectors, for which the respective sanitary measures were initially recognized as equivalent for trade purposes are listed in Annex V. This Annex also lists other sectors for which the parties apply differing sanitary measures and have not concluded an assessment of equivalence. The model attestation for the official health certificate for animals is prescribed in Annex VII.
10 See ibid Art 10, Annex VI.
11 See ibid Art 11 and Annex VIII A and B.
12 See ibid Art 12.
13 See ibid Art 13.
14 See ibid Art 15 and Annex X. See also Art 14.
15 Ibid Art 16.
16 Ibid Art 18(4).
17 See Commission of the European Communities, Proposal for a Council Decision on the conclusion of the Agreement on Mutual Recognition in relation to Conformity Assessment, Certificates and Markings between the European Community and Australia, and Proposal for a Council Decision on the conclusion of the Agreement on Mutual Recognition in relation to Conformity Assessment between the European Community and New Zealand, COM(1998) 179 final (98/0126(ACC), 98/0127(ACC), Brussels, 24.3.1998.

Index

619